EVOLO
SKYSCRAPERS
3

eVolo

CREDITS

EDITOR-IN-CHIEF

CARLO AIELLO

EDITORS

PAUL ALDRIDGE

NOÉMIE DEVILLE

RAMI SARABI

ANNA SOLT

JUNG SU LEE

Library of Congress Cataloging-in-Publication Data Available.

ISBN: 978-1-938740-22-0

Manufactured in China

Evolo, Inc.
6363 Wilshire Blvd. Suite 311
Los Angeles, CA 90048

www.evolo.us

CONTENTS

3
NEW
FRONTIERS

INTRODUCTION

THE SUBMISSIONS REACT TO THE CONTEMPORARY PROBLEMS OF URBAN LIVING INCLUDING EXPONENTIAL INCREASE IN POPULATION, SCARCITY OF NATURAL RESOURCES, SOCIAL DIVISIONS, AND ENVIRONMENTAL THREATS, AMONG OTHERS.

This book is the third publication in a series dedicated to showcase the best submissions to the annual *eVolo Skyscraper Competition*. Each year *eVolo Magazine* makes a call to architects, designers, and urbanists around the globe to explore new ideas for vertical living. The projects received are not traditional skyscrapers by any means but instead they are deep investigations on many aspects of contemporary architecture and urbanism. The six main areas of study are technological advances, sustainability, exploration of uncharted territories, social solutions, new aesthetics, and urban strategies. The submissions react to the contemporary problems of urban living including exponential increase in population, scarcity of natural resources, social divisions, and environmental threats, among others. The proposed solutions are seldom simple; they are multi-layered endeavors, far from current architectural agenda, envisioning the future of our cities, and potentially redefining the way in which we live, work, and play in urban areas.

One of the most interesting aspects of these projects is the number of functions that they address. Single-program solutions are no longer relevant. These works are explorations on mixed-use programs – the idea of transforming a vertical structure into a vertical city that shelters and provides all the necessary infrastructure and amenities to their inhabitants. In some examples even vertical farms are imagined along manufacturing, processing, and recycling plants seamlessly integrated with the rest of the required programs.

The ever increase of population and migration to urban areas in conjunction with the dramatic environmental problems of our time have fueled the imagination of designers that are constantly looking for new territories to inhabit. The exploration of underwater and outer space colonization are two of the most recurrent topics. Although these projects face hundreds of technical problems, they are laying the first stones for future visionaries to solve.

The *Skyscraper Competition* is also an opportunity for dialogue and critique. Each year, the results selected from over a thousand submissions, are eagerly awaited and shared by hundreds of media outlets around the globe. This phenomenon provides an opportunity to reach other areas of knowledge that contribute to the architectural discourse. A sense of disbelief is a first reaction towards many of the projects, which seem to be way ahead of our time, sometimes even categorized as science fiction. A more profound investigation reveals the complexity of the projects and the potential for their ideas to become our future. These skyscrapers are not finished concepts but a collage of theories and solutions, which enable further investigations.

The one hundred fifty projects showcased in this book are the best submissions received in 2014, 2015, and 2016 selected by an international Jury of renowned architects, designers and theorists. The members of the Jury are: Wiel Arets, John Beckmann, Matias Del Campo, Thom Faulders, Massimiliano Fuksas, Michael Hansmeyer, Richard Hassell, Michael Hensel, Alvin Huang, Lisa Iwamoto, Wong Mun Summ, Kas Oosterhuis, Tom Price, Fernando Romero, Craig Scott, Marcelo Spina, Benedetta Tagliabue, and Dan Wood.

eVolo – to study, to develop, to evolve, to fly away...

JURORS

WIEL ARETS is a Dutch architect, theorist, urbanist, industrial designer, and the dean of the Illinois Institute of Technology's College of Architecture in Chicago, USA. He studied at the Eindhoven University of Technology, graduating in 1983, and founded Wiel Arets Architects in the same year. From 1995-2002 he was dean of the Berlage Institute in Rotterdam, where he introduced the idea of 'progressive-research' and co-founded the school's architectural journal named HUNCH.

JOHN BECKMANN founded Axis Mundi in 2004. He received a Bachelor of Fine Arts in Environmental Design from Parsons School of Design. During his studies, he apprenticed with master minimalist Joseph P. D'Urso and, after graduating, collaborated with various other design luminaries. Throughout his career he has honed an astute understanding of the intersections between architecture, design and contemporary art. Beckmann's honors include a grant from the Graham Foundation for Advanced Studies in the Fine Arts (1998) and a McDowell Colony Fellowship (2010). He both edited and contributed to The Virtual Dimension: Architecture, Representation and Crash Culture (Princeton Architectural Press, 1998), one of the first books to grasp the implications of digital technologies on the fields of architecture and design. Beckmann has also been a visiting critic at Yale School of Architecture, Pratt Institute and Parsons the New School for Design, and he has been a featured guest on Bloomberg TV and LX-TV's Open House.

MATIAS DEL CAMPO studied architecture at the University of Applied Arts Vienna, Austria, where he graduated with distinction. Together with Sandra Manninger he founded the Architecture Office SPAN in 2003. Apart from his role as founder and principal of SPAN, his academic qualifications include an appointment as visiting Professor at the DIA, Dessau Institute of Architecture (Dessau, Germany), the ESARQ, Universitat Internacional de Catalunya, in Barcelona, Spain, a lecturer position at the University of Pennsylvania, UPenn, USA. In fall 2013 he was appointed as Associate Professor of Architecture at Taubman College, University of Michigan. In 2008 and 2010 he served as curator for the ABB, Architecture Biennale Beijing. His main projects include: The Austrian pavilion at Shanghai EXPO 2010; The Microblur project, commissioned by Microsoft Austria and The Austrian Winery Boom, exhibition design for ACF, New York, commissioned by the Architecture Center Vienna. In 2012 the work of SPAN was on show at the Venice Architecture Biennale. In 2013 the work of Matias del Campo and Sandra Manninger was on display at the 9th Archilab Exhibition of the FRAC Center in Orleans France, Naturalising Architecture. His work is part of the permanent collection of FRAC Orleans, the MAK in Vienna and the Albertina, Vienna.

THOM FAULDERS works at the intersection of commissioned architecture, speculative design research, permanent public art installations and international museum and gallery exhibitions. Directed by architect Thom Faulders, the multi-disciplinary practice believes that the design of today's built the environment can be positioned as an open condition: a responsive medium formed in direct exchange with active contextual phenomena and dynamic perceptual tactics. With a focus on new production methodologies and innovative material applications, the projects embed architecture with spatial variability that sync stability with change, and are informed through and defined by investigations into emergent behaviors of complex systems. Participation in leading international museum and gallery venues includes the FRAC Centre Orleans in France, Oslo Triennale, SOMarts Cultural Center San Francisco, San Francisco Museum of Modern Art, New York Museum of Modern Art, New York Center for Architecture, San Francisco Museum of Craft and Design, UC Berkeley Art Museum, Art Institute of Chicago, Fondazione La Triennale di Milano, Lisbon International Biennale, Maison de l'Architecture et de La Ville, Kunstlerhaus Vienna, Wattis Institute for Contemporary Art San Francisco, and is included in the permanent architecture and design collections at the FRAC Centre Orleans and San Francisco Museum of Modern Art. Awards include AIA New Practices Award, AIA Building Awards, Emerging Architect Award from the Architecture League of New York, SFMOMA Experimental Design Award, Society of Environmental Graphic Design Award, Private Plots International Design Awards, Winning Competition Award SF Bay Conservation & Development Commission, Miami Bienal + Beach Competition Award, plus others.

MASSIMILIANO FUKSAS of Lithuanian decent was born in Rome in 1944. He graduated in Architecture from the University of Rome "La Sapienza" in 1969. Since the eighties he has been one of the main protagonists of the contemporary architectural scene. He has been Visiting Professor at a number of universities such as: Columbia University in New York, the École Spéciale d'Architecture in Paris, the Akademie der Bildenden Künste in Wien, the Staatliche Akademie der Bildenden Künste in Stuttgart. From 1998 to 2000 he directed the "VII Mostra Internazionale di Architettura di Venezia":

า 1 Bermuda 2 Bosnia and Herzegovina 3 Brazil 20 Bulgaria 5 Burma 2 Canada 68 Chile 4 China 146
El Salvador 1 Finland 3 France 65 Georgia 2 Germany 28 Ghana 2 Greece 15 Grenada 1 Guatemala 1
ว Kuwait 4 Latvia 1 Lebanon 9 Lithuania 1 Macau 1 Macedonia 1 Malaysia 11 Mexico 28 Moldova 1
ico 11 Qatar 2 Romania 17 Russia 43 Saudi Arabia 3 Scotland 2 Serbia 12 Singapore 14 Slovakia 3
sia 1 Turkey 18 Ukraine 15 United Arab Emirates 3 United Kingdom 86 United States 292 Vietnam 8

1 TECHNOLOGICAL ADVANCES

HIGH-RISE CITY AT NET

Marios C. Phocas
George Tryfonos
Nicky Nicolaou

Cyprus

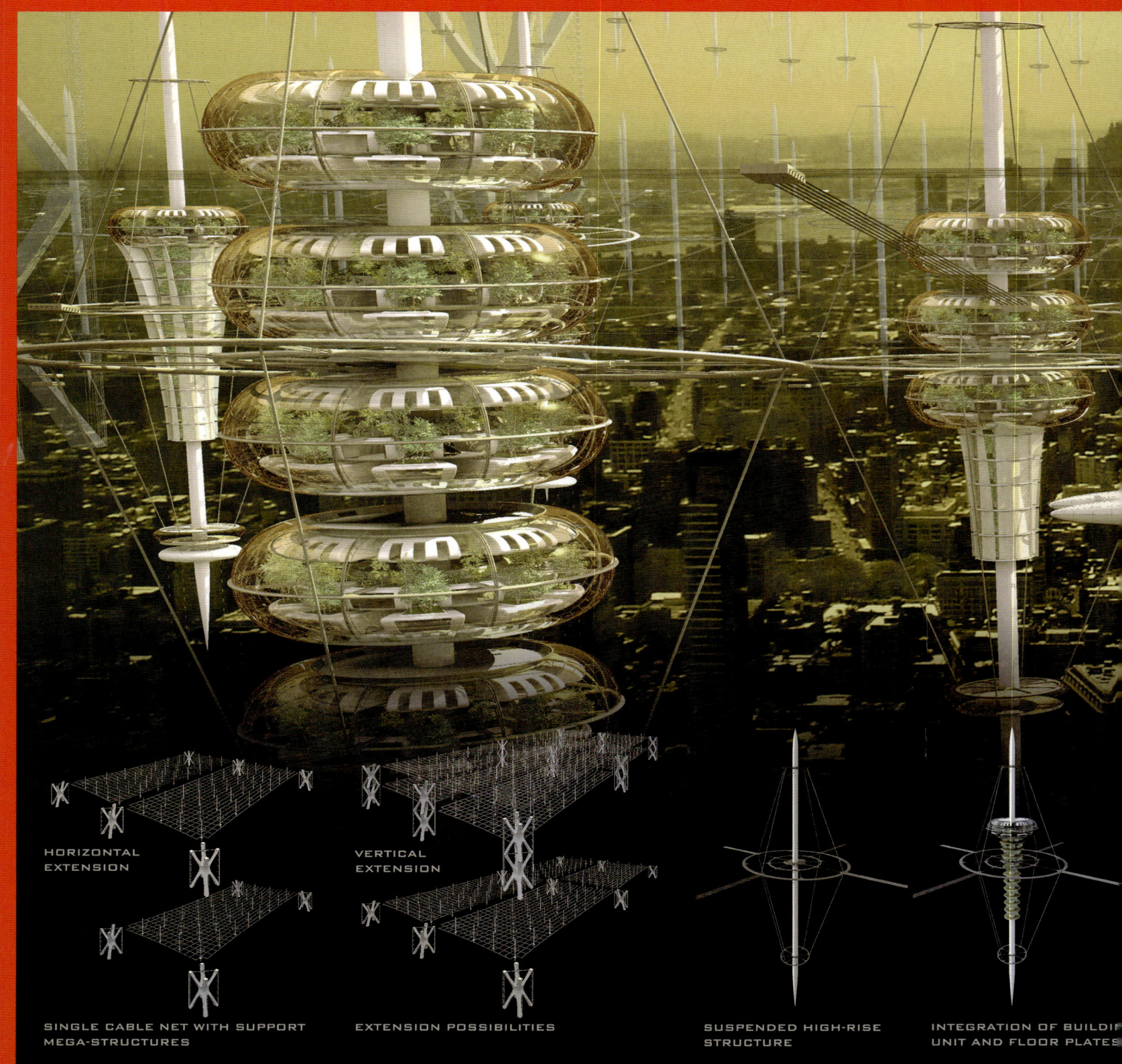

HORIZONTAL
EXTENSION

VERTICAL
EXTENSION

SINGLE CABLE NET WITH SUPPORT
MEGA-STRUCTURES

EXTENSION POSSIBILITIES

SUSPENDED HIGH-RISE
STRUCTURE

INTEGRATION OF BUILDI
UNIT AND FLOOR PLATES

The proposed High-Rise City at Net addresses aspects of globalization, flexibility, adaptability, technology advances, sustainability and modes of interdisciplinary aspects in the design of high-rise buildings in the 21st Century. The proposed inhabited, floating, urban layers act as regeneration mechanisms of minimal physical intervention with the existing contemporary city characterized by scarcity of natural resources and infrastructure, exponential increase of inhabitants, pollution and lack of usage diversity and expandability. In addition, a creation of dynamic and adaptive communities over the height is envisioned, capable of intelligent interconnectivity and growth.

Sustainability features of the design derive from the adaptive integration of private, public and green areas, the minimization of the structure's self-weight, the integration of environmentally friendly transportation

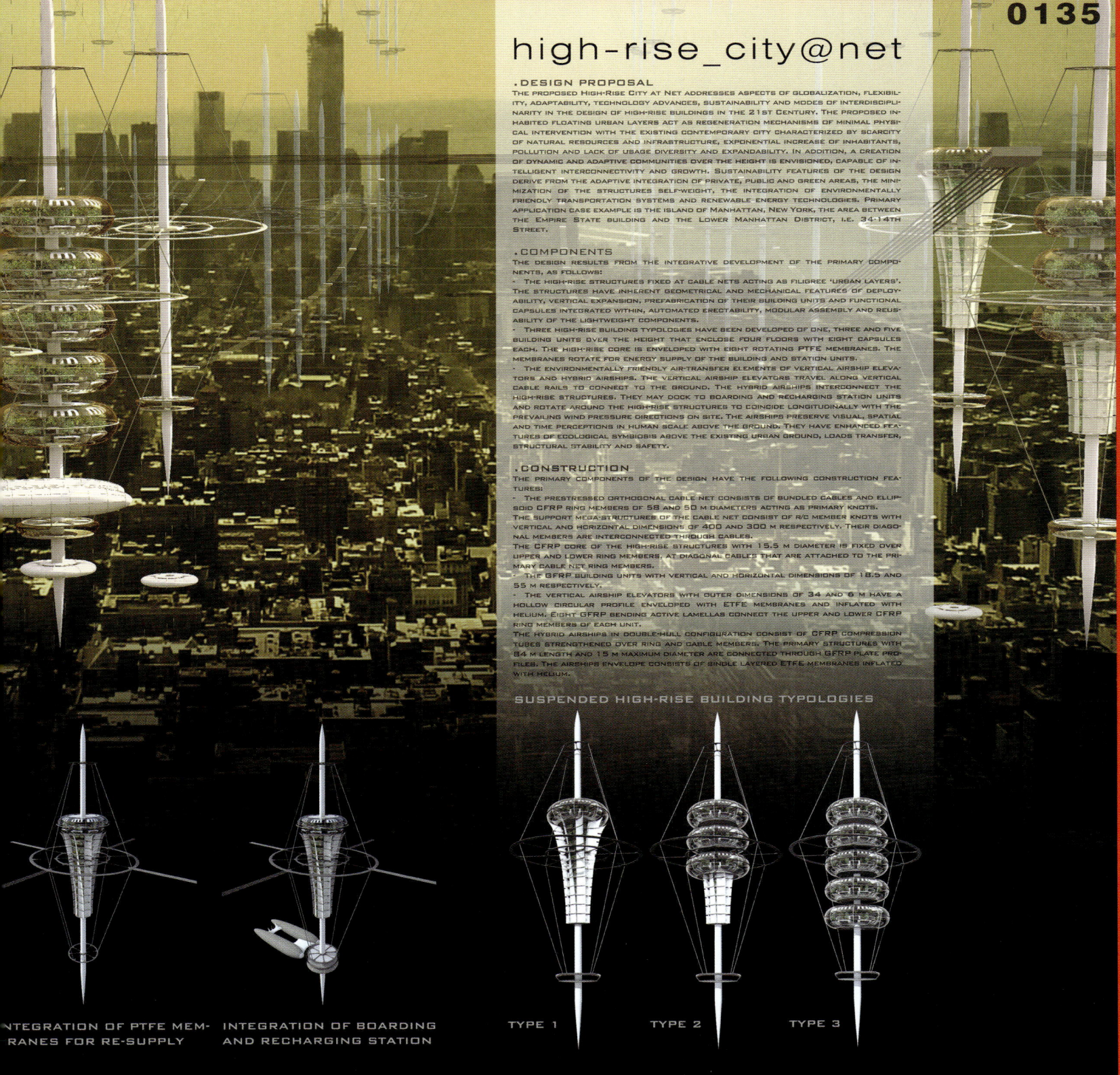

0135

high-rise_city@net

.DESIGN PROPOSAL

THE PROPOSED HIGH-RISE CITY AT NET ADDRESSES ASPECTS OF GLOBALIZATION, FLEXIBILITY, ADAPTABILITY, TECHNOLOGY ADVANCES, SUSTAINABILITY AND MODES OF INTERDISCIPLINARITY IN THE DESIGN OF HIGH-RISE BUILDINGS IN THE 21ST CENTURY. THE PROPOSED INHABITED FLOATING URBAN LAYERS ACT AS REGENERATION MECHANISMS OF MINIMAL PHYSICAL INTERVENTION WITH THE EXISTING CONTEMPORARY CITY CHARACTERIZED BY SCARCITY OF NATURAL RESOURCES AND INFRASTRUCTURE, EXPONENTIAL INCREASE OF INHABITANTS, POLLUTION AND LACK OF USAGE DIVERSITY AND EXPANDABILITY. IN ADDITION, A CREATION OF DYNAMIC AND ADAPTIVE COMMUNITIES OVER THE HEIGHT IS ENVISIONED, CAPABLE OF INTELLIGENT INTERCONNECTIVITY AND GROWTH. SUSTAINABILITY FEATURES OF THE DESIGN DERIVE FROM THE ADAPTIVE INTEGRATION OF PRIVATE, PUBLIC AND GREEN AREAS, THE MINIMIZATION OF THE STRUCTURE'S SELF-WEIGHT, THE INTEGRATION OF ENVIRONMENTALLY FRIENDLY TRANSPORTATION SYSTEMS AND RENEWABLE ENERGY TECHNOLOGIES. PRIMARY APPLICATION CASE EXAMPLE IS THE ISLAND OF MANHATTAN, NEW YORK, THE AREA BETWEEN THE EMPIRE STATE BUILDING AND THE LOWER MANHATTAN DISTRICT, I.E. 34-14TH STREET.

.COMPONENTS

THE DESIGN RESULTS FROM THE INTEGRATIVE DEVELOPMENT OF THE PRIMARY COMPONENTS, AS FOLLOWS:
- THE HIGH-RISE STRUCTURES FIXED AT CABLE NETS ACTING AS FILIGREE 'URBAN LAYERS'. THE STRUCTURES HAVE INHERENT GEOMETRICAL AND MECHANICAL FEATURES OF DEPLOYABILITY, VERTICAL EXPANSION, PREFABRICATION OF THEIR BUILDING UNITS AND FUNCTIONAL CAPSULES INTEGRATED WITHIN, AUTOMATED ERECTABILITY, MODULAR ASSEMBLY AND REUSABILITY OF THE LIGHTWEIGHT COMPONENTS.
- THREE HIGH-RISE BUILDING TYPOLOGIES HAVE BEEN DEVELOPED OF ONE, THREE AND FIVE BUILDING UNITS OVER THE HEIGHT THAT ENCLOSE FOUR FLOORS WITH EIGHT CAPSULES EACH. THE HIGH-RISE CORE IS ENVELOPED WITH EIGHT ROTATING PTFE MEMBRANES. THE MEMBRANES ROTATE FOR ENERGY SUPPLY OF THE BUILDING AND STATION UNITS.
- THE ENVIRONMENTALLY FRIENDLY AIR-TRANSFER ELEMENTS OF VERTICAL AIRSHIP ELEVATORS AND HYBRID AIRSHIPS. THE VERTICAL AIRSHIP ELEVATORS TRAVEL ALONG VERTICAL CABLE RAILS TO CONNECT TO THE GROUND. THE HYBRID AIRSHIPS INTERCONNECT THE HIGH-RISE STRUCTURES. THEY MAY DOCK TO BOARDING AND RECHARGING STATION UNITS AND ROTATE AROUND THE HIGH-RISE STRUCTURES TO COINCIDE LONGITUDINALLY WITH THE PREVAILING WIND PRESSURE DIRECTIONS ON SITE. THE AIRSHIPS PRESERVE VISUAL, SPATIAL AND TIME PERCEPTIONS IN HUMAN SCALE ABOVE THE GROUND. THEY HAVE ENHANCED FEATURES OF ECOLOGICAL SYMBIOSIS ABOVE THE EXISTING URBAN GROUND, LOADS TRANSFER, STRUCTURAL STABILITY AND SAFETY.

.CONSTRUCTION

THE PRIMARY COMPONENTS OF THE DESIGN HAVE THE FOLLOWING CONSTRUCTION FEATURES:
- THE PRESTRESSED ORTHOGONAL CABLE NET CONSISTS OF BUNDLED CABLES AND ELLIPSOID CFRP RING MEMBERS OF 58 AND 50 M DIAMETERS ACTING AS PRIMARY KNOTS. THE SUPPORT MEGA-STRUCTURES OF THE CABLE NET CONSIST OF R/C MEMBER KNOTS WITH VERTICAL AND HORIZONTAL DIMENSIONS OF 400 AND 300 M RESPECTIVELY. THEIR DIAGONAL MEMBERS ARE INTERCONNECTED THROUGH CABLES.
THE CFRP CORE OF THE HIGH-RISE STRUCTURES WITH 15.5 M DIAMETER IS FIXED OVER UPPER AND LOWER RING MEMBERS. AT DIAGONAL CABLES THAT ARE ATTACHED TO THE PRIMARY CABLE NET RING MEMBERS.
- THE GFRP BUILDING UNITS WITH VERTICAL AND HORIZONTAL DIMENSIONS OF 18.5 AND 55 M RESPECTIVELY.
- THE VERTICAL AIRSHIP ELEVATORS WITH OUTER DIMENSIONS OF 34 AND 6 M HAVE A HOLLOW CIRCULAR PROFILE ENVELOPED WITH ETFE MEMBRANES AND INFLATED WITH HELIUM. EIGHT GFRP BENDING ACTIVE LAMELLAS CONNECT THE UPPER AND LOWER CFRP RING MEMBERS OF EACH UNIT.
THE HYBRID AIRSHIPS IN DOUBLE-HULL CONFIGURATION CONSIST OF CFRP COMPRESSION TUBES STRENGTHENED OVER RING AND CABLE MEMBERS. THE PRIMARY STRUCTURES WITH 54 M LENGTH AND 15 M MAXIMUM DIAMETER ARE CONNECTED THROUGH GFRP PLATE PROFILES. THE AIRSHIPS ENVELOPE CONSISTS OF SINGLE LAYERED ETFE MEMBRANES INFLATED WITH HELIUM.

SUSPENDED HIGH-RISE BUILDING TYPOLOGIES

INTEGRATION OF PTFE MEMBRANES FOR RE-SUPPLY   INTEGRATION OF BOARDING AND RECHARGING STATION   TYPE 1   TYPE 2   TYPE 3

systems, and renewable energy technologies. A primary application case example is the island of Manhattan, New York, the area between the Empire State building and the Lower Manhattan District, i.e. 34-14th Street. The design results from the integrated development of the primary components, as follows.

The high-rise structures fixed at cable nets acting as filigree 'urban layers'. The structures have inherent geometrical and mechanical features of deployment, vertical expansion, prefabrication of their building units and functional capsules integrated within, automated building, modular assembly and reusability of the lightweight components.

Three high-rise building typologies have been developed of one, three, and five building units over the height that enclose four floors with eight capsules each. The high-rise core is enveloped with eight

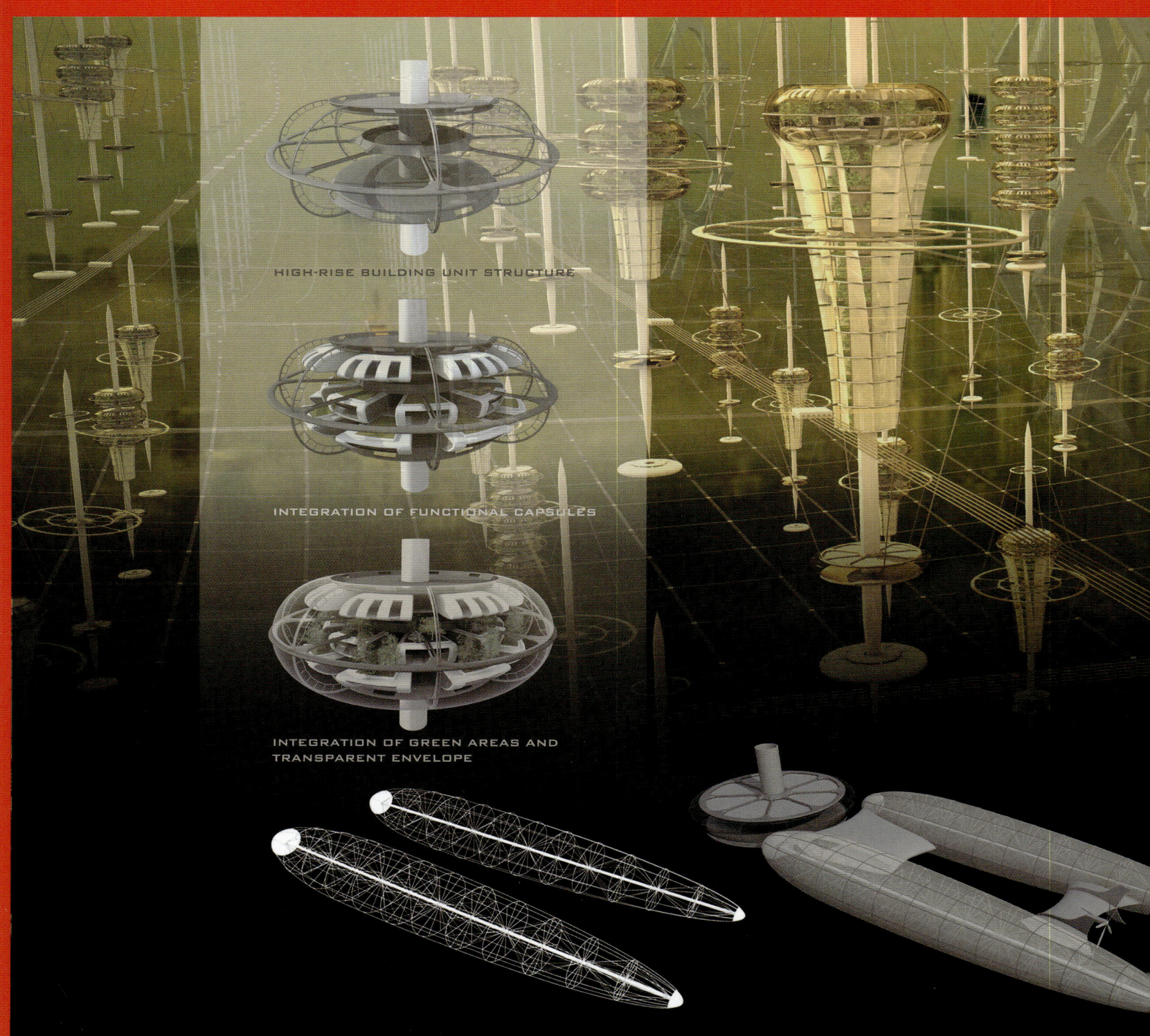

HIGH-RISE BUILDING UNIT STRUCTURE

INTEGRATION OF FUNCTIONAL CAPSULES

INTEGRATION OF GREEN AREAS AND
TRANSPARENT ENVELOPE

PRIMARY HYBRID AIRSHIP STRUCTURE:
STRENGTHENING COMPRESSION TUBE WITH RING AND CABLE MEMBERS

HYBRID AIRSHIP AT HIGH-RISE BOARDING
AND RECHARGING STATION

rotating PTFE membranes. The membranes rotate for energy supply of the building and station units. The environmentally friendly air transfers elements of vertical airship elevators and hybrid airships. The vertical airship elevators travel along vertical cable rails to connect to the ground. The hybrid airships interconnect the high-rise structures. They may dock to boarding and recharging station units and rotate around the high-rise structures to coincide longitudinally with the prevailing wind pressure directions on site.

The airships preserve visual, spatial and time perceptions in human scale above the ground. They have enhanced features of ecological symbiosis above the existing urban ground, loads transfer, structural stability and safety.

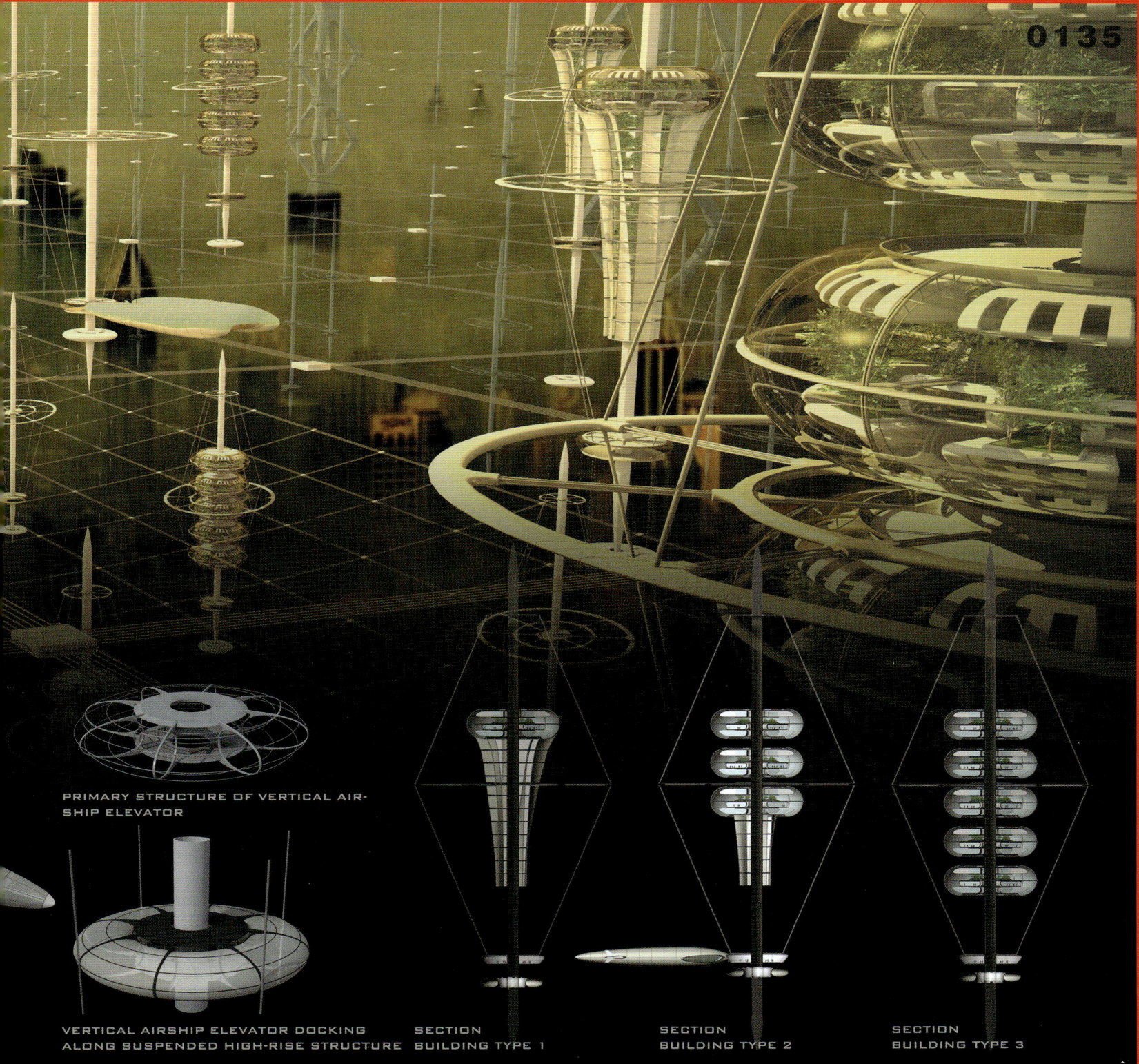

PRIMARY STRUCTURE OF VERTICAL AIR-SHIP ELEVATOR

VERTICAL AIRSHIP ELEVATOR DOCKING ALONG SUSPENDED HIGH-RISE STRUCTURE

SECTION BUILDING TYPE 1

SECTION BUILDING TYPE 2

SECTION BUILDING TYPE 3

LIQUEFACTOWER

Eric Nakajima

New Zealand

LIQUEFACTOWER The Sinking City

Case

The city of Christchurch had been greatly damaged when the New Zealand's second largest city was hit by a destructive earthquake on February 2011. In the case of Christchurch, soil liquefaction was the main cause of damage which meant that deep saturated soil pre-existed beneath the city that liquefied and destabilized the surface during the rumble. **The effects were commonly described as "sinking" as the buildings, automobiles and roads simply sunk into the ground** as though the ground turned liquid. As a result, over 100,000 homes were damaged and citywide infrastructures requiring repair.

Since New Zealand lie on the fault line of two continental plates, more large earthquakes are expected in the near future. a debate struck arguing that it is not worth it to rebuild the city on the same soil since most of land had been marked as "high liquefaction potential" zone, therefore, the effort to stabilize soil conditions (with methods such as soil compaction) should rather be focused on shifting the city centre to a safer location with a lower potential of liquefaction. Due to this unstable soil conditions of greater Christchurch, the recovery has been slow and much of the city is still inoperable even after 2 years had passed.

High Liquefica

With bigger and worse natural disasters appearing on the news with no signs of slowing down, we need to rethink how cities should rebuild. When a city is destroyed, it is a sign that the city's infrastructure is not suitable for the environmental conditions of that particular location. With so much variation of inherent environmental properties around the globe, why do we globalize a singular infrastructural system?

Christchurch, New Zealand is one city that has recently been devastated by an earthquake. With citywide liquefaction destroying infrastructure, it is clear that the typical method of construction is not suited for such soil condition.

The immediate response by the city is to artificially condition the soil for better building surface, but this method of forcing nature to take form of an ideal environment to perpetuate the same construction

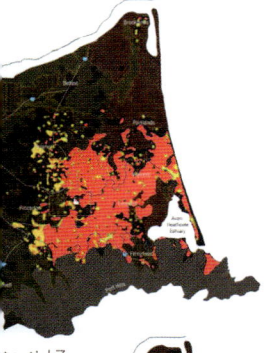

tential Zone

Concept

History will tell us that humans have evolved from species that adapted to the surrounding environment into species that condition the environment to suit our needs. we flatten mountains, make artificial islands, and even wipe out forests just to provide ourselves a place to build. Therefore, **fighting against nature has become our evolutionary response.** Rather than adapting our infrastructural systems, we resort to altering nature to accommodate our traditional methods. Christchurch will need to undergo conditioning of the deeper layers of its soil using various compaction techniques, just to be able to reconstruct buildings on the surface. However, this phenomenon of environmental conditioning is inefficient, destructive and energy consuming. We have focused our energy away from adaptation to preservation (of culture), but with the rapidly changing forces of nature and ongoing disasters ahead, **we will inevitably need to focus back on adaptation in order to preserve our existence.**

The concept is to simply adapt to the environment rather than fighting against it. If deep and unstable soil is undesirable for structure on the surface, then a structural system that benefit from the loose soil will not only eradicate the need to condition the environment but also eliminate the fear of future earthquakes. The architectural concept exploits the effect of earthquakes and **artificially generate liquefaction to burrow or 'sink' the city deep into the ground,** literally adapting into the environmental conditions.

"It is not the strongest of the species that survives, nor the most intelligent that survives. It is the one that is the most adaptable to change."

0182

technique seems time consuming and wasteful.

The proposal is a system that adapts into the current environmental conditions without the need for tweaking, alteration or correction. For the new city, unstable soil becomes a necessity and not a burden as the structure buries and sinks into the ground by exploiting the phenomenon of liquefaction. This project becomes an example of rethinking adaptation by responding to the nature of site without being constrained by traditional methods.

The project is designed as a cylindrical excavation with housing and infrastructure placed on the perimeter walls. The living units are conceived as modular elements that extend outwards depending on their use and size. The result is a random pattern that allows a play of light and shadow while craeting voids

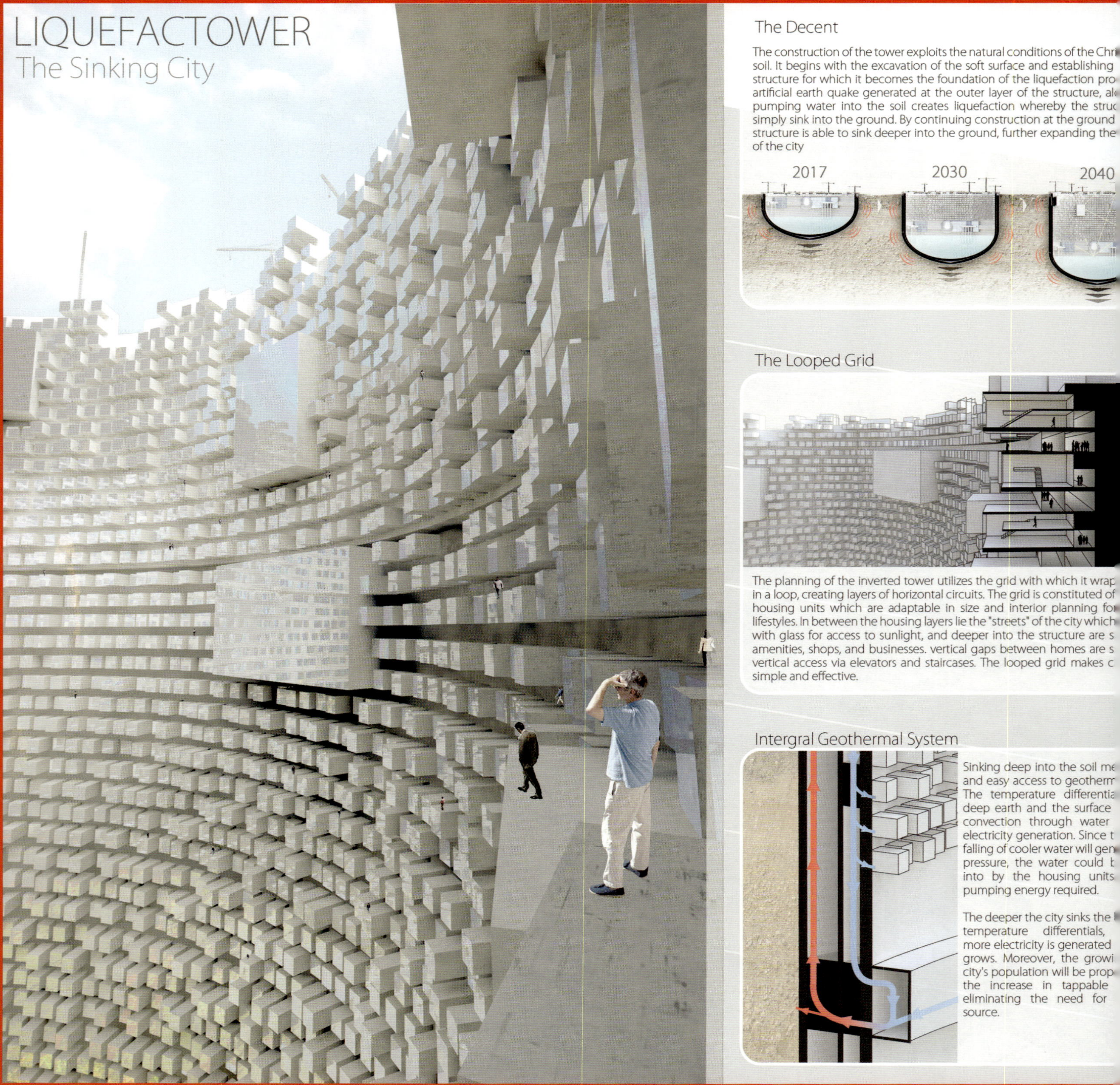

LIQUEFACTOWER
The Sinking City

The Decent

The construction of the tower exploits the natural conditions of the Chri soil. It begins with the excavation of the soft surface and establishing structure for which it becomes the foundation of the liquefaction pro artificial earth quake generated at the outer layer of the structure, ale pumping water into the soil creates liquefaction whereby the struc simply sink into the ground. By continuing construction at the ground structure is able to sink deeper into the ground, further expanding the of the city

The Looped Grid

The planning of the inverted tower utilizes the grid with which it wrap in a loop, creating layers of horizontal circuits. The grid is constituted of housing units which are adaptable in size and interior planning fo lifestyles. In between the housing layers lie the "streets" of the city which with glass for access to sunlight, and deeper into the structure are s amenities, shops, and businesses. vertical gaps between homes are s vertical access via elevators and staircases. The looped grid makes c simple and effective.

Intergral Geothermal System

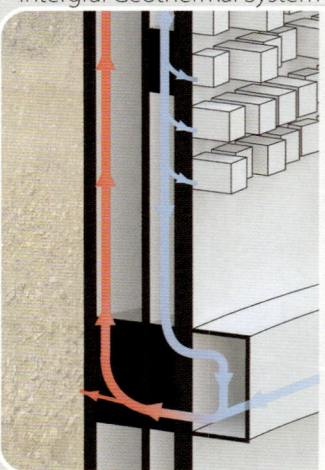

Sinking deep into the soil me and easy access to geotherm The temperature differentia deep earth and the surface convection through water electricity generation. Since t falling of cooler water will gen pressure, the water could t into by the housing units pumping energy required.

The deeper the city sinks the temperature differentials, more electricity is generated grows. Moreover, the growi city's population will be prop the increase in tappable eliminating the need for source.

to be used as recreational areas. Larger blocks serve as localized activity centers that are interconnected to inner vertical and horizontal circulations.

    The project is designed to be built in a series of phases, with each phase going deeper until completed in 2040. The bottom of the prject will serve as a manmade water reservoir equipped with an internal geothermal system. The maximum depth of the project depends on a series of factors including population density requirements, ideal light penetration, and projected growth.

0182

0m

100m

200m

300m

400m

500m

600m

Localized Activity Centre

Activity centres will become the focal points for city life, recreation and business.

These mixed use centres are constructed following the vertical grid so the location and size can be adaptable depending on the demands of the people.

The Loop has a unique feature of making the whole city visible to everyone, creating a hightened sense of unity and involvement.

AEG (Artificial Earthquake Generator)

AEG Shell Anatomy

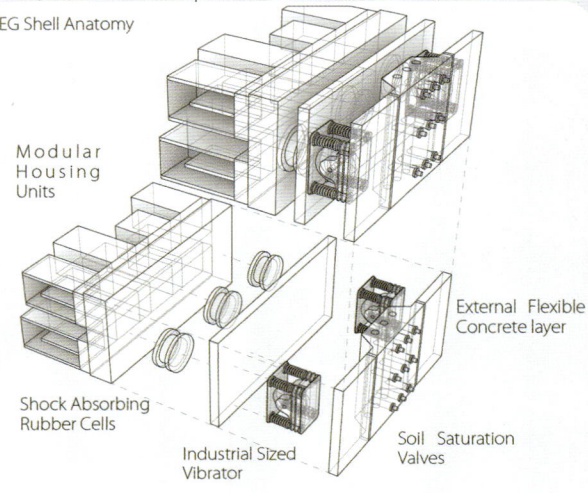

Modular Housing Units

External Flexible Concrete layer

Shock Absorbing Rubber Cells

Industrial Sized Vibrator

Soil Saturation Valves

The AEG shell consists of centrally controlled vibrators which transfers seismic energy through flexible outer shell. Since Liquefaction is more likely to occur in saturated soil, the water valves pumps additive water into the soil creating optimum liquefaction. To ensure the vibration energy is not transferred to the inner city structure, an absorption layer with rubber cells are wedged between the city and AEG.

HYPER-SPEED VERTICAL TRAIN HUB

Christopher Christophi
Lucas Mazarrasa

United Kingdom

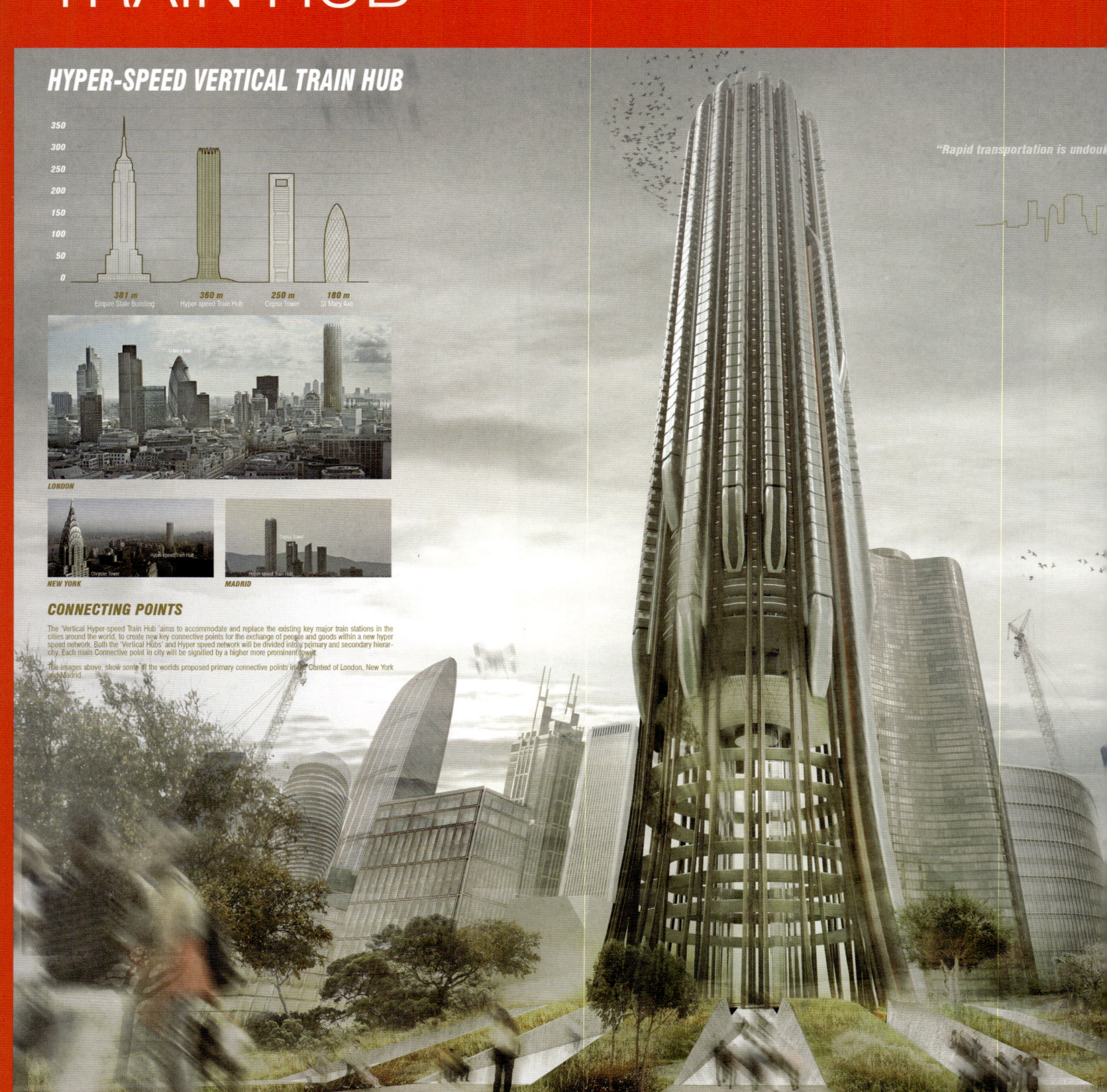

HYPER-SPEED VERTICAL TRAIN HUB

350
300
250
200
150
100
50
0

| 381 m | 350 m | 250 m | 180 m |
| Empire State Building | Hyper-speed Train Hub | Cepsa Tower | St Mary Axe |

LONDON

NEW YORK　　Chrysler Tower

MADRID

CONNECTING POINTS

The 'Vertical Hyper-speed Train Hub' aims to accommodate and replace the existing key major train stations in the cities around the world, to create new key connective points for the exchange of people and goods within a new hyper speed network. Both the 'Vertical Hubs' and Hyper speed network will be divided into a primary and secondary hierarchy. Each main Connective point in city will be signalled by a higher more prominent tower.

The images above, show some of the worlds proposed primary connective points in the Context of London, New York and Madrid.

"Rapid transportation is undou

The Hyper-Speed Vertical Train Hub, aims to resolve the inevitable challenges that cities will face by 2075, and offers a deliverable and sustainable solution for the future of the transport generation.

As the world's population dramatically increases, the demand for goods, natural resources, foods, fuel and land would have increased significantly by 2075. The majority of the future's population will gravitate towards living in megacities, increasing the pressure and competition for adjacent suburban land, therefore forcing cities to explore more innovative forms of public transport.

The essence of time is already an invaluable representation for the technological revolution. Smart phones, video calls are already cemented into society as mandatory modes of communication. However, our proposal will not only simplify time, it will reduce CO_2 emissions, increase energy security and revolutionize

international trading relations. The project will become a 'repeatable' piece of infrastructure that can be implemented to support any city around the world, connecting to a new Hyper Speed under and over ground network, with trains covering an average distance of 300 miles in 30 minutes.

The Hyper-Speed Vertical Train Hub aims to replace existing flagship train stations and create new key connective points for the exchange of people and goods with the new hyper speed network. The proposal will 'flip' the traditional form and function of the current train station design vertically, and re-form it into a cylindrical mass to increase the towers train capacity. This tall cylindrical form aims to eliminate the current impact that traditional stations have currently on land use, therefore returning the remaining site mass back to the densely packed urban Mega City. This remaining land will surround the base of the tower forming a

6 ROOF TOP PLAZA

As an extension of the of parks below, a Green Rooftop plaza will also be placed at the top of the tower which will create another large recreational and performance space for the public; it will allow passengers to enjoy outdoor space and views of the city whilst they await arrival of their trains.

7 ATRIUM

The Atrium space will be the main circulation space for the passengers through the tower. Each floor will contain a variety of shops, stalls, and further supporting services. The three Terminals throughout the tower divides the Atrium into three parts.

8 PARK REGENERATION

The Base of the tower will become an extension of the surrounding newly formed park. A raised platform which surrounds the tower, will act as a green barrier to the void which accommodates the train's movement into the network of underground tunnels. A series of bridges will travel above this void and become the main connective extension points from the park into the Vertical Hub's 'Green Lobby'. The lobby will act as the main arrival and departure point for pedestrian.

9 CROSS SECTION

10 LIFT STRATEGY

The lifts are divided into three cores which surround the Atrium. Within each of the three cores, there are a total of 6 lifts. Two of these lifts are Shuttle Lifts, which Stop at every main floor of the 3 Terminals, as well as the ground floor and the Green Roof Top plaza. The Further 4 lifts in each core will serve the terminal floors separately. These lifts will only travel between the floors of its designated terminal, to ensure a more efficient vertical movement of people throughout the Hub.

11 PUBLIC TOWER

This proposal will be the first 'skyscraper' that will become fully accessible and designed solely for public use, a dream that could be one step closer to reality.

12 TRAIN CARRIA

13 TRAIN CARRIA

large urban park, leading towards to the base of the Hyper-Speed Vertical Hub. Passengers will travel into the main lobby allowing travellers to ascend through the atrium and through the platforms and onto the carriages. The trains will create a dynamic and kinetic facade, one that will be continuously evolving and responsive to the workings of the vertical hub, a language that can be read by the whole city. As the train travels and transitions from its horizontal formation, and ascends up the facade vertically, the carriages will pivot similar to that on a 'Ferris wheel', allowing the passengers within the carriage to remain in an upright position and facing towards the cityscape. The carriages will be supported by a magnetic structure located at either side, eliminating the need for rails beneath, and allowing the carriages and its passengers to connect to the tower.

HYPER-SPEED VERTICAL TRAIN HUB

0276 02

Each carriage will contain 10 people composed of two rows of seats which face each other and maximising views of the landscape when travelling. The proportions of the carriage are designed in a cubical form to enable it work in both vertical (when docked) and in horizontal position when travelling.

FERRIS WHEEL

As the train travels and transitions from its horizontal formation, and ascends up the facade vertically, the carriages will pivot similar to that on a 'Ferris wheel', allowing the passengers within the carriage to remain in an upright position and facing towards the cityscape. The carriages will be supported by a magnetic structure located at either side, eliminating the need for rails beneath and allowing for the carriages and its passengers to connect to the tower. .

DYNAMIC ELEVATION
The trains will create a dynamic and kinetic facade, one that will be continuously evolving and responsive to the workings of the Vertical hub, a language that can be read by the whole city

THE INJECTOR

Luca Pedrielli
Paolo Alborghetti

Italy

valleys for water
accumulation

the injector

dunes as shelters
for wind storms

Desertification is a phenomenon that ranks among the greatest environmental challenges of our time. Although desertification can include the encroachment of sand dunes on land, degradation of dryland ecosystems by human activities and by climate change.

The injector seeks to trigger processes of reappropriation of adverse territories for human survival, especially desert environments(instead of common natural ground consuming inhabitation processes) through innovative methods for processing matter, thanks to the biggest renewable energy source we can exploit : the sun.

Nowadays we're facing with issues of energy production and raw material deficiency. The project exploit the potential of desert resources, where energy and substrate material are abundant. The main project potential lays in its productive core, composed by platforms and machines for 3D sand - sinter . The blades, that compose the facade ,can be dynamically oriented to optimize solar energy harvesting and to reflect and converge sun rays to the core tower , where the sintering takes place. This machine prints minimal living modules from sand silica (in the form of quartz) that can be stored in stations inside the tower structure. The sintering machine also creates sand structures at the bottom of the tower and covered areas (oasis) in the desert where the living modules can be placed and benefit of the conditions provided by these structures (shadows, air flow circulation, humidity accumulation) obtaining basic conditions for trees and plants prosperity and diffusion.

The Injector is a framework that can be built out of site. Initially assembled as pure structure with only body skin and sinter machine, it can be then moved to the site, where, thanks to its mobile arms, it can orient itself for optimal sun energy capture.

The project suggest a shift in the way we conceive hi-rise building, our understanding of this typology in relation with the concept of living, inhabitation and sustainability.

The skyscraper itself is no more a process outcome, an object that stores permanently users life. instead it becomes a process trigger, a machine that produces the conditions for living, combining clean energy and innovative production methodologies that involves the usage of in-site materials (sand silica).

Desertification is a phenomenon that ranks among the greatest environmental challenges of our time. Although desertification can include the encroachment of sand dunes on land, it mainly consists of the degradation of dry land ecosystems by human activities and by climate change.

The injector seeks to trigger the processes of re-appropriation of adverse territories for human survival, especially desert environments, instead of common natural ground consuming inhabitation processes, through innovative methods for processing matter, thanks to the biggest renewable energy source we can exploit - the sun.

Nowadays we are faced with issues of energy production and raw material deficiency. The project exploits the potential of desert resources, where energy and substrate material are abundant.

0496

The Injector
Sand-scraper framework for desert reappropriation

Impact of desertification

Desertification is a global issue, with serious implications worldwide for biodiversity, eco-safety, poverty eradication, socio-economic stability and sustainable development.
Drylands are already fragile. As they become degraded, the impact on people, livestock and environment can be devastating. Some 50 million people may be displaced within the next 10 years as a result of desertification.
The issue of desertification is not new though — it played a significant role in human history, contributing to the collapse of several large empires, and the displacement of local populations. But today, the pace of arable land degradation is estimated at 30 to 35 times the historical rate.

Desertification and Poverty

Some two billion people depend on ecosystems in dry land areas, 90% of whom live in developing countries.
A downward spiral is created in many underdeveloped countries where overpopulation causes pressure to exploit drylands for farming. These marginally productive regions are overgrazed, the land is exhausted and groundwater is overdrafted.
When rural land becomes unable to support the local population the result is mass migrations to urban areas.
The increased frequency and severity of droughts resulting from projected climate change is likely to further exacerbate desertification.

Sand solar sinter

In the deserts of the world two elements dominate - sun and sand. The former offers a vast energy source of huge potential, the latter an almost unlimited supply of silica in the form of quartz. Silicia sand when heated to melting point and allowed to cool solidifies as glass. This process of converting a powdery substance via a heating process into a solid form is known as sintering and has in recent years become a central process in design prototyping known as 3D printing or SLS (selective laser sintering). These 3D printers use laser technology to create very precise 3D objects from a variety of powdered plastics, resins and metals - the objects being the exact physical counterparts of the computer-drawn 3D designs inputted by the designer. By using the sun's rays instead of a laser and sand instead of resins, Markus Kaiser had the basis of an entirely new solar-powered machine and production process for making glass objects that taps into the abundant supplies of sun and sand to be found in the deserts of the world.

The main project potential lies in its productive core, composed by platforms and machines for a 3D sand-sinter. The blades that make up the facade can be dynamically oriented to optimize solar energy harvesting and to reflect and converge sunrays to the core tower, where the sintering takes place. This machine prints minimal living modules from sand silica, in the form of quartz, which can be stored in stations inside the tower structure. The sintering machine also creates sand structures at the bottom of the tower and covered areas like an oasis in the desert where the living modules can be placed and benefit from the conditions provided by these structures, such as shadows, air flow circulation, humidity accumulation, while obtaining basic conditions for trees and plants prosperity and diffusion.

The Injector is a framework that can be built out of site. Initially assembled as pure structure with only

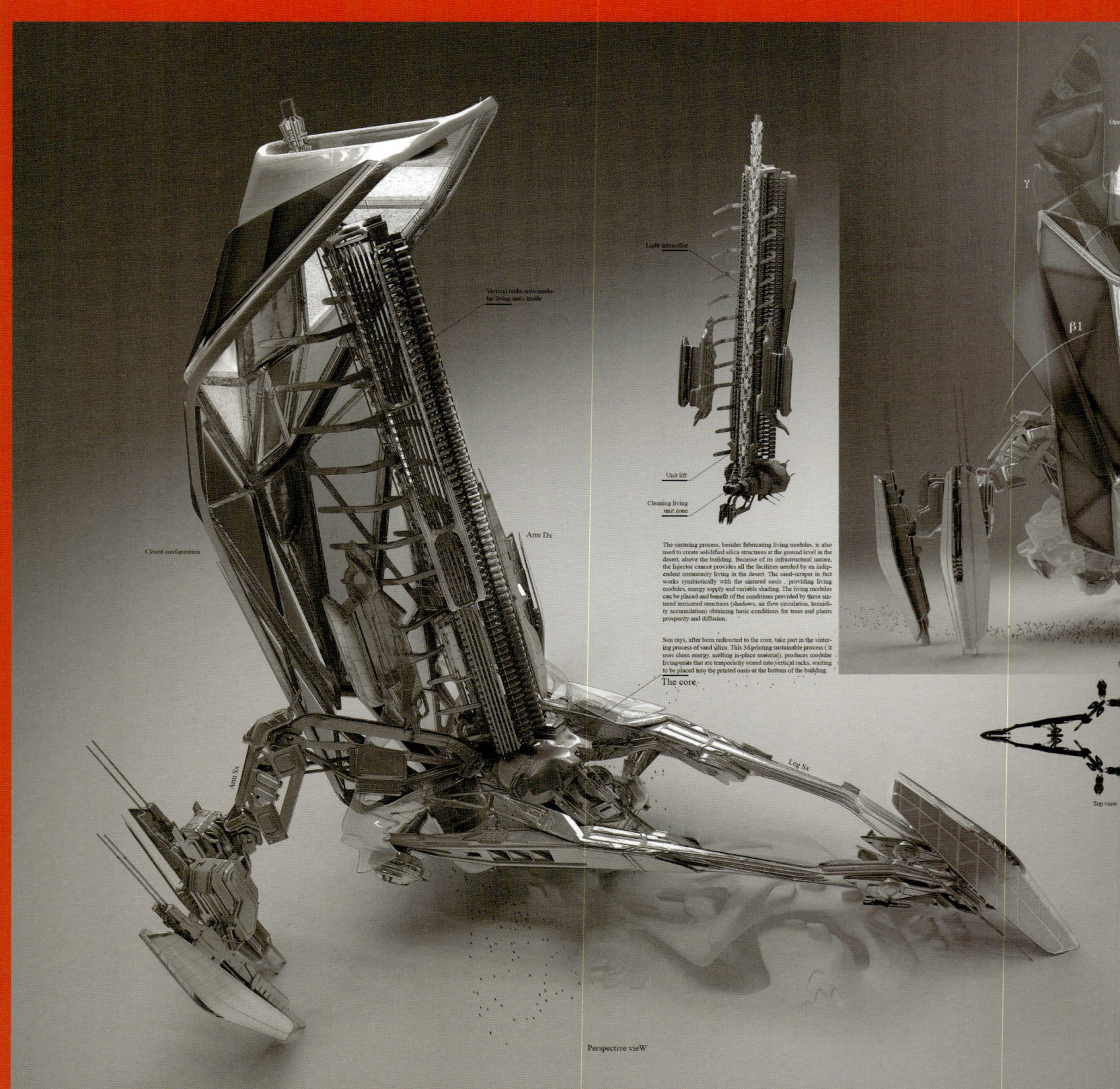

body skin and sinter machine, it can be then moved to the site, where, thanks to its mobile arms, it can orient itself for optimal sun energy capture.

The project suggests a shift in the way we conceive high-rise building, our understanding of this typology in relation with the concept of living, inhabitation, and sustainability.

The skyscraper itself is no more a process outcome, an object that permanently stores its users' life. Instead, it becomes a process trigger, a machine that produces the conditions for living, combining clean energy and innovative production methodologies that involve the usage of on-site materials like sand silica.

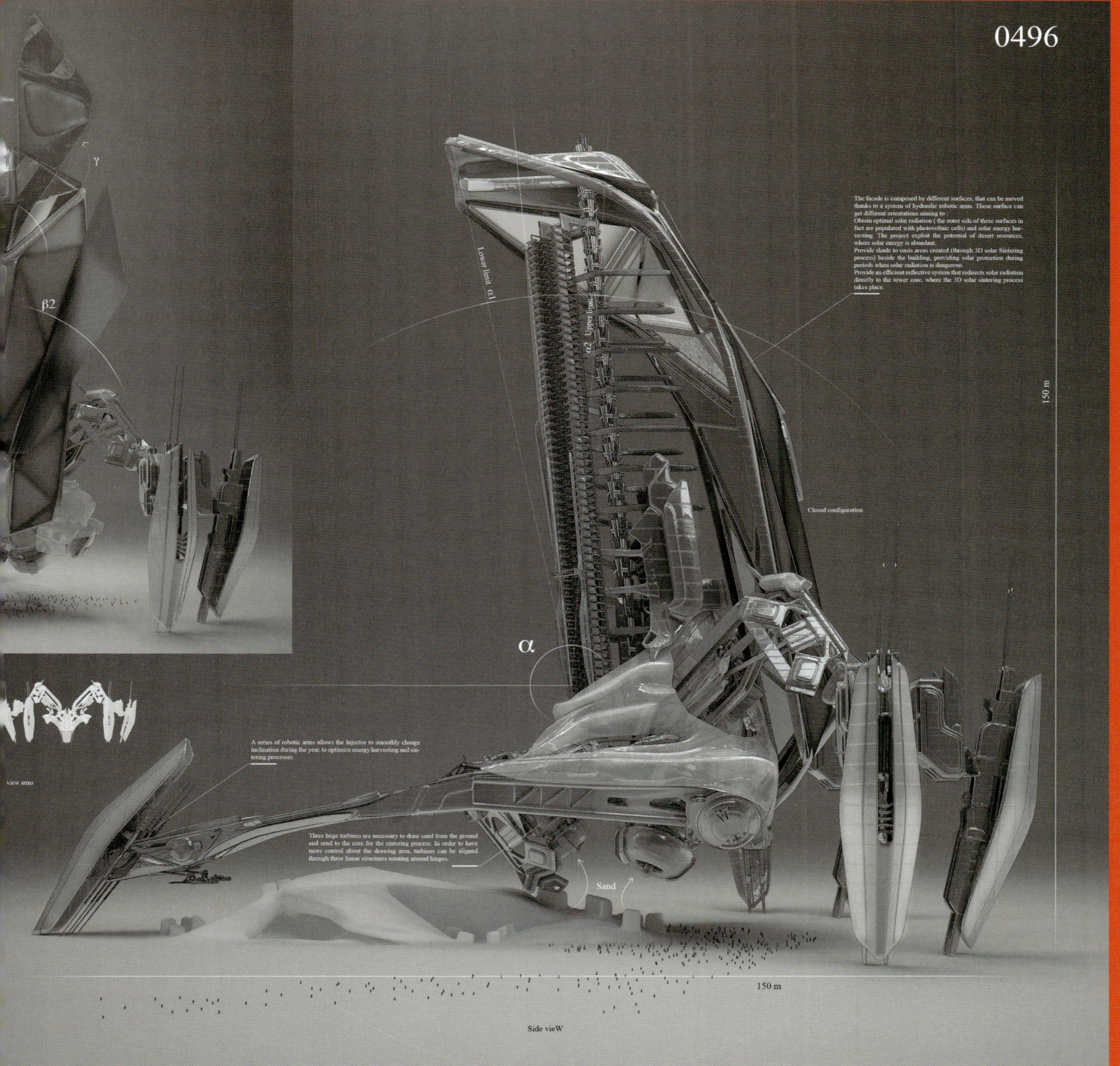

QUAKE CANOPY

Glen Marquardt
Ian Miley
Aleksis Bertoni

United States

QUAKE CANOPY

ACCORDING TO A STUDY BY THE U.S. GEOLOGICAL SURVEY, CALIFORNIA HAS A 99.7 PERCENT CHANCE OF EXPERIENCING A 7.0 MAGNITUDE OR LARGER EARTHQUAKE IN THE NEXT 25 YEARS. IN DANGEROUS PROXIMITY TO THE VOLATILE HAYWARD AND SAN ANDREAS FAULTS, SAN FRANCISCO INARGUABLY HAS THE HIGHEST RISK FOR DEVASTATING AMOUNTS OF INFRASTRUCTURAL DAMAGE IN THE CASE OF A LARGE EARTHQUAKE. TO PRE-EMPTIVELY ANTICIPATE AND REMEDY THE DAMAGE, A NETWORK OF SELF-SUFFICIENT SUPERSTRUCTURES WILL BE CONSTRUCTED ON AND AROUND THE SAN FRANCISCO PENINSULA. PRE-QUAKE, THEY WILL FUNCTION AS ENERGY GENERATORS (SOLAR, WIND, GEOTHERMAL) AND ADDRESS THE EVER-INCREASING DEMAND FOR REAL ESTATE AND HOUSING; PROVIDING MAXIMUM AMOUNTS OF BUILDING POTENTIAL WITH MINIMAL FOOTPRINTS.

SAN FRANCISCO

PROJECTED LOSSES   SOIL LIQUEFACTION VULNERABILITY   SPECULATIVE NETWORK ARRANGEMENT

THE SUPERSTRUCTURAL LAYERED EXOSKELETON, CORE, DEEP PILES, AND EXCESS LATERAL BRACING ENSURE THE STRUCTURES WILL REMAIN STANDING WHEN THE 'BIG ONE' DOES HIT SAN FRANCISCO. THE UPPER LAYER OF THE NETWORK IS CONNECTED, ALLOWING FOR STRUCTURAL CODEPENDENCE AND SUPPORT BETWEEN THE STRUCTURES. AT THE TIME OF THE QUAKE, PIEZOELECTRIC (MOTION GENERATED ELECTRICITY) CABLES HARVEST THE MAXIMUM AMOUNT OF USABLE ENERGY TO IMMEDIATELY POWER RESCUE, RELIEF AND RECONSTRUCTION EFFORTS. TO ALLOW FOR INCREASED HABITATION OF THE CANOPY AS RECOVERY CONTINUES, A TERTIARY TENSILE SYSTEM OF CABLES AND POST-TENSIONED SLABS CAN SUPPORT A NUMBER OF CONSTRUCTION METHODS, ALLOWING FOR AS-NEEDED DEVELOPMENT OF HOUSING, FARMING, AND OTHER INFRASTRUCTURAL NECESSITIES, EFFECTIVELY SERVING AS THE FRAMING FOR A NEW, POST-QUAKE CITY.

ENERGY GENERATION

AGRICULTURE
CROPS AND GREENERY OCCUPY THE EXTERIOR RING AND TOP CANOPY WITH ACCESS TO MAXIMUM SUNLIGHT

SOLAR
FIELD OF MECHANIZED MIRRORS ON THE CANOPY SURFACE TRACK THE SUN, REFLECTING SOLAR RADIATION TOWARDS AN ULTRACAPACITY PHOTOVOLTAIC RECIEVER ATOP THE CENTRAL SPIRE

WIND
THE STRUCTURAL EXOSKELETON SUPPORTS A NET OF MICROTURBINES, HARVESTING WIND ENERGY AND SHIELDING THE INTERIOR

SEISMIC
AT EACH STRUCTURE'S BASE IS A PIEZOELECTRIC GENERATOR SUPPORTING A NETWORK OF UNDERGROUND MOTION SENSITIVE CABLES

GEOTHERMAL
GEOTHERMAL PUMPS EXTEND ALONG STRUCTURAL PILES DEEP INTO EARTH'S CRUST

According to a study by the U.S. Geological Survey, California has a 99.7 percent chance of experiencing a 7.0 magnitude or larger earthquake in the next 25 years.

In dangerous proximity to the volatile Hayward and San Andreas faults, San Francisco inarguably has the highest risk for devastating amounts of infrastructural damage in the case of a large earthquake. To preemptively anticipate and remedy the damage, a network of self-sufficient superstructures will be constructed on and around the San Francisco peninsula. Pre-quake, they will function as energy generators (solar, wind, geothermal) and address the ever-increasing demand for real estate and housing; providing maximum amounts of building potential with minimal footprints.

The superstructure layered exoskeleton, core, deep piles, and excess lateral bracing ensure the

structures will remain standing when the 'big one' does hit San Francisco. The upper layer of the network is connected, allowing for structural codependence and support between the structures.

At the time of the quake, piezoelectric (motion generated electricity) cables harvest the maximum amount of usable energy to immediately power rescue, relief and reconstruction efforts. To allow for increased habitation of the Canopy as recovery continues, a tertiary tensile system of cables and post-tensioned slabs can support a number of construction methods, allowing for as-needed development of housing, farming, and other infrastructural necessities, effectively serving as the framing for a new city.

The height of the structures will be calibrated according to housing and farming needs. The idea is that this network will provide enough infrastructure for San Francisco's growth in the next 30 years.

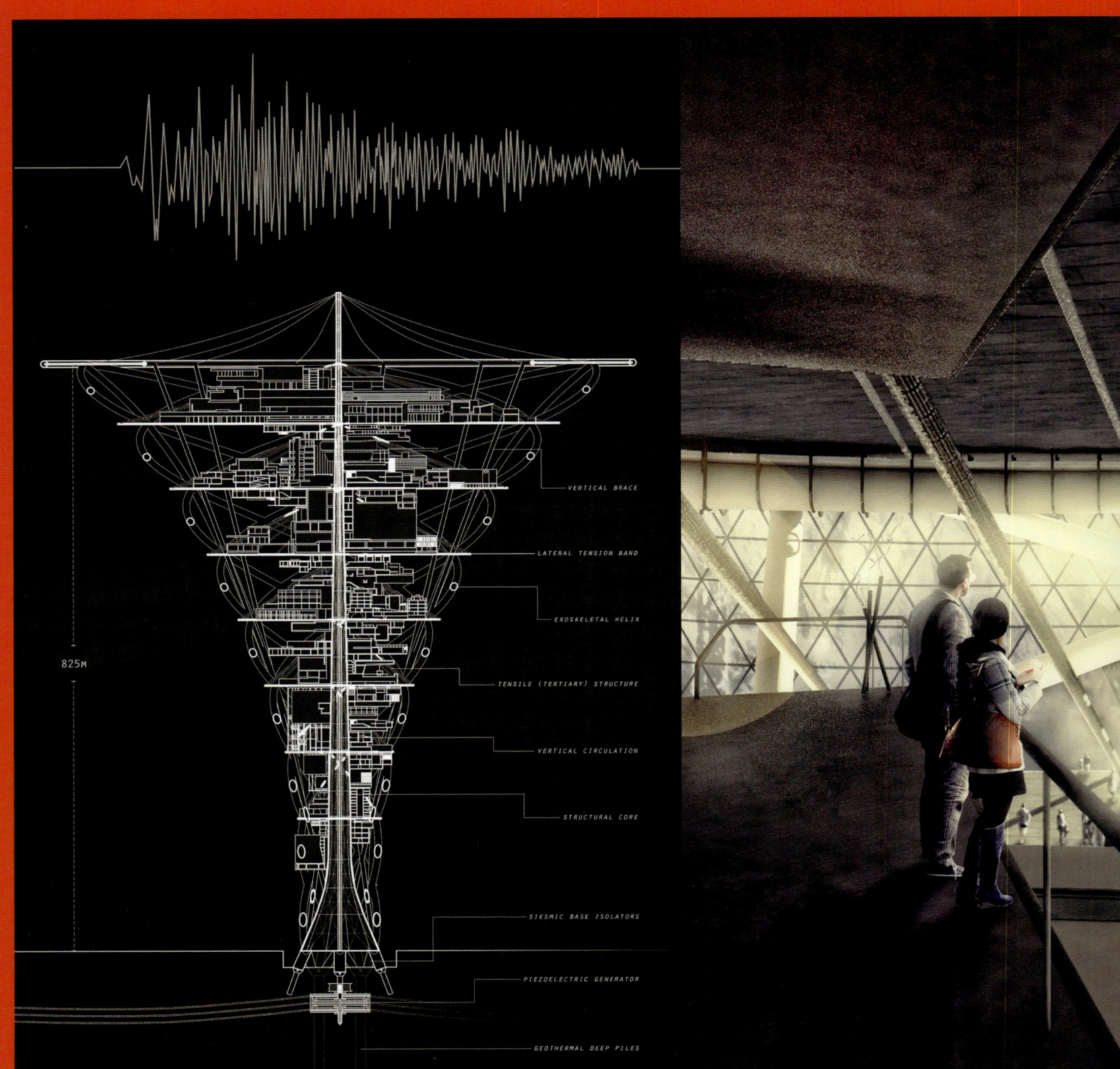

Inside the towers residents and city dwellers will enjoy various recreational parks and commercial areas. The towers will work as small interconnected cities, fully dependable on their own in terms of eneregy and food production. When combined as a network they will provide the surplus resources to the city. In case of emergencies, the habitable spaces will be transformed to help in the prompt recovery of the city.

SAND BABEL

Qiu Song
Kang Pengfei
Bai Ying
Ren Nuoya
Guo Shen

China

Sand Babel is a group of ecological structures designed as scientific research facilities and tourist attractions for the desert. The structures are divided into two parts. The first part, above ground, consists of several independent structures for a desert community while the second part is partially underground and partially above ground connecting several buildings and creating a multi-functional tube network system.

The main portion of each building is constructed with sand, sintered through a solar-powered 3D printer. The top structures are based on the natural phenomena called tornadoes and mushroom rocks, which is very common in deserts. It utilizes a spiral skeleton structure, which is tall, straight and with strong tension, to meet the requirements of residential, sightseeing and scientific research facilities. The dual funnel model not only improves cross-ventilation, but also generates water condensation atop the

SAND BABEL

SOLAR-POWERED 3D PRINGTING TOWER

0656

Background

When we first visited the Sahara Desert in southern Algeria and saw a seemingly boundless expanse of sand further than the eye could see, we thought of the planet Akrrakis from the movie Dune. As a designer, not a science fiction movie director, my initial instinct to transform the desert led us to begin a feasibility study on constructing man-made residences in the desert. In our view, this not only increases the amount of living space available for mankind, but also protects against the ever-increasing threat of desertification.

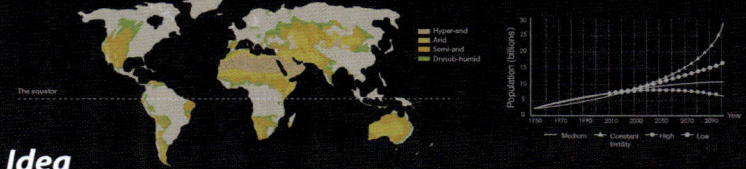

Idea

Thanks to advances in manufacturing technology, specifically in the form of Solar-sintering 3D Printers, our design may one day come to fruition. In my eyes, sand is a perfect building material – it has stable chemical and strong physical properties and is resistant to weathering. The sand is our thermoplastic powder and the ample sunlight of the Sahara is our inexhaustible source of energy. Sand and sunlight, these are the sources of Sand Babel.

3D Printing & Structure

Solar Energy +3D Printer + Sand ⎯⎯ Sintering / Building ⎯⎯→ Sand Babel

Sand Babel, which is a group of ecological structures, is built in the vastness of desert, serves the purposes of both scientific inquiry and sightseeing. The structures are divided into two parts. The first part is above ground part that consists of many independent structures and forms a well-proportioned Desert Community. The other part is underground and surface, which is connected by buildings, and creates a multi-functional tube network system.

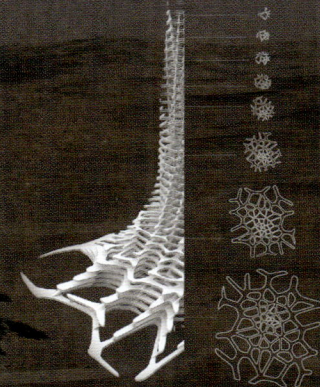

The main portion of each building is constructed by the material made from the sintered sand through a solar-powered 3D printer. The form of the aboveground structures are designed based on nature phenomena of desert called Tornadoes and Mushroom Rocks. It utilizes a spiral skeleton structure, which is tall, straight and with strong tension, to meet the requirements of residential, sightseeing and scientific research. The Dual Funnel Model not only improves cross-ventilation inside, but also generates condensation water at the top of structures based on the temperature difference between ground and above higher. Then the collected condensation water supplies the Sand Babel. The net structure for the portion of underground and surface is similar to tree roots. This design not only helps to fix flowing sand dunes in place such as structures is rooted, but also facilitates communication among the buildings.

Green Architecture

Sand Babel is also a future Green Architecture in light of its sustainable development. It harnesses local resources by using 3D printing technology to turn sand into building materials, thus cost of construction materials and transportation is dramatically reduced. It also helps to solve he problem of sand dune stabilization effectively. In addition, with intension to have a zero carbon footprint, the buildings utilize temperature difference to create internal airflow and water vapor condensation, and use solar energy, wind energy, plus temperature difference to generate clean energy for the complex.

Sand Babel can be called as wonderful flower of desert. It opens up new series of thoughts and establishes a new model to harness desert for mankind.

structures based on temperature differences. The net structure for the portion of underground and surface is similar to tree roots. This design not only helps to keep flowing sand dunes in place but also facilitates communication among the buildings.

Over time, the construction of several buildings will create a complex network in the desert that will serve as the blueprint for new cities. These cities will emerge from a carefully articulated grid that will subdivide areas according to use, proximity with other areas, and environmental data. The new city would inherit a DNA to grow in the most efficient and sustainable way. Soon, portions of these arid regions would be transformed into lushed slef-sustainable environments.

Gradually new buildings will emerge and new networks will be created. A series of new cities will then

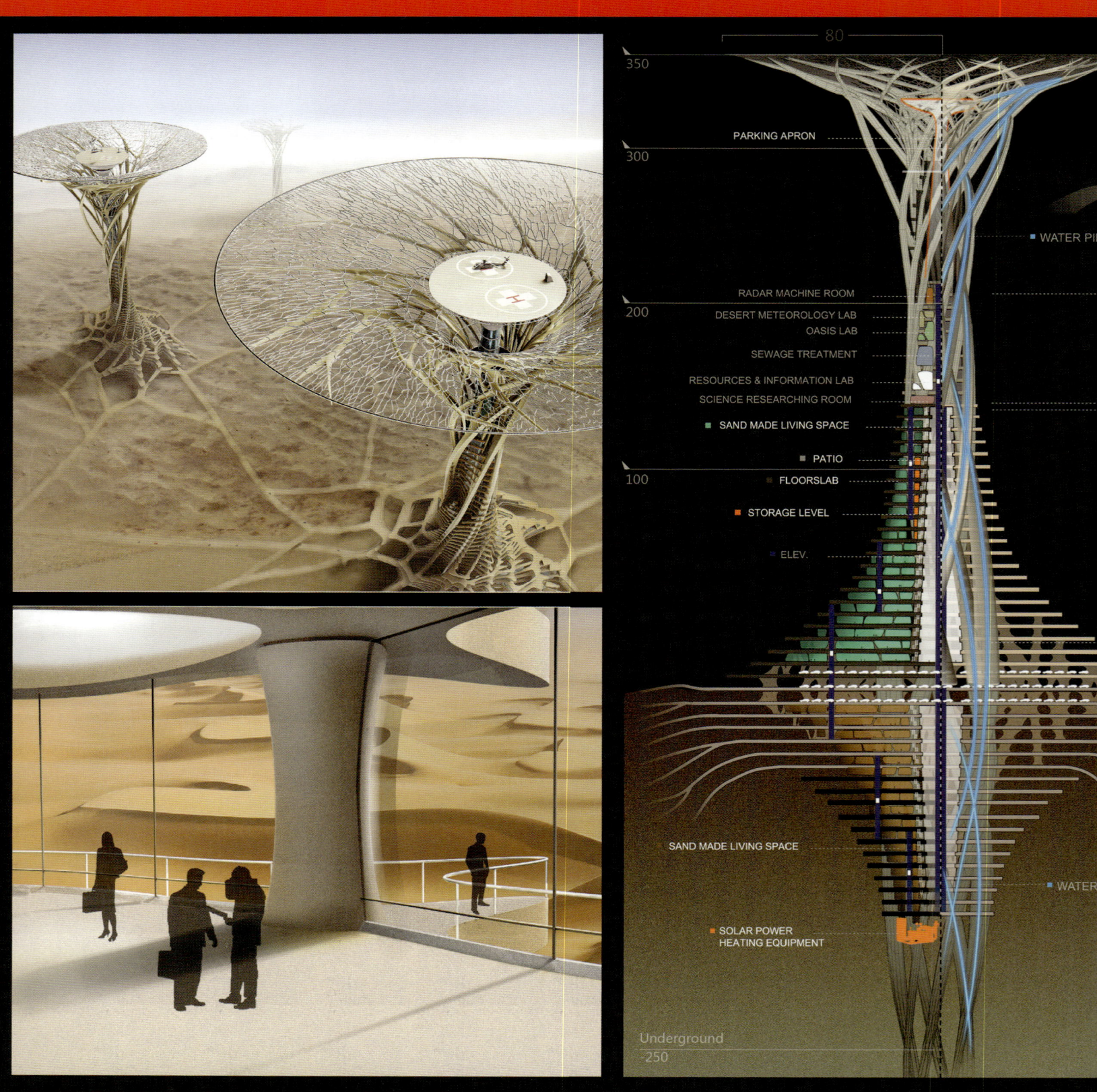

be interconnected and large portions of inhabitable deserts will be occupied. These 3-D printed towers are the first step in a series of changes needed to ptovide new cities to the world's ever growing poplution. The big difference bewteen Sand Babel and traditional cities is that these communities would be 100% sustainable and self-sufficient - true cities for the 21st Century ready for the exploration and transformation of new territories. Similar concepts could be used to terraform planets in the distant future -conceptual proposals from NASA explore these ideas.

0656

SAND BABEL

SOLAR-POWERED 3D PRINGTING TOWER

WATER PIPE & BRACKET

EMERGENCY GENERATING SET & WATER MANAGEMENT

LIFT PLATFORM & OBSERVATION

RESTAURANT

SIGHTSEEING & REPAIR PLATFORM

AIR CORRIDOR

TOURISM & ACTIVITY SPACE

NTIFIC
IRY PART

G PART

▶ Condensate-gathering Net
Collecting Condensate Water in the Top of Building
Transporting and Storing the Condensate Water

▶ Solar-powered 3D Printing Technology & Mesh-form Sand Fixation StructureStructure
Preventing Sand to Move
Rooting Buildings
Constructing Channels of Buildings

▶ Helix-form Dual Funnel Model
Enhancing the Building Interior Air Circulation

Based on the temperature control system of termite nest, the hollow structure utilizes the temperature difference between high and low altitudes to create warm air flow upwards, enough to hold asund nets. Combined with the stable triangular shape of the main body, the hollow structure will make the entire building safe and study, and also contributes to air circulation.

Reducing the Building External Wind Drag
Conducive to Reinforce the Building Structure

Hot Air

BAMBOO FOREST

Thibaut Deprez

France

BAMBOO FOREST

When skyscrapers and scaffoldings achieve symbiosis

Used as a traditional building material in numerous regions of the world, bamboo is now only used for the construction of buildings in Asia's great megalopolises. In this context, it was used for the scaffolding of five of the greatest skyscrapers in the world. It continues to be used for other buildings, without for all that being restored to its historical use. It could be otherwise because, by making these scaffoldings permanent, the presence of bamboo at the heart of the cities could be renewed. Moreover, it would endow the buildings with new qualities.

STARTING CONSTRUCTION

Light and resistant, bamboo is traditionally used as a building material in numerous regions around the globe. Over time, its allocation was somewhat modified, especially in Asia. Henceforth, within great cities, it is restricted to being used as a building construction support. In this way, it was used for the scaffolding of five of the greatest skyscrapers in the world.

Bamboo scaffolding served the splendor of these constructions, but also contributed to the erection of many much more modest towers. These towers make us feel ill at ease because of the harshness and coldness of their frontages. The virtually infinite stacking of identical stories annihilates all human expressions and interactions. Abruptly cloned, these towers produce oppressing dormitory towns.

The stance of this project is set up around the observation of the harshness of these towers and to

1. CONCEPT

Once the buildings are completed, bamboo scaffoldings are dismantled and reassembled elsewhere. They let appear cold and harsh standardized residential blocks. By contrast, the scaffoldings that raise them present interesting patterns and shapes, due to the variability proper to their self-building properties. They would be an appreciable alternative to the harshness of these buildings. Developed in resonance with the building they erect, they could enhance them with new qualities at a lesser cost while respecting conventional building techniques. Indeed, since the scaffolding is absolutely necessary to the edification, its original conception doesn't imply any excessive additional cost.

Deployed on new buildings, bamboo scaffoldings could also be integrated to more ancient ones, using the load-bearing capacity reserves of reinforced concrete. In this way, for each building, a distinctive form of second skin made of bamboo could be found by analysing the load-carrying capacity of the building while confronting it with other criteria, notably sunshine, size and near neighbourhood.

0733

?

SHANGHAI SUBURBS

LIFELESS ENVIRONMENT

RUCTION   CONSTRUCTION PHASE FINISHED   BUILDING COMPLETED   CLONING PHASE   SUBURBS TEXTURE

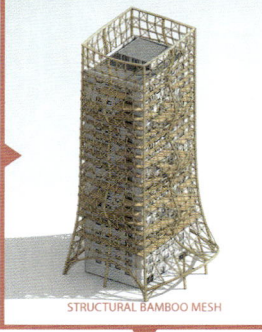

MAKING SCAFFOLDINGS PERMANENT !

SCAFFOLDINGS AS TERRACE SUPPORTS   STRUCTURAL BAMBOO MESH

VARIATIONS ACCORDING TO PARAMETERS
BUILDING TYPOLOGY, CLIMATE DATA, URBAN CONTEXT, FORMAL IDENTITY

suggest a solution.

The project offers to use bamboo scaffoldings as a driving force to promote the revival of these buildings. By making them permanent and inseparable from the construction. They endow the towers with an external surface which the inhabitants can directly claim and where life can expand. They produce a net which can be fashioned according to the circumstances, specific to each building and give each one a true identity.

They promote the emergence of authentic vertical gardens in places where density does not allow the establishment of horizontal gardens. Furthermore, they favor the stabilization of structures during earthquakes and support an ecological production of energy - towers and bamboo scaffoldings achieve

2. ADVANTAGES OF BAMBOO

Used in numerous regions of the globe (Asia, America, Africa, Oceania), bamboo presents surprising qualities which have made it a popular building material since time immemorial.

	COMPRESSION STRENGTH	TENSILE STRENGTH	YOUNG MODULUS
BAMBOO	200 MPa	70 Mpa	13500 MPa
PINE	100 MPa	50 Mpa	12000 MPa
CONCRETE	5 MPa	25 Mpa	17000 MPa
STEEL	400 MPa	400 MPa	200000 MPa

Just like grass, corn or wheat, bamboo is a plant in the grass family Poaceae. It has unique structural characteristics that can be linked with those of trees. With a flexural modulus (Young's modulus) of about 13500 MPa, an ultimate tensile strength of around 200 MPa and an ultimate compressive strength of 70 MPa, bamboo has a resistance superior to the most commonly used woods in construction (pine, Douglas fir, oak). It is also superior to standard concrete in tensile and compressive strength. Thanks to its nature, bamboo is structurally viable for the edification of buildings.

It has another advantage as compared to wood and concrete: its ability to withstand very high accidental external constraints, which is rather interesting in a region of the world where earthquakes are both frequent and intense.

It is light (mass density: 700 kg/m3; concrete: 2500 kg/m3), hence easy to transport and apply. Ingrained in various construction cultures, its traditional and unique know-how has allowed the development of numerous applications, houses, churches, bridges, hydraulic infrastructures, etc.

7 years   30 to 50 years

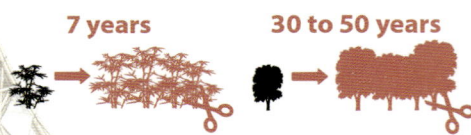

Thanks to a very high growth rate (certain species can grow at a rate of a meter per day), it is quickly available. It typically takes around 7 years to harvest bamboo, as opposed to 30 to 50 years for trees. Bamboo has a productive capacity as a building material which is 20 times superior to that of trees and a better energy efficiency (energy balance of steel: 1500 MJ/m3; cement: 240 MJ/ m3, wood: 80 MJ/m3, bamboo: 30 MJ/ m3).

+30% CO_2 captured   **+30% O_2** produced

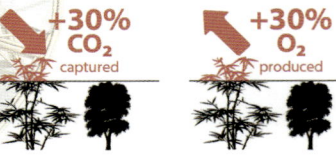

Its incredible ability to capture CO2 and to produce O2 (almost 30% superior to deciduous trees) as well as its role in soil regeneration and remediation contribute to demonstrating its ecological qualities.
Even if it appears to be naturally less sensitive to water and insect related damage, bamboo needs to be treated in order to improve its longevity. Natural techniques have been developed to satisfy this requirement. In this way, it can meet the standards of sustainable construction.

3. ADVANTAGES FOR THE

Bamboo scaffoldings provide numerous ternal surface the inhabitants can direct open to all kinds of individual or collecti

With their distinctive shapes developed aesthetics and identity.

They reinstate bamboo as a building ma

Another advantage is that they particip bamboos act as bracings and carries a strength that can be sought as a respons

The introduction of plants in the buildin mizes noise pollution and allows water t mitted to a first filtration and is then rei

Finally, bamboo scaffoldings increase th wind turbines, solar panels and photovo

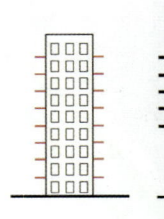

TERRACES   BUIL

STANDARD BUILDING

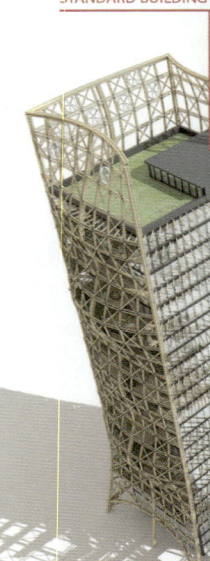

symbiosis.

With the construction of this secondary bamboo skin, the original facade of these buildings could be transformed into a more porous entity to allow visual and physical connections with the city. The interstitial space beween the old and new skins is a tremendous opportunity to be exploited, not only as green areas, but as a chance to examine a new set of programs that could emerge in these conditions.

Visually, they would transform the cities into friendlier environments while providing an opportunity to expand and explore their own identity.

G / BENEFITS OF PERMANENT SCAFFOLDING

the edifice it is built against. They extend the building with an ex-
ate. This surface, in between the walls of the building and the net, is
ging gardens, shade terraces, small sports fields, religious altars, etc.

nique context proper to each building, they define their very own

big cities and bridge the gap between tradition and innovation.

stability of the building. Indeed, the intersected mesh structure of
lateral loads due to wind. This interweaving also defines a reserve
thquake.

anging gardens contributes to the reduction of air pollution, mini-
rally. As water follows the building's pockets of vegetation, it is sub-
e water system.

surface for energy production. They act as a mounting support for

ILITY   WATER FILTRATION   ENERGY PRODUCTION

MBOO BEAMS

WIND TURBINES AND PHOTOVOLTAIC
CELLS ON FLEXIBLE FABRIC

VEGETATED TERRACES

BAMBOO MESH

4.   ADVANTAGES FOR THE CITY

Bamboo scaffoldings produce the Asian megalopolis. They follow its evolution and make its mutations perceptible. They are ephemeral, transitory structures. By becoming permanent, they persistently bring a new texture to the city. Updated at the heart of the cities, bamboo positions itself as an alternative to concrete, steel and glass. It links the city to its history and to the territory. It allows the continuation of an ancestral know-how and exposes it to ever more inventive applications.

Bamboo scaffoldings can be used as individual or collective vertical gardens where lack of space doesn't allow them to be established on the ground. They are then set up in areas with a high built-up density where they act as real lungs.

Finally, the emergence of new uses at the heart of the bamboo net institutes a new centrality for the building. With its double skin, the tower becomes a point of focus from which both city and life can unfold.

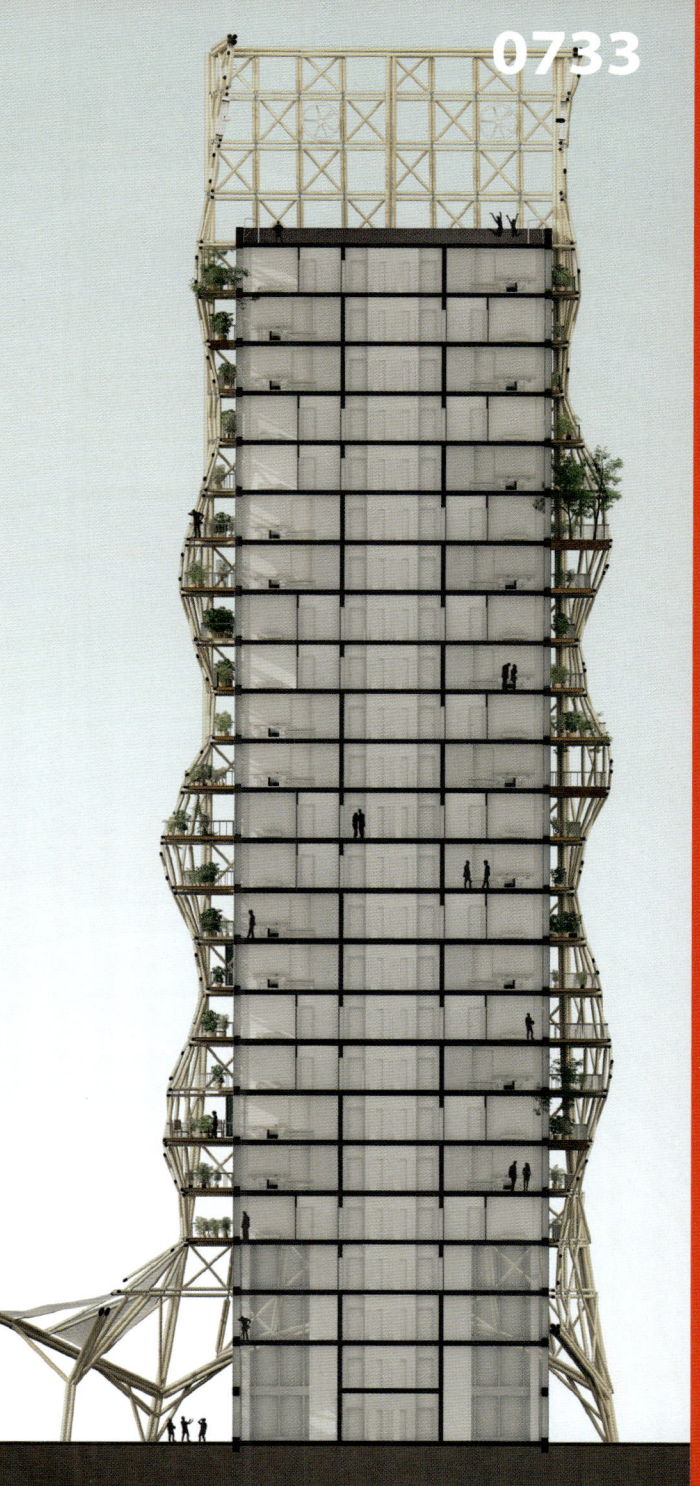

0733

URBAN ALLOY TOWER

Matt Bowles
Chad Kellog

United States

A. B. C.

ALLOY SYSTEMS:

1. Unlike concrete structures that benefit from a very regular floor to floor height because of the need to reuse form-work, steel structures can efficiently be constructed with each unique member cut by an automated system.
2. GPS systems can handle geometric complexity of the overall structure via locating each member during the erection process.
3. Cantilevers – favorable strength to weight ratio allowing large cantilevers and small footprints
4. High recycled content and positive life cycle analysis
Unitized Curtain Wall System:
1. With the rapid acceleration of automated manufacturing processes, mass customization and automated assembly has begun, and will replace traditional building techniques.
2. Precision
3. Slender structural profile - maximizes views and daylight
4. Ability to efficiently Unitize

PLAN

ELEVATION

The combination of escalating land prices and the acceleration of city migration have made urban renewal based modes of densification unfit for the contemporary city. Urban Alloy is the symbiotic repurposing of the air rights above transportation corridors in New York. Urban planners have long touted the benefits of greater housing density near public transportation hubs - Urban Alloy proposes the advancement of this idea by locating the system directly on the intersections between surface and elevated train lines. We have chosen the intersection of the LIRR and the 7 trains as a test case.

The paradigm of one-size fits all is obsolete. Urban citizens want diverse living situations where they can work, play, eat and rest within a pedestrian zone. As technology creates the market desire and a conditioning for personalization, society is more willing to pay a premium for spaces that are tailored to

INTER-MODAL ATRIUM

URBAN ALLOY

#0806

The most dynamic cities of the 21st century, such as New York, are anthropomorphic alloys that act as engines for innovation and social cohesion. These cities, with their continually evolving demographics, will forge the dynamic societies of the future. With the rapid rise of near instantaneous communication, a city's' livability has gained prominence as an attractor for top minds. In order to secure its future as the leading global center, New York needs to continue to grow in smart ways. We see the opportunity to draw the energy of Manhattan out into the four other boroughs without disrupting existing land use. We propose a residential typology rooted in the remnant spaces surrounding the intersection of transportation infrastructure, such as elevated train lines and freeway interchanges. With the proposed design and specified materials, we aim to optimize a heterogeneous and highly linked set of living environments capturing the air rights above these systems.

SUMMER SUN

WINTER SUN

HORIZONTAL SHADING

COMPOSITE SHADING ALGORITHM

MORNING SUN   AFTERNOON SUN

VERTICAL SHADING

SECTIONAL PERSPECTIVE

their particular needs. The towers' design facilitates a continuous blend of program and space types that are accommodated by a spectrum of floor heights and enclosure conditions.

The skin concept reflects a desire to optimize shading and day lighting performance on the surface of a complex volume. The surface of the towers transitions from a cylindrical to a triangular extrusion across its height in relation to the blend in floor heights. A composite or alloy of multiple flexible systems is required to optimize a skin in which every point has a unique environmental exposure. The system developed for this structure is deployed on a grid that follows the geometric directionality of the surface. At each intersection of the grid the normal of the surface is analyzed against its optimal solar shading and daylight transmitting requirements. An authored algorithm then generates vertical and horizontal fin profiles that blend with

TYPICAL LIVING SPACE

LIVING

The combination
the acceleration
urban renewal
unfit for the co
is the symbiotic
above transport
Urbanist's have
greater housing
tation hubs - U
vancement of t
directly on the
and elevated tra
intersection of
test case. The p
obsolete. Urban
situations where
rest within a pe
creates the ma
for personalizat
pay a premium
their particular
describing the v

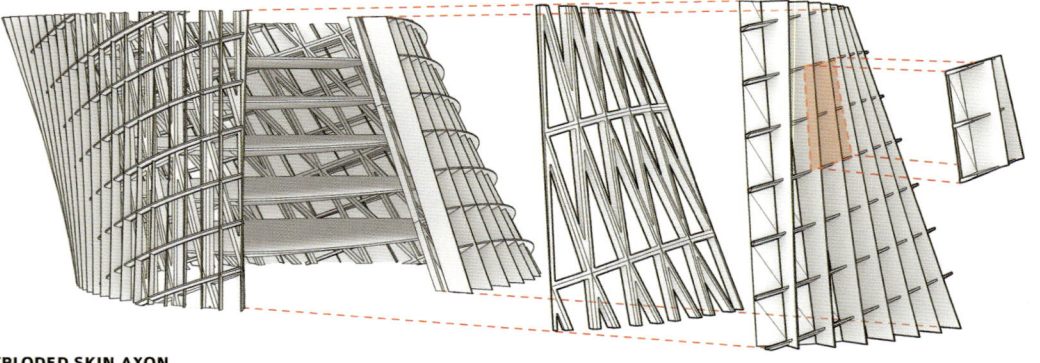

EXPLODED SKIN AXON

OPTIMIZED SHELL

The skin concept reflects a desire to optimize shading and daylighting performance on the surface of a complex volume. The surface of the towers transition from a cylindrical to a triangular extrusion across it's height in relation to the blend in floor heights. A composite or alloy of multiple flexible systems is required to optimize a skin in which every point has a unique environmental exposure. The system developed for this structure is deployed on a grid that follows the geometric directionality of the surface. At each intersection of the grid the normal of the surface is analyzed against its optimal solar shading and daylight transmitting requirements. An authored algorithm then generates vertical and horizontal fin profile that blends with profiles at adjacent intersections. The result is an optimized system of decorative metal fins that are unique but fabricated with the same logic and process.

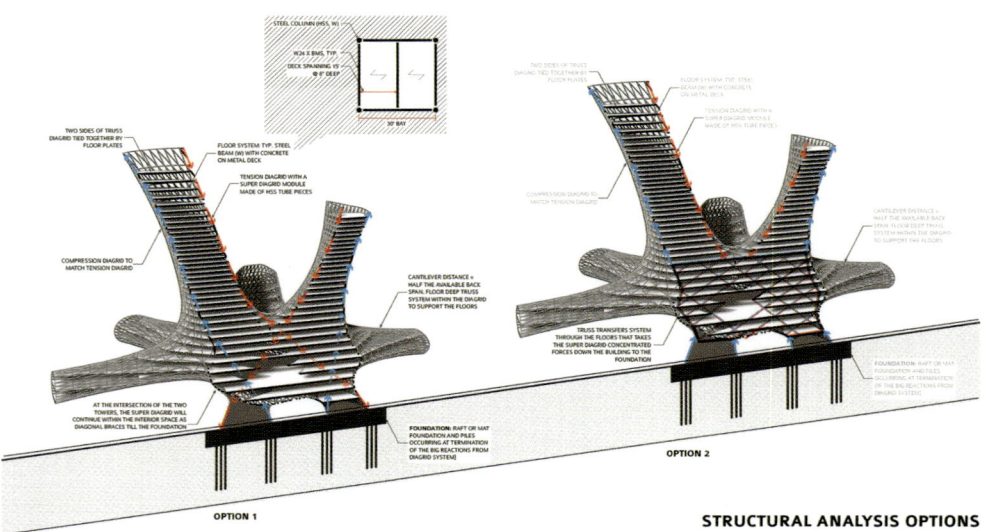

OPTION 1   OPTION 2

STRUCTURAL ANALYSIS OPTIONS

profiles at adjacent intersections. The result is an optimized system of decorative metal fins that are unique but fabricated with the logic and process described below.

The steel diagrid structural system can efficiently be constructed with each unique member cut by an automated system. GPS systems can handle the geometric complexity of the overall structure via locating each member during the erection process. Cantilevers benefit from a favorable strength to weight ratio allowing large cantilevers and small footprints. With a high-recycled content and positive life cycle analysis the unitized curtain wall system will also be fabricated with rapid automated manufacturing processes. Precision and slender structural profile that maximizes views and daylight skin the entire building.

#0806

PROGRAM BLEND

EXCERPT FLOOR PLANS

PLAN KEY

LIVING 1
BEDROOM 2
FOYER 3
BATH 4
SERVICE 5
STUDY 6
STORAGE 7
MEDIA 8
STUDIO 9
CORE 10

NEW NOMADS

Wang Xinyuan
Ye Zhaodan

China

As cities change and develop, the lifestyle of people today is more and more close to becoming "mobile" in and of itself. And many cities are faced with the practical problem of residents preforming continuous migration. We believe that cities in the future will be mostly inhabited by these mobile, nomadic types. These "nomads" live to provide for oneself in the completely ephemeral, relative time by using up resources of their environments for their work or personal needs, etc. And once life in a certain place no longer serves an appeal, and the original city has overwhelmed you, dare you leave? To become a nomad? To live in a completely different environment? Humans have this dream, but seldom do they realize it.

Many "nomads" hovering in the air, can settle in any place, with a variety of aircraft shuttle in the middle. A "nomad" is almost a neighborhood, where each block has a lake, surrounded by terraced gardens. In

0074
NEW NOMADS:life is elsewhere

The design conception

Along with the change of the development mode of city ,The life of people today is more and more close to a "mobile" way. And many city are faced with the practical problem of residents of the continuous migration. City fixed in one place has been unable to adapt to the future development, and with the growth of population problems arise such as excessive resource consumption, environmental pollution etc.
We believe that the future of the city will show not fixed nomadic state. The city is relatively concentrated in a "nomad", the "nomad" can fly in the air, and replace different settlements. It is provide for oneself in the relative time, and can obtain supplies from the settlement . on the basis of resource environment, work needs or something else, "nomads" are gathered here to form city, also the overall relocation does not destroy the surface environment.

Fixed city is not suitable for living?
The big city has brought many problems_ pollution heat is not easy to diffusion, poor environmental quality; traffic congestion in the city, people more and more indifferent relationship; etc.

NEW NOMADS:life is elsewhere
When the original life no longer give you power, the original city has overwhelmed you, dare you instead? Become a nomad :live in elsewhere? Humans have this dream, but people dare to dream.

Application the theory that high speed rotating superconductor has gravity field effect to realize the anti gravity flight, pushing the air-craft in level flight with Lorenz, let the human realize the dream of NEW NOMADS

The flowing magnetic ultra fluid in red coil , drives by outer coil, ultra fluid rapid counter clockwise flow,on the basis of hand rotation theorem, generated an upward magnetic thrust..

addition to the apartment complex, there are shops, kindergartens, beauty salons, recreational facilities, parks, ponds and other facilities city residents use daily. The lake, within the city, acts as a natural water collector that collects rainwater, which, after the purification, can supply daily family and farmland irrigation needs. There is a large wind power generator, which acts as the main source of energy on the outside of the "nomad." And in the open spaces inside the city, there are tree wind generators, which power the city's lighting. Nutrients from the atmosphere, water, soil and other natural resources, are absorbed into the ecological system through the photosynthesis of green plants, flowing in a variety of biological and ecological ecosystems, eventually returning to the environment, to complete a cycle. The collective travel between each nomad uses a maglev train using among the stars, where a single trip can use a single

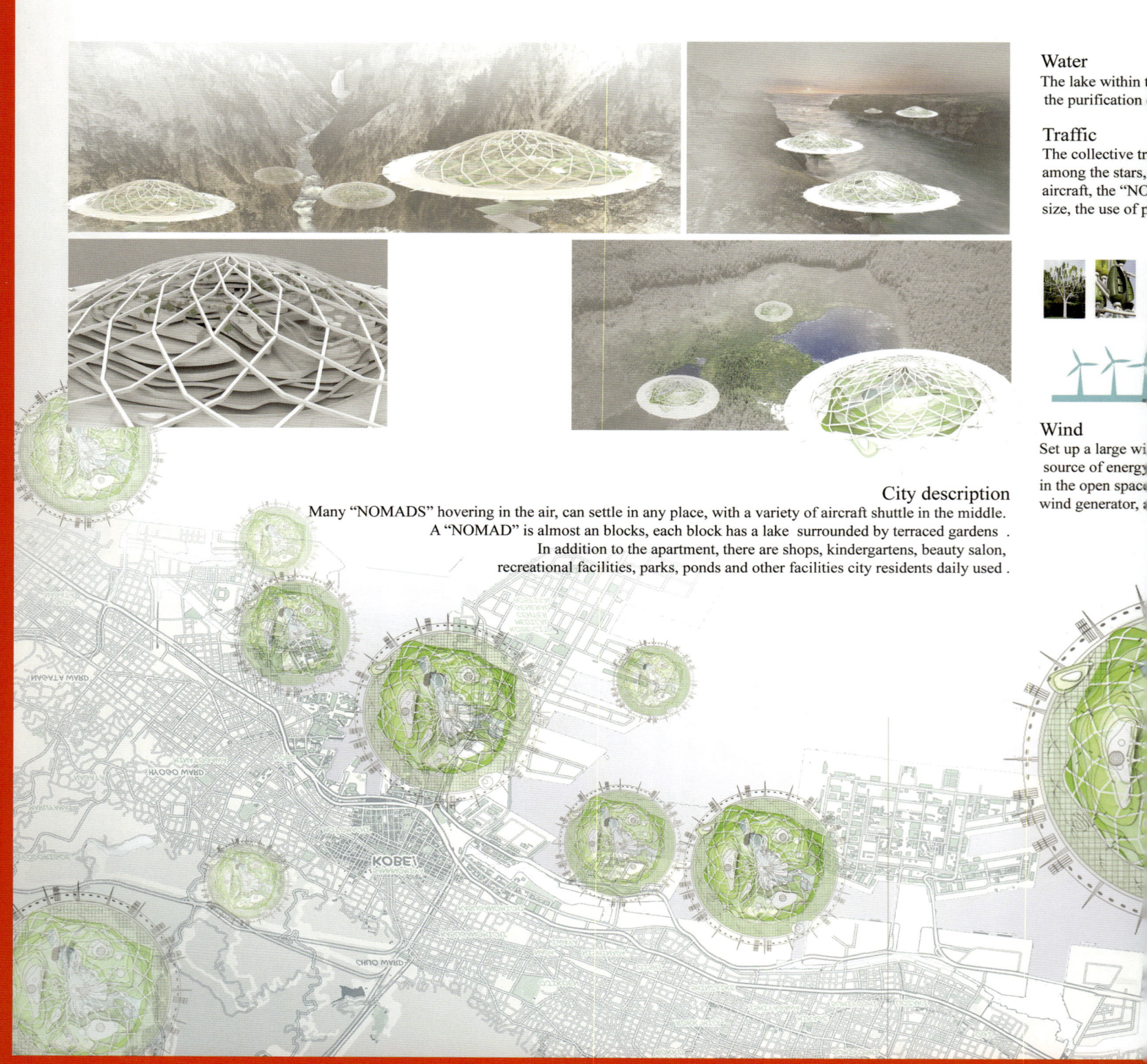

Water
The lake within t
the purification

Traffic
The collective tr
among the stars,
aircraft, the "NC
size, the use of p

Wind
Set up a large wi
source of energy
in the open space
wind generator, a

City description

Many "NOMADS" hovering in the air, can settle in any place, with a variety of aircraft shuttle in the middle.
A "NOMAD" is almost an blocks, each block has a lake surrounded by terraced gardens.
In addition to the apartment, there are shops, kindergartens, beauty salon,
recreational facilities, parks, ponds and other facilities city residents daily used.

aircraft, the "nomad" is generally a block size, and the use of pedestrian traffic can occur inside it.

The nomad consists of three parts, from top to bottom, the living layer, the driver layer and supply layer. The living layer is an island arranged with patches of flat farmland around the terraced surface models to meet the aspirations of the people close to nature, as in the middle there is a lake, water collection, domestic water, landscape lake, etc. The naturally lit part of the island consists of people's daily living, with internal space as daily offices and entertainment. Then the driving layer is divided into an isolation layer and a power layer, which can provide the impetus for their flight. The supply layer is formed only after settlement offers soilless cultivation space, and exchanges energy and substances with the surface within the appropriate range.

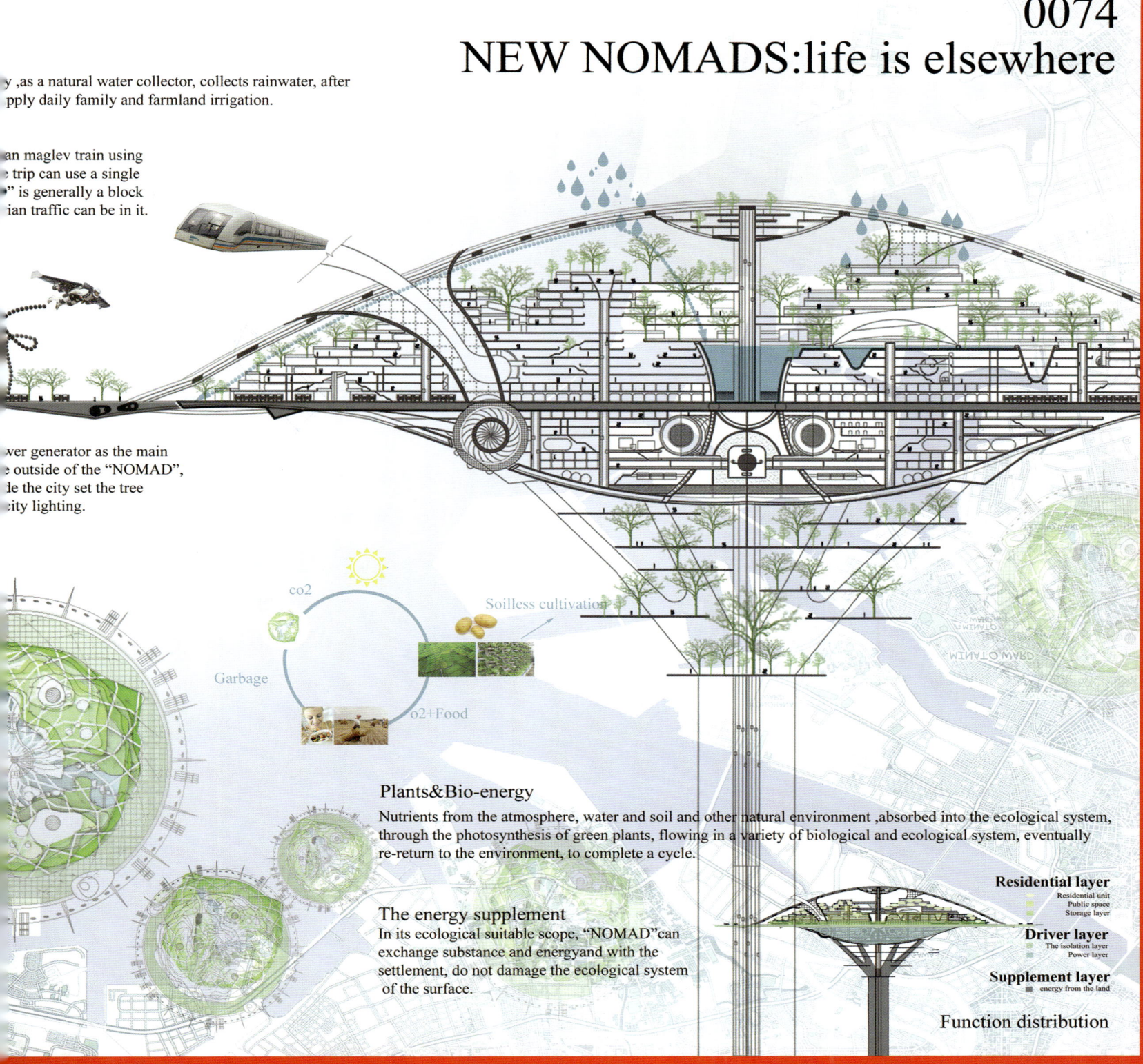

0074
NEW NOMADS:life is elsewhere

y ,as a natural water collector, collects rainwater, after
pply daily family and farmland irrigation.

an maglev train using
trip can use a single
" is generally a block
ian traffic can be in it.

ver generator as the main
outside of the "NOMAD",
le the city set the tree
city lighting.

co2

Soilless cultivation

Garbage

o2+Food

Plants&Bio-energy
Nutrients from the atmosphere, water and soil and other natural environment ,absorbed into the ecological system, through the photosynthesis of green plants, flowing in a variety of biological and ecological system, eventually re-return to the environment, to complete a cycle.

The energy supplement
In its ecological suitable scope, "NOMAD"can exchange substance and energyand with the settlement, do not damage the ecological system of the surface.

Residential layer
Residential unit
Public space
Storage layer

Driver layer
The isolation layer
Power layer

Supplement layer
energy from the land

Function distribution

GEODESIC SKYSCRAPER

Caterina Sposato

Italy

SITE LOCATION: Queens is the largest in area and second in population of the districts of New York City. The urban district has a strictly regular mesh with orthogonal streets and a dense grid. The corridor of Roosevelt Avenue, is currently running through the place and particularized the area due to the presence of elevated subway and major prospects who have lived and colored by the different ethnic groups. This site is currently being criticized as a poor place, suffering, with tensions at the social level due to the mixture of different populations concentrated on the same axis that little complement and not relate to each other.

SCENARIO:

Global warming and the rising level of the ocean waters will lead to the disappearance of cities like New York, Boston and Miami.
As early as 2100 some of the major cities present on the American coast could be submerged and uninhabitable, according to the latest data on climate change. It's time to think seriously about the future and to change course.
To bring to the fore the problem is a new study published in an article that appeared in the pages of the prestigious scientific journal Proceedings of the National Academy of Sciences (PNAS), which carries the title of "The Sea-Level Commitment Multimillennial of Global Warming". From the experts' forecasts show that, because of CO_2 emissions and global warming, the sea level will rise by 20 cm to 2 meters within the next 100 years and from 4 to 9 meters within the next 2,000 years.
Experts have calculated that the levels of marine waters will rise to 2 meters per degree centigrade which will result in a higher global temperatures.
How many degrees will rise atmospheric temperatures? According to an article that appeared recently in the journal Nature Climate Change, temperatures will rise by at least 2 degrees Celsius by 2100. This seems to make inevitable a significant rise in sea level over the next 2000 years.

What are the areas most at risk? Experts have made a map of the areas of

Global warming and the rising level of the ocean waters could cause in 2100 some of the major cities on the American coast to be completely submerged and uninhabitable. It's time to think seriously about the future and to change course. To bring forth the problem is a new study published in "The Sea-Level Commitment Multimillennial of Global Warming". From the experts' forecasts, it is hypothesized that because of CO_2 emissions and global warming, the sea level will rise by 20cm to 2 meters within the next 100 years. Experts have calculated that the levels of marine waters will rise to 2 meters per degree centigrade, which will result in higher global temperatures. How many degrees will raise atmospheric temperatures? According to an article that appeared recently in the journal Nature Climate Change, temperatures will rise by at least 2 degrees Celsius by 2100. This seems to make a significant rise in sea level inevitable over the

QUEENS · NEW YORK · U.S.A. · 2100

next 2000 years. What are the areas most at risk?

How will the world look like in 2100? And what will happen in Queens? In the near future we will have to deal with global warming, the depletion of resources essential to survival, and the decline of today's lifestyle quality. The waters will flood coastal cities and big cities; hurricanes and bad weather will reach powers of destruction never before experienced. And in terms of people, many will be forced to move in every corner of the earth in order to feel protected, to find food, to defend themselves and survive. So all is lost? Maybe not, because the future depends on how we intend to use today's technological innovations that we have available and that mark our era of growth and decline.

The challenge is that the 3km in diameter project is to save the people of Queens, bringing together

the different ethnic groups through the struggle for survival; ensuring an ideal microclimate with its shape through the evaporation of water flood; and protecting against environmental disasters, such as hurricanes, storms, heat waves. Inside the dome is created a lifestyle ideal: the circumference of the base allows the connection with the city; to purify floodwaters that will be reused, and to dispose of waste. As one moves up from the base, there are paths that vertically connect the various urban centers of the dome with residences, services, food production, urban parks. The cover is used as a photovoltaic surface and some arms using wind power of storms and hurricanes in 2100, which will have a capacity greater than 70% compared to those of today. Geodesic Skyscraper aims to be an example of a solution to a problem that will invest the entire globe in the next century.

QUEENS · NEW YORK · U.S.A. · 2100

NEW INTERVETION

WATER FLOODING

POROUS ENERGY TOWER

Yusuke Takahashi

Japan

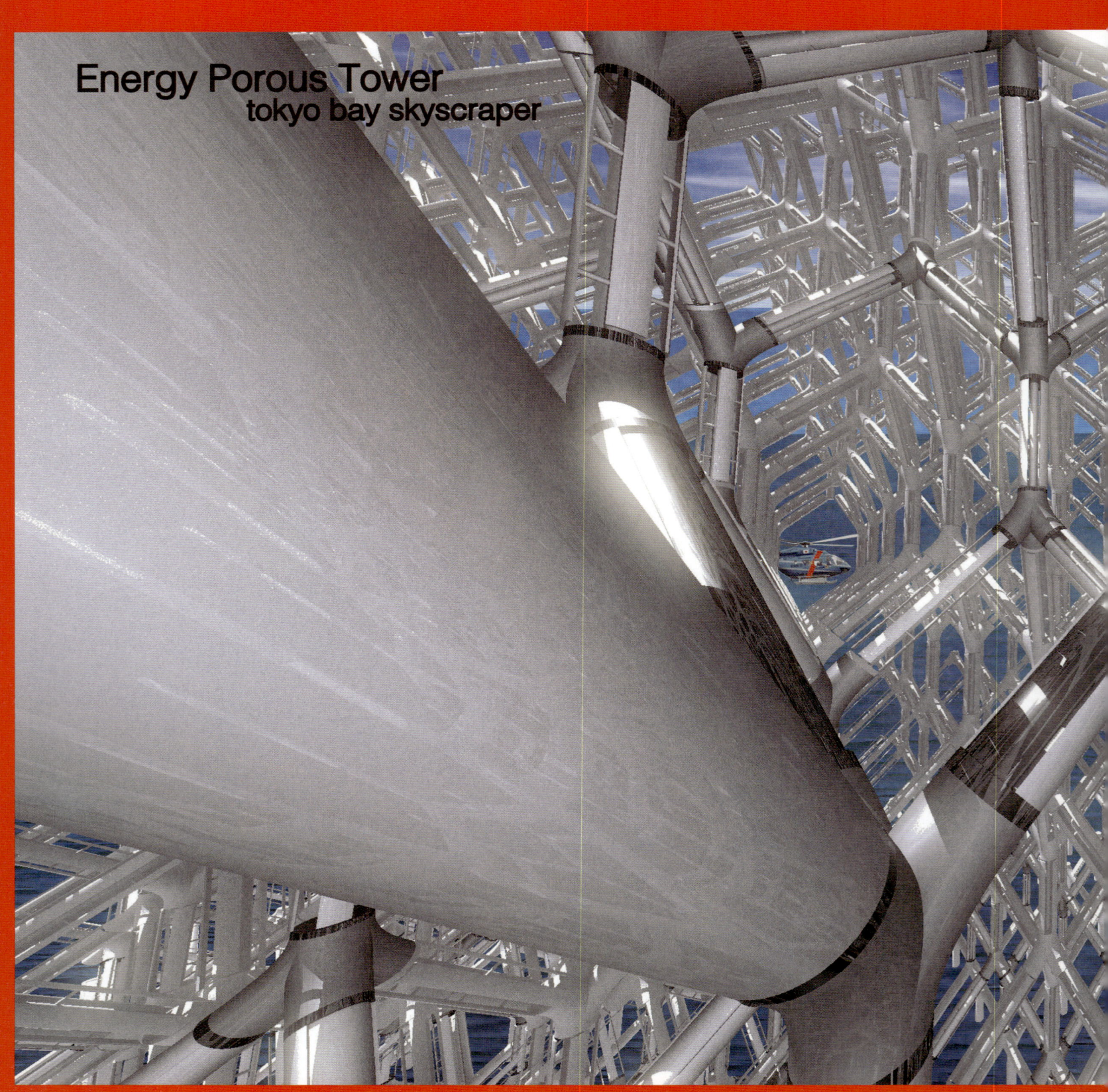

Energy Porous Tower
tokyo bay skyscraper

Japan consumes large amounts of electricity when compared to many other countries across the globe. Thermal power plants, hydroelectric power plants, and nuclear power plants generate the most of this electricity. But now it is necessary to reconsider these methods of power generation against environmental problems and the risk of nuclear power plant disasters, like that in Fukushima, as a turning point. So in this project I propose an energy plant, which can generate electricity only using renewable energy instead of conventional power generation methods.

If you research about electric consumption in Japan, you will notice that Tokyo accounts for over 10% of all electric consumption in Japan. The area of Tokyo is the second smallest in Japan, but Tokyo consumes so much electricity nevertheless because of the great population density of the city. In such a

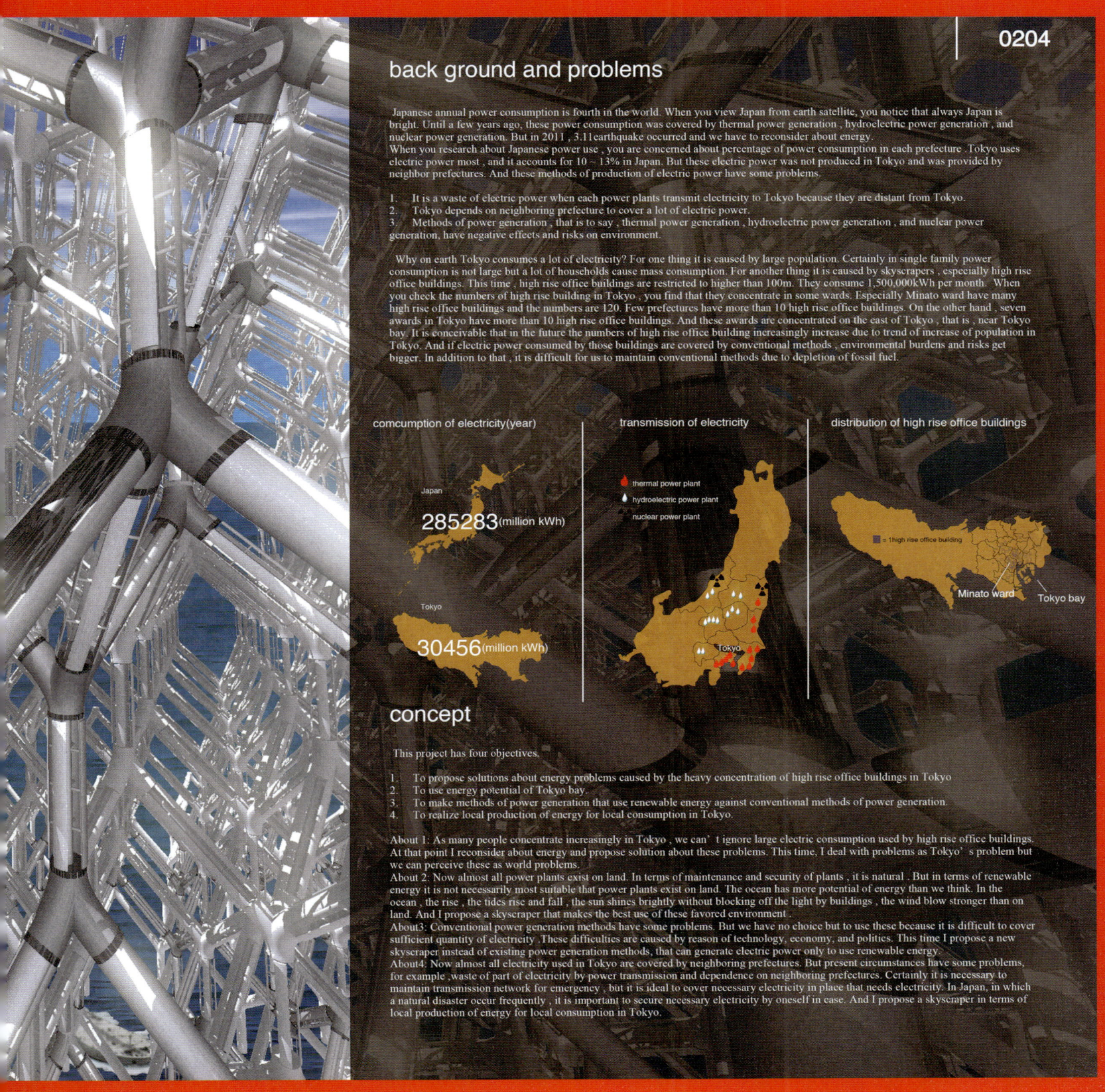

0204

back ground and problems

Japanese annual power consumption is fourth in the world. When you view Japan from earth satellite, you notice that always Japan is bright. Until a few years ago, these power consumption was covered by thermal power generation , hydroelectric power generation , and nuclear power generation. But in 2011 , 3.11earthquake occurred and we have to reconsider about energy.
When you research about Japanese power use , you are concerned about percentage of power consumption in each prefecture .Tokyo uses electric power most , and it accounts for 10 ~ 13% in Japan. But these electric power was not produced in Tokyo and was provided by neighbor prefectures. And these methods of production of electric power have some problems.

1. It is a waste of electric power when each power plants transmit electricity to Tokyo because they are distant from Tokyo.
2. Tokyo depends on neighboring prefecture to cover a lot of electric power.
3. Methods of power generation , that is to say , thermal power generation , hydroelectric power generation , and nuclear power generation, have negative effects and risks on environment.

Why on earth Tokyo consumes a lot of electricity? For one thing it is caused by large population. Certainly in single family power consumption is not large but a lot of households cause mass consumption. For another thing it is caused by skyscrapers , especially high rise office buildings. This time , high rise office buildings are restricted to higher than 100m. They consume 1,500,000kWh per month. When you check the numbers of high rise building in Tokyo , you find that they concentrate in some wards. Especially Minato ward have many high rise office buildings and the numbers are 120. Few prefectures have more than 10 high rise office buildings. On the other hand , seven awards in Tokyo have more than 10 high rise office buildings. And these awards are concentrated on the east of Tokyo , that is , near Tokyo bay. It is conceivable that in the future the numbers of high rise office building increasingly increase due to trend of increase of population in Tokyo. And if electric power consumed by those buildings are covered by conventional methods , environmental burdens and risks get bigger. In addition to that , it is difficult for us to maintain conventional methods due to depletion of fossil fuel.

comcumption of electricity(year)

Japan
285283 (million kWh)

Tokyo
30456 (million kWh)

transmission of electricity

● thermal power plant
● hydroelectric power plant
● nuclear power plant

Tokyo

distribution of high rise office buildings

■ = 1 high rise office building

Minato ward   Tokyo bay

concept

This project has four objectives.

1. To propose solutions about energy problems caused by the heavy concentration of high rise office buildings in Tokyo.
2. To use energy potential of Tokyo bay.
3. To make methods of power generation that use renewable energy against conventional methods of power generation.
4. To realize local production of energy for local consumption in Tokyo.

About 1: As many people concentrate increasingly in Tokyo , we can't ignore large electric consumption used by high rise office buildings. At that point I reconsider about energy and propose solution about these problems. This time, I deal with problems as Tokyo's problem but we can perceive these as world problems.
About 2: Now almost all power plants exist on land. In terms of maintenance and security of plants , it is natural . But in terms of renewable energy it is not necessarily most suitable that power plants exist on land. The ocean has more potential of energy than we think. In the ocean , the rise , the tides rise and fall , the sun shines brightly without blocking off the light by buildings , the wind blow stronger than on land. And I propose a skyscraper that makes the best use of these favored environment.
About3: Conventional power generation methods have some problems. But we have no choice but to use these because it is difficult to cover sufficient quantity of electricity .These difficulties are caused by reason of technology, economy, and politics. This time I propose a new skyscraper instead of existing power generation methods, that can generate electric power only to use renewable energy.
About4: Now almost all electricity used in Tokyo are covered by neighboring prefectures. But present circumstances have some problems, for example ,waste of part of electricity by power transmission and dependence on neighboring prefectures. Certainly it is necessary to maintain transmission network for emergency , but it is ideal to cover necessary electricity in place that needs electricity. In Japan, in which a natural disaster occur frequently , it is important to secure necessary electricity by oneself in case. And I propose a skyscraper in terms of local production of energy for local consumption in Tokyo.

situation, a problem occurs. It is electric consumption by high-rise office buildings. Electric consumption by high-rise office buildings over 100m is equivalent to about 7000 houses. In Tokyo, Minato ward has more than 100 such office buildings. Porous Energy Tower can cover all electric consumption by these high-rise office buildings in Tokyo.

Porous Energy Tower has 5 distinctive features. First is its ocean megastructure. This plant is located on Tokyo bay where has a huge potential of energy harvesting. Second is its renewable energy. This plant generates electricity out of 4 different kinds of renewable energy, such as solar, wind, wave, and tide. Third is its porous structure. This structure can absorb and harvest large amount of renewable energy efficiently. Fourth is its modular system. This large-scale plant is formed by a simple modular system. And finally, it

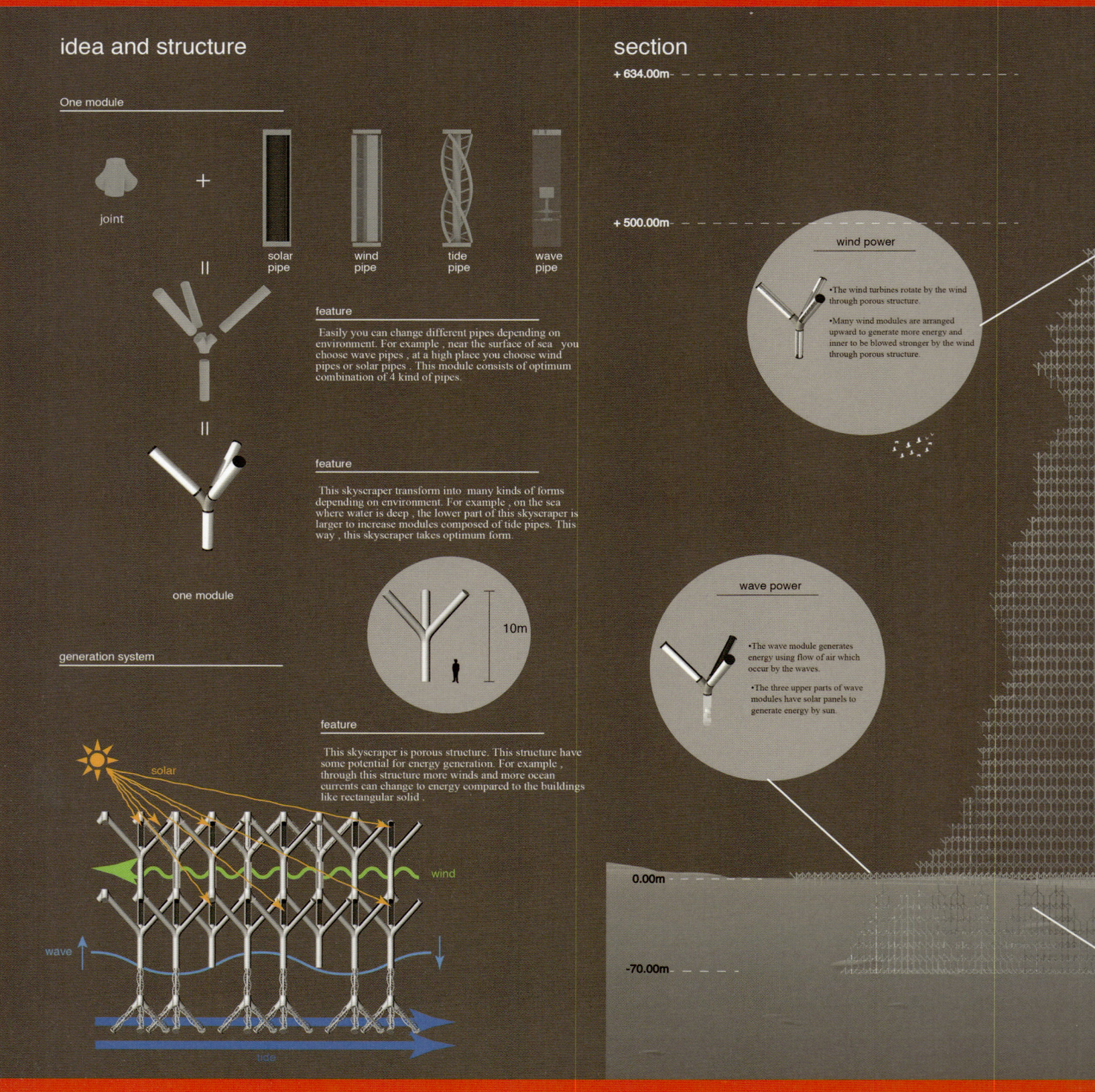

idea and structure

One module

joint

+

solar pipe   wind pipe   tide pipe   wave pipe

feature

Easily you can change different pipes depending on environment. For example , near the surface of sea you choose wave pipes , at a high place you choose wind pipes or solar pipes . This module consists of optimum combination of 4 kind of pipes.

feature

This skyscraper transform into many kinds of forms depending on environment. For example , on the sea where water is deep , the lower part of this skyscraper is larger to increase modules composed of tide pipes. This way , this skyscraper takes optimum form.

one module

10m

generation system

solar

wind

wave

tide

feature

This skyscraper is porous structure. This structure have some potential for energy generation. For example , through this structure more winds and more ocean currents can change to energy compared to the buildings like rectangular solid .

section

+ 634.00m

+ 500.00m

wind power

•The wind turbines rotate by the wind through porous structure.

•Many wind modules are arranged upward to generate more energy and inner to be blowed stronger by the wind through porous structure.

wave power

•The wave module generates energy using flow of air which occur by the waves.

•The three upper parts of wave modules have solar panels to generate energy by sun.

0.00m

-70.00m

has great adaptability as this plant transforms to optimal shape depending on its circumstances.

How does the structure generate all this energy? The project is designed as a series of steel tubes that interconnect between them to create a large-scale structure. The main building block is a four leg unit that connects with other pieced with three legs while the fourth is used to connect a distinct electricty generator system. At the top of the strcuture, solar panels are used while wind turbines occupy the mid leveles. At the bottom, underwater, water trubines are used to harvest clean eneregy from tides and waves.

The size of the entire strcuture could increase or decrease according to Tokyo's needs.

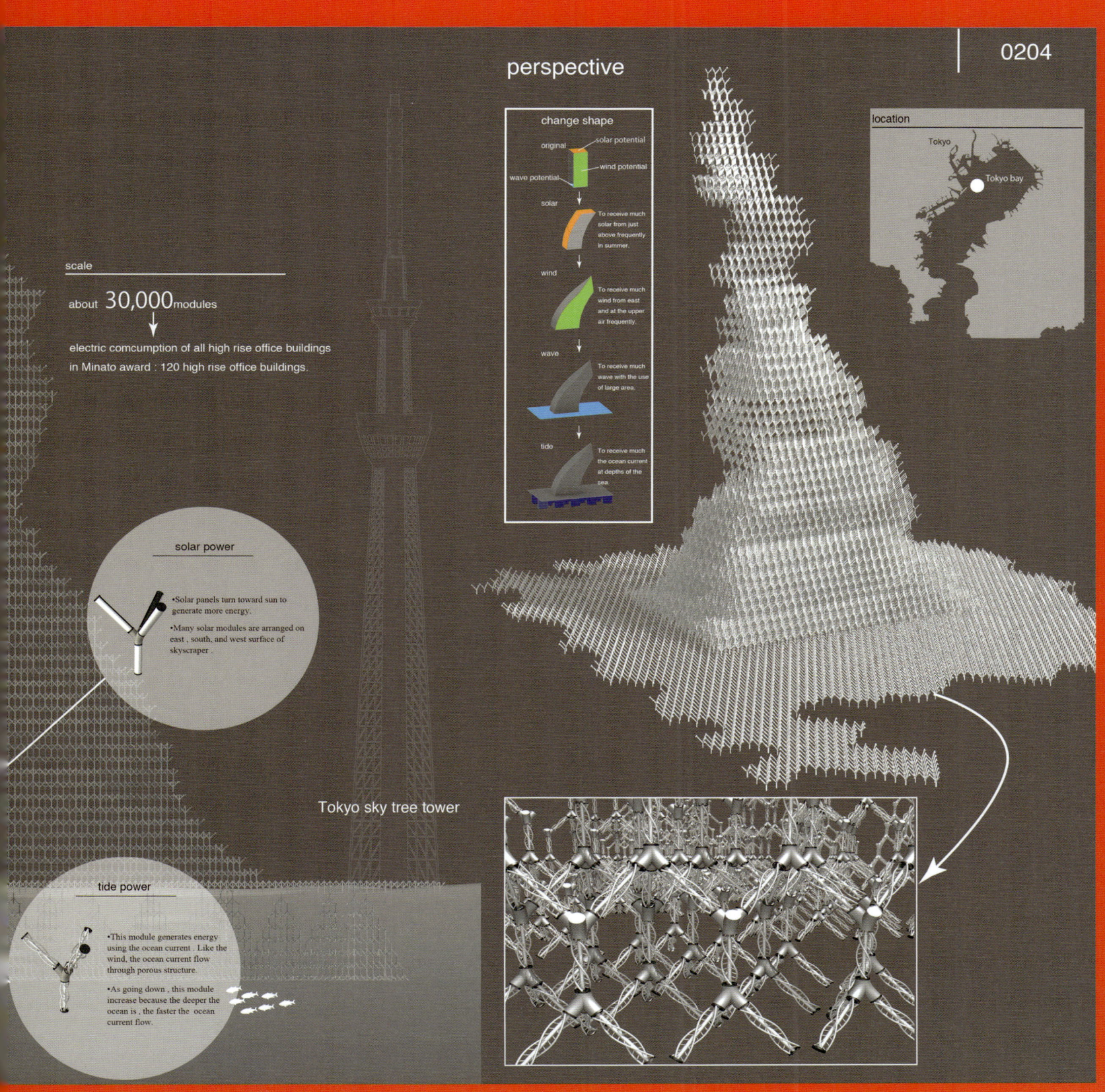

perspective

0204

change shape

original — solar potential

wave potential — wind potential

solar — To receive much solar from just above frequently in summer.

wind — To receive much wind from east and at the upper air frequently.

wave — To receive much wave with the use of large area.

tide — To receive much the ocean current at depths of the sea.

location

Tokyo

Tokyo bay

scale

about **30,000** modules

electric comcumption of all high rise office buildings in Minato award : 120 high rise office buildings.

solar power

•Solar panels turn toward sun to generate more energy.

•Many solar modules are arranged on east , south, and west surface of skyscraper .

Tokyo sky tree tower

tide power

•This module generates energy using the ocean current . Like the wind, the ocean current flow through porous structure.

•As going down , this module increase because the deeper the ocean is , the faster the ocean current flow.

EUTHANASIA

Yahia
Ghonemy
Fathi
Zoz
Nabrawy
Maghalawy
Menshawy

Egypt

EUTHANASIA
using inner power of the nature to solve its problems

For some patients, medical therapy is 95% psychological and it depends on his inner power. Applying the same rule to nature, can we use the inner power of nature to solve its problems?

Gulf Stream is called the engine of world atmosphere. It connects four of five global oceans exchanging water with each other. It is also called the " thermohaline " system, where "thermo" refers to heat and "haline" refers to the salt content of water. The gulf stream transfers heat with a speed of 2 meters per second and a carrying a load of 100,000,000 cubic meters per second of water, ending with a waterfall of 15 kilometers width and 4 kilometers height and that makes it the largest waterfall on earth. The waterfall carries over 17,000,000 cubic meters per second, which is 15 times more than what all rivers over the world carry. It acts as an engine for the Gulf Stream that gives it the power and speed necessary for its trip.

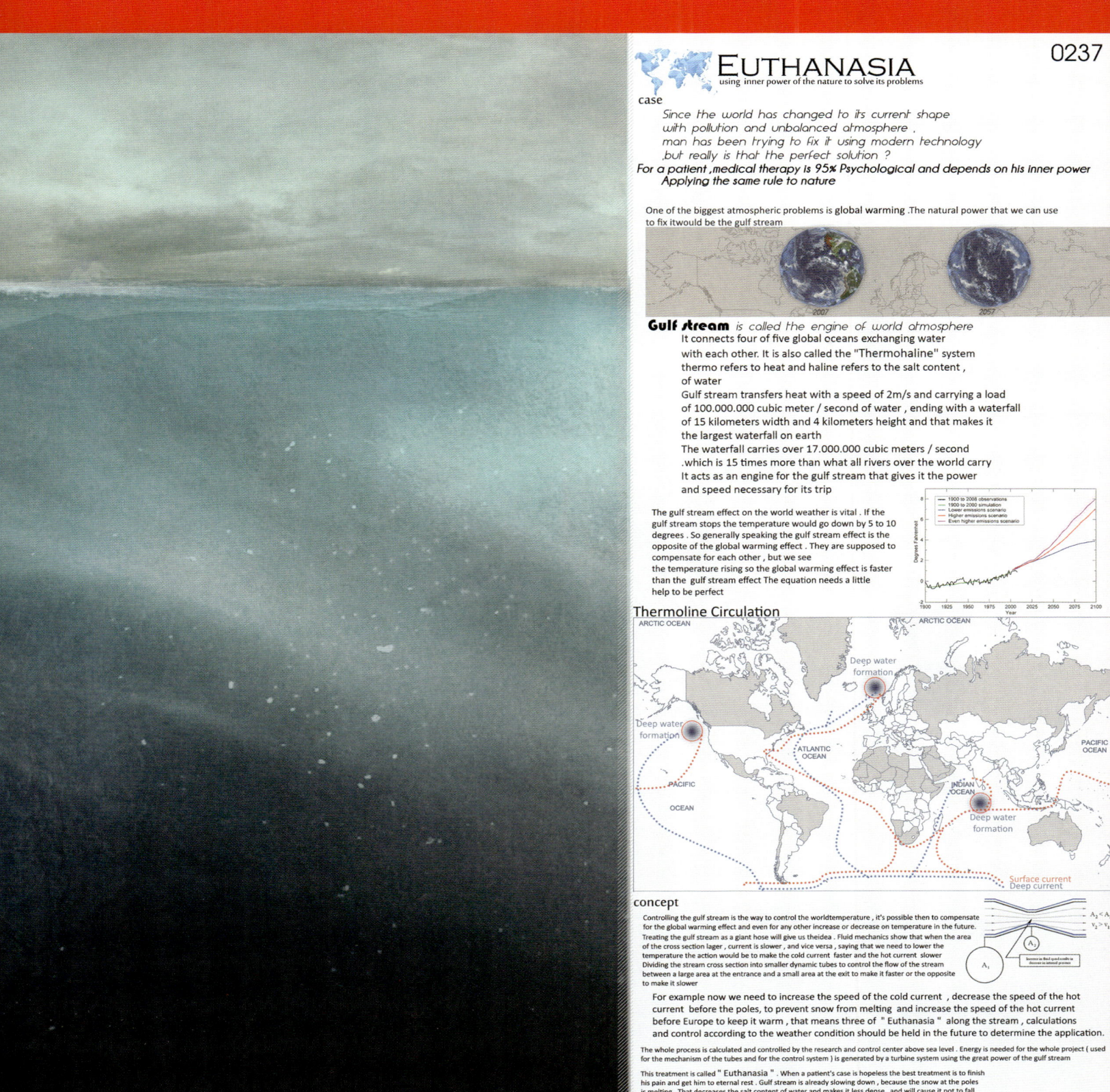

EUTHANASIA
using inner power of the nature to solve its problems

0237

case

Since the world has changed to its current shape with pollution and unbalanced atmosphere, man has been trying to fix it using modern technology, but really is that the perfect solution?
For a patient, medical therapy is 95% Psychological and depends on his inner power Applying the same rule to nature

One of the biggest atmospheric problems is global warming. The natural power that we can use to fix it would be the gulf stream

Gulf stream is called the engine of world atmosphere
It connects four of five global oceans exchanging water with each other. It is also called the "Thermohaline" system thermo refers to heat and haline refers to the salt content, of water
Gulf stream transfers heat with a speed of 2m/s and carrying a load of 100.000.000 cubic meter / second of water, ending with a waterfall of 15 kilometers width and 4 kilometers height and that makes it the largest waterfall on earth
The waterfall carries over 17.000.000 cubic meters / second .which is 15 times more than what all rivers over the world carry
It acts as an engine for the gulf stream that gives it the power and speed necessary for its trip

The gulf stream effect on the world weather is vital . If the gulf stream stops the temperature would go down by 5 to 10 degrees . So generally speaking the gulf stream effect is the opposite of the global warming effect . They are supposed to compensate for each other , but we see the temperature rising so the global warming effect is faster than the gulf stream effect The equation needs a little help to be perfect

Thermoline Circulation

concept

Controlling the gulf stream is the way to control the worldtemperature , it's possible then to compensate for the global warming effect and even for any other increase or decrease on temperature in the future.
Treating the gulf stream as a giant hose will give us theidea . Fluid mechanics show that when the area of the cross section lager , current is slower , and vice versa , saying that we need to lower the temperature the action would be to make the cold current faster and the hot current slower
Dividing the stream cross section into smaller dynamic tubes to control the flow of the stream between a large area at the entrance and a small area at the exit to make it faster or the opposite to make it slower

For example now we need to increase the speed of the cold current , decrease the speed of the hot current before the poles, to prevent snow from melting and increase the speed of the hot current before Europe to keep it warm , that means three of " Euthanasia " along the stream , calculations and control according to the weather condition should be held in the future to determine the application.

The whole process is calculated and controlled by the research and control center above sea level . Energy is needed for the whole project (used for the mechanism of the tubes and for the control system) is generated by a turbine system using the great power of the gulf stream

This treatment is called " Euthanasia " . When a patient's case is hopeless the best treatment is to finish his pain and get him to eternal rest . Gulf stream is already slowing down , because the snow at the poles is melting . That decreases the salt content of water and makes it less dense , and will cause it not to fall in the waterfall to start over . So gulf stream is coming to an end We will use " Euthanasia " for a better future

The Gulf Stream effect on the world weather is vital. If the Gulf Stream stops the temperature would go down by 5 to 10 degrees. So generally speaking the Gulf Stream effect is the opposite of the global warming effect. They are supposed to compensate for each other, but we see the temperature rising so the global warming effect is faster than the Gulf Stream effect. The equation needs a little help to be perfect.

Treating the Gulf Stream as a giant hose will give us the idea. Fluid mechanics show that when the area of the cross section larger, current is slower, and vice versa, saying that we need to lower the temperature the action would be to make the cold current faster and the hot current slower. Dividing the stream cross section into smaller dynamic tubes to control the flow of the stream between a large area at the entrance and a small area at the exit to make it faster or the opposite to make it slower.

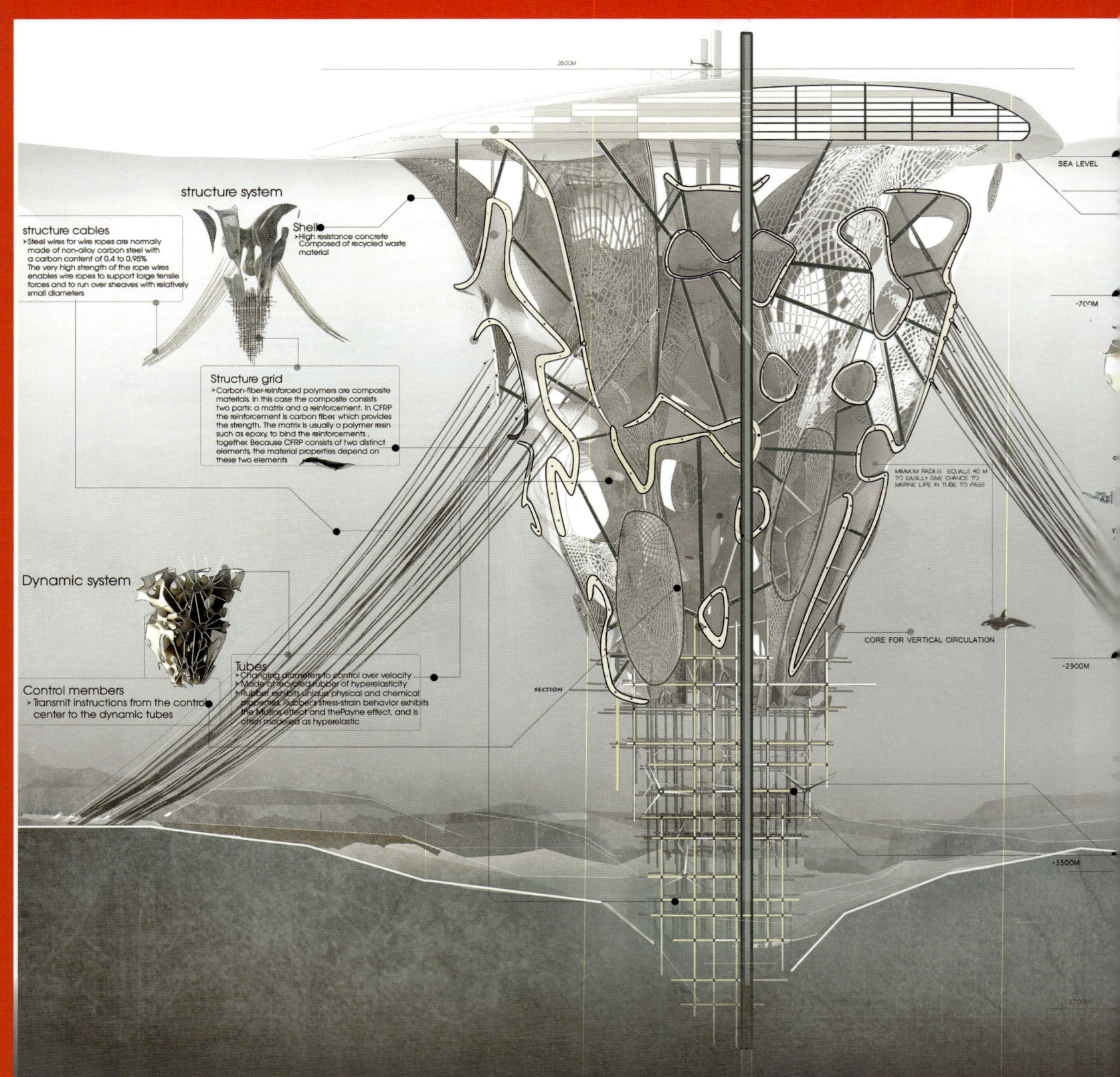

structure system

structure cables
›Steel wires for wire ropes are normally made of non-alloy carbon steel with a carbon content of 0.4 to 0.95%
The very high strength of the rope wires enables wire ropes to support large tensile forces and to run over sheaves with relatively small diameters

Shell
›High resistance concrete
Composed of recycled waste material

Structure grid
›Carbon-fiber-reinforced polymers are composite materials. In this case the composite consists two parts: a matrix and a reinforcement. In CFRP the reinforcement is carbon fiber which provides the strength. The matrix is usually a polymer resin such as epoxy, to bind the reinforcements . together Because CFRP consists of two distinct elements the material properties depend on these two elements

Dynamic system

Control members
›Transmit instructions from the control center to the dynamic tubes

Tubes
›Changing diameters to control over velocity
›Material recycled rubber of hyperelasticity
Rubber exhibits unique physical and chemical properties Rubber's stress-strain behavior exhibits the Mullins effect and thePayne effect, and is often modeled as hyperelastic

SEA LEVEL

2600M

-700M

MINIMUM RADIUS EQUALS 40 M TO EASILY GIVE CHANCE TO MARINE LIFE IN TUBE TO PASS

A2

CORE FOR VERTICAL CIRCULATION

-2900M

SECTION

-3500M

-3700M

For example now we need to increase the speed of the cold current, decrease the speed of the hot current before the poles, to prevent snow from melting and increase the speed of the hot current before Europe to keep it warm, that means three of " Euthanasia " along the stream, calculations and control according to the weather condition should be held in the future to determine the application.

The whole process is calculated and controlled by the research and control center above sea level. Energy needed for the whole project (used for the mechanism of the tubes and for the control system) is generated by a turbine system using the great power of the Gulf Stream.

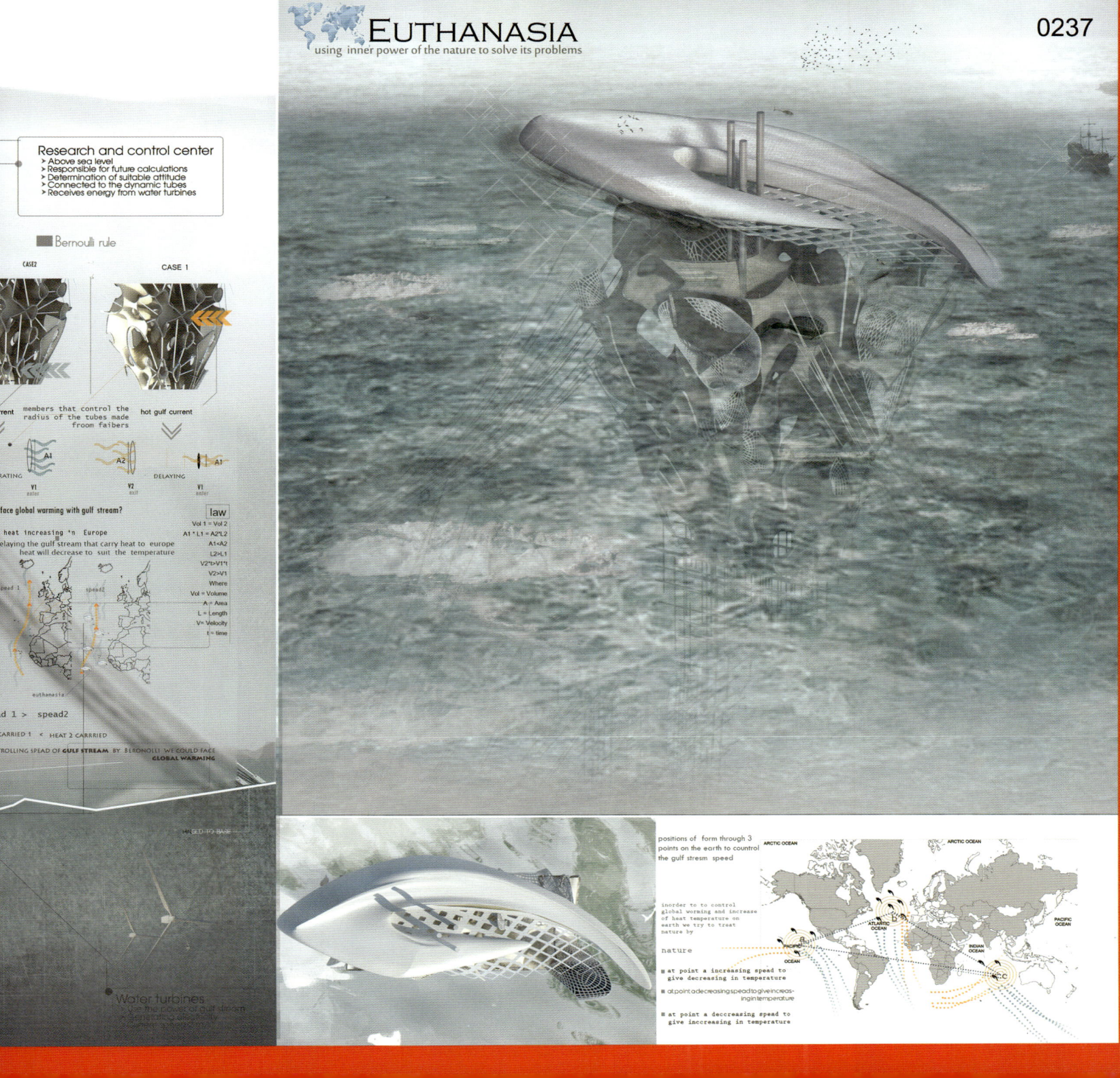

CLOUD CITY

Gilberto Baroni Junior
Rafael Santos Ferraz
Rodolfo Parolin

United States
Brazil

CLØUD C1TY

//scenario

In 1970, it was the first time that the word INTERNET was used, but just in the beggining of the 90s it was popularized. Now, just 25 years later, we have a world of 50 petabytes in the cloud surrounding us. In this last decade the virtual world is not only growing, but becoming each day more real. We are testifying internet companies without no big physical structure becoming much more valuable than big heavy industries.

Many of us spend more time in the virtual environment than in the real world. Our daily routine is based on the web, from getting any sort of information, do transactions, interact with others or just for entertainment. It is also possible to notice that people create two identities in these two worlds: differents but complementaries.

This boundary between worlds is becoming each day more blurred but we still have some barriers.

//location

Japan is well known as a technology pioneer in virtual experience. That is why we choose TOKYO as the perfect city for the first CLOUD. The japanese culture have many references to the virtual reality, making them better prepared to emerge inside this new life experience.

tokyo> japan

//concept

real

CLOUD

virtual

Reality and virtuality in one dimension. This is the purpose of The CLOUD, created to put an end to the boundaries between these two aparently different worlds. The result: a new universe of perception, the interaction between your inner being, the architecture that surrounds you, the environment around you and people with who you conect. A responsive experience. The interaction between people and construction, in a continuous exchange of human emotions and databytes, through the materialization of data.

//the architect

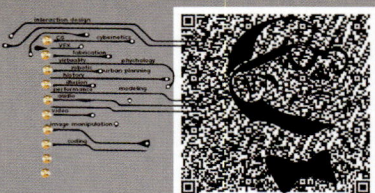

The architect work will be to codify each aspect of human personality and translate it into spaces according to the user internet profile, designing a different experience depending his behavior pattern. The building architecture will also respond to the city personality and natural environment. His challenge is not an easy task, hum? But that's what architects do today, this will be just a new level of challenge!

//the device

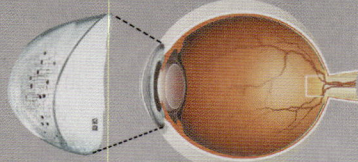

The PORTAL LENS are the portal for your dream. With the bounce of your head your contact lens will recharge just like any watch in your wrist. The screen in the lens have a full eye resolution of 576megapixels and it's semi-transparent, so you can look into the eyes.

//the system

‹modules›

‹buiding services›

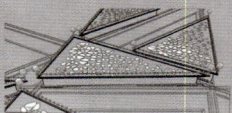

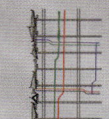

The building have a facade composed by modules. Each module have cameras, light sensors and tracking lights. They move to balance the confort of the interior, based on the information collected by the sensors crossed with users data welfare.

Pipes, HVAC systems are physically shown and virtually hidden. Facilitating the maintenance, and reducing costs and waste of materials in finishings.

‹interior layout›

‹physical structure›

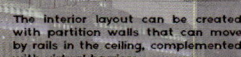

The interior layout can be created with partition walls that can move by rails in the ceiling, complemented with virtual barriers.

The structure is physically present, matter of the existing reality and static. The virtual ambient can be arranged within its limits and its appearance can be blurred within the VR. Typologies like pillars, slabs, pipes, escalators, glass, restrooms are all physically present and help to assure security and privacy.

Architecture inside the virtual world has a lot to be explored as the barriers between the current concepts of real and virtual are on the verge of becoming one new hybrid, the conception of a unified reality.

Investigating these new concepts and possibilities of dimensions, we realize a new perspective of interaction between us and our surrounding spaces, pushing our experiences deeper, establishing a never imagined before responsive conversation with the construction of the world around us.

This last decade showed us how real the virtual world can be: our own identities being formed by virtual and real information mixed together; our ideas being printed in 3D material and showing us new possibilities of work. New forms to explore the construction of reality. The examples are various. The virtual and the real. The two into one.

YOUR PORTAL LENS ARE DEACTIVATED!

0354

facade trackers
Lighted trackers are responsable to allow the lens to read the exactly position to render the virtual, even at night.

facade panels
The panels are the module that carries all the equipements and components, such as: lighing sensors, cameras and facade tracks and envolve the facade of the building.

light sensors
The sensors capture the light in the facade to adjust render with the natural lighting and collecting data to adjust environmental comfort.

cameras
The cameras scan a 360 degrees environment, making possible the replacement of the geometry, with the background

In 1970 the word "internet" was used for the first time. At the beginning of the 90's, the term is popularized. Only 25 years later after that: we have a world of 50 petabytes in a big cloud of information. At this growing rate, what does the future holds for us? Transformation. Reality and virtuality in one dimension.

This is the purpose of The cloud, created to put an end to any remaining boundaries. The result is a new universe of perception, the interaction between our inner being, the environment around us and people we are connected to, all combined together, giving shape to a unique and individual visualization of the architecture of life.

The cloud, made to make you the master of your atmosphere, the controller of your welfare, collecting and managing data and generating results. Inputs based in a complex network, however easily represented

by a simple triangle of ideas. On one side is the user, which includes all his account data, his possible interests and needs. On another side is the community, his cultural background, his neighbors data and city momentary events. The environment completes the triangle, the result of nature´s influence and the energy around us, our needs and desires included.

Based on the behaviour of the user, the program generates a cluster graph of the relationship between the user and his neighbours' parameters. With this neural network set, flocking agents fly over this map attracted by the user last thoughts and actions, focusing in certain areas. The cluster parameters inside those areas are triggered, feeding the program with the necessary information to develop the building architecture for that single user in real time.

YOUR PORTAL LENS ARE ACTIVATED!

0354

AQUAKINETICS

Gen Sugiyama

Canada

AQUAKINETICS

AquaKinetics is a tower that responds to rain and the fluctuating water use of the occupants. The site is located in the heart of downtown Vancouver, Canada. While the city is well known for its lack of sunshine and abundance of rain, it is lesser known for its summer draught and floods that occur due to an aging infrastructure that can't keep up with the city's rapid growth. Aquakinetics dynamically absorbs water, alleviating the stress on the city's storm system while also celebrating the abundance of rain, both for the occupants and the public.

concept:

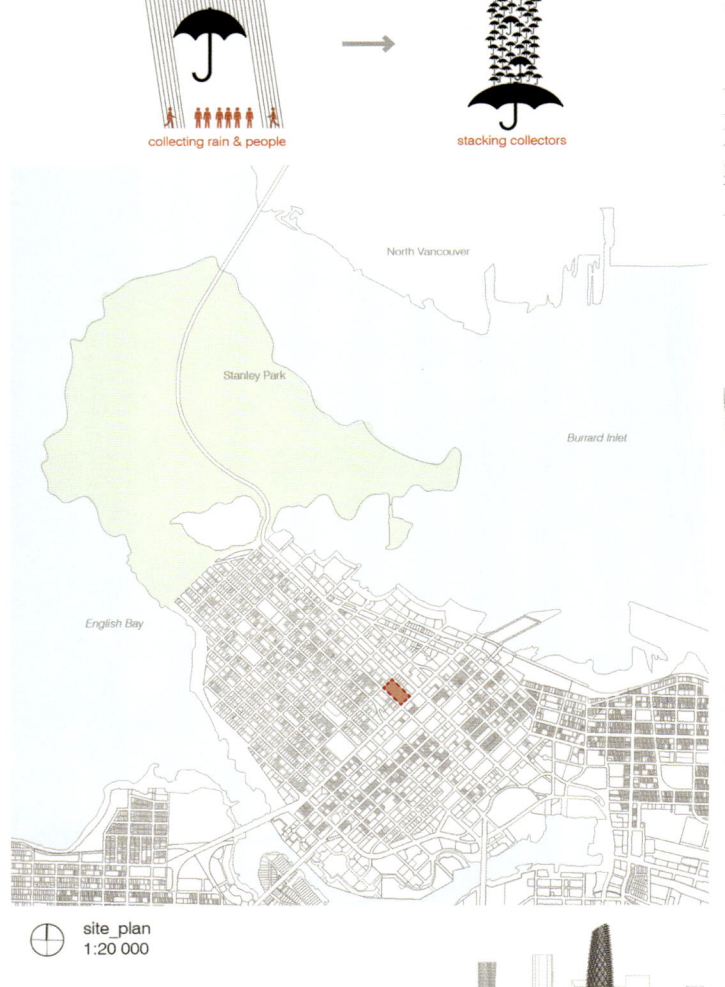

collecting rain & people   stacking collectors

site_plan
1:20 000

urban_section: west-east
1:5000

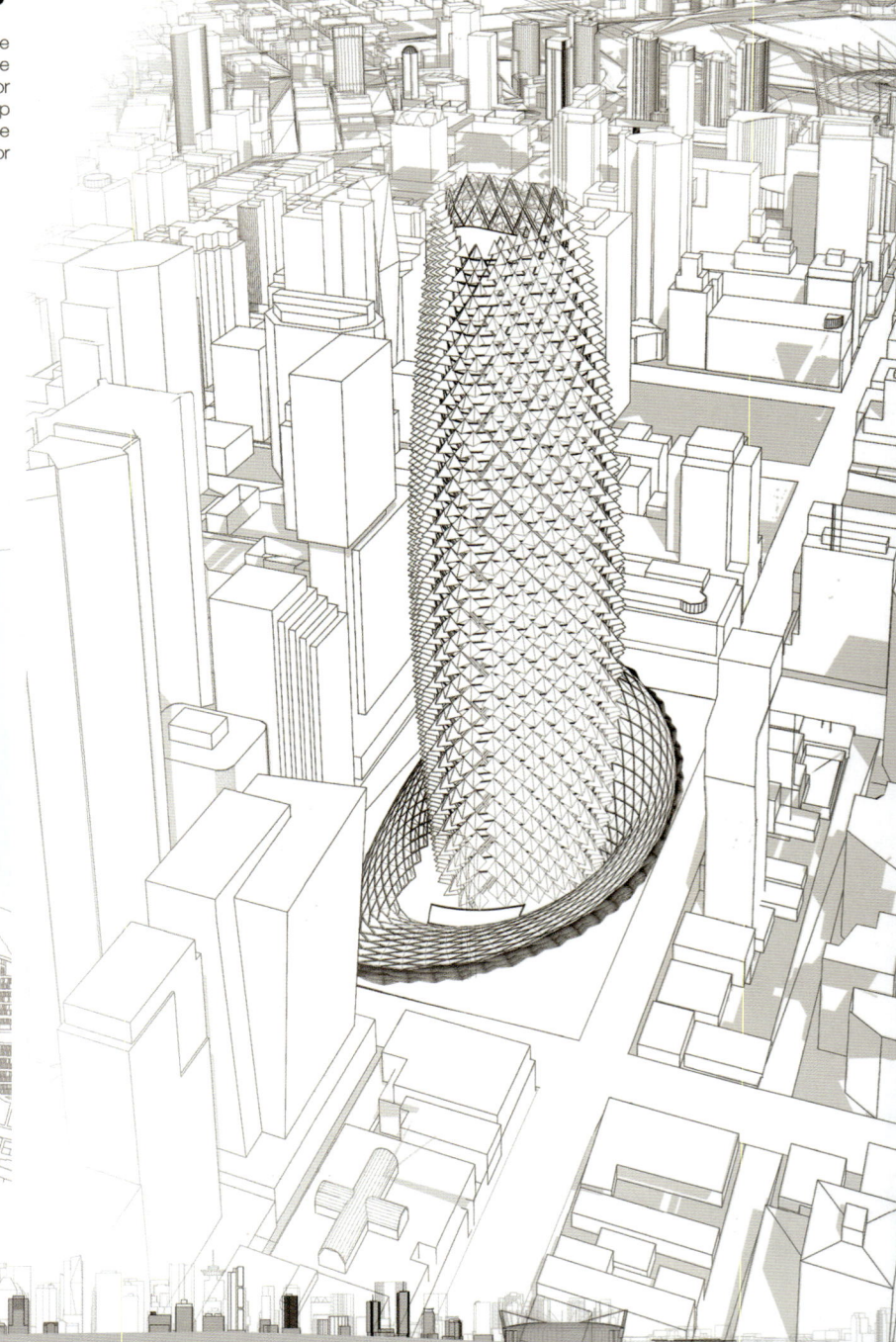

AquaKinetics is a tower that responds to rain and the fluctuating water use of the occupants. The site is located in the heart of downtown Vancouver, Canada. While the city is well known for its lack of sunshine and abundance of rain, it is lesser known for its summer draught and floods that occur due to an aging infrastructure that can't keep up with the city's rapid growth.

Aquakinetics dynamically absorbs water, alleviating the stress on the city's storm system while also celebrating the abundance of rain, both for the occupants and the public.

The façade is comprised of a white flexible fabric that collects water. As rainwater is collected the canopy slowly opens, allowing rain to then be collected by the canopies below. A collection tank and filtration system is located every six floors, providing non-potable water for the units. As water is extracted

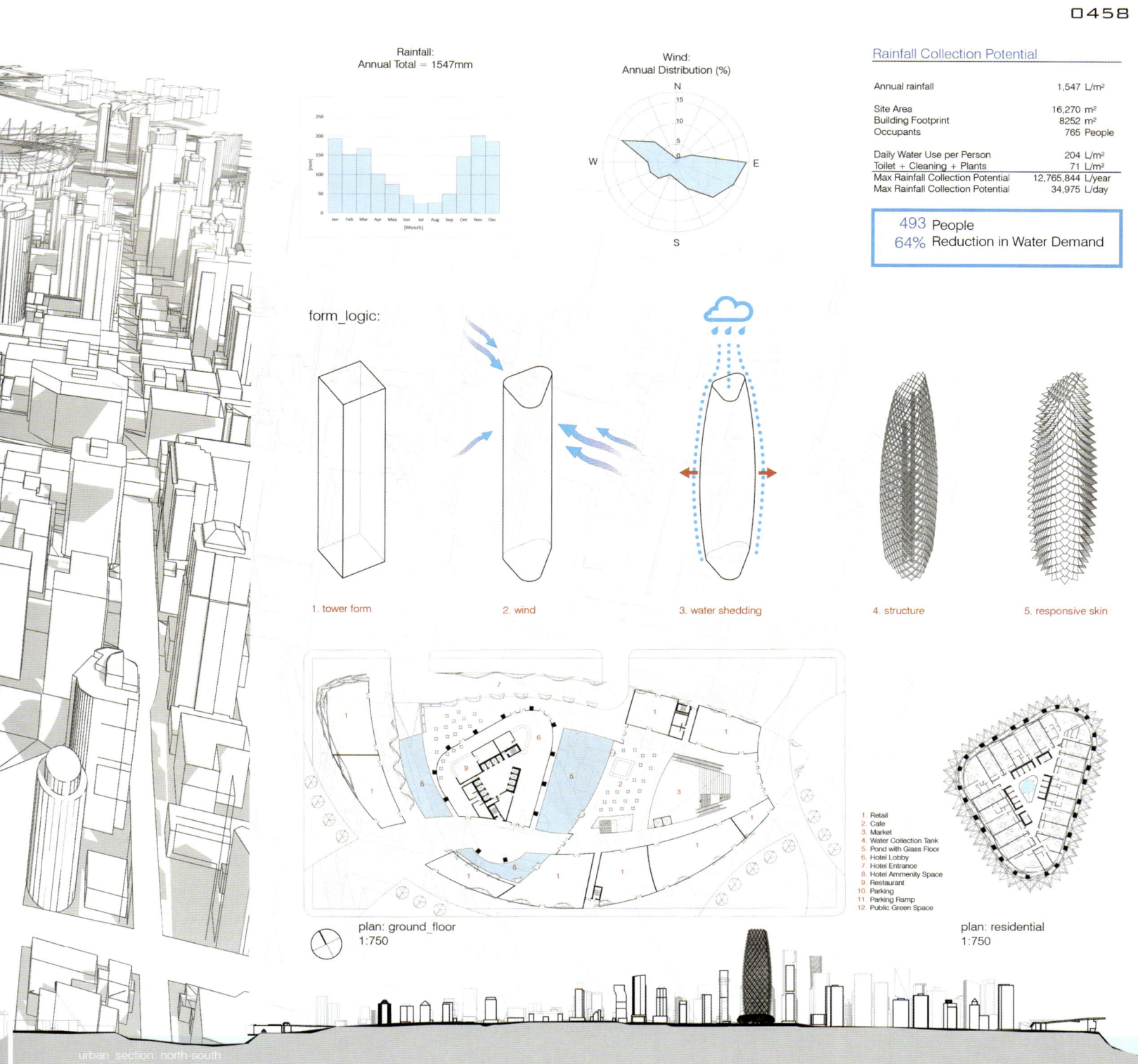

0458

Rainfall:
Annual Total = 1547mm

Wind:
Annual Distribution (%)

Rainfall Collection Potential

Annual rainfall	1,547 L/m²
Site Area	16,270 m²
Building Footprint	8252 m²
Occupants	765 People
Daily Water Use per Person	204 L/m²
Toilet + Cleaning + Plants	71 L/m²
Max Rainfall Collection Potential	12,765,844 L/year
Max Rainfall Collection Potential	34,975 L/day

493 People
64% Reduction in Water Demand

form_logic:

1. tower form   2. wind   3. water shedding   4. structure   5. responsive skin

1. Retail
2. Cafe
3. Market
4. Water Collection Tank
5. Pond with Glass Floor
6. Hotel Lobby
7. Hotel Entrance
8. Hotel Ammenity Space
9. Restaurant
10. Parking
11. Parking Ramp
12. Public Green Space

plan: ground_floor
1:750

plan: residential
1:750

urban_section: north-south
1:5000

from the tank, the canopy begins to close to allow the collection process to occur again. The remaining water is transfered to water tanks at the bottom of the structure. These tanks are equipped with filtering systems to make water potable. At the end, the water is transfered to the city's potable water grid.

The residential units are double story to optimize the façade size and to define ownership. The canopies that overlap four adjacent units are controlled by the system and cannot be overridden. This system of control and override provides users with complete control of their desired use while retaining a fluid and elegant dynamic façade from the exterior.

The tower is erected on a a five-storey plinth dedicated to commercial and recreational areas. This plinth surrounds the tower and connects to the city in a vertical and horizontal way.

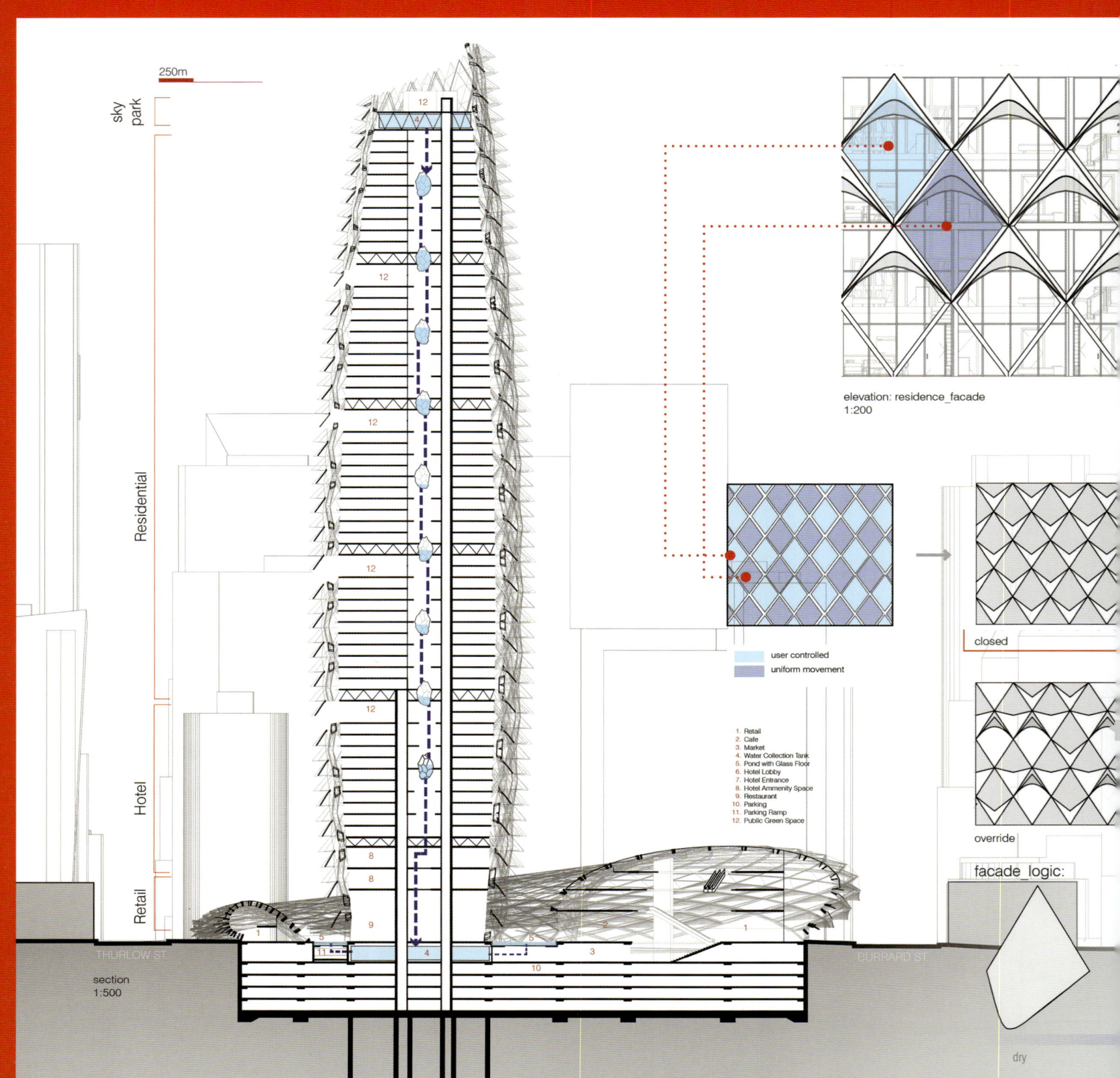

elevation: residence_facade
1:200

user controlled
uniform movement

1. Retail
2. Cafe
3. Market
4. Water Collection Tank
5. Pond with Glass Floor
6. Hotel Lobby
7. Hotel Entrance
8. Hotel Ammenity Space
9. Restaurant
10. Parking
11. Parking Ramp
12. Public Green Space

closed

override

facade_logic:

dry

section
1:500

The tower structure follows a dimond diagrid with opennings as large as two stories allowing unobstructed views to the city from every residence. The residences are spacious and offer an open floor plan for customization.

Every ten floors, two floors are dedicated to auxiliary and recreational programs. Floor plates opened to the inner core and to the outer facade to create an efficient cross ventilation throughout the entire building.

The first few floors of the tower are dedicated to hotel and retail.

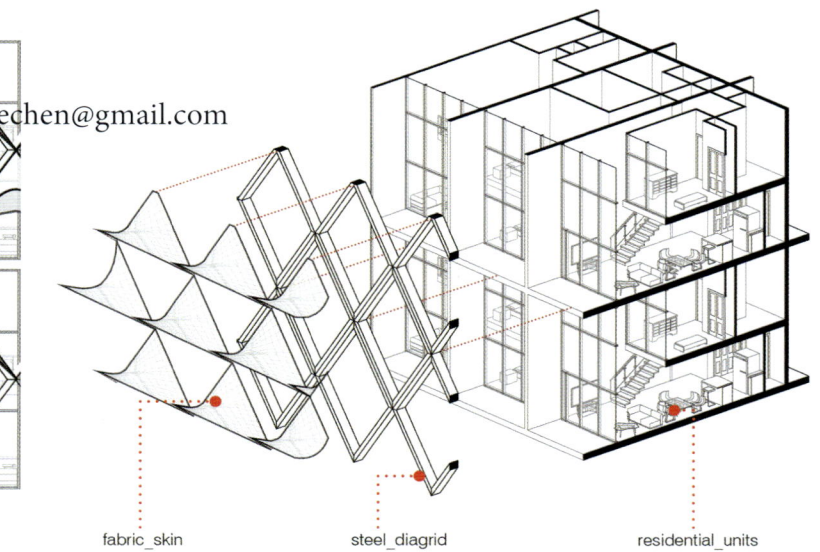

lechen@gmail.com

fabric_skin   steel_diagrid   residential_units

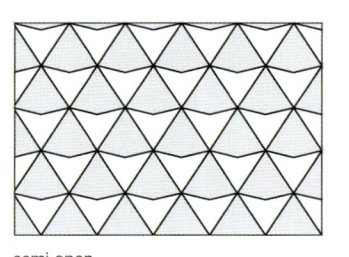

semi-open

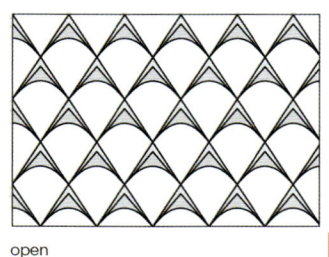

open

facade_system:

The facade is comprised of a white flexible fabric that collects water. As rain water is collected the canopy slowly opens, allowing rain to then be collected by the canopies below. A collection tank and filtration system is located every six floors, providing non-potable water for the units. As water is extracted from the tank, the canopy begins to close to allow the collection process to occur again.

The residential units are double storey to optimize the facade size and to define ownership. The canopies that overlaps four adjacent units are controlled by the system and cannot be overridden. This system of control and override provides users with complete control of their desired use while retaining a fluid and elegant dynamic facade for the exterior.

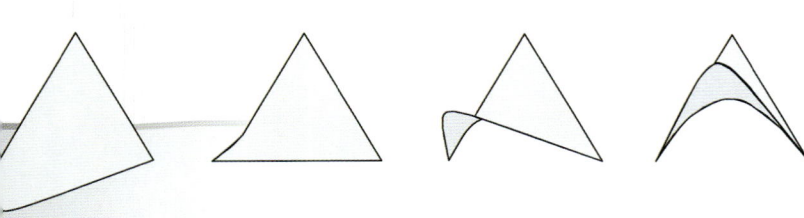

wet

0458

interior: residential

interior: retail_atrium

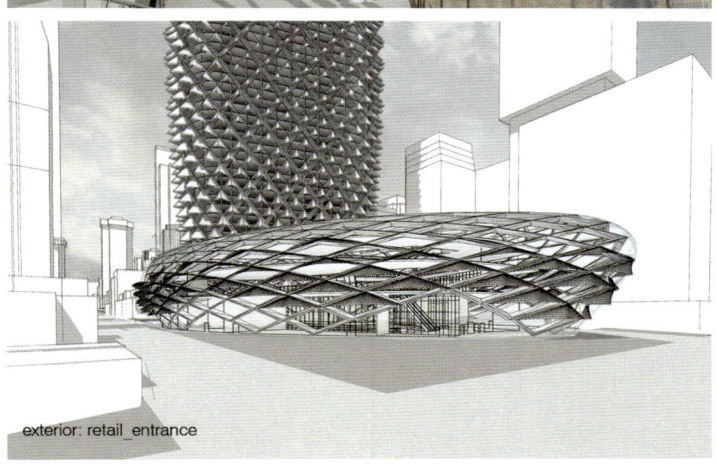

exterior: retail_entrance

A HAVEN IN TEHRAN'S SKY

Hasan Bazzaz Zadeh
Sohrab Pirani
Mohammad Heydari
Elmira Keshavarz Haddad

Iran

A HAVEN IN TEHRAN'S SKY

ABSTRACT

"Based on the geolog
near Tehran is extrem
of the quake canno
hazard and probable
gists and seismologi
Whereas earthquake
ral disasters. Tehran
aspects prove it as a

Magnitude: 7 - 9 on t
Death tolls: over than
Casualties: 1,000,000
Destruction: between

Despite this horrible
not been logical. So
gerous and very pre
faults. Especially 3
North Tehran fault, w
Our design intends
hazardous districts.
as a haven.
This skyscraper star
Not only by the weig
field. It would be pro
source and recycled
as a safety sign in the
itants are sure about

Based on geological science, a severe earthquake occurrence near Tehran is extremely possible. Although the strength and time of the quake cannot be predicted we are able to estimate the hazard and probable destructions to prepare for it. Whereas earthquakes are the most destructive among all the natural disasters. The Tehran earthquake would be a large tragedy. Some predicted aspects prove it as catastrophic, being a magnitude 7-9, killing over 200,000 people, and destroying almost half of the buildings and infrastructure of the city. This skyscraper stands on the fault and sticks two sides together. Not only by the weight force, especially with the electromagnetic field. It would be produced by façade photocells and geothermal energy as an electricity source and recycled metal as the material. Therefore, it would work as a safety sign in the neighborhood. Until it works properly, inhabitants are sure about having a safe and peaceful life.

0700

science, a severe earthquake occurrence conclusive. Though the strength and time predicted we are able to estimate the ructions to prepare for it" Claimed geolo-

the most destructive among all the natu-
quake would be tragedy. Some predicted
strophic earthquake.

chter scale
,000 people

50% of buildings and structures

mation, the urban growth in Tehran has
than 8,000,000 citizens are living in dan-
us districts. And they are threatened by
e faults, Masha fault, South Rey fault,
are main earthquake locations.

ovide safe neighborhoods in extremely
e function and location of the skyscraper

n the fault and sticks two sides together.
rce, especially with the electromagnetic
d by façade photocells as an electricity
l as the material. Therefor it would work
hborhood. Until it works properly, inhab-
ng a safe and peaceful life...

ENTRY

The strategy used in this project, provides the opportunity to use the waste and apparently useless materials to stabilize and consolidate the fault's area. It tries to use renewable and clean energies to promote Tehran's development with regard to the obstacles and difficulties presented. The important point in this scheme is the dual use of energy in buildings. That provides residents' daily uses and the required electricity to strengthen the fault condition. Another noticeable point of the scheme is the green parts of the skyscraper. In addition to providing edible supplies for residents, especially in emergency occasions, it would create a micro-climate inside the structure. According to the height of the skyscraper and allocating a part of each floor to the garden, project tries to create a sustainable climate place. In this regard, among crossing up the floors, oxygen density reduction would happen. So by managing the green areas it tries to

abstract explanation of concept

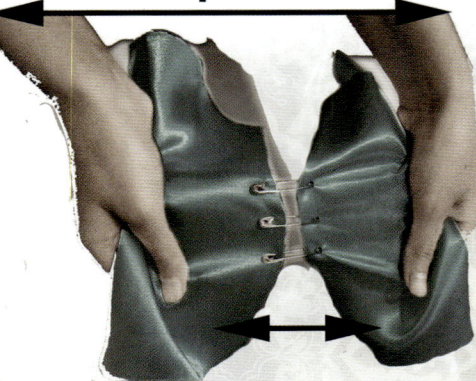

The Strategy used in this project, provides the opportunity to use the waste and apparently useless materials to stabilize and consolidate the fault's area.

This strategy tries to use renewable and clean energy to promote develop of Tehran with regard to the obstacles and difficulties presented. In addition to creating a safe zone during earthquake and providing a vibrant and dynamic urban environment in the region this project intends to be as a model for the development of other fault zones similar conditions.

The important point in this scheme is dual use of energy in buildings. That provides resident's daily uses and the required electricity to strengthen the fault condition. Multi-functional features were attended by ancient architecture as a solution. And this feature is an appropriate response to the current situation in under developing countries.

Another noticeable point of the scheme is the green parts of the skyscraper. In addition to providing edible supplies for residents, especially in emergency occasions, it would create a micro-climate inside the structure. According to the height of the skyscraper and allocating a part of each floor to the garden, project tries to create a sustainable climate place.

In this regard, among crossing up the floors, oxygen density reduction would happen. So by managing the green areas it tries to control the amount of oxygen in the air.

As a conclusion, this designed skyscraper is a safe haven in different hazardous situations such as earthquakes and worse climatic conditions. When there is safety and piece, growth and development is possible.

1 In order to stabilize and strengthen two sides of the fault, as a basic way to ensure area's safety, concrete injection -perpendicular to the fault's wall- would be an appropriate and effective method. To make a reinforced concrete wall.

2 **3** In addition to using reinforced concrete, there is another effective method to stabilize faults. This project's innovation is the use of electromagnetic field to stick two sides of the fault together. And the material is Tehran's daily wastes. And molten metal is the main aim. So after collecting and sorting wastes, metals should be extracted and then be melted. Finally it would be used to cover the walls of the fault

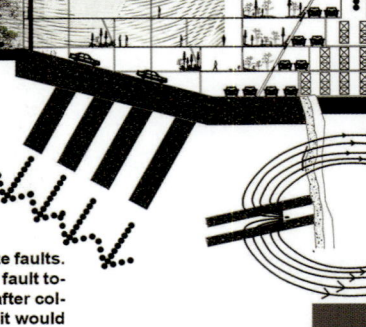

control the amount of oxygen in the air.

In order to stabilize and strengthen two sides of the fault, as a basic way to ensure area's safety, concrete injection, perpendicular to the fault's wall, would be an appropriate and effective method. To make a reinforced concrete wall. In addition to using reinforced concrete, there is another effective method. This project's innovation is the use of electromagnetic field to stick two sides of the fault together. The material is Tehran's daily waste. The final step of the process is using the produced electricity to make a strong electromagnetic field between two sides of the fault. So the next destination of electricity is a generator that transfers it to the metallic walls of the fault and makes them electrically charged.

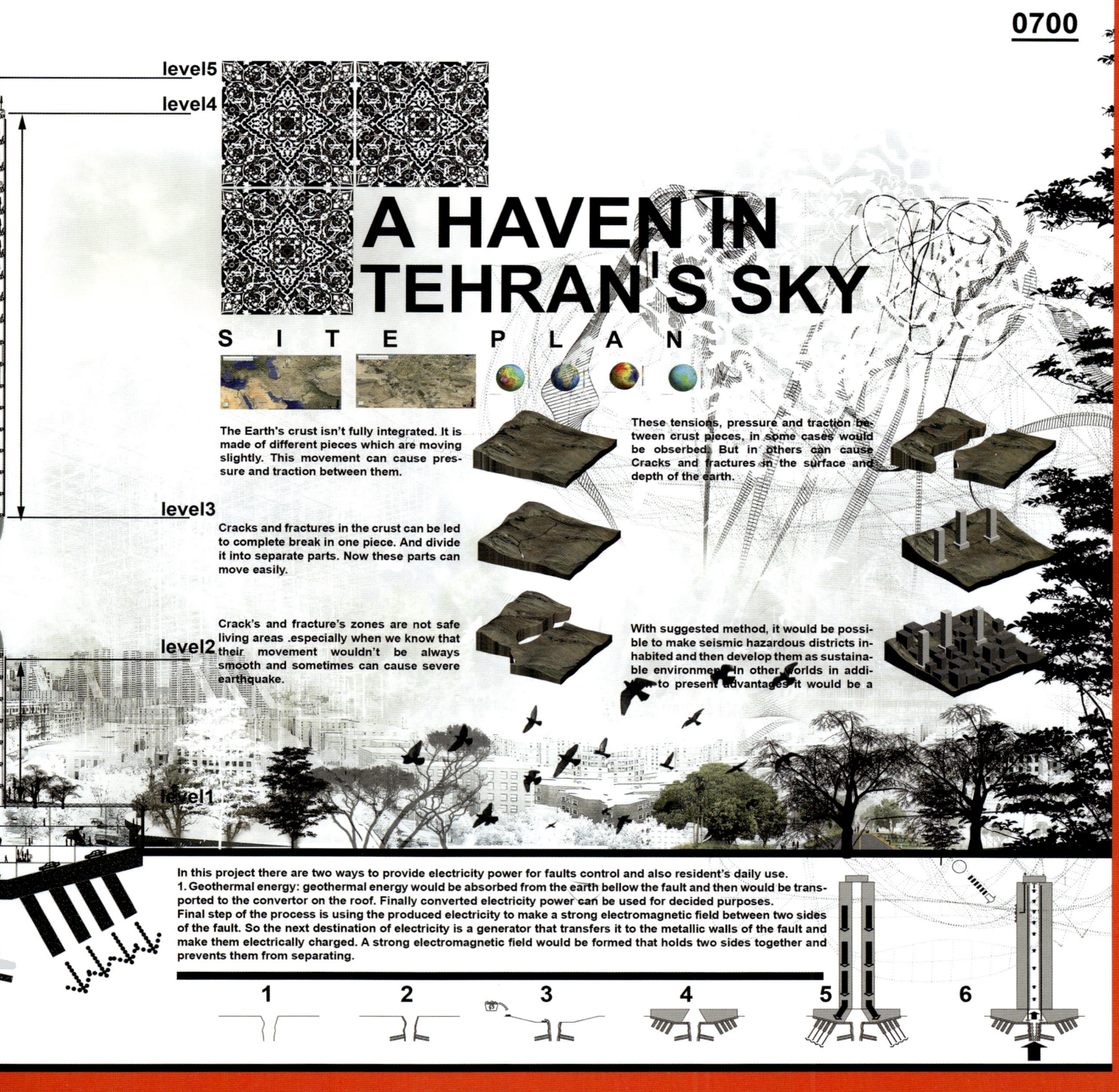

0700

A HAVEN IN TEHRAN'S SKY

S I T E   P L A N

level5
level4
level3
level2
level1

The Earth's crust isn't fully integrated. It is made of different pieces which are moving slightly. This movement can cause pressure and traction between them.

These tensions, pressure and traction between crust pieces, in some cases would be obserbed. But in others can cause Cracks and fractures in the surface and depth of the earth.

Cracks and fractures in the crust can be led to complete break in one piece. And divide it into separate parts. Now these parts can move easily.

Crack's and fracture's zones are not safe living areas .especially when we know that their movement wouldn't be always smooth and sometimes can cause severe earthquake.

With suggested method, it would be possible to make seismic hazardous districts inhabited and then develop them as sustainable environment. In other worlds in addition to present advantages it would be a

In this project there are two ways to provide electricity power for faults control and also resident's daily use.
1. Geothermal energy: geothermal energy would be absorbed from the earth bellow the fault and then would be transported to the convertor on the roof. Finally converted electricity power can be used for decided purposes.
Final step of the process is using the produced electromagnetic field between two sides of the fault. So the next destination of electricity is a generator that transfers it to the metallic walls of the fault and make them electrically charged. A strong electromagnetic field would be formed that holds two sides together and prevents them from separating.

1   2   3   4   5   6

DANDELION VESSEL

Wei Ke Li
Sgeng Jiang
Xing Chun Zhi Zhang

China

Nowadays, there is a group of people who are out of the society, because of living in remote areas, the traffic is not convenient and they are gradually isolated from the outside world. Poor medical and traffic standards result into the reduction of local population. Located in the central area of North Guangxi Rongshui County, the area is 50 km long and 30-35 km wide, with general height of 1500 m. The Mount Yuanbaoshan is 2081 m above sea level and it is the third highest mountain in Guangxi province. In this valley, people who live in poverty are difficult to communicate with the outside world. In recent years, natural disasters have become worse, but it takes too long time to escape from the town. So when the nature disaster come or the people get sick, they are sentenced to death, so we have to solve the problem. There is a river flows through the valley, the river is the source of the water for the local people. Usually, the

0080

amount of water is relatively stable, but the water tends to rise when the rainfall becomes large. If the it keeps raining, the water level will become higher and higher, resulting in floods, landslides and other natural disasters. There have been many villagers loss their life for this reason. We thought of making a 'master assembling station'. When natural disasters occur, every household can reach the station by the device of the refugees, which prepared for every house quickly. The "station" has many small units for people to live in. In this way we can avoid life's loss in a better way. In the small container, we provide a place for the villagers to rest and reside in. Even when there is no disaster, the villagers also can go to any places where has medical treatment or

Other facilities by the devices we designed. The behavior of station looks like dandelion, so we call it

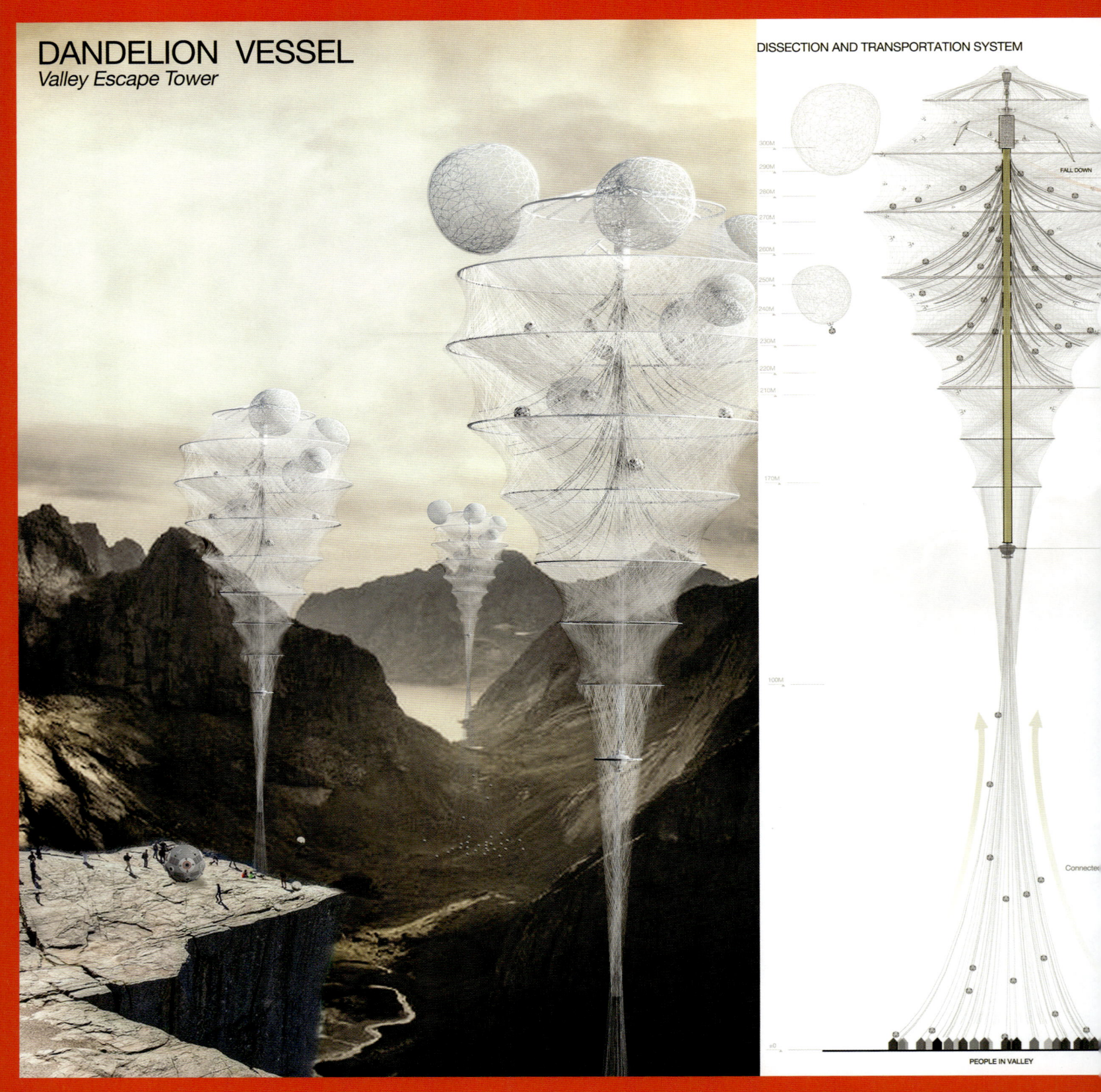

DANDELION VESSEL
Valley Escape Tower

DISSECTION AND TRANSPORTATION SYSTEM

'dandelion vessel'. We made it possible to combine these villages and to transport the people from the bottom to the master station which can transfer the people who are in emergency while contacting with the outside environment very well. So that people can adapt to nature better, rather than to reform the natural.

The master station' is made by membrane and tensile, every house will given a rescues unit which can rise to the station when they need. And the surface of the 'master station' is made of strings and tensile, and the membrane will be inflated to a inflation balloon units which can link to rescue units to get away form station.

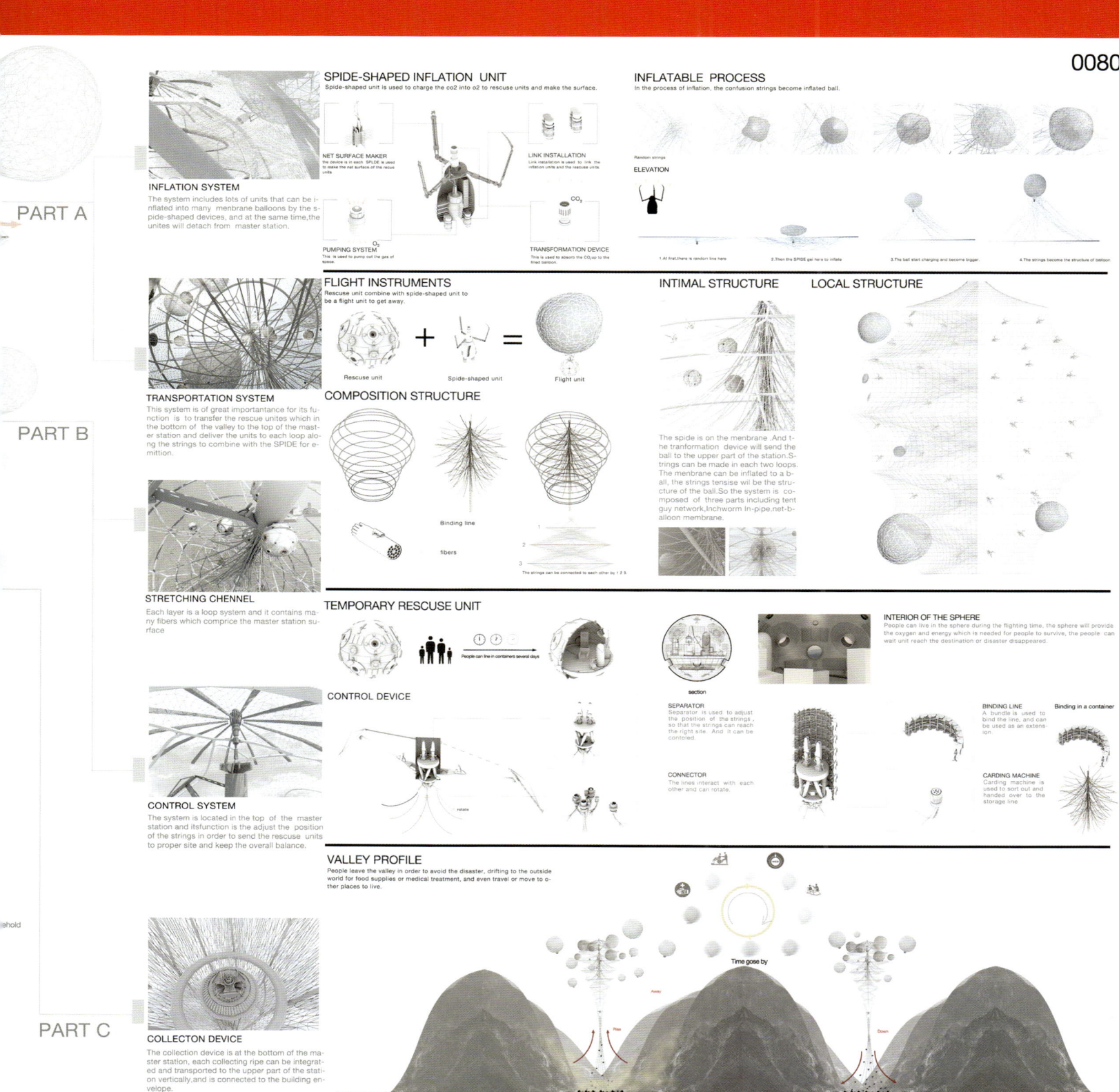

LOGISTICS REVOLUTION: DRONES HUBE

Ge Feiran
Zhuang Changming
Xue Songnan
Xue Han
Huang Ying

China

LOGISTICS REVOLUTION———DRONES HUB

That is often the case. Waves of online shopping always make the logistics crash: packages are piled up mountain-high in the mail station; couriers shuttle among the streets without a rest. Even though the logistics companies work so hard, packages can still hardly be sent to customers timely. Why is this always the case? Firstly, the development of e-commerce causes the booming up of the on-line trade, which contributes the goods, movement more frequently and faster. This gives the enormous pressure on logistics system. Secondly, rapid urbanization makes the urban larger and higher and also the road more crowded. This situation will become even more dramatic in the following years.

Up to the year 2030 the road transportation is about to double - compared to 2015. Longer distance and higher buildings as well as crowded street prevent the couriers' way to deliver. To catch up with steps

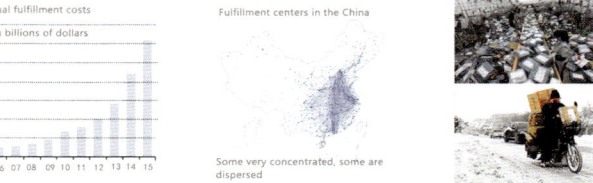

0178

Situations of the logistic

That is often the case. Waves of online shopping always make the logistics crash: packages are piled up mountain-high in the mail station ; couriers shuttle among the streets without a rest . Even though the logistics companies work so hard, packages can still hardly be sent to customers timely. Why might this always be the case?

Firstly, the development of e-commerce causes the booming up of the on-line trade, which contributes the goods movement more frequently and faster. This gives the enormous pressure on logistics system.
Secondly , rapid urbanization makes the urban larger and higher and also the road more crowded . This situation will become even more dramatic in the following years . Up to the year 2030 the road transportation is about to double - compared to 2015. Longer distance and higher buildings as well as crowded street prevent the couriers' way to deliver.

Annual fulfillment costs
In billions of dollars

Fulfillment centers in the China

Some very concentrated, some are dispersed

Strategy of revolution

To catch up with steps of e-commerce and urbanization, a brand new mode of logistics should be established.Compared with the traditional one, the new mode must be more comprehensive.
The logistics-net system should be established in the whole area. Such system is composed of "node" and "line" . The "node" is the "logistics-skyscraper" which is built in each city and responsible to machine, storage, packing, sorting and transportation . While the "line" is the "underground-pipeline" system which is used to connect logistics skyscrapers in each city and transport packages among skyscrapers.
The logistics-skyscraper integrates the source and need of the city which improves the efficiency while the underground-pipeline system forms the dedicated line of package which increases the speed of goods movement and keep the goods safely.
When it comes to the delivery from company to customer, the UAV should be taken into consideration. UAVs could provide major relief for inner cities, taking traffic off the roads and into the skies. So far, payloads are limited but a network of UAVs could nevertheless support first and last-mile logistics networks.

Mapping the drone highway system

Exelis is close to unveiling a low-altitude aircraft surveillance software system, Symphony RangeVue that could help drones to fly beyond the line of sight of the operator.

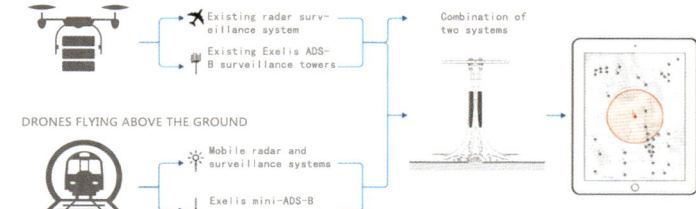

DRONES FLYING ABOVE THE GROUND

→ Existing radar surveillance system
→ Existing Exelis ADS-B surveillance towers
Combination of two systems

DRONES FLYING ABOVE THE GROUND

→ Mobile radar and surveillance systems
→ Exelis mini-ADS-B ground relay stations

1. Goods and signals are transmitted from the respective aircraft or drone to various surveillance towers.

2. The goods are then sent to the system Data from the drones are also sent to this air traffic control towers.

3. Users can then see a moving map that tracks aircraft around the drone on a laptop.

Two kinds of system

The underground-pipeline system
The pipelines are the dedicated traffic system of packages and connect logistic skyscrapers to form the net system. Since the type of goods are different, we classify the pipes into certain types to transport certain goods which can insure the safety and efficiency.

The UAV and capacity in-box
The UAV carrying package lifts from the logistics skyscraper, flies through the city, and finally delivers the package into customer's balcony. To ensure the accuracy of delivery , there is a capacity inbox in each balcony equipping with an qr code scanner . When the uav arrives, it scan the qr code to make sure the package is delivered. Such transporting system releases the traffic pressure on road and shorten the time of delivery.

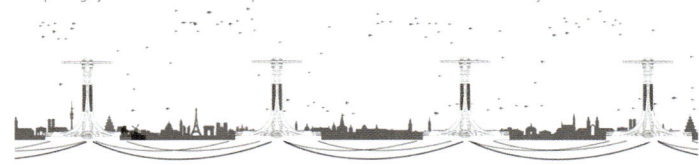

of e-commerce and urbanization, a brand new mode of logistics should be established. Compared with the traditional one, the new mode must be more comprehensive.

The logistics-net system should be established in the whole area. Such system is composed of "node "and "line". The "node" is the "logistics-skyscraper" which is built in each city and responsible to machine, storage, packing, sorting and transportation. While the "line" is the "underground-pipeline" system which is used to connect logistics skyscrapers in each city and transport packages among skyscrapers.

The logistics-skyscraper integrates the source and need of the city which improves the efficiency while the underground-pipeline system forms the dedicated line of package which increases the speed of goods movement and keep the goods safely.

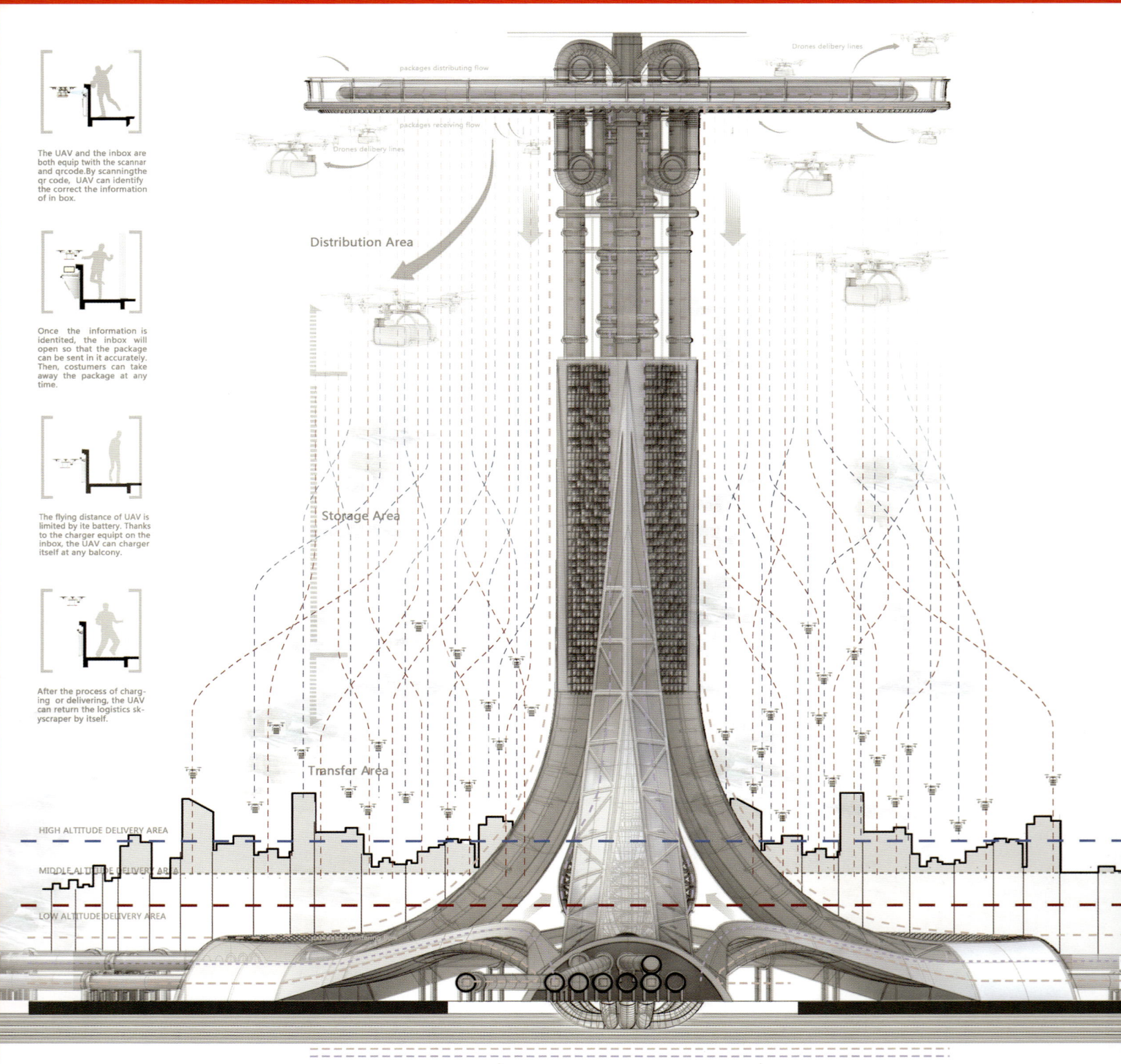

The UAV and the inbox are both equip twith the scannar and qrcode.By scanningthe qr code, UAV can identify the correct the information of in box.

Once the information is identited, the inbox will open so that the package can be sent in it accurately. Then, costumers can take away the package at any time.

The flying distance of UAV is limited by ite battery. Thanks to the charger equipt on the inbox, the UAV can charger itself at any balcony.

After the process of charging or delivering, the UAV can return the logistics skyscraper by itself.

When it comes to the delivery from company to customer, the UAV should be taken into consideration. UAVs could provide major relief for inner cities, taking traffic off the roads and into the skies. So far, payloads are limited but a network of UAVs could nevertheless support first and last-mile logistics networks.

ART A

[Distribution system]
The distribution system consists of delivery pipes and returned packages pipes.On the top of the hub centre, all distribution pipes radiate from the centre transportation pipes to the surrounding stretch. The drones will enter the hub through retractable doors and load the ordered packages after unloding the returned packages. The returned packages will be sent into special pipes that connected to the downward collecting-distributing center.

Distribution level perspective

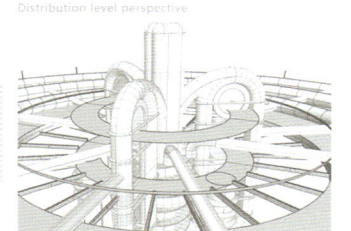

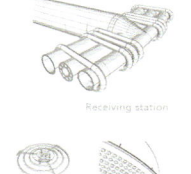

Receiving station

Wheel diverter retractable entrance

Experimental Pilot

0178

POPULATION:79.6 MILLION
AREA : 102,600 KM²

In 2015,there are 22.9 billion packages deliveried in Jiangsu province.

MAIN CITIES
MINOR CITIES
NEW SYSTEM

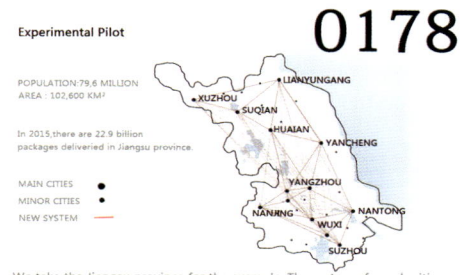

We take the Jiangsu province for the example. The system of new logitics net connects main cities by underground-pipes and UAVs. Through this logistics net , packages can be transported from on place to another in this province fast and safety.

ART B

[Order picking system]
This system is for highly efficient order picking. Packages and shipping units in the pipes will be calculated accurately in advance; picked products are placed directly into the shipping unit . This system will combine with a collation method such as zone picking, compact picking or integrated picking and systems such as pick-to-light (P2L), voice picking and RFID scanning.

Components

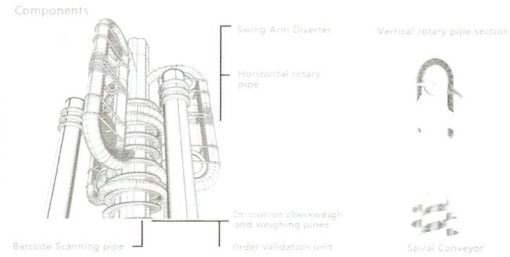

Swing Arm Diverter

Vertical rotary pipe section

Horizontal rotary pipe

In-motion checkweigh and weighing pipes

Barcode Scanning pipe

order validation unit

Spiral Conveyor

The delivery system is composed of a large number of UAVs. The uavs take off from the logistics skyscraper and carry packages to each customer's department punctually and accurately . This system relieves the pressure of the city traffic and saves the manpower.

ART C

[Automated storage and retrieval system]
An efficient AS/RS system will track where product are stocked, which suppliers they come from, and the length of time they are stored. By analyzing such data, this system can control inventory levels and maximize the use of warehouse space, which also improves organization of the contents of a warehouse. This system also enables a seamless link to order processing and logistics management in order to pick, pack, and ship product out of the facility.

Automated warehouse perspective

Transportation between the layers

Storage rack   Guide rails
portble belt conveyor

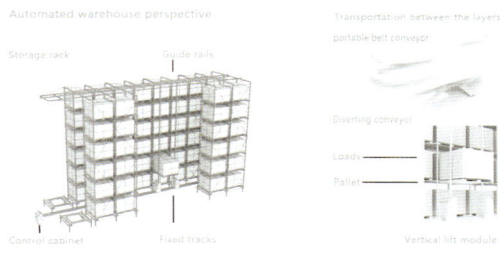

Diverting conveyor

Loady

Pallet

Control cabinet   Fixed tracks

Vertical lift module

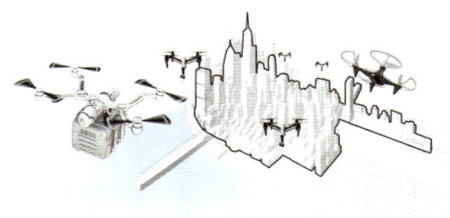

BLUELINE   REDLINE

Range:50km   Range:50km
Payload:10kg   Payload:10kg
Wingspan:2m   Wingspan:4m

x20   x200
x50
Total:10 Litres   x1.54

There are two sizes of UAV used in the delivery system. The smaller one can fly 50 kilometers diatance, carrying regular sized package. The larger one can fly 100 kilometers distance with package no more than 100kg.

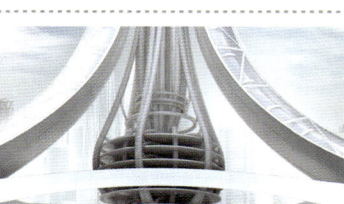

[Parcel automatic sorting system]
As soon as the packages have arrived at their final destinations , further transport will be provided by vertical and horizontal pipes . The system will use crosssed pipes pass through the package to the destination pipe crossings.

Sorting pipeline perspective

Telescopic sorting pipe

Barcode Printer

Labeling pipe

Wheel and axle

Curve conveyor

Packaging pipe

Roller conveyor

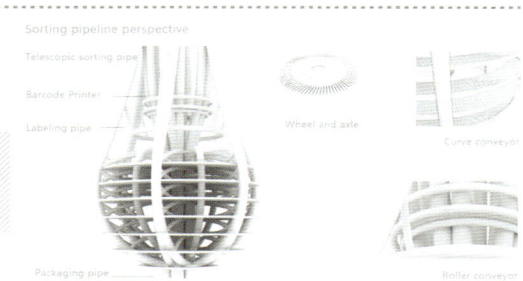

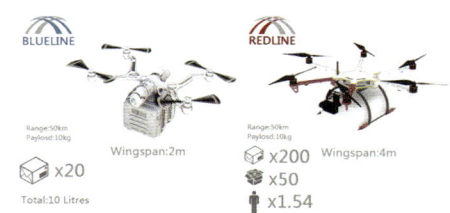

ART D

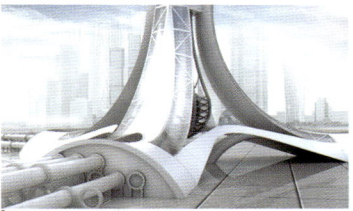

[Pipe transportation system]
Packages will be transported into the distribution hub via ground and underground pipe network from other cities.Streams of goods will roll with a highspeed towards their final destination .

Transportation pipe section

Magnets

Negative rail

Positive rail   Armature

Hub 1   Hub 2

Reduced-pressure tubes

Top speed 750mph

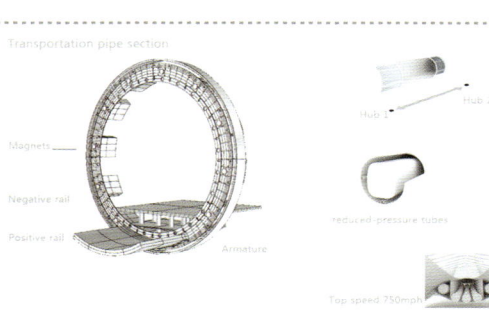

ART E

A CORE ISSUE AGAINST SMOG

Fangshuo Liu
Xiaoyu Wu
Jin Che
Shoda Tomoki
Pablo Bernar Fernández-Roca

China
Spain

A "CORE" ISSUE AGAINST SMOG

THE NEW URBAN AIR INFRASTRUCTURE

The human activities' byproducts, such as the piston effect of the metro and elevators and the stack effect of the dominating skyscrapers within the metropolis, are generally unexplored due to the ignorance of the severity of the environmental situation. Based on the fact that the smog problem within Chinese metropolis always concurs with the lack of air flow due to meteorological reasons, this design intends to utilize these passive energies as the source of urban air-flow.

By a careful analysis of our site——LUJIAZUI area and the discovery of the never-changing core structure system behind the ever-changing facades of the skyscrapers, our team arrived at the conclusion that designing a new core prototype could be of great value not just to the incorporation of these passive energies mentioned above into the great war against smog, but also to the education of the entire population.

Beside the traditional functions of a core such as the stairs, the, the toilets, the shafts and the elevators, this new core prototype includes this very core urban issue of AIR. Passive airflows from subways, elevators, atriums and stacks are intentionally conducted through a serious of carefully designed spaces and devices, so that the dangerous pollutants in the atmosphere can be absorbed by the mature and energy efficient methods, including centrifuge, wet deposition, HEPA, phytoremediation, and low voltage adsorption. Meanwhile more public and green spaces are created along this process, so that everyone within and without this building can interact with it to get more awareness of the air situation.

With the smog becoming a national issue, the government and the citizens in China are forced to fight together. FAR policies can be adopted to encourage the developers to apply this new core prototype which benefits the city, making such bold architectural adventure more sensible.

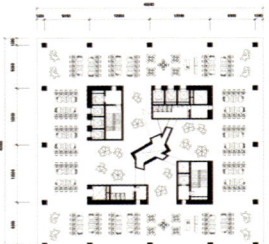

Base Core Plan +120 m

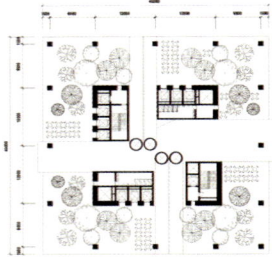

Base Core Plan +85 m

25 x 25 x 200

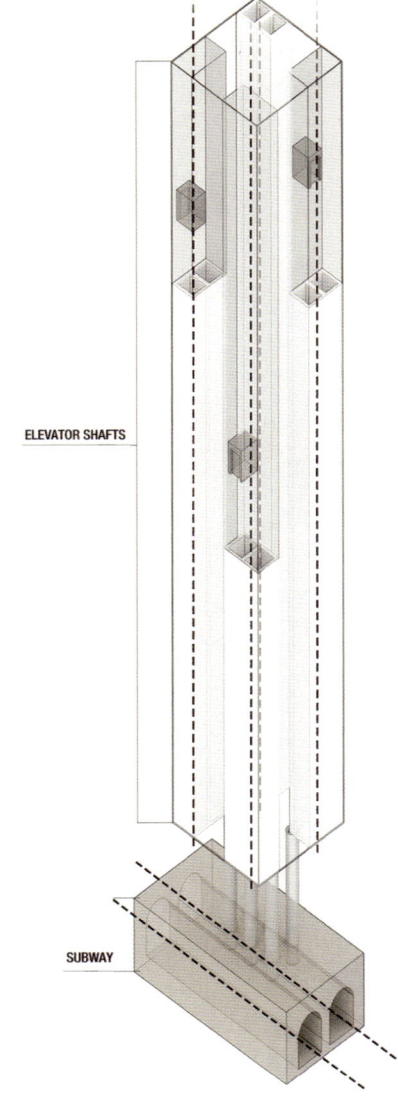

ELEVATOR SHAFTS

SUBWAY

ELEVATOR SHAFT + SUBWAY

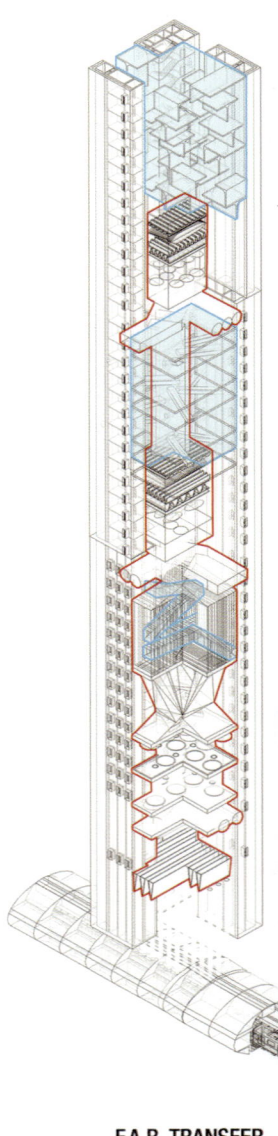

F.A.R. TRANSFER

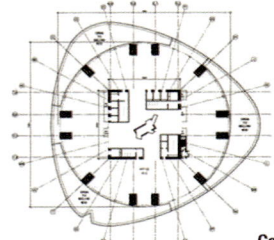

Core type 1

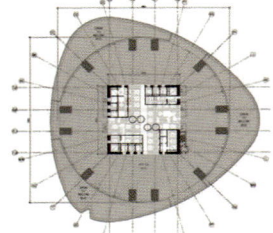

Core Type 2

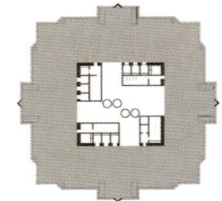

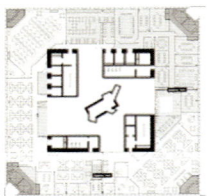

Core Type 3

Chinese cities are facing the worst environmental problem in recent years. The air quality is at the lowest levels and suspended particles are a constant threat to the overall population.

This project seeks to redirect polluted air into purifying systems located in the building core of the tallest skyscrapers. The idea is based on the fact that the lack of airflow is one of the main reasons of smog accumulation. This design utilizes passive energies to create an urban airflow.

The first iteration of modified skyscrapers would be located in the city of Shanghai. The building cores would still retain their basic programs including stairs, elevators, and restrooms but a new set of massive ducts would be designed to catch polluted air by energy efficient methods such as centrifuge systems, wet deposition, phytoremediation, and low voltage adsorption.

0218

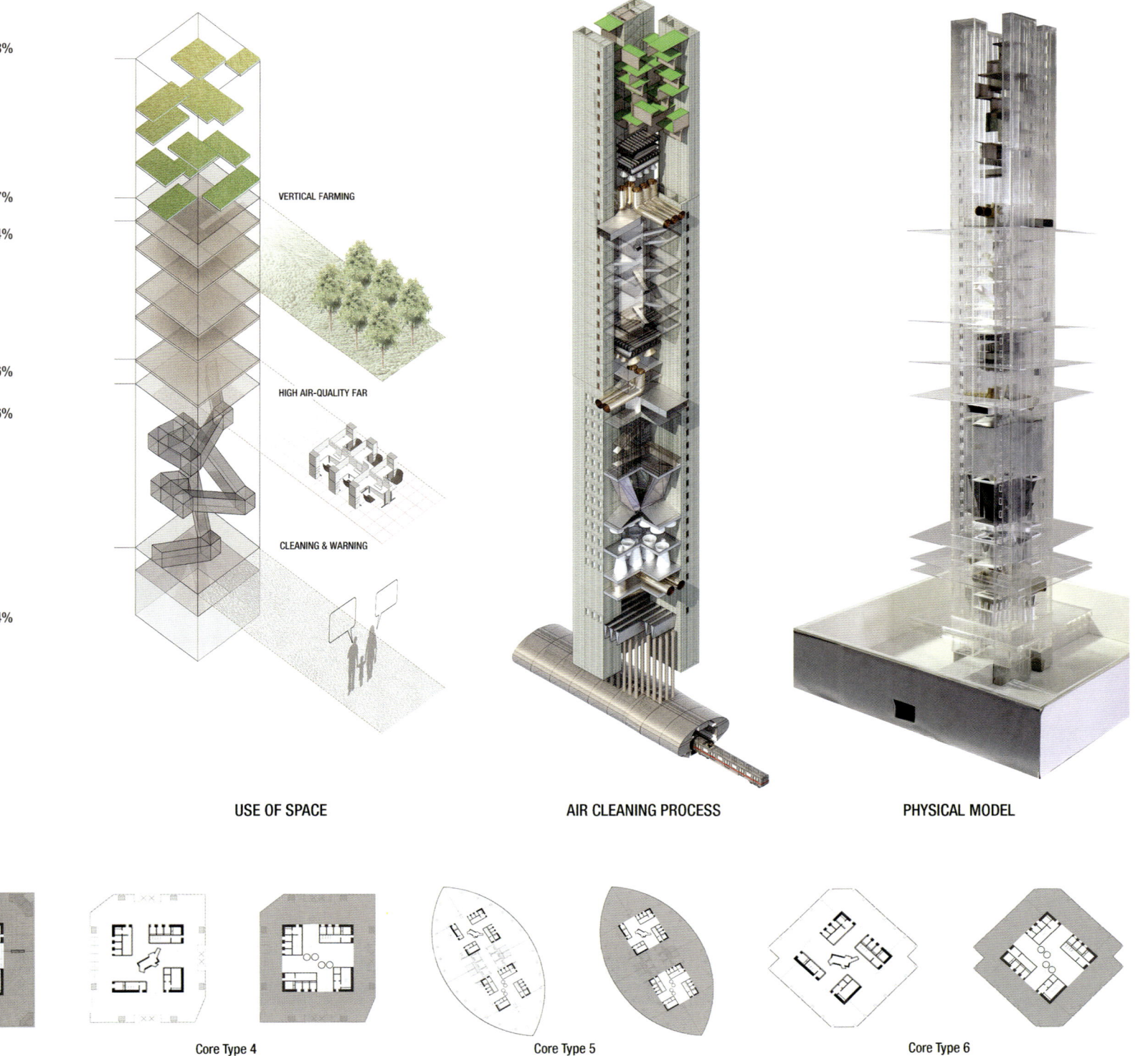

USE OF SPACE   AIR CLEANING PROCESS   PHYSICAL MODEL

VERTICAL FARMING

HIGH AIR-QUALITY FAR

CLEANING & WARNING

73%
27%
54%
46%
26%
74%

Core Type 4   Core Type 5   Core Type 6

Meanwhile, more green areas accessible to the public will be connected with the air-cleansing ducts at different levels.

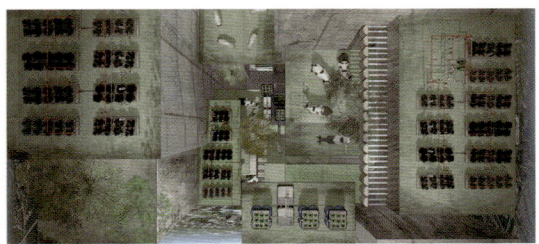

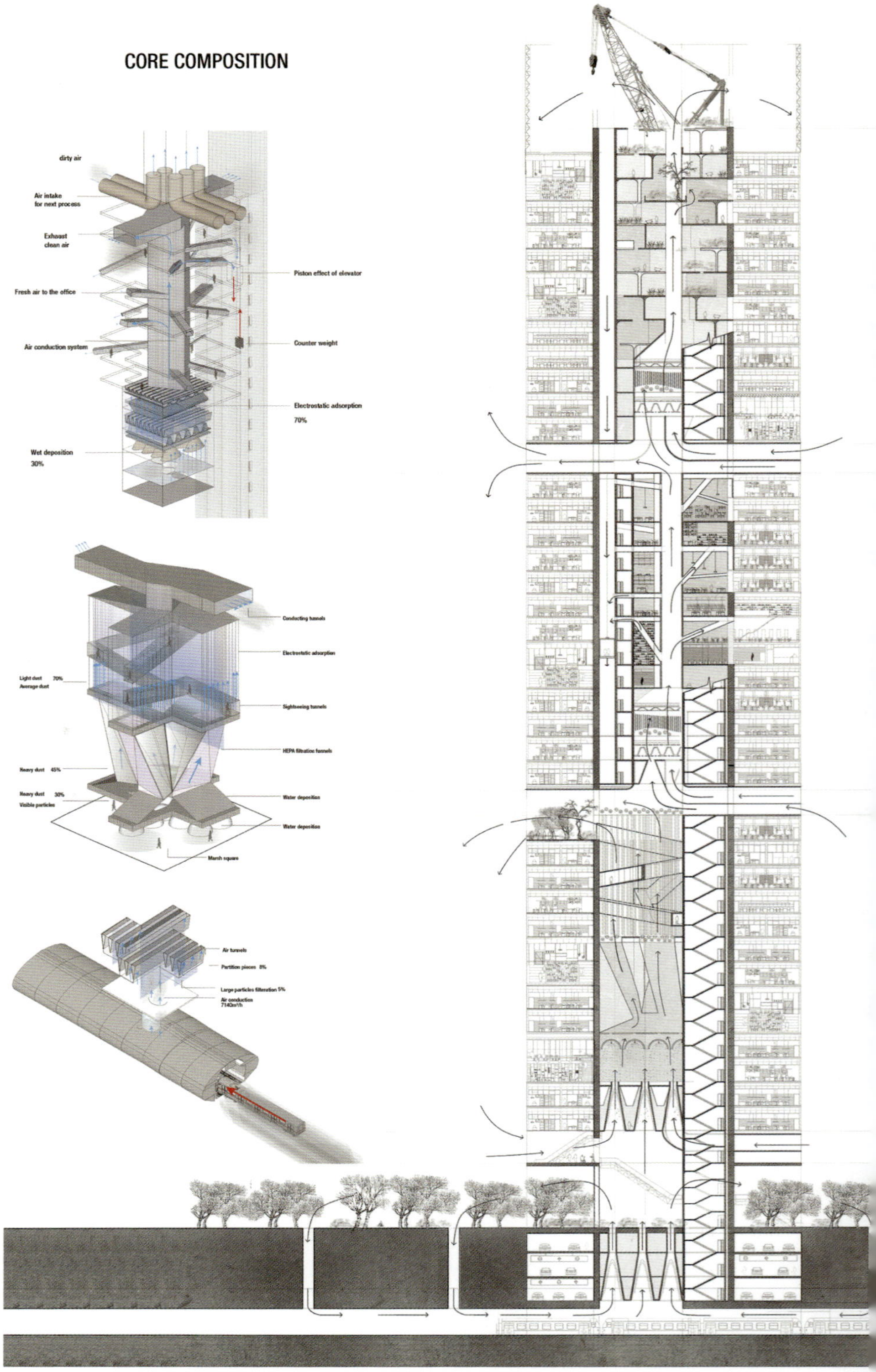

CORE COMPOSITION

AIR CLEANING PROCESS

Vertical farm

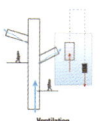

Ventilation

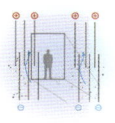

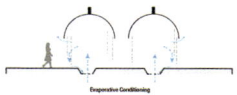

Evaporative Conditioning

HEPA filter

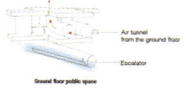

Ground floor public space

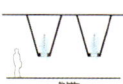

Air lobby

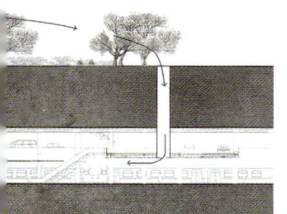

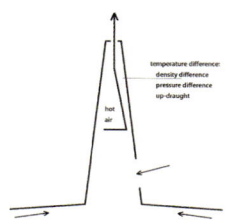

temperature difference
density difference
pressure difference
up-draught

hot air

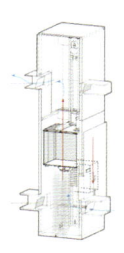

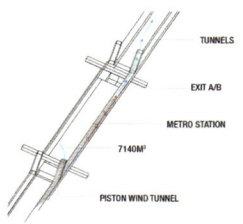

TUNNELS

EXIT A/B

METRO STATION

7140M³

PISTON WIND TUNNEL

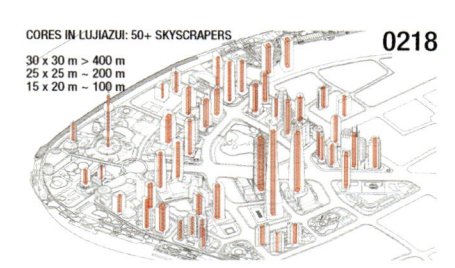

CORES IN LUJIAZUI: 50+ SKYSCRAPERS

30 x 30 m > 400 m
25 x 25 m ~ 200 m
15 x 20 m ~ 100 m

0218

NEW SHANGHAI   OLD SHANGHAI

94

DATA TOWER:
DATA CENTER IN
ICELAND

Valeria Mercuri
Marco Merletti

Italy

3RD PLACE / 2016

DATA TOWER
Future Data Center in Iceland

CASE

Data is proliferating: every transaction, entry, email, every clicking on mouse is stored by somebody in a server somewhere we don't even see. Annual global IP traffic will pass the zettabyte threshold by the end of 2016, and will reach 2 zettabytes per year by 2019.
Considering this, the problem in the next future will be to find a place to store these data.

A Data Center is the physical location hosting different servers used by many types of companies, it is used to store and process all the information we generate every day.
In the future, data and consequently the number of data centers will continue to grow, as well as their impact on the environment.
Today data centers consume a lot of energy and have a large carbon footprint: servers absorb a lot of electrical power and they need to be constantly cooled down to avoid overheating problems.

The solution for the future is hosting data centers where the power is clean and the costs are low. For this reason some companies have been started to think about Iceland.

SITE LOCATION

Iceland is a strategic location for data centers for 3 reasons:
- Location: its placement between Europe and the U.S. means that companies can run their web services for both continents in one location;
- Renewable energy sources: Iceland can offer data center services powered by 100% clean energy (hydropower and geothermal) for the same price or less than web services powered by fossil fuel-based grids in other locations;
- Climate: Iceland's proximity to the Arctic Circle allows to exploit cold temperatures and a fresh natural breeze that could be used to cool down the servers avoiding the costs of a traditional cooling system.

CONCEPT

Our project is a vision of how could it be a future green data center located in Iceland.
A data center is often a large industrial building without a significant architectural connotation, a big anonymous container.
The main issue of our project is to investigate a new morphological solution that could represent both the complexity and the importance of the building into which we keep our data.
Above all, we conceive the data center's configuration in order to maximize the use of the available renewable energies and also to allow the re-use in a sustainable way.

1 Zettabyte
= 1 billion TerabBytes
= 75 billion 16GB-size iPad

2016 88.4 EB data per month
= 17 billion 5GB HD movies

2019 168.0 EB data per month
and 3.9 billion internet users
(≈ 51% world population)

3 networked devices
per capita

Global IP traffic
growth diagram:
annual growth rate
= 23 % from 2014
to 2019

1% - 2% of all energy worldwide
is dedicated to Data Centers

BIG DATA = CO$_2$

Free cooling

Energy production:
75% hydropower
25% geothermal

100 % Renewable Energy

The largest data centers in the world range between 35.000 m² and 100.000 m² taking up a lot space.
On the contrary, we propose a vertical data center both to reduce the occupied space and to favour the use of natural and renewable resources.

The use of computing data is exponentially expanding: every Internet log, email, and even every mouse click is stored in a server. Annual global IP traffic will pass the zettabyte threshold by the end of 2016, and will reach two zettabytes per year by 2019. Considering this alarming numbers, a serious problem in the near future will be to design a place to store all this information. The solution for the future is hosting data centers where the power is clean and the costs are low. For this reason some companies have been started to think about Iceland. Iceland is a strategic location for 3 reasons. Location: its placement between Europe and the U.S. means that companies can run their web services for both continents in one location. Renewable energy sources: Iceland can offer data center services powered by 100% clean energy (hydropower and geothermal) for the same price or less than web services powered by fossil

0356 - 1

fuel-based grids in other locations. Climate: Iceland's proximity to the Arctic Circle allows exploiting cold temperatures and a fresh natural breeze that could be used to cool down the servers avoiding the costs of traditional cooling systems. Our project is a vision of how could a future green data center located in Iceland be. A data center is often a large industrial building without a significant architectural connotation, a big anonymous container. The main issue of our project is to investigate a new morphological solution that could represent both the complexity and the importance of the building into which we keep our data. Above all, we conceive the data center's configuration in order to maximize the use of the available renewable energies. The tower is conceived as a giant 3D motherboard with a cylindrical shape. On the external façade all the hardware components are secured. The interior void is a technical space with a

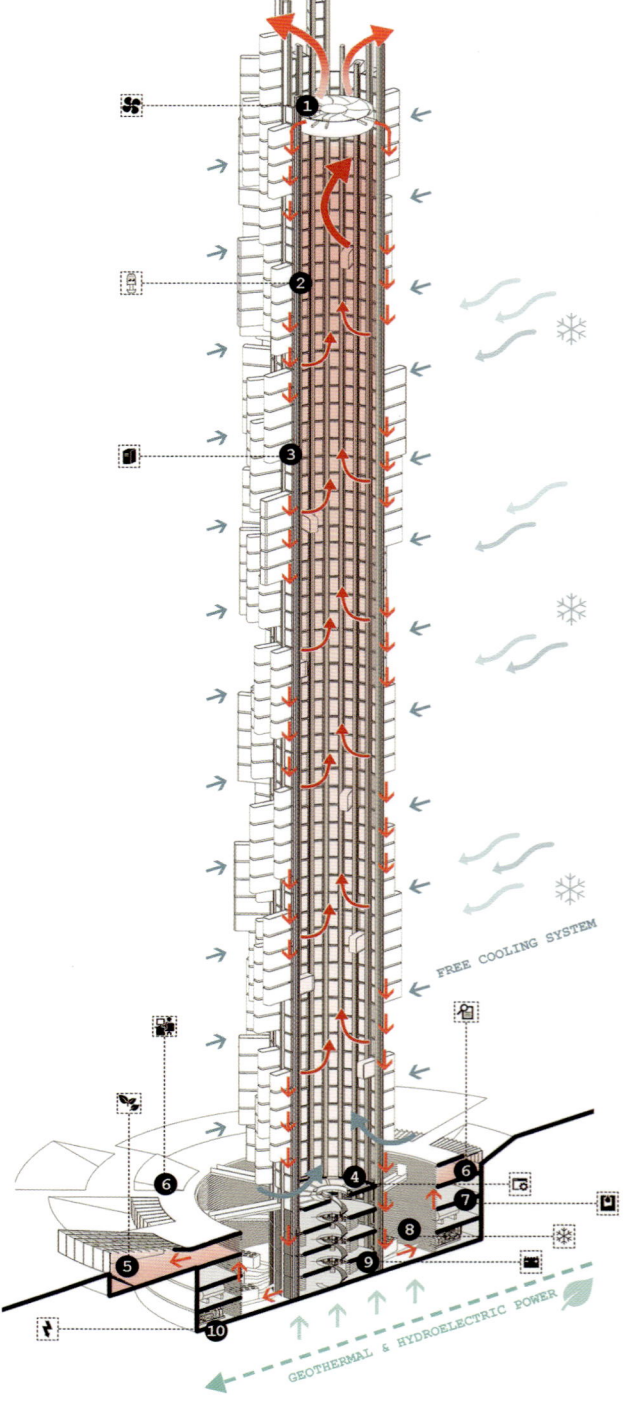

FREE COOLING SYSTEM

GEOTHERMAL & HYDROELECTRIC POWER

double function: first, it is the main air duct of the cooling system, and second it is a space where the pods can be moved to the ground floor, during the maintenance and the upgrade phases. Similar to a desktop computer, a huge cooling fan on the top of the tower activates a natural chimney effect, in which each pod takes the natural fresh air from the outside and releases the warm air inside. A part of this air is expelled from the top of the tower and another part is re-used to heat the laboratories and the greenhouses situated in the basement. During the winter the warm air released by the server could be used to heat the houses in the surrounding neighborhood. The modern data center is a building in continuous evolution just like a computer motherboard where components are always replaced and updated -the façade of the tower is adaptable and in continuous evolution; in fact, depending on necessity, the density and the position of the pods can freely change increasing the height of the tower.

0356 - 2

WER CONCEPT

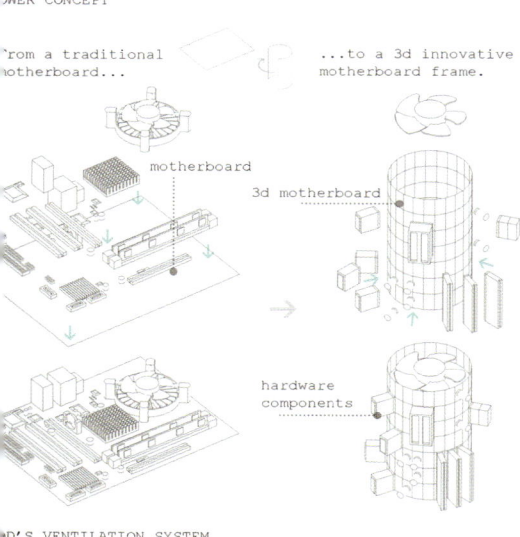

from a traditional motherboard...   ...to a 3d innovative motherboard frame.

motherboard

3d motherboard

hardware components

D'S VENTILATION SYSTEM

(interior)   (exterior)

pod

acks+servers

D'S MECHANICAL HANDLING SYSTEM

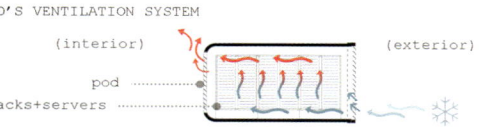

pod   steel structure

WER CONFIGURATION (65 storeys - H 300 m)

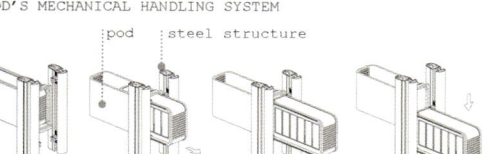

pod 4 racks

pod 5 racks

pod 6 racks

pod 7 racks

pod 8 racks

different types of pods

60% = 240.000 servers

100% = 400.000 servers

The tower is designed to grow over time: other pods can be added up to fill the availables slots on each floor.

The building can also grow in height, a 300 m tower is already able to host up to 400.000 servers, more than the bigger Data center in the world.

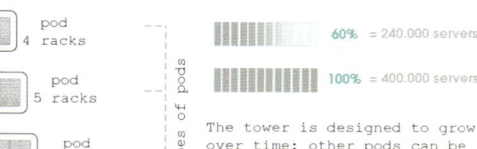

ooling fan

teel structure

od

ontrol Station

reenhouses

6 Laboratories & offices

7 Ice cold-water 4°C

8 Turbo-cooling units

9 Batteries

10 Diesel generators

VENTILATION SYSTEM / FREE COOLING

The cooling system is accomplished by an 100% ambient air: the fresh natural breeze is captured and conveyed into each pod to cool down the servers (= free cooling).

A particle filtration monitoring system guarantees that the natural air which flows into each pod is clean.

The heated air coming from each pod then goes toward the large central void and rises: part of it is recovered and re-used to heat the laboratories and a series of greenhouses surrounding the tower, while the rest is expelled by a cooling fan.

DATA STORAGE SYSTEM / PODS

The tower consists of a hollow cylindrical body supported by 24 steel pillars, to which are externally fastened the pods.

According to the need, tower can grow over the time, other pods can be added in order to achieve a smart scalability.

A control station is used to check each server and if an intervention is needed, a mechanical handling system carries the pod to the ground level where the technicians can operate.

RENEWABLE ENERGY

The basement hosts all the equipment rooms, the laboratories and the greenhouses.

The electricity required to run the entire building comes directly from Iceland's dual source grid, geothermal and hydroelectric.
In this way it is possible to have low cost, highly available and 100% green power.

In the basement there are also redundant heat rejection system that can be used if the needed rises (for example during the summer) and a backup power infrastructure design to run continuously in the case of an interruption to the already reliable sources of renewable energies.

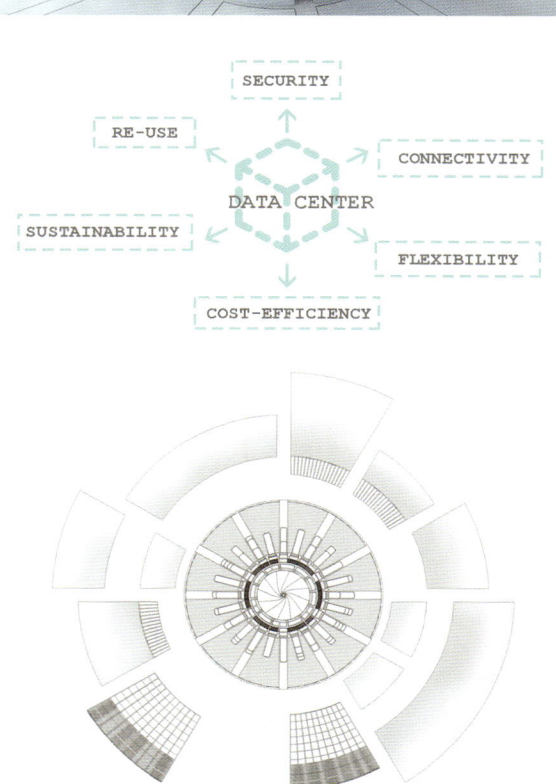

SECURITY

RE-USE

CONNECTIVITY

DATA CENTER

SUSTAINABILITY

FLEXIBILITY

COST-EFFICIENCY

ANGEL RING

Liu Gang
Qian Ren
Liu Jinrui

China

With the development of economy and technology, skyscrapers are booming around the world. But when encountering unexpected natural disasters and man-made emergencies, it is very difficult for the people on the top floors to evacuate using emergency stairs. How to evacuate to the ground safely is a big problem for those who are working and living in the upper floors of skyscrapers. Although the skyscraper fire scene in the history is shocking, the trend of building higher skyscrapers is irreversible.

With the development of economy and technology, the skyscraper has increasingly become a sophisticated machine. This design is inspired by the rocket escape tower and the space X Falcon9 retrievable rocket. Without prejudice to the internal functions and external morphology, solve the escape problem of people in the upper part of skyscrapers when meeting a fire accident by nesting an "Angel

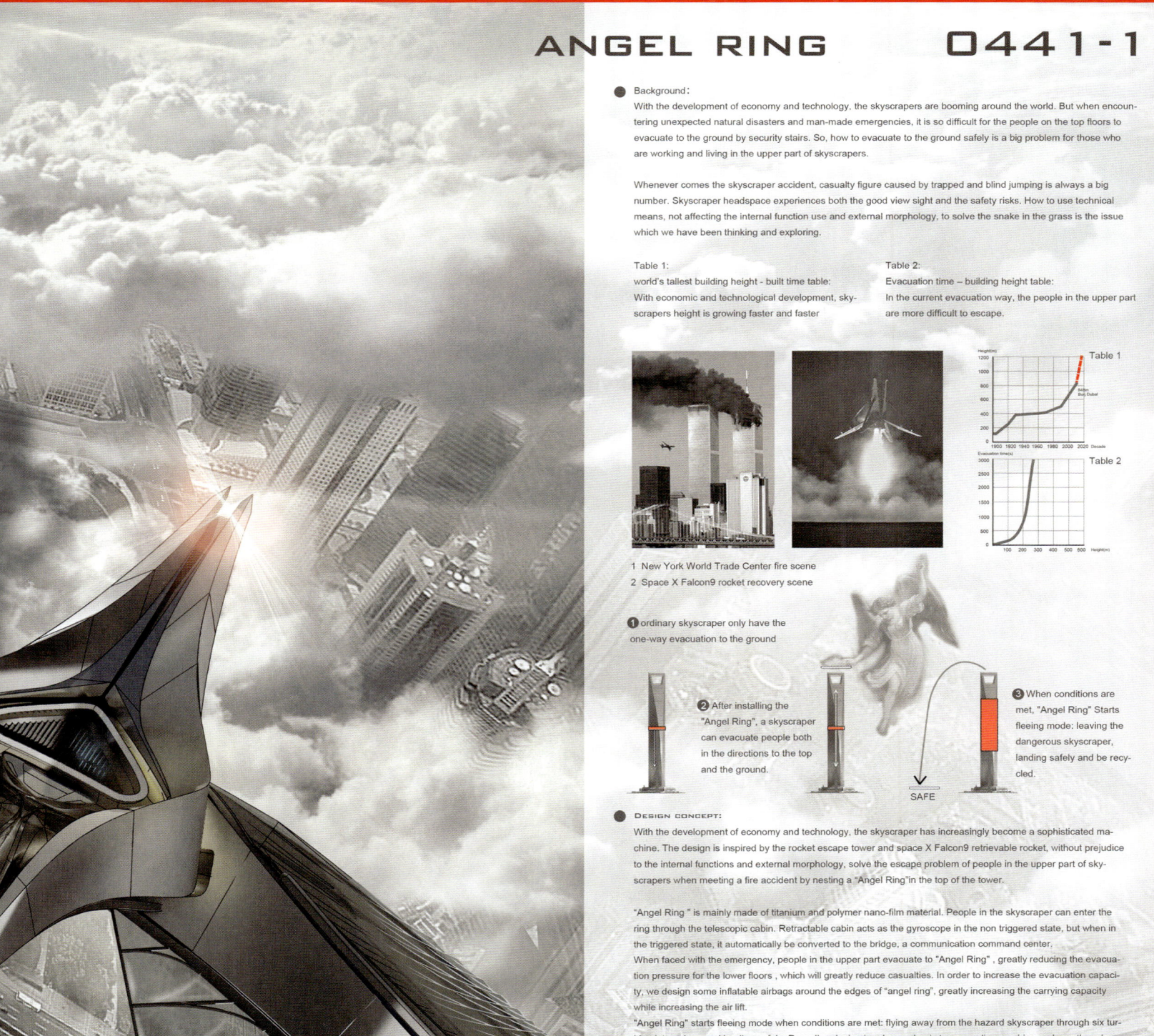

ANGEL RING   0441-1

● Background：
With the development of economy and technology, the skyscrapers are booming around the world. But when encountering unexpected natural disasters and man-made emergencies, it is so difficult for the people on the top floors to evacuate to the ground by security stairs. So, how to evacuate to the ground safely is a big problem for those who are working and living in the upper part of skyscrapers.

Whenever comes the skyscraper accident, casualty figure caused by trapped and blind jumping is always a big number. Skyscraper headspace experiences both the good view sight and the safety risks. How to use technical means, not affecting the internal function use and external morphology, to solve the snake in the grass is the issue which we have been thinking and exploring.

Table 1:
world's tallest building height - built time table:
With economic and technological development, skyscrapers height is growing faster and faster

Table 2:
Evacuation time – building height table:
In the current evacuation way, the people in the upper part are more difficult to escape.

Table 1

Table 2

1 New York World Trade Center fire scene
2 Space X Falcon9 rocket recovery scene

❶ ordinary skyscraper only have the one-way evacuation to the ground

❷ After installing the "Angel Ring", a skyscraper can evacuate people both in the directions to the top and the ground.

SAFE

❸ When conditions are met, "Angel Ring" Starts fleeing mode: leaving the dangerous skyscraper, landing safely and be recycled.

● DESIGN CONCEPT:
With the development of economy and technology, the skyscraper has increasingly become a sophisticated machine. The design is inspired by the rocket escape tower and space X Falcon9 retrievable rocket, without prejudice to the internal functions and external morphology, solve the escape problem of people in the upper part of skyscrapers when meeting a fire accident by nesting a "Angel Ring"in the top of the tower.

"Angel Ring " is mainly made of titanium and polymer nano-film material. People in the skyscraper can enter the ring through the telescopic cabin. Retractable cabin acts as the gyroscope in the non triggered state, but when in the triggered state, it automatically be converted to the bridge, a communication command center.
When faced with the emergency, people in the upper part evacuate to "Angel Ring" , greatly reducing the evacuation pressure for the lower floors , which will greatly reduce casualties. In order to increase the evacuation capacity, we design some inflatable airbags around the edges of "angel ring", greatly increasing the carrying capacity while increasing the air lift.
"Angel Ring" starts fleeing mode when conditions are met: flying away from the hazard skyscraper through six turbine jet engines and landing safely. Recycling design in advance leads to a recycling machine and greatly reduce the manufacturing cost.

Ring" in the top of the tower. The Angel Ring is mainly made of titanium and polymer nano-film material. People in the skyscraper can enter the ring through the telescopic cabin. When faced with the emergency, people in the upper part evacuate to the Angel Ring greatly reducing the evacuation pressure for the lower floors, which will greatly reduce casualties. In order to increase the evacuation capacity, we design some inflatable airbags around the edges that greatly increasing the carrying capacity while increasing the airlift.

Connection & Control System

The telescopic cabin consists of four parts: the connecting pipe, passage tube, lift-jet engine and the empennage. The connecting pipe can stretch to connect the skyscraper via the hydraulic system. The lift-jet engine works with the empennage to provide power when the ring is fleeing.

ANGEL RING

THE RING BRIDGE

06

Connecting Pipe   Passage tube

Connection & Control System(CCS)
The bridge is the main part of the "Angel R the control center. On the other hand, it is tween the skyscraper and the ring. It cons necting pipe, passage tube, lift-jet engine connecting pipe can stretch to connect the lic system. The passage tube transports p the ring. The lift-jet engine works with th power when the ring is fleeing.

03

02

ELEVATION

01

Balanced System & Energy System

In peacetime, the Angel ring works as a sightseeing corridor. The ETFE film in the center catches the upwind produced by the skyscraper, so the ring can stay in the air. We have six left-jet engines all controlled by the central computer so that every engine can adjust the jet volume to keep the ring horizontally. The material of the ring is titanium alloy to make it as light as possible.

Fleeing System

When the accident has happened, people who are in the upper floor of the skyscraper can get into the Angel ring to escape. In order to improve the efficiency of rescue, the wings will open so that the Angel ring can hold as many people as possible. There are inflatable airbags inside the wings. When the wings open, the bags will blow up to provide a safety place for people.

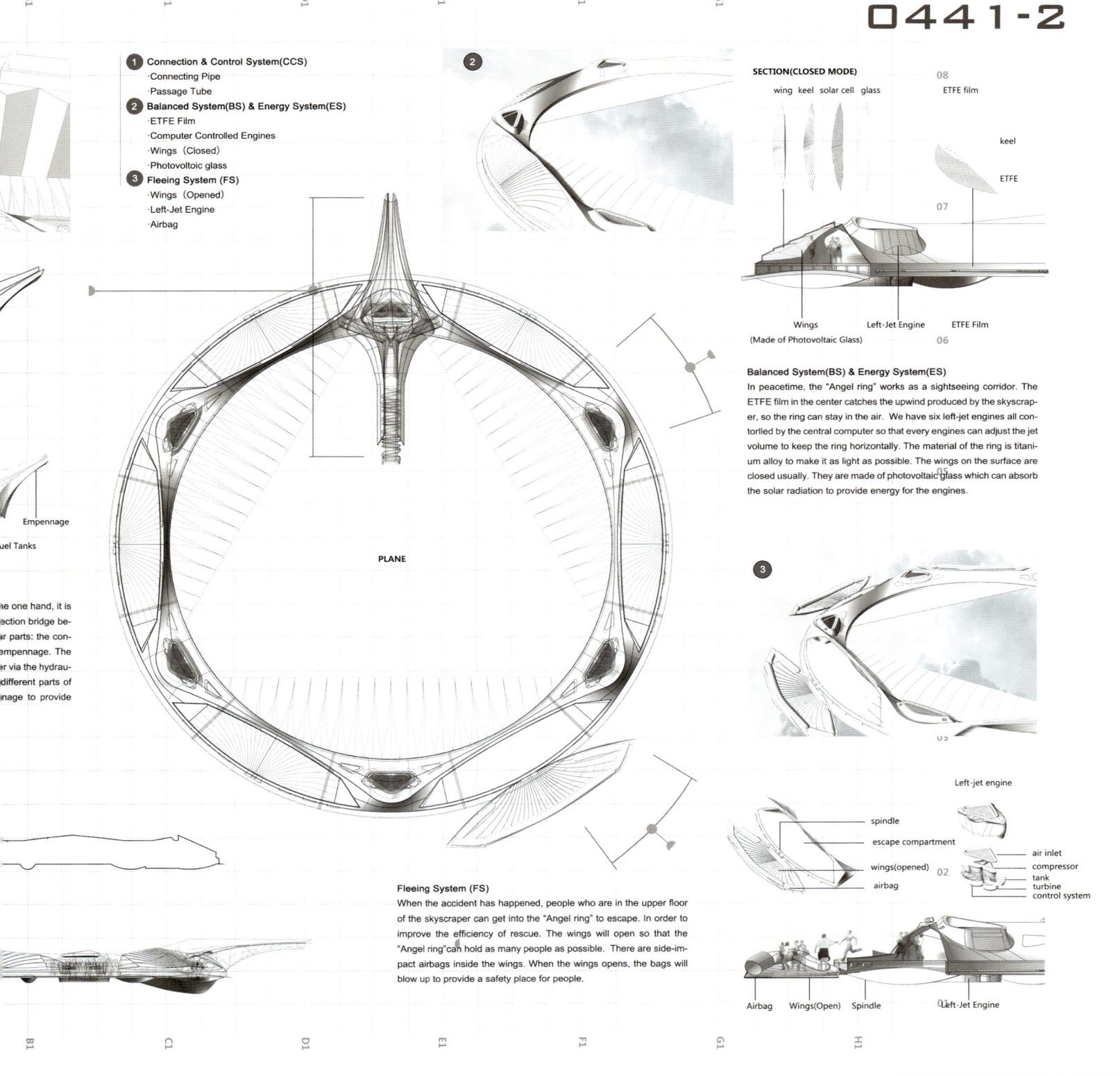

0441-2

1 Connection & Control System(CCS)
· Connecting Pipe
· Passage Tube
2 Balanced System(BS) & Energy System(ES)
· ETFE Film
· Computer Controlled Engines
· Wings (Closed)
· Photovoltoic glass
3 Fleeing System (FS)
· Wings (Opened)
· Left-Jet Engine
· Airbag

Empennage

uel Tanks

e one hand, it is
ection bridge be-
r parts: the con-
empennage. The
r via the hydrau-
different parts of
nage to provide

PLANE

SECTION(CLOSED MODE)

wing keel solar cell glass

08

ETFE film

keel

ETFE

07

06

Wings   Left-Jet Engine   ETFE Film
(Made of Photovoltaic Glass)

Balanced System(BS) & Energy System(ES)

In peacetime, the "Angel ring" works as a sightseeing corridor. The ETFE film in the center catches the upwind produced by the skyscraper, so the ring can stay in the air. We have six left-jet engines all contorlled by the central computer so that every engines can adjust the jet volume to keep the ring horizontally. The material of the ring is titanium alloy to make it as light as possible. The wings on the surface are closed usually. They are made of photovoltaic glass which can absorb the solar radiation to provide energy for the engines.

Left-jet engine

spindle
escape compartment
wings(opened) 02
airbag

air inlet
compressor
tank
turbine
control system

Fleeing System (FS)

When the accident has happened, people who are in the upper floor of the skyscraper can get into the "Angel ring" to escape. In order to improve the efficiency of rescue. The wings will open so that the "Angel ring"can hold as many people as possible. There are side-impact airbags inside the wings. When the wings opens, the bags will blow up to provide a safety place for people.

Airbag Wings(Open) Spindle   Left-Jet Engine

CLOUD CRAFT: RAINMAKING SKYSCRAPER

Michael Militello
Amar Shah

United States

CLOUD CRAFT
Cloud Seeding & Weather Modification in the 21st Century

California Drought

As populated and metropolised as some parts of California are, the truth is, most of California is an arid semi-desert, with a climate similar to that of the North African Plain. About 65 percent of the state receives less than 20 inches of rainfall per year, most of that in the winter months. Droughts are a recurring feature of California's climate, and the current four-year period starting from the fall of 2011 has been the driest in history since recordkeeping began in 1895. So much so that Governor Brown declared a statewide drought emergency in January 2014, establishing an interagency drought response team.

California is in fact the world's fifth-largest supplier of food. Most farming in California depends on irrigation, which usually accounts for about 80% of the state's human water use. In 2014 growers lost about 6.6 million acre-feet of surface water and 2.2 billion dollars because of the drought. California, much like the rest of the planet, is in dire need of immediate rain and snowfall, long-term water conservation and storage strategies for the future, and responsible architectural designs that incorporate innovative technologies to help preserve the earth's environment, before it is too late . . .

Cloud Seeding

Even in areas with very low humidity, there's at least some water in the sky and clouds. Clouds contain supercooled liquid water vapor. A rainstorm happens after moisture collects around naturally occurring particles in the air, causing the air to reach a level of saturation at which point it can no longer hold in that moisture. Cloud seeding essentially helps that process along, providing additional "nuclei" around which water condenses. These nuclei can be salts, dry ice, or silver iodide which are all effective because their crystalline structural forms are similar to that of ice. The water vapor molecules combine with the crystals to induce freezing nucleation, resulting in larger water droplets.

Cloud seeding has been around for many decades and used throughout the world in various strategies. China used cloud seeding in Beijing just before the 2008 Olympic Games in order to clear the air of pollution. Farmers in the midwestern United States shoot flares of silver iodide out of planes to help spur rainfall in that region. It is more and more becoming a popular weather modification tool to help combat drought, famine, pollution, solar radiation, etc.

CALIFORNIA DROUGHT LEVELS
Abnormally Dry Moderate Drought Severe Drought Extreme Drought Exceptional Drought

2011   2012   2013   2014   2015

PERCENTAGES OF L.A. WATER SUPPLY SOURCES

LA AQUEDUCT	COLORADO RIVER AQUEDUCT	CALIFORNIA STATE WATER PROJECT
50%	42%	26%

OWENS VALLEY   LA AQUEDUCT

SEEDING PROCESS ON A CUMULUS CLOUD

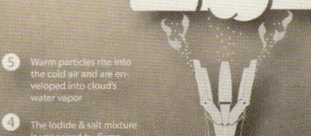

3 Cumulus marine cloud formed over the ocean passes overhead

2 Salt is mixed with iodide chemical to create a particle mixture

1 Ocean water naturally evaporates from desalination pools at the base and remaining salt is syphoned up the tower to mixing stations

5 Warm particles rise into the cold air and are enveloped into cloud's water vapor

4 The iodide & salt mixture is vaporized by flame and sprayed into atmosphere as particles

7 The artificial nuclei from the salt & iodide particles attract more water vapour within the cloud and combine to create larger droplets

6 Iodide & salt crystals have almost the same shape and form of ice crystals within clouds

10 Rainwater harvesting nets mounted in the tower catch condensation and precipitation, storing water for the farms

9 Precipitation turns to snow in colder atmospheres and rainfall in warmer areas. Entire precipitation process can last as quick as 10 min.

8 The combined larger ice crystal droplets within the cloud become heavier and eventually cause precipitation

EVAPORATION & DESALINATION   SEEDING   NUCLEATION   PRECIPITATION

Droughts are a recurring feature of California's climate, and the current four-year period starting from the fall of 2011 has been the driest in history since recordkeeping began in 1895. California, much like the rest of the planet, is in dire need of immediate rain and snowfall; long-term water conservation and storage strategies for the future; and responsible architectural designs that incorporate innovative technologies to help preserve the earth's environment, before it is too late. Looking to the sky can be a solution. Cloud seeding has been around for many decades and used throughout the world in various strategies. China used cloud seeding in Beijing just before the 2008 Olympic Games in order to clear the air of pollution. Farmers in the midwestern United States shoot flares of silver iodide out of planes to help spur rainfall in that region. Clouds contain super-cooled liquid water vapor. A rainstorm happens after moisture collects

0522

around naturally occurring particles in the air, causing the air to reach a level of saturation at which point it can no longer hold in that moisture. The process of cloud seeding essentially provides additional "nuclei" around which water vapor molecules condense in the cloud. These nuclei can be salts, dry ice, or silver iodide, which are all effective because their crystalline structural forms are similar to that of ice. The water vapor molecules combine with the added crystals to induce freezing nucleation, resulting in larger heavier water droplets and eventual precipitation. The architectural concept imagines a future earth where cloud seeding has become the standard process to modify and manipulate the weather. Cloud seeding can result in many positive environmental outcomes including temperature control, flooding prevention, decreasing pollution, dispersing fog, and deflecting solar radiation. But for the purposes of California, it is mainly used

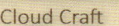

CLOUD FARMS

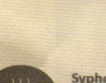
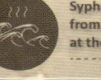

Cloud Craft

The architectural concept imagines a future earth where cloud seeding has become the standard process to modify and manipulate the weather. Cloud seeding can result in many positive environmental outcomes including temperature control, flooding prevention, decreasing pollution, dispersing fog, and deflecting solar radiation. But for the purposes of California, it is mainly used for irrigation and rainfall to combat droughts and famine.

Towers are erected near the coast so as the lower marine layer clouds pass overhead, they can be seeded at different times and intervals, causing precipitation to occur in as little as 10 minutes. After years of practice, scientists have been able to pinpoint the exact amount and timing of release of chemical mixtures in order to manipulate the path of a cloud after seeding and predict where the rainfall will occur. Thus, rainfall is dispersed or "doled out" to cities and towns further inland that are suffering from drought.

The towers themselves take on the aesthetics of a tree. Cloud pylons are mounted at the top of the tower, each individually capable of storing and releasing the seed mixture. Great limbs stretch to the sky, cloud farms grow like fungi off these limbs. The upper levels of the tower act as a self-sustaining community- the cloud pylons jettison the salt + iodide mixture into the air forcing the clouds to precipitate. The cable netting catches the rainfall and syphons it down to irrigate the farms. And the farms in turn provide food for the community. Residential flats line the cloud pythons, housing the farmers and workers of the tower.

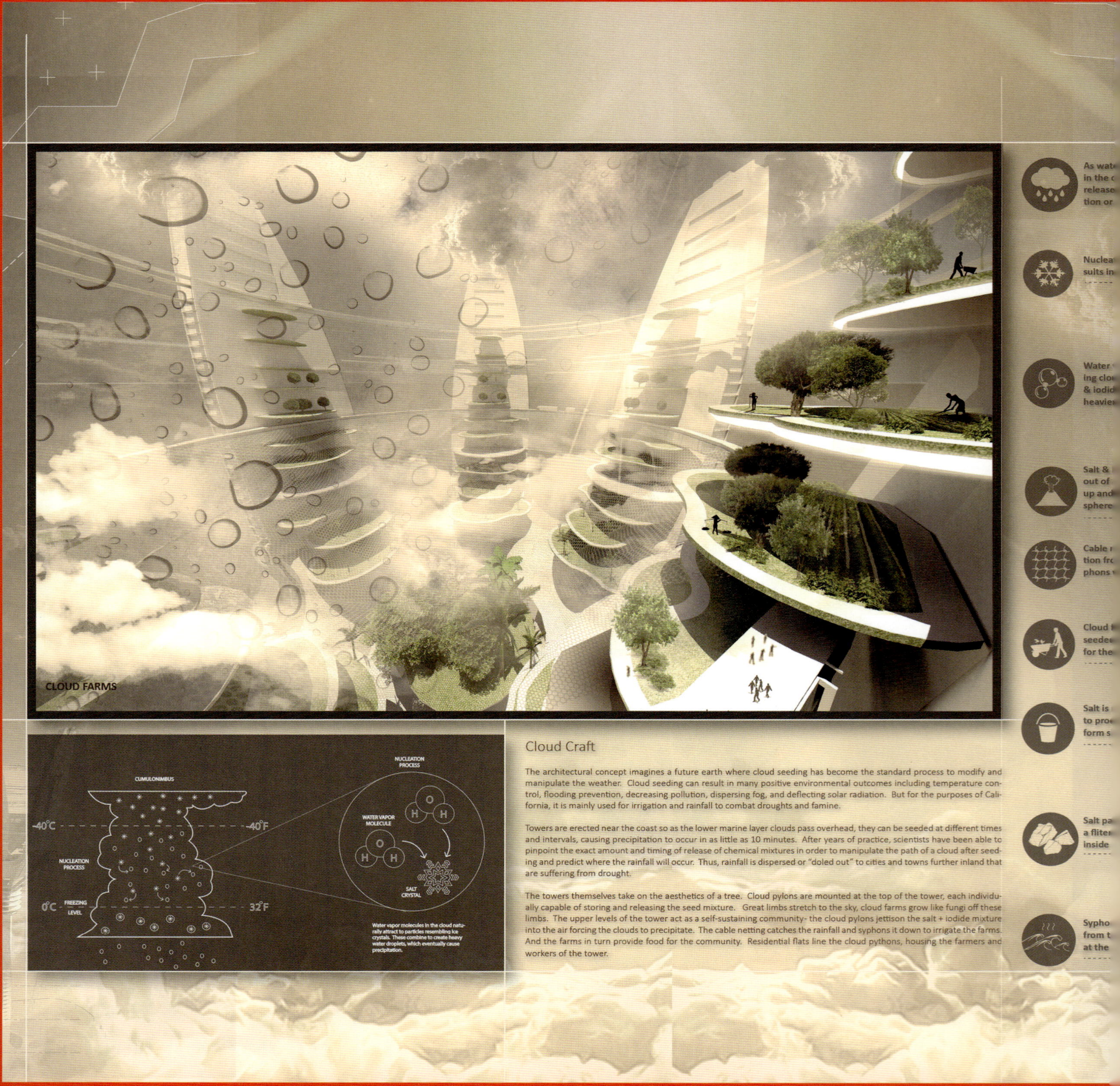

for irrigation and rainfall to combat droughts and famine. Towers are erected near the coast so as the lower marine layer clouds pass overhead, they can be seeded at different times and intervals, causing precipitation to occur in as little as 10 minutes. After years of practice, scientists have been able to pinpoint the exact amount and timing of release of chemical mixtures in order to manipulate the path of a cloud after seeding and predict where the rainfall will occur. The towers themselves take on the aesthetics of a tree. Great limbs stretch to the sky; cloud farms grow like fungi off these limbs. The upper levels of the tower act as a self-sustaining community – the cloud seeders jettison the salt + iodide mixture into the air forcing the clouds to precipitate. The cable netting catches the rainfall and syphons it down to irrigate the farms. And the farms in turn provide food for the community. Residential flats line the cloud pythons, housing the farmers and workers of the tower.

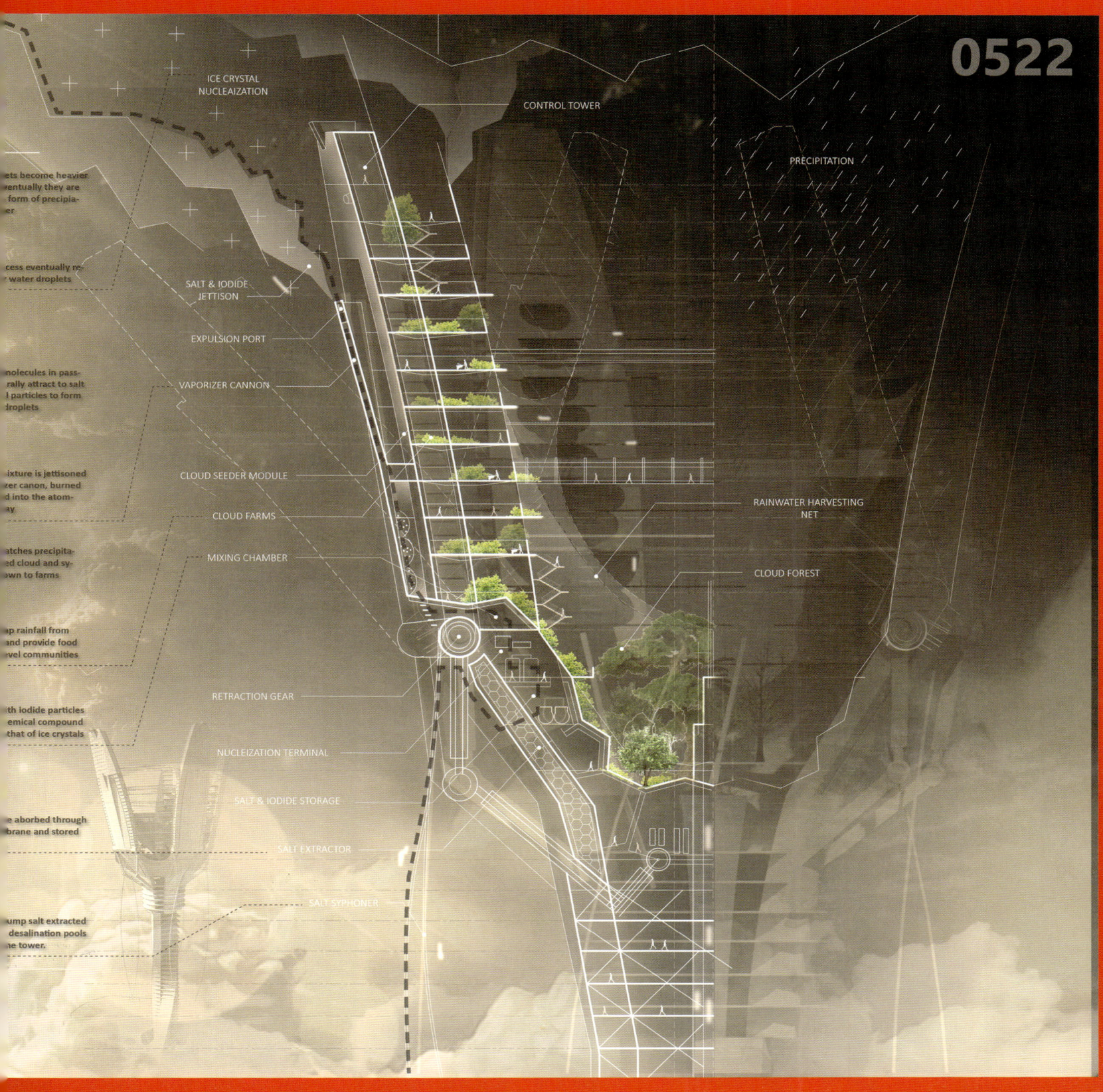

0522

ICE CRYSTAL NUCLEAIZATION

CONTROL TOWER

PRECIPITATION

...ts become heavier ...entually they are ...form of precipita... ...r

...cess eventually re... ...water droplets

SALT & IODIDE JETTISON

EXPULSION PORT

VAPORIZER CANNON

...molecules in pass... ...rally attract to salt ...l particles to form ...droplets

CLOUD SEEDER MODULE

...ixture is jettisoned ...er canon, burned ...d into the atom... ...ay

CLOUD FARMS

RAINWATER HARVESTING NET

...atches precipita... ...ed cloud and sy... ...own to farms

MIXING CHAMBER

CLOUD FOREST

...ap rainfall from ...and provide food ...vel communities

RETRACTION GEAR

...th iodide particles ...emical compound ...that of ice crystals

NUCLEIZATION TERMINAL

...e aborbed through ...brane and stored

SALT & IODIDE STORAGE

SALT EXTRACTOR

...ump salt extracted ...desalination pools ...e tower.

SALT SYPHONER

THE HIVE: DRONE SKYSCRAPER

Hadeel Ayed Mohammad
Yifeng Zhao
Chengda Zhu

United States

2ND PLACE / 2016

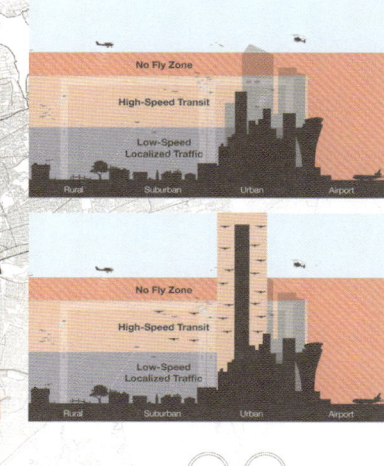

Drone technology, adopted by many large corporations, has become a leading trend in the field of fast-delivery, aerial mapping, commercial advertising, government inspection, and film making. As more and more people live on internet-based lifestyles, these "small flying robots" could easily become an ordinary part of future everyday life.

However, legal restrictions on the navigation of drones are currently standing in the way of drastically broadening the use of drones in various aspects of our daily lives. No-fly zones and conditions to maintain visibility with the drone at all times are two of the main constraints.

"The Hive" is an infrastructure project that can better meet the emerging demand for incorporating advanced Drone technology into daily life in New York City. The project aims to create a central control terminal that hosts docking and charging stations for personal or commercial drones in the center of Manhattan. The current air-zoning regulations are to be re-shaped in a vertical highway model around a tower. This centrally-controlled model will be more appealing to the legislative sector as it adheres to the concerns about regulating drone traffic. The primary location of the building does not only gather the commercial power of Manhattan, but also stands away from the no-fly-zones set by the FAA (Federal Aviation Administration).

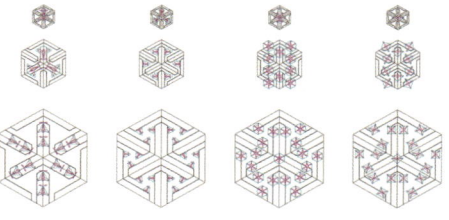

Derived configurations

Classification of drone models

Drone technology, adopted by many large corporations, has become a leading trend in the field of fast-delivery, aerial mapping, commercial advertising, government inspection, and filmmaking. As recent years have witnessed a rise in the development of drone technology, several major corporations, such as Amazon, DHL and Walmart, have begun investigating the use of drones in high-speed delivery service. The demand for high-speed drone delivery is estimated to increase continuously in the upcoming years. However, legal restrictions on the navigation of drones are currently standing in the way of drastically broadening the use of drones in various aspects of our daily lives. The Hive is an infrastructure project that can better meet the emerging demand for incorporating advanced Drone technology into daily life in New York City. The project was proposed as an alternative asset argument for the usage of the land on 432

0577

Park Avenue, the project aims to create a central control terminal that hosts docking and charging stations for personal or commercial drones (unmanned aerial vehicles) in the center of Manhattan. The current air-zoning regulations are to be re-shaped in a vertical highway model around a tower. This centrally controlled model will be more appealing to the legislative sector as it adheres to the concerns about regulating drone traffic. The Modules on the façade are designed to fit nine different types of drones, categorized by the shape and scale of their landing fixtures (point, bar or ring). A sequential study of how to categorize non-uniformed industry products into modular fixed architectural structures was conducted through a series of simplification of the geometries and articulations of the forms. The different sizes and geometry of the drone paired with different size and geometry of the module result in a variety of configurations. To provide

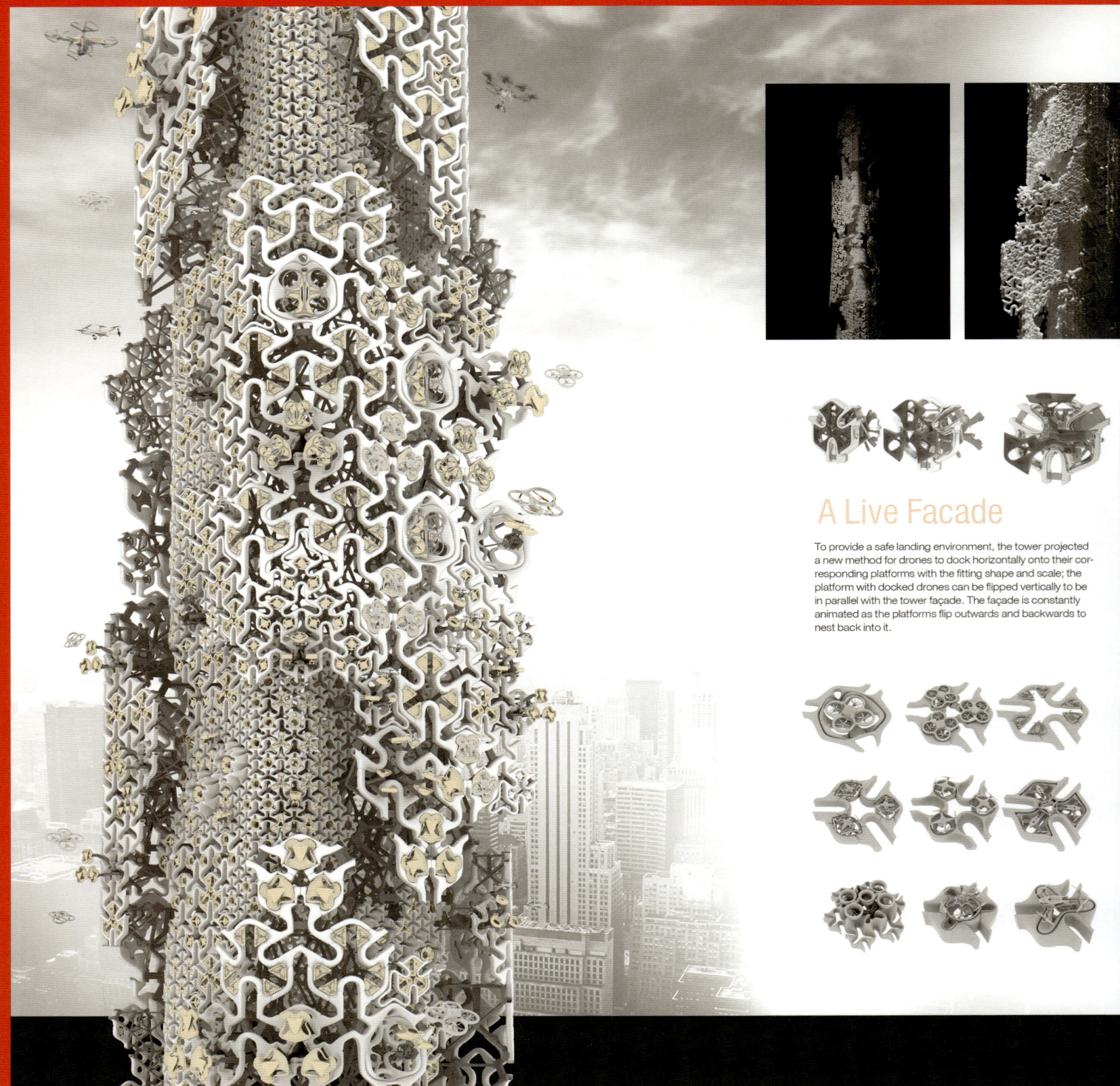

A Live Facade

To provide a safe landing environment, the tower projected a new method for drones to dock horizontally onto their corresponding platforms with the fitting shape and scale; the platform with docked drones can be flipped vertically to be in parallel with the tower façade. The façade is constantly animated as the platforms flip outwards and backwards to nest back into it.

a safe landing environment, the tower projected a new method for drones to dock horizontally onto their corresponding platforms with the fitting shape and scale; the platform with docked drones can be flipped vertically to be in parallel with the tower façade. The façade is constantly animated as the platforms flip outwards and backwards to nest back into it. The overall organization of the façade uses layering as means to maximize surface area, with two overlapping exterior layers and an inner layer. A hierarchy is established, as the size of drones and modules is smaller in the inner layer creating a more intricate interior that can be accessed by the smallest drones by a major opening in the façade. The transparency of the tower changes constantly, while the tenants of the building-the drones fly in and out. The flickering lights of the battery station behind each module help with navigation and also indicate the occupancy percentage of the building as well.

0577

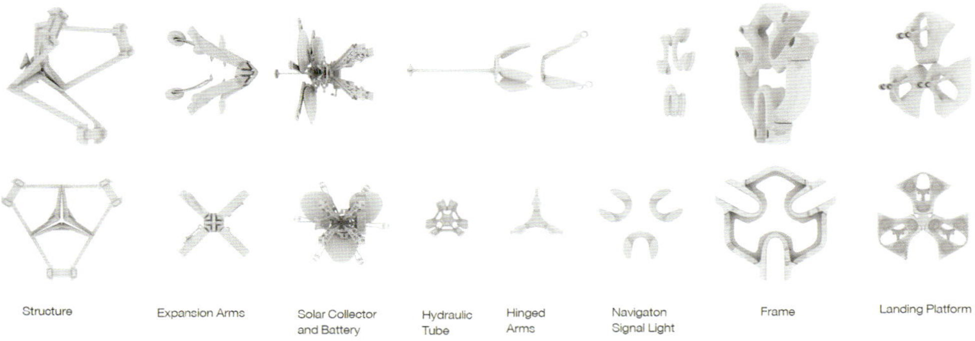

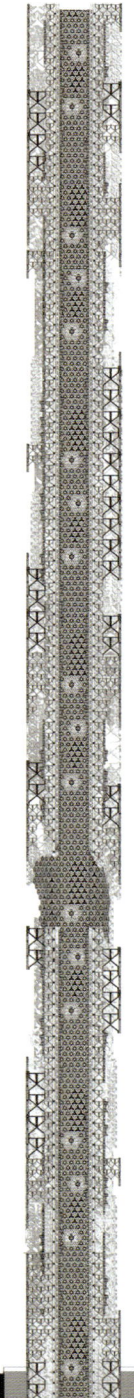

Structure | Expansion Arms | Solar Collector and Battery | Hydraulic Tube | Hinged Arms | Navigaton Signal Light | Frame | Landing Platform

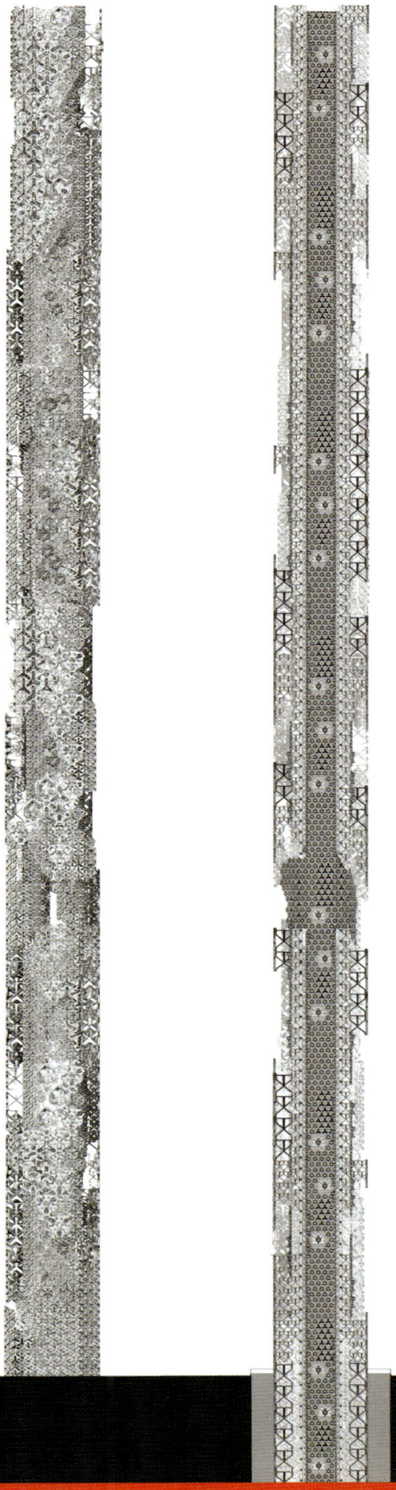

MAJUNGA TOWER

Jean-Paul Viguier Et Associes,
Architecture Et Urbanisme

France

REINVENTED TOWER

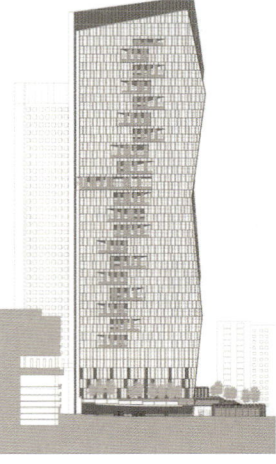

SOUTHERN FACADE

ONE OF THE FIRST SKETCHES

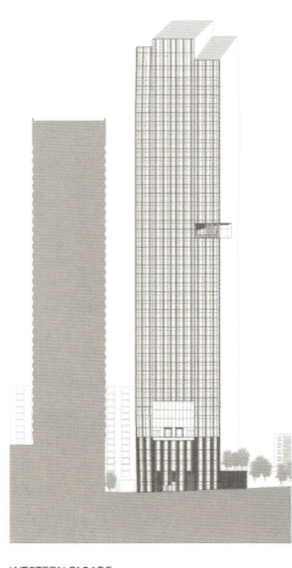

WESTERN FACADE

For us, towers bring back childhood emotions. It's the Gulliver effect, the competition that has always existed between towers: constantly striving to be taller, more unique, give more panoramic views from the top, and nowadays, be more environmentally friendly. Made up of three vertical blocks, each slightly different from the other, this tower is like a giant tropical plant whose stem thickens as it grows during the rainy season. Monotony is suppressed by the geometric variation of each floor. Repetition remains an exercise for the rigor and inventiveness it requires. The building envelope has a double skin of glass, which allows the occupants to open the windows and feel less closed in. Natural air can circulate inside, reducing power consumption for air conditioning. Between these two layers, a space was created for a garden on each floor with a living space. A piece of natural earth, the garden introduces in the tower a

0687

LEVEL ELEVATOR BLOCK

LEVEL ELEVATOR BLOCK

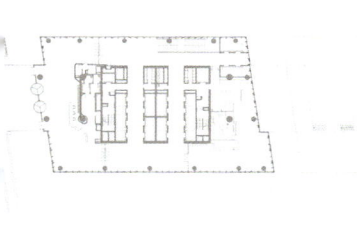

ADE LEVEL (main entrance)

A LOGGIA OR A BALCONY ON EVERY FLOOR

OPENING WINDOW PANELS

LUMINOUS AND TRANSPARENT FLOOR LANDINGS

This tower is a completely reinvented office ...ling that fits perfectly into life and the city. ...ear departure from the monolithic architec- ...of previous-generation office buildings, ...open, living and environmentally-friendly. ...unique exterior, consisting of three verti- ...strips differing slightly in shape, placed side- ...de, creates lines that suggest movement. ...like a plant whose stem has been gradual- ...ickened under the effects of the climate. ...high ceilings, all-glass facades and ...es that are open to the outdoors, give ...impression of volume and celebrate a ...freer, more informal art of working. ...s also an environmental breakthrough, ...to the measures taken to decrease en- ...consumption inside the building."

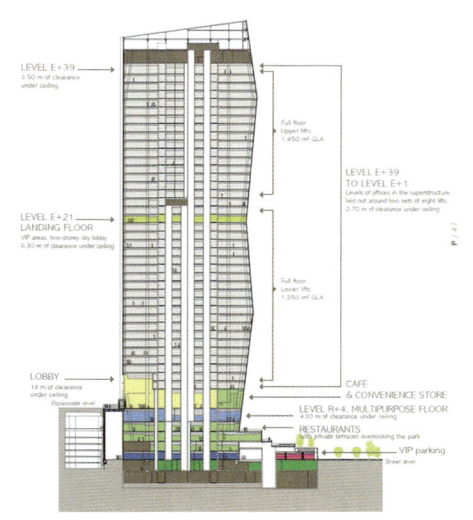

ORGANISATION

familiar element, adapted to the scale of the users. Without wanting to dominate, this tower is designed as a bridge between the universe of the child and that of adults in their daily office environment.

A very high environmental quality tower. The double skin facade offers numerous benefits: plenty of natural daylight floods into the offices, but they are also protected by an integrated sunshade system. Energy consumption is thereby cut both for lighting and air-conditioning. The facade materials used are: glass for the window frames and sills, and aluminum for the joinery and opaque components of the facades. Balconies and loggias (southern façade), often associated with domestic construction, here make an appearance in a tertiary building. These spaces provide employees with access to free air and an opportunity to enjoy the feeling of being outside. They add quality to their workspace.

REMARKABLE GREEN SPACES

Monumental painting commissioned. The bulk of the Tower's 97,000 tons are anchored on four pillars underneath the entrance hall space. Imperceptible to the observer, the center of the building's static forces is located between these pillars, forming an area charged with an invisible energy. This "void" was to be the essential source of inspiration for the artist's work, having been commissioned in March 2013 to complete a monumental painting for the new structure. Fascinated by scientists' claims that only 5% of the Universe's total mass is visible, she set out to uncover an archetypal form expressing this dynamic, however inaccessible to our senses. In concrete terms, she has sought to capture in the act of painting the forces at play between the load and weightlessness characterizing the Tower. The work was conceived to mirror the energies exerting their power over the space and occupy the 8 × 13-meter wall facing the main entrance, between two of the four foundational pillars.

0687

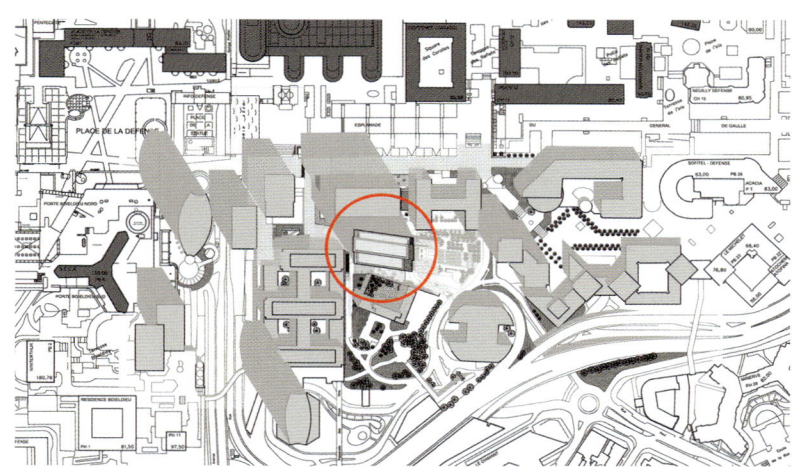

LOCATION IN THE HEART OF THE DISTRICT

A MONUMENTAL PAINTING
IN THE MAIN ENTRANCE

SUSTAINABLE SKYSCRAPER ENCLOSURE

Soomin Kim
Seo-Hyun Oh

South Korea

RE-COVER

Biochemical corporation with Botany Lab for co-existence

Cities are closely related to human society, culture and political environment. They faced extreme changes due to technical developments after industrial revolution and metropolitanization caused by population increase. Artificial environment, cities, offered diversity of opportunities and new lifestyles which humans comforted themselves with. However, this benefit that which derived from developments under mechanical, deterministic perspective, jeopardized the balance and harmony of natural environment. Capitalism, while making possible the forming of megacities, also brought severe side-effects such as economic polarization and social imbalance. Once expected to guarantee prosperity of human lives, human technics and systems, are now even considered as threats to human and natural environment, and the coexistence between human communities. Architecture of the past reflected the overheated technologies in competition of developments and selfish gene of capital. However, as the question of coexistence and balance is brought to the surface nowadays, how will the generation's idea change this selfish gene and what kind of form will modern architecture will take as its phenotype?

Modern cities have faced extreme changes due to developments of the Industrial Revolution and the urban sprawl caused by population increase. These artificial environments offer a diversity of opportunities and new lifestyles. However, this benefit jeopardized the balance and harmony with the natural environment. Architecture of the past reflected the overheated technologies in competition of developments and selfish gain of capital. However, as the question of coexistence and balance is brought to the surface, how will this generation's idea change this selfish gain and what kind of form will modern architecture take as its phenotype? Today, 54% of the world population live urban based lives, megacities of population over 10 million keep increasing. Skyscrapers were born from the necessity to disperse dense complexity of horizontal cities by vertically expanding and reconstructing, in order to make a more effective use of

Recovered Skyscraper

UN predicts that by 2050, the world population will go over 9 billion, which is nearly 2 billion more than present. Cities will be overcrowded in due to accept this change in population, which makes experts believe that demand for skyscrapers will continue to increase. However, these demands are in contradiction with the social and environmental problems that could be caused if the Megacities like NYC continue to spend the energy and resources in this rate. Thus, to satisfy these demands, we need to have a new, sustainable model for a sky-scraper.

If the 20C's skyscrapers followed the logic of develop-ment and growth, the new model should be following the law of recovery and coexistence. Currently most of the NYC's areas are already in use, and it would take a great deal of energy and resources to try starting over entirely like in 20C. The new model will use conventional build-ings as a new resources, and it will find a new usage for them and give them purposes for the future using only the slightest efforts on building acts. The newly born buildings will use and self-produce eco-friendly energy in sustainable cycle, so that they can co-exist with the environment instead of opposing it. With the new model, the capitals will have a new frontier in front of them as they implement shared values within the public, and the skyscrapers, once a symbol of polarization of capital and public, will make a transition to a symbol of co-exist-ence.

Diagram of Co-existence System in Re-Cover

$
Human Equality   Ecological Harmony
Market   Lab
Port
Community Well-Being

" RE-COVER "

① Skin   ② Structure   ③ Platform

① Interface between Nature and Energy Purifying System
  - Capture Solar Energy and Harvest Rainwater

② Energy Purifying System
  - Control Skin to Produce and Store Nature Energy

③ Climate Adjusted Zone
  - Botanic Life Growth Using Eco-Energy

Megacities and Skyscrapers

0711

At this present, where 54% of world population live urban based lives, megaci-ties of population over 100 million keep increasing. It is estimated that in year 2050, almost 70% of people around the world will be living in cities.
Skyscrapers were born from the necessity to disperse dense complexity of horizontal cities by vertically expanding and reconstructing, in order to make a more effective use of scarce land. Moreover, many cities and nations pas-sionately competed in building more skyscrapers since they were often taken as outcomes of their economic success. As result, from year 1930, when the fever to build more skyscrapers had peaked, to the present, skyscrapers have become common type of architecture in megacities around the world.

Population of the World (1950-2050)   Increase of Completed Skyscrapers

20th century New York and the Empire State Building

New York, which had become somewhat modern due to 19th century great immigration and city developments, had emerged as the new center of world industry in early 20th century. State of the art technology and highly concen-trated capital turned New York into city of skyscrapers. The Empire State, completed in 1930 becoming the world's highest man-made structure, was imprinted into the mind of people as the symbol of prosperity and a great leap towards success. This piece of architecture visualized the harsh competing nature of capitalism itself, which is the driving force of the idea. Simultaneous-ly, making a scenery that even shows the severe polarization of capital, shabby slum streets of the city in contrast to the world's tallest building.

World's Tallest Building Timeline

NYC's Status as Megacity

As the population in the urban area continues to increase, the efficient usage of energy and resources are becoming a main concern in 21st Century's urban planning. The urban areas in earth, which just account for just 1% of the Earth surface, uses 75% of the total energy, and responsible for 80% of green gas emission. This shows how the city residents are using more energy than any other area. It was found that New York City, which developed into the first Megacity to have population more than 10 million in 1950, uses the most excessive energy and resources amongst all the Megacities.

Megacity Resource as a Percentage of World Values   Total Energy Use

scarce land. State of the art technology and highly concentrated capital turned New York into the city of skyscrapers. The Empire State, completed in 1930 becoming the world's highest man-made structure, was imprinted into the mind of people as the symbol of prosperity and a great leap towards success Simultaneously, making scenery that even shows the severe polarization of capital. The urban areas in earth, which just account for just 1% of the Earth surface, uses 75% of the total energy, and responsible for 80% of green gas emission. It was found that NYC, which developed into the first megacity to have population more than 10 million in 1950, uses the most excessive energy and resources amongst all the megacities. UN predicts that by 2050, the world population will go over 9 billion. Cities will be overcrowded in due to accept this change in population, which makes experts believe that demand for skyscrapers

The perpendicular-structured garden will provide differentiated experiences from linear gardens of past to NY's citizens. "Re-cover" 's unique position enables companies to have optimized infrastructure for botanical research and at the same time have accessibility to network for enterprising efforts.

Biochemical corporation with Botany Lab for co-existe

"Re-Cover" is an architectural model to achieve mutually benefi co-existence between the capital, environment, and public. model, which grants a new function to an aged Empire States build the heart of New York, self-produces and consumes eco-frier energy. Solar energy absorbed from transparent integument is use optimize greenhouse environment. Simultaneously, electricity ger ated from sunlight and rain water harvested from integument is a used as resources to adjust environment. In the gardening platf generated in this way, it can cultivate various kinds of plants aro the world, and it will serve as meaningful resources in researc concerning the preservation of variety in plants.

Company and Environment

Companies should make a transition to a mutually-beneficial relat ship with Nature from a one-way relationship in which the compa exploit the nature unilaterally. In "Re-Cover", companies inves researches for restoration of greenery and diversity of plants, and the results as necessary data for providing new services for cust ers and generating profits. "Re-cover" 's unique position enables c panies to have optimized infrastructure for botanical research an the same time have accessibility to network for enterprising effort

Environment and Society

"Re-cover" 's research area will serve as botanical garden for p as well as employees. The perpendicular-structured garden will vide differentiated experiences from linear gardens of past to NY's zens. Research results will be posted to visitors real-time to awareness to public about nature's current status.

Society and Company

A foundation for coexistence between the economic values fo companies and social values for the public will be earned with the plementation of "Re-Cover". Companies can provide values that be shared with other stakeholders in order to sustain the profit stay competitive. In turn, public can use the services and goods the companies to provide necessary fund for companies to vigoro engage furthermore, thus completing cycle of coexistence Re-cover can provide.

will continue to increase. However, these demands are in contradiction with the social and environmental problems that could be caused if the megacities like NYC continue to spend energy and resources at this rate. Thus, to satisfy these demands, we need to have a sustainable model for a skyscraper. If skyscrapers in the 20th Century followed the logic of development and growth, the new model should be following the law of recovery and coexistence. The model will use conventional buildings as resources, and it will find a new usage for them and give them purposes for the future using only the slightest efforts on building acts. The newly born buildings will use and self-produce eco-friendly energy in sustainable cycle, so that they can co-exist with the environment instead of opposing it. With the model, the capitals will have a new frontier in front of them as they implement shared values within the public, and the skyscrapers, once a symbol of polarization of capital and public, will make a transition to a symbol of co-existence.

Section View

Botany Lab and Park

Research area will serve as botanical garden for public.

Garden Island

Adequate condition will be provided to all plants on each platform.

Greenhouse Environment

Greenhouse is an environment adequate for plant growth.

Specimens Delivery Drone

Specimens from platform will be managed by drones. Drones will take care of monitoring of specimens as well as artificial fertilization between specimens. The samples needed for researches will also be gathered by drones, delivered to the lab in form of capsule.

Function of Skin

0711

"Re-cover" converts energy from nature to usable energy, and uses it to form an environment adequate for plant growth. The Skin of "Re-Cover" is a collection of sensory devices that can recognize climate information such as humidity and temperature and use these information to adjust inner environment. The central AI processes weather information gathered from inner and outer sensors to manage each platform of plants accordingly.

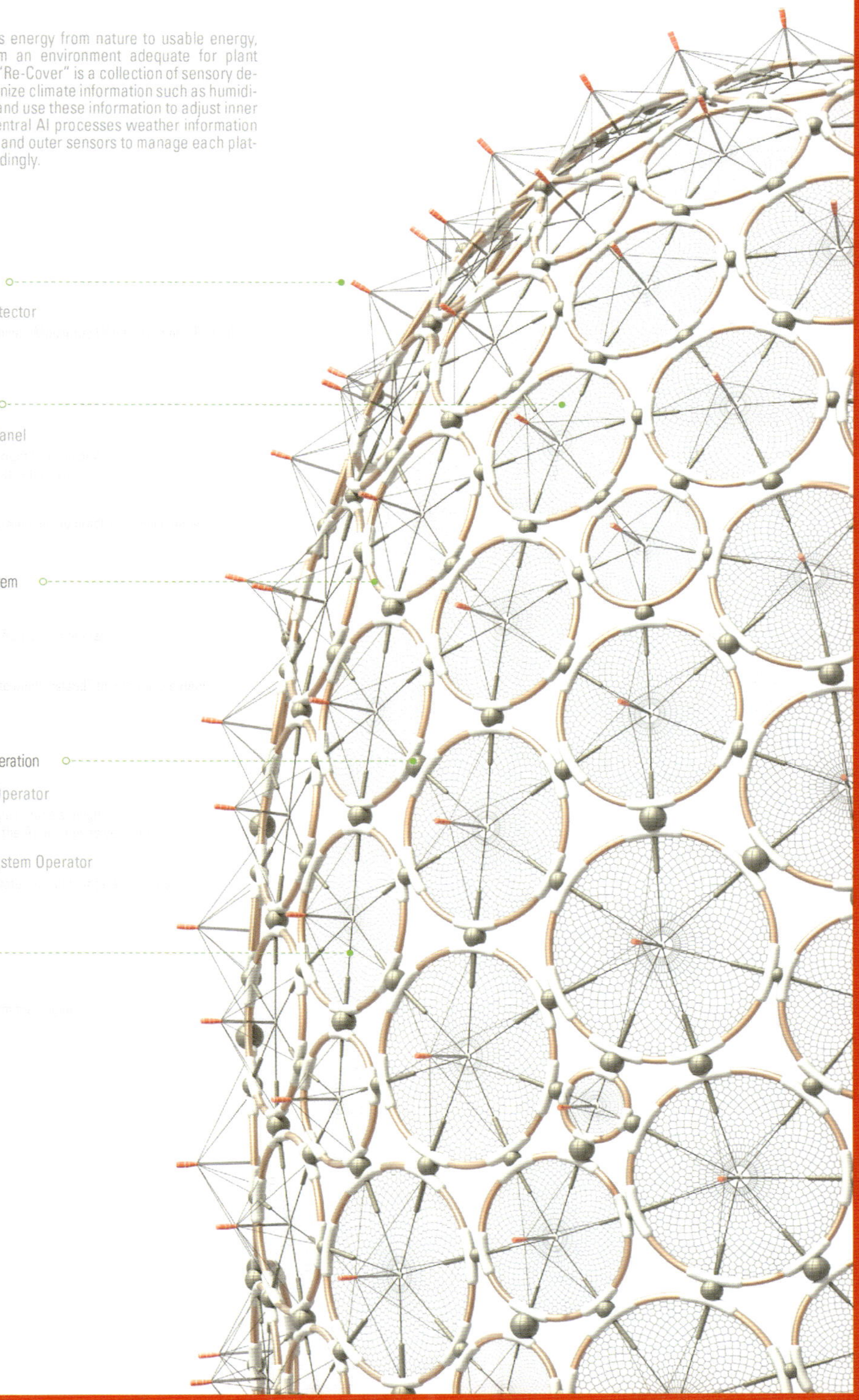

Microclimate Sensor
Climatic Element Detector

Cellular Skin Panel
Solar Photovoltaic Panel

Rainwater Collector

Water Circulation System
Purifying Filter

Circulation Pipe

Engine for Physical Operation
Cellular Skin Panel Operator

Water Circulation System Operator

Wire
Driving Part

ALTA VISTA HABITABLE FOG WATER TOWERS

Fergus Knox

United Kingdom

Alta Vista will be one of several inhabited water towers to be built within the Sunset District of San Francisco. The proposal is an inhabited public infrastructure and prototype housing: self sufficient, off-grid living that harnesses its energy from natural resources and pays back into the grid. Recently San Francisco and the state of California suffered their worst drought on record. In January 2015 for the first time in 165 years, no measurable rainfall was recorded. California leads the way in recognizing the peril that faces the planet, and has already imposed drought control measures such as hose pipe bans, daily water usage recommendations and efficiency requirements for toilets and taps. This drought, unfortunately, wont be the last or the worst. San Francisco has an unexploited water resource available in the ubiquitous fog. If this could be harnessed to augment the city's water supply, it could be of great benefit. The prevailing

Pacific onshore wind regularly and reliably blows the condensed fog layer into the Sunset District, San Francisco's most westerly and foggiest neighborhood. The proposed Alta Vista towers positioned in the fog layer will condense and collect San Francisco's fog. This fog water will be used for both the sanitary, and energy needs of the building. The building will collect solar energy from above the fog layer, which it will use to convert the collected fog water into hydrogen gas using electrolysis. The hydrogen gas will act as an energy store from which during foggy periods the houses will be powered using hydrogen fuel cells. Each house will be constructed from lightweight materials to allow for large cantilevers and minimal supporting structure. From street level when shrouded by fog the structure should be barely perceivable, the lightweight structures reach up and disappear into the fog to support the suspended housing above.

ALTA VISTA HABITABLE FOG WATER TOWERS
- San Fransico, USA

Fog Illumination

Illumination plays a crucial role in the experience of the house. As the users sense of vision is obscured by the fog, the house distorts and manipulates their experience. The user is disorientated as the house rotates through the fog. Living spaces feel isolated and intimate as the fog rolls past their windows. At foggy times, natural daylight is diffuse, casting an even shadowless white light. The transparent materials and white structural supporting structure blur the boundaries of cloud and building. During sunny conditions the many skins and transparent layers of the house diffuse and fracture the light, casting an even fog like light. At night or in dense fog, the membranes are lit transforming the building into a floating light-box.

Night Time Illumination

At night the translucent nature of the building allows the skin to be illuminated in an unusual and interesting way. The rooms illuminate inside the membrane, and create bright light boxes at the openings. Spotlights illuminate fog pools on the underside creating glowing diffuse orbs floating in the sky. At foggy times when observing from street level viewers can track distinctive glowing patches move across the sky as the building rotates.

Transparent frog constructed from layers of translucent membranes

The design circumnavigates the city's strict planning restrictions and 'Anti-manhattanization movement' petition (against the rise of tall buildings) by building above San Francisco's habitual fog layer. The building intends to simulate these fog's effects with its chosen materials, each selected to enhance the occupants' experience. Each tower will cater for various family demographics with a four, three, two and one bed house in each. Houses will be carefully orientated to amplify feelings of occlusion and remoteness, changing position at different hours of the day carefully counterbalanced by collected water. The city's unusual topography channels and directs the fog through the city, over hilltops and down streets. It's not uncommon to see the fog rolling down the city's hills. A new skyscraper typology unique to San Francisco will embrace the city's unique climate and provide new housing and a public water facility to the city.

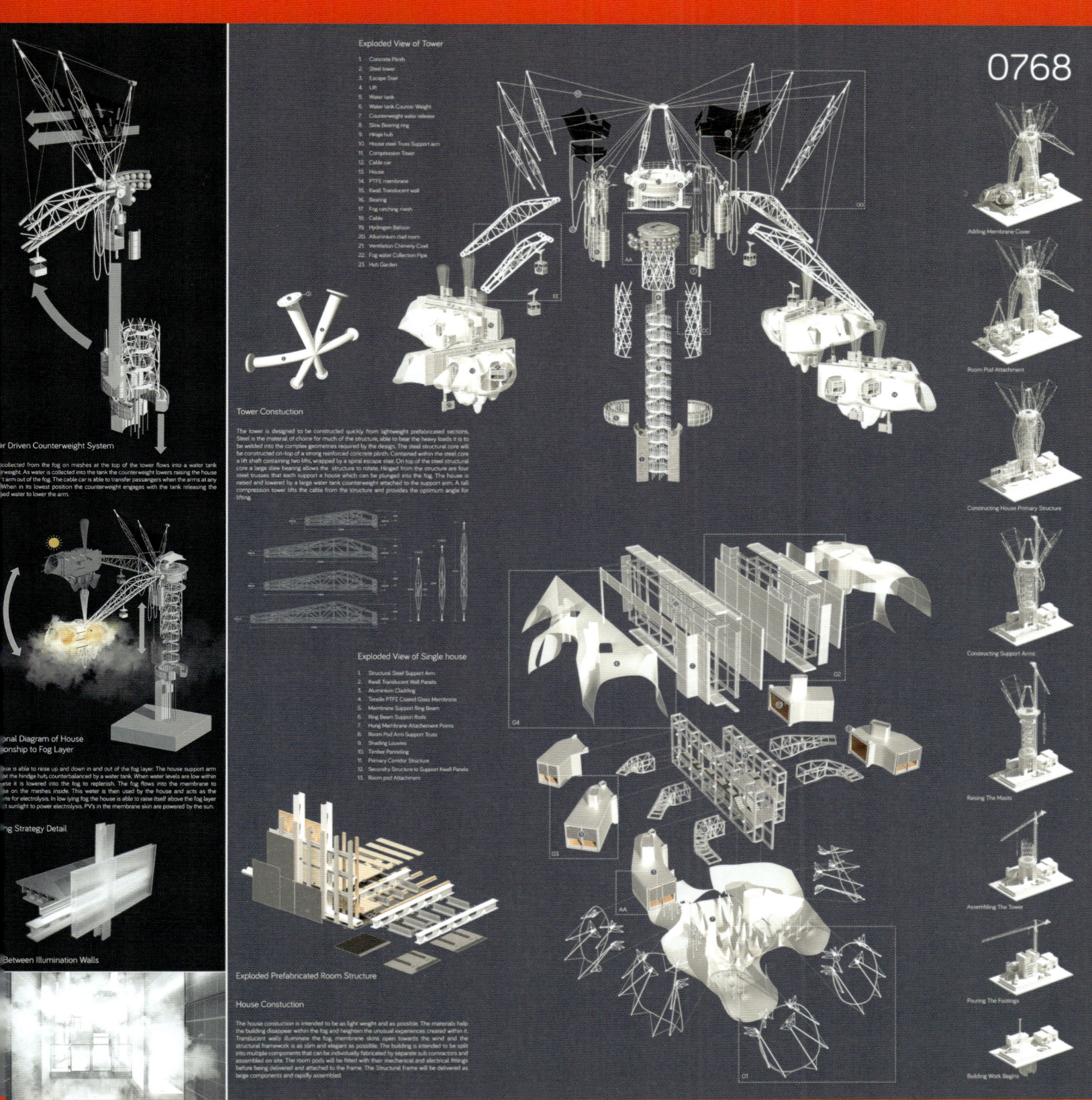

ECOLOGICAL URBANISM 2

WINGS OF ASPERGES

Takwan Bae
Changhee Lee
Yoonseok Park

South Korea

0090

WINGS OF ASPERGES
The Earth Humidifying Tower for the Hydrological Cycle

Recently, numbers of natural disasters due to climate changes have increased throughout the world. Desertification is a phenomenon seen frequently around the world where desert like climates widens abnormally. Sahel region in the southern Africa for instance, has not encountered rainy season since 1960s. As a result, underground water has dried up, drying out green plants, which eventually led to death of thousands of animals. On the other hand, the rates of devastating floods are increasing from heavy rain throughout the world. Just recently, South East Asian countries such as Philippines and Indonesia suffered from heavy rain that led to landslides and destruction of buildings.

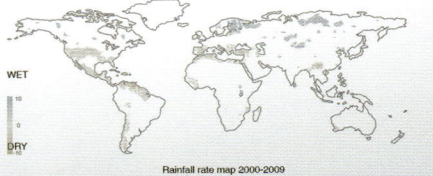

Rainfall rate map 2000-2009   Rainfall rate map 2050-2059

Drought in Brazil, 2010   Drought in Darfur, Sudan, 2013   Flood in Huang He River, China, 2012   Flood in Pakistan, 2013

The chart described the desertification areas and flooded areas due to the heavy rain increased every years. According to this, two thirds of the land would be changed to the anomaly climate area in 2050. For this reason, global organizations try to solve this climatic problem, however this climatic change was already appeared at several places and it should be more seriously. Unfortunately, this climatic problem would damage to the nature more seriously since it tend to spread thorough the urban and rural area. Moreover, these kind of phenomenon spread to the nature too rapidly to restore it.

Damaged Hydrological Cycle

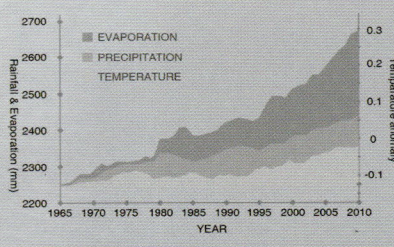

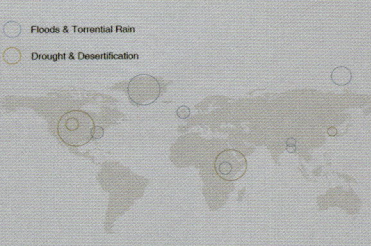

Precipitation and evaporation according to the temperature   Extreme weather 25 June-5 July, 2012

This phenomenon about getting flooded and a drought which is comes from a problem of hydrologic cycle is observed in specific area with precipitation increase or decrease in other area. The important point of it is that amount of evaporation increasing in the air. In the desert area, quantity of evaporation exceed mean value meanwhile it is increased due to the deconstruction of nature by the production activity of mankind. For excessive amount of evaporation, desertification is in effect in some area while others have a flood for excessive amount of vapor.

Therefore, there should be 'the Key' for the repair the cycle.

Rain, the Key of Damaged Cycle

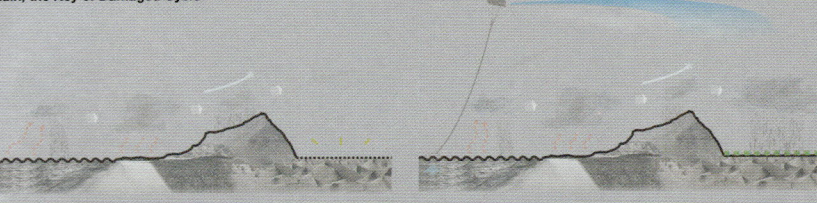

More rain is necessary in desertified regions and less rain in flooded regions. Simply put, controlling the rain is the key solution to the entire problem. Increasing amount of saturated water vapor in the cloud is crucial in increasing the rate of rain. On the other hand, cutting off saturated water vapor in the frequently flooded region will lead to less rain. After all, if we are able to turn water vapors traveling from desertified region to flooded region into rain in advance, desertification and disastrous floods could be solved at the same time.

Therefore, we propose skyscraper system that could produce rain by releasing water vapors.

Recently, numbers of natural disasters due to climate change have increased throughout the world. Desertification is a phenomenon seen frequently around the world where desert-like climates widen abnormally.

   Sahel region in southern Africa, for instance, has not encountered a single rainy season since the 1960s. As a result, underground water has dried up, drying out green plants, which has eventually led to death of thousands of animals.

   On the other hand, the rates of devastating floods are increasing from heavy rain throughout the world. Just recently, South East Asian countries such as the Philippines and Indonesia suffered from heavy rain that led to landslides and the destruction of buildings.

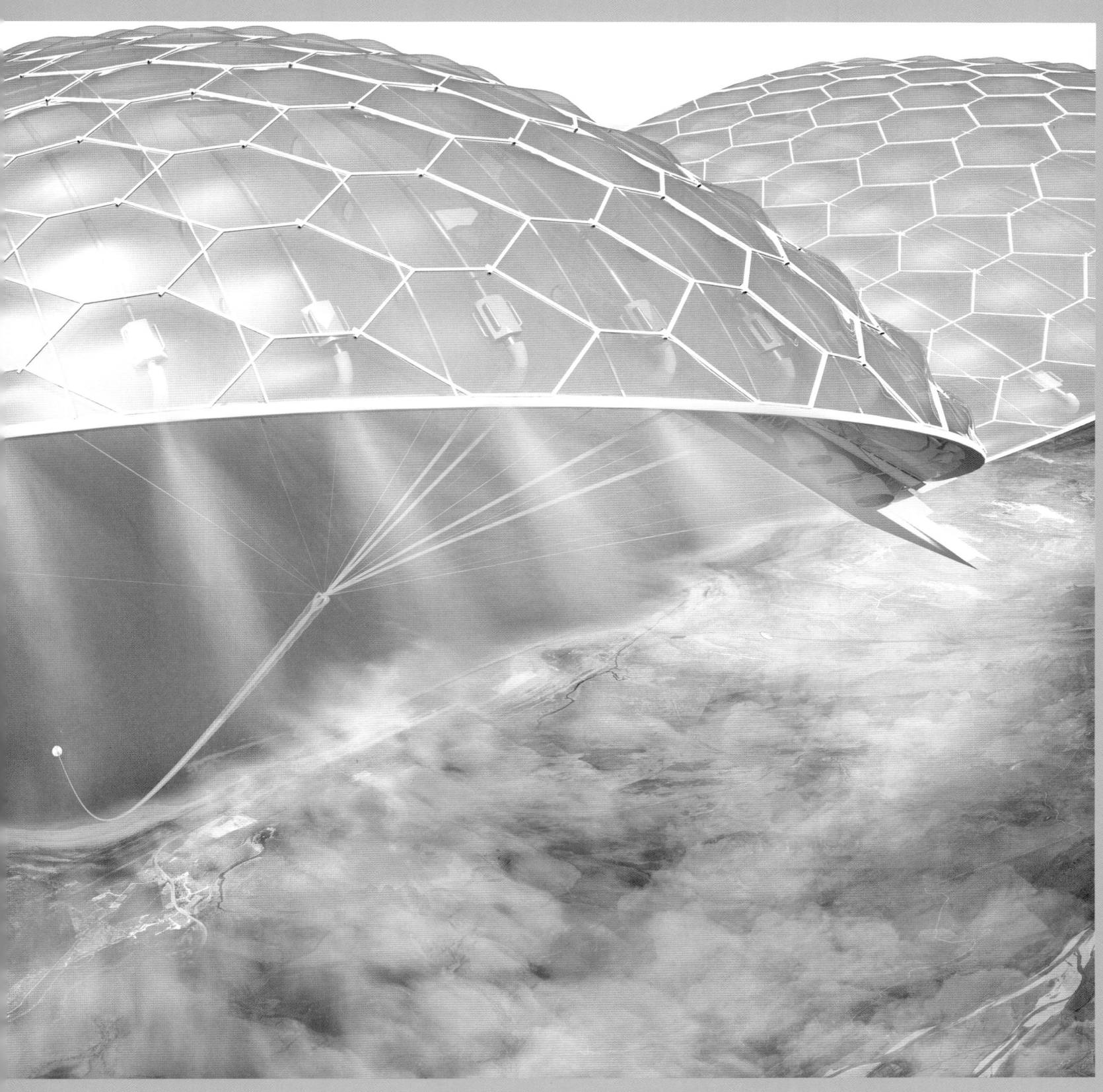

More rain is necessary in desert regions and less rain in flooded regions. Simply put, controlling the rain is the key solution to the entire problem. Increasing the amount of saturated water vapor in the clouds is crucial in increasing the rate of rain.

On the other hand, cutting off saturated water vapor in frequently flooded regions will lead to less rain. After all, if we are able to turn water vapor traveling from desert regions to flooded regions into rain in advance, desertification and disastrous floods could be solved at the same time. Therefore, we propose a skyscraper system that could produce rain by releasing water vapor.

Three factors were considered in arranging the building. The first factor is atmospheric circulation between desert regions and flooded regions. Our structure's site is in the midst of the atmospheric

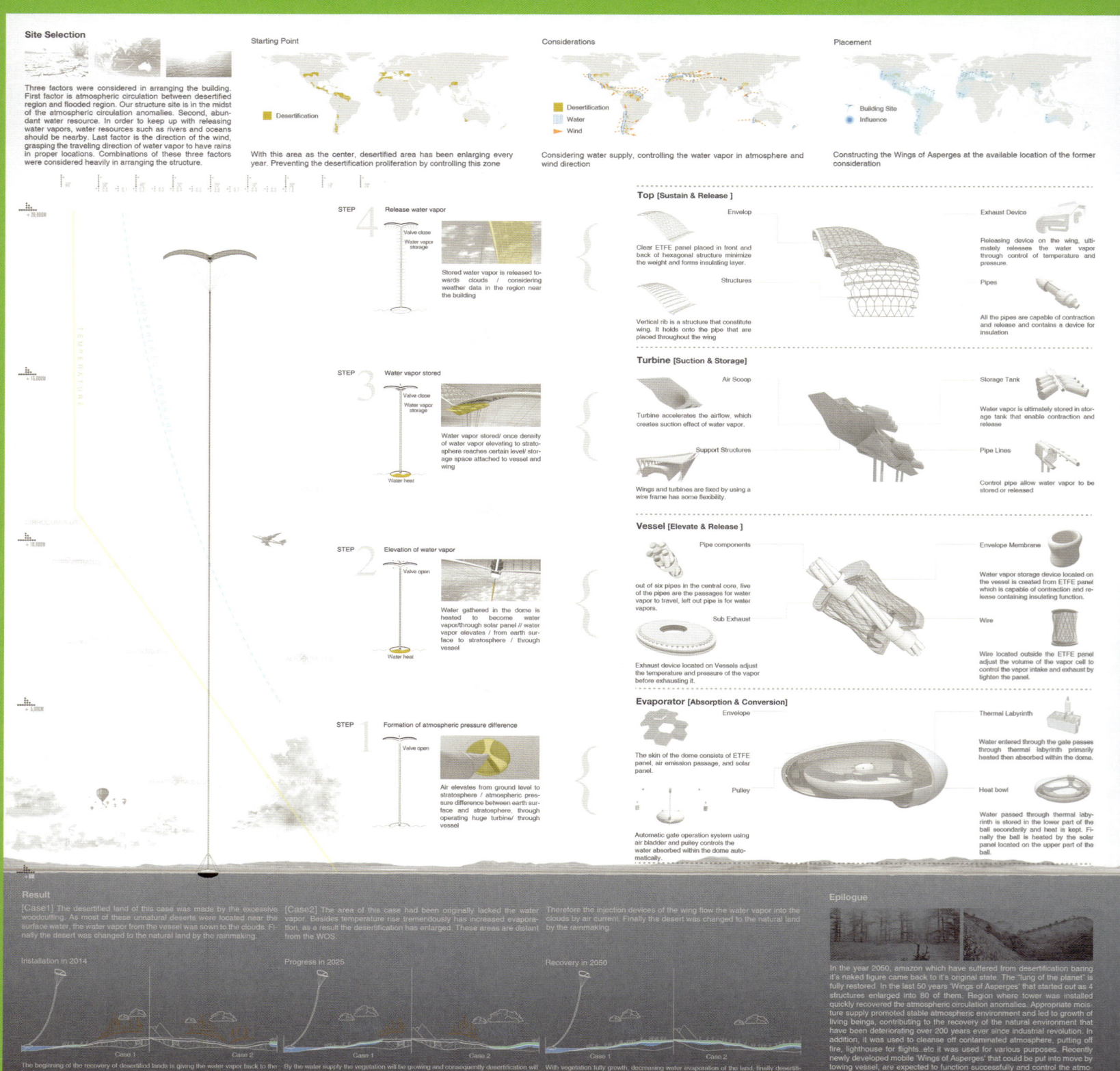

circulation anomalies. Second, a necessity for the project is abundant water resources. In order to keep up with the released water vapor, water resources such as rivers and oceans should be nearby. The last factor is the direction of the wind, grasping the traveling direction of water vapor to have rain in the proper locations. Combinations of these three factors were considered heavily in arranging the structure.

SEAWER SKYSCRAPER

Sung Jin Cho

South Korea

Let's flush them all into the

SEAWER

THE GARBAGE SCRAPER ON THE OCEAN

ISSUE

"25% of our planet is a toilet that never flushes."   Charles Moore

The smaller Western Garbage Patch

The Eastern Garbage Patch contains estimated plastic concentrations of 5.1kg/km², six times the concentrations of zooplankton

Globally, millions of tons of trash enter the ocean each year. Between 60 and 80 percent of it is land-based and the rest is from ocean-based operations. Plastic constitutes 90 percent of all trash floating in the world's oceans. Due to ocean currents, this plastic waste collects in particular areas of our global ocean. Such a region of accumulated plastic debris is the North Pacific Subtropical Gyre, where the prevailing ocean currents have created a large mass of very small particles of plastics, which have resulted in a "plastic soup" to which commonly referred as the Great Pacific Garbage Patch(GPGP). GPGP is twice the size of Texas and contains six times more plastic than plankton biomass. As plastic does not biodegrade, it poses a threat to thousands of marine animals. Charles Moore, the discoverer of the GPGP, said "It's a toilet that never flushes, but just keeps accumulating."

PROBLEMS OF PLASTIC

SOURCE: Algalita Marine researchFoundation, GREENPEACE

Plastic never biodegrades, it doesn't break down into natural substances. However, it goes through a photodegradation process, split into ever smaller and smaller parts, which are still plastic. Most of the plastic debris floats below the surface at depths of up to 10 meters. Albatross can mistake floating debris for food, while smaller particles closely resemble zooplankton and enter the ocean food chain when they are eaten by jellyfish. Trash in the ocean kills more than one million seabirds and 100,000 marine mammals and turtles each year through ingestion and entanglement.

CONCEPT

"Let's punch a drainage hole in the Ocean, then flush them all!"

SEAWER proposes to install a huge drainage hole whose size is 550 meters in diameter and 300 meters in depth, in the middle of GPGP and flushes polluted water through SEAWER. SEAWER engulfs all kinds of floating trashes filled with seawater. SEAWER has five layers of baleen filters which separate particles and fluid. When the ocean garbage and plastic debris pass through the baleen filters, they are sorted and collected by size, weight, and type. The plastic particles collected from filters, are taken to a recycling plant at the top of SEAWER for reproducing. The seawater filtered out impurities is settled in a large clarifier at the bottom of SEAWER for purification. Finally, cleaned seawater is released to the ocean.

KAWOOSHHHH !!!

Globally, millions of tons of trash enter the ocean each year. Between 60 and 80 percent of it is land-based and the rest is from ocean-based operations. Due to ocean currents, this plastic waste collects in particular areas of our global ocean. Such a region of accumulated plastic debris is the North Pacific Subtropical Gyre, where the prevailing ocean currents have created a large mass of tiny particles of plastics, which have resulted in a "plastic soup" commonly referred as the Great Pacific Garbage Patch (GPGP).

GPGP is twice the size of Texas and contains six times more plastic than plankton biomass. As plastic does not biodegrade, it poses a threat to thousands of marine animals.

Seawer proposes to install a huge drainage hole 550 meters in diameter and 300 meters in depth in

the middle of the GPGP. The project would engulf all kinds of floating trash filled with seawater. Seawer consists of five layers of baleen filters, which separate particles and fluids. The plastic particles collected from filters are taken to a recycling plant atop of the structure while seawater is filtered and stored in a large sedimentation tank at the bottom to be further cleaned and released into the ocean.

The three secttions of the building; hydroelectric power plant, plastic recycling facility, and water purification facility are codependant. In order for them to properly work each section needs to opperate perfectly.

In addition, the structure will serve as a marine research laboratory and potentially as a tourist destination. The top portion of the project was designed to allow trees to grow and create a small forest

Plastic Recycling Facility

SEAWER provides an efficient, practical, and feasible solution to clean up GPGP. Vacuuming seawater mixed with plastic debris as a whole, SEAWER can collect, sort, recycle, and reproduce ocean debris faster than ever before. SEAWER has a recycling capacity of 135 tons of plastic garbage per day and 50,000 tons per annum. It means that SEAWER can clean 100,000km² of ocean surface each year.

Water Purification Facility

SEAWER purifies contaminated seawater. The surface seawater moves vertically downwards through five layers of baleen filter for removing plastic particles. At the bottom floor of SEAWER, purification facility cleans and desalinates dirty seawater such as filtered seawater, ballast water, and water outflow from hydro turbines. Desalinated water goes up to the residence area on the top floor for human consumption and irrigation. Clean seawater is discharged into the ocean.

in the middle of the Pacific Ocean. This section is also equipped with solar panels and at the center a lighthouse serves as a beacon for humanity in an attempt to reverse the enviornmental problems that we have caused during the last two centuries. This strsucture is a monument of hope for future generations and a reminder of the problems that our world currently faces.

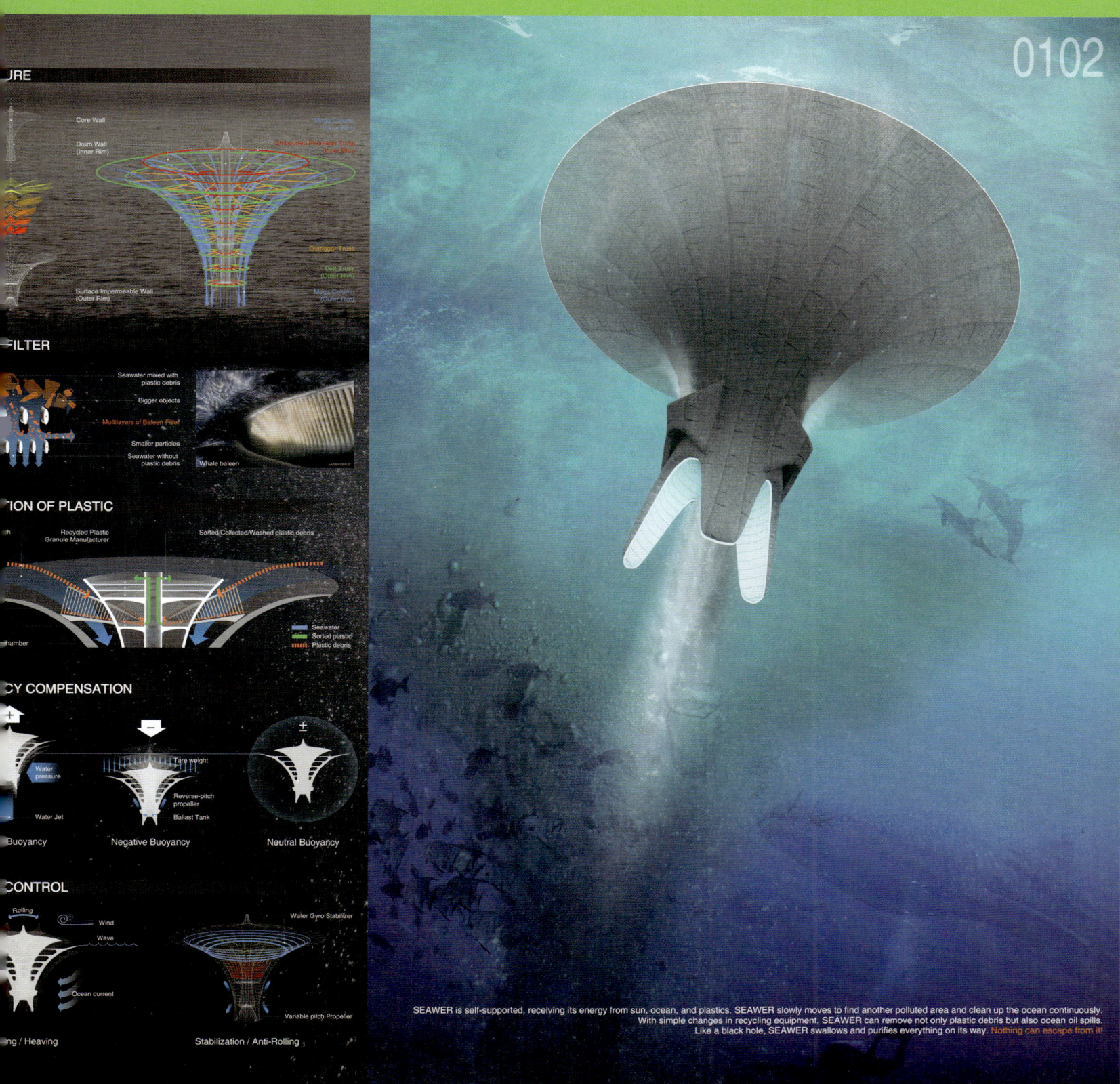

SEAWER is self-supported, receiving its energy from sun, ocean, and plastics. SEAWER slowly moves to find another polluted area and clean up the ocean continuously. With simple changes in recycling equipment, SEAWER can remove not only plastic debris but also ocean oil spills. Like a black hole, SEAWER swallows and purifies everything on its way. Nothing can escape from it!

FOGWATER STATION

Olivier Dauce
Alban Denic

France
United States

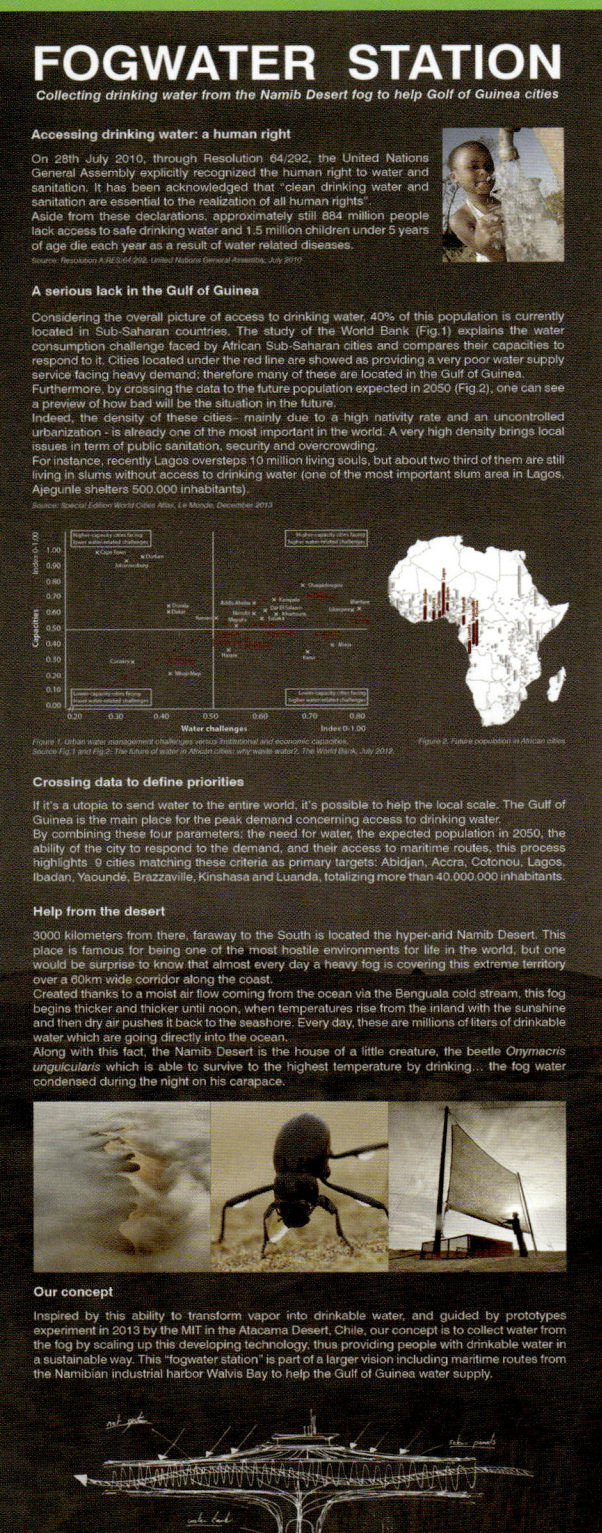

FOGWATER STATION
Collecting drinking water from the Namib Desert fog to help Golf of Guinea cities

Accessing drinking water: a human right

On 28th July 2010, through Resolution 64/292, the United Nations General Assembly explicitly recognized the human right to water and sanitation. It has been acknowledged that "clean drinking water and sanitation are essential to the realization of all human rights".
Aside from these declarations, approximately still 884 million people lack access to safe drinking water and 1.5 million children under 5 years of age die each year as a result of water related diseases.
Source: Resolution A/RES/64/292, United Nations General Assembly, July 2010

A serious lack in the Gulf of Guinea

Considering the overall picture of access to drinking water, 40% of this population is currently located in Sub-Saharan countries. The study of the World Bank (Fig.1) explains the water consumption challenge faced by African Sub-Saharan cities and compares their capacities to respond to it. Cities located under the red line are showed as providing a very poor water supply service facing heavy demand; therefore many of these are located in the Gulf of Guinea.
Furthermore, by crossing the data to the future population expected in 2050 (Fig 2), one can see a preview of how bad will be the situation in the future.
Indeed, the density of these cities– mainly due to a high nativity rate and an uncontrolled urbanization - is already one of the most important in the world. A very high density brings local issues in term of public sanitation, security and overcrowding.
For instance, recently Lagos oversteps 10 million living souls, but about two third of them are still living in slums without access to drinking water (one of the most important slum area in Lagos, Ajegunle shelters 500.000 inhabitants).
Source: Special Edition World Cities Atlas, Le Monde, December 2013

*Figure 1. Urban water management challenges versus institutional and economic capacities.
Source Fig.1 and Fig.2: The future of water in African cities, why waste water?, The World Bank, July 2012.* *Figure 2. Future population in African cities*

Crossing data to define priorities

If it's a utopia to send water to the entire world, it's possible to help the local scale. The Gulf of Guinea is the main place for the peak demand concerning access to drinking water.
By combining these four parameters: the need for water, the expected population in 2050, the ability of the city to respond to the demand, and their access to maritime routes, this process highlights 9 cities matching these criteria as primary targets: Abidjan, Accra, Cotonou, Lagos, Ibadan, Yaoundé, Brazzaville, Kinshasa and Luanda, totalizing more than 40.000.000 inhabitants.

Help from the desert

3000 kilometers from there, faraway to the South is located the hyper-arid Namib Desert. This place is famous for being one of the most hostile environments for life in the world, but one would be surprise to know that almost every day a heavy fog is covering this extreme territory over a 60km wide corridor along the coast.
Created thanks to a moist air flow coming from the ocean via the Benguela cold stream, this fog begins thicker and thicker until noon, when temperatures rise from the inland with the sunshine and then dry air pushes it back to the seashore. Every day, these are millions of liters of drinkable water which are going directly into the ocean.
Along with this fact, the Namib Desert is the house of a little creature, the beetle *Onymacris unguicularis* which is able to survive to the highest temperature by drinking... the fog water condensed during the night on his carapace.

Our concept

Inspired by this ability to transform vapor into drinkable water, and guided by prototypes experiment in 2013 by the MIT in the Atacama Desert, Chile, our concept is to collect water from the fog by scaling up this developing technology, thus providing people with drinkable water in a sustainable way. This "fogwater station" is part of a larger vision including maritime routes from the Namibian industrial harbor Walvis Bay to help the Gulf of Guinea water supply.

Inspired by the ability to transform vapor into drinkable water, and guided by the prototypes experiment in 2013 by MIT in the Atacama Desert in Chile, our concept is to collect water from the fog by scaling up this developing technology, thus providing people with drinkable water in a sustainable way.

This "fogwater station" is part of a larger vision including maritime routes from the Namibian industrial harbor Walvis Bay to help the Gulf of Guinea water supply.

The project is designed as a T and consists of three main components. The top bar is the heart of the proposal, where the fog is captured and accumulated as water. This enormous bar works as a sandwich in which the interior open layers are equipped with hundreds of cylinders with fine meshes that capture fog from the athmosphere. In addition, the top layer is equipped with phovoltaic panels for solar energy

0212

harvesting. The control room is also located in this area, excatly at the top center of the project.

The middle portion of the project, the shaft or mast serves as primary structure and also contains housing units in the perimeter. These units enjoy unubstructed views towards the landscape. Finally, the space located underneath the canopy will be transformed into a new habitat.

The idea is that a serires of towers would be built and these new habitats would create a new urban identity and provide a place to live for the inhabitants of the region.

While other proposals to capture fog have been developed, this project is the first to imagine it at a large scale. A scale large enough to transform an arid region into a lush environment. The surplus water could then be transported to other areas where water collection from fog is impossible. In summary,

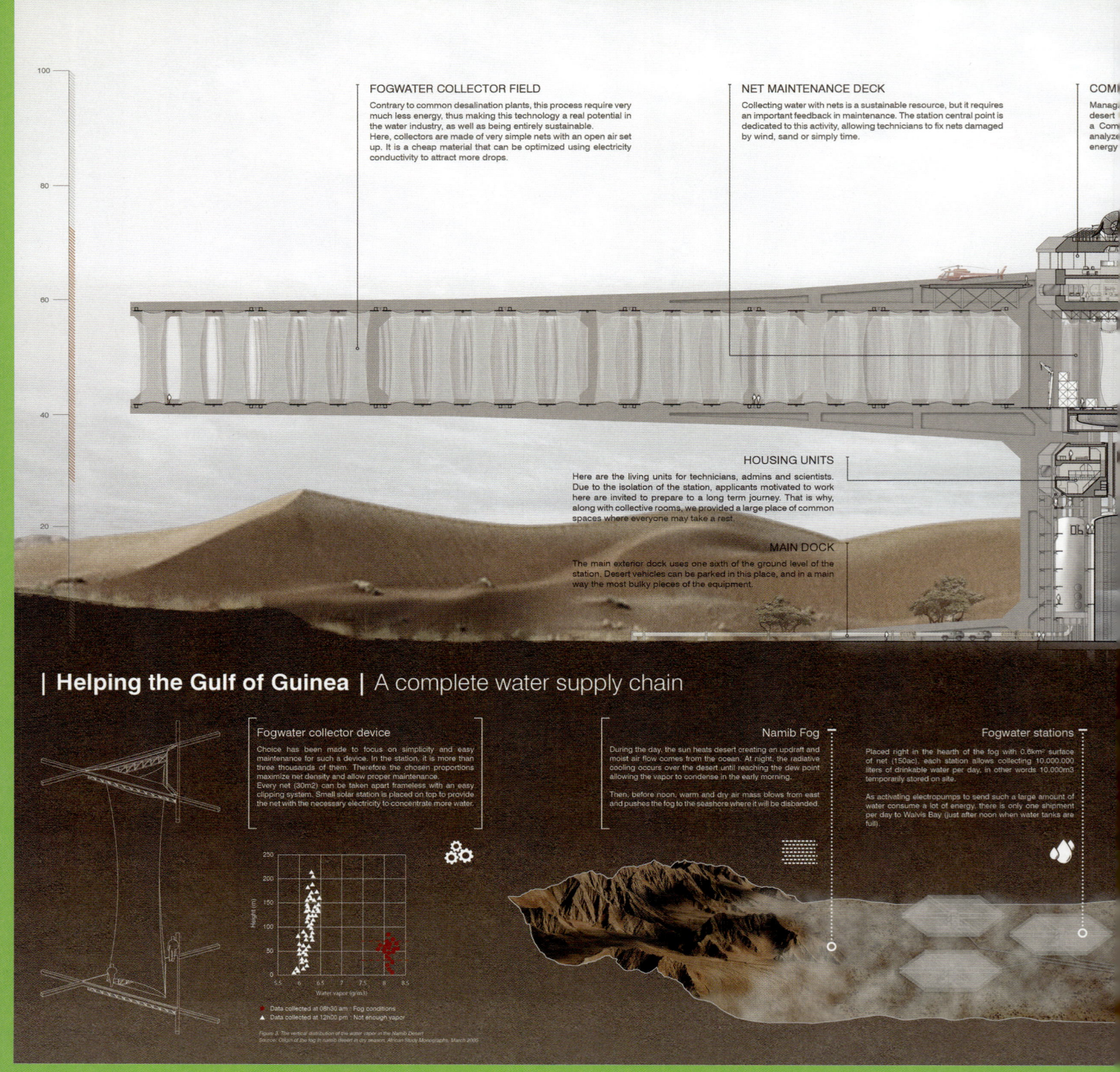

FOGWATER COLLECTOR FIELD
Contrary to common desalination plants, this process require very much less energy, thus making this technology a real potential in the water industry, as well as being entirely sustainable.
Here, collectors are made of very simple nets with an open air set up. It is a cheap material that can be optimized using electricity conductivity to attract more drops.

NET MAINTENANCE DECK
Collecting water with nets is a sustainable resource, but it requires an important feedback in maintenance. The station central point is dedicated to this activity, allowing technicians to fix nets damaged by wind, sand or simply time.

COMM
Manage
desert
a Com
analyze
energy

HOUSING UNITS
Here are the living units for technicians, admins and scientists. Due to the isolation of the station, applicants motivated to work here are invited to prepare to a long term journey. That is why, along with collective rooms, we provided a large place of common spaces where everyone may take a rest.

MAIN DOCK
The main exterior dock uses one sixth of the ground level of the station. Desert vehicles can be parked in this place, and in a main way the most bulky pieces of the equipment.

| **Helping the Gulf of Guinea** | A complete water supply chain

Fogwater collector device
Choice has been made to focus on simplicity and easy maintenance for such a device. In the station, it is more than three thousands of them. Therefore the chosen proportions maximize net density and allow proper maintenance.
Every net (30m2) can be taken apart frameless with an easy clipping system. Small solar station is placed on top to provide the net with the necessary electricity to concentrate more water.

Namib Fog
During the day, the sun heats desert creating an updraft and moist air flow comes from the ocean. At night, the radiative cooling occurs over the desert until reaching the dew point allowing the vapor to condense in the early morning.

Then, before noon, warm and dry air mass blows from east and pushes the fog to the seashore where it will be disbanded.

Fogwater stations
Placed right in the hearth of the fog with 0.6km² surface of net (150ac), each station allows collecting 10.000.000 liters of drinkable water per day, in other words 10.000m3 temporarily stored on site.

As activating electropumps to send such a large amount of water consume a lot of energy, there is only one shipment per day to Walvis Bay (just after noon when water tanks are full)

Data collected at 08h30 am : Fog conditions
Data collected at 12h00 pm : Not enough vapor

the structure would provide a new opportunity for the region with the hopes to improve many other arid areas nearby.

Research laboratories will be an important program of the project. Academics will have the opportunity to experience and analyze the transformation of the area. They will be able to quantify the used resources and propose new and more efficient ways to replicate the system in other parts of the world.

0212

& CONTROL ROOM

h a technical installation in the middle of the n easy thing. That is why there is in each station & Control room where all data are synced and her control, fog density, quantity of liters collected, nption, water leak prevention, etc.

LABORATORIES

The Namib Desert is a unique place on earth. Species incredibly adapted to survive to this hostile environment like the *Onymacris unguicularis, Welwitschia mirabilis*, etc. The station is able to host up to five scientist teams who desired to make long-term studies, providing them with laboratories, housings and conviviality spaces.

SOLAR PANELS

The Namib Desert has a very high rate of sunshine all throughout the year. Solar panels powered the entire station, especially for daily use, water pumps, and electrifying nets during the fog period. Indeed, if 1 square meter can collect 3 liters of water, adding electricity and the yield is six times as much!

SAFETY HABITAT

The station frame, thought as a canopy, creates a safety environment for local species, especially during the very dry season when temperatures can reach up to 40°C in the desert. Then, the station provides animals with shadows, fresh air, and of course drinking water.

Bottling plant

ecuperated in the factory, water needs to be quickly ned in order to stay drinkable. o, we use two systems: the first one stores water in e tanks and the second directly in 20L per bottles.

wo approaches aim to answer different needs. Bottles de to be directly accessible to people once the ship in the city, and portable tanks are made to be sent into terland by train or trucks to reach isolated villages.

Recycling and wastewater treatment plant

A first issue in maritime transport is for ships to find a way not to come back empty. Furthermore, water infrastructures and services aren't enough developed in cities: the same for plastic recycling.

That is why we include in the water supply chain a last move, the recycling of bottles and wastewater; once the ship come back to the port, we offload and recycled them for thereafter feeding back the cycle.

Operating by ships

Transportation by land is too risky. Indeed, going from Namibia to the Gulf of Guinea means passing through difficult geographic areas. Furthermore, this way is crossing seven different borders with potential insecurity or conflicts.

To avoid these troubles, we reuse the ancient colonial port of Walvis Bay as a launching base. At this moment, water is loaded in ships and sent for a 2.5 days trip.

CLIMATOLOGY TOWER

Yuan-Sung Hsiao
Yuko Ochiai
Jia-Wei Liu
Hung-Lin Hsieh

Japan

Climatology Tower: Healthy Climatology for the city

If one feels ill, you may need to seek medical assistance.
If the city is sick, what will we do for it?
Healthy Climatology in the urban environment is an indicator
for a safe living - protecting civic health in the city.

If you feel sick, you seek medical assistance. If the city is sick, what should we do? The Climatology Tower is a proposed skyscraper designed as a research center that evaluates urban meteorology and corrects the environment through mechanical engineering. The skyscraper analyzes microclimates within cities as a result of the use of industrial materials, the accumulation of buildings, and the scarceness of open spaces.

In order to maintain a healthy environment for the city, two main strategies are employed: The environmental control system consists of evaluation and operational programs. Evaluation programs inspect city climates through a variety of factors such as insolation, radiation, and thermal coverage. Collected data is compared with humidity levels and then mechanical systems respond to reduce or

0255

Society is concerned about current levels of environmental damage, resulting from increased pollution in the modern city. But to what extents are considerations of the microclimate's effects on urban spaces. Cities, such as Tokyo and NY, are now full of industrial materials such as concrete, metal and glazing, and create a sub-climate between buildings and empty blocks. Factors from these environments, such as air, moisture and temperature directly affect human health. While toxic substances of air pollution are highly considered in relation to health, one does not always such damaging factors in the

moisture within the air. According to medical research, Asthma is caused by over humidity (70-90% watery air) and contains a high density of bacteria. Additionally, dry environments cause skin allergies and circulation diseases. The Climatology Tower therefore, is a skyscraper which is based on a research centre, aiming to evaluate the urban meteorology. Through mechanical engineering, the tower intelligently responds and adjusts to reform a safe environment throughout. Recorded climate data can additionally be associated with medical research for public health, preventing flu and infections.

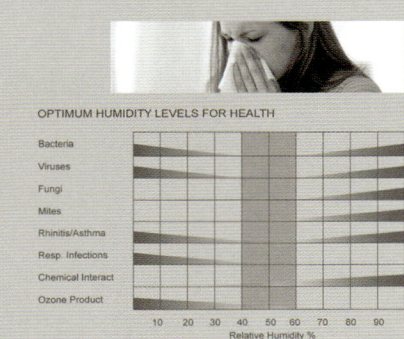

OPTIMUM HUMIDITY LEVELS FOR HEALTH

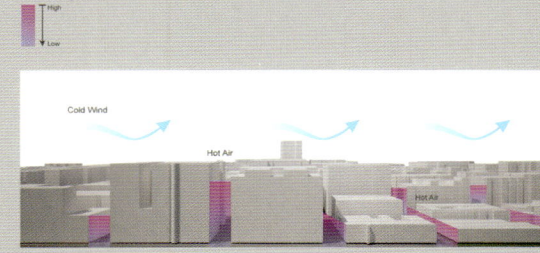

Microclimate in the City:

Key Strategies:

In order to maintain a healthy environment for the city, two main strategies are employed:

1. Environmental control engineering:
The environmental control system consists of evaluation and operational programs. Evaluation programs inspect city climates through a variety of factors such as Insolation, radiation and thermal coverage. Collected data is compared with humidity levels and then responds in a balanced stabilisation, reducing or increasing to optimise environmental conditions. These processes will combine automatic mechanisms with physical circulation to achieve better atmosphere.

2. Information expression:
In addition to automatically adjusting to optimal environmental conditions, data is transferred from a control centre to extensive city departments, giving opportunity to ultimately maintain a healthy environment throughout the entire city. This can benefit entire communities, notifying all of present and upcoming environmental hazards and conditions. Climatic information is also displayed publicly, though digital networks, notifying the public on maintaining certain conditions, to preserve both energy and health.

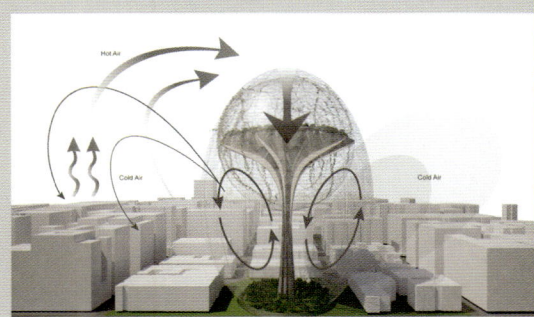

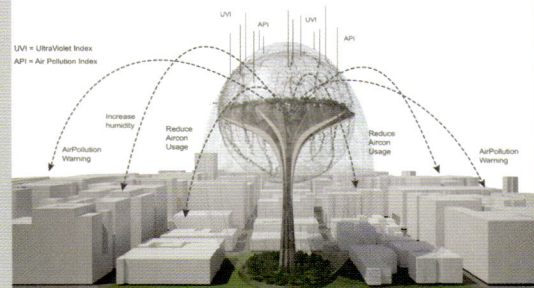

increase the levels to optimal environmental conditions.

In addition to automatically adjusting to optimal environmental conditions, data is transferred from a control center to extensive city departments, giving opportunity to ultimately maintain a healthy environment throughout the entire city. This can benefit entire communities, notifying all of present and upcoming environmental hazards and conditions. Climatic information is also displayed publicly, though digital networks, notifying the public on maintaining certain conditions, to preserve both energy and health.

In terms of architecture and engineering, this structure takes the form of a cup. A flat area atop is designed as a floating garden above the city. It is supported by a central column that contains a water

Functional Programmes:

The following examples indicate operations in various aspects of the Climatology Tower, including programmes such as a research centre and mechanical department.

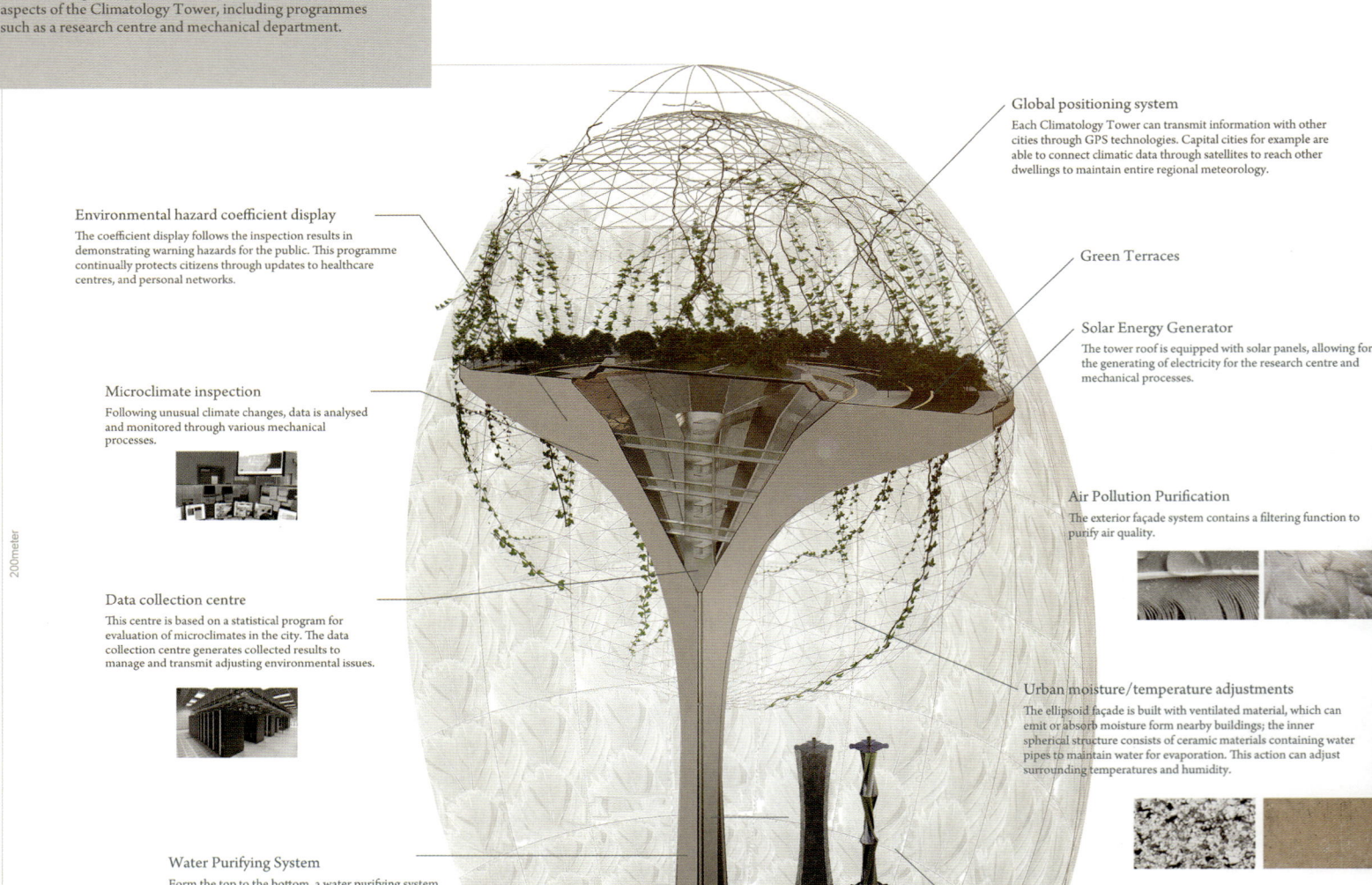

Environmental hazard coefficient display
The coefficient display follows the inspection results in demonstrating warning hazards for the public. This programme continually protects citizens through updates to healthcare centres, and personal networks.

Microclimate inspection
Following unusual climate changes, data is analysed and monitored through various mechanical processes.

Data collection centre
This centre is based on a statistical program for evaluation of microclimates in the city. The data collection centre generates collected results to manage and transmit adjusting environmental issues.

Water Purifying System
Form the top to the bottom, a water purifying system uses gravitation forces in principle to clean the water resources form the natural precipitation.

200meter

Green Terraces
Based on top and at the bottom of the tower, these terraces are designed to create air circulation in between tower blocks.

City Botanic Garden

Education Centre

Global positioning system
Each Climatology Tower can transmit information with other cities through GPS technologies. Capital cities for example are able to connect climatic data through satellites to reach other dwellings to maintain entire regional meteorology.

Green Terraces

Solar Energy Generator
The tower roof is equipped with solar panels, allowing for the generating of electricity for the research centre and mechanical processes.

Air Pollution Purification
The exterior façade system contains a filtering function to purify air quality.

Urban moisture/temperature adjustments
The ellipsoid façade is built with ventilated material, which can emit or absorb moisture form nearby buildings; the inner spherical structure consists of ceramic materials containing water pipes to maintain water for evaporation. This action can adjust surrounding temperatures and humidity.

Air Conditioning
Centrally to the tower is an air conditioning unit which is equipped with a turbine for increasing air circulation.

Urban climatology research centre
Natural circulation and mechanical systems:
Public Space

purification system. The whole structure is enclosed by a clear membrane that allows solar penetration while creating an interior micro-climate. This new environment will inject fressh into the city and will provide green recreational areas for its inhabitants. These areas will be located at the gound level and at the urban forest at the top.

A series of these mega-structures could be combined to create a network of sustainable "lungs" for highly polluted metropolitan regions.

0255

Natural circulation and mechanical systems:
Based from natural circulation theories, these mechanical devices adjust moisture levels, making automatic modifications to reach optimum environmental conditions from the research centre.

Urban climatology research centre
This department is based on the city's climate collection and distribution of analysis to professional programmes. All research data is integrated into a library system, where various generic typologies are available for further utilization. The research centre also connects with local medical institutions and health departments.

Public Space
The ground floor provides public access for citizens. On this level, the education centre runs healthy living courses, demonstrating health issues between society and the urban environment.
-City Botanic Garden
-Education Centre

HYPER-FILTER SKYSCRAPER

Umarov Alexey

Russia

THE HYPER FILTER

One of the greatest problems that the world is facing today is that of environmental pollution, increasing with every passing year and causing grave and irreparable damage to the Earth.

Environmental pollution can be divided into the following types: Local, Regional and Global.

This process is considered as an evidence of atmosphere recourses finiteness and it shows limits of the natural atmosphere self-regeneration. However sharp increasing pollution has reached the level of self-regeneration inability and even stepped over this border.

Under nowadays level of pollution harmful substances from air pollution source spread over dozens and hundred kilometers. The term "pollution source" itself means a lot. A whole region and even a country can represent a single pollution source. By now some important problems of anthropogenic Earth pollution have appeared. They are as follows:
1. Possible climate changes caused by technogenic warmth, carbon dioxide and volatile solids emission to the atmosphere.
2. The Earth ozone layer damage possibility connected with freons, nitrogen oxides and some other environmental contaminants.
3. Global environment pollution from radioactive material, heavy metals and pesticides shows harmful impact on the ecology system.
4. The problem of water pollution from atmosphere precipitation, stream flow, ground and water transport.
5. Problems of atmospheric transfer and acid rain.

The Hyper Filter project is designed to solve the regional air pollution problem. Located in big cities between skyscrapers surrounded by busy traffic roads, stations and factories The Hyper Filter "inhales" polluted by CO2, harmful gases air and "exhales" clear concentrated O2. Atmosphere air warmth is expected to sustain The Hyper Filter building in working conditions. The building envelope structure is designed to provide proportional clear air emission to the over-building space. Thr external envelope with long pipe-filters keeps temperature balance of the building. All the released harmful substances are moved on uptake to holders. Then they are divided into reservoirs for future use in construction and chemical industry.

0368

GENEVA

The Hyper Filter Skyscraper recognizes the threat of environmental pollution to Earth. Under today's levels of pollution, harmful substances spread over hundreds of kilometers and a whole region and even a country could represent a single pollution source.

The Hyper Filter Skyscraper is designed to inhale carbon dioxide and other harmful gases in cities and exhale concentrated oxygen. The skin of the project is made out of long pipe filters that ensure the cleaning process. While clean air is released to the atmosphere, all the harmful substances are stored for use in the chemical industry.

Seen as urban dandelions, the towers unique shape is derived from an anlysis to optimize their footprint and air-filtering surface. The towers are narrow at the bottom to maximize solar exposure to

the city below. As the tower rises, its diameter also increases and gradually reduces itself at the top. The entire facade is covered with large-scle filaments or tubes that serve as air filters. The iiner core is void and serves as a funnel to move and exhale clean air.

The design is purely an infrastructure piece without any inhabitable spaces. The aggregation of towers would create a cluster capable of filtering a great portion of the polluted air. This system could be replicated in major cities around the globe. Its success relies on creating these clusters working together as a big lung. A single tower wold not be sufficient to make a noticable impact.

At night the towers would light up the sky and serve as beacons or urban markers. The size of each tower is also variable depending on its unique location within the city and in reponse to the severity of

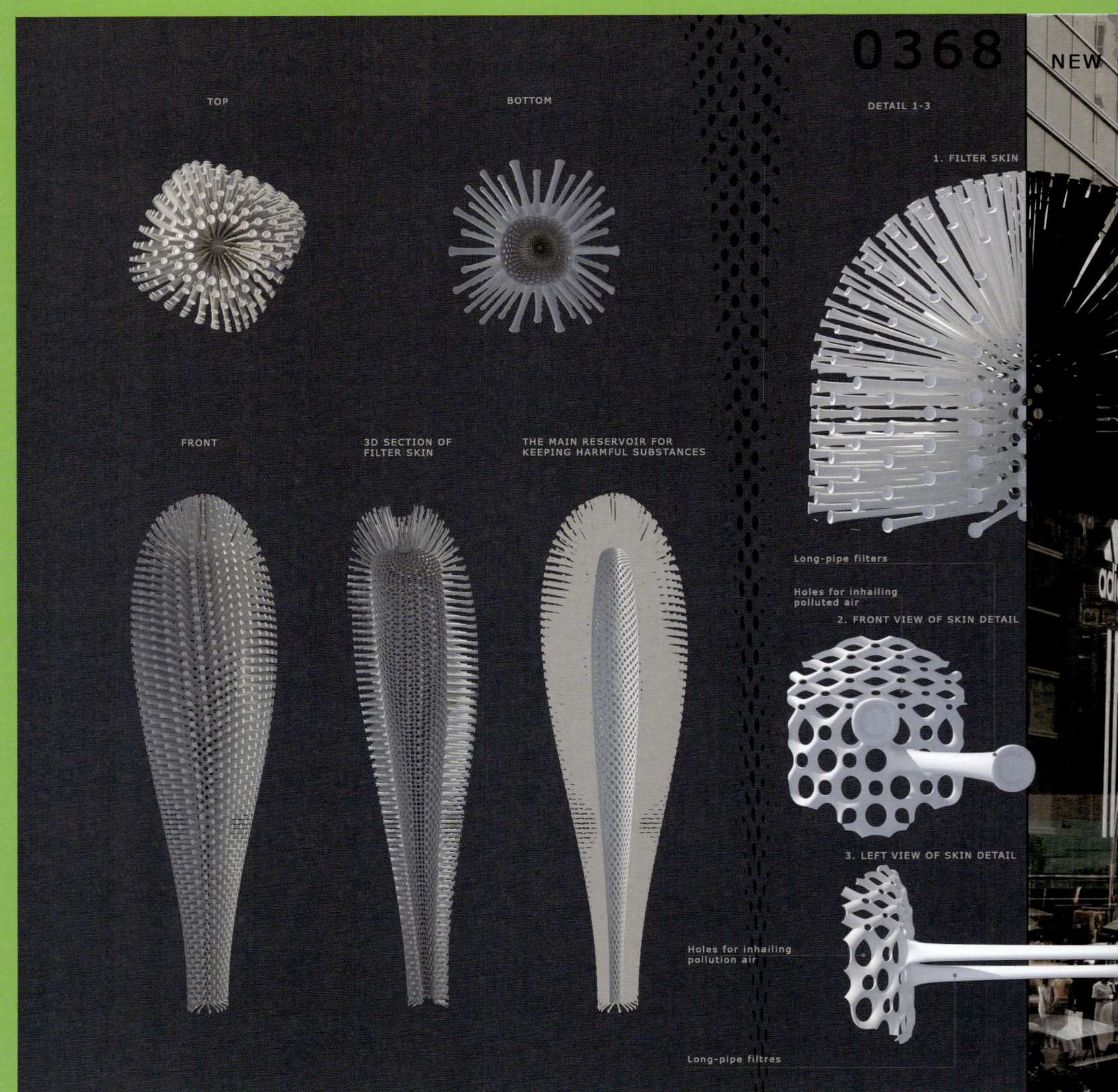

TOP

BOTTOM

DETAIL 1-3

0368

NEW

1. FILTER SKIN

FRONT

3D SECTION OF FILTER SKIN

THE MAIN RESERVOIR FOR KEEPING HARMFUL SUBSTANCES

Long-pipe filters

Holes for inhailing polluted air

2. FRONT VIEW OF SKIN DETAIL

3. LEFT VIEW OF SKIN DETAIL

Holes for inhailing pollution air

Long-pipe filtres

pollution.

The tower is designed as a steel structure anchored to a reinforced concrete foundation. The air filters are made of space-grade aluminum. A fine mesh is inserted at the tip of each filament to filter air particles and chemicals. The filtering process uses a standard techology applied at a large scale.

It is estimated that by 2030 more than 70% of the world population will live in an urban area. This rapid urbanization will lead to more polluted cities expanding at breaking neck speeds. These towers offer a potential solution to allow urban sustainable growth.

SKYSCAPE

Lifeng Lin
Lanmuzhi Yang
Le Luo

United States

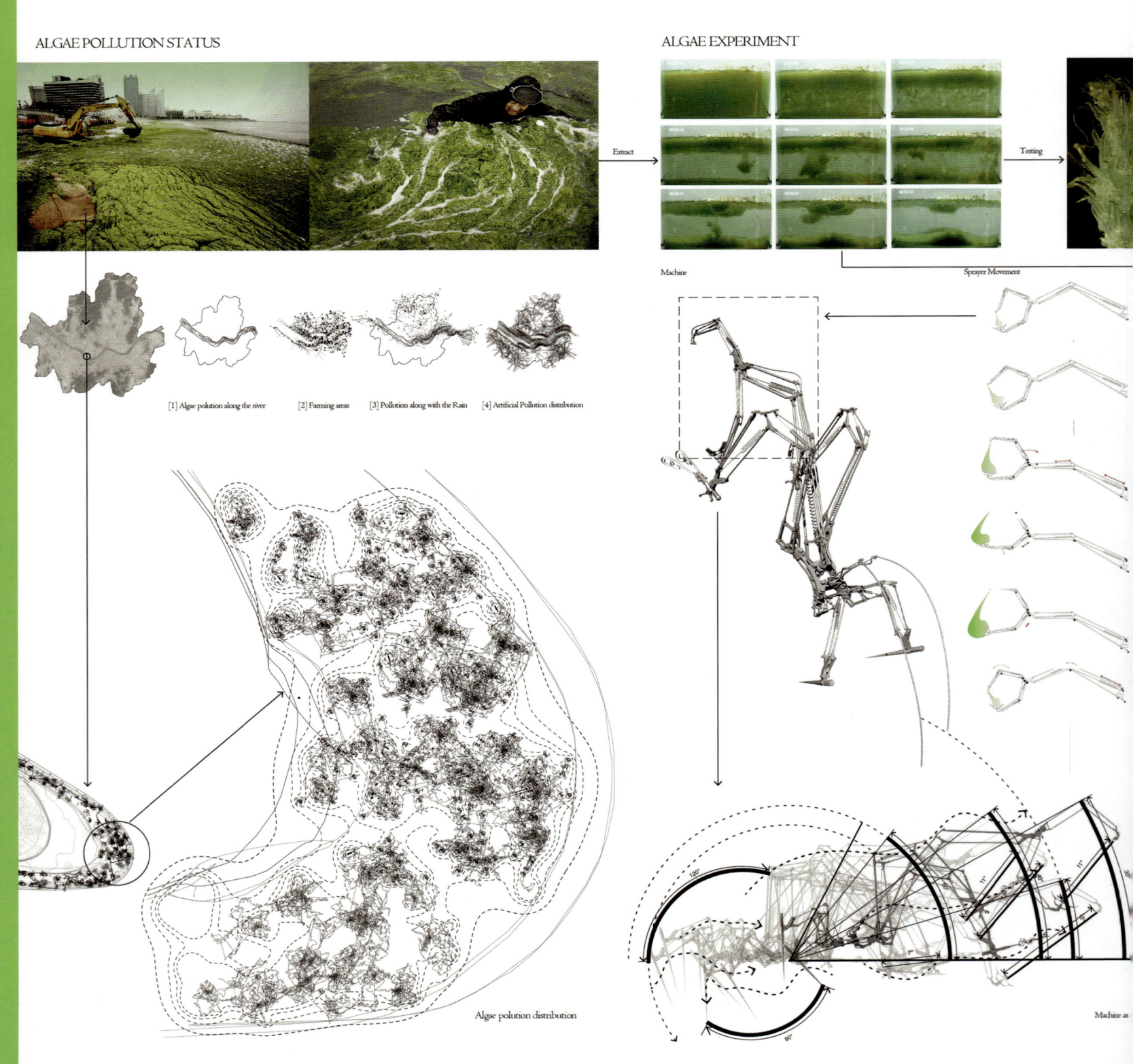

ALGAE POLLUTION STATUS

ALGAE EXPERIMENT

Extract

Testing

[1] Algae polution along the river   [2] Farming areas   [3] Pollution along with the Rain   [4] Artificial Pollution distribution

Machine

Sprayer Movement

Algae polution distribution

Machine as

There are two phenomena in the future that interest us most, one is the algae pollution in many coastal cities, which will become a severe problem and the other is the surge of high-tech, intelligent machines being produced at great speeds. As architects, we are given the task of thinking of these two things as a combination.

The natural pollution of algae grows unscrupulously because of the over-fertilization from farmers, eutrophication from the land, and massive excretion from livestock. A traditional way to deal with algae is to collect them and dry them, and then burn them, which leads to more pollution.

Now we are treating these algae in a brilliant way. We are using the high-tech product- an intelligent machine - to extract the algae from the polluted water and convert it into a buildable material named

BUILDING ALGAE

0570-01
RECYCLE-BUILDED IN HIGH-TECH

A New SKYSCRAPER
----SKY (LAND) SCAPE

'algae glue.' The machine will work following a designed trajectory to build a skyscraper, which is not a traditional skyscraper by any means. Because this skyscraper can be a remarkable place in these cities and it can serve multiple functions in addition to being merely a building, now it becomes a landscape, and we call it Skyscape.

As long as the pollution is evading the cities, the machine keeps building. You will never see the process stop unless the pollution is over. The process is a permanent equilibrium, because the system will not disappear, the machine just maintains the system and keeps doing, redoing and re-redoing until the abolishment of pollution, while simultaneously reminding inhabitants of pollutions grave effects upon visiting it.

BIRD-VIEW

The new green areas will be used for recreational activities. From city parks to urban forests they will provide fresh air to the congested urban environment. In time, the green clusters will be large enough to transform the cityscape and stop air pollution. Until the environment is clean, the system will continue expanding vertically and horizontally.

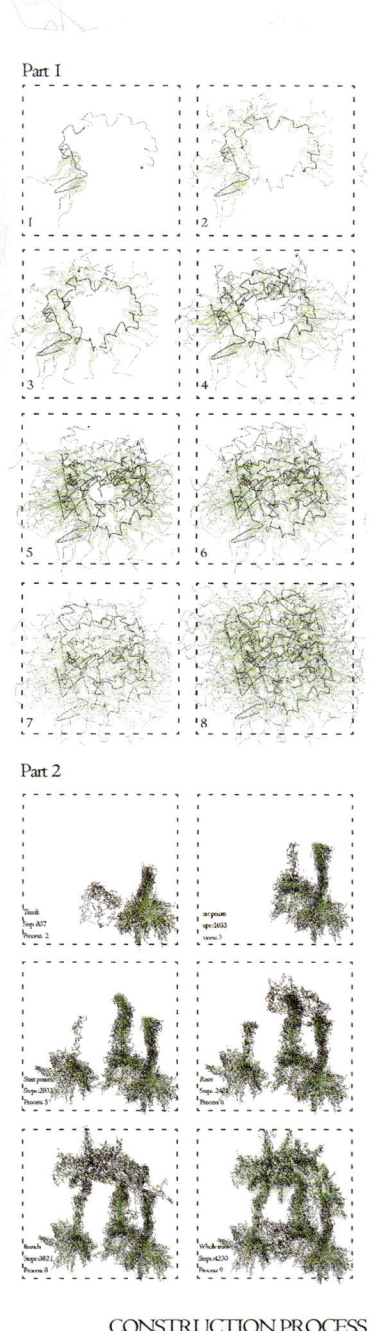

Part 1

Part 2

CONSTRUCTION PROCESS

0570-2
RECYCLE BUILDED IN HIGH-TECH

A New SKYSCRAPER
——SKYLANDSCAPE

FRAGMENT IN FUTURE

GREEN GENERATOR

Kim Wan
Sul Ah Lee
Jin Ho Choi
Jong Gil Park
Ja Ram Kim
Han Seung Cho
Dogyun Kim
Yeong Seon Son
Jong Hyuk Kim

South Korea

Green Generator

Air purifier for water about famine

The fundamental cause of desertification that has been progressing in Africa is starvation. 33% of the population in Africa suffers from malnutrition and 70% struggles to make ends meet through agriculture and stock farming. They are damaging grounds and forests for production of food and firewood. This destruction of nature makes the progression of desertification faster, eventually; it makes it more difficult to solve starvation with decreasing fruitful soil. In order to solve problems of starvation and desertification, we suggest the resolution to produce purified drinking water and water for production of crops.

For sustainable supplies of water, we come up with the idea of using air. Moisture in air can be the key to producing water. Hot air that has risen by convection is put into contact with a cooling fan that is in the top of the building. The difference of temperature creates dew condensation at the top of

0620

Background

Desertification, according to UNCCD refers to the process that dry or semi-dry lands, or semi-swamps become increasingly arid because of the climate change and human activities. Devastation of land leads to low quality of soil, water shortage, decreased production of farming, decrease of biodiversity, and accelerated famine and drought. Especially, land degradation is a main factor to accelerate global warming increasing carbon emission of soils. Desertification has progressed at an alarming rate all over the world. Every year, 6 milion hectare area is becoming desertificated, and the causes of desertification are diverse.

Desertification of Africa

Africa is vulnerable to desertification and drought. Over 60% areas in Africa belong to dry regions. Excessive cultivation and graze conducted through habitants in dry areas, forest clearing, inappropriate management of soil, and the absence of system for soil and water preservation make decertification of Africa worse. Every year, 15thousands hectares of tropical rain forests are disappearing because of agriculture, livestock grazing.

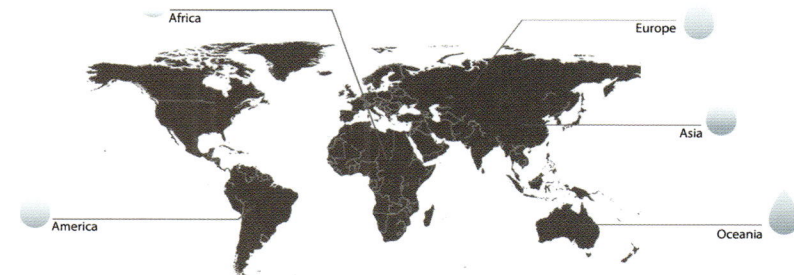

Starvation that causes from desertification

The fundamental cause of desertification that has been progressing in Africa is starvation. 33% of population in Africa suffers from malnutrition and 70% struggles to make ends meet through agriculture and stock farming. They are damaging grounds and forests for production of food and firewood. This destruction of nature make the progression of desertification faster, eventually, it make more difficult to solve starvation with decreasing fruitful soil. In order to solve problems of starvation and desertification, we suggest the resolution to produce purified drinking water and water for production of crops.

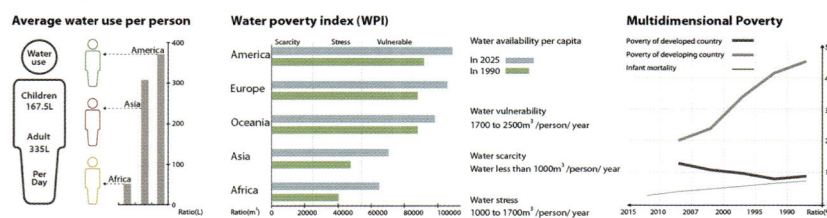

Concept

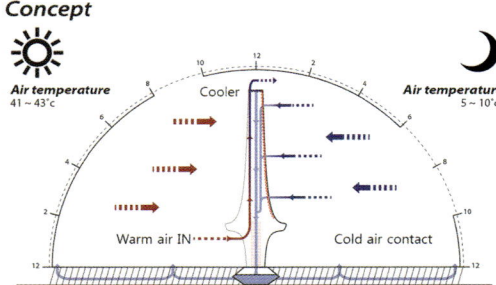

For sustainable supplies of water, we come up with the idea of using air. Moisture in air can be the key to producing water. Hot air that is risen by convection contacts with cooling pan that is in the top of the building. The difference of temperature creates dew condensation at the top of the building, and pans in the bottom of it, allows to generate water continually keeping making water enter the building. Moreover, it is possible to create water at night using the hot air that is made in daytime, in the building. The inside of building consists of low heat conductivity material and the outside; high heat conductivity. Therefore, water can be generated by dew condensation that happens by the difference of temperature; cold air of desert at night and hot air inside building. We propose sustainable water generator that create water utilizing the condition of desert and innovative systems.

Plans for the sustainable future

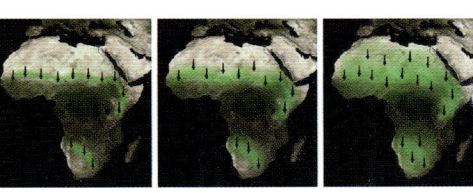

We suggest to establish the building in area of desertification in Africa. Through this building that produces water, people are able to get purified drinking water and crops that grow from water. There is a irrigation system below the building and it makes crops grow through supplied water.
The building starts to be set up at the severe desertification in Africa and spread to modest dry regions in Africa in the future. We propose this plan for sustainable life of Africa. This building would become a significant solution for starvation and water shortage problems that Africa has by providing drinking water and crops.

the building, and pans in the bottom of it, and allows the constant generation of water. Moreover, it is possible to create water at night using the hot air that is made in daytime, in the building. The inside of building consists of low heat conductivity material and the outside; high heat conductivity. There is an irrigation system below the building and it makes crops grow through supplied water.

The building has four water generation systems. First is the air-cooling generator. This is the system to correct hot air that is entered through pan in the bottom of the building, and has air coolant that makes dew condensation. Through this process water is created when raised hot air contact with coolant. Sloped roof let produced water to flow to the bottom easily.

Second is the air web generator. The facade consists of double skin window and web pipe. Pipes are

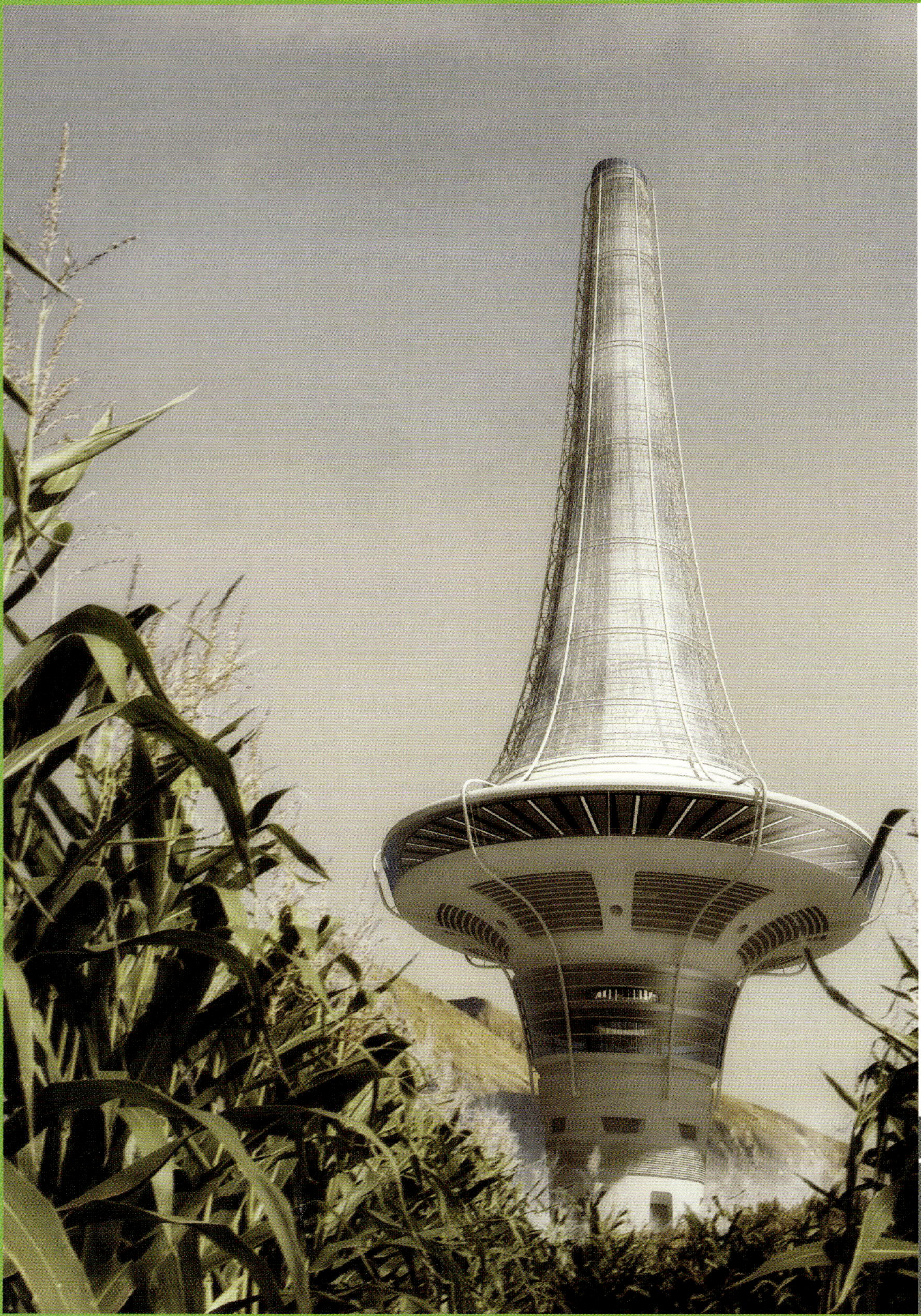

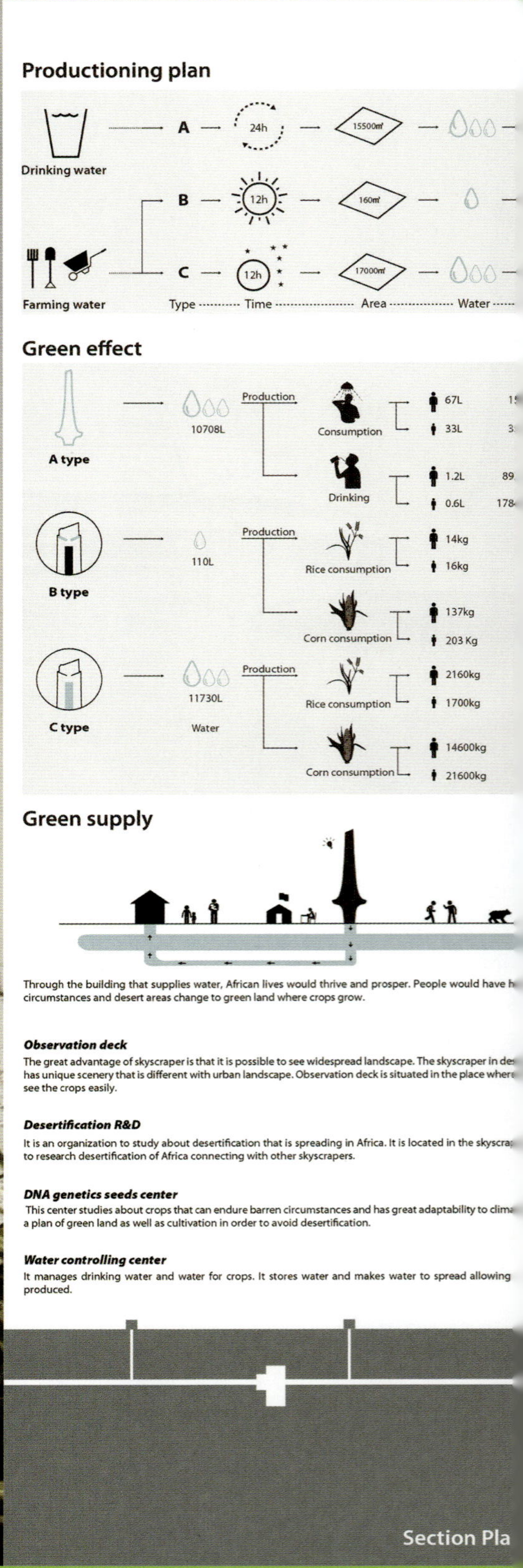

Productioning plan

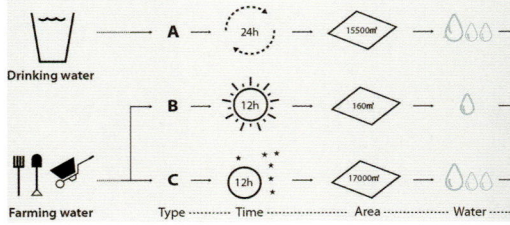

Green effect

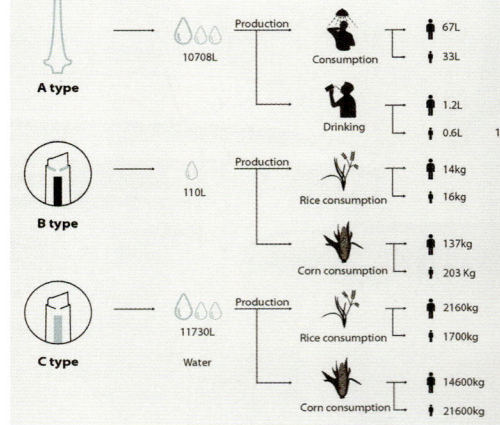

Green supply

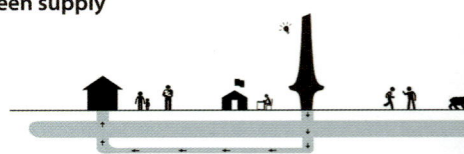

Through the building that supplies water, African lives would thrive and prosper. People would have h... circumstances and desert areas change to green land where crops grow.

Observation deck
The great advantage of skyscraper is that it is possible to see widespread landscape. The skyscraper in des... has unique scenery that is different with urban landscape. Observation deck is situated in the place where... see the crops easily.

Desertification R&D
It is an organization to study about desertification that is spreading in Africa. It is located in the skyscra... to research desertification of Africa connecting with other skyscrapers.

DNA genetics seeds center
This center studies about crops that can endure barren circumstances and has great adaptability to clima... a plan of green land as well as cultivation in order to avoid desertification.

Water controlling center
It manages drinking water and water for crops. It stores water and makes water to spread allowing... produced.

Section Pla

made of Zeolite stone, which has low heat conductivity. Dew condensation happen through temperature differential between hot air of outside window and cold air of pipes. Third is the purification system. The high-rise building has the function to create dew through temperature differential between coolant of roof and hot air of desert, and collect the water making it flow the structure to the bottom. Since Zeolite, which is installed in pipes, has purified function, flowing water on the structure is purified. And fourth is the ventilation system. He fan aspirates hot air from the outside filling the building with hot temperature. Hot air that is entered through fan is raised to the top and touch with coolant. Through this principal, water is generated.

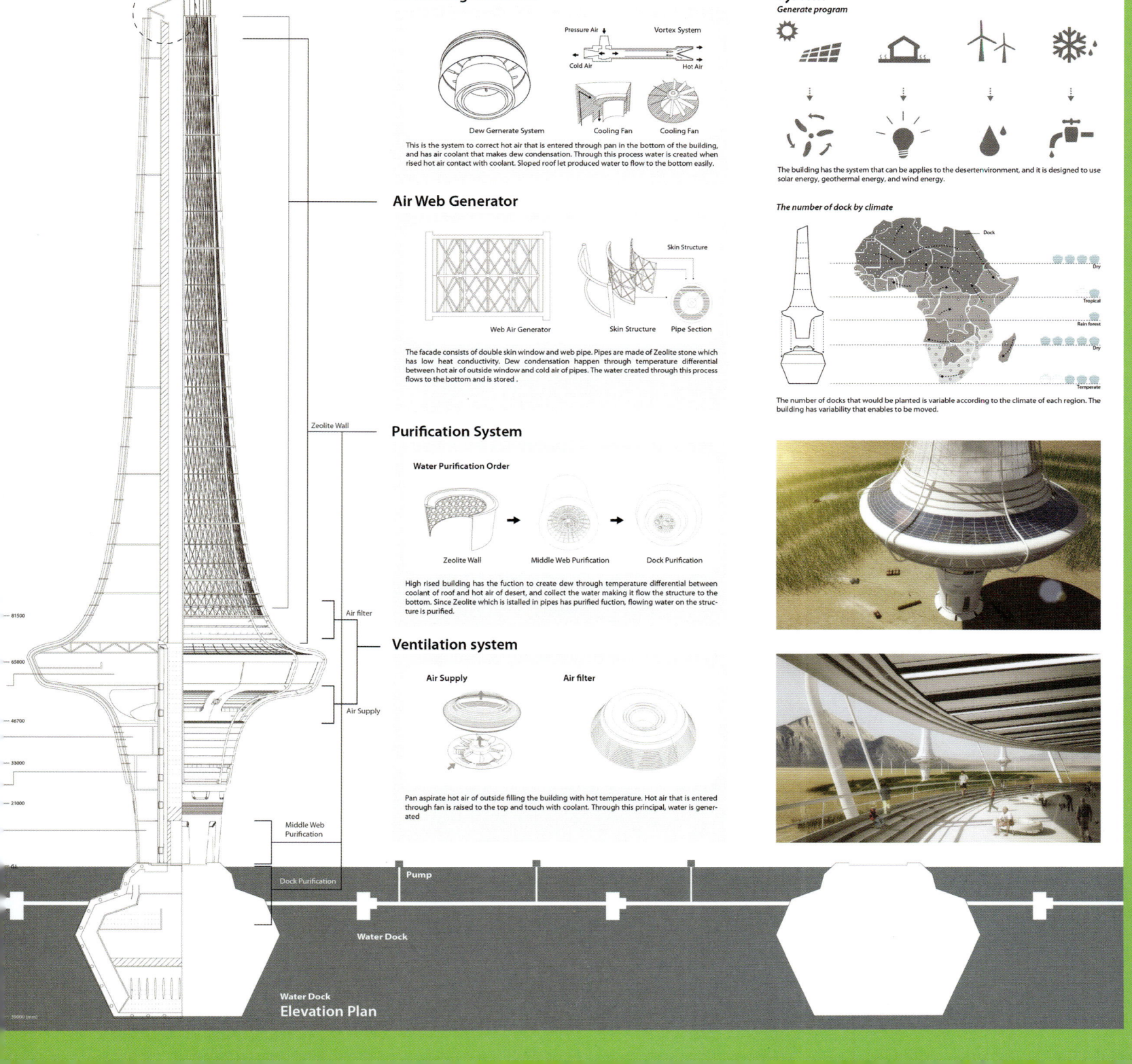

0620

Air Cooling Generator

Dew Gernerate System   Cooling Fan   Cooling Fan

This is the system to correct hot air that is entered through pan in the bottom of the building, and has air coolant that makes dew condensation. Through this process water is created when rised hot air contact with coolant. Sloped roof let produced water to flow to the bottom easily.

Air Web Generator

Web Air Generator   Skin Structure   Pipe Section

The facade consists of double skin window and web pipe. Pipes are made of Zeolite stone which has low heat conductivity. Dew condensation happen through temperature differential between hot air of outside window and cold air of pipes. The water created through this process flows to the bottom and is stored .

Purification System

Water Purification Order

Zeolite Wall   Middle Web Purification   Dock Purification

High rised building has the fuction to create dew through temperature differential between coolant of roof and hot air of desert, and collect the water making it flow the structure to the bottom. Since Zeolite which is istalled in pipes has purified fuction, flowing water on the structure is purified.

Ventilation system

Air Supply   Air filter

Pan aspirate hot air of outside filling the building with hot temperature. Hot air that is entered through fan is raised to the top and touch with coolant. Through this principal, water is generated

System
Generate program

The building has the system that can be applies to the desertenvironment, and it is designed to use solar energy, geothermal energy, and wind energy.

The number of dock by climate

The number of docks that would be planted is variable according to the climate of each region. The building has variability that enables to be moved.

Zeolite Wall

Air filter

Air Supply

Middle Web Purification

Dock Purification

Pump

Water Dock

Water Dock
Elevation Plan

RAINFOREST GUARDIAN SKYSCRAPER

Jie Huang
Jin Wei
Qiaowan Tang
Yiwei Yu
Zhe Hao

China

RAINFOREST GUARDIAN ///////////////////

PROBLEM
Purveyors of water, consumers of carbon, treasure houses of species, the Amazon Rainforest is a ecological miracles, referred to as the lungs of the Earth. During the last decades of accidental forest fires, the Amazon Rainforest has fragility. Fires have burned 3 percent of Amazon rainforest in 12 years, according to NASA's observation. Compared with over-logging and over-grazing, forest fires not only are typical of unexpectedness, uncertainty and complexity. laws and policies. Due to the vicious cycle caused by serious ecological destruction, the self-adjustment ability of the rainforest is getting too weak to recover from the fire injury. It is essential for us to help the rainforest in the role of skyscraper is designed as "the guardian of rainforests", capable of prevent, monitor and combat fire activities.

SITE LOCATION
Our skyscrapers are arranged along the edge of the rainforest area, making sure that it make least damage to the forest. The distance between two towers is based on a reasonable firefighting time.

The site is in the southeastern Amazon, in the Brazilian states of Mato Grosso

FIRE PROBLEM OF THE SITE
Satellite and ground observations from NASA show evidence of frequent fires burning in the Xingu River Basin, especially at some rainforest frontier areas. One reason is that the ecological system of these boundary regions is fragile and more vulnerable to fire activities. The other is that the regional distinct dry season when little or no rain falls is also an important cause of fire frequency in the dry season.

Number of Fires (1999-2010) from NASA

AVERAGE TEMPERATURE OF MATO
Previously Mato Grosso has the high

CONCEPT
Acting as infrastructure targeting at forest fires, "Rainforest guardian" is introduced into the forest frontier of the Amazon. For the reason that the boundary is the most weak parts of the Amazon rainforest and needed special prote reducing damages to the natural environment as far as possible. The height of "the guardian" is above the canopy level, depended on the rainforest height. The outlook of the guardian is large in the top and small in the bottom, as a c certain trees. The essential function is centered on the large top of the building in order to limit the damages to the forest land. The "aerial root" dropped down from the top makes the building "invisible" in the rainforest. "Rainforest guardian" stand still at the forest frontier, preventing the fire effectively by capturing the rain water in rainy season and irrigating the land in the dry season. In the case of fire, "the firefighters" on the top are alarmed , detac fly to the scene of the fire and put out the fire with collected water. "Rainforest guardian" is not only a skyscraper with important function, but also a warning tower that remind inhabitants of the boundary existence and the importance

The Rainforest Guardian Skyscraper consists of a water tower, a forest fire station, a weather station, and scientific research and education laboratories. It stands still at the Amazon's frontier, preventing fires effectively by capturing rainwater in the rainy season and irrigating the land in the dry season.

The lotus-shaped water tower is capable of capturing rainwater directly. The collected water is filtered and stored in spare reservoirs. Using capillarity combined with active energy, the aerial roots with a distinct sponge-structure can absorb and store the excess water without disturbing the Amazon's ecosystem.

In the case of fire, firefighters fly to the scene and extinguish the fire with the collected water. In addition, the Guardian Skyscraper provides special scientific research laboratories for scientists to

0665

monitor the climate change and the ecosystem stability. The laboratories also act as exhibition spaces for tourists to create environmental awareness.

The Rainforest Guardian Skyscraper utilizes a steel diagrid as main structural component. The intricate mesh allows long spans and the ability to surpass in height the great Amazon trees with a relatively small footprint. The idea is to minimize the impact on the surface and maximize the water collection capabilities.

The water is conveniently stored in filaments or vertical reservoirs along the entire perimeter of the tower. This allows to use gravity when water pressure is needed to extinguish fires. The canopy serves to functions. First, it collects rainwater. Second, it accommodates a research floor and observatory with

RAINWATER COLLECTION SYSTEM

The rainwater collection system is based on two parts, one on the roof and the other on the ground. Most of the water is collected from the roof, which go through a simple filter system and then is stored in a big reservoir. This part of water is mainly used for both fire-fighting. The "aerial roots" can also store a large amount of water which is mainly used for irrigating the land arround. However, these two parts of water can complement each other if necessary.

PROCESS 1

Step 1. Rainwater drop on the roof.
Step 2. Simply filtered the water to make sure it will not jam the sprays.
Step 3. Store the water in the reservoir.
Step 4. Transfer the water to the temporary reservoir.

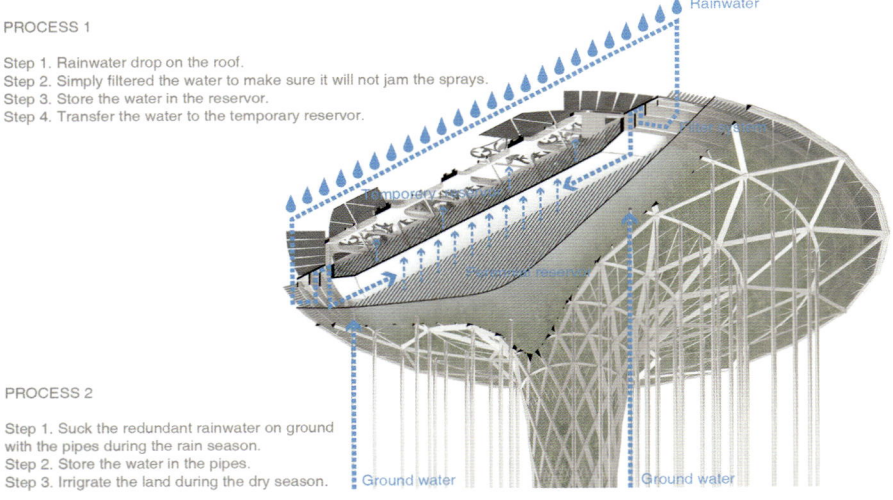

PROCESS 2

Step 1. Suck the redundant rainwater on ground with the pipes during the rain season.
Step 2. Store the water in the pipes.
Step 3. Irrigate the land during the dry season.

THE "AERIAL ROOT"

"Aerial roots" is a piping system with a combination function of absorbing, delivering and storing water. Using the capillarity combined with the active energy, this system can not only absorb and store the excess run-off water, but also deliver the water back to the land when it is necessary. The operation mechanism of this system is just like the function of plant's aerial roots, which transport water in the outer layer and store water in the inner layer.

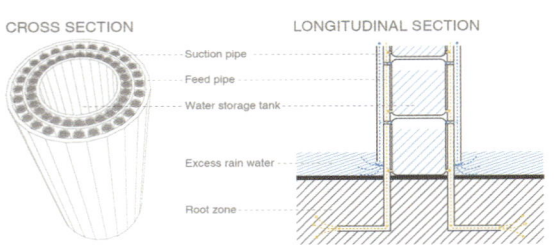

CROSS SECTION   LONGITUDINAL SECTION   FORM COMPARATION

Suction pipe
Feed pipe
Water storage tank
Excess rain water
Root zone

Step 1. Build a big water tank in site to store excess rainwater.

Step 2. Separate it into some small ones to make less influence to the forest.

Step 3. Make them tall and slender enough to "disappear" in the forest.

THE EXTINGUISHMENT PROCESS

Rainwater is collected in the reservors and the "Firefighters" to be ready for extinguishment. T has a particular detecting area and can react much quickly than the GPS system, which can n

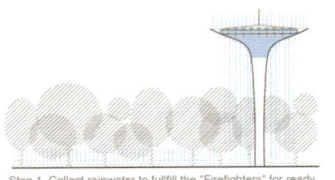
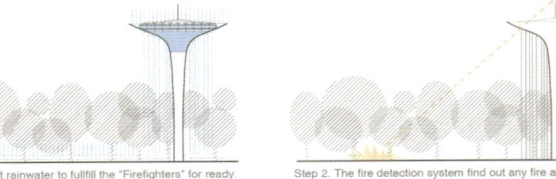

Step 1. Collect rainwater to fullfill the "Firefighters" for ready.

Step 2. The fire detection system find out any fire and into an alarm condition.

THE WATER-CYCLE REGULATING PROCESS

The other important function of "Rainforest guardian" is capturing the surplus rainfall in the ra the dry season, the water is delivered back to irrigate the land. This artificial stored-delivered as well as fix up the degradation of natural water-cycle ability.

RAIN SEASON   DRY SEASON

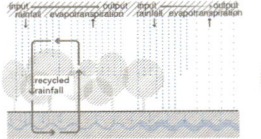
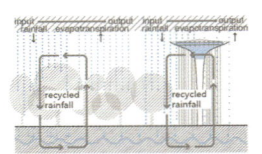
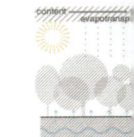

The edge area of rainforest is losing its ability to control the water-cycle.

"Rainforest guardian" can play as a similar role to help regulate the water-cyce.

The edge area is and to catch fire.

THE "RAINFOREST FIREFIGHTERS"

"Firefighters" is an small-size aircraft that used to extinguish the fire directly. It contains a retractable "needle" which can suck and spray water, it looks like a dandelion seed in the a can reach to the fire even through the canopies is too thick to get through.

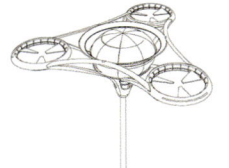
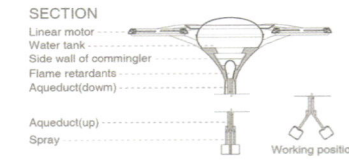

SECTION
Linear motor
Water tank
Side wall of commingler
Flame retardants
Aqueduct(down)
Aqueduct(up)
Spray
Working position

SECT
Side wa

Superch
Eddy cu
Nozzle

RAINFOREST GUARDIAN ////////////////////////////

360 degrees unobstructed views of the Amazon Rainforest. This structure could be replicated in various locations to create a network that protects the entire Amazon region.

The Rainforest firefighters consist of a group of drones equipped with a water storage filament. This filament will connect to the towers to collect water and would spray it above fires. The drones are controllled directly from the tower to minimize human casualties.

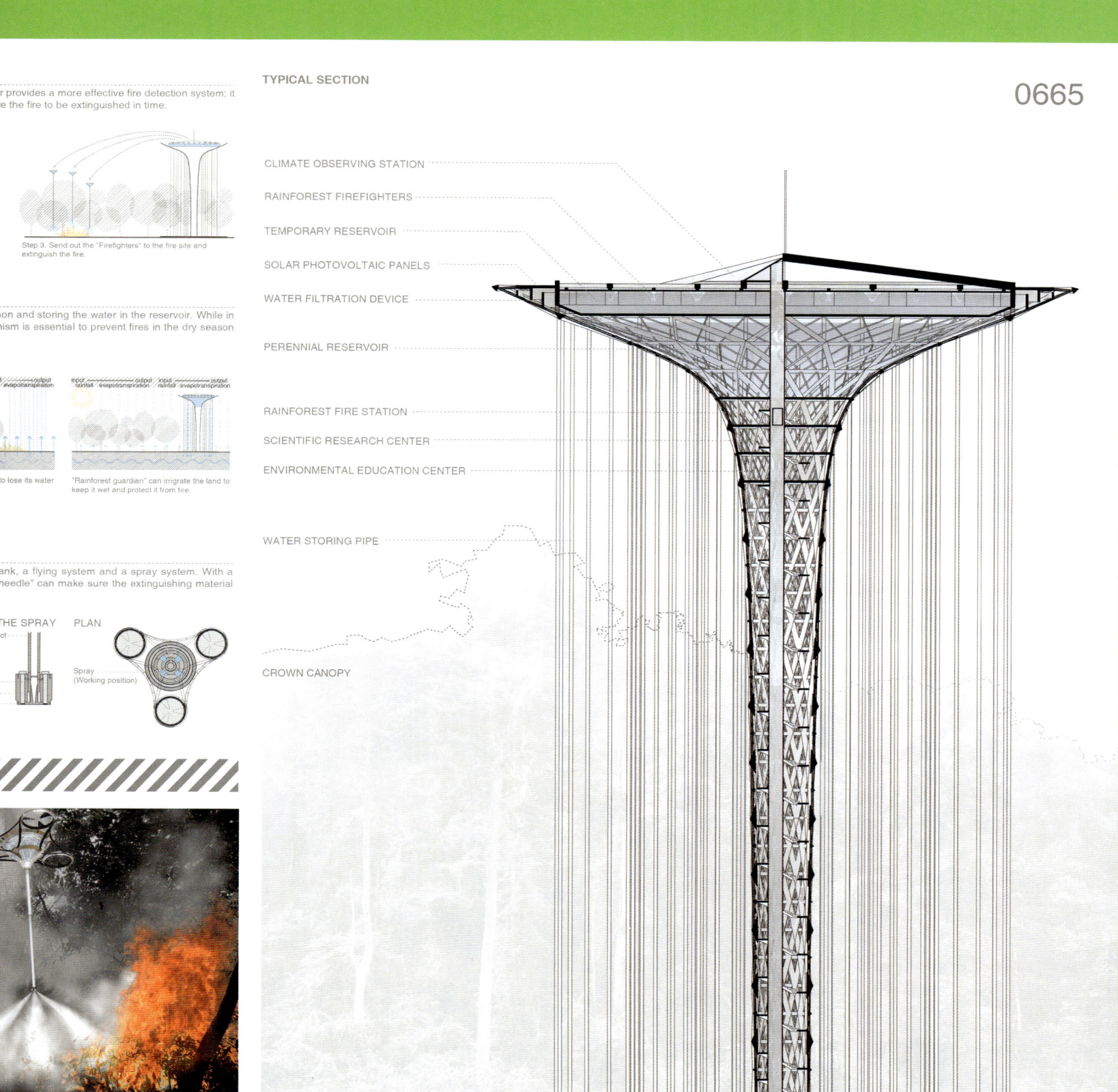

TYPICAL SECTION

0665

...er provides a more effective fire detection system: it ...re the fire to be extinguished in time.

Step 3. Send out the "Firefighters" to the fire site and extinguish the fire.

...son and storing the water in the reservoir. While in ...nism is essential to prevent fires in the dry season

...to lose its water   "Rainforest guardian" can irrigate the land to keep it wet and protect it from fire.

...ank, a flying system and a spray system. With a ...needle" can make sure the extinguishing material

THE SPRAY   PLAN

Spray
(Working position)

CLIMATE OBSERVING STATION

RAINFOREST FIREFIGHTERS

TEMPORARY RESERVOIR

SOLAR PHOTOVOLTAIC PANELS

WATER FILTRATION DEVICE

PERENNIAL RESERVOIR

RAINFOREST FIRE STATION

SCIENTIFIC RESEARCH CENTER

ENVIRONMENTAL EDUCATION CENTER

WATER STORING PIPE

CROWN CANOPY

INFILL AQUIFER

Jason Orbe-Smith

United States

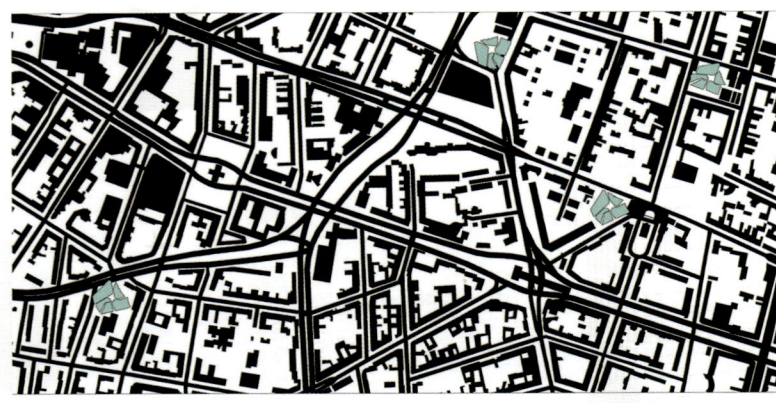

INFILL AQUIFER

The Infill Aquifer aims to reconnect the built world with the natural environment in order to create healthy and thriving urban ecosystems.

The project does this by re-establishing the ground plane as a vital component of urban building design. The Infill Aquifer is a floating mass, exposing the ground and soil to natural processes while accommodating the density required by growing cities and world populations. The Infill Aquifer is an optimistic proposal that humanity and nature can coexist and flourish.

Densely urban environments have many rich and positive qualities. The ability to gather together large populations generates great advantages in creativity and commerce, education, technology and social interaction. However urban environments also often lack other features that enhance quality of life; features such as open space, recreation, green vegetation, a calm atmosphere, and the organic and inorganic processes of nature.

The project targets two main concerns facing us now and in the near future: the quality and quantity of new open space to build, live and work; and issues surrounding water usage and rights. The Infill Aquifer is designed as a regeneration and rehabilitation program for groundwater supplies within a city while maintaining its functionality as a usable building.

The Infill Aquifer is both a singular building design as well as an integral component of a larger ecological network. They are strategic pinpoints that can be located within a city as surface parking lots and underutilized pieces of land are redeveloped. With each new infill, the network in the region strengthens and grows, increasing the diversity of composition of the city and aiding in the health of the aquifer and hydrologic cycles. Cities that begin to implement infill aquifers can have the benefits of water security, increased green space, improved air quality and improved quality of life for the inhabitants.

The Infill Aquifer is as an achievable step in the conversion of our cities from static, sprawling monoliths towards active, vibrant and sensitive ecologies.

CONTEXTUAL MASSING

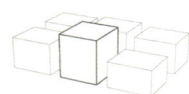 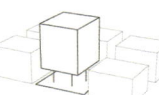  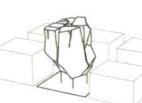

TYPICAL URBAN DEVELOPMENT
Dense, primarily hardscape environment. Design is often predicated on returns on financial investment at the expense of the health of the local ecology.

ELEVATED MASS
Building volume lifted, freeing and exposing the earth. Natural processes such as vegetated ground cover, evapotranspiration and groundwater recharging are able to continue functioning.

CARVED MASS
External environmental factors such as sun, wind and prevalent rain directions shape the building mass. Programmatic requirements and intended building use further develop the mass.

FRACTURED MASS
The overall mass is cracked and fractured allowing water to pass through easily or be stored for future use. These fissures also bring light, air and exhaust cavities deep into the mass, allowing the building to breathe naturally.

INFILL AQUIFER HYDROLOGY

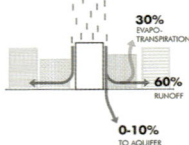 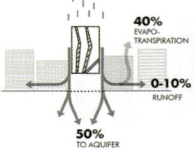 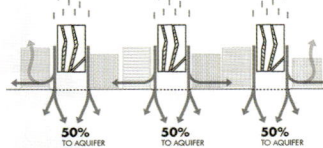

TYPICAL URBAN ENVIRONMENT
In a typical urban development, the majority of water that falls on a site will rush over the hardscape as runoff. 30% evaporates in the air and nearly no water reached the underground water supply.

INFILL AQUIFER ENVIRONMENT
By elevating the building, the ground's natural processes are improved. 50% of water now reaches the aquifer and 40% returns to the air. Less than 10% now leaves the site as runoff.

NETWORKED AQUIFERS
As more infill projects are completed, the health of the groundwater continues to improve and replenish. 50% of water that falls on each location will now reach the aquifer.

POROSITY

The Infill Aquifer is a porous mass as seen through the figural qualities of the section.

The amount, direction and variation of the fractures are dependent on the building's site location and weather as well as on the program. Large cracks allow heavy water to flow though and off of the building while smaller veins funnel water into storage and purification tanks.

The deep crevices, folded planes and environmental features of the building can create a unique experience for the occupant as they move through the spaces.

The Infill Aquifer aims to reconnect the built world with the natural environment in order to create healthy and thriving urban ecosystems.

The project does this by re-establishing the ground plane as a vital component of urban building design. The Infill Aquifer is a floating mass, exposing the ground and soil to natural processes while accommodating the density required by growing cities and world populations. The Infill Aquifer is an optimistic proposal stating that humanity and nature can coexist and flourish.

Densely urban environments have many rich and positive qualities. The ability to gather together large populations generates great advantages in creativity and commerce, education, technology, and social interaction. However urban environments also often lack other features that enhance quality of

life; features such as open space, recreation, green vegetation, a calm atmosphere, and the organic and inorganic processes of nature.

The project targets two main concerns facing us now and in the near future: the quality and quantity of new open space to build, live and work; and issues surrounding water usage and rights. The Infill Aquifer is designed as a regeneration and rehabilitation program for groundwater supplies within a city while maintaining its functionality as a usable building.

The Infill Aquifer is both a singular building design as well as an integral component of a larger ecological network. They are strategic pinpoints that can be located within a city as surface parking lots and underutilized pieces of land are redeveloped. With each new infill, the network in the region

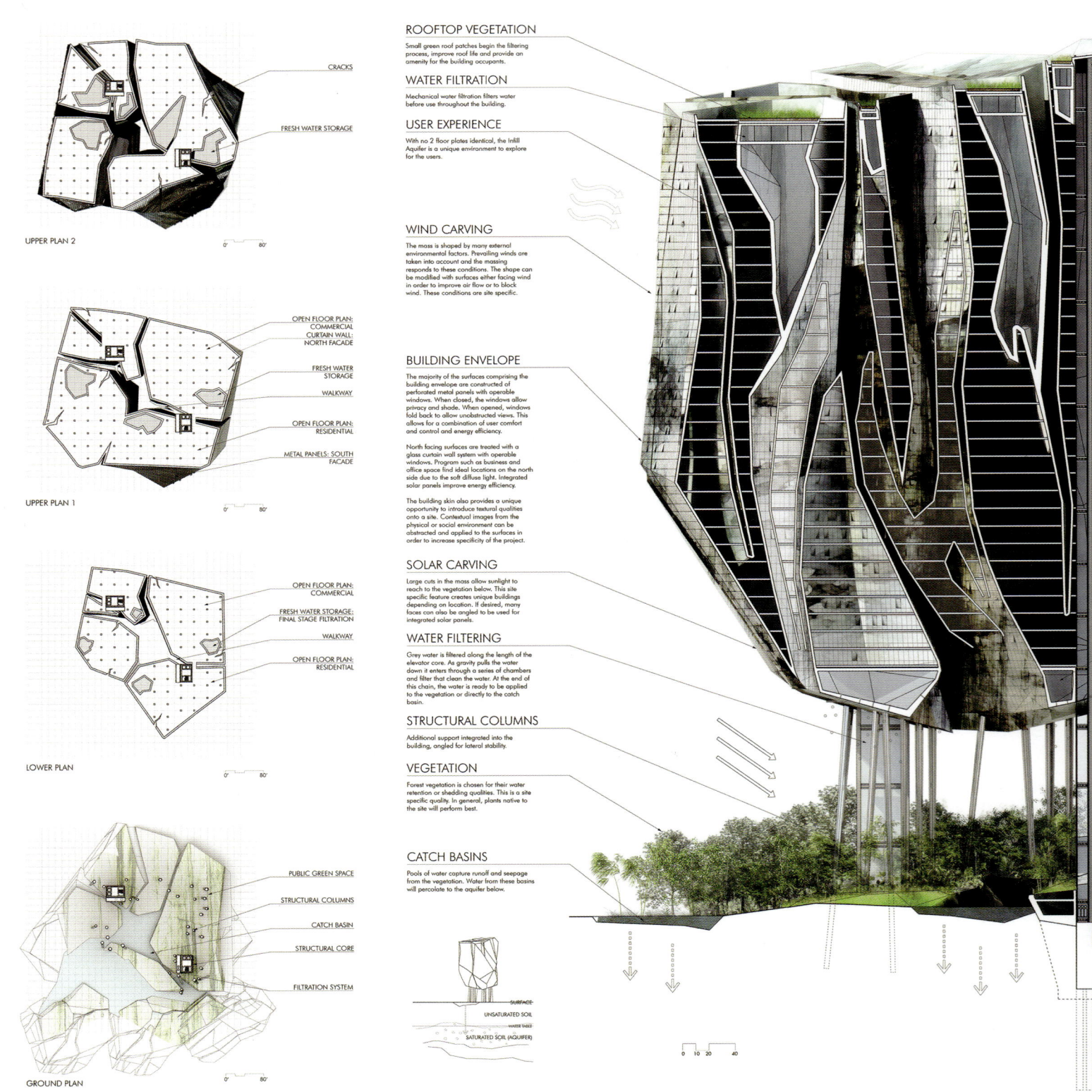

strengthens and grows, increasing the diversity of composition of the city and aiding in the health of the aquifer and hydrologic cycles. Cities that begin to implement infill aquifers can have the benefits of water security, increased green space, improved air quality and improved quality of life for the inhabitants.

The Infill Aquifer is as an achievable step in the conversion of our cities from static, sprawling monoliths towards active, vibrant and sensitive ecologies.

MECHANICAL EQUIPMENT
Covered mechanical equipment improves component life and the appearance of the building.

FRESH WATER STORAGE
Several large water storage units are located throughout the building. The amount of water needed for the building is based on estimated building usage, per person usage, occupancy type, local weather conditions, length of dry season, etc. An economical balance between these factors results in the sizing of fresh water containers. Each building is therefore uniquely specific to their site and needs. Many areas in the building allow you to touch the walls of the water tanks.

CONSUMPTION
The building maintains an equilibrium balance between stored water and water being used. The building acts as a sponge or a porous stone, keeping fresh water available for individual use. As water is used, fresh water is drawn from within the system and the storage tanks. Grey water is sent below to be recycled. Black water is sent to the city infrastructure or to bio-remedial plants.

THERMAL
The thermal qualities of water make it an ideal filler in locations where thermal mass are desired. This helps the building maintain its ambient temperature. The water can also can be used for radiant floor heating/cooling.

CRACKS
Cracks in the building mass create pockets where fresh air can reach individual units. Units can also exhaust air into the cracks. The cracks also serve to funnel and collect water into the storage compartments. The size, placement and prominence of cracks are a result of environmental and programmatic conditions.

GREY WATER STORAGE
As greywater is used, it is stored in containers waiting to be filtered through the elevator core filtering system. The size of the holding tanks is dependent on the building use and occupancy type.

FRESH WATER STORAGE
Excess freshwater that goes beyond the needs of the building are stored in order to water the vegetation below using the rain nozzles. The storage of freshwater is calibrated to the demands of the ecosystem and types of plants below.

RAIN NOZZLES
Nozzles on the underside of the building create a misty rain that falls below when watering is required.

GROUND FLOOR
The ground floor has a minimal parking area accessible from the alley. The project relies heavily on public transportation, bikes and car share.

FOUNDATION
The Infill Aquifer uses efficient, small and deep foundations. They provide a solid support with minimal environmental impact.

FOUNDATION SOIL
The soil surrounding the foundations is composed of graded and engineered compacted sand and gravel that dispels water rapidly from the foundation.

AQUIFER
Water percolates through the layers of earth until it reaches the porous rock of the aquifer. With time the health of the local aquifer can be greatly improved.

DESERTSCRAPER

Afshin Koupaei
Mona Zand
Mohammad Soleimani
Behnaz Shamsaei

Iran

DESERTSCRAPER

DESERTIFICATION

The study by the United Nations University suggests climate change is making desertification the greatest environmental challenge of our times. Desertification is a type of land degradation in which a dry land region becomes increasingly arid, losing its bodies of water, vegetation and wildlife. Drylands occupy approximately 40-41% of Earth's land area and are home to more than 2 billion people. It has been estimated that some 10-20%of drylands are already degraded, the total area affected by desertification being between 6 and 12 million square kilometres, that about 1-6% of the inhabitants of drylands live in desertified areas, and that a billion people are under threat from further desertification.

PROJECTED FUTURE ARIDITY BY NATIONAL CENTER FOR ATMOSPHERIC RESEARCH (NCAR)
(ASOLD DAI: DROUGHT UNDER GLOBAL WARMING, 2010)

DESERTS

A land which is poor in rainfall and its mean potential evapo-transpiration reaches 100 times of yearly rainfall at low geographical latitudes. It is very poor in water and vegetation, and is inflicted with severe water and wind erosions.

KAVIR (SALT DESERT)

A piece of land under an intense influence of salt that no organic plants , which are salt resistant, can grow on it. However, non-organic salt resistant and alkai-resistant plants (tamarix, alhadj camelerum, salsola) might grow on it. Kavirs become cultivable only when they are rendered utilized through operations like creating drainage networks, parceling, and washing the salts away.

RESPONSE

In order to prevent desertification, a network of habitats which grow on the outskirts of kavirs (salt fields) in a serial and chain style is to be employed. The vitality of each center is guaranteed through preserving it's connection with others. Each habitat, DESERTSCRAPER , acts as a micro-climate to provide the inhabitants with comfort conditions despite the severe weather of the deserts. Consequently, considering a skyscraper is reasonable due to its height which causes a total separation with outside and a pressure difference that make the formation of clouds and rainfalls possible. Each DESERTSCRAPER behaves as an independant ecosystem, offering and supporting a whole life cycle and livelihood.

All factors in kavir regions which are considered to be inappropriate for life (burning sun, severe winds, lands affected gravely by salt, salinated supplies of water, huge hills and masses of wind sand around kavirs) can be used in the best manner toward improving the living conditions and economic, social and cultural development.Moreover , they are of great potential for construction of DESERTSCRAPER.

Global map of wind and solar energy
Iran - Kerman - Kavir Lut

FORMATION

In order to overcome the severe conditions, one should not fight against them, but should go along with them and benefit. The very main purpose of DESERTSCRAPER is to benefit from what nature offers in dry lands in order that use them in mega scale to form the architecture. This approach concludes in an **emergent self-organizing** system that has a dynamic exchange with its environment, and forms based on the natural stimuli.All exist in Kavir are sand, wind, sunlight, salt and salt-resistant plants. And all used in the manufacturing of DESERTSCRAPER and its metabolism is sand, wind, sunlight, salt and salt-resistant plants, as the same. As wind blows, it carries the piles of sand, which in the case of facing plants accumulate around them and form the nebkhas. Thats the start of the DESERTSCRAPER formation.

Different types of sand dunes can be formed according to the direction of winds in the selected region. In proposed site of this project Kavir-e Lut, wind blows in two opposite directions, each in a specific season. That results in the formation of DESERTSCRAPER

April - May - June   July - August - September

October - November - December   January - February - March

April - May - June   July - August - September

October - November - December   January - February - March

Desertification is the biggest environmental challenge of our time, as the United Nations University mentioned. Dry lands occupy approximately 40-41% of Earth's land area and are home to more than 2 billion people.   Desertification is a type of land degradation in which a dry land region becomes increasingly arid, losing its bodies of water, vegetation and wildlife. Some of the causes are the removal of vegetation by drought, climatic shifts, deforestation, overexploitation of land, and unsustainable irrigation and unsustainable use of scarce natural resources.

   In order to prevent desertification, a network of habitats, which grow on the outskirts of kavirs, or salt fields, in a serial, and chain style is to be employed. The vitality of each center is guaranteed through preserving its connection with the others. For each habitat, Desertscraper acts as a microclimate to

0770

provide the inhabitants with comfort conditions despite the severe weather of the deserts. Consequently, considering a skyscraper is reasonable due to its height which causes a total separation with outside and a pressure difference that make the formation of clouds and rainfalls possible, Each deserscraper behaves as an independent ecosystem, offering and supporting a whole life cycle and livelihood.

The response to the fabrication of Desertscraper is achieved by utilizing a composite system consists of three main components - tamarix, soil and halite - each plays a distinct role in forming the final structural system. These components seem ubiquitous in dry lands, which are the targets of Desertscraper.

A hyperaccumulator is a plant capable of growing in soils with very high concentrations of metals,

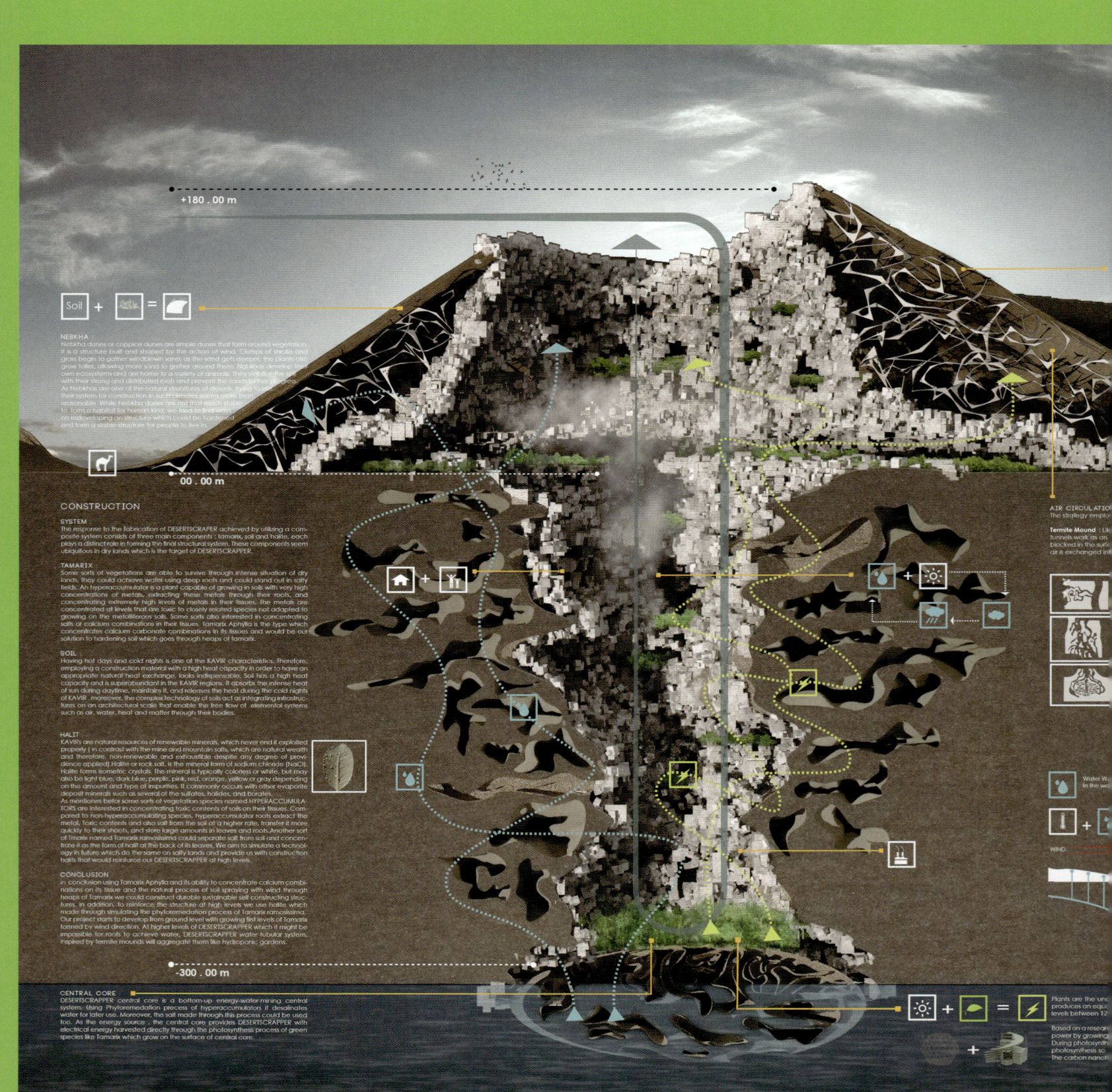

extracting these metals through their roots, and concentrating extremely high levels of metals in their tissues. Some sorts also interested in concentrating salts or calcium combinations in their tissues. Tamarix Aphylla is the type, which concentrates calcium carbonate combinations in its tissues and would be our solution to hardening soil, which goes through heaps of tamarix.

Halite, or rock salt, is the mineral form of sodium chloride, or NaCl. Halite forms isometric crystals. Some sorts of vegetation species named hyperaccumulators are interested in concentrating toxic contents of soils on their tissues as the form of halite. We aim to simulate a technology in the future, which does the same on salty lands, and provide us with construction halite that would reinforce our Desertscraper at high levels.

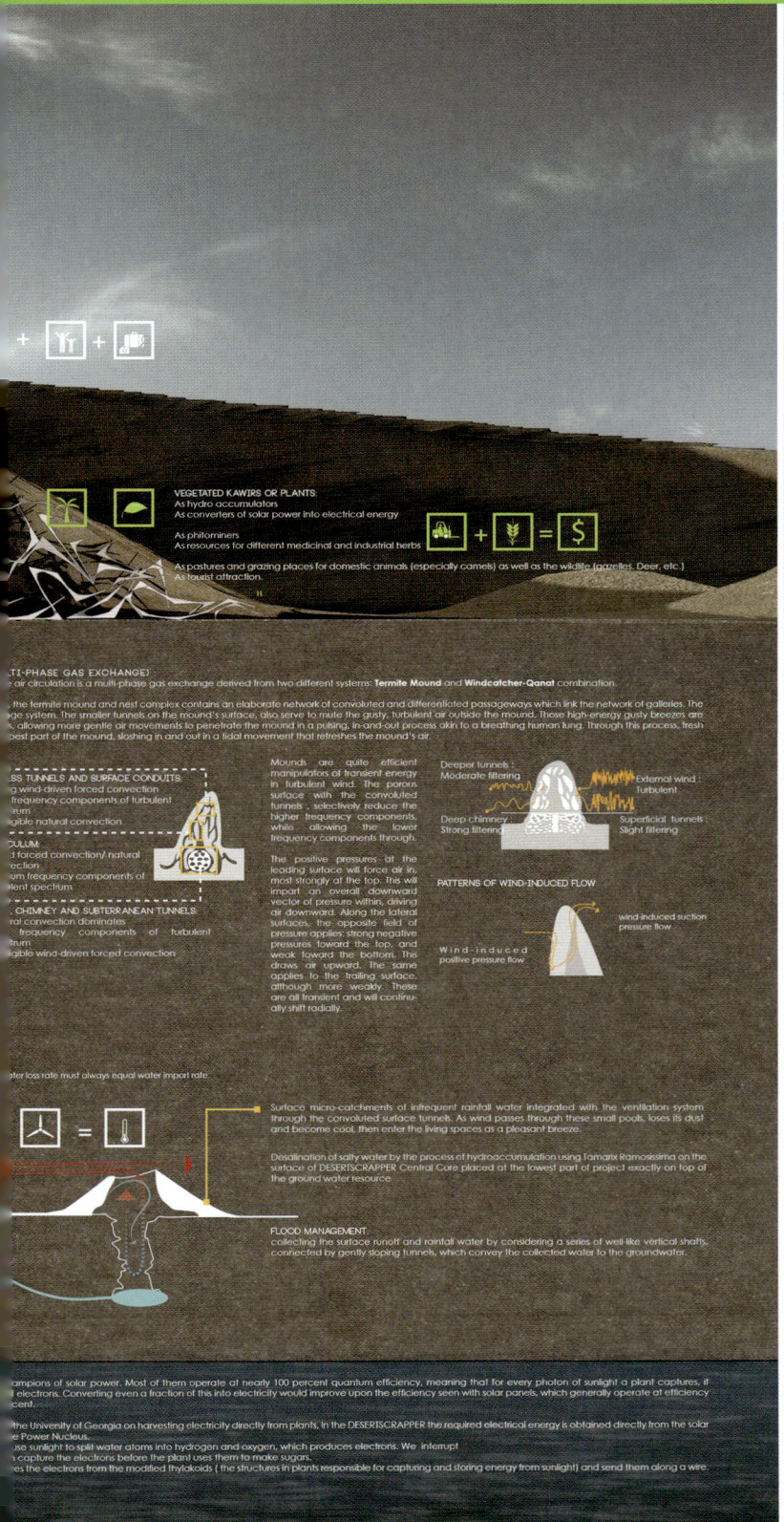

0770

BIO-PYRAMID

Arianna Armelli
Colin Joyce
Salvador Juarez
Ishaan Kumar
Wagdy Moussa
David Sepulveda
Wesley Townsend

United States

BIO-PYRAMID

GIZA: REVERSING DESERTIFICATION

BACKGROUND

SEEN FROM SPACE, THE MAJORITY OF THE EARTH'S SURFACE IS COVERED BY OCEANS – THAT MAKES UP 71% OF THE SURFACE OF THE EARTH, WITH THE REMAINING 29% FOR LAND. BUT WHAT PERCENTAGE OF THE EARTH'S LAND SURFACE IS DESERT? DESERTS ACTUALLY MAKE UP 33%, OR 1/3RD OF THE LAND'S SURFACE AREA. DESERTIFICATION IS YET ANOTHER CONSEQUENCE OF CLIMATE CHANGE THAT TAKES A GREAT TOLL ON BIODIVERSITY, NATURAL RESOURCES AND, ULTIMATELY, THE LIVES OF PEOPLE WHO INHABIT DRYLANDS. ALONG WITH MEASURES TO CURB AND COMPENSATE IT, THERE ARE SEVERAL SOLUTIONS FOR BRINGING LIFE BACK TO ARID LANDS. IT IS CALLED "REVERSING DESERTIFICATION", AND IT HAS A GREAT DEAL TO DO WITH PERMACULTURE. PERMACULTURE IS THE DEVELOPMENT OF AGRICULTURAL ECOSYSTEMS INTENDED TO BE SUSTAINABLE AND SELF-SUFFICIENT.

"YOU CAN SOLVE ALL THE WORLD'S PROBLEMS IN A GARDEN." - GEOFF LAWTON

THE LARGEST NON-POLAR DESERT IN THE WORLD IS THE SAHARA DESERT, A SUBTROPICAL DESERT IN NORTHERN AFRICA; IT COVERS A SURFACE AREA OF ABOUT 3.5 MILLION SQUARE MILES. JUST TO PUT THAT INTO PERSPECTIVE IT IS AS BIG AS THE UNITED STATES OF AMERICA, ONLY DIFFERENCE IS THAT DESERTIFICATION AND LAND DEGRADATION INCREASES ABOUT 12 MILLION HECTARES EACH YEAR, THE SIZE OF NEW YORK STATE!

IRONICALLY, WHERE THE SAHARA DESERT ENDS IS WHERE AGRICULTURE STARTED, ANCIENT EGYPT – CAIRO. THE CIVILIZATION OF ANCIENT EGYPT WAS INDEBTED TO THE NILE RIVER AND ITS DEPENDABLE SEASONAL FLOODING. THE RIVER'S PREDICTABILITY AND THE FERTILE SOIL ALLOW THE EGYPTIANS TO BUILD AN EMPIRE ON THE BASIS OF GREAT AGRICULTURAL WEALTH. EGYPTIANS ARE CREDITED AS BEING ONE OF THE FIRST GROUPS OF PEOPLE TO PRACTICE AGRICULTURE ON A LARGE SCALE. THIS IN RETURN CREATED SUCH MONUMENTAL CITIES LIKE GIZA THAT FEATURES THE GREAT SPHINX AND PYRAMID CONSTRUCTED AROUND 2584 BC WHICH IS THE RESTING PLACE OF THE EGYPTIAN PHARAOH KHUFU. THIS IS THE LARGEST OF THE THREE PYRAMIDS THAT MAKE UP THE GIZA NECROPOLIS, ALONG WITH THE PYRAMIDS OF KHAFRE AND MENKAURE. ALL THESE FACTS LEAD TO THE SAME RE-OCCURRING ISSUES THAT WE DEAL WITH IN TODAY'S PROGRESS TO EVOLVE NOT ONLY TECHNOLOGICALLY BUT SOCIALLY AS A HUMAN RACE. WE PUT TOO MUCH EMPHASIS ON MATERIALITY, CONSUMPTION AND TOURISM AND NOT ENOUGH BACK TO THE POINT OF ORIGIN FROM THE INSIDE OUT.

CONCEPT

OUR PROJECT "BIO-PYRAMID" PROPOSES THAT WE THROW AWAY THE STATUS-NORM ON HISTORIC PRESERVATION/ TOURISM AND CREATE A SUPER-HYBRID OF RE-ACTIVATING AREAS THAT TRULY MAKE A GLOBAL DIFFERENCE. "BIO-PYRAMID" IS A NON-CONVENTIONAL SKYSCRAPER THAT NOT ONLY OPERATES AS A "BIO-SPHERE" BUT ALSO AS A GATEWAY FROM CAIRO ACROSS THE SAHARA DESERT; LINKING A SUSTAINABLE ARMATURE TO REVERSE DESERTIFICATION FROM A MONUMENTAL TO SMALL NOMADIC SCALE. THIS PROPOSAL IS NOT ONLY A VIABLE ECONOMICAL GAIN FOR CITIES LIKE GIZA AND CAIRO BUT ALSO STANDS AS AN ARCHITECTURAL ECO-TECHNO STATEMENT THAT MIXED-USE TYPOLOGIES ARE MORE RELEVANT AS WE DIVERSE GLOBALLY AND SUSTAINABLY. WITH OVER POPULATION AND CONSUMPTION ON THE RISE WE NEED TO FIND A WAY TO MERGE DIFFERENT TYPOLOGIES

"THE PAST, LIKE THE FUTURE, IS INDEFINITE AND EXISTS ONLY AS A SPECTRUM OF POSSIBILITIES."

- STEPHEN HAWKING

GEOMETRIC EVOLUTION

 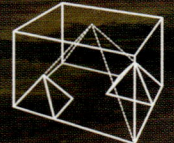 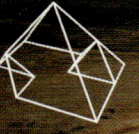 

ANCIENT   MAXIMIZE   VOID   INTERGRATE

GEOMETRY HAS ALWAYS BEEN A CRITICAL DRIVING FORCE SINCE ANCIENT TIMES TO NOW. WE CAN TRACE DIFFERENT ARCHITECTURAL MOVEMENTS FROM FUNCTION FOLLOWS FORM OR FORM FOLLOWS FUNCTION, TO THE ABSTRACT RANDOMNESS OF TODAY'S TECHNOLOGICAL CAPABILITIES. WE CAN ALSO JUSTIFY CERTAIN TYPOLOGICAL SKYSCRAPERS BEING CERTAIN FUNCTIONS AND SHAPES THROUGH CLIMATE, FINANCE, ART, POLITICS, TOURISM, ETC., BUT WE RARELY EXPLORE THE CAPABILITIES OF MORPHING SEVERAL DISCIPLINES INTO ONE. BIO-PYRAMID DOES JUST THAT, IT IS AN EVOLUTIONARY MORPHISMS OF THE ANCIENT PYRAMIDS + MODERN SKYSCRAPER + BIO-SPHERE. THE SECOND LAYER TO THIS COMPLEX HYBRID IS THAT IT SERVES A SECOND AGENDA, IN THAT WE DO NOT ONLY CONSIDER THIS A HISTORIC PRESERVATION PROJECT BUT ALSO STRIVES TO DE-CENTRALIZE TOURISM AND ACTUALLY FUNCTION AS A "LIVING MACHINE" BACK TO ITS LOCAL COMMUNITIES. BIO-PYRAMID INVESTIGATES THE RELATIONSHIPS BETWEEN ARCHITECTURE, URBANISM, LANDSCAPE, HISTORIC PRESERVATION AND TECHNOLOGY WITH AN EMPHASIS ON USING ENVIRONMENTAL PERFORMANCE AS A GENERATOR FOR ARCHITECTURAL FORM.

Seen from space, the majority of the Earth's surface is covered by oceans – that makes up 71% of the surface of the Earth, with the remaining 29% for land. But what percentage of the Earth's land surface is desert? Deserts actually make up 33%, or 1/3rd of the land's surface area. Desertification is yet another consequence of climate change that takes a great toll on biodiversity, natural resources and, ultimately, the lives of people who inhabit dry lands. Along with measures to curb and compensate it, there are several solutions for bringing life back to arid lands. It is called "reversing desertification", and it has a great deal to do with permaculture. Permaculture is the development of agricultural ecosystems intended to be sustainable and self-sufficient.

Our project "Bio-Pyramid" proposes that we throw away the status-norm on historic preservation/

0080

EVOLUTIONARY
TIMELINE

ANCIENT CITY
2584 BC

MEDIVAL CITY
397-1882 AD

MODERN CITY
1981-2015 AD

BIO CITY
2099 AD

tourism and create a super-hybrid of reactivating areas that truly make a global difference. "Bio-Pyramid" is a non-conventional skyscraper that not only operates as a "bio-sphere" but also as a gateway from Cairo across the Sahara Desert; linking a sustainable armature to reverse desertification from a monumental to small nomadic scale. This proposal is not only a viable economical gain for cities like Giza and Cairo, but also stands as an architectural eco-techno statement that mixed-use typologies are more relevant as we diverse globally and sustainably. With overpopulation and consumption on the rise we need to find a way to merge different typologies

Geometry has always been a critical driving force since ancient times to now. We can trace different architectural movements from function follows form or form follows function, to the abstract

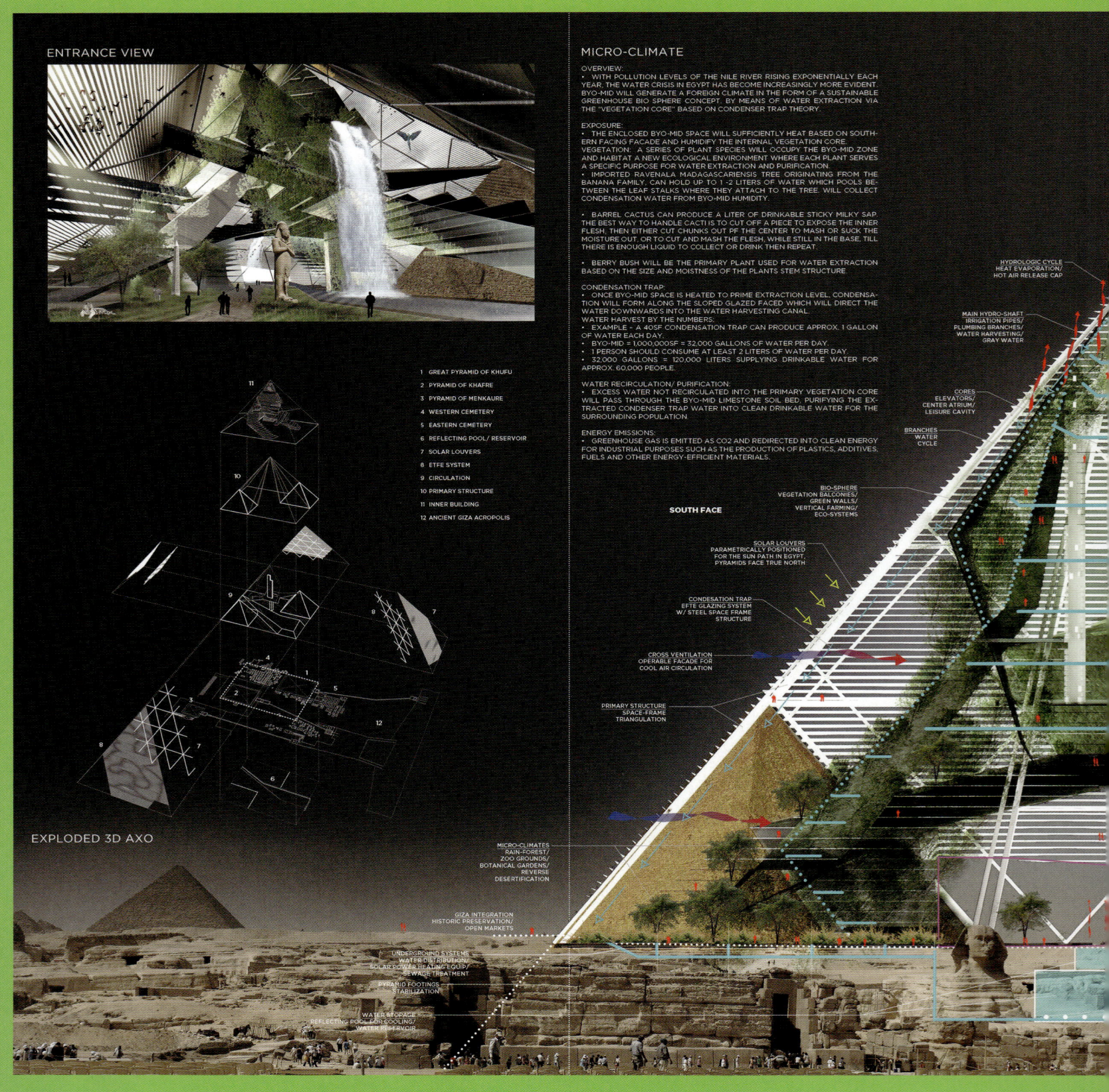

randomness of today's technological capabilities. We can also justify certain typological skyscrapers being certain uses and shapes through climate, finance, art, politics, tourism, etc., but we rarely explore the capabilities of morphing several disciplines into one. Bio-pyramid does just that, it is an evolutionary morphism of the ancient pyramids + modern skyscraper + bio-sphere. The second layer to this complex hybrid is that it serves a second agenda, in that we do not only consider this a historic preservation project, but it also strives to de-centralize tourism and actually function as a "living machine" back to its local communities. Bio-pyramid investigates the relationships between architecture, urbanism, landscape, historic preservation and technology with an emphasis on using environmental performance as a generator for architectural form.

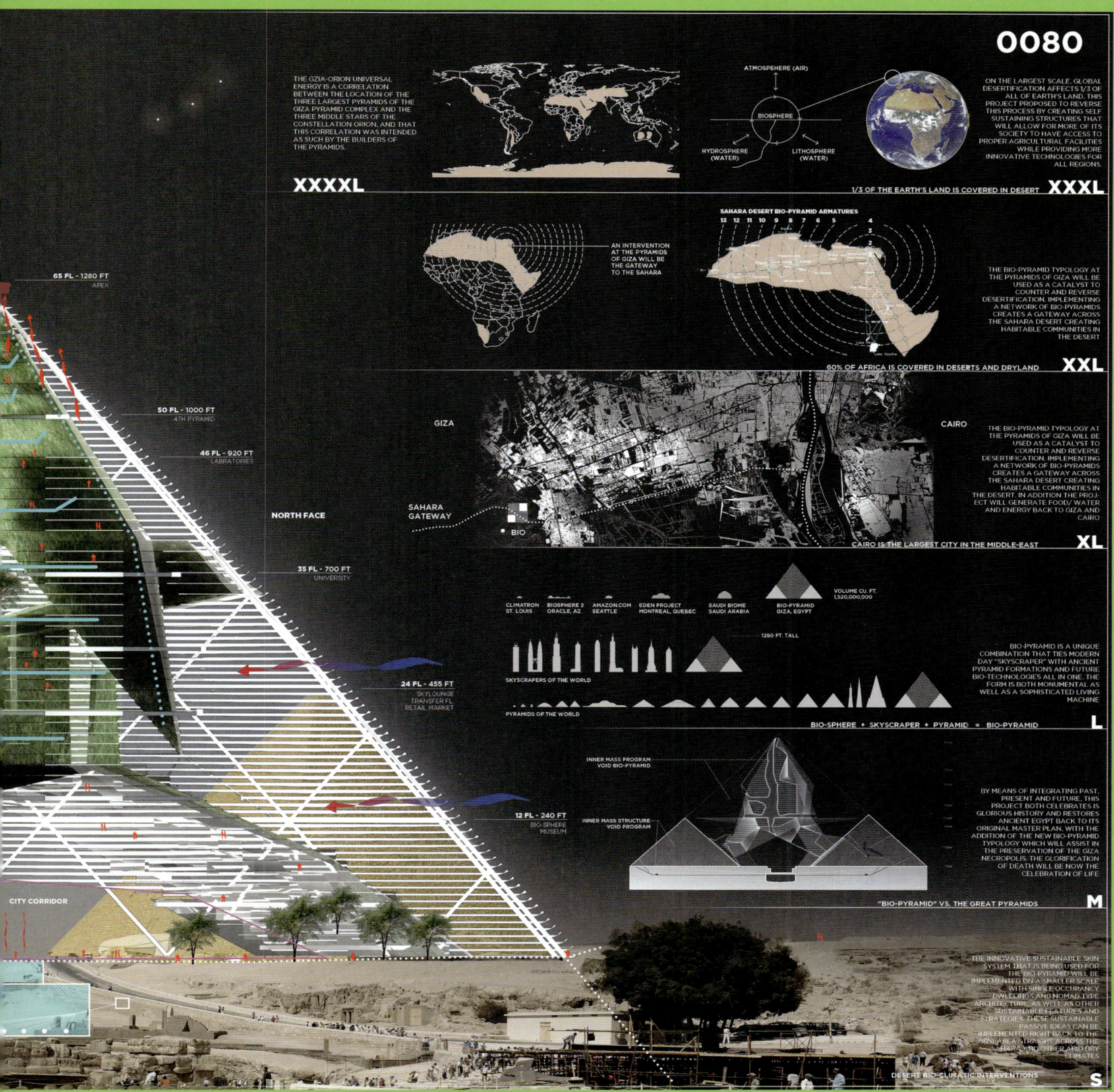

ELECTROMAGNETIC POLLUTION FREE ZONE

Maryam Fazel
Hossein Montazery
Maryam Safari

United Kingdom

Electromagnetic Pollution-Free Zone:
(De-toxication + Non-radiation)

Together with rapid industrialization, Increased urbanization has resulted in high levels of environmental pollutants with a consequent impact on human health. Presence of high levels of chemical (e.g. polycyclic aromatic hydrocarbon (PAHs)) and physical (e.g. strong electromagnetic fields (EMFs)) contaminants in the environment has resulted in two major types of pollutions that need serious attention due to their subsequent health hazards.

In this project we aim to tackle these two major environmental issues through the use of a combinational strategy. Incorporating phytoremediation (the use of plants to remediate pollutants) into a design made from special shielding (composite-polymer-skin) results in simultaneous mitigation and reduction of both pollutions. In this system transgenic plants with the ability to degrade chemical contaminants will be planted into a composite-polymer-skin that in turn act as a shield to exposure to high levels of EMFs. This strategy creates a cleaner environment with reduced levels of chemical and physical pollutants in the immediate surroundings of the building.

Recently, presence of high levels of electromagnetic pollution in the environment has raised debates and concerns in developing countries. This in particular is due to possible health hazards of exposure to electromagnetic fields or satellite jamming. These health risks have recently become under the scope of environmental researchers, building scientists and material specialists.

To create de-toxicated environment With regards to these concerns, harnessing unwanted exposure to (RF fields, EMR, EMF), we are implementing material and design strategies that help to transform the built environment into a healthier place to live.

Current research on electromagnetic pollution mitigations suggests alternative methods to shield, absorb or reflect back the waves through material solutions such as polyetherimide composite foams or some forms of polymer.

in a combinational strategy, we are taking this one step further and hypothesize a material that has two interrelated functions; a shielding canopy to protect interior spaces from EMR/EMF, and at the same time, capable of de-toxicating air through Phytoremediation.

Phytoremediation is considered as being efficient, eco-friendly and cost effective. Compared to some microorganisms such as bacteria and fungi which utilise chemical contaminants as a source of energy, plants have little inherent ability to phytodegrade pollutants. However, they can be improved for phytoremediation by transferring genes from external sources (e.g. transferring genes encoding enzymes for degradation of xenobiotics such as polycyclic aromatic hydrocarbon (PAHs), benzene-toluene-ethylbenzene-xylene (BTEX), chlorophenols etc. from fungi into plants). Consequently, pollutants can be phytodegraded to non-toxic metabolites or completely mineralized into carbon dioxide, nitrate, ammonia, chlorine etc. by transgenic plants. Plants have the advantage of being able to grow independently using sunlight water and inorganic ions. They are not only robust in growth, but also are a renewable resource and can be utilised for in situ bioremediation.

In this project we aim to create and utilise transgenic plants that are able to remove pollutants from the surrounding environment. To do this, genes involved in degradation of pollutants will be isolated from fungi (e.g. from Cunninghamella elegans and/or white-rot fungi with ability to degrade and transform many environmental pollutants such as PAHs, benzo[a]pyrene etc.) and introduced into candidate plants (e.g. Leuceana, poplar tree) using direct DNA methods of gene transfer (e.g. particle gun bombardment). Following genetic confirmation of the insertion and expression of the new inserted gene into the plant genome, the new transgenic plant with enhanced bioremediation ability will be planted into specially designed spaces made of specific EMF shielding polymer.

In this project we aim to tackle two major environmental issues through the use of a combinational strategy. Incorporating phytoremediation (the use of plants to remediate pollutants) into a design made from special shielding (composite-polymer-skin) results in simultaneous mitigation and reduction of both pollutions. In this system transgenic plants with the ability to degrade chemical contaminants will be planted into a composite-polymer-skin that in turn acts as a shield to exposure to high levels of EMFs. This strategy creates a cleaner environment with reduced levels of chemical and physical pollutants in the immediate surroundings of the building.

Recently, presence of high levels of electromagnetic pollution in the environment has raised debates and concerns in developing countries. This in particular is due to possible health hazards of exposure to

0   1   1   7

electromagnetic fields or satellite jamming. These health risks have recently become under the scope of environmental researchers, building scientists and material specialists.

To create de-toxicated environment with regards to these concerns, harnessing unwanted exposure to (RF fields, EMR, EMF), we are implementing material and design strategies that help to transform the built environment into a healthier place to live. Current research on electromagnetic pollution mitigations suggests alternative methods to shield, absorb or reflect back the waves through material solutions such as polyetherimide composite foams or some forms of polymer. In a combinational strategy, we are taking this one step further and hypothesize a material that has two interrelated functions; a shielding canopy to protect interior spaces from EMR/EMF, and at the same time, capable of de-toxicating air through

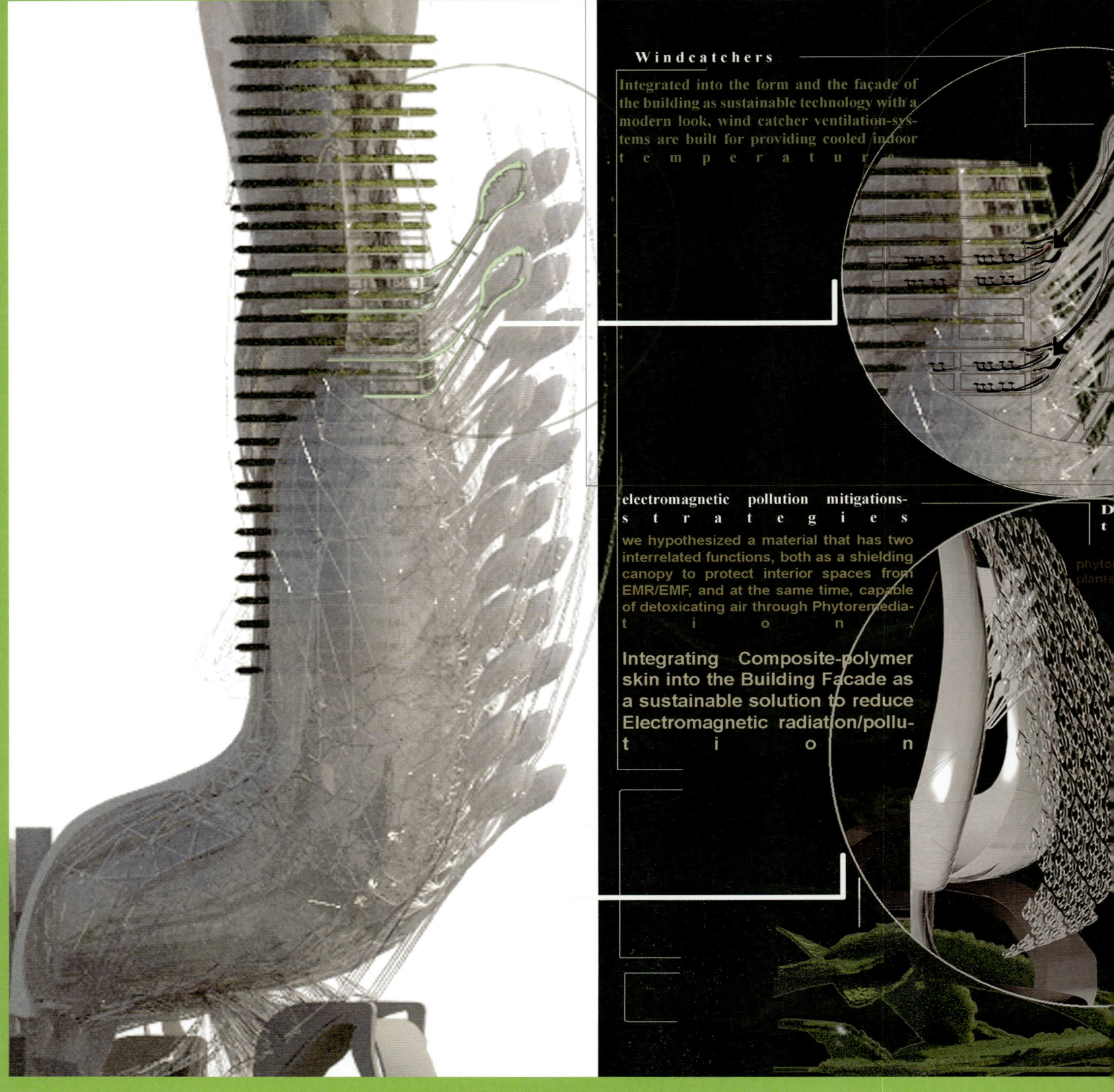

Windcatchers

Integrated into the form and the façade of the building as sustainable technology with a modern look, wind catcher ventilation-systems are built for providing cooled indoor temperature

electromagnetic pollution mitigations-
s t r a t e g i e s

we hypothesized a material that has two interrelated functions, both as a shielding canopy to protect interior spaces from EMR/EMF, and at the same time, capable of detoxicating air through Phytoremedia-
t i o n

Integrating Composite-polymer skin into the Building Facade as a sustainable solution to reduce Electromagnetic radiation/pollu-
t i o n

Phytoremediation.

   In this project we aim to create and utilise transgenic plants that are able to remove pollutants from the surrounding environment. To do this, genes involved in degradation of pollutants will be isolated from fungi (e.g. from Cunninghamella elegans and/or white-rot fungi with ability to degrade and transform many environmental pollutants such as PAHs, benzo[a]pyrene etc.) and introduced into candidate plants (e.g. Leuceana, poplar tree) using direct DNA methods of gene transfer (e.g. particle gun bombardment). Following genetic confirmation of the insertion and expression of the new inserted gene into the plant genome, the new transgenic plant with enhanced bioremediation ability will be planted into specially designed spaces made of specific EMF shielding polymer.

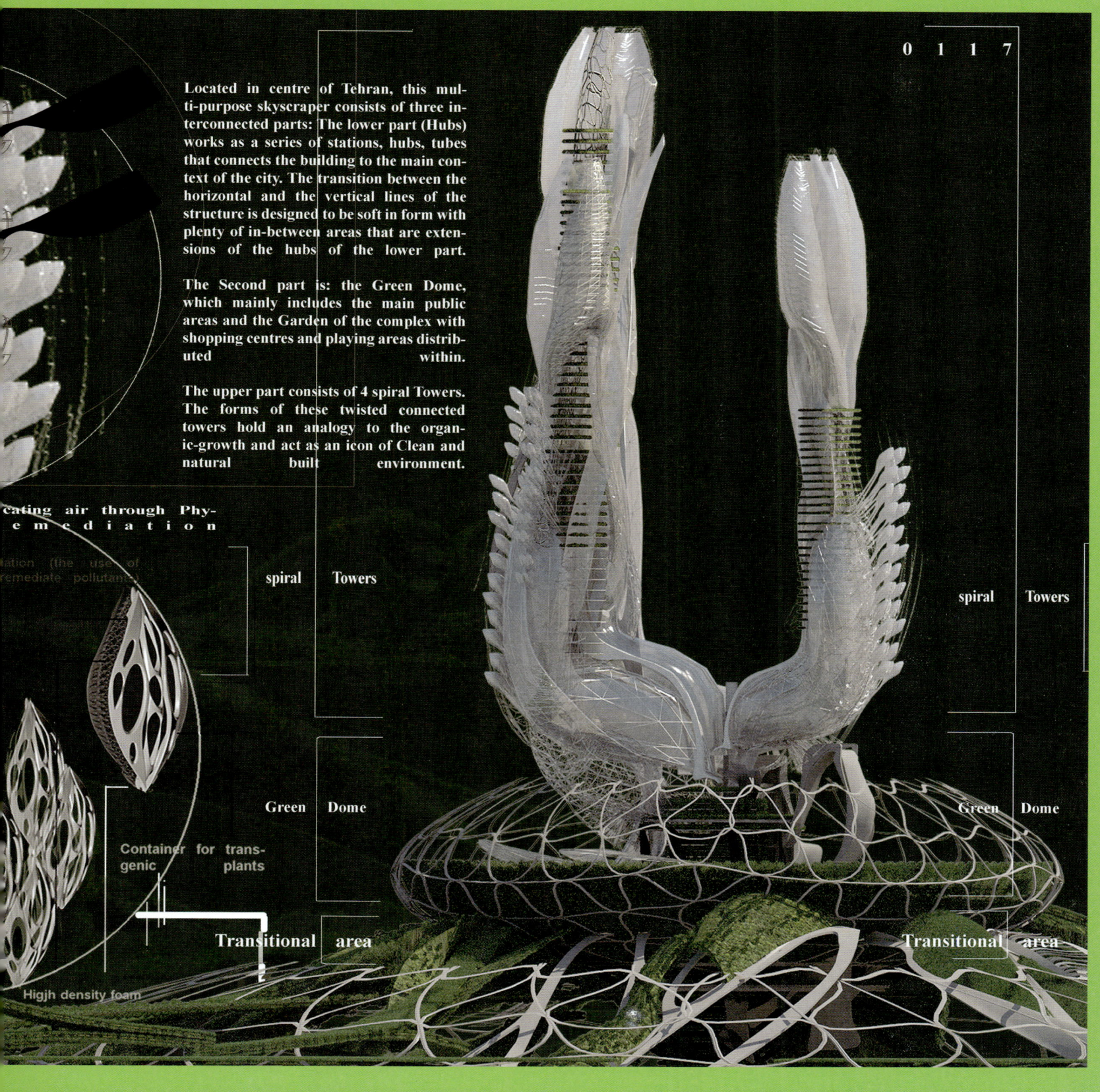

0 1 1 7

Located in centre of Tehran, this multi-purpose skyscraper consists of three interconnected parts: The lower part (Hubs) works as a series of stations, hubs, tubes that connects the building to the main context of the city. The transition between the horizontal and the vertical lines of the structure is designed to be soft in form with plenty of in-between areas that are extensions of the hubs of the lower part.

The Second part is: the Green Dome, which mainly includes the main public areas and the Garden of the complex with shopping centres and playing areas distributed   within.

The upper part consists of 4 spiral Towers. The forms of these twisted connected towers hold an analogy to the organic-growth and act as an icon of Clean and natural   built   environment.

cating air through Phy-
e m e d i a t i o n

ation (the use of
remediate pollutant)

spiral   Towers

spiral   Towers

Green   Dome

Green   Dome

Container for trans-
genic

Transitional   area

Transitional   area

Higjh density foam

NOAH OASIS

Ma Yidong
Jiang Zhe
Qin Zhengyu
Zhu Zhonghui

China

With the increasing demand of energy resources and the exhaustion of inland petroleum, the exploitation of marine ecosystems seems inevitable. The drastic development of offshore rigs, however, comes with the great potential risk of oil spills, which will endanger the entire marine bionetwork tremendously for decades. The clean up of spills, however, is still inefficient and time-consuming.

Our design transforms the original rigs into vertical bio-habitats, which aim to exert instant responses to oil spills, restore damaged ecosystems, and offer all beings shelter from future disasters. The original rig will become a reaction center, where the spilled oil will be converted into a catalyst and building materials, as well as a recreational center and research facility. The underwater structure will be attached to pipes with a floater at the end. Our strategy could be divided into the following three periods of time.

0144

NOAH OASIS
RIG TO VERTICAL BIO-HABITAT

Number of offshorre rigs worldwide as of 2014

With the exhaustion of inland energy, offshore rigs have become an important way of acquiring petroleum resource. Statistics have shown a strong demand for deep-water rigs. The underwater oil will remain a mainstream energy resource in the predictable future. Meanwhile, with the development of technology, these offshore rigs have gone further and further into the sea. Many previous intact marine areas will soon be exploited by the development.

180 North Sea
140 Persian Gulf
176 Far East Asia
229 Gulf of Mexico (U.S.)
93 Mexico
105 Western Africa
109 Brazil
187 Southeast Asia

The Current Status of Petroleum Pollution of the Ocean

The drastic development of offshore rigs comes with the great potential risk of oil spill, which will endanger the whole ecosystem tremendously for decades. It will also greatly affect the marine related industry nearby and leave us vulnerable for the climate change. Throughout history, several great incidents, such as the leak in Gulf of Mexico, China south sea etc., have caused lives of millions marine animals and their damage would take decades to recover. The clean up of the spill, however, is still inefficient and time-consuming.

1,227,600
600,353
194,485
10,000

Oil Spills-1901 to present

Ecological Damage of Petroleum Pollution

Brown pelicans often dive into the oil because the slick makes the water look calmer. If they are coated in oil, they will be unable to regulate their temperatures, leading to hypothermia.

Plankton, tiny immobile organism at the base of the food chain, can be killed by chemically dispered oil.

Sea turtles are threatened or endangered. Some have already washed up ashore, and with numbers already low, it would be harder to rebuild the population.

Dolphins, which often follows boats to play, have been following response crews, getting near the slicks.

Shrimp are more vulnerable to oil and chemical dispersants because they are stationary, while some adult fin fish populations may be mobile.

Fish larvae are most at risk. Bluefin tuna, spawning near the spill, are of particular concern. The Gulf of Mexico, for example, is one of the only two nurseries in the world for bluefin tuna.

Sperm whales, which spend most of their time diving for prey, may come up in the slick as they reach the surface to breathe.

Design Concept

The original rig may pollute the sea environment at any time. However, with the purpose of preventing potential oil spill and habiting marine animals, the oil rig will be transformed into a prosperous "tree", whose root absorbs the oil spill and change it into fertilizers. Its trunk and leaves will become shelter for animals. The once polluted oil rig will eventually become an oasis for the eco-system.

Key Strategy

When an oil spill happens, the root like tunnels will immediately spread out over the polluted area as an instant response to control the oil from further pollution. The tunnel will absorb the petroleum over the sea into the oil tank, where the pollution oil will be transformed into fertilizer for coral to booster its growth over the tunnel. Meanwhile, the oil will also be transformed into plastic and several observatory tower will be built in this building material with the help of 3d printing. After all the contamination is transformed, the original rig will become a prosperous eco-habitat.

First, there is the short-term strategy including absorption of spilled oil. When an oil spill incident happens, the floaters at the end of each pipe will immediately absorb the spilled oil covering the surface of the sea as an instant response.

Second comes the medium-term strategy of establishing a habitat for marine life and migrating birds. The collected oil will be transported through the root-like pipes underwater to the central processor attached to the original rig, where the crude oil will be converted into a catalyst for coral reef and produce plastic as building material.

The catalyst will be transported back to the pipe to booster the growth of coral reef on its surface and the plastic will become the building material of the plastic-twig structure with the help of 3D printing

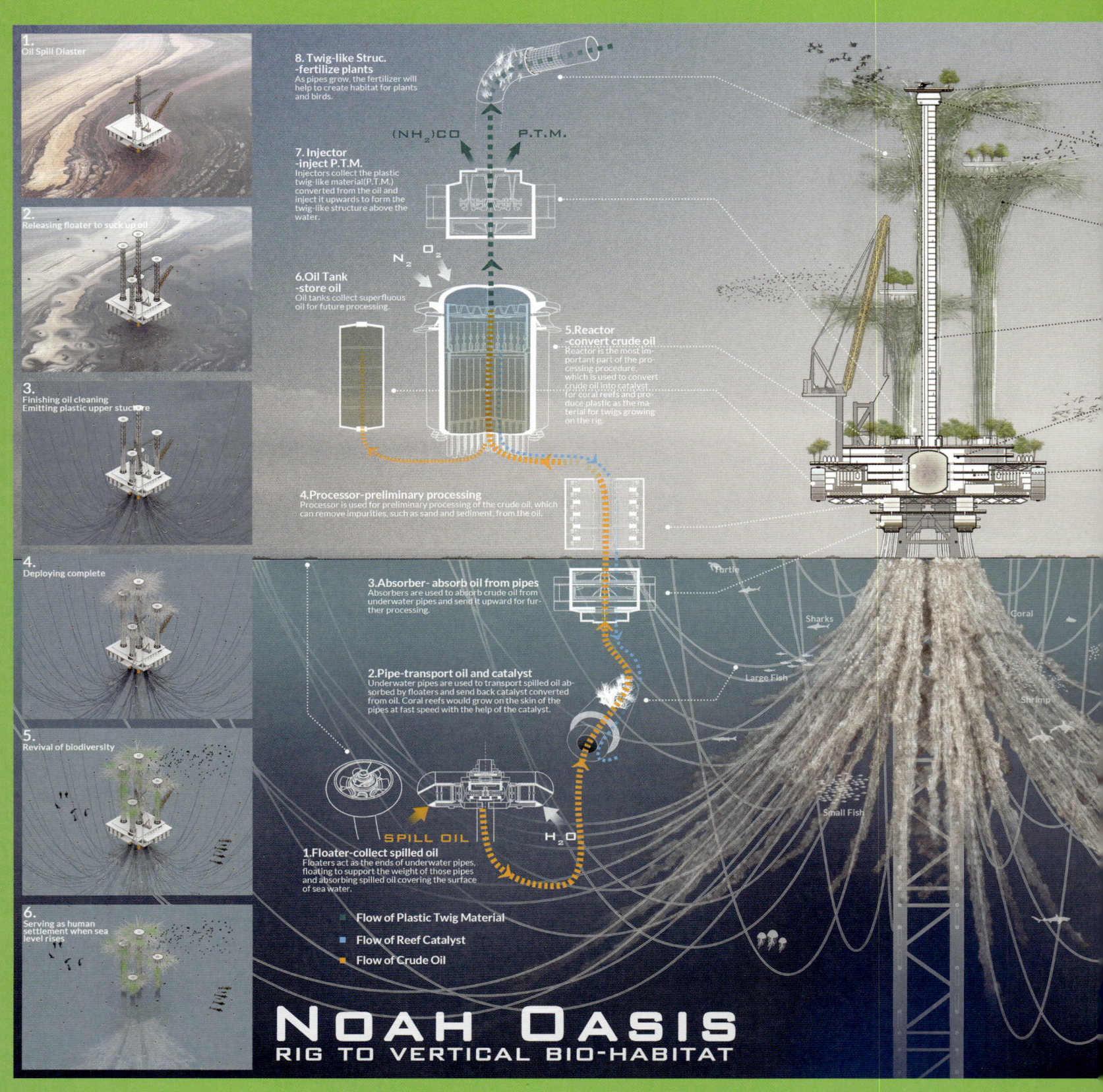

and the injector. In this way, the project will become a vertical bio-habitat and help revive the biodiversity. Finally, there is the long-term strategy, or shelter from future disasters. Ultimately, when the sea level rises to a disastrous degree, the twig like structure would continue to remain above the sea level. Then the oilrig will become the Noah Oasis.

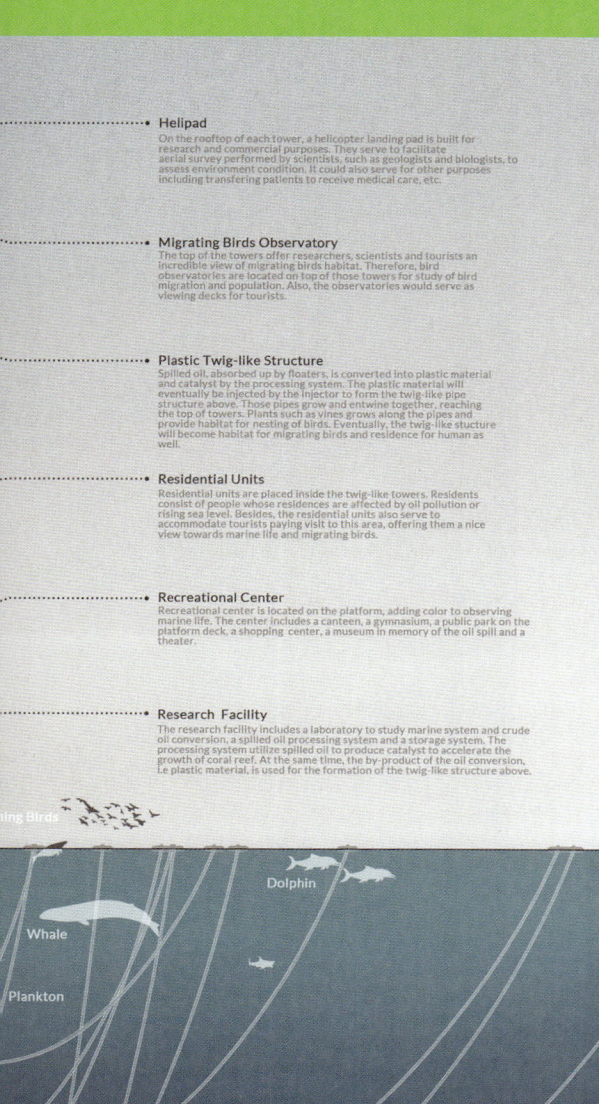

Helipad
On the rooftop of each tower, a helicopter landing pad is built for research and commercial purposes. They serve to facilitate aerial survey performed by scientists, such as geologists and biologists, to assess environment condition. It could also serve for other purposes including transfering patients to receive medical care, etc.

Migrating Birds Observatory
The top of the towers offer researchers, scientists and tourists an incredible view of migrating birds habitat. Therefore, bird observatories are located on top of those towers for study of bird migration and population. Also, the observatories would serve as viewing decks for tourists.

Plastic Twig-like Structure
Spilled oil, absorbed up by floaters, is converted into plastic material and catalyst by the processing system. The plastic material will eventually be injected by the injector to form the twig-like pipe structure above. Those pipes grow and entwine together, reaching the top of towers. Plants such as vines grows along the pipes and provide habitat for nesting of birds. Eventually, the twig-like structure will become habitat for migrating birds and residence for human as well.

Residential Units
Residential units are placed inside the twig-like towers. Residents consist of people whose residences are affected by oil pollution or rising sea level. Besides, the residential units also serve to accommodate tourists paying visit to this area, offering them a nice view towards marine life and migrating birds.

Recreational Center
Recreational center is located on the platform, adding color to observing marine life. The center includes a canteen, a gymnasium, a public park on the platform deck, a shopping center, a museum in memory of the oil spill and a theater.

Research Facility
The research facility includes a laboratory to study marine system and crude oil conversion, a spilled oil processing system and a storage system. The processing system utilize spilled oil to produce catalyst to accelerate the growth of coral reef. At the same time, the by-product of the oil conversion, i.e plastic material, is used for the formation of the twig-like structure above.

0144

SKY-MENDING TREE

An Rongrong
Ren Xiaohui

China

[BACKGROUND]

The ozone layer refers to a region of Earth's stratosphere that absorbs most of the Sun's UV radiation. It is a protection of the earth. A steady decline of about 4% per decade in the total volume of ozone in Earth's stratosphere , and a much larger springtime decrease in stratospheric ozone over Earth's polar regions,which is called the ozone hole .This phenomenon has attracted the global attention. The almost 70% reduction of the ozone column observed in the austral spring over Antarctica first was reported in 1985 and it is still continuing.Now Ozone depletion has occurred in many parts of the world, such as New Zealand, Australia, South Africa, Peru, Brazil, etc. The Antarctica pole, the Arctic pole and the Qinghai-Tibet Plateau are the most serious regions.

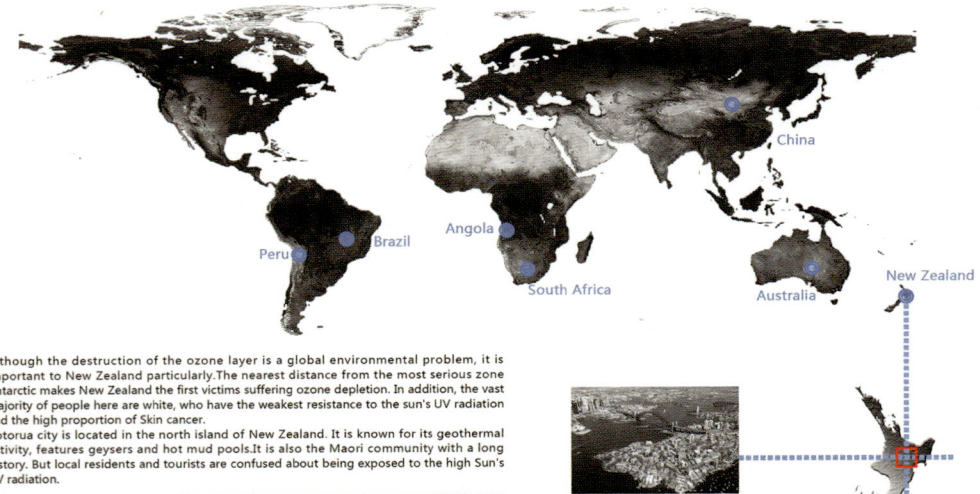

Although the destruction of the ozone layer is a global environmental problem, it is important to New Zealand particularly.The nearest distance from the most serious zone Antarctic makes New Zealand the first victims suffering ozone depletion. In addition, the vast majority of people here are white, who have the weakest resistance to the sun's UV radiation and the high proportion of Skin cancer.
Rotorua city is located in the north island of New Zealand. It is known for its geothermal activity, features geysers and hot mud pools.It is also the Maori community with a long history. But local residents and tourists are confused about being exposed to the high Sun's UV radiation.

Rotorua, New Zealand

| 1982 NIMBUS7 | 1987 NIMBUS7 | 1992 NIMBUS7 | 1997 EPTOMS |
| 2002 EPTOMS | 2007 OMI | 2012 OMI | 2012 OMPS |

200 250 300 350 400

Ozone layer depletion will increase surface UVB levels, which could lead to damage, including skin cancer and cataract. Scientists have estimated that a one percent decrease in stratospheric ozone would increase the incidence of skin cancer by 2%. Besides, an increase of UV radiation would cause crop yields.

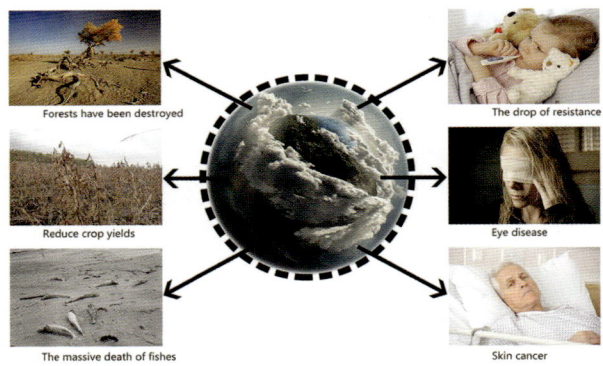

Forests have been destroyed

Reduce crop yields

The massive death of fishes

The drop of resistance

Eye disease

Skin cancer

[CONCEPT]

In China, there is an ancient mythology,called Mending the sky by Nuwa. In ancient times, the four corners of the sky collapsed and the world with its nine regions separated. Then a goddess ,Nuwa melted rocks of five colours and used them to mend the cracks in the sky.
Plants can absorb carbon dioxide and release oxygen through photosynthesis , keeping the air balanced.
Now,we take the mythology of sky-mending as the essence, the form of tree as the appearance. These skyscrapers can produce ozone and release it to the stratosphere, repairing the ozone hole step by step,keeping the stratosphere stable.Ozone layer will be completely healed oneday ,thus we can achieve the goal of "mending the sky".

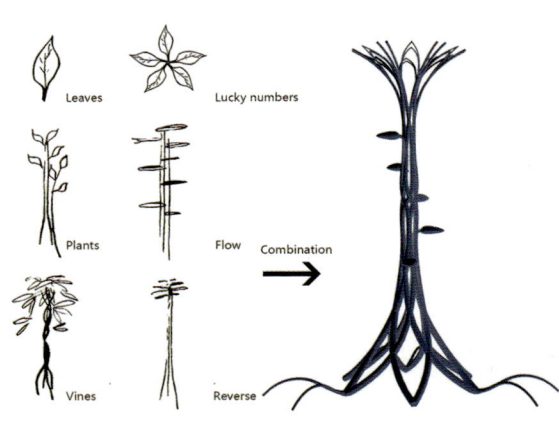
Leaves   Lucky numbers

Plants   Flow   Combination

Vines   Reverse

[CIRCULATION]

Circulation system is based on the principle that oxygen can convert into ozone the condition of high voltage. Oxygen is obtained by the electrolysis of water, the same time, we can also get hydrogen. Hydrogen will be used as the traction one bubble", leading them into the stratosphere.
The abundant underground thermal energy in Rotorua region can provide ele for the building, especially for the need high voltage of ozone.
In addition, we also focus on the multi-function use of ozone. The urban sewa be transported to the underground sewage treatment plant. Here, the sewage purified by ozone into clean water. The clean water can be reduced to oxygen drogen by electrolysis ,it can also be used to irrigate plants in the botanical ga

$$2H_2O \longrightarrow 2H_2 + O_2$$
$$3O_2 \longrightarrow 2O_3$$

H_2O

Electrolysis

H_2 O_2 High voltage   Geother energy

Traction

O_3

Storage → Release   Sewage treatmen

H_2O & Nitro

Plants

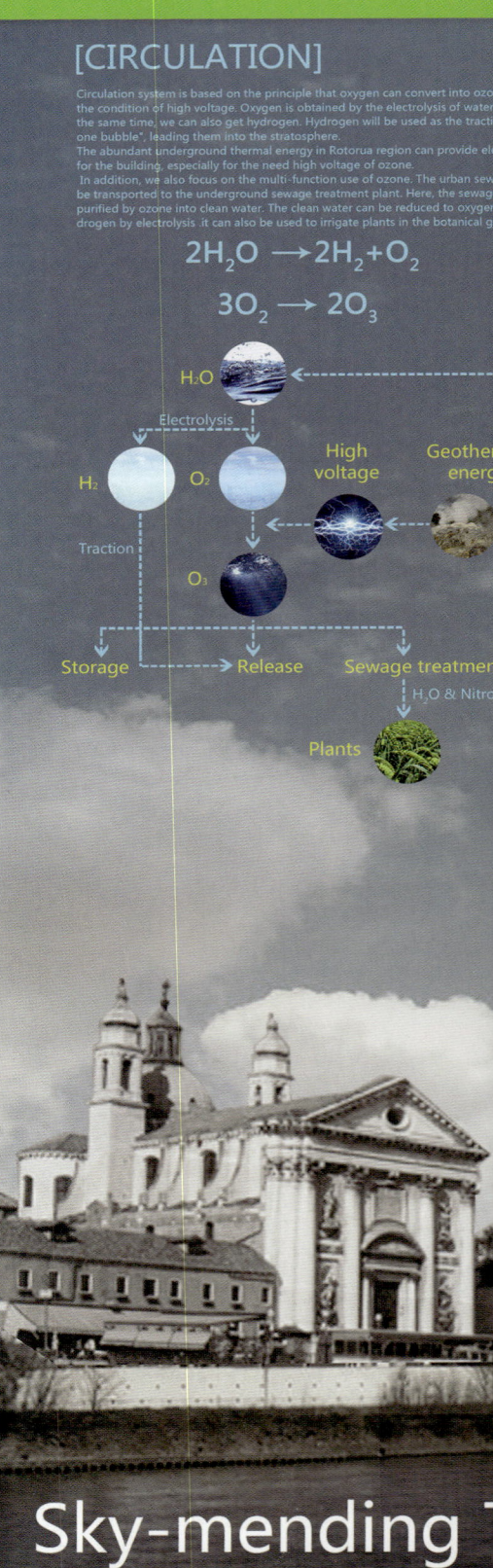

Sky-mending

The hole in the ozone layer has already attracted the global attention of goverments and private organizations. Although the destruction of the ozone layer is a global environmental problem, it is important to New Zealand in particular .The nearest distance from the most serious puncture zone near the Antarctic makes New Zealand the first victims suffering ozone depletion.

In China, there is an ancient myth, called "Mending the sky by Nuwa." In ancient times, the four corners of the sky collapsed and the world with its nine regions separated. Then a goddess, Nuwa, melted rocks of five colors and used them to mend the cracks in the sky.

Sky-mending Tree is a group of ecological structures designed as producing scientific ozone research facilities and tourist attractions. The structures are divided into two parts. The first part, above ground, is

0166

the main structure of the skyscraper, which imitates the morphology of the tree, while the second part is the system of geothermic and water purification underground.

The main portion of each building is the discharged ball. High voltage discharge inside the ball converts the oxygen into ozone. With the help of "molecular sieves", ozone, which has a bigger molecular volume and larger mass, is separated, and then transported to the top.

Ozone produced by these skyscrapers is released to the stratosphere, repairing the ozone hole step by step, keeping the stratosphere stable. Ozone layer will be completely healed one day, thus we can achieve the goal of "mending the sky".

The tower is designed as a series of steel tubes that intertwine to create a structural mesh. This

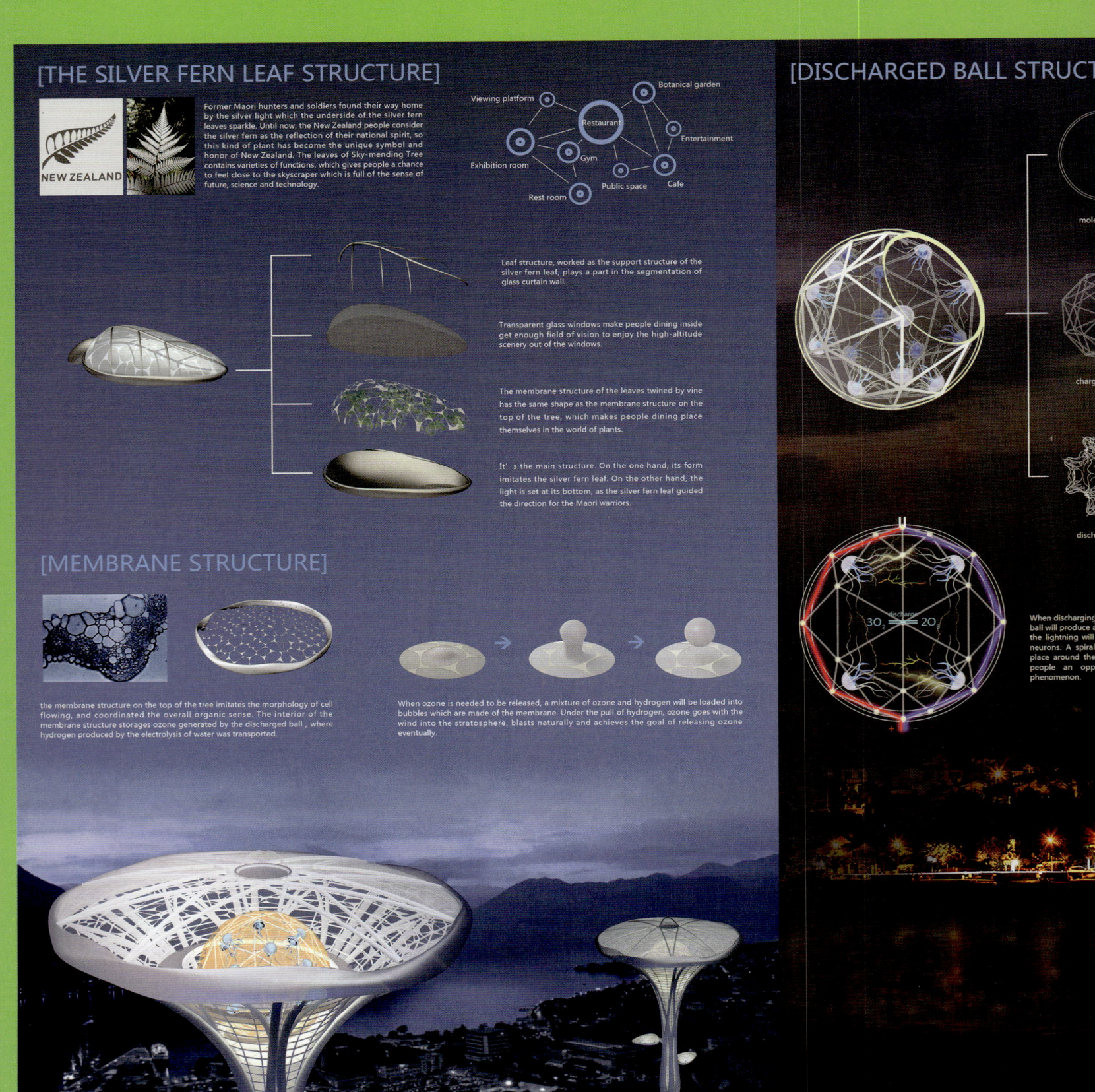

[THE SILVER FERN LEAF STRUCTURE]

NEW ZEALAND

Former Maori hunters and soldiers found their way home by the silver light which the underside of the silver fern leaves sparkle. Until now, the New Zealand people consider the silver fern as the reflection of their national spirit, so this kind of plant has become the unique symbol and honor of New Zealand. The leaves of Sky-mending Tree contains varieties of functions, which gives people a chance to feel close to the skyscraper which is full of the sense of future, science and technology.

Viewing platform — Botanical garden — Restaurant — Entertainment — Exhibition room — Gym — Rest room — Public space — Cafe

Leaf structure, worked as the support structure of the silver fern leaf, plays a part in the segmentation of glass curtain wall.

Transparent glass windows make people dining inside get enough field of vision to enjoy the high-altitude scenery out of the windows.

The membrane structure of the leaves twined by vine has the same shape as the membrane structure on the top of the tree, which makes people dining place themselves in the world of plants.

It's the main structure. On the one hand, its form imitates the silver fern leaf. On the other hand, the light is set at its bottom, as the silver fern leaf guided the direction for the Maori warriors.

[MEMBRANE STRUCTURE]

the membrane structure on the top of the tree imitates the morphology of cell flowing, and coordinated the overall organic sense. The interior of the membrane structure storages ozone generated by the discharged ball, where hydrogen produced by the electrolysis of water was transported.

When ozone is needed to be released, a mixture of ozone and hydrogen will be loaded into bubbles which are made of the membrane. Under the pull of hydrogen, ozone goes with the wind into the stratosphere, blasts naturally and achieves the goal of releasing ozone eventually.

[DISCHARGED BALL STRUCT

mole

chargi

disch

$3O_2$ — $2O_3$

When discharging ball will produce the lightning will neurons. A spiral place around the people an oppe phenomenon.

mesh opens and closes to create facade openings for the interior. The openings vary depending on the program and required light exposure. As you move up along the main column a series of platforms are encountered. Each platform is designated for a specific use, including leisure activities and an observatory. At the bottom of the tower, the structural lattice creates four buildings at each corner. These structures are seen as roots holding the tower to the ground and provide auxiliary programs to the city.

0166

Under the help of "molecular sieves", ozone which has the bigger molecular volume and the larger mass is separated, and then transports to the top.

In the framework of the discharged ball, the positive and negative wires are accessed along the longitude in turn. They are insulated from each other, and charge nearby neurons.

Adjacent neurons are charged successively. As the adjacent two have opposite charge, they can generate the discharge reaction, which converts the oxygen into ozone.

THE UNEXPECTED AURORA IN CHERNOYBL

Zhang Zehua
Song Qiang
Liu Yameng

China

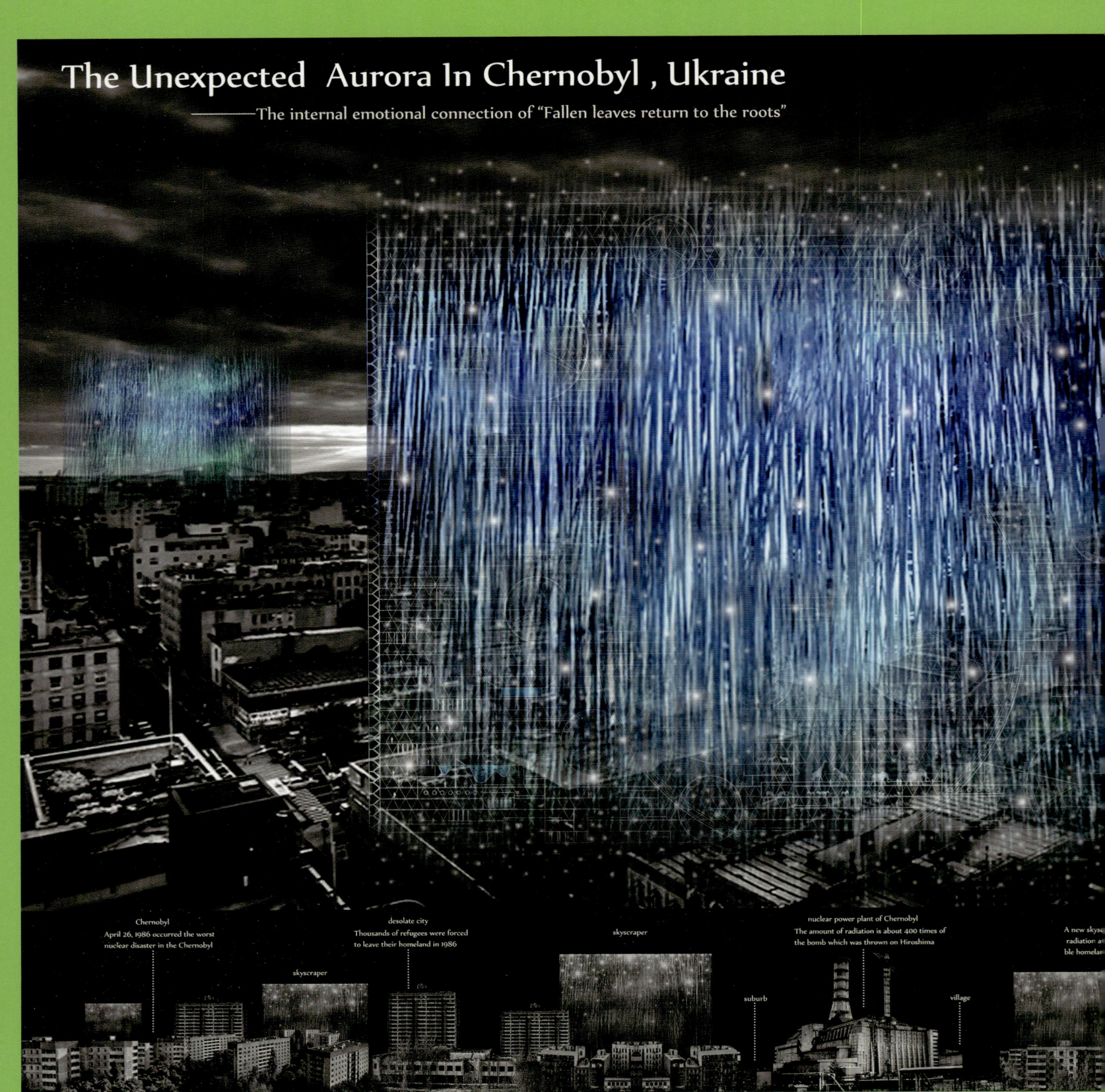

The Unexpected Aurora In Chernobyl , Ukraine
——— The internal emotional connection of "Fallen leaves return to the roots"

Chernobyl
April 26, 1986 occurred the worst
nuclear disaster in the Chernobyl

desolate city
Thousands of refugees were forced
to leave their homeland in 1986

skyscraper

nuclear power plant of Chernobyl
The amount of radiation is about 400 times of
the bomb which was thrown on Hiroshima

A new skyscr
radiation a
ble homelan

skyscraper

suburb

village

On April 26, 1986, the fourth reactor of Chernobyl's nuclear power plant exploded, and the amount of radiation that resulted from it was about 400 times greater than the energy from the atomic bomb dropped in Hiroshima. About seven million people were forced to leave their homes in two days without any chance to say goodbye to their present life.

But not everyone accepts the arrangement of fate. The negative effects of radiation have been defeated by a large group of settlers, more and more people are returning to their homeland in the restricted area, but now with a diferent perspective towards the risks they face. They survived some the harshest environments in the 20th century, from the Great Famine in Ukraine in 1930s, which sent millions of people to death, to the atrocities of the Nazis in 1940's. Therefore, the Chernobyl accident

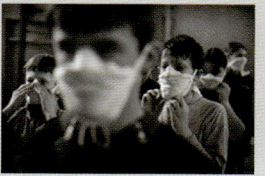

0205-1

So forgettable, so engraved. Time dating back to April 26, 1986 ,a quiet night.With a big bang , the fourth reactor which is located in the Chernobyl nuclear power plant exploded , the amount of radiation is about 400 times of the atomic bomb which is dropped on the Hiroshima .There are about seven million people were forced to leave their homeland in two days,they even had no time to say goodbye to their present life.

But not everyone accepts the arrangement of fate. The negative effects of radiation have been defeated by a large group of settlers , more and more people are returning to their homeland which located in the restricted area, what can be sure is that they use a different way to look at the risk which they bear .They survived from the harshest environments in the 20th century,Stalin caused the Great Famine in Ukraine in 1930s,which caused millions of people to death, they also experienced the atrocities of the Nazis in 1940s . Therefore , after the Soviet government is stable for years , the Chernobyl incident happen , they do not want to leave because of the enemy which is invisible .There is a kind of heroic toughness and frank reality in their character. Motherland is motherland, they will never leave.

For the people who return to the motherland , home is no longer a transitory concept ,it is a force even to resist the radiation, they no longer bear the pain of homesick. Their spirit will let us review the meaning of the relative risk and grab a kind of internal emotional contact of motherland——Fallen leaves return to the roots,return to the origin.

Purpose:
This project aims to build a skyscraper for them, the air purification equipment and water purification equipment are contained in the skyscraper,the solar power is used to provide energy for internal devices.the skyscraper is just like a Garden of Eden,it provide a safe habitat for people in the dangerous regions, a new and safe life will start from here.

Principle:
Nuclear radiation is consisted of three particles, α, β andγ. In the atomic nucleus, electron will absorb the radiation and give out light when it promoted from lower energy level to higher energy level. Fluorescent plates are used to construct the facade of the skyscraper to shield and use the radiation , which create a safe and stable living environment for people inside.

digital analysis

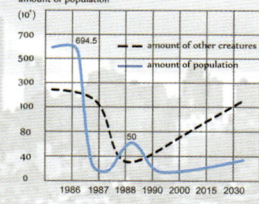

regional present situation

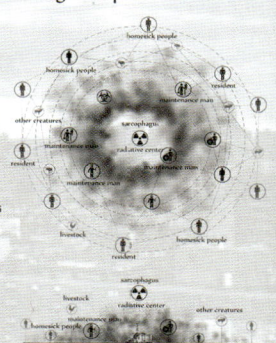

Before the Chernobyl disaster , there are 6.9 million people existed in the near area.
More than 500 thousand people participated in the rescue in 1986.
According to the investigative data,some of the refugees have come back to their homeland which are in the forbidden region.
At the same time ,the species of other creatures are also increasing.
For those who return, home is no longer a short-lived concept,It is a strength, even to resist radiation

The normal data of nuclear radiation is 20 msv,the real data is 600 thousand times compared with the normal data in 1986.
Since the 1986,the data of nuclear radiation has declined at a high speed. According to the investigative,the data of nuclear radiation is 744 msv in the 2015.
According to the United Nations,it still need 60 years to make the data of nuclear radiation decrease to a normal level,but it can not stop people from going home.

The maintenance men are constructing the new sarcophagus to replace the old one.
people who come back are living in the area 10 km from the radiation center.

Pripyat
The city close to Chernobyl ,which is used to settle down the refugee

came at a time of relative peace, making it harder for people to leave their homes. The inhabitants of the city thus have an innate heroic toughness and frank reality in their character.

For the people who return, home is no longer a transitory concept, it is a force to resist the radiation. Their spirit will let us review the meaning of the relative risk and grab a kind of internal emotional connection to one's hometown - Fallen leaves return to the roots

This project aims to build a skyscraper for them with air purification equipment and water purification equipment contained in the skyscraper. In addition, solar power is used to provide energy for internal devices. The skyscraper is just like a Garden of Eden, a new and safe life will start from here.

Nuclear radiation consists of three particles, and in the atomic nucleus, electrons will absorb the

radiation and give out light when it is promoted from a lower energy level to a higher energy level. Fluorescent plates are used to construct the facade of the skyscraper to shield and use the radiation, which create a safe and stable living environment for people inside.

Although not safe at the moment it is estimated that in a few years radiation level will drop to acceptable conditions and more people will return to the city. The creation of this skyscraper allow for acceptable infrastructure to exist at the time of their return.

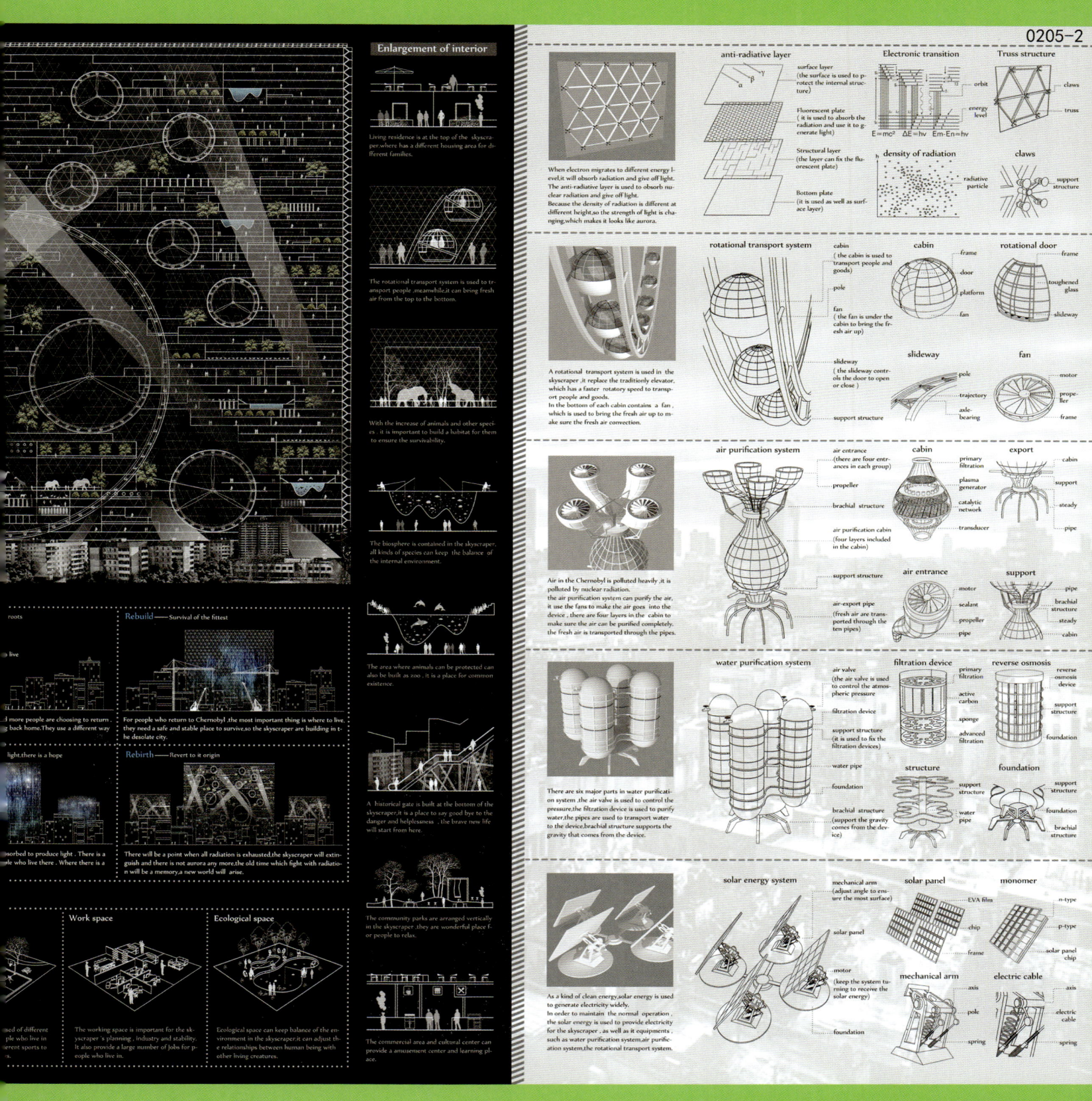

ESSENCE

Ewa Odyjas
Agnieszka Morga
Konrad Basan,
Jakub Pudo

Poland

1ST PLACE / 2015

"Essence"

Away from everyday routines, in a city center, a secret garden as a building, combining both: an architecture and a nature is proposed. The main goal of the project is to position non-architectural phenomena in a dense, urban fabric, by using the building as a neutral background. An inspiration rooted in the nature allowed to form a representation of external worlds in a shape of the vertical structure. Overlapping landscapes like an ocean, a jungle, a cave, a waterfall, so on and so forth, tend to stimulate diverse and complex range of sensual experiences - not only visual, but also acoustic, thermal, olfactory, kinesthetic, etc. A group of basic elements used as requisites in the design process contain results of some of the environmental processes. They translate the building through an impression — a roam-like experience.

Huge open floor
cropped by the
to 30 meters abo
up to surround
structure. The
into 11 various
environmentally
Three among the
to control all the

The sequence of
of routes dedica
proposals inspire
acclaimed geogra

Concept diagram

Functional diagram 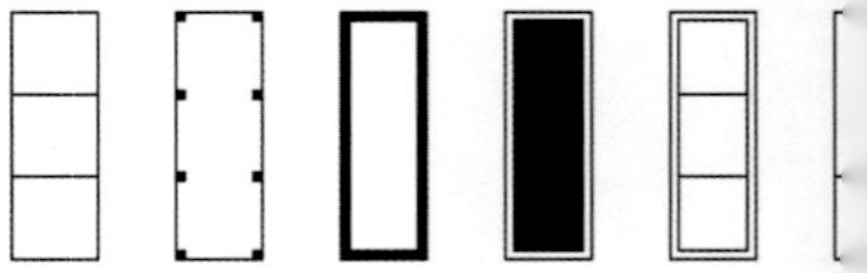   **Circulation diagram**

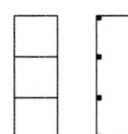   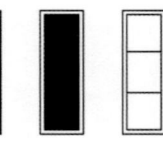

| Scale (300m x 100m) | Circulation cores | Additional facilities | Basic function (landscapes) |

Urban Context

ESSENCE

Away from everyday routines while still in a city center, a secret garden disguised as a building combining both an architecture and a nature is proposed. The main goal of the project is to position non-architectural phenomena in a dense, urban fabric by using the building as a neutral background. An inspiration rooted in nature allowed for the formation of a representation of external worlds in the shape of the vertical structure.

　　　Overlapping landscapes like an ocean, a jungle, a cave, a waterfall, so on and so forth, tend to stimulate a diverse and complex range of sensual experiences - not only visual, but also acoustic, thermal, olfactory, kinesthetic, etc. A group of basic elements used as requisites in the design process contain results of some of the environmental processes. They translate the building through an

Longitudinal section

0307

ms spectacular entrance area,
, a gigantic fish tank lifted up
und and a group of columns set
while supporting the building
y of the building is divided
. They are meant to form an
sequence open to the public.
tain technical facilities in order
d conditions.

apes might become a variable set
rent shades of adventure. Some
r representatives of historically
veries are possible.

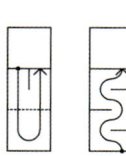

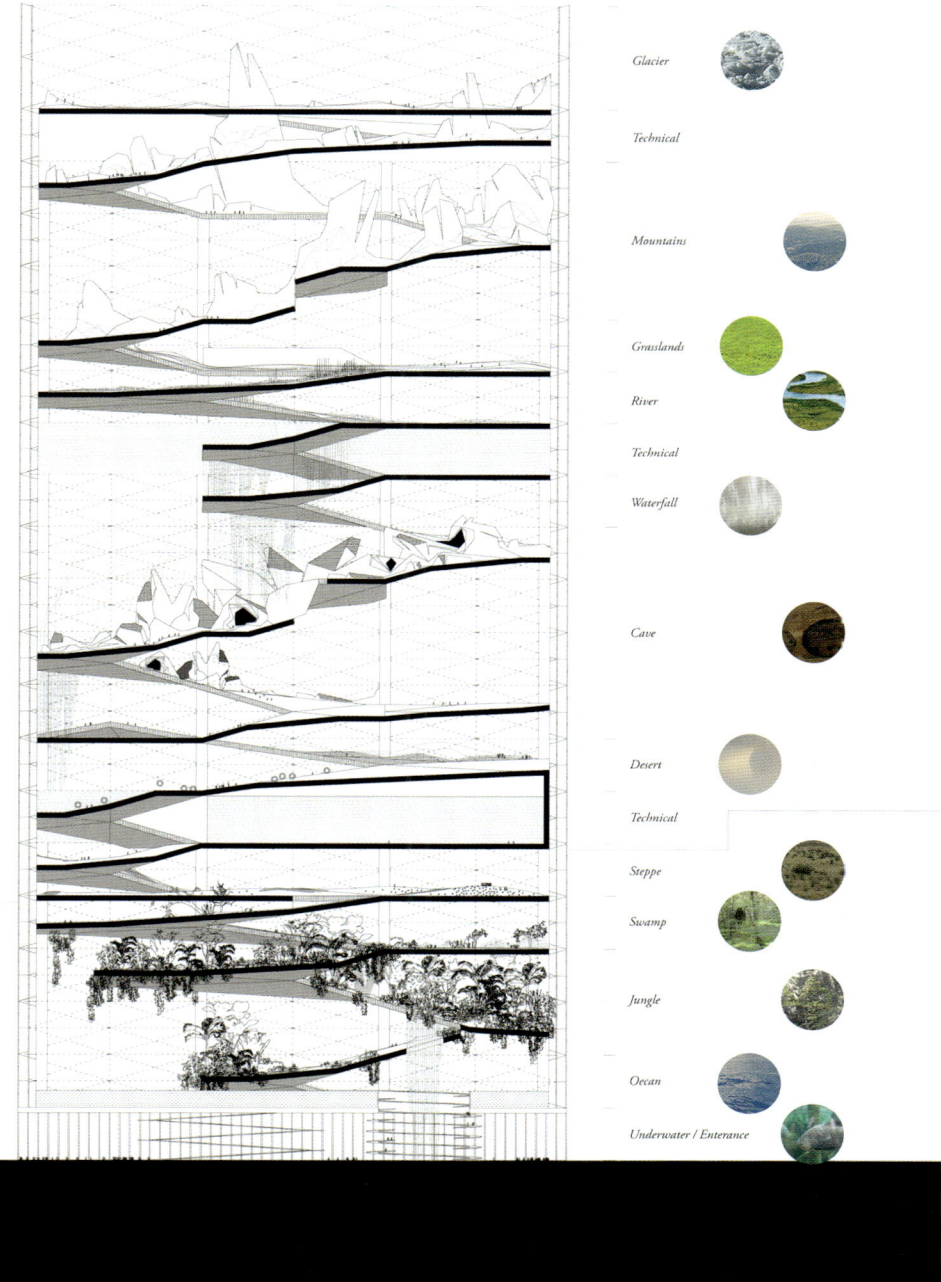

Glacier

Technical

Mountains

Grasslands

River

Technical

Waterfall

Cave

Desert

Technical

Steppe

Swamp

Jungle

Oecan

Underwater / Enterance

0   10   20   50

impression – a roam-like experience.

Essence Skyscraper was designed for New York City or any other large metropolitan area. The main idea is to provide a unique natural enclosure to congested cities. This is a place where people can escape from their daily routines into a fascinating natural environment with distinct seasonal conditions. You can explore all of them or only spend a few minutes in one of them. This type of architectural and environmental relationship will promote the well being of the inhabitats. Presenting the ecosystems in a vertical setting allows for a small footprint and maximum density.

A huge open floor plan forms a spectacular entrance area, cropped by the water floor, a gigantic fish tank lifted up to 30 meters above the ground and a group of columns set up to surround the plaza, while

Landcape 0 *Underwater / Enterance*

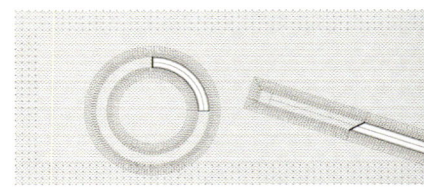

Landcape 1 *Ocean*

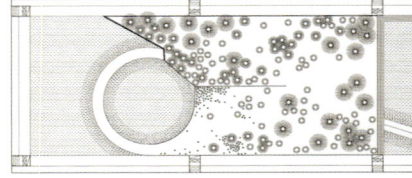

Landcape 2 *Jungle*

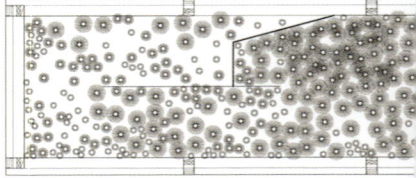

Landcape 3 *Swamp*

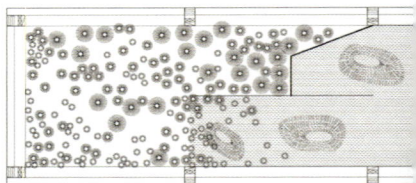

supporting the building structure. The main body of the building is divided into 11 various landscapes. They are meant to form an environmentally justified sequence open to the public. Three among them contain technical facilities in order to control all the necessary conditions.

The sequence of the landscapes might become a variable set of routes dedicated to different shades of adventure. Some proposals inspired by major representatives of historically acclaimed geographic discoveries are possible.

0307

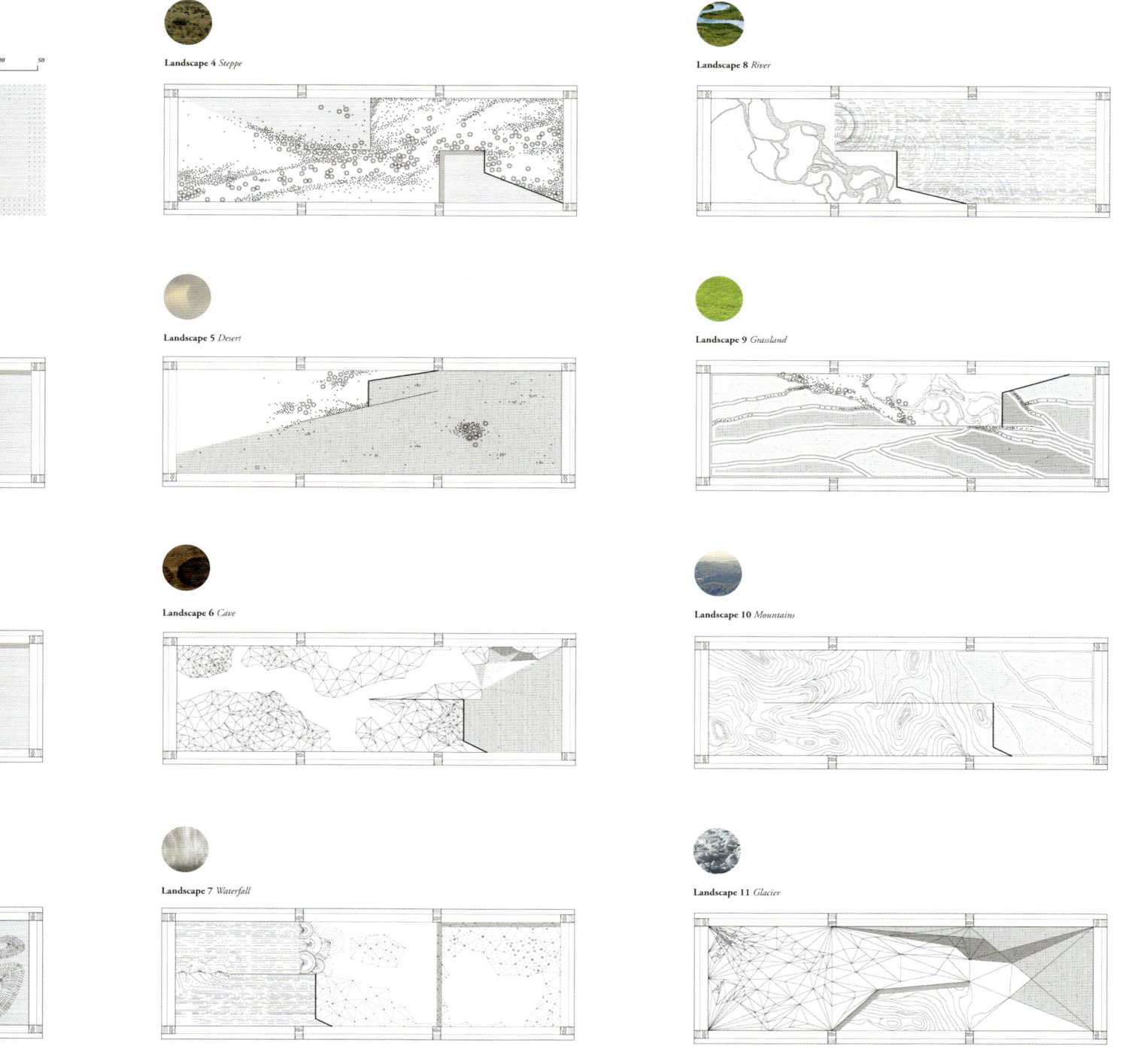

Landscape 4 *Steppe*

Landscape 5 *Desert*

Landscape 6 *Cave*

Landscape 7 *Waterfall*

Landscape 8 *River*

Landscape 9 *Grassland*

Landscape 10 *Mountains*

Landscape 11 *Glacier*

TOWER OF REFUGE

Qidan Chen

China

Because of a growing amount of threats from the alternation of the natural growth pattern causing the deterioration of the global environment, combined with the excessive harvesting of living creatures, more and more species of animals and plants are now endangered on the Earth. How to maintain species diversity has become a crucial issue in our "modern" world.

Endless reports of deforestation, city sandstorms, unpredictable deaths of elephants and brutal hunting of whales keep coming into the public eye, while human beings are focusing on constructing their survival fortresses and exploring potential habitats in outer space instead. However, could we slow down the pace and ensure our future generations could have the same experience about this blue planet as we did?

TOWER OF REFUGE
THREATENED SPECIES PROTECTION

Because of facing threat from alternation of the natural growth pattern, deterioration of the global environment and excessive harvesting of the living creatures, more and more species of animals and plants are now endangered on the Earth. How to maintain species diversity has become a crucial issue.

PROPOSAL

Endless reports of deforestation, city sandstorms, unpredictable death of elephants and brutal hunting of whales keep coming into the public eyes, while human beings are focusing on constructing their survival fortress and exploring potential habitat outer space. However, could we slow down the pace and ensure our future generations could have the same experience about this blue planet, and even the blue sky before industrial era?

INITIAL IDEA

Before rehabilitating successfully the livable environment and climate, or finding out artificial reproduction methods of all species, human have to build up a Noah's ark, which guarantees the provision of three elements of life: sunlight, air and water. Meanwhile, enough soil and food are essential for growth and reproduction.

CONCEPT

According to the IUCN Red List of Threatened Species, species are classified into nine groups:
• Extinct   [EX]
• Extinct in the Wild   [EW]
• Critically Endangered [CR]
• Endangered   [EN]
• Vulnerable   [VU]
• Near Threatened   [NT]
• Least Concern   [LC]
• Data Deficient   [DD]
• Not Evaluated   [NE]

Based on these basic concepts, scheme about Tower of Refuge has come out. Tower as a huge refuge, likes a self-operating machine serving all survival conditions. It can obtain and filter water and air, reallocate sunlight and transform solar energy for tower using.

The tower is divided into three sections, in the air, on the ground and in the water for corresponding to survival needs of varied species. Small cubes are classified into six groups accumulating on structural frame. All of them can be rearranged for specified environment and climates.

CE EN VU PT

Tower of refuge is not a machine for endangered species survival, but an experimental micro-city alluding humans' interstellar battle.

Before successfully rehabilitating the livable environment and climate, or finding out artificial reproduction methods for all species, humans have to build up a "Noah's ark," which guarantees the provision of three elements of life: sunlight, air and water. Meanwhile, enough soil and food are essential for growth and reproduction.

According to the IUCN Red List of Threatened Species, species are classified into nine groups: extinct, extinct in the wild, critically endangered, endangered, vulnerable, near threatened, least concern, data deficient, and not evaluated.

Based on these basic concepts, the scheme Tower of Refuge has been created. The tower as a huge refuge likens itself to a self-operating machine serving all survival conditions. It can obtain and filter

water and air, reallocate sunlight, and transform solar energy for consumption by the tower itself.

The Tower of Refugee will store the DNA information of all living creatures on the planet with the intention of bringing back to life species currently threatened by our irrational consumption of our planet's natural resources. The ark is completely self-sufficient and is capable of harvesting solar and wind energy. It also filters contaminated water and restores balance to fragile ecosystems.

AIR

AIR ABSORBER

AIR FILTER SYSTEM   AIR TANK

SUNLIGHT

SOLAR ENERGY PANEL

AIR TANK   AIR TANK

WATER

WATER TANK

CHEMICAL FILTRATION   PHYICAL FILTRATION

ENERGY

POLLUTION MONITOR

FOOD DISPENSER   WATER ABSORBER

AIR MONUMENT

Shi Yuqing
Hu Yifei
Zhang Juntong
Sheng Zifeng
He Yanan

China

CONCEPT

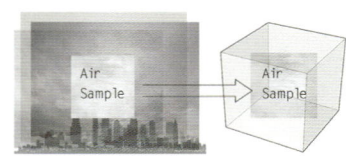

1. In the process of atmosphere research, compared with insufficient data collection from current tests, direct air sampling owns more significance over the aspect of a comprehensive research on the existing circumstance.

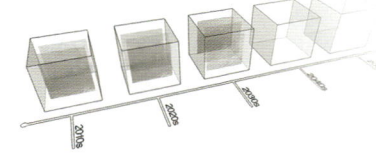

2. With the passage of time, the collection of air samples will increasingly gain significance, benefitting human being in the future.

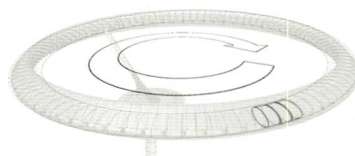

3. Air Monument will store the air samples in chrono-logical order, in resemblance with document files, constituting a huge atmosphere data base.

4. The main volume floats hi generation and pneumatic st Air Monument will survive civilization even when the

Nowadays, there is a growing problem in global climate. Studies on atmospheric components provide possibilities for people to learn the laws of climate change. However, detected datum does not include all the components of the atmosphere. We hope in this monumental building, there will be a possibility to get atmosphere samples automatically every year, and store the samples.

As time passes, the building will become a library to study the change in atmospheric components. In the meantime, future techniques will allow for a more thorough study of the atmosphere, providing better ways to respond to climate change.

Since the industrial revolution, with more fuel usage, more biomass burning, and more motor vehicle exhaust, the concentration and distribution of both regional and global atmospheres have changed

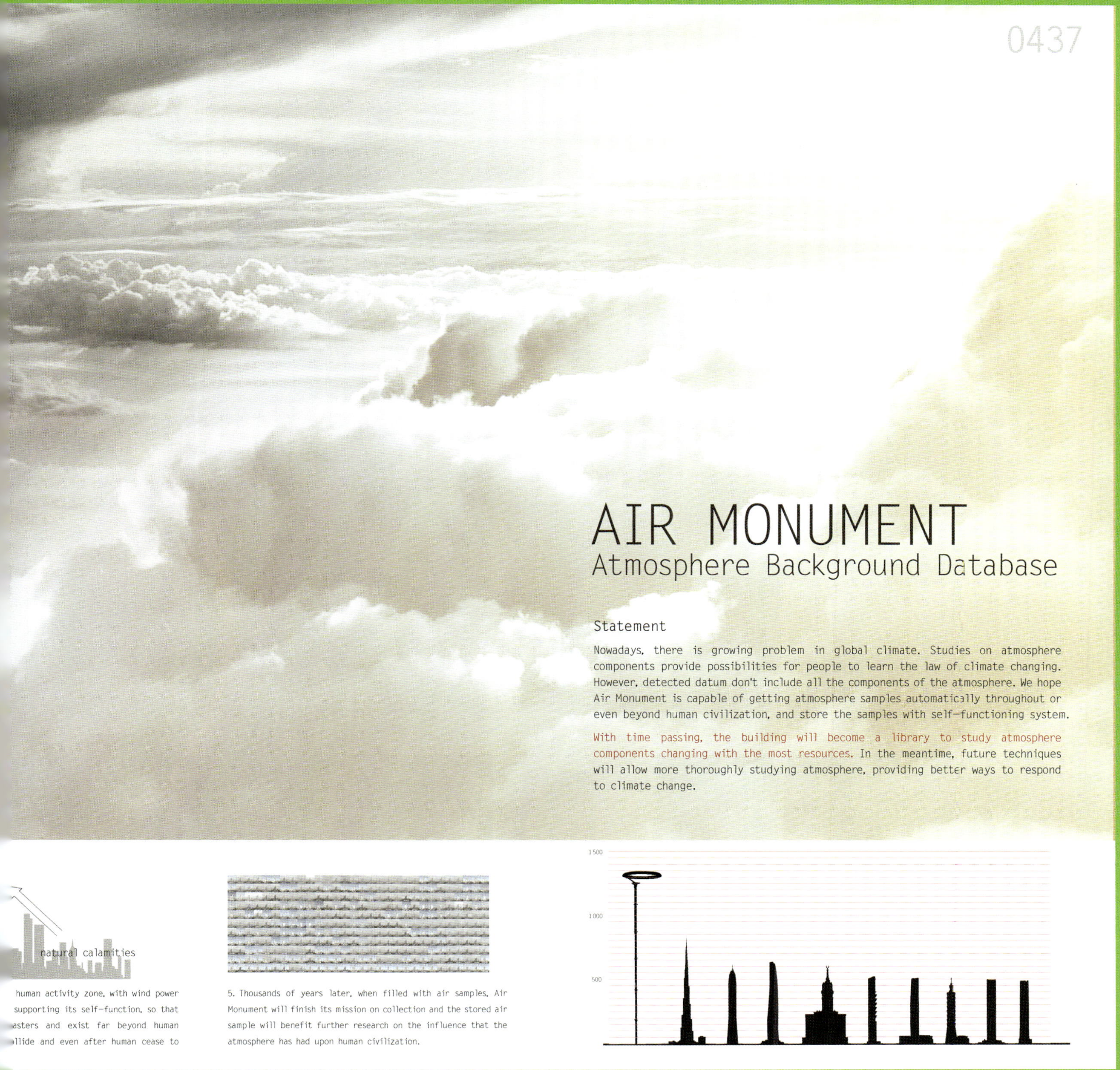

0437

AIR MONUMENT
Atmosphere Background Database

Statement

Nowadays, there is growing problem in global climate. Studies on atmosphere components provide possibilities for people to learn the law of climate changing. However, detected datum don't include all the components of the atmosphere. We hope Air Monument is capable of getting atmosphere samples automatically throughout or even beyond human civilization, and store the samples with self—functioning system.

With time passing, the building will become a library to study atmosphere components changing with the most resources. In the meantime, future techniques will allow more thoroughly studying atmosphere, providing better ways to respond to climate change.

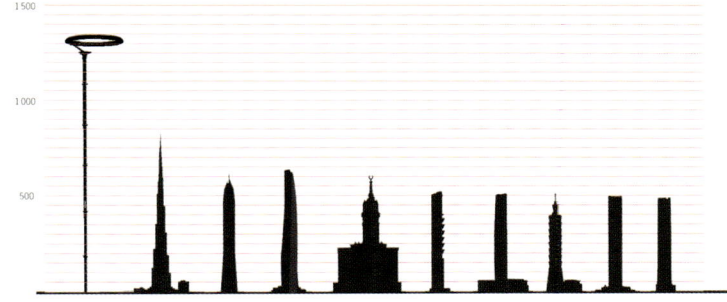

natural calamities

human activity zone, with wind power supporting its self-function, so that asters and exist far beyond human llide and even after human cease to

5. Thousands of years later, when filled with air samples, Air Monument will finish its mission on collection and the stored air sample will benefit further research on the influence that the atmosphere has had upon human civilization.

quite obviously. And that leads to problems like global warming, ozone depletion, acid deposition, air quality going down and so on, which have extreme effects on the earth's environment and ecosystems, and puts a huge threat to human development. Therefore, carrying on long-term steady observation of atmosphere components and its relevant qualities is essential for learning atmosphere components and its changing process.

It's not enough for studies on atmosphere components to only rely on clearly recording and studying datum. Earth atmosphere components are really complex, including solidities, fluids, and gas, with complicated physicochemical properties. There is limited datum from detecting existing air samples. And there is possibility that some unknown substances make much difference during climate changing

ETERNITY

The ring floats high above human activity zone, with wind power generation and pneumatic structure, supporting its self-function, so that Air Monument will survive any disasters and exist far beyond human civilization even when the worlds collide and even after human cease to exist.

BACKGROUND

Atmosphere components study is very important
Since the industrial revolution, with more fuel use, more biomass burning, more motor vehicle exhaust, the concentration and distribution of both regional and global atmosphere have changed observably. And that leads to problems like global warming, ozone depletion, acid deposition, air quality going down and so on, which have much effect on earth environment and ecosystems, and put huge threat to human development. Therefore, the observation and study of atmosphere components is quite important. Carrying on long-term steady observation of atmosphere components and its relevant qualities is essential for learning atmosphere components and its changing process. Such based studies on atmosphere components changing law, and responding to climate change and disasters, is one of the essential issues of achieving the unity of man and nature both nowadays and in the future

Air samples are more important than datum
It's not enough for studies on atmosphere components to only rely on clearly recording and studying datum. Earth atmosphere components are really complex, including solidities, fluids, and gas, with complicated physicochemical properties. There are limited datum from detecting existing air samples. And there is possibility that some unknown substances make much difference during climate changing process but could not be detected for now. Therefore, air samples are the most comprehensive data resources. Today's scientific researches often need early air samples. Nowadays these samples usually come from polar deposits. Although these samples are precious few and hard to define a particular year, they still help scientists study greenhouse gas concentration changes for the past 200 years. Modern advanced techniques also helped discover atmosphere component like hydro fluorocarbon, which were not paid attention to before.

Caution of scie
Human behaviors
There were many
River Valley smo
photochemical s
decades, there
happening, whic
activities. In t
growing concern
environment, it'
that scientific
life. Thus, to s
them.

process but could not be detected for now. Therefore, air samples are the most comprehensive data resources.

Human behavior has had large impacts on atmospheric components and global climate change. In recent decades, there are constant droughts, floods, higher temperatures, rainstorms and sandstorms happening, which are all closely related to atmospheric components changing due to human activities. In the 21st century, even if governments and scientific institutes have shown growing concerns over environmental problems, without public consciousness and action towards protecting the environment, it's still not optimistic that there will be an improvement towards atmosphere pollution.

0437

TECHNOLOGY NODE

Function Layer

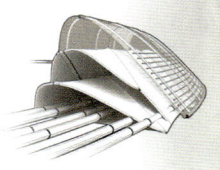

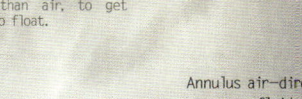

Suspension devices:

The skyscraper choose a suspension structure system considering maximized storage years, away from complicated ground environment and disaster chances. The suspension devices are provided by the gasbags inside the circle, filled with helium which is lighter than air, to get enough buoyancy to float.

Auto-run devices:

The outer skin is divided into two layers. Through the aerodynamic-formed design of the inner groove, high-altitude wind is led into of the vertical axis wind turbine inside the circle. Auto-run devices guarantee the skyscraper could still function even when human beings are extinct, until the air samples are abundantly collected.

Storage devices:

The storage of atmosphere samples involves non-light, steady temperature, steady pressure and other relevant environmental conditions. The storage devices are arranged in chronological order. The air gathering jar is connected by silica gel airway tube and sampling devices, for atmosphere sampling use. According to different atmosphere sampling requirements, there are atmosphere components jar and atmospheric particle jar.

Sampling devices:

According to the air assessment from each part of the circle, the atmosphere sampling devices will choose the optimized sampling site. The assessment structure consists of concentration meter, anemoscope, etc. The collecting component includes getter pump and vacuum pump, delivering samples through vacuum pipeline to each storage device which represent a certain time.

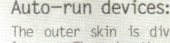
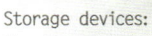
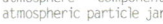

Annulus air-directing fluid design

Detachable from the main body after disaster damage

Research Center and atmosphere sampling devices

Sampling height(every 250 meters, every 1.3℃ down, with top circle height 1300 meters)

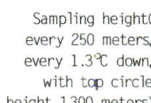

anagement should be called to the public.
arge impacts on atmosphere components and global climate change.
s air pollution events all around the world in history, such as Meuse
c in Belgium in 1930, which has caused 63 deaths. And in 1952, the
London has cause 4000 people to death within four days. In recent
tant drought, flood, high temperature, rainstorm and sand storm
losely related to atmosphere components changes due to human
century, even if governments and scientific institutes have shown
ronmental problems, without public consciousness of protecting the
ot so optimistic of improving atmosphere pollution. There is reason
ches of improving the environment is too far away from everyday
entific work to the public in a better way, is essential to alarm

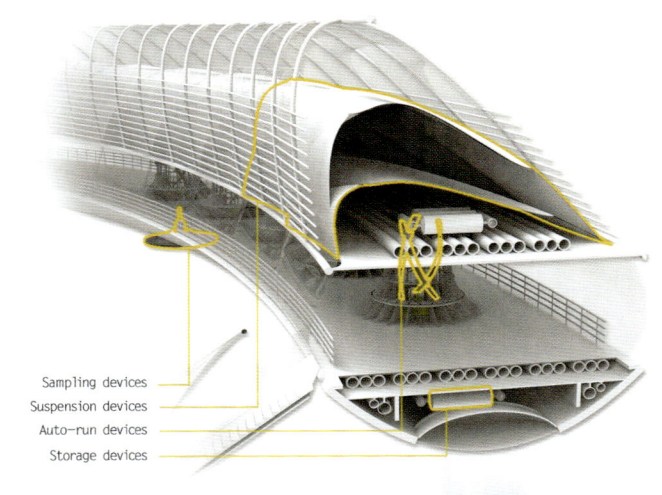

Sampling devices
Suspension devices
Auto-run devices
Storage devices

AQUAPONICS-SCRAPER

Leo Octora
Hendry Hermawan Supartan

Indonesia

THE RESERVOIR AT RISK AND GOVERNMENT'S EFFORTS

Pluit reservoir is one of the largest reservoir, located in North Jakarta, Indonesia. Because of the reservoir's lip area occupied by the slums, then trivialization occurs slowly and followed by transition in function by 20 hectares of a total of 80 hectares of land that is supposed to be a water storage reservoir. Besides water plants like eceng gondok/ water hyacinth grow sporadic and uncontrolled resulting almost the entire surface of the lake covered. Consequently every rainy season come severe flooding, outbreaks of disease and deployment of waste. To overcome this, in mid-2013 the local government of Jakarta held a thorough revitalization by changing the slum into a city park partially and dredging the lake's bottom. But these efforts are inadequate. Social problems then occur related to the relocation of slums. Mostly they can not adapt to new situation and lost livelihoods. In addition the native ecosystems need to be repaired.

before   *timeline*   after

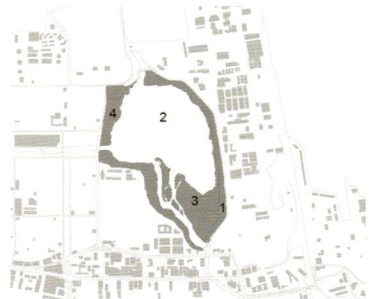

1. URBAN SLUMS   2. POLLUTED WATER   3. WATER HYACINTH   4. PLUIT RESERVOIR PARK

URBAN REVITALIZATION CONCEPT

 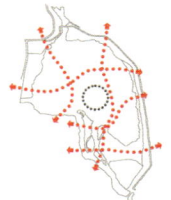 

RELOCATION OF THE DWELLING & EXPANDING EXISTING PARK AROUND RESERVOIR PERIMETER   NEW CONNECTION   NEW COMMUNAL SPACE

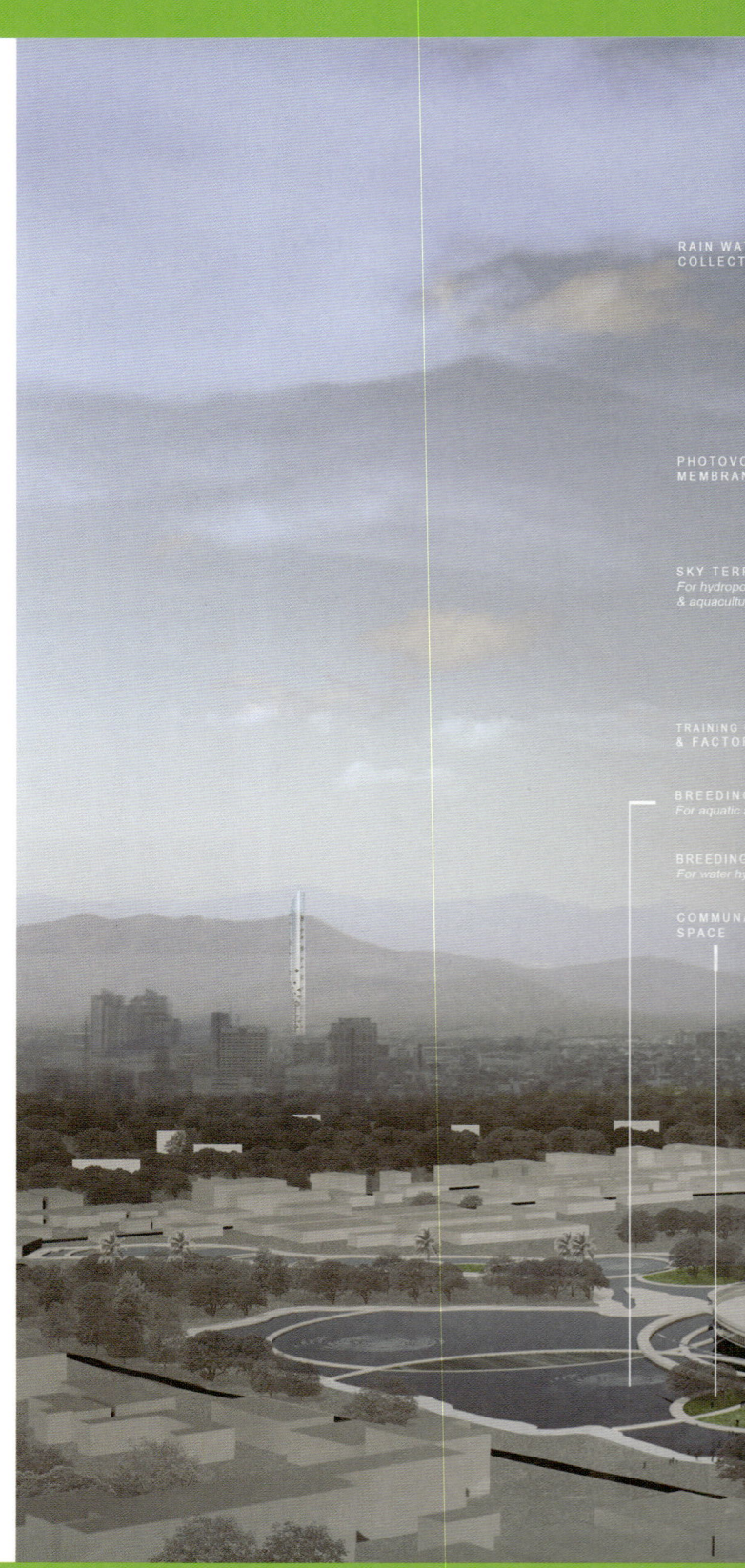

RAIN WATER COLLECTO

PHOTOVOT MEMBRANE

SKY TERRA
For hydropon & aquaculture

TRAINING C & FACTOR

BREEDING
For aquatic an

BREEDING
For water hya

COMMUNA SPACE

Jakarta is the capital of Indonesia and has become South-East Asia's largest megacity. Being in a short time magnets for immigrants and spurred the emergence of an area called Kampung within the city. The Kampung 'village' in the area of Jakarta, is often associated with informality, poverty, and remembrance of rural tradition. For those who are uneducated, unskilled laborers and poor living in slums. It is likely that many of these people reside illegally on riverbanks, empty lots and flood canal system. One cf which is the Pluit reservoir.

Pluit reservoir is one of the largest reservoirs, located in north Jakarta. Because of the reservoir's lip area occupied by the slums, then trivialization occurs slowly and followed by transition in function by 20 hectares of a total of 80 hectares of land that is supposed to be a water storage reservoir. Besides

0 4 5 6

A Q U A P O N I C - S C R A P E R

A MUTUALISTIC ECO DESIGN: AN ANSWER BETWEEN URBAN SLUMS AND WATER BASIN AREAS

The design of Aquaponics - Scraper is adapted from food production system called aquaponics. This system combine conventional aquaculture (raising aquatic animal such as fish, snails) with hydroponics (cultivating plants in water) in symbiotic environment. Aquaponics consists of two main parts, the aquaculture part for raising aquatic animals and the hydroponics part for growing plants. In an aquaponics system, water from an aquaculture system is fed to hydroponic system, where the excretions from aquatic animals are used by the plants as nutrients. The water is recirculated back to aquaculture system.

This aquaponics system is then thoroughly implemented in the form of skyscraper, where the main components of the system become an architectural elements which is devided vertically. The reservoir act as a giant rearing embankment for local fish.

This can be used as a prototype for restructuring other reservoir.

WIND TURBINES

PHOTOVOTAIC PANEL

water plants like eceng gondok and other wild plants grow sporadic and uncontrolled resulting almost the entire surface of the lake covered. Consequently every rainy season come severe flooding, outbreaks of disease and deployment of waste. To overcome this, in mid-2013 the local government of Jakarta hold a thorough revitalization by changing the slum into a city park and dredging the lake's bottom. But these efforts are inadequate.

The design of Aquaponic – Scraper is adapted from food production system called aquaponics. This system combine conventional aquaculture (raising aquatic animals such as fish, snails with hydroponics (cultivating plants in water) in a symbiotic environment. Aquaponics consists of two main parts, the aquaculture part for raising aquatic animals and the hydroponics part for growing plants. In an

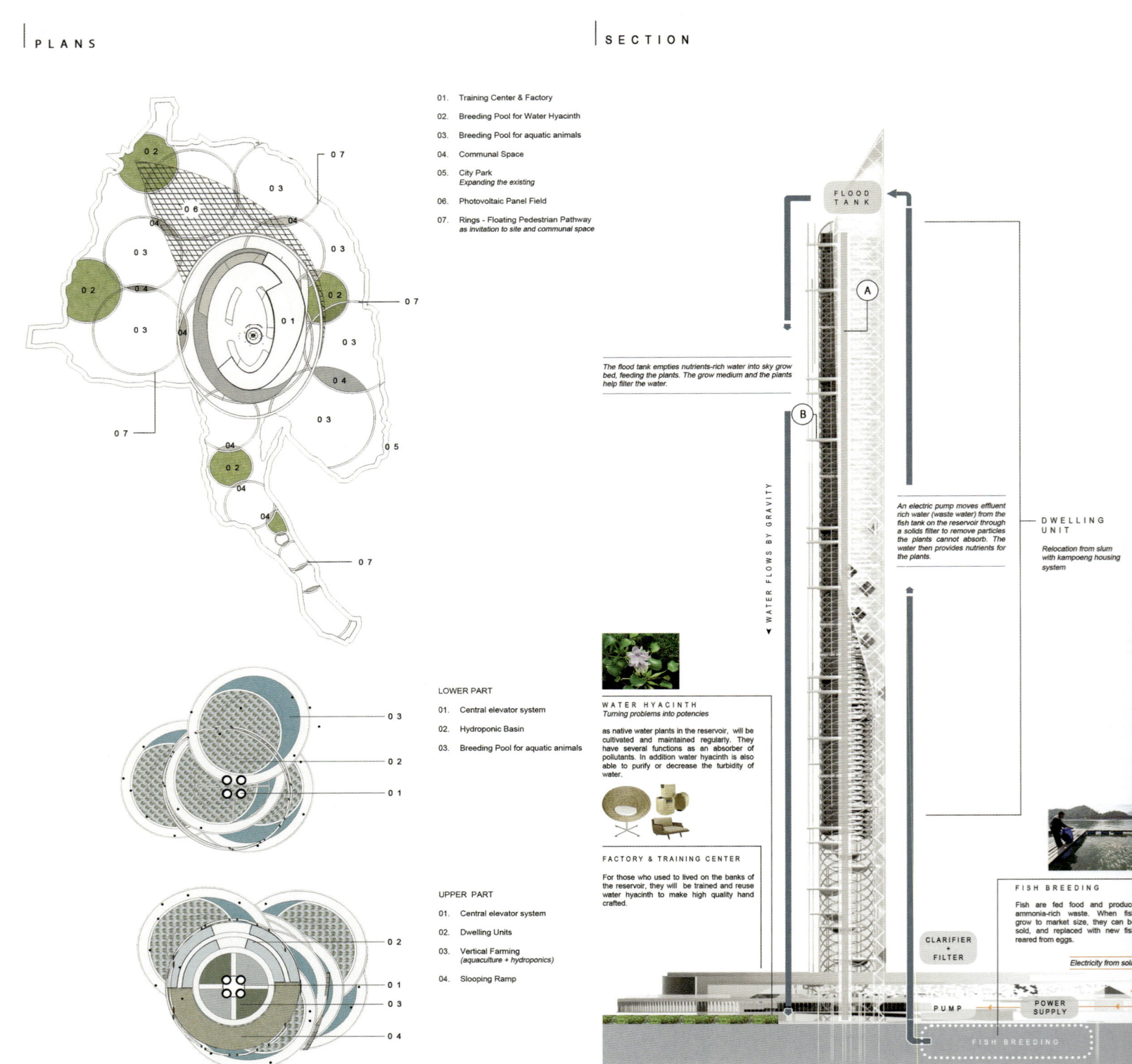

PLANS

01. Training Center & Factory
02. Breeding Pool for Water Hyacinth
03. Breeding Pool for aquatic animals
04. Communal Space
05. City Park
    Expanding the existing
06. Photovoltaic Panel Field
07. Rings - Floating Pedestrian Pathway
    as invitation to site and communal space

LOWER PART
01. Central elevator system
02. Hydroponic Basin
03. Breeding Pool for aquatic animals

UPPER PART
01. Central elevator system
02. Dwelling Units
03. Vertical Farming
    (aquaculture + hydroponics)
04. Slooping Ramp

SECTION

FLOOD TANK

The flood tank empties nutrients-rich water into sky grow bed, feeding the plants. The grow medium and the plants help filter the water.

A

B

◀ WATER FLOWS BY GRAVITY

An electric pump moves effluent rich water (waste water) from the fish tank on the reservoir through a solids filter to remove particles the plants cannot absorb. The water then provides nutrients for the plants.

DWELLING UNIT

Relocation from slum with kampoeng housing system

WATER HYACINTH
Turning problems into potencies

as native water plants in the reservoir, will be cultivated and maintained regularly. They have several functions as an absorber of pollutants. In addition water hyacinth is also able to purify or decrease the turbidity of water.

FACTORY & TRAINING CENTER

For those who used to lived on the banks of the reservoir, they will be trained and reuse water hyacinth to make high quality hand crafted.

FISH BREEDING

Fish are fed food and produce ammonia-rich waste. When fish grow to market size, they can be sold, and replaced with new fish reared from eggs.

CLARIFIER + FILTER

Electricity from sola

PUMP

POWER SUPPLY

FISH BREEDING

aquaponics system, water from an aquaculture system is fed to hydroponic system, where the plants as nutrients use the excretions from aquatic animals. The water is recirculated back to aquaculture system.

A sophisticated zero energy consumption vertical transport system called a pneumatic vacuum elevators are used in the building. Without cables or piston air pressure above and beneath the elevator cab becomes the key to transporting. As the elevator cab go left or right (sideways), the linear induction motors help to make it possible. A metro system is like a commuter train. The rotating circulation makes cabs come continuous, so that passengers do not have to wait long.

VERTICAL TRANSPORTATION

PNEUMATIC VACUUM ELEVATOR

Sophisticated zero energy consumption vertical transport system called a pneumatic vacuum elevator are used in the building. Without cables or piston air pressure above and beneath the elevator cab are the key to transporting.

Electricity runs through these steel comes from vertical farming on each floor and and also from floating aquapods that scattered in every part of the building.

These energy will be used to operate the elevator.

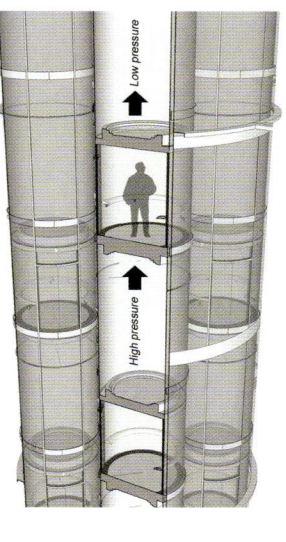

METRO SYSTEM ELEVATOR ▶

Continuous loop to support vertical mass transportation for dwelling purpose. As the elevator cab go left or right (sideways), the linear induction motors help to make it possible.

LOOPING RAMP

The circular ramp provides direct access to each floor within the building and act as a transfer canal to supplies the need of micro-aquaponics system. Pipes are installed along the ramp's path and dwelling units are connected one another.

PERSPECTIVE

▲
PLACE MAKING
Integrating existing park with building communal space that float above the reservoir.

Working space intergrated with public space and elevated aquaponics pods ▶

B

FLOATING AQUAPOD
as Micro Aquaponic System

01. Water pipe covering the structure inside

02. Rearing tank
the tanks for raising and feeding the fish

03. Settling basin
a unit for catching uneaten food and detached biofilms, and for settling out fine particulates

04. Biofilter
a place where the nitrification bacteria can grow and convert ammonia into nitrates, which are usable by the plants

05. Hydroponics subsystem
the portion of the system where plants are grown by absorbing excess nutrients from the water

MESOCYCLONE

Gwak Min-Hwan
Jeong Ji-Na

South Korea

Since the industrial revolution, human fossil energy use created a change in the climate system, which has been growing exponentially. This global warming is accelerating the reduction of radiation emitted out of the earth. Earth's average temperature during the 21st century may potentially rise up to 6 celsius degrees.

Due to the extreme changes of global weather there are many problems such as environmental pollution, depletion of the ozone layer, respiratory disease, and lightning damage. As a result, life is threatened. The future generation to come will be able to expand the regional impacts of sea level rise, subtropical deserts with increased temperatures due to global warming, and all of this is expected to make life for mankind extremely difficult.

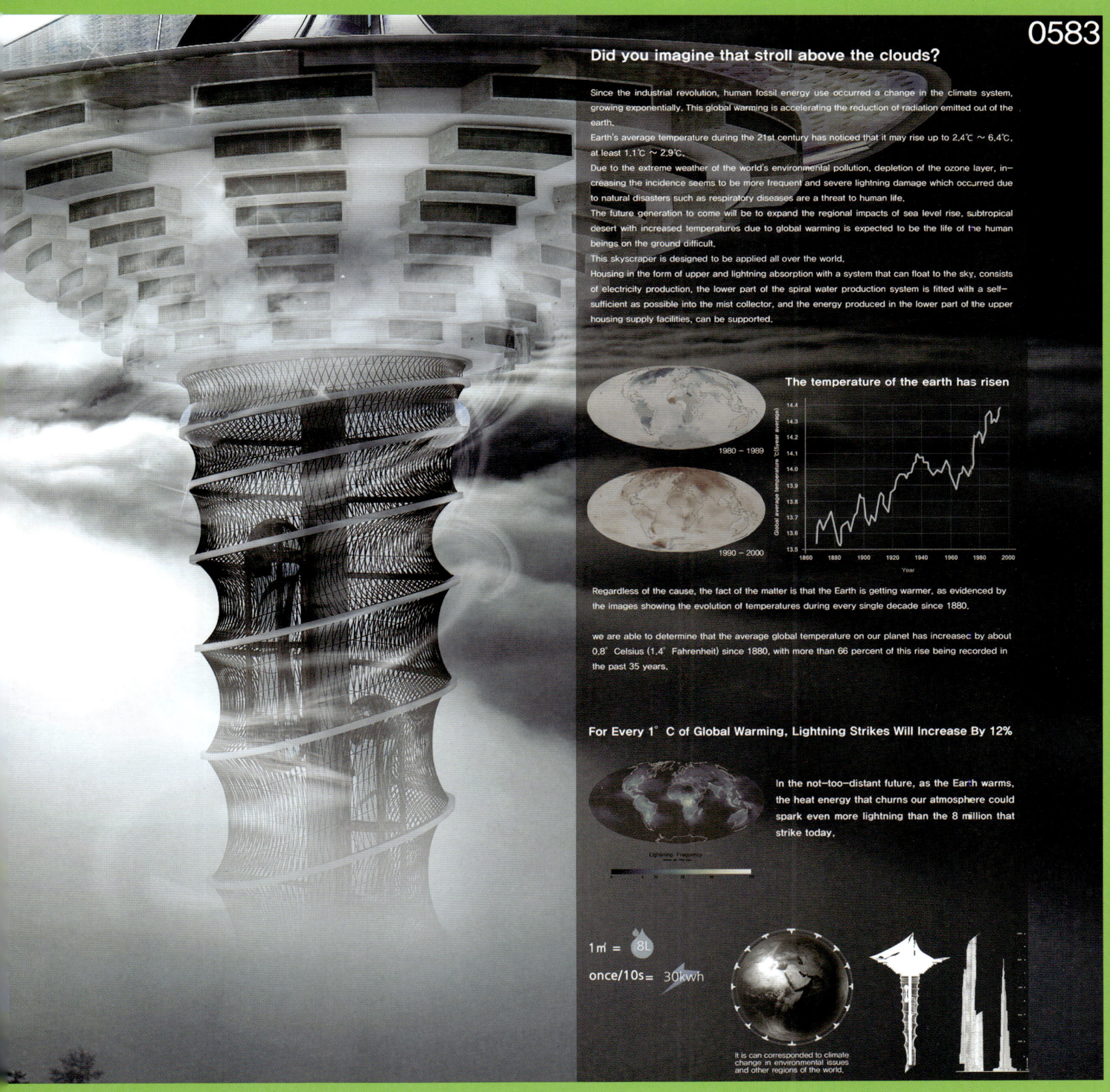

The lower part of the spiral skyscraper is self-sufficient and has three distinctive features. First, the skyscraper consists of a permeable mesh structure. This is a technique for collecting the water passed through the fog in the air called "fog nets". The mists of water droplets to pass through the net, which are then stored on top of the water tank. Second, the skyscraper has a large heating fan. This fan helps the temperature be maintained to the ideal setting. The temperature of the cloud has an unsuitable environment. The heating fan allows the warm air to enter the interior of the skyscraper, and cold air to move outside of the building. Third, It absorbs lightning and makes electricity. Lightning has hundreds of millions of volts and hundreds of thousands of amperage in current.

When lightning strikes or clouds discharge, to the amount of electricity appears to be equivalent to

about 300Kb. In a summer thunderstorm, because the discharge phenomenon occurs once every ten seconds, it is intended to have the power generation capacity of a medium-range power plant.

At this time, the skyscraper can store the generated electric current in an electric charger of huge capacity. Electricity stored in the electric charger is supplied to the skyscraper's upper levels.

The stored electricity supply powers the heating fan to warm the housing; water is supplied from the mist produced by upper collector. This project is one of the solutions for improving the human living environment of the future and to evade more severe environmental pollution. This skyscraper is self-sufficient and has the potential to become a new typology for building.

0583

Using the principle of electrical induction lightning rod

positive charge
negative charge
ng strikes,
erved at a time
erstorms, thun-
station. During
tem is used to
useful energy,
ding.

Housing

The higher at altitude causes a damage caused by bad air, such as dust particles and PH levels, Membrane structure enclosed by the housing will serve to filter it in the concentration of PH dark.

He

Public area

Condenser

above Clouds temperature is minus 20 ℃, therefore humans are difficult to live, therefore, The building is must do Temperature controlled by oneself, and Using a convection heating fan keeps the temperature.

CARBON FILTER

Electric charger

The skyscraper is consists of a permeable mesh structure. This is a technique for collecting the water passed through the fog in the air called a "fog nets".

Collector

It absorbs lightning and make use of electricity.
The number of deaths caused by lightning accident is increasing every year. through the absorbing, lightning accidents are prevented and can produce the electricity by lightning and clouds discharge.

Self-sufficient living above the clouds are possible when supplied with water by the water vapor in clouds.

RE-GENERATOR

Gabriel Munoz Moreno

United States

The constant change and growth of the human population that we are experiencing these days produce a collateral damage in the natural ecosystems where the cities stand all around the world. Today's building and urban systems that do not take into account the natural environment where they are built produce this damage.

The expected and rapid population growth for the first half of the 21st century, propelled especially by the developing countries, results in a need to research about alternatives to today's building methods in order to provide construction tools and guides that make urban growth compatible with the preservation of our environment.

Moreover, there is strong evidence in the power of architecture to change the future of our cities and

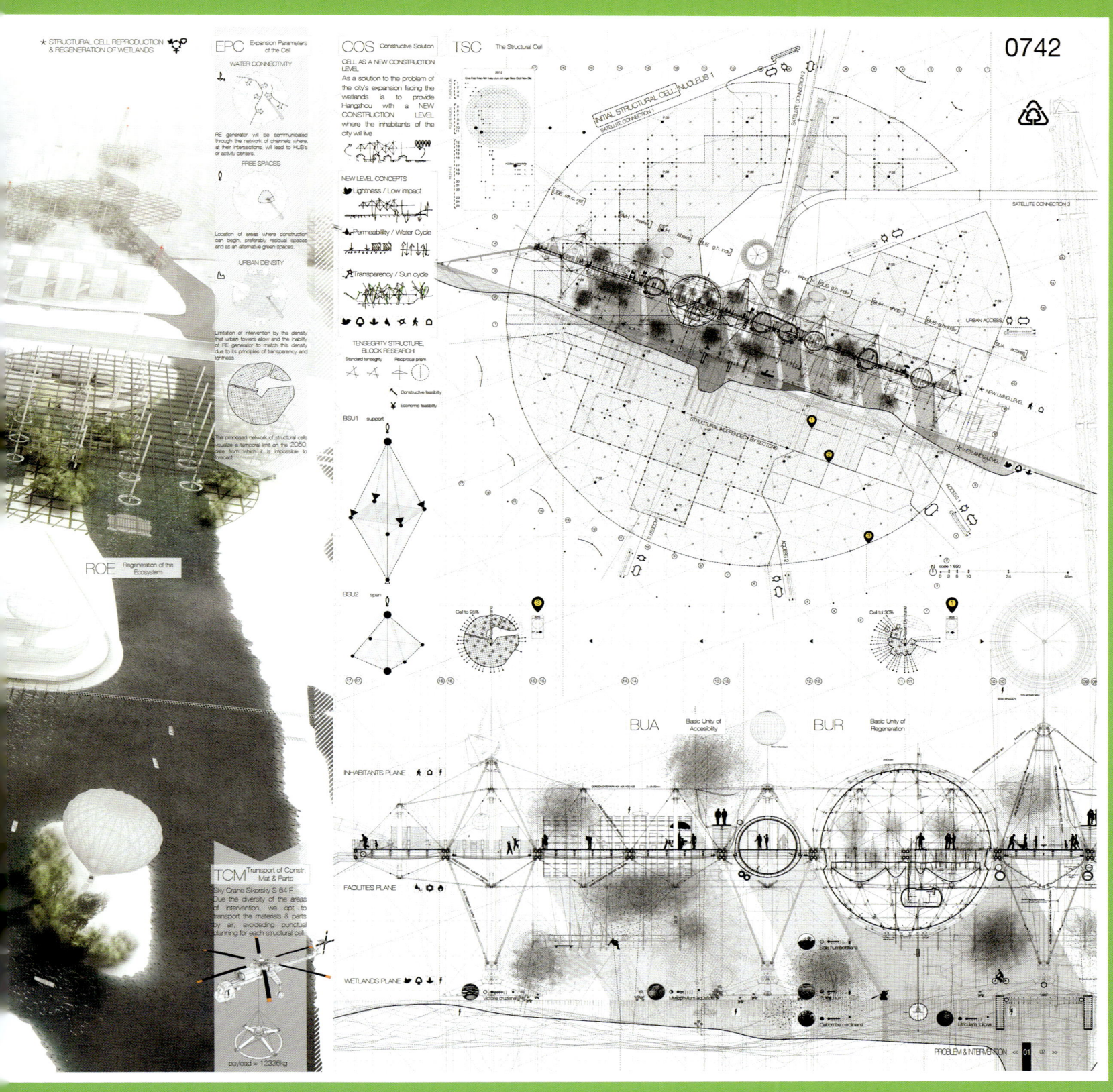

generations, and with that, our thinking and behavior towards an understanding between the places that we inhabit and our ways of living in them.

The project stems from the analysis of the population growth of Hangzhou, China. The direct consequence observed was the partial destruction of the ecosystem on which the city stands, the wetlands. The construction system used so far does not support them. In China, and all around the world, the population will continue growing, and the continued use of the current construction system will end up destroying entire ecosystems.

As a solution to this, a new construction system is proposed that is organized, distributed, and expands as cells throughout the city. This cell is elevated above the ground, to make way for the

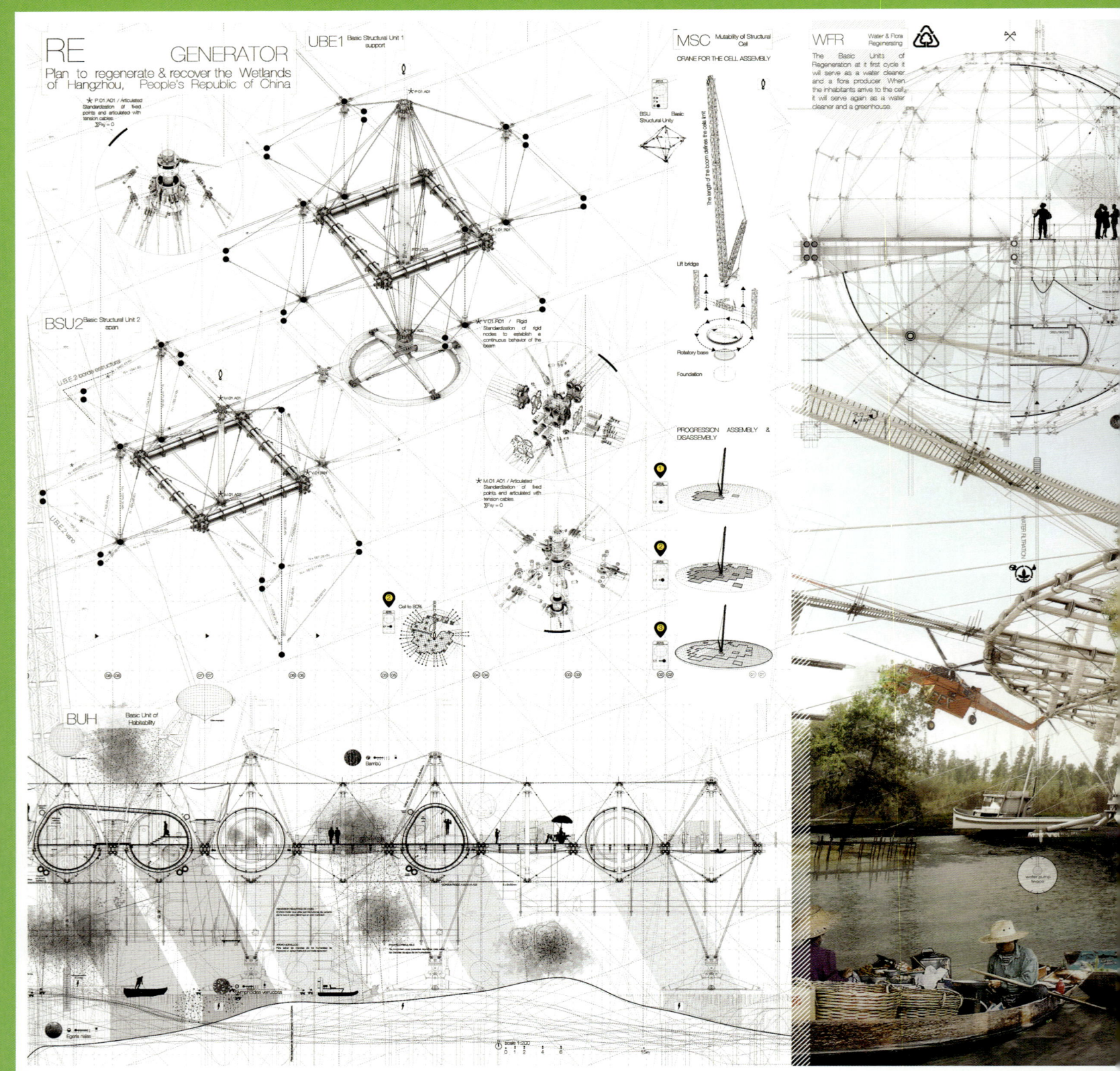

recovery of the wetlands. To do so, it should be translucent and permeable, without disrupting the natural cycles of the sun, air and water, which allows for the natural regeneration of any ecosystem.

Furthermore, the cell is supplied with different "inputs" to make possible the habitability and the cleaning of the wetlands, using its waste to encourage self-sufficiency. These mimic different parts of natural cells and enables our construction cell to be a living element, a system in constant change and growth, regenerating the ecosystems, in this case, the wetlands of Hangzhou.

NEZA YORK TOWERS

Israel López Balan
Gabriel Mendoza Cruz
Ana Saraí Lombardini Hernández
Yayo Melgoza Acuautla

Mexico

Ciudad Nezahualcóyotl or more commonly Ciudad Neza, is a city and municipality of State of Mexico adjacent to the northeast corner of Mexico City. In the 20th Century, the land on which Ciudad Neza sits was under Lake Texcoco and uninhabited. Successful draining of the lake in the early 20th Century created new land, which the government eventually sold into private hands. Today Ciudad Neza is a sprawling city of over one million entirely with modern buildings. As Mexico City continues to pull water from the aquifer below, its ground is sinking. While subsidence has been stabilized in the city center, many parts of the metropolitan area continue to sink. Some parts like Ciudad Neza have sunk more than 30 feet during the last century. Mexico City puts a lot of effort to stop the sinking. In some locations it has caused the sewage lines to become slanted - resulting in the lines running backward. Consequently,

0072

NEZA YORK TOWERS

HOW DO WE STOP THE SINKING OF MEXICO CITY
AND ITS WATER SYSTEM CRISIS?

the city struggles with flooding during the rainy season. Emergency pumping stations have been built to maintain extraction capacity, but a major solution is still needed. The water difficulties have become a vicious circle: as the city grows, more water is pumped from the aquifer. As more is pumped, the city sinks further. The sinkage ruptures more underground water pipes, sending fresh water gushing into the sewers, aggravating the shortage, requiring more water to be pumped from the aquifer, and so on.

If Mexico City receives significant pluvial precipitation at a total rate of 215 m3/s, pluvial water is partly responsible for the urban flooding problem in rainy season, but rainwater harvesting could be part of the solution for people living in Ciudad Neza. Here, rainfall is heaviest, and the area is sufficient to collect and store water to reduce costs. In the other hand, the total amount of wastewater treated by public

ANTI – SINKING SYSTEM FOR A CITY

SCENARIO 1- NEZA YORK

Ciudad Nezahualcóyotl or more commonly Ciudad Neza, is a city and *municipality* of State of Mexico adjacent to the northeast corner of Mexico's Federal District it is thus part of the Mexico City Metropolitan Area. In the 20th century, the land on which Ciudad Neza sits was under Lake Texcoco and uninhabited. Successful draining of the lake in the early 20th century created new land, which the government eventually sold into private hands. However, public services such as adequate potable water, electricity and sewerage were lacking until after the area was made an independent municipality in 1963. Today Ciudad Neza is a sprawling city of over one million entirely with modern buildings.

Until the 2000s, most migrants from Mexico to the United States, especially to places like New York, were from poor rural areas. However, since the turn of the century, another wave of immigrants is coming from poor urban areas such as Ciudad Neza. These immigrants tend to be younger and better educated than their rural counterparts, and tend also to keep separate from them. This is bringing into existence a new Mexican subculture called "Neza York" distinguished by dress, speech and the likelihood of learning English. Businesses with names like Tacos Neza and Neza Grocery have appeared in New York City.

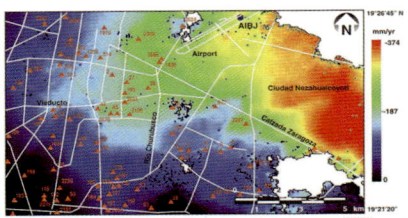

SUBSIDENCE MAP OF MEXICO CITY, CIUDAD NEZA, THE MOST AFFECTED

POPULATION
1.140.540   DENSITY 18000 PEOPLE PER SQUARE KILOMETER   UNDERUTILIZED PUBLIC SPACES

CIUDAD NEZA'S URBAN FABRIC

SCENARIO 2 - SUBSIDENCE

As Mexico City continues to pull water from the aquifer below, its ground is sinking. The subsidence that results from groundwater extraction is a problem all over the world, but is especially dramatic in Mexico City. The aquifer has been under increasing pressure over the last several decades as the city's population has skyrocketed. Additionally, the city is mostly constructed atop layers of clay and highly permeable sand and gravel — the type of ground most liable to collapse as water is pulled out.
While subsidence has been stabilized in the city center, many parts of the metropolitan area continue to sink. Some parts like Ciudad Neza have sunk more than 30 feet during the last century.

SCENARIO 3 – VICIOUS CIRCLE

Today the most serious damage is occurring underground, where the collapsing subsoil continues to rupture sewer lines, subway tunnels, and potable water pipes. Because the subsidence is not uniform, it has caused hundreds of millions of dollars in damage to buildings and other structures over the years, especially in the colonial-era city center.
Mexico City puts a lot of effort to stop the sinking. In some locations it has caused the sewage lines to become slanted - resulting in the lines running backward. Consequently, the city struggles with flooding during the rainy season. Emergency pumping stations have been built to maintain extraction capacity, but a major solution is still needed.
The water difficulties have become a vicious circle: as the city grows, more water is pumped from the aquifer. As more is pumped, the city sinks further. The sinkage ruptures more underground water pipes, sending fresh water gushing into the sewers, aggravating the shortage, requiring more water to be pumped from the aquifer, and so on.

SUBSIDENCE EFFECTS IN MEXICO CITY'S DOWNTOWN

DESIGN CONCEPT

If Mexico City receives significant pluvial precipitation at a total rate of 215 m3/s, pluvial water is partly responsible for the urban flooding problem in rainy season, but rainwater harvesting could be part of the solution for people living in Ciudad Neza. Here, rainfall is heaviest, and the area is sufficient to collect and store water to reduce costs.

In the other hand, the total amount of wastewater treated by public wastewater treatment plants is 10 m3/s and all the treated wastewater is reused. At the present time, reused water is utilized to fill recreational lakes and canals (54%), to irrigate agricultural areas and parks over a total area of 6,500 ha (31%), cooling in industry (8%), diverse commercial activities (5%) and to recharge the aquifer (only 2%).

With all this in mind, the proposal is to replace gradually the network of small storm sewers in Ciudad Neza with a rainwater system collector that converge in recreational lakes on the surface, where towers emerge as large natural filters for rainwater storage; and treatment plants with absorption wells for underground injection. Following this system, floods will decrease because drainage system of the city will not be saturated in rainy season, and after treated water is injected directly into the aquifer, the sinking will stop.

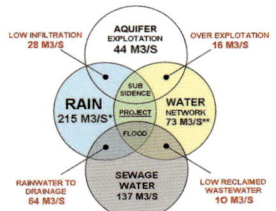

LOW INFILTRATION
28 M3/S   AQUIFER EXPLOTATION 44 M3/S   OVER EXPLOTATION 16 M3/S

RAIN
215 M3/S*   SUBSIDENCE PROJECT FLOOD   WATER NETWORK 73 M3/S**

RAINWATER TO DRAINAGE 64 M3/S   SEWAGE WATER 137 M3/S   LOW RECLAIMED WASTEWATER 10 M3/S

MEXICO CITY WATER USE

*EVAPORATION = 118 M3/S - TO RIVERS = 5 M3/S
** FROM CUTZAMALA SYSTEM = 29 M3/S

BUILDIN

Soil from
to build a
collection

1

wastewater treatment plants is 10 m3/s and all the treated wastewater is reused. At the present time, reused water is utilized to fill recreational lakes and canals (54%), to irrigate agricultural areas and parks over a total area of 6,500 ha (31%), cooling in industry (8%), diverse commercial activities (5%) and to recharge the aquifer (only 2%). With all this in mind, the proposal is to replace gradually the network of small storm sewers in Ciudad Neza with a rainwater system collector that converge in recreational lakes on the surface, where towers emerge as large natural filters for rainwater storage; and treatment plants with absorption wells for underground injection. Following this system, floods will decrease because drainage system of the city will not be saturated in rainy season, and after treated water is injected directly into the aquifer, the sinking will stop.

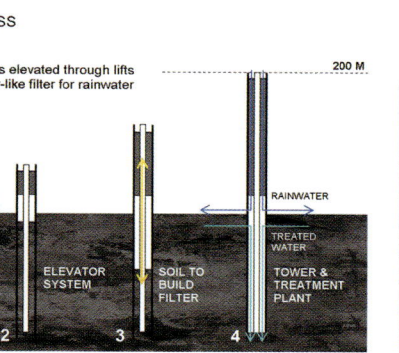

s elevated through lifts
-like filter for rainwater

200 M

RAINWATER

TREATED
WATER

2   3   4
ELEVATOR   SOIL TO BUILD   TOWER &
SYSTEM   FILTER   TREATMENT
                           PLANT

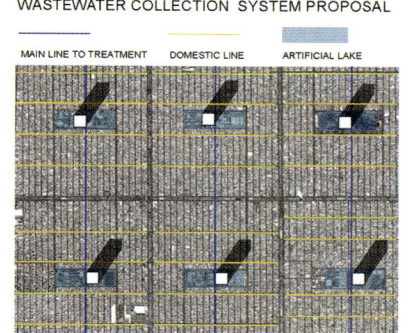

WASTEWATER COLLECTION SYSTEM PROPOSAL

MAIN LINE TO TREATMENT   DOMESTIC LINE   ARTIFICIAL LAKE

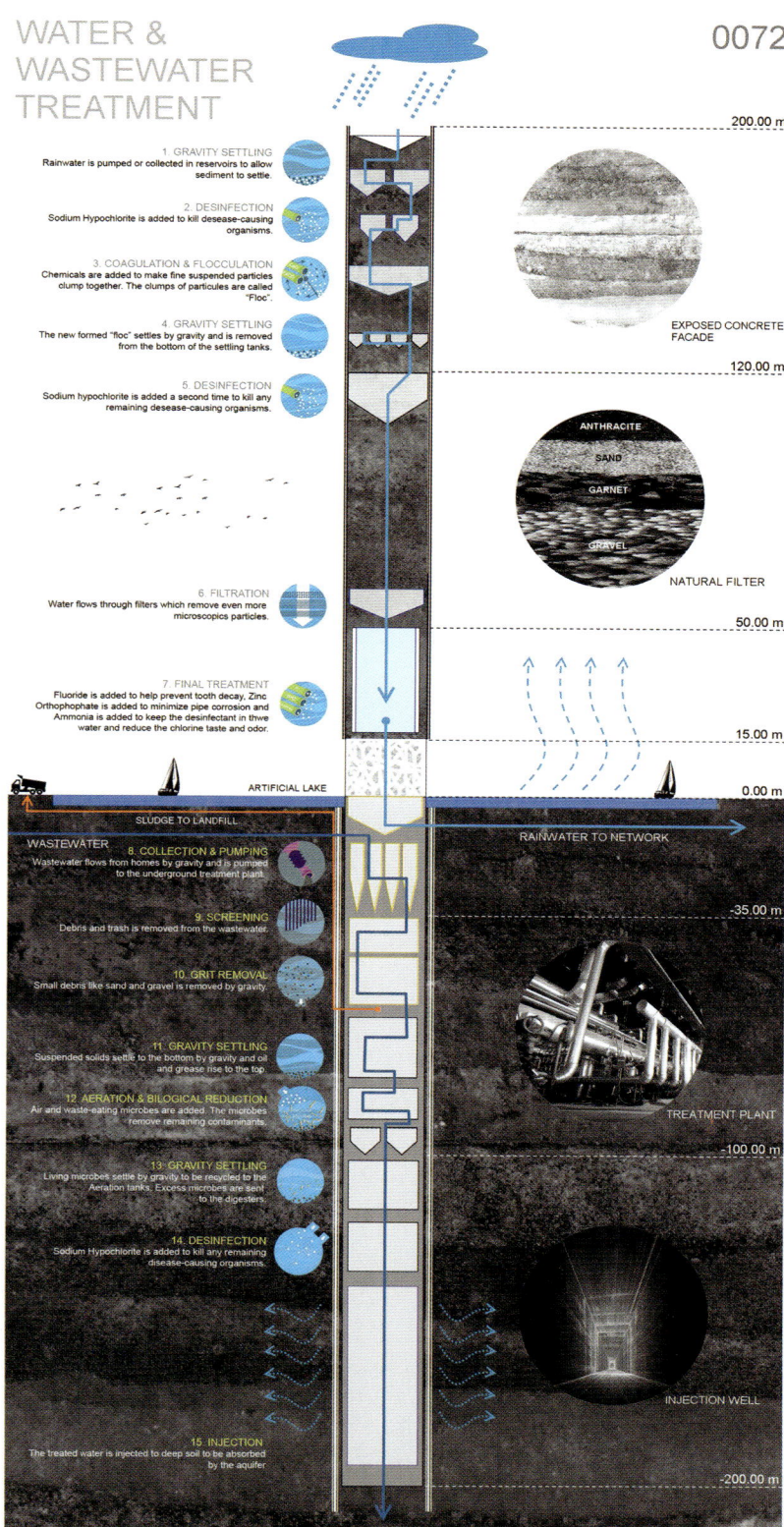

WATER &
WASTEWATER
TREATMENT

0072

200.00 m

1. GRAVITY SETTLING
Rainwater is pumped or collected in reservoirs to allow sediment to settle.

2. DESINFECTION
Sodium Hypochlorite is added to kill disease-causing organisms.

3. COAGULATION & FLOCCULATION
Chemicals are added to make fine suspended particles clump together. The clumps of particles are called "Floc".

4. GRAVITY SETTLING
The new formed "floc" settles by gravity and is removed from the bottom of the settling tanks.

5. DESINFECTION
Sodium hypochlorite is added a second time to kill any remaining desease-causing organisms.

6. FILTRATION
Water flows through filters which remove even more microscopics particles.

7. FINAL TREATMENT
Fluoride is added to help prevent tooth decay, Zinc Orthophophate is added to minimize pipe corrosion and Ammonia is added to keep the desinfectant in thwe water and reduce the chlorine taste and odor.

EXPOSED CONCRETE FACADE

120.00 m

ANTHRACITE
SAND
GARNET
GRAVEL

NATURAL FILTER

50.00 m

15.00 m

ARTIFICIAL LAKE

0.00 m

SLUDGE TO LANDFILL

RAINWATER TO NETWORK

WASTEWATER   8. COLLECTION & PUMPING
Wastewater flows from homes by gravity and is pumped to the underground treatment plant.

9. SCREENING
Debris and trash is removed from the wastewater.

10. GRIT REMOVAL
Small debris like sand and gravel is removed by gravity.

11. GRAVITY SETTLING
Suspended solids settle to the bottom by gravity and oil and grease rise to the top.

12. AERATION & BIOLOGICAL REDUCTION
Air and waste-eating microbes are added. The microbes remove remaining contaminants.

13. GRAVITY SETTLING
Living microbes settle by gravity to be recycled to the Aeration tanks. Excess microbes are sent to the digesters.

14. DESINFECTION
Sodium Hypochlorite is added to kill any remaining disease-causing organisms.

-35.00 m

TREATMENT PLANT

-100.00 m

INJECTION WELL

15. INJECTION
The treated water is injected to deep soil to be absorbed by the aquifer.

-200.00 m

AIR-STALAGMITE

Changsoo Park
Sizhe Chen

United States

AIR-STALAGMITE

AIR-STALAGMITE is a type of highrise formation that rises from the ground of the site with air pollution due to the accumulation of atmospheric particulates deposited on the ground from polluted air.

Air-Stalagmite is a skyscraper designed for the most polluted areas in the world. This project recognized the environmental problems originated after the Industrial and Technological Revolutions – two centuries of a very high consumption of natural resources around the globe.

This skyscraper has two main functions. First, it serves as a beacon that acknowledges an extremely high pollution problem. Second, it is designed to filter contaminated air while capturing suspended air particles.

Basically, the skyscraper is equipped with a large vacuum placed at the bottom of the building that sucks polluted air to be cleaned by a series of air filters located on the higher levels. These particles are then accumulated and used as building material to keep constructing the skyscraper. Each filament

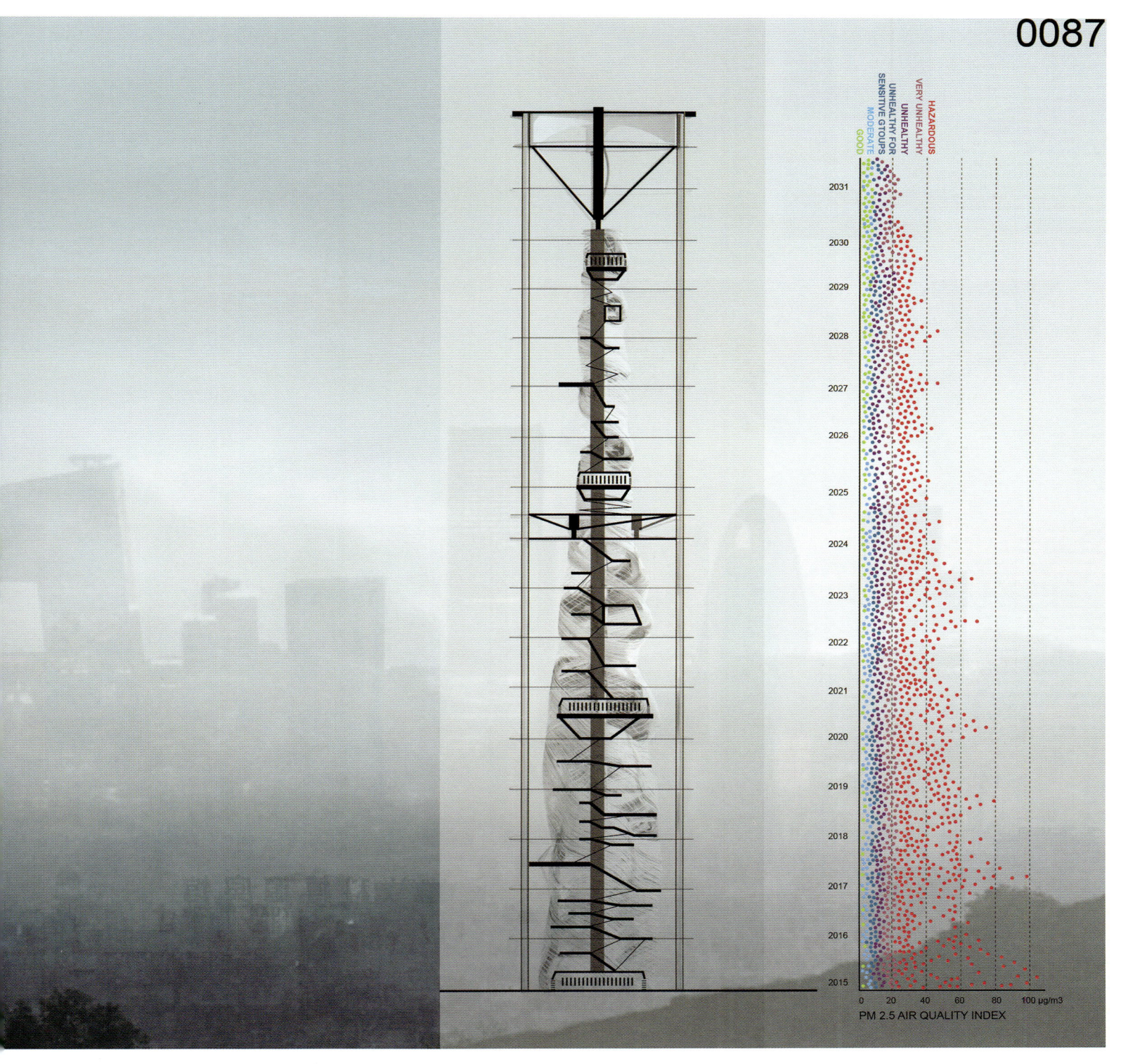

0087

on the building's façade represents a year – a similar concept to tree trunk rings in which each ring represents a year in the life of the tree.

Since the Industrial Revolution, the development of many technologies had made the consumption of the Earth's natural resources. At that time, the revolution was happened through using resources and making and consuming products in the limited space. But globalization revolution, happened in the late 20th century, has made it possible to move resource quickly all over the world. Furthermore, it has accelerated usage of the Earth's resource by making and consuming of products rapidly and broadly. However, this acceleration has created global warming and environmental pollution as the trade. Since the damage is coming back to us, we need an alarm that can serve as a beacon to tell the degree of risk.

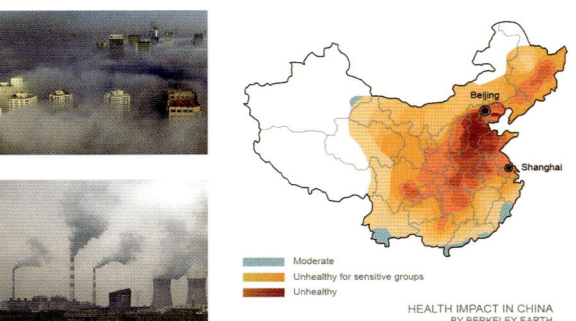

HEALTH IMPACT IN CHINA
BY BERKELEY EARTH

Moderate
Unhealthy for sensitive groups
Unhealthy

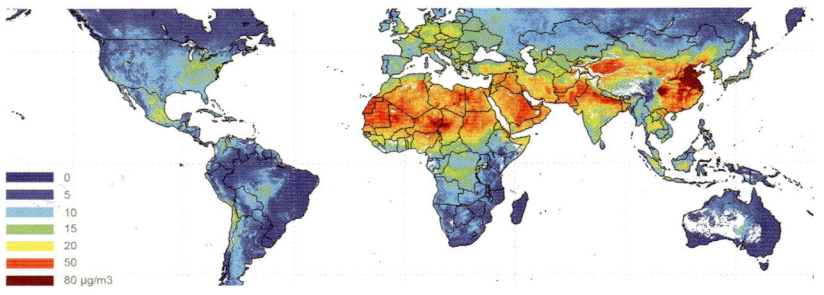

0
5
10
15
20
50
80 µg/m3

WORLD SATELLITE-DERIVED PM 2.5
BY NASA

Smog is introduced into the tower through the vacuumed fan mounted in the each bottom part. Filtered clean air is discharged to the outside through the perforated area in the each upper part of the tower. Atmospheric particulates which have impacts on climate and precipitation that adversely affect human health are accumulated and reused as composited building material with concrete. With developed carbon capture and storage technique and 3D printing method, Beacon tower is constructed over a time. Its shape and height expresses site specific air pollution index for the year as tree ring represents the weather of the year. Starting to reduce the environmental pollution problem is started from its recognition.

TREE RING
Living records of climate

AIR-STALAGMITE
Living record of air pollution

AIR-STALAGMITE

STALAGMITE

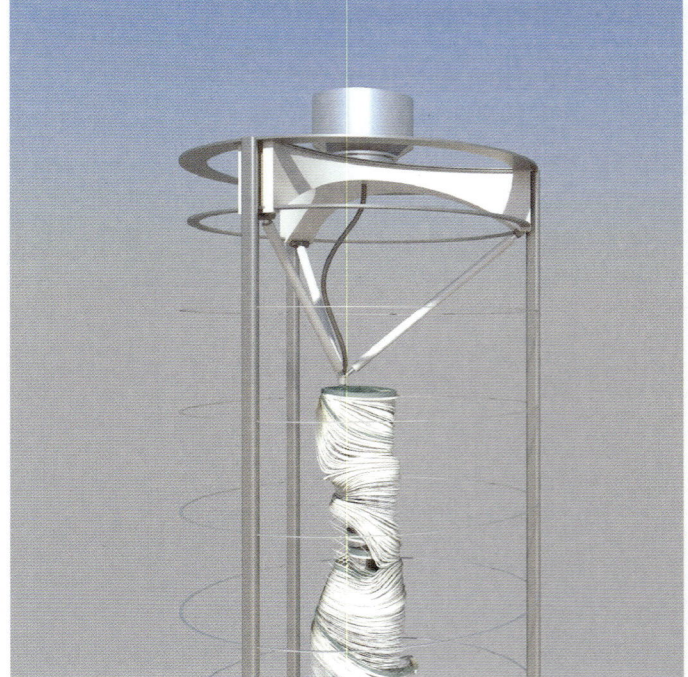

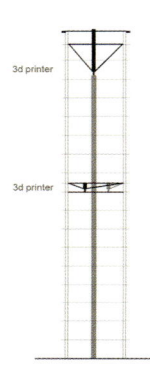

3d printer

3d printer

CORE & STRUCTURE

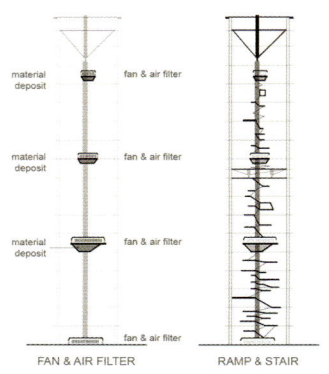

material deposit — fan & air filter

material deposit — fan & air filter

material deposit — fan & air filter

fan & air filter

FAN & AIR FILTER

RAMP & STAIR

SKIN

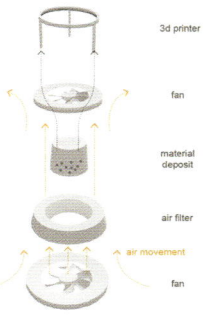

3d printer

fan

material deposit

air filter

air movement

fan

COMPONENT

0087

HANOI VERTICAL QUARTER

M Architects Ltd.
Minh Phuc Nguyen
Linh Phuong Phan

Vietnam

HANOI
VERTICAL
QUARTER

HANOI

A city inside the river, is a sanctuary and special City. It is not only a Capital of Vietnam, it is a place where histories throughout different eras have met, where all Cultural and Historical values have converged and which has been inhabited since at least 3000 BC

THE OLD QUARTER OF HANOI

Witnessing the ups and downs of Vietnam history, Hanoi has evolved significantly from its Core – The Old Quarter. This Quarter initially started with 36 Streets with each street had its name reflected the business trading happening on the street. This is one of many unique points of Hanoi. Some of the streets currently still reflect that such as: Steel street, Silk street. Hanoian is very proud of the Old Quarter. Especially, families those that have been living here for many generations, those who called the Old Quarter was the Cradle of Culture.

Streets in old quarter

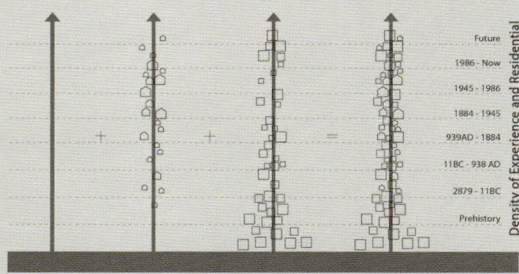
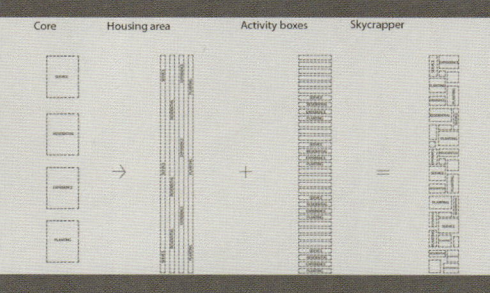

Life in old quarter

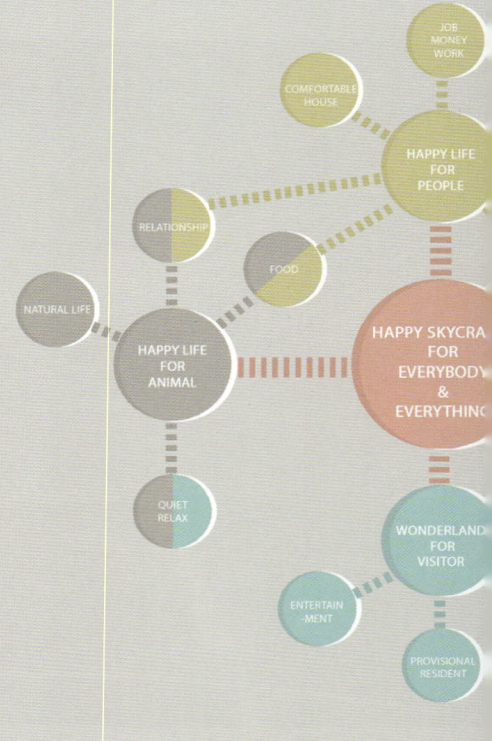

A HAPPY TOWER COMES HANOI VERTICAL OLD QUARTER

Hanoi nowadays is a big Capital which is comparable to London, UK. However, the expansion has up the gaps and to reduce density from the City centre since then. However, due to unready infra of leaving a large area of new parts of Hanoi in very much poor conditions in a terms of people's to trade, work, and live. This has become a serious fact for a thousand year old Capital. Together w scribed through population density, types of professions, building's functions and infrastructure trades as well as tourists, famous for its street activities within a human scaled street covered by

Future
1986 - Now
1945 - 1986
1884 - 1945
939AD - 1884
11BC - 938 AD
2879 - 11BC
Prehistory

Density of Experience and Residential

Core   Housing area   Activity boxes   Skycrapper

Functionality   Vertical functionality   Horizontal functionality   Regional functionality

IDEA
Facade reflect the history and function
The Experience and Residential area are arranged diffuse along the building
Creating fully-equipped sections
Creating interaction between the local residents here and guest

WEST LAKE

OLD QUARTER

SITE
Location 3 km from old quarter
A highlight point inside the Red river, connecting all historic sites

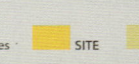
SITE

Hanoi, a city inside the river, is a sanctuary and special city. It is not only the capital of Vietnam but also a place where histories throughout different eras have met, where all cultural and historical values have converged and which has been inhabited since at least 3000 BC. Hanoi has evolved significantly from its core – The Old Quarter. This Quarter initially started with 36 streets with each street had its name reflected the business trading happening on the street. This is one of many unique points of Hanoi. Some of the streets currently still reflect that such as: Steel street, Silk street, Paper Craft street. Hanoian is very proud of the Old Quarter. Especially, families those have been living here for many generations, those who called the Old Quarter the cradle of culture.

Hanoi nowadays is a big capital and comparable to London, UK. However, the expansion has been done much faster than living conditions of people. This has caused tremendous problem of leaving a large area of new

much faster than living conditions of people. This has caused tremendous problem
ell as infrastructure. There have been a lot of new urban developments started to fill
onditions in the new expansion areas, people still pull themselves into the city centre
anization, the Core of Hanoi has become more complex. The complexity could be de-
uarter is still the most important Centre of the City attracting a lot of businesses and
f trees along both sides.

0189

parts of Hanoi in very much poor conditions in terms of people's lives as well as infrastructure. There have been a lot of new urban developments started to fill up the gaps and to reduce density from the City center since then. However, due to unready infrastructure conditions in the new expansion areas, people still pull themselves into the city center to trade, work, and live. This has become a serious fact for a thousand year old capital. The Old Quarter is still the most important Centre of the City attracting a lot of businesses and trades as well as tourists, famous for its street activities within a human scaled street covered by two rows of trees along both sides.

The Tower is stemmed from an idea of bringing the horizontal density of Hanoi to a vertical living space and still reflecting all beautiful aspects of an Old Quarter and a busy city center. The Tower is expected to be a Happy Tower where people will live their lives with full of joys, experience good facilities and where tourists could come

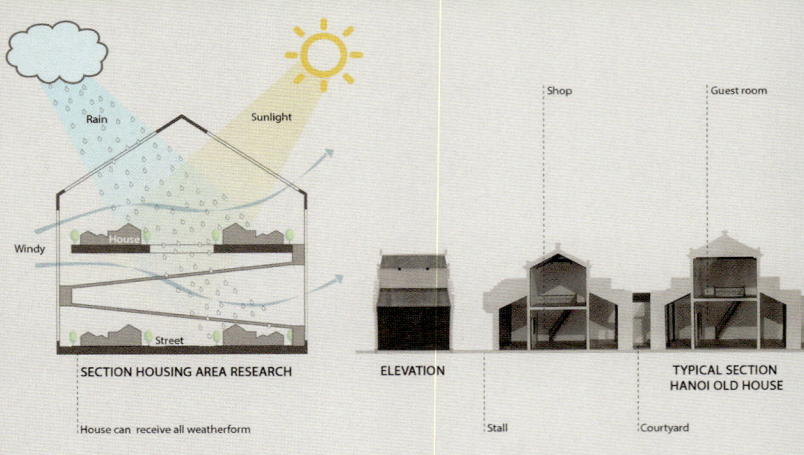

SECTION HOUSING AREA RESEARCH   ELEVATION   TYPICAL SECTION HANOI OLD HOUSE

House can receive all weatherform   Stall   Courtyard

A SMALL DISTRICT OF THE OLD QUARTER
It's not just a bland copy of Old Quarter's terrace or a construction with full facilities, it is also a place with profoundness, a dependable home for human relationship as well as the relationship between human and nature; to preserve and flourish cultures, lifestyles and habits that cumulated

EXPERIENCE BOX
Regenerative historical space
Create the habitat for animals
Serve visitors

PV FIBRE
as a cell of body
harvest energy from sun, rain
as chlorophyll of leaves,
absorb toxic air and regeneration fresh air

PLACES OF INTERESTS, WHERE VISITORS COME AND EXPERIENCE HI
They will find different atmosphere, different experiences starting from Prehistory, to French invasion period till the current status

FIBRE BOX: ACTIVITIES SERVICE FOR CUSTOMERS - REENACMENT TRAVEL HISTORY
An artificial environment was created, plants and animals here will be able to grow in the most natural way

Pure water
Pure Air
Heat energy
Green energy

Heat

Pure water   Heat energy   Energy
Pure Air   Energy tree

Tunnel connect all box and house area
Transporting energy provide for skyscraper from root to tip

AN OPEN PARK FOR PUBLIC AS THE BASE OF THE QUARTER
Attracting spontaneous visitors

and experience Hanoi's History through different eras. The Tower is also an ambition of future architecture, which is integrated with potential technologies to provide an uplifting sustainable living condition.

The Tower is a combination of modules, which reflect Hanoi urban density in a better way. Two types of modules are created: Experience and Residential. The Experience is distributed along the Tower right from ground level to the Top.

A great Core in the center connects all modules. This Core is not only for vertical transportation; it is where technologies are integrated in order to transform energy collected from the Experience's solar fiber and the residential cladded PV fibers. Besides, it could self-collect energy from the earth and ground water. In addition, modules also are connected by horizontal connections acting like pathways or water tubes.

0189

FUTURE

1986 - NOW

1945 - 1986

FRENCH PROTECTORATE (1884 - 1945)

LATE DYNASITIC EPOCH (939 - 1884)

THE LONG ECLIPSE: CHINESE MILLENNIUM
(11BC - 938AD)

EARLY DYNASTIC EPOCH (2879 - 11BC)

PREHISTORY

THE VALLEY OF THE GIANTS

Eric Randall Morris
Galo Canizares

United States

THE VALLEY OF THE GIANTS

2100 A.D.

Located north of Tindouf, Algeria, the Valley of the Giants is the largest oasis in Northern Africa. However, this was not always the case. In the early 21st century, the area was mostly dust. Water was scarce, and the only inhabitants were nomadic tribes like the Tuareg people. As global conflicts grew and their impact rippled over several continents, demand for refugee housing and temporary settlements increased in the area. Frustrated, the country's government decided that they needed to build something; a permanent solution to the temporal problems which kept piling up. They needed something that addressed the influx of immigrants, the desertification of the area, and changing cultural diversity; something beyond a quick-fix.

Architecture was the solution. But not a contingency plan; rather, a catalyst. The proposal was not to build temporary shelters or redesign a city from scratch, but instead to use infrastructure and ecology to jumpstart and augment already existing environmental and cultural systems. The concept was simple: a series of towers that would (1) house plant-spores, (2) produce, collect, and treat water, and (3) pollinate the surrounding landscape, catalyzing the production of an oasis in the region. The structures themselves had to be of an immense scale in order to effect significant change; thus they were designed as 1km tall, thin, cylinders. In addition to their independent functions, a new network of underground pipes was implemented to facilitate the creation of pools and wells. Within 20 years, the area would drastically transform from a barren landscape into the Valley of the Giants.

Today it is home to both permanent residents and traveling nomads. The oasis extends far to the base of the Anti Atlas Mountains in Morocco, and south to the city of Tindouf. The new urban development is a mixture of traditional Tuareg tents, permanent clay huts, and contemporary dwellings. Politics and social life have their ups and downs, but there hasn't been a major conflict in the area since the time before the Giants. The structures themselves are still functional. They tower over the villages like keepers of the land. Some communities have even invented their own stories of how the Giants came, suggesting a new mythology and awareness of these mysterious structures.

Located north of Tindouf, Algeria, the Valley of the Giants is the largest oasis in Northern Africa. However, this was not always the case. In the early 21st century, the area was mostly dust. Water was scarce, and the only inhabitants were nomadic tribes like the Tuareg people. As global conflicts grew and their impact rippled over several continents, demand for refugee housing and temporary settlements increased in the area.

    Frustrated, the country's government decided that they needed to build something; a permanent solution to the temporal problems which kept piling up. They needed something that addressed the influx of immigrants, the desertification of the area, and changing cultural diversity; something beyond a quick-fix.

0405

Architecture was the solution. But not a contingency plan; rather, a catalyst. The proposal was not to build temporary shelters or redesign a city from scratch, but instead to use infrastructure and ecology to jumpstart and augment already existing environmental and cultural systems. The concept was simple: a series of towers that would (1) house plant-spores, (2) produce, collect, and treat water, and (3) pollinate the surrounding landscape, catalyzing the production of an oasis in the region. The structures themselves had to be of an immense scale in order to effect significant change; thus they were designed as 1km tall, thin, cylinders. In addition to their independent functions, a new network of underground pipes was implemented to facilitate the creation of pools and wells. Within 20 years, the area would

drastically transform from a barren landscape into the Valley of the Giants.

Today it is home to both permanent residents and traveling nomads. The oasis extends far to the base of the Anti Atlas Mountains in Morocco, and south to the city of Tindouf. The new urban development is a mixture of traditional Tuareg tents, permanent clay huts, and contemporary dwellings. Politics and social life have their ups and downs, but there hasn't been a major conflict in the area since the time before the Giants. The structures themselves are still functional. They tower over the villages like keepers of the land. Some communities have even invented their own stories of how the Giants came, suggesting a new mythology and awareness of these mysterious structures.

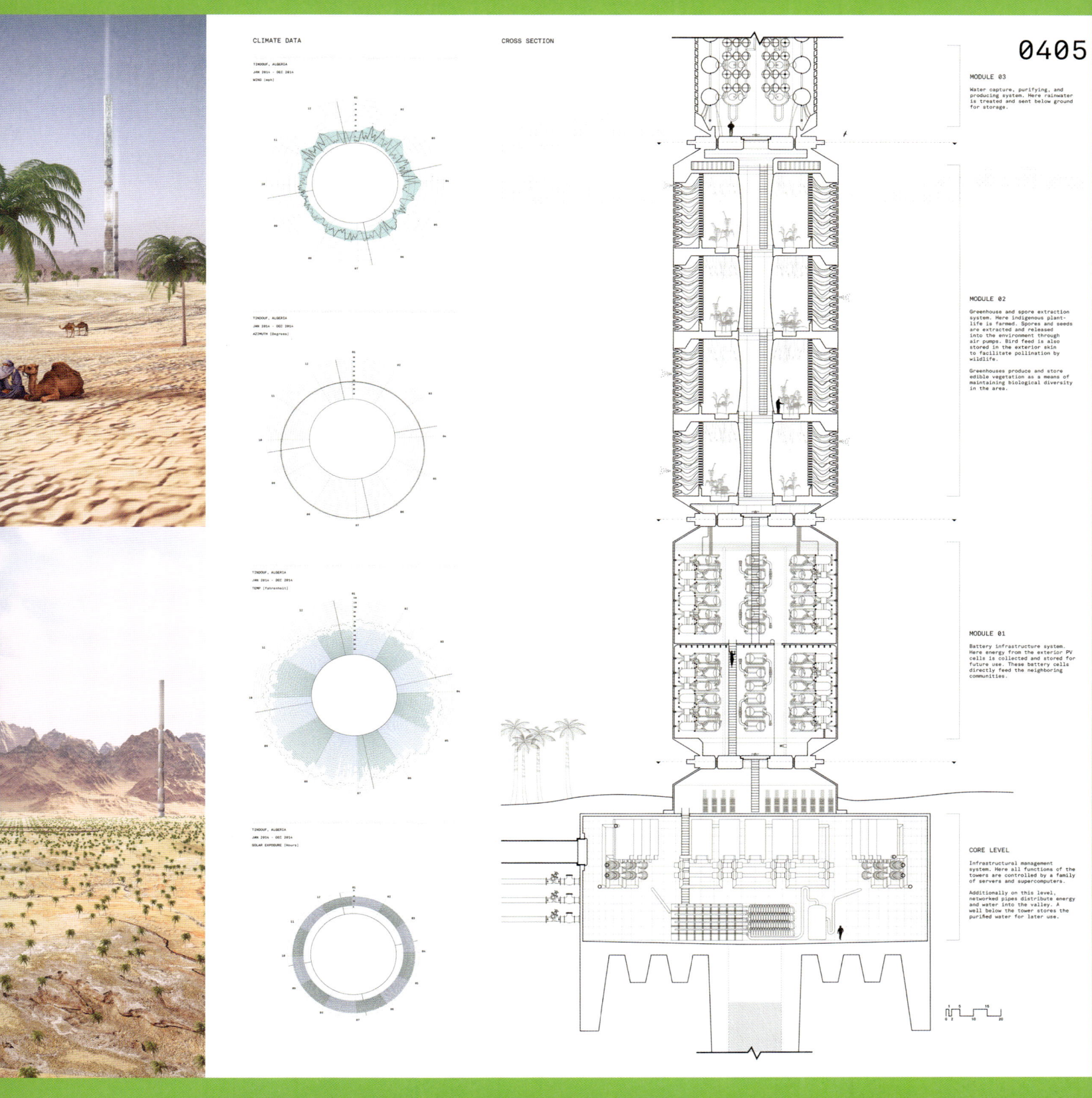

CLIMATE DATA

CROSS SECTION

0405

MODULE 03

Water capture, purifying, and producing system. Here rainwater is treated and sent below ground for storage.

MODULE 02

Greenhouse and spore extraction system. Here indigenous plant-life is farmed. Spores and seeds are extracted and released into the environment through air pumps. Bird feed is also stored in the exterior skin to facilitate pollination by wildlife.

Greenhouses produce and store edible vegetation as a means of maintaining biological diversity in the area.

MODULE 01

Battery infrastructure system. Here energy from the exterior PV cells is collected and stored for future use. These battery cells directly feed the neighboring communities.

CORE LEVEL

Infrastructural management system. Here all functions of the towers are controlled by a family of servers and supercomputers.

Additionally on this level, networked pipes distribute energy and water into the valley. A well below the tower stores the purified water for later use.

NOAH'S INDEX

Chua Lawrance
Ian Cheah
Victor Phoo

Malaysia

PROJECT NOAH'S INDEX NX

2030
Mega-cities in existence exceeded 50 numbers over a century. Over 2 billions of the world populations are living in slums now.

1930s

1930
Establishment of the first mega-city housing more than 8 millions of the population. The world has entered the great metropolitan era.

2050

2050
Discontent among urban dwellers raises the tension between different social status groups. Cities are falling into chaos; rebellions are rising in the slums; armed intervention started.

The degradation of the world's natural habitat and ecosystems has compromised the ability of nature to keep sustaining life. Given some of the examples of environmental issues such as overpopulation, urban sprawl, loss of diversity and habitat destruction, these aggravating factors of causing world destruction are so serious that none can be taken lightly. These environmental issues are the chained reactions of one and another and we cannot take any of this as a single event. Despite countermeasures are being introduced at different stages of any given crisis, the negative factors always weigh heavier on the scale than the resolution that is actually designed to control these crisis from worsening. In the history, establishment of mega-city has effectively tackled the rapid growth of population. Unfortunately, unplanned mega-cities rose in the last decades are turning into slums due to the lack of proper

0429 01

"Degradation"

The degradation of the world's natural habitat and ecosystems has compromised the ability of the nature to sustain life. Given some of the examples of environmental issues such as overpopulation, urban sprawl, loss of diversity and habitat destruction, these aggravating factors of causing world destruction are so serious that none can be taken lightly. These environmental issues are the chained reactions of one and another and we cannot take any of this as a single event.

"Loss of biodiversity; extinction"

In order to break the cycle of the issue, our team has studied the timeline and envisioned what will happen in the future if those aforementioned issues are not being addressed and solved appropriately and immediately. Albert Einstein once quoted, 'Mankind will not survive the honeybees' disappearance for more than five years'. Therefore, we strongly believe that uncontrolled urban sprawl will eventually lead to the loss of biodiversity and if this remains unmanaged, it will be the most devastating crisis causing extinction in the future.

"Into the future"

By understanding the importance of the biodiversity, we divert from the predicted timeline to initiate our proposal - Project Noah's Index(NX) which will house the genes of the nature and become a breeding bed and hope for the dying future. The concept of the project derives from the story of Noah's Ark on how prevention and salvation can be achieved. Our objectives are to enlist, preserve, and regenerate the biodiversity through the establishment of the project to serve as a genetic chamber for the future.

"Concept & idea"

The concept of the project derives from the story of Noah's Ark on how disastrous natural phenomenons can be prevented and salvation can be achieved. Our project will serve as the ark for both mankind and the nature to sail forward a better future. Through the establishments of the project, our objectives are to enlist, preserve, and regenerate the biodiversity to serve as a genetic chamber for the future.

infrastructures and other social factors. These issues will soon lead to breeds discontent among urban dwellers, leading to high crime rates. In our opinion, expansion and establishment of mega-cities still fail to accommodate the rising population and causes more urban sprawls. By understanding the importance of the biodiversity, we divert from the predicted timeline to initiate our proposal - Project Noah's Index (NX) which will house the genes of the nature and become a breeding bed and hope for the dying future. The concept of the project derives from the story of Noah's Ark on how prevention and salvation can be achieved. Our objectives are to enlist, preserve, and regenerate the biodiversity through the establishment of the project to serve as a genetic chamber for the future.

Project NX will consist of full-fledged R&D towers located at different sites away from the population.

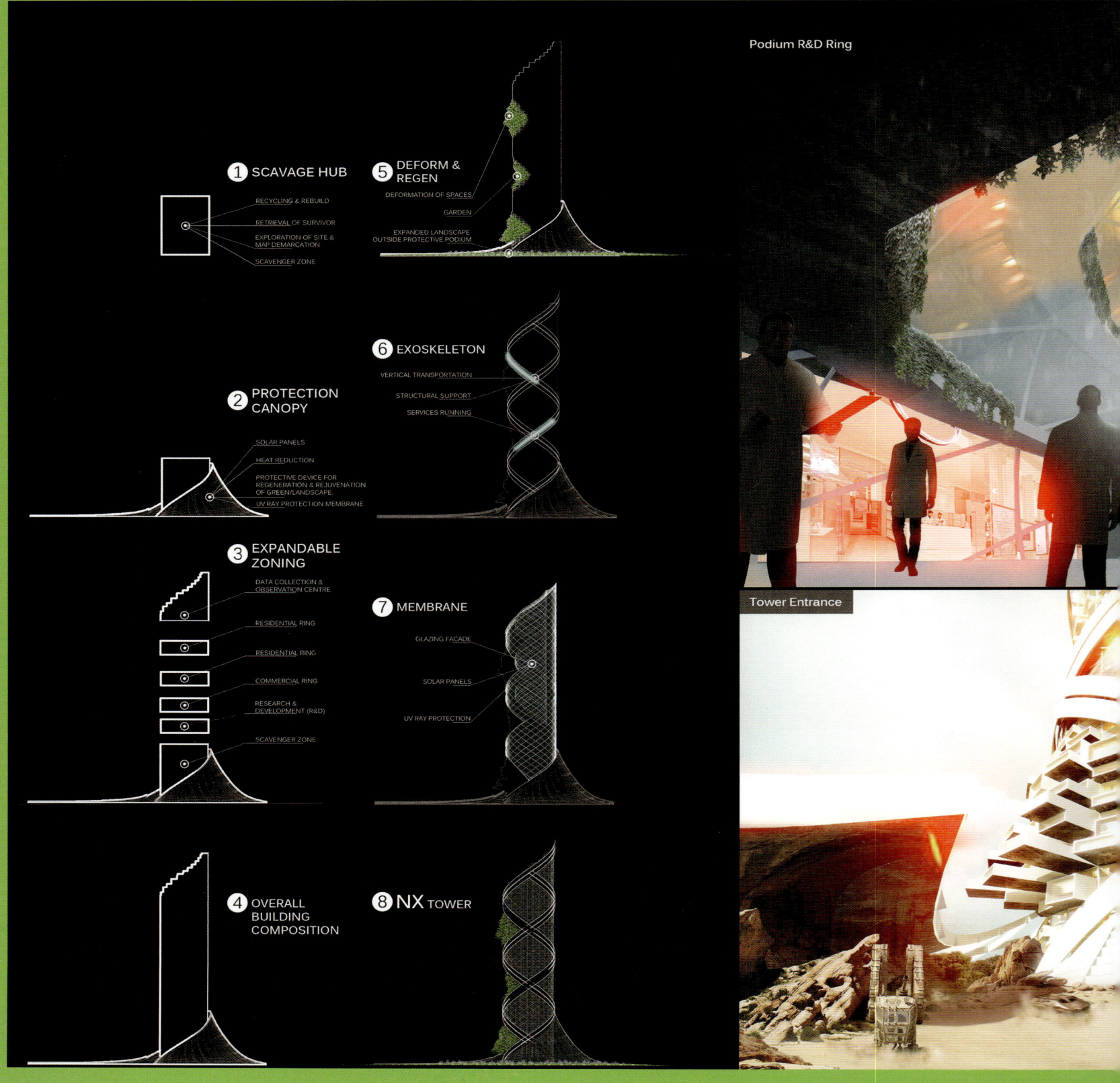

Isolated and barren lands are potentially the best sites to explore the full potential of the project. Each site will establish their unique set of program based on the respective site condition; the standard sequence will always include but not limited to expedition, sampling, research, restoration, and lastly, regeneration. Through the program, the tower will be reactivating and transforming the barren land into a green oasis. The towers will house both R&D labs as well as the technical facilities required to restore the environment. Should any of the predicted future happened; the residential rings on the higher levels will eventually serve as the new refuge shelter for mankind. Project NX will be the legacy from the story, executing the duty in a larger scale with the capability to capture all the genetic codes, hence the name, Index.

0429 02

Inner Canopy Regenerated Green

THE URBAN VILLAGE

Kuwalsanam Chintala

India

THE URBAN VILLAGE
CELEBRATION OF FOOD WITH CELEBRATION OF LIFESTYLE
The project explores the idea of a **self sustaining** agrarian village in the midst of the hybrid urban context.

ANALYSIS

- 1998
- 2014
- 2031

Development trend and polpulation growth in Mumbai over the yeas.

Food Distribution markets In Mumbai Mapped Along The Railways Network

The above diagrams show the areas with the major strain in each wards and its impact area for food availability in mumbai.

PLANTING, MANAGEMENT, HARVESTING — PRODUCTION — PROCESSING — WASHING, DRYING, CANNING, FREEZING

COMPOSTING, REUSE — WASTE MGNT — DISTRIBUTION — STORAGE, LOGISTICS, TRUCKING, RAIL, SHIP

COOKING, MEALS, SLOW FOOD, EVENTS — CONSUMPTION — MARKETING — FARMERS MARKET, COOPS, RETAIL, DIRECT, PANTRIES

FOOD SYSTEM

FOOD SYSTEM'S RELATION TO OTHER PROGRAMS

FESTIVALS, PUBLIC TRANSPORTATION, RECREATION, MUNICIPAL UTILITIES, REGIN, DINING, EDUCATION, BICYCLE COMMUTING, WORK, RECYCLING

DESIGN DETAIL CONSTRUCTION:

SERVICE SYSTEM

Edible facade which changes with the consumption of the food the building takes

max height 40 mtrs

HARVESTING FLOOR

HARVESTING BINS AND GERMINATION TRAY

Section Showing Facade Farm : Vertically Integrated Green

CABLE GUIDES ON OUTER CURTAIN

SWIVEL CLAMP

NFT TRAY WITH HOLES FOR PLANTS

FACADE DETAILS: Vertical farming details

plants add moisture and warmer, fresh humidified air enters offices

hotter air is exhausted to exterior

plant rows adjusted so sunlight cannot penetrate into the building

plant rows adjusted to allow sunlight to penetrate

fresh air

plants shade interior

evapotranspiration of plant cools air

Act as thermal buffer

Summer operation - Sunny, warm and dry day

Winter operation - cold, sunny dry day

INTERACTIONS BETWEEN FACADE FARM AND HVAC OPERATION

LIFESTYLE

SUBSIDARY PROGRAM

FARMERS MARKET / AFFORDABLE PRODUCE MARKETS / FOOD DISTRIBUTION CENTERS

PRODUCTION — PROCESSI

WASTE MGMT — DISTRIBU

HEALTHY FOOD ACCESS — FOOD SYSTEM

CONSUMPTION — MARKETI

FOOD BANK / DROP IN MEALS — FOOD SKILLS

COMMUNITY GARDENS
COMMUNITY KITCHENS   SYSTEMS EDUCATIO

PLAY

Main Food Loop: The main food sys the subsidary programs all confined with work and play

CONCEPTUAL DEVELOPM
Each and every program has specific fo tribution centers are placed in the cente efficiently throughout the structure. The then distributed throughout the city from

ELEVATI

The design proposal was inspired by an additive system of the self-sustaining village, which fulfills the urban needs of a scarce food resource. The vertical urban village aims on sustaining the parasitical food system of the city along with providing a healthier lifestyle amidst social and cultural interactions into a productive driven form for the mundane and hectic urban city life. The proposal uses architecture as a possibility of solving major concerns and problems in the world. The design is an intervention within the urban environment investigating the relationship between the alimentary, architecture, and urbanism. Since cities are biggest consumer of food. Lack of productive land, food insecurity, uncontrolled urban growth, unstable food market, and a general lack of knowledge of food growing and preparations have become primary food issues. The design integrates live work play with alimentary into the activities of a

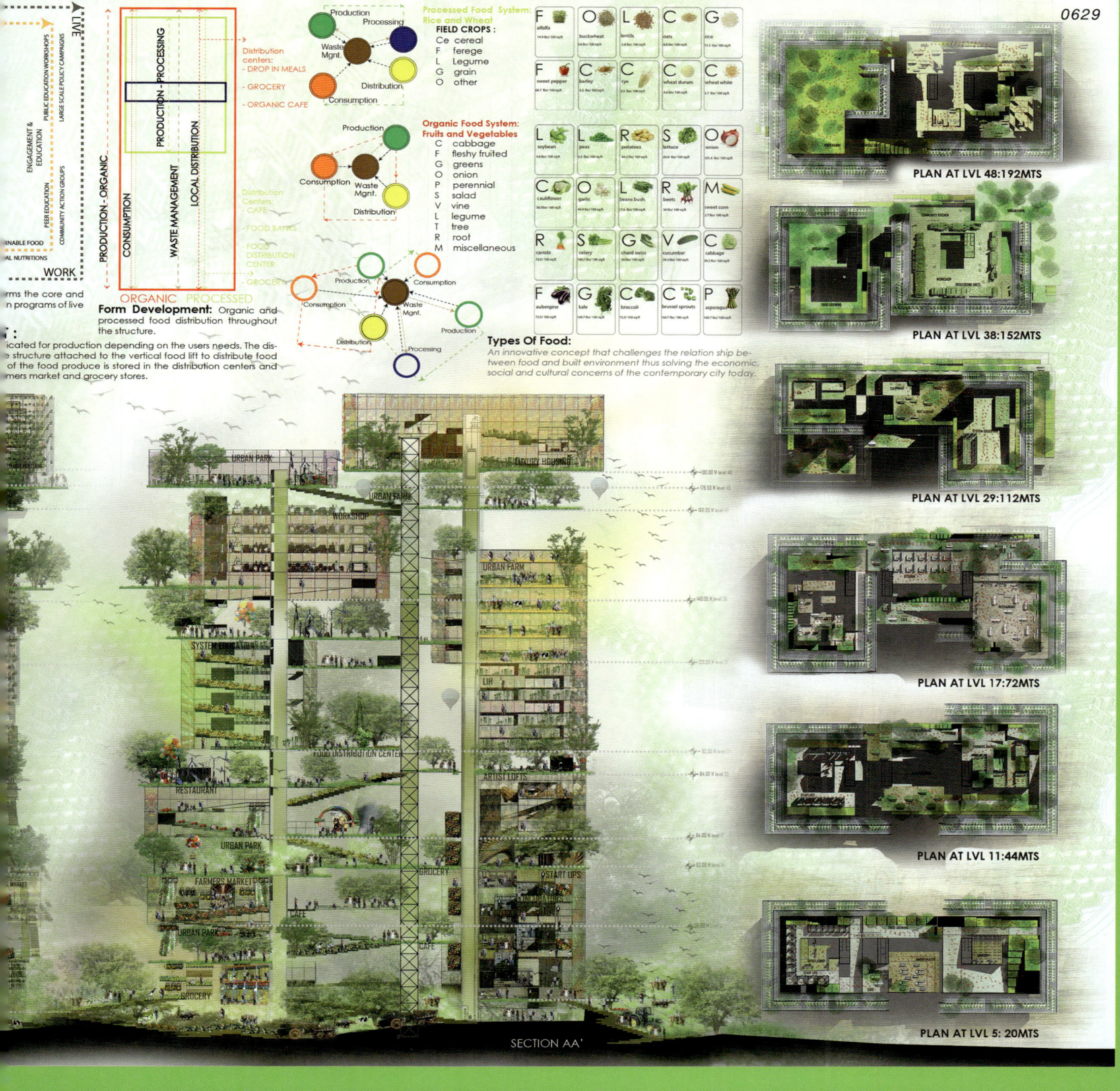

productive landscape. The site is located on an abandoned mill land, key area of urban growth straining the existing food system in Mumbai city.

The design intends to communicate, educate and provide an economically favorable environment for urban agriculture integrated with the healthier lifestyle of people. The strategy led to use the parameters of the food system from farming + harvesting, post-harvesting handling, processing + warehouse, retailers + distributors, consumers, to waste management as the main driver for the generation of the form and develop seamless integration with the city pattern with food efficiency into architecture. The Urban Village refers to a dynamic system having input and output within a loop of constant feedback. Thus becomes a central element representing the culture of the city. Based on various calculations on

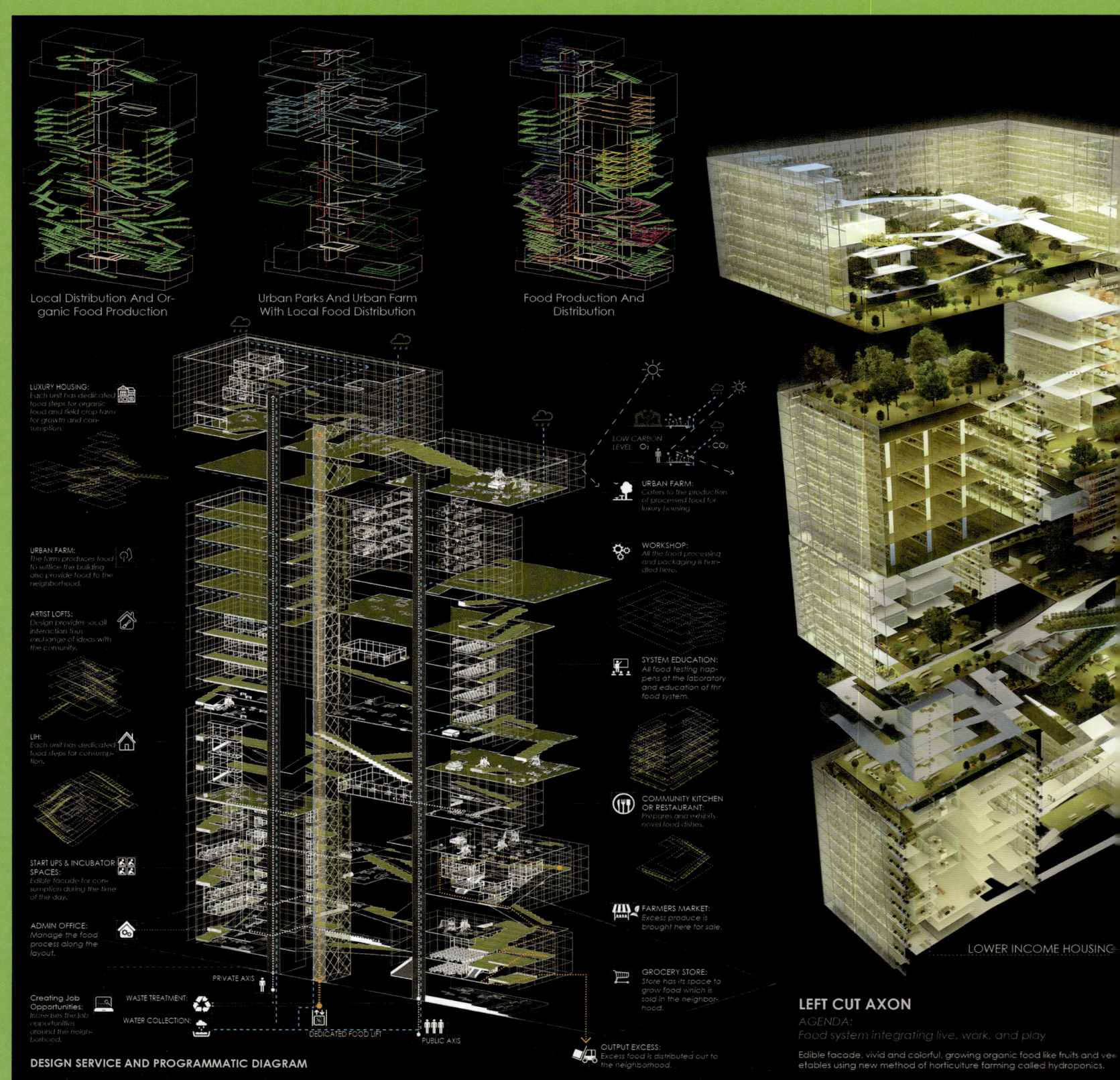

Local Distribution And Organic Food Production

Urban Parks And Urban Farm With Local Food Distribution

Food Production And Distribution

LUXURY HOUSING:
Each unit has dedicated food steps for organic food and field crop farm for growth and consumption.

URBAN FARM:
The farm produces food to suffice the building also provide food to the neighborhood.

ARTIST LOFTS:
Design provides social interaction thus exchange of ideas with the community.

LIH:
Each unit has dedicated food steps for consumption.

START UPS & INCUBATOR SPACES:
Edible facade for consumption during the time of the day.

ADMIN OFFICE:
Manage the food process along the layout.

Creating Job Opportunities:
Increases the job opportunities around the neighborhood.

WASTE TREATMENT:

WATER COLLECTION:

PRIVATE AXIS

DEDICATED FOOD LIFT

PUBLIC AXIS

LOW CARBON LEVEL O₂   CO₂

URBAN FARM:
Caters to the production of processed food for luxury housing

WORKSHOP:
All the food processing and packaging is handled here.

SYSTEM EDUCATION:
All food testing happens at the laboratory and education of the food system.

COMMUNITY KITCHEN OR RESTAURANT:
Prepares and exhibits novel food dishes.

FARMERS MARKET:
Excess produce is brought here for sale.

GROCERY STORE:
Store has its space to grow food which is sold in the neighborhood.

OUTPUT EXCESS:
Excess food it distributed out to the neighborhood.

DESIGN SERVICE AND PROGRAMMATIC DIAGRAM

LOWER INCOME HOUSING

LEFT CUT AXON

AGENDA:
Food system integrating live, work, and play

Edible facade, vivid and colorful, growing organic food like fruits and vegetables using new method of horticulture farming called hydroponics.

the available area production land and taking an average of the food consumed by the designed 10 percent of the produce remains surplus to be distributed thus becoming an additive living. The design integrates edible facade, vivid and colorful, growing organic food like fruits and vegetables using novel method of horticulture farming called hydroponics. Each and every program has specific food space dedicated for production depending on the user's needs. The distribution centers are placed in the center of the structure attached to the vertical food lift to distribute food efficiently throughout the structure. The excess of the food produce is stored in the distribution centers and then distributed throughout the city from the farmers market and grocery stores.

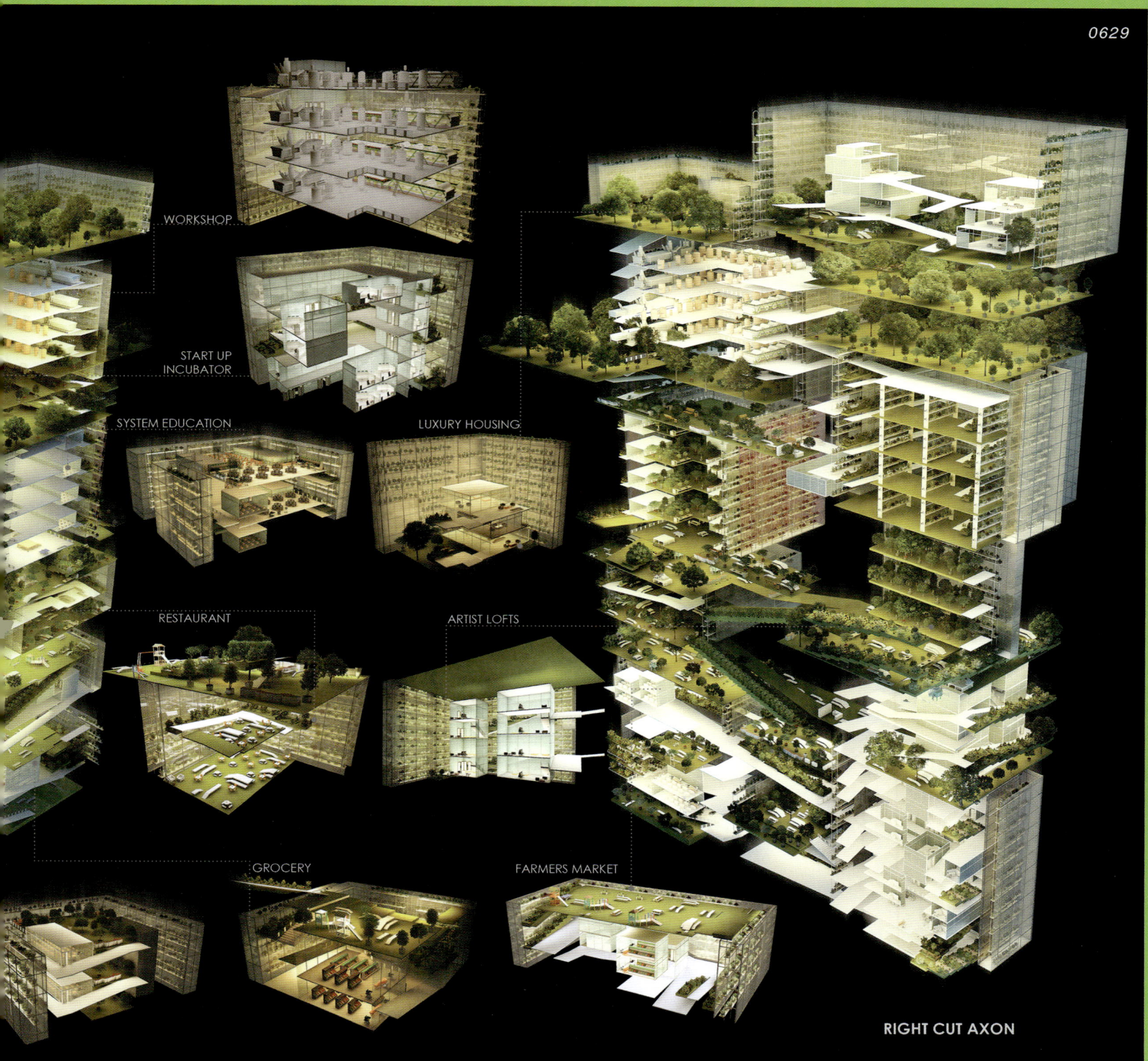

0629

WORKSHOP

START UP INCUBATOR

SYSTEM EDUCATION

LUXURY HOUSING

RESTAURANT

ARTIST LOFTS

GROCERY

FARMERS MARKET

RIGHT CUT AXON

FOOD BECOMING POWERFUL ELEMENT OF SOCIAL INTERACTION, ALONG WITH ENHANCING THE ECONOMIC AND CULTURAL GROWTH OF THE CONTEMPORARY CITY.

OASIS

Soyeon Park
Sukyung Kim

South Korea

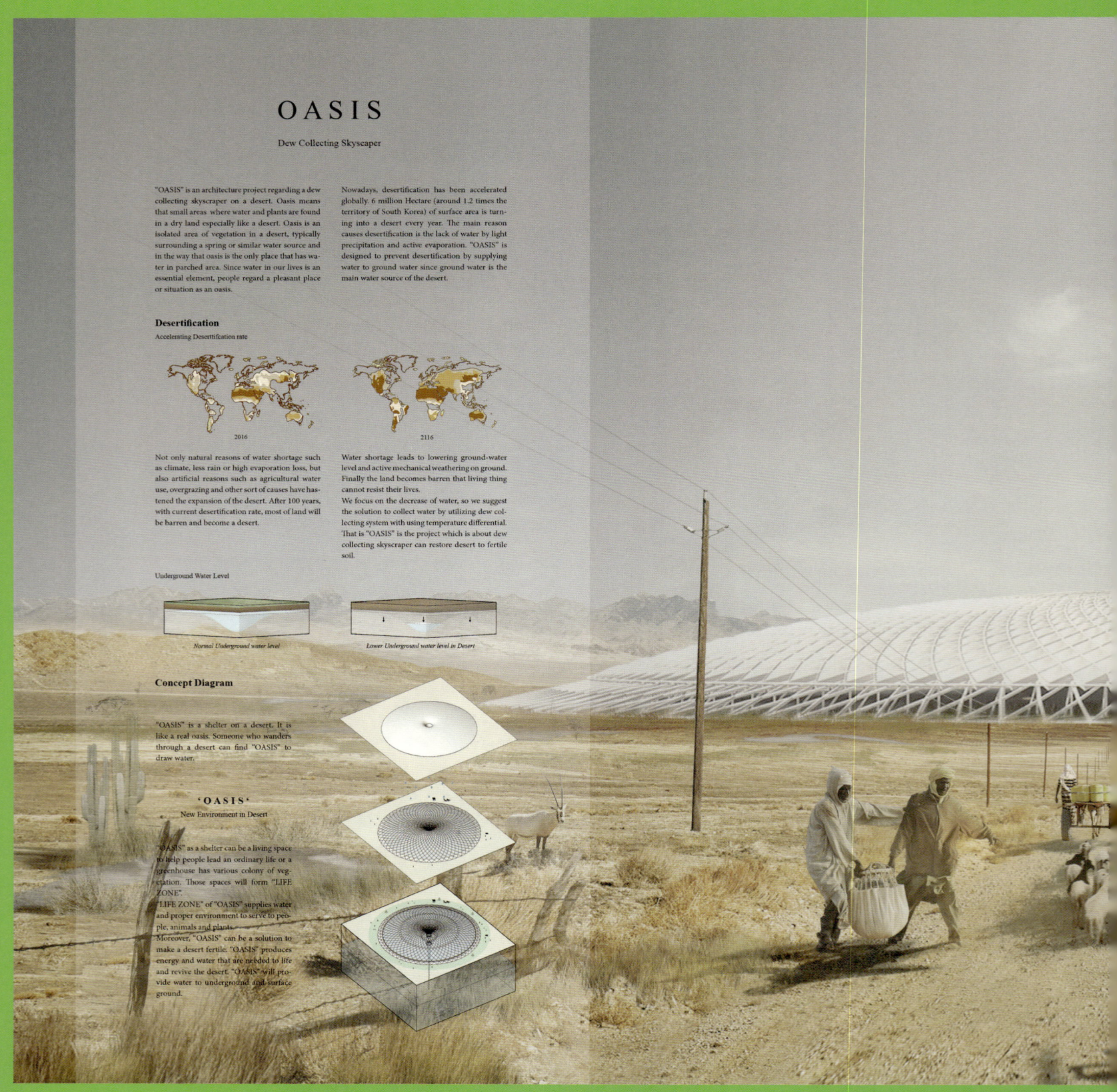

OASIS

Dew Collecting Skyscaper

"OASIS" is an architecture project regarding a dew collecting skyscraper on a desert. Oasis means that small areas where water and plants are found in a dry land especially like a desert. Oasis is an isolated area of vegetation in a desert, typically surrounding a spring or similar water source and in the way that oasis is the only place that has water in parched area. Since water in our lives is an essential element, people regard a pleasant place or situation as an oasis.

Nowadays, desertification has been accelerated globally. 6 million Hectare (around 1.2 times the territory of South Korea) of surface area is turning into a desert every year. The main reason causes desertification is the lack of water by light precipitation and active evaporation. "OASIS" is designed to prevent desertification by supplying water to ground water since ground water is the main water source of the desert.

Desertification

Accelerating Desertification rate

2016

2116

Not only natural reasons of water shortage such as climate, less rain or high evaporation loss, but also artificial reasons such as agricultural water use, overgrazing and other sort of causes have hastened the expansion of the desert. After 100 years, with current desertification rate, most of land will be barren and become a desert.

Water shortage leads to lowering ground-water level and active mechanical weathering on ground. Finally the land becomes barren that living thing cannot resist their lives.
We focus on the decrease of water, so we suggest the solution to collect water by utilizing dew collecting system with using temperature differential. That is "OASIS" is the project which is about dew collecting skyscraper can restore desert to fertile soil.

Underground Water Level

Normal Underground water level

Lower Underground water level in Desert

Concept Diagram

"OASIS" is a shelter on a desert. It is like a real oasis. Someone who wanders through a desert can find "OASIS" to draw water.

'OASIS'
New Environment in Desert

"OASIS" as a shelter can be a living space to help people lead an ordinary life or a greenhouse has various colony of vegetation. Those spaces will form "LIFE ZONE".
"LIFE ZONE" of "OASIS" supplies water and proper environment to serve to people, animals and plants.
Moreover, "OASIS" can be a solution to make a desert fertile. "OASIS" produces energy and water that are needed to life and revive the desert. "OASIS" will provide water to underground and surface ground.

Oasis is an architecture project regarding a dew-collecting skyscraper on a desert. Oasis means that small areas where water and plants are found in a dry land especially like a desert. Oasis is an isolated area of vegetation in a desert, typically surrounding a spring or similar water source and in the way that oasis is the only place that has water in parched area. Since water in our lives is an essential element, people regard a pleasant place or situation as an oasis.

Oasis is a shelter on a desert. It is like a real oasis. Someone who wanders through a desert can find Oasis to draw water.

Oasis as a shelter can be a living space to help people lead an ordinary life or a greenhouse has various colony of vegetation. Those spaces will form life zone. Moreover, Oasis can be a solution to make a

0684

desert fertile. Oasis produces energy and water that are needed to life and revive the desert. Oasis will provide water to underground and surface ground. The water will be provided to underground, surface and the Life Zonethat has 3 kinds of terrestrial community. Three kinds of Life Zones are the Savanna area, the Forest area and the Human area.

Originally, dew is water in the form of droplets that appears on thin, exposed objects in the early morning or evening due to condensation. As the exposed surface cooled by radiating its heat, atmospheric moisture condenses resulting in the formation of water droplets.

These units constitute the whole system of Oasis Each unit operates to produce the dew and keep proper temperature of this architecture. The water made from this panel system is collected at center

place continuously.

At first, the vapor in the air is captured by Oasis multi-panel system by utilizing temperature differential. The water is produced to prevent desertification.

In the second place, the water generated from the air is collected and used at Life Zone Inner space of Oasis can be hospitable to life. Also the water gathered from fine pipe lines store the central water tank.

Finally, the water is stored the central water tank of Oasis and then the water is transported to ground water. The ground water level will be higher gradually. Eventually, the ground will be fertile and have natural power.

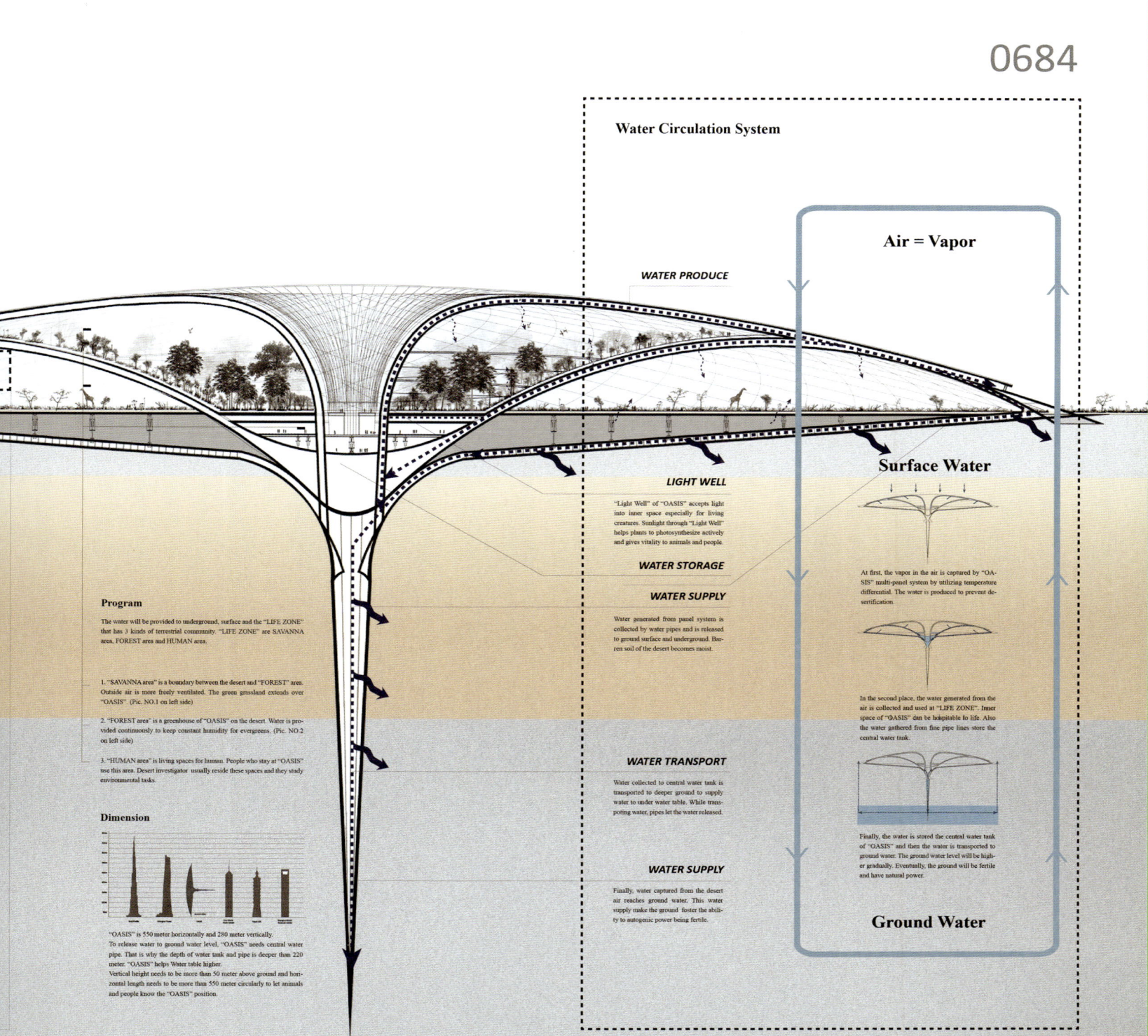

0684

Water Circulation System

Air = Vapor

WATER PRODUCE

Surface Water

LIGHT WELL

"Light Well" of "OASIS" accepts light into inner space especially for living creatures. Sunlight through "Light Well" helps plants to photosynthesize actively and gives vitality to animals and people.

At first, the vapor in the air is captured by "OA-SIS" multi-panel system by utilizing temperature differential. The water is produced to prevent desertification.

WATER STORAGE

WATER SUPPLY

Water generated from panel system is collected by water pipes and is released to ground surface and underground. Barren soil of the desert becomes moist.

In the second place, the water generated from the air is collected and used at "LIFE ZONE". Inner space of "OASIS" dan to hospitable to life. Also the water gathered from fine pipe lines store the central water tank.

Program

The water will be provided to underground, surface and the "LIFE ZONE" that has 3 kinds of terrestrial community. "LIFE ZONE" are SAVANNA area, FOREST area and HUMAN area.

1. "SAVANNA area" is a boundary between the desert and "FOREST" area. Outside air is more freely ventilated. The green grassland extends over "OASIS". (Pic. NO.1 on left side)

2. "FOREST area" is a greenhouse of "OASIS" on the desert. Water is provided continuously to keep constant humidity for evergreens. (Pic. NO.2 on left side)

3. "HUMAN area" is living spaces for human. People who stay at "OASIS" use this area. Desert investigator usually reside these spaces and they study environmental tasks.

WATER TRANSPORT

Water collected to central water tank is transported to deeper ground to supply water to under water table. While transporting water, pipes let the water released.

Finally, the water is stored the central water tank of "OASIS" and then the water is transported to ground water. The ground water level will be higher gradually. Eventually, the ground will be fertile and have natural power.

Dimension

"OASIS" is 550 meter horizontally and 280 meter vertically. To release water to ground water level, "OASIS" needs central water pipe. That is why the depth of water tank and pipe is deeper than 220 meter. "OASIS" helps Water table higher. Vertical height needs to be more than 50 meter above ground and horizontal length needs to be more than 550 meter circularly to let animals and people know the "OASIS" position.

WATER SUPPLY

Finally, water captured from the desert air reaches ground water. This water supply make the ground foster the ability to autogenic power being fertile.

Ground Water

BABEL
SKYSCRAPER

Nathakit Sae-Tan
Prapatsorn Sukkaset

Thailand

This is an imaginary future, where resources of nature have been used and reclaimed exhaustively by the greed of man to the point of irreversible damage. Spanning across the landscape by human intervention, until there is no more nature left for the upcoming generations to see. In those days where the impermanence of concrete can not withstand the true forces of nature, the solid ground is soon to be covered by earth, minerals and eventually the green, growing on top are the woods that would stem deep and span miles and miles, beyond the imagination of mankind. We build these super structures that would spread throughout the city, as if they were grains of seeds that would uncontrollably grow, taking back what was once theirs.

0691

EXPERIMENTAL SITE SELECTION

CONCEPTUAL INTERPRETATION

MAIN ROUTES CONNECTING PARTS OF BANGKOK

IRRIGATION NETWORK

GREEN AREA

EXPERIMENTAL SITE POSSIBILITIES/
CRITERIA: CLOSED TO COMMUNITIES & WATERSOURCE

NETWORK OF WATER IS FORMED CONNECTING THE ARCHITECTURE

THE SPREAD OF FORESTRY AREA FROM THE CITY, BACK TOWARDS THE EXISTING GREEN

FORM STUDY

INSPIRED BY HOW WE SEE THE MOUNTAIN AS ARCHITECTURE, THE FORM OF MOUNTAIN IS INTEGRATED WITH THE UPDRAFT TOWER, BY PULLING THE FORM VERTICALLY UPWARD; THE GREEN EVENTUALLY GROWING FROM THE BASE, CLIMBING UP TOWARDS THE PEAK.

SKYSCRAPPER PHASES

TIME-BASED ARCHITECTURE

During the prior phases, the architecture only contains the mountain-shaped base and vertical columns, which would eventually grow into some kind of Eden, a relaxing park and food bank, for the organic vegetables and rice. The architecture itself is time-based and would change dramatically through the years.

GROWTH TIMELINE

PHASE I   PHASE II   PHASE III   PHASE IV

VEGETABLE FOOD BANK

RECREATIONAL PARK

VERTICAL LIVING

HABITANTS TRAVEL TO THEIR UNITS BY DRONES

When the forces of nature is too strong for men to resist, we would have to learn how to cope with nature in order to co-exist with the earth, occupying less surface on ground as much as possible, tall vertical super structure is the proposed solution. The Babel skyscraper can accommodate food security and living space for both nature and human. To achieve this, the architecture is designed with a concept of the emergence twisting parametric mountain, seamlessly flow with the geometric skyscraper. The building is designed with only floors to provide the vertical spaces; with open plan and inside void, providing ventilation. The Babel skyscraper is located in many sites around Bangkok. People visiting and living there will once again experience the natural habitat; bringing back the intimate bond we once have being so close to nature. The homogenizing of concrete landscape had us forgotten our relationship

01 WETLAND ENTRACE

02 INSIDE VOID

03 ROOF TOP

04 FARMING/ VEGETATION

05 DRONE TRASPORTING

06 LOBBY

07 HABITANTS

with nature. This future is to re-imagine these connections and visualize them. This connection would also form a more intimate symbiotic relationship between nature and humans. During the first phases, the architecture only contains the mountain-shaped base and vertical columns, which would eventually grow into an Eden, a relaxing park and food bank, for the organic vegetables and rice. The architecture itself is time-based and would change dramatically through the years. And in the times where human can no longer walk the earth, this skyscraper is where humans can depend on as inhabitants, traveling up and down by drones, a technology of the future, which we foresee. This set of skyscrapers would be a symbol for the cruelty we've done to nature, and what we have to pay back; including how human should adapt in order to survive.

05

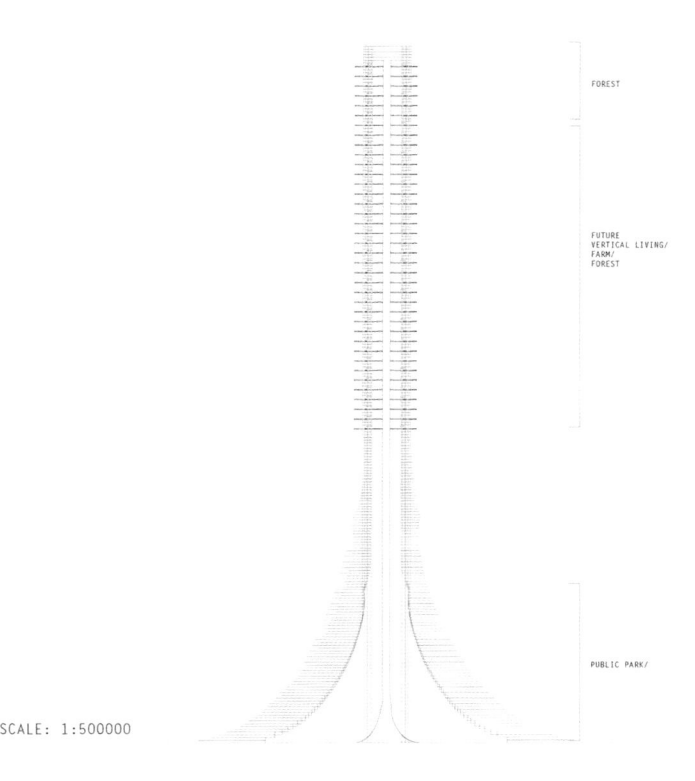

0691

MASTER PLAN
EXPERIMENTAL SITE A
13°44'53.1"N 100°29'41.7"E

FOREST

FUTURE
VERTICAL LIVING/
FARM/
FOREST

PUBLIC PARK/

SCALE: 1:500000

BABEL

In the imagined future, where we plant structures that would spread out the green throughout the city, as if they were grains of seeds that would uncontrollably grow, taking back what was once theirs, resources of land has been used extensively by the greed of man, spanning across human intervention until there is no more land left for the upcoming generations to reclaim. In those days where the impermanence of concrete can not withstand the true forces of nature, the solid ground is soon to be covered by earth, minerals and eventually the green, growing on top are the woods that would stem deep and span miles and miles, beyond the imagination of mankind.

Here, we design skyscrapers, with nature as the main user and human as parasites of the planet, struggling to survive and camouflage, living towards the very end of the race.

06

07

THE KITE

Andreev Dmitriy
Maximov Ivan
Elitsa Stephanie

Russia

Every year a tornado takes hundreds of lives and causes billions of dollars in usher. Every year, these figures become larger. Even though humanity cannot prevent the appearance of the elements, but it can control it. One of the reasons of this disaster is global warming, wich affects opposite phases of what is known as the El Niño-Southern Oscillation (ENSO) cycle. The ENSO cycle is a scientific term that describes the fluctuations in temperature between the ocean and atmosphere in the east-central Equatorial Pacific (approximately between the International Date Line and 120 degrees West).

La Niña is sometimes referred to as the cold phase of ENSO and El Niño as the warm phase of ENSO. These deviations from normal surface temperatures can have large-scale impacts not only on ocean processes, but also on global weather and climate. These fluctuations are the reason of

0785

THE KITE

Every year a tornado takes hundreds of lives and causes billions of dollars in uscher. Every year, these figures become larger. Even though humanity can not prevent the appearance of the elements, but it can control it.

Tornadoes. The research showed that ENSO affects tornado and hailstorm frequency by influencing the position of the jet stream over North America. El Niño weakens the surface winds that carry warm, most air from the Gulf of Mexico over Texas and neighboring states. La Niña, in contrast, concentrates hot, humid air over the region. The heat and humidity over the southern Plains states sets up a strong north-south temperature gradient, which in turn favors storm formation. For the most people this problem might sound unfamiliar, it is because of concentration of the storm in a specific areas.

    The key principle of system performance is a progressive motion of a sail resisting the wind subject to its direction. Restraining guy roosts are electromagnets levitating over a electromagnetic platform. The electromagnet structure is underground.

KITE MODE

THE REASONS

I. GLOBAL WARMING → II. LA NINO EL NINO VIOLATION

LA NIÑA

EL NIÑO

III. TORNADO BECOMES STRONGER

PER YEAR

500 - 3000 of lives

10 - 200 blns$

600 - 4000 sq. km

LOCATION

USA. 1000 sq. miles of Tornado valley.

Tornado Alley is a colloquial term for the area of the United States where tornadoes are most frequent. Although the boundaries of Tornado Alley are not clearly defined, its core extends from northern Texas, Oklahoma, Kansas, into Nebraska.

TIMELINE

The Kite — Stable mode

Strong winds / Weak winds — Cyclone appearance

Spinning along horizontal axis / Updraft — Tornado swirl flow

Extremum — Setting the sail from the extremum

Setting the sail / Extremum — Tornado appearance

Kite mode

Sail destructing the tornado

Tornade dissipation

The structural element subjected to the incoming airflow is activated like a kite. The scale is a architectural element of a building cluster of 150 x 150 meters. The colossal area of the structure allows for generation of clean energy by oscillating harmonic motions. Motion interference from edges to the center and backwards allows for the use of perpetual motion.

CALM MODE

0785

Sailing boat
The key principle of system performance is a progressive motion of a sail resisting the wind subject to its direction.

Hoverboard
Restraining guy roosts are electromagnets levitating over a electromagnetic platform. The electromagnet structure is underground.

Flap
The structural element subjected to the incoming air flow is activated like a kite.

Master grid
The scale is a architectural element of a building cluster of 150 x 150 meters.

Stingray
The colossal area of the structure allows for generation of clean energy by oscillating harmonic motions.

Kite
Motion interference from edges to the center and backwards allows for the use of perpetual motion. The fundamental architectural character.

Nanometal
The most durable and flexible strain/compression-resistant material.

MECHANICS LOCAL

FORM GLOBAL

STRUCTURE LOCAL

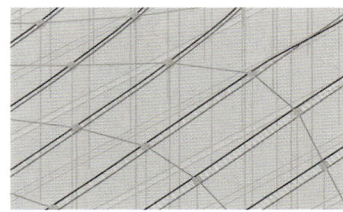

ABSORBER SKYSCRAPER

Na Sangho
Kim Mingyun
Lim Hyunjun

South Korea

Human Catastrophe

Think again about Human catastrophe in detail, it is that 'huge group of people' lose home and are propelled into 'narrow space' by the disaster mentioned above. The most worried and terrible thing of Natural disasters or wars, terrorism is secondary disaster, Human catastrophe. It eliminates house that people live in stable, makes the refugees and even threaten other people living commonplace. And then the group of homeless might stay in narrow area, it could be changed to slum and there would exist a criminal who exploited the panic situation. These people are massive, get panicked and they are moving constantly to find a place to survive.

1)Massive group of people
2)Unpredictable direction of refugees.
This Human Catastrophe with two features is going to occur over and over again,
so it is duty of our humanity to prepare for this Catastrophe.

DISASTER   PANIC   OUT OF CONTROL   CRIME / ECONOMIC CRISIS / VIOLATION / ANARCHY

Substitute to Law of conservation of motion

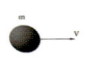  

Momentum =mV   Stick together at inelastic collision situation   Momentum=(M+m)v

PROCESS OF INELASTIC COLLISION

So we tried to substitute the two features (Massive group of people, Unpredictable direction of refugees) for 'momentum' which used in physics. The momentum is expressed by the mass(m) and velocity(v). Let's substitute 'Massive group of refugees' for 'm' and 'Moving velocity to find new home' for 'v'. Then refugees(Human Catastrophe) can be considered the momentum mv, and our mission is to make the momentum as close to zero causing various problems. But since the momentum with refugees is preserved by the law of conservation of motion, it should share the momentum by the collision with other objects. Also we need to make velocity almost zero because of its large mass. So we need some building which have large mass that can take in refugee's momentum. And that will be an inelastic collision. However, this building is followed by a number of constraints.

Constraints

First, the building is not only simply increases the mass. If the building expands widely, we should use the large space for unpredictable disasters. Besides, it could make large area to slum. So we have first constraints that the building must have not only small space but also large mass.

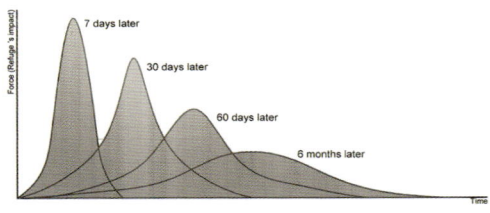

7 days later
30 days later
60 days later
6 months later

We must also not only consider the momentum but also 'time'(t). Human Catastrophe doesn't occur gradually It is massive momentum that occurs by sudden disaster. In physics, momentum is equal to the impulse that multiplication of Force (F) and Time (t). Momentum generated in a short time has a huge Force. So we defined again momentum to impulse. The influence by refugees occurred can be defined F and the time that stay in the building can be defined t. If refugee occur and come to the building, it must receive the Force (F) at one time. As time goes by, let the people who become stable get out, then the Force is reduced and the building can get smaller gradually. Likewise, building performs a little task usual time. And it needs to get biggerin short time to receive refugee's impact also needs to get smaller gradually when they become stable.

B-2

C-1

ABS
HANDLING 1

Three years old child who died alone at the beach, woman who becomes broker's se
Lately Syrian refugee crisis have been showing a num
The refugee is a secondary disaster after primary disaster
The secondary disaster is like a refugee, over population expansion of slum wi

Three years old child who died alone at the beach, woman who becomes broker's sexual slave because of her husband's immigration, the wire barrier in Greece, group sexual crime of Cologne City, lately Syrian refugee crisis have been showing a number of problems. 'The Refugee' itself is not the primary problem, which itself occurs. 'The refugee' is a secondary disaster after primary disaster. The primary disaster is such as earthquake, volcano eruption, tsunami, war and terror. The secondary disaster is like a refugee, over population, expansion of slum, which is a humanistic problem.

Think again about Human catastrophe in detail, it is that 'huge group of people' lose home and are propelled into 'narrow space' by a disaster. The most worried and terrible thing of natural disasters or wars, terrorism is secondary disaster, Human catastrophe. It eliminates house that people live in

stable, makes the refugees and even threaten other people living commonplace. And then the group of homeless might stay in narrow area, it could be changed to slum and there would exist a criminal who exploited the panic situation.

We have two constraints. First, building performs a little task usual time. Second, it needs to get bigger in short time to receive refugee's impact also needs to get smaller gradually when they become stable. Detail of the process is on first board.

In conclusion, our building shape has to become big in short time and also become small gradually at disaster situation. But in normal state, it just performs disaster management center. We found the idea, which can perform above every function. It is Hot-air Balloon. It's one unit. The list is on first board that

STRUCTURE

Our crane is important as hot-air balloon. It can be built upward really fast speed.
And it performs three important roles. First, it can go upward by itself. Next is lifting anything. The last one is put the deck plate which is the path of people. And all the materials are on the sixth floor. In roof floor, hot-air balloon is launched.

Lifting Facility

Installing Deckplate

Self Leveling

Water & drainage facility

Cable dispersion

Secondary Electric transformer

Winding the wire cable

Water supply facilities

Air inlet ducts

It is a machinery room at basement. There exists HVAC system, Water & Drainage system.
First, HVAC system is related to wire cable. In normal state, wire is winded in the system box.
But in disaster situation, it is stretched out to the envelope. Water & drainage system has two stream lines.
Purification and sewage line that supply water and drain sewage.

Housing Unit (Toilet & Shower)

A-2

-3

B-1

Sector Unit (SES & Hospital)

Sector Unit (Toilet & Shower)

B-3

Sector Unit (Public Peace)

GARDEN

4-6F SUPPORT FACILITY

3F HEADQUATER

2F HOSPITAL

1F TEMPORARY SHELTER

URBAN INFRA

MACHANICAL AREA

the hot air balloon how to perform certain functions.

We made a building by hot-air balloon as follows. First, envelope is air film structure and it is not stretched at normal state. When refugees occur, air film consisting of several layers of air tubes are blow up by injection of air and heat. This is connected with wire that involved electricity line and air conditioner duct and it opened together. At the same time, 9 Luffing tower cranes increase themselves and build deck plate, which people can walk. Finally, hot-air balloons (stored at 5~6 floor) are launched on the roof. It will be connected with electric wire and become to shelter. This process has to be done quickly. It is designed by tower cranes and hot-air balloon, which can be installed within 24 hours.

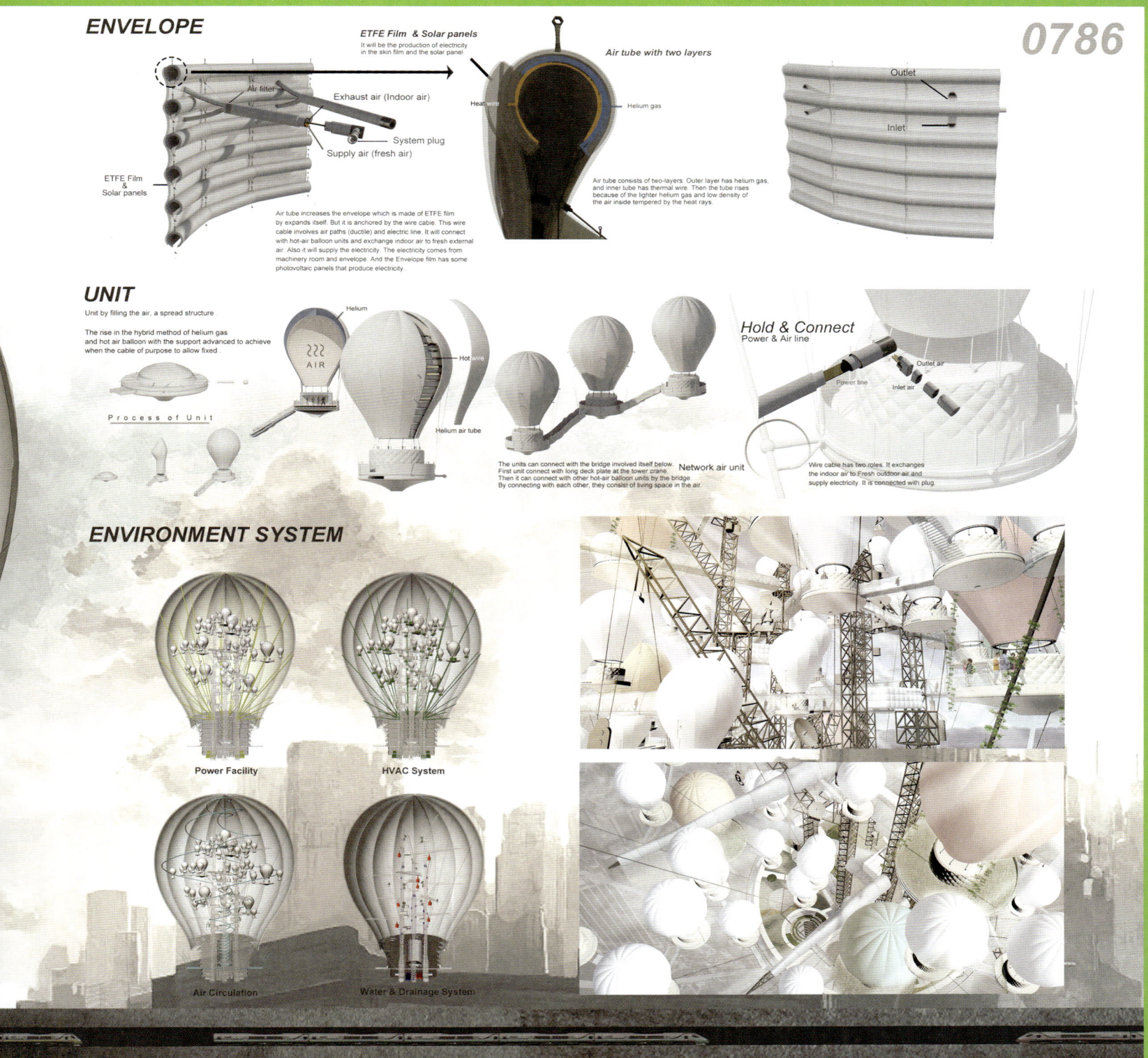

ENVELOPE

0786

ETFE Film & Solar panels
It will be the production of electricity in the skin film and the solar panel

Air tube with two layers

Air filter
Exhaust air (Indoor air)
System plug
Supply air (fresh air)

ETFE Film & Solar panels

Heat wire
Helium gas

Outlet
Inlet

Air tube increases the envelope which is made of ETFE film by expands itself. But it is anchored by the wire cable. This wire cable involves air paths (ductile) and electric line. It will connect with hot-air balloon units and exchange indoor air to fresh external air. Also it will supply the electricity. The electricity comes from machinery room and envelope. And the Envelope film has some photovoltaic panels that produce electricity.

Air tube consists of two-layers. Outer layer has helium gas, and inner tube has thermal wire. Then the tube rises because of the lighter helium gas and low density of the air inside tempered by the heat rays.

UNIT

Unit by filling the air, a spread structure

The rise in the hybrid method of helium gas and hot air balloon with the support advanced to achieve when the cable of purpose to allow fixed.

Process of Unit

Helium
AIR
Hot wire
Helium air tube

Hold & Connect
Power & Air line

Power line
Outlet air
Inlet air

The units can connect with the bridge involved itself below. First unit connect with long deck plate at the tower crane. Then it can connect with other hot-air balloon units by the bridge. By connecting with each other, they consist of living space in the air

Network air unit

Wire cable has two roles. It exchanges the indoor air to Fresh outdoor air and supply electricity. It is connected with plug

ENVIRONMENT SYSTEM

Power Facility

HVAC System

Air Circulation

Water & Drainage System

NEW FRONTIERS 3

PROTEUS

Patrick Chopson

United States

PROTEUS
RETURN TO A NOMADIC WAY OF LIFE

Fundamentally, there was a certain promise, pervasive in the 50s and 60s that an ever increasing level of innovation would continue forever. People believed in flying cars, electric vehicles, fusion power, and colonization of Mars by the year 2000. Engineers and architects became the new keepers of the public trust. Yet, that promise of progress was broken. People and electronics conspired to create a society that betrayed that promise. Technological progress was a failure by engineers and architects. People stopped believing and started saying "maybe never". Instead of the best and the brightest striving to solve the great problems of the age, they submitted their genius to the world of finance and for a generation we suffered from mother to mothers.

Into this beginning of the 21st century, this face of base true truth modified directly into a society preoccupied with finance and progress wealth delights in the cheap glow of social media and fears to please pays at the Great Recession has awakened the young creative class. No longer do young people automatically assume that wealth comes from finance. A generation is realizing the technology is within reach to realize the forgotten dreams of their parents. The age has dawned when we, the youth of this country, ask "not why not?". Formerly old job descriptions are changing, as well. Institutionalized science is being disrupted by a rising creative class un-intimidated by big business. Also known as the maker movement, this new class learned first to create their own content on the internet. Now they are leading the charge forward into the manufacturing 2.0 revolution. Mass customization and inexpensive 3d printing are beginning to offer unprecedented access to manufacturing by lowering barriers of entry. No longer will expensive production cycles and mass production runs be needed to achieve low prices and high quality. This disruptive new technology is beginning to release an explosion of creativity that fundamentally alters the nature of labor, manufacturing, and finance.

To move beyond this reactive state, one must develop a way of understanding design in terms of the dynamic historical interplay between the "control" and the "market". Thus, one may posit that there are two systems of architecture on this planet. On the one hand, is classicism. A system of architecture I define as an approach which fetishizes the act of building. An architecture of power and control filled with axial relationships and the concretization of the functions of the state. Classicism diminishes agency and builds to create an immobile monument to its creator. Set against classicism, is the architecture of the meshwork. Meshwork design integrates with the landscape bending to the unique constraints of the context rather than imposing alien forms and values. This is a plastic architecture. This is a mobile architecture representing the destabilizing forces of the world.

But why should it be mobile? Many architecture theories begin with the primitive hut, or the woven wall of the nomad. If one is to create a mythical state of man beyond the reach of time, then his "natural" state is one of an explorer. Gathering his resources as he pushes back the edges of the known universe, early mankind was a race of explorers. They settled the Polynesian Islands on ships. They swept across the uninhabited plains of North America in search of "Prehistoric" game. They penetrated Africa with its multitude of dangers.

Yet as the edges of that universe were encountered, mankind began the unnatural process of building cities as fortification against other men. Stationary fortifications negated the life of living from the land and necessitated farming. The benefits of the static life were clear. Increased numbers led to more ideas and greater technology. However, not all ideas and goods could be obtained from one city alone. Trading networks developed to spread goods and gradually the city became the meeting place of goods and ideas. In turn, these ideas gave rise to the industrial age with factories that required vast numbers of people to operate the machines.

For some time now, it is increasingly obvious that all of the trends of technology are leading toward a world of ever increasing automation. With the decentralization caused by three-dimensional printing and most manual task performed by robots, what will be the place of mankind in this new century? The old need for cities to be immobile centralized collections of people, goods, and manufacturing do not exist. On the contrary, the only need for humans will be in the creation of new ideas. So they must live together. However, they are no longer tied to fixed locations for resources. It is time for humans to resume their nomadic ways from the distant past. On Mars, adoption of this new way of living and building is adopted by default for there are no traditional cities to hold mankind back. Now humans can travel from resource to resource pushing back edges of the known universe limited only by their collective creativity.

The year is 2040, mankind is radically altering the way they collectively inhabit space on Mars. Automation, 3d printing, and resource constraints are freeing humans to return to their natural nomadic state. A new kind of mesh work architecture imbued with vision, unrestrained invention, technical rigor, and mobility has risen to the challenge. This is a call to action. This is a call to anticipate the future of architecture. A future visualized through a blend of practical constraints, theory, and a narrative. This is the Proteus Colony. This is technological urbanism.

| 2030 | 2033 | 2035 | 2038 | 2039 |

PROTEUS GROWTH PROGRESSION

The year is 2040. Driving forces in technology, politics, and finance are spurring humanity to colonize Mars. A new way of living is developing that is returning man back to his natural nomadic state through automation, 3D printing, and resource constraints.

The Proteus colony resides at the inflection point where humans abandon the sedentary ways of a decadent Earth and return to a life of mobility and exploration. This is technological urbanism.

Proteus is a nomad city; its architecture is conceived entirely for functional purposes. It can be seen as an enormous cloud of infrastructure – a post-apocalyptic city conceived only for our survival. Exhaust vents and building cranes are a constant reminder, a hint about the different functions of this machine; a building designed to extract natural resources from new planets in an attempt to colonize them. The

0061

2040

MAPS OF MARS. RESOURCE CONCENTRATIONS DICTATE TRAVEL ACROSS THE SURFACE IN SEARCH OF WATER AND RAW MATERIALS

production of water and food for its inhabitants is a primary activity within its multiple layers. The creation of space is reduced to the most simple and efficient formula. The interior is also equipped with living quarters and some recreational spaces that mimic spatial condition on Earth - a reminder of where we came from and what we need to do to go back to our origins.

A network of cities would gradually create extensive settlements that through the use of terraforming activities could potentially transform a lifeless planet like Mars into a new lush environment for future generations.

The change would be slow but achievable in a few hundred generations.

At the moment the project is a reminder of the struggles that future generations will need to

A civilization constrained to a single planet is doomed to collapse, chaos, and the destruction of mankind.

FRONT ELEVATION

DRIVING FORCES FOR MARS COLONIZATION

AXON VIEW

COLONY FLOATS ABOVE THE GROUND WITH THE AID OF QUANTUM SUPERCONDUCTING MAGNETS FITTED WITH LONG LIFE ION ENGINES.

LARGE SCALE RESOURCE MINING

1 TITANIUM ORE SMELTING - MAIN ECONOMIC DRIVER OF COLONY

ELEVATION - THE PROTEUS COLONY IS 4 KM LONG AND GROWING

overcome if we do not stop the irrational and rapid destruction of our planet. It is much easier to put a solution now than to try to change the course of an entire planet with the suffering of hundreds of generations.

5 COMMAND CENTER OF THE COLONY

0061

2 CENTRAL MARKET NODE - ECLETIC MIX OF COLONISTS FROM EARTH

3 COLONY GROWS INCREMENTALLY BY ROBOTIC ASSEMBLY

4 TYPICAL LIVING UNIT - COLONIST RETAIN MEMORY OF EARTH

CLOUDSOURCE TOWER

Jonsun Lee
Misun Lee
Peter Suen

United States

CLOUDSOURCE TOWER
MEETING DATA, ENERGY & SPATIAL NEEDS THROUGH THE CLOUD

CONTEXT // THE INCREASING DEMAND FOR DATA, ENERGY AND SPACE
Our society thirsts for data, energy and space. Enormous server farms struggle to keep pace with "big data" and our digital needs. Non-renewable energy sources and our aging power grid face uncertainty. And our buildings are inflexible and contribute to an unsustainable condition. How can we integrate these three driving forces to create a synergistic new future?

CONCEPT // INVERT & INTEGRATE
Currently our data and energy needs are supplied in a horizontal and centralized manner. We *invert* this existing condition to vertically integrate data and energy with building structure. Servers float above using kites which efficiently harvest renewable energy in high altitude. Tethered by fiber, these strands weave together below to create a flexible structural envelope. This literal cloud of data and power creates an efficient and resilient new building typology.

INTEGRATE

01001010010
11101010010
01001001010
11101010011

CLOUD POWER   CLOUD DATA

INVERT   **INVERT**

POWER PLANTS   SERVER FARMS

POWER GRID   FIBER NETWORK

BENEFITS // DATA, ENERGY & STRUCTURAL SYNERGY
The three main components, kites, servers and fiber, benefit from this inversion and integration. The kites gather more renewable energy in altitude than what is available at ground level. Servers operate efficiently in the cooler temperatures in the sky. Fiber, as the bridge between the cloud and the building, bundle together to form rigidized cores that weave around program spaces below.

CLOUD SERVERS:
IMPROVED PERFORMANCE

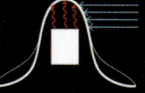

Servers produce a large amount of waste heat. Cooler temperatures in altitude help servers operate more efficiently.

KITE GENERATORS:
EFFICIENT ENERGY HARVEST

Wind at higher altitudes is steadier, more persistent and of higher velocity. This results in an exponential increase in the power available in wind. Low temperatures and a cleaner atmosphere also improve photovoltaic performance. A piezoelectric core in the tether can also generate electricity through the tension and mechanical stress exerted on the fibers.

FIBER OPTIC TETHERS:
FLEXIBLE STRUCTURAL WEAVE

The tethers transmit both data and energy from the kites to the building below. These fibers are also woven together to create a flexible yet strong building envelope.

The system uses multi-functional kites to harness a variety of energy. Rotating fins gather high-altitude wind power through airborne wind turbines. The kite surface is also a blend of flexible photovoltaics, allowing the capture of solar energy.

The fiber optic tethers utilize a piezoelectric core that converts the stress and strain on the tether into electric charge. The kites can maintain positions within the cloud canopy using their wind-generation fins. In addition, the push & pull of the canopy can be converted into electricity using piezoelectric materials within the tethers.

Computer servers are attached underneath the kites and run on the power generated by the kites. The servers are integrated with the wind turbine generator to provide a high-capacity source of data

0469

DISTRIBUTED DATA & POWER

Our digital needs are growing exponentially. Social media, the web, and big data are all contributing to this growth. If we continue on this centralized path, the servers of tomorrow will be much larger than stadiums.

By distributing server farms in a localized manner, we protect our networks from attack and also reduce high operation costs.

Like server farms, centralized power plants are also vulnerable. Our power grid struggles during peak usage, and is often damaged by natural disasters. Distributing power generation in a renewable and robust manner can alleviate these infrastructural problems.

Solar

Wind

Tension

storage. The high temperature heat by-product of the servers is both offset by the cooler high-altitude temperatures and utilized to provide additional lift for the kite as a tethered balloon. Data communication is achieved through the fiber optic tether.

The kite tethers are aggregated to form structural bundles, which are woven to create an envelope. The woven structural envelope allows the system to wrap and easily accommodate a variety of spaces. The detail shown in the panel submissions here shows a library, auditorium and green spaces, which are combined within the Cloudsource Tower.

From the street, the Cloudsource tower appears as a fine veil that covers the sky. It is an elegant solution to power our cities with renewable energy. At the same time it offers an iconic design and

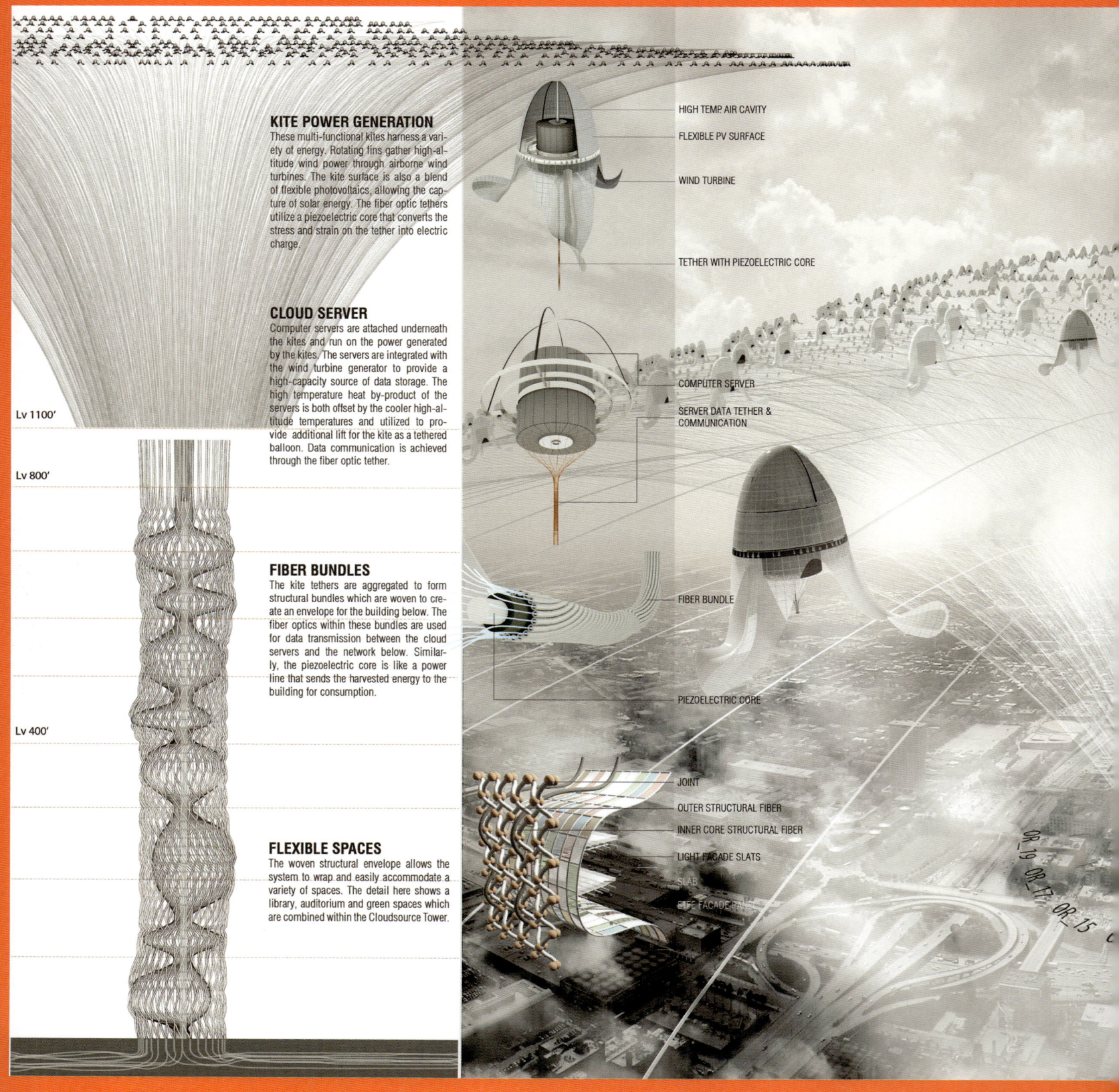

KITE POWER GENERATION
These multi-functional kites harness a variety of energy. Rotating fins gather high-altitude wind power through airborne wind turbines. The kite surface is also a blend of flexible photovoltaics, allowing the capture of solar energy. The fiber optic tethers utilize a piezoelectric core that converts the stress and strain on the tether into electric charge.

CLOUD SERVER
Computer servers are attached underneath the kites and run on the power generated by the kites. The servers are integrated with the wind turbine generator to provide a high-capacity source of data storage. The high temperature heat by-product of the servers is both offset by the cooler high-altitude temperatures and utilized to provide additional lift for the kite as a tethered balloon. Data communication is achieved through the fiber optic tether.

FIBER BUNDLES
The kite tethers are aggregated to form structural bundles which are woven to create an envelope for the building below. The fiber optics within these bundles are used for data transmission between the cloud servers and the network below. Similarly, the piezoelectric core is like a power line that sends the harvested energy to the building for consumption.

FLEXIBLE SPACES
The woven structural envelope allows the system to wrap and easily accommodate a variety of spaces. The detail here shows a library, auditorium and green spaces which are combined within the Cloudsource Tower.

Lv 1100'
Lv 800'
Lv 400'

HIGH TEMP. AIR CAVITY
FLEXIBLE PV SURFACE
WIND TURBINE
TETHER WITH PIEZOELECTRIC CORE
COMPUTER SERVER
SERVER DATA TETHER & COMMUNICATION
FIBER BUNDLE
PIEZOELECTRIC CORE
JOINT
OUTER STRUCTURAL FIBER
INNER CORE STRUCTURAL FIBER
LIGHT FACADE SLATS
SLAB
LIFE FACADE PANEL

habitable spaces at its core. Residential areas are located in the mid floors while the bottom floors are reserved for commercial and recreational activities.

The main structure consists of a fine steel lattice that weaves up creating a diamond-like pattern with large openings that allow unobstructed views to the city. The open floor plan also allows for a great variety of living spaces.

0469

FIBER BUNDLE MOVEMENT
The kites can maintain positions within the cloud canopy using their wind-generation fins. In addition, the push & pull of the canopy can be converted into electricity using piezoelectric materials within the tethers.

AUDITORIUM   GREEN SPACE   LIBRARY

ENDLESS BABEL

Andreas Zuhr

Germany

Genesis 11:1 - 4

2 As people moved eastward,they found a plain and settled there.
3 They said to each other, "Come, let's make bricks and bake them thorough-
hly." They used brick instead of stone,and tar for mortar.
4 Then they said, "Come, let us build ourselves a city, with a tower that rea-
ches to the heavens, so that we may make a name for ourselves; otherwise we
will be scattered over the face of the whole earth."

The Tower of Babel - the myth of the first tower - the ideal skyscraper.
A sign of Humanity's ambition and achievement, first depicted by
Pieter Bruegel the Elder.

The Tower of Babel could never be built. Mankind still dreams of a
supernatural building reaching to the sky.

But...what if Mankind had not abandoned this dream?
What architectural visions would have nurtured it?

This Tower absorbs the unbuilt visions of the great masters. It is a
journey through time and height. It is the story of Mankind, its technological achievements, its memories of its past and its dreams of its
future....and it continues............Pieter Bruegel (1563-) - Giovanni Battista Piranesi (1758-) - Claud Nicolas Ledoux (1773-) - Etienne-Louis
Boulee (1784-) - Karl Friedrich Schinkel (1816-) - John Soane (1818-
) - Joseph Michael Gandy (1830-) - Charles Robert Cockerell (1848)
- Tony Garnier (1901-) - Antonio San't Elia (1914-) - Wladimir Tatlin
(1919-) - Bruno Taut (1919-) - Ivan Lenidov (1927-) - Georgy Krutikov
(1928-) - Frank Lloyd Wright (1934-) - Le Corbusier (1935-) - Buckminster Fuller (1959-) - Cedric Price (1962-) - Archigram (1964-)
- Superstudio (1967-) - Lebbeus Woods (2004-) - Peter Cook (2013-)

-------------------------- the Tower - like the Future
- NEVER ENDS.

ENDLESS BABEL

HEIGHT = 000m HEIGHT = 100m HEIGHT = 200m HEIGHT =

1600 1650

The Tower of Babel, as a myth, portrays the ideal skyscraper. It was a beacon of humanity's ambition and achievement, first depicted by Pieter Bruegel the Elder.

The Tower of Babel could never be built. Mankind still dreams of a supernatural building reaching to the sky. But...what if mankind had not abandoned this dream? What architectural visions would have nurtured it?

This tower absorbs the unsubstantiated visions of the great masters. It is a journey through time and height. It is the story of mankind, its technological achievements, its memories of its past and its dreams of its future...and it continues.

At the ground level, the skyscraper is presented as an interpretation of Bruegel's Tower of Babel.

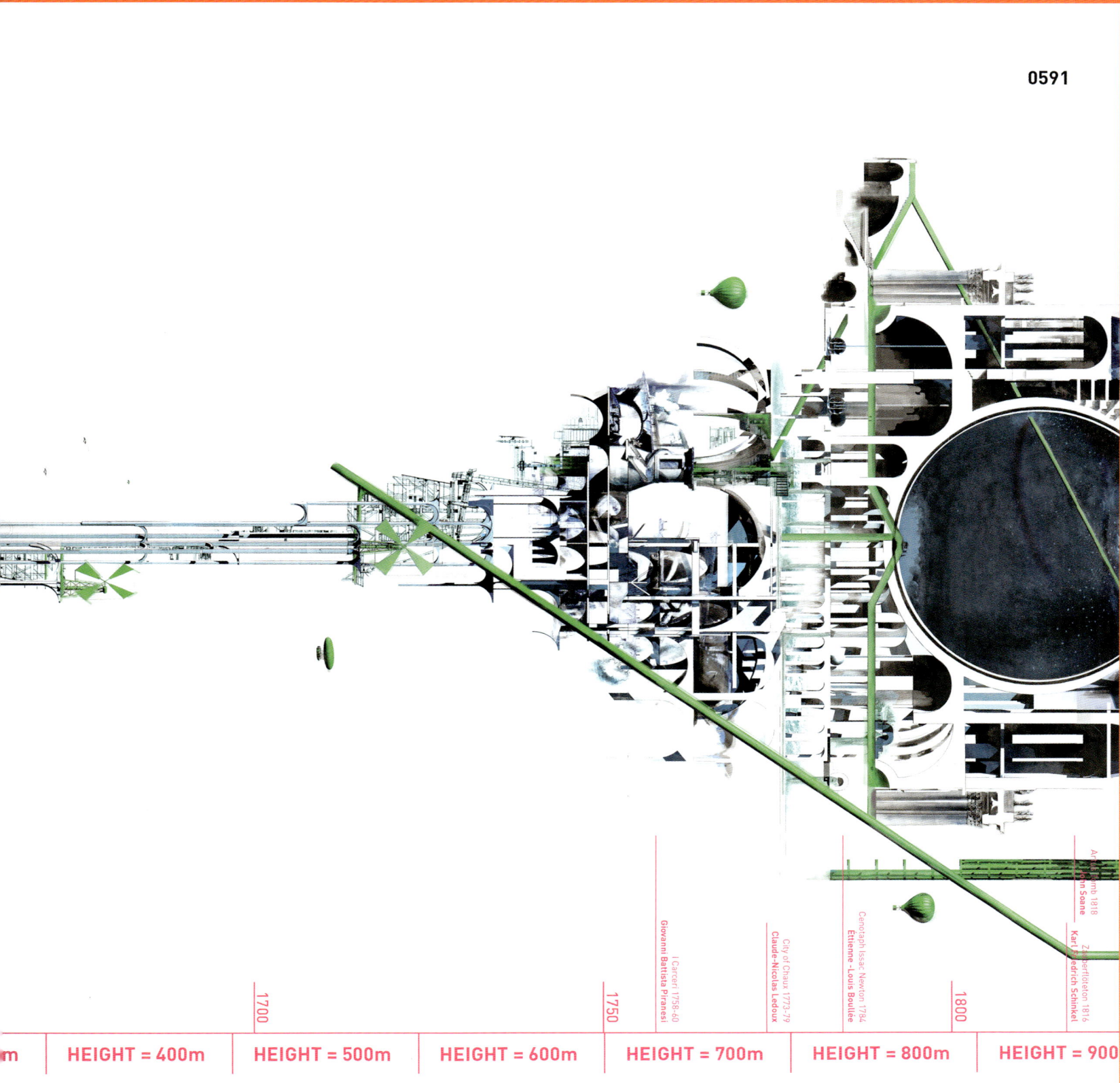

0591

I Carceri 1758-60
Giovanni Battista Piranesi

City of Chaux 1773-79
Claude-Nicolas Ledoux

Cenotaph Issac Newton 1784
Etienne-Louis Boullée

Archer Tomb 1818
Sir John Soane

Zauberflöten 1816
Karl Friedrich Schinkel

1700   1750   1800

m | HEIGHT = 400m | HEIGHT = 500m | HEIGHT = 600m | HEIGHT = 700m | HEIGHT = 800m | HEIGHT = 900

As the tower reaches for the sky, we encounter a condensed history of architecture. It is a journey through some of the most important and iconic architectural periods. Examples of these structures include a basilica from the renaissance or a dome from Rome's Pantheon. This project is almost a schizophrenic vision of Man's ability to transform space and evoke its spirituality. This is not a functional skyscraper but an allegorical representation of mankind.

The use of a green strcutural ribbon serves as a connector between all the different structures. The sky is reached and humankind spiriuatl ambition is satisfied. Inhabitants can make a spiritual journey that commences on the ground and as you move higher and encounter all these spaces your connection to reality disappears. It is a voyage that takes people through a collective sub-consciousness. There is

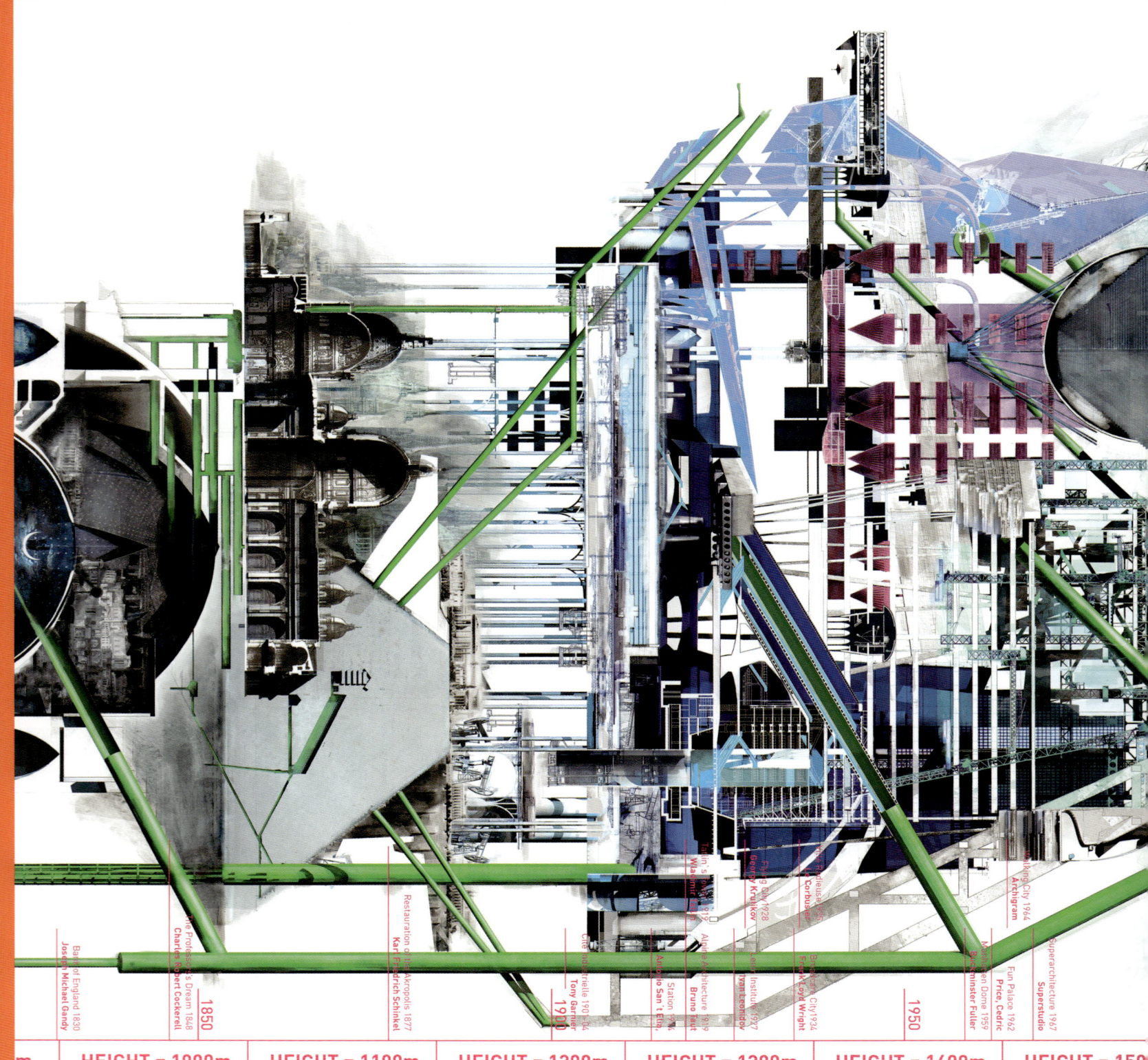

Bank of England 1830
Joseph Michael Gandy

The Professor's Dream 1848
Charles Robert Cockerell

1850

Restauration of the Acropolis 1877
Karl Friedrich Schinkel

Cité industrielle 1901-04
Tony Garnier

1900

Station 1914
Antonio San't Elia

Berlin's Dream 1919
Wassmuth

Algiers Architecture 1919
Bruno Taut

Flying City 1928
Georgy Krutikov

Ural Institute 1927
Ivan Leonidov

Broadacre City 1934
Frank Lloyd Wright

Dôme 1955
Le Corbusier

Manhattan Dome 1959
Buckminster Fuller

1950

Fun Palace 1962
Price, Cedric

Walking City 1964
Archigram

Superarchitecture 1967
Superstudio

| m | HEIGHT = 1000m | HEIGHT = 1100m | HEIGHT = 1200m | HEIGHT = 1300m | HEIGHT = 1400m | HEIGHT = 150 |

a need for discovery and interpretation where spirit and mind come to peace and find a way to move forward in the endless journey of time.

There is an emphasis on trip, the movement from one spiritual level to another. Reaching the higher levels require a self guidance through your own being and its resonance to the collective mind and its surrealistic vision of space.

0591

HEIGHT = 1700m | HEIGHT = 1800m | HEIGHT = 1900m | HEIGHT = 2000m | HEIGHT = 2100m

DELICATE PAGODA

Meng Zhang
Meng Zhao

United States

DELICATE PAGODA
TOWER Polluted Water Purification & Groundwater Regeneration

FOREWORD

When crossing YongDing river in Beijing, a strange odor assaulted the nostrils, the quality of water is decreasing recently. People's activities seems like killing themselves to pollute and waste the water source. If we do not cherish our water resource, our **TEARS** must be the last water of our earth.

ISSUE

The trend of water pollution is becoming more and more serious, especially in earth's surface water of Beijing, China, the result of environment agency shows that rivers expected 9 no-water rivers, all 50 rivers have a over-fulfilled productive quota, most of these is consisted with **EXTRA O, N, P.**

The most of pollution comes from people living and industry, and 17% of dirty water do not treated and discharge directly. Facilities for water treatment of the industries in the boundary of city and suburb, which is not elegible so that make the dirty water flowing into and destroy the river, even it has some droppings, finally the quality of water contaminated and become seriousness.

As we all know, Beijing is also one the most lack of water city in the world, the data in 2003 indicated that the natural water of Beijing only has 37 billion square meter, which is on the 10% of percapita in China and on the 2.5% of per capital in the world. According to the internationally recognized standards, Per-capita water resources occupies less than 1000 cubic meter belongs to **THE SEVERE WATER SHORTAGE AREA.** So Beijing is face with serious storage shortage of water in the world.

The water supply channel in Beijing mainly consists with two parts: **SURFACE WATER AND GROUNDWATER.** surface water supplied by rivers in the city and the situation of delivery. In surface water supply must be under the premise of the trend of population increase, when the breaking population in Beijing, China, the **WATER SUPPLY BURDEN** is increasing.

1. The pollution of surface water, recently the ground water is damaged by a sever **INDUSTRIAL POLLUTION**, most of dirty water without any processing sewage into chanals directly. These water also used for agricultural irrigation.
2. The reduction of groundwater, in the 50s and 60s, groundwater resources' exploitation is in a small amount, since the '70s, the **GROUNDWATER RESOURCE EXPLOITATION** is in a **LARGE GROWING** year by year, and the groundwater became one of the main water source in Beijing.

SOLUTION

The function of **DELICATE PAGODA** in ancient China is pray water for people, while at recently, facing with the pollution of water source, We still help to build a Delicate Pagoda for **PURIFICATION AND REGENERATION** of water in the future.

To sum up, the Beijing city is failure to be make perfect the water supply system, and the water is hard to recycle. So we consider and rethink about this atmosphere then make a design which is use skyscraper to build a exhaustive solution to solve the pollution and the current situation of water shortage. Create Delicate Pagoda -- a warer purification skyscraper to purify the industrial waste water in the river, after **4** purification treatment from the surface to the sky: **PRECIPITATION, DECOMPOSITION, FILTER AND RE-FILTER,** will eventually put the clean water return to the ground surface and underground area, one part is considered recycle the ground surface water and the other part is considered supple the lacking groundwater. During the process of the purification, decomposition of organic fertilizer which comes from the waste water also can used into each layer with green plant irrigation in the skyscraper, or other need of agricultural area.

BRINE ELECTROLYSIS
$2H_2O \rightarrow 2H_2 \uparrow + O_2 \uparrow$

FILTER — PART C

RE-FILTER — PART D

A SEPARATION LAYER FOR EXCHANGE CIRCULATION

DECOMPOSITION — PART B

PRECIPITATION

RETURNED CLEAR WATER

When crossing the Yong Ding River in Beijing, a strange odor arose; the quality of water is decreasing recently due to people's lack of environmental awareness. The trend of water pollution is becoming more and more serious; especially in the surface water of Beijing, China, the result of an environment agency study shows that the river is laced with copious amounts of Oxygen, Nitrogen, and Phosphorus.

Most pollution comes from people and industry, and 17% of dirty water used is not treated, and rather just discharges directly. Facilities for water treatment in the boundary of Beijing cannot treat the water in outside of the precincts, making the water flowing into the Yong Ding River extremely dirty, thus destroying the river.

As we all know, Beijing is one of the worst cities in the world in regards to water reserve, with data in

2003 indicating that the natural water of Beijing comprises only 37 billion square meters, which is 10% of the per-capita rate in China and 2.5% of per capita rate in the rest of the world

The water supply channel in Beijing mainly consists with two parts, surface water and groundwater. Rivers in the city supply surface water, but with sever population growth in Beijing, surface water supply cannot possibly keep up with demand. The pollution of surface water, along with the damage of ground water by severe industrial pollution, is fed into canals directly, without any filtering process. This contaminated water is what is used for agricultural irrigation. The reduction of has been getting worse in large part year by year, since the 1970's, as it remains one of the most important water supplies for Beijing.

DELICATE PAGODA
TOWER POLLUTED WATER PURIFICATION & GROUNDWATER REGENERATION

In ancient China, the function of Delicate Pagoda was to allow people to pray for solid water supply. We hope to create a modern-day Delicate Pagoda where people can help ensure the circulation of water and its ability to exist into the future. This project will create a water purification skyscraper, used to purify the industrial waste water in the river, after 3 purification treatments from the surface to the sky - precipitation, decomposition, and re-filter. Thus will eventually return clean water to the ground surface and underground. One part of the building is designated towards recycling the ground surface water and the other part is used to replenish the lacking groundwater supply. During the process of the purification, decomposition of organic fertilizer, which comes from the wastewater, can also be used in each layer with green plant irrigation in the skyscraper.

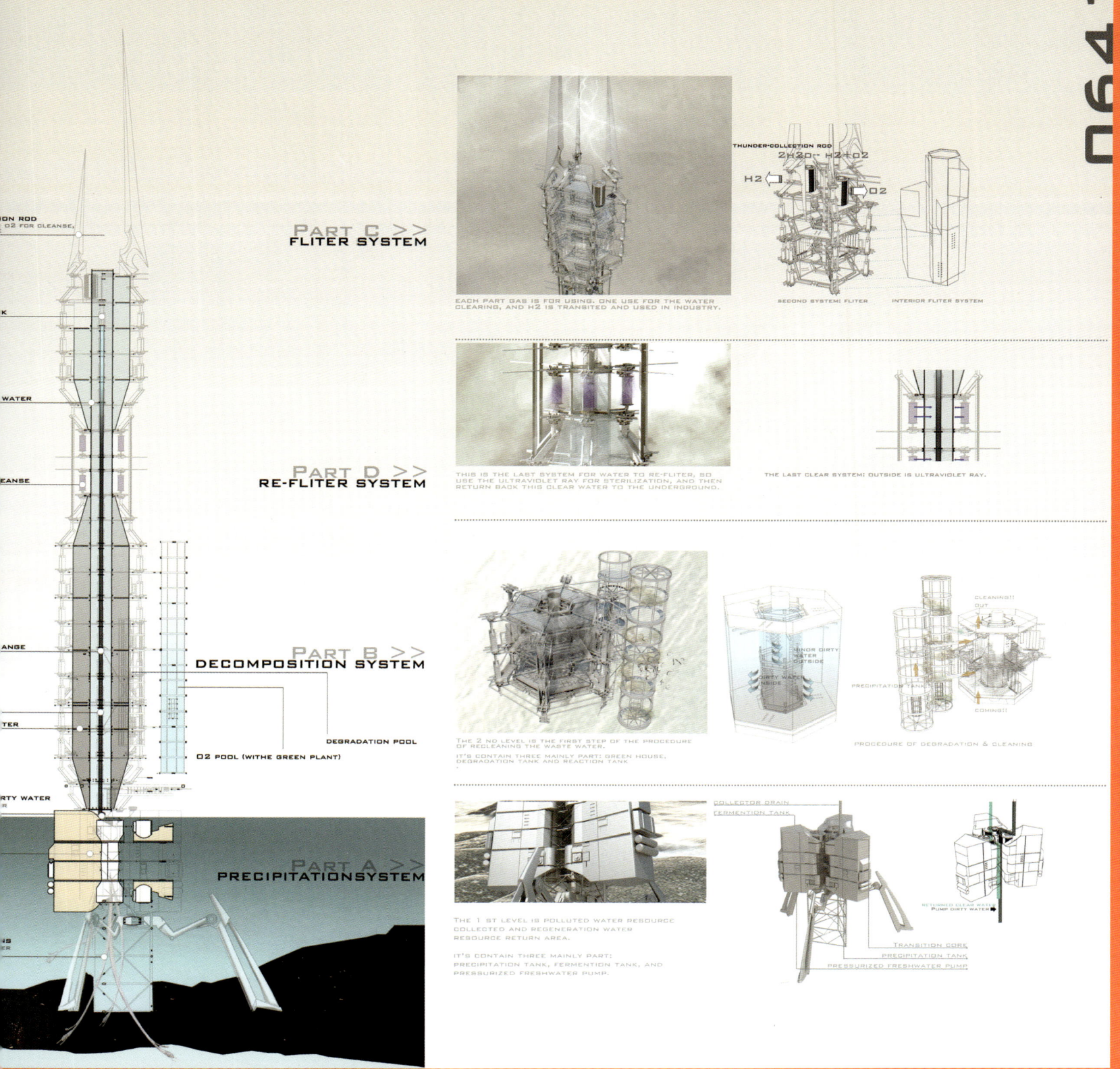

PART C >>
FLITER SYSTEM

EACH PART GAS IS FOR USING. ONE USE FOR THE WATER CLEARING, AND H2 IS TRANSITED AND USED IN INDUSTRY.

THUNDER-COLLECTION ROD
2H2O = H2+O2

SECOND SYSTEM: FLITER   INTERIOR FLITER SYSTEM

PART D >>
RE-FLITER SYSTEM

THIS IS THE LAST SYSTEM FOR WATER TO RE-FLITER, SO USE THE ULTRAVIOLET RAY FOR STERILIZATION, AND THEN RETURN BACK THIS CLEAR WATER TO THE UNDERGROUND.

THE LAST CLEAR SYSTEM: OUTSIDE IS ULTRAVIOLET RAY.

PART B >>
DECOMPOSITION SYSTEM

DEGRADATION POOL

O2 POOL (WITHE GREEN PLANT)

THE 2 ND LEVEL IS THE FIRST STEP OF THE PROCEDURE OF RECLEANING THE WASTE WATER.
IT'S CONTAIN THREE MAINLY PART: GREEN HOUSE, DEGRADATION TANK AND REACTION TANK

PROCEDURE OF DEGRADATION & CLEANING

PART A >>
PRECIPITATION SYSTEM

THE 1 ST LEVEL IS POLLUTED WATER RESOURCE COLLECTED AND REGENERATION WATER RESOURCE RETURN AREA.

IT'S CONTAIN THREE MAINLY PART: PRECIPITATION TANK, FERMENTION TANK, AND PRESSURIZED FRESHWATER PUMP.

A VISION FOR YEAR 2800

Luis Longhi
Christian Bottger
Carla Tamariz

Peru

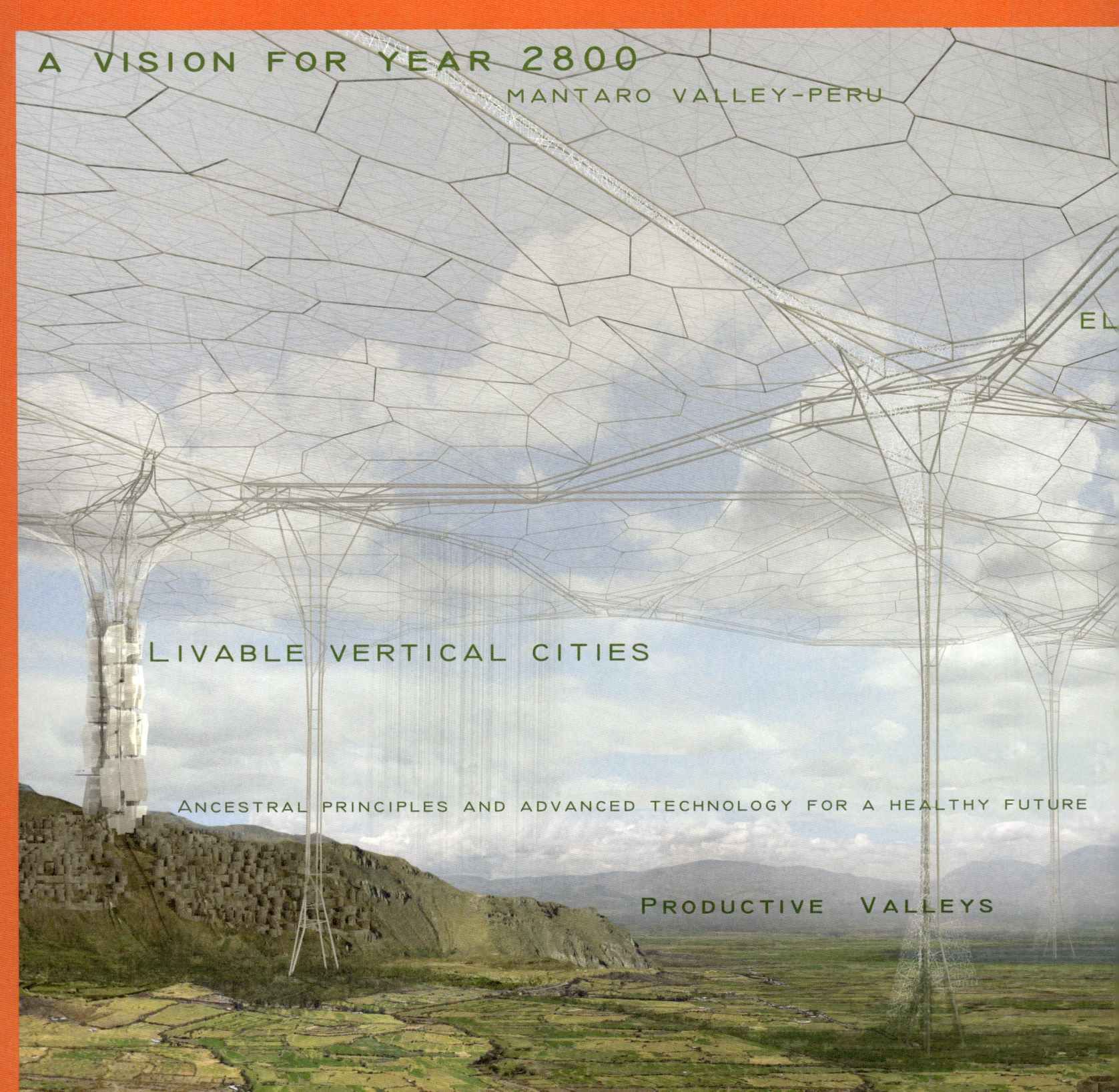

A VISION FOR YEAR 2800
MANTARO VALLEY–PERU

EL

LIVABLE VERTICAL CITIES

ANCESTRAL PRINCIPLES AND ADVANCED TECHNOLOGY FOR A HEALTHY FUTURE

PRODUCTIVE VALLEYS

Both pre-Columbian and later Incan civilizations were very strict in the use of their land, flat surfaces were used exclusively for agriculture, while hills were occupied by their architecture. With Spanish colonization came new ways of life, most of them not as respectful to nature as the previous civilizations. Creation of new cities took place near rivers and constructions were built mostly on flat surface.

The selected site is Mantaro River Valley located at the Andes of Peru near Lima (10 million people) capital and the biggest city of the country. Since the creation of Lima in 1535, Mantaro Valley has been it's more important source of food and water. Nowadays 30% of the flat land of the valley is occupied by cities, studies show that by year 2035 it will increase to 90%, this fact along with overpopulation both at the Valley and in Lima, will cause serious problems of survival.

VERTICAL CITIES AS GENERATORS OF
...VATED MEMBRANES

CONTROL OF NATURAL PHENOMENA

0707

The project suggests the recovery of flat land for agriculture, the relocation of buildings to the hills by moving existing cities to the mountains as it used to be in ancestral times allowing flat surfaces to be dedicated exclusively to agriculture.

High-rise structures will grow as extensions of the occupied hills, like morphological extensions of the Andes, creating vertical cities.

The structures of those vertical cities will support elevated membranes which will act as filter for the UV high radiation, with Peru having the highest level of UV radiation in the world, as well as a system for massive solar energy, accumulation and distribution of water. Important function of the elevated membrane is to generate microclimates to contribute for a perfect environment by controlling natural

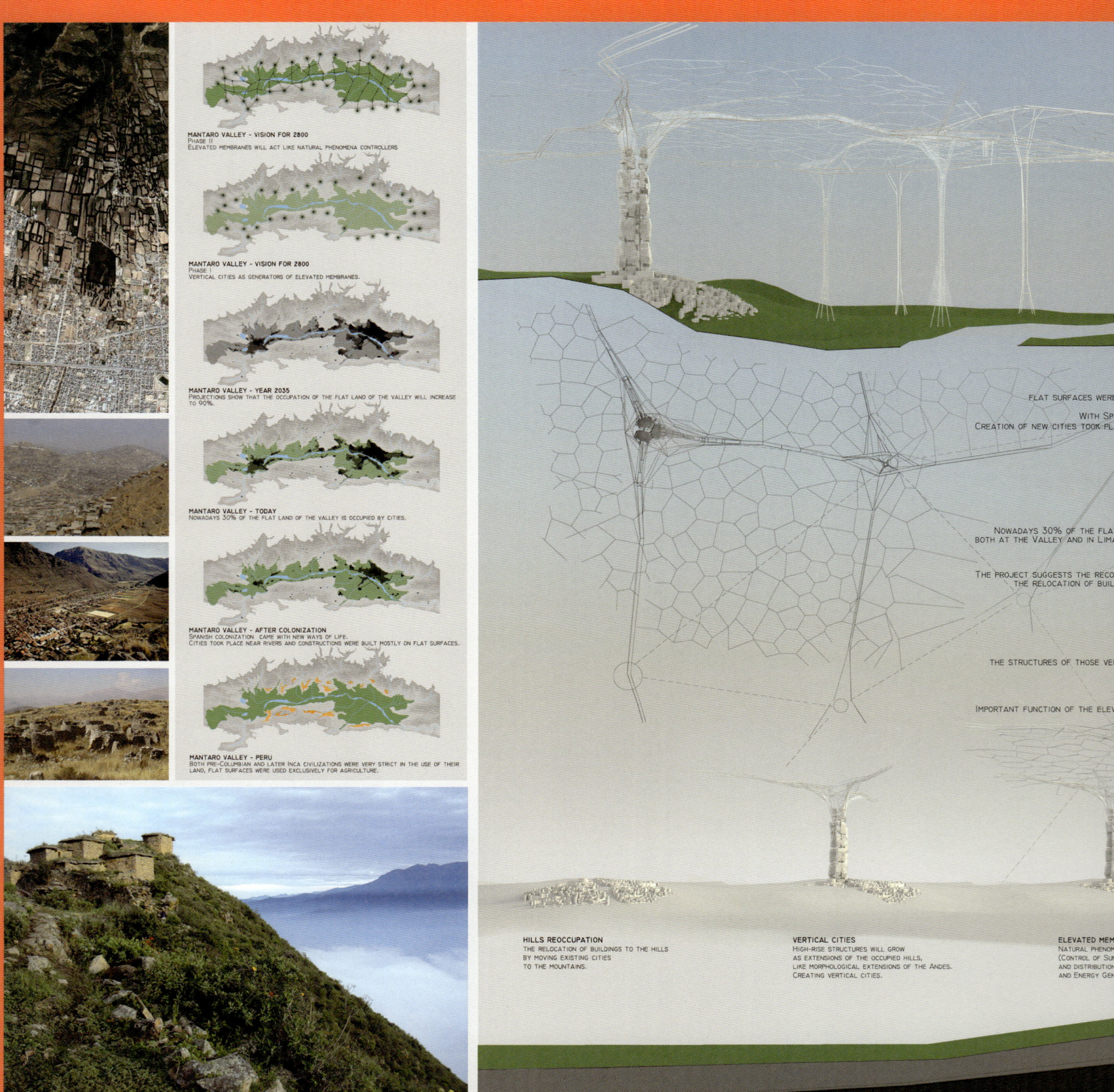

MANTARO VALLEY - VISION FOR 2800
Phase II
Elevated membranes will act like natural phenomena controllers.

MANTARO VALLEY - VISION FOR 2800
Phase I
Vertical cities as generators of elevated membranes.

MANTARO VALLEY - YEAR 2035
Projections show that the occupation of the flat land of the valley will increase to 90%.

MANTARO VALLEY - TODAY
Nowadays 30% of the flat land of the valley is occupied by cities.

MANTARO VALLEY - AFTER COLONIZATION
Spanish colonization came with new ways of life.
Cities took place near rivers and constructions were built mostly on flat surfaces.

MANTARO VALLEY - PERU
Both pre-columbian and later Inca civilizations were very strict in the use of their land, flat surfaces were used exclusively for agriculture.

FLAT SURFACES WERE
WITH SPAN
CREATION OF NEW CITIES TOOK PLAC

NOWADAYS 30% OF THE FLAT
BOTH AT THE VALLEY AND IN LIMA,

THE PROJECT SUGGESTS THE RECOVE
THE RELOCATION OF BUILDI

THE STRUCTURES OF THOSE VERT

IMPORTANT FUNCTION OF THE ELEVA

HILLS REOCCUPATION
THE RELOCATION OF BUILDINGS TO THE HILLS
BY MOVING EXISTING CITIES
TO THE MOUNTAINS.

VERTICAL CITIES
HIGH-RISE STRUCTURES WILL GROW
AS EXTENSIONS OF THE OCCUPIED HILLS,
LIKE MORPHOLOGICAL EXTENSIONS OF THE ANDES.
CREATING VERTICAL CITIES.

ELEVATED MEMB
NATURAL PHENOME
(CONTROL OF SUN
AND DISTRIBUTION
AND ENERGY GENE

phenomena, like rain, wind, and sun intensity, in order to maintain a productive Valley for centuries to come.

The construction of several towers will create a network of inhabitable spaces in the sky. The canopy of each tower will expand to physically connect between them similar to neuron cells. This grid will serve as a communication device and will also be equipped with photovoltaic cells and kinetic sensors to harvest solar and wind energy.

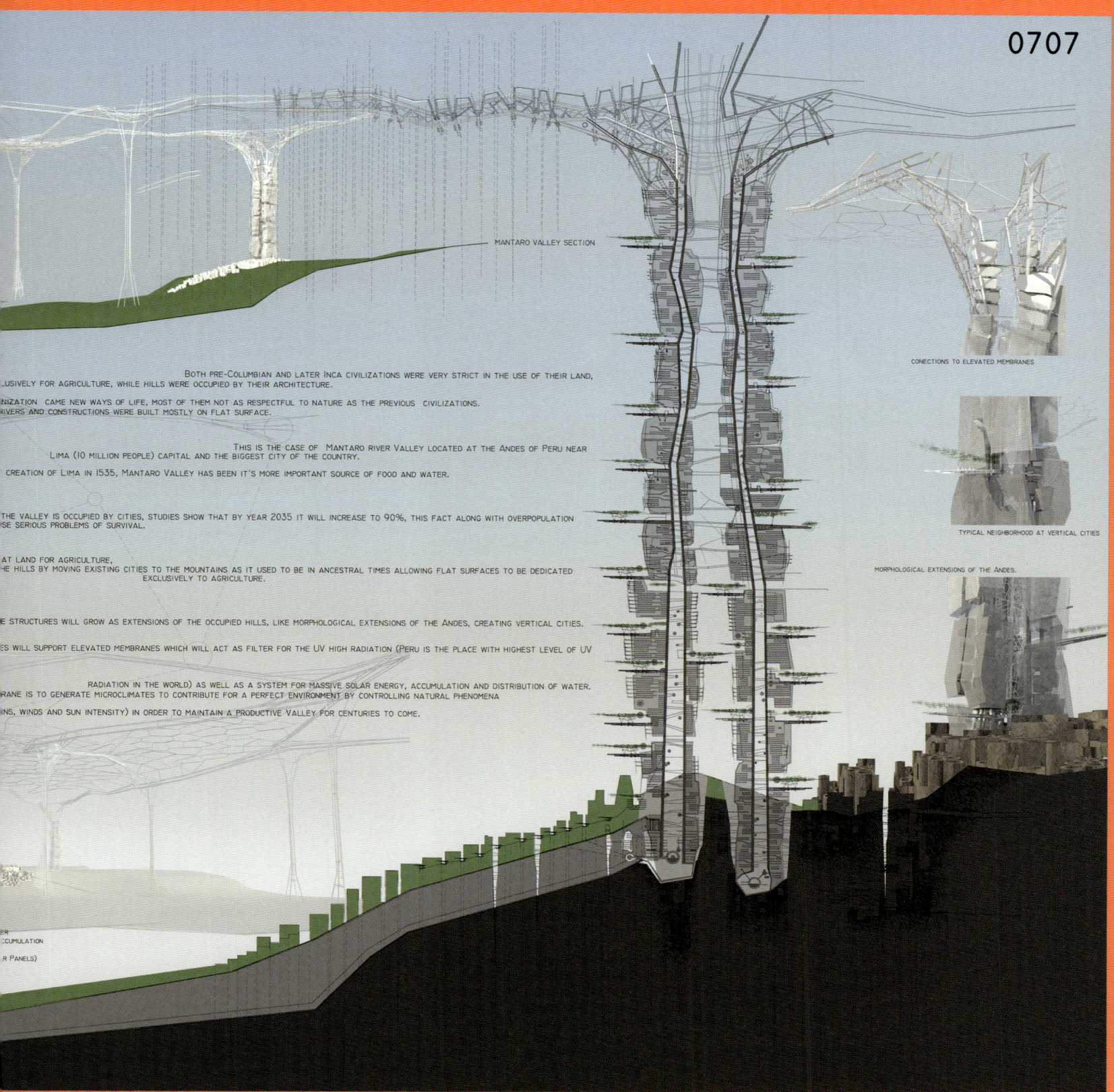

0707

MANTARO VALLEY SECTION

BOTH PRE-COLUMBIAN AND LATER INCA CIVILIZATIONS WERE VERY STRICT IN THE USE OF THEIR LAND,
...LUSIVELY FOR AGRICULTURE, WHILE HILLS WERE OCCUPIED BY THEIR ARCHITECTURE.

...NIZATION CAME NEW WAYS OF LIFE, MOST OF THEM NOT AS RESPECTFUL TO NATURE AS THE PREVIOUS CIVILIZATIONS.
...RIVERS AND CONSTRUCTIONS WERE BUILT MOSTLY ON FLAT SURFACE.

THIS IS THE CASE OF MANTARO RIVER VALLEY LOCATED AT THE ANDES OF PERU NEAR
LIMA (10 MILLION PEOPLE) CAPITAL AND THE BIGGEST CITY OF THE COUNTRY.

...CREATION OF LIMA IN 1535, MANTARO VALLEY HAS BEEN IT'S MORE IMPORTANT SOURCE OF FOOD AND WATER.

...THE VALLEY IS OCCUPIED BY CITIES, STUDIES SHOW THAT BY YEAR 2035 IT WILL INCREASE TO 90%, THIS FACT ALONG WITH OVERPOPULATION
...ISE SERIOUS PROBLEMS OF SURVIVAL.

...AT LAND FOR AGRICULTURE,
...HE HILLS BY MOVING EXISTING CITIES TO THE MOUNTAINS AS IT USED TO BE IN ANCESTRAL TIMES ALLOWING FLAT SURFACES TO BE DEDICATED
EXCLUSIVELY TO AGRICULTURE.

...E STRUCTURES WILL GROW AS EXTENSIONS OF THE OCCUPIED HILLS, LIKE MORPHOLOGICAL EXTENSIONS OF THE ANDES, CREATING VERTICAL CITIES.

...ES WILL SUPPORT ELEVATED MEMBRANES WHICH WILL ACT AS FILTER FOR THE UV HIGH RADIATION (PERU IS THE PLACE WITH HIGHEST LEVEL OF UV

RADIATION IN THE WORLD) AS WELL AS A SYSTEM FOR MASSIVE SOLAR ENERGY, ACCUMULATION AND DISTRIBUTION OF WATER.
...RANE IS TO GENERATE MICROCLIMATES TO CONTRIBUTE FOR A PERFECT ENVIRONMENT BY CONTROLLING NATURAL PHENOMENA
...INS, WINDS AND SUN INTENSITY) IN ORDER TO MAINTAIN A PRODUCTIVE VALLEY FOR CENTURIES TO COME.

CONECTIONS TO ELEVATED MEMBRANES

TYPICAL NEIGHBORHOOD AT VERTICAL CITIES

MORPHOLOGICAL EXTENSIONS OF THE ANDES.

...ER
...CUMULATION
...R PANELS)

NOT JAWS

Marcos Ortega Davila

Spain

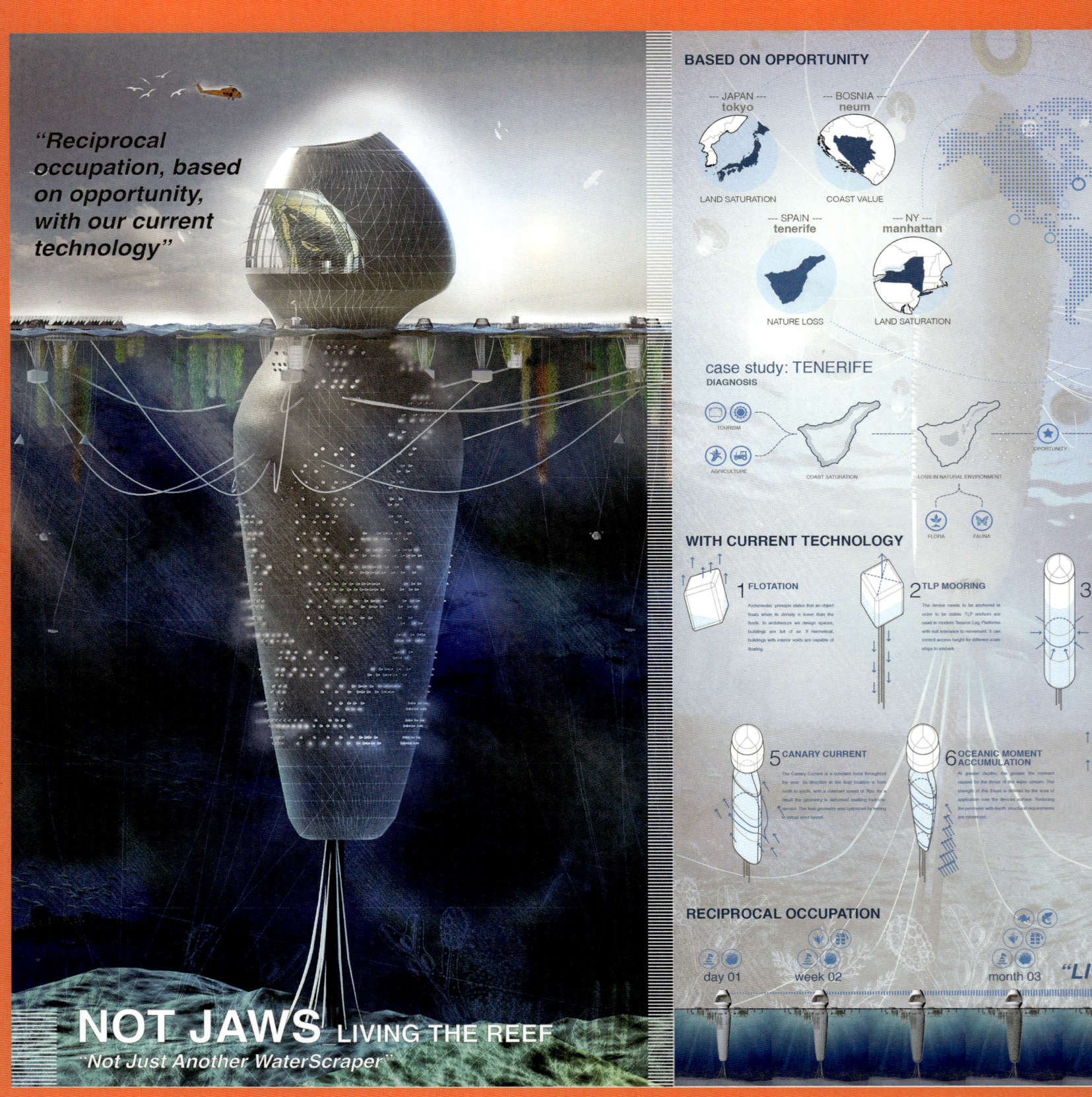

"Reciprocal occupation, based on opportunity, with our current technology"

NOT JAWS LIVING THE REEF
"Not Just Another WaterScraper"

BASED ON OPPORTUNITY

--- JAPAN --- tokyo   --- BOSNIA --- neum
LAND SATURATION   COAST VALUE

--- SPAIN --- tenerife   --- NY --- manhattan
NATURE LOSS   LAND SATURATION

case study: TENERIFE
DIAGNOSIS

TOURISM   OPPORTUNITY

AGRICULTURE   COAST SATURATION   LOSS IN NATURAL ENVIRONMENT

FLORA   FAUNA

WITH CURRENT TECHNOLOGY

1 FLOTATION
2 TLP MOORING
3

5 CANARY CURRENT
6 OCEANIC MOMENT ACCUMULATION

RECIPROCAL OCCUPATION

day 01   week 02   month 03   "LI

The conquest of the ocean has always been a dream for mankind. Throughout history, technical advances have enabled man to navigate the ocean and learn about it. Today, technology allows us to take a new step in this dream, and there are different areas of opportunity worldwide. Today, the conquest of the sea can be, not just a dream, but rather an advantage.

The proposal is Not Jaws. Unlike Spielberg's shark, the device does not intend to be aggressive or dangerous. It seeks a reciprocal occupation of the environment. Its target is the necessary coexistence of humans with the natural environment in a time when we are more aware than ever that we cannot be Jaws.

This coexistence is based on its supply archipelago, which acts as a seed of life in a technological

device. Its islands, which initially serve only to supply the device, become biological catalysts that propagate marine flora and attract fish and fauna. In the ocean, the big fish always eats the small one, so eventually the device´s hull, or exoskeleton, would become an ecosystem of artificial origin.

The biggest challenge that presented the proposal was the technical challenge. Technical rigor was the key to generate a strong project, so it had the collaboration of technical specialists in offshore projects to ensure a reasonable technical basis. There have been tests of virtual wind tunnel to optimize forms to specific site conditions, besides other analysis.

In addition, the project incorporates other techniques as the design of a courtyard, or belly, and mouth to feed light interior spaces. A convex mirrors system covering the whole belly reflects light to

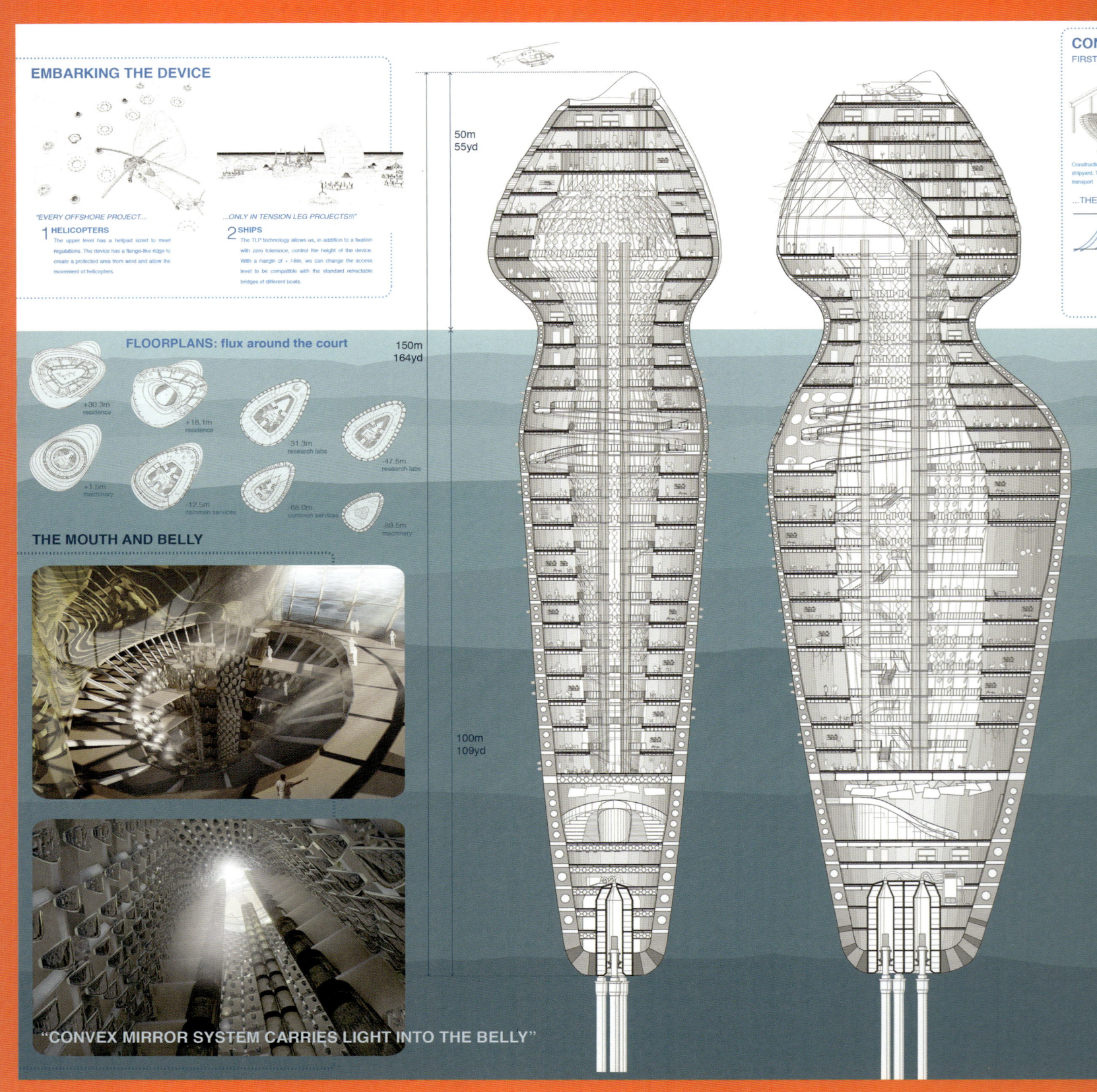

EMBARKING THE DEVICE

"EVERY OFFSHORE PROJECT...

1 HELICOPTERS

2 SHIPS

...ONLY IN TENSION LEG PROJECTS!!!"

FLOORPLANS: flux around the court

THE MOUTH AND BELLY

"CONVEX MIRROR SYSTEM CARRIES LIGHT INTO THE BELLY"

50m / 55yd

150m / 164yd

100m / 109yd

allow the deeper areas to be well illuminated. This, together with a passive ventilation system trough the belly and mouth after injecting air from the exoskeleton, makes the proposal more than just another waterscraper.

JCTION AND ASSEMBLY PROCESS

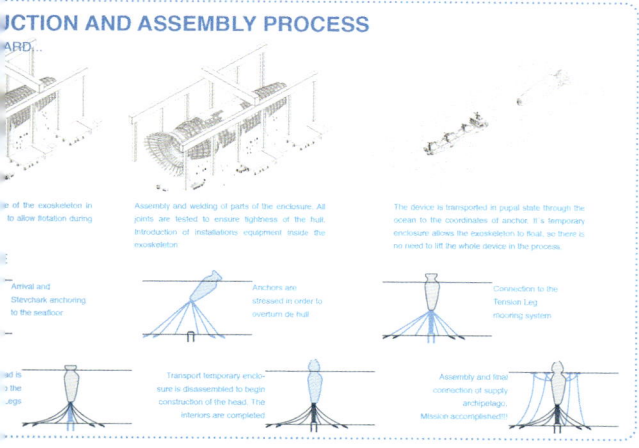

HE EXOSKELETON: HULL, STRUCTURE AND INSTALLATIONS

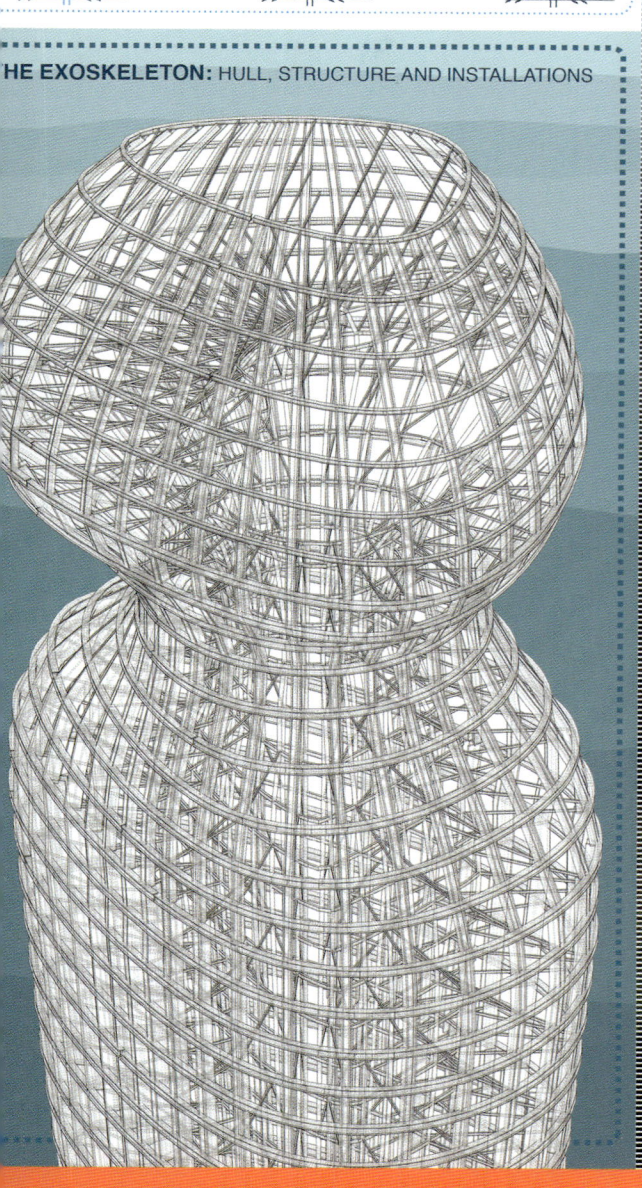

"Its current technology that actually works".
The Offshore Engineer.

0719

"Even its not something to invest in this moment, it gives valuable clues on what to expect in future naval industry".
The Civil Engineering Faculty Professor.

"Awesome".
The Friend.

NOT JAWS_LIVING THE REEF
"Not Just Another WaterScraper"

SUCTION TOWER

Myung Duk Chung

United States

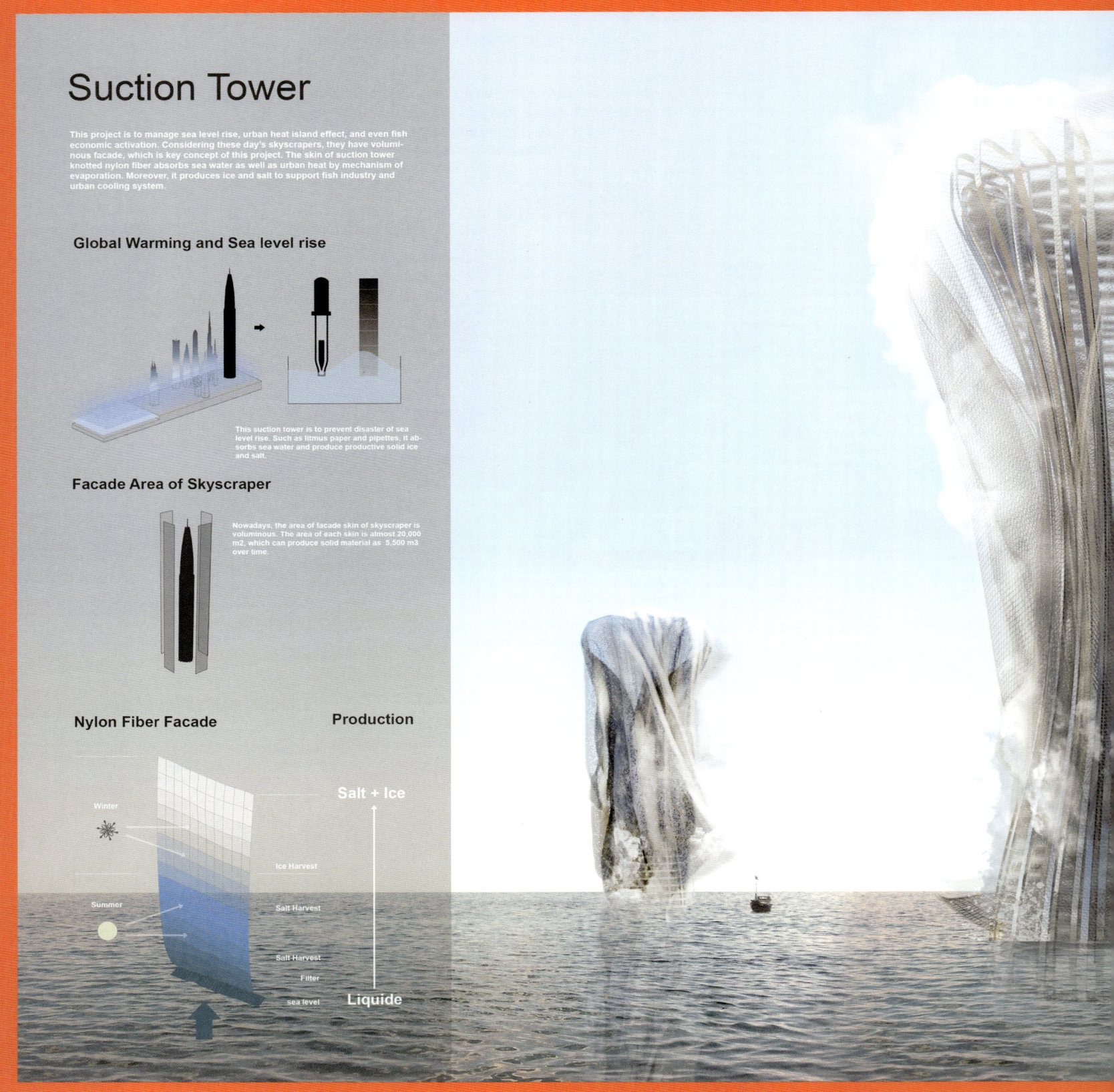

Suction Tower

This project is to manage sea level rise, urban heat island effect, and even fish economic activation. Considering these day's skyscrapers, they have voluminous facade, which is key concept of this project. The skin of suction tower knotted nylon fiber absorbs sea water as well as urban heat by mechanism of evaporation. Moreover, it produces ice and salt to support fish industry and urban cooling system.

Global Warming and Sea level rise

This suction tower is to prevent disaster of sea level rise. Such as litmus paper and pipettes, it absorbs sea water and produce productive solid ice and salt.

Facade Area of Skyscraper

Nowadays, the area of facade skin of skyscraper is voluminous. The area of each skin is almost 20,000 m2, which can produce solid material as 5,500 m3 over time.

Nylon Fiber Facade

Production

Winter

Summer

Salt + Ice

Ice Harvest

Salt Harvest

Salt Harvest

Filter

sea level

Liquide

This project is used to manage sea level rise, urban heat island effect, and even fish economic activation. Considering today's skyscrapers, the area of façade skin of skyscraper is voluminous. For example, the area of each skin is almost 20,000 m2, which can produce solid materials, such as ice and salt, as approximately 5,500 m3 over time.

    Firstly, sea level rise is a serious problem to urban areas within the pacific islands. Therefore, the skin of Suction Tower knotted with nylon fiber can easily absorb sea water. Once the water is absorbed, it goes through evaporation, which absorbs urban heat and produces salt.

    Moreover, as the surface of the façade is exposed to the cold air in winter, it is possible to form ice. The important relationship between ice and salt is that salt is beneficial in reducing the freezing point

0845

of ice. Therefore, ice blocks mixed with salt are transported to city and stored in a frigid basement for summer season. Also, they support the fish industry since ice and salt are indispensable to keep fish fresh.

Finally, the form of the tower follows the natural elements, such as wind, sun, and sea level. The façade, made with nylon fiber, is flexible and has the possibility to form a diverse amount shape according to humidity, temperature, and seasonal change.

The Suction Tower rises from the sea as a series of vertical filaments that serve as structure and connectors to the nylon skin. This veil gives the tower an almost ethereal aspect that blends with environment. There is a play of light passing through the veil and creating visual discrepancies in the

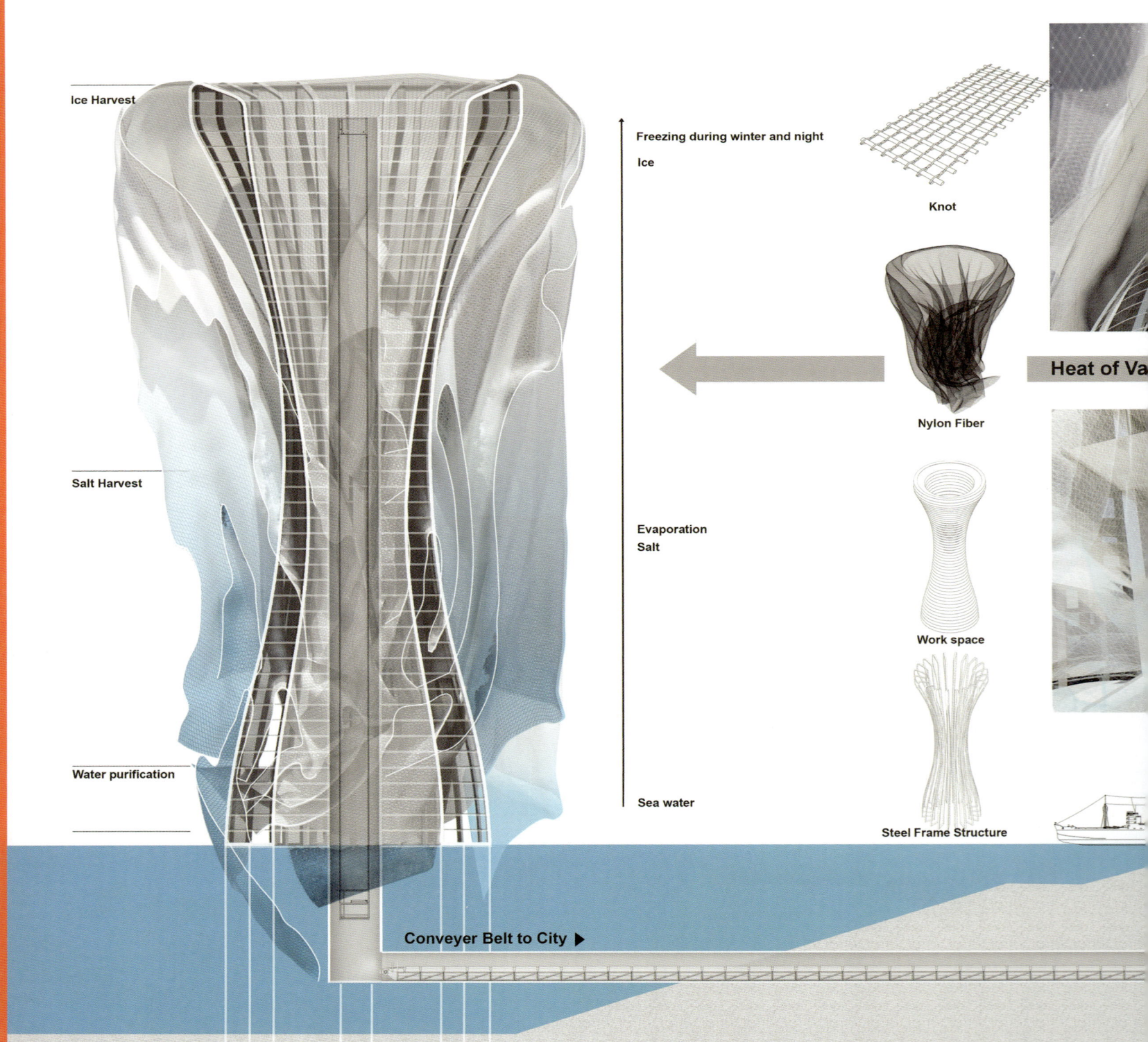

horizon while marking an iconic building. The vapors expelled from the tower also create a translucency effect that changes dramatically with the light exposure at different times during the day.

0845

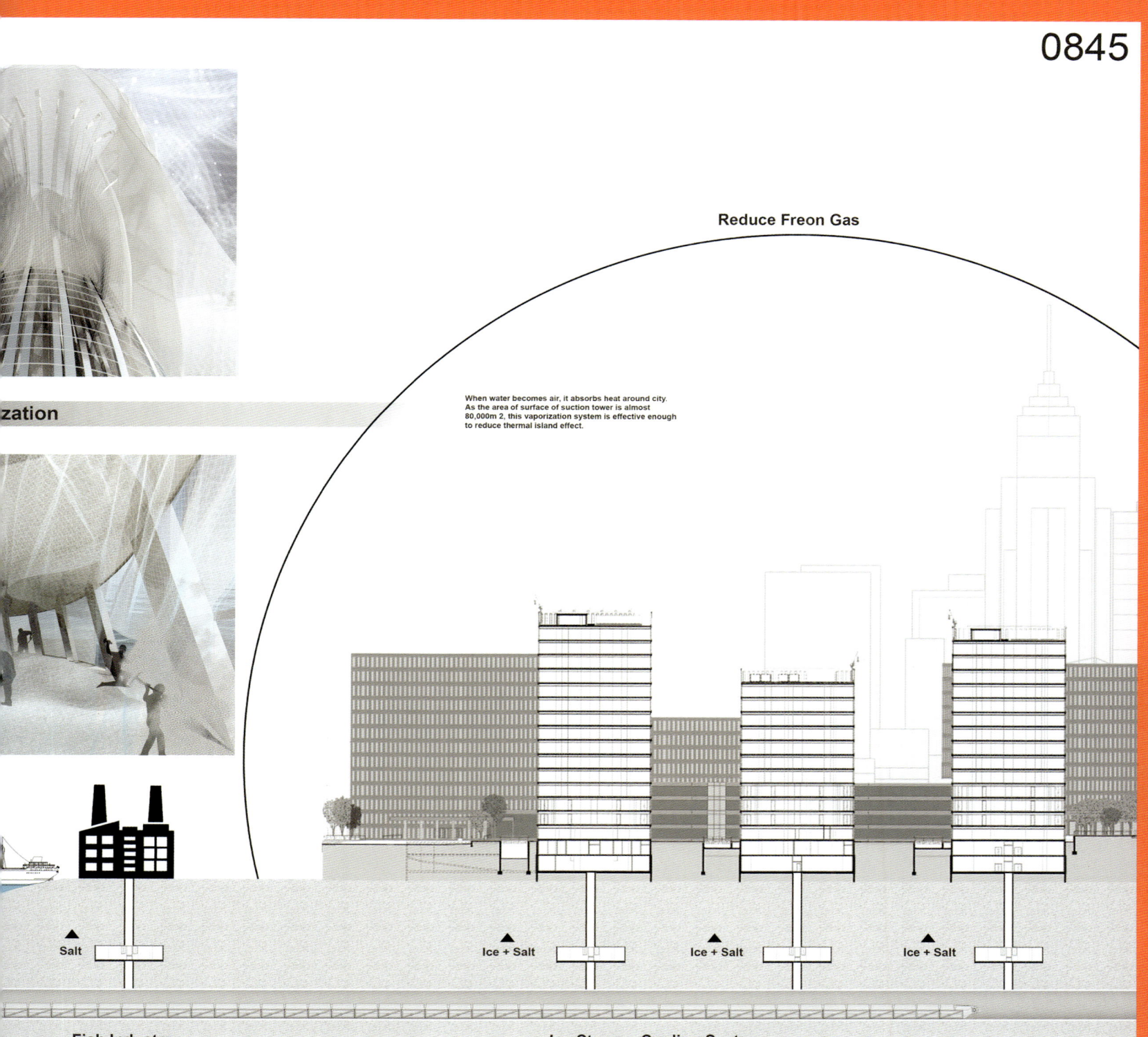

Reduce Freon Gas

When water becomes air, it absorbs heat around city. As the area of surface of suction tower is almost 80,000m 2, this vaporization system is effective enough to reduce thermal island effect.

zation

Salt

Ice + Salt   Ice + Salt   Ice + Salt

Fish Industry

Ice and salt are indispensable in fish industry in order to keep fishes fresh. Produced salt and ice from suction tower will improve fish industry and market economy.

Ice Storage Cooling System

Ice blocks and salts produced during winter and night are stored in storage under city buildings and support cooling system. This system replaces air-conditioning system which has produced Freon Gas. Moreover, the salt is good to decrease freezing point of ice.

EXPLORING ARCTIC

Nikolay Zaytsev
Elizaveta Lopatina

Russia

DIKSON /

This project is based on a complete transformation of an Arctic hub port. It is necessary to create comfortable working and living environments in the Northern Sea Route transport infrastructure. The initial idea is to design a separate anthropogenic microcosm, detached from the harsh Arctic environment, but based on the dynamic equilibrium between people and nature. The structure of the proposed building is similar to structures in nature; the earth's crust, and the structure of usual human perception. Symbolically, the imaginative solution consists of two main parts: a square of "man-made" land and circles of supporting celestial pillars. The result of the design is a single "horizontal skyscraper" high-rise building bearing all the functions of a port city, with the possibility of expanding.

The aim of the project is to increase the population of Dikson City from 674 to 5,000 by attracting

multifunctional complex in Dikson harbor
new   social   utopia / EXPLORING ARCTIC

people with various skills from all over the Russian Federation. The proposed building is a multifunctional complex that can replace the existing, ruined port city. Two distinct types of housing are created - housing for permanent workers with families and housing for temporary workers. Residential and public areas are augmented with large green recreational areas. For this purpose, the project employs natural and artificial lighting, since the Polar Night lasts three and a half months in this region.

One of the top priority tasks of this project is to redefine the energy supply of the city and the region as a whole. It requires switching from scarce fossil fuels to more environmentally friendly energy sources. In Dikson, the most available and abundant energy sources are wind and tidal power. The output capacity of designed wind and tidal power plants could reach up to 500 MW, which is enough to power

a city double the size of St. Petersburg. Water supply is another important aspect to reach sustainable development. Because of the small amount of fresh water available, the project involves the use of desalination plants and rainwater harvesting. The green zones' irrigation systems use water coming from the water recycling system. The proposed building is deliberately separated from the harsh environment, and at the same time is transparent and lightweight. The internal building's space is visually exposed to the Kara Sea, Dikson Island, and the mainland.

This project is expected to renovate the region's development, attracting both government and private investors, and to become a key point in global transport infrastructure. In this case, the project would be the beginning of a comprehensive Arctic exploration.

rainwater harvesting

0048

oculus

offices

hospital

housing for temporary workers

apartment block
168 040 m²

128 000 m²

public areas
63 500 m²

offshore wind generators

parking
93 000 m²

logistics

desalination plants

wind farm
100 000 m²

tidal power plants

NORTH PATH LEVIATHAN

Suleymanov Arsen
Anastasiya Lapina

Russia

GLOBAL MEAN SEA LEVEL / IPCC 4th report

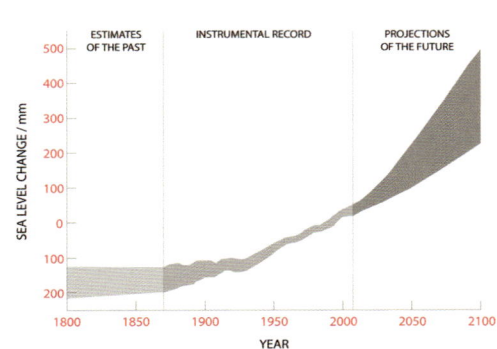

LEVIATHAN North-Path

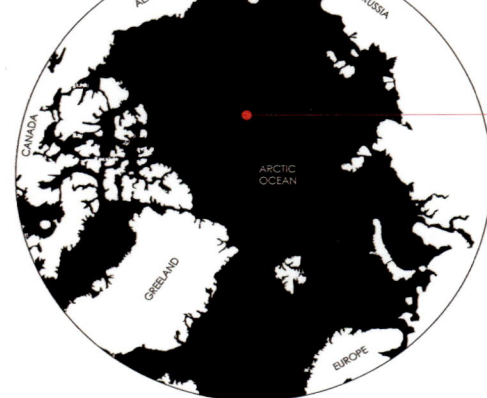

MAP-INVERSION

shows the "water to land" ratio.

Do not forget about GLOBAL WARMING and increasing WATER LEVEL -> huge UNUSED SPACE.

That is why our CONCEPT located in such undeveloped place.

And that is why the MAIN problems OUR PROJECT solves is: ECONOMIC and TRANSPORT issues, ICE- melting and CO2-excess.

Let's start with the fact that the Arctic - a huge area of the globe on the map represents a perfect circle whose area varies from 21 to 27 million square feet. km. In general, it is accepted to include areas stretching from the North Pole to the Arctic Circle and the northern boundary of the tundra. In the Arctic includes margin of North America and Eurasia(the five countries - Russia, Norway, Denmark, the United States and Canada) and adjacent oceanic expanses - the northern areas of the Pacific and Atlantic Oceans, plus the Arctic Ocean completely. The Arctic also holds 1/5 of the Earth's water supply.

Contrary to popular misconception that the Arctic - it's entirely severe frosts, the climate is diverse and is soft enough in the summer, when the Arctic and organize the major tours and amateur expeditions.

For the Arctic climate is characterized by long cold winters and short cool summers in moderation. The average July temperature ranges from -10 ° C in the polar regions and +10 ° C on the northern borders of the continent. This is quite a comfortable climate due to large bodies of water: the ocean water can not be cooled below -2 ° C and thus supports a moderate temperature in the region.

Increased solar radiation - a feature of the Arctic, because during the polar day the sun does not set at all. This should definitely be taken into account, going to the Arctic: you definitely need a sunscreen with a high SPF.

Winter in the Arctic, the thermometer drops to the level of -10 ° C in the mainland to -40 ° C as it approaches the North Pole. Strong gusty winds and blizzards.

Polar summer tundra nesting millions of migratory birds. In the seas of the Arctic live seals, walruses and several species of cetaceans: baleen whales, narwhal, beluga and killer whales. Climate change threatens many Arctic animals with extinction.

But we decided to place an object in the most difficult and problematic area: in the central part - the Arctic Basin, a region deep basins (up to 5527 m) and underwater ridges. Single physiographic regions of the Earth. One of the dangers - icebergs, high waves, fog and ice multimeter .. Arctic ice are essential to Earth's climate system. Ice cap reflects the sun's rays and thus prevents overheating the planet. In addition, the Arctic ice play an important role in the systems of water circulation in the oceans. Many experts suggest that in the XXI century in the summer most of the water area of the Arctic will be completely ice-free, and it will open up new prospects for the carriage of goods. And now passes through the Arctic cross-polar air bridge (the shortest route between North America and Asia) and the Northern Sea Route - the shortest sea route between East Asia and Europe or A Polar Route is an aircraft route across the uninhabited polar ice cap regions.

The Arctic is comparatively clean, although there are certain ecologically difficult localized pollution problems that present a serious threat to people's health living around these pollution sources. Due to the prevailing worldwide sea and air currents, the Arctic area is the fallout region for long-range transport pollutants, and in some places the concentrations exceed the levels of densely populated urban areas. An example of this is the phenomenon of Arctic haze, which is commonly blamed on long-range pollutants. Another example is with the bioaccumulation of PCB's (polychlorinated biphenyls) in Arctic wildlife and people.

Burj Khalifa
(horizontal)

Eiffel Tower
(vertical)

5500 m

SMART COLUMNS

FORMFINDING

AIRPORT

SEAPORT

ARCH
for functions
and sustainability

SKYLIGHTS ar
for internal
public park

LEVIATHAN North-Path

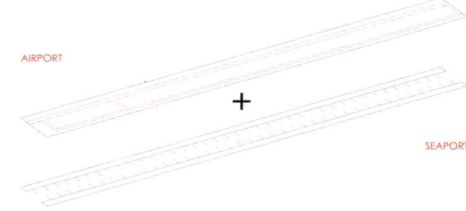

MAIN FUNCTIONS

HORIZONTAL-SKYS

Arctic sea ice is melting rapidly, and within the next decade the effects of global warming may transform the Polar region from an inaccessible frozen desert into a seasonally navigable ocean. The summer of 2011 saw a record 33 ships, carrying 850,000 tons of cargo navigate the Northern Sea Route (NSR) off Russia's northern coast. This year's shipping season may see up to 1.5 million tons of cargo, as Germany's Alfred Wegener Institute predicts the NSR to be ice-free and passable for ships by early summer. The North West Passage (NWP), first ice-free in 2007, and the Transpolar Sea Route (TSR) may also open up to shipping traffic over the coming decades. Over the past decades the Arctic has witnessed a much faster than anticipated decline of sea ice and the continuation of this trend will transform the Arctic Ocean into a navigable seaway over the coming decades. Yet due to the region's

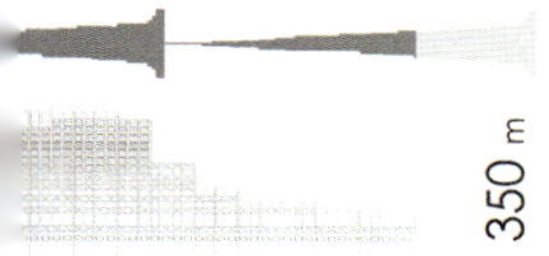

0139

350 m

ZONING SCHEME: the basic functions of the airport and port are set statically. The rest are on mobile construction.

CONTROL CENTER   AIRPORT   CENTRAL PARK   HOLDING   SOCIAL FUNCTIONS   STORAGE   PORT

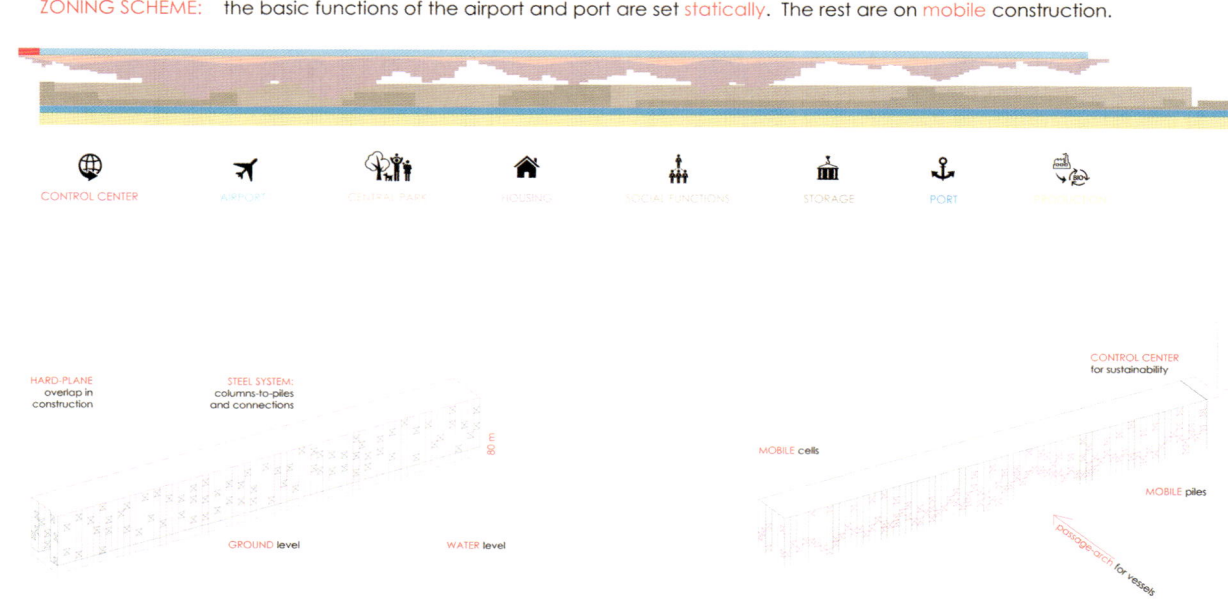

HARD-PLANE
overlap in
construction

STEEL SYSTEM:
columns-to-piles
and connections

CONTROL CENTER
for sustainability

350 m

80 m

MOBILE cells

MOBILE piles

HEIGHT
for functions
and sustainability

GROUND level   WATER level

passage-arch for vessels

CONCEPT   best CONSTRUCTIVE solution 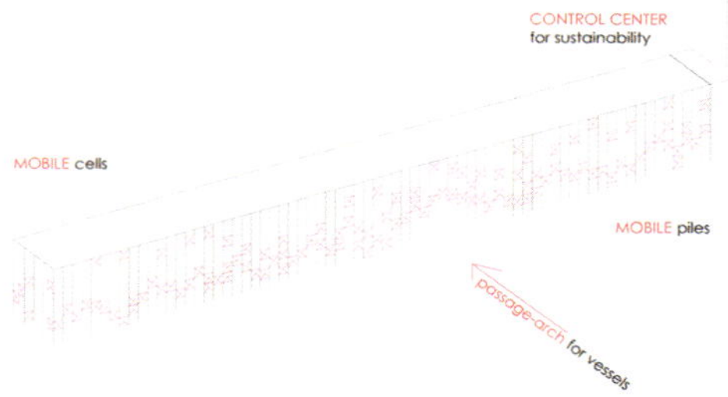   by WEATHER-changing system

unique navigational and economic challenges Arctic shipping will, for the foreseeable future, only be cost effective for a limited number of operators. The Transpolar Sea Route (TSR) represents the most direct route for trans-Arctic shipment but has yet to attract significant commercial interest, as multi-year ice remains a formidable obstacle for most of the Arctic-shipping season. Trans-Arctic shipping, regardless of the actual route used, will not serve as a substitute for existing shipping routes, but will instead be supplemental and provide additional capacity for a growing transportation volume. For the foreseeable future, the limited seasonal window for trans-Arctic voyages must be taken into account in any projections. Nonetheless, the development of Arctic offshore hydrocarbon resources and related economic activities will result in an improved integration of the Arctic economy in global trade patterns.

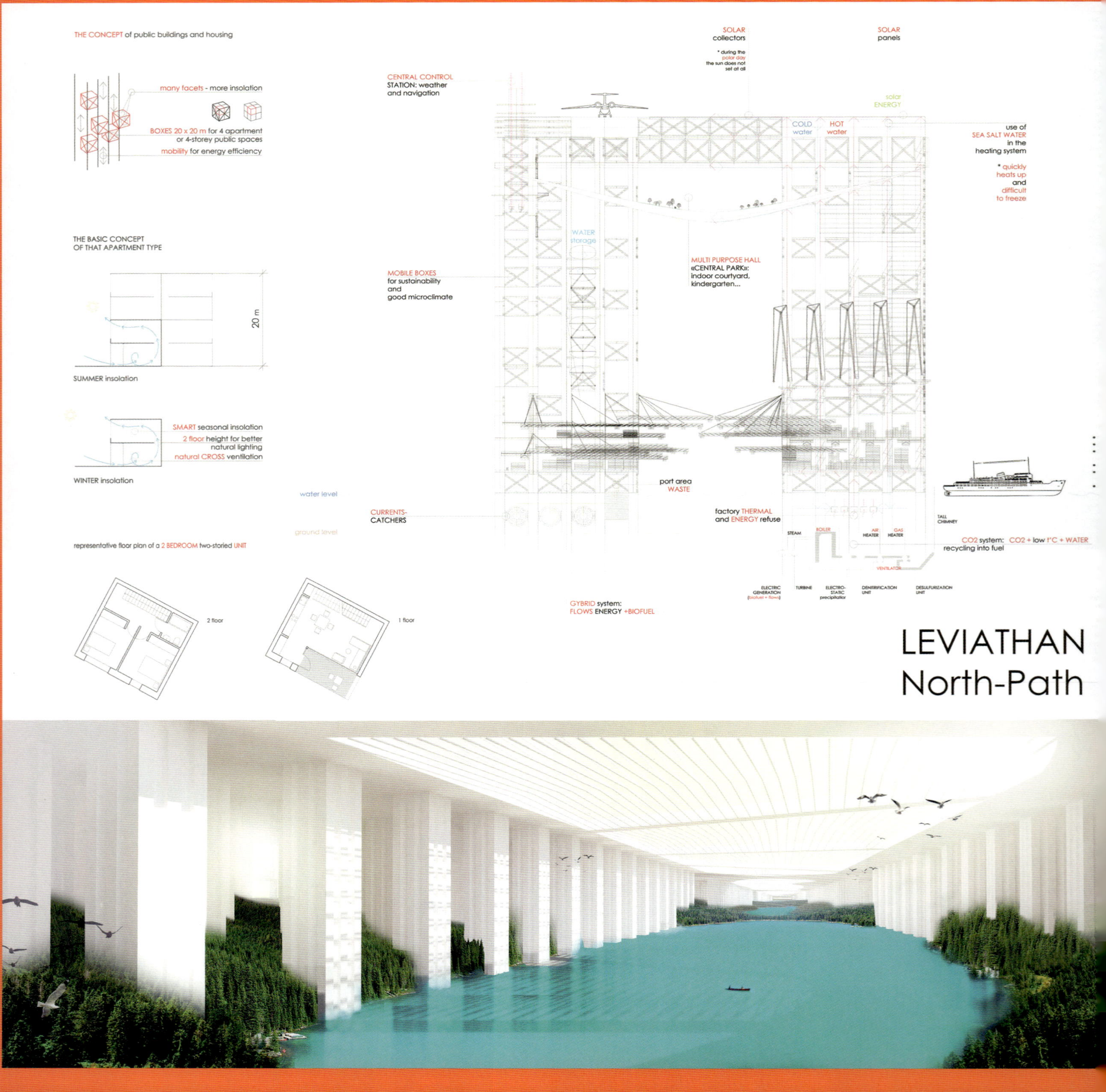

THE CONCEPT of public buildings and housing

many facets - more insolation

BOXES 20 x 20 m for 4 apartment or 4-storey public spaces

mobility for energy efficiency

THE BASIC CONCEPT OF THAT APARTMENT TYPE

20 m

SUMMER insolation

SMART seasonal insolation

2 floor height for better natural lighting

natural CROSS ventilation

WINTER insolation

water level

ground level

representative floor plan of a 2 BEDROOM two-storied UNIT

2 floor

1 floor

CENTRAL CONTROL STATION: weather and navigation

SOLAR collectors

* during the polar day the sun does not set at all

SOLAR panels

solar ENERGY

COLD water HOT water

use of SEA SALT WATER in the heating system

* quickly heats up and difficult to freeze

WATER storage

MOBILE BOXES for sustainability and good microclimate

MULTI PURPOSE HALL «CENTRAL PARK»: indoor courtyard, kindergarten...

CURRENTS-CATCHERS

port area WASTE

factory THERMAL and ENERGY refuse

STEAM BOILER AIR HEATER GAS HEATER

TALL CHIMNEY

CO_2 system: CO_2 + low t°C + WATER recycling into fuel

VENTILATION

ELECTRIC GENERATION (biofuel + flows) TURBINE ELECTRO-STATIC precipitator DENITRIFICATION UNIT DESULFUREZATION UNIT

GYBRID system: FLOWS ENERGY +BIOFUEL

LEVIATHAN
North-Path

The idea of our Project is to provide Arctic Zone with marine infrastructure - the three primary demands for shipping services being moving natural resources out of the region, supplying goods to communities, and tourism; an airport where passenger volumes on intercontinental flights are low, but cargo traffic is expanding rapidly, and new routes are in demand; a community, as extracting resources without creating community near the place of extraction is the best recipe for ecological disaster; an efficient industry to provide arctic zone and future projects with products; an energy system based on half oil and gas extraction half on using wind, current and solar energy and producing resources from carbon dioxide; eco-control of all activities in Arctic; a supplement of offshore oil and gas production; and control of releasing carbon dioxide from melting permafrost pushing oil and gas production on a new high and eco-safe level.

nception is integrated into the environment:
transparent and unobtrusive, pass-through,
, capacious and unusual.

esult, good conditions for improving energy
cy. Huge flat roof allows using of solar collectors
nels. For victory over the rigorous climate - wide
one implemented in MULTIPUROSED HALL
l park" with good microclimate, indoor
rd, kindergarten... Large percentage of energy
from undercurrents. Our "currents –catchers"
at the level of warm water t'C. Huge CO2
ulation in Arctic ice and in the atmosphere has
he creation of a plant for processing CO2 into
ough a long recovery process. the synthesis of
ol - that requires a low temperature and water).
er, the plant loses a lot of heat during "CO2-
cture", so we use these losses for heating pipes
water for heating all the building. Sea water
urities: salt crystals. It is difficult to freeze and
p quickly! Also we have a hybrid system with a
tion biofuels-biogas station of debris.

ic constructive concept – vertical connections,
d pillars. They provide mobility of construction:
to different functions of our project from the
o the Industry area, from the Central park to the
atial boxes 20x20 move vertically, depending on
conditions and the approaching ships. The
station is equipped with a powerful navigation
and a weather station. Plus, we have clearance
for the future elevation of the water level...
nore in the construction of piles a pipe-system
d which heats buildings, supports Park's green-
mate. For fluid heating – solar-collectors, the
a heat from the industry and port zones. We
the energy, heat and condensate of
ent and refrigeration of underwater industrial
heating public spaces of the complex. Also we
eservoir of water- system.

g-architecture concept - small blocks: good
nate, lighting and natural-ventilation,
able living-area. The frame construction with
crete partitions and eco-materials. Using of
in on the glazing system of public areas and
ted shutters for living: the principle is in the oil
on and contraction with the temperature
g, so oil pushes or takes-in a stock in special
c cylinders.

can even depict the application of heat by
of hoods, and, for example, to heat this heat
d elevator components since we are talking
e air, which probably is not good from a public
he living lodge.

important thing to make people really want to
ate in the ecology of our "city" and around the
housing. We need to use psychological
es and bring that feeling from childhood.

have provided:

nentally friendly waste-free production.
nental marketing
capital in the environmental field and effective
on.
nental insurance.
nental management and environmental
on.
l reports and inventories of natural resources.

urpose - to transform a former military
ture into a leisure time & cultural focal point -
on one hand of triggering urban
opment & social cooperation and on the other
attract citizens & tourists?

e trying to rethink a skyscraper into a multi-
chitectural element:

scale - combine the basic necessary
and a public comfort -"horizontal
unity skyscraper".

ole project will match energetic and
nmental sustainability criteria. Energetic
vironmental sustainability will be achieved
cleverly distributing functions and wisely
materials, techniques and building solutions
in order to attenuate environmental impact.
r, it is possible to take care of energetic
ction (i.e. from renewable sources) in order to
/ totally cover the project's overall energetic
tion.

0139

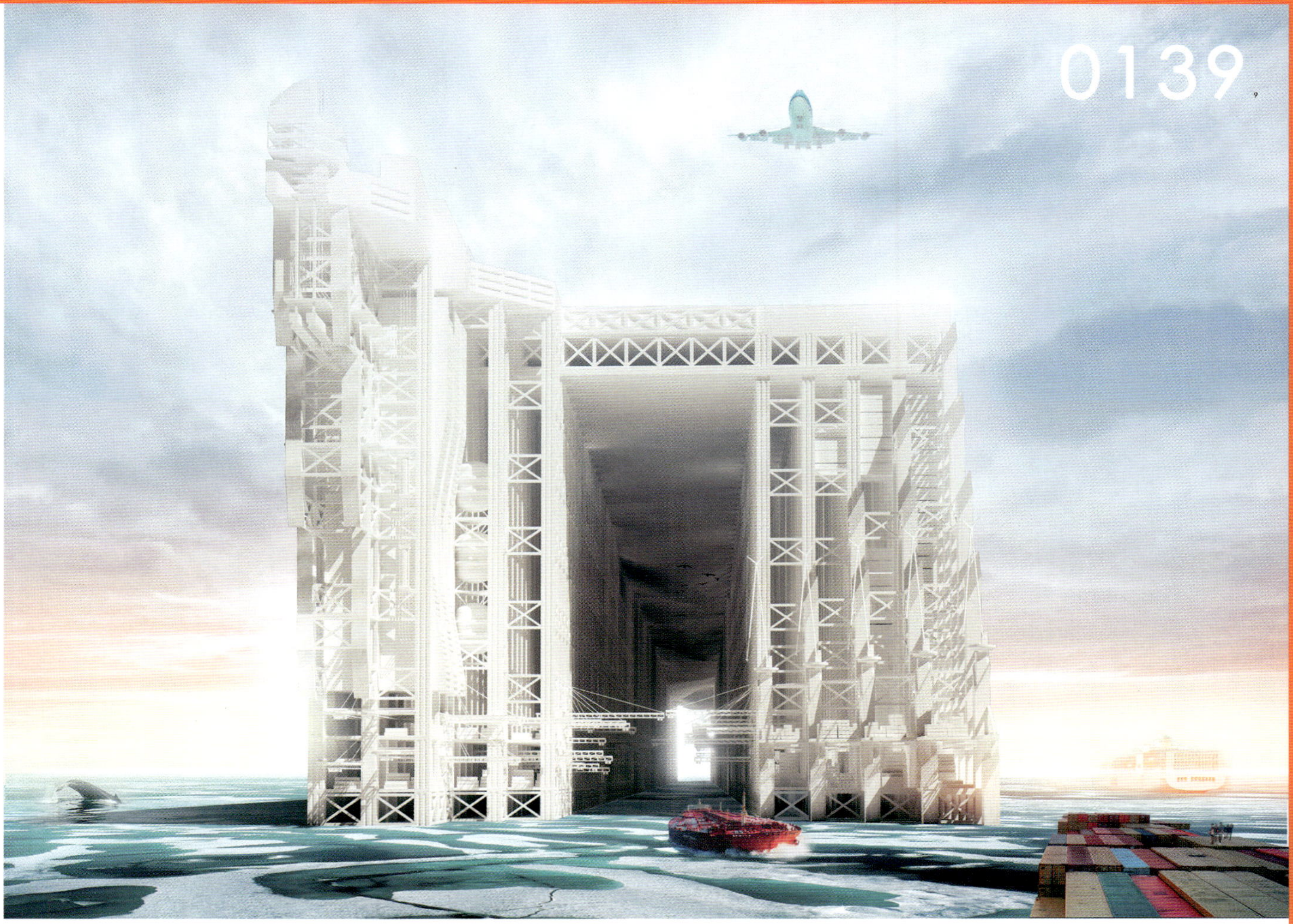

WHERE GLOBAL WARMING IS GOING?

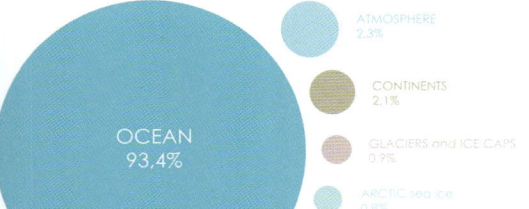

OCEAN
93,4%
ATMOSPHERE
2,3%
CONTINENTS
2,1%
GLACIERS and ICE CAPS
0.9%
ARCTIC sea ice
0.8%
GREENLAND ice sheet
ANTARCTIC ice sheet
0.2%

Energy efficiency and eco-friendship of HOUSING DEVICE

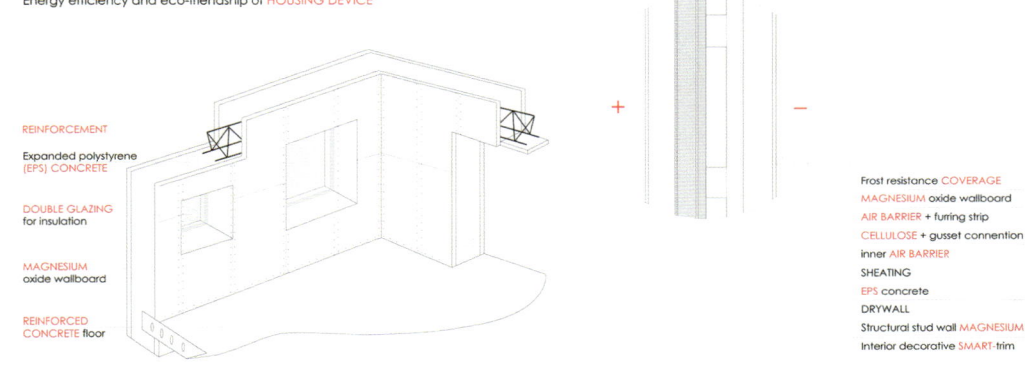

REINFORCEMENT
Expanded polystyrene (EPS) CONCRETE
DOUBLE GLAZING for insulation
MAGNESIUM oxide wallboard
REINFORCED CONCRETE floor
+
–
Frost resistance COVERAGE
MAGNESIUM oxide wallboard
AIR BARRIER + furring strip
CELLULOSE + gusset connention
inner AIR BARRIER
SHEATING
EPS concrete
DRYWALL
Structural stud wall MAGNESIUM
Interior decorative SMART-trim

TRITON

Amit Bura
Jack Marston
Mateusz Wlosek

United Kingdom

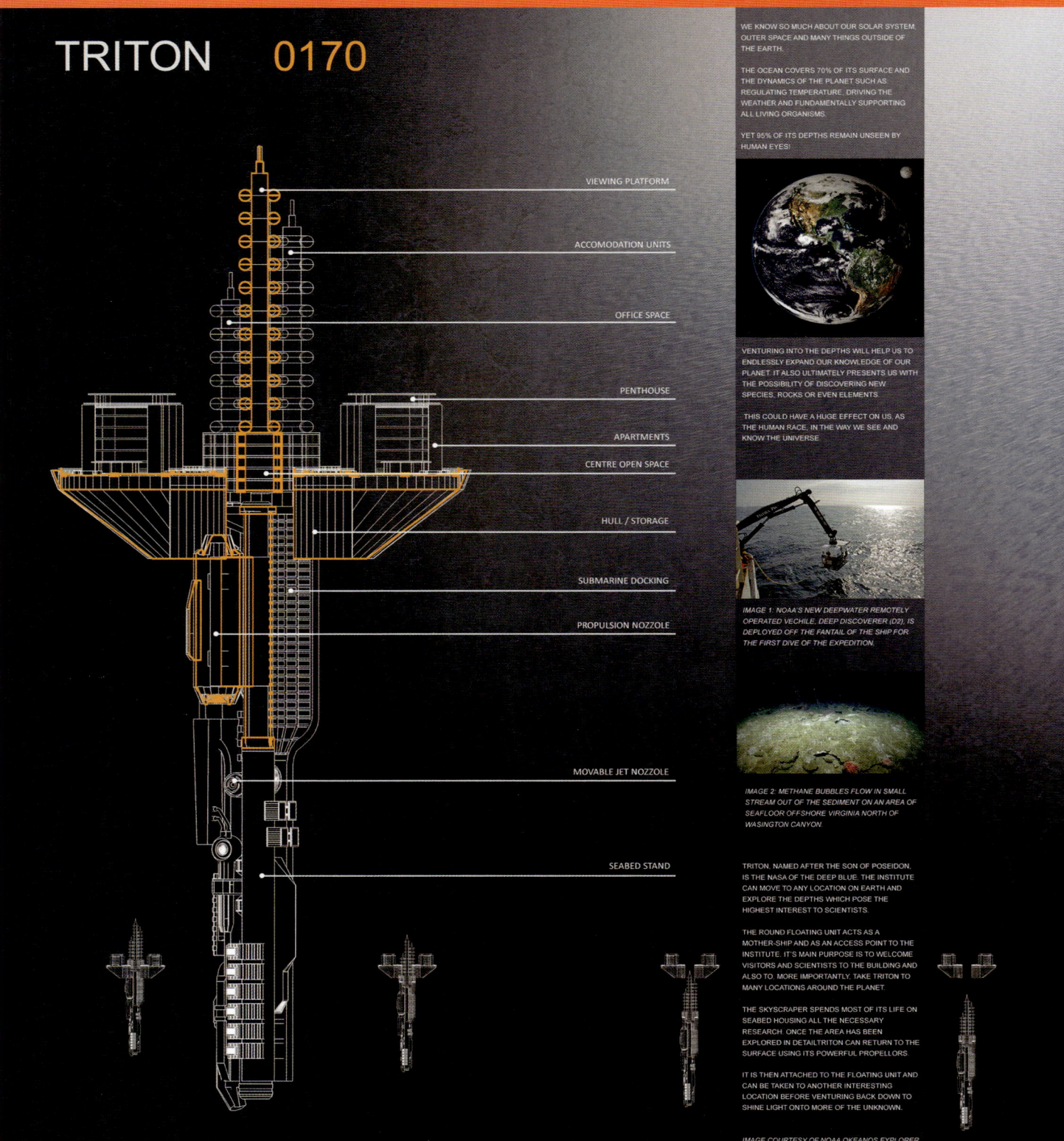

TRITON   0170

VIEWING PLATFORM

ACCOMODATION UNITS

OFFICE SPACE

PENTHOUSE

APARTMENTS

CENTRE OPEN SPACE

HULL / STORAGE

SUBMARINE DOCKING

PROPULSION NOZZOLE

MOVABLE JET NOZZOLE

SEABED STAND

WE KNOW SO MUCH ABOUT OUR SOLAR SYSTEM, OUTER SPACE AND MANY THINGS OUTSIDE OF THE EARTH.

THE OCEAN COVERS 70% OF ITS SURFACE AND THE DYNAMICS OF THE PLANET SUCH AS: REGULATING TEMPERATURE, DRIVING THE WEATHER AND FUNDAMENTALLY SUPPORTING ALL LIVING ORGANISMS.

YET 95% OF ITS DEPTHS REMAIN UNSEEN BY HUMAN EYES!

VENTURING INTO THE DEPTHS WILL HELP US TO ENDLESSLY EXPAND OUR KNOWLEDGE OF OUR PLANET. IT ALSO ULTIMATELY PRESENTS US WITH THE POSSIBILITY OF DISCOVERING NEW SPECIES, ROCKS OR EVEN ELEMENTS.

THIS COULD HAVE A HUGE EFFECT ON US, AS THE HUMAN RACE, IN THE WAY WE SEE AND KNOW THE UNIVERSE

IMAGE 1: NOAA'S NEW DEEPWATER REMOTELY OPERATED VECHILE, DEEP DISCOVERER (D2), IS DEPLOYED OFF THE FANTAIL OF THE SHIP FOR THE FIRST DIVE OF THE EXPEDITION.

IMAGE 2: METHANE BUBBLES FLOW IN SMALL STREAM OUT OF THE SEDIMENT ON AN AREA OF SEAFLOOR OFFSHORE VIRGINIA NORTH OF WASINGTON CANYON.

TRITON, NAMED AFTER THE SON OF POSEIDON, IS THE NASA OF THE DEEP BLUE. THE INSTITUTE CAN MOVE TO ANY LOCATION ON EARTH AND EXPLORE THE DEPTHS WHICH POSE THE HIGHEST INTEREST TO SCIENTISTS.

THE ROUND FLOATING UNIT ACTS AS A MOTHER-SHIP AND AS AN ACCESS POINT TO THE INSTITUTE. IT'S MAIN PURPOSE IS TO WELCOME VISITORS AND SCIENTISTS TO THE BUILDING AND ALSO TO. MORE IMPORTANTLY, TAKE TRITON TO MANY LOCATIONS AROUND THE PLANET.

THE SKYSCRAPER SPENDS MOST OF ITS LIFE ON SEABED HOUSING ALL THE NECESSARY RESEARCH. ONCE THE AREA HAS BEEN EXPLORED IN DETAILTRITON CAN RETURN TO THE SURFACE USING ITS POWERFUL PROPELLORS.

IT IS THEN ATTACHED TO THE FLOATING UNIT AND CAN BE TAKEN TO ANOTHER INTERESTING LOCATION BEFORE VENTURING BACK DOWN TO SHINE LIGHT ONTO MORE OF THE UNKNOWN.

IMAGE COURTESY OF NOAA OKEANOS EXPLORER PROGRAM, 2013 NORTHEAST U.S. CONYPNS EXPEDITION.

We know so much about our solar system, distant space and outer earth. A vast ocean covers 70% of our planet's surface. The dynamics of this planet such as: temperature, weather and the support of all living organisms depend upon it. Yet 95% of its depths remain unseen by human eyes!

Venturing into the depths can helps us to tremendously expand our knowledge of the Earth and ultimately present us with the possibility of discovering new species, rocks or even elements. This could have a huge effect on us, as the human race; in the way we see and know the universe.

Triton, named after the son of Poseidon, is the NASA of the deep blue. The institute can move to any location on the globe and explore the depths, which interest scientists. The round floating unit acts as a mother ship and as an access point for the institute. Its main purpose is to welcome visitors and

scientists to the building providing a open green space far out in the ocean. More importantly, it is to take triton to various locations around the planet. The skyscraper spends most of its life on the seabed, housing all the necessary equipment and people to carry out that is bound to become, and breakthrough research. Once an area has been extensively explored triton can return to the surface using its powerful propellers. It is then attached to its counterpart and can be taken to another area of interest before voyaging back down to shine light onto more of the unknown.

It is our aim to map the oceans as accurately as we have mapped our lands, with species of plants, bacteria, fish and rock. With many scientists living down on the ocean floor on a daily basis discoveries made will be ten-fold more efficient and useful. Allowing the seabed itself to become a laboratory will

THE ROVER DISCOVER: A FIELD OF BED FORMS OR RIPPLES ON A FLAT AREA OF KELVIN SEAMOUNT. GEOLOGISTS AND OCEANOGRAPHERS CAN LEARN A LOT ABOUT THE CURRENT CONDITIONS OF AN AREA BY STUDYING THE SIZE AND SHAPE OF THE RIPPLES.

CLOSE-UP OF METHANE HYDRATE OBSERVED AT A DEPTH OF 1,055 METERS, NEAR WHERE BUBBLE PLMES WERE DETECTED.

TODAY A TRIP DOWN TO BEDROCK IS VERY INEFFICIENT. A SEMI-PERMANENT STRUCTURE ON THE SEABED WILL BRING THE VAST POSSIBILITIES AND DISCOVERIES HIDING IN THE DARK TO THE FINGERTIPS OF:

BIOLOGISTS
ARCHAEOLOGISTS
PHYSICISTS
GEOLOGISTS
CHEMISTS

TRITON:

AS MUCH AS THE TRITON IS DESIGNED FOR THE SEA ENTHUSIAST THE DESIGN IS ALSO AIMED TOWARDS PROVIDING A HIGH QUALITY LIVING SPACE. AS WITH UNIQUE LANDSCPAPE THE USERS WILL ALSO BE ABLE TO ENJOY THE ULTIMATE UNDISTRUBED ASPECTS TOWRDS THE OCEAN. THE ICONIC ROUND INNER TUBE SHAPE IS CONTSTRUCTED WITH PURE GLASS AND STEE STRUCTURE TO ALLOW UNDISTURBED VIEW. AUTOMATIC BLINDS WILL PROVIDE THE SHADING. THE STRUCTURE IS MADE UP OF TWO MAIN COMPONENTERS A CIRCULAR FLOATING BASE WHICH ACTS AS A MEANS OF TRANSPORT FOR THE INSTITURE AND ALSO AS THE HUB OF THE BUILDING ON THE SURFACE.

THE HIGHEST OF THE 3 TOWERS HOUSES THE PENTHOUSES, WHEREAS THE TOP FLOOR IS DESIGNED TO BE A VIEWING PLATFORM FOR THE VISITORS. THE PART OF THE TOWER ALSO SHARES THE ROLE OF DATA SURVIALLANCE AND NAVIGATION OF THE TRITORN.THE STAINLESS STEEL TUBES THAT SUPPORTS THE FLOOR PROVIDE THE STRUCTURE AND IS THE CIRCULATION CORE FOR THE FLATS LABS AND OFFICES. TRITORN FLOATS AS A UNIT INTO SEA.

THE SKYSCRAPER THEN DETACHES FROM THE BASE AND SWIMS TO THE SEABED, RESHEARCH IS CARRIED OUT OVER A PERIOD OF MONTHS BEFORE IT FLOATS BACK UP TO ITS COUNTERPART TO BE TAKEN TO ANOTHER LOCATION.

undoubtedly to maximise the possibilities for the development of new technologies and inventions like it has never been done before.

It must be stressed that increasing our understanding of the ocean realm will help us understand the dynamics of our seas at greater depth, aid in the development of countless new technologies and help unlock the secrets of the ocean.

BOAT ENTRANCE

PUBLIC SEATING

OPENING BRIDGE

RESEARCH LABS

CIRCULATION TUBES

APARTMENTS

LANDSCAPING / GREENARY

BOAT ENTRANCE

PUBLIC SEATING

OPENING BRIDGE

OPEN WATER

APARTMENTS

LANDSCAPING

TRITON   0170

WEATHER DOCTOR

Taehan Kim
Seungji Lee
Yujin Ha

South Korea

SCENARIO 1(2033 A.D.): Conversation between Air Traffic control (ATC) and Weather Doctor (WD)

0 : 25 : 30
ATC : WD this is ATC ,

WD : Good Morning , ATC! This is WD. How Can we help you today?

00 : 26 : 10
ATC : WD, what's the weather status in the next half hour ?

WD: ATC , The weather has chances of dense fog and hail around the Airport!!

00 : 27 : 10 ATC : WD, Flight MH333, MH301 and MH378 are about to land in next 20 minutes.

WD: ATC, ok, what you want us to do?

00 : 27 : 55 ATC : WD, Please hold the phenomenon for next 20 minutes for safe landing at the airport.

WD : ATC, Give us 2 minutes !!

00 : 28 : 15 ATC : WD, OK !

00 : 34 : 15 WD: ATC , Hail and fog has been delayed for next 20 minutes !

ATC : WD, Alright, Good Night.

00 : 34 : 30 WD : ATC , Good Night !

SCENARIO 2(2033 A.D.): Conversation between Coast gaurd(CG) and Weather Doctor (WD)

17 : 05 : 30 : WD : CG , This is WD , this is an urgent broadcast !

CG : WD, This is CG California , what's the matter ?

17 : 06 : 10 WD : CG, There is a hurricane heading towards the Coast of California at SECTOR 13 , kindly evacuate in the next half hour and leave the shore clear ?

CG: WD ,Evacuation is not possible in next 30 minutes can u delay the hurricane for 2 hours for safe evacuation ?

17 : 07 : 10 WD : CG ,Alright we are making efforts to impede the Storm and delay the outcomes, in the mean time kindly evacuate

CG: WD, ok, Evacuation Procedure started and is Underway!

17 : 25 : 55 WD: CG the hurricane intensity has been mitigated for safe evacuation time!!

18 : 55 : 55
CG : Coast Secure!!

18 : 56 : 15 WD: CG, ok, Guard town till further notice!

CG : WD, Alright!

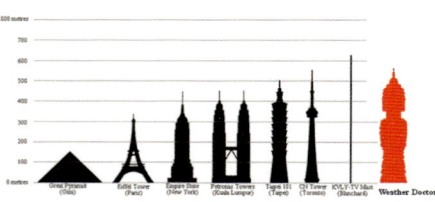

Weather Doctor

The Weather modification programme.

Mother Nature has always remained powerful and at times dangerous in terms of weather situation it creates on Planet Earth. Yet it yield life in many different form. We design our habitats keeping in mind adversity of its behavior. Till now we never have proper control on Weather situations. Life on Earth have faced major disastrous consequence arises from bad Weather which include Drought, Hail, Strom, Hurricanes, Tornado, Fog, Lightning. If we know how electricity builds up and spreads in the atmosphere, we can also prevent death and damage caused by lightning strikes. Weather modifiers were trying to produce rain in drought-afflicted areas, mitigate hail damage by preventing hailstones from growing so large, or disperse fog banks around airports. Effort to keep nature at bay isn't new, but to succeed controlling the weather as per our need is really a difficult question to be answered....

Study of earth's environment has become major importance among the scientist throughout the world. Large number of research and intuition have come up to understand how environment behaves. Project Storm fury, Project Cirrus or Project Baton etc has deployed to understand weather phenomenon. Still we are unable to make it adaptive in nature.

The Weather Modification Operations and Research Board United States government, promote research into weather modification. Carrying the development further, we have tried to envisage the project which actually does so.
  Proposed project intended to provide substantial Weather Modification Programme to control weather in a suitable way which would be beneficial for the habitation in an around world. We do not intent to change weather drastically, but to protect ourselves from its disastrous consequence. For this, Project dated 2033 citing to have a developed technology for controlling weather as per our need, our project requires to build a skyscraper to accommodate our experimental lab, research facilities, weather monitoring center etc.

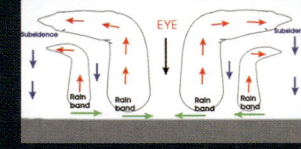

Typical cyclone formation

Concept

In 2033, Project Weather Doctor has come up solving weather related issue. This project is the heart of chaos theory, a set of scientific principles describing highly complex weather systems, where small changes in initial conditions radically change the final results. Our project can be located in any part of world where cities have to face major shift in climatic conditions. This project aims to control many aspect of weather considered which is disastrous in nature. Below mention are aspects which our skyscrapers require have control over the same.

1. Cloud seeding.
2. Fog prevention.
3. Strom prevention.
4. Hurricane modification.
5. Tornado prevention
6. Hail/snow prevention.
7. Prevent tornadoes formation.
8. Prevent Acidic deposition in Air to improve air quality.
9. Control tropical Cyclone.

Project also aims to:
• Capture Electricity from atmosphere.
• Harvest Lightning energy.
• Increase ozone production in atmosphere for protection against Sun's Ultraviolet rays.
• Monitor Carbon monoxide & Carbon dioxide emission responsible for green house effect.

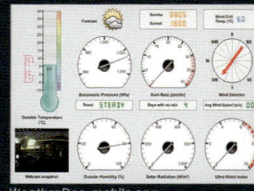

Weather Doc. mobile app.

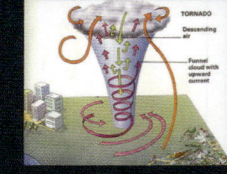

Tornado formation diagram

It was unknown at first that the juvenile yet ingenious imagination of touching and catching a cloud would bring balance to Earth.

    Mankind, despite its remarkable advancements, could not for once surpass the greatness of nature. In the face of devastating floods and droughts, our best attempts resulted in the mere building of dams and planting of trees. But one day, the abnormalities of climate started to exhibit signs of balance.

    This balance came from the redistribution of clouds. Capturing then releasing the clouds from where they are abundant to scarce, started to change the color of the planet Earth. The arid, yellow deserts transformed into lush environments full of life and diverse vegetation. Changes in the nature were only the start of all the other transformations to follow.

0239

The Weather Doctor is a skyscraper that controls weather in multiple ways. It is equipped with cloud seeding properties. The top of the skyscraper is designed to release particles of silver iodide to help in the creation of new clouds. Rockets filled with liquid nitrogen are kept in the skyscraper to be launched at the epicenter of hurricanes or tropical cyclones. The liquid nitrogen will reduce evaporation, the process that drives hurricane formation.

The skyscraper is also equipped with a powerful solar beam to heat the atmosphere in front of tornados to divert their path. The lower section of the skyscraper contains fog collectors to store atmosphere's water.

Finally the Weather Doctor is also equipped with tools to harvest lightning energy through a ionized

Cloud Seeding
Today skyscraper has reached up to the clouds. Cloud seeding is a technique to enhance precipitation. . Cloud seeding entails spraying small particles, silver iodide onto clouds directly from the top of the tower. Alternately using laser on the top of the tower works by stripping electrons from the atoms in the air, forming positively charged particles that help generate tiny "seeds" around which ice or rain drops can grow. The particles become heavy enough to fall as rain or snow. Water releases heat as it freezes, warmed air rises. Updrafts lift moist air into cloud making more snow.

Hurricane Modification
A tropical cyclone is a rapidly rotating storm system characterized by a low-pressure center, strong winds, and a spiral arrangement of thunderstorms that produce heavy rain. They derive their energy through the evaporation of water from the ocean surface, which ultimately recondenses into clouds and rain when moist air rises and cools to saturation.
Rockets filled with liquid nitrogen or with a thin layer of biodegradable oil are fired from the tower onto the sea to deprive the hurricane of heat energy. Using non-toxic oil slicks to calm the surface of the ocean and prevent formation of the ocean spray that eventually evolves into a hurricane i.e. literally pouring oil onto troubled waters. This will reduce evaporation, the process that drives hurricane formation.

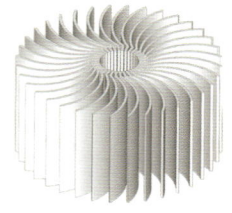

Rotating fan for capturing So2 & No from atmoshpere

Tornado prevention
Tornado needs both a cold, rainy downdraft and a warm updraft. The tower would collect solar energy, transform it into microwaves, and send a beam. The beams would be focused on cold downdrafts, heating them or Divert the path of a hurricane by heating the atmosphere in front of it, presumably with the aforementioned microwave satellites, or with a giant orbiting mirror that reflects the sun's energy

Fog prevention
Fog is caused by tiny water droplets suspended in the air. Anti-fog agents are chemicals that prevent the condensation of water in the form of small droplets on a surface which resemble fog. This chemical cloud can be disbursed from the tower into the surrounding atmosphere to clear Fog.

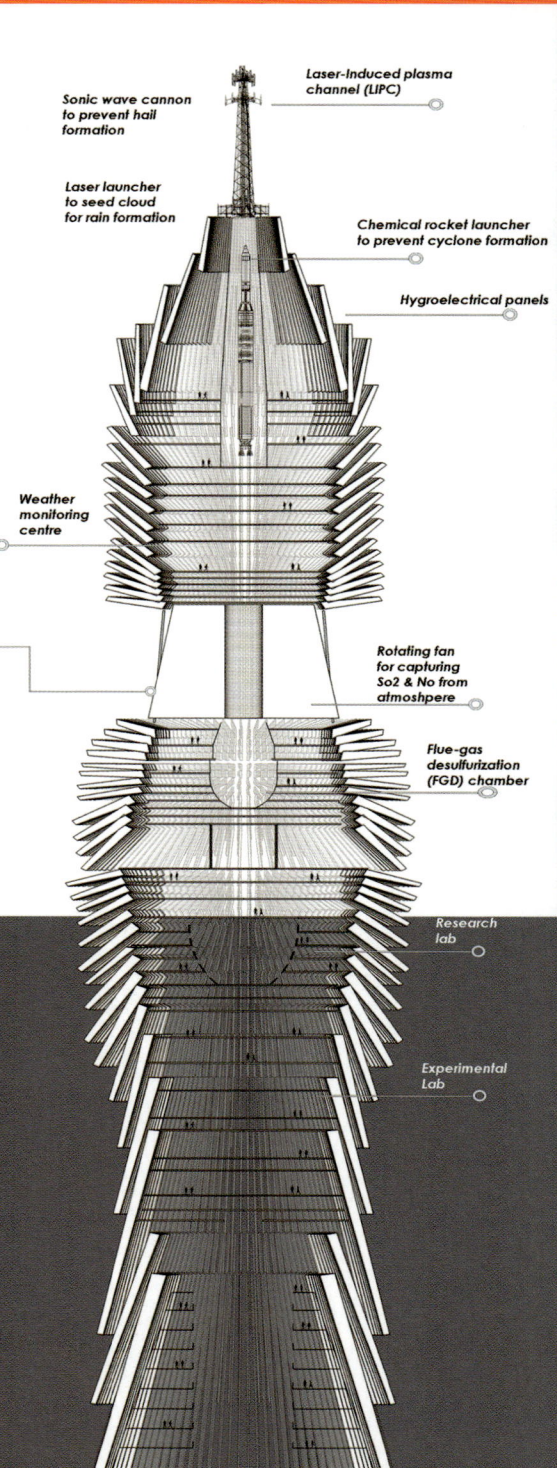

Sonic wave cannon to prevent hail formation

Laser-Induced plasma channel (LIPC)

Laser launcher to seed cloud for rain formation

Chemical rocket launcher to prevent cyclone formation

Hygroelectrical panels

Weather monitoring centre

Rotating fan for capturing So2 & No from atmoshpere

Flue-gas desulfurization (FGD) chamber

Research lab

Experimental Lab

Hail/snow prevention.
Cannon on the top of tower sends sonic waves up to 50000 feet in the air to keep hailstones from forming. It automatically activates when its own weather radar system detects conditions favorable for the formation of hail. It fires every 5.5 seconds, making a sound we know can be heard at least five miles away.

Harvesting Lightning energy
A laser-Induced plasma channel (LIPC) used to allow lightning to strike in a predictable location. A high power laser used to form an ionized column of gas, which would act as an atmospheric conduit for electrical discharges of lightening, which would direct the lightening to a ground station for harvesting. By arranging porphyrin dye molecules on a clay surface using the "Size-Matching Effect," an energy transfer efficiency of approximately 100%

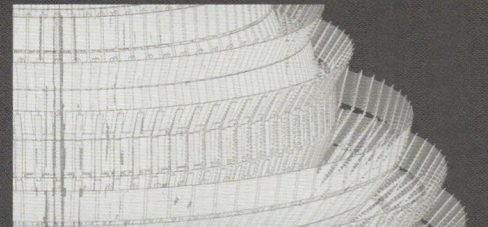

Prevent Acidic deposition in Air to improve air quality
Acid deposition is a general name for a number of phenomena, namely acid rain, acid fog and acid mist. Use of Coal, oil, gas and mainly industrial production, the SO2&NOx, drives the ph value of atmosphere under 5.6 Large rotating fan blades will suck surrounding air into the chamber which will use flue-gas desulfurization (FGD) to remove sulfur-containing gases from their stack gases. . A wet scrubber is basically a reaction tower equipped with a fan that extracts smoke, stack gases from atmosphere into the tower. Lime or limestone in slurry form is also injected into the tower to mix with the stack gases and combine with the sulfur dioxide present. The calcium carbonate of the limestone produces pH-neutral calcium sulfate that is physically removed from the scrubber. That is, the scrubber turns sulfur pollution into industrial sulfates. Filtered air is sent back into the atmosphere which improves air quality.

Increase ozone production in atmosphere for protection against Sun's Ultraviolet rays.
Method of generating ozone relies on applied energy to break the bonds holding the oxygen atoms in a molecular form, allowing them to dissociate and then re-form as ozone
Corona discharge is the condition created when a high voltage passes through an air gap. In the case of ozone production, this high voltage transfers energy for the breaking of the O2 molecule, allowing the formation of a 3-atom oxygen molecule - ozone.

SE

OZGEN OZ
which will r
duction of
which is ge
panels whi
general ele
verted bac

column of gas that would attract lightning during electric storms. The strategic location of a cluster of these skyscrapers could transform arid regions into lush environments while others will prevent natural disasters and collect energy. One third of the skyscraper will house the research and experimental labs that would provide the opportunity to keep exploring renewable energy ideas and natural disaster preventions. There is no specific location for the Weather Doctor, it was designed to be built in any place around the world.

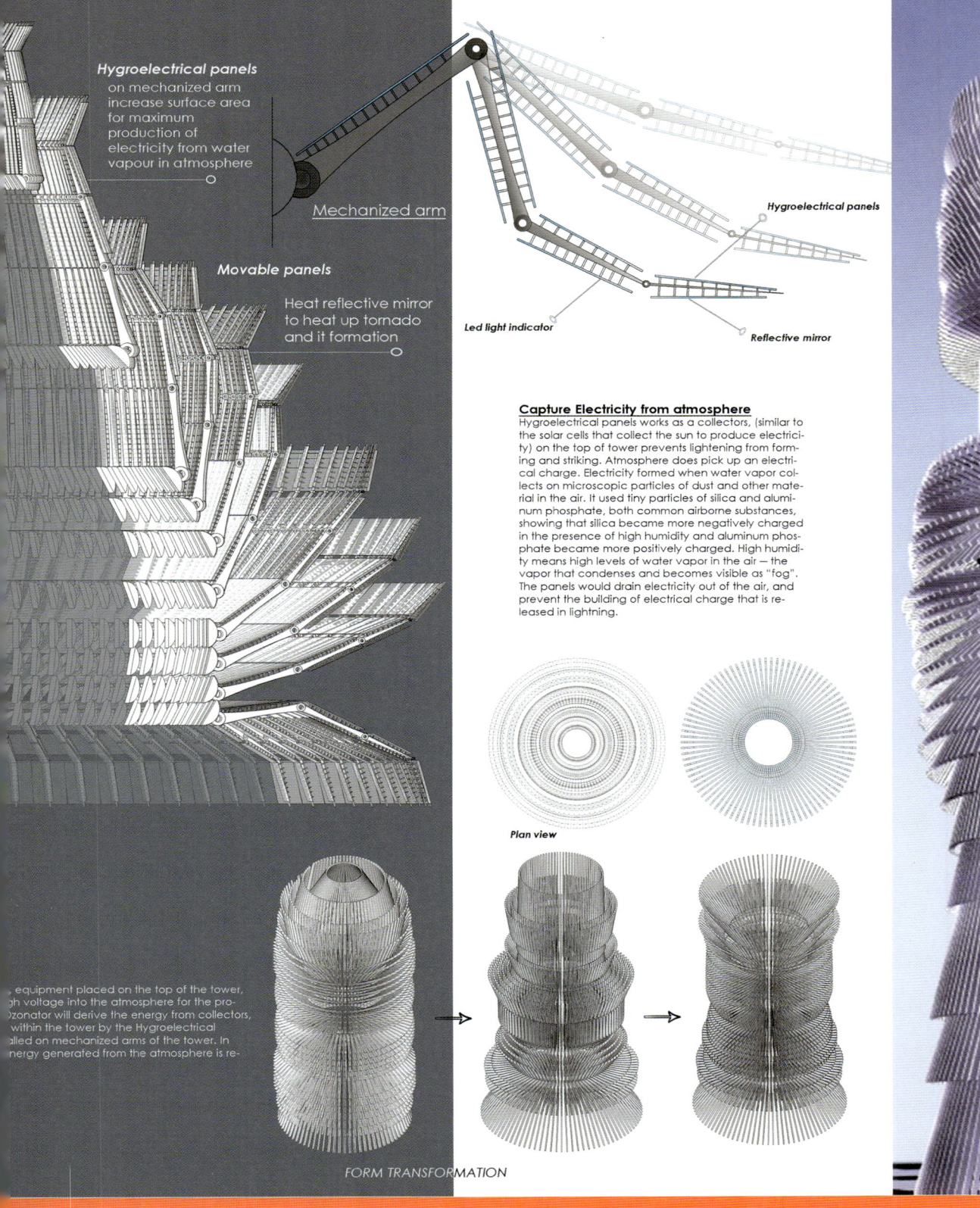

Hygroelectrical panels
on mechanized arm increase surface area for maximum production of electricity from water vapour in atmosphere

Mechanized arm

Movable panels
Heat reflective mirror to heat up tornado and it formation

Led light indicator

Hygroelectrical panels

Reflective mirror

Capture Electricity from atmosphere
Hygroelectrical panels works as a collectors, (similar to the solar cells that collect the sun to produce electricity) on the top of tower prevents lightening from forming and striking. Atmosphere does pick up an electrical charge. Electricity formed when water vapor collects on microscopic particles of dust and other material in the air. It used tiny particles of silica and aluminum phosphate, both common airborne substances, showing that silica became more negatively charged in the presence of high humidity and aluminum phosphate became more positively charged. High humidity means high levels of water vapor in the air — the vapor that condenses and becomes visible as "fog". The panels would drain electricity out of the air, and prevent the building of electrical charge that is released in lightning.

Plan view

0239

...equipment placed on the top of the tower, ...h voltage into the atmosphere for the pro- ...zonator will derive the energy from collectors, ... within the tower by the Hygroelectrical ...alled on mechanized arms of the tower. In ...nergy generated from the atmosphere is re-

FORM TRANSFORMATION

CLOUD CAPTURE

Hitesh Kamdar
Parappa Jabin
Meghana Asalekar
Himanshu Chandak
Ruchika Bora
Amruta Landekar
Kalyani Mukhate
Kirti Verma

India

Neither did we know at first that the juvenile yet ingenious imagination of touching and catching the cloud would bring balance to the Earth...

CLOUD CAPTURE
_ STATE OF EQUIBILIUM

The mankind, despite their remarkable advancements, could not for once surpass the greatness of nature. In the face of devastating floods and droughts, our bests were mere building of dams and planting of trees. But one day, the abnormalities of climate started to exhibit signs of balance.

Mother Nature has always remained powerful and at times dangerous in terms of the weather situation it creates on Planet Earth. Yet it yields life in many different forms. We design our habitats keeping in mind adversity of its behavior. Until now, we have never had proper control on weather situations. Life on Earth has faced major disastrous consequences arising from bad weather, which include drought, hail, storms, hurricanes, tornadoes, fog, and lightning. If we know how electricity builds up and spreads in the atmosphere, we can also prevent death and damage caused by lightning strikes. Weather modifiers were trying to produce rain in drought-afflicted areas, mitigate hail damage by preventing hailstones from growing so large, or disperse fog banks around airports. Effort to keep nature at bay isn't new, but to succeed controlling the weather as per our need is really a difficult question to be answered.

0241

Capturing then releasing the clouds from where they are affluent to scarce started to change the color of the planet Earth. The arid-yellow deserts transformed themselves as fresh green. Neither did we know at first that the uvenile yet ingenious imagination of walking and catching the cloud would bring balance to the Earth.

BACKGROUND

_ Why should we bring the balance of cloud?

Since rain comes from the cloud, to balance the precipitation, we need to redistribute cloud. So if we can br-ing the balance of cloud's distribution, the precipitation also can be balanced. And this balance would bring the earth's overall stability.

_ Why are clouds formed out of balance?

Sea surface temperature   water vapor

The equator is the most heated part of the Earth. The Sun's heat causes a great amount of water evaporation of equator's ocean. This huge amount of water vapor forms cloud and leads to rain 10,000ml a year in this a-rea. This climate system makes the humid equator stay humid and the arid desert stay arid. Accordingly, as l-ong as the location of the equator is not changed, the climate system cannot avoid this unchangeable clim-ate structure.

DISASTER CIRCULATION

Every year, regional precipitation imbalance raise problems of economic loss, devastation of ecosystem, incr-ease of daily stress. Coastal areas suffer from excessive amount of rain and snow, on the other hand, many of the inland areas suffer from droughts. Even worse, the drought turns into desertification. 2 percent of grassl-and becomes desert every year, which means the size of the desert that is already over the 1/10 of the entire land will become even bigger and bigger. Dust from increasing desert area causes sandy dust phenomena and makes cities and people ill. Also, recently cities have been suffering from sinkholes which are caused by the imbalance of subterranean water. Cities using up too much subterranean water to solve the water probl-ems by floods and droughts, the subterranean water dried up. Drying up of subterranean water can cause s-oft ground and eventually make sinkholes occur. If we cannot solve the causes of these chain disasters, man-kind, one day might be end up being collapsed.

STRATEGY

1. Cloud Capture only captures moist clouds. The reason it captures clouds is that collecting rain or mist is la-rgely dependent on the weather at that time. Cloud Capture is an active system that does not wait for rain or mist, but it finds where the water is affluent and capture the water, in this case, clouds.

2. Cloud Capture moves to the water-stressed region with captured clouds. When they arrive at the target ar-ea, it changes the vapor of clouds into water and let them down as rain.

Study of earth's environment has become of major importance amongst the scientific field throughout the world. Large numbers of research institutions have come up to understand how environment behaves. Project Storm Fury, Project Cirrus, or Project Baton, etc. have all been deployed to understand the weather phenomenon. Still we are unable to make it adaptive in nature. Carrying the development further, we have tried to envision the project, which actually does so. The proposed project intended to provide substantial Weather Modification Programs to control weather in a suitable way, which would be beneficial for the habitation in and around the world. We do not intend to change weather drastically, but to protect ourselves from its disastrous consequence. For this, project, dated to 2033, citing to have a developed technology for controlling weather as per our need, our project requires to the building

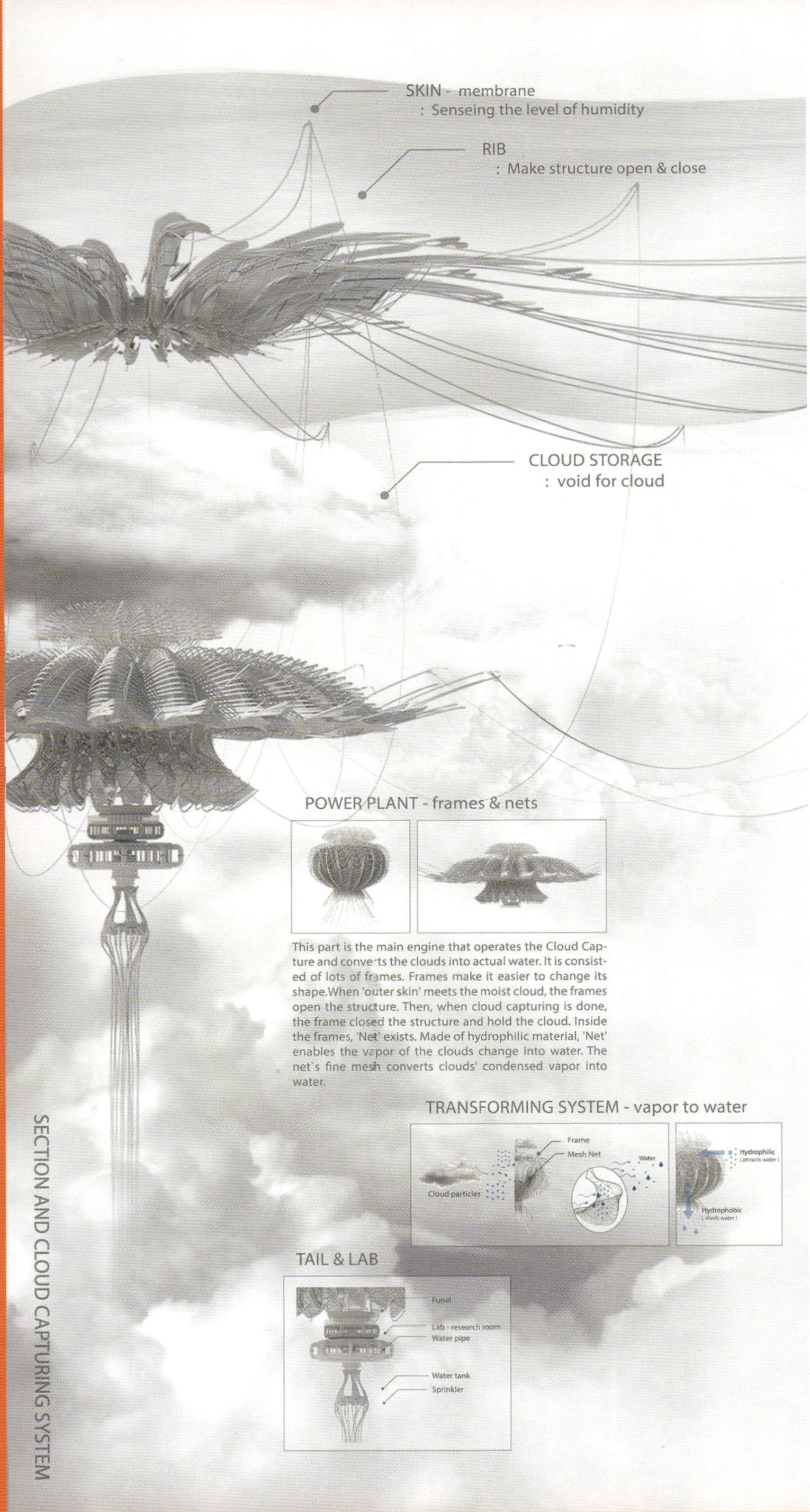

SKIN - membrane
: Senseing the level of humidity

RIB
: Make structure open & close

CLOUD STORAGE
: void for cloud

CIRCULAR SYSTEM OF CLOUD CAPTU

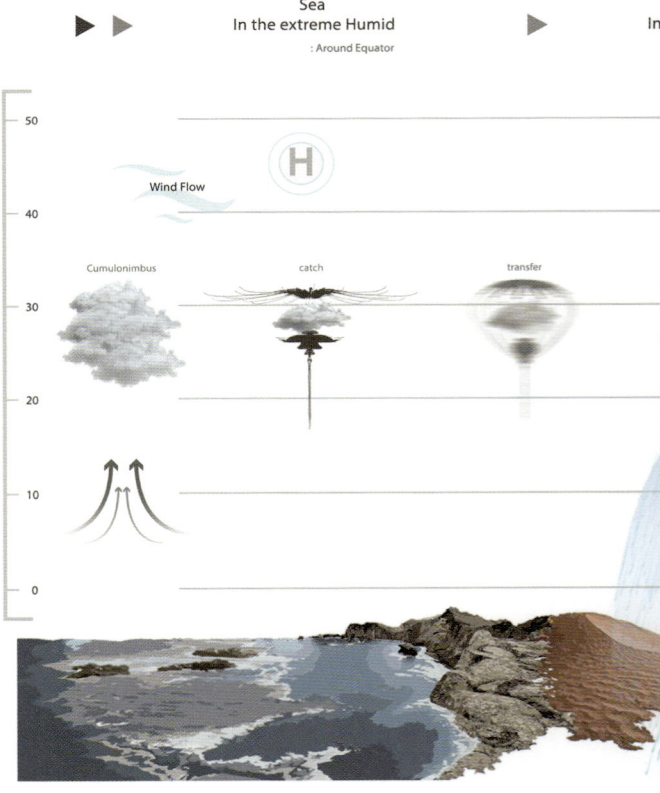

Sea
In the extreme Humid
: Around Equator

In

Wind Flow

50

40

Cumulonimbus   catch   transfer

30

20

10

0

POWER PLANT - frames & nets

This part is the main engine that operates the Cloud Capture and converts the clouds into actual water. It is consisted of lots of frames. Frames make it easier to change its shape. When 'outer skin' meets the moist cloud, the frames open the structure. Then, when cloud capturing is done, the frame closed the structure and hold the cloud. Inside the frames, 'Net' exists. Made of hydrophilic material, 'Net' enables the vapor of the clouds change into water. The net's fine mesh converts clouds' condensed vapor into water.

TRANSFORMING SYSTEM - vapor to water

Frame
Mesh Net
Water
Hydrophilic
(attracts water)

Cloud particles

Hydrophobic
(sheds water)

TAIL & LAB

Funnel
Lab - research room
Water pipe

Water tank
Sprinkler

of a skyscraper to accommodate our experimental lab, research facilities, weather monitoring center, etc. In 2033, Project Weather Doctor has come up solving the weather related issue. This project is the heart of chaos theory, a set of scientific principles describing highly complex weather systems, where small changes in initial conditions radically change the final results. Our project can be located in any part of world where cities have faced major shift in climatic conditions. This project aims to control many aspects of weather considered disastrous in nature. Following are the weather aspects in over which the skyscraper controls - cloud seeding, fog prevention, storm prevention, hurricane modification, tornado prevention, hail/snow prevention, preventing tornadoes' formation, preventing Acidic deposition in the air to improve air quality, and the controlling of tropical cyclones.

0241

SKYLINK

Alexandre Voegele
Eric Geraud

France

SKYLINK A first step towards infinity

The access to space currently requires a large amount of energy, generates a high concentration of orbital debris and is neither regular, nor reliable. However leaving the atmosphere is the essential step in the realization of any space project of great extent.

We propose to create the first section of an Earth-Space link allowing freeing itself from the force of gravity. This connection will be similar to a regular rail, air or sea transportation line. It will serve an orbital hub, starting point of a new page in the space history.

True "umbilical cord" between Man and his home planet, it will provide a solution to the problems of waste, energy and transportation. It will also be an incubator for the future space dreams.

PROBLEMATICS

Which are the major difficulties of the space access?

Current space launcher vehicles are not adapted for mass transportation. Three major issues emerge in establishing an Earth-Space link.

WASTE
A clean and mastered space is the challenge of any galactic project. If man wants to develop Earth-Space exchanges, Earth orbit should not be saturated with waste.
According to Kessler's syndrome, a chain reaction is at work. Collisions between debris are multiplying, which increases the number of polluting objects. Thus the proportion of debris will continue to grow and putting object into orbit from Earth will become impossible if man continues his space activity with conventional launchers.

CONNECTION
There is currently no regular "link" between Earth and Space equivalent to the passengers and goods transportation by land, sea or air.
Unlike the airline industry, the space transportation does not flight between predefined locations or along known line and landing zones are random.
In addition, take-off and landing phases are much more delicate and risky than for any other means of transportation.

ENERGY
The current propulsion system by chemical reaction is basic compared to other technologies of the space industry. It has many risks when firing and appears polluting. A booster rocket is a consumable vehicle; almost all of its mass is dedicated to its propulsion. This expensive energy process has a huge impact on spacecraft's costs and the shipment capacities are thereby very limited.

SITE

Where to establish the project?

OCEAN
The project is located in international waters, a maritime neutral space favorable to the production of energy and resources required for its functioning. The ocean also allows to serve it easily and widely whatever the using nations.

EQUATOR
The equatorial location allows using the slingshot effect. This area also benefits from updrafts increasing the upper limit of the atmosphere and it is not topped by a jet stream that may affect the stability of the device. Finally, it's the area that receives the most solar energy.

AFRICA
The optimum location is in an area without natural diseases in the South of Benin. The African continent is in full development and has huge energy, human and economic potentials. The project would raise it at the same level as the others.

SPACE JUNK
Some facts on space pollution

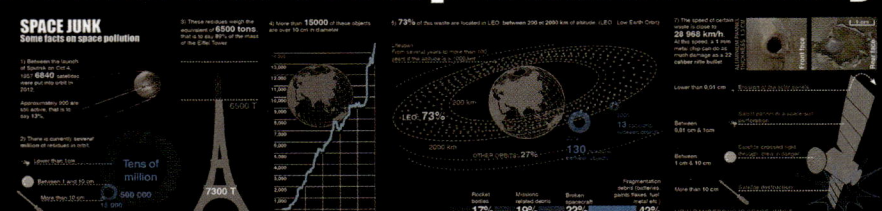

CONNECTION
Inventory of the flows between the Earth and Space

TRAIN = 15 000T   CONTAINER SHIP 197 000T

9/100

ENERGY
situation of space transport

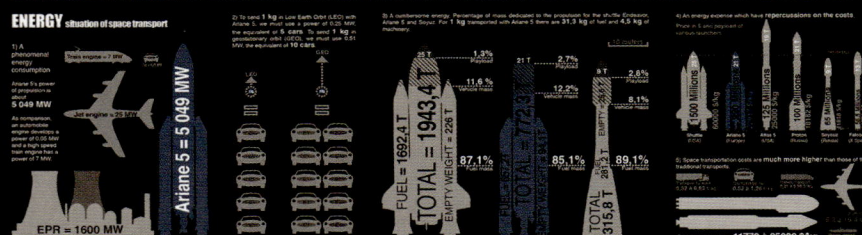

THE EQUATOR, IDEAL FOR WINDS

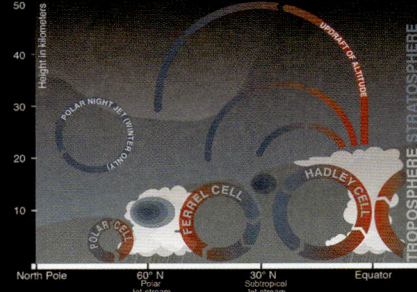

THE EQUATOR, IDEAL FOR PASSIVE ENERGY

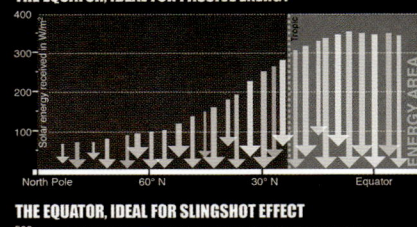

THE EQUATOR, IDEAL FOR SLINGSHOT EFFECT

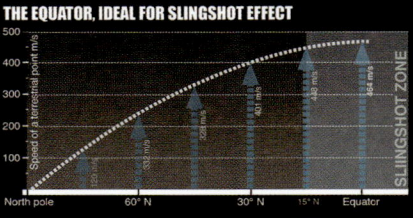

PROJECT SITE

LEGEND International waters Exclusive economic zone

SPACE ELEVATOR PRINCIPLE

A space elevator is a proposed type of transportation system from an Earth surface into an orbit by a cable with one end attached near the equator and the other end in space beyond geostationary orbit at 36 000 km of altitude. The system is maintained by a counterweight located at 91000 km. The competing forces of gravity, stronger at the lower end, and the centrifugal force, stronger at the upper end, would result in the cable being held up, under tension, and stationary over a single position on Earth. Once deployed, the cable would be ascended repeatedly by mechanical means to reach orbit.

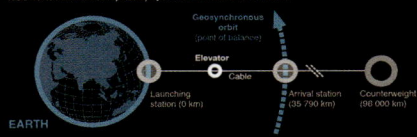

SOLAR TOWER PRINCIPLE

A solar tower uses the greenhouse effect and the chimney effect to activate turbines that generate electricity. The difference of pressure & temperature between the bottom and the top generates an upward airflow; the warm air lighter than cold air rises.

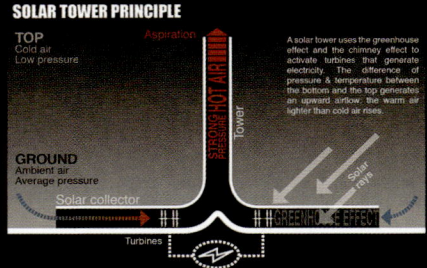

OCÉANE - GENERAL VIEW

OCEANE PERSPECTIVE SECTION

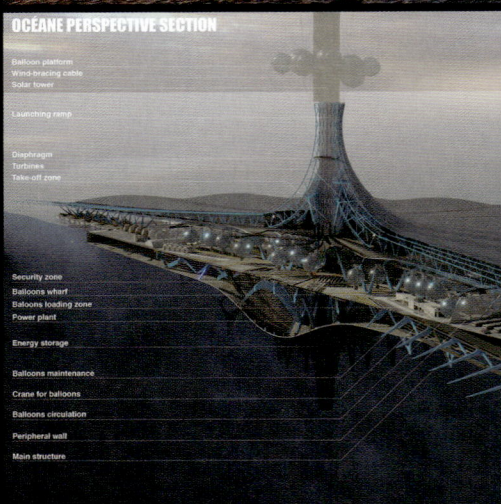

TOP VIEW OF THE TOWER

The access to space currently requires a large amount of energy, generates a high concentration of orbital debris, and is neither regular, nor reliable. However leaving the atmosphere is the essential step in the realization of any space project of great extent.

We propose to create the first section of an Earth-Space link allowing freedom from the force of gravity. This connection will be similar to a regular rail, air or sea transportation line. It will serve as an orbital hub, a starting point of a new page in space history. Powered by the sun, water, and air, Skylink faces the great climatic challenges and enables the creation of a reliable, clean and regular Earth-Space connection.

A true "umbilical cord" between Man and his home planet, it will be the first stretch of an intergalactic

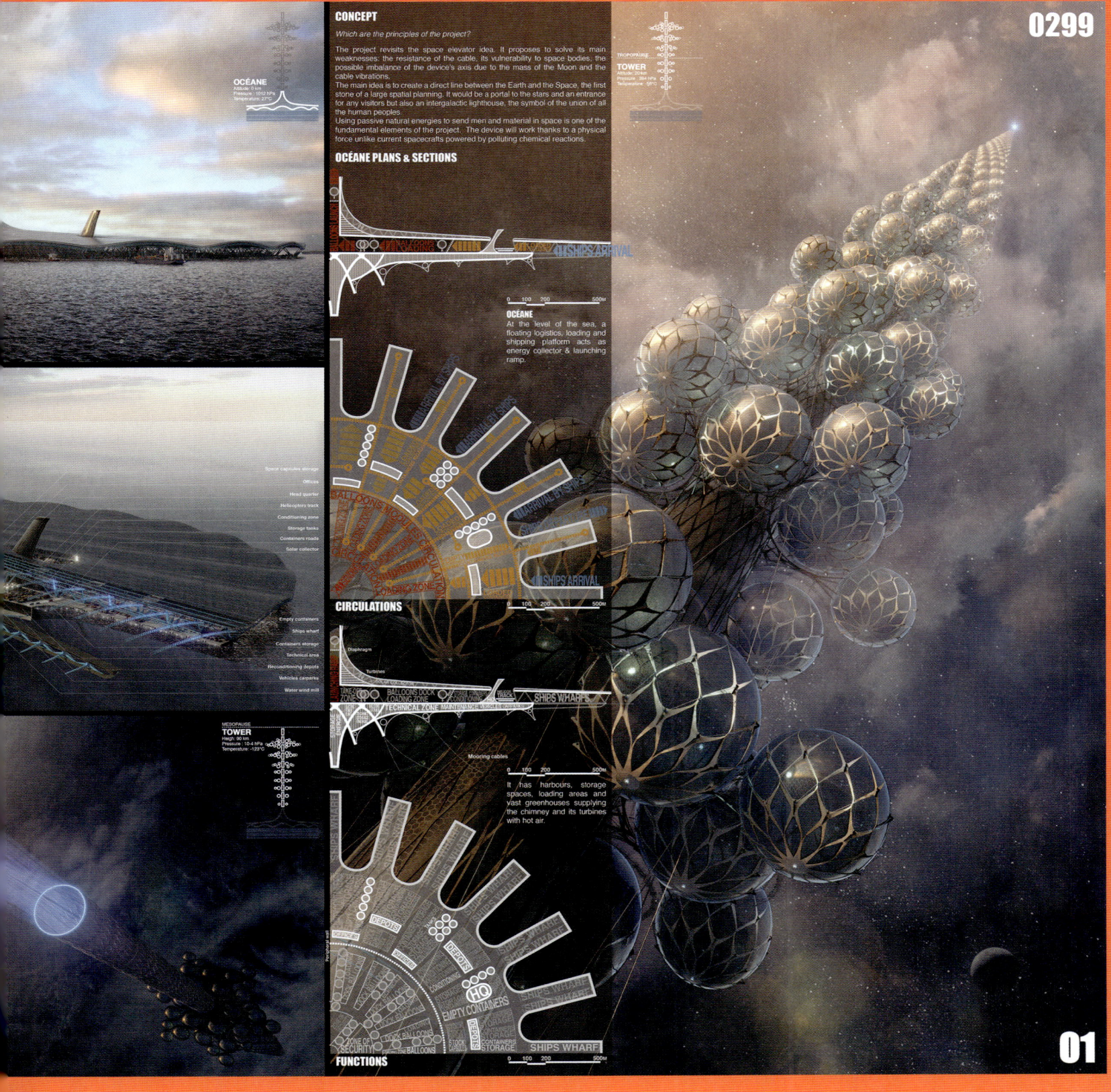

TECHNOLOGICAL ADVANCES   ECOLOGICAL URBANISM   NEW FRONTIERS

300

line, the first step of mankind to a veritable access to the universe. The universe is a common good of humanity according to the Outer Space Treaty of 1967. A great scientific and technical international program with a unifying power is thus essential for the success of the project.

Skylink opens new prospects for travel and discovery. It's a vessel for imagination that catalyses the major space projects to come. It's up to anyone to get on with his or her dreams.

The Skylink is designed as two circular mega-platforms connected by a linear structure. The first platform would be erected in the ocean while the second will be located in outer space. The link between the two would serve as a futuristic elevator into space. Pod-like spaceships will travel inside this tube at great speeds. Additional pods would cluster around the linear structure and will serve as auxiliary spaces

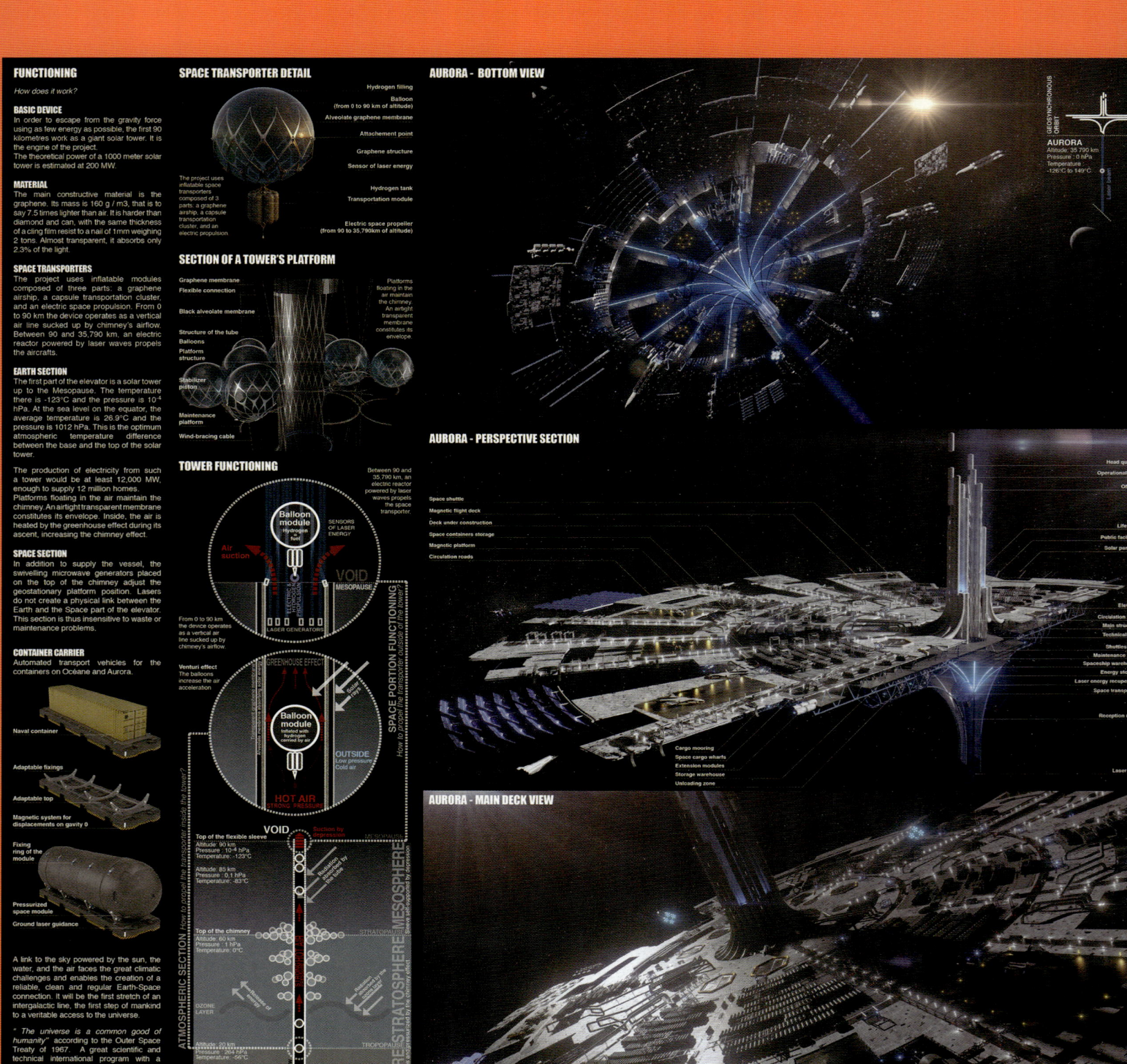

until needed for travel.

A permanent connection to outer space would allow using resources for research and development of new technologies instead of dedicating these funds for spaceship construction capable of reaching outer space on their own. The pace of exploration would also be dramatically increased establishing a new era for mankind.

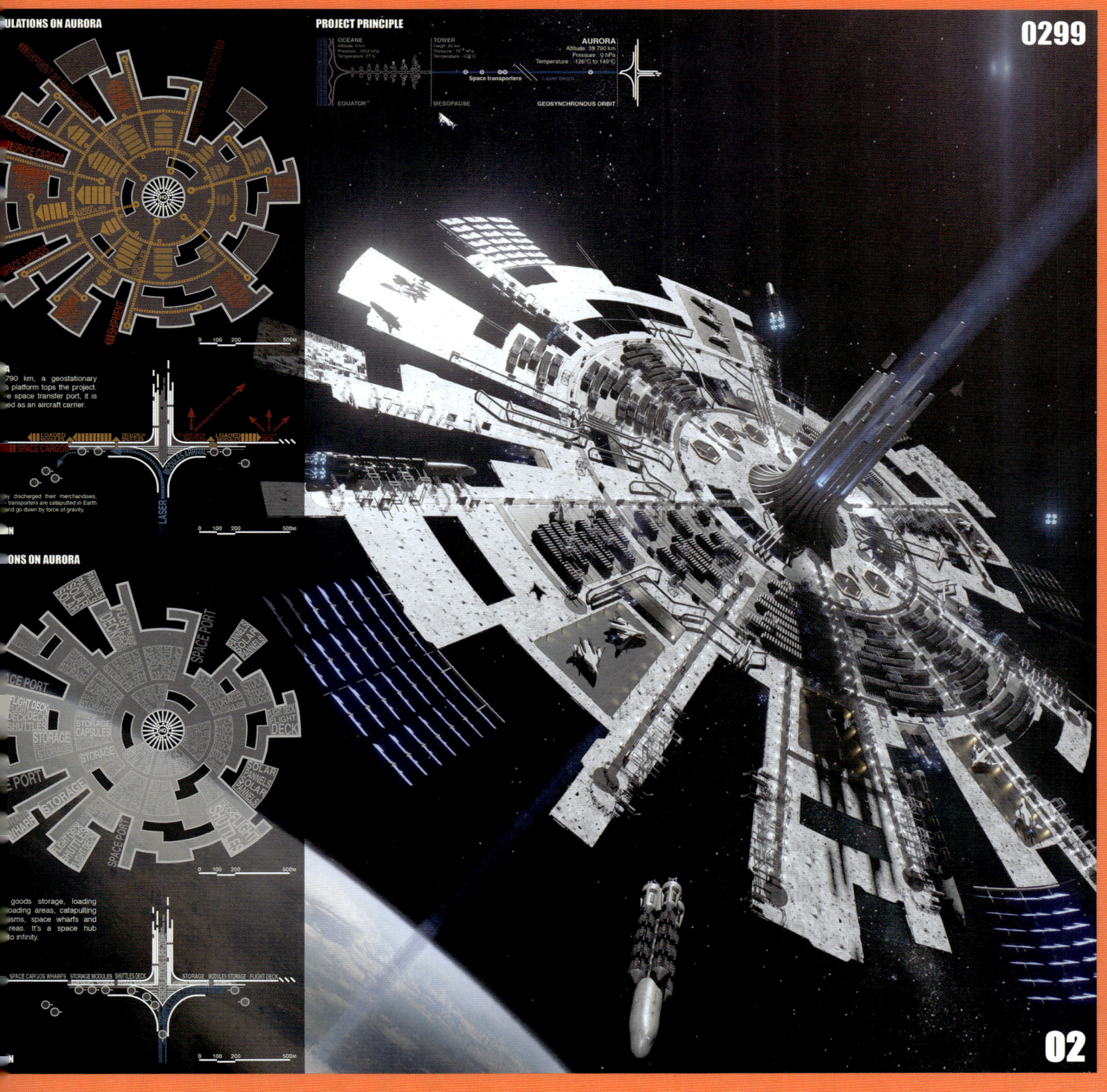

CLOUD PORT

Adam Sogel

Czech Republic

I started with this topic during my study exchange program in Finland, when I was participating in course called Lost in Transit. I tried to find a solution to present problems in aerial transportation, which has to be done in a more radical way.

I am an industrial designer, so I wanted to come up with a concept according to my study field. I ended up with a solution, which solves almost every asked problem. The answer is to give the airport a new dimension, to build it straight in the sky above the city. It seems to be a crazy idea, which is totally out of logic, but in my draft it started to make sense. After studying new technologies and materials, it seems to be feasible in the near future. New materials such as graphene, open amazing capabilities, which were unimaginable ten years ago, are now starting to be a part of our daily lives.

0410

The concept of a floating building above the city solves problems with connections between flights and domestic/city transportation. The whole design supports using the renewable resources and mitigates the impacts of air transportation on the environment. It improves the parts of flight such as landing and takes off, which is the least effective and produces most of the harmful emissions. The other advantage is, that this kind of airport doesn't need any land, which is very scarce in the biggest cities.

There are many questions and challenges in these visionary concepts. For example, how does one create construction, which is light and tough enough to flow in the air? How does one use the most effective technologies to support the renewal energy, good economy of operation, environment and safety? I tried to answer all of there question in my master thesis.

CLOUD PORT - CONCEPT OF FLOATING AIRPORT ABOVE THE CITY

Concept description:
Object with diameter: 800-1500m, hight: 100-150m
Floating 2-3km above the city, due to filling with Hellium
Connection with elevators with main points in the city, such as main station
Anchoring wires works as guiding lines for elevators

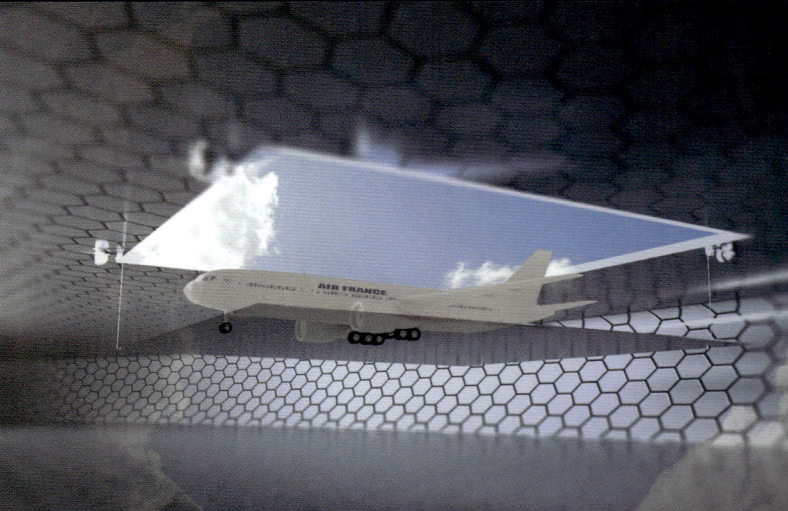

Landing and take off surface
- multiple take offs or landings in one time
- magnetic catapults helps speeding
- 360° landing according to weather conditions
- runway could work as a power station

runway and hangar
- after landing airplane will be hidden under runway
- movement of planes is controlled automatically in hangar
- runway and hangar is heated to prevent frosting

Writing this statement I tried to attract the attention to the problems of the near future, which mankind will face, but also to suggest possible solutions to these challenges. It is important to be aware of upcoming problem with the growing society and come up with unorthodox solutions, which young designers could take into account. The crucial part of any project like this is the technical and technological progress.

0410

main advantages:
- No land needed!
- Use of existing infrastructure and multiple access points
- Eliminate the negative consequences of air transportation: less harmfull emisions, limit the noice pollution, better fuel economy

elevators for passangers
- maglev principle (magnetic levitation)
- speed up to 70km/h
- time of transport: 2-3min
- energy recovery
- diameter of each capsule: 3-5m

used material: GRAPHENE
- graphene is futuristic material, which is made of carbon atoms built into hexagon structure
- 200x tougher than steel, but very light
- perfect electric conductor (suitable for photovoltaic cells)
- translucent, heat condactive, elastic

2045+ TOWER

Ioana Galie
Florin Jude
Iustin Roceanu

Romania

2045+ TOWER

Ray Kurtzweil

In his book The Singularity Is Near (2005), Ray Kurtzweil predicts that by the year 2045 artificial intelligence (A.I.) will surpass the brainpower equivalent of all human brains combined. Among Ray Kurzweil's many honors, he is the recipient of the National Medal of Technology, was inducted into the National Inventors Hall of Fame, holds twenty honorary Doctorates, and honors from three U.S. presidents.

Our Vision

Based on his predictions, in our vision of 2045+ the A.I. will takeover many of the current tasks done by human beings in all fields of activity. In this new world, the architect's role is to closely coordinate with the A.I., much like a conductor coordinates with the orchestra. The Human + A.I team's main challange will be to develop ways to enhance human life. The architectural structures of the future, spawned by this new generation of super-architects, will not only cover human basic needs such as shelter/food/clean water/energy, but will actually have to go far beyond these limits and, in a sense, become integral to the human society of the future.

Technological advances in all industries will develop at an exponential rate, leading to a new type of human society and new requirements for the structures we design. For instance, technological advances in hydroponics, vertical farming systems and robotic harvesting will mean that, at a minimum, all buildings will be able to grow food for their inhabitants in a self sustaining, autonomous manner, yielding crops at a much faster and more predictable rate than traditional farming. Implemented on a large scale, this can help immensely in eradicating world hunger.

Advances in 3D printing will allow new materials to emerge, completely generated by A.I. from their chemical structure to their actual production with 3D printing equipment (also A.I. designed and manufactured). Designing and continuously optimizing all these highly sophisticated systems will be a task completely undertaken by the A.I.;

The human partner will set the goals and the A.I. will find the optimum solutions to achieve them. Humans will become part of the A.I. universe and gradually merge with the machine, interacting on a much deeper (perhaps even subconcious) level with the structures they design and inhabit, becoming an interconnected part of them.

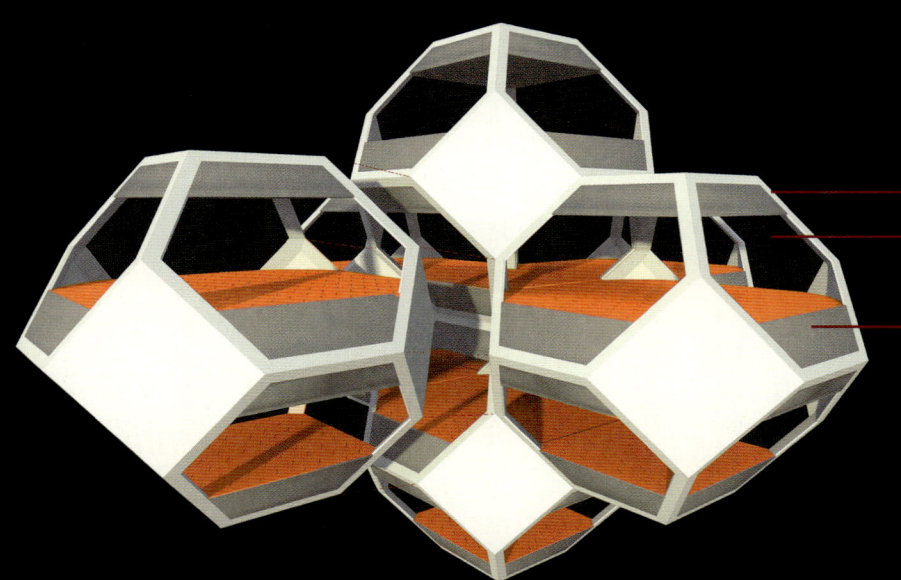

+ PREFABRICATED MODULES THAT ARE BUILT, DELIVERED AND ASSEMBLED BY A.I. CONTROLLED DRONES. EACH MODULE INTERLOCKS PERFECTLY WITH THE ONES IN ITS IMMEDIATE VICINITY AND CAN RECEIVE A WIDE ARRAY OF FUNCTIONS. IN THIS CASE, THE MODULE IS A TRUNCATED OCTAHEDRON.

+ 3D PRINTED STRUCTURAL FRAME OF ULTRA-LIGHTWEIGHT, ULTRA-STRONG METAL ALLOY, CHEMICALLY ENGINEERED BY A.I.

+ GLASS PANELS MADE OF INTELLIGENT GLASS THAT INCORPORATE A VAST ARRAY OF SENSORS, RADIATION PROTECTION LAYERS, ADVANCED OLED TECHNOLOGY GRIDS AND CLEAR PHOTOVOLTAIC CELLS, ALLOWING THE TOWER TO PRODUCE MANY TIMES THE ENERGY IT NEEDS. THE EXTRA ENERGY PRODUCED IS FED INTO THE CITY GRID.

+ INTERCHANGABLE FACADE PANELS:

THEIR CONFIGURATION AND POSITIONING IS A TASK FOR THE A.I., WHICH WILL CONSIDER ALL FACTORS SUCH AS THE GEO-LOCATION OF THE STRUCTURE, PREVAILING WINDS, ETC.

+ FILTERING PANELS - SELF-CLEANING MICROSTRUCTURES THAT DECONTAMINATE THE AIR BY ABSORBING CO2 AND OTHER POLLUTANTS AND PRODUCE CLEAN AIR. THE EMERGENCE OF THESE TECHNOLOGIES CAN BE A STARTING POINT IN DEVELOPING A STRATEGY TO INTEGRATE HIGH-RISE STRUCTURES INTO AN EFFORT OF GLOBAL ATMOSPHERIC CLEAN-UP.

+ WATER COLLECTION PANELS - CAPTURING AND FILTERING WATER EITHER FROM VAPORS AND/OR RAIN.

In his book The Singularity Is Near (2005), Ray Kurtzweil predicts that by the year 2045 artificial intelligence (A.I.) will surpass the brainpower equivalent of all human brains combined. Among Ray Kurzweil's many honors, he is the recipient of the National Medal of Technology, was inducted into the National Inventors Hall of Fame, holds twenty honorary Doctorates, and honors from three U.S. presidents.

Based on his predictions, in our vision of 2045+ the A.I. will takeover many of the current tasks done by human beings in all fields of activity. In this new world, the architect's role is to closely coordinate with the A.I., much like a conductor coordinates with the orchestra. The Human + A.I team's main challenge will be to develop ways to enhance human life. The architectural structures of the future, spawned by this

0739

new generation of super-architects, will not only cover human basic needs such as shelter/food/clean water/energy, but will actually have to go far beyond these limits and, in a sense, become integral to the human society of the future.

Technological advances in all industries will develop at an exponential rate, leading to a new type of human society and new requirements for the structures we design. For instance, technological advances in hydroponics, vertical farming systems and robotic harvesting will mean that, at a minimum, all buildings will be able to grow food for their inhabitants in a self sustaining, autonomous manner, yielding crops at a much faster and more predictable rate than traditional farming. Implemented on a large scale, this can help immensely in eradicating world hunger.

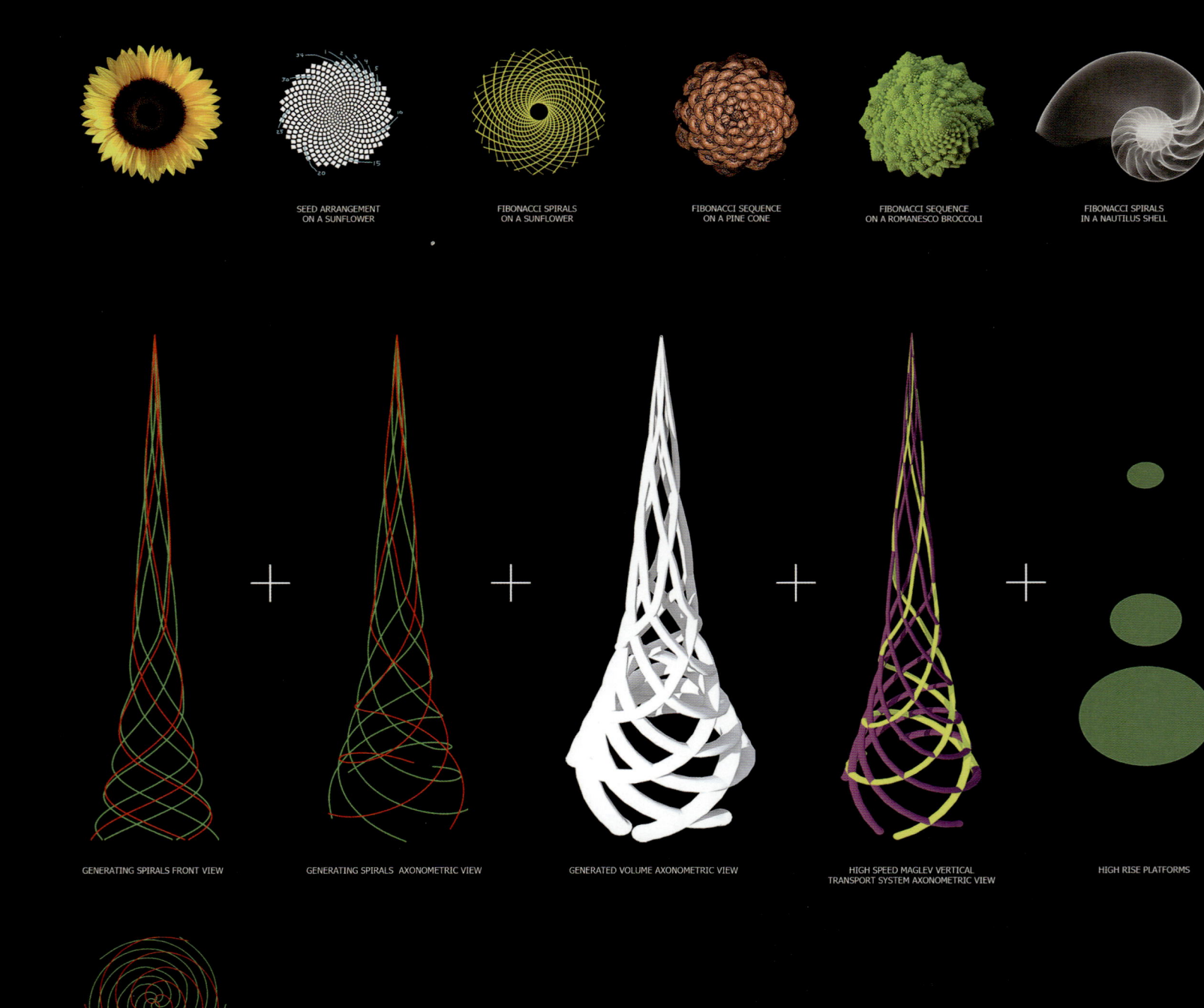

SEED ARRANGEMENT
ON A SUNFLOWER

FIBONACCI SPIRALS
ON A SUNFLOWER

FIBONACCI SEQUENCE
ON A PINE CONE

FIBONACCI SEQUENCE
ON A ROMANESCO BROCCOLI

FIBONACCI SPIRALS
IN A NAUTILUS SHELL

GENERATING SPIRALS FRONT VIEW

GENERATING SPIRALS AXONOMETRIC VIEW

GENERATED VOLUME AXONOMETRIC VIEW

HIGH SPEED MAGLEV VERTICAL
TRANSPORT SYSTEM AXONOMETRIC VIEW

HIGH RISE PLATFORMS

GENERATING SPIRALS PLAN VIEW

+ ARRANGEMENT OF MODULES FOLLOWS PATTERNS OBSERVED IN NATURE - IN THIS PARTICULAR CASE, THE FIBONACCI SPIRAL; IN PLAN, THE SPIRALS FOLLOW THE PATTERN OF DISTRIBUTION OF SEEDS ON A SUNFLOWER, WHILE ON THE VERTICAL AXIS THEY FOLLOW THE PATTERNS SEEN IN THE GROWTH OF PINE CONES. DISTRIBUTING THE MODULES IN THIS MANNER ENSURES EXCELLENT NATURAL LIGHTING AND VENTILATION OF THE ENTIRE STRUCTURE.

THE FIBONACCI NUMBERS ARE NATURE'S NUMBERING SYSTEM. THEY APPEAR EVERYWHERE IN NATURE, FROM THE LEAF ARRANGEMENT IN PLANTS, TO THE PATTERN OF THE FLORETS OF A FLOWER, THE BRACTS OF A PINECONE, OR THE SCALES OF A PINEAPPLE.

+ A.I. DESIGNED AND DISTRIBUTED AQUAPONICS FARMS POPULATE THE TOWER. AUTOMATED ROBOTIC FARMING AND HARVESTING WILL ENSURE OPTIMUM EFFICIENCY IN CROP YIELDING. YEAR ROUND, THE BUILDING PRODUCES ITS OWN SUPPLY OF FRESH VEGETABLES, FISH, POULTRY AND HERBS.

Advances in 3D printing will allow new materials to emerge, completely generated by A.I. from their chemical structure to their actual production with 3D printing equipment (also A.I. designed and manufactured). Designing and continuously optimizing all these highly sophisticated systems will be a task completely undertaken by the A.I.;

The human partner will set the goals and the A.I. will find the optimum solutions to achieve them. Humans will become part of the A.I. universe and gradually merge with the machine, interacting on a much deeper (perhaps even subconscious) level with the structures they design and inhabit, becoming an interconnected part of them.

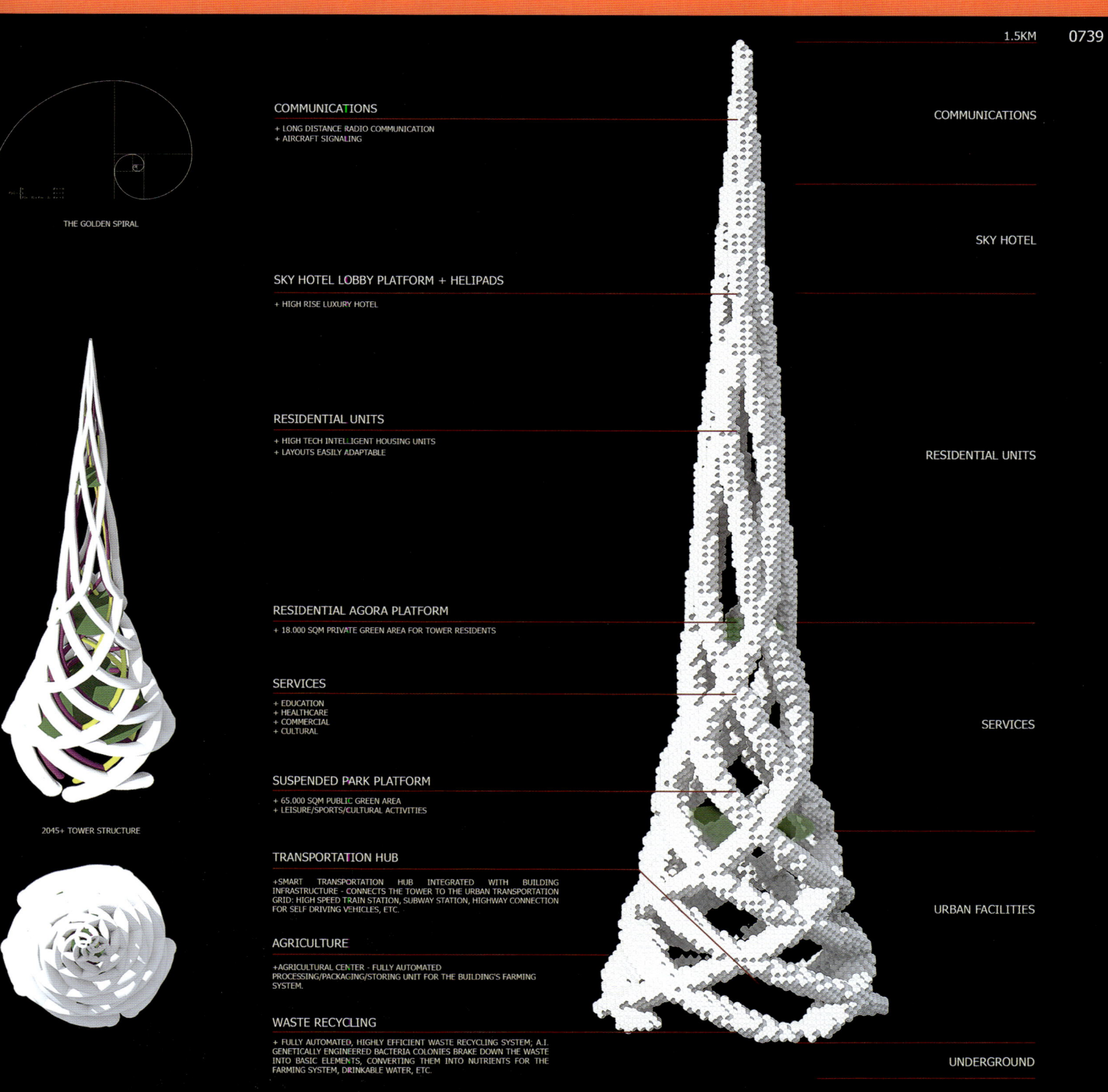

THE GOLDEN SPIRAL

2045+ TOWER STRUCTURE

1.5KM   0739

COMMUNICATIONS

+ LONG DISTANCE RADIO COMMUNICATION
+ AIRCRAFT SIGNALING

SKY HOTEL LOBBY PLATFORM + HELIPADS

+ HIGH RISE LUXURY HOTEL

RESIDENTIAL UNITS

+ HIGH TECH INTELLIGENT HOUSING UNITS
+ LAYOUTS EASILY ADAPTABLE

RESIDENTIAL AGORA PLATFORM

+ 18.000 SQM PRIVATE GREEN AREA FOR TOWER RESIDENTS

SERVICES

+ EDUCATION
+ HEALTHCARE
+ COMMERCIAL
+ CULTURAL

SUSPENDED PARK PLATFORM

+ 65.000 SQM PUBLIC GREEN AREA
+ LEISURE/SPORTS/CULTURAL ACTIVITIES

TRANSPORTATION HUB

+SMART TRANSPORTATION HUB INTEGRATED WITH BUILDING INFRASTRUCTURE - CONNECTS THE TOWER TO THE URBAN TRANSPORTATION GRID: HIGH SPEED TRAIN STATION, SUBWAY STATION, HIGHWAY CONNECTION FOR SELF-DRIVING VEHICLES, ETC.

AGRICULTURE

+AGRICULTURAL CENTER - FULLY AUTOMATED PROCESSING/PACKAGING/STORING UNIT FOR THE BUILDING'S FARMING SYSTEM.

WASTE RECYCLING

+ FULLY AUTOMATED, HIGHLY EFFICIENT WASTE RECYCLING SYSTEM; A.I. GENETICALLY ENGINEERED BACTERIA COLONIES BRAKE DOWN THE WASTE INTO BASIC ELEMENTS, CONVERTING THEM INTO NUTRIENTS FOR THE FARMING SYSTEM, DRINKABLE WATER, ETC.

COMMUNICATIONS

SKY HOTEL

RESIDENTIAL UNITS

SERVICES

URBAN FACILITIES

UNDERGROUND

PLANTAGE:
THE SKY HANGER

Michal Ganobjak
Martin Koiš

Slovakia

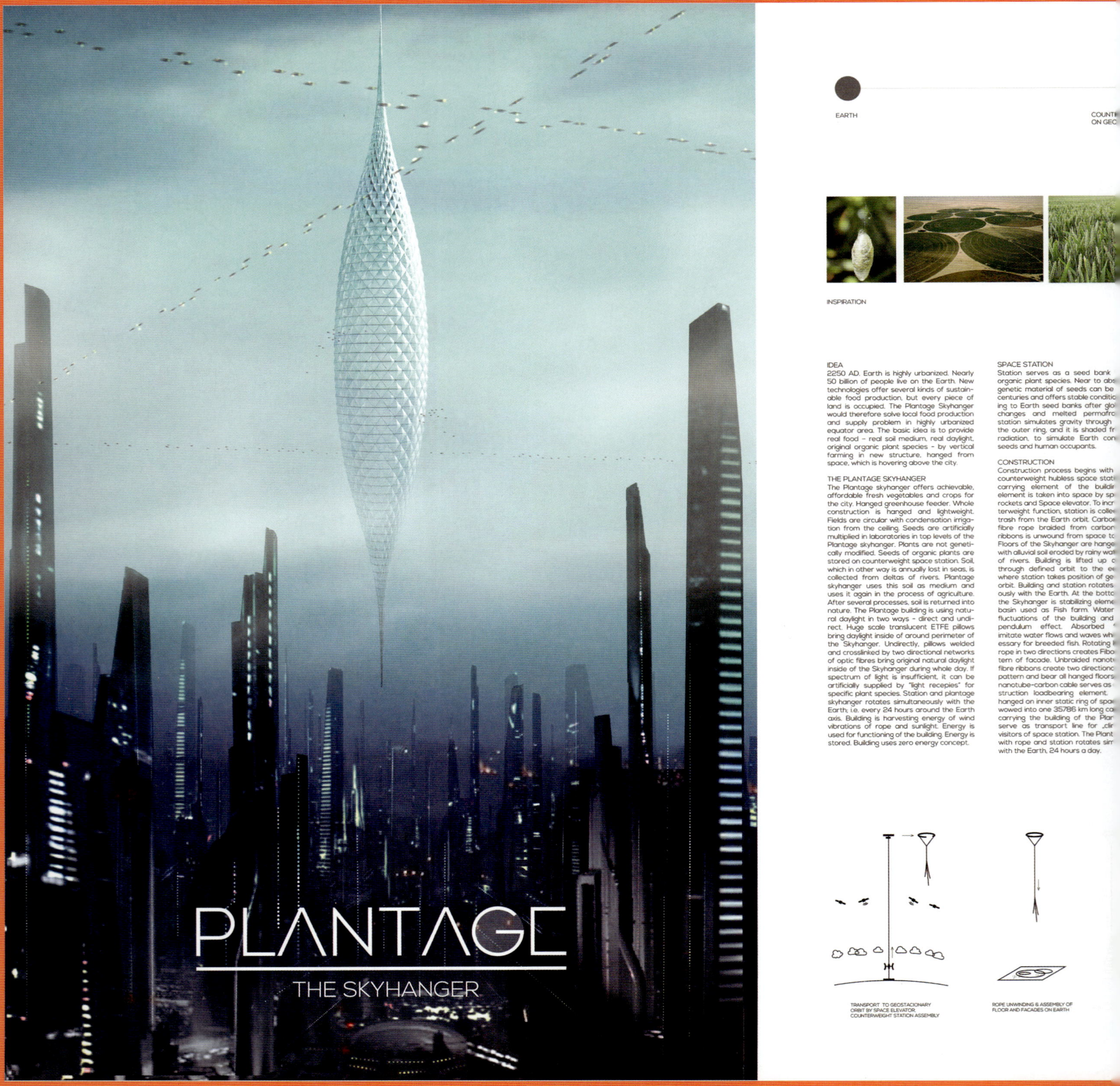

EARTH   COUNTRI
ON GEO

INSPIRATION

IDEA

2250 AD. Earth is highly urbanized. Nearly 50 billion of people live on the Earth. New technologies offer several kinds of sustainable food production, but every piece of land is occupied. The Plantage Skyhanger would therefore solve local food production and supply problem in highly urbanized equator area. The basic idea is to provide real food – real soil medium, real daylight, original organic plant species - by vertical farming in new structure, hanged from space, which is hovering above the city.

THE PLANTAGE SKYHANGER

The Plantage skyhanger offers achievable, affordable fresh vegetables and crops for the city. Hanged greenhouse feeder. Whole construction is hanged and lightweight. Fields are circular with condensation irrigation from the ceiling. Seeds are artificially multiplied in laboratories in top levels of the Plantage skyhanger. Plants are not genetically modified. Seeds of organic plants are stored on counterweight space station. Soil, which in other way is annually lost in seas, is collected from deltas of rivers. Plantage skyhanger uses this soil as medium and uses it again in the process of agriculture. After several processes, soil is returned into nature. The Plantage building is using natural daylight in two ways - direct and undirect. Huge scale translucent ETFE pillows bring daylight inside of around perimeter of the Skyhanger. Undirectly, pillows welded and crosslinked by two directional networks of optic fibres bring original natural daylight inside of the Skyhanger during whole day. If spectrum of light is insufficient, it can be artificially supplied by "light recepies" for specific plant species. Station and plantage skyhanger rotates simultaneously with the Earth, i.e. every 24 hours around the Earth axis. Building is harvesting energy of wind vibrations of rope and sunlight. Energy is used for functioning of the building. Energy is stored. Building uses zero energy concept.

SPACE STATION

Station serves as a seed bank of organic plant species. Near to abs genetic material of seeds can be centuries and offers stable conditio ing to Earth seed banks after glo changes and melted permafro station simulates gravity through the outer ring, and it is shaded fr radiation, to simulate Earth con seeds and human occupants.

CONSTRUCTION

Construction process begins with counterweight hubless space stati carrying element of the buildir element is taken into space by sp rockets and Space elevator. To incr terweight function, station is colle trash from the Earth orbit. Carbor fibre rope braided from carbon ribbons is unwound from space to Floors of the Skyhanger are hange with alluvial soil eroded by rainy wat of rivers. Building is lifted up a through defined orbit to the e where station takes position of ge orbit. Building and station rotates ously with the Earth. At the botto the Skyhanger is stabilizing eleme basin used as Fish farm. Water fluctuations of the building and pendulum effect. Absorbed imitate water flows and waves whessory for breeded fish. Rotating rope in two directions creates Fibotem of facade. Unbraided nanotfibre ribbons create two directionpattern and bear all hanged floorsstruction loadbearing element. nanotube-carbon cable serves as hanged on inner static ring of spawowed into one 35786 km long cacarrying the building of the Plaserve as transport line for "climvisitors of space station. The Plantwith rope and station rotates simwith the Earth, 24 hours a day.

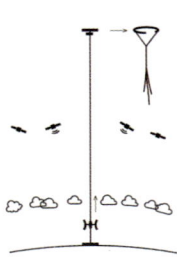

TRANSPORT TO GEOSTATIONARY
ORBIT BY SPACE ELEVATOR.
COUNTERWEIGHT STATION ASSEMBLY

ROPE UNWINDING & ASSEMBLY OF
FLOOR AND FACADES ON EARTH

PLANTAGE
THE SKYHANGER

2250 AD. Earth is highly urbanized with 50 billion people living on the planet. New technologies offer several kinds of sustainable food production, but every piece of land is occupied. The Plantage Skyhanger would therefore solve local food production and supply problem in highly urbanized areas. The basic idea is to provide real food – real soil medium, real daylight, original organic plant species - by vertical farming in a new structure, hanged from space, which is hovering above the city.

The Plantage Skyhanger offers achievable, affordable fresh vegetables and crops for the city. Hanged greenhouse feeder. Whole construction is hanged and lightweight. Fields are circular with condensation irrigation from the ceiling. Seeds are artificially multiplied in laboratories in the top levels. Plants are not genetically modified. Seeds of organic plants are stored on counterweight space station. Soil, which in

0077

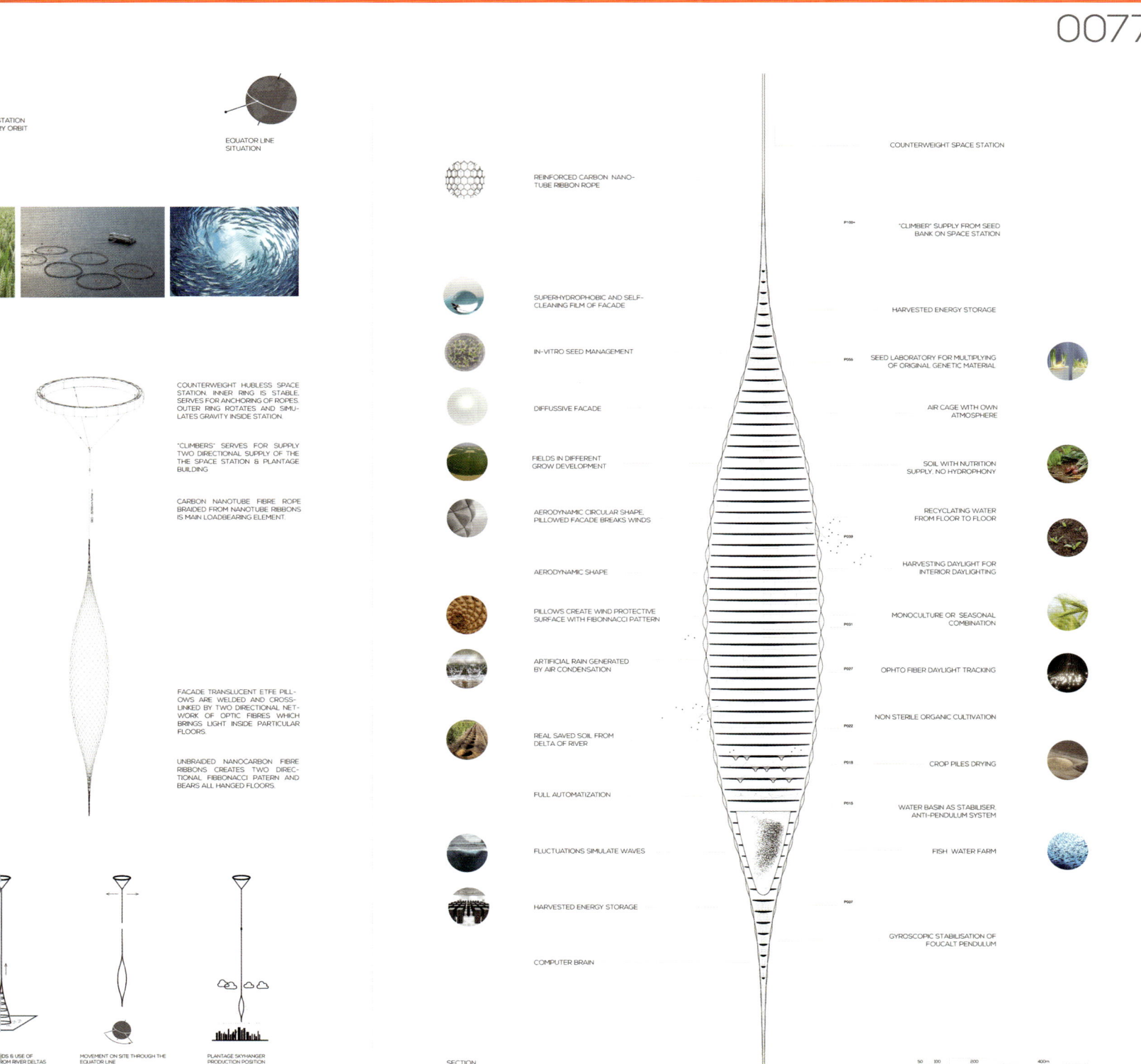

other way is annually lost in seas, is collected from deltas of rivers. Plantage skyhanger uses this soil as medium and uses it again in the process of agriculture. After several processes, soil is returned into nature. The Plantage building is using natural daylight in two ways - direct and indirect. Huge scale translucent ETFE pillows bring daylight inside of around perimeter of the Skyhanger. Indirectly, pillows welded and cross-linked by two directional networks of optic fibers bring original natural daylight inside of the Skyhanger during whole day. If spectrum of light is insufficient, "light recipes" for specific plant species can artificially supply it.

The Space Station serves as a seed bank for original organic plant species. Near to absolute zero, genetic material of seeds can be stored for centuries and offers stable condition comparing to Earth

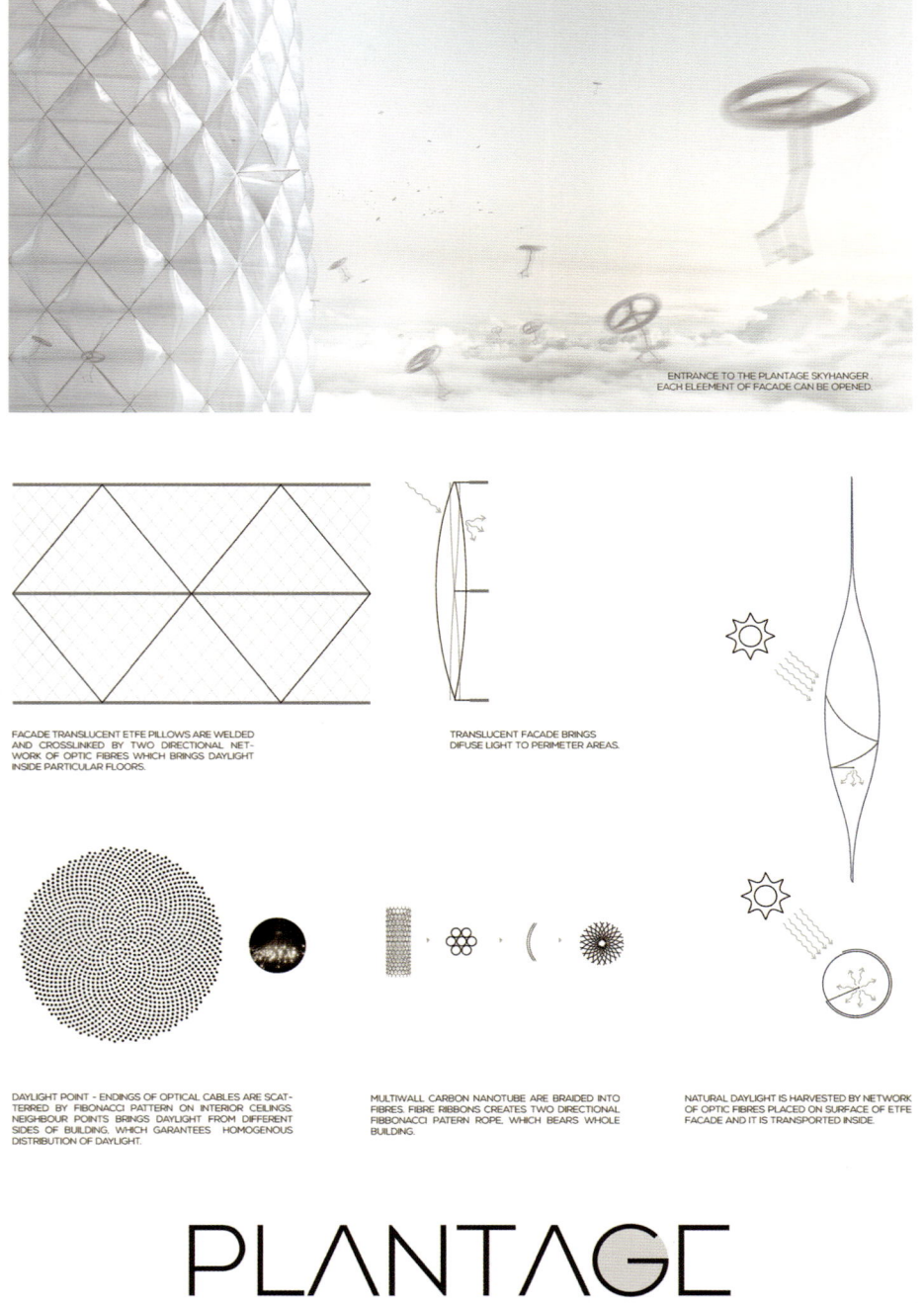

ENTRANCE TO THE PLANTAGE SKYHANGER. EACH ELEEMENT OF FACADE CAN BE OPENED.

FACADE TRANSLUCENT ETFE PILLOWS ARE WELDED AND CROSSLINKED BY TWO DIRECTIONAL NET-WORK OF OPTIC FIBRES WHICH BRINGS DAYLIGHT INSIDE PARTICULAR FLOORS.

TRANSLUCENT FACADE BRINGS DIFUSE LIGHT TO PERIMETER AREAS.

DAYLIGHT POINT - ENDINGS OF OPTICAL CABLES ARE SCAT-TERRED BY FIBONACCI PATTERN ON INTERIOR CEILINGS. NEIGHBOUR POINTS BRINGS DAYLIGHT FROM DIFFERENT SIDES OF BUILDING, WHICH GARANTEES HOMOGENOUS DISTRIBUTION OF DAYLIGHT.

MULTIWALL CARBON NANOTUBE ARE BRAIDED INTO FIBRES. FIBRE RIBBONS CREATES TWO DIRECTIONAL FIBBONACCI PATERN ROPE, WHICH BEARS WHOLE BUILDING.

NATURAL DAYLIGHT IS HARVESTED BY NETWORK OF OPTIC FIBRES PLACED ON SURFACE OF ETFE FACADE AND IT IS TRANSPORTED INSIDE.

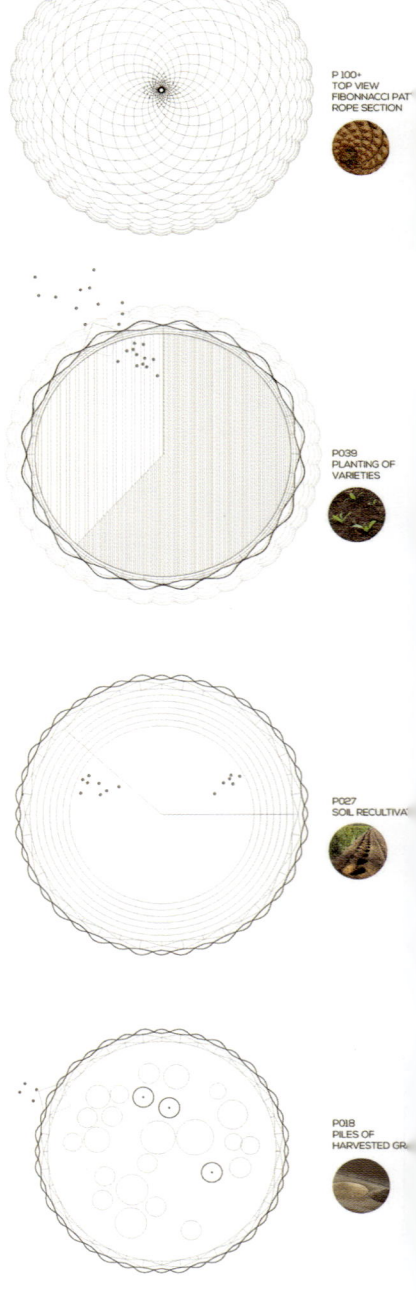

P 100+
TOP VIEW
FIBONNACCI PAT'
ROPE SECTION

P039
PLANTING OF
VARIETIES

P027
SOIL RECULTIVA'

P018
PILES OF
HARVESTED GR'

SELECTED FLOORPLANS

PLANTAGE
THE SKYHANGER

seed banks after global climate changes and melted permafrost. Space station simulates gravity through rotation of the outer ring, and it is shaded from cosmic radiation, to simulate Earth conditions for seeds and human occupants.

The construction process begins with building of counterweight hubless space station, which is carrying element of the building. Station element is taken into space-by-space shuttle rockets and Space elevator. To increase counterweight function, station is collecting space trash from the Earth orbit. Carbon nanotube fibre rope braided from carbon nanotube ribbons is unwound from space to the Earth. Floors of the Skyhanger are hanged and filled with alluvial soil eroded by rainy waters in delta of rivers.

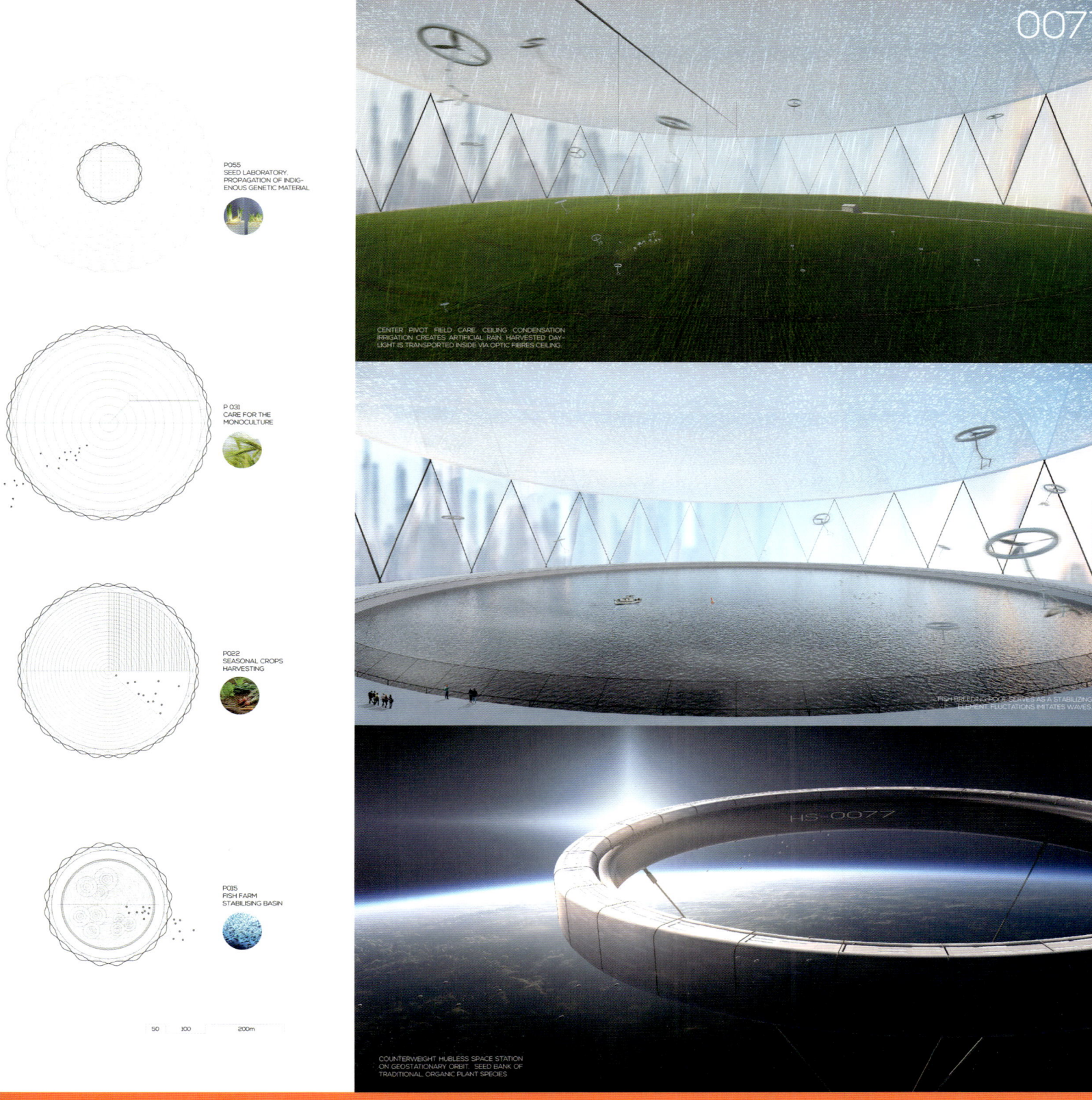

0077

P055
SEED LABORATORY,
PROPAGATION OF INDIG-
ENOUS GENETIC MATERIAL

P031
CARE FOR THE
MONOCULTURE

P022
SEASONAL CROPS
HARVESTING

P015
FISH FARM
STABILISING BASIN

50   100   200m

CENTER PIVOT FIELD CARE. CEILING CONDENSATION IRRIGATION CREATES ARTIFICIAL RAIN. HARVESTED DAYLIGHT IS TRANSPORTED INSIDE VIA OPTIC FIBRES CEILING.

FISH BREEDING POOL SERVES AS A STABILIZING ELEMENT. FLUCTATIONS IMITATES WAVES.

HS-0077

COUNTERWEIGHT HUBLESS SPACE STATION ON GEOSTATIONARY ORBIT. SEED BANK OF TRADITIONAL ORGANIC PLANT SPECIES

FLOATING HOUSING

GuoChao Deng
Jiong Lin
You Zhou
Yang Li
GuoFu Wang
XiaoLong Liu

China

Reincarnation-Future Sea Slum

Design background:

In the process of urbanization in Nigeria, the gap between the rich and the poor is widening gradually,which makes a large number of homeless people gathered in Gamma cocoa community and turned this community into a slum on the sea. It is a very extreme case in the process of urbanization in Africa.There is no traditional road, no land as well as modern architecture,but it has developed into a plum of about 200000 people.Surrounded by foul smelling of the sea,creaky wooden houses are everywhere,and each wooden houses are crammed six to ten people who are completely ignored by the government.In the official map, Nigeria along the coast are uninhabited, including Gamma cocoa community.

Now the Gamma cocoa community may become the real unmanned area at any time. It's possible that the region be swallowed up by the sea thanks to the rise of sea level caused by Global warming.Faced with such a situation,the government only adopt a measure of demolitions.There are no resettlement measures as well as subsidies,as a result,a great quantity of people became homeless and are scattered on various parts of Africa.

Problems that exist in Gamma cocoa community:

1.Serious lack of community function:there is no public space in Gamma cocoa community just like the traditional community.In the meantime,the community infrastructure is inadequate.For example,there is no hospital in the community so residents can't get timely treatment when they are sick.There is also a serious problem in the education.Schools are temporary substandard housing,but even in that case,the number of classrooms is limited,causing many students unable to receive education.What's more,there is no Electric Power Facility owing to the lack of land.

2.Poor living environment of the community:people can not handle the waste of daily life with a lack of land so they have to pour it into the sea,which leads to serious pollution,and in turn makes the living environment unhealthier.Meanwhile,the main source that local residents rely on is from the polluted sea,so people are suffering a serious shortage of nutrition.

3.Inadequate safe water: the lack of simple and convenient traffic has brought great inconvenience to the residents' life,especially in terms of safe water.People have to transport safe water by fishing boat from several miles away while there is rainwater to drink.

In the process of urbanization in Nigeria, the gap between the rich and the poor is widening gradually, which makes a large number of homeless people gathered in Gamma cocoa community and turned this community into a slum on the sea. It is a very extreme case in the process of urbanization in Africa. There is no traditional road, no land as well as modern architecture, but it has developed into a slum of about 200,000 people. Surrounded by foul smelling of the sea, creaky wooden houses are everywhere, and each wooden house are crammed six to ten people who are completely ignored by the government. In the official map, Nigeria along the coast is uninhabited, including Gamma cocoa community.

Now the Gamma cocoa community may become the real unmanned area at any time. It's possible that the region be swallowed up by the sea thanks to the rise of sea level caused by Global warming.

0090

.Dangerous living condition:the community may become a real unmanned area due to the rise of sea level.What's more,most of the local housing for residents is built by wood,thus some security risks may exist.

.There is no guarantee of human rights:In the official map, Nigeria along the coast are uninhabited,the government regards residents as rubbish and can throw them away at any time.The local government never take resettlement measures after demolition,leading to a great quantity of homeless slum.

Design concept:

.According to the present situation of the Gamma cocoa community, we put forward a proposal,we try to improve the dilemma by architecture.We will centralize the original tiled slums in high-rise buildings,which can not only solve the waste and pollution problems of the sea caused by traditional flat sea slum but also create a better, more secure and healthier living environment for the poor in the slum.

Fantasy after construction:

We use architecture to rebuild hope,we use architecture to construct a new Gamma cocoa community. The original residents can directly carry their houses to our high-rise buildings,there is no need to rebuild,only need a little transformation.We use local materials and adopt the traditional way of construction to make residents feel a sense of belonging when they move to high-rise buildings.We purify deep sea water to people living in our building,we also have a complete set of waste recycling mechanism so that our buildings can handle the waste and be self-sufficient.Our high-rise buildings provide a more complete and healthier community function.Residents will not only possess a private balcony,but they can own a lager public space to communicate, recreation and entertainment.Let's imagine a scene: you can enjoy the beautiful sunset on your balcony after dinner,you can also choose

The local government compares us to waste

Faced with such a situation, the government only adopts a measure of demolitions. There are no resettlement measures as well as subsidies, as a result, a great quantity of people became homeless and are scattered on various parts of Africa.

We use architecture to rebuild hope; we use architecture to construct a new Gamma cocoa community The original residents can directly carry their houses to our high-rise buildings, there is no need to rebuild, only need a little transformation. We use local materials and adopt the traditional way of construction to make residents feel a sense of belonging when they move to high-rise buildings. We purify deep sea water to people living in our building, we also have a complete set of waste recycling mechanism so that our buildings can handle the waste and be self-sufficient. Our high-rise buildings

Central Park: in order to improve the community cohesion and life quality, we set up a Central Park in the middle so that residents can have activities like communication, recreation and entertainment. At the same time a lot of plants have been planted here.

Growing region: In order to improve the variety of people's food, we provide residents with their own growing region to plant food.

Pipeline for transporting methane: deliver the purified bio-gas to the distribution station and then the distribution station distribute bio-gas to each household.

Conduit for conveying water: After the purification of drinking water it can be sent to the drinking water distribution station and then the distribution station distribute drinking water to each household.

SWRO DEVICE: desalinate sea water using the theory of dialysis and filter out some toxic substances in the meantime and turn the sea water into fresh water for drinking. At the same time utilize salt that desalinated from seawater.

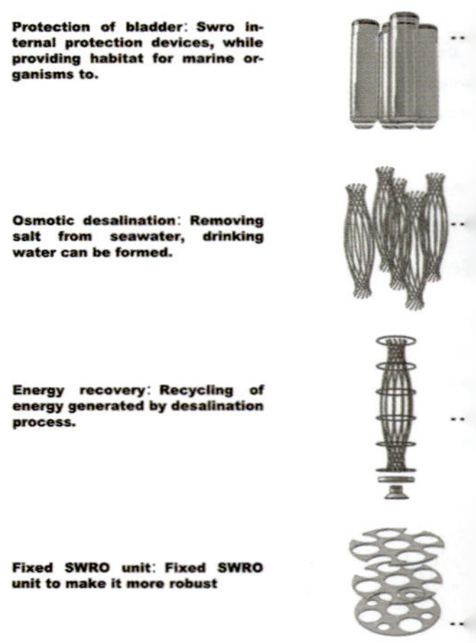

Protection of bladder: Swro internal protection devices, while providing habitat for marine organisms to.

Osmotic desalination: Removing salt from seawater, drinking water can be formed.

Energy recovery: Recycling of energy generated by desalination process.

Fixed SWRO unit: Fixed SWRO unit to make it more robust

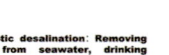

provide a more complete and healthier community function. Residents will not only possess a private balcony, but they can own a lager public space for communication, recreation and entertainment. Let's imagine a scene: you can enjoy the beautiful sunset on your balcony after dinner; you can also choose to chat with friends or take a walk in the center park. To conclude, we hope to improve residents' living condition and unite them to construct a "desperate slum" into a "hopeful slum" by their own hand through our buildings.

Reincarnation-Future Sea Slum   0090

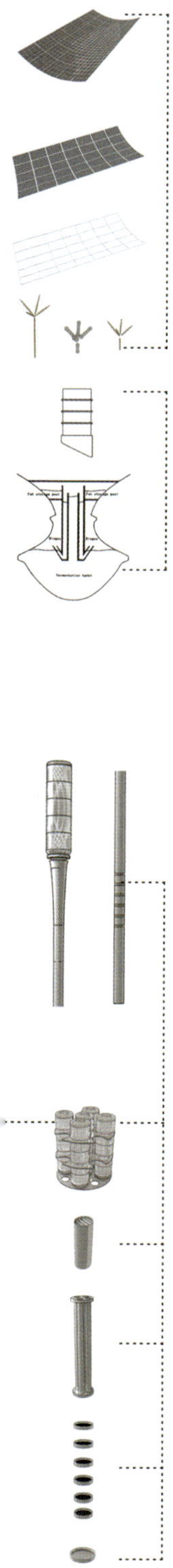

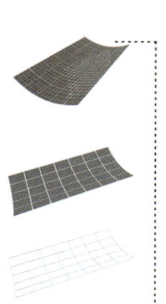

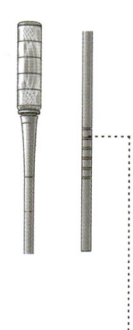

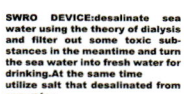

Solar energy system: In order to allow the entire building to achieve self-sufficiency,we choose to use solar energy system,we also take residents into account to provide them with power system so they can have a healthier living environment.

Solar panels:we adopt transparent solar glass panels.

fixation construct: Fix solar panels on buildings

Supporting structure: The force of the whole building is realized through the wooden hinge

Biogas purification:use this device to purify biogas.

Biogas system:to handle the waste in daily life,we use bioga circulation system to decompost metabolites and use the fertilizer to fertilize plant,after that,the biogas can be used in daily life and achieve the circulatory system in the buildings,

Working principle of methane tank:when the biogas is produced in the methane tank,methane in gas storage increases and pressure increases,force the liquid level in the main pool to drop and extrude a part of the liquid into the water pressure chamber.When people turn on the stove,The pressure in the biogas tank gradually decrease,waste liquid in hydraulic room continue to flow back into the main pool.In this way continuously to produce

Seawater Purification System:to cope with the problem of the safety of drinking water in community,our design draws sea water from the deep sea and purify sea water into drinking water through Desalination of sea water can be purified into drinking water.At the same time, these water absorption tubes can also provide a habitat for the underwater creatures.

SWRO DEVICE:desalinate sea water using the theory of dialysis and filter out some toxic substances in the meantime and turn the sea water into fresh water for drinking.At the same time utilize salt that desalinated from seawater.

Security Filter:protect water purification system and ensure that the water quality meets the water purification standards at the same time.

Precision Filter:use precision filter to filter out some toxic Substances and disinfect seawater.

Milti-medium Filter:use milti-medium filter to filter out some of the smaller impurities in the seawater.

Water Inlet Filter:filter out large impurities through the filter to prevent large impurities sucked into the suction pipe and cause clogging

VANGUARD SKYSCRAPER

Zacc Israel Renia

Philippines

Amid the backdrop of a world still torn by the ravages of war, the Vanguard slashes like a bolt of lightning through the skyline, breaking many records and—quite literally—reaching new heights.

Funded by a philanthropist with a heart set at changing the way people think of war, the Vanguard is a homage to the unparalleled valor of every soldier fighting for the country. The 1000-feet building, which stands directly in the middle of a walled city, serves as a military base camp, a residential space, a museum, a training ground, and a burial, all at once. It is solar-paneled all over, and has its own rain collectors and wind turbines, thus making the most of renewable energy sources.

At first sight, the Vanguard, a soldier itself, stands steady and strong, conquering even the limits of gravity, seismic activity, and the wind. It is made of kind of reinforced heavy-duty military grade steel and concrete, making extra certain that it strictly follows its no-compromise approach to safety and durability. Finally, it features modules that are able to repair itself when damaged, with the help of a high-performance system of robotic arms working together to employ the smoothest, most efficient restoration technique.

With a team of architects, engineers, and scientists, what was once a dream project blatantly ignored and disregarded by experts and media alike is now a reality that does not need to boast or beg just to be noticed. The Vanguard is not just an architectural and engineering stroke of genius in steel and concrete. It is a sight and a light in itself. It does not hold any pretense—but is, rather, straightforward in its mission to inspire people to resist, to make war against war.

Despite its astute, stern appearance, the Vanguard shows vulnerability through its open, modular structure. It pays tribute to a soldier's undying spirit—their determination to continue the fight despite being hurt and gravely wounded.

Most significantly, however, the Vanguard is unique in that it banks on the vulnerability of its inhabitants by reinforcing in them a lifestyle that is simple and sincere. Soldiers are forced to live with their families and colleagues, helping them foster better working relations and more harmonious relationships with each other. In doing so, the Vanguard reveals the oft-overlooked, yet most important aspect of warfare: that every soldier gets their strength and courage, ultimately, from their love for their family and their country.

Amid the backdrop of a world still torn by the ravages of war, the Vanguard slashes like a bolt of lightning through the skyline, breaking many records and—quite literally—reaching new heights. Funded by a philanthropist with a heart set at changing the way people think of war, the Vanguard is homage to the unparalleled valor of every soldier fighting for the country. The 1000-feet building, which stands directly in the middle of a walled city, serves as a military base camp, a residential space, a museum, a training ground, and a burial, all at once. It is solar-paneled all over, and has its own rain collectors and wind turbines, thus making the most of renewable energy sources. At first sight, the Vanguard is a soldier itself. It stands steady and strong, conquering even the limits of gravity, seismic activity, and the wind. It is made of tons of reinforced heavy-duty military grade steel and concrete, making extra certain that it

0150

strictly follows its no-compromise approach to safety and durability. Finally, it features modules that are able to repair it when damaged, with the help of a high-performance system of robotic arms working together to employ the smoothest, most efficient restoration technique. With a team of architects, engineers, and scientists, what was once a dream project blatantly ignored and disregarded by experts and media alike is now a reality that does not need to boast or beg just to be noticed. The Vanguard is not just an architectural and engineering stroke of genius in steel and concrete. It a sight and a fight in itself. It does not hold any pretense—but is, rather, straightforward in its mission to inspire people to resist, to make war against war.

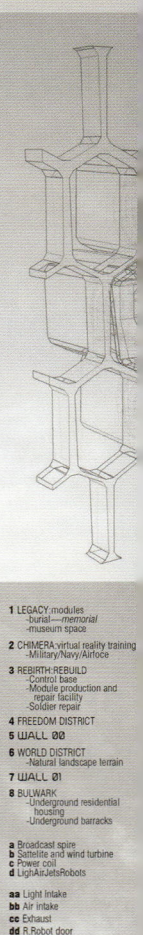

(Excerpt from a military soldier's audio recording, dated 18 November 2070)

I woke up today feeling a lot more anxious than usual. And then, like a jolt of shock straight to the heart, I remembered: it's been sixteen years since the third world war ended. Sixteen years since the most horrific combat and bloodshed in history ruined our faith in attaining peace at all. Sixteen years since millions of lives and houses, families and friendships were shattered—never to be found nor restored again.

It's been sixteen years since we lost all hope. Or at least, that's what we thought.

We were wrong.

Sixteen years was long enough to create a revolution: the Vanguard—my base camp, my shield, my refuge...my home. The Vanguard has been receiving generally good feedback among my colleagues because of the motivations and ambitions behind it. I can't help but feel really proud. I'm proud of what we, as soldiers, have become because of it.

I noticed we have become more eager and enthusiastic in fulfilling our mandate to serve the people. Since the Vanguard is an all-in-one military skyscraper, it saves us a lot of time, money and effort. Military trainings are now more exciting knowing that our families are literally just there with us, only several floors away.

I'm already on my 30-hour mark in flying school. In the middle of the training, I suddenly missed my daughter. I remembered she have always wanted to ride a plane! How I wished she was there with me during training.

Our commanding officers have become easier to approach, and communication of plans and tactics have become faster than ever. During lunch today, I observed Officer Ravi dined with us—for the first time. He was smiling and talking to our colleagues. It was a pleasure to see. I hope he sustains his happy temperament, because honestly, it suits him better.

What I like most about serving—and living—in the Vanguard is that it doesn't only make us great soldiers; it also makes us great friends, and great persons in general. We have learned to laugh at each other's jokes. We have learned to cry without fear of being judged. We have learned to appreciate simple joys. We have learned to inspire and become inspired by one another.

In short, we have learned what it feels to be alive.

What more could we ask, really? The Vanguard provides everything for us and the country. There's just some kind of enigma in this building I couldn't quite translate into words. Perhaps it's because it's a life-saver. Or...a love-saver? Ah.

It's a war-saver.

1 LEGACY modules
  -burial—memorial
  -museum space

2 CHIMERA virtual reality training
  -Military/Navy/Airforce

3 REBIRTH REBUILD
  -Control base
  -Module production and
   repair facility
  -Soldier repair

4 FREEDOM DISTRICT

5 WALL 00

6 WORLD DISTRICT
  -Natural landscape terrain

7 WALL 01

8 BULWARK
  -Underground residential
   housing
  -Underground barracks

a Broadcast spire
b Satellite and wind turbine
c Power coil
d LightJetsRobots

aa Light intake
bb Air intake
cc Exhaust
dd R Robot door

VANGUARD

Despite its astute, stern appearance, the Vanguard shows vulnerability through its open, modular structure. It pays tribute to a soldier's undying spirit—their determination to continue the fight despite being hurt and gravely wounded. Most significantly, however, the Vanguard is unique in that it banks on the vulnerability of its inhabitants by reinforcing in them a lifestyle that is simple and sincere. Soldiers are forced to live with their families and colleagues, helping them foster better working relations and more harmonious relationships with each other. In doing so, the Vanguard reveals the oft-overlooked, yet most important aspect of warfare: that every soldier gets their strength and courage, ultimately, from their love for their family and their country.

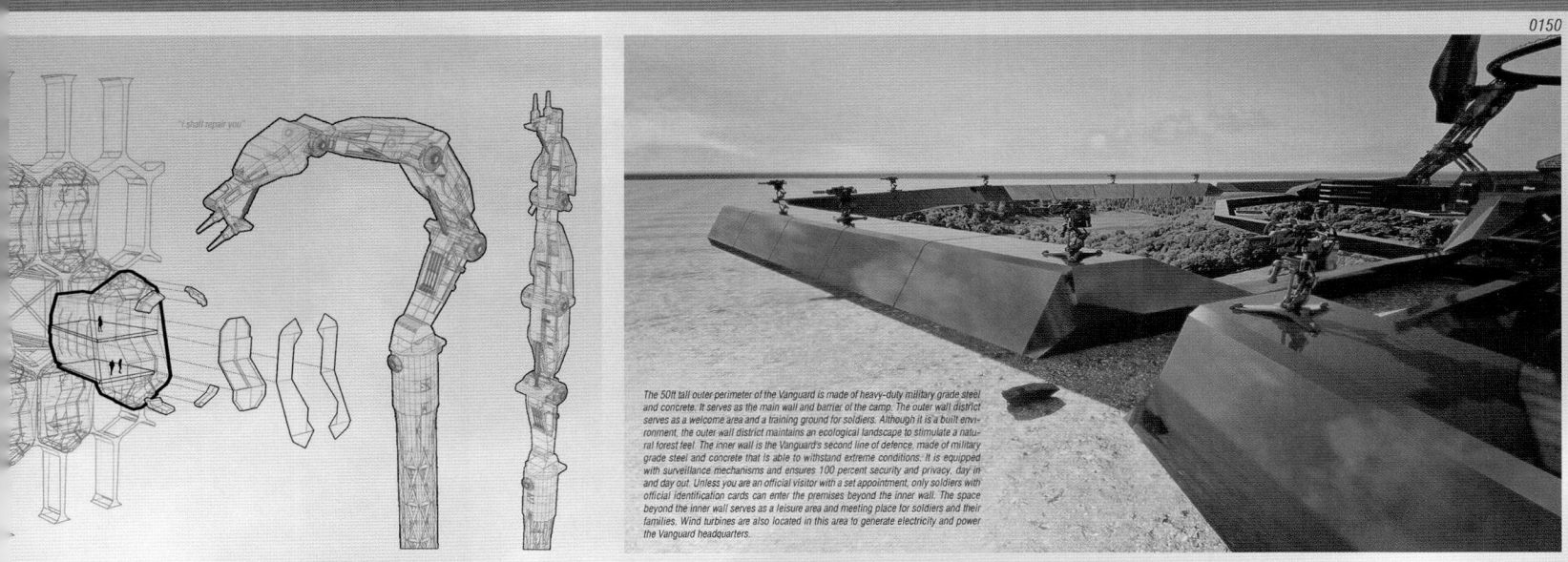

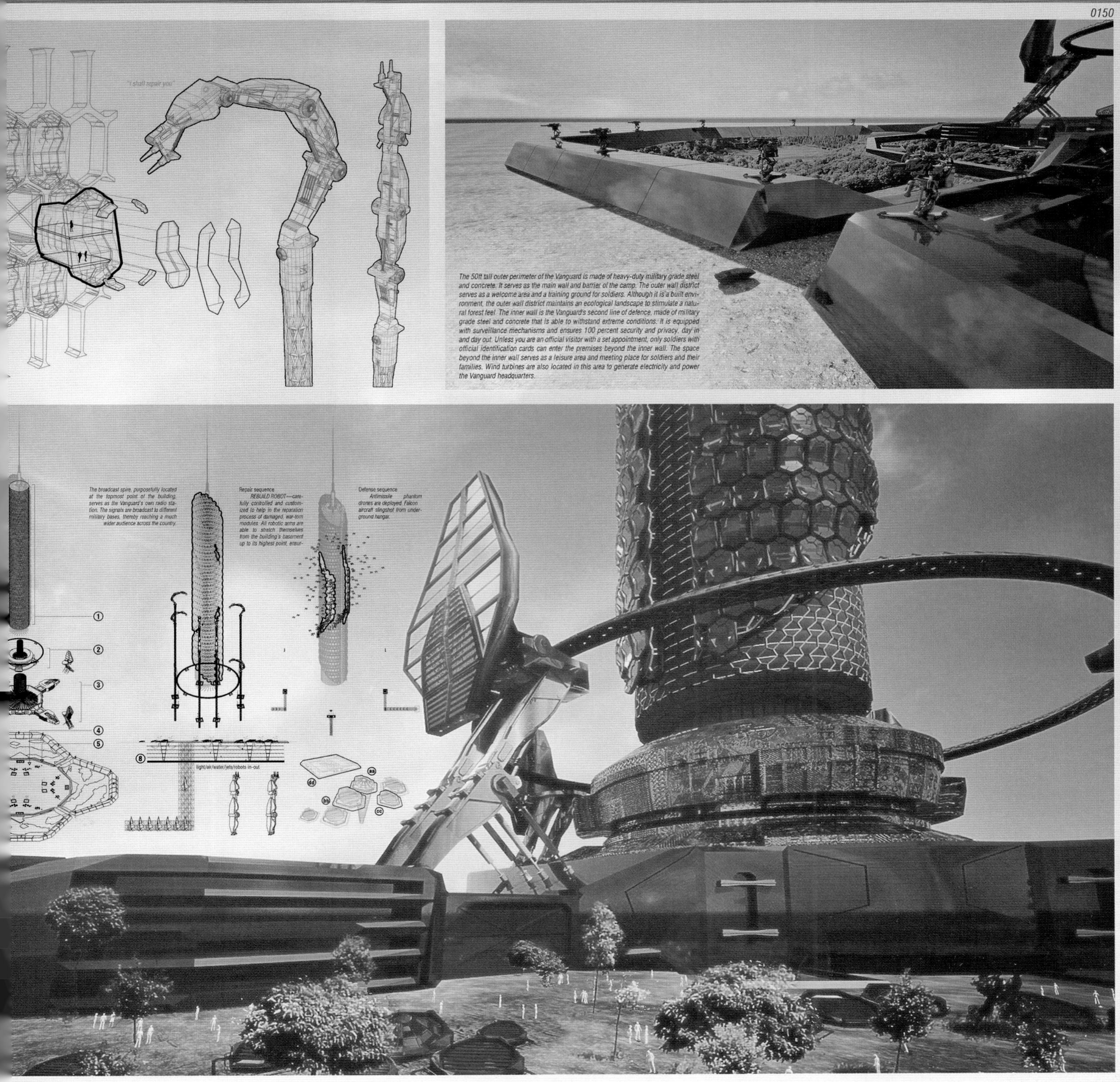

0150

The 50ft tall outer perimeter of the Vanguard is made of heavy-duty military grade steel and concrete. It serves as the main wall and barrier of the camp. The outer wall district serves as a welcome area and a training ground for soldiers. Although it is a built environment, the outer wall district maintains an ecological landscape to stimulate a natural forest feel. The inner wall is the Vanguard's second line of defence, made of military grade steel and concrete that is able to withstand extreme conditions. It is equipped with surveillance mechanisms and ensures 100 percent security and privacy, day in and day out. Unless you are an official visitor with a set appointment, only soldiers with official identification cards can enter the premises beyond the inner wall. The space beyond the inner wall serves as a leisure area and meeting place for soldiers and their families. Wind turbines are also located in this area to generate electricity and power the Vanguard headquarters.

"I shall repair you"

The broadcast spire, purposefully located at the topmost point of the building, serves as the Vanguard's own radio station. The signals are broadcast to different military bases, thereby reaching a much wider audience across the country.

Repair sequence
REBUILD ROBOT—carefully controlled and customised to help in the reparation process of damaged, war-torn modules. All robotic arms are able to stretch themselves from the building's basement up to its highest point, ensur-

Defense sequence
Antimissile phantom drones are deployed. Falcon aircraft slingshot from underground hangar.

light/air/water/jets/robots in-out

AQUARIUM TRINITY

Quah Zheng We
Jethro Koi Lik Wai

Malaysia

AQUARIM TRINITY

DESIGN ISSUE

Coral reefs are now endangered.

Coral reefs are complex mosaic of marine plants and animals. Supporting up to two million species of marine life, the biodiversity richness making itself a rival to tropical rain forest. Similarly, the reefs play an important roles in balancing the ecosystem in the water. The polyps within coral control the content of carbon dioxide in the water by turning them into limestone shell. Besides biologically beneficial to mankind, coral reefs generate sizeable economy values as many relies on them as a source of food, income and medicine.

Despite being significantly important in many ways, there is minimal effort shown in protecting them from threats from human and natural disturbances; resulting in a permanent loss of 27% coral area and 30% more are at the brink of disappearing in coming years according to a research funded by WWF.

This underwater paradise is slowly being destroyed by actions such as the practice of uncontrolled, destructive fishing methods, oil spills, pollution (from domestic and industrial wastes, fertilizers, and pesticides), anchor damage, untreated or improperly treated sewage, and land runoffs are serious threats to the delicate reefs. Global Warming causes significant temperature increases in waters in which corals inhabit. This rise in sea temperature creates a very stressful living enviroment for the coral reef. Coral Reefs respond to such stresses by ejecting necessary symbiotics within themthat provide vital nourishment to the coral. This ejection leads to a loss of pigmentation in the coral reef, this is known as coral bleaching

DESIGN STATEMENT

The Aquarim Trinity is a design proposal that aims to rejuvenate destroyed coral reefs by reproducing millions of existing coral species. While attempts to reproduce coral is evident on land, the ideal coral breeding location remains to be its natural habitat, the ocean. The architecture intervention introduces a mega-skeletal vertical coral farm that extended across euphotic to dysphotic. The reason of which is to create the heights that cater for a conducive environments for different species with respective height adaptiveness.

Subsequent to propagating endangered species on the platform of tower farm, Aquarim Trinity focuses on coral regional rejuvenation whereby upon matured the corals will be released and dispersed further afield to develop a new colony, assimilating mushroom spore reproduction system. To compliment the growth, human footprint is restricted to a manoeuvrable research in such instance to minimize their impact.

Consolidating all coral species in a tower as it may seem, the new architecture typology is truly about restoring ocean to the state it used to be and it shall serve as a towering statement to mankind about the dying state of the forgotten lungs in ocean.

Coral reefs are now endangered; they are a complex mosaic of marine plants and animals. Supporting up to two million species of marine life, the biodiversity richness even rival tropical rain forests. Similarly, the reefs play an important role in balancing ocean ecosystems. The polyps within coral control the content of carbon dioxide in the water by turning them into a limestone shell.

Despite being significantly important in many ways, there is minimal effort shown in protecting them from humans and natural disturbances; resulting in a permanent loss of 27% coral area and a 30% more are at the brink of disappearing in coming years according to the World Wide Fund for Nature.

This underwater paradise is slowly being destroyed by actions such as the practice of uncontrolled, destructive fishing methods, oil spills, pollution (industrial wastes, fertilizers, and pesticides), anchor

0292

damage, untreated or improperly treated sewage, and land runoffs. Global Warming causes significant temperature increases in waters in which corals inhabit. This rise in sea temperature creates a very stressful living environment for the coral reef. Coral Reefs respond to such stresses by ejecting necessary symbiotic within them. This ejection leads to a loss of pigmentation in the coral reef, known as coral bleaching

The Aquarim Trinity is a design proposal that aims to rejuvenate destroyed coral reefs by reproducing millions of existing coral species. While attempts to reproduce coral is evident on land, the ideal coral breeding location remains to be its natural habitat, the ocean. This architecture intervention introduces a mega-skeletal vertical coral farm.

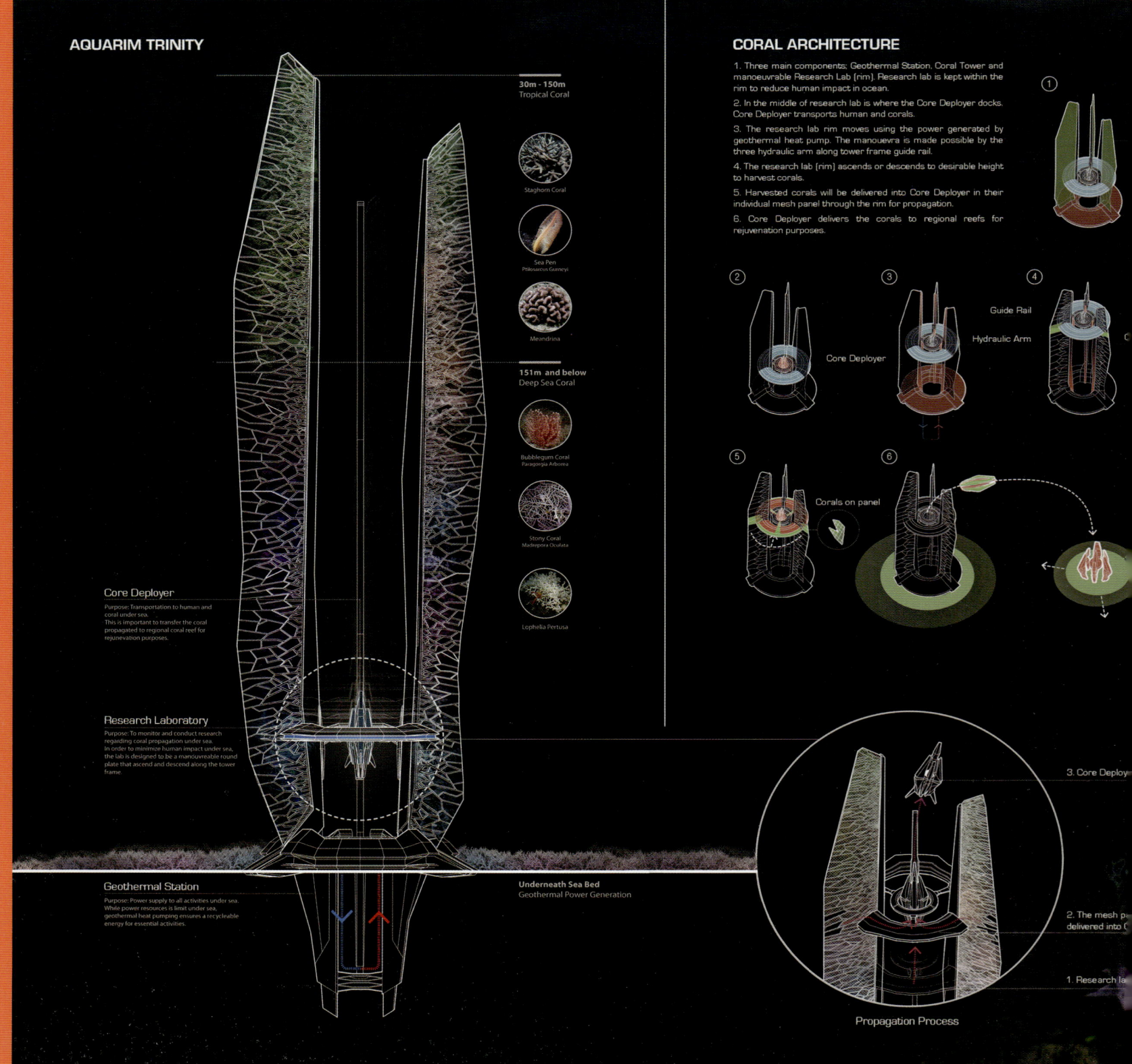

AQUARIM TRINITY

30m - 150m
Tropical Coral

Staghorn Coral

Sea Pen
Ptilosarcus Gurneyi

Meandrina

151m and below
Deep Sea Coral

Bubblegum Coral
Paragorgia Arborea

Stony Coral
Madrepora Oculata

Lophelia Pertusa

Core Deployer
Purpose: Transportation to human and coral under sea.
This is important to transfer the coral propagated to regional coral reef for rejunevation purposes.

Research Laboratory
Purpose: To monitor and conduct research regarding coral propagation under sea.
In order to minimize human impact under sea, the lab is designed to be a manouvreable round plate that ascend and descend along the tower frame.

Geothermal Station
Purpose: Power supply to all activities under sea.
While power resources is limit under sea, geothermal heat pumping ensures a recyclable energy for essential activities.

Underneath Sea Bed
Geothermal Power Generation

CORAL ARCHITECTURE

1. Three main components; Geothermal Station, Coral Tower and manoeuvrable Research Lab (rim). Research lab is kept within the rim to reduce human impact in ocean.

2. In the middle of research lab is where the Core Deployer docks. Core Deployer transports human and corals.

3. The research lab rim moves using the power generated by geothermal heat pump. The manouevra is made possible by the three hydraulic arm along tower frame guide rail.

4. The research lab (rim) ascends or descends to desirable height to harvest corals.

5. Harvested corals will be delivered into Core Deployer in their individual mesh panel through the rim for propagation.

6. Core Deployer delivers the corals to regional reefs for rejuvenation purposes.

Guide Rail

Hydraulic Arm

Core Deployer

Corals on panel

3. Core Deploy

2. The mesh p
delivered into C

1. Research la

Propagation Process

Subsequent to propagating endangered species on the platform of tower farm, Aquarim Trinity focuses on coral regional rejuvenation in which mature corals will be released and dispersed to develop a new colony, following mushroom spore reproduction system. To compliment the growth, human footprint is restricted to a maneuverable research lab to minimize their impact. Consolidating all coral species in a tower creates a new architecture typology that is truly about restoring ocean to the state it used to be and it shall serve as a towering statement to mankind about the dying state of the forgotten ocean lungs.

0292

Coral Farm

Research Lab

hermal Station

rm

e Deployer expanded

rals goes on coral propagation.

h corals grow on will be
oyer through the rim.

cends to desirable harvesting heights.

RE-BALANCE SEASCRAPER

Jia Yue
Shi Yuqing
Wang Haoyu
Li Zhibin
He Run
Yu Songqiao

China

REEBALANCE

Desic
El Nino
Moreo
great
vulner
mode
Vertica
In the
reefs,
enviro

Desic
We ra
ecosy
close
growt
(ocea
circula

Top oceanic scientists around the world are documenting how fast coral reefs around the world are shrinking. Coral reefs are one of the most important resources on earth, both as an ecological landscape and as a resource to humans. Also, as vividly called "tropical marine desert oasis", it has a high biological diversity. They provide a variety of biological resources, and have great environmental functions. Besides, reflected in the marine biological diversity effects, it turns into a natural barrier of coastal engineering, with marine scientific research.

However in recent decades, out of suffering the dual pressures of men and nature the coral reef ecosystem is facing serious degradation. Data shows that over the past few decades, more than a quarter of the global coral reef has been degraded. Scholars estimate that within the next 20 years at

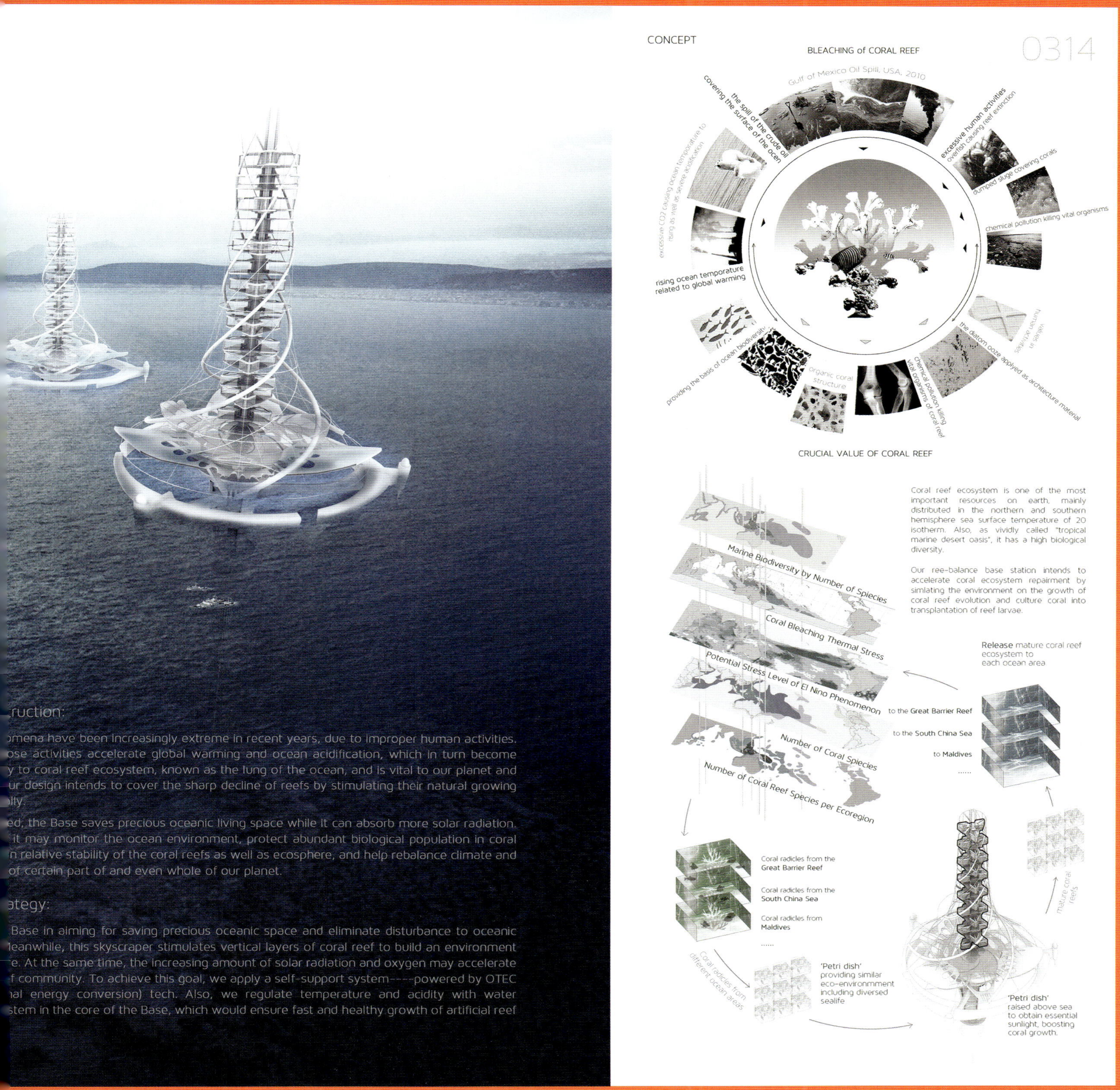

CONCEPT

0314

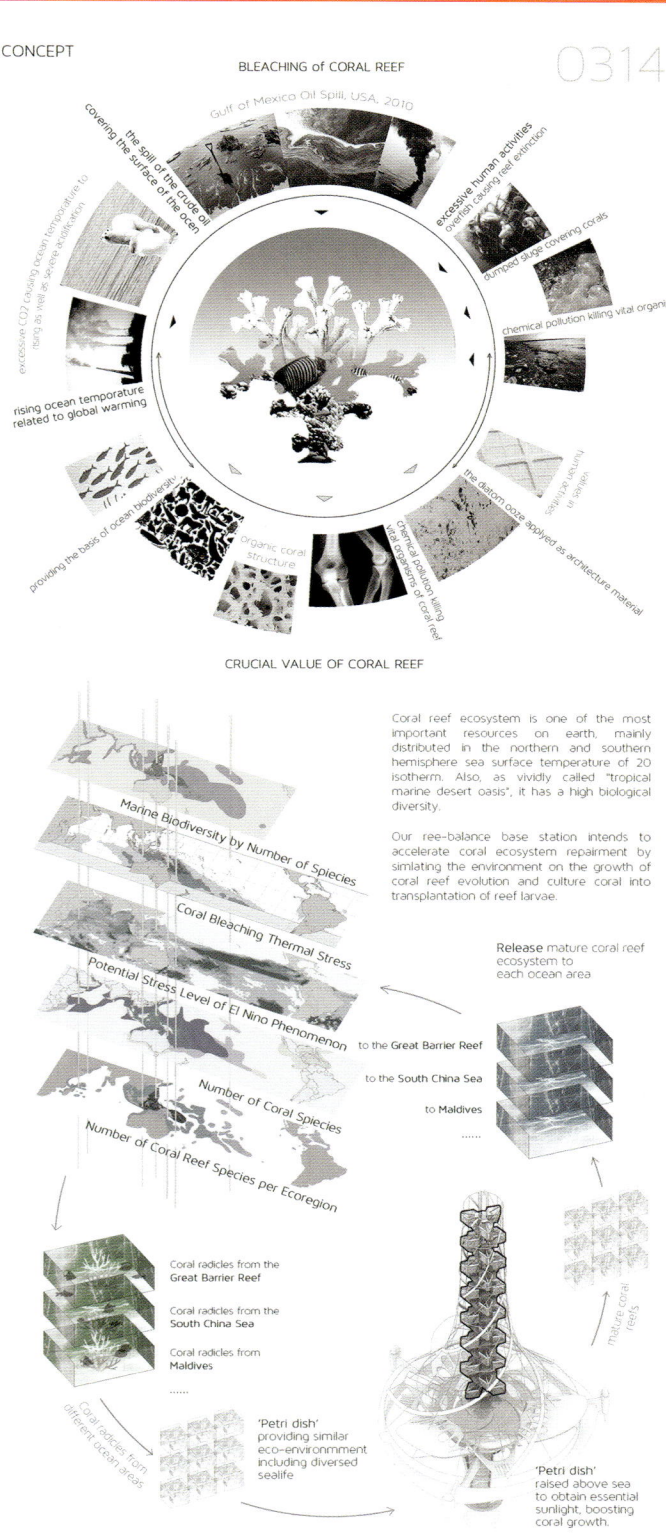

BLEACHING of CORAL REEF

Gulf of Mexico Oil Spill, USA, 2010

CRUCIAL VALUE OF CORAL REEF

Coral reef ecosystem is one of the most important resources on earth, mainly distributed in the northern and southern hemisphere sea surface temperature of 20 isotherm. Also, as vividly called "tropical marine desert oasis", it has a high biological diversity.

Our ree-balance base station intends to accelerate coral ecosystem repairment by simlating the environment on the growth of coral reef evolution and culture coral into transplantation of reef larvae.

Marine Biodiversity by Number of Spiecies

Coral Bleaching Thermal Stress

Potential Stress Level of El Nino Phenomenon

Number of Coral Spiecies

Number of Coral Reef Species per Ecoregion

Release mature coral reef ecosystem to each ocean area

to the Great Barrier Reef

to the South China Sea

to Maldives

......

Coral radicles from the Great Barrier Reef

Coral radicles from the South China Sea

Coral radicles from Maldives

......

'Petri dish' providing similar eco-environment including diversed sealife

'Petri dish' raised above sea to obtain essential sunlight, boosting coral growth.

ruction:

menma have been increasingly extreme in recent years, due to improper human activities. ose activities accelerate global warming and ocean acidification, which in turn become y to coral reef ecosystem, known as the lung of the ocean, and is vital to our planet and ur design intends to cover the sharp decline of reefs by stimulating their natural growing lly.

ed, the Base saves precious oceanic living space while it can absorb more solar radiation. it may monitor the ocean environment, protect abundant biological population in coral n relative stability of the coral reefs as well as ecosphere, and help rebalance climate and of certain part of and even whole of our planet.

ategy:

Base in aiming for saving precious oceanic space and eliminate disturbance to oceanic leanwhile, this skyscraper stimulates vertical layers of coral reef to build an environment e. At the same time, the increasing amount of solar radiation and oxygen may accelerate f community. To achieve this goal, we apply a self-support system----powered by OTEC nal energy conversion) tech. Also, we regulate temperature and acidity with water stem in the core of the Base, which would ensure fast and healthy growth of artificial reef

least another quarter will disappear and in the next 40 years most of Southeast Asian coral reefs will be gone. If this situation continues to deteriorate, most of coral reef resources of the globe will disappear in this century.

A lot of research has been made by the international coral reef rebalancing plan. However, the general ecological restoration strategy is mainly based on two kinds of reproduction of coral; most importantly, regulating the water temperature and salinity, and adjusting the water depth and illumination conditions. Using vertical stratification, the project simulates shallow marine layers of a coral reef ecosystem growth zone.

To be eco-friendly, the project has to be self-supporting. The stability of the project needs height,

BACKGROUND

Coral reefs are some of the most diverse and valuable ecos reefs support more species per unit area than any other m cluding about 4,000 species of fish, and hundreds of ot id-base and atmospheric balances are interconnected wil profound impact to the ecosphere of earth. Meanwhile, at of coral reefs are shrinking worldly. 80% are bleaching whi out protection, corals will dead out by 2100.

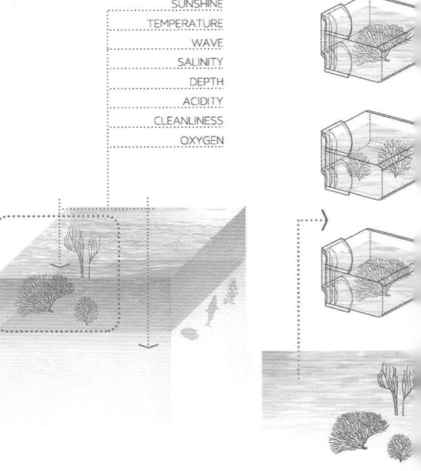

The growth of coral is closely related to the seawater tem perature for coral growth is 25-28 °C,while less than 13 °C and the optimum salinity is 36 ‰.Besides, the optimum a The growth of coral is also affected by the transmittance growth, and within 20m the growth of coral is the most p is 50 -70m, but not form the reef. So cultivate coral can b surface, the coral will interference other marine organism with the solution of lifting the seawater. Taking advantag Meanwhile, in order to ensure adequate sunlight, the dish propriate nutrients and get growth necessities in the time

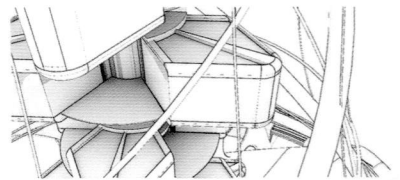

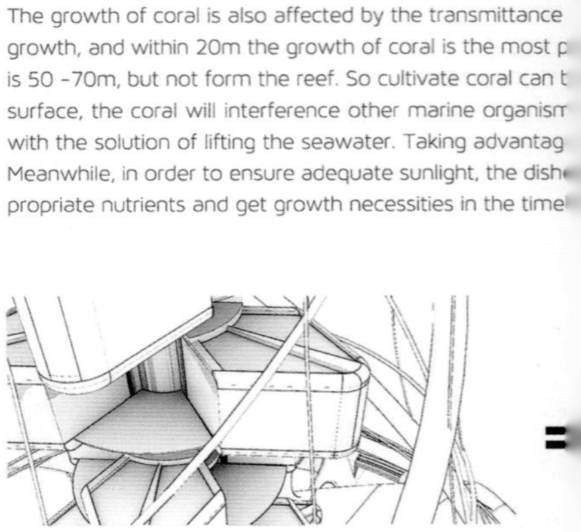

Vertical coral culture system, every 'petri dish' maintain a favorable living condition for the coral to grow rapidly, each dish is connected by tubes to supervise the condi- tion inside as well as exchanging materials with the out- side sea water to grow those corals. each level has three dishes, and they are arranged seperately to gain enough light to grow.

which is also essential for OTEC generating systems. The steam travels up a pipe into a turbine, where it generates electricity. The steam then condenses back to water and travels down to another heat exchanger this one cooling the liquid with cold seawater from lower depths. From here, a pump brings it back up to the first heat exchanger, and the system continues on.

0314

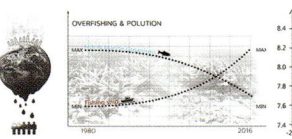
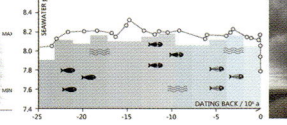

The rate of decline is quite fast. Coral reefs have been subjected to a wide spectrum of disturbances and there have been current global mass extinctions. Coral reef is vulnerable and its disturbances have ranged from infrequent El Nino to frequent human activities, such as shipping. Both of them are fatal to reef eco-system, in turn to the Mother Nature as a whole. In ,some perticular regions, like Caribbean coral reef, they have declined since the 1970s from a 50% cover of live corals to 8%. Consequently, it has been argued that the decline of coral reefs is both syptom and incentive of global environmental deterioration process and the key to reverse the trend.

Coral ecosystems are a source of food for millions, protect coastlines from storms and erosoion, provide habitat, spawning and nursery grounds for economically important fish species, provide jobs and income to local economies from fishing, recreation, and tourism, are a source of new medicines, and are hotspots of marine biodiversity. other than that, the coral reef is a perfect source of building material and human-affinity artificial bone. Besides, laboratory research is another major value of coral reef.

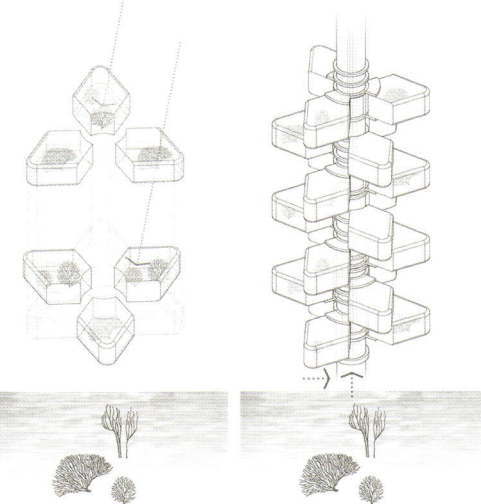

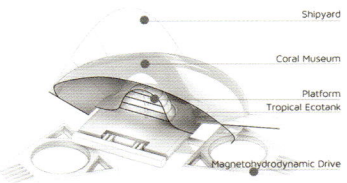

Shipyard
Coral Museum
Platform
Tropical Ecotank
Magnetohydrodynamic Drive

Structure of the propeller is hollow and flanges of the shipyard are raised to release the surface of the sea for working boats and Shallow sea creatures.

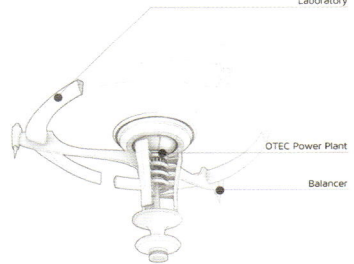

Laboratory

OTEC Power Plant

Balancer

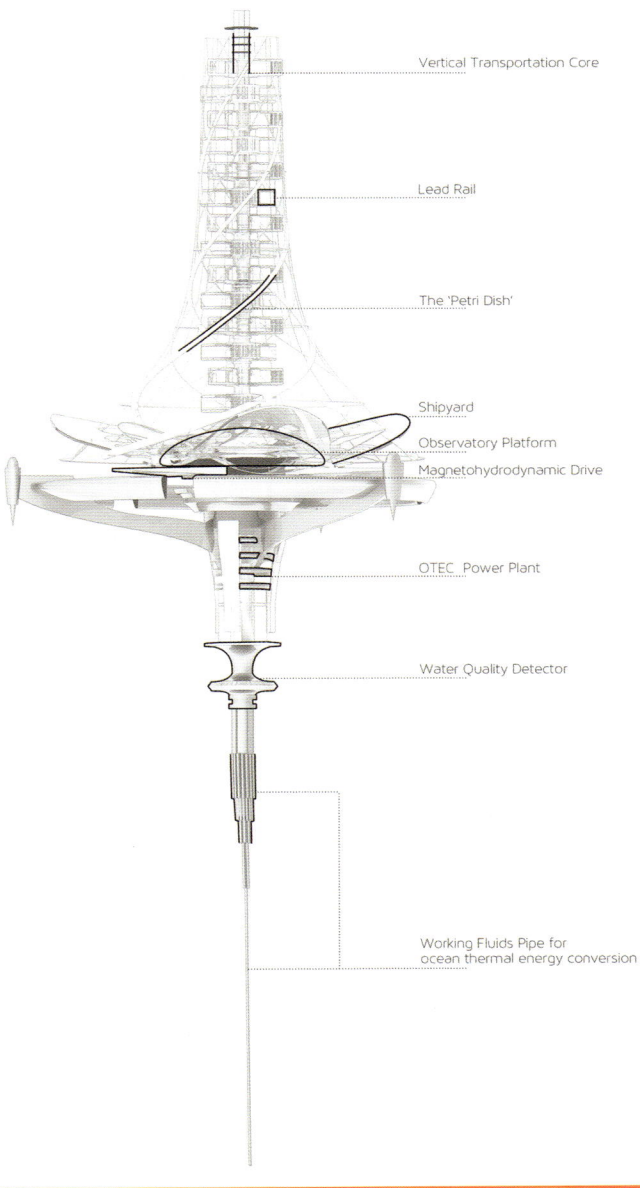

Vertical Transportation Core

Lead Rail

The 'Petri Dish'

Shipyard
Observatory Platform
Magnetohydrodynamic Drive

OTEC Power Plant

Water Quality Detector

Working Fluids Pipe for
ocean thermal energy conversion

, salinity, water depth, solar radiation and light conditions. The optimum tem-
ve 36 °C leads to death. Coral adapts to salinity ranges from 27 ‰ to 40 ‰,
of dissolved oxygen in the water is 4.5 - 5.0ml / L;
Depth of coral growth can be 70m, generally within 50m is suitable for coral
us. Individual species and individuals can grow with the transmittance of light
ved only in the thin layer of ocean surface. If we cultivate a large area on sea
ad to the destruction of marine ecological balance. Therefore, we came up
erent height, we can get numerous different growing environments for coral.
fferent planes are staggered. We also use transmission tubes to transport ap-
ust the living environment according to the corresponding index indicators.

OTEC plant is located in the core of the under-
sea hub aboratory while factories of byproduct
such as artificial skeletons, chemical products
and gesso material produced by coral itself to
build dam to protect coral reefs in the open environment.

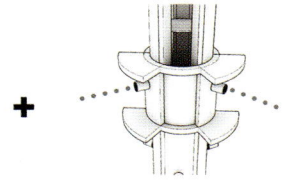
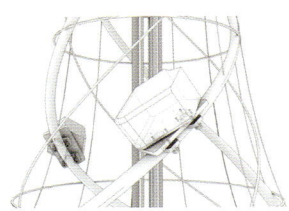

eme for the petri dish, many linear
es are dispatched out of the con-
rd facing the inside core structure.
er structures offer places for coral
on and also detect the living con-
n the dishes as well as offering
the researchers.

Main core structure offer platform for
the petri dishes outside with trake on it
making the sdjustment of the equipment more convenient, the transmission tube come out from the core
structure, linking the petri dish outside,
circulating the water in the dish.

Parts of the lead rail : the enclosed structure is
installed outside the architecture, interspersed
with which are tracks that used to transport
coral reef dishes. The constant curvature can
slow down the speed of transport in order to
prevent negative effects on coral reefs and
buildings that causing by travelling too fast.

LEGACY PLANETSCRAPER

Klaudio Muça
Ani Safaryan
Enrico Vito Sciannameo
Maria Luisa Vittorelli

Albania
Armenia
Italy

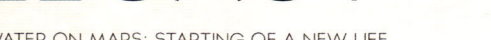

LEGACY

WATER ON MARS: STARTING OF A NEW LIFE

Challenge

The growing influence of mankind in the environment has led to a new geological era, the Anthropocene calling into question the future of life on planet Earth. Overpopulation, pollution, lack of resources, global warming, natural disasters are only some of the factors that characterize this new epoch.
Trying to think of a future far from our home seems now a key concern. Various public and private space companies are currently planning missions to Mars. Recent observations provide the strongest evidence yet that liquid water flows intermittently on its present-day surface.

Concept

Legacy is the skyscraper that attempts to learn from our mistakes and to investigate how we could adapt the present life on earth in a context such as that of Mars.
It is with a profound sense of respect and through research and experiments that we can approach a world that does not belong to us.
The idea is to create different gradients of interactions between terrestrial life and the martian environment.
Recently, planetary scientists detected hydrated salts on these slopes at Hale crater, corroborating their original hypothesis that the streaks they saw are indeed formed by liquid water. The skyscraper is planned to be located on the area close to the crater assuming that there is evidence of the presence of underground water. The idea is to reach the layer of the crust of Mars until the aquifers and to bring water into the surface.

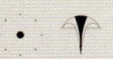

central core   buffer zone   context

Materials

A lightweight inflatable dome could be carried aboard a craft, along with a disassembled 3D printer with a tall, telescoping arm. The printer would mix Martian soil together with a soluble glue to be sprayed over the inflated dome. Once dried, the inner dome can be deflated and used for the next structure, then linked with short inflatable tunnels. In terms of design, the dome would be more aerodynamic in an atmosphere of high winds and harsh conditions.

 mars soil

 soluble glue

 3d printer

The growing influence of mankind in the environment has led to a new geological era, the Anthropocene calling into question the future of life on planet Earth.

Overpopulation, pollution, lack of resources, global warming, natural disasters are only some of the factors that characterize this new epoch. Trying to think of a future far from our home seems now a key concern. Various public and private space companies are currently planning missions to Mars. Recent observations provide the strongest evidence yet that liquid water flows intermittently on its present-day surface.

Legacy is the skyscraper that attempts to learn from our mistakes and to investigate how we could adapt the present life on earth in a context such as that of Mars. It is with a profound sense of respect

0497

and through research and experiments that we can approach a world that does not belong to us. The idea is to create different gradients of interactions between terrestrial life and the Martian environment.

"Today we have touched Mars. There is life on Mars, and it us—extensions of our eyes in all directions, extensions of our mind, extensions of our heart and soul have touched Mars today. That's the message to look for there: We are on Mars. We are the Martians!"-Ray Bradbury

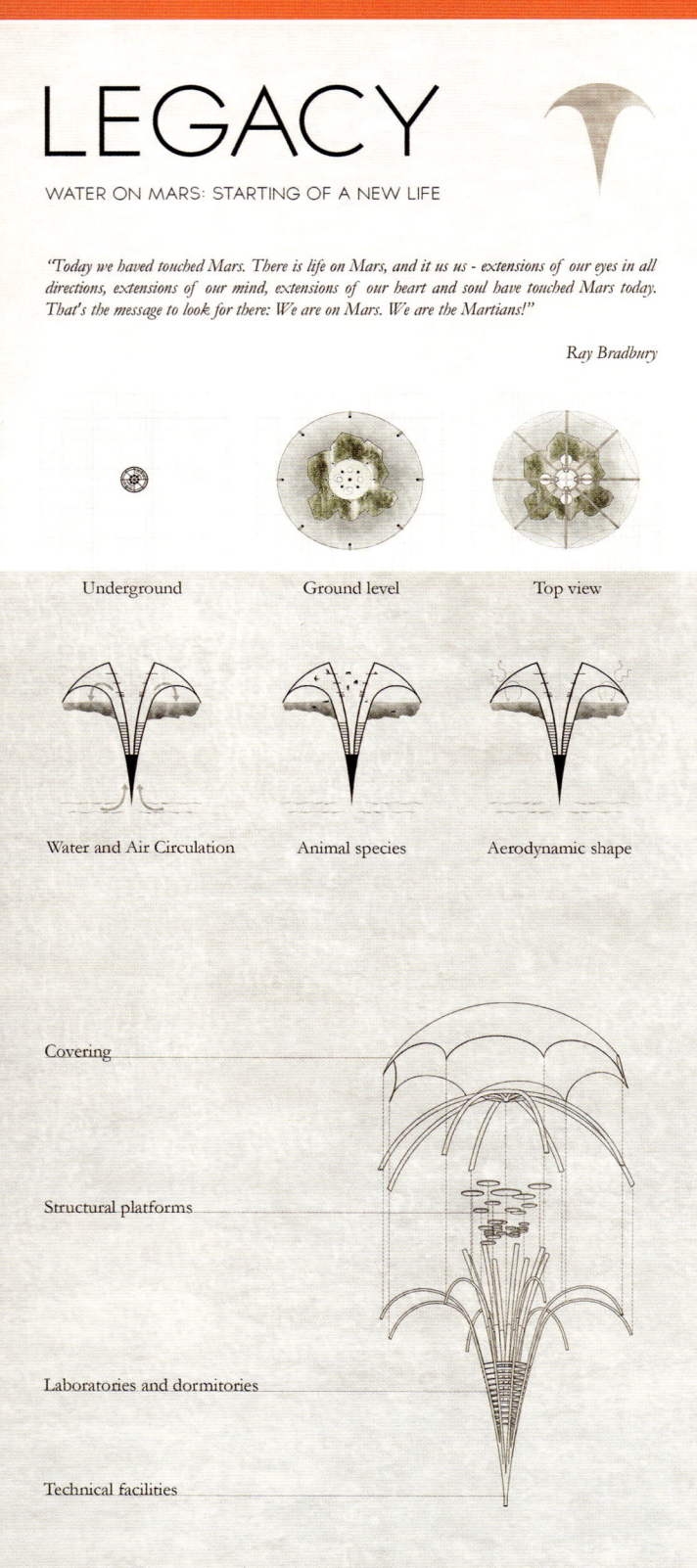

LEGACY

WATER ON MARS: STARTING OF A NEW LIFE

"Today we haved touched Mars. There is life on Mars, and it us us - extensions of our eyes in all directions, extensions of our mind, extensions of our heart and soul have touched Mars today. That's the message to look for there: We are on Mars. We are the Martians!"

Ray Bradbury

Underground   Ground level   Top view

Water and Air Circulation   Animal species   Aerodynamic shape

Covering

Structural platforms

Laboratories and dormitories

Technical facilities

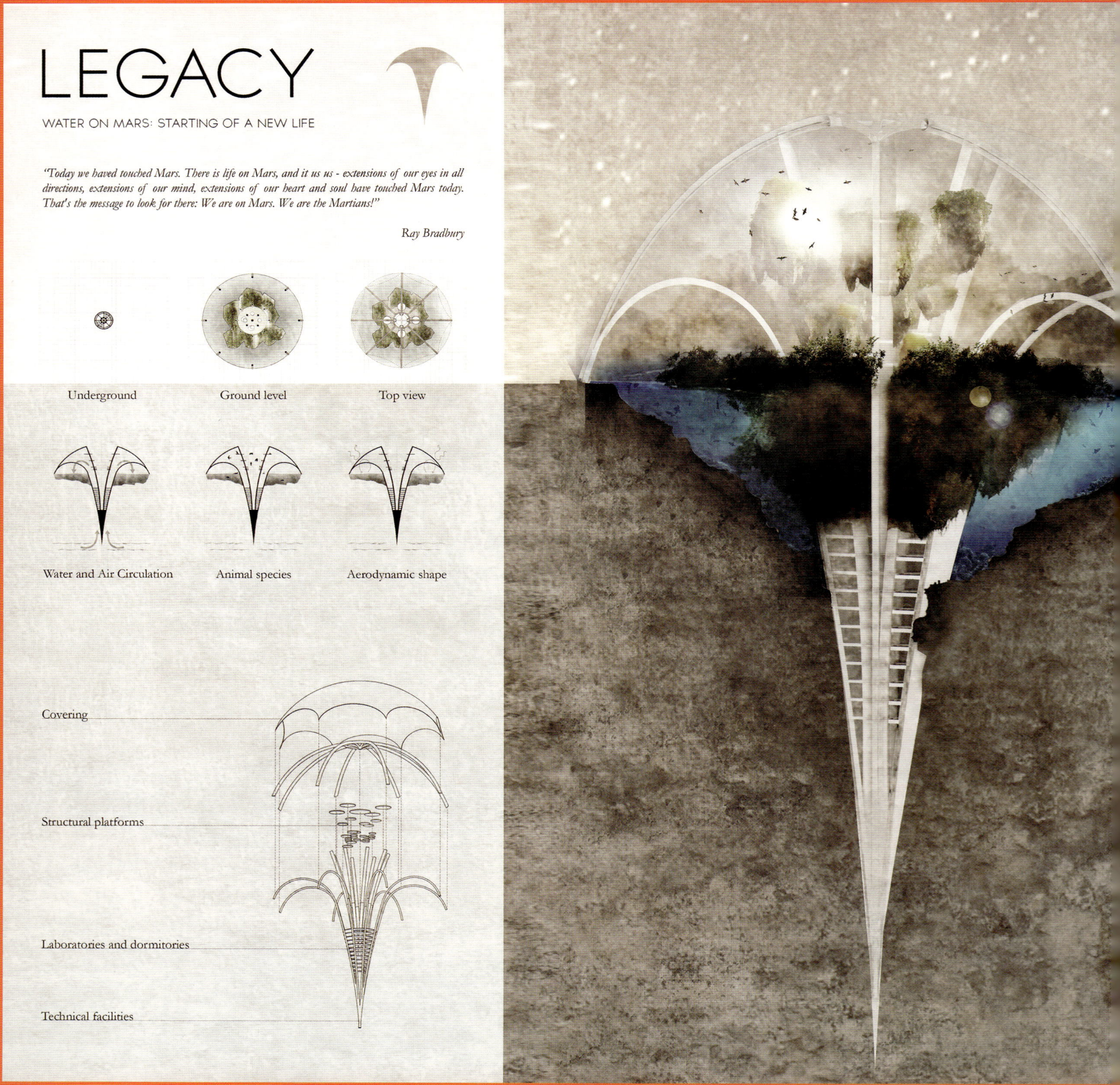

0497

GLOBAL
COOLING

Paolo Venturella
Cosimo Scotucci

Italy

Our planet is going through the irreversible process of global warming, and even if various strategies have been planned to solve the problem, none of them provided a solution. This is causing natural disasters all over the planet. The temperature all around the planet is increasing making the ice in the pole melt. Only a "global strategy" can be adopted.

To cool down the temperature a huge greenhouse is placed in between the sun and us. This works according the same principle of the "solar tower". Thanks to the accumulation of heat in the glazed structure, air flows naturally from hot to cold generating rapid and strong flows. These flows bring hot air far from the Earth cooling down the temperature of the whole globe. The airflows restore better climate conditions and moreover generate renewable energies by wind turbines placed inside the structures. The

0747

GLOBAL COOLING

Our planet is going through the irreversible process of global warming, and even if various strategies have been planned to solve the problem, none of them provided a solution.
This is causing natural disasters all over the planet. The temperature all around the planet is increasing making the ice in the pole melt.
Only a "global strategy" can be adopted.
To cool down the temperature a huge greenhouse is placed in between the sun and us.
This works according the same principle of the "solar tower". Thanks to the accumulation of heat in the glazed structure, air flows naturally from hot to cold generating rapid and strong flows. These flows bring hot air far from the Earth cooling down the temperature of the whole globe.
The air flows restore better climate conditions and moreover generate renewable energies by wind turbines placed inside the structures.
The structure act either on climate conditions and on energy production.
Furthermore this structure creates an amazing and surprising effect. Since it has to solve a problem for the entire planet, its dimension is overscaled. It has to be a unique and continuous structure, placed in a single point, and cantilever on both sides. It results as a tangent object on the planet.
It touches the ground in a unique point, and for this reason it is perceived in different ways from different parts of the world.
On the Equator it looks an horizontal element while from the poles it looks a vertical one.
The impressive structure allow to solve a critical question and works mantaining perfect climate conditions and providing clean energy for all.

EARTH   SUN

structure acts either on climate conditions or on energy production.

    Furthermore this structure creates an amazing and surprising effect. Since it has to solve a problem for the entire planet, its dimension is over scaled. It has to be a unique and continuous structure, placed in a single point, and cantilever on both sides. It results as a tangent object on the planet. It touches the ground in a unique point, and for this reason it is perceived in different ways from different parts of the world. On the Equator it looks a horizontal element while from the poles it looks a vertical one. The impressive structure allows solving a critical question and works maintaining perfect climate conditions and providing clean energy for all.

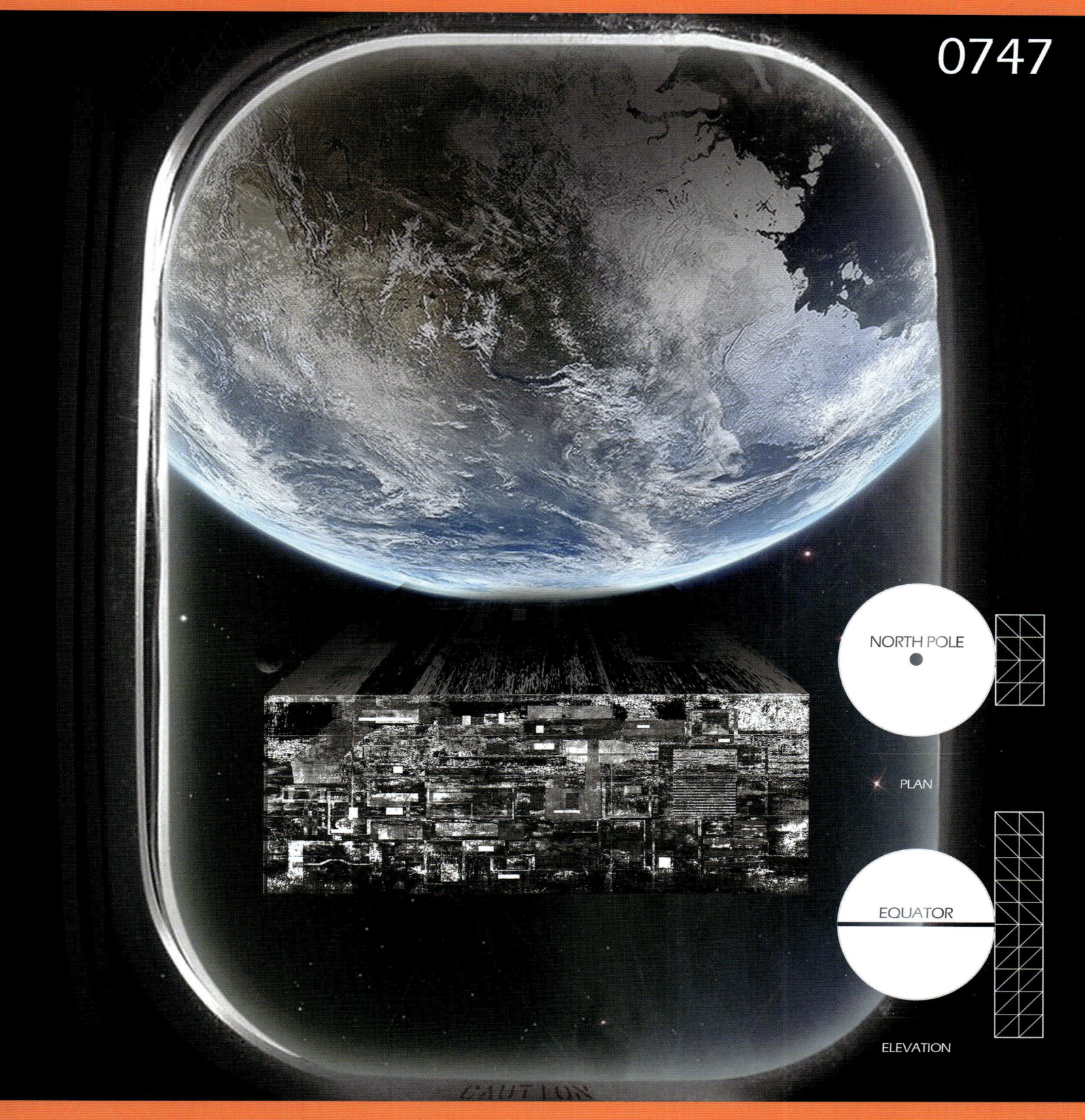

0747

NORTH POLE

PLAN

EQUATOR

ELEVATION

4 SOCIAL SOLUTIONS

HERE AFTER

Tsang Aron Wai Chun

Hong Kong

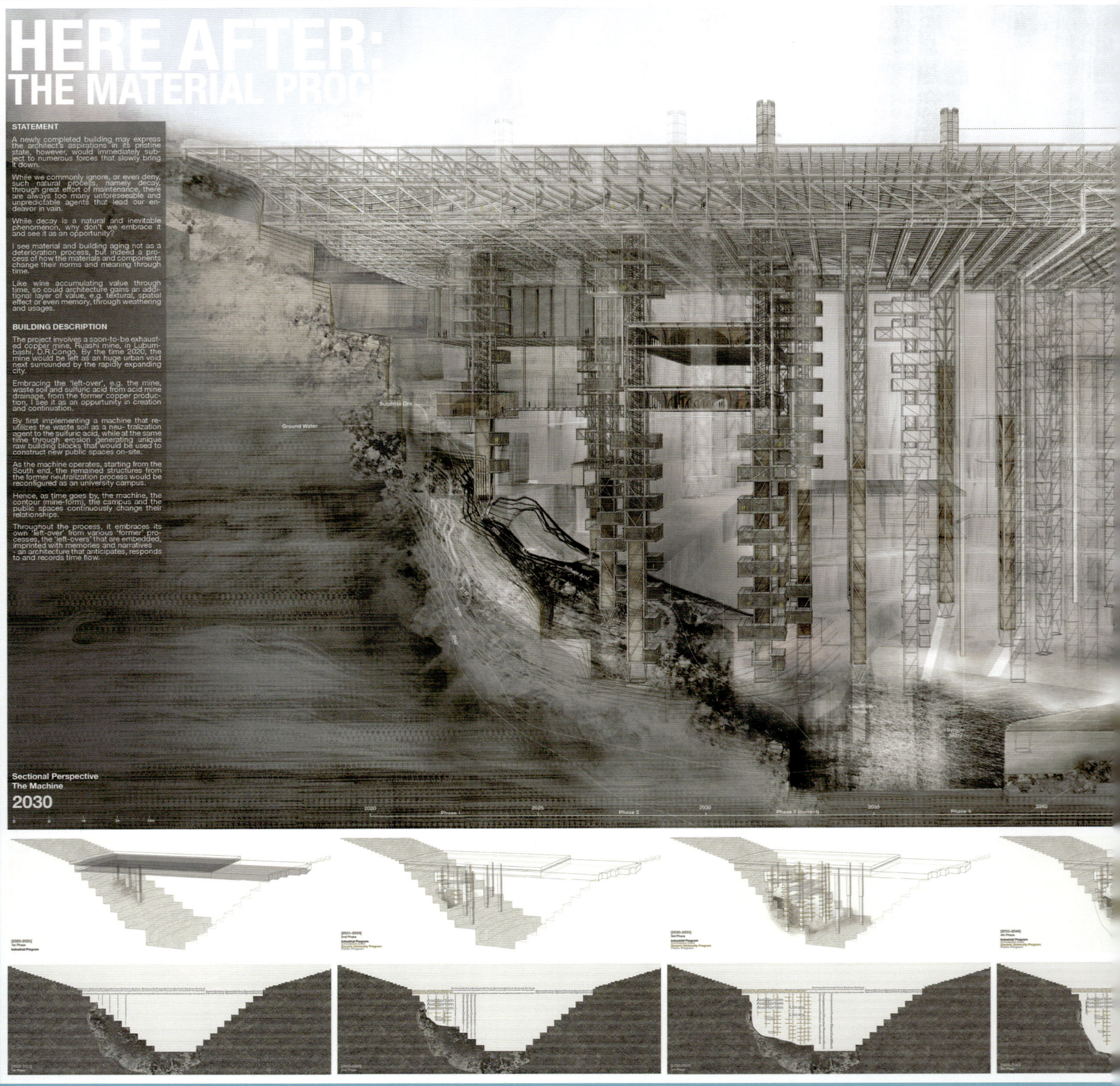

HERE AFTER: THE MATERIAL PROCESS

STATEMENT

A newly completed building may express the architect's aspirations in its pristine state, however, would immediately subject to numerous forces that slowly bring it down.

While we commonly ignore, or even deny, such natural process, namely decay, through great effort of maintenance, there are always too many unforeseeable and unpredictable agents that lead our endeavor in vain.

While decay is a natural and inevitable phenomenon, why don't we embrace it and see it as an opportunity?

I see material and building aging not as a deterioration process, but indeed a process of how the materials and components change their norms and meaning through time.

Like wine accumulating value through time, so could architecture gains an additional layer of value, e.g. textural, spatial effect or even memory, through weathering and usages.

BUILDING DESCRIPTION

The project involves a soon-to-be-exhausted copper mine, Ruashi mine, in Lubumbashi, D.R.Congo. By the time 2020, the mine would be left as an huge urban void next surrounded by the rapidly expanding city.

Embracing the 'left-over', e.g. the mine, waste soil and sulfuric acid from acid mine drainage, from the former copper production, I see it as an oppurtunity in creation and continuation.

By first implementing a machine that re-utilizes the waste soil as a neu- tralization agent to the sulfuric acid, while at the same time through erosion generating unique raw building blocks that would be used to construct new public spaces on-site.

As the machine operates, starting from the South end, the remained structures from the former neutralization process would be reconfigured as an university campus.

Hence, as time goes by, the machine, the contour (mine-form), the campus and the public spaces continuously change their relationships.

Throughout the process, it embraces its own 'left-over' from various 'former' processes, the 'left-overs' that are embedded, imprinted with memories and narratives — an architecture that anticipates, responds to and records time flow.

Sectional Perspective
The Machine
2030

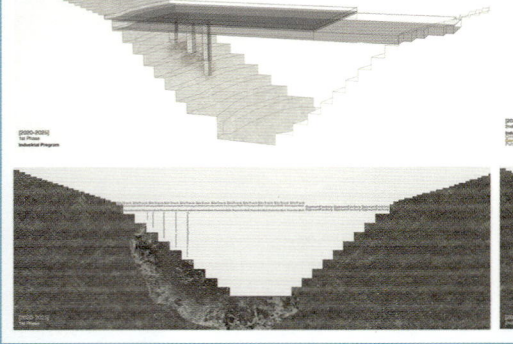 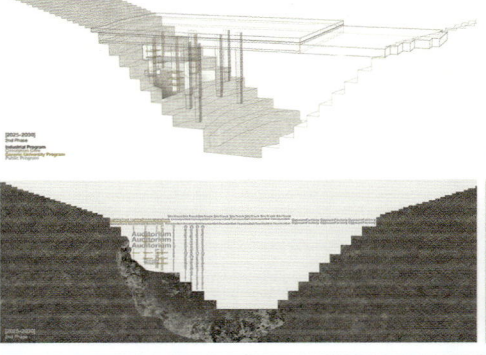 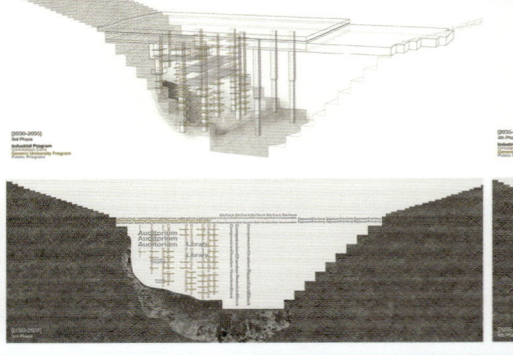 

The project is designed in the Ruashi copper mine in Lubumbashi, Congo, which is predicted to stop production in 2020. The mine would then be abandoned and left as an enormous urban void surrounded by a rapidly expanding city.

The Here After project seeks to make use of the left over space, waste soil, and sulfuric acid from the mine drainage and former copper production. A machine will reuse the waste soil to neutralize the sulfuric acid, which, in turn, will be used to erode the land in order for it to be used as raw buildings blocks for the project.

As the machine operates, starting from the South end, the remaining structures from the neutralization process would be reconfigured as a university campus. Throughout the building process

the contour, the campus, and the public spaces would continuously change their relationships and form. The main idea behind this project is to use a tridimensional wireframe structure to cover the full opening of the former copper mine. This structure would be used to support hanging skyscrapers that will drop into the open pit.

The tridimensional structure will also contain the main infrastructure including power and water lines. Its openness would allow direct sunlight to penetrate the lower levels and each hanging skyscraper would be designed to accommodate different programs including housing, offices, and recreational areas.

Horizontal structures, bridges between skyscrapers would create connections between them and

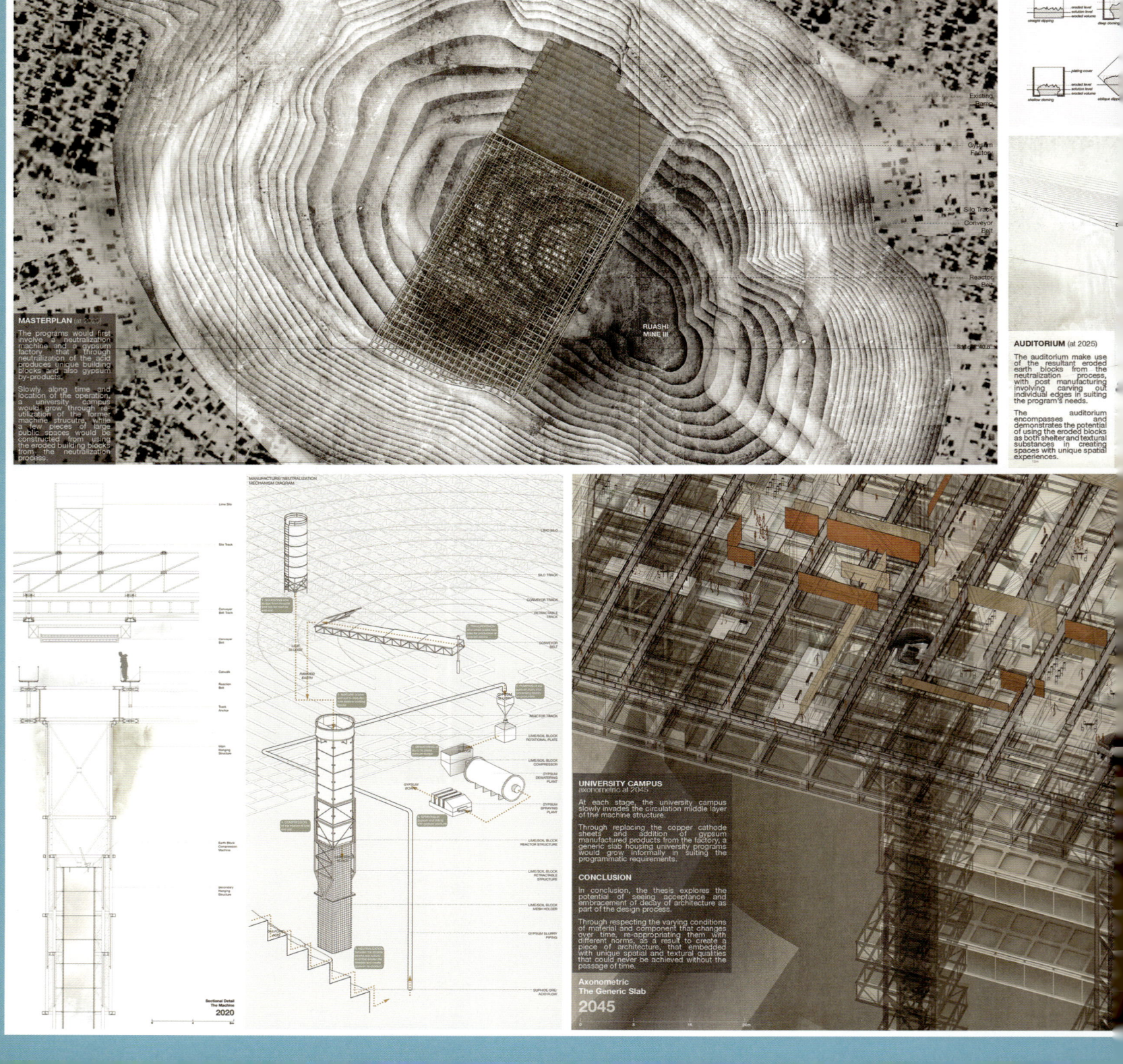

provide additional public programs.

It could be said that the project would become a small city in its own right. It will be able to provide its inhabitants with all the necessary resources and amenities for a prosperous life.

The massive stepping retaining walls of the former mine will be repurposed as a green landscape. The horizontal areas at different levels would be used as recreational parks and sports fields while the bottom of the mine could be filled up with subterranean water and serve as lake and reservoir.

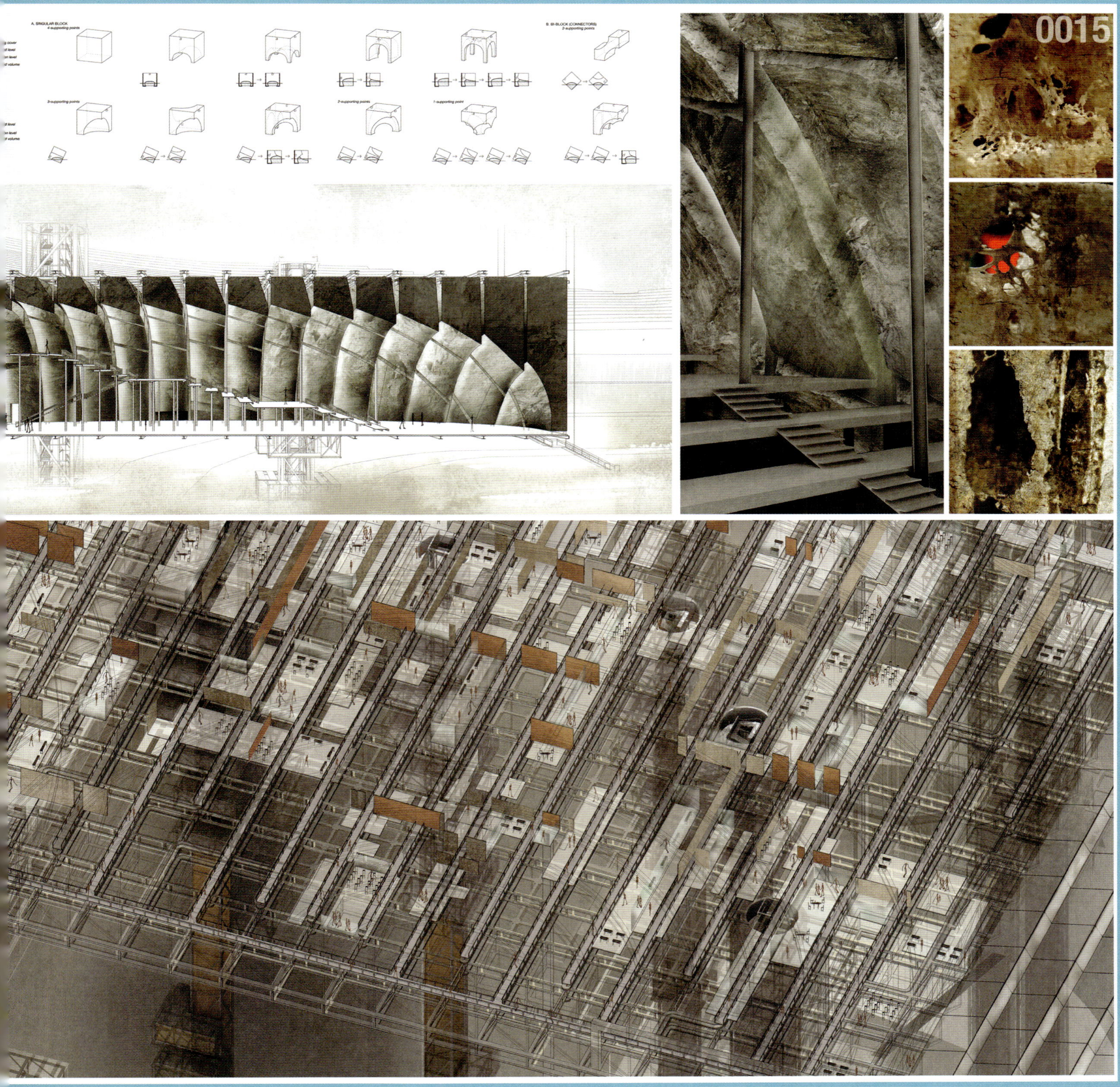

THE BLOSSOM TOWER

Perkins+Wills
Anthony Fieldman

United States

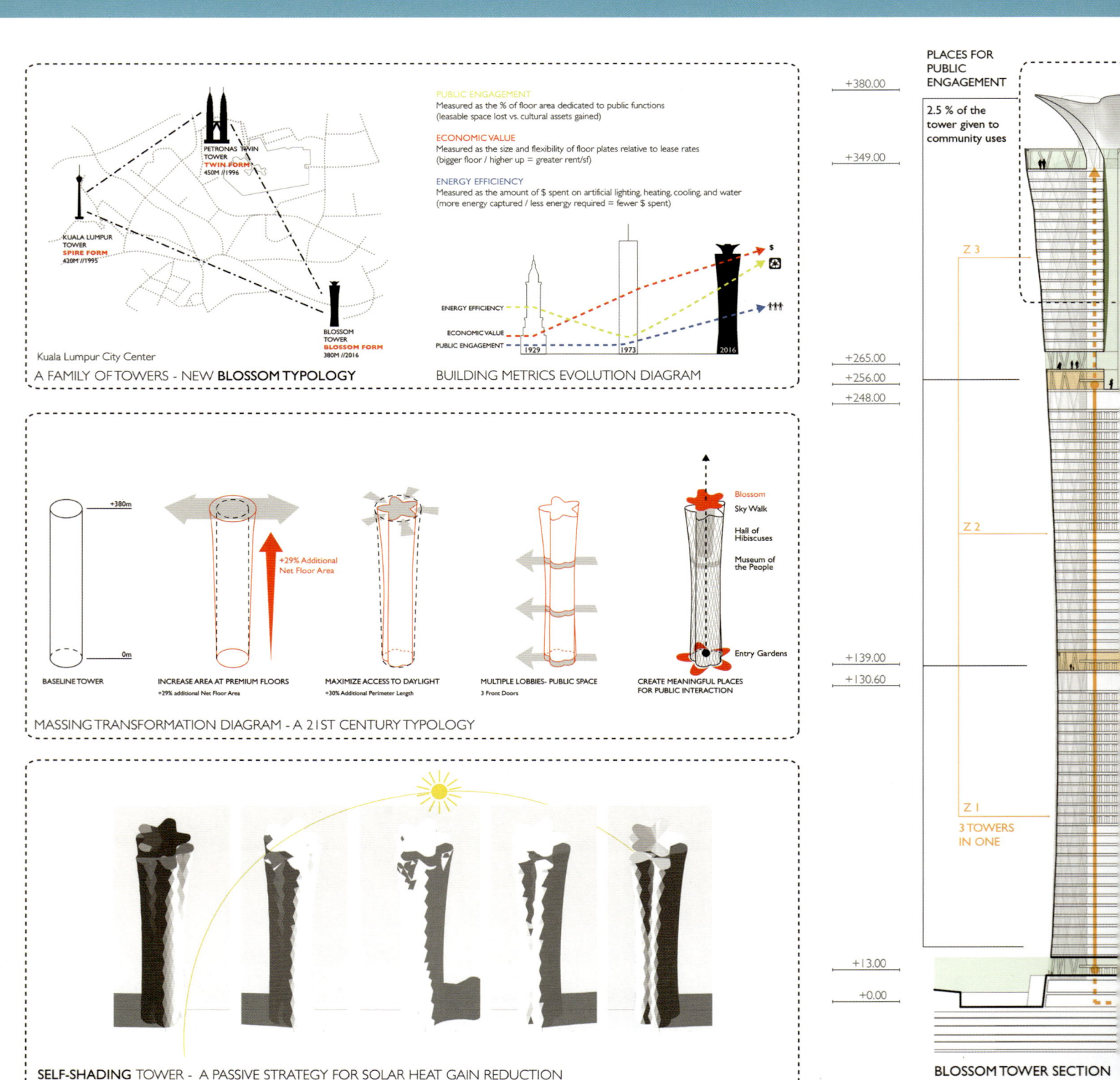

PUBLIC ENGAGEMENT
Measured as the % of floor area dedicated to public functions
(leasable space lost vs. cultural assets gained)

ECONOMIC VALUE
Measured as the size and flexibility of floor plates relative to lease rates
(bigger floor / higher up = greater rent/sf)

ENERGY EFFICIENCY
Measured as the amount of $ spent on artificial lighting, heating, cooling, and water
(more energy captured / less energy required = fewer $ spent)

PETRONAS TWIN TOWER
TWIN FORM
450M //1996

KUALA LUMPUR TOWER
SPIRE FORM
420M //1995

BLOSSOM TOWER
BLOSSOM FORM
380M //2016

Kuala Lumpur City Center
A FAMILY OF TOWERS - NEW **BLOSSOM TYPOLOGY**

ENERGY EFFICIENCY
ECONOMIC VALUE
PUBLIC ENGAGEMENT
1929   1973   2016
BUILDING METRICS EVOLUTION DIAGRAM

+380m
0m
BASELINE TOWER

+29% Additional Net Floor Area
INCREASE AREA AT PREMIUM FLOORS
+29% additional Net Floor Area

MAXIMIZE ACCESS TO DAYLIGHT
+30% Additional Perimeter Length

MULTIPLE LOBBIES- PUBLIC SPACE
3 Front Doors

Blossom
Sky Walk
Hall of Hibiscuses
Museum of the People
Entry Gardens
CREATE MEANINGFUL PLACES FOR PUBLIC INTERACTION

MASSING TRANSFORMATION DIAGRAM - A 21ST CENTURY TYPOLOGY

SELF-SHADING TOWER - A PASSIVE STRATEGY FOR SOLAR HEAT GAIN REDUCTION

PLACES FOR PUBLIC ENGAGEMENT

2.5 % of the tower given to community uses

+380.00
+349.00

Z 3

+265.00
+256.00
+248.00

Z 2

+139.00
+130.60

Z 1
3 TOWERS IN ONE

+13.00
+0.00

BLOSSOM TOWER SECTION

The Blossom Tower in Kuala Lumpur has created an opportunity for Malaysia to lead the world in defining the 21st Century tower - uniting social, commercial and environmental agendas in a new symbol for Malaysian cultural ambitions. Kuala Lumpur has several icons, among them the KL Tower and Petronas Twin Towers; each employs a well-known typology (a sky needle and twin gateway, respectively) that contributes a strong and defining silhouette to the skyline that adds to Malaysia's assets. Yet, there is room for a third icon – one that builds on sustainable leadership, using one of nature's perfect engines as its highly functioning symbol. The Blossom Tower takes its form from Malaysia's national flower, the Hibiscus, for a number of reasons. Expanding in size over its height, the tower announces its presence in the sky – not by poking it, like its neighbors, but by reaching up,

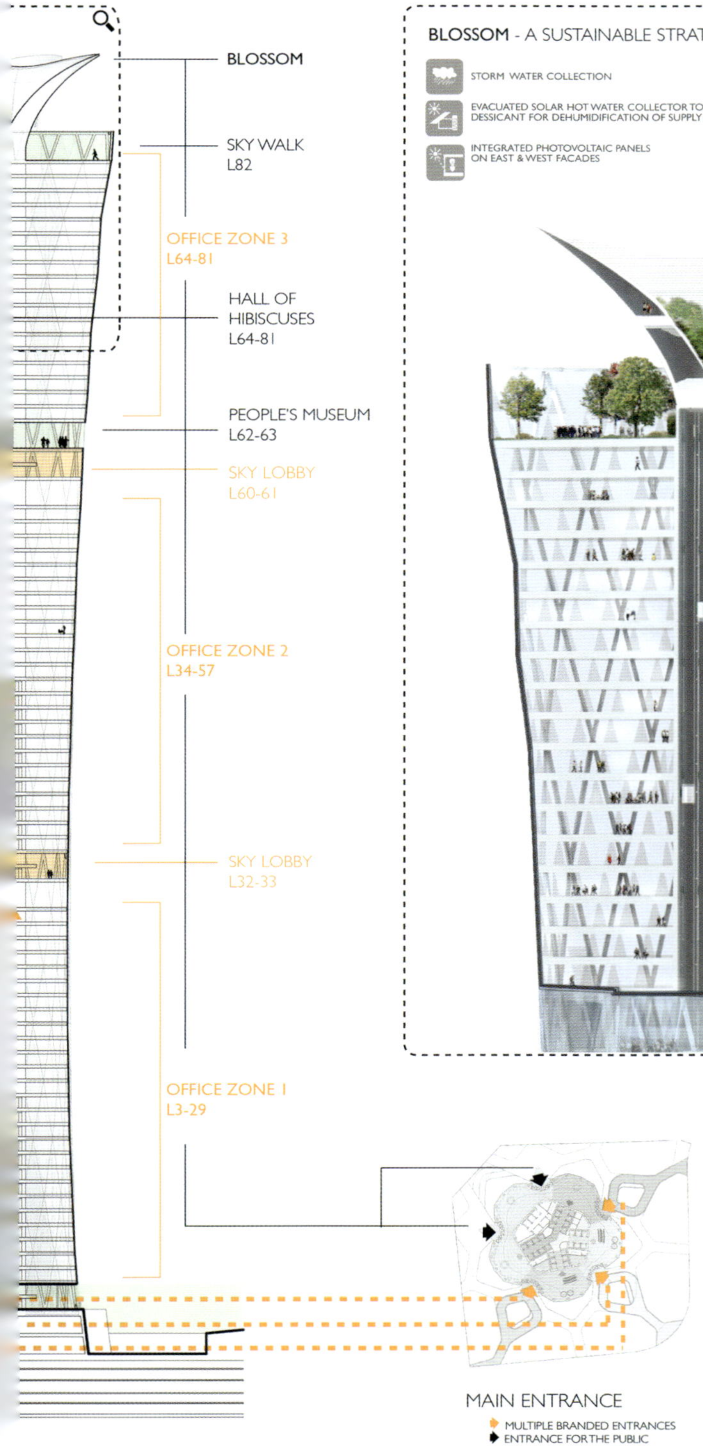

BLOSSOM

SKY WALK
L82

OFFICE ZONE 3
L64-81

HALL OF
HIBISCUSES
L64-81

PEOPLE'S MUSEUM
L62-63

SKY LOBBY
L60-61

OFFICE ZONE 2
L34-57

SKY LOBBY
L32-33

OFFICE ZONE 1
L3-29

MAIN ENTRANCE

◆ MULTIPLE BRANDED ENTRANCES
▲ ENTRANCE FOR THE PUBLIC

BLOSSOM - A SUSTAINABLE STRATEGY

STORM WATER COLLECTION

EVACUATED SOLAR HOT WATER COLLECTOR TO RECHARGE
DESICCANT FOR DEHUMIDIFICATION OF SUPPLY AIR

INTEGRATED PHOTOVOLTAIC PANELS
ON EAST & WEST FACADES

PV Panels on East
and West facades

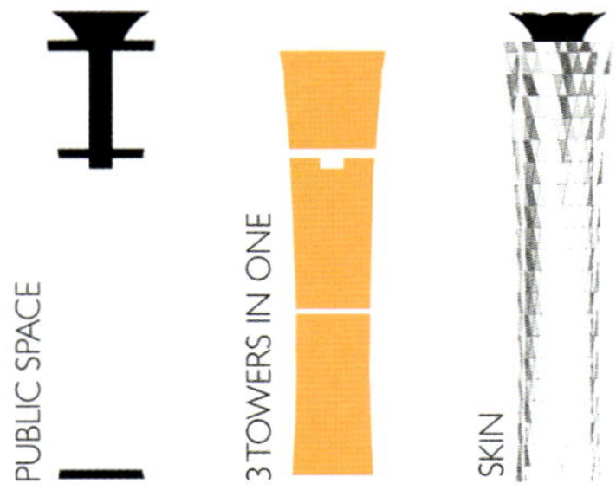

PUBLIC SPACE

3 TOWERS IN ONE

SKIN

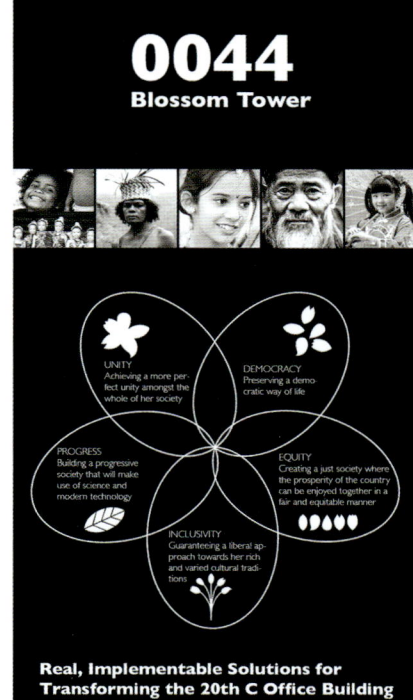

0044
Blossom Tower

UNITY
Achieving a more per-
fect unity amongst the
whole of her society

DEMOCRACY
Preserving a demo-
cratic way of life

PROGRESS
Building a progressive
society that will make
use of science and
modern technology

EQUITY
Creating a just society where
the prosperity of the country
can be enjoyed together in a
fair and equitable manner

INCLUSIVITY
Guaranteeing a liberal approach towards her rich
and varied cultural traditions

Real, Implementable Solutions for Transforming the 20th C Office Building

The Blossom Tower in Kuala Lumpur has created an opportunity for Malaysia to lead the world in defining the
21st Century tower – uniting social, commercial and environmental agendas in a new symbol for Malaysian cultural ambitions.

The tower, like Malaysia's national flower, the Hibiscus,
expands in size over its height, reaching up to embrace
and harness power. Its petals spanning over a 75m
radius, the Blossom collects the sun's energy over 100%
of its surfaces via solar hot water collection tubes. Paired
with on-site desiccants, the petals capture enough heat
energy to dehumidify the entire tower's air supply. Additional PV panels are located on the east and west facades, where the yield is greater than 40 watts/sm. 10%
additional shade is created by the undulation of the
tower's form in addition to the shade from the structure's broad reaches that protect visitors to the Sky
Walk (observation deck) and the tower roof itself, from
the greatest daily energy loads. Lastly, storm water is
transferred to a cistern 20 stories below to irrigate
on-site landscape, including the Hall of Hibiscuses.

In addition, this formal strategy provides 26% more
commercial lease area and perimeter windows at the
top, creating financial value for investors and tenant businesses where views, daylight and visibility are best. 2.5%
of the tower is dedicated to public uses, including a
sculpture park and outdoor performance spaces at the
tower base; a new Museum of People inside the tower
devoted to the guiding principles of the Rukun Negara;
and a Sky Walk and café atop the crown; the latter two
connected by a 20-story tall vertical living garden, the
Hall of Hibiscuses.

The ethos outlined above resonates well with Malaysia's
seminal social contract - the Rukun Negara - which describes a society that embraces the unity, democracy
and inclusivity of its people; the equitable sharing of its
economic and natural resources; and the advancement
of its progressive, modern leadership for society as a
whole.

BOARD 1

outstretched, to embrace and harness power. Like the crown of a flower, the top floor of the tower has 29% more area than its base, capturing maximum solar energy and water for use in the tower's systems. The Blossom Tower is designed for people, profit and the planet, reflecting an emerging awareness that our buildings must deliver value beyond simple economics - that they must speak to the highest aspirations of society. In this context, Blossom Tower creates social value for a complex and varied people by allocating 2.5% of the tower toward public uses, including a sculpture park and outdoor performance spaces at the tower base; a new Museum of People inside the tower devoted to the guiding principles of the Rukun Negara; and a Sky Walk and cafe atop the crown; the latter two connected by a 20-story tall Hall of Hibiscuses - a vertical, living garden celebrating the national flower of Malaysia.

GROUND FLOOR
+0m

PLAZA LEVEL
+13m

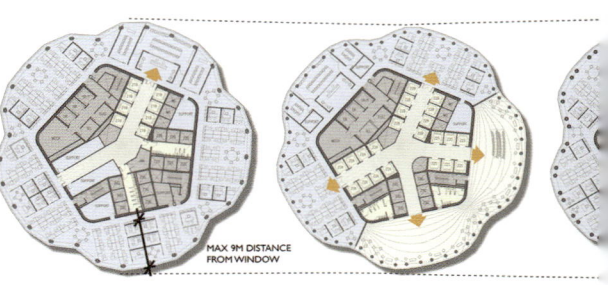

MAX 9M DISTANCE
FROM WINDOW

OFFICE TYPICAL ZONE I   OFFICE TYPICAL SKY LOBBY   OFFICE
+23m/+130.60m   +139m   +150m

Crowning the tower, the innovative Blossom is an iconic and optimistic symbol that speaks to the aspirations of the tower's environmental leadership agenda by performing several sustainable functions. With its petals spanning over a 75m radius, the Blossom collects the sun's energy over 100% of its surfaces via solar hot water collection tubes. Paired with on-site desiccants, the petals capture enough heat energy to dehumidify the entire tower's air supply. Additional PV panels are located on the east and west facades, where the yield is greater than 40 watts/sm. 10% additional shade is created by the undulation of the tower's form in addition to the shade from the structure's broad reaches that protect visitors to the Sky Walk (observation deck) and the tower roof itself, from the greatest daily energy loads. Lastly, storm water is transferred to a cistern 20 stories below to irrigate on-site landscape, including the Hall of Hibiscuses.

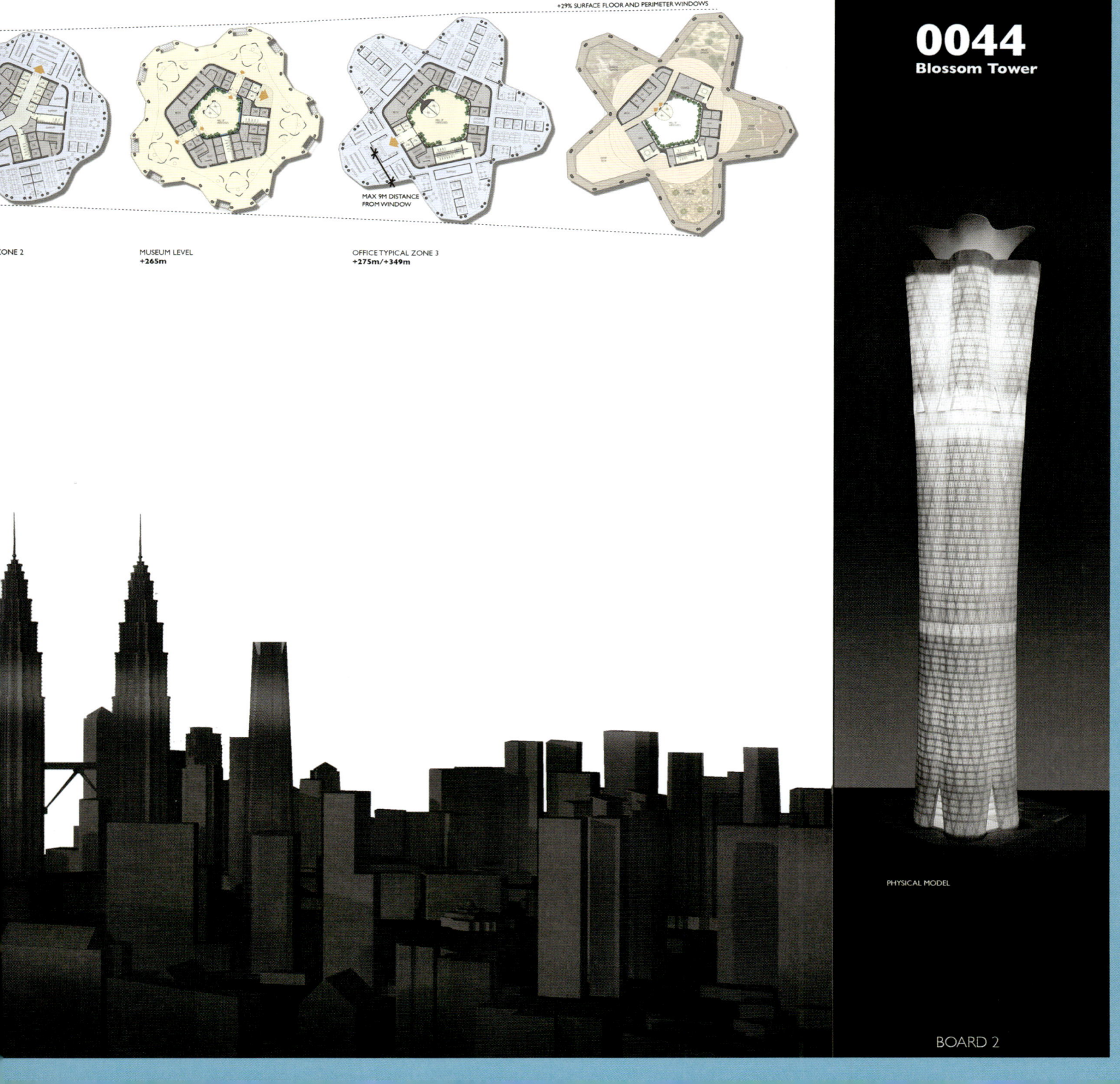

+29% SURFACE FLOOR AND PERIMETER WINDOWS

ZONE 2

MUSEUM LEVEL
+265m

MAX 9M DISTANCE
FROM WINDOW

OFFICE TYPICAL ZONE 3
+275m/+349m

0044
Blossom Tower

PHYSICAL MODEL

BOARD 2

NEW YORK CIRCUS

José Antonio Carrillo Andrada

Spain

This project focuses attention towards contemporary circus and directs it towards the future. Fellini announced the obsolescence of the traditional circus in his film I clown, 1971: "The circus does not make sense in today's society". The circus has diversified and nurtures the arts and techniques that work the corporeal, the set design, poetry, fantasy, etc. but lacks of a 'circus concept' for future generations". This project aims to establish various strategies to unify concepts and diversify options for the adaptation and survival of the circus in a sustainable way.

New York Circus does so by diversifying its strategies into three categories. The first being mutations, where circus species are catalogued from combinations of physical qualities and the infrastructure of the traditional circus. The circus is forced to mutate in order to survive itself with some "supernatural"

New York 0218
Circus

CIRCUS 2014

This project puts gaze in contemporary circus and directs it towards the future. The obsolescence of the traditional circus was announced by Fellini in his film I clown, 1971: "The circus does not make sense in today's society". The circus has diversified and nurtures the arts and techniques that work the corporeal, the set design, poetry, fantasy, etc. but lacks of a 'circus concept' for future generations". This project aims to establish various strategies to unify concepts and diversify options for the adaptation and survival of the circus in a sustainable way.

THREE STRATEGIES FOR A SURVIVAL

MUTATIONS: circus species catalogued from combinations of physical qualities and the infrastructure of the traditional circus. The circus is forced to mutate in order to survive itself with some "supernatural" powers.

SUPERHEROES: the city as a stage, meaning an exchange of artistic languages and technology. Specialized architecture will have the ability to offer shows that ordinary buildings could never achieve.

HYBRIDS: (Graft: Application of a piece of living somewhere in the city so as to produce an organic union taking advantage of the increased resistance of the foot used against genetic drift introduced by sexual reproduction of an architectural model). Combinations make space more open, flexible, versatile, informal and ambivalent. The circus itself is considered an intruder, an antitype in harmony with the host body in order not to cause rejection.

OCCUPATION, PARASITISM AND GRAFTING

Attested stages in constant architectural suspense: the site does not exist as such. The ownership of the street, airspace and infrastructure constructed the building just as Philippe Petit build the show helped by a steel wire and a pole. The balance between reality and utopia breaks with the circus typological past and links the continent and content with new rituals.

CIRCUS BUILDING

The Circus will be an untypical embryo that develops its own race, mythology, time and language. The culture of the circus was generated without architecture. Now, building a self-sufficient cosmos in which the known circus disappears allows its survival.

powers. The second is superheroes, where the city acts as a stage, allowing for an exchange of artistic languages and technology. Specialized architecture will have the ability to offer shows that ordinary buildings could never achieve. The third is hybrids as combinations make space more open, flexible, versatile, informal and ambivalent. The circus itself is considered an intruder, an antitype in harmony with the host body in order not to cause rejection.

The site does not merely exist as attested stages in constant architectural suspense. The ownership of the street, airspace, and infrastructure are what construct the building, just as Philippe Petit built his circus using only a steel wire and a pole. The balance between reality and utopia breaks with the circus typological past and links the content with new rituals.

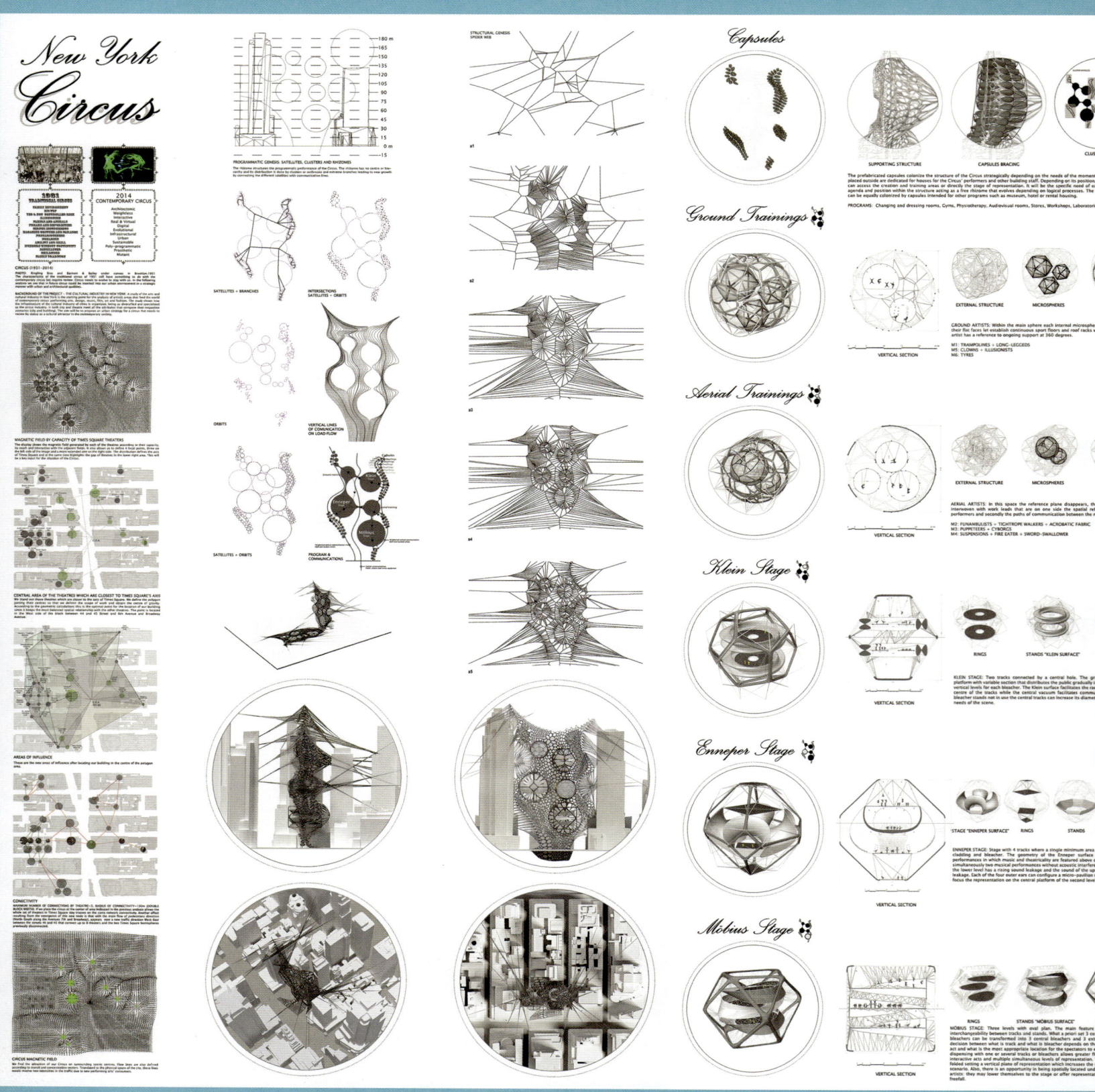

The Circus will be an atypical embryo that develops its own race, mythology, time, and language. The culture of the circus was generated without architecture. Now, building a self-sufficient cosmos in which the known circus disappears is what actually allows for its survival.

A study of the arts and cultural industry in New York is the starting point for the analysis of artistic areas that feed the world of contemporary circus: performing arts, design, music, film, art, and fashion. The aim will be to propose an urban strategy for a circus that aims to renew its status as a cultural attraction in the contemporary society.

21ST CENTURY CLASSICAL SKYSCRAPER

John Houser
Parke MacDowell

United States

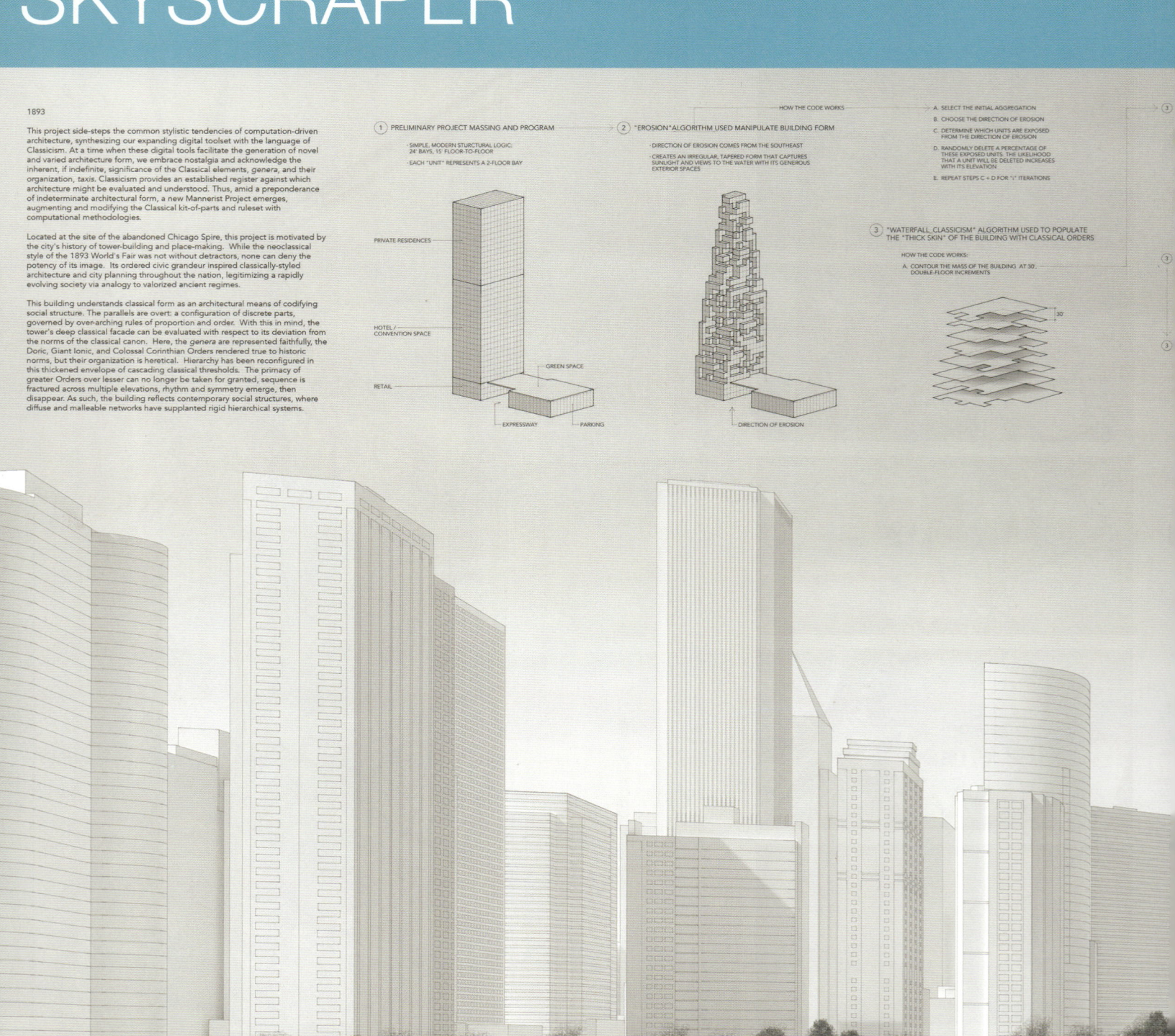

1893

This project side-steps the common stylistic tendencies of computation-driven architecture, synthesizing our expanding digital toolset with the language of Classicism. At a time when these digital tools facilitate the generation of novel and varied architecture form, we embrace nostalgia and acknowledge the inherent, if indefinite, significance of the Classical elements, genera, and their organization, taxis. Classicism provides an established register against which architecture might be evaluated and understood. Thus, amid a preponderance of indeterminate architectural form, a new Mannerist Project emerges, augmenting and modifying the Classical kit-of-parts and ruleset with computational methodologies.

Located at the site of the abandoned Chicago Spire, this project is motivated by the city's history of tower-building and place-making. While the neoclassical style of the 1893 World's Fair was not without detractors, none can deny the potency of its image. Its ordered civic grandeur inspired classically-styled architecture and city planning throughout the nation, legitimizing a rapidly evolving society via analogy to valorized ancient regimes.

This building understands classical form as an architectural means of codifying social structure. The parallels are overt: a configuration of discrete parts, governed by over-arching rules of proportion and order. With this in mind, the tower's deep classical facade can be evaluated with respect to its deviation from the norms of the classical canon. Here, the *genera* are represented faithfully, the Doric, Giant Ionic, and Colossal Corinthian Orders rendered true to historic norms, but their organization is heretical. Hierarchy has been reconfigured in this thickened envelope of cascading classical thresholds. The primacy of greater Orders over lesser can no longer be taken for granted, sequence is fractured across multiple elevations, rhythm and symmetry emerge, then disappear. As such, the building reflects contemporary social structures, where diffuse and malleable networks have supplanted rigid hierarchical systems.

① PRELIMINARY PROJECT MASSING AND PROGRAM

- SIMPLE, MODERN STURCTURAL LOGIC:
  24' BAYS, 15' FLOOR-TO-FLOOR
- EACH "UNIT" REPRESENTS A 2-FLOOR BAY

PRIVATE RESIDENCES

HOTEL / CONVENTION SPACE

GREEN SPACE

RETAIL

EXPRESSWAY   PARKING

② "EROSION" ALGORITHM USED MANIPULATE BUILDING FORM

- DIRECTION OF EROSION COMES FROM THE SOUTHEAST
- CREATES AN IRREGULAR, TAPERED FORM THAT CAPTURES SUNLIGHT AND VIEWS TO THE WATER WITH ITS GENEROUS EXTERIOR SPACES

DIRECTION OF EROSION

HOW THE CODE WORKS

A. SELECT THE INITIAL AGGREGATION

B. CHOOSE THE DIRECTION OF EROSION

C. DETERMINE WHICH UNITS ARE EXPOSED FROM THE DIRECTION OF EROSION

D. RANDOMLY DELETE A PERCENTAGE OF THESE EXPOSED UNITS. THE LIKELIHOOD THAT A UNIT WILL BE DELETED INCREASES WITH ITS ELEVATION

E. REPEAT STEPS C + D FOR "i" ITERATIONS

③ "WATERFALL_CLASSICISM" ALGORITHM USED TO POPULATE THE "THICK SKIN" OF THE BUILDING WITH CLASSICAL ORDERS

HOW THE CODE WORKS:

A. CONTOUR THE MASS OF THE BUILDING AT 30', DOUBLE-FLOOR INCREMENTS

This project side-steps the common stylistic tendencies of computation-driven architecture, synthesizing our expanding digital toolset with the language of Classicism. At a time when these digital tools facilitate the generation of novel and varied architecture form, we embrace nostalgia and acknowledge the inherent, if indefinite, significance of the Classical elements, genera, and their organization.

   Classicism provides an established register against which architecture might be evaluated and understood. Thus, amid a preponderance of indeterminate architectural form, a new Mannerist Project emerges, augmenting and modifying the Classical kit-of-parts and rule set with computational methodologies.

   Located at the site of the abandoned Chicago Spire, this project is motivated by the city's history of

tower-building and place-making. While the neoclassical style of the 1893 World's Fair was not without detractors, none can deny the potency of its image. Its ordered civic grandeur inspired classically-styled architecture and city planning throughout the nation, legitimizing a rapidly evolving society via analogy to valorized ancient regimes.

This building understands classical form as an architectural means of codifying social structure. The parallels are overt: a configuration of discrete parts, governed by over-arching rules of proportion and order. With this in mind, the tower's deep classical facade can be evaluated with respect to its deviation from the norms of the classical canon. Here, the genera are represented faithfully, the Doric, Giant Ionic, and Colossal Corinthian Orders rendered true to historic norms, but their organization is heretical.

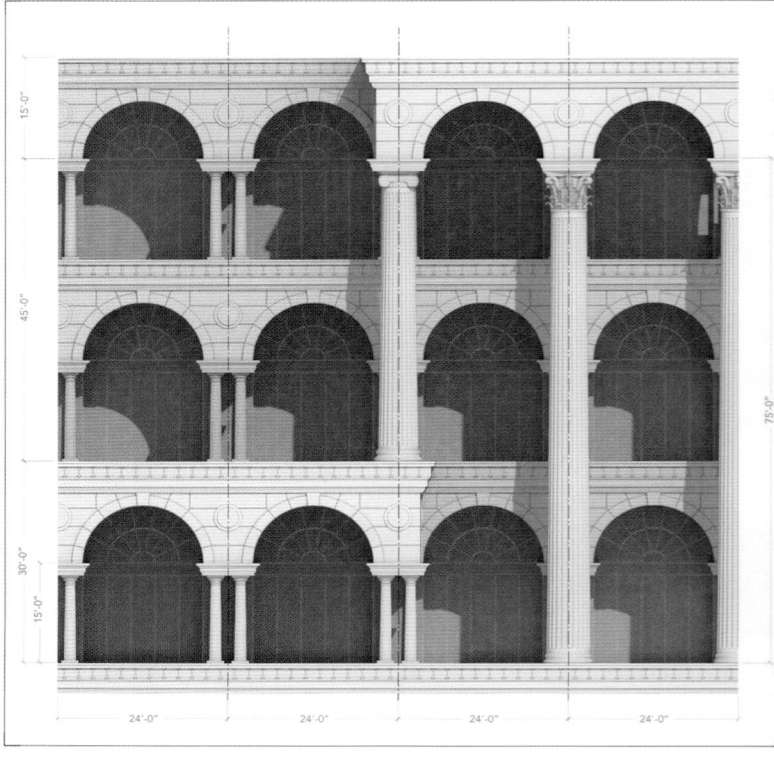

Hierarchy has been reconfigured in this thickened envelope of cascading classical thresholds. The primacy of greater Orders over lesser can no longer be taken for granted, sequence is fractured across multiple elevations, rhythm and symmetry emerge, then disappear. As such, the building reflects contemporary social structures, where diffuse and malleable networks have supplanted rigid hierarchical systems.

PROJECT BLUE

Yang Siqi
Zhan Beidi
Zhao Renbo
Zhang Tianshuo

China

CASE

When the whole world witness the miracle of chinese economy, and when the whole society is drunk by the quality of life rising as time goes by, the frequent appearance of hazy weather have pulled the alarm and make people realize that the name of 'factory of the world' costs China a really fat price. Recently, hazy weather has attacked several Chinese cities and PM2.5 is at the bottom of all these troubles. Atmospheric particulate matter – also known as particulates or particulate matter (PM) – are tiny pieces of solid or liquid matter associated with the Earth's atmosphere. They are suspended in the atmosphere as atmospheric aerosol, a term which refers to the particulate/air mixture, as opposed to the particulate matter alone. Some components of the aerosol are toxic and harmful to human being. And PM2.5 is now becoming an international problem.

The AQI index of two cities in recent 25 days

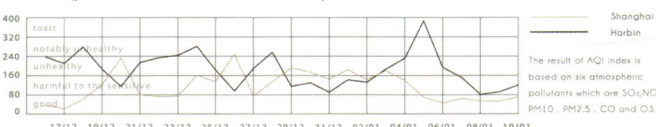

Shanghai
Harbin

The result of AQI index is based on six atmospheric pollutants which are SO_2, NO_2, PM10 , PM2.5 , CO and O3

CONCEPT

In the background of sharply industrial development, PM2.5 is becoming a severe environmental problem day by day and causes hazy weather condition all over the world. In case commonplace 'Treatment After Pollution' situation, re-use of the polluted waste has more social significance than protection. Our solution is to transform PM2.5 particles into green energy and solute the problem of air pollution and realize resources re-use at the same time. First, we upside down the traditional cooling tower and exhaust device. Then we connect the 'mirror image' of exhaust device to the underground pipe network of heating area while using part of the heat of exhaust gas to assist the indoor heat system. The gas heat could take the place of coal burning heat. The remaining gas would ascend to our floating transforming device through a central pipe. In the transforming device, We proceed a Systematic project consisted of Multitubular bag flue gas desulfurization method and Cyclic reduction method system could produce Sulfur and Nitrogen. At the next stage, we compound surplus carbon monoxide with filtered rain steam to produce water coal (Carbon monoxide and hydrogen mixtures).Then the device would transfer water coal into methane which is a kind of green energy through a low pressure reaction called low pressure efficient methanation.

Transforming the smog into liquid methane which is a kind of usable clean energy.The final stage of the project is transferring the liquid methone to ground fueling station through multiple pipes then fuel charging to environmental vehicles.

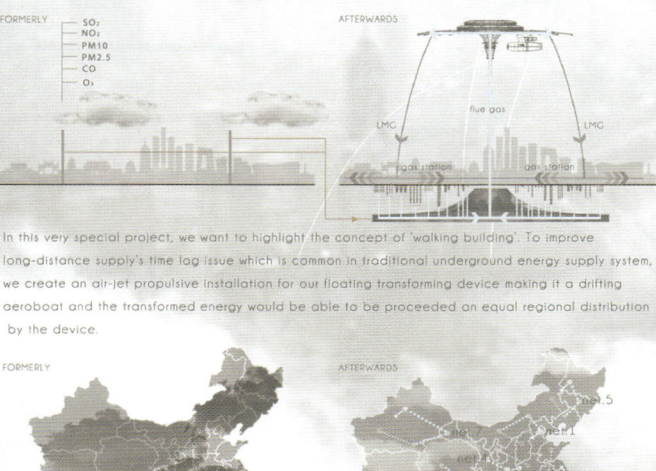

In this very special project, we want to highlight the concept of 'walking building'. To improve long-distance supply's time lag issue which is common in traditional underground energy supply system, we create an air-jet propulsive installation for our floating transforming device making it a drifting aeroboat and the transformed energy would be able to be proceeded an equal regional distribution by the device.

China's explosive economy has left the world in awe but the country is paying a big price as the "factory of the world" is getting polluted at an alarming speed. Chinese cities are now characterized by an unhealthy hazy weather as the result of large amounts of suspended particles in the air.

The purpose of Project Blue is to transform suspended particles into green energy by creating an enormous upside-down cooling tower with a multi-tubular cyclic desulfurization system that produces nitrogen and sulfur. When both elements are combined with the atmospheres surplus of carbon monoxide the result is water coal that would later be transformed in methane and used as green energy through a low-pressure reaction called low pressure efficient mathanation - a physical-chemical process to generate methane from a mixture of various gases out of biomass fermentation or thermo-chemical

0473

BLUE
CREATING GREEN ENERGY

gasification.

The building consists of three main areas. The first part is the foundation, which will also be used as underground power storage. The second section is the main shaft that will support the top structure. This shaft is a wireframe structure made of titanium and reinforced ceramics. Tubular pipes will also transport the energy to the storage facility. Finally the top portion of the structure will house the desulfurization towers and complimentary systems including a heating circle and the reaction shell.

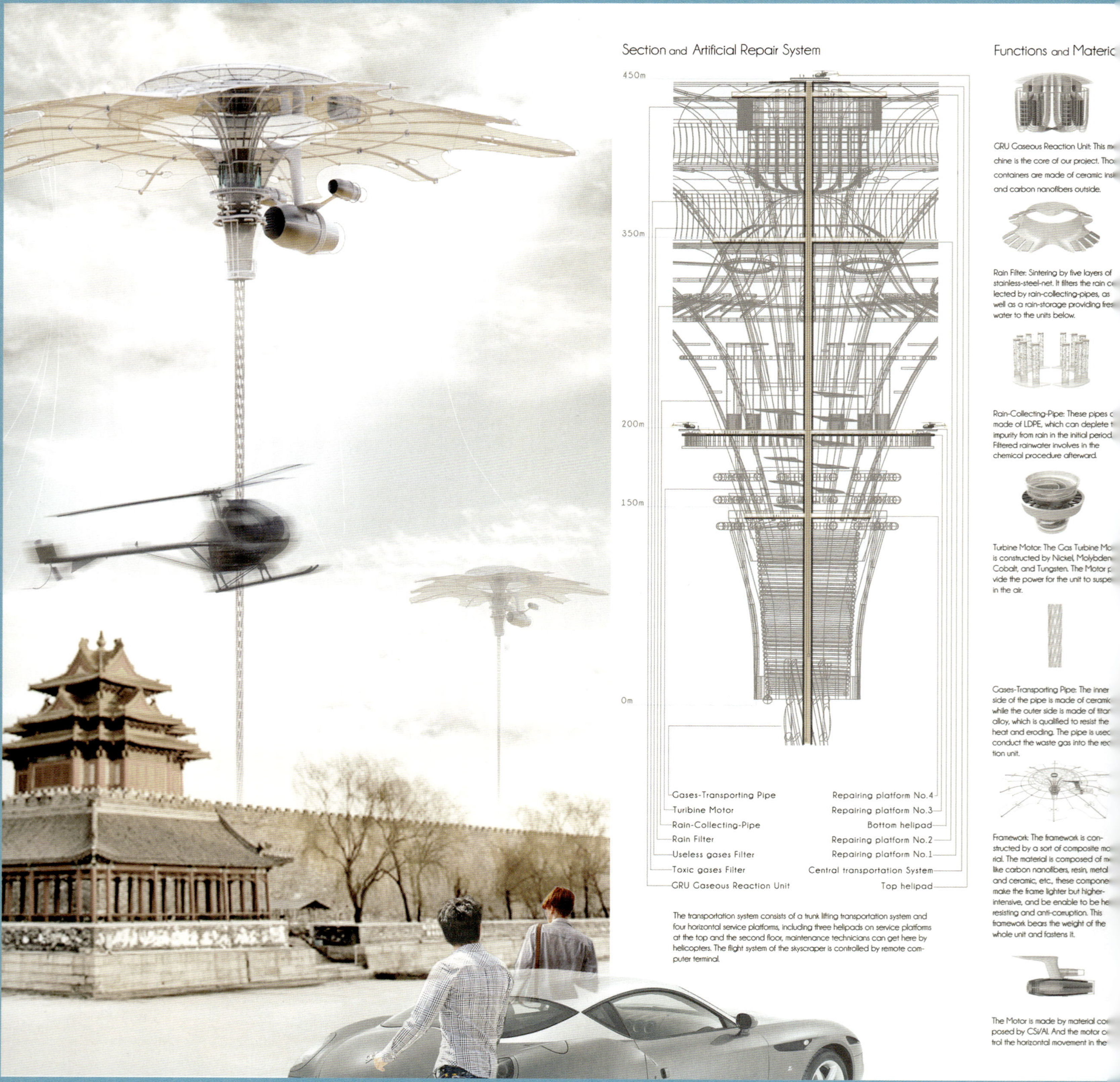

Section and Artificial Repair System

450m

350m

200m

150m

0m

Gases-Transporting Pipe	Repairing platform No.4
Turbine Motor	Repairing platform No.3
Rain-Collecting-Pipe	Bottom helipad
Rain Filter	Repairing platform No.2
Useless gases Filter	Repairing platform No.1
Toxic gases Filter	Central transportation System
GRU Gaseous Reaction Unit	Top helipad

The transportation system consists of a trunk lifting transportation system and four horizontal service platforms, including three helipads on service platforms at the top and the second floor, maintenance technicians can get here by helicopters. The flight system of the skyscraper is controlled by remote computer terminal.

Functions and Materia[l]

GRU Gaseous Reaction Unit: This m[a]chine is the core of our project. Tho[se] containers are made of ceramic insi[de] and carbon nanofibers outside.

Rain Filter: Sintering by five layers of stainless-steel-net. It filters the rain c[ol]lected by rain-collecting-pipes, as well as a rain-storage providing fres[h] water to the units below.

Rain-Collecting-Pipe: These pipes [are] made of LDPE, which can deplete t[he] impurity from rain in the initial period. Filtered rainwater involves in the chemical procedure afterward.

Turbine Motor: The Gas Turbine Mo[tor] is constructed by Nickel, Molybden[um], Cobalt, and Tungsten. The Motor p[ro]vide the power for the unit to suspe[nd] in the air.

Gases-Transporting Pipe: The inner side of the pipe is made of ceramic while the outer side is made of titan[ium] alloy, which is qualified to resist the heat and eroding. The pipe is used [to] conduct the waste gas into the rea[c]tion unit.

Framework: The framework is constructed by a sort of composite ma[te]rial. The material is composed of m[a]like carbon nanofibers, resin, metal and ceramic, etc., these compone[nts] make the frame lighter but higherintensive, and be enable to be he[at] resisting and anti-corruption. This framework bears the weight of the whole unit and fastens it.

The Motor is made by material co[m]posed by CSI/Al. And the motor c[on]trol the horizontal movement in the

0473

GRU Gaseous Reaction Unit

The gaseous reaction takes place in the kernel units(the transforming device) placed above the central pipe. Each of the Unit consists of three parts, which are a reaction shell, a heating reaction circle and a esembling of desulfteration towels. These complicate devices provide a safe and efficient container for the reaction process. The production of the reactions inside the kernel can be finally used in public transportations and heating system. As the kernel floating, we supply the gas stations and power stations in a brand new way. We send the fuel through multiple long, flexible pipes to the ground, and collect toxic gases through a central pipe in the meantime.

There are two reaction processes in each one of the unit. Down below is a reduction reaction, which is a reaction that the gases desulfured and detoxified. Meanwhile the redundant Carbon Monoxide can be used as the fuel to opreating our "SKYSCRAPER". The products from down below, like Hydrogen, Carbon Monoxide, can be used in the upper part of the Unit. Up in the shell is where the product fuel finally being producted. With the help of Sun Light and the low pressure at the high altitude, the reaction would become more efficient and energy-saving than thoes in the normal factories down on the ground. And this is why we launch our SKYSCRAPER up to the sky and let it float through clouds.

In comparing with the normal energy industry, besides the factors mentioned before, our SKYSCRAPER has some other superiorities. First, our SKYSCRAPER provides a spacious container for a massive reaction. The higher reactants concentration, the greater efficiency, but the potential safety hazard would be rising in the meantime. So this kind of massive reaction is not safe in a workshop on the ground, especially those in the city or near residence. Besides, through this reaction device, we actually prevent the massive discharge from the ground energy factories. As our transforming device can travel between cities, many small and low efficient local energy factories can be took away. So it is easier to control the air condition.

We simply apply simple chemical reactions in our kernel. At a high altitude, the atmosphere components themselves will be the best catalyst. And above all is how we make the kernel safer and more eco-friendly.

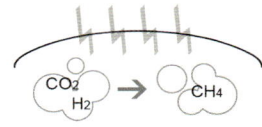

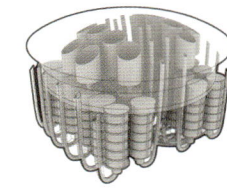

The Shell is transparent so the sunligh can be easily let in and provide energy to the reaction, which is called solar catalysis. The shell is where the Process of Methane Producing takes place. Under the low pressure beneath the shell, the whole reaction accelerates and runs in a high efficiency. The fuel is finally formed here.

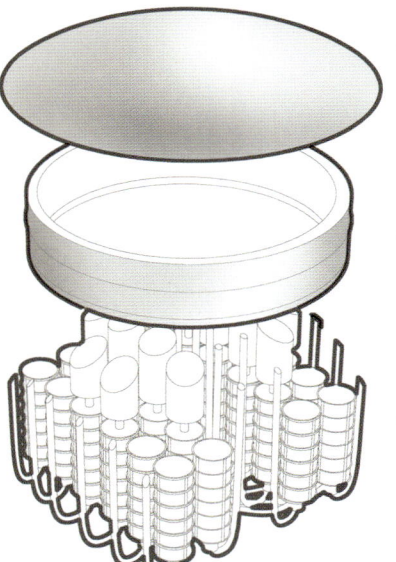

Reaction Shell

Where the Process of Methane Producing takes place. Because of the low pressure beneath the shell, the whole reaction accelerates and runs highly efficiently.

$$CO + 3H_2 \longrightarrow CH_4 + H_2O$$
$$2CO + 2H_2 \longrightarrow CH_4 + CO_2$$

Heating Circle

This Circle provides a stable reaction environment acting the same way like Controlling Bars acted in Nuclear Process. The whole reaction can be stopped by simply cooling down the heating circle.

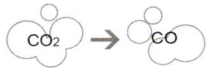

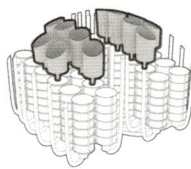

Under a High Temperature and Pressure circumstance, the CO_2 molecules become unstable and finally crack into CO molecules, which is stabler and smaller. This decomposition reaction provides the Reagents that are conducted to the Desulfurization Towers.

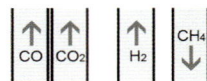

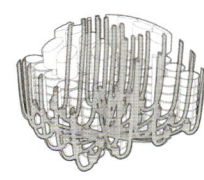

These complex pipes are severed as blood vessels to the transforming device, transporting different gases to different reaction containers. The Pipes are made of synthetic material, which provide a complete air-tight and high-pressure travel tunnel 'internal environment'.

Desulfurization Towers

Where the Desulfurization and Puration processes take place. These Towels are the cores in reusing gases. Inside these towels can the toxic substances be seperated and reused.

$$CO_2 \longrightarrow CO$$
$$SO_2 \xrightarrow{CO} S$$
$$NO_x \xrightarrow{CO} N_2$$

GRU Gaseous Reaction Unit

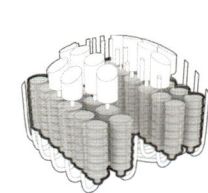

The Gases we collect from fog and hazy are quite toxic. The bottom of the CRU is called desulfurization towers. These towers are where the Desulfurization and Puration processes take place. Meanwhile, the toxic substances could be seperated and reused.

HUNTING PM2.5 PARTICLES AND CREATING GREEN ENERGY PROJECT BLUE

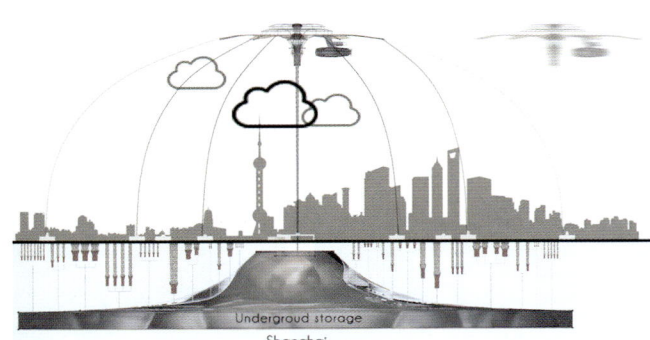

Underground storage
Shanghai

Working and Walking process

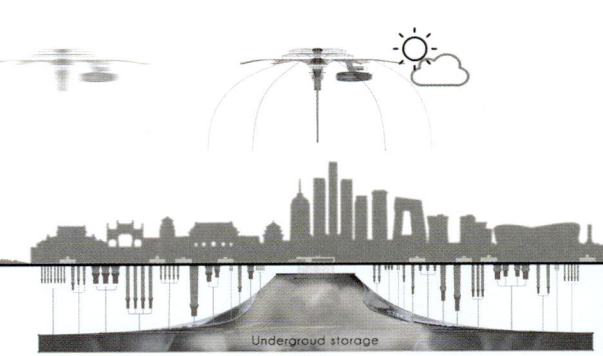

Underground storage
Beijing

AERO-CITY TOWERS II

Layton Reid

United Kingdom

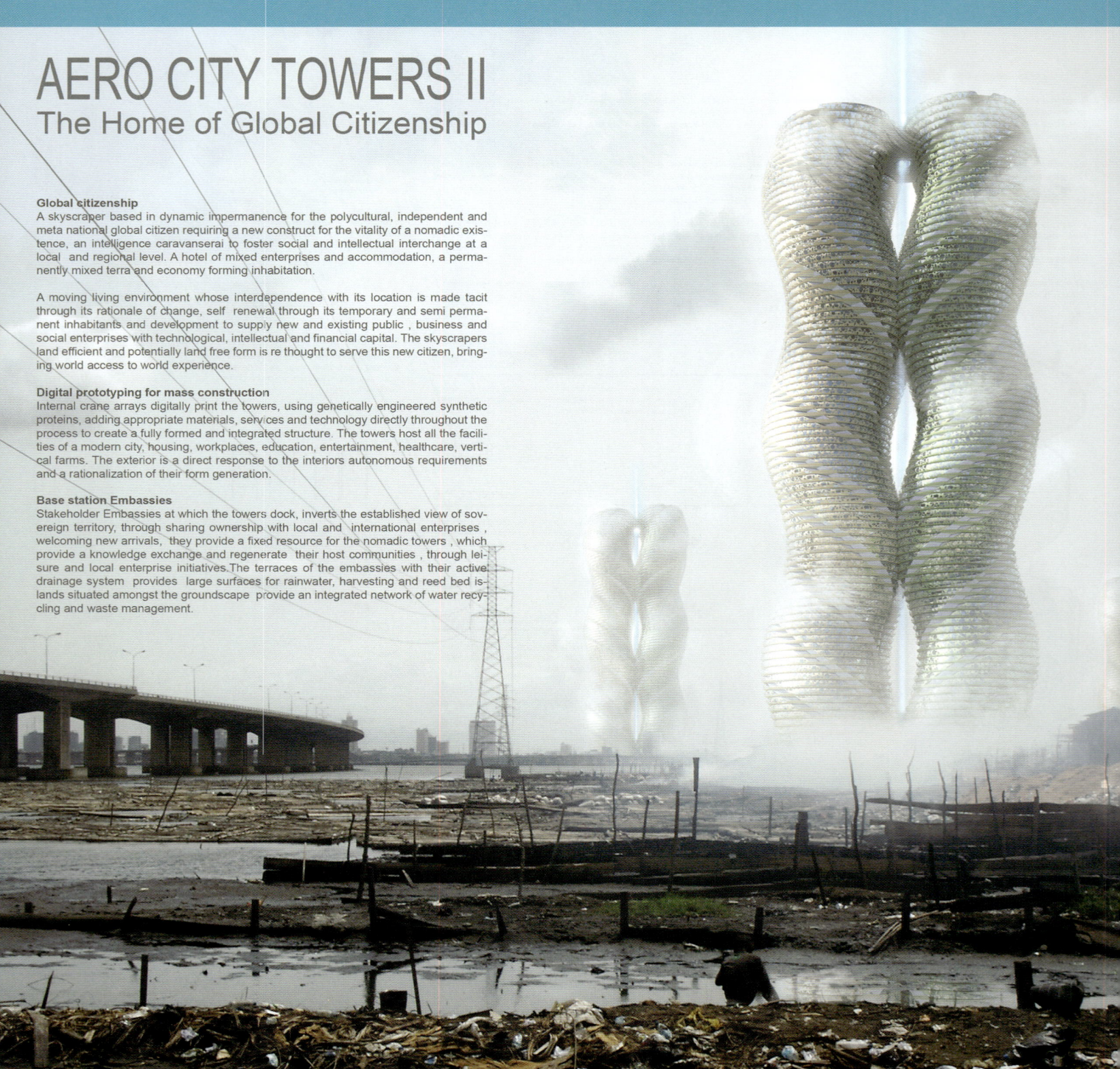

AERO CITY TOWERS II
The Home of Global Citizenship

Global citizenship
A skyscraper based in dynamic impermanence for the polycultural, independent and meta national global citizen requiring a new construct for the vitality of a nomadic existence, an intelligence caravanserai to foster social and intellectual interchange at a local and regional level. A hotel of mixed enterprises and accommodation, a permanently mixed terra and economy forming inhabitation.

A moving living environment whose interdependence with its location is made tacit through its rationale of change, self renewal through its temporary and semi permanent inhabitants and development to supply new and existing public , business and social enterprises with technological, intellectual and financial capital. The skyscrapers land efficient and potentially land free form is re thought to serve this new citizen, bringing world access to world experience.

Digital prototyping for mass construction
Internal crane arrays digitally print the towers, using genetically engineered synthetic proteins, adding appropriate materials, services and technology directly throughout the process to create a fully formed and integrated structure. The towers host all the facilities of a modern city, housing, workplaces, education, entertainment, healthcare, vertical farms. The exterior is a direct response to the interiors autonomous requirements and a rationalization of their form generation.

Base station Embassies
Stakeholder Embassies at which the towers dock, inverts the established view of sovereign territory, through sharing ownership with local and international enterprises , welcoming new arrivals, they provide a fixed resource for the nomadic towers , which provide a knowledge exchange and regenerate their host communities , through leisure and local enterprise initiatives.The terraces of the embassies with their active drainage system provides large surfaces for rainwater, harvesting and reed bed islands situated amongst the groundscape provide an integrated network of water recycling and waste management.

Internal cranes array the digitally printed towers, using genetically engineered synthetic proteins, adding appropriate materials, services and technology directly throughout the process to create a fully formed and integrated structure.

The towers host all the facilities of a modern city, housing, workplaces, education, entertainment, healthcare, and vertical farms. The exterior is a direct response to the interiors autonomous requirements and a rationalization of their form generation. Stakeholder Embassies at which the towers dock, inverts the established view of sovereign territory, through sharing ownership with local and international enterprises, welcoming new arrivals, they provide a fixed resource for the nomadic towers, which provide a knowledge exchange and regenerate their host communities, through leisure and local

0619

Bamboo permeable living skin/ brise soleil

Solar Collectors

Solomonic column structure and Parans intigration

Light wells

Elevated Landscape containing public facilities

Site strategy zoned reed bed filtration park

enterprise initiatives. The terraces of the embassies with their active drainage system provides large surfaces for rainwater, harvesting and reed bed islands situated amongst the ground-scape provide an integrated network of water recycling and waste management. The form takes its inspiration from both the traditional heat shedding structural tower forms of African traditionally devised women's braided hair and vortex shedding strakes optimizing efficient airflow systems. Whilst allowing the four towers to interconnect at three points over their 120 floor height.

The towers form accelerates the existing airflow aided by ram jet turbines within the atria, and base to provide levitating thrust. Pelamis breakwater wave energy production, vertical photovoltaic array, rooftop heat transfer pools, and coastal heat transfer, atrium turbines, inter-floor turbines inhabit the floor voids

AERO CITY
The Home of Glo

Solomonic tower form
The form takes its inspiration from both the tr forms of African traditionally devised wome strakes optimizing efficient airflow systems connect at three points over their 120 floor he

Sustainable energy generation
The towers form accelerates the existing air atria, and base to provide levitational thrust. I tion, vertical photovoltaic array, rooftop heat atrium turbines, inter floor turbines inhabit the ing low out put electricity for domestic/ reside are integrated into the hollow edges of the floo the plan.
The vertical farm, will be a general direct sou age the use of local expertise in the productio

Skin
The need for solar shading and the braided h organic bamboo mesh whose qualities are determined by the internal arrangement of sp possibility of seasonal self propagation, crea

Gyroscopes
The levitational properties of gyroscopes are vide direction.

World sites
The sites are selected to bring the first and th benefits of using hitherto unknown areas, re global economy and add the potential to dev forlorn. The first is in Lagos, Sangotedo, in region.

Primary arterial roads

Secondary access to towers

Integrated Master Plan with promenade to wave energy generation

Transport
Main Road
Tram Station
Car Park

Surrounding Use
Commercial
Education
Retail / Hospitality
Residential Expansion

Surrounding Use
Green Pedestrian Link
Reed Beds

Typical apartment plan

Structure form integration

Air flow diagram

Structure form integration

Pelamis offshore wind generator

Pelamis inter-floor system

recirculating air and generating low out put electricity for domestic/residential use. Parans fiber optic sun collectors are integrated into the hollow edges of the floor plates. Providing natural light deep into the plan.

The vertical farm, will be a general direct source of self-sufficient produce, and encourage the use of local expertise in the production of specialist produce.

The need for solar shading and the braided hair concept have generated an integrated organic bamboo mesh whose qualities are akin to a cellular structure, with openings determined by the internal arrangement of spaces. This permeable living skin has the possibility of seasonal self-propagation, creating a green loading protective barrier.

KNOCKING ON HEAVEN'S DOOR

Fayza Alshaalan

Jordan

knocking on heaven's door
Al Zaatari refugee camp skyscraper

There is a mystical and majestic beauty that is contained within the essence of a snowflake. Flawless, each geometrically designed flake is one masterpiece of nature's symphony. With the fall of each snowflake, as it gracefully and graciously makes its way from the heavens to the earth, comes a moment of rejoice. With the fall of each snowflake, earth's white blanket of purity stretches from one corner to another, kissing every tree, every flower, every street lamp along its way. I am mesmerized by nature's gift however my thoughts fog rapidly, like the cloud of unclarity that builds along my window. I am reminded that where there is beauty there is also pain. I am reminded of Al Zaatari camp, a place not too far off, a place much less fortunate.

Jordan hasn't witness this kind of harsh weather conditions since 1992, streets were blocked and people where alarmed to go out except in a case of an emergency. The very next day we hear about the death of nine children in Al Zaatari, nothing in the news to verify it but the word seemed to be very believable.
Images of tents blown away or trenched in water, children shivering, and moms crying where all over the internet.

AL Zaatari Camp

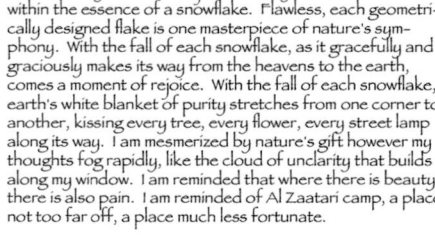

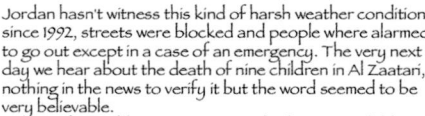

An hour and a half away from the comfort of my home, Al Zaatari camp is "home" to over 120,000 Syrian refugees half of which are children. As Jordan's first official Syrian refugee camp, the world's second largest, the camp which is rapidly growing to accommodate an overflow of Syrian refugees, projects conditions that make it anything but home. The jordanian government has graciously opened its arms and welcomed all refugees from around the world; Circassians, Palestinians, Iraqis and of course Syrians, however with very limited resources, there is only so much they can do to accommodate their refugee guests.

Set amongst a forbidding desert terrain, the camp lacks proper water, sanitation, and hygiene facilities. Waste management, adequate drinking water points, toilets, and showers are a concern as they are located far from tents. These temporary living quarters are constraining because the refugees are not allowed access to construction resources and therefore cannot build on the site. Adding onto that, an unsafe setting where organized crime, rape, vandalism, and a disregard for the law are the norm; Al Zaatari Camp is the face of an unacceptable living condition where poverty is rampant throughout.

A majority of refugees, who have escaped their countries and are now desperately in need of escaping the harsh and unacceptable living conditions of the camp. The refugees would literally kill to get out of the camp, some are even ready to go back to Syria, preferring to die in war rather than suffer a different kind of war away from their home lands. The end of the Syrian crisis is no where near, and Al Zaatari Camp continues to sink. If the Syrian refugees can't find solace on earth, should they be knocking on heaven's door? There is an Arabian proverb which reads: "like being hanged between the skies and the ground," which implies a state of instability and lack of direction because one can neither go back nor move forward.

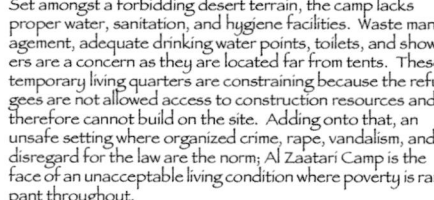

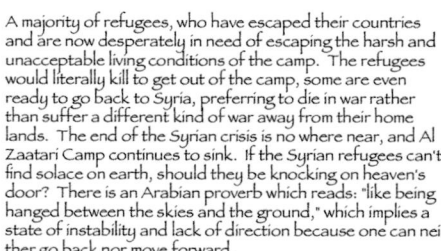

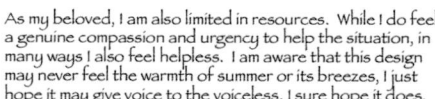

As my beloved, I am also limited in resources. While I do feel a genuine compassion and urgency to help the situation, in many ways I also feel helpless. I am aware that this design may never feel the warmth of summer or its breezes, I just hope it may give voice to the voiceless. I sure hope it does.

Jordan hasn't witnessed this kind of harsh weather conditions since 1992, streets were blocked and people where warned not to go outside except in the case of an emergency. One day we hear about the death of nine children in Al Zaatari, nothing in the news to verify it but the word seemed to be very believable. Images of tents blown away or trenched in water, children shivering, and moms crying were all over the Internet.

An hour and a half away from the comfort of my home, Al Zaatari camp is "home" to over 120,000 Syrian refugees, half of whom are children. As Jordan's first official Syrian refugee camp and the world's second largest, the camp, which is rapidly growing to accommodate an overflow of Syrian refugees, projects conditions that make it anything but home. The Jordanian government has graciously

opened its arms and welcomed all refugees from around the world; Circassians, Palestinians, Iraqis and of course Syrians. However, with very limited resources, there is only so much they can do to accommodate their refugee guests. Set amongst a forbidding desert terrain, the camp lacks proper water, sanitation, and hygiene facilities, which are all usually located far from tents. These temporary living quarters are constraining because the refugees are not allowed access to construction resources and therefore cannot build on the site. Adding onto that, an unsafe setting where organized crime, rape, vandalism, and a disregard for the law are the norm; Al Zaatari Camp is the face of unacceptable living conditions where poverty is rampant throughout.

A majority of refugees have escaped their countries and are now desperately in need of escaping

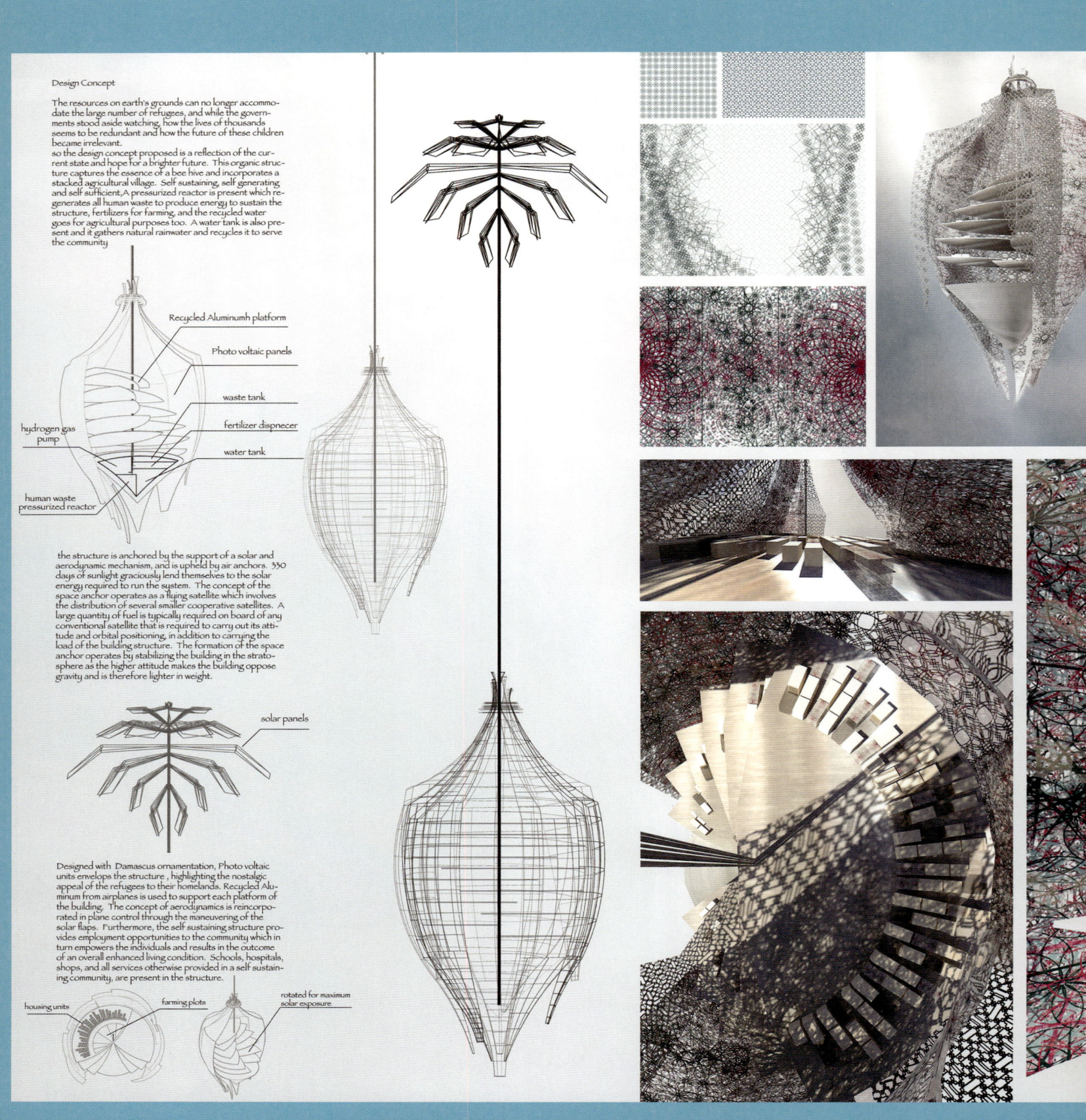

Design Concept

The resources on earth's grounds can no longer accommo-date the large number of refugees, and while the govern-ments stood aside watching, how the lives of thousands seems to be redundant and how the future of these children became irrelevant.
so the design concept proposed is a reflection of the cur-rent state and hope for a brighter future. This organic struc-ture captures the essence of a bee hive and incorporates a stacked agricultural village. Self sustaining, self generating and self sufficient, A pressurized reactor is present which re-generates all human waste to produce energy to sustain the structure, fertilizers for farming, and the recycled water goes for agricultural purposes too. A water tank is also pre-sent and it gathers natural rainwater and recycles it to serve the community

Recycled Aluminumh platform
Photo voltaic panels
waste tank
hydrogen gas pump
fertilizer dispnecer
water tank
human waste pressurized reactor

the structure is anchored by the support of a solar and aerodynamic mechanism, and is upheld by air anchors. 330 days of sunlight graciously lend themselves to the solar energy required to run the system. The concept of the space anchor operates as a flying satellite which involves the distribution of several smaller cooperative satellites. A large quantity of fuel is typically required on board of any conventional satellite that is required to carry out its atti-tude and orbital positioning, in addition to carrying the load of the building structure. The formation of the space anchor operates by stabilizing the building in the strato-sphere as the higher attitude makes the building oppose gravity and is therefore lighter in weight.

solar panels

Designed with Damascus ornamentation, Photo voltaic units envelops the structure , highlighting the nostalgic appeal of the refugees to their homelands. Recycled Alu-minum from airplanes is used to support each platform of the building. The concept of aerodynamics is reincorpo-rated in plane control through the maneuvering of the solar flaps. Furthermore, the self sustaining structure pro-vides employment opportunities to the community which in turn empowers the individuals and results in the outcome of an overall enhanced living condition. Schools, hospitals, shops, and all services otherwise provided in a self sustain-ing community, are present in the structure.

housing units   farming plots
rotated for maximum solar exposure

the harsh and unacceptable living conditions of the camp. The refugees would literally kill to get out of the camp, some are even ready to go back to Syria, preferring to die in war rather than suffer a different kind of war away from their homeland. The end of the Syrian crisis is nowhere near, and Al Zaatari Camp continues to sink. If the Syrian refugees cannot find solace on earth, should they be knocking on heaven's door? There is an Arabian proverb, which reads, "like being hung between the skies and the ground," which implies a state of instability and lack of direction because one can neither go back nor move forward.

THE TREE

Gensler
MIR

United States
Norway

THE TREE

A TIMELINE TO SURVIVAL / A PLAN TO RECOLONIZE DEVASTATED LANDS

DESTRUCTION

The 21st century is witnessing the largest human migration in history. Mankind is fleeing the countryside for the vague promises of "modern" city living, leaving desolation in its wake. From the irradiated wastelands of Fukushima and Chernobyl to the battlefields of the Middle East to the oil-devastated Niger Delta, humans are being forced away from nature and pushed into cities that are inhumanly designed; row upon row of concrete forms layered in pollution with no access to clean air, water, and landscape. How can this desperate flow be reversed? The Tree resolves the balance between the devastation old world cities wreak while providing a home to the billions looking for new way of life. In only five years, The Tree turns dead empty land into an oasis for new beginnings.

REGROWTH

MINUTE 01

The seed is activated by its context, the form of its growth driven by the pollution it encounters. A Radiation Tree evolves differently from a Chemical Tree, which evolves differently from an Oil Tree ... when planted, nano fusion machines absorb the local pollution, transforming it into the raw materials required to fuel growth. The more polluted the region, the faster and taller the tree grows ...

WEEK 01

With accelerating growth the tree spirals upwards as it sucks filth from the devastated ground. Its surroundings start to show the first signs of change with oil and radiation levels dropping ...

MONTH 01

Now over 1000m tall, The Tree enters its second growth phase, internal mechanics shift and pollution seekers bifurcate and multiply into refinery and storage zones. The Tree's growth accelerates, but now its environmental recycling capacity has started to exceed the native pollution. Its growing volume is utilized to refine and store the reservoir of raw building materials it will need in its next growth phase ...

YEAR 01

Topping out at 4,500m, The Tree has cleaned its surroundings and now starts to grow the first of its two different types of seed. Drawn from an extensive DNA bank local types of flora and fauna are created to refill then clean, yet empty environment. The tree rebuilds the local ecosystem, devastation becomes barren rock becomes savanna grasses becomes forests and streams triggering Stage Three.

STAGE 01 - SITE PURIFICATION

AIR PURIFICATION

CHEMICAL + RADIATION PURIFICATION

WATER PURIFICATION

STAGE 02 - SEED GENERATION / BUILDING A NEW CITY

REFINED MATERIALS STORED INTERNALLY

INTERNAL SEED MANUFACTURING

SEEDING NEW CITY

The 21st century is witnessing the largest human migration in history. Mankind is fleeing the countryside for the vague promises of "modern" city living, leaving desolation in its wake. From the irradiated wastelands of Fukushima and Chernobyl to the battlefields of the Middle East to the oil-devastated Niger Delta, humans are being forced from nature and pushed into cities that are inhumanly designed; row upon row of concrete forms layered in pollution with no access to clean air, water, and landscape. How can this desperate flow be reversed? The Tree resolves the balance between the devastation old world cities wreak while providing a home to the billions looking for new ways of life. In only five years The Tree turns dead, empty land into an oasis for new beginnings.

In week one, with accelerating growth the tree spirals upwards as it sucks filth from the devastated

0632

+4,000M

+3,000M

+2,000M

+1,000M

+0M

YEAR 05
DESIGNATION: 1_0045
AGE: 5.76 YEARS
LOCATION: AFGHANISTAN
POPULATION: 2.376 MILLION
GROWTH: 17,600 / MONTH

ground. Its surroundings start to show the first signs of change with chemical or radiation levels dropping …

In week 2, now over 1000m tall, The Tree enters its second growth phase, internal mechanics shift and pollution soakers bifurcate and multiply into refinery and storage zones. The Tree's growth accelerates, but now its environmental recycling capacity has started to exceed the native pollution. Its growing volume is utilized to refine and store the reservoir of raw building materials it will need in its next growth phase …

After year 1, topping out at 4,500m, The Tree has cleansed its surroundings and now starts to grow the first of its two different types of seed. Drawn from an extensive DNA bank local types of flora and fauna are created to refill the clean yet empty environment. The tree rebuilds the local ecosystem;

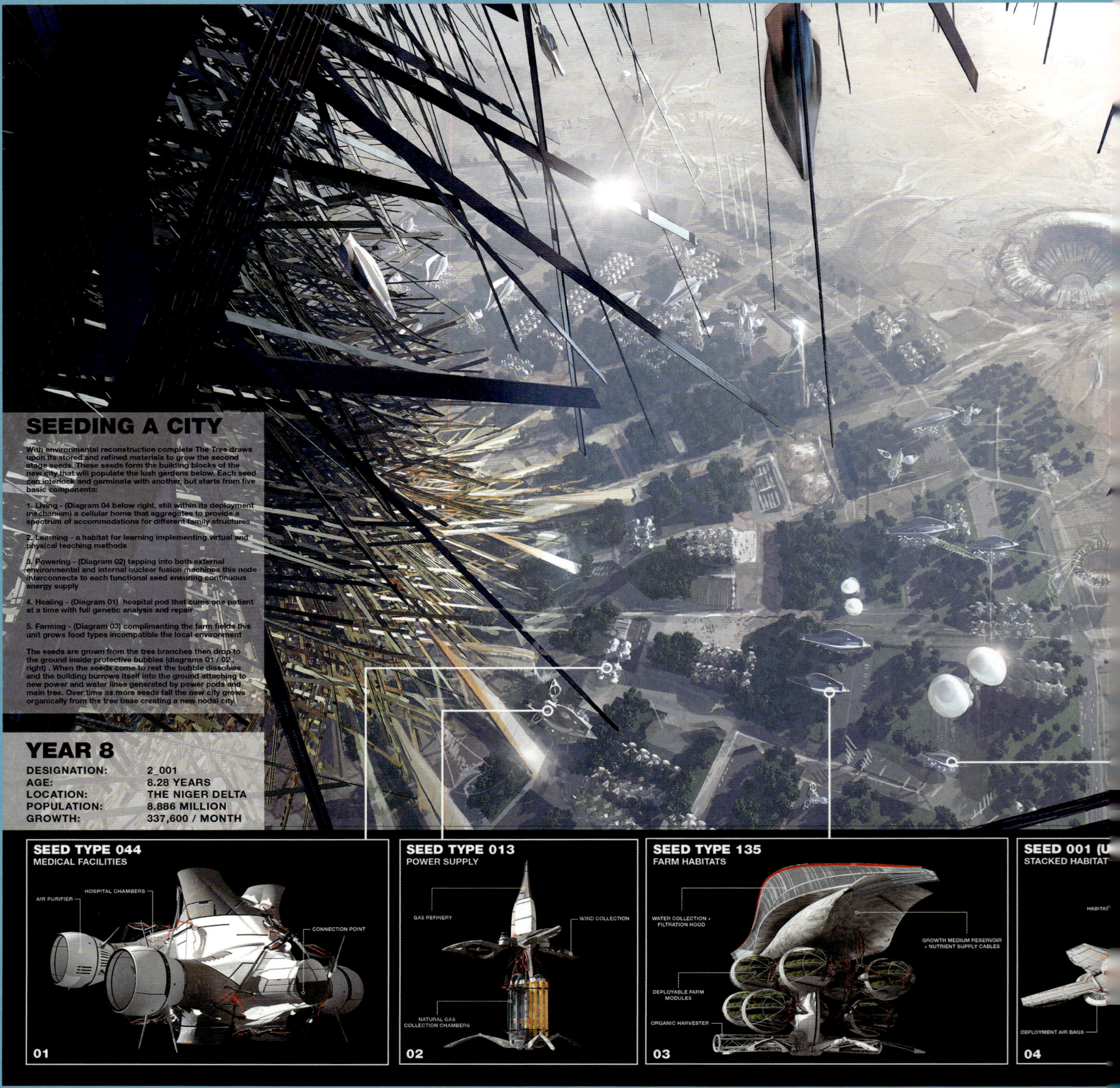

SEEDING A CITY

With environmental reconstruction complete The Tree draws upon its stored and refined materials to grow the second stage seeds. These seeds form the building blocks of the new city that will populate the lush gardens below. Each seed can interlock and germinate with another, but starts from five basic components:

1. Living - (Diagram 04 below right, still within its deployment mechanism) a cellular home that aggregates to provide a spectrum of accommodations for different family structures

2. Learning - a habitat for learning implementing virtual and physical teaching methods

3. Powering - (Diagram 02) tapping into both external environmental and internal nuclear fusion machines this node interconnects to each functional seed ensuring continuous energy supply

4. Healing - (Diagram 01) hospital pod that cures one patient at a time with full genetic analysis and repair

5. Farming - (Diagram 03) complimenting the farm fields this unit grows food types incompatible the local environment

The seeds are grown from the tree branches then drop to the ground inside protective bubbles (diagrams 01 / 02, right). When the seeds come to rest the bubble dissolves and the building burrows itself into the ground attaching to new power and water lines generated by power pods and main tree. Over time as more seeds fall the new city grows organically from the tree base creating a new nodal city.

YEAR 8

DESIGNATION:	2_001
AGE:	8.28 YEARS
LOCATION:	THE NIGER DELTA
POPULATION:	8.886 MILLION
GROWTH:	337,600 / MONTH

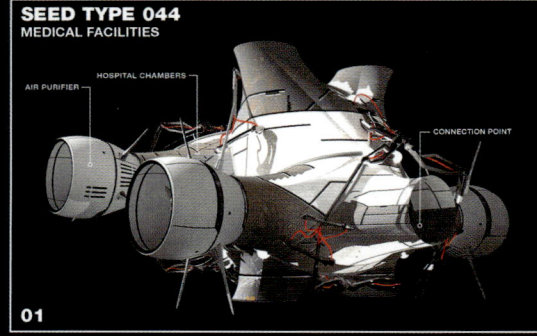

SEED TYPE 044
MEDICAL FACILITIES

AIR PURIFIER
HOSPITAL CHAMBERS
CONNECTION POINT

01

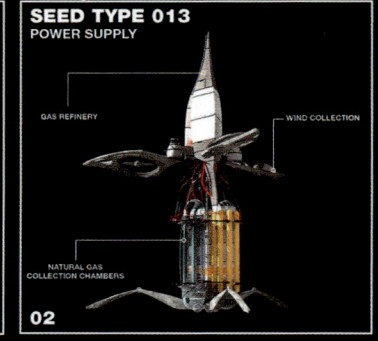

SEED TYPE 013
POWER SUPPLY

GAS REFINERY
WIND COLLECTION
NATURAL GAS COLLECTION CHAMBERS

02

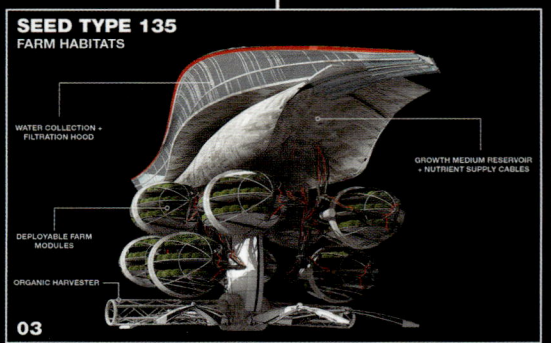

SEED TYPE 135
FARM HABITATS

WATER COLLECTION + FILTRATION HOOD
GROWTH MEDIUM RESERVOIR + NUTRIENT SUPPLY CABLES
DEPLOYABLE FARM MODULES
ORGANIC HARVESTER

03

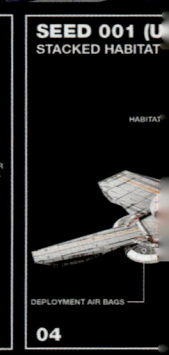

SEED 001 (U
STACKED HABITAT

HABITAT

DEPLOYMENT AIR BAGS

04

devastation becomes barren rock, becomes savanna grasses, becomes forests and streams triggering
 After year 5, with environmental reconstruction complete The Tree draws upon its stored and refined materials to grow the second stage seeds. These seeds form the building blocks of the new city that will populate the lush gardens below. Each seed can interlock and germinate with another, but starts from five basic components: Living - a cellular home that aggregates to provide a spectrum of accommodations for different family structures, Learning - a habitat for learning implementing virtual and physical teaching methods, Powering - tapping into both external environmental and internal nuclear fusion machines this node interconnects to each functional seed ensuring continuous energy supply, Healing - hospital pod that cures one patient at a time with full genetic analysis and repair, Farming - complimenting the farm fields this unit grows food types incompatible the local environment.

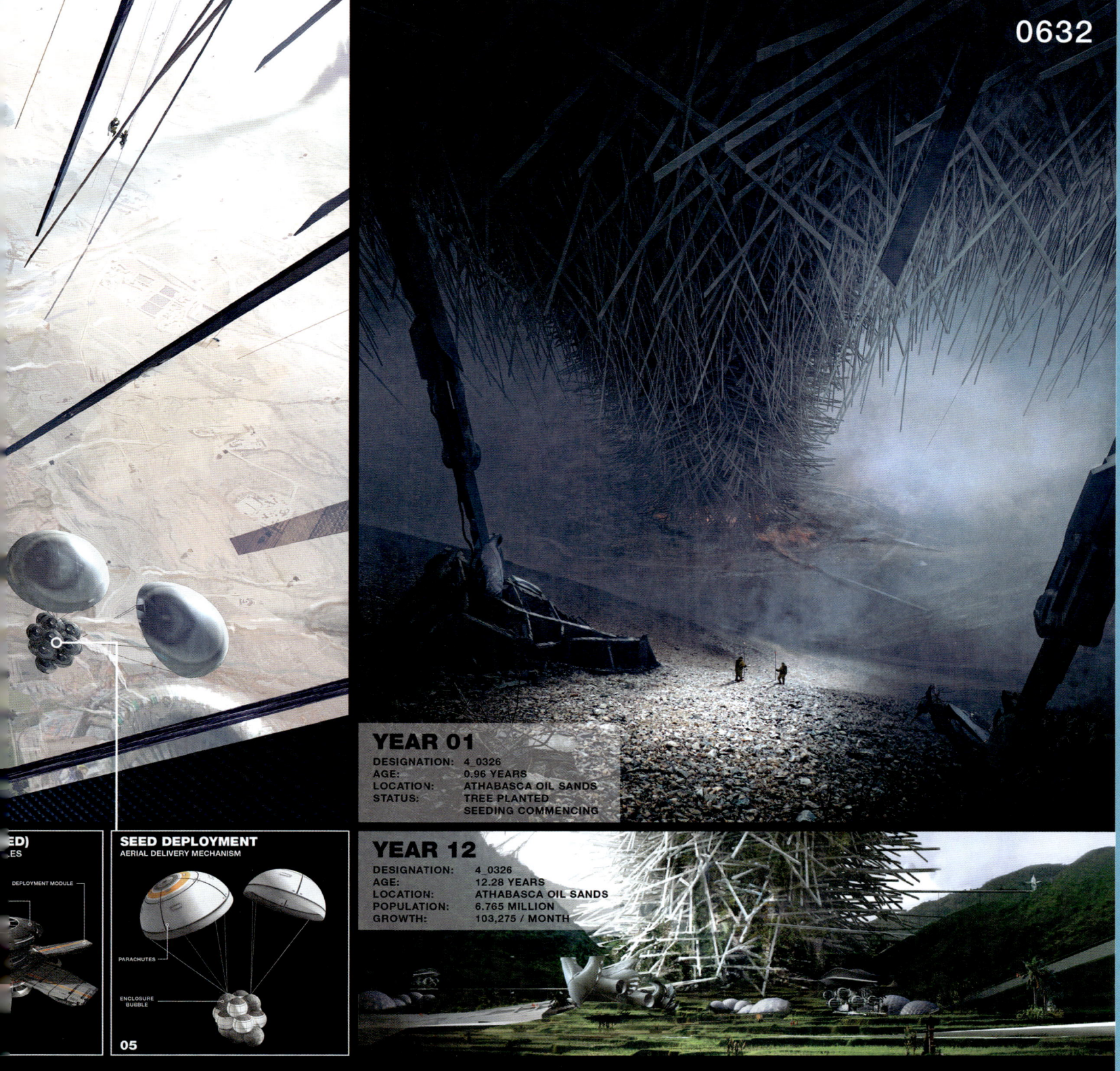

0632

YEAR 01
DESIGNATION: 4_0326
AGE: 0.96 YEARS
LOCATION: ATHABASCA OIL SANDS
STATUS: TREE PLANTED
 SEEDING COMMENCING

SEED DEPLOYMENT
AERIAL DELIVERY MECHANISM

DEPLOYMENT MODULE

PARACHUTES

ENCLOSURE
BUBBLE

05

YEAR 12
DESIGNATION: 4_0326
AGE: 12.28 YEARS
LOCATION: ATHABASCA OIL SANDS
POPULATION: 6.765 MILLION
GROWTH: 103,275 / MONTH

THE RHIZOME

Daniel Fernández Flórez
Mariana Vilela Betto
Rolf Türme

Spain
Switzerland

THE RHIZOME - A MULTIFUNCTIONAL BUILDING FOR THE WINTER OLYMPIC

Height   +10m   +20m

Lenght   SKI ENTRY RAMP   ENTRY & CAFÉ   RETAIL & EQUIPMENT RENTAL   WINTER SPORTS SCHOOL   MUSEUM   OFFICES   HOTEL

Gilles Deleuze and Félix Guattari used the term "rhizome" and "rhizomatic" to describe elements that allows multiple and non-hierarchical entries and exit points in their structure.

"The principal characteristics of a rhizome: unlike tress or their roots, the rhizome connects any point to any other point, and its traits are not necessarily linked to traits of the same nature; it brings into play very different regimes of signs, and even nonsign states. A rhizome has no beginning or end; it is always in the middle, between things, interbeing, intermezzo."

A Thousand Plateaus: Capitalism and Schizophrenia (1980) Gilles Deleuze and Félix Guattari

CONCEPT AND PLACE

The building is located in the high snowy mountains of any auspicious place to host a Winter Olympic Games.

The project is conceived as the Deleuzian rhizomatic thinking. It emerges among snow covered pines as a winding stripe, entangling over itself along its 6km lenght, evoking the soulful sensuality of natural structures, but also the footprints left over human displacements - randomly left in a space of circulation, as the curves skiers trace on snow.

The slenderness of the band (9m) and supports provides the necessary transparency to – as rhizomatic structure –blur the boundaries between outside and inside.

Program Diagram

+120.00m
+113.50m
+104.61m
+81.72m
+32.83m
+12.43m

PROGRAM

The Rizoma building is a necessary icon for the W[...] where people meet, sleep and train every day. It [...] spa for the Olympic audience, apartments for at[...] cafeteria, retail and equipment rental, winter sp[...] museum and, as a main feature, its soft slopes.
The linear 6km of the Rizoma building grow and br[...] high with a slope of 2%. The 54'000m2 of indoo[...] as a DNA band, so that the building has no be[...] Rhizome, could grow indefinitely.

CIRCULATION AND ROOF

The circulation is produced by a system similar to [...] like a funicular train around the façade, allowing a[...] building.

To access the roof top there is a circular core of 10m [...] lifts and emergency stairs, connecting the ground fl[...] of the roof allowing skiers to descend the 6km [...] the ground low.

"Make rhizomes, not roots, never plant! Don't sow, gr[...] one or multiple, be multiplicities! Run lines, never pl[...] the point into a line!"

A Thousand Plateaus: Capitalism and Schi[...]
Del[...]

Gilles Deleuze and Félix Guattari used the term "rhizome" and "rhizomatic" to describe elements that allow multiple and non-hierarchical entries and exit points in their structure. The building is located in the high snowy mountains of any auspicious place to host a Winter Olympic Games.

The project is conceived as the Deleuzian rhizomatic thinking. It emerges among snow covered pines as a winding stripe, entangling over itself along its 6km length, evoking the soulful sensuality of natural structures, but also the footprints left over by human displacements - randomly left in circulation spaces, as the curves skiers trace on snow.

The slenderness of the band (9m) and supports provides the necessary transparency to – as a rhizomatic structure –blur the boundaries between outside and inside.

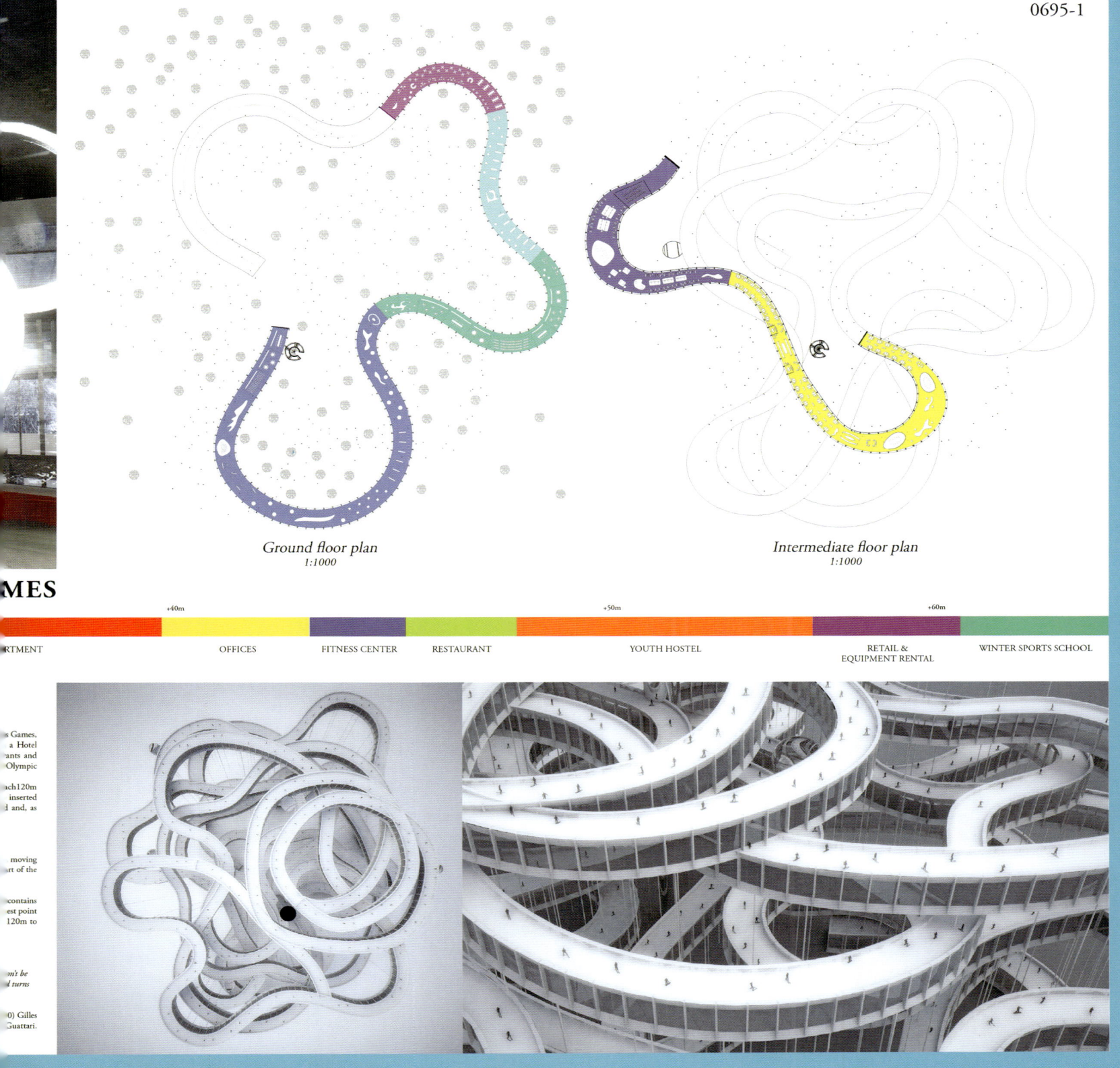

0695-1

Ground floor plan
1:1000

Intermediate floor plan
1:1000

MES

+40m   +50m   +60m

RTMENT   OFFICES   FITNESS CENTER   RESTAURANT   YOUTH HOSTEL   RETAIL &   WINTER SPORTS SCHOOL
                                                                                          EQUIPMENT RENTAL

s Games,
a Hotel
ants and
Olympic

ach120m
inserted
d and, as

moving
rt of the

contains
est point
120m to

n't be
d turns

0) Gilles
Guattari.

The Rhizome building is a necessary icon for the Winter Olympics Games, where people meet, sleep and train every day. It comprehends a Hotel spa for the Olympic audience, apartments for athletes, restaurants and cafeteria, retail and equipment rental, winter sports school, Olympic museum and, as a main feature, its soft slopes.

The linear 6km of the Rhizome building grow and branch out to reach120m high with a slope of 2%. The 54'000m2 of indoor program are inserted as a DNA band, so that the building has no beginning or end and, as Rhizome, could grow indefinitely.

The circulation is provided by a system similar to the ski cabins, moving like a funicular train around the façade, allowing access to any part of the building. To access the roof top there is a circular core of

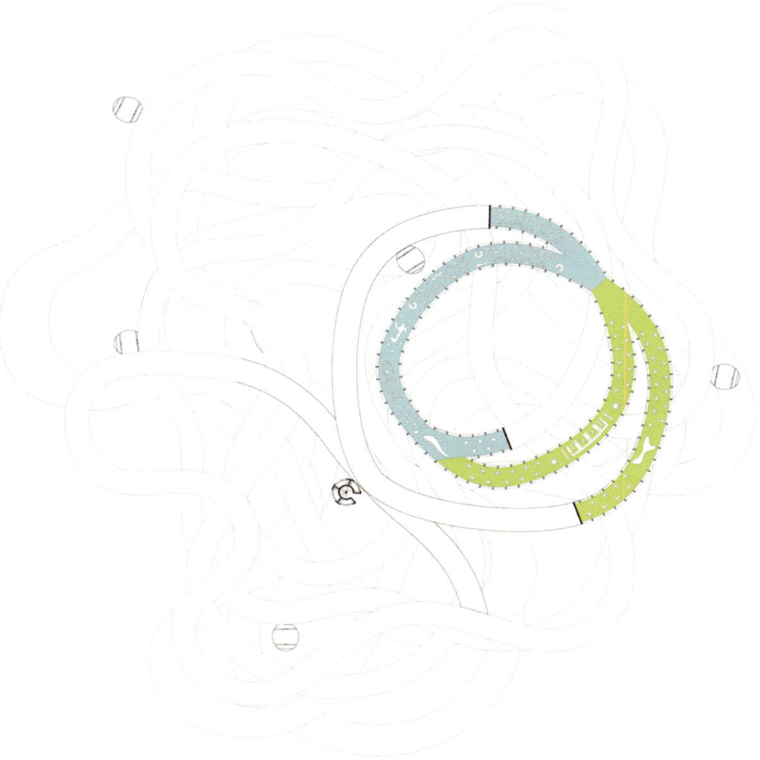

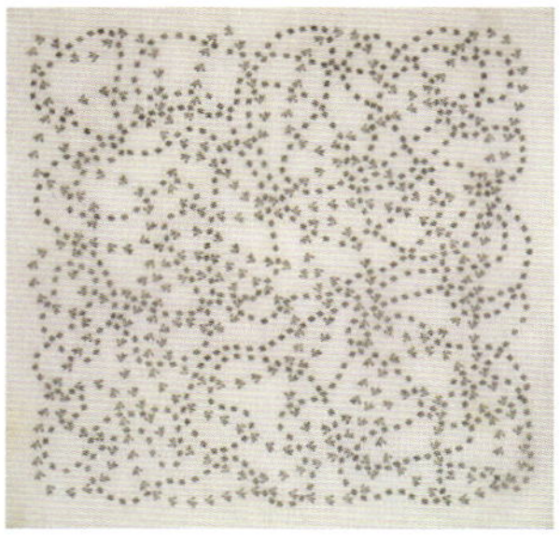

"People", 1982, León Ferrari.

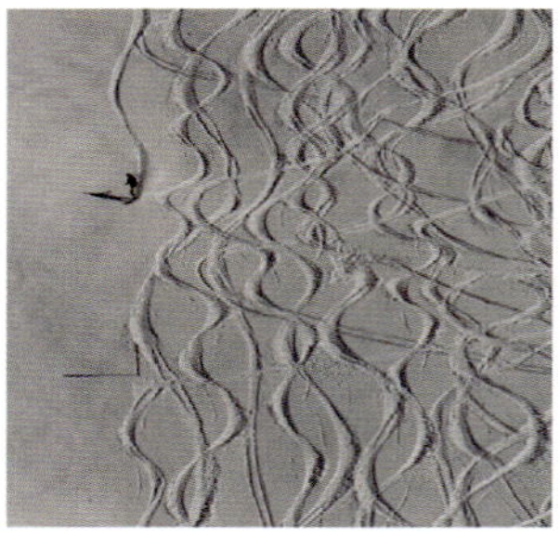

Ski tracks, anonymous.

Top floor plan
1:1000

References

+70m	+80m	+90m	+100m
OFFICES	APARTMENTS	HOTEL & SPA	ROOF TO

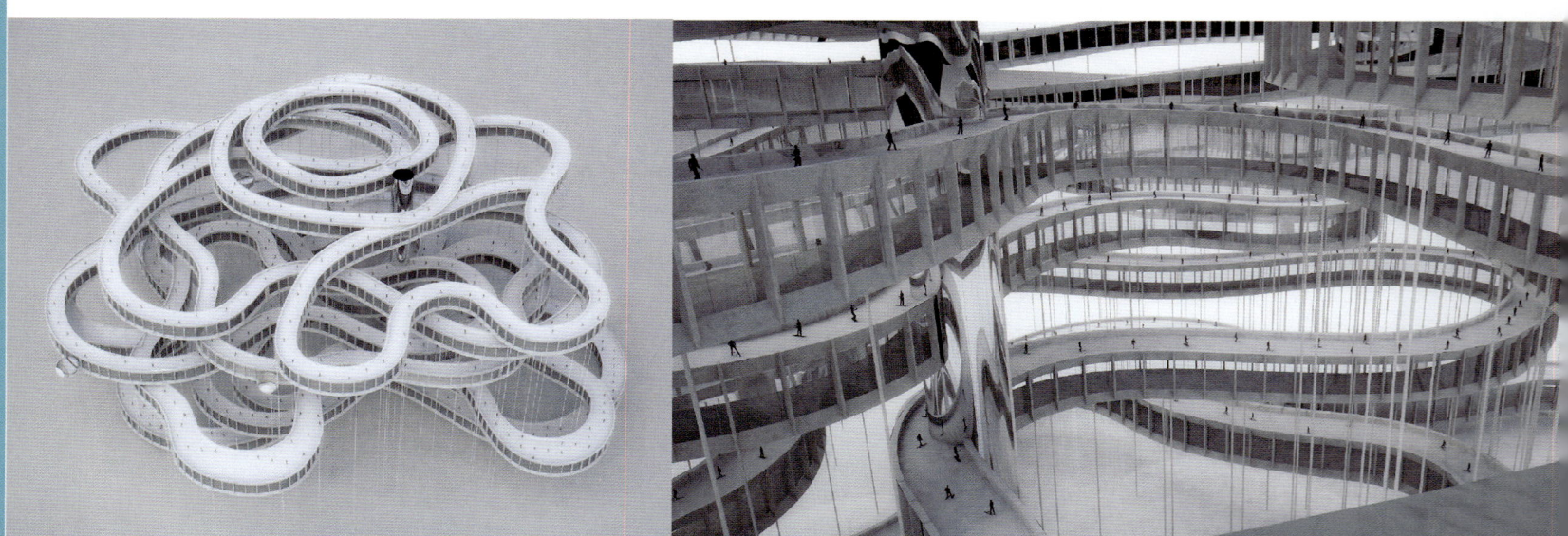

10m diameter which contains lifts and emergency stairs, connecting the ground floor to the highest point of the roof allowing skiers to descend the 6km slope, dropping 120m to the ground floor.

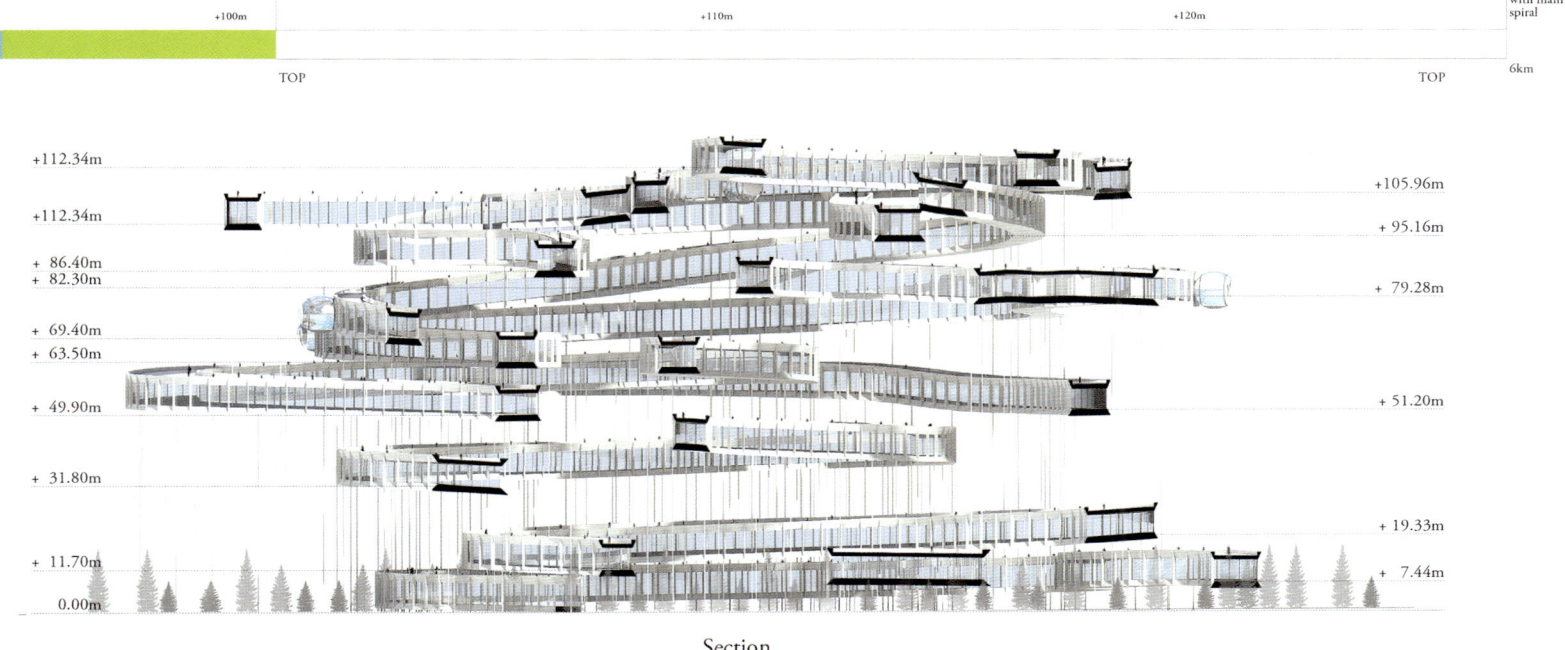

111m Top Height Ground Floor
Spiral Bifurcation

+110m
Reconnects with main spiral

+100m   +110m   +120m

6km

RANT   TOP   TOP

+112.34m   +105.96m

+112.34m   + 95.16m

+ 86.40m
+ 82.30m   + 79.28m

+ 69.40m
+ 63.50m

+ 49.90m   + 51.20m

+ 31.80m

+ 19.33m

+ 11.70m   + 7.44m

0.00m

Section

BODY-BUILDING

Maciej Nisztuk

Poland

BODY-BUILDING
Inhumanity memorial

IN THE 20TH CENTURY, 980 MILLION PEOPLE DIED DUE TO DARK SIDE OF HUMAN NATURE.

177 MILLION DUE TO IDEOLOGY, 142 MILLION DUE TO MURDER, 132 MILLION DUE TO WAR.

DURING THE LAST HUNDRED YEARS 250 MAJOR MILITARY CONFLICTS TOOK PLACE ACROSS THE GLOBE, 41 ONGOING.

The World we live in feeds on divisions. When things go wrong, humanity begins to divide and look for a scapegoat, an imaginary cause of evil. 20th century shows this pattern in a distinct way. Current global economic crisis is the most recent reason for the emergence of social divisions, both at the macro and micro scale. In a world like this a cult of the Stranger appears. The Stranger is one who does not fit to the image of a statistical citizen. It can be anyone, depending on the needs and circumstances: a Jew, a homeless, a gypsy, an immigrant, black, white, yellow, red, rightist, leftist, anarchist... .

History shows numerous examples of the use of architecture in the sick way: Nazis concentration camps and Jewish ghettos, Japanese death camps, Soviet Gulags. Also architecture is often used as a tool to form a New Human: Socrealism, Nazi architecture of thousand-year Reich, Gothic churches, North Korean splendor…

It was something normal in medieval Europe, to create spatial structures which served as a warning to the society: gallows, pillory, public place of execution.

We are currently in a 'Neo' age of technology, new economics, globalization and the global village where people live closer to each other, engaging in a more complex environment than ever, causing the social divisions to become more frequent and severe. If architecture can be seen as the echo of the era, under this rule, we can get to the point where we begin to create buildings - anti-monuments of humanity, memorials of incompatible beliefs or canons of beauty. Architecture changes along with the world in which it exist, but the fundamental mechanisms of human nature does not.

The Structure

Steel structure tower filled with "gabions" of human remains. Decompose over time. Monument of human idealisms, anti-monument of the body cult, monument of murderers, disposal site of society members who are uncomfortable: homeless, gypsies, blacks, homosexuals, religious dissenters…

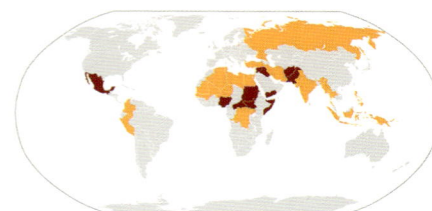

WORLD MAP
ongoing armed conflicts
(source wikipedia.org)

In the 20th century, 980 million people died due to the dark side of human nature - 177 million due to ideology, 142 million due to murder, 132 million due to war. During the last hundred years 250 major military conflicts took place across the globe, 41 ongoing.

In the world we live in feeds on divisions. When things go wrong, humanity begins to divide and look for a scapegoat, an imaginary cause of evil. The 20th century shows this pattern in a distinct way. The current global economic crisis is the most recent reason for the emergence of social divisions, both at the macro and micro scale. In a world like this, a cult of the 'stranger' appears. The 'stranger' is one who does not fit to the image of a statistical citizen. It can be anyone, depending on the needs and circumstances: a Jew, a homeless, a gypsy, an immigrant, black, white, yellow, red, rightist, leftist,

0736-1

anarchist, etc.

History shows numerous examples of the use of architecture in the sick way: Nazis concentration camps and Jewish ghettos, Japanese death camps, Soviet Gulags. Also architecture is often used as a tool to form a New Human: Socrealism, Nazi architecture of thousand-year Reich, Gothic churches, and North Korean splendor.

It was something normal in medieval Europe, to create spatial structures, which served as a warning to the society: gallows, pillory, and public places of execution.

We are currently in a 'Neo' age of technology, new economics, globalization and the global village where people live closer to each other, engaging in a more complex environment than ever, causing

SIDE VIEW
with construction outline

the social divisions to become more frequent and severe. If architecture can be seen as the echo of the era, under this rule, we can get to the point where we begin to create buildings - anti-monuments of humanity, memorials of incompatible beliefs or canons of beauty. Architecture changes along with the world in which it exists, but the fundamental mechanisms of human nature do not.

A steel structure tower filled with "gabions" of human remains that decompose over time. Monument of human idealisms, anti-monument of the body cult, monument of murderers, and disposal sites of society members who are uncomfortable: homeless, gypsies, blacks, homosexuals, and religious dissenters, etc.

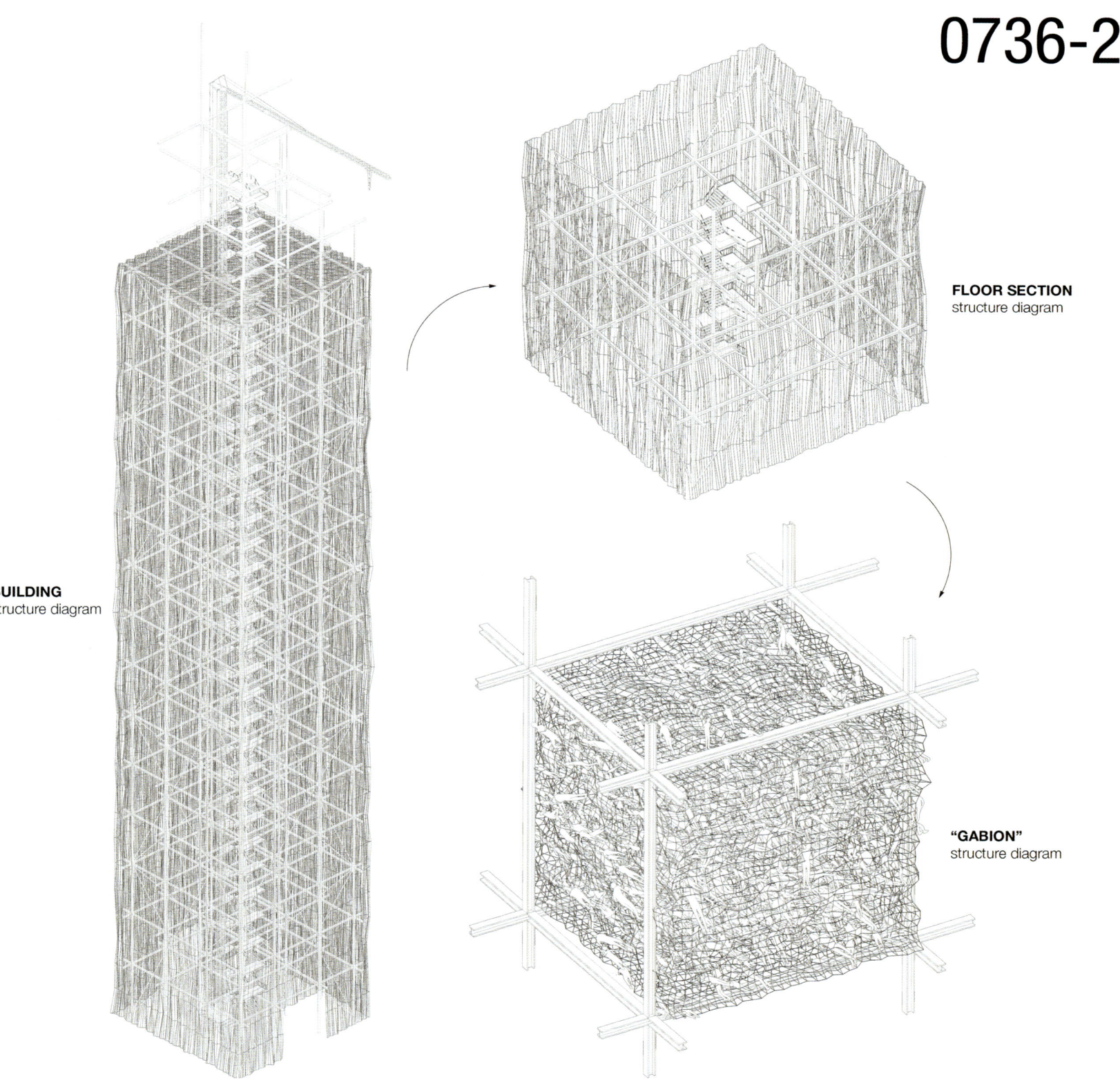

0736-2

FLOOR SECTION
structure diagram

BUILDING
structure diagram

"GABION"
structure diagram

REFUGEE SKYSCRAPER

Hani Shata
Mohanned Iskanderani

Saudi Arabia

REFUGEE SKYSCRAPER

The objective of "Refugee Scraper" proposal is to address the refugee camps situation and status. Camps usually occupy a massive area on host countries soil which drain its infrastructure and utilities and raises many social and security concerns and threats. What we tried to achieve in this proposal, is a vertical confide solution to the refugee camps. The tower is not only concerned with resolving the issue of size but also towards the health and safety of tenants. Refugee scraper proposes a flexible affordable system that can be assembled anywhere in the world.

The major component of the refugee scraper, is the tensile structure which was designed to create a web system. The tensile is prefabbed, assembled and folded before it gets to the site. The system is created in a way that functions like an inverted umbrella and is easy to deliver and assemble once the steel structure is finished and set in place. The web system will only enclose the outside skin, and the inner faces "cells" will have the opportunity to merge, creating different space articulations and forms depending on the function and number of inhabitants. The outer skin will act as a toxic gas filter and protector from all natural causes as rain, wind and sun and in case of emergencies from smoke and chemical gases.

The Zaatari refugee camp that is located in Jordan is being occupied with over 81,000 people as of July 2014. It's about 1.3 sq mil. It was founded in 2012 after the Syrian crisis war. Its population started with 15,000 as of 2012 and grew more than four times as much in 2-3 years. With everything happening around the Middle East and most of the world, a new urban solution is needed to resolve the refugee camps crises.

Traditional camps |
1,500,000 sqm offering homes for
81,000 refugees

Refugee scraper |
600,000 sqm offering homes for
81,000 refugees

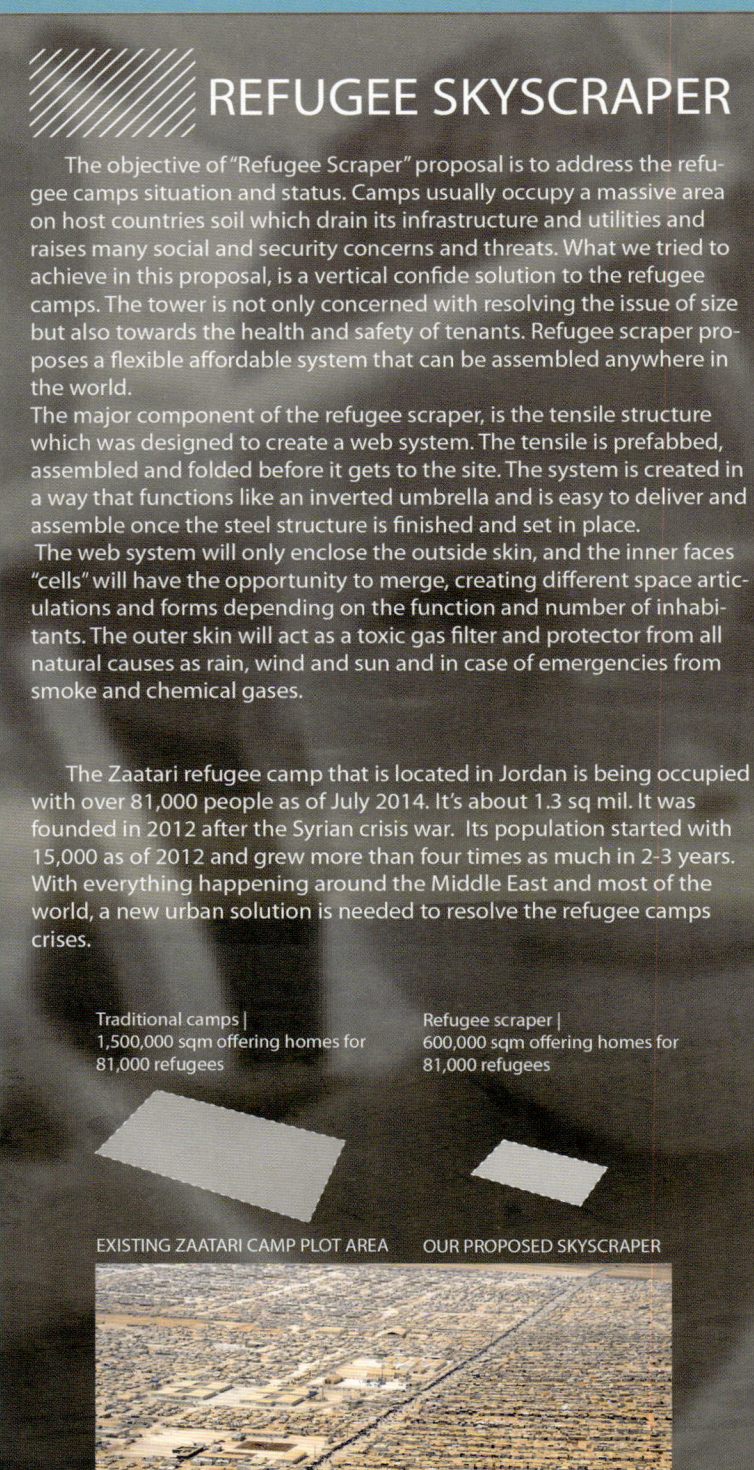

EXISTING ZAATARI CAMP PLOT AREA   OUR PROPOSED SKYSCRAPER

PLATONIC SOLID LAYERS

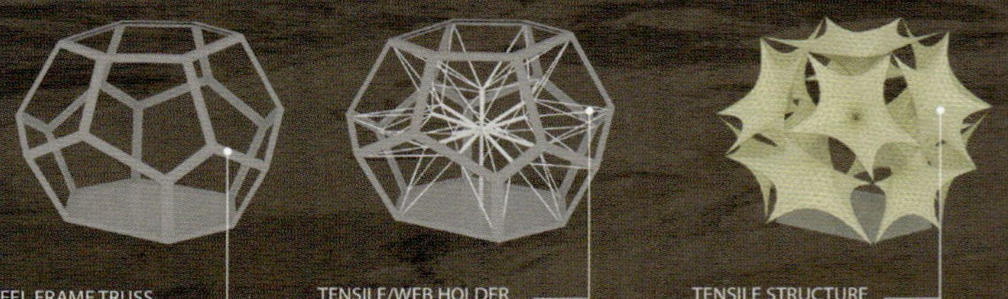

STEEL FRAME TRUSS   TENSILE/WEB HOLDER   TENSILE STRUCTURE

MENA has been a troubled zone since 1948 and the number of refugees has been increasing ever since. The situation started to become a real threat and burden on adjacent and host countries' infrastructure, economies and security. The objective of "Refugee Skyscraper" proposal is to address the refugee camps situation and status. Camps usually occupy a massive area on host countries soil, which drain its infrastructure and utilities and raise many social and security concerns and threats. What we tried to achieve in this proposal is a vertical confide solution to the refugee camps. The tower is not only concerned with resolving the issue of size but also towards the health and safety of tenants. Refugee scraper proposes a flexible and affordable system that can be assembled anywhere in the world.

The major component of the "Refugee Skyscraper" is the tensile structure, which was designed to

0070

NIC SOLID ASSEMBLY TIME LINE

Web holder/adjuster

Steel pcle connecting the tensile back with the beam

The web system can completely shut off to elemenate any threats from reaching the tenants such as chemical toxic gases or natural causes like rain, sand storms or wind.

The web system surface act as a gas mask protecting the tenants from any harm

create a web system. The tensile is prefabricated, assembled and folded before it gets to the site. The system is created in a way that functions like an inverted umbrella and is easy to deliver and assemble once the steel structure is finished and set in place.

The steel cells will be prefabricated and assembled with a crane on site. The web system will only enclose the outside skin, and the inner faces, or "cells" will have the opportunity to merge, creating different space articulations and forms depending on the function and number of inhabitants. The outer skin will act as a toxic gas filter and protector from all natural causes as rain, wind and sun and in case of emergencies from smoke and chemical gases. The web system was designed to provide maximum flexibility and adaptability to be hosted on different surface, spaces and structures to provide damaged

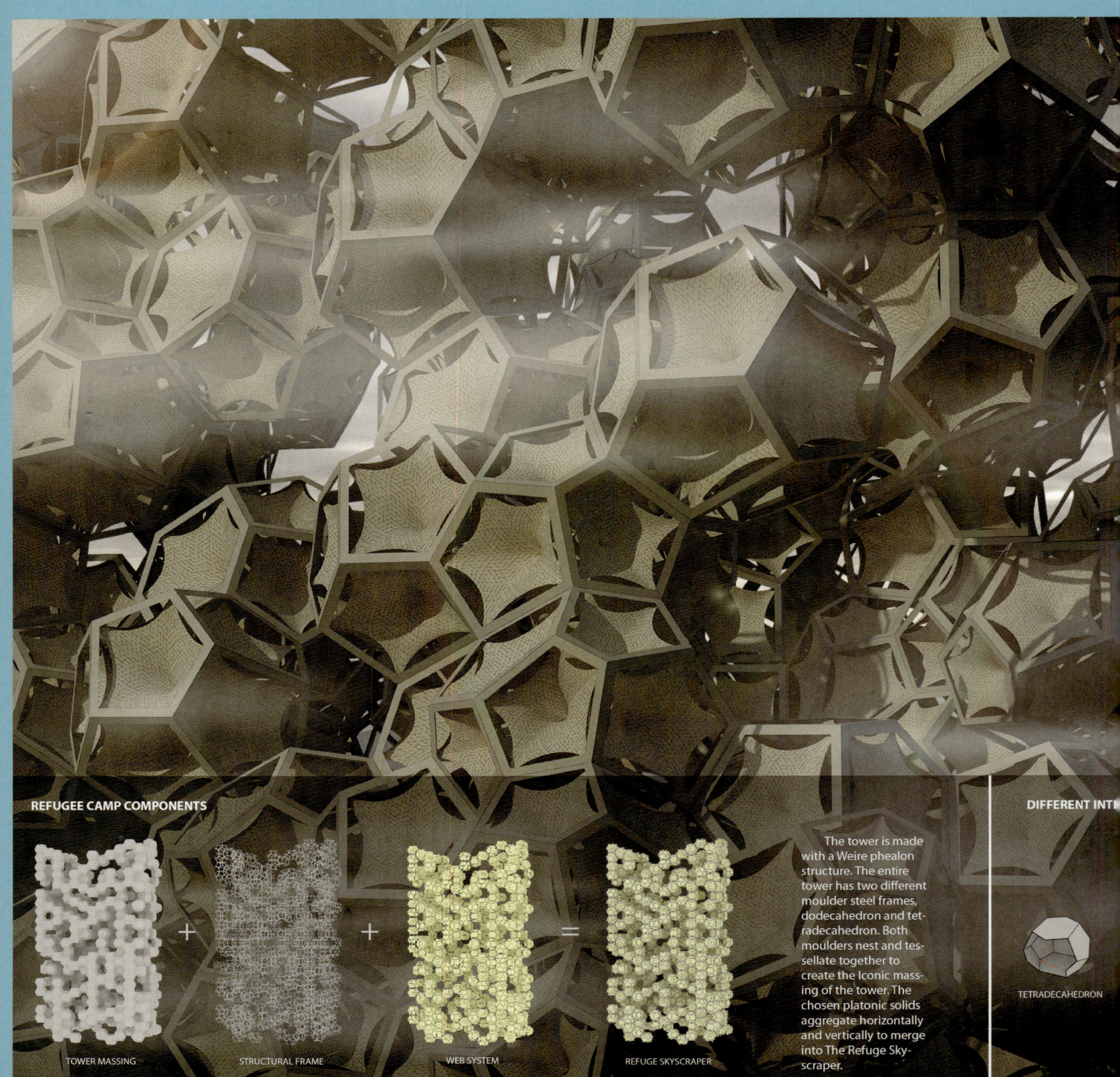

REFUGEE CAMP COMPONENTS

TOWER MASSING   STRUCTURAL FRAME   WEB SYSTEM   REFUGE SKYSCRAPER

The tower is made with a Weire phealon structure. The entire tower has two different moulder steel frames, dodecahedron and tetradecahedron. Both moulders nest and tessellate together to create the Iconic massing of the tower. The chosen platonic solids aggregate horizontally and vertically to merge into The Refuge Skyscraper.

DIFFERENT INT

TETRADECAHEDRON

buildings with a safe enclosure to benefit from existing infrastructure and minimize the need to immigrate.
The Zaatari refugee camp that is located in Jordan is being occupied with over 81,000 people as of July 2014. It's takes p an area of only 1.3 square miles. It was founded in 2012 after the beginning of the Syrian civil war. Its population started with 15,000 as of 2012 and grew more than four times as much in 2-3 years. With everything happening around the Middle East and most of the world, a new urban solution is needed to resolve the refugee camps crises. The tower is made with a Weaire Phelanstructure. The entire tower has two different modular steel frames, dodecahedron and tetra decahedron. Both modules nest and tessellate together to create the Iconic massing of the tower. The chosen platonic solids aggregate horizontally and vertically to merge into The Refugee Skyscraper.

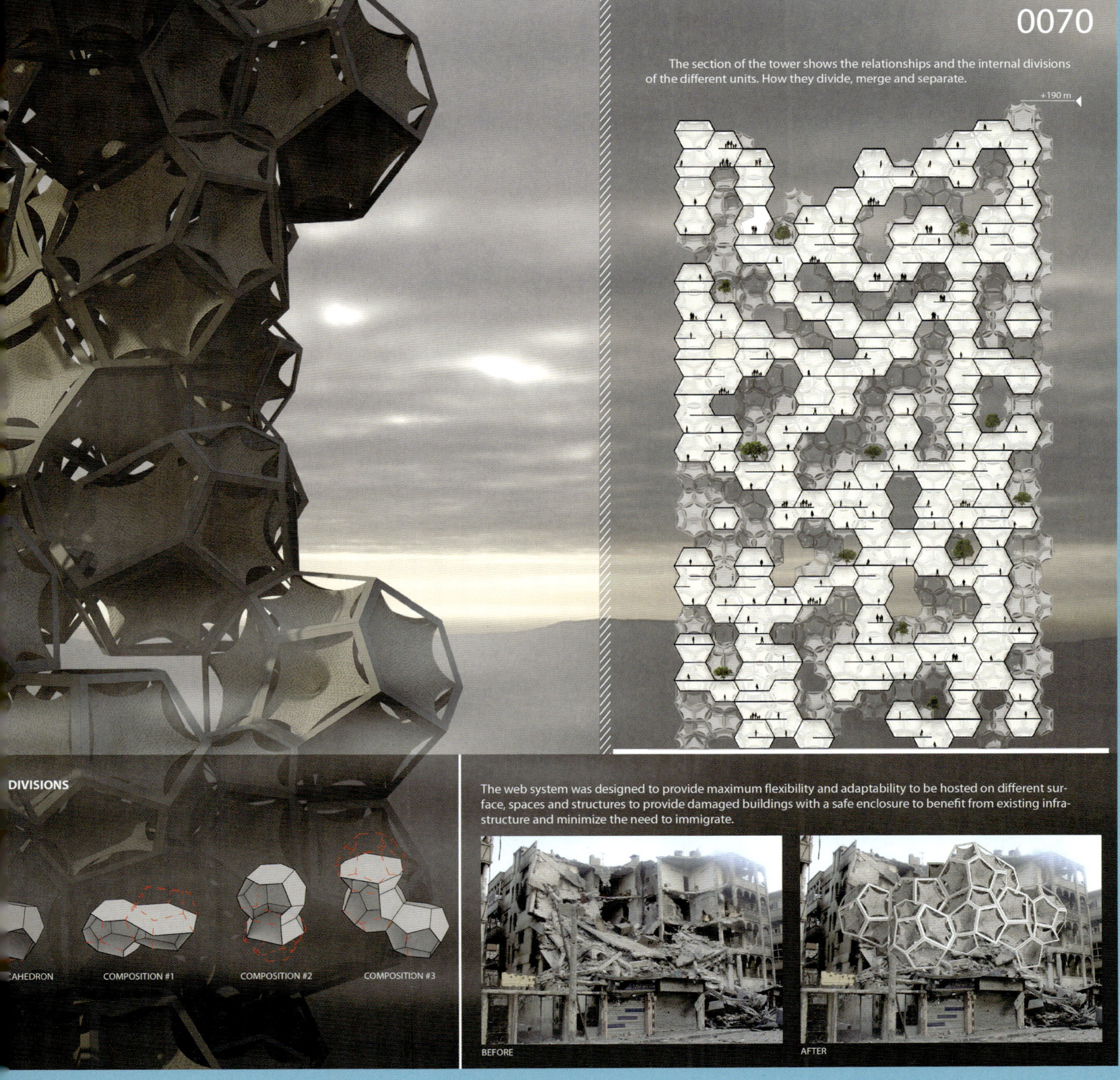

0070

The section of the tower shows the relationships and the internal divisions of the different units. How they divide, merge and separate.

+190 m

DIVISIONS

AHEDRON   COMPOSITION #1   COMPOSITION #2   COMPOSITION #3

The web system was designed to provide maximum flexibility and adaptability to be hosted on different surface, spaces and structures to provide damaged buildings with a safe enclosure to benefit from existing infrastructure and minimize the need to immigrate.

BEFORE   AFTER

AFTERLIFE

Shiqi Ma
Ruizhi Wang

China

Humans are all going through a serious challenge of life and death in overcrowded cities. With population explosion and birth of super-cities, cities are facing huge survival challenges, like the reduction of available land and lack of cemeteries within cities, which will make it more and more difficult to provide everyone with a final resting space.

In many countries, death affects the spiritual line of a family. It is natural that the graveyard becomes a permanent building and be located in local area. But this land cannot be used by the living. Consequently, cemeteries begin to swallow more and more green land within cities.

Before 2050, there will be no more land available to be exploited as cemeteries in big cities like London and New York. The dead will be forced to move out from cities and the living will lose the chance

AFTERLIFE   0079

Connecting the living and the dead in a new way

Identity of death worldwide

Human are all going through a serious challenge of life and death in metropolitans. With population explosion and appearance of supercity, cities are facing huge challenges for survival--reducing of available land and lacking of cemeteries within cities will make it more and more difficult to provide everyone with a resting pure-land equally.

Super density cemetery in Hongkong, each tomb costs for 30 million dollars, and the price is still growing;New Orleans,crowded tombs occupy green land;Vertical tombs pile in mountains in Petah Tikva.

Problem

1. In many countries,death affects spiritual line of a family.It is natural that graveyard becomes a permanent building and be located in local area. But those land can not be used by the living.Consequently, cemeteries began to swallow more and more green land within cities.

2. Before 2050, there will be no more land available to be exploited as cemetery in big cities like London and New York. The dead will be forced to move out from cities and the living will lose the chance to cherish the departed. A graveyard within cities will become a luxury for future humans.

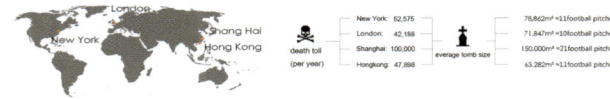

Site

This high-rise building is designed exclusively for super density city worldwide, and is located at super density areas like Macao and HongKong.There is no possibility for bucolic graveyard in HongKong.Graveyard needs to extend to higher floor to meet the demand of 600,000 people.

Concept

Consequently ,vertical tomb is destined to become an inevitable trend .In traditional culture ,graveyard is a dead land (negative space),its nature cannot be changed by simple verticality.Afterlife offers a container to store the dead's memory recource,switching the negative space into an energetic communicating space.

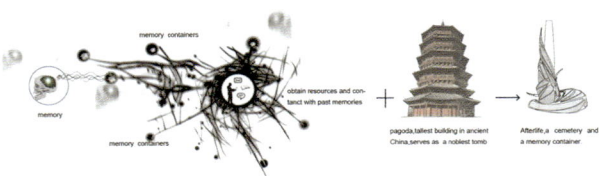

Memory container

The meaning of building begins with a container to store memory of the dead and a place to communicate with the living. If there is a membrane which can store memory and exchange energy, memory of the dead can be stored into chips and membranes, and their memory can not only communicate with their families, but also be a city information resource library,people can obtain instructive resources from memory bank ,which makes the living benefit a lot.

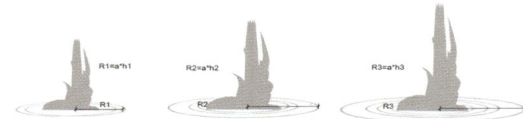

Afterlife acts as memory storage to serve near community; building height(h) depends on service radius(r) of the tower.

Dead land to living land, city energy resource

Vertical graveyard which was just used for memorizing becomes active because of storage of human memory and information, and it turns into a information sharing and checking platform—city memory library.Countless leaves which contain chips of memory grow up along with core-tube, and radius of information spread and service increases gradually along with height.

These leaves can also act as collectors of city resource, using advanced materials to transform sunlight to electricity.

to cherish the departed. A graveyard within cities will become a luxury for future humans.

Consequently, vertical tombs are destined to become an inevitable trend, In traditional culture, a graveyard is a negative space, and its nature cannot be changed by simple verticality. Afterlife offers a container to store the dead's memory resource, switching the negative space into an energetic communicating space.

The purpose of the building begins with a container to store the memory of the dead and a place to communicate with the living. If there is a membrane which can store memory and exchange energy, memory of the dead can be stored into chips and membranes, and their memory can, not only communicate with their families, but also be a city information resource library, where people can obtain

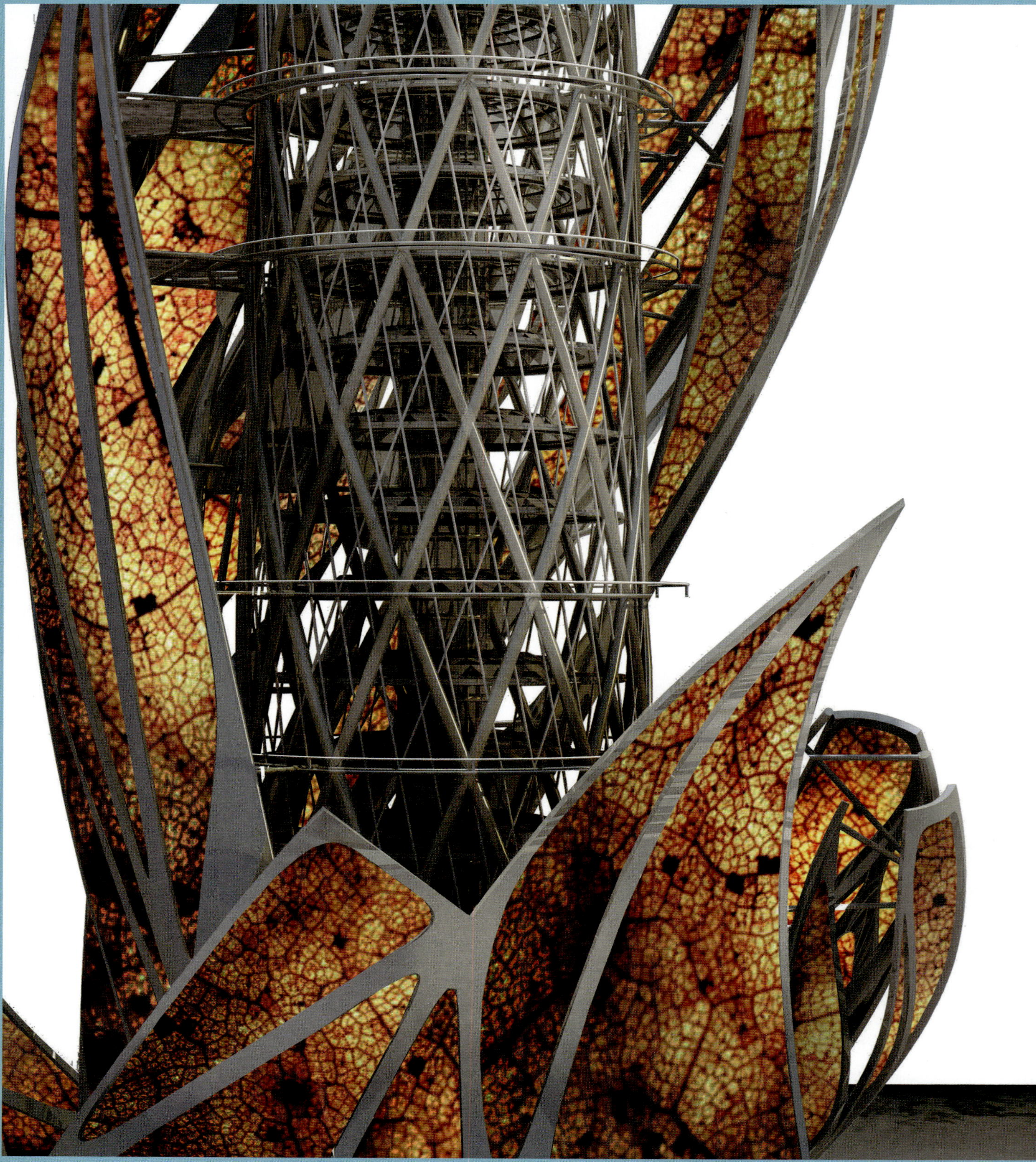

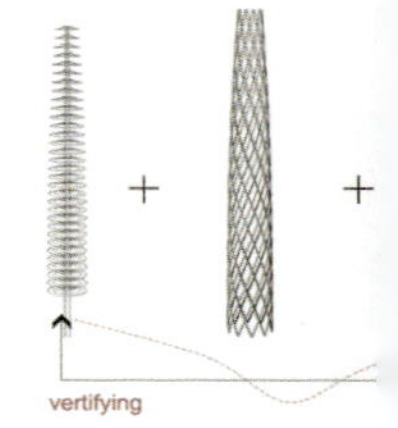

vertical tombs   main structure

+   +

vertifying

Memories are safe Vertical tombs
"inside leaves" and conveyed to tom

Air Cemetery People are buried
and solace.

Air Cemetery People are buried
sunshine through the "leaves",gives

← **Energy to the city**

memories and ashes f

instructive resources from memory banks, which can benefit the living quite a lot.

A vertical graveyard, which was just used for memorializing, becomes active because of its storage of human memory and information, and it turns itself into an information sharing and checking platform – a city memory library. Countless leaves, which contain chips of memory, grow along with core-tube, and a radius of information spreads and service increases gradually along with height. These leaves can also act as collectors of city resources, using advanced materials to transform sunlight into electricity.

0079

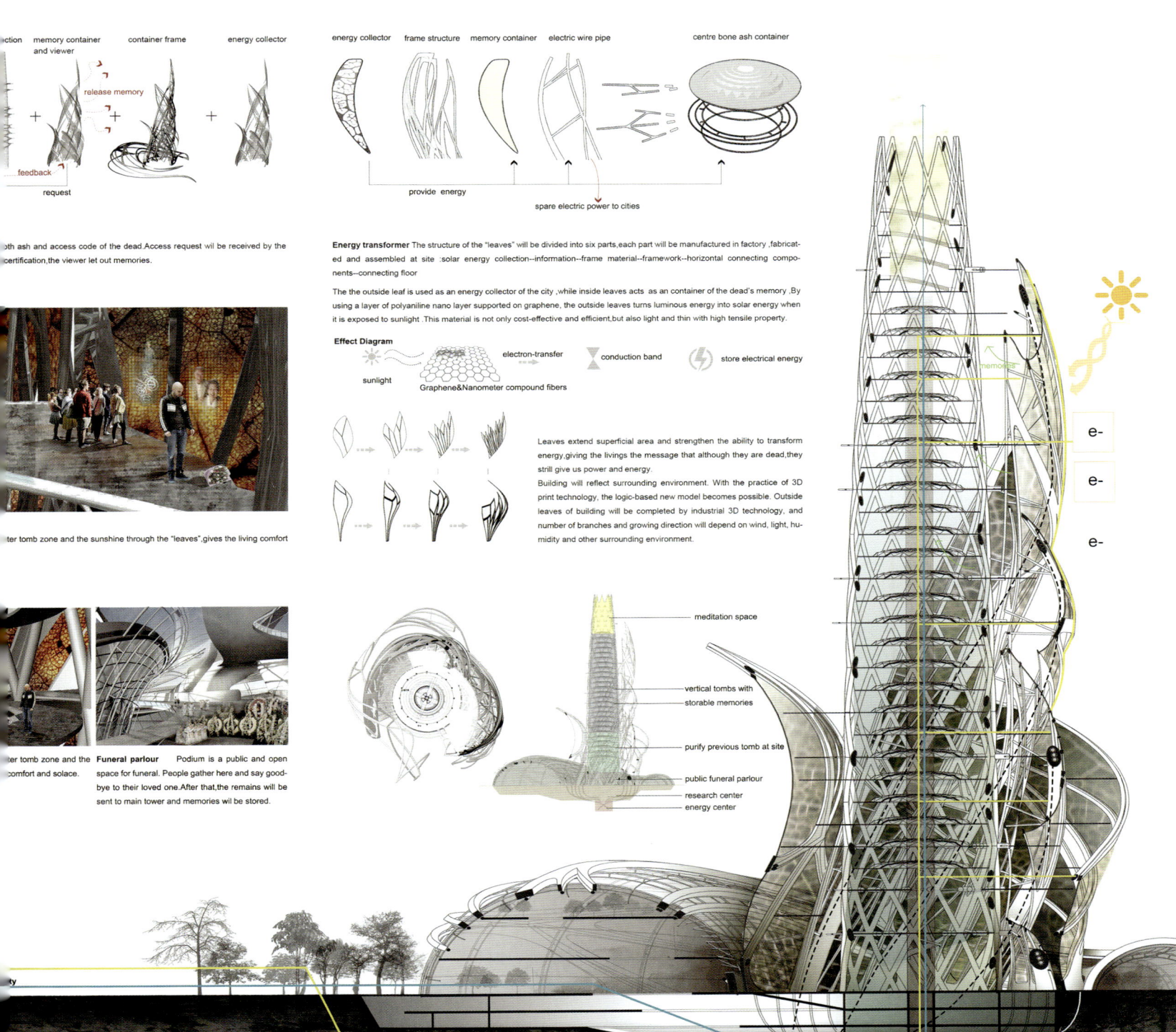

memory container and viewer   container frame   energy collector

release memory

feedback

request

both ash and access code of the dead.Access request will be received by the certification,the viewer let out memories.

energy collector   frame structure   memory container   electric wire pipe   centre bone ash container

provide energy

spare electric power to cities

Energy transformer The structure of the "leaves" will be divided into six parts,each part will be manufactured in factory ,fabricated and assembled at site :solar energy collection--information--frame material--framework--horizontal connecting components--connecting floor

The the outside leaf is used as an energy collector of the city ,while inside leaves acts as an container of the dead's memory ,By using a layer of polyaniline nano layer supported on graphene, the outside leaves turns luminous energy into solar energy when it is exposed to sunlight .This material is not only cost-effective and efficient,but also light and thin with high tensile property.

Effect Diagram

electron-transfer   conduction band   store electrical energy

sunlight   Graphene&Nanometer compound fibers

Leaves extend superficial area and strengthen the ability to transform energy,giving the livings the message that although they are dead,they strill give us power and energy.

Building will reflect surrounding environment. With the practice of 3D print technology, the logic-based new model becomes possible. Outside leaves of building will be completed by industrial 3D technology, and number of branches and growing direction will depend on wind, light, humidity and other surrounding environment.

ter tomb zone and the sunshine through the "leaves",gives the living comfort

ter tomb zone and the   **Funeral parlour**   Podium is a public and open
comfort and solace.   space for funeral. People gather here and say goodbye to their loved one.After that,the remains will be
sent to main tower and memories will be stored.

meditation space

vertical tombs with
storable memories

purify previous tomb at site

public funeral parlour
research center
energy center

e-

e-

e-

INVISIBLE PERCEPTION: SHANTY-SCRAPER

Suraksha Bhatla
Sharan Sundar

India
United Kingdom

2ND PLACE / 2015

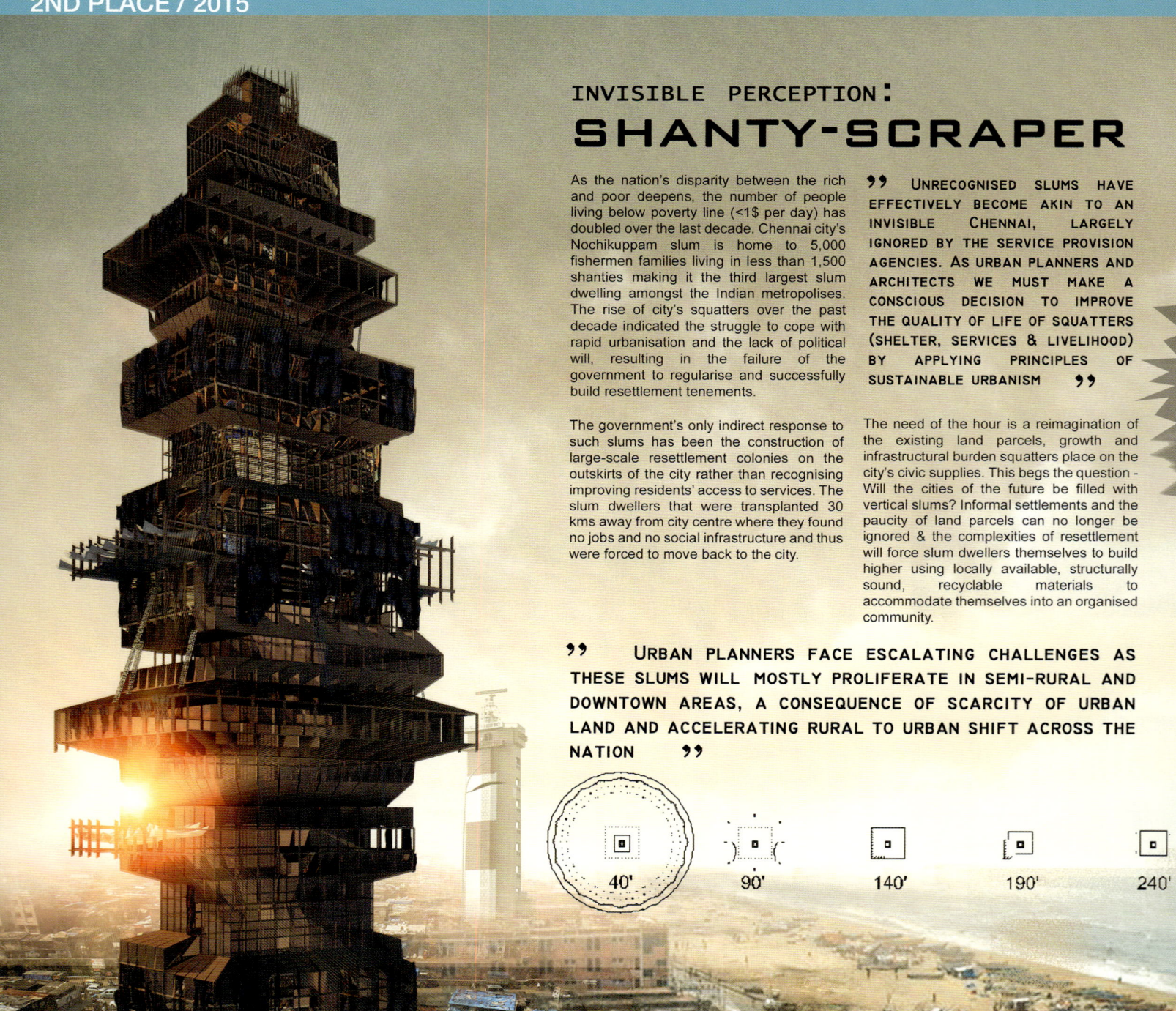

INVISIBLE PERCEPTION:
SHANTY-SCRAPER

As the nation's disparity between the rich and poor deepens, the number of people living below poverty line (<1$ per day) has doubled over the last decade. Chennai city's Nochikuppam slum is home to 5,000 fishermen families living in less than 1,500 shanties making it the third largest slum dwelling amongst the Indian metropolises. The rise of city's squatters over the past decade indicated the struggle to cope with rapid urbanisation and the lack of political will, resulting in the failure of the government to regularise and successfully build resettlement tenements.

The government's only indirect response to such slums has been the construction of large-scale resettlement colonies on the outskirts of the city rather than recognising improving residents' access to services. The slum dwellers that were transplanted 30 kms away from city centre where they found no jobs and no social infrastructure and thus were forced to move back to the city.

" UNRECOGNISED SLUMS HAVE EFFECTIVELY BECOME AKIN TO AN INVISIBLE CHENNAI, LARGELY IGNORED BY THE SERVICE PROVISION AGENCIES. AS URBAN PLANNERS AND ARCHITECTS WE MUST MAKE A CONSCIOUS DECISION TO IMPROVE THE QUALITY OF LIFE OF SQUATTERS (SHELTER, SERVICES & LIVELIHOOD) BY APPLYING PRINCIPLES OF SUSTAINABLE URBANISM "

The need of the hour is a reimagination of the existing land parcels, growth and infrastructural burden squatters place on the city's civic supplies. This begs the question - Will the cities of the future be filled with vertical slums? Informal settlements and the paucity of land parcels can no longer be ignored & the complexities of resettlement will force slum dwellers themselves to build higher using locally available, structurally sound, recyclable materials to accommodate themselves into an organised community.

" URBAN PLANNERS FACE ESCALATING CHALLENGES AS THESE SLUMS WILL MOSTLY PROLIFERATE IN SEMI-RURAL AND DOWNTOWN AREAS, A CONSEQUENCE OF SCARCITY OF URBAN LAND AND ACCELERATING RURAL TO URBAN SHIFT ACROSS THE NATION "

40'   90'   140'   190'   240'

Pragmatically, building adequate amounts of resettlement housing to house all slum-dwellers in India will simply take too long, require vast amounts of land and cost the city 1 billion rupees. Moreover, many residents do not necessarily desire such housing: reports indicate that nearly 20 % of allotted homes are vacant and 50 per cent of the original beneficiaries are no longer living in them, subletting them instead. Clearly, this was due to the fact that slum dwellers were transplanted 30 kilometers away from city center where they found no jobs and no social infrastructure and thus were forced to move back to the city. A far more reasonable strategy would be to implement the Tamil Nadu Slum Clearance Act in the spirit that it was written, and start to recognize slums and improve them in situ. The sky-high rentals in Chennai's downtown and the fight for survival in India's slums such as Nochikuppam are increasingly

blurring the lines between center and periphery. Urban planners face escalating challenges as these slums will mostly proliferate in semi-rural and downtown areas, a consequence of scarcity of urban land and accelerating rural to urban shift across the nation. Unrecognized slums have effectively become akin to an invisible Chennai, largely ignored by the service provision agencies. As urban planners and architects we must make a conscious decision to improve the quality of life of squatters (shelter, services & livelihood) by applying principles of sustainable urbanism. The need of the hour is a re-imagination of the existing land parcels, growth and infrastructural burden squatters place on the city's civic supplies. This begs the question - Will the cities of the future be filled with vertical slums? Informal settlements and the paucity of land parcels can no longer be ignored & the complexities of resettlement will force slum dwellers themselves to build higher using locally available, structurally sound, recyclable materials

accommodating themselves into organized communities. Shanty-Scraper aspires to provide a unique solution for the fishermen of Nochikuppam located at Marina bay beach. The vertical squatter structure predominately is comprised of post-construction debris such as pipes and reinforcement bars that crucially articulate the structural stability. Recycled corrugated metal sheets, regionally sourced timber & thatch mold the enclosure of each dwelling profile and lend to their vernacular language. The double height semi enclosures serve as utility yards & social gathering spaces. The vertical transportation is fragmented into multiple plank lifts that are constructed from a simple mechanically driven lever & pulley contraption. The rhythmic timber lattice membrane structure at the ground level, houses the public seafood market, & forms the first level of defense against future tsunamis.

0131-2

INVISIBLE PERCEPTION:

SHANTY-SCRAPER

Shanty Scraper aspires to provide a unique solution for the fishermen of Nochikuppam. The vertical squatter structure predominately comprises of post construction debris such as metal pipes & reinforcement bars that crucially articulate the structural stability. Recycled corrugated metal sheets, in situ concrete adobe blocks, regionally sourced timber & thatch mould the enclosure of each dwelling profile and lend to their vernacular language.

The concept is driven by the masses, their demand for social spaces, growing sporadically & random in character emulating the settlement pattern of Nochipakkam.

99 ANTICIPATED AS A SELF-BUILD PROJECT THIS TOWER EPITOMISES THE SUSTAINABLE VERNACULAR URBANISM OF THE NEW ERA. **99**

These low cost, low-tech, low embodied materials not only positively impact the city's recycling policy but also provides respite to the excessive dependence on glass as seen in modern archtypes.

The architecture congregates into the market place, where local fishermen sell their catch.

99 IT IS A VIBRANT CONCLAVE OF THE HAVE-NOTS AND THE URBAN COMMUNITY THAT MUTUALLY UNITE IN COMMERCE **99**

The circular timber braced lattice structure is elevated with roped abutments, fastened to the ground. The tensile roof conjugates into an array of enclosed sloping posts that form the circular framework and contribute to the rhythmic constitution. Above grade, the social cores exist in the peripheral corridors overlooking the sea. These double height semi enclosures serve as utility yards as well as social hubs.

The vertical transportation is comprised of fragmented multiple ladders that intra link communities. Plank lifts are constructed from a simple mechanically driven lever & pulley contraption that ferry the slum dwellers to the top. The pinnacle culminates into an unfinished spire, allowing room for future expansion.The high rise typology also serves as a vantage point for the fishermen to gauge high risk waters during potential emergencies.

99 THE PINNACLE CULMINATES UNFINISHED, GIVEN FUTURE EXPANSION. THE HIGH RISE TYPOLOGY SERVES AS A VANTAGE POINT FOR THE FISHERMEN TO GAUGE HIGH RISK WATERS & EMERGENCIES. **99**

VERNACULAR SKY-TERRACE

KHZNH Studio

Amir Izzat Adnan
Nur Farhanah Saffie

Malaysia

Vernacular Sky-Terrace

Presentation of Issues

City populations are growing faster than the city infrastructure can adapt. The world's cities are growing because of population shift especially concerning rural to city areas in search of jobs and other opportunities in hopes for improvement of lives and creating better future for the younger generations. Along with the growth and expansion of cities, comes the rise in environmental issues and problems. It comes to the role of future architects, planners and developers to achieve green and sustainable strategies where modern buildings can rely on new forms of energy.

Horizontal Skyscrapers as Possible Solution

Although most skyscrapers provide solutions of catering the density of population with the spaces they provided as compared to the available space on land, it is highly argued that they do not provide good street-level experience that hence, totally disconnect the street cultures from vertical structures. This disconnection has led to the difficulties, in a case of high-rise apartment living, for families to experience the community living where the proximity to other facilities available in street culture is higher instead of being constrained in the walls and perimeter of the vertical structures they live in.

The exploration of horizontal skyscraper aims to offer dwellers a maximum recreational experience almost as much as living on the ground or surface of the streets. This horizontal skyscraper is building a community where neighborhood qualities and everyday life practices are carried through. People relate to these living environments as part of their identity and, thus, neighborhood community living becomes personally meaningful and relevant. In fact, studies have shown that people who live in close-knit communities are statistically safer and less likely to be burglarized.

Program Identification

Family Oriented
Resident Facilities
Recreation
Green Tech

Aim Land Use Percentage

53% Residential
22% Commercial Unit
23% Public Facility
2% Office Unit

Architecture Profil

KHZNH Studio-Vernacular Sky-Terrace

By honoring the culture of the nature setting, the Vernacular Sky-Terrace invites visionary ideas for Kampung Baru to become a better city without 'touching' the existing fabric. The basic idea for this project is to elevate the existing site and improvise. The decision of hovering over the existing site is inspired by the aims to create one community consisting of office spaces, apartments, commercial area and public landscape also to generate the largest possible green space open to the public, right in the heart of Kuala Lumpur city.

The overall design comprises of three primary components. They are structure and services, staggered modules and pitched roofs. Firstly, structure and services, which are large supports equipped with ducts carrying service functions that include water, electric, plumbing, and air conditional supply,

0195-01

Vernacular Sky-Terrace

which is transferred from the land up into the building. Next, the module, which is arranged in staggered manner. The arrangement is responsible to maximize the view as well as to prevent overshadowing the area below. This also allows different programs being implied through different levels. The third component of the building is the pitched roof. The triangle prism shape of the roof relates to the traditional Malay house roof characteristic, emerging with the site below.

In term of programs, Vernacular Sky-Terrace is simply divided into public spaces and private spaces. The public area consists of a community park and garden, retail, shops, and a lake, which completes the artificial ecosystem within the building. On the other hand, the private spaces include apartment units, which are restricted for the residences and service controls, which are accessible only by the administration.

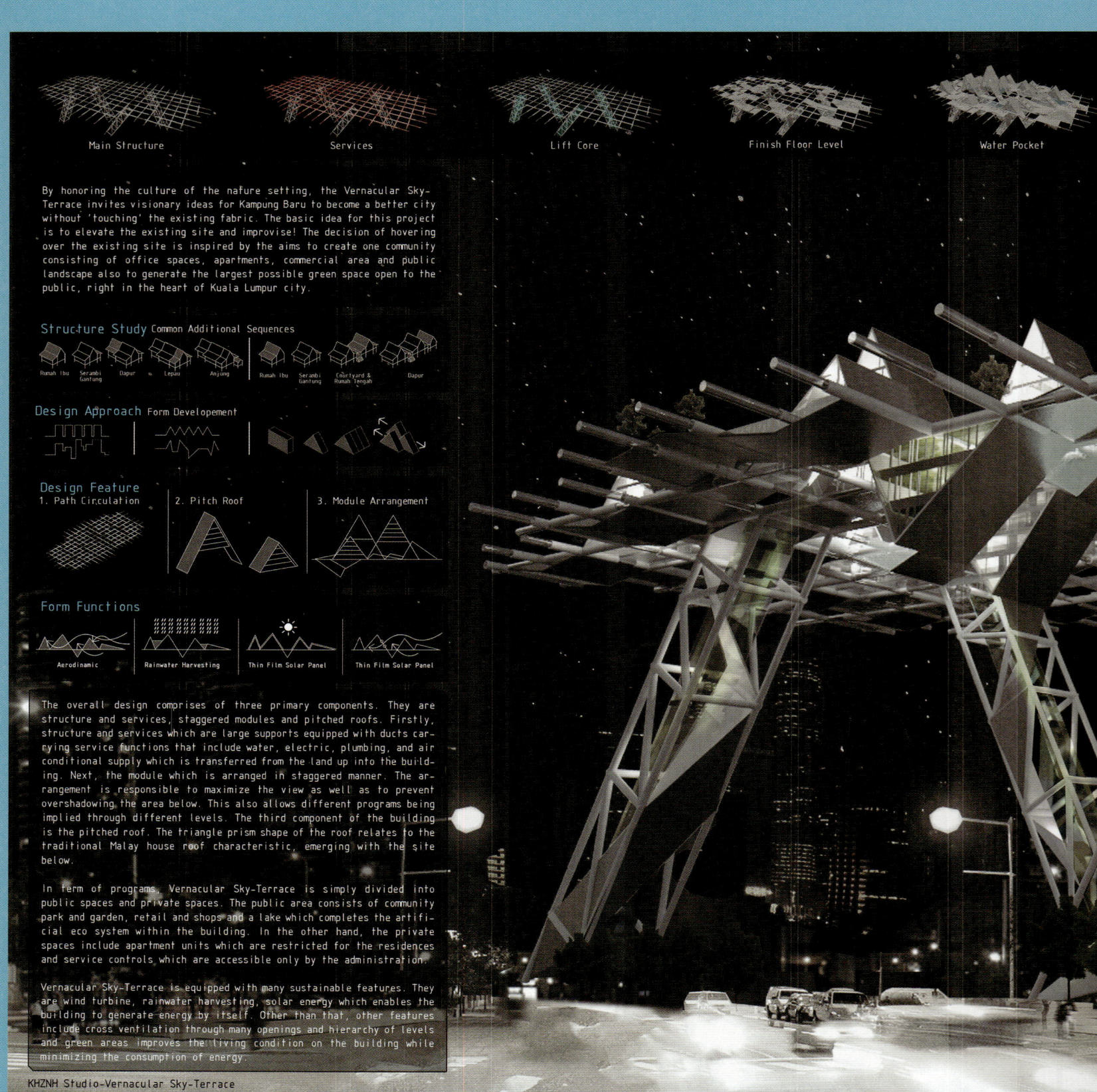

Main Structure   Services   Lift Core   Finish Floor Level   Water Pocket

By honoring the culture of the nature setting, the Vernacular Sky-Terrace invites visionary ideas for Kampung Baru to become a better city without 'touching' the existing fabric. The basic idea for this project is to elevate the existing site and improvise! The decision of hovering over the existing site is inspired by the aims to create one community consisting of office spaces, apartments, commercial area and public landscape also to generate the largest possible green space open to the public, right in the heart of Kuala Lumpur city.

Structure Study Common Additional Sequences

Rumah Ibu   Serambi Gantung   Dapur   Lepau   Anjung   Rumah Ibu   Serambi Gantung   Courtyard & Rumah Tengah   Dapur

Design Approach Form Developement

Design Feature

1. Path Circulation   2. Pitch Roof   3. Module Arrangement

Form Functions

Aerodinamic   Rainwater Harvesting   Thin Film Solar Panel   Thin Film Solar Panel

The overall design comprises of three primary components. They are structure and services, staggered modules and pitched roofs. Firstly, structure and services which are large supports equipped with ducts carrying service functions that include water, electric, plumbing, and air conditional supply which is transferred from the land up into the building. Next, the module which is arranged in staggered manner. The arrangement is responsible to maximize the view as well as to prevent overshadowing the area below. This also allows different programs being implied through different levels. The third component of the building is the pitched roof. The triangle prism shape of the roof relates to the traditional Malay house roof characteristic, emerging with the site below.

In term of programs, Vernacular Sky-Terrace is simply divided into public spaces and private spaces. The public area consists of community park and garden, retail and shops and a lake which completes the artificial eco system within the building. In the other hand, the private spaces include apartment units which are restricted for the residences and service controls which are accessible only by the administration.

Vernacular Sky-Terrace is equipped with many sustainable features. They are wind turbine, rainwater harvesting, solar energy which enables the building to generate energy by itself. Other than that, other features include cross ventilation through many openings and hierarchy of levels and green areas improves the living condition on the building while minimizing the consumption of energy.

KHZNH Studio-Vernacular Sky-Terrace

Vernacular Sky-Terrace is equipped with many sustainable features. There are wind turbines, rainwater harvesting, and solar energy, which enable the building to generate energy by itself. Other than that, additional features include cross ventilation through many openings and hierarchy of levels and green areas improves the living condition on the building while minimizing the consumption of energy. Apart from personal usage like socializing and entertainment, the Internet has contributed so much in aiding global development as a whole, especially through the economy. In conjunction with Vernacular Sky-Terrace, we came up with the idea to associate the potential of Internet with its development. The idea is to allow access for the clientele (developer, architect, entrepreneur etc.) to an interface, which is responsible for real time planning of the project, which includes land expansion, upgrading of structure, and choosing the residential units/floor based on provided modules for purchase.

0195-02

Green & Community Area   Residential   Commercial   Vistas   Respond to Climate

Internet as Technological Injections

Apart from personal usage like socializing and entertainment, the internet had contributes so much in aiding global development as a whole especially economy. In conjunction with Vernacular Sky-Terrace, we came up with the idea to associate the potential of internet with its development. The idea is to allow access for the client (developer, architect, entrepreneur etc.) to an interface which is responsible for real time planning of the project which includes land expansion, upgrade of structure or choosing the residential units/floor based on provided module for purchase. This will attract more users in investing in the project as well as expanding possibilities for its growth.

REMINISCENCE

Panitnan Patanayindee
Eakapob Huangthanapan

Thailand

Reminiscence
MOUNT MERU

What is the point of living when one is oblivion to the essence of one's life.
In the future era, technological advancements and globalized norms spread
throughout the globe. Human could find ways to prevent and solve phenomenon
considered threats to mankind. Through fast-paced developments, people can finally
feel safe with a promising future where environmental problems and such are no
longer dreadful apprehension but an obsolete anxiety of the past. Digital advancement becomes a part of human life. Everything is within our reach and people strive
less to live. People thought to be
salvaged from the past conjecture of future decays and continue to find ways to
commit the everlasting betterment, physically...

The project reminiscence Mount Meru represents the mythical Mountain Meru,
believed to be the ancient center of the universe and the world. The mountain's
geometry and concept were long implied within the Buddhist architecture and
fostered within the cultural fabric of Thailand. The built structure is no ordinary
skyscraper as it also resembles the revitalized trend of temple among the jungles of
man-made environment. In the period wherephysical superficiality is being prioritized
over the mind. The period when Thailand tight knots of spiritual cultures starts to
loosen with people's mental states fluctuate within the fast-paced global developments. The reminiscence of Mount Meru served to function as what the
traditional temple did during the period of moral deterioration, a place of spiritual
refuge.

In recent years people have strived their best to construct skyscrapers that impress
and satisfy the physical needs. The project Reminiscence Mount Meru is a skyscraper
that value the preservation of traditional cultures, especially with its site in Thailand,
and enhances beyond physical impressions and could possibly towards the
enlightenment of an
individual's spirit.

PLAN

The project Reminiscence: Mount Meru represents the mythical Mountain Meru, believed to be the ancient center of the universe and the world. The mountain's geometry and concept were long implied within the Buddhist architectural typology and fostered within the cultural fabric of Thailand. The built structure is no ordinary skyscraper, as it also resembles the revitalized trend of temple among the jungles of man-made environment. In the period where physical superficiality is being prioritized over the mind, he period when Thailand tight knots of spiritual cultures starts to loosen with people's mental states fluctuate within the fast-paced global developments, the Reminiscence of Mount Meru serves to function as what the traditional temple did during the period of moral deterioration, a place of spiritual refuge.

   The project consists of three major compositions, which are the core tower, the outer shells and the

0298

intertwining curves of circulation. Also on ground levels are areas provided for traditional festive events and a sanctuary for animals. As Eastern philosophy states, all living things should be appreciated and human beings should not think of themselves as superior. The erected inner tower provides an area for temple ceremonies and complexes, in the upper floor, some areas for meditation are provided. Living in the digital era, people strive less to survive with the aids of technological gadgets and appliances. People use less of their brains and occupy too much information within their heads. The act of meditation is proved to aid and enhance the brain's activities. The structure has an intertwining route of pathways for individuals to walk with careful consciousness. It is wrapped with segments of shells that seclude the individuals from the outside world. The pathways also represent the journey of life in circular movement

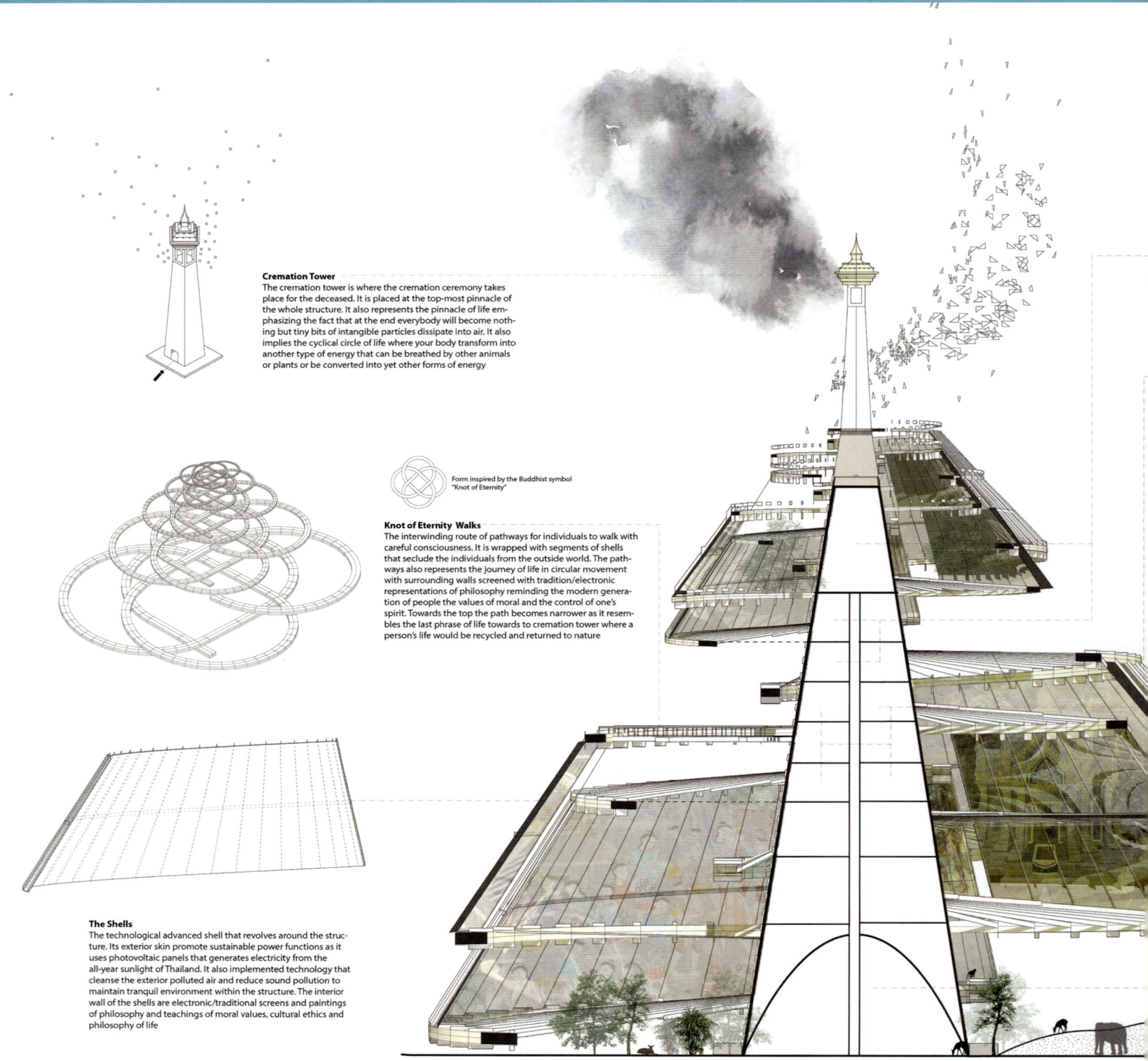

Cremation Tower
The cremation tower is where the cremation ceremony takes place for the deceased. It is placed at the top-most pinnacle of the whole structure. It also represents the pinnacle of life emphasizing the fact that at the end everybody will become nothing but tiny bits of intangible particles dissipate into air. It also implies the cyclical circle of life where your body transform into another type of energy that can be breathed by other animals or plants or be converted into yet other forms of energy

Form inspired by the Buddhist symbol "Knot of Eternity"

Knot of Eternity Walks
The interwinding route of pathways for individuals to walk with careful consciousness. It is wrapped with segments of shells that seclude the individuals from the outside world. The pathways also represents the journey of life in circular movement with surrounding walls screened with tradition/electronic representations of philosophy reminding the modern generation of people the values of moral and the control of one's spirit. Towards the top the path becomes narrower as it resembles the last phrase of life towards to cremation tower where a person's life would be recycled and returned to nature

The Shells
The technological advanced shell that revolves around the structure. Its exterior skin promote sustainable power functions as it uses photovoltaic panels that generates electricity from the all-year sunlight of Thailand. It also implemented technology that cleanse the exterior polluted air and reduce sound pollution to maintain tranquil environment within the structure. The interior wall of the shells are electronic/traditional screens and paintings of philosophy and teachings of moral values, cultural ethics and philosophy of life

with surrounding walls screened with tradition/electronic representations of philosophy reminding the modernized generation of people the value of morals and the control of one's own spirit. Towards the top, the path becomes narrower as it resembles the last phase of life towards the cremation tower where the cremation ceremony takes place for the deceased. It is placed at the top-most pinnacle of the whole structure. It also represents the pinnacle of life emphasizing the fact that, at the end, everybody will become nothing but tiny bits of intangible particles dissipated into the air. It also implies the cyclical circle of life where your body transforms into another type of energy that can be breathed by other animals or plants or be converted into yet other forms of energy. An emphasis that a person's life would be recycled and returned to nature.

Temple Complex & Sacred artifacts
Mostly the upper floors are space occupied by traditional temple complexes that combined together all the horizontal locations of temple facilities into vertical temple complex.

Representation of the mythical Mount Meru

Meditation center & Research
A lot of interior spaces are provided as areas for meditation. As later meditation is proved to help enchance brain activities. The activity is being promoted as an important routine for the deteriorating brains of modernized generations. There is also research center on meditation and brain activities.

Ceremonial Hall
The multi-purpose hall but mostly a space where traditional ceremonies are held

Traditional Buddhist Chedi /Stupa

Animal Sanctuary
Not only is this place a spiritual sanctuary for human but it is also as well for the animals. As to fulfill the Eastern philosophy of valuing all living things as precious lives not only human being as the superior

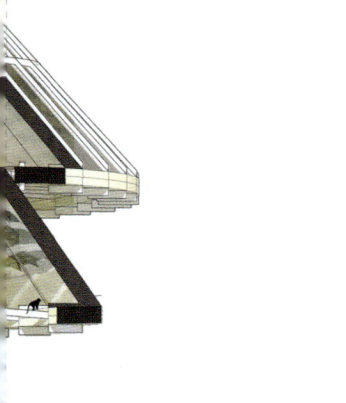

The Reminiscene of Mount Meru

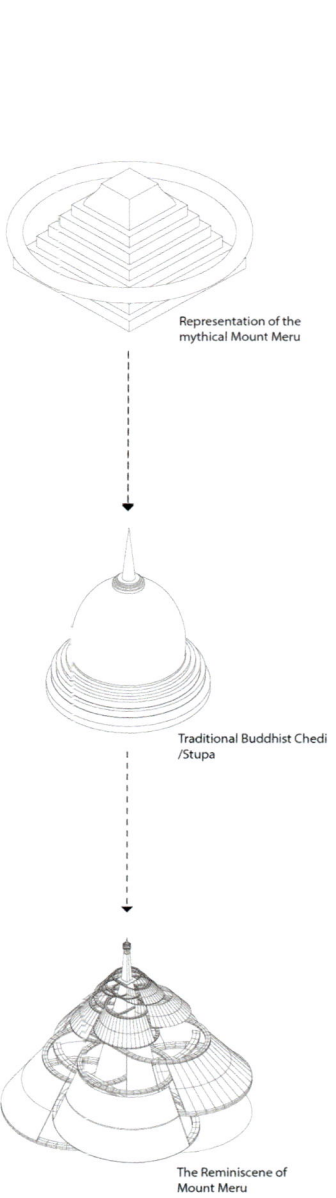

0298

LIMESTONE SKYSCRAPER

Jethro Koi Lik Wai
Quah Zheng Wei

Malaysia

DESIGN STATEMENT

Limestone hills that are mined are doomed to suffer total annihilation, or become remnance of a souless terrain. This design approach seeks to intervene the process of mining, turning it into a mere "site clearance and earthwork" phase to allow buildings to be erected within, adapting to the sophisticated and ever so beautiful terrain of the karsk topography. This in turn, creates a building within a mountain, harnessing the natural resources of existing stones and minerals on site to be used as the construction materials eg. marble, travertine. The Architecture serves as a compliment to the monolithic beauty in its original state, bringing a different life and purpose to the mining hill sites.

Li Jiang River, Guilin China,

SCENIC BEAUTY

Karsk Topography, commonly known as Li____ soluble rocks such as limestone, dolomite, ____ ated with hills and downland, and occurs in ____ derground drainage systems with sinkhole ____

A trip to these areas will allow one to witne____ minding ourselves of a higher power scapie____ als forms interesting textures and surface____

Notable karsk topographies are located at ____ Forest, Madagascar.

DEATH OF OUR M

These towering natural monuments withs____ stances. Mining of these substances not ____ as flash floods and landslides. Therefore, ____ mining the natural resources.

Limestone has numerous uses: as a build____ pigment or filler in products such as tooth____

Limestone hills that are mined are doomed to suffer total annihilation, or become remnants of a soulless terrain. This design approach seeks to intervene the process of mining, turning it into a mere "site clearance and earthwork" phase to allow buildings to be erected within, adapting to the sophisticated and ever so beautiful terrain of the Karsk topography.

These towering natural monuments withstood the tests of time, until humans begin to mine their substances. Mining of these substances not only creates an eye sore, it also increases calamities such as flash floods and landslides. Therefore, it is vital that proper treatment has to be applied upon mining of the natural resources.

Limestone materials have numerous uses: mainly as building materials, as aggregate for the base of

b Halong Bay, Vietnam

e Hills, is a landscape formed from the dissolution of sum over millions of years. They are usually associ- with other sedimentary rocks, characterized by un- s, and caves.

ealithic monuments arranged in a natural setting, re- eauty of this earth. As the precipitation of the miner- ls to be tourist attractions.

River, Guilin China, Viet Nam, Halong bay and Karst

NTAINS

ests of time, until humans begin to mine their sub- es an eye sore, it also increases calamities such at proper treatment has to be applied upon

al, as aggregate for the base of roads, as white paints, and as a chemical feedstock.

ARCHITECTURE INTERVENTION

The confrontation of architecture and limestone hills provides unprecedented oppurtunities in space exploration. Far beyond the conventional floorplate, limestone architecture derives new spatial experience and programs through intergration of rocky surface and architecture

While caves are known for low sun light illumination which often thwart the growth of most vegetations, this architecture begs to differ. Utilizing multiple blocks massing which allows sun penetration between blocks, the buildings provide green living environment for the residents besides recovering hillside vegetaion. Other than that, it also mitigates limestone mountain surface erosion.

Water is easily sourced contextually, which implies greater wastage. In this case, grey water will be utilized to water the surface vegetation while waste water will be treated and discharge to nearby plants.

REGISTRATION NUMBER : 0351

SKY COMMUNITY DECK

BIRD NEST FARM

VERTICAL SURFACE PLANTATION

WELLBEING DECK

CAVE ROCK CLIMBING

LANDSCAPE DECK

GREY WATER RUN-OFF

RESIDENTIAL SPACE

LEISURE MALL

MOUNTAIN URBAN SQUARE

LAKESIDE PARK

TREATED WATER DISCHARGE

roads, as white pigment or filler in products such as toothpaste or paints, and as a chemical feedstock. This in turn, creates a building within a mountain, harnessing the natural resources of existing stones and minerals on site to be used as the construction materials eg. marble, travertine.

The architecture serves as a compliment to the monolithic beauty in its original state, bringing a different life and purpose to the mining hill sites.

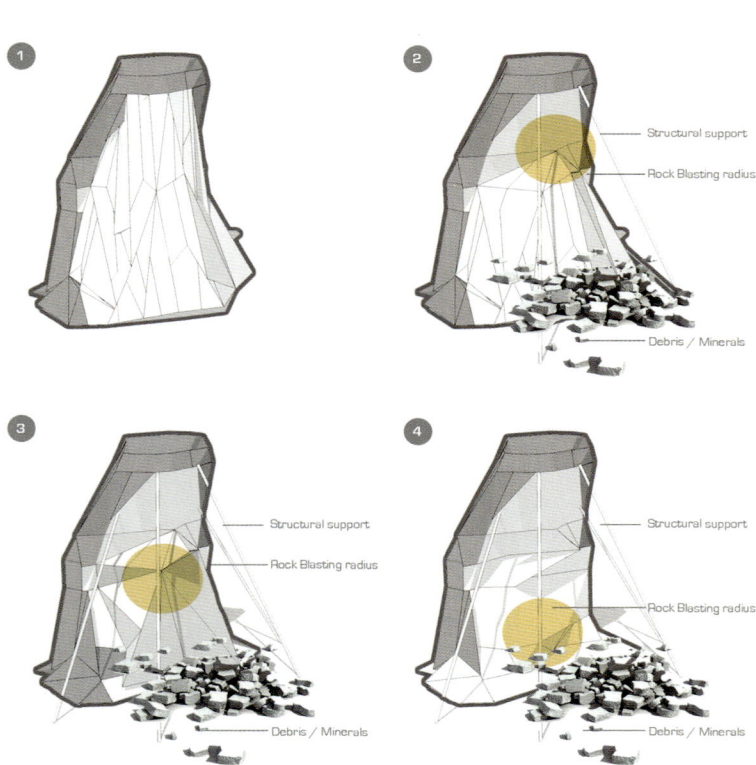

LIMESTONE MINING

[1] Suitable limestone hill designated for limestone mining

[2] Reinforced rods are used to support the peak of the mountain.
First sequence of controlled blasting is right below the structural rod support.

[3] Blasting proceeds to the centre of the hill. More structural rods are introduced to prevent the hill from collapsing.

[4] Final blasting is at the foot of the hill, Mineral and rocks are transported

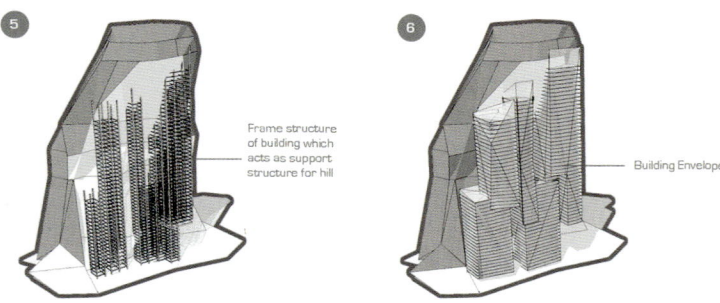

LIMESTONE ARCHITECTURE

[5] The empty shell of the limestone hill is then reinforced with steel structures which acts as the frame structure of the building

[6] Building envelope is then installed onto the frame structure creating beautiful spaces underneath the limestone.

CONCEP SCALABILITY

The concept of re-using any limestone mining site can be further explored to different types of monolithic mountains as well as mountain belts with architecture that truly adapts itself to the surrounding terrain. However, it is imperative that proper planning of limestone mining has to take place to create a city-scape of monumental buildings.

REGISTRATION NUMBER: 0351

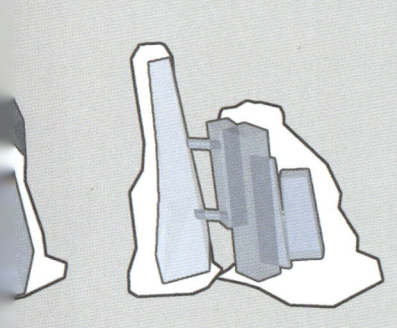
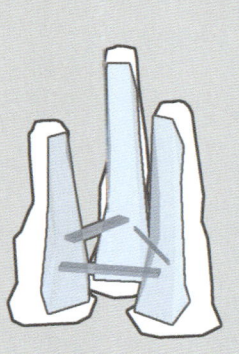

MAREA

Brittany Cameron

Canada

View into St John Harbour. The series of towers in the water act as the creates a picturesque and iconic gateway into the city.

MAREA

Marea, meaning tidal, is a skyscraper located in the future hyperdense city of St. John, NB. Due to the increased need for oil export, the town has a possibility to expand rapidly. Instead of expanding outwards, Marea addresses notions of vertical hyperdensity as well as using the areas natural resources for energy generation.

The most direct route from the cultural centre to the industrial centre in St. John is across the Bay of Fundy. To accommodate the increase in population density, the most efficient method of mass transportation is a gondola system. The towers required for the gondola create an opportunity to develop a vertical city, part of which spans across the Bay of Fundy.

Tidal power is one of the most effective and underused methods of energy generation. The Bay of Fundy, with 10m tidal differentials offers extreme opportunities to generate vast amounts of renewable energy. Marea capitalizes on the tidal energy of the bay of Fundy, providing electricity to the tower and the surrounding community. It is both residential and commercial, offering live-work opportunities and easy access to rapid transit

South-West elevation

Commercial Centre

St John Harbour

Bay of Fundy

Marea

Industrial Centre

North-East elevation

The year is 2030 and St. John New Brunswick is expanding rapidly due to its ideal location for oil and LNG export. Instead of expanding outwards, the possibility of a vertical city is considered. Marea, meaning tidal, is a skyscraper that forms one of the gondola towers connecting the cultural centre to the industrial centre in St. John. Marea addresses notions of vertical hyper density, as well as using the areas natural resources for energy generation.

When considering hyper density, it is also important to consider both land and water. A network system across the Bay of Fundy and St. John Harbor would cut commute times for workers in half. Additionally, a network spanning across the water allows for skyscrapers to be created in the water that are no longer isolated, but part of a new, innovative and efficient city. The most efficient transportation

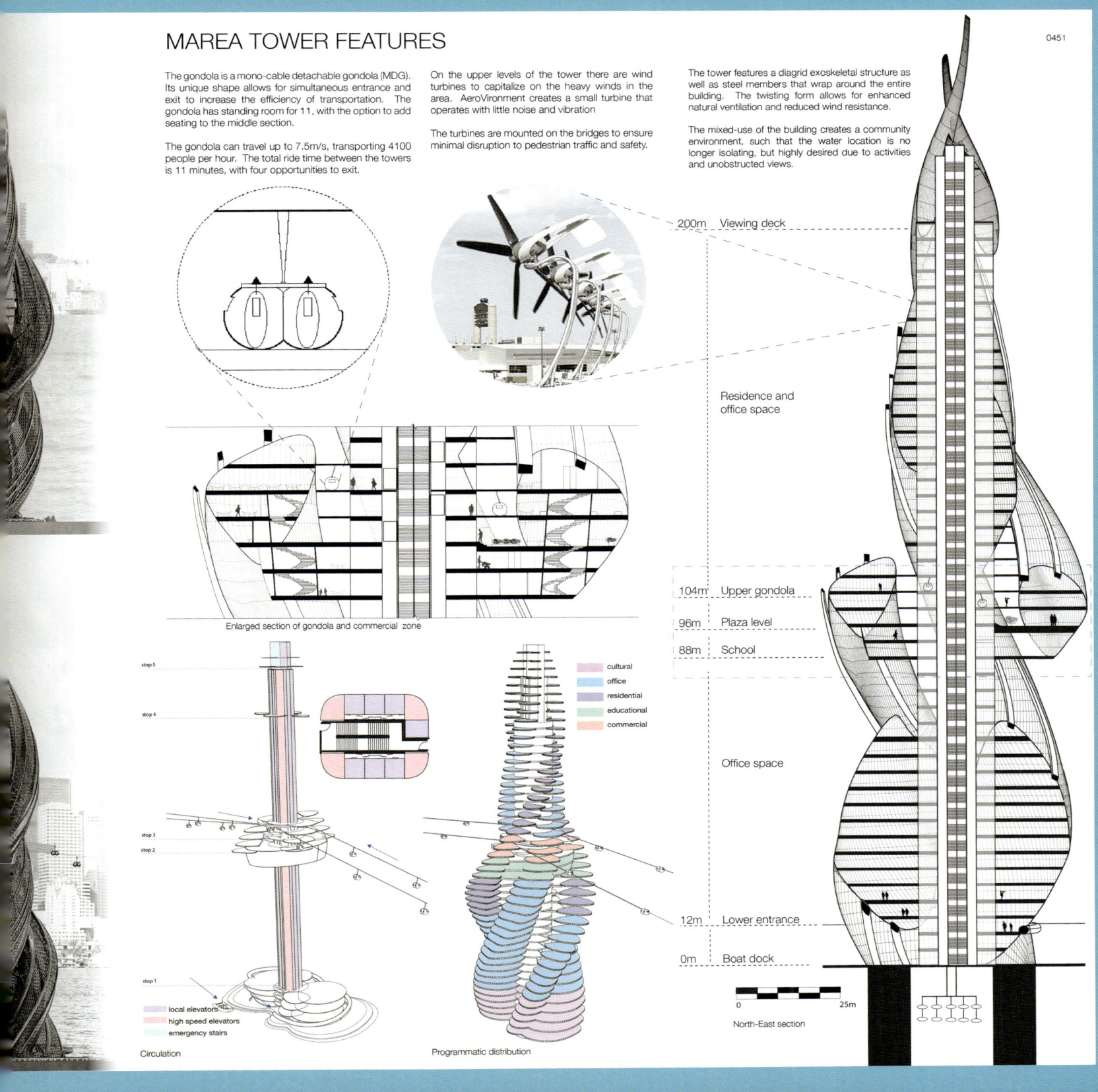

MAREA TOWER FEATURES

0451

The gondola is a mono-cable detachable gondola (MDG). Its unique shape allows for simultaneous entrance and exit to increase the efficiency of transportation. The gondola has standing room for 11, with the option to add seating to the middle section.

The gondola can travel up to 7.5m/s, transporting 4100 people per hour. The total ride time between the towers is 11 minutes, with four opportunities to exit.

On the upper levels of the tower there are wind turbines to capitalize on the heavy winds in the area. AeroVironment creates a small turbine that operates with little noise and vibration

The turbines are mounted on the bridges to ensure minimal disruption to pedestrian traffic and safety.

The tower features a diagrid exoskeletal structure as well as steel members that wrap around the entire building. The twisting form allows for enhanced natural ventilation and reduced wind resistance.

The mixed-use of the building creates a community environment, such that the water location is no longer isolating, but highly desired due to activities and unobstructed views.

200m   Viewing deck

Residence and office space

Enlarged section of gondola and commercial zone

104m   Upper gondola

96m   Plaza level

88m   School

cultural
office
residential
educational
commercial

Office space

stop 5

stop 4

stop 3
stop 2

12m   Lower entrance

0m   Boat dock

stop 1

local elevators
high speed elevators
emergency stairs

0   25m

North-East section

Circulation

Programmatic distribution

vessel across the water would be a new, high speed gondola. The gondola design takes technology from around the world and integrates it into a high speed, mass transport system.

The Bay of Fundy is also unique in that it has the highest tides in the world. 10m tidal differentials would allow the entire city to be powered by the tide. One tower alone could power up to 4000 homes. Marea capitalizes on the tidal energy of the Bay of Fundy, providing electricity to the tower, the gondola system and the surrounding community.

Marea is innovative in program and design. The tower could be considered a small community. Residents have the ability to live and work within the tower. Residential and commercial zones are integrated, allowing new opportunities for interaction. Additionally, there is a school and many cultural

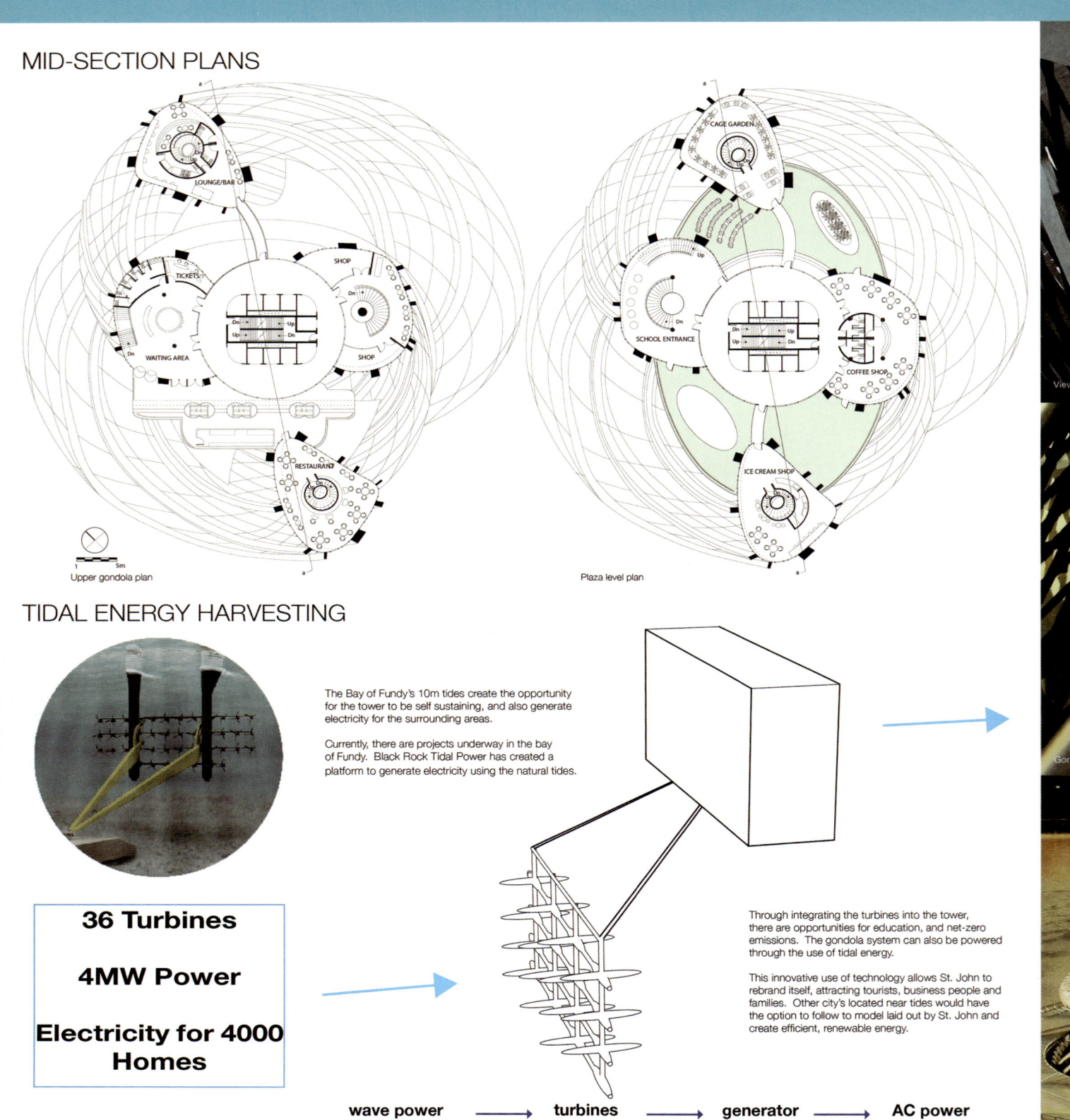

MID-SECTION PLANS

Upper gondola plan

Plaza level plan

View from the plaza

Gondola and plaza

Base of the tower

TIDAL ENERGY HARVESTING

The Bay of Fundy's 10m tides create the opportunity for the tower to be self sustaining, and also generate electricity for the surrounding areas.

Currently, there are projects underway in the bay of Fundy. Black Rock Tidal Power has created a platform to generate electricity using the natural tides.

Through integrating the turbines into the tower, there are opportunities for education, and net-zero emissions. The gondola system can also be powered through the use of tidal energy.

This innovative use of technology allows St. John to rebrand itself, attracting tourists, business people and families. Other city's located near tides would have the option to follow to model laid out by St. John and create efficient, renewable energy.

36 Turbines

4MW Power

Electricity for 4000 Homes

wave power ⟶ turbines ⟶ generator ⟶ AC power

and commercial experiences. The design allows the tower to be a beacon in the water. Its iconic nature, similar to that of a piece of driftwood rising out of the water, acts as the gateway to the community. The design is also efficient and innovative, considering minimizing wind resistance and maximizing air circulation.

DRILLSHIP DAM

Kyung Sun Min
Ju Hyun Byun

South Korea

DRILLSHIP DAM

: Infrastructure to maintain homeostasis

Case : International River

In 2006 the defence minister of U.K. warned that, there would be violent and political clashes related to water within 20~30 years time as there the desertification has been going along here and there globally because of the global warming.

Recently the importance of water has been growing in the international society due to the global worming, so there has been political disputes between nations related to water and the core of these disputes are the international river. The international river is the river flows though multi nations or the border of multi nations, and all over the world more than 300 rivers flow through more than 2 nations, and 35~40% of world population of more than 50 nations is living in the basin of international river.

As multi nations shares the international river there are various concerns. The most common case of international river dispute is the dam construction of upper river country, that would reduce the water flow to lower river country, and this may create the secondary problems such as environmental contamination, ecosystem change, and increase of disease. The examples are the Tigris river, the Euphrates river, the Nile river, the Indus river and the Mekong river.

River of conflict : Mekong River

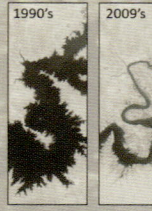

1990's   2009's

The Mekong river is the base of tens of million of Indo-China peninsula people, that supplies water for irrigation, allows fishing for living. So it is the river of lifeline. The Mekong river is the base of so many residents of China, Thailand, Laos, Myanmar and Cambodia. Today the Mekong river is the triggering point of disputes, river of thirst, no more lifeline.

China, locates at upper region of the Mekong river, has constructed 2 large dams in 1996 and 2003 to prepare the drought and flood, and two more dams in 2010. This dam construction by China makes severe reduction of water flow to lower river nations, Laos, Myanmar, Vietnam, Thailand and Cambodia, so that they have faced the problems of water contamination, disease and ecosystem change by severe draught. So this dispute between upper river nation and lower river nations caused by dam construction of upper Mekong river becomes a trouble of international society.

Using an abandoned oil rig (Drillship)

The drillship is a special ship to drill the bottom of sea for oil exploration and divided into two groups, for coastal use and deep sea use. The average life time of the drillship is 20~25 years, and more than 1,500 drillships are abandoned in the international waters near around U.S.A.. Further more about 4,000 drillships are going to stop its operation within this century. These drillships, abandoned or planned to stop operation, have many problems for their future usage. It costs huge money to dismantle these abandoned drillship, but it would create environmental contamination as well as to be a heavy dummy on the sea difficult to remove.

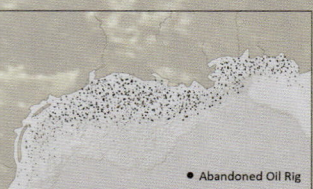

● Abandoned Oil Rig

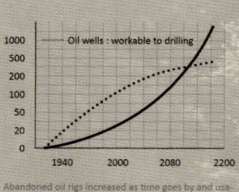

Oil wells : workable to drilling

Abandoned oil rigs increased as time goes by and usable oil wells increase relatively decreased.

Concept

It is utilizing the abandoned drillships, thousands all over the world. The drillship is movable and the possibility of recycling facilities are very high. This our proposal can solve the disputes between nations sharing international water, and provide a new possibility of reusing the abandoned drillship which has to be a garbage on the sea.

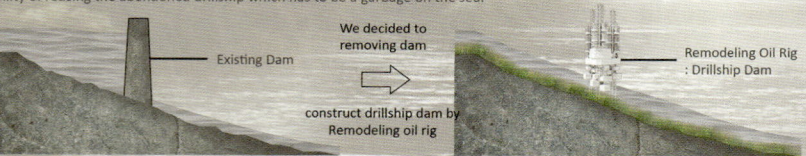

Existing Dam

We decided to removing dam

construct drillship dam by Remodeling oil rig

Remodeling Oil Rig : Drillship Dam

Recently the importance of water has been growing in the international society due to the global warming, so there has been political disputes between nations related to water and the core of these disputes are the international river. The most common case of international river dispute is the dam construction of upper river country, that would reduce the water flow to lower river country, and this may create the secondary problems such as environmental contamination, ecosystem change, and increase of disease. The Mekong river is the base of tens of million of Indo-China peninsula people, that supplies water for irrigation, allows fishing for living. So it is the river of lifeline. The Mekong River is the base of so many residents of China, Thailand, Laos, Myanmar and Cambodia. Today the Mekong River is the triggering point of disputes, river of thirst, no more lifelines. China, locates at upper region of the

0489

Mekong river. has constructed 2 large dams in 1996 and 2003 to prepare the drought and flood, and two more dams in 2010. This dam construction by China makes severe reduction of water flow to lower river nations, Laos, Myanmar, Vietnam, Thailand and Cambodia, so that they have faced the problems of water contamination, disease and ecosystem change by severe draught. So this dispute between upper river nation and lower river nations caused by dam construction of upper Mekong River becomes a trouble of international society. To solve this international river dispute, we are here proposing completely new type of dam that can replace the function of dam required by mankind, which is the fundamental reason of the international river dispute. The facilities are discarded drillship, more than a thousand over the world. We have named the facility as Drillship Dam. The biggest advantage of Drillship Dam is natural circulation of the water, which purifies the water and discharges or stores certain quantity continuously,

Drillship Dam's ecological effect

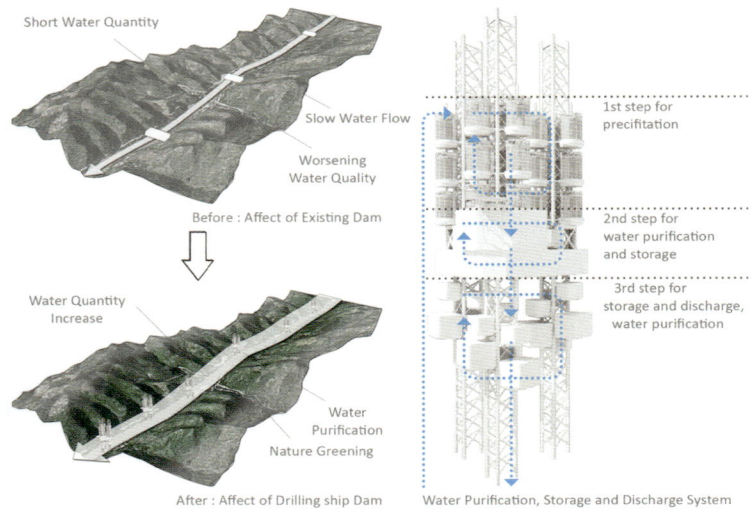

Short Water Quantity

Slow Water Flow

Worsening Water Quality

Before : Affect of Existing Dam

Water Quantity Increase

Water Purification

Nature Greening

After : Affect of Drilling ship Dam

1st step for precipitation

2nd step for water purification and storage

3rd step for storage and discharge, water purification

Water Purification, Storage and Discharge System

Storage Type

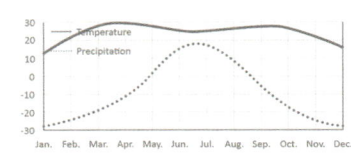

Considering the specific environmental conditions of the Mekong river basin, tropical monsoon climate, big difference of rain fall between rainy season and dry season, the discharging water quantity can be controlled by season.

For the dry season, to prepare the low water flow of Mekong river the type should be capable to discharge large volume of water. In this type most of modules are taking discharging system.

Type 1

On the contrary for the rainy season, the water flow of Mekong river is high, so to prepare the risk of flood the water discharge is minimized and water storage type module is increased. In this season most of modules are closing water exit and storing water.

Type 2

Drillship Dam System

Precipitation System

To purify the pumped water this part takes settling function. Settling is the first step of purification process, by settling impurities in the water, dissolving oxygen and uv sterilizing by ultra violet lay. By locating this facility at very high position, the water can be exposed to very strong ultra violet lay. The precipitate is to be dried to make it solid, then can be used as fuel for power plant. The water after settling will be pipe to filtering system.

House for Victim

Imbalance of a rate of flow by international dams cause lots of nature disaster. It causes many victims as well and Drillship Dam is systematized for victims from nature disaster and has dwelling function where they can live in. Housing features of Drillship Dam for victims are comprised of prototypes which can accommodate people from a few numbers to a large family.

Filtering System

This filtering section was for the sea water storage space in old drillship. In this process the water shall pass through multiple layers of micro particles. So it needs very large space and this space is suitable.

Water storage and Discharge System

This part is to store and discharge water section. So the most important function of dam. Each module has a power system for forced circulation, and control discharging water volume according to the average water level of river so that to keep certain water level of the river as well as flexible control of discharging water to prepare the seasonal change such as flood or draught.

House for Victim

Imbalance of a rate of flow by international dams cause lots of nature disaster. It causes many victims as well and Drillship Dam is systematized for victims from nature disaster and has dwelling function where they can live in. Housing features of Drillship Dam for victims are comprised of prototypes which can accommodate people from a few numbers to a large family. Imbalance of a rate of flow by international dams cause lots of nature disaster. It causes many victims as well and Drillship Dam is systematized for victims from nature disaster and has dwelling function where they can live in. Housing features of Drillship Dam for victims are comprised of prototypes which can accommodate people from a few numbers to a large family.

so that it can control the water flow of the river flexibly and remove the contamination possibility of stored water. And Imbalance of a rate of flow by international dams cause lots of nature disaster. It causes many victims as well and Drillship Dam is systematized for victims from nature disaster and has dwelling function where they can live in. Housing features of Drillship Dam for victims are comprised of prototypes, which can accommodate people from a few numbers to a large family. Imbalance of a rate of flow by international dams cause lots of nature disaster. It causes many victims as well and Drillship Dam is systematized for victims from nature disaster and has dwelling function where they can live in. The Drillship Dam can solve not only the dispute between nations caused by the international river but also provide more useful and eco-friendly life to mankind and ailing environment.

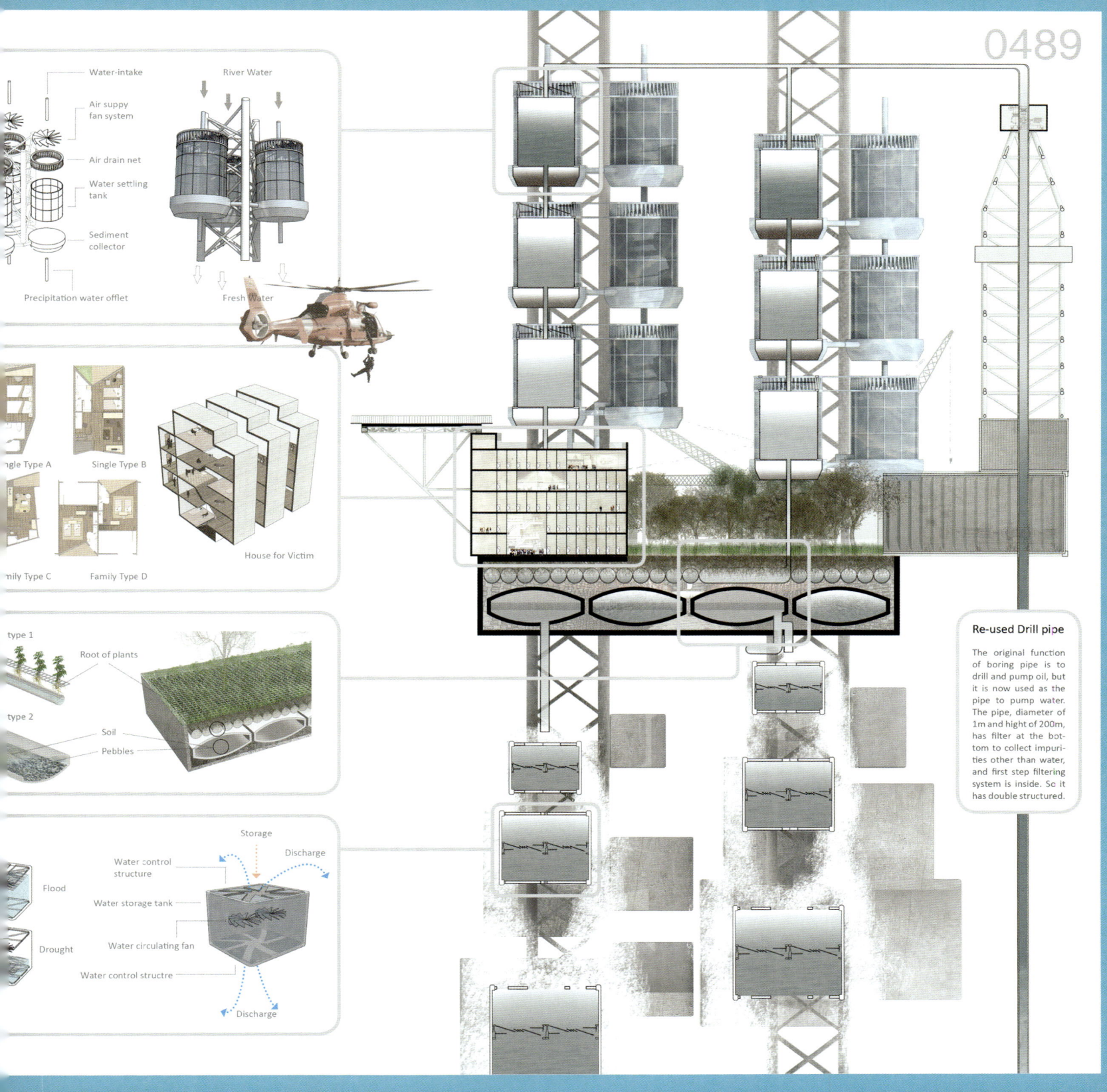

0489

Water-intake
River Water
Air suppy fan system
Air drain net
Water settling tank
Sediment collector
Precipitation water offlet
Fresh Water

Single Type A
Single Type B
Family Type C
Family Type D
House for Victim

type 1
Root of plants
type 2
Soil
Pebbles

Storage
Discharge
Water control structure
Flood
Water storage tank
Water circulating fan
Drought
Water control structre
Discharge

Re-used Drill pipe

The original function of boring pipe is to drill and pump oil, but it is now used as the pipe to pump water. The pipe, diameter of 1m and hight of 200m, has filter at the bottom to collect impurities other than water, and first step filtering system is inside. So it has double structured.

REBUILDING OF THE VALLEY

Du Xinchi
Dong Xiaohuan

China

Case

In June 2003, the Three Gorges Dam was completed. A hydropower station with maximum power output in the world was born. The primary purpose of this construction is to control the flood. The second one is to provide power for the upper and middle reaches of the Yangtze River. The third one is to reduce the transportation cost from Shanghai to Chongqing to improve the trade efficiency. Although the Three Gorges Dam has brought huge profits to China, it also cause many irreparable problems.

Immigration

During the period of 2003-2009, the level of upstream water had reached 175m from 60m. This change resulted in 113 million people who had lived a long time there facing the 'migration' problem. Losing and gaining both took place in front of the immigrants. Many of them had shed tears.

Landscape

The completion of the Three Gorges Dam, along with the rising of the water level, has led this natural river become a huge artificial lake. The landscape of the steep valley has disappeared. Meanwhile, the poem which had been spread for hundreds of years describing the landscape couldn't be verified anymore. These are the painful lost of the Chinese civilization.

Conservation

The Yangtze River is well known as the birthplace of the Chinese civilization. The Three Gorges area once had created Daxi Culture, Bachu Culture and more. A large number of unearthed culture relics have showed the history of China and the wisdom of chinese ancestors. Thanks to those relics, people nowadays can know their ancestors better and also experienced the greatness of Chinese culture. But with the impoundment of the Three Gorges, many cultural relics would be buried in the bottom of the river forever, and we would lose the chances to learn about our own culture.

The Three Gorges project had also changed the fate of local animals and plants. There were many kinds of rare animals in the reservoir area of the Three Gorges. Bai Jitun which lived in the Yangtze River for 2500 million years had now on the verge of extinction. The Three Gorges project would even affect the existence and spread of an architectural from called Diaojiaolou.

Concept

Based on problems listed above, we decided to present the concept of rebuilding the canyon to solve these problems.

Rebuild

Through abstracting the canyon landscape, we extracted the image of Canyon ridge and then represented it to rebuild in a modern way and restore the steep feature of the Canyon.

No Pressure Container

We use the 'non pressure vessel' techniques to protect the relics under the river, which had been already used in the 'White Crane Ridge underwater museum' project. Its principle is to build protective structures around the outboard of the relics. Through using the filtering device to provide water, the internal and external pressure can reach a dynamic balance. Also, we build channels in the structure to let tourists to visit.

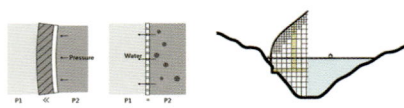

Pile Dwellings（吊脚楼）

The whole construction will use the form of Diaojiaolou. We abstract the chuandou wooden frame structure form and then use it in the framework construction of the whole struction. The residential units and public units are formed through connecting the wooden frames. In additon, we solve the immigrant issue by restoring Diaojiaolou and original ecological living style of the immigrants in the residential units

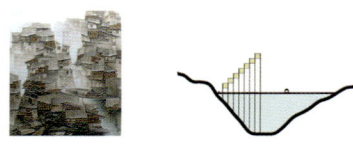

Being the world's largest hydropower station, the Three Gorges Dam has brought in huge profits to the nation, while simultaneously causing a series of difficult problems including the issue of immigration, disappearance of canyon scenery, and the protection of cultural relics and local creatures. In order to solve the aforementioned issues, we present the concept of "rebuilding the valley."

Our scheme is to abstract the landscape through extracting one side of the ridge curve of the canyon and using large-scale membrane structures to simulate the valley, so as to build a modern 'mountain' which combines with the original one to restore the steepness in the canyon landscape.

The form of 'Rebuilding valley' will use the principle of Chuandou wood frame in which the frames will form the entire structure through connecting the lateral-connected beams in series. In our scheme, the

0523

REBUILDING OF THE VALLEY

abstracted curves will form the main frame, which will be arranged together at regular intervals and be connected by the lateral-connected wood structures.

　　We decided to choose the traditional form of Diaojiaolou in Xiangxi in our design. Together with the large-scale membrane, the main frame will form the giant Diaojiaolou. The lateral-connected wooden frames will form multiple basic units after linking with one another. Public units and residential units will be divided according to their sizes. In the residential units, miniature Diaojiaolou are constructed so that the original life of the immigrants can be recovered. In addition, reserves for local animals and plants are set in the public units according to their relative functions. The Interactions between both kinds of units add a sense of depth and richness to the space to make our scheme even more remarkable.

REBUILDING OF THE VALLEY

There are reserves and research center of relics on the bottom layer of the whole construction. We use the techniques called 'non-pressure vessel' to protect the relics. Through utilizing the filtering device to provide water, the internal and external pressure can reach the dynamic balance. We also provide vertical transportations and platforms at the same time, so that it cannot only serve as spots to visit, but also protect the spiritual beliefs of the local residents.

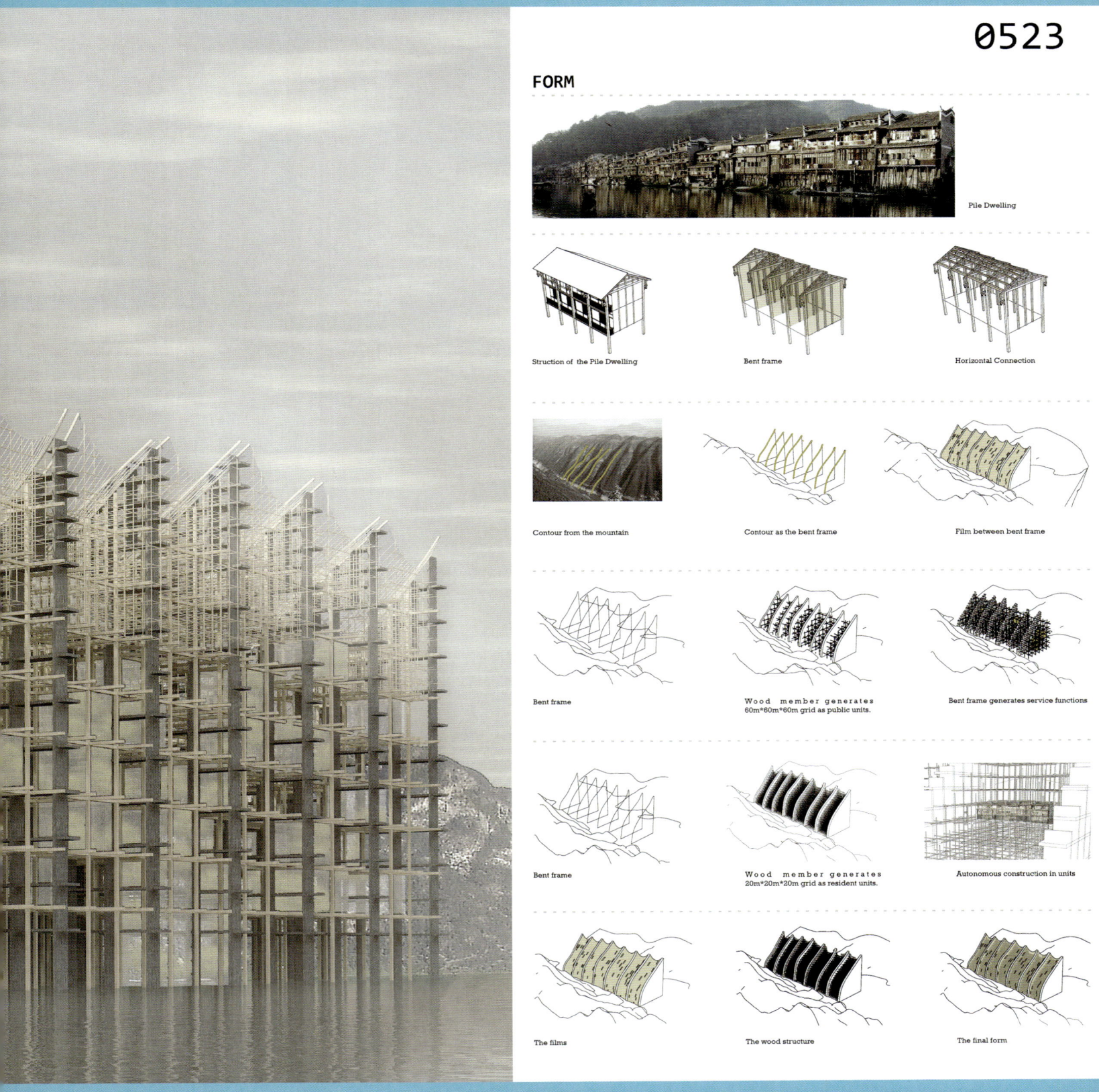

0523

FORM

Pile Dwelling

Struction of the Pile Dwelling

Bent frame

Horizontal Connection

Contour from the mountain

Contour as the bent frame

Film between bent frame

Bent frame

Wood member generates 60m*60m*60m grid as public units.

Bent frame generates service functions

Bent frame

Wood member generates 20m*20m*20m grid as resident units.

Autonomous construction in units

The films

The wood structure

The final form

EFFULGANT CHAMBER OF HUMAN SPIRIT

Yegor Svillar

Russia

The world has experienced a series of crises, disasters and its consequences throughout the 20th and 21st centuries, and coupled with the skewing of anthropological thought through the dynamic changes of human essence within such environment, as a result — defocalization of identity of the modern person with his objectives and guidelines undermined

The main and most widespread `illness` of the 20th century — depression — was replaced by the paranoia of the 21st. Often unconscious, it alters the landscapes of human presence as seen through incorrect eyeglasses.

This project is a response to the observed changes of the modern man, and to his inherent spatial perception; one that is illuminated by the morbid glow of paranoia.

The new spaces of modernity are spaces of war, strife, overpopulation, consumption, survival, gain, ideology and control. The suggested solution — space of mental and spiritual activities correlated with the fundamental task given to human beings, namely spiritual ascent and experience.

The suggested solution — a monastery.

From the very beginning we had this goal in our sights, — as a man who carefully holds a bowl full of water in his hands, — allowing us to focus on the idea without unnecessary distractions. We were free from the constraints of stylistic and construction trends, social and "green" (sustainable) pathos, ideologies, cultural allusions, digital formalism (as well as other numerous `isms`), and most importantly — the presence of architect`s ego and `genius`.

This conscious adherence to austerity has crystallized the way of spatial organization of the structure, allowing the monastery to grow isotropically to match the required capacity — while respecting the monastic dichotomy of solitude and cohesion (relatedness).

The accumulator of spiritual energy and power of hundreds of men this project create the setting for the erection of a `building` whose triumphant height is by far unattainable by any highest surrounding skyscraper, and the `building` we talking about is an **effulgent chamber of human spirit**.

The world has experienced a series of crises, disasters and its consequences throughout the 20th and 21st centuries, and coupled with the skewing of anthropological thought through the dynamic changes of human essence within such environment, as a result — defocalization of identity of the modern person with his objectives and guidelines undermined. The main and most widespread "illness" of the 20th century — depression — was replaced by the paranoia of the 21st. Often unconscious, it alters the landscapes of human presence as seen through incorrect eyeglasses. This project is a response to the observed changes of the modern man, and to his inherent spatial perception; one that is illuminated by the morbid glow of paranoia. The new spaces of modernity are spaces of war, strife, overpopulation, consumption, survival, gain, ideology and control. The suggested solution — space of mental and

0682

Typical cell interior organisation

3.75 m

2.5 m

spiritual activities correlated with the fundamental task given to human beings, namely spiritual ascent and experience. The suggested solution — a monastery. From the very beginning we had this goal in our sights, — as a man that carefully holds a bowl full of water in his hands, — allowing us to focus on the idea without unnecessary distractions. We were free from the constraints of stylistic and construction trends, social and "green" (sustainable) pathos, ideologies, cultural allusions, digital formalism (as well as other numerous `isms`), and most importantly — the presence of architect's ego and `genius`. This conscious adherence to austerity has crystallized the way of spatial organization of the structure, allowing the monastery to grow isotropically to match the required capacity — while respecting the monastic dichotomy of solitude and cohesion (relatedness).

The accumulator of spiritual energy and power of hundreds of men this project create the setting for

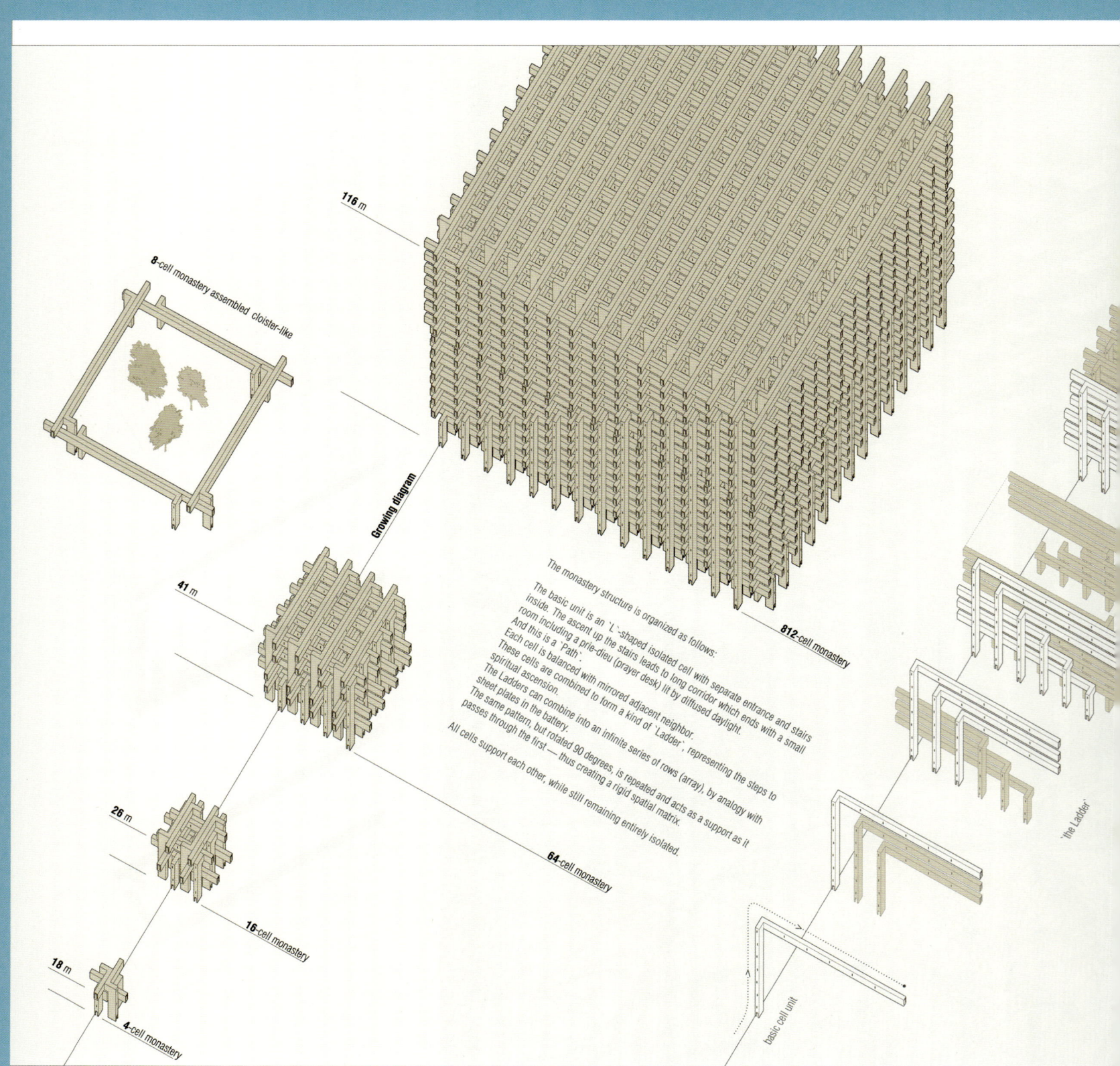

8-cell monastery assembled cloister-like

116 m

Growing diagram

41 m

812-cell monastery

The monastery structure is organized as follows:

The basic unit is an `L`-shaped isolated cell with separate entrance and stairs inside. The ascent up the stairs leads to long corridor which ends with a small room including a prie-dieu (prayer desk) lit by diffused daylight.

And this is a `Path`.

Each cell is balanced with mirrored adjacent neighbor.

These cells are combined into a kind of `Ladder`, representing the steps to spiritual ascension.

The Ladders can combine into an infinite series of rows (array), by analogy with sheet plates in the battery.

The same pattern, but rotated 90 degrees, is repeated and acts as a support as it passes through the first — thus creating a rigid spatial matrix.

All cells support each other, while still remaining entirely isolated.

26 m

64-cell monastery

18 m

16-cell monastery

4-cell monastery

`the Ladder`

basic cell unit

the erection of a `building` whose triumphant height is by far unattainable by any highest surrounding skyscraper, and the `building` we talking about is an effulgent chamber of human spirit. The basic unit is an `L`-shaped isolated cell with separate entrance and stairs inside. The ascent up the stairs leads to long corridor, which ends with, a small room including a prie-dieu (prayer desk) lit by diffused daylight. Each cell is balanced with mirrored adjacent neighbor. These cells are combined to form a kind of Ladder, representing the steps to spiritual ascension. The Ladders can combine into an infinite series of rows (array), by analogy with sheet plates in the battery. The same pattern, but rotated 90 degrees, is repeated and acts as a support as it passes through the first — thus creating a rigid spatial matrix. All cells support each other, while still remaining entirely isolated.

0682

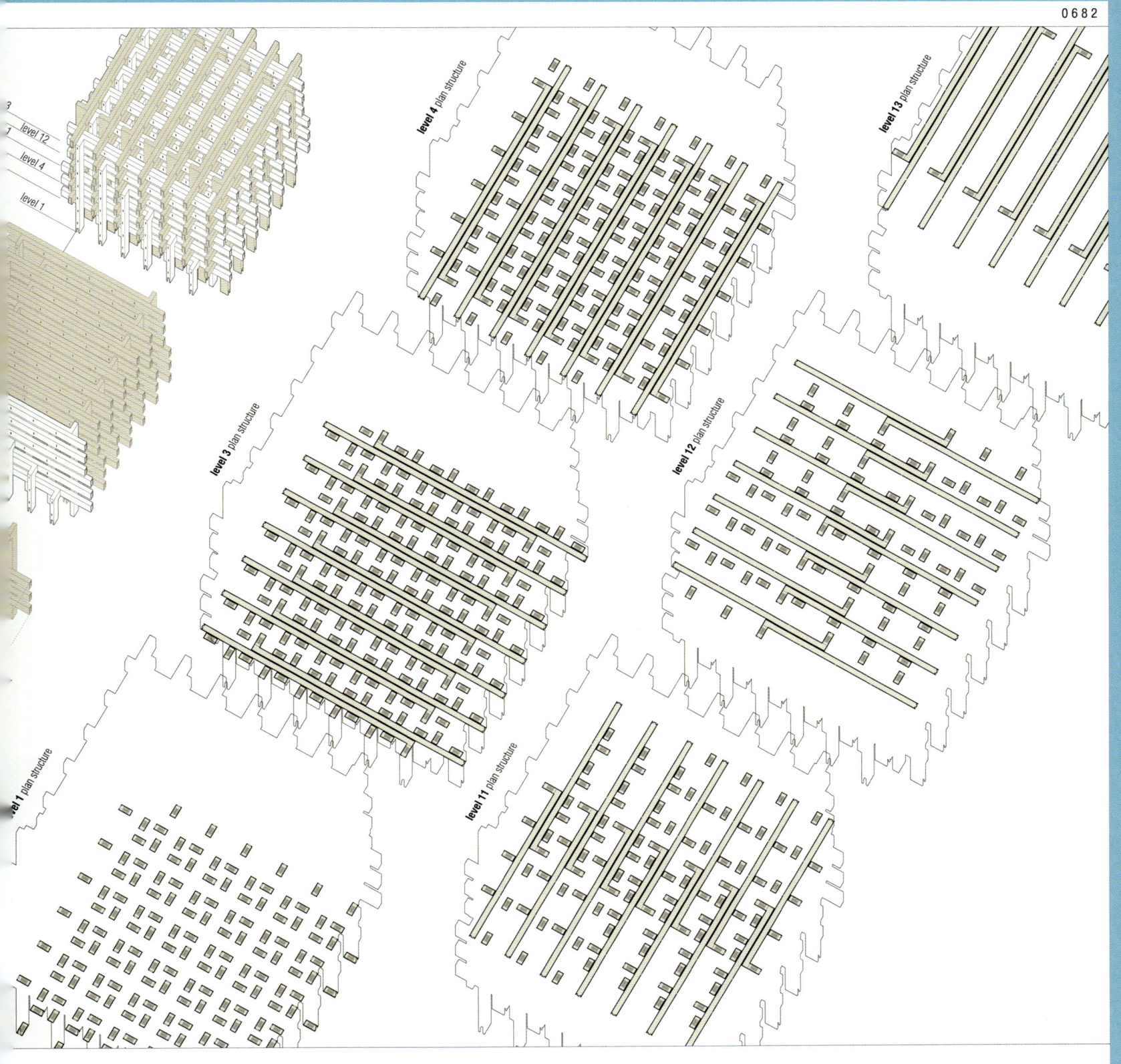

TRANS-PITAL: SPACE RESPONSIVE HOSPITAL

Chen Linag
Jia Tongyu
Sun Bo
Wang Qun
Zhang Kai
Choi Minhye

China

TRANS-PITAL
DEFERMATION HOSPITAL

BACKGROUND

GERMANY
It provides an incentive for the best doctors to move to urban areas where there are more high earners who can afford private sickness funds. As a result, rural regions struggle.

ITALY
Italians by and large regard health as a priority. And it shows up in one of the highest life expectancies in the world. In 2012, according to the World Bank, the average newborn Italian could expect to live to the age of 83 – the same as in Switzerland or Japan.
The provision of health services varies widely from one part of Italy to another.

CHINA
As Chinese citizens grow older and wealthier, they are also burdened by a rise in pollution, smoking, obesity and other public-health hazards.
Chinese authorities have been embracing other, more innovative ideas to improve the system: new technologies, private investment, new training regimens for doctors – in short, redoubling their speed just to keep up the pace.

AMERICA
The private and public systems that overlap in some areas, and leave gaps in others, make the US the country that spends the most per capita and as a percentage of GDP of any country in the world, but paradoxically consistently last among comparable nations in measures of quality of coverage such as infant mortality.

EGYPT
A system that doesn't know how to manage itself.

INDIA
All India Institute of Medical Sciences (AIIMS) in New Delhi- Mazes of dingy corridors, outdated equipment and filthy wards where linens are absent and rats run freely greet the desperately poor and sick patients seeking care. In the lobby of one of New Delhi's swanky corporate hospitals, wealthy patients from around the world sip lattes as they wait for doctors in brightly lit waiting rooms, complete with cleaners, attendants and stacks of glossy magazines.

BRAZIL
Reflecting this very unequal society, there is a huge gap between standards of private and public care. Regional disparities are even more glaring. Residents of the poorest state, Maranhão, have barely a quarter of the spend per head as the inhabitants of wealthy Rio de Janeiro.

SOUTH AFRICA
With the world's biggest HIV caseload, rampant tuberculosis (TB) and rising obesity, South African healthcare is under unique strain.

DESIGN STATEMENT

Concept

WHY IS HOSPITAL?
The medical and health organization of a country includes the country's security and improves the health of the people, the treatment of diseases and injuries of persons, organizations, systems and processes. The hospital plays a very important role in the system. However, the world is generally encountered in the case of lack of hospitals to serve the patients, at the same time, the chaos of the hospital streamline is not convenient for patients to use.

The problems mentioned above are reflected many places in the world, such as Europe, Asia and America......

WHY IS A DEFERMATION HOSPITAL?
Aiming at these two problems, we put forward a concept of defermation hospital.

A hospital, which is easy to assemble, which can reflect the society, which can show the BMI from the morphology of itself, which can be interpreted by the patients by the QR code.

Morphological changes can be suitable for various terrain environments, at the same time according to the functional requirements to change in morphology.

Our hospital
The medical building tries to solve the medical problems, so that the building can reflect the urban living conditions of the urban human settlements directly. The building collected within 10 km radius of the residents health data, which is reflected from the building surfaces directly, and the internal function (inpatient, emergency treatment, medical technology, and the outpatient which contains 50 departments) consistently.

Patients arrive at the hospital, and enter the core tube directly to the emergency treatment and the out-patient departments directly. The patients who need the in-patient treatment will transfer to the wards. The idea of the hospital is that the patient does not have to move by themselves, according to the motion track, the wards can move to where it should go to, like the out-patient space for further consultation with a doctor instead. However, if there is not too many patients of any department, the space for the out-patient and in-patient will be folded to form a rehabilitation garden space.

Technology

HOW IS IT LIKE?
The whole building is divided into a frame, a core tube structure, a large assembled body which is an independent department module and a small mobile body which is a medical cubic module inside the large assembled body.

HOW DOES IT TRANSFORM?
The small medical cubic module could move on the track in and among the large assembled bodies to form the body of the independent department.

Driving device
It is the mechanism that drives the actuator to move, according to the command signal sent by the control system, the module moves with the aid of the power element. It is the input of the electrical signal, the output of the line and the angular displacement.

Detecting device
It is a real-time detection of movement and work, according to the need to feed back to the control system, and sets the information after the comparison, the implementation of the organization to adjust, to ensure that the action is in accordance with the requirements of the scheduled.

Control system
One is centralized control, which is the total mechanical control by a microcomputer to complete. The other is decentralized (level) control, which uses multiple computers to share the control.

WHAT IS THE DRIVING FORCE OF DEFERMATION?
Energy conversion from nature: solar and wind energy mainly.

PREDICTION

MAX
ECI (Environmental Comprehensive Index)
SSI (Social Security Index)
BMI (Body Mass Index)
NHI (National Health Index)
MAX

AIR POLLUTION 2015   AGING 2035   SUDDEN INFECTIOUS DISEASES 2055   EARTHQUAKE 2075   HEALTHY PHYSICAL THERAPY 2095

The medical building can reflect the urban ECI, SSI, BMI and NHI through the surface and the form of itself. All the datas about health and environment are collected by the big data analysis.

The medical and health organization of a country includes the country's security and improves the health of the people, the treatment of diseases and injuries of persons, organizations, systems and processes. Hospitals plays a very important role in the system. However, the world is generally encountered in the case of lack of hospitals to serve the patients, at the same time, the chaos of the hospital streamline is not convenient for patients to use.

A space and tectonic responsive hospital is easy to assemble and reflects today's society. It shows the BMI from the morphology of itself. Morphological changes can be suitable for various terrain environments, at the same time according to the functional requirements to change in morphology.

0025

Patients arrive at the hospital, and enter the core tube directly to the emergency treatment and the outpatient departments directly. The patients who need the in-patient treatment will transfer to the wards. The idea of the hospital is that the patient does not have to move by himself, according to the motion track, the wards can move to where it should go to, like the outpatient space for further consultation with a doctor instead. However, if there are not too many patients of any department, the space for the outpatient and in-patient will be folded to form a therapy garden space.

The whole building is divided into a frame, a core tube structure, a large assembled body, which is an independent department module, and a small mobile body, which is a medical cubic module inside the large assembled body.

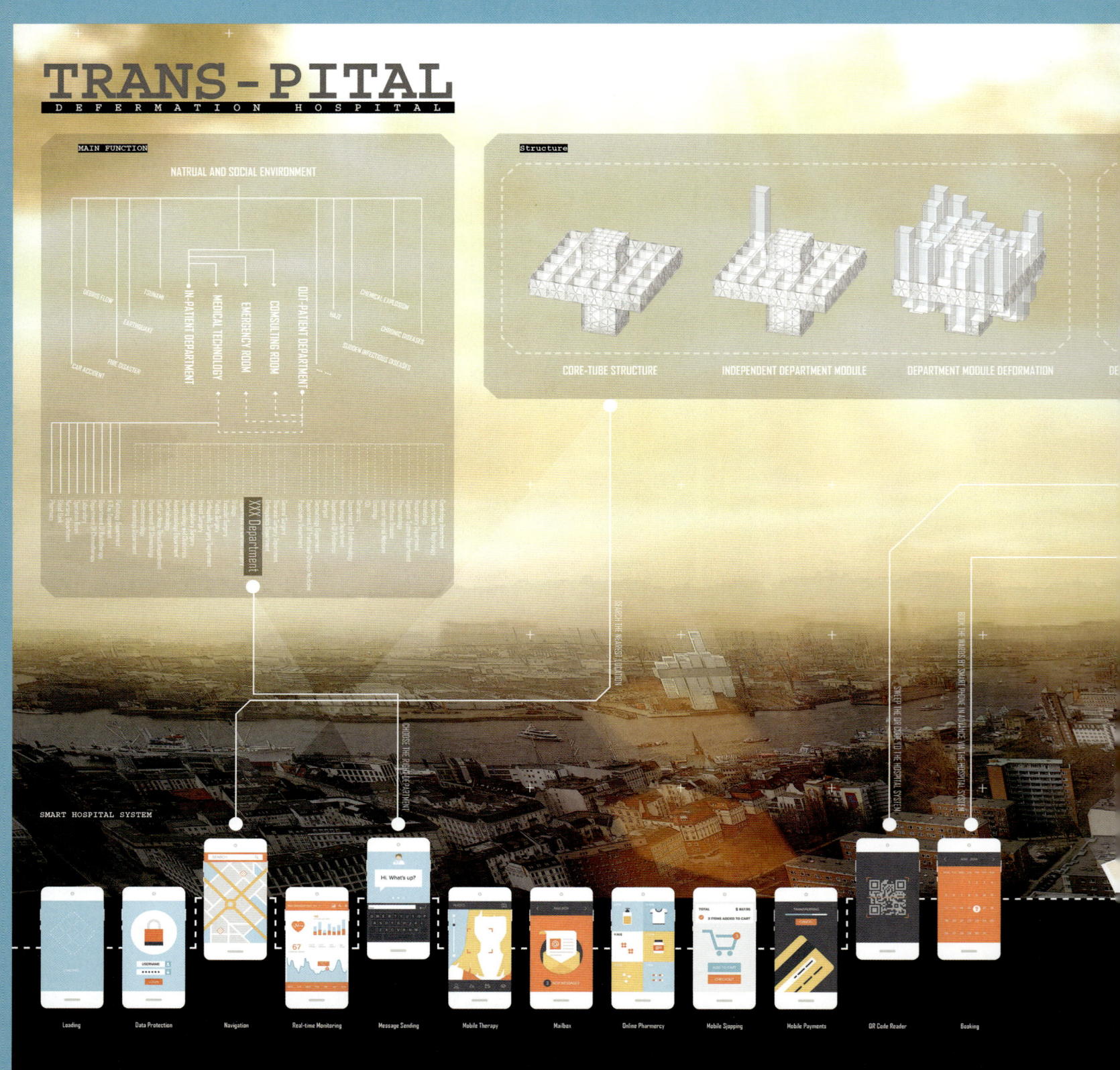

The small medical cubic module could move on the track in and among the large assembled bodies to form the body of the independent department. It is the mechanism that drives the actuator to move, according to the command signal sent by the control system, the module moves with the aid of the power element. It is the input of the electrical signal, the output of the line and the angular displacement.

It is a real-time detection of movement and work, according to the need to feed back to the control system, and sets the information after the comparison, the implementation of the organization to adjust, to ensure that the action is in accordance with the requirements of the scheduled.

One is centralized control, which is the total mechanical control by a microcomputer to complete. The other is decentralized (level) control, which uses multiple computers to share the control.

0025

INTEGRATION INFORMATION DISPLAY AT THE BOTTOM OF THE DEPARTMENT MODULE DRONE LANDING PLATFORM FOR FIRST-AID AT THE TOP OF THE DEPARTMENT MODULE

NT MODULE DEFERMATION MEDICAL CUBIC MODULE

MEDICAL CUBIC MODULE COMBINATION IN AND AMONG DEPARTMENT MODULES THE FREE SPACE BECOMES THE THERAPY GARDEN FOR THE PATIENTS

5MX5M MEDICAL CUBIC MODULE

VARIETY COMBINATION TYPES OF 5MX5M MEDICAL CUBIC MODULES IN THE DEPARTMENT MODULE

MANUFACTURING REGENERATION

Jamie Evans
Matthew Jones
Yasmin Giles
Alistair Wood

United Kingdom

Department of Choco

Town of Nóvita

Colombia has the second highest population of internally displaced people [IDP] in the world, behind only Syria. The Norwegian Refugee Council's Internal Displacement Monitoring Centre estimated the total to be at least 5,700,000, 11.5% of the national population, and has been labelled an "invisible crisis" by the UNHCR (United Nations High Commissioner for Refugees, 2015). It is generally agreed that the direct reason for this vast displacement is the ongoing civil war that has plagued Colombia for over a decade. Though relatively low in intensity, the asymmetric nature of the conflict being fought between the Colombian government, crime syndicates and left-wing guerrillas such as the Revolutionary Armed Forces of Colombia (FARC), and the National Liberation Army (ELN), the duration of the hostilities has resulted in great loss and disruption. The influence of powerful drug cartels has added greater complexity

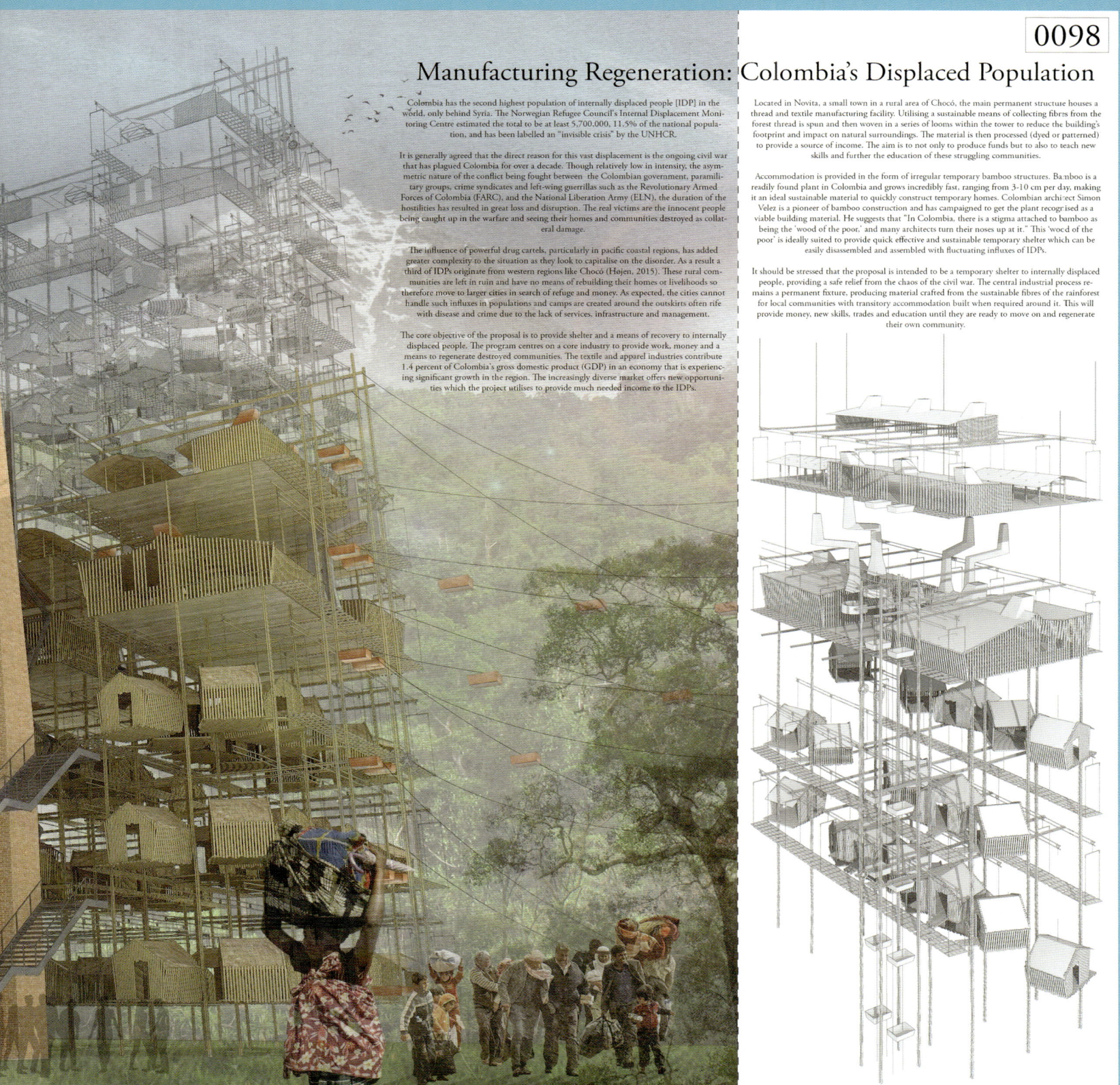

0098

Manufacturing Regeneration: Colombia's Displaced Population

Colombia has the second highest population of internally displaced people [IDP] in the world, only behind Syria. The Norwegian Refugee Council's Internal Displacement Monitoring Centre estimated the total to be at least 5,700,000, 11.5% of the national population, and has been labelled an "invisible crisis" by the UNHCR.

It is generally agreed that the direct reason for this vast displacement is the ongoing civil war that has plagued Colombia for over a decade. Though relatively low in intensity, the asymmetric nature of the conflict being fought between the Colombian government, paramilitary groups, crime syndicates and left-wing guerrillas such as the Revolutionary Armed Forces of Colombia (FARC), and the National Liberation Army (ELN), the duration of the hostilities has resulted in great loss and disruption. The real victims are the innocent people being caught up in the warfare and seeing their homes and communities destroyed as collateral damage.

The influence of powerful drug cartels, particularly in pacific coastal regions, has added greater complexity to the situation as they look to capitalise on the disorder. As a result a third of IDPs originate from western regions like Chocó (Højen, 2015). These rural communities are left in ruin and have no means of rebuilding their homes or livelihoods so therefore move to larger cities in search of refuge and money. As expected, the cities cannot handle such influxes in populations and camps are created around the outskirts often rife with disease and crime due to the lack of services, infrastructure and management.

The core objective of the proposal is to provide shelter and a means of recovery to internally displaced people. The program centres on a core industry to provide work, money and a means to regenerate destroyed communities. The textile and apparel industries contribute 1.4 percent of Colombia's gross domestic product (GDP) in an economy that is experiencing significant growth in the region. The increasingly diverse market offers new opportunities which the project utilises to provide much needed income to the IDPs.

Located in Novita, a small town in a rural area of Chocó, the main permanent structure houses a thread and textile manufacturing facility. Utilising a sustainable means of collecting fibres from the forest thread is spun and then woven in a series of looms within the tower to reduce the building's footprint and impact on natural surroundings. The material is then processed (dyed or patterned) to provide a source of income. The aim is to not only to produce funds but also to teach new skills and further the education of these struggling communities.

Accommodation is provided in the form of irregular temporary bamboo structures. Bamboo is a readily found plant in Colombia and grows incredibly fast, ranging from 3-10 cm per day, making it an ideal sustainable material to quickly construct temporary homes. Colombian architect Simon Velez is a pioneer of bamboo construction and has campaigned to get the plant recognised as a viable building material. He suggests that "In Colombia, there is a stigma attached to bamboo as being the 'wood of the poor,' and many architects turn their noses up at it." This 'wood of the poor' is ideally suited to provide quick effective and sustainable temporary shelter which can be easily disassembled and assembled with fluctuating influxes of IDPs.

It should be stressed that the proposal is intended to be a temporary shelter to internally displaced people, providing a safe relief from the chaos of the civil war. The central industrial process remains a permanent fixture, producing material crafted from the sustainable fibres of the rainforest for local communities with transitory accommodation built when required around it. This will provide money, new skills, trades and education until they are ready to move on and regenerate their own community.

to the situation as they look to capitalise on the disorder. As a result a third of IDP's originate from western regions like Chocó (Højen, 2015). These rural communities are left in ruin and have no means of rebuilding their homes or livelihoods so therefore move to larger cities in search of refuge and money. The central objective of the proposal is to provide shelter and a means of recovery to internally displaced people. The program centres on a core industry to provide work, money and a means to regenerate destroyed communities. The textile and apparel industries contributed 1.4 percent of Colombia's gross domestic product (GDP) in an economy that is experiencing significant growth in the region. This diverse market offers new opportunities which the project utilises to provide much needed income to the IDPs. Located in Novita, a small town in a rural area of Chocó, the main permanent structure houses a thread

Collection of fibres from rainforest along network of pulleys

Sorting debris from fibres

Produced thread fed into loom to create fabric

The process of manufacturing the material is integral to the recovery of the displaced pe (left) fibres are sorted at the top and bottom of the tower and fed into the mechanism looms and produced material run up to dying stations where the residents are allowed are learning new useful skills as well as reciving education and materials to sell on or c erate their old community.

and textile manufacturing facility. Utilising a sustainable means of collecting fibres from the forest thread is spun and then woven in a series of looms within the tower to reduce the building's footprint and impact on natural surroundings. The material is then processed (dyed or patterned) to provide a source of income. Accommodation is provided in the form or irregularly built, temporary bamboo structures. Bamboo is a readily found plant in Colombia and grows incredibly fast, making it an ideal sustainable material to quickly construct temporary homes. This 'wood of the poor', as named by the pioneering Columbian architect Simon Valez, who specialises in its use, is ideally suited to provide quick effective and sustainable temporary shelter which can be easily disassembled and assembled with fluctuating influxes of IDP's.

The plan integrates continuously changing towers of bamboo, temporary accomadation around the permanent industrial structure. Fibres are collected in the surrounding forest to be spun into thread and woven to create materials to dye. The dyes are created by forage materials from the forest as well as the bamboo from which the accomadation is constructed.

0098

Dying and patterning material to be sold or used for personal craft to sell

Integrated schools, leaarning academic and trade skills

through the tower. Starting at the base The thread is woven in the suspended n for sale. Throughout their stay they they are able to return home to regen-

Community grows before moving back to regenerate their home

SUBURBIA REDUX SKYSCRAPER

Jia le Ren
Yu Chen Zhou

China

movement

Skyscraper provides posibilities for people to use the upper space between different buildings. The main goal of this project is to resolve the transportation issue due to the congested urban space and precipitious natural terrain. In order to arrive at the destination directly regardless of topography constraint, the removable unit which is also an inherent part of architecture play a multi-funtion role. The dynamic, transparent visual exterior of architecure emerged cause of the movment of unit which is meant to bring kinesthetic experiences. Adding the forth axis time to achitecture is the root of design.

The high density slim scaffold structure that can be comprehensive as a homogeneous medium, each structure grid fix one unit, different array and combination forms 10 types traditional courtyard space with different scale of extensity, approach to generate diverse and complex atomosphere of life. From moment hence, People can reduce the contact with the ground, life is processing in the air.

concept diagram

plan

This skyscraper provides possibilities for people to use the upper space between different buildings. The main goal of this project is to resolve the transportation issue due to the congested urban space and precipitous natural terrain. In order to arrive at the destination directly regardless of topography constraint, the removable unit, which is also an inherent part of architecture, plays a multi-function role.

The dynamic, transparent visual exterior of architecture emerged cause of the movement of unit, which is meant to bring kinesthetic experiences. Adding the forth axis time to architecture is the root of design.

The high density slim scaffold structure that can be comprehensive as a homogeneous medium, each structure grid fix one unit; different array and combination forms 10 types traditional courtyard

space with different scale of extensity, approach to generate diverse and complex atmosphere of life. From moment hence people can reduce the contact with the ground life is processing in the air.

MASLOW WALL

Dingming Wang
Yucen Fan
Haolin Zhu

China

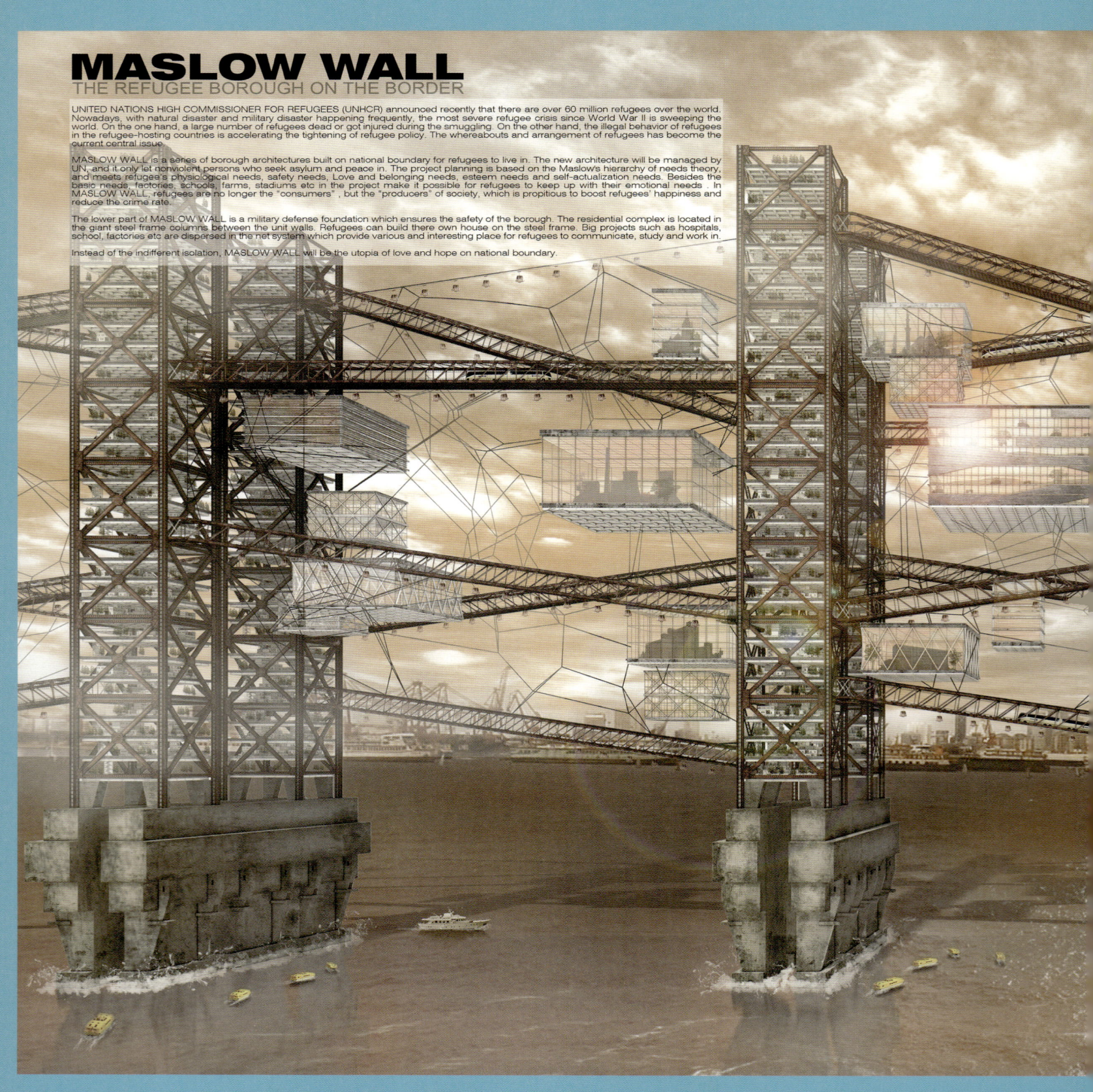

MASLOW WALL
THE REFUGEE BOROUGH ON THE BORDER

UNITED NATIONS HIGH COMMISSIONER FOR REFUGEES (UNHCR) announced recently that there are over 60 million refugees over the world. Nowadays, with natural disaster and military disaster happening frequently, the most severe refugee crisis since World War II is sweeping the world. On the one hand, a large number of refugees dead or got injured during the smuggling. On the other hand, the illegal behavior of refugees in the refugee-hosting countries is accelerating the tightening of refugee policy. The whereabouts and arrangement of refugees has become the current central issue.

MASLOW WALL is a series of borough architectures built on national boundary for refugees to live in. The new architecture will be managed by UN, and it only let nonviolent persons who seek asylum and peace in. The project planning is based on the Maslow's hierarchy of needs theory, and meets refugee's physiological needs, safety needs, Love and belonging needs, esteem needs and self-actualization needs. Besides the basic needs, factories, schools, farms, stadiums etc in the project make it possible for refugees to keep up with their emotional needs . In MASLOW WALL, refugees are no longer the "consumers" , but the "producers" of society, which is propitious to boost refugees' happiness and reduce the crime rate.

The lower part of MASLOW WALL is a military defense foundation which ensures the safety of the borough. The residential complex is located in the giant steel frame columns between the unit walls. Refugees can build there own house on the steel frame. Big projects such as hospitals, school, factories etc are dispersed in the net system which provide various and interesting place for refugees to communicate, study and work in.

Instead of the indifferent isolation, MASLOW WALL will be the utopia of love and hope on national boundary.

The United Nations High Commissioner for Refugees (UNHCR) announced recently that there are over 60 million refugees over the world. Nowadays, with natural and military disaster happening frequently, the most severe refugee crisis since World War II is sweeping the world. All men are created equal. Refugees are unfortunately born in countries ruined by natural disasters or wars, but under no circumstances their right to live should be deprived. Where is appropriate to construct new homeland for refugees to protect them from discrimination and distrust? How to create a place that not only meets refugees' needs for living but also enable them to start a new life with confidence and skills? The whereabouts and arrangement of refugees has become the current central issue.

0566

Maslow Wall is a series of borough architectures built on national boundary for refugees to live in. The UN will manage the new architecture, and will only let in nonviolent persons who seek asylum and peace. The project planning is based on the Maslow's hierarchy of needs theory, and meets refugee's physiological needs, safety needs, love and belonging needs, esteem needs and self-actualization needs. Besides the basic needs, factories, schools, farms, stadiums etc; in the project make it possible for refugees to keep up emotionally.

In Maslow Wall, refugees are no longer the consumers, but the producers of society, which is propitious to boost refugees' happiness and reduce the crime rate. The lower part of Maslow Wall is a military defense foundation, which ensures the safety of the borough. Troops can be based in the mega

MASLOW WALL
THE REFUGEE BOROUGH ON THE BORDER

● case

Problem 1: Number of refugees & Refugee migration
There are over 60 million refugees over the world, many of which choose to flee to other countries for asylum. Countries in Europe, America, Asia and Australia have accepted a large number of refugees actively or passively. However, the high crime rate of refugees makes it difficult for refugee-hosting countries to accept and arrange them. Meanwhile, massive numbers of refugees died in the shipwrecks and other accidents during migration and smuggling, which is saddening to us as human beings.

1	3	4
2		5

1. Refugees are fleeing on an overloaded boat.
2. Workers are distributing relief food to the starving refugees.
3. Children are brought up in awful environment.
4. A Syria child died on the Turkey Beach, of which the body is highly decomposed.
5. Refugee are waiting in queue for clean water.

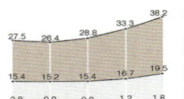

Country	Illegal Resident 2014	Illegal Resident 2015 Jan.-Mar
Syria	74723	12907
Kosovo	10900	11970
Afghanistan	23393	7920
Morocco	25239	7078
Albania	20283	8603
Ukraine	16744	4492
Iraq	7777	3751
Eritrea	34477	3734

refugees who recieved new identity
refugees looking for asylum
total amount of refugees
refugees remained in their own country

The composition of refugees in Europe is complex, and the amount is larger and larger by year.

| 1 | 2 | |
| 3 | | |

1. Changes in the number of refugees in the world
2. The nationality and number of illegal immigrants
3. The number of asylum seekers in Europe in the last five years

2015 Illegal immigration routes in the EU

Problem 2: The deteriorating relationship between refugees and refugee-hosting countries

1	3	4
2		5

1. A demonstration consists of residents protesting at accepting refugees.
2. Armed police trying to control riot.
3. A refugee is robbing the store of food.
4. Graffiti painted on the wall calling for the expulsion of refugees.
5. The police is keeping a mob under control.

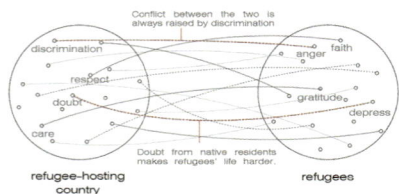

Conflict between the two is always raised by discrimination

discrimination — faith — anger
respect — doubt — gratitude — depress
care

Doubt from native residents makes refugees' life harder.

refugee-hosting country   refugees

The relationship between refugees and refugee-hosting countries is always one of the international focus. On one hand, some refugees are able to live normally in the new country. On the other hand, refugees with depress and contradiction are possibly to commit aggressive behavior which disturb the social stability of refugee-hosting countries. The influx of refugees even gave rise to violent racism, which caused collective criminal behavior and made the residents of refugee-hosting countries hate them more.

● concept

Problem 1: Whereabouts to arrange refugees
All men are created equal. Refugees are unfortunately born in countries ruined by natural disasters or wars, but under no circumstances their right to live should be deprived. Transfer refugees from the disadvantaged who accept help to contributors of society should be our common goal.
Where is appropriate to construct new homeland for refugees to protect them from discrimination and distrust? How to create a place not only meet refugees' needs for living but also enable them to start a new life with confidence and skills? These two questions are the key to solve refugee problem.

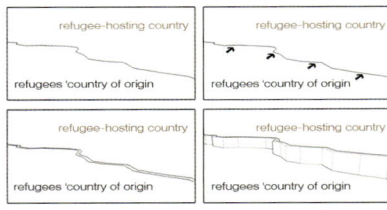

Refugees have crossed the border for asylum, while they met many obstacles in new life. The integration of refugees and original residents brings noticeable difficulties both to the two group. Therefore, we chose to build the MASLOW WALL, a refugees' borough on the border, to create an independent place for refugees to live in.

Problem 2: How to provide refugees with opportunities to create new life
It's an indisputable fact that all men are created equal, refugees deserve opportunities to earn better life. But since discrimination, doubt and other factors, it's always difficult for refugees to find satisfying jobs and raise a family. Based on the Maslow's hierarchy of needs theory, MASLOW WALL managed to meets refugee's physiological needs, safety needs, Love and belonging needs, esteem needs and self-actualization needs.

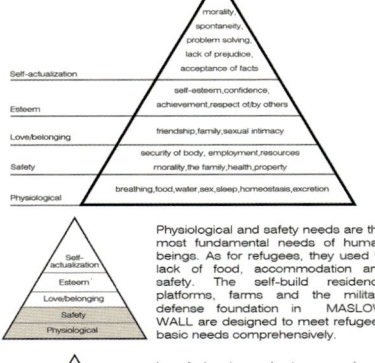

Self-actualization — morality, spontaneity, problem solving, lack of prejudice, acceptance of facts
Esteem — self-esteem, confidence, achievement, respect of/by others
Love/belonging — friendship, family, sexual intimacy
Safety — security of body, employment, resources, morality, the family, health, property
Physiological — breathing, food, water, sex, sleep, homeostasis, excretion

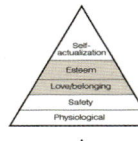

Physiological and safety needs are the most fundamental needs of human beings. As for refugees, they used to lack of food, accommodation and safety. The self-build residence platforms, farms and the military defense foundation in MASLOW WALL are designed to meet refugees basic needs comprehensively.

Love/belonging and esteem needs are advanced needs which distinguish the meaning of life and survival. If we merely meet refugees' basic need, they'll be helped objects. The parks, schools, hospitals, theaters and other entertainment and office place in MASLOW WALL offer opportunities for refugees to satisfy their psychological

Self-actualization is the highest need, the satisfaction of which is beneficial for refugees' transformation to the contributors of society, factories and other public infrastructure can offer more employment opportunities to the borough, and more opportunity for refugees to improve themselves.

● structure explosion

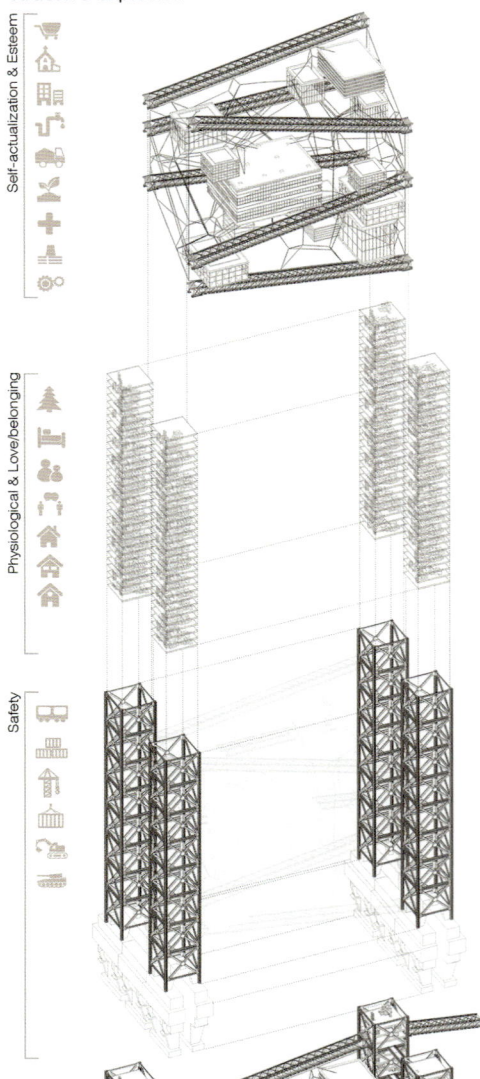

Self-actualization & Esteem

Physiological & Love/belonging

Safety

● scenes in

Steel cable syste bridges and funct three-dimensiona provide service comprehensively. every where they

The structure of t mega steel-frame connected by st traffic channels. steel-frame colun

The trestle bridge of transverse traffi they also connect are subways in th facilities, which convenient.

The skyscraper to enable reside like. The strength the platforms a Meanwhile the n of the residential

The lower part of ensures the safe foundation of oc holes .

foundation of concrete with watchtowers and machine guns firing holes. The residential complex is located in the giant steel frame columns between the unit walls. The skyscraper provides refugees with self-build residence platforms to enable residents in the borough to build their own house. Big projects such as hospitals, school, factories etc. are dispersed in the steel cable net system in the functional units, which provide various and interesting place for refugees to communicate, study and work in and meet refugees' needs comprehensively.

Instead of the indifferent isolation, Maslow Wall will be the utopia of love and hope on national boundary.

rough

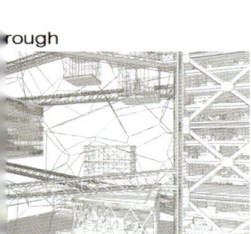

...ect the residential complexes, trestle ... as a whole. The functional units contain ...ctories, hospitals, school, markets, etc to ...borough and meet resident's needs ...ys and cable cars, residents can get to ...borough.

...per consists of two layers. Two row of ...with residential complexes in it are mainly ...trestle bridges, which also work as the ...cable systems also connected all the ...hole.

...the residential complexes is the main part ...ough. Besides the residential complexes, ...entertainment units in the borough. There ...dges as residents' main public transport ...traffic in the borough efficient and

...gees with self-build residence platforms ...brough to build their own house as they ...r columns located in the four corner of ...n structural support of the borough. ...elevators are main vertical transportation

...er is a military defense foundation which ...ough. Troops can be based in the mega ...watchtowers and machine guns firing

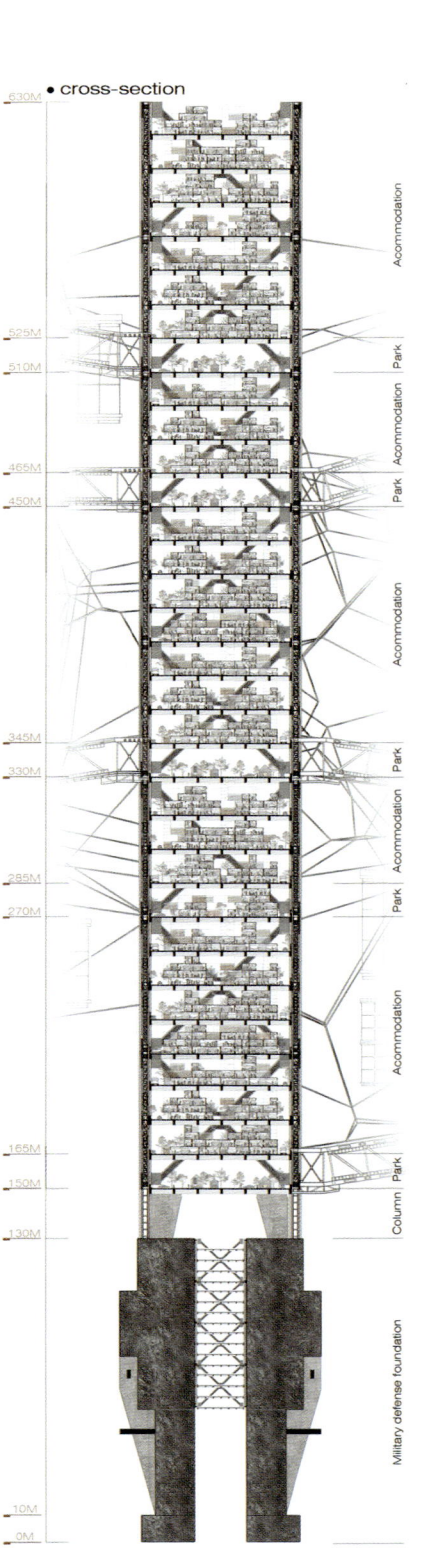

• cross-section

630M
525M
510M
465M
450M
345M
330M
285M
270M
165M
150M
130M
10M
0M

Acommodation
Park
Acommodation
Park
Acommodation
Park
Acommodation
Park
Acommodation
Park
Acommodation
Column   Park
Military defense foundation

0566

URBAN TENT

Woo Min Lee
Kan Min Yoo
Justin Baek
Tamin Song

New Zealand

While the use of glass in skyscrapers has proliferated, contemporary skyscrapers are effectively closed off from the environment. Since its inception, the use of closed and artificially controlled interior environments have caused large strains on the planet's resources; have made these buildings homogenous experientially; and have also caused sicknesses related to this over-reliance on air-conditioning. Modern humans now live, work, play and learn in towers with the outside as if it were wallpaper: despite it snowing outside, the occupants feel no cold; nor feel any heat during a hot summer's day. The Urban Tent seeks to change this static typology by reutilizing the traditional tent concept: a breathable skin that adapts for multiple environmental settings without resorting to air-conditioning. Using innovations in smart fabric technology, such as the UHMWP fabric (ultra-high-

0603

URBAN TENT

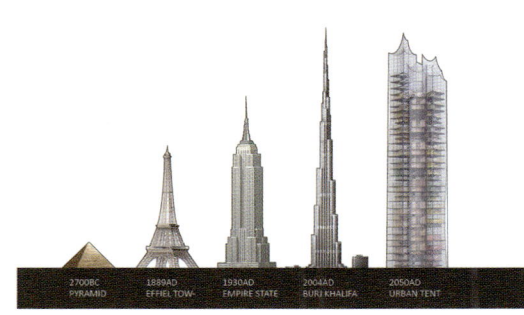

While the use of glass in skyscrapers has proliferated, contemporary skyscrapers are effectively closed off from the environment. Since its inception, the use of closed and artificially controlled interior environments have caused large strains on the planet's resources; have made these buildings homogenous experientially; and have also caused sicknesses related to this over-reliance on air-conditioning. Modern humans now live, work, play and learn in towers with the outside as if it were wallpaper: despite it snowing outside, the occupants feel no cold; nor feel any heat during a hot summer's day. While comfort is of importance, this comfort-craziness has driven more and more advanced air-conditioning technology creating buildings that no longer open up to the nature's seasonal changes and are the same all year round.

A NEW KIND OF SKYSCRAPER: THE URBAN TENT

The Urban Tent Skyscraper seeks to change this static typology by reutilising the traditional tent concept: a breathable skin that adapts for multiple environmental settings without resorting to air-conditioning. Using innovations in smart fabric technology, such as the UHMWP fabric (ultra-high-molecular-weight-polyethylene), the Urban Tent Skyscraper can do more than traditional tent fabrics with its dynamic properties of transparencies, porosities, insulations, tensions, strengths and plasticity. The design for the Urban Tent Skyscraper is conceived as being more like the human skin with an outer porous fabric membrane around the outside of the building, like the epidermis, and different additional inner layers of fabric-walls around all the interior rooms and in particular spaces creating multiple temperatures and different layers of interior conditions within the whole building. Consequently, occupants can then choose to be in zones of different comfort and temperatures which also creates an opportunity for co-existence of different trees and plants. People can be enjoying the winter without feeling too cold in the outer zones, or feeling warm by being inside one of the warmer inner layer fabric rooms. The outside and inside fabric work together in a way that it creates different environmental conditions and different micro-climates on the inside of the building so that the harsh outside natural environment is filtered into the building in different amounts in different zones of the interior.

URBAN TENT IN SEOUL

The Urban Tent skyscraper is envisioned to work well in a site like in Seoul where there are four extreme seasons: hot summers, freezing-cold winters, chilly autumns and warm springs. In order to adapt to these radical changes, the tower is capable of opening and closing, like traditional tent mechanisms, to change not only the macro-climate of the tower but also the micro-climates inside. In summer, the tower's outer and inner fabric walls can open up so that natural ventilation can occur throughout; spring and autumn can have varying levels and interior rooms opened and closed depending on each floor levels' requirements; and in winter the tower's fabric is fully closed with additional ice-capturing to increase insulation capacity (like an igloo).

THE VISION

Because of these varying micro-climates inside the tower, rather than completely cutting people off from nature, the tower begins to bridge people closer to nature. We feel that as technology advances, the architecture should follow suit to enhance the sense of experience and integration to nature so that the daily lives can also be equally enriched; redefining the fundamental concept of shelter in architecture to that of not only protection from but integration to nature. Owing to the design's multiple climate zones inside, this tower is essentially mixed-use. The architecture is a new spatial experience of ephermal beauty like that of nature: it changes with sunlight, captures shadows and warps with the wind. Inside people can see the new beauty of living on a changing building, rather than that of a static normal airtight building. We imagine that this kind of design will allow for many more different kinds of activity and experiences to occur in daily life of the building as people are moved closer to nature, even in an urban environment.

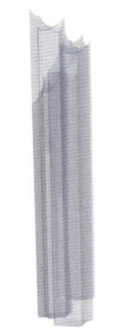

FLEXIBLE OUTER ENVELOPE:
A BREATHABLE SKIN TO CONTROL THE OVERALL BUILDING ENVIRONMENT

+

MICROCLIMATE INNER ZONES:
LAYERING OF FABRIC WALLS CREATING ZONES OF DIFFERENT CLIMATES FOR PEOPLE AND TREES

+

EXISTING CONTEXT:
UTILISES LANDSCAPE FROM BELOW, AND BRIDGES ENVIRONMENT TO BUILDING

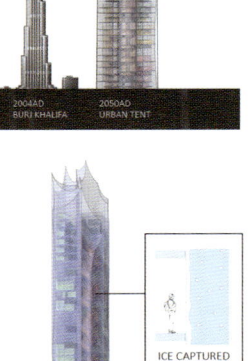

ICE CAPTURED FOR ADDED INSULATION

WINTER
INNER FABRIC WITH MORE WARMER TEMPERATURES INSIDE

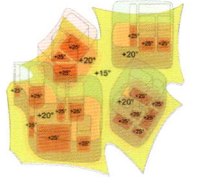

FABRIC LIFTED FOR SHADING AND COOLING

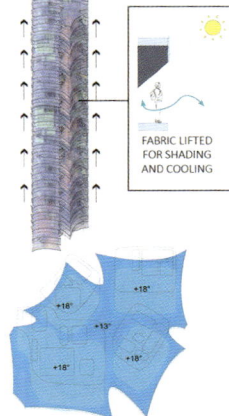

SUMMER
COOLS BY HAVING THE FABRIC WALLS ALL OPEN UP TO THE ENVIRONMENT

molecular-weight-polyethylene), the Urban Tent Skyscraper can do more than traditional tent fabrics with its dynamic properties of transparencies, porosities, insulations, tensions, strengths and plasticity. The design for the Urban Tent Skyscraper is conceived as being more like the human skin with an outer porous fabric membrane around the outside of the building, like the epidermis, and different additional inner layers of fabric-walls around all the interior rooms and in particular spaces creating multiple temperatures and different layers of interior conditions within the whole building. Consequently, occupants can then choose to be in zones of different comfort and temperatures, which also creates an opportunity for co-existence of different trees and plants. The outside and inside fabric work together in a way that it creates different environmental conditions and different micro-climates on the inside of the

AUTUMN

WINTER

MULTIPLE STRENGTHS AND PLASTICITY

LOW STRENGTH, FLEXIBLE

HIGH STRENGTH, STIFF

MULTIPLE POROSITY AND TENSIONS

HIGH TENSION

MID TENSION

LOW TENSION

MULTIPLE TRANSPARENCIES

DIFFERENT LEVELS OF PRIVACY

building so that the harsh outside natural environment is filtered into the building in different amounts in different zones of the interior. The Urban Tent is envisioned to work well in a site like in Seoul where there are four extreme seasons: hot summers, freezing-cold winters, chilly autumns and warm springs. In order to adapt to these radical changes, the tower is capable of opening and closing, like traditional tent mechanisms, to change not only the macro-climate of the tower but also the micro-climates inside. In summer, the tower's outer and inner fabric walls can open up so that natural ventilation can occur throughout; spring and autumn can have varying levels and interior rooms opened and closed depending on each floor levels' requirements; and in winter the tower's fabric is fully closed with additional ice-capturing to increase insulation capacity.

SPRING

SUMMER

MULTIPLE COLOURS AND OVERLAP

OFFICE & RETAIL

SCHOOL

CULTURAL

CIRCULATION

DIFFERENT COLOURS FOR DIFFERENT FUNCTIONS

SECTION AND PLAN

The Urban Tent's plan and section aim to provide the occupants a sense of wide openness and continuous flow in the interior. Unlike contemporary skyscrapers which are locked to a single repeating floor level, the Urban Tent creates a sense of continuity from one floor to another throughout the whole building with each floor being different in shape. Good amount of double and triple height spaces in the design contribute to a variety of circulation, spatial experience and drama in both horizontal and vertical directions. This means that in certain places people can feel connected to other levels. It is like a continuous landscape which climbs throughout the building

1. PARK (EXTERIOR)
2. PUBLIC AREA
3. PUBLIC AUDITORIUM
4. RETAIL STORES, RESTAURANTS, CAFES & OFFICES
5. BATHROOM
6. STUDENT SERVICES
7. MEETING ROOM
8. OFFICES
9. ART GALLERY
10. LECTURE THEATRES
11. STUDENT STUDY AREAS
12. STUDENT WORK EXHIBITION SPACE

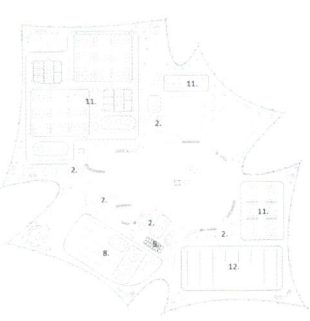

FOURTH FLOOR

SECOND FLOOR

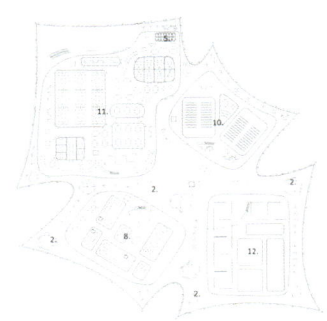

THIRD FLOOR

GROUND FLOOR

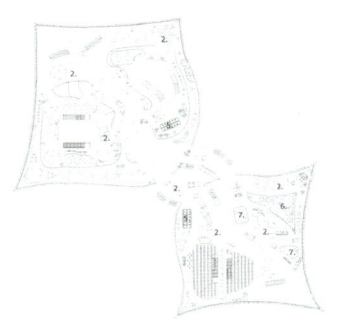

FIRST FLOOR

VERTICAL SHANGHAI

Yuta Sano
Eric Nakajima

Australia

VERTICAL SHANGHAI

Hyperlocal Monument of the Global Housing Crisis

Problem

It is apparent that throughout history, diversity fuels innovation and progress. Many studies show that multi-lingual individuals are better at problem solving, and multi-cultural societies spark new ideas and provoke critical thinking. Reversibly, lack of diversity and variation will stunt our imagination. This is also true with spatial environments as lack of diverse spaces that we inhabit everyday will hinder our capabilities to be more imaginative and creative. Globalization is therefore a phenomenon that has indisputably aided the advancement of our civilization by cross pollinating ideas, culture and tradition around the world, however, the benefits of globalization will foreseeably expire shortly if we are not careful with how we progress.

> "Diversity is not a characteristic of life; it is a condition necessary for life... like air and water."
>
> *Barry Lopez*

Today, in the midst of a housing crisis where 70% of the world's population is expected to be living in cities by 2050, building high density apartments to accommodate mass migration and population growth is a natural response to the demands our economy is facing. To solve this global crisis, we have banded together through free trade of goods and knowledge to provide efficient building solutions by standardizing construction materials, techniques and spatial configurations. Although it may be effective, as a result, repetitive and standardized apartments are being built all over the world irrespective of its location, and living spaces categorized into types to meet the image of modern living. No matter how idealistic this temporary solution may be, this type of *'Global Modernization'* is a slow devolution of our race as it sets a standard of a unified cultural norm and irradiates diversity through socio-global expectations.

China is an extreme example of 'Global Modernization'. Within a few decades, China has assimilated cities by rapidly building high density apartments, and more often than not, by demolishing old towns and structures that are rich in local culture and tradition. This careless rapid urbanization is not only wiping out historical artifacts but also eliminating opportunity for diversity in the future. Local, cultural, and spatial diversity is a necessity for enlightenment and enriching progress, therefore we must ask ourselves "is global unification worth the extinction of local characteristics?"

Old City of Shanghai
■ High Density Developm

1990

Today

Concept

Shanghai is suffering from an urbanization syndrome where local and traditional values are neglected in the name of modernization. Within a few decades, the old City of Shanghai is systematically being demolished to make room for highways and high-rise apartments with little regard to the hundreds of years of cultural history that has defined the lifestyle of its inhabitants. The people of old Shanghai are given two choices: either adapt their lifestyle to the modern expectations or move out of the city. Traditional Chinese lifestyles have developed through its opportunistic culture. Since the modernized duality of infrastructure and function does not exist, spaces are not designed to accommodate but they are accommodated with design.

The Tower
The concept
old structures
demolished s

'VERTICAL SHANGHAI' is not a vertical city, but merely a hyperlocal response to our global housing crisis.

Power lines /trees branches are also clothing lines, steps can be a place of communal gatherings, and sidewalks are an extension of home. Since the idea of territory and the ambiguity of private/ public space are uniquely local, these characteristics are lost though modernized western forms.

The concept of 'VERTICAL SHANGHAI' is to vertically recreate and enhance the traditional lifestyles of old Shanghai through understanding the opportunistic nature of local culture, moreover, *it is a monument that preserves the unique identity of local history.*

Internal intercon

It is apparent that throughout history, diversity fuels innovation and progress. Many studies show that multi-lingual individuals are better at problem solving, and multi-cultural societies spark new ideas and provoke critical thinking. Reversibly, lack of diversity and variation will stunt our imagination. This is also true with spatial environments, as lack of diverse spaces that we inhabit everyday will hinder our capabilities to be more imaginative and creative.

Globalization is therefore a phenomenon that has indisputably aided the advancement of our civilization by cross-pollinating ideas, culture and tradition around the world, however, the benefits of globalization will foreseeably expire shortly if we are not careful with how we progress.

2030

2050

...thesis to the ongoing developments. Rather than simply demolishing the ...ICAL SHANGHAI is gradually constructed from combining fragments of ...s with modern technology.

0630

Today, in the midst of a housing crisis where 70% of the world's population is expected to be living in cities by 2050, building high-density apartments to accommodate mass migration and population growth is a natural response to the demands our economy is facing. To solve this global crisis, we have banded together through free trade of goods and knowledge to provide efficient building solutions by standardizing construction materials, techniques and spatial configurations.

Although it may be effective, as a result, repetitive and standardized apartments are being built all over the world irrespective of its location, and living spaces categorized into types to meet the image of modern living. No matter how idealistic this temporary solution may be, this type of 'Global Modernization' is a slow devolution of our race as it sets a standard of a unified cultural norm and

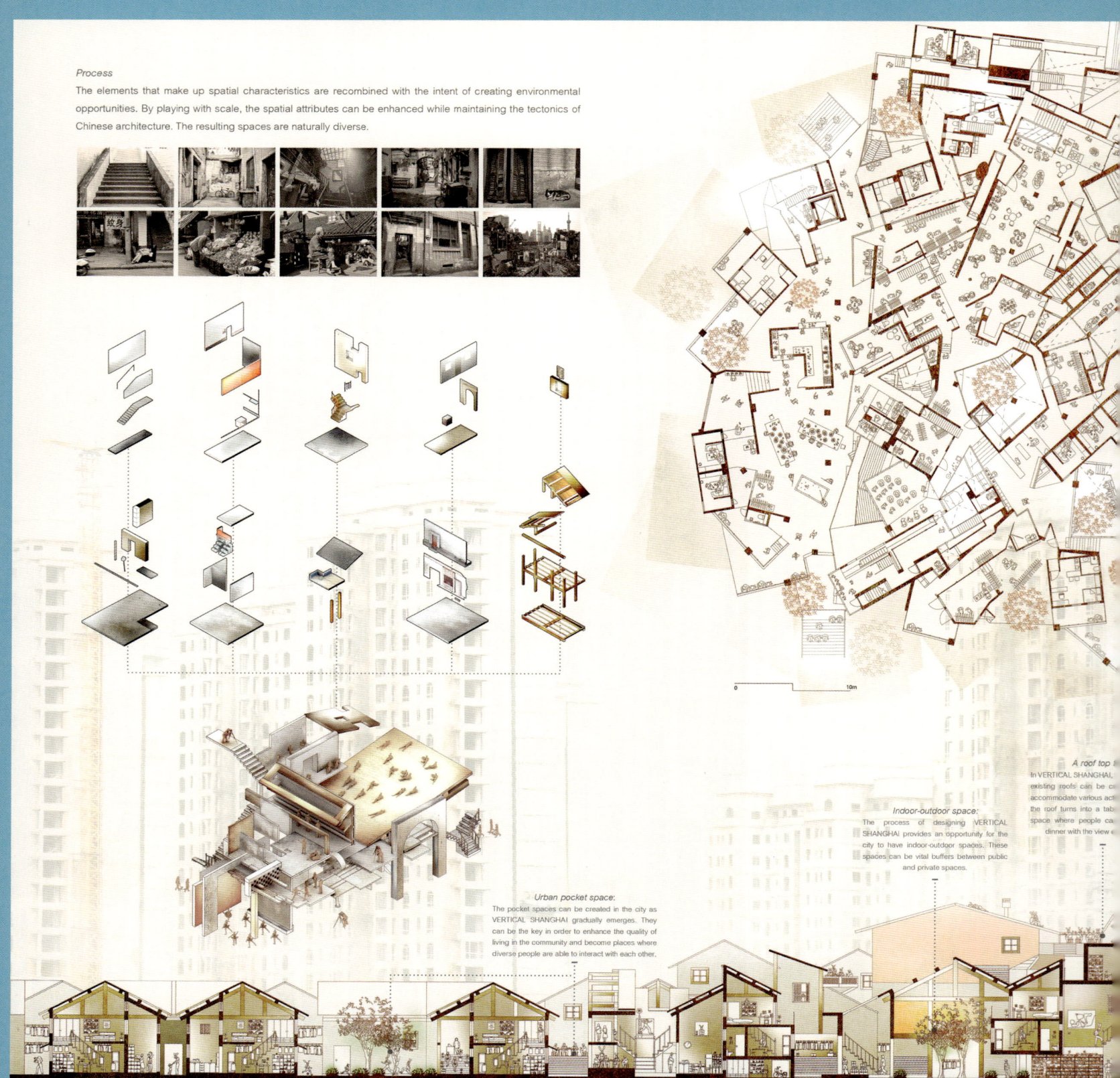

Process

The elements that make up spatial characteristics are recombined with the intent of creating environmental opportunities. By playing with scale, the spatial attributes can be enhanced while maintaining the tectonics of Chinese architecture. The resulting spaces are naturally diverse.

Urban pocket space:
The pocket spaces can be created in the city as VERTICAL SHANGHAI gradually emerges. They can be the key in order to enhance the quality of living in the community and become places where diverse people are able to interact with each other.

Indoor-outdoor space:
The process of designing VERTICAL SHANGHAI provides an opportunity for the city to have indoor-outdoor spaces. These spaces can be vital buffers between public and private spaces.

A roof top
In VERTICAL SHANGHAI, existing roofs can be accommodate various activities the roof turns into a table space where people can dinner with the view

0   10m

irradiates diversity through socio-global expectations.

China is an extreme example of 'Global Modernization'. Within a few decades, China has assimilated cities by rapidly building high-density apartments, and more often than not, by demolishing old towns and structures that are rich in local culture and tradition. This careless rapid urbanization is not only wiping out historical artifacts but also eliminating opportunity for diversity in the future. Local, cultural, and spatial diversity is a necessity for enlightenment and enriching progress, therefore we must ask ourselves "is global unification worth the extinction of local characteristics?"

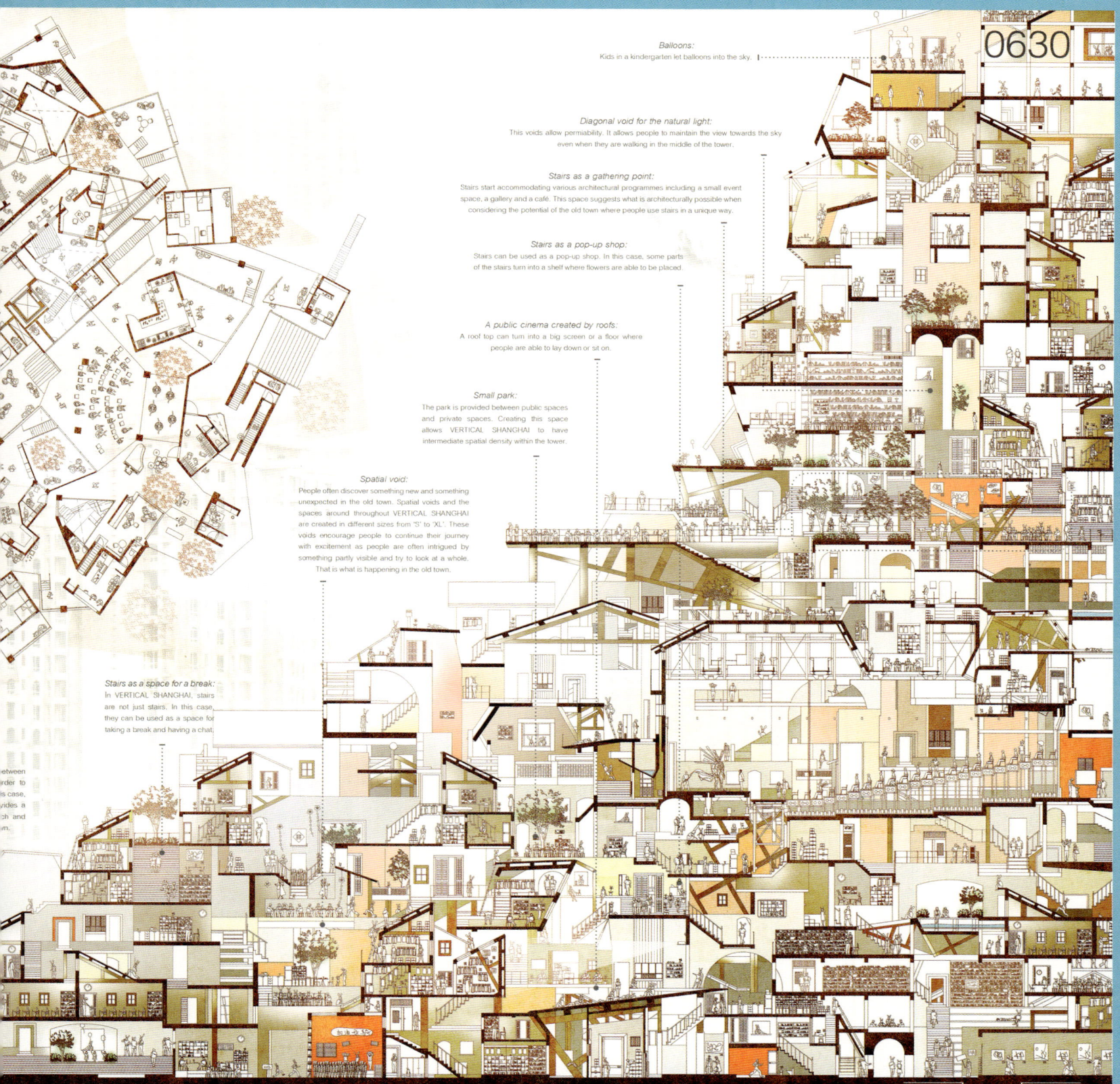

Balloons:
Kids in a kindergarten let balloons into the sky.

Diagonal void for the natural light:
This voids allow permiability. It allows people to maintain the view towards the sky even when they are walking in the middle of the tower.

Stairs as a gathering point:
Stairs start accommodating various architectural programmes including a small event space, a gallery and a café. This space suggests what is architecturally possible when considering the potential of the old town where people use stairs in a unique way.

Stairs as a pop-up shop:
Stairs can be used as a pop-up shop. In this case, some parts of the stairs turn into a shelf where flowers are able to be placed.

A public cinema created by roofs:
A roof top can turn into a big screen or a floor where people are able to lay down or sit on.

Small park:
The park is provided between public spaces and private spaces. Creating this space allows VERTICAL SHANGHAI to have intermediate spatial density within the tower.

Spatial void:
People often discover something new and something unexpected in the old town. Spatial voids and the spaces around throughout VERTICAL SHANGHAI are created in different sizes from 'S' to 'XL'. These voids encourage people to continue their journey with excitement as people are often intrigued by something partly visible and try to look at a whole. That is what is happening in the old town.

Stairs as a space for a break:
In VERTICAL SHANGHAI, stairs are not just stairs. In this case, they can be used as a space for taking a break and having a chat.

0630

15m

HOMELAND

Dylan Zhou
Songkai Liu

United States

The war fire destroyed so many historical architecture sites. This is so unacceptable for architects and historians all around the world. However, we didn't found a way to preserve them.

Famous archaeologist Khaled al-Assad from Syria dedicated his life to the preservation of the history Refugees are now the most serious problem in Europe.

Lacking of the infrastructure and having difficulty in finding jobs have caused many problems; they want to return to their homeland. Due to some political reasons, it has created antagonistic relationships in the Europe. The symbol of the homeland remains in the top of the skyscraper, follows the steps of refugees. The lower part of the building provides the refugees with community centers and supply station during special times. It is a skyscraper can be placed anywhere.

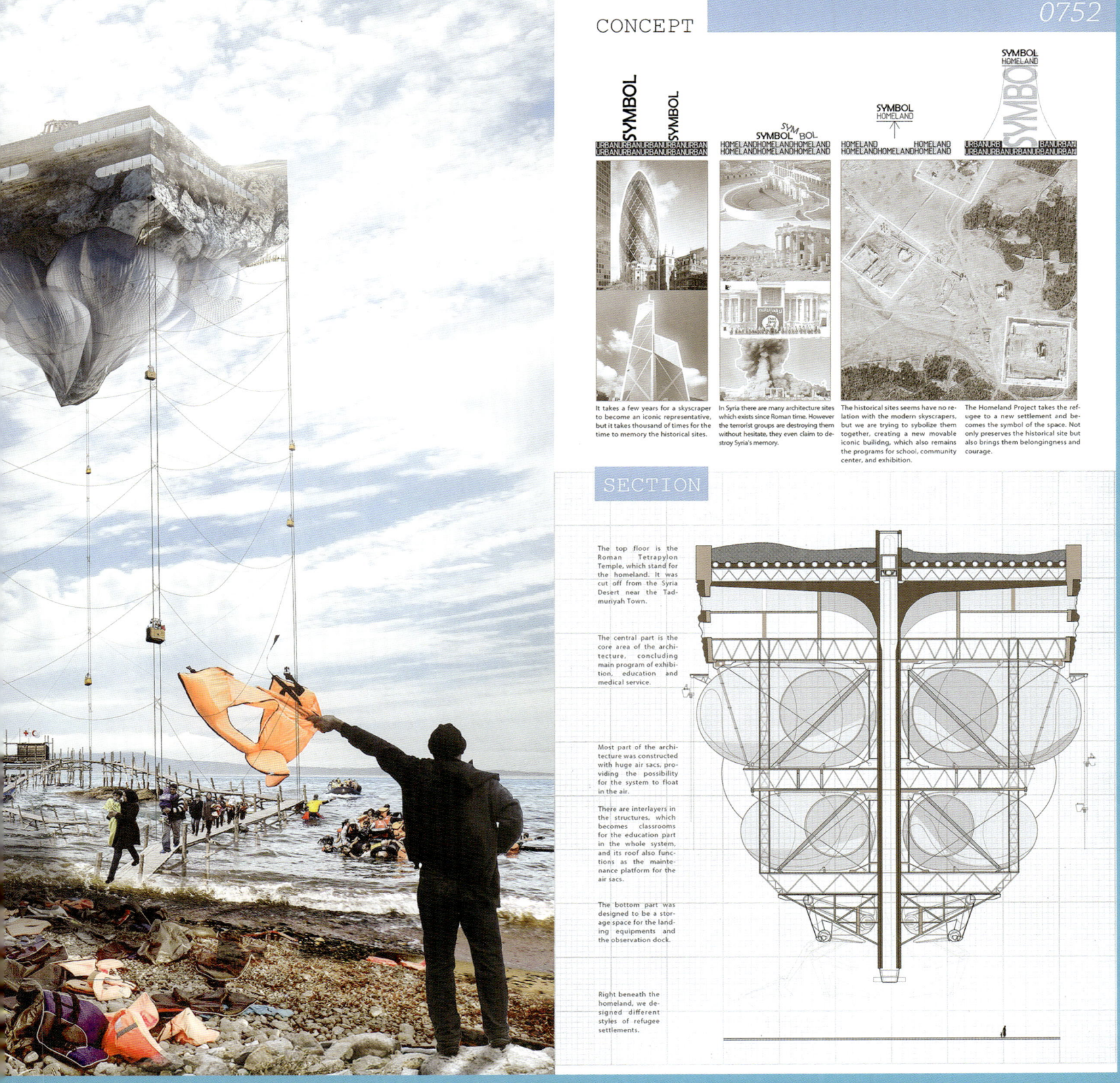

CONCEPT

0752

It takes a few years for a skyscraper to become an iconic representative, but it takes thousand of times for the time to memory the historical sites.

In Syria there are many architecture sites which exists since Roman time. However the terrorist groups are destroying them without hesitate, they even claim to destroy Syria's memory.

The historical sites seems have no relation with the modern skyscrapers, but we are trying to sybolize them together, creating a new movable iconic building, which also remains the programs for school, community center, and exhibition.

The Homeland Project takes the refugee to a new settlement and becomes the symbol of the space. Not only preserves the historical site but also brings them belongingness and courage.

SECTION

The top floor is the Roman Tetrapylon Temple, which stand for the homeland. It was cut off from the Syria Desert near the Tadmuriyah Town.

The central part is the core area of the architecture, concluding main program of exhibition, education and medical service.

Most part of the architecture was constructed with huge air sacs, providing the possibility for the system to float in the air.

There are interlayers in the structures, which becomes classrooms for the education part in the whole system, and its roof also functions as the maintenance platform for the air sacs.

The bottom part was designed to be a storage space for the landing equipments and the observation dock.

Right beneath the homeland, we designed different styles of refugee settlements.

Like a lighthouse from their homeland, bringing the refugees courage and confidence.

H O M E L A N D

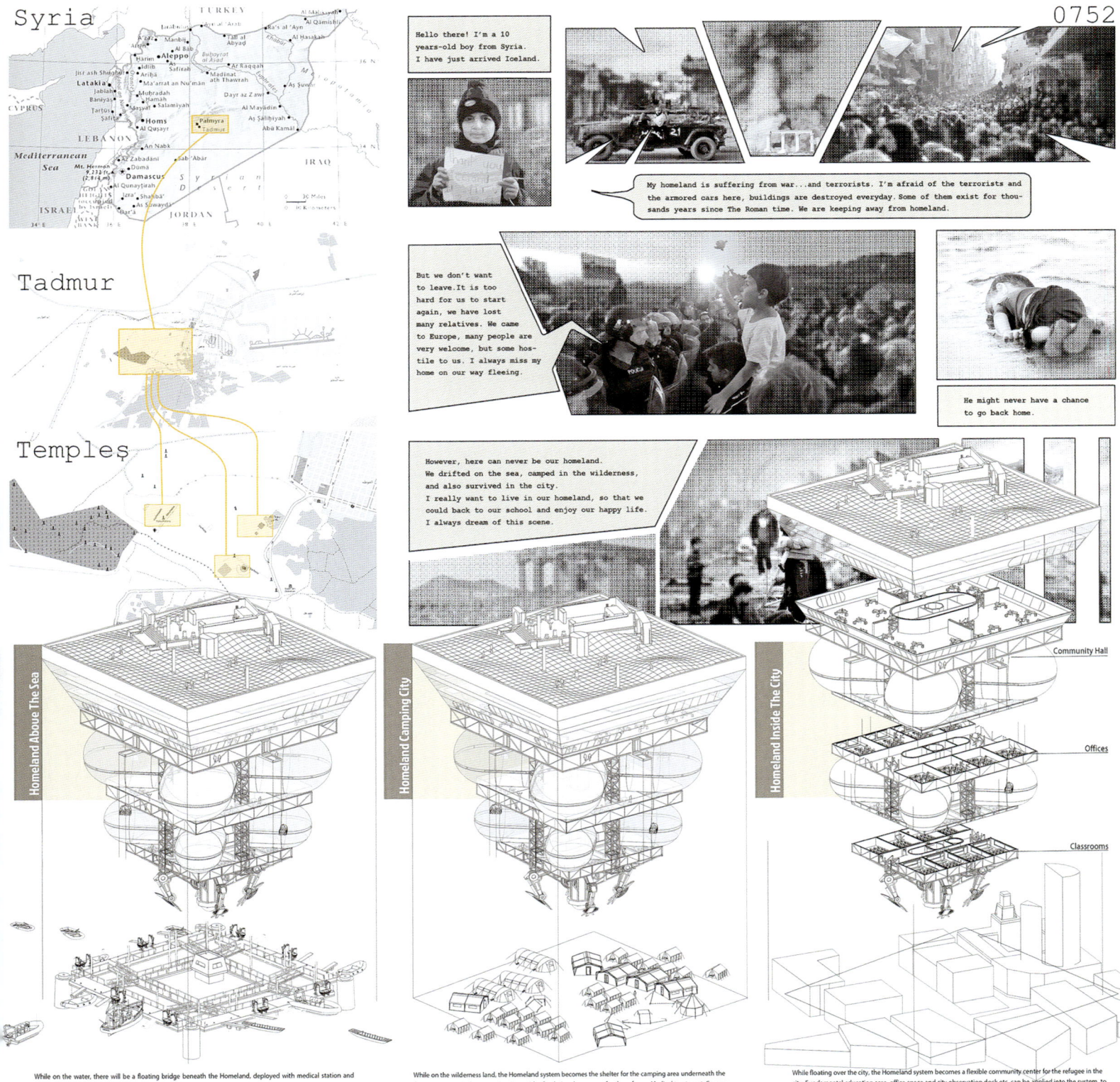

Syria

Tadmur

Temples

0752

Hello there! I'm a 10 years-old boy from Syria. I have just arrived Iceland.

My homeland is suffering from war...and terrorists. I'm afraid of the terrorists and the armored cars here, buildings are destroyed everyday. Some of them exist for thousands years since The Roman time. We are keeping away from homeland.

But we don't want to leave. It is too hard for us to start again, we have lost many relatives. We came to Europe, many people are very welcome, but some hostile to us. I always miss my home on our way fleeing.

He might never have a chance to go back home.

However, here can never be our homeland. We drifted on the sea, camped in the wilderness, and also survived in the city. I really want to live in our homeland, so that we could back to our school and enjoy our happy life. I always dream of this scene.

Homeland Aboue The Sea

Homeland Camping City

Homeland Inside The City

Community Hall

Offices

Classrooms

While on the water, there will be a floating bridge beneath the Homeland, deployed with medical station and rescue ships for refugee from the center. This system cooperates with the floating architecture, forming into the Skyscraper over the water, providing signals for the refugee far away.

While on the wilderness land, the Homeland system becomes the shelter for the camping area underneath the floating system. At the same time, it provides fundational programs for the refugee: Medical treatment, Communication, Supply, and Security.

While floating over the city, the Homeland system becomes a flexible community center for the refugee in the city. Fundamental education area, office space and city observation dock etc. can be applied into the system, to create financial connect with the city.

5

MORPHOTECTONIC
AESTHETICS

450

PILLARS OF FLUX

Keremcan Kirilmaz
Erdem Batirbek

Turkey

Upon analyzing today's busiest ports, it is clear that the port capacity / port area ratio is unacceptable in terms of trade efficiency and social city life. Vast, horizontal spaces, recklessly occupied by conventional ports, are broken and re-arranged into vertical storage volumes by Pillars of Flux. In order to maximize freight capacity, berths of the Pillars are designed in a triangular orientation. This double-sided berth network only needs 1.5 km2 as an optimal working area. To create a fully self-sustaining freight complex; wave turbines on sub-sea berth columns, solar panels, and wind turbines on pillar façade are used. The relationship between the pillars and the city is only on a transportation basis. This results in a fully automated port system that works fast and sustainably, respecting the city life and surrounding sea-life. Although the capacity and efficiency of a single pillar of flux are higher than the busiest ports of today,

0034

SEA FREIGHT COMPRISES 90% OF THE WORLD TRADE. DESPITE ITS INTRIGUING SYSTEMS & IMPRESSION, IT IS THE CHEAPEST, GREENEST AND MOST EFFICIENT FORM OF LOGISTICS ON EARTH, BUT TODAY'S FREIGHT ESTABLISHMENTS OUTDATED TECHNOLOGIES & PREMISES DESPERATELY NEED A RADICAL FUTURE MODERNIZATION. PILLARS OF FLUX BRING THIS MODERNIZATION BY RENOVATING THE RELATIONSHIP BETWEEN PORT AND CITY NETWORKS. OF THESE PILLARS DECONSTRUCTS THE PORT'S CONFINEMENT TO THE CITY BY RELOCATING THE PORT ON THE OCEAN & ENABLE THE GROWTH IN TRADE CAPACITY WHILE LIBERATING THE PORT AREA TO CREATE ADDITIONAL LIVABLE RECREATIONAL SPACES FOR CITIZENS.

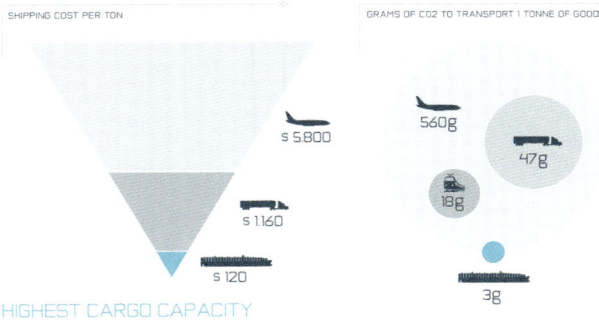

CHEAPEST SHIPPING
SHIPPING COST PER TON

$ 5.800
$ 1.160
$ 120

LESS POLLUTING
GRAMS OF CO2 TO TRANSPORT 1 TONNE OF GOODS / KM

560g
47g
18g
3g

HIGHEST CARGO CAPACITY
IN TONS

79.850 TONS
34 TONS
25 TONS

UPON ANALYZING TODAY'S BUSIEST PORTS, PORT CAPACITY / PORT AREA RATIO IS UNACCEPTABLE IN TERMS OF TRADE EFFICIENCY & SOCIAL CITY LIFE. VAST & HORIZONTAL SPACES RECKLESSLY OCCUPIED BY CONVENTIONAL PORTS ARE BROKEN & RE-ARRANGED INTO VERTICAL STORAGE VOLUMES BY PILLARS OF FLUX

PORT CAPACITY (MILLION TEU/YEAR) – PORT AREA (km²)
*TEU = TWENTY-FOOT EQUIVALENT CONTAINER UNIT

	CAPACITY	AREA	CAPACITY / AREA COEFFICIENT
PILLARS OF FLUX	30.5M TEU	1.5 km²	20
SHANGHAI	32.5M TEU	7.5 km²	4
SINGAPORE	31.6M TEU	9.5 km²	3.3
HONG KONG	25.3M TEU	5 km²	5
ROTTERDAM	13.6M TEU	52 km²	0.3

IN ORDER TO MAXIMIZE FREIGHTER CAPACITY, BERTHS OF THE PILLARS ARE DESIGNED IN A TRIANGULAR ORIENTATION. THIS DOUBLE-SIDED BERTH NETWORK ONLY NEEDS 1.5 KM² AS AN OPTIMAL WORKING AREA. TO CREATE A FULLY SELF-SUSTAINING FREIGHT COMPLEX; WAVE TURBINES ON SUB-SEA BERTH COLUMNS, SOLAR PANELS & WIND TURBINES ON PILLAR FAÇADE ARE USED.

DIMENSIONS & SUSTAINABILITY

> 30 BERTHS
> 150 CRANES

BERTHS

1.25 km

1.25 km
TOP VIEW

SOLAR PANELS
WIND TURBINES
WAVE TURBINES
ENERGY CELLS

SOLAR PANELS
WIND TURBINES
WAVE TURBINES
WAVE TURBINES

THE RELATIONSHIP BETWEEN PILLARS AND THE CITY IS ONLY ON A TRANSPORTATIONAL BASIS. THIS RESULTS IN A FULLY AUTOMATED PORT SYSTEM THAT WORKS FAST & SUSTAINABLY, RESPECTING THE CITY LIFE AND SURROUNDING SEA-LIFE. ALTHOUGH CAPACITY & EFFICIENCY OF A SINGLE PILLAR OF FLUX IS HIGHER THAN THE BUSIEST PORT OF TODAY; TOTAL CONTAINER CAPACITY CAN BE INCREASED THROUGH A NETWORK OF PILLARS. RELEASE A CITY MIGHT REQUIRE MORE THAN ONE PILLAR. THERE WILL ALWAYS BE NEW HORIZONS AS LONG AS THERE IS A PILLAR OF FLUX ON THE HORIZON.

PILLARS – CITY LINK

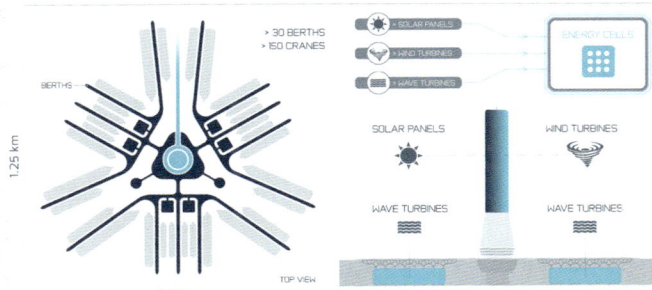

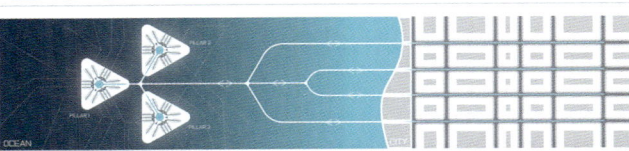

total container capacity can be increased through a network of pillars - in case a city might require more than one pillar.

Container flux shaft is the core of the Pillar that is designed for autonomous organization of smart containers through the structure. Courier-to-city, city-to-courier, and courier-to-courier container traffic is provided with the help of the peripheral units of this flux system. Inside this shaft, specially designed concentrically oriented lifters, those have multiple axis of motion, which are able to control the flow of containers of the Pillar. Central lifters can organize 40' containers whilst outer-layer lifters can operate on 20' ones on both directions. Façade modules of the Pillars are designed to be repetitive, modular and eco-friendly. These modules are made of sand from sea floor that is 3D-printed in an Inspection Center between berth arms. A protective coating layer is sprayed on these modules for environmental

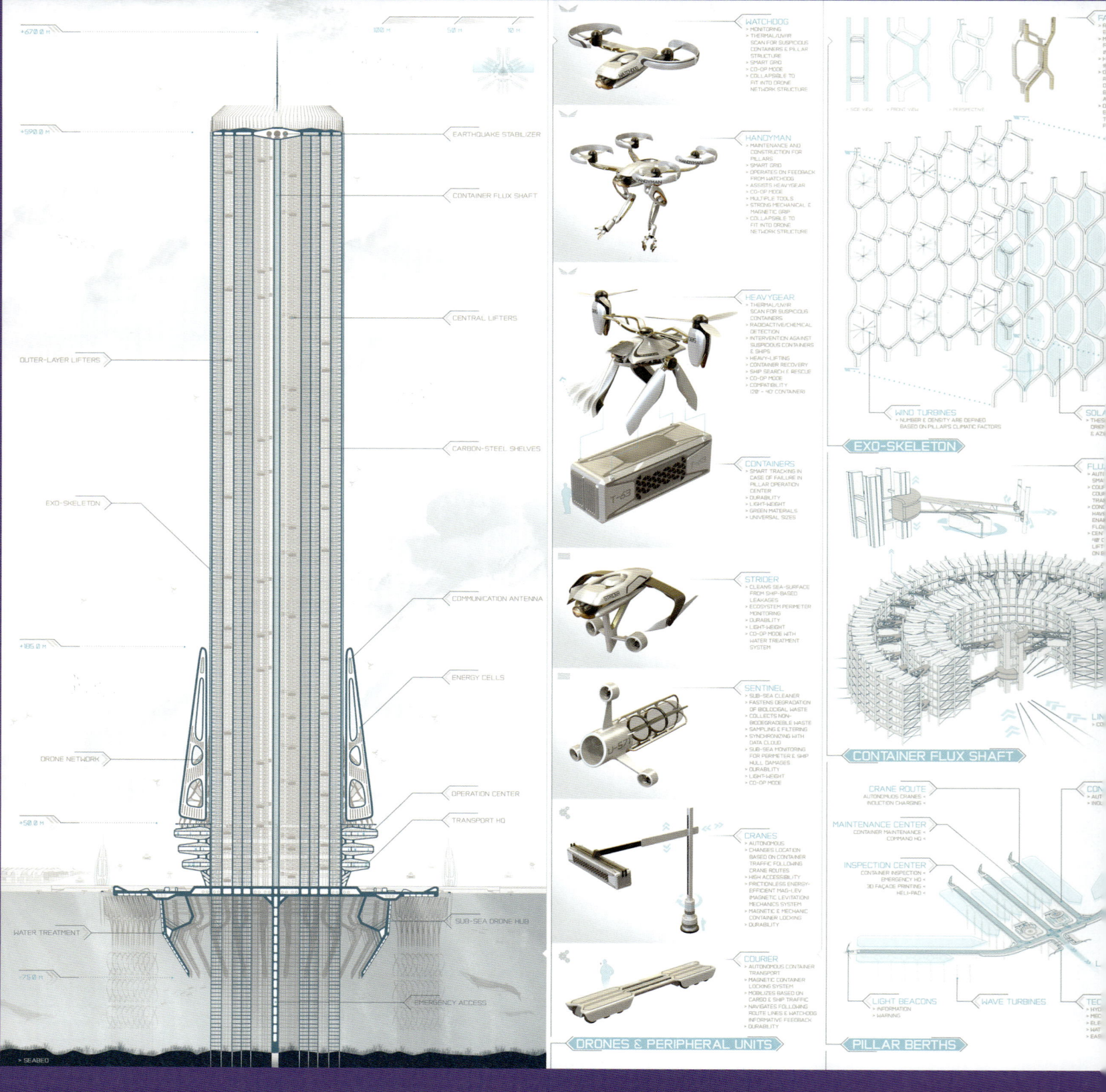

and weather protection. The drone, Handyman, transports and installs these modules. Damaged façade modules are released into the sea for the dissolving of the biodegradable sand adhesive & coating. Integrated solar panels and wind turbines in these façade modules provide sustainable energy for Pillars. The double hull design of the exo-skeleton enables twofold sustainable energy production. Pillars function and do maintenance through employing various types of air and water drones to avoid human error, work injuries and to increase speed. Watchdog drones monitor the facility and cargo through various sensors. Based on Watchdog's feed, Handyman drones are deployed to install or repair damaged parts of Pillars and berths; or Heavygears are deployed to take suspicious or fallen cargo to Inspection Center and handle other heavy loads. Strider drones monitor and clean sea surface from pollution, while Sentinels take care of pollution under the sea-surface and check ships for hull damage.

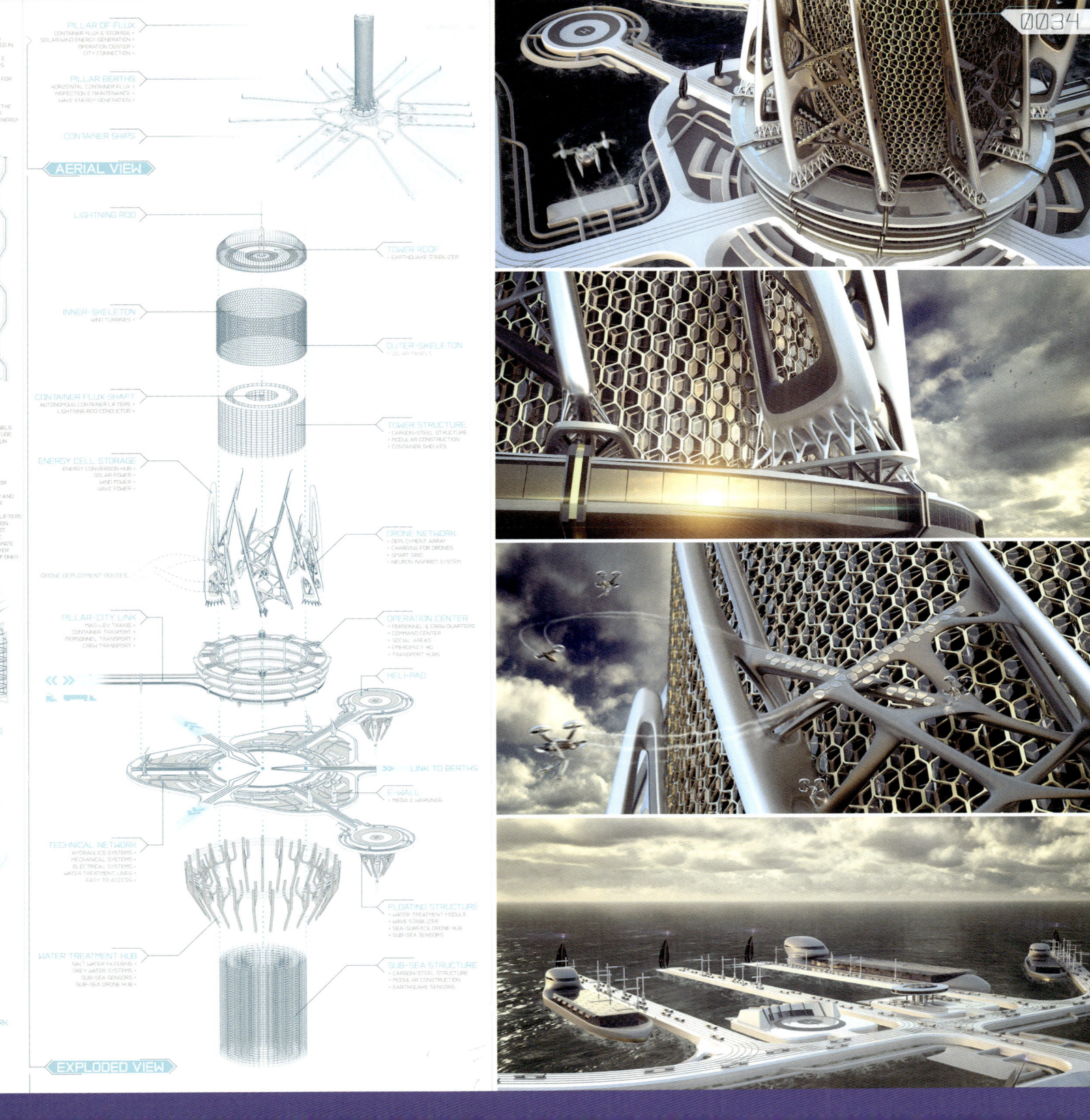

WASTELAND RECLAIMER

Pavel Pavlov Tsochev
Alexander Antoniev Todorov
Snezhina Slavi Aleksieva
Maria Ivanova Dimitrova

Bulgaria

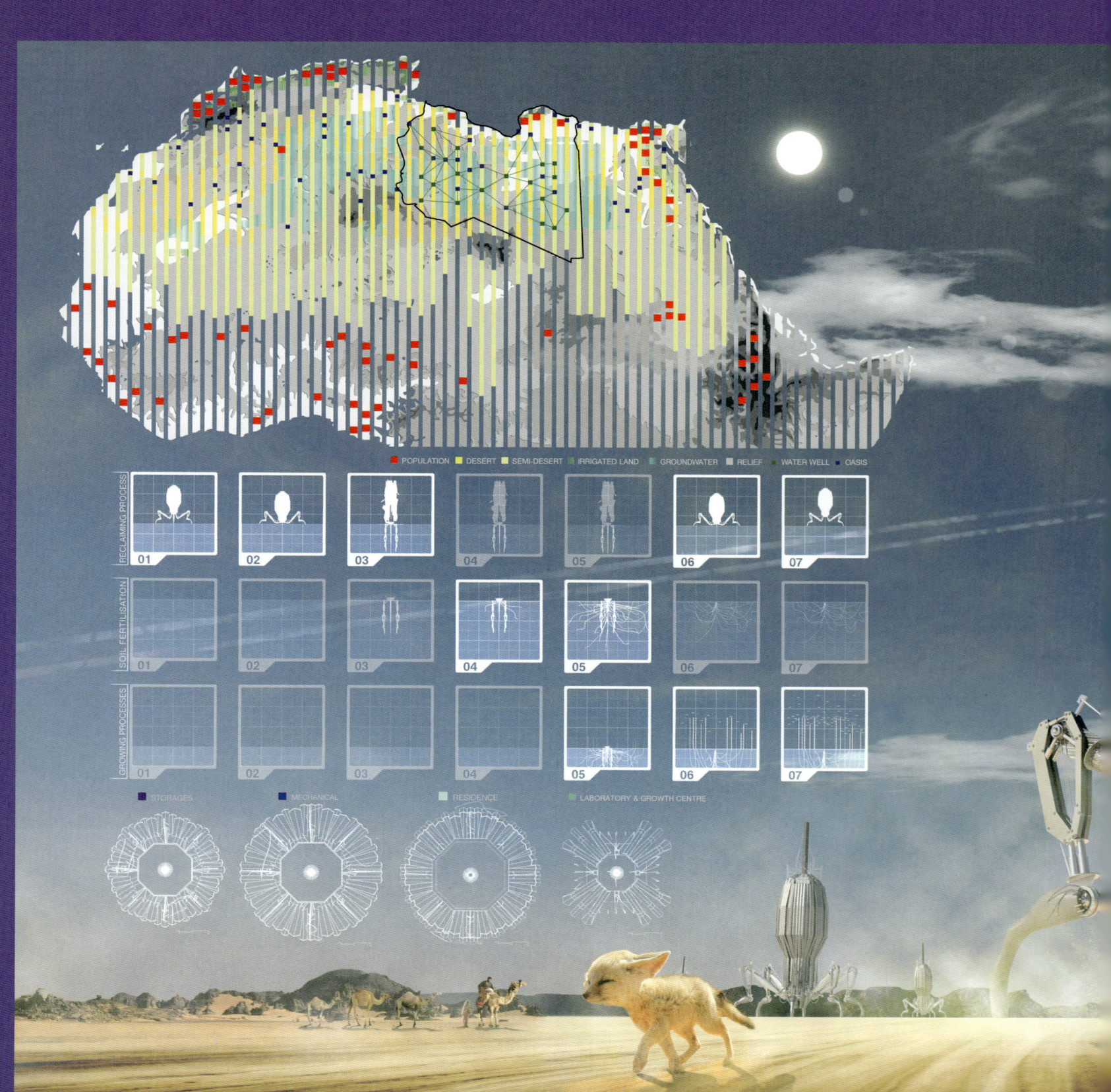

Wasteland Reclaimer is a dynamic high-rise structure, meant to perform in the hostile environment of the Sahara desert. Instead of investing human potential in search of ways for creating habitats in outer space, Wasteland Reclaimer offers new scientific horizons, by handing researchers a set of powerful tools for modeling the microclimate. Creating livable environment in regions with progressive loss of soil fertility has both ecological and social impacts. Climate change leads to poverty and unstable political situations, reducing all possibilities for local initiatives aiming to prevent natural disasters. Wasteland Reclaimer is a mobile, energy self-sufficient unit, which can temporarily be attached to different locations to trigger processes of soil fertilization and microclimate ameliorations. Its variable volume enables the project to perform a variety of tasks including transportation, drilling, anchoring, storing and sheltering.

0088

The process of reclaiming wastelands consists of several successive steps that Wasteland Reclaimer executes – searching for water, choosing a location, settling down, implanting nano-technologies into the soil, and detaching from the ground in order to leave space for the growing superstructures. Underground works involve site excavation, placing vats, injecting codes, and stimulating molecular growth. The self-evolving superstructures of the nano-cable clusters penetrate the soil, leading to the ionizer's growth. Ionizers create artificial nano-clouds, responsible for the condensation of vaporized water quantities. Once a process of condensation is triggered, the further development of the system will be enhanced to evolve to a sustainable habitat. Charging the weather with ions increases fresh water through rainfall enhancement. The atmosphere contains ten times as much fresh water as all the

INDUSTRIAL ENVIRONMENT

OBSERVATION LEVEL

RECREATION, FITNESS
LEASURE, SPORTS

MAINTAINANCE FLOOR

MOSS GROWTH, PLANTING
AREA WITH TECHNICAL
SUPPORT LEVELS

RESIDENCE FOR
SCIENTISTS WORKING
IN THE "RECLAIMER"

LIBRARY, DAYROOMS,
KITCHEN, DINING AREA

MACHINE ROOM

CLEANROOMS
EXPERIMENTIAL
RESEARCHES

STORAGES

LABORATORIES FOR
NANOPRODUCTION

MAINTAINANCE FLOOR

GROWTH CENTER

WATER TANKS
HYDRAULICS
MECHANICAL

GRAVEL

CROSS-BEDDED
SANDSTONE

SHALE AND CLAY

BASEMENT COMPLEX

GROUNDWATER

BEDROCK

PROJECT DEVELOPMENT OVER TIME

EVOLO
FORMATION
OF THE IDEA

THE ERA OF
NANOTECHNOLOGY

WELCOME TO MACHINE
WORLD

2004   2005 2006 2007 2008 2009 2010 2011 2012 2013   2014   2015 2016 2017 2018 2019 2020 2021 2022

lakes and rivers in the world combined. Moisture condenses around the charged dust. This turns into clouds, which produce the rain. Wasteland Reclaimer has two major modes of performing its duty – as a high-rise anchored structure and as a mobile compact unit. When soil-fertilizing works are running, most of the activities are performed deep underground. This leads to the necessity of anchoring the structure, while the levels above ground assure technical support, energy gathering, storage, and living spaces. The mobile mode of Waste Reclaimer faces the needs of the researching processes. Wasteland Reclaimer's spatial strategies are based on the presumption that the north rim of the Sahara desert could be reclaimed under the Mediterranean climate influence. The planning framework targets Libya as its strategic location, with physical assets that have the potential to evolve.

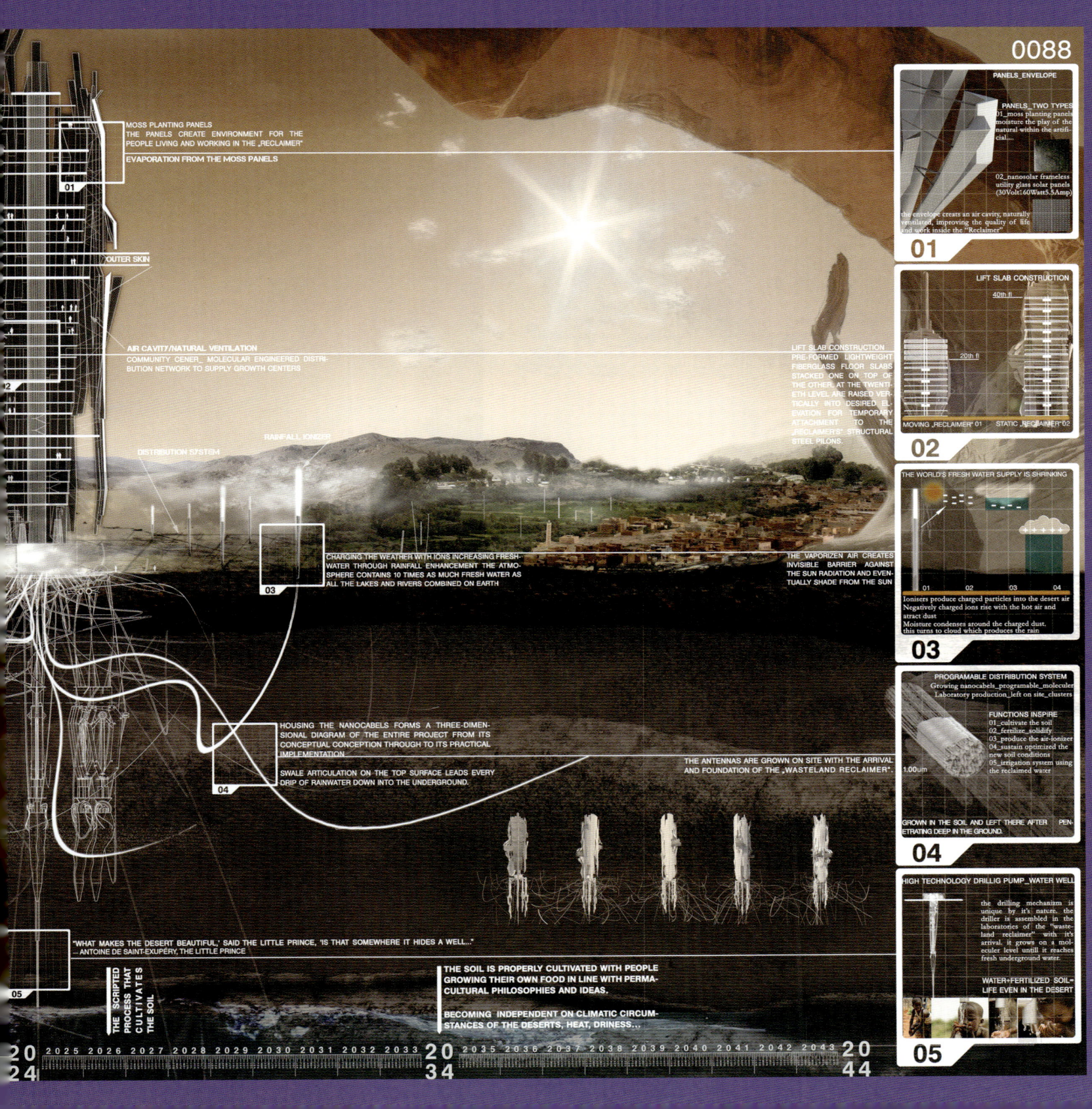

LAUNCHSPIRE

Henry Smith
Adam Woodward
Paul Attkins

United Kingdom

C A E L U M A P T U S

A cylindrical matrix of super tall structure centred on a electromagnetic vertical accelerator used to eliminate the hydrocarbon dependency of aircraft during take-off. The radical re-interpretation of the skyscraper format provides hyper density and an organic adaptive habitat.

Introduction

Human Settlement has its roots in movement; historically this aggregation occurred at crossroads, passes through difficult terrain and points of transit from rivers and seas to land. The nucleation of these settlements around geographical focal points coupled with ingenuity and technical development has led to our vertical metropolises and a trend in city dwelling.

Commercial air travel is celebrating its centenary in 2014 and over the last 100 years aviation has made an unprecedented impact on the way people can experience an interconnected and relatively open world.

Over the last four decades the real cost of air travel has fallen by about 60% and the number of travellers increased tenfold. Last year worldwide air passengers passed three billion for the first time, and are forecast to rise to 3.6 billion by 2016. This year demand for air travel is expected to grow by six per cent. According to statistics supplied by IATA, every 60 seconds worldwide, 52 aircraft take off, 5,700 passengers board aeroplanes, and $12.1m (£7.3m) worth of cargo is delivered.

Looking ahead, we can see that in 2050 aviation is predicted to fly 16 billion passengers and 400 million tonnes of cargo.
We must be able to manage that with sustainable technologies and efficient infrastructure.
The economic importance of 'Hub' airports has influenced the current growth of cities worldwide with Dubai a prime example of how an international Hub airport can generate enormous growth despite its inhospitable geographic location.

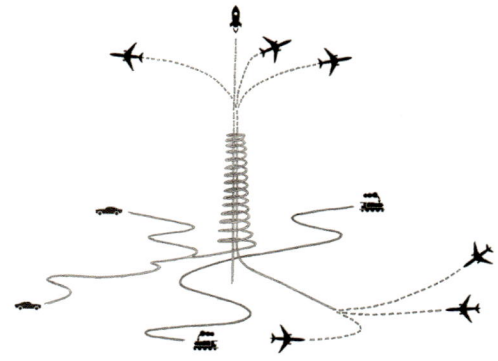

Design Intent/Focus

The future of Aviation is anticipated to rely on energy dense hydro carbon fuels to provide the power required to make flight possible. On short flights, as much as 25% of the total fuel consumed is used during take-off. The most fuel-efficient route length for airlines is 4,300 kilometres, roughly a flight from Europe to the U.S. East Coast. About 45 percent of all flights in the European Union cover less than 500 kilometres.

An electromagnetic vertical accelerator, utilising the technological principles developed at CERN's LHC and maglev train propulsion, provides a method for commercial aircraft to be accelerated to cruising speed using renewable electrical energy sources from ground based infrastructure. The longer the accelerator and greater exit velocity resulting in the aircraft being closer to cruising altitude. This creates a need for a super tall structure that is advantageous due to improvements in aviation efficiency, not as an iconic expression of supremacy.

A cylindrical matrix of super tall structure centered on an electromagnetic vertical accelerator to eliminate the hydrocarbon dependency of aircraft during takeoff. The radical re-interpretation of the skyscraper format provides hyper density in an organic and adaptive habitat. Commercial air travel is celebrating its centenary in 2014 and over the last 100 years aviation has made an unprecedented impact on the way people can experience an interconnected and relatively open world. Looking ahead, we can see that in 2050 aviation is predicted to fly 16 billion passengers and 400 million tones of cargo. We must be able to manage that with sustainable technologies and efficient infrastructure. The future of Aviation is anticipated to rely on energy dense hydrocarbon fuels to provide the power required to make flight possible. On short flights, as much as 25% of the total fuel consumed is used during takeoff. The

0275 - 01

most fuel-efficient route length for airlines is 4,300 kilometers, roughly a flight from Europe to the U.S. East Coast. About 45 percent of all flights in the European Union cover less than 500 kilometers. An electromagnetic vertical accelerator, utilizing the technological principles developed at CERN's LHC and maglev train propulsion, provides a method for commercial aircraft to be accelerated to cruising speed using renewable electrical energy sources from ground based infrastructure. The longer the accelerator and greater exit velocity resulting in the aircraft being closer to cruising altitude. This creates a need for a super tall structure that is advantageous due to improvements in aviation efficiency, not as an iconic expression of supremacy. We propose a new methodology of 'spiral tube' structure that ensures a habitable floor plate depth and simple pedestrian movement throughout the structure, whilst providing an overall cross-sectional width to overcome stability issues. The structural solution is born out of a

Space Exploitation
The progression of the human race will eventually involve the exploitation and colonisation outside of earths finite resources.
Over the last 20 years UK based Reaction Engines has been developing SABRE (Synergetic Air-Breathing Rocket Engine).
A new engine class that can operate in both air-breathing and rocket modes enabling aircraft to operate easily at speeds of up to five times the speed of sound or fly directly into Earth orbit. The vertical mass accelerator will aid the efficiency of vehicles destined for Earth's orbit by providing propulsion that would otherwise require additional fuel to be carried on board.
Unmanned spacecraft would be able to withstand acceleration far greater than the limitations of human occupied vehicles and could utilise the full power of the accelerator to transport materials at much greater speeds and efficiencies of ascent.

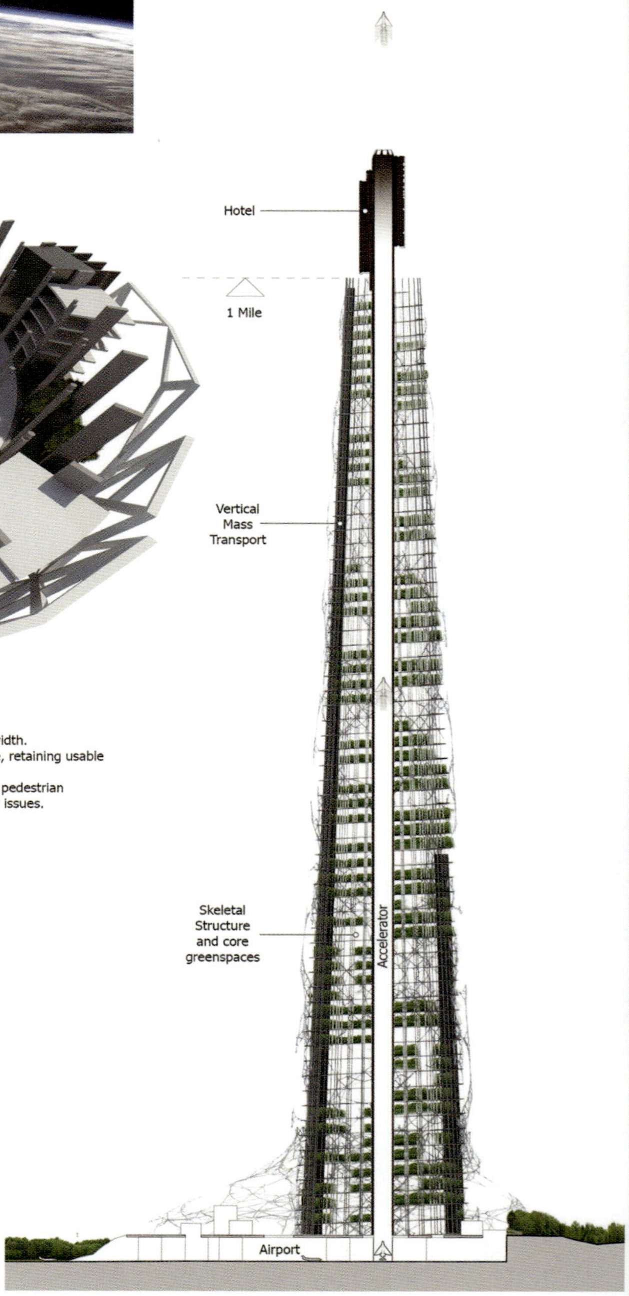

Vertical Mass Transport

Hotel

1 Mile

Vertical Mass Transport

Skeletal Structure and core greenspaces

Accelerator

Structure
The limit of a buildings structural height using known technologies and materials is down to slenderness and width.
The buttressed approach is the current method that the worlds super tall structures use to overcome this issue, retaining usable floor plate depth and maintaining structurally rigidity.
We propose a new methodology of 'spiral tube' structure that ensures a habitable floor plate depth and simple pedestrian movement throughout the structure, whilst providing a large overall cross-sectional width to overcome stability issues.

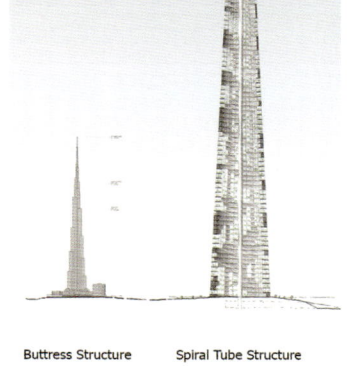

Structural Inspiration   Buttress Structure   Spiral Tube Structure

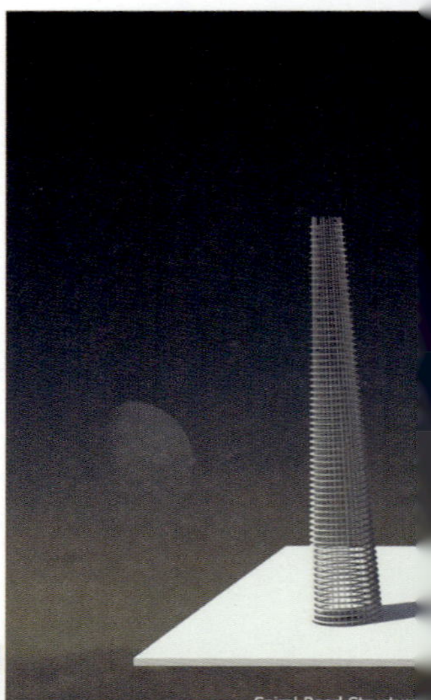

Airport

Spiral Road Structure
Tube Grid

desire to reinvigorate the 'core and floor plate' model of high-rise buildings. By creating a continuous street of privately owned 'plots' of habitation the development and evolution of the towers inhabitation becomes organic and specifically tailored to provide for the people that live within the tower. The use of plots would be governed by a democratic planning system to ensure the building serves its occupants well. Schools, hospitals, commercial, residential uses would be interspersed throughout the tower with approximately one third of all Plots to be public green spaces, nature reserves and farm land. Due to the scale of the building different climates would be experienced at various levels of the structure housing various wildlife and crop species, whilst also being natural devices for internal climate control. The concept is essentially a helical version of the classic urban grid environment.

0275 - 02

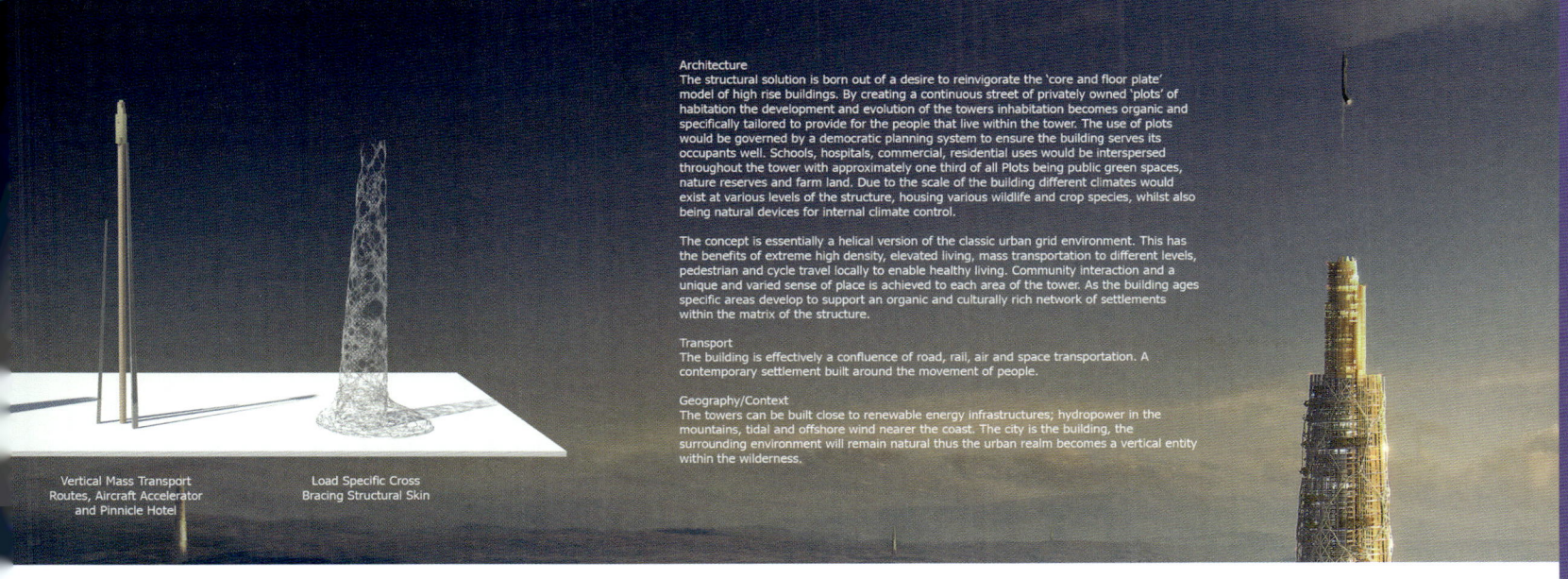

Vertical Mass Transport
Routes, Aircraft Accelerator
and Pinnicle Hotel

Load Specific Cross
Bracing Structural Skin

Architecture
The structural solution is born out of a desire to reinvigorate the 'core and floor plate' model of high rise buildings. By creating a continuous street of privately owned 'plots' of habitation the development and evolution of the towers inhabitation becomes organic and specifically tailored to provide for the people that live within the tower. The use of plots would be governed by a democratic planning system to ensure the building serves its occupants well. Schools, hospitals, commercial, residential uses would be interspersed throughout the tower with approximately one third of all Plots being public green spaces, nature reserves and farm land. Due to the scale of the building different climates would exist at various levels of the structure, housing various wildlife and crop species, whilst also being natural devices for internal climate control.

The concept is essentially a helical version of the classic urban grid environment. This has the benefits of extreme high density, elevated living, mass transportation to different levels, pedestrian and cycle travel locally to enable healthy living. Community interaction and a unique and varied sense of place is achieved to each area of the tower. As the building ages specific areas develop to support an organic and culturally rich network of settlements within the matrix of the structure.

Transport
The building is effectively a confluence of road, rail, air and space transportation. A contemporary settlement built around the movement of people.

Geography/Context
The towers can be built close to renewable energy infrastructures; hydropower in the mountains, tidal and offshore wind nearer the coast. The city is the building, the surrounding environment will remain natural thus the urban realm becomes a vertical entity within the wilderness.

VERNACULAR VERSATILITY

Yong Ju Lee

United States

1ST PLACE / 2014

VERNACULAR VERSATILITY

CONTEMPORARY ADAPTATION OF KOREAN TRADITIONAL ARCHITECTURE

Hanok is an antonym of western house and a synonym of Korean style house. A Hanok is defined by its exposed wooden structural system and tiled roof. The curved edge of the roof can be adjusted to control the amount of sunlight entering the house. The core structural element is a wooden connection named Gagu, which is located below the main roof system where the column meets the beam and girder and it is fastened without the need of additional components such as nails – this connection is the main aesthetic characteristic of traditional Korean architecture.

Historically this structural system has been developed exclusively in plan, applied only to one-story residences. However, as various modeling software have been recently developed, there are more opportunities to apply this traditional system into complex high-rise structures that meet contemporary

0302

KOREAN TRADITIONAL WOODEN STRUCTURE SYSTEM -"HANOK"

Hanok is defined as antonym of western house and synonym of house of Korean style. *Hanok* is featured by its own wooden structure system and tiled roofs. The edge of *Hanok*'s curvy roofs accomplishes its strong formal gesture. The lengths of the roof edge can be adjusted to control the amount of sunlight that enters the house.
The form and structure consisted of wood is exposed in exterior and interior of this system. The core structural element is wooden connection - *Gagu*, right under the roof where column meets beam and girder without additional fastener such as nail. And this connection also characterizes aesthetic of Korean traditional architecture.

Historically this structure system has been developed exclusively in plan, applied only to one-story residence, even there were some higher unoccupiable structures with this system as a religious symbol. However, as various modeling softwares have been developed recently, there are more opportunities to apply this traditional system into complex high-rise structure to meet contemporary purposes and programs. *Vernacular Versatility* can open a new chapter of possibility to bring this hundreds-year-old tradition to present day with high-resolution intelligence and beauty.

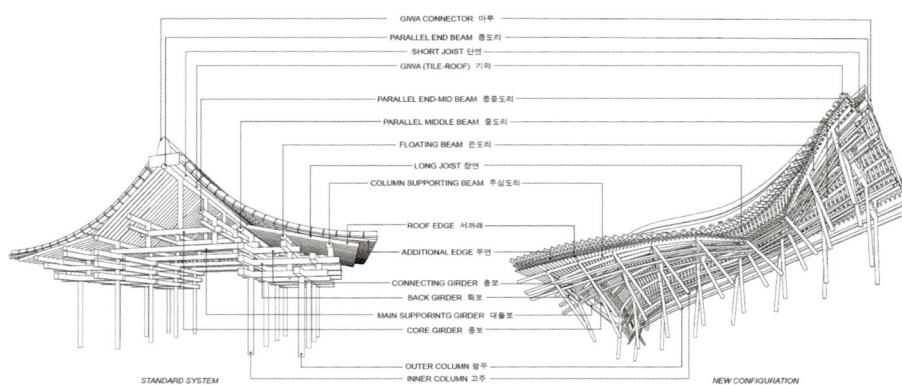

purposes and programs. Vernacular Versatility can open a new chapter of possibilities to bring this hundreds-year-old tradition to present day with high-resolution intelligence and beauty.

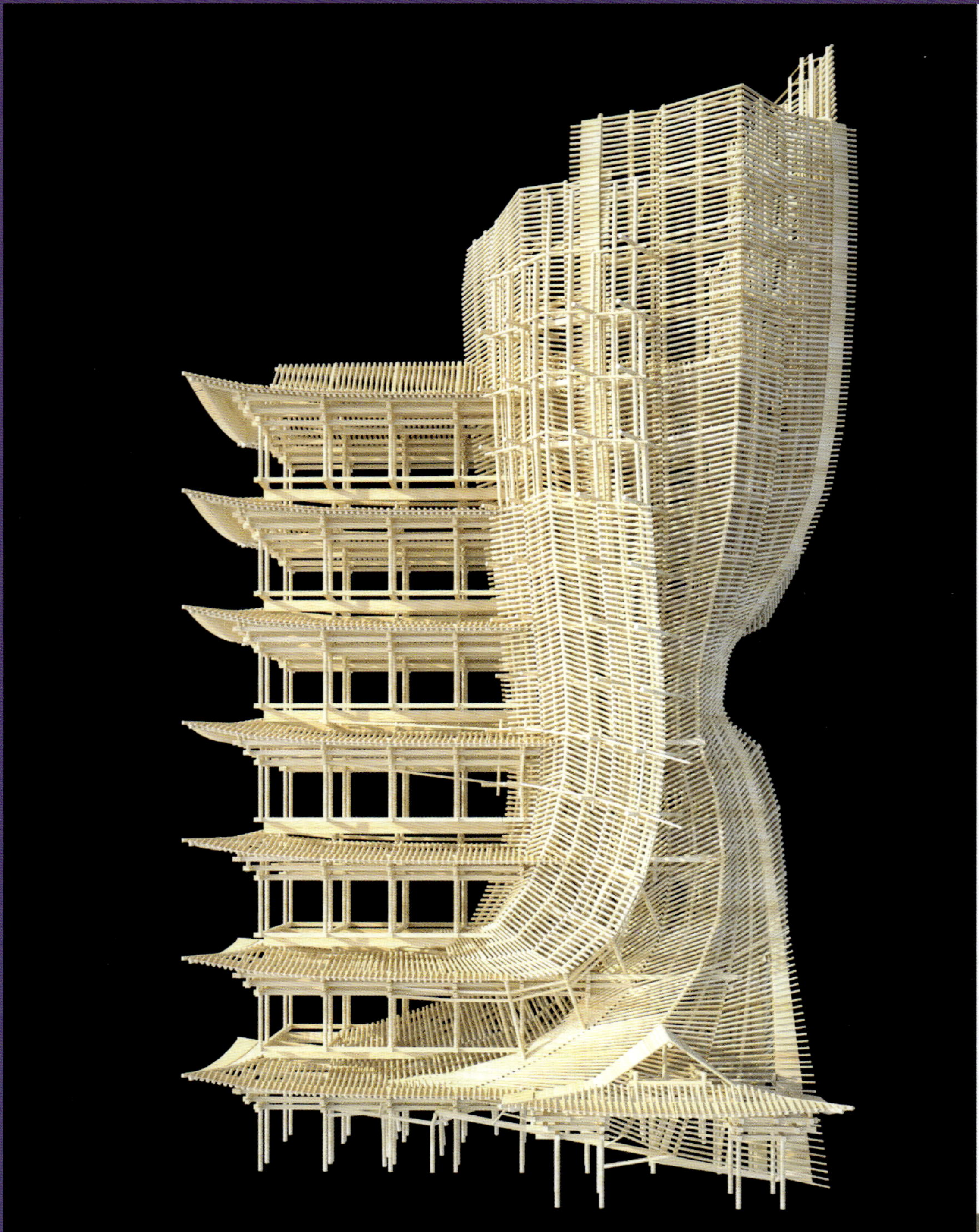

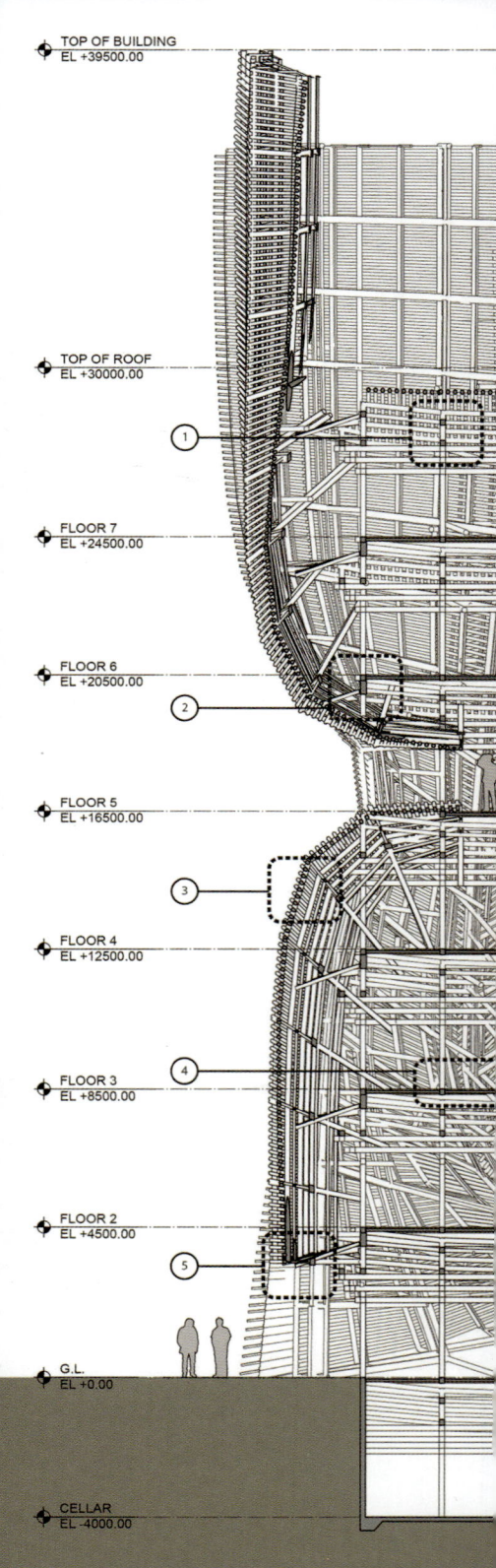

TOP OF BUILDING
EL +39500.00

TOP OF ROOF
EL +30000.00

①

FLOOR 7
EL +24500.00

FLOOR 6
EL +20500.00

②

FLOOR 5
EL +16500.00

③

FLOOR 4
EL +12500.00

④

FLOOR 3
EL +8500.00

FLOOR 2
EL +4500.00

⑤

G.L.
EL +0.00

CELLAR
EL -4000.00

After 1970's, with urban development, modern apartment had overwhelmed Korean built environment and *Hanok* was disappeared in every town. However, the value of *Hanok* has been highlighted from 2000s the efficient of its eco-friendly function and healing effectiveness has been emphasized. Today, the number of people who try to move in *Hanok* is growing rapidly to cure the diseases such as atopy or asthma which is mainly caused by environment. *Hanok* takes only 0.77% yet in whole buildings oh Korea (2008).
This proposal is located in one of the busiest districts in Korea, employed by commercial and residential purpose like neighbor buildings. While people use this building in their routines, its exceptional vision will attract people's attention and stimulate their interest in traditional architecture. Moreover, it will eventually be absorbed into people's everyday lives.

0302

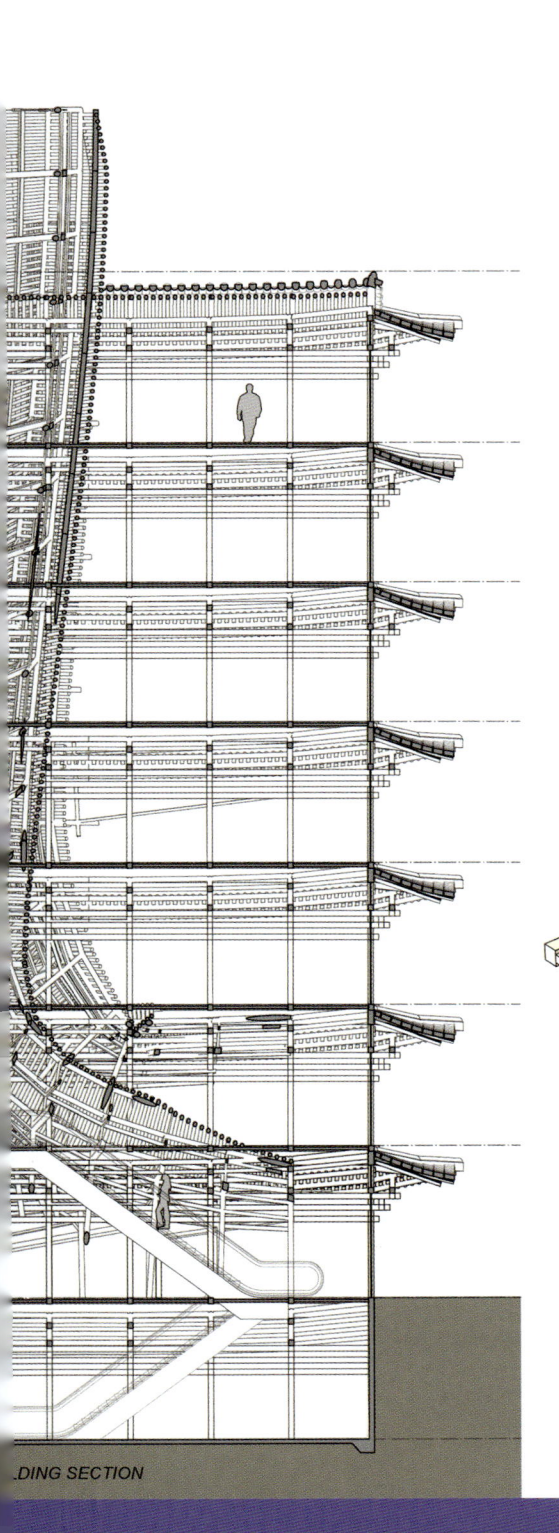

.DING SECTION

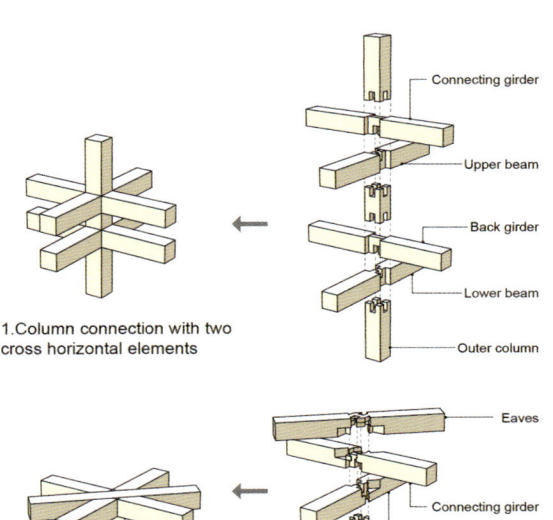

Connecting girder
Upper beam
Back girder
Lower beam
Outer column

1. Column connection with two cross horizontal elements

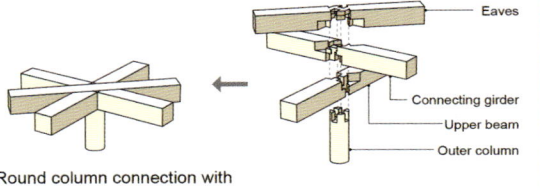

Eaves
Connecting girder
Upper beam
Outer column

2. Round column connection with three cross horizontal elements

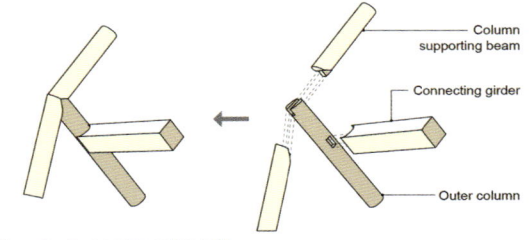

Column supporting beam
Connecting girder
Outer column

3. Round column connection with point-meeting horizontal elements

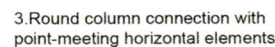

Back girder
Lower beam
Slab

4. Slab connection with two horizontal elements

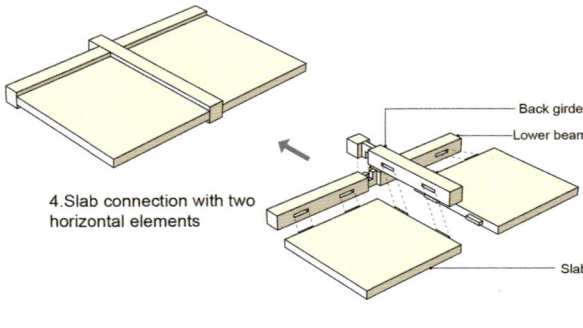

Lower beam
Back girder

Inner column
Outer column

5. End connection

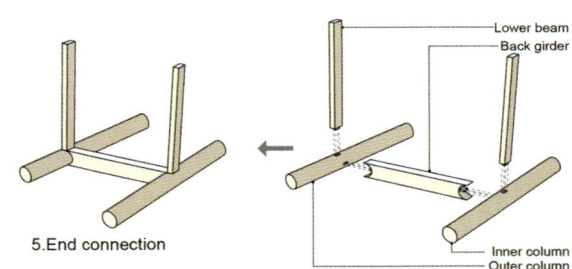

WOODEN CONNECTION -"GAGU"

STANDARD SYSTEM, 3D PRINTING

TRANSFORMATION, 3D PRINTING

NEW ADAPTATION, 3D PRINTING

PROPOGATE

YuHao Liu
Rui Wu

Canada

3RD PLACE / 2014

PROPAGATE tower grows.
carbon assimilating structure

Carbon capture is an emerging practice aimed at capturing and containing greenhouse gases to mitigate its net availability in the atmosphere. However, existing carbon capture practices use the method of point capture, capturing carbon gases at the source, requiring a significant initial investment in additional facilities, infrastructure, and maintenance of underground storages. Hence the implementation of point capture method may directly and indirectly contribute to a significant sum of greenhouse gases through construction, material production and processing, in addition to the contingencies associated with underground storage. Current research on carbon gases suggest alternative method of capture, such as air capture through carbon-philic resins and material processes that reform carbon dioxide into solid construction material. Taking this one step further, we hypothesized a material capable of assimilating

0612

Challenge

Carbon capture is an emerging practice aimed at capturing and containing greenhouse gases to mitigate its net availability in the atmosphere. However, existing carbon capture practices use the method of point capture, capturing carbon gases at the source, requiring a significant initial investment in additional facilities, infrastructure, and maintenance of underground storages. Hence the implementation of point capture method may directly and indirectly contribute to a significant sum of greenhouse gases through construction, material production and processing, in addition to the contingencies associated with underground storage.

Current research on carbon gases suggest alternative method of capture, such as air capture through carbon-philic resins and material processes that reform carbon dioxide into solid construction material. Taking this one step further, we hypothesized a material capable of assimilating carbon dioxide as a means to self-propagation. Employing such a material allows air capture of carbon dioxide and the resultant production of a solid construction material capable of supporting load.

Channeling its properties, we propose a skyscraper that grows.

Concept

By constructing a simple vertical grid scaffold as a framework, we are given control to the extent and underlying structure of the skyscraper. Required ingredients for material propagation are supplied through the scaffold, while its actual pattern of growth is defined by environmental factors such as wind, weather, and the saturation of carbon dioxide within the immediate atmosphere. Thus each resulting structure is sui generis in its formal expression while maintaining a regular spatial organization for ease of occupation and adaptation.

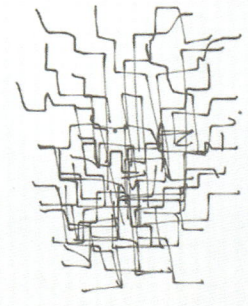

Various circulation methods can be employed depending on the need, and retrofitting of circulation enables the occupation of individuals. Naturally, clusters of habitation will emerge with the circulation access at its center, with each structure able to accommodate multiple circulation access and clusters. As occupied spaces increase, varying access can be linked to form lifted streetscapes between a multiplicity of clusters. While programmatic attributions are left undefined and inherently open to occupying individuals, the open structural framework allows tetris-like stacking and up to six directions to extend existing space. The regularity of its physical form guarantees the ease and accessibility of occupation, attracting and inspiring new methods of habiting within the skyscraper. Given the three-dimensional freedom of occupying space, new forms of social interaction may also emerge as a result.

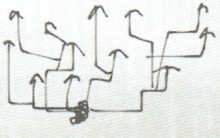

Unlike conventional skyscrapers which rely on steel frame and concrete casting, the proposed skyscraper suggests a more environmental conscious construction method, an alternative mode of occupation and ownership, and possibly a distinct organization of social relationships.

carbon dioxide as a means to self-propagation. Employing such a material allows air capture of carbon dioxide and the resultant production of a solid construction material capable of supporting load. Channeling its properties, we propose a skyscraper that grows. By constructing a simple vertical grid scaffold as a framework, we are given control to the extent and underlying structure of the skyscraper. Required ingredients for material propagation are supplied through the scaffold, while its actual pattern of growth is defined by environmental factors such as wind, weather, and the saturation of carbon dioxide within the immediate atmosphere. Thus each resulting structure is sui generis in its formal expression while maintaining a regular spatial organization for ease of occupation and adaptation. Various circulation methods can be employed depending on the need, and retrofitting of circulation enables the occupation of individuals. Naturally, clusters of habitation will emerge with the circulation access at its center, with

Diagrams

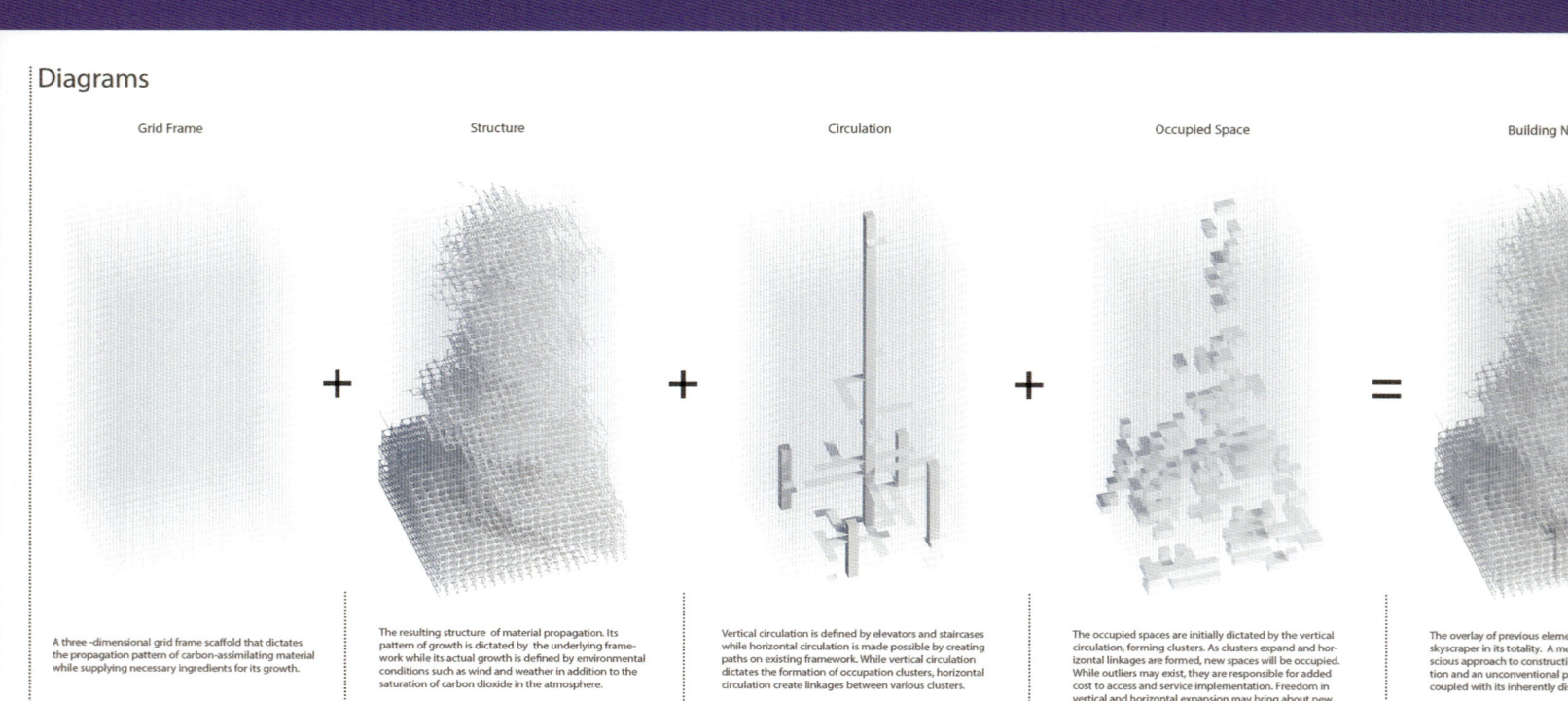

| Grid Frame | Structure | Circulation | Occupied Space | Building Name |

A three -dimensional grid frame scaffold that dictates the propagation pattern of carbon-assimilating material while supplying necessary ingredients for its growth.

The resulting structure of material propagation. Its pattern of growth is dictated by the underlying framework while its actual growth is defined by environmental conditions such as wind and weather in addition to the saturation of carbon dioxide in the atmosphere.

Vertical circulation is defined by elevators and staircases while horizontal circulation is made possible by creating paths on existing framework. While vertical circulation dictates the formation of occupation clusters, horizontal circulation create linkages between various clusters.

The occupied spaces are initially dictated by the vertical circulation, forming clusters. As clusters expand and horizontal linkages are formed, new spaces will be occupied. While outliers may exist, they are responsible for added cost to access and service implementation. Freedom in vertical and horizontal expansion may bring about new social dynamics.

The overlay of previous elements of skyscraper in its totality. A more en scious approach to construction th tion and an unconventional patter coupled with its inherently distinct

Interior

each structure able to accommodate multiple circulation access and clusters. As occupied spaces increase, varying access can be linked to form lifted streetscapes between a multiplicity of clusters. While programmatic attributions are left undefined and inherently open to occupying individuals, the open structural framework allows tetris-like stacking and up to six directions to extend existing space. The regularity of its physical form guarantees the ease and accessibility of occupation, attracting and inspiring new methods of habiting within the skyscraper. Given the three-dimensional freedom of occupying space, new forms of social interaction may also emerge as a result. Unlike conventional skyscrapers, which rely on steel frame and concrete casting, the proposed skyscraper suggests a more environmental conscious construction method, an alternative mode of occupation and ownership, and possibly a distinct organization of social relationships.

Section

The section illustrates a possible way of occupying the proposed skyscraper through the overlay of all key elements.

Regularity is emphasized while vertical circulation dictates the central axis of the structure.

While most individual spaces are enclosed, paths for horizontal circulation may be open to the environment.

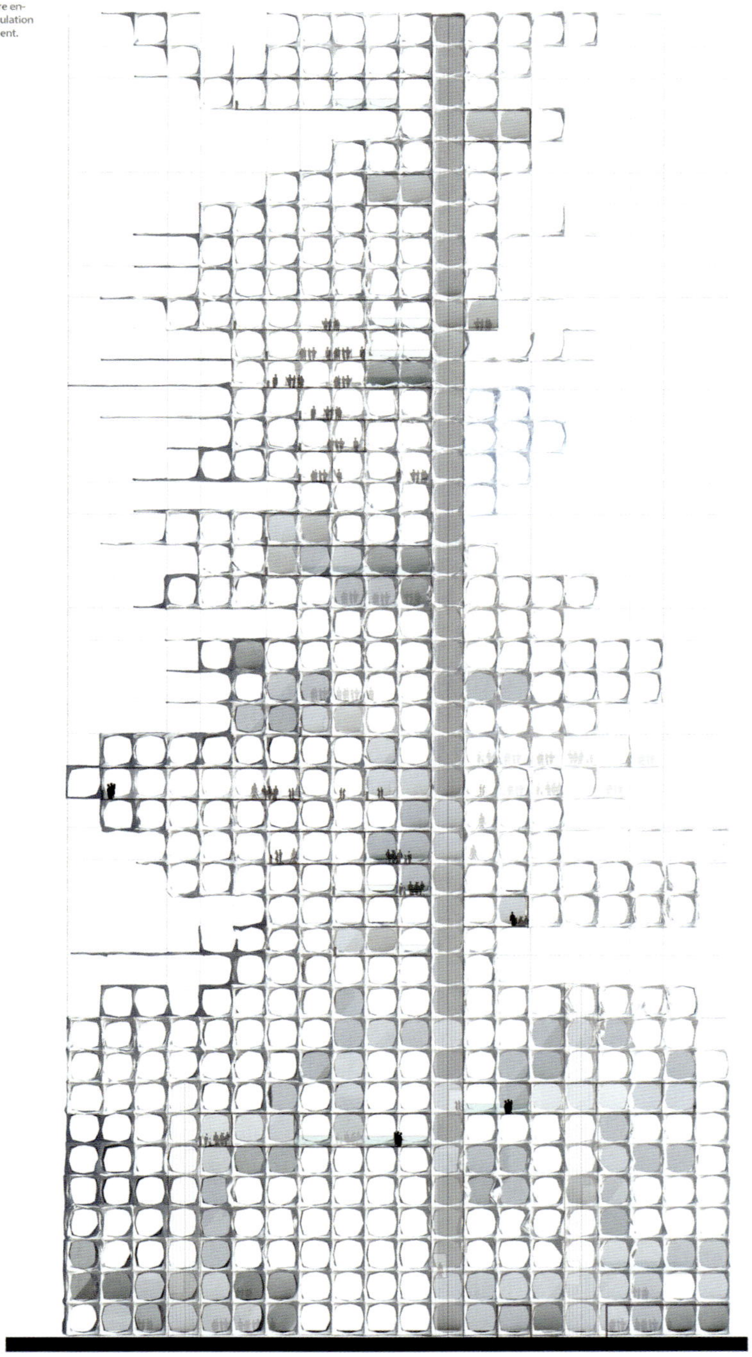

Structural Growth

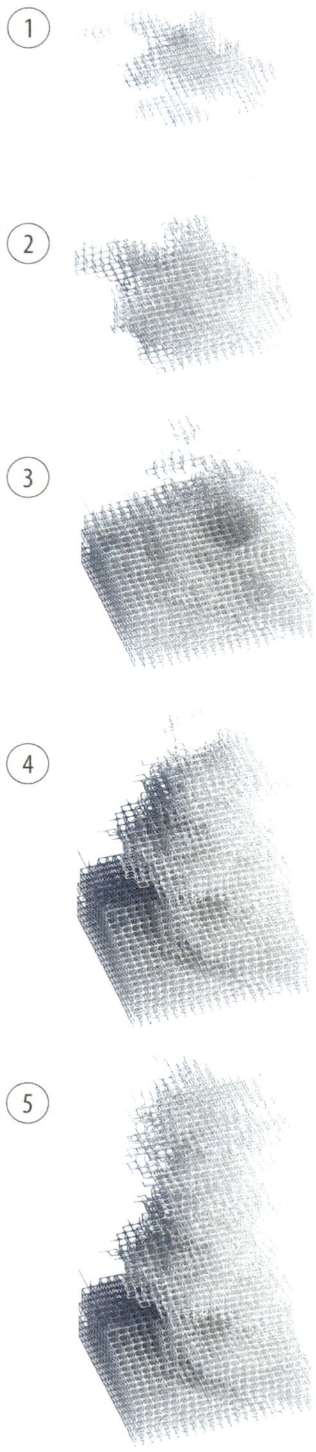

0612

① ② ③ ④ ⑤

PLEXUS TOWER

Chris Thackrey
Steven Ma
Bao An Nguyen Phuoc
Christos Koukis
Matus Nedecky

United States

Aerial View +>> Approaching Helicopter

orth Perspective +>> From Hong Kong Vi

The PleXus Tower emerges from the banks of the West Hong Kong Harbor as a distribution of disjointed structures, initially finding itself amidst the neighboring ferry terminal. The structure starts out as distributed pods reaching out to connect with the city's transportation fabric, accepting traffic from the water in the form of boats, ferries, and other water vehicles. This misfit arrangement of structural pods weaves into alignment with the Macau terminal to greatly increase the scale of the transportation hub. Bridged together by connected pipelines over the water, these pods work in harmony with the existing Macau Ferry Terminal to expediently move people towards the inner structure. This assembly forms a podium for the first segment of the tower, which emerges as a parking structure accessible from the highway network tangent to the tower. Located at the water's edge next to the Macau Ferry Terminal,

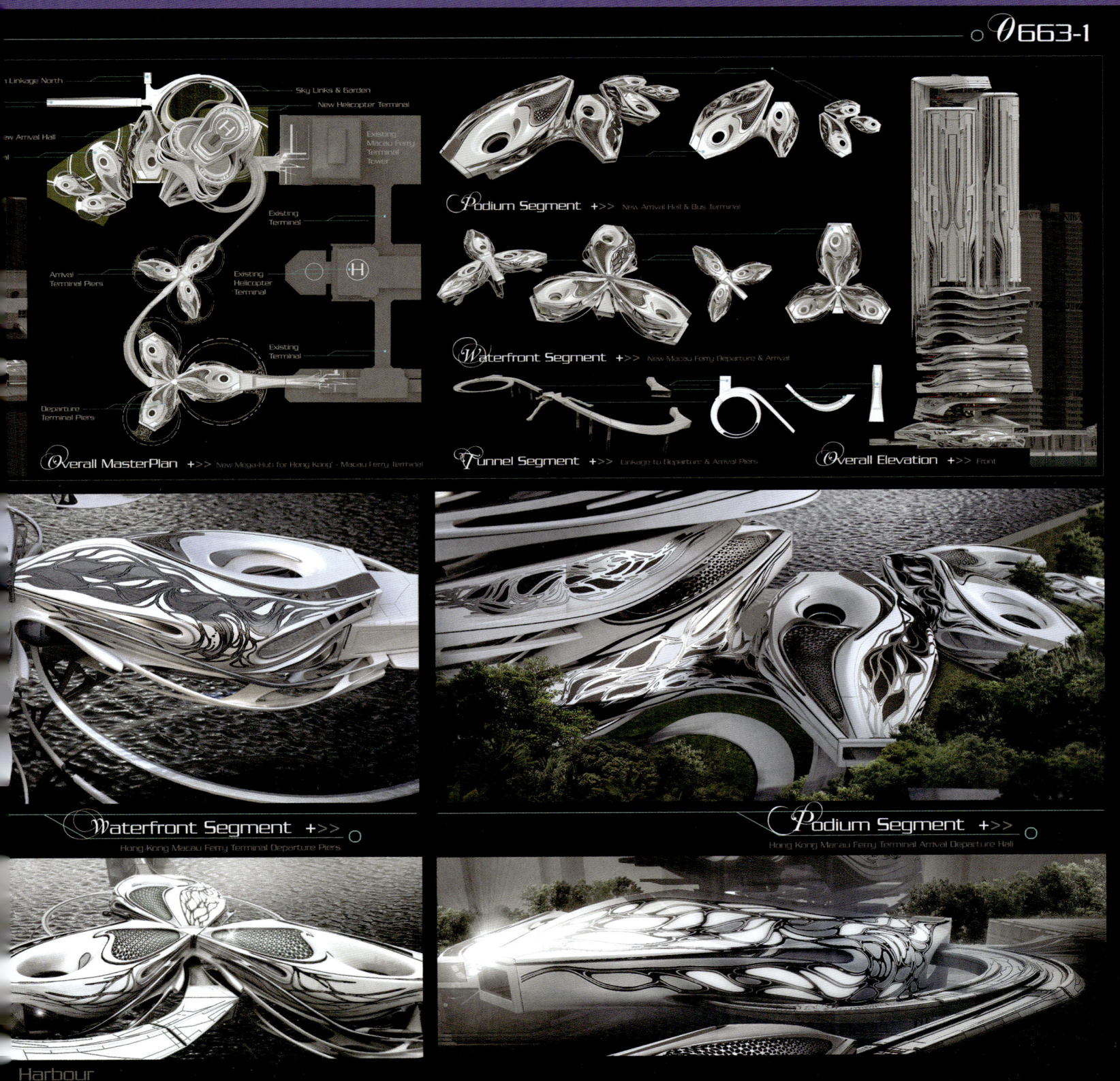

the tower's design varies in both its circulation and organization to control the speed at which it receives and negotiates the flow of traffic to optimize movement around and inside the structure. As you move inward from the receiving pods, the main structure begins to evolve its own function. First is a horizontal parking structure on the lower levels of the main building, which emerges as a parking structure accessible from the connected highway network to efficiently receive car traffic. As you move up the main structure, business and shopping space is available, all accessible by car to the highest level of the tower. The upper reaches of the towers are set aside for residential space, high above the noise of the city, providing a living area that incorporates spectacular views of the dynamic city skyline. A heliport on top of the structure can receive air traffic from above. The solid form on the south side of the main tower receives solar energy during the day, providing power to the building. The skin is breathable with

Horizontal Segment +>> v

plexus

South Perspective +>> From Sheung Wan H

numerous openings designed to overlap each other, undulating throughout, allowing carbon dioxide to easily filter out from the designated parking areas on the lower levels. Each parking level will also utilize foliage to further filter carbon dioxide from the air helping to reduce pollution in Hong Kong. The PleXus tower was conceived as a segmented, but highly connected network of major transportation functions, as well as housing conventional program. The shift in the way the tower design is read, as well as in the functionality of each segment, provides greater programmatic control. Residential is accessible yet private, parking is convenient, and circulation through the ground-level public space is able to provoke interest. At night, lights will glow from the panels, reminding us of the connections these segments share as well as blending in with Hong Kong's unique night skyline.

EIDOS

Carlo Bailey
Lorenzo Villaggi

United States

EIDOS:
OR WHEN DESIRE BECOMES MATTER

Concept

Eidos is a prototypical self-sufficient community based sometime in the near future. The project seeks to manage difference and individualism within spatial collectivity. Additive manufacturing technologies (7-axis 3D printing robots) are employed to facilitate a housing complex that is the physical manifestation of its inhabitants wants, executed within a rigid rule-set of constraints that allow for maximum autonomy and expression. The rule-set consists of a set of algorithms, a "DNA" structure programmed into the robots which feed both environmental and the inhabitant's desires as inputs to enable the construction of units and the building's infrastructure. The rules become manifest both at the macroscopic scale - apartments, lot size, distance between units, maximum and minimum floor area - and at the the microscopic scale - walkways, fenestration, room sizes etc.

Organization & Massing

The organization of the complex wants to be as generic and uniform as possible, with the least amount of input from the architect's hand. The sun's movement across the site was analyzed to define the optimum placement of light wells and breaks in the grid to minimize shadows and bring light to the ground plane. Cuts in the massing and grid are introduced on the ground to provide connections through to adjacent city blocks and extend the Manhattan grid. The market-place is located on the ground floor with the school lying on the two floors above. The communal areas are strategically located adjacent to the four vertical circulation cores and are intertwined with the housing units throughout the remaining floors of the complex.

Building

The housing complex consists of a tubular steel mega-structure (the only explicit trace of the architect's hand). It has the combined function of being the tracks that the robots run along and the (infra)structure that upholds the housing units. The 8' x 8' grid relentlessly exhausts the horizontal plane across the site and is constantly expressed throughout the project - piercing bedrooms, living rooms and at times visible on unit facades. The grid however changes to a 16' x 16' spacing in the spaces of production and school areas. Each inhabitant is assigned a given lot area when joining the community (which can be expanded or contracted depending on need and availability of space); the inhabitant is then free to request any architectural style to her house and spatial configuration. The housing units are printed using a concrete + polymer composite with varying chromatic tones. Each detail is reproduced with fidelity and high resolution.

Program

The public program of Eidos consists of educational facilities that train those who want to learn design tools and rapid fabrication skills, a market-place for those who sell locally produced 3D printed goods, and communal areas which provide a generic space where the manufacturing and production of goods can be practiced informally. The inward looking communal areas seek to counter the "private single-balcony" typology and encourage community activities and shared spaces. A degree of economical and cultural autonomy will be achieved by the community thanks to a resilient form of production and adaptable spatial conditions over time.

Eidos according to Anonomy

While entering Eidos from Park avenue, Anonomy walks through the market. It appears to him as the physical manifestation of desire, the expression of commodified impulses. He recognizes the space as a black hole that objectively absorbs every form of lust, from the most depraved passions to the purest inclinations. Every vender is a potential collaborator, every product is a mirror revealing the cultural disposition of the surrounding neighbourhoods inhabitants. As a transient resident of East Harlem - frequently flys back to Dakar - Anonomy's unit is a simple studio apartment. Emulating the smooth futuristic curves of a Star Trek interior, Anonomy believes 90 degree corners are last century and wants his clients to think him a forward thing man.

Eidos according to Lucille

The backdrop of the bazaar, the long steel members of the structure, are for Lucille reminiscent of the bald-cypress trees that grow along the Congaree River in North Carolina. As she walks along the pedestrian paths, she imagines it as the riverbed, and the tide of people ebbing and flowing amongst the floodplain as the water that both submerges and washes away the sediment in the bazaar. Haggling, bartering, shouting and, sometimes fighting to gain the upper hand in a transaction of desire. For her own home, Lucille never wanted anything other than a stable environment to raise her children. The desire for of a mid-century ranch house aesthetic in uptown Manhattan, is vivid in the details of the 3d printed sandstone that simulates and fakes the materials of her place of origin. Lucille reconfigured the existing walls, with ornaments that she always wanted but that she could never afford. Here Architecture follows desire. And her current one is to change the location of certain rooms and walls, in order to accommodate the frequent visits of her grandchildren, usually lost contemplating the unpredictable organic movements of the machines.

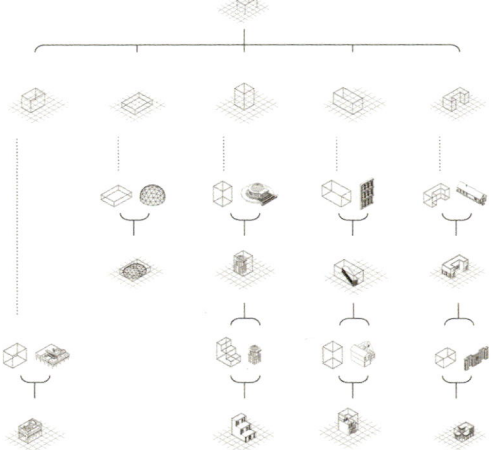

Above: housing unit hybridization - diagram indicates the limitless possibilties of housing styles and growth; that are a combination of inhabitants desires and prescribed lot size

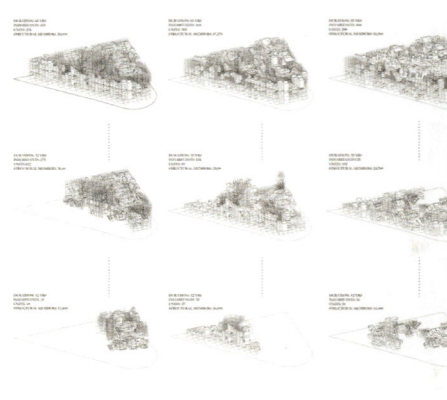

Above: Eidos growth scenerios - showing the potential varying configurations the housing complex assume over time

Above: site plan - oblique view looking from below, showing the circulaiton walkways, spaces of production and housing units.
Right: Elevation - close-up of the megastructure

Eidos is a prototypical self-sufficient community based sometime in the near future. The project seeks to manage difference and individualism within spatial collectivity. Additive manufacturing technologies (7-axis 3D printing robots) are employed to facilitate a housing complex that is the physical manifestation of its inhabitants wants, executed within a rigid rule-set of constraints that allow for maximum autonomy and expression. The rule-set consists of a set of algorithms; a "DNA" structure programmed into the robots which feed both environmental and the inhabitant's desires as inputs to enable the construction of units and the building's infrastructure. The rules become manifest both at the macroscopic scale - apartments, lot size, distance between units, maximum and minimum floor area - and at the microscopic scale - walkways, fenestration, room sizes etc. The sun's movement across the site was analysed to

0693

define the optimum placement of light wells and breaks in the grid to minimize shadows and bring light to the ground plane. Cuts in the massing and grid are introduced on the ground to provide connections through to adjacent city blocks and extend the Manhattan grid. The market place is located on the ground floor with the school lying on the two floors above. The communal areas are strategically located adjacent to the four vertical circulation cores and are intertwined with the housing units throughout the remaining floors of the complex. The housing complex consists of a tubular steel mega-structure (the only explicit trace of the architect's hand). It has the combined function of being the tracks that the robots run along and the infrastructure that upholds the housing units. The 8' x 8' grid relentlessly exhausts the horizontal plane across the site and is constantly expressed throughout the project -

Above: market-place
Right: combined urban section and ground floor plan showing the marketplace

Above: looking north along walkway
Below: classroom of the educational facility

Right: axonmetric showing educational facility, market-place and housing units

piercing bedrooms, living rooms and at times visible on unit facades. The grid however changes to a 16' x 16' spacing in the spaces of production and school areas. Each inhabitant is assigned a given lot area when joining the community (which can be expanded or contracted depending on need and availability of space); the inhabitant is then free to request any architectural style to her house and spatial configuration. The housing units are printed using a concrete + polymer composite with varying chromatic tones. Each detail is reproduced with fidelity and high resolution. The public program of Eidos consists of educational facilities that train those who want to learn design tools and rapid fabrication skills, a market-place for those who sell locally produced 3D printed goods, and communal areas which provide a generic space where the manufacturing and production of goods can be practiced informally.

PLASTIC MODEL

Hee Seung Yoon
Tae Youn Lee

South Korea
Philippines

DESIGN STUDIO

LEE TAE YOUN | YOON HEE SEUNG

We imagine in the distant future, a world without design drawings, a society in which everyone has a home of his or her choice; homes, which are already prefabricated in a factory. This is a future where we can buy space like a buying a car.

The problems with today's society are the expensive costs of construction and the rise of home prices. Therefore, someone who does not have the capital cannot buy house nor can they save money for their future.

Individuals will assemble the product, which is produced by companies and governments. This space can be removable or detachable like a toy, and all products have product number. Hence the product will be advertised on television and. This attributes to the mass appeal and access of the

0798-1

PLASTIC MODEL
SPACE OF PRODUCT

BACKGROUND
we are dreaming of in Distant future from Interesting thought.
A world without design drawings. Society in which everyone has a home of their choice. house which already made from factory. The future that we can buy space like a buying a car.
The problem with today's society is expensive construction costs and House prices rise. Therefore, someone who do not have capital can not buy house in the society and and they will not able to save money for their future.
Individuals will assemble the Product which produced by companies and governments for Making their house. This space can be removable or detachable like a toy, and all product have product number. Hence the product will show on the tv and media as a advertisement. a lot of people are able to buy the product which produced by factory. Therefore, the product will improve for people in Distant future.

SPACE OF PRODUCT

product.

Now, users who do not have time to create design drawings, and those who cannot understand them will be able to create their own homes to their very own liking. This idea also changes the roles of the designers and architects. When they work on designing, they do not have to concentrate on making design drawings, and thus have more free time allocated to creative design.

In addition the variability of the materials and plastics used as building mediums, and they allowance of recycling the mediums, means the homes can be fabricated and installed just about anywhere. And the lightweight nature of this building type means skyscrapers can be vertically stacked with ease.

DESIGN STUDIO

LEE TAE YOUN | YOON HEE SEUNG

798-2

SEMBLY PROCESS

...use it is a direct impact to the user, such as performance and safety of the product,
...e be used in assembling by assembly instructions exactly.
...on Breakage Before assembly, cannot be replaced due to damage.

PLASTIC MODEL
SPACE OF PRODUCT

① ASSEMBLY PLAN1

② ASSEMBLY PLAN2

③ FINISHED PRODUCT

④ COMBINATION

EFSF-INTERIOR
MADE IN KOREA

A DEAL DRAWING

ROBOT ARM

Anymore User do not have to use Design drawings
which can not understand because the Design drawings would change like a manual for assembly.
As well as this idea would change the future for the Designer and architect. when they work designing, they
do not have to Concentrate for making a Design drawings. Therefore, they can have the time which for Creative design.
In another aspect of we can get the benefit that the Materials of plastic can make Various forms so we can live
to any places.
this product is not heavy so it can help that we can build
skyscraper easily at any where as a Various functions.

① ASSEMBLY PLAN1

② ASSEMBLY PLAN2

③ BACK PLAN

④ FINISHED PRODUCT

MADE IN KOREA
WB

SPACE OF PRODUC

CYBERTOPIA

Egor Orlov

Russia

3RD PLACE / 2015

Future of an archit

Cybertopia. Death of analogous cities

Program blocks of the skyscraper

A complex space structure of the future megapolis made from reality and fairytale generates a more complicated structure of the city. Spaces of these "fairytales" have a large number of physical and mechanical laws that are alien to real space. An ability to fly over or move from one planet to another one, to pass through the walls during system bugs makes the city more complicated. Cyberspace, full of hallucination and bugs - components of its own habitat, has moved into a real megapolis that is being formed and organized simultaneously in the digital and physical space. Tomorrow, we expect a completely different topography of the city. It will be a map, which includes cyber worlds with intrinsic geography, laws of physics, qualities, and even its own residents. It is as though landscapes of computer games have woven into the city space becoming an integral part. The spatial structure of a skyscraper

0019

ture space

Profound scrutinizing
Bay of the skyscraper's city

International blocks of the skyscraper's city

Communications in the Hollywood

Card file of elements and components

Bay of the skyscraper's city

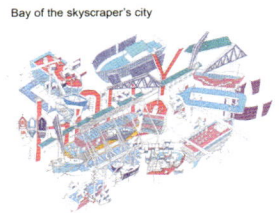

International blocks of the skyscraper's city

Communications in the Hollywood

is also flexible and mobile. The entire complex is formed as a round frame structure, on which cranes move, completing and moving whole blocks of the complex. The part of the frame structure can be sorted all at once upon completion of the region of a housing estate or intentionally to remain invested with a framework for the potential possibility of further transformation and change in the future. The whole, completed regions of a housing estate can move to a separate sector in order "not to disturb" nor "not to constrain" further building, or can be interspersed directly into the frame structure for transformation of a programmatic palette or its intended consolidation. Huge ships all at once become part of this block of the skyscraper, its organic communication and spatial cell. Its decks are temporary squares of the city, and the scaffolding of its streets. On them, inhabitants move. Having sated, the ship "sails" into the next journey and on arrival in the new port city, leaving indefinitely the dusty megalopolis

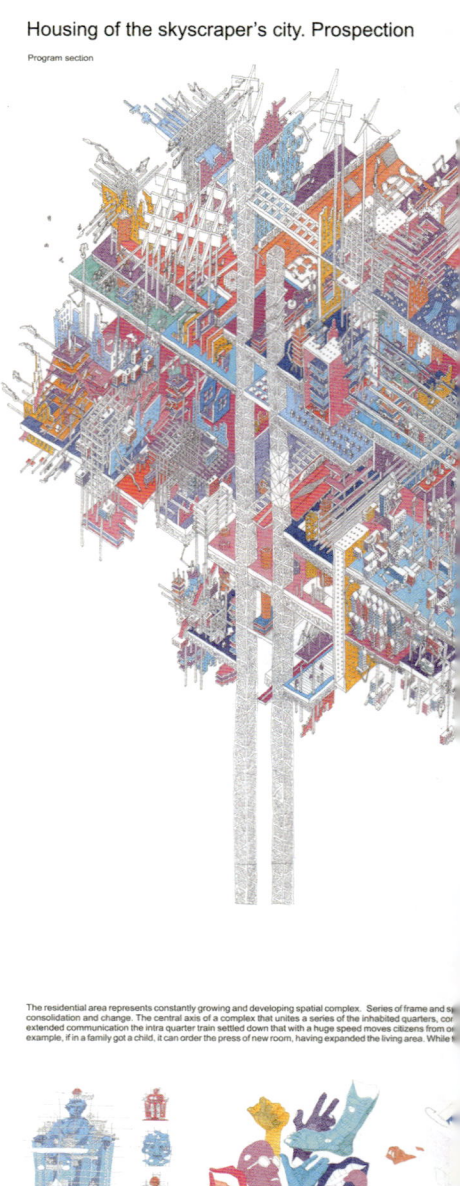

Housing of the skyscraper's city. Prospection

Program section

The residential area represents constantly growing and developing spatial complex. Series of frame and consolidation and change. The central axis of a complex that unites a series of the inhabited quarters, extended communication the intra quarter train settled down that with a huge speed moves citizens from example, if in a family got a child, it can order the press of new room, having expanded the living area. While

Yes, we CAN!

port, joins a new structure as the spatial block. Main decks of the ships are covered with numerous weaving installations, where highly skilled immigrant workers start weaving goods for the city. Other ships serve as suppliers of a material for housing that is constructed here. It is a new format of the city street, new public space in a hyper dense and dynamic urban environment. The residential area of the skyscraper represents constantly growing and developing spatial complexes. Series of framing and spatial elements, printed by a 3D printer or by drone construction, carry out a role of structures for the subsequent local consolidation and change. The central axis of a complex that unites a series of the inhabited quarters comprises of a monorail, on which moves the printer, which is printing out, and in some cases erasing spatial structures.

0019

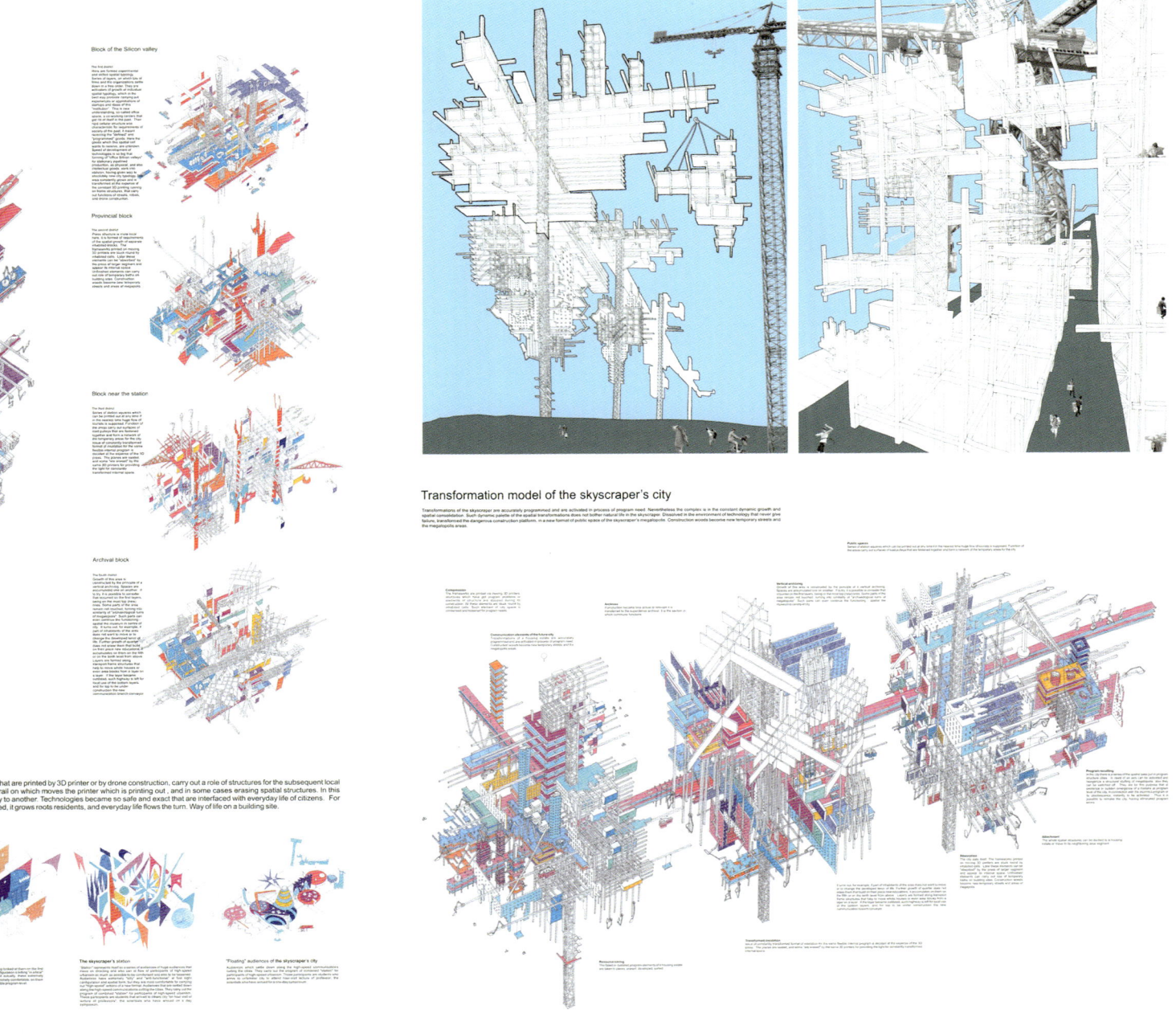

Transformation model of the skyscraper's city

THE ARK

Razvan Barsan
Alexandru Duca
Alexandru Solomon
Simona Dinescu

Romania

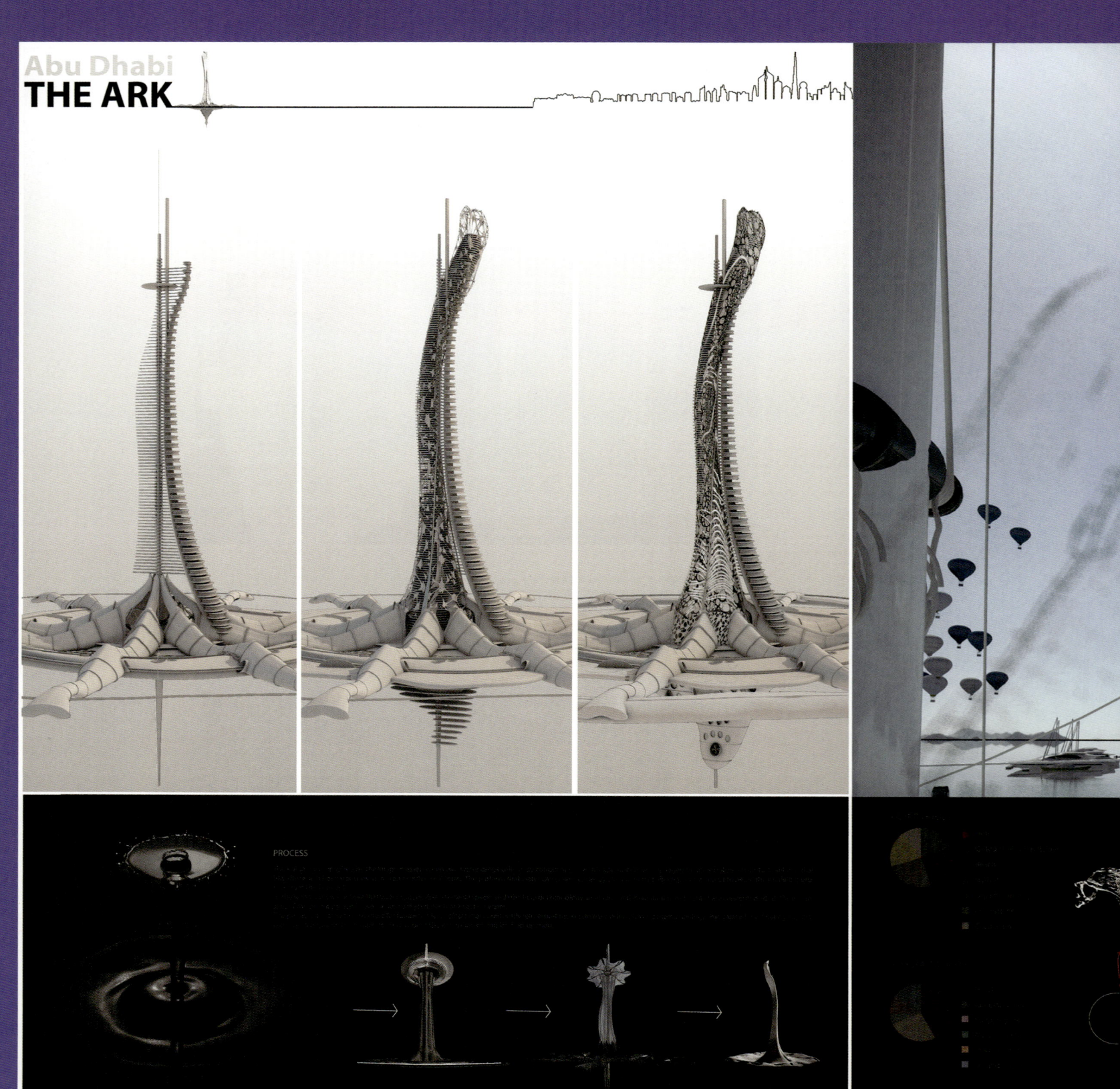

The volume was inspired by the shape created when two water drops collide. By conducting several experiments we managed to immortalize a sculptural volume that has afterwards been transposed into an architectural form. The patterns that water can shape, either by carving or by colliding, motivated us to begin the modeling process from this concept. At the same time, we believe that water can provide habitable spaces with the help of technology, ingenuity and imagination. As scientists are concerned about the expansion of the planetary ocean, we created a skyscraper that floats on water.. Although we`ve chosen Abu Dhabi as the original location for the skyscraper, the island can be moved about the planetary ocean with the help of massive ships thanks to the submerged volume that sustains the entire tower. Due to its high level of self-sufficiency, the island can be relocated across the ocean`s surface, in

0190

GLOBAL SCALE

LANDMARK

either high-populated or isolated areas. The skyscraper is located strategically into the main harbor of Abu Dhabi. This idle setting places the hotel in a coherent context, allowing it to contribute to the city's identity and notoriety. The hotel continues the skyline of the city whilst enriching its architectural value and emphasizing its modern appearance. Therefore, the tower becomes a landmark for Abu Dhabi, reinforcing its status of international city. A subtle dialogue starts between the city and the floating skyscraper, as the inhabitants of the city can admire the skyscraper from various points across the bay, while the visitors of the hotel can enjoy a panoramic view of Abu Dhabi. The skyscraper integrates naturally into the landscape, giving the impression that it rises above the waves from the depths of the ocean, just like the seamount chains nearby. The exterior shell is composed of three layers that define a double-skin facade covered in an LED layer that brightens the building at night. The first layer has a

Abu Dhabi
THE ARK

structural role. A spider-web made of carbon fiber models the shape of the building, while at the same time creating spectacular views from the inside. The second skin is translucent, allowing natural light to flood the interior spaces. A part of the green areas on the island recreate ecosystems from the five continents in order to express the tower`s global nature. The nature preservation centers located here monitor the fauna and flora from the island and from under the sea. Some of the green areas are used for farming, thus providing typical foods from different parts of the world. The hotel offers a unique experience to its visitors, allowing them to get to know better the world that we live in. In a dry area water is a valuable resource, therefore the tower integrates purified water processed on the on-site plant into the functioning of the ecosystems. Clean water is also used for farming.

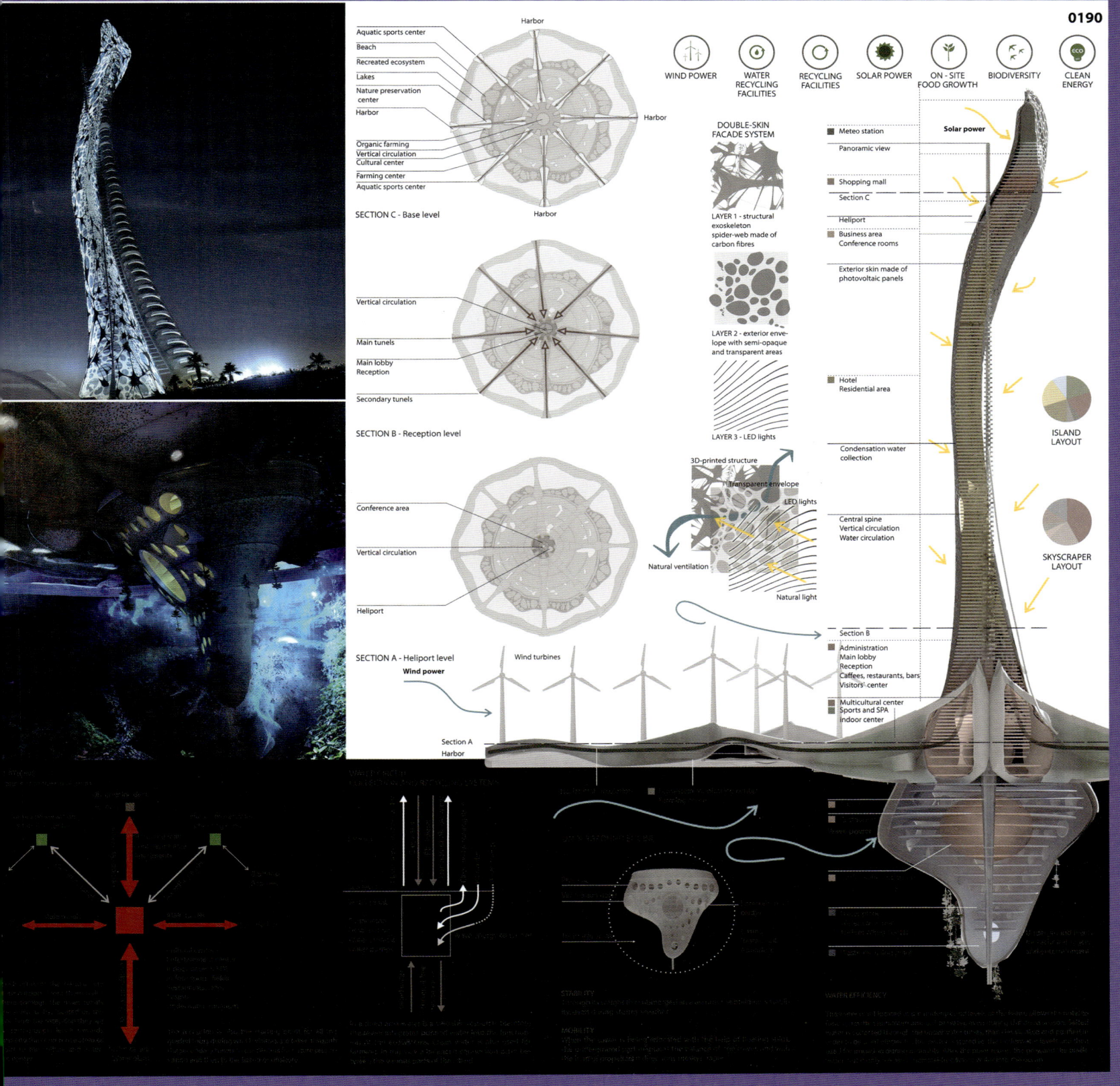

PLAY THE SYSTEMS   Samuel Kim

United States

TRANSITION POINT TO DTLA

The fundamental concept of 'play the systems' begins with the interpretation of architecture as a character rather than a medium. Game theorists Katie Salen and Eric Zimmerman describe the term 'play' as the "free movement within a more rigid structure". 'Play' requires the willingness of the player to submit to the rules of a structure, providing an input for a crafted system. However, such free movement is ultimately governed by the intrinsic qualities and characteristics of the player. How does architecture 'freely' move?

    This exploration is driven particularly by the observance of systems that emerge out of various professions and/or are revealed in different moments of nature. Specific to this case is the weaire-phelan structure, which currently seems to be the solution to the 'kelvin problem', a problem that asks

LOBBY

0219

PLAY THE SYSTEMS

THE FUNDAMENTAL CONCEPT OF 'PLAY THE SYSTEMS' BEGINS WITH THE INTERPRETATION OF ARCHITECTURE AS A CHARACTER RATHER THAN A MEDIUM. GAME THEORISTS KATIE SALEN AND ERIC ZIMMERMAN DESCRIBE THE TERM 'PLAY' AS THE "FREE MOVEMENT WITHIN A MORE RIGID STRUCTURE". 'PLAY' REQUIRES THE WILLINGNESS OF THE PLAYER TO SUBMIT TO THE RULES OF A STRUCTURE, PROVIDING AN INPUT FOR A CRAFTED SYSTEM. HOWEVER, SUCH FREE MOVEMENT IS ULTIMATELY GOVERNED BY THE INTRINSIC QUALITIES AND CHARACTERISTICS OF THE PLAYER. HOW DOES ARCHITECTURE 'FREELY' MOVE?

THIS EXPLORATION IS DRIVEN PARTICULARLY BY THE OBSERVANCE OF SYSTEMS THAT EMERGE OUT OF VARIOUS PROFESSIONS AND/OR ARE REVEALED IN DIFFERENT MOMENTS OF NATURE. SPECIFIC TO THIS CASE IS THE WEAIRE-PHELAN STRUCTURE WHICH CURRENTLY SEEMS TO BE THE SOLUTION TO THE 'KELVIN PROBLEM'. A PROBLEM THAT ASKS WHAT THE MOST IDEAL STRUCTURE IS. THIS STRUCTURE ANSWERS BY MAXIMIZING THE VOLUME WITHIN EACH CELL WHILE MINIMIZING THE SURFACE AREA.

THE PROJECT IS THE RESULT OF THE OBSERVANCE OF ARCHITECTURE (SKYSCRAPER) AS IT PLAYS THIS SYSTEM.

ENTRY TO BUILDING

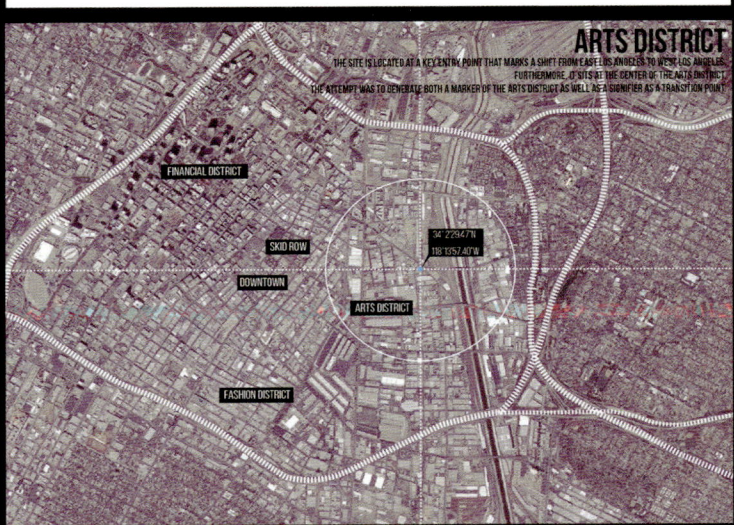

ARTS DISTRICT

THE SITE IS LOCATED AT A KEY ENTRY POINT THAT MARKS A SHIFT FROM EAST LOS ANGELES TO METRO LOS ANGELES. FURTHERMORE, IT SITS AT THE CENTER OF THE ARTS DISTRICT. THE ATTEMPT WAS TO GENERATE BOTH A MARKER OF THE ARTS DISTRICT AS WELL AS A IDENTIFIER AS A TRANSITION POINT

FINANCIAL DISTRICT

SKID ROW

DOWNTOWN

ARTS DISTRICT

FASHION DISTRICT

ENTRY TO ARTS DISTRICT

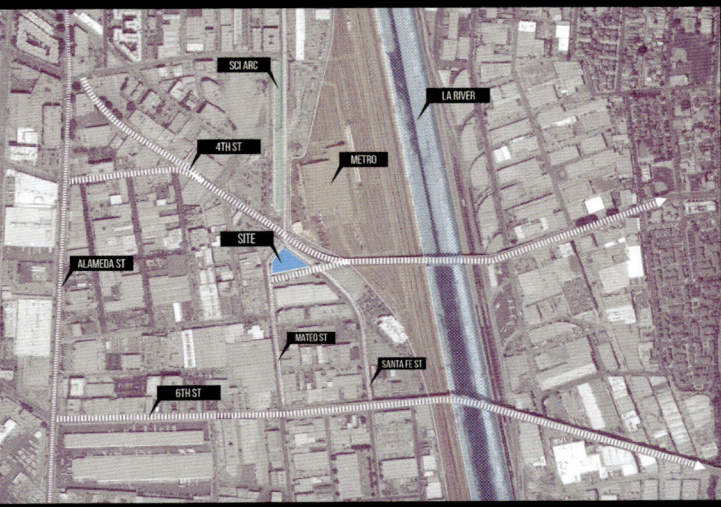

SCI ARC

LA RIVER

4TH ST

METRO

SITE

ALAMEDA ST

MATEO ST

SANTA FE ST

6TH ST

what the most ideal structure is. This structure answers by maximizing the volume within each cell while minimizing the surface area. The project is the result of the observance of architecture (skyscraper) as it plays this system.

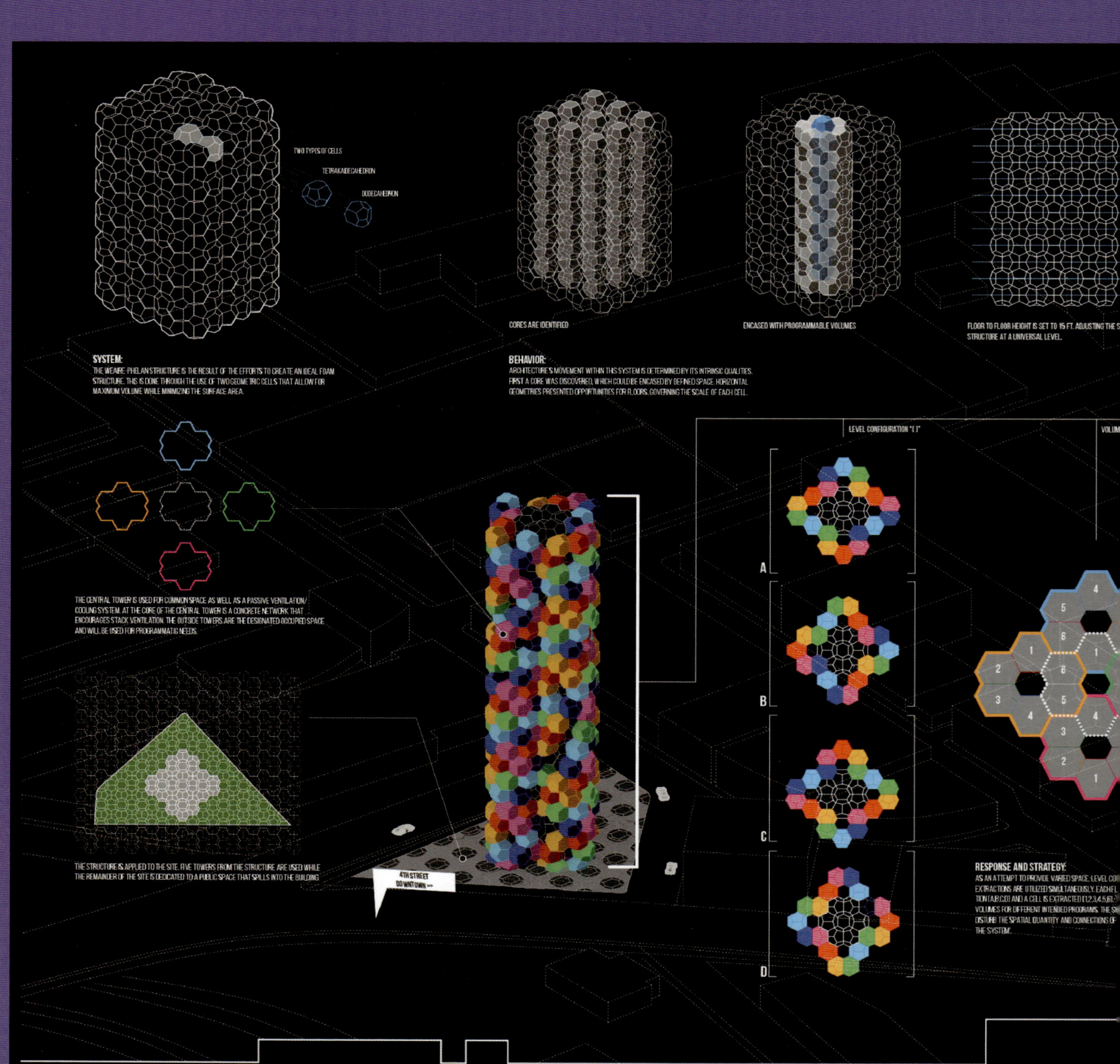

SYSTEM:
THE WEAIRE-PHELAN STRUCTURE IS THE RESULT OF THE EFFORTS TO CREATE AN IDEAL FOAM STRUCTURE. THIS IS DONE THROUGH THE USE OF TWO GEOMETRIC CELLS THAT ALLOW FOR MAXIMUM VOLUME WHILE MINIMIZING THE SURFACE AREA.

BEHAVIOR:
ARCHITECTURE'S MOVEMENT WITHIN THIS SYSTEM IS DETERMINED BY ITS INTRINSIC QUALITIES. FIRST A CORE WAS DISCOVERED, WHICH COULD BE ENCASED BY DEFINED SPACE. HORIZONTAL GEOMETRIES PRESENTED OPPORTUNITIES FOR FLOORS, GOVERNING THE SCALE OF EACH CELL.

TWO TYPES OF CELLS

TETRAKAIDECAHEDRON

DODECAHEDRON

CORES ARE IDENTIFIED

ENCASED WITH PROGRAMMABLE VOLUMES

FLOOR TO FLOOR HEIGHT IS SET TO 15 FT. ADJUSTING THE S... STRUCTURE AT A UNIVERSAL LEVEL.

THE CENTRAL TOWER IS USED FOR COMMON SPACE AS WELL AS A PASSIVE VENTILATION/ COOLING SYSTEM. AT THE CORE OF THE CENTRAL TOWER IS A CONCRETE NETWORK THAT ENCOURAGES STACK VENTILATION. THE OUTSIDE TOWERS ARE THE DESIGNATED OCCUPIED SPACE, AND WILL BE USED FOR PROGRAMMATIC NEEDS.

THE STRUCTURE IS APPLIED TO THE SITE. FIVE TOWERS FROM THE STRUCTURE ARE USED WHILE THE REMAINDER OF THE SITE IS DEDICATED TO A PUBLIC SPACE THAT SPILLS INTO THE BUILDING.

4TH STREET
DOWNTOWN >>

LEVEL CONFIGURATION "L1"   VOLUM...

A

B

C

D

RESPONSE AND STRATEGY:
AS AN ATTEMPT TO PROVIDE VARIED SPACE, LEVEL CO... EXTRACTIONS ARE UTILIZED SIMULTANEOUSLY. EACH L... TION (A,B,C,D) AND A CELL IS EXTRACTED (1,2,3,4,5,6)... VOLUMES FOR DIFFERENT INTENDED PROGRAMS. THE SI... DISTURB THE SPATIAL QUANTITY AND CONNECTIONS OF THE SYSTEM.

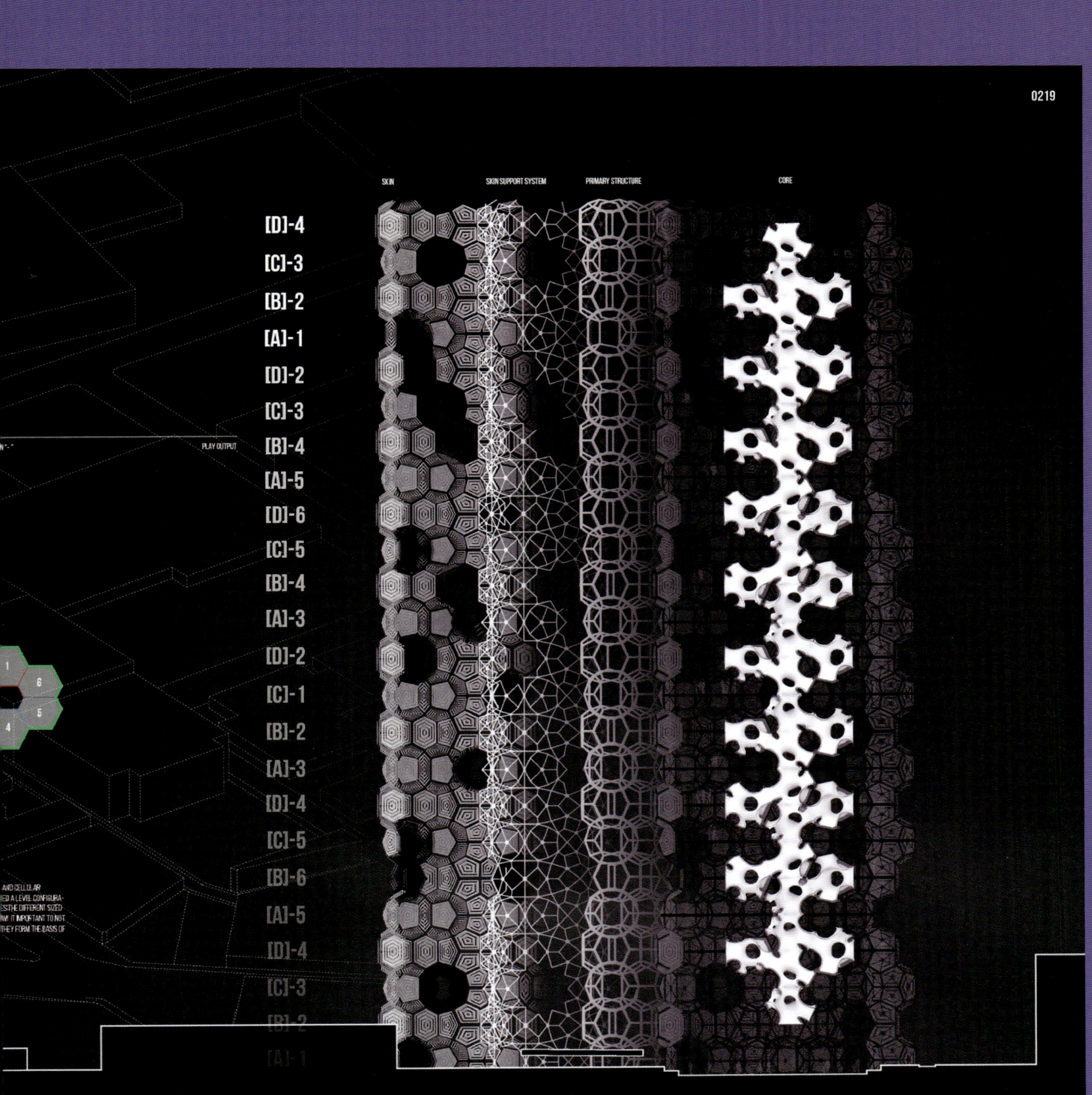

0219

SKIN   SKIN SUPPORT SYSTEM   PRIMARY STRUCTURE   CORE

[D]-4
[C]-3
[B]-2
[A]-1
[D]-2
[C]-3
[B]-4
[A]-5
[D]-6
[C]-5
[B]-4
[A]-3
[D]-2
[C]-1
[B]-2
[A]-3
[D]-4
[C]-5
[B]-6
[A]-5
[D]-4
[C]-3
[B]-2
[A]-1

PLAY OUTPUT

AND CELLULAR
ED A LEVEL CONFIGURA-
ES THE DIFFERENT SIZED
W IT IMPORTANT TO NOT
THEY FORM THE BASIS OF

24 HOUR TOWER

Honghao Deng,
Xuesong Zhang
Liwan Zhang

China

Our project is a prospect and attempt of a future architecture, which will be in E-business, rapidly constructed and industrialized. The fictional construction company mentioned in our boards as well as this article, 24 Hours Tower Co., provides services including architecture customization and rapid construction. Customers can just place an order on the website like shopping at an online retailer.

Based on the paper garland's idea, we designed a collapsible building composed by folding units, so that the building rate can be lifted sharply. We also designed the customizing, delivering, and building mode. Our two boards showed the customers' user interface under our operation mode of customizing buildings. The skyscraper showed there is a prototype of our idea.

Want a skyscraper on your property tomorrow? Login into www. 24hour-tower.com and customize

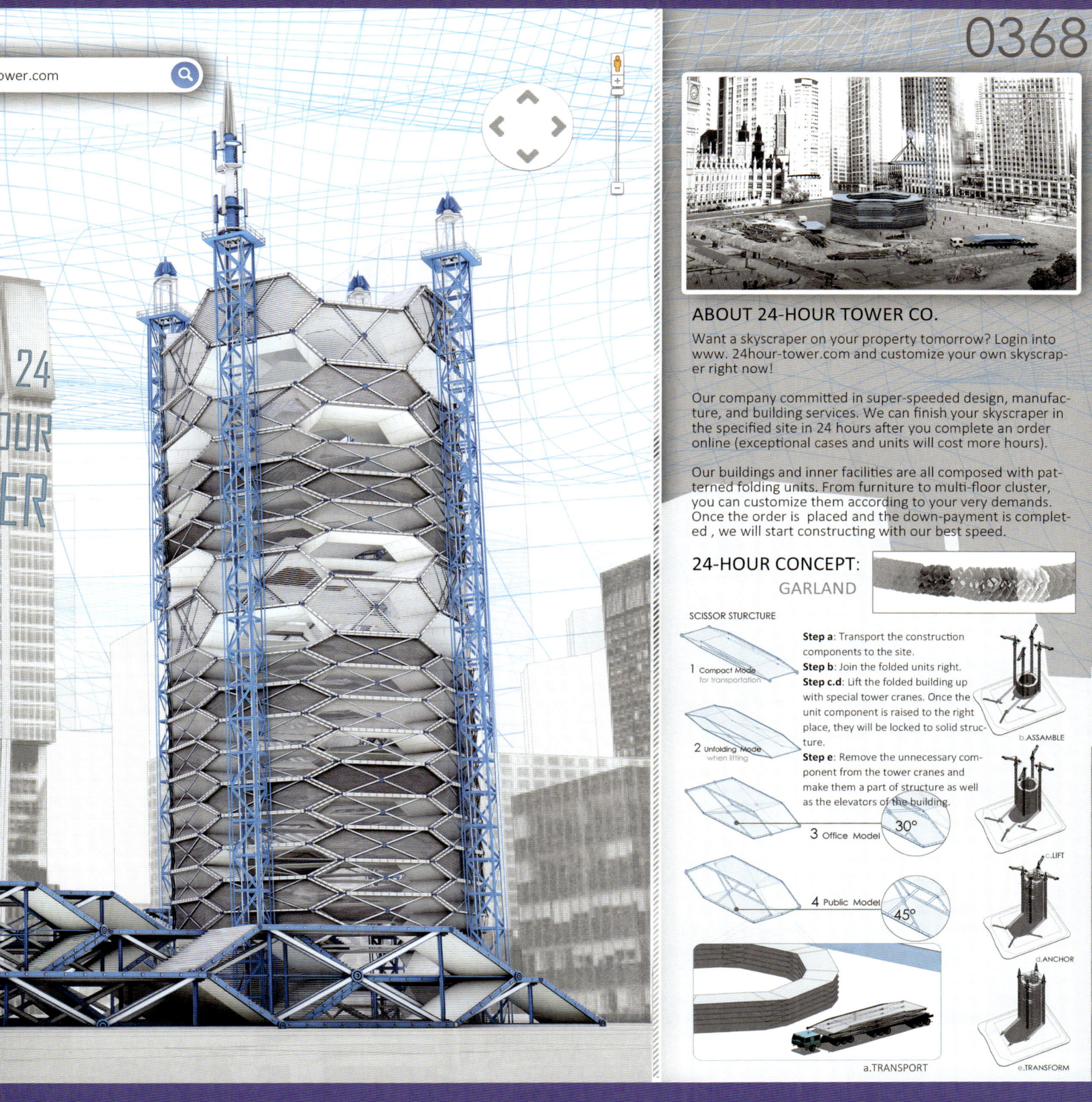

0368

ABOUT 24-HOUR TOWER CO.

Want a skyscraper on your property tomorrow? Login into www. 24hour-tower.com and customize your own skyscraper right now!

Our company committed in super-speeded design, manufacture, and building services. We can finish your skyscraper in the specified site in 24 hours after you complete an order online (exceptional cases and units will cost more hours).

Our buildings and inner facilities are all composed with patterned folding units. From furniture to multi-floor cluster, you can customize them according to your very demands. Once the order is placed and the down-payment is completed, we will start constructing with our best speed.

24-HOUR CONCEPT:
GARLAND

SCISSOR STURCTURE

1 Compact Mode for transportation

2 Unfolding Mode when lifting

3 Office Model   30°

4 Public Model   45°

Step a: Transport the construction components to the site.
Step b: Join the folded units right.
Step c.d: Lift the folded building up with special tower cranes. Once the unit component is raised to the right place, they will be locked to solid structure.
Step e: Remove the unnecessary component from the tower cranes and make them a part of structure as well as the elevators of the building.

b.ASSAMBLE

c.LIFT

d.ANCHOR

a.TRANSPORT

e.TRANSFORM

your own skyscraper right now!

Our company committed in super-speed design, manufacturing, and building services. We can finish your skyscraper in the specified site in 24 hours after you complete an order online (exceptional cases and units will take more hours to complete).

Our buildings and inner facilities are all composed with patterned folding units. From furniture to multi-floor cluster, you can customize them according to your very demands. Once the order is placed and the down payment is completed, we will start constructing with our fastest speed.

Based on the paper garland's idea, we designed collapsible facility units with folding furniture and office equipment. Step 1 is to have the customer place the order. Step 2 is to transport the construction

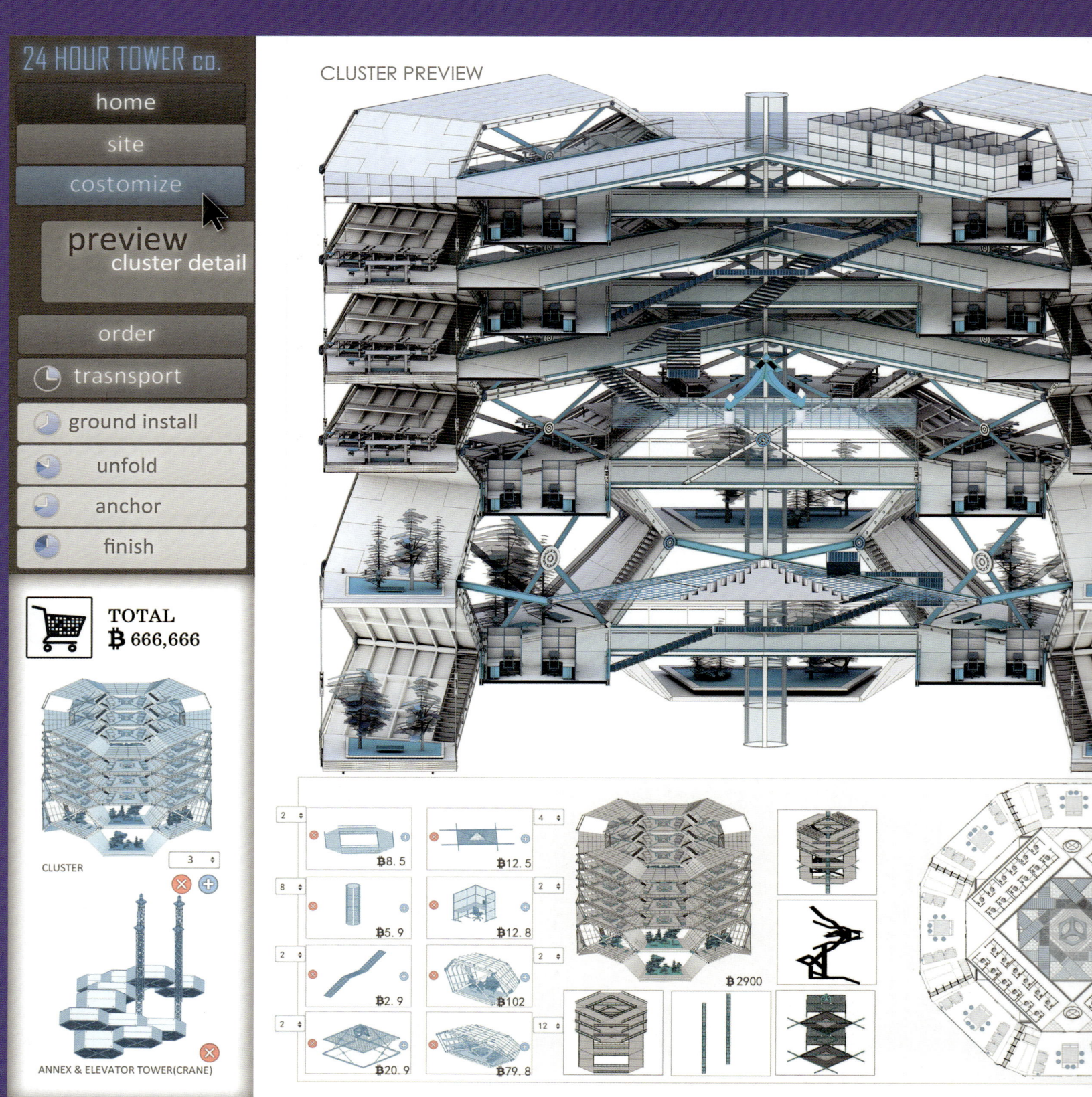

24 HOUR TOWER CO.

home
site
costomize

preview
cluster detail

order
transnport
ground install
unfold
anchor
finish

TOTAL
฿ 666,666

CLUSTER   3

ANNEX & ELEVATOR TOWER(CRANE)

CLUSTER PREVIEW

2   ฿8.5
4   ฿12.5
8   ฿5.9
2   ฿12.8
2   ฿2.9
2   ฿102
2   ฿20.9
12   ฿79.8

฿2900

components to the site. Step 3 is to join the folded units right. Step 4 is to lift the folded building up with dedicated tower cranes. Once the unit component is raised to the right place, they will be locked to solid structure. Step 5 is to remove the unnecessary component from the tower cranes and make them a part of structure as well as the elevators of the building.

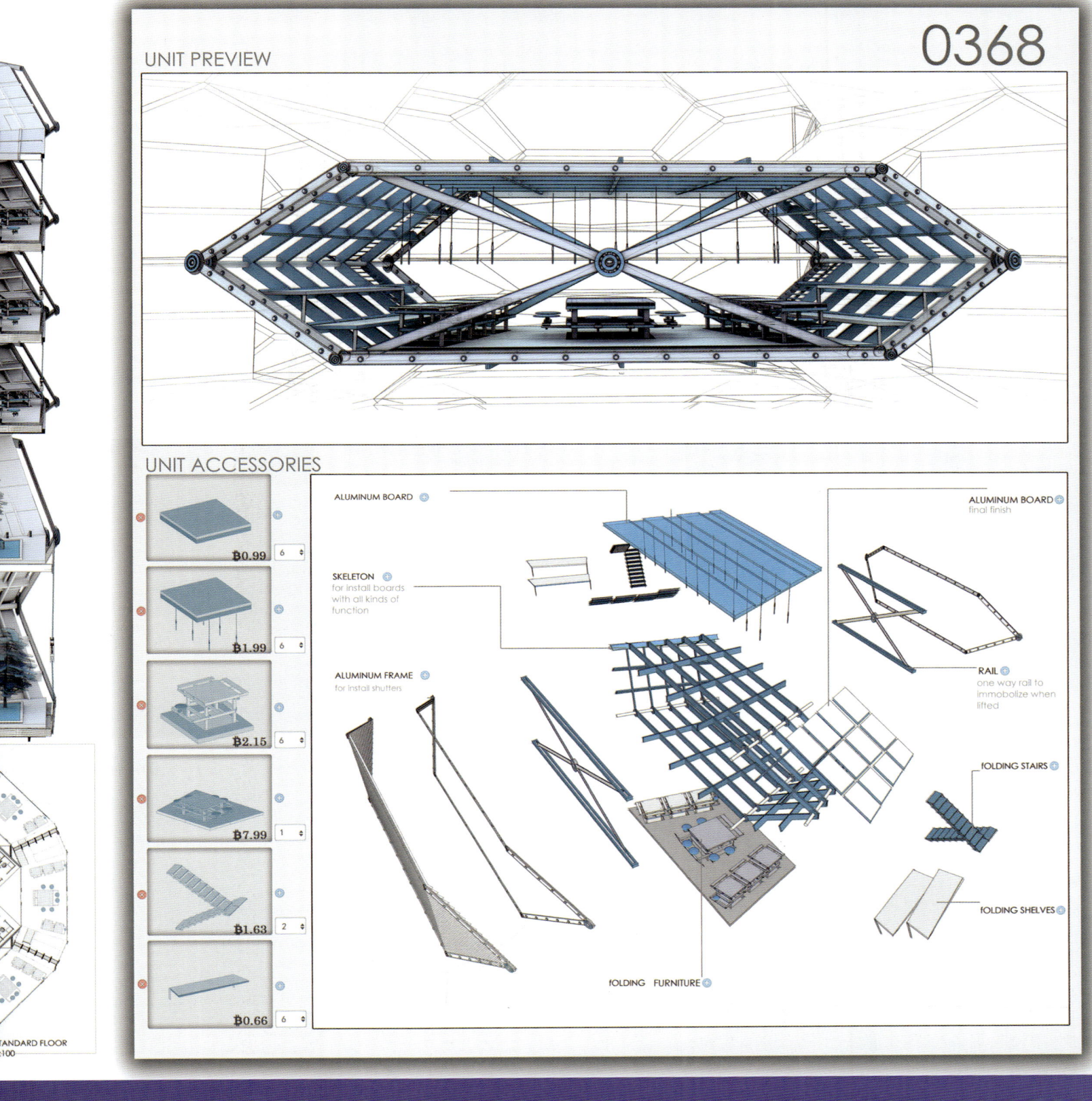

UNIT PREVIEW

0368

UNIT ACCESSORIES

฿0.99   6

฿1.99   6

฿2.15   6

฿7.99   1

฿1.63   2

฿0.66   6

ALUMINUM BOARD

ALUMINUM BOARD
final finish

SKELETON
for install boards
with all kinds of
function

ALUMINUM FRAME
for install shutters

RAIL
one way rail to
immobilize when
lifted

FOLDING STAIRS

FOLDING SHELVES

FOLDING FURNITURE

STANDARD FLOOR
1:100

PUDONG MIXED-USE TOWER

Milad Showkatbakhsh
James Maldonado

United States

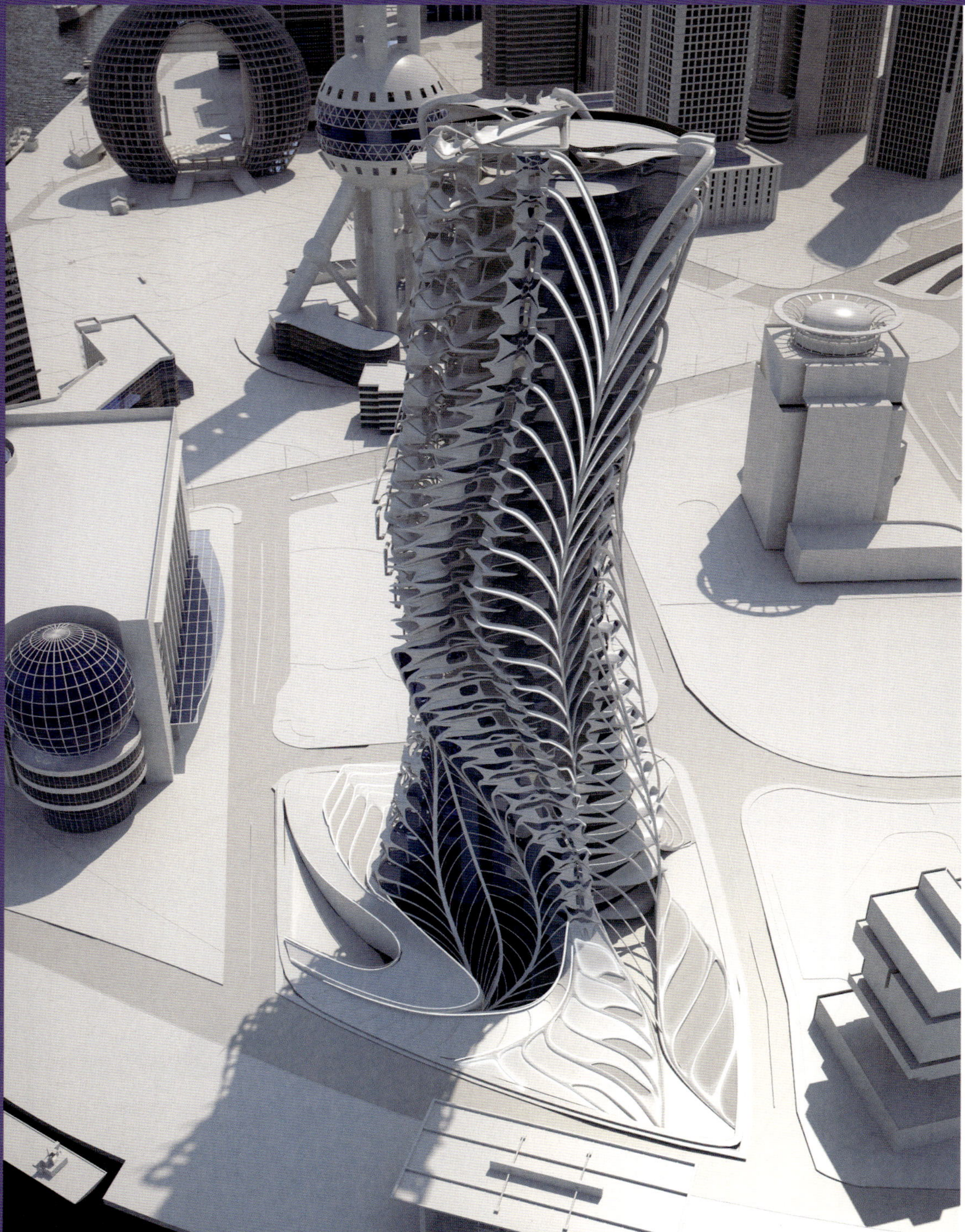

The Design process started with analysing a natural transformational system. Group use more structural were two most considerable attributes that drive the system and units.

As a mixed - use tower with recreational programs on top, It is important to pay attention to the night use of the tower. Based on the group's decision, tower will be transformed to a recreational spot at the nights with respect to the offices. There are several and separate accesses to the recreational parts during the night time. Tower at the day time has its regular function .offices and recreational parts both are open.

The Pudong Mixed Use Tower is located at the rivers edge in a district highly occupied by tourist attractions and businesses. The focus of this building is all about attribute driven spaces that split open as the program changes vertically. For the design process, analyses were made focusing on the metamorphosis of the frog, from an egg to a mature adult. Extractions of certain attributes were gathered, throughout its transformation, and were replicated and interpreted into three-dimensional units. At the end of this process, five different units were created. The units transform from an enclosed surfaced based model to a skeletal and more structural unit. The transformation is made complete through the stacking and connecting of the transforming units, creating four different spines.

The program for the tower directly correlates with the attributes of the units. Accordingly, the units

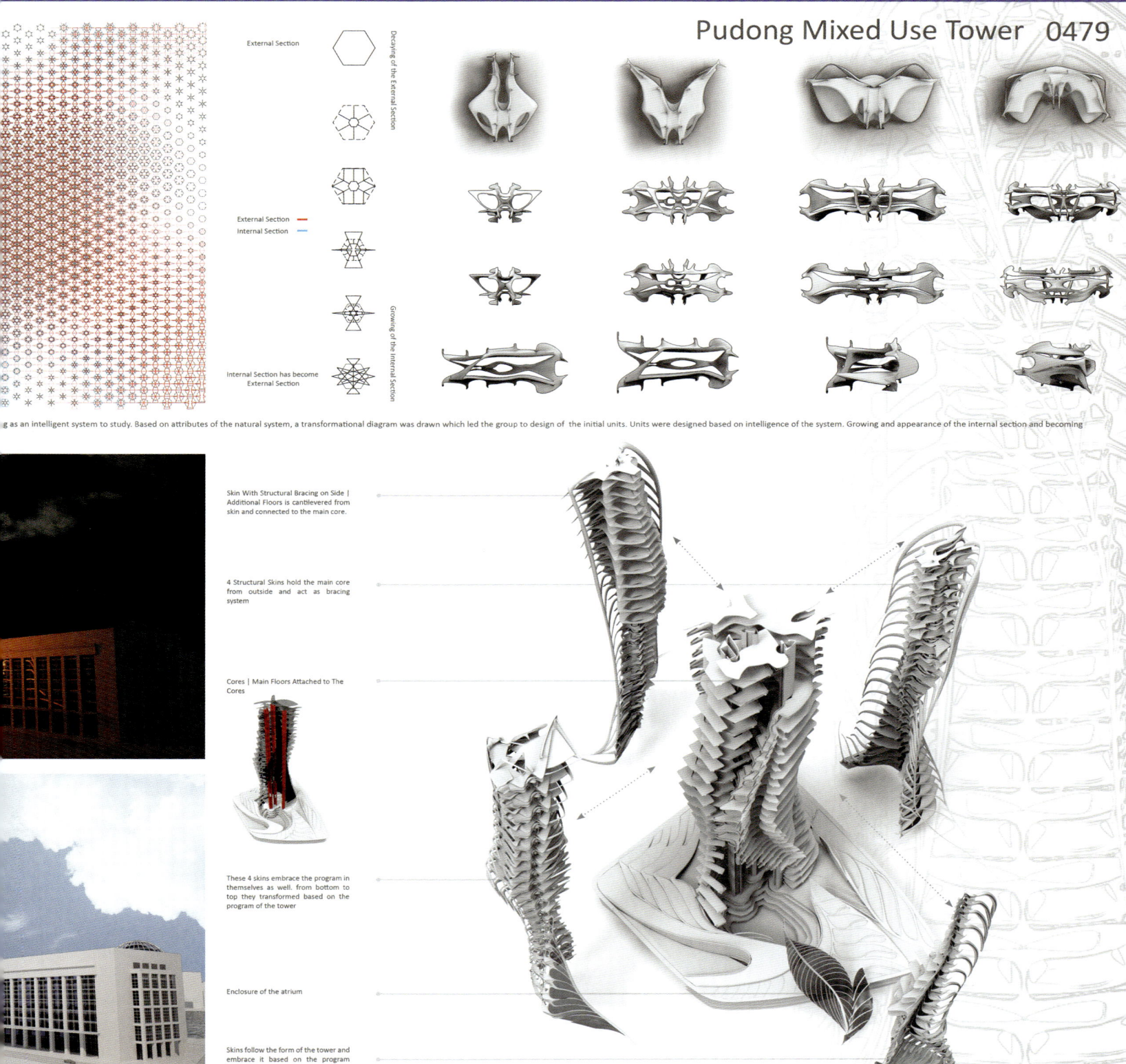

Pudong Mixed Use Tower   0479

External Section

Decaying of the External Section

External Section ⎯
Internal Section ⎯

Growing of the Internal Section

Internal Section has become External Section

g as an intelligent system to study. Based on attributes of the natural system, a transformational diagram was drawn which led the group to design of the initial units. Units were designed based on intelligence of the system. Growing and appearance of the internal section and becoming

Skin With Structural Bracing on Side | Additional Floors is cantilevered from skin and connected to the main core.

4 Structural Skins hold the main core from outside and act as bracing system

Cores | Main Floors Attached to The Cores

These 4 skins embrace the program in themselves as well. from bottom to top they transformed based on the program of the tower

Enclosure of the atrium

Skins follow the form of the tower and embrace it based on the program behind them

transform from open spaces to a gradient of enclosures and privacies. The open spaces, which serve as retail, are located on the bottom portion of the tower while the middle portion, which is more private, serve as offices. The upper portion of the tower, which is more enclosed, serves as recreational space. Inherent within the intelligence of our transformative system is a focus on the visually open aspects of our circulation. From the ground floor up the occupants can see the negative space consistently recede as their eye moves to the top, thus connecting our floor plates together. Observation elevators, which ride on the exterior of their shafts, allow the occupant to view the spaces that surround them and provide consistent views of the river. Tying all these ideas together the spines/units attach to the elevator cores, which serve as structural cores, and the spines connect together via bracing on the exterior skin, which

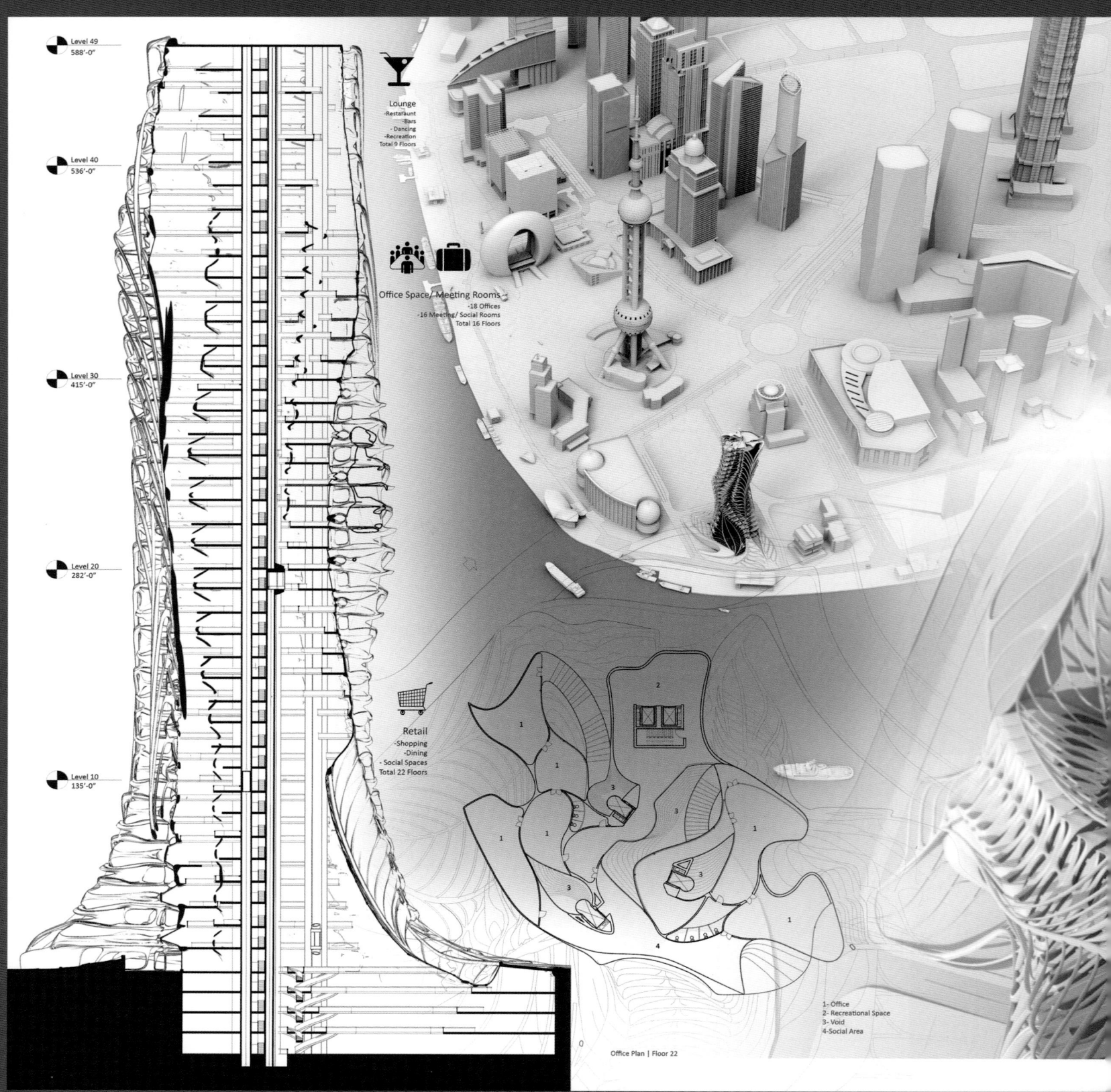

Level 49
588'-0"

Level 40
536'-0"

Level 30
415'-0"

Level 20
282'-0"

Level 10
135'-0"

Lounge
-Restaraunt
-Bars
-Dancing
-Recreation
Total 9 Floors

Office Space/ Meeting Rooms
-18 Offices
-16 Meeting/ Social Rooms
Total 16 Floors

Retail
-Shopping
-Dining
- Social Spaces
Total 22 Floors

1- Office
2- Recreational Space
3- Void
4-Social Area

0

Office Plan | Floor 22

creates a unique structural situation. Thus cores and the cantilevering floor plates hold up the center portion of the tower or units are held up by an exoskeleton. Unifying the project with the context is also another focus. The highlight of landscape is the connection between the ground and the atrium. By sinking the atrium glass into the subfloor a more cohesive connection to the landscape was created. Curved terrascaping offers seating arrangements, which creates social interaction. The transformational spines terminate into the landscape while still serving as clear cues on where entrances are located. Pudong is known for its extravagant use of lights. At nighttime the tower transforms into a recreational scene, with lounge spaces, a club scene and bars. Simultaneously, the tower lights will turn on and light up the interior and the exterior of the building.

South Elevation

East Elevation

Pudong Mixed Use Tower 0479

Atrium view from bottom to top at night when tower transforms to a recreational center

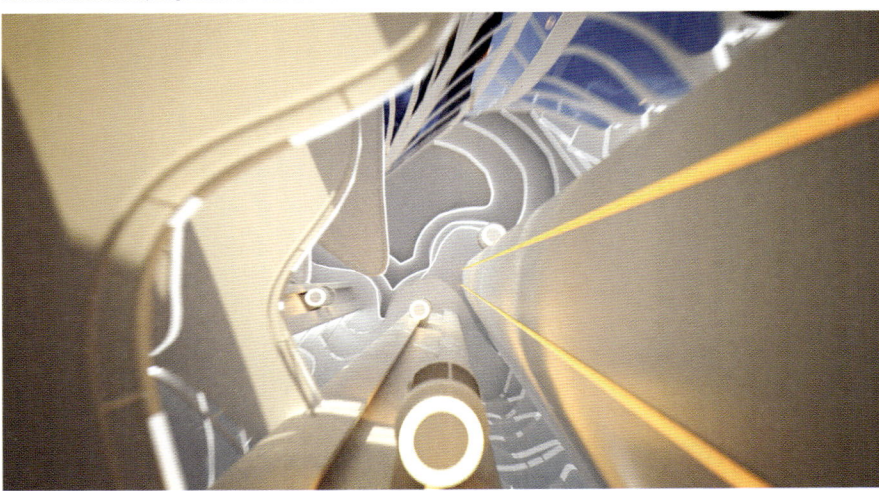

Atrium view from top to bottom during its office hours.

URMIANA

Seyed Rouzbeh Mirhosseini
Zahra Balador
Milad Rezazadeh
Saba Sultan Qurraie
Adib Khaeez
Armin Rangani

Iran

Urmiana

Introduction:

Lake Urmia is located in Azerbaijan which is the northwestern region of Iran. Lake Urmia has 102 islands, which has been registered as a protected area and a Nature reserve by UNESCO. The lake is in the forest, which is due to the specific ecological conditions, a beautiful natural landscape. Large shallow Bed of the lake has created a proper environment for different birds such as flamingos, pelicans and a complete ecosystem for other Animal species like deer. According to the legislation passed by MAB in 1356 this lake is one of the international biosphere reserves in the world, but these ecosystems are going to be destroyed. Lake Urmia is the largest inland lake in Iran and is the world's second largest brine lake. The lake is in danger of becoming dry and over the past 13 years the level of the lake has been reduced 6 meters. According to officials of the environmental organizations, reduction of rainfall, low irrigation efficiency in the catchment area of the lake and not allowing enough water to meet the biological needs of the rivers leading into the lake are booster factors of the desertification crisis of the region. Experts have expressed if the lake become dry temperate climate will change into tropical climate with salt winds therefore ecosystem will change. But no serious attempt has been made to save the lake.
Considering locating the lake on the lower levels compared to the land around the lake, there is a very beautiful and extensive view of the lake. In this area there is a wide view from one side to the lake and on the other side the surrounding mountains which is framed by the towers. The beautiful colors of the lake bed with a glint of sunlight on the salt lake has increased a natural scenic beauty of the region. Tower of polyhedral modules that are connected like crystals of salt lake has been raised from the salty lake bed as a salty rock, which has connected the salty lake to the sky. According to the salt crystal structures tower is in a harmony with the lake, in this landscape the pink color of the salt lake and the green color of the pistachio gardens are composed beautifully with the grey and sky blue of the background.
Seven similar towers are located in this site. These seven locations are at the confluence of previous rivers' paths. In fact, these locations are as a source for producing rain in the shallow part of the lakes which is the edge of the existing lake.

1984 2014 Locating 2040

Formal concept:

The basic idea of the project is the structure of the salt and how sediments are created. Modules are formed around a core and raised.

Functional Concept:

Finding a site was in response to a crisis. Urmia Lake is one of the most important and yet in crisis in Iran. Crisis of water shortages and drought in the region has many consequences for the inhabitants of the region. In this project we have tried to take advantage of the area's indigenous energy production capacities to create energy for rain production in the region. The first feature is abundant amounts of salt. Urmia Lake is a natural salt lake which has the ability to produce energy on a large scale. In addition to this capacity, we can produce a lot of energy from solar cells and microalgae bioreactors. Eventually the energy that is produced in addition to support the needs of the tower, create sound waves to produce rain which is the real job of the tower. Producing rain is the most important long-term strategies for revitalization of the Lake Urmia.

Solar Energy

Rain Production

Sound Waves

Salt

Power Tower

Revitalization of the Lake

Since Lake Urmia was registered in UNESCO due to drought there has been a reduction of the tourists. Considering the characteristics of the area we should find a way to our two main objectives which are revitalize the lake and get rid of the drough crisis.

Potentials of this region can be pointed out as follows:

1. Salt saturated lake: this lake has many therapeutic properties.
2. The use of natural solar salt pool: the gradient of temperature and saturation has the potential of generating energy for the project.

0500

Urmia Lake
2014 - 4:32 pm

3. The use of salt as a material: low cost and abundant amount can make salt a good choice to be composed with the other substances and make a material for the project.

4. There are many clouds in this area: we have enough clouds to produce rain by using the sound waves and to prevent the sequences of the drought.

Identify the main stakeholder of the project:

1. UNESCO: Registration of the lake as a prestigious and historic lake.
2. People living in Urmia region: Inactive area because of the drought.

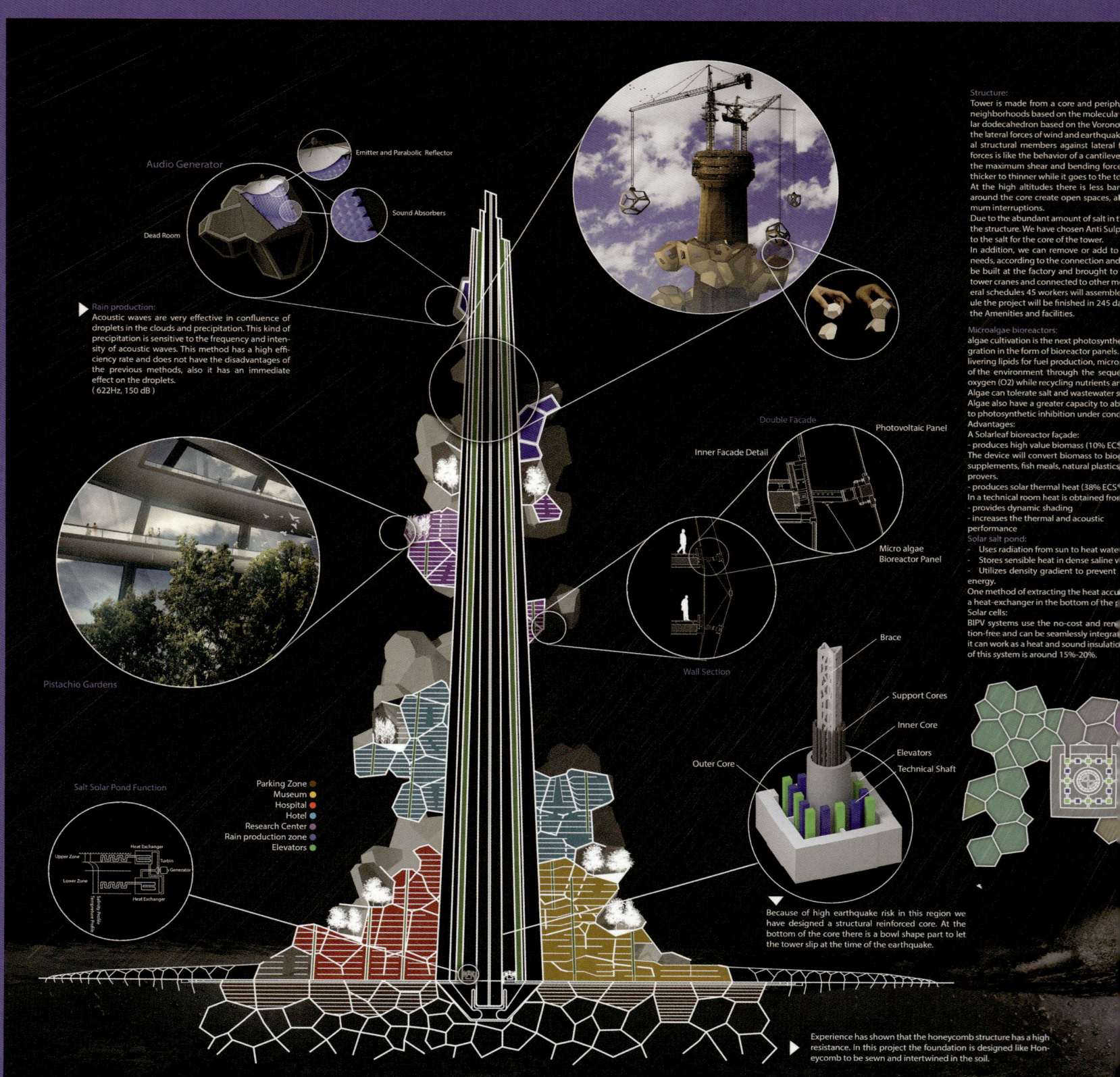

3. Farmers: salt particles are spread all over the region and will destroy the agricultural fields.
4. Domestic and foreign tourists: reduction of the tourists because of drying the lake.
5. Patients: reduction of the potentials of the lake for the therapeutic goals.

0500

...ules. The constituent modules form the
... of the salt. Permanent link of non-regu-
...m, improves the tower's stability against
...se the performance of three-dimension-
...havior of the tower against the lateral
...erefore at the foot of the tower, there is
...sult the form of the tower change from

...st the wind. Modules with spiral form
...ind to pass along the tower with mini-

... should use a special kind of material for
...ent and Anti-corrosion additives against

...ules in the future due to the residents'
...of each module. Modules are planned to
...ith 18-wheel trailers, then taken up by
...th screw and nuts. According to the gen-
...odule in 2 days. In proposed early sched-
...nd night) with the maximum capacity of

...ven system primed for architectural inte-
...ve a fast reproduction rate. Besides de-
...capable of actively improving the health
...f carbon-dioxide (CO2) and production
...ally cleaning waste water in this process.
...nd thereby greatly reduce freshwater use.
...than land plants, and are also not prone
...ntense sunlight.

...ual biomass is used for food, nutritional
...ls, pharmaceuticals,fertilizers and soil im-

...changer.

...e heat flow and therefore store thermal

...t the bottom of a solar pond is by laying
...e form of a series of parallel pipes.

...ar energy to generate electricity pollu-
...uildings to reduce installation costs, also
...ten energy payback time. The efficiency

- Lobby
- Salon
- Restaurant
- Kitchen
- Coffe shop
- Hotel rooms
- Garden
- Elevators
- Technical

Urmia Lake
2040 - 11:36 pm

DEEP SKINS

Yongsu Choung
Ge Zhang
Chuanjingwei Wang

South Korea
China

View from W57th Street

Shark skin

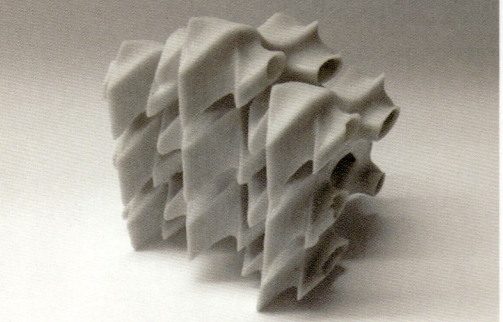

Prototype, 3d printing

Ne

The s
tectu
placi
much
skys

This
desig
the r
skin,
pecia
inner
being

The
and
the t
cordi
are v
The
com
throu

In th
how
pied
panc
one
whe
the te

As s
of the
up th
vary
as it
tacul

The skyscraper is one architectural typology that is still under the strong influence of the Modernist architectural movement. Generally, a skyscraper is limited to flat floors for efficiency of construction and glass façades for placing a premium on the expansive vistas of the city below. Therefore, skyscrapers have not changed very much since their introduction, unlike other types of architecture, since the height and the transparency of skyscrapers are the absolute standards to determine their values in this era. This project avoids the typical skyscraper constraints and aims to create a new archetype. Instead of approaching the design with an existing architectural methodology, the design is approached to from the skin. To be precise, the research focused on, not a skin of an existing architecture per se, but a skin of living organism, a shark skin, in order to adopt its system for a façade design. The analysis of the

0537

DEEP SKINS

pology of Skyscraper in NYC by Adaptation of Organism

per is one of the type of architecture which is still under the strong influence of Modern archi-
erally, a skyscraper is limited to flat floors for efficiency of construction and glass façades for
nium on expansive vistas of the city below. Therefore, skyscrapers have not changed very
their introduction unlike other types of architecture, since the height and the transparency of
are the absolute standards to determine their values in this era.

avoids the typical skyscraper and aims to create a new typology. Instead of approaching the
an existing architectural methodology, the design is approached from the skin. To be precise,
focused on, not on a skin of an existing architecture but, a skin of living organism, a shark
r to adopt its system for a façade design. The analysis of the configuration of a shark skin, es-
it is formed in macro and micro scales has led to the idea of 'Deep Skins' in which, different
es of the tower is derived from various skin types. The idea of Deep Skins has a potential of
ped to the scale of a tower.

d building is located on 157 West 57th street in Manhattan, New York City, between the 6th
avenues. The layout of programs follows that of a typical tower in New York City. However,
composed of accumulated volumes transformed from a prototype, instead of flat floors, ac-
e programs. The resulting design stands as a towering interlocks of tightly packed units that
eyond the norm and yet provides a desirable level of privacy and intimacy simultaneously.
f intimacy from the interlocking and from the billowing interiority introduces a new sense of
or a type of structure that is bound to be highly liquid and mobile in terms of occupancy
s existence.

e, the idea of Deep Skins is about intimacy as much as it is about vistas, or precisely, about
ach the vistas that are invaluable. Like in a conventional skyscraper, the inhabitants and
investors would admire the vistas, but instead of simply panning across a homogeneous
om floor to floor, they are looking out from round apertures that cantilever out midair, urging
further, with more embrace towards the physicality of the tower itself. While highly energetic
om the west 58th street towards the base and the streets, calm moments are found towards
he facades facing its adjacent neighbors.

sections, such consistent attitude of viewing is attended towards vistas created in the core
tself where vertical volumes of great heights can be found and in the large opening a midway
that functions as an outdoor sky lobby. While manifold like floor plates and billowing walls
al experiences, the attitude of approaching vistas unites the tower looking out and looking in
rtically. The idea of this tower is a counterpoint to the much ingrained transparent and species of glass towers that are perpetuated throughout the modern skyscraper architecture.

Hotel

Office

View from W57th Street

configuration of a shark skin, especially how it is formed in macro and micro scales, has led to the idea of 'Deep Skins' in which, different inner volumes of the tower are derived from various skin types. The idea of Deep Skins has a potential of being developed to the scale of a tower. The proposed building is located on 157 West 57th street in Manhattan, New York City, between the 6th and the 7th avenues. The layout of programs follows that of a typical tower in New York City. However, the tower is composed of accumulated volumes transformed from a prototype, instead of flat floors, according to the programs. The resulting design stands as a towering interlocking of tightly packed units that are varied beyond the norm and yet provide a desirable level of privacy and intimacy simultaneously. The sense of intimacy from the interlocking and from the billowing interiority introduces a new sense of community for a type of structure that is bound to be highly liquid and mobile in terms of occupancy throughout its existence.

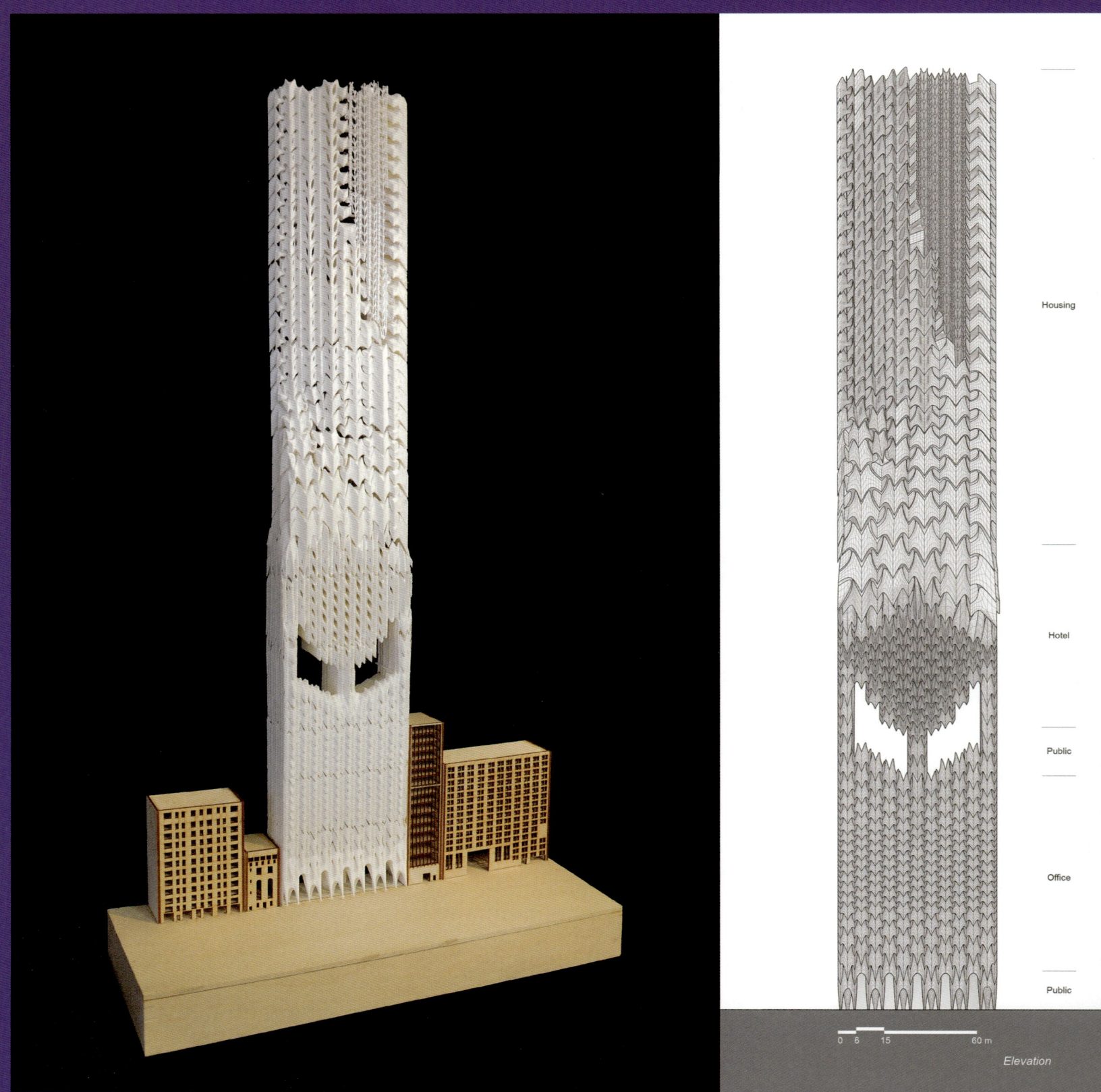

Housing

Hotel

Public

Office

Public

0　6　15　　　　　60 m

Elevation

In that sense, the idea of 'Deep Skins' is about intimacy as much as it is about vistas, or more precisely, about how to approach the vistas that are invaluable. Like in a conventional skyscraper, the inhabitants and pied-à-terre investors would admire the vistas, but instead of simply panning across a homogeneous panorama from floor to floor, they are looking out from round apertures that cantilever out midair, urging one to step out further, with more of an embrace towards the physicality of the tower itself. While highly energetic when seen from West 58th street towards the base and the streets, calm moments are found towards the top and the facades facing its adjacent neighbors. Such a consistent attitude of viewing is attended towards vistas created in the core of the tower itself where vertical volumes of great heights can be found, and an outdoor sky lobby located in the large opening midway up the tower.

0537

Section

View from W58th Street

510

FUTURE COLLECTIVISM

David Tajchman
Luc Izri

France

FUTURE COLLECTIVISM

INTEGRATING VERTICAL FARMING AND SHARED VEHICLES IN A COLLECTIVE LIVING IN THE MEDITERRANEAN AREA

This mixed use high-rise is about integrating vertically the specificities of living in a mediterranean environment, developing the three-dimensionality of an hybrid program that is usually subject to an urban horizontal sprawl, and breaking the limits between traditional stacked slabs. Beyond the fact to build tall or super-tall, the proposal experiments the vertical setting of a topological geometry, that welcomes local natures and technologies, and results into a tower that is spiraling, endless and flourishing.

Using the social typology of a kibbutz as a vehicle for investigation, this tower takes inspiration into the Israeli version of agricultural co-housing. Parallel to this investigation is a study on the technique of urban agriculture which can be applied to the site in the horizontal and vertical dimensions. The result is a synthesis of the two that will allow us to explore the potential of integrating collective living with urban agriculture. What would the product be like when people begin to take responsibility for the growing of their own food? Or when the separation between architecture and agriculture blends into a single entity?

The Gran Mediterraneo tower is located in a White City, name given by the Unesco proclaiming it as World Cultural Heritage site, where low-rise constructions from the1930s belong to the Art-Deco and Bauhaus movements. The citation recognized the unique adaptation of modern international architectural trends to the cultural, climatic, and local traditions of the city. We were inspired by the curves of the concrete painted white predominant in the city and decided to pay tribute to this plasticity, finding a specific topological geometry to build with white concrete dyed. The curvy concrete extends to the public space, integrating its geometry into a ground parametrical arabesque based on the circle proliferation. Aiming to become an architectural landmark for the city skyline and perhaps for the Middle-Eastern Mediterranean area, searching for a specific architectural identity that is a cultural mix of Orient and Occident.

The site, located in a Mediterranean City, is the biggest pedestrian public space in the city, symbolic, circular and designed by Brazilian architect Oscar Niemeyer in the 1970s. Surrounded by a repetitive brutalist building, the plaza is nowadays being gentrified, becoming a hub for luxury boutiques. Located midway between the freeway and the beach, in a residential area, this proposal is an opportunity to re-design components of an urban farming and its applications and, to investigate the social characteristics of a kibbutz and how we can apply this collective community into an urban environment already congested with car traffic and gated community high-rises.

This collective scheme is extended to the development of a shared car system for the city. Driverless, shared and electrical vehicles as a futuristic symbol of freedom and social equity. The tower features a car-silo equipped with robotic car-parking, emerging from the plaza underground. This vertical car-park is a response to the current lack of parking lots in the city and the inadaptation of the city to its rising number of vehicles. The tower acts as the first metropolitan station for regular and driverless vehicles as well as an electrical station for vehicles to charge batteries.

Mediterranean Nature combined with concrete and vehicles are the three components of this high-rise, merging ecological needs with local technological inventions in the process of building as well as in the building life and usage. Co-housings, co-working, co-moving, and vertical farming constitute the collective spirit in the Gran Mediterraneo, translated into programmatic landscapes all along the tower's height.

Integrating vertical farming and shared vehicles in a collective living in the Mediterranean area

This mixed use high-rise is about integrating vertically the specificities of living in a mediterranean environment, developing the three-dimensionality of an hybrid program that is usually subject to an urban horizontal sprawl, and breaking the limits between traditional stacked slabs. Beyond the fact to build tall or super-tall, the proposal experiments the vertical setting of a topological geometry that welcomes local natures and technologies, and results into a tower that is spiraling, endless and flourishing.

Using the social typology of a kibbutz as a vehicle for investigation, this tower takes inspiration into the Israeli version of agricultural co-housing. Parallel to this investigation is a study on the technique of urban agriculture, which can be applied to the site in the horizontal and vertical dimensions. The result is

a synthesis of the two that will allow us to explore the potential of integrating collective living with urban agriculture. What would the product be like when people begin to take responsibility for the growing of their own food? Or when the separation between architecture and agriculture blends into a single entity?

The Gran Mediterraneo tower is located in a White City, name given by the Unesco proclaiming it as World Cultural Heritage site, where low-rise constructions from the1930s belong to the Art Deco and Bauhaus movements. The citation recognized the unique adaptation of modern international architectural trends to the cultural, climatic, and local traditions of the city. We were inspired by the curves of the concrete painted white predominant in the city and decided to pay tribute to this plasticity, finding a specific topological geometry to build with white concrete dyed. The curvy concrete extends to the public space, integrating its geometry into a ground parametrical arabesque based on the circle

THE NEW PEDESTRIAN PLAZA

THE CAR SILO EMERGING FROM THE UNDERGROUND IS SURROUNDED BY A VERTICAL MEDITERRANEAN PARK

THE CAR SILO IS A STATION FOR CHARGING ELECTRICAL BATTERIES, WHERE AU

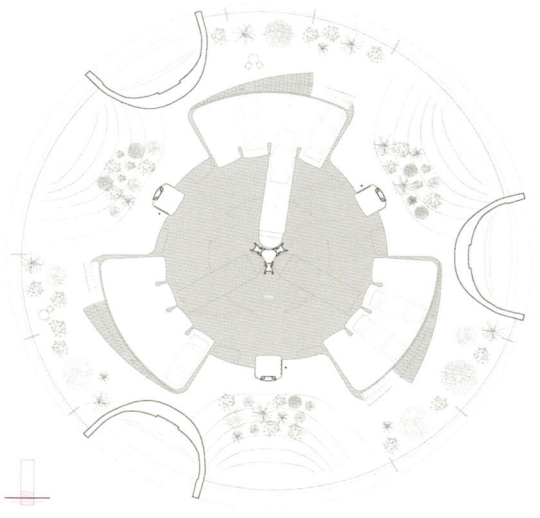

SHAPED CAR SILO AND VERTICAL MEDITERRANEAN PARK

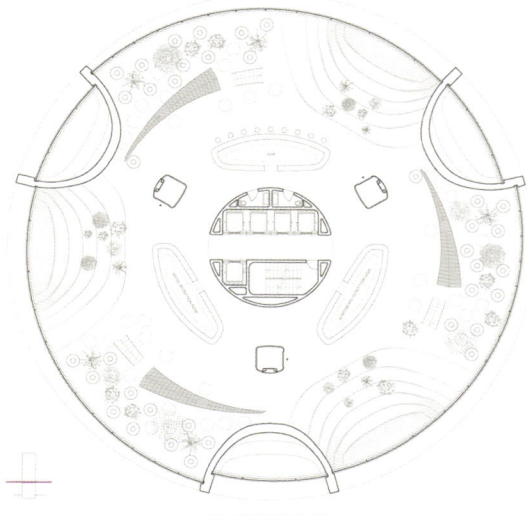

ELEVATED RESIDENTIAL LOBBY

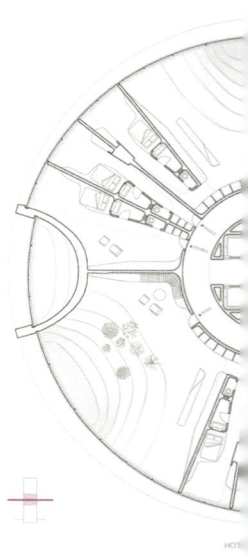

HOT

proliferation. Aiming to become an architectural landmark for the city skyline and perhaps for the Middle-Eastern Mediterranean area, searching for a specific architectural identity that is a cultural mix of Orient and Occident.

This collective scheme is extended to the development of a shared car system for the city. Driverless, shared and electrical vehicles as a futuristic symbol of freedom and social equity. The tower features a car-silo equipped with robotic car-parking, emerging from the plaza underground. This vertical car-park is a response to the current lack of parking lots in the city and the inadaptation of the city to its rising number of vehicles. The tower acts as the first metropolitan station for regular and driverless vehicles as well as an electrical station for vehicles to charge batteries.

GRAN MEDITERRANEO 0143

INSIDE A HOTEL SUITE

PLATFORMS PARK REGULAR CARS AND SHARED DRIVERLESS VEHICLES

INSIDE A RESIDENTIAL COLLECTIVE KITCHEN

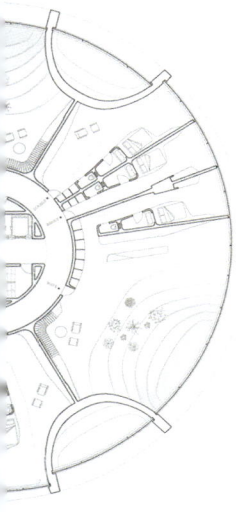

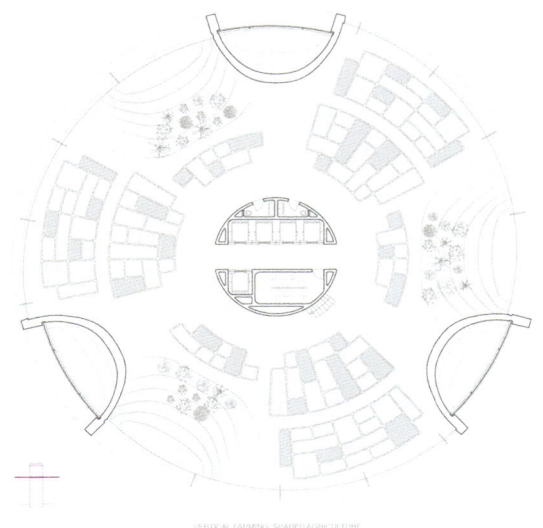

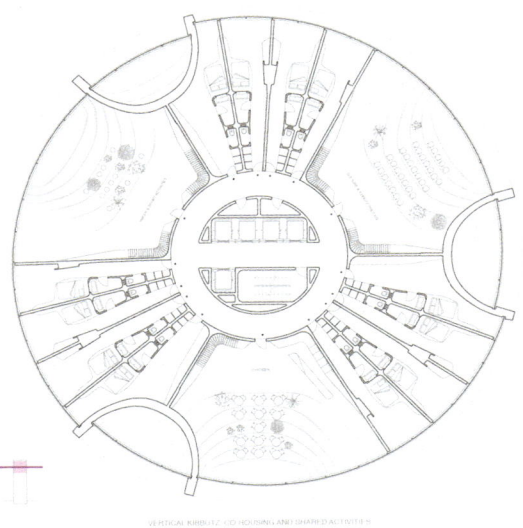

THRIVING CLUSTER   Luisa Roth

Spain

THRIVING
CLUSTER

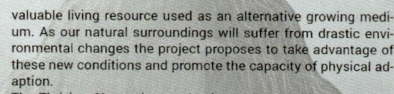

The world we live in is transforming due to the environmental consequences of climate change. Prospectively the expected rise of sea level among other complications will strongly affect our way of living. At the same time we are experiencing the most drastic demographic shift in history. Due to population increase and global migration humanity will soon be forced to acquire new living territories and develop adaptive and sustainable design solutions for different environmental conditions.

The Thriving Cluster project seeks to explore the potential of high rising architecture in emerging territories to provide new habitats for climate refugees. The structure is based on productive cellular modules which agglomerate according to particular local circumstances and therefore becomes adaptable to prospective shifts in a post apocalyptic environment.

The project aims to foster a symbiotic relation between a modular system and altering landscapes which are influenced by climate changes such as tropical cliffs. The complex structure is inspired by a coral type named Astroides Calycularis, a colonial coral genus which clusters along certain surface formations. The skyscraper consists of various self-assembling units hosting infrastructures for energy and food production, waste management and habitation. The cells themselves are 3D printed from recycled plastics taken from the garbage floating in the ocean. The shell itself functions as an infrastructure for water purification and biofuel production based on a complex system of pipes and pockets filled with algae. The skin surface is physically maximized to enhance the system's efficiency.

The interior volumes serve as containers for fish and algae farming to ensure sufficient food and biofuel supply. Habitation capsule can be plugged in additionally to provide spaces for public and private usage as well as for maintenance purposes. The Thriving Cluster takes advantage of garbage as a sustainable construction material and saltwater as a renewable and valuable living resource used as an alternative growing medium. As our natural surroundings will suffer from drastic environmental changes the project proposes to take advantage of these new conditions and promote the capacity of physical adaption.

The Thriving Cluster is an adaptive and productive landscape establishing an efficient zero-waste system and answering global needs for self-sustaining habitats in emerging territories suffering from climate changes.

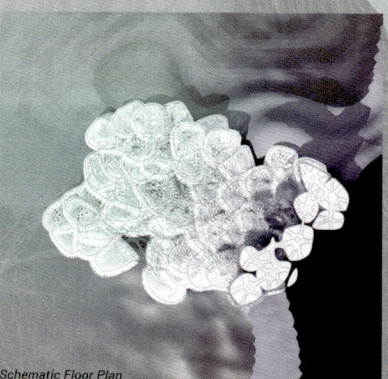

Schematic Floor Plan

The world we live in is transforming due to the environmental consequences of climate change. Prospectively the expected rise of sea level among other complications will strongly affect our way of living. At the same time we are experiencing the most drastic demographic shift in history. Due to population increase and global migration humanity will soon be forced to acquire new living territories and develop adaptive and sustainable design solutions for different environmental conditions.

The Thriving Cluster project seeks to explore the potential of high rising architecture in emerging territories to provide new habitats for climate refugees. The structure is based on productive cellular modules which agglomerate according to particular local circumstances and therefore becomes adaptable to prospective shifts in a post apocalyptic environment. The project aims to foster a symbiotic

0488

relation between a modular system and altering landscapes, which are influenced by climate changes such as tropical cliffs. The complex structure is inspired by a coral type named Astroides Calycularis, a colonial coral genus that clusters along certain surface formations. The skyscraper consists of various self-assembling units hosting infrastructures for energy and food production, waste management and habitation. The cells themselves are 3D printed from recycled plastics taken from the garbage floating in the ocean. The shell itself functions as an infrastructure for water purification and biofuel production based on a complex system of pipes and pockets filled with algae. The skin surface is physically maximized to enhance the system's efficiency. The interior volumes serve as containers for fish and algae farming to ensure sufficient food and biofuel supply. Habitation capsule can be plugged in

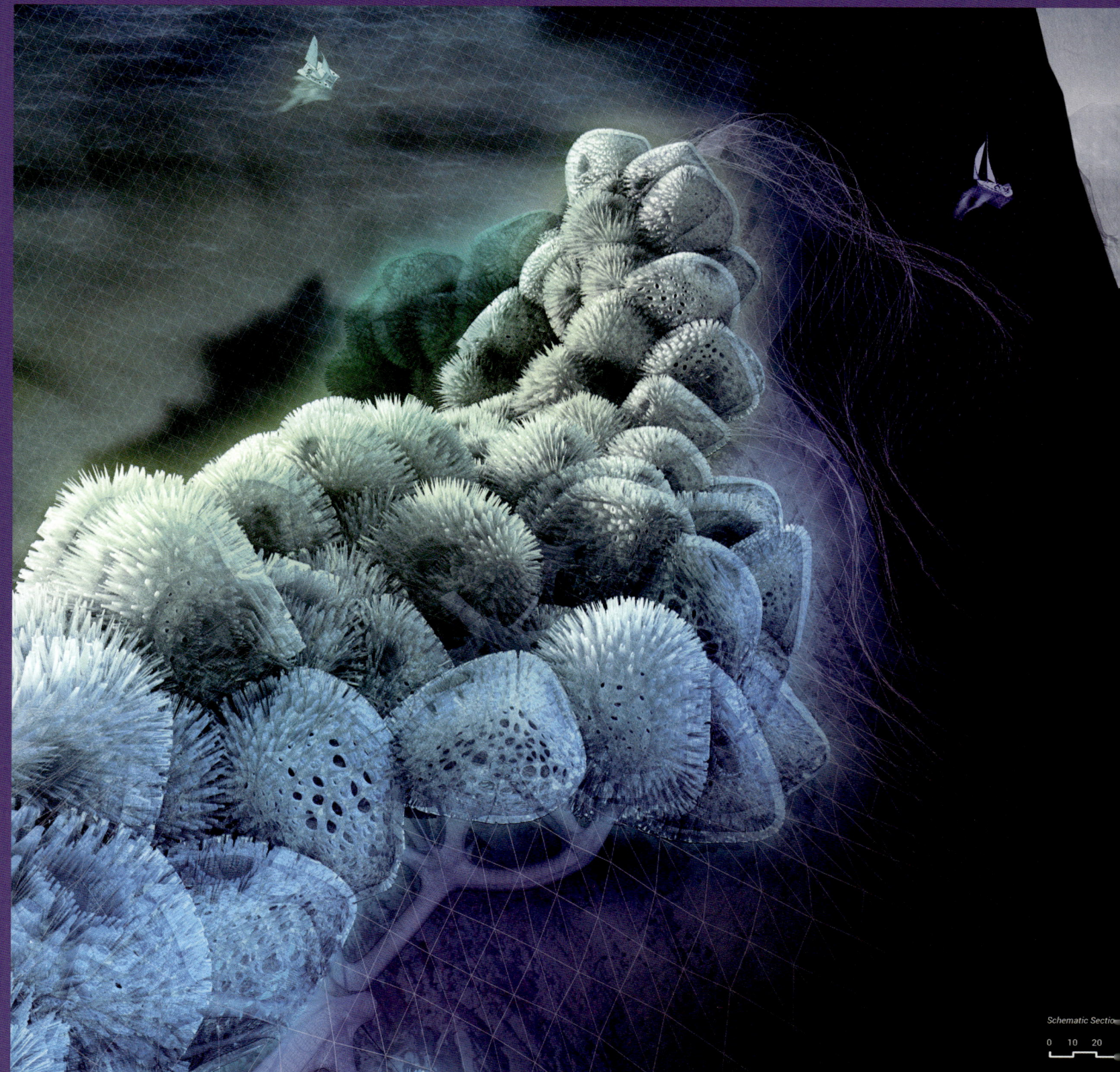

Schematic Section

0   10   20

additionally to provide spaces for public and private usage as well as for maintenance purposes.

The Thriving Cluster takes advantage of garbage as a sustainable construction material and saltwater as a renewable and valuable living resource used as an alternative-growing medium. As our natural surroundings will suffer from drastic environmental changes the project proposes to take advantage of these new conditions and promote the capacity of physical adaption. The Thriving Cluster is an adaptive and productive landscape establishing an efficient zero-waste system and answering global needs for self-sustaining habitats in emerging territories suffering from climate changes.

0488

3D PRINTED CAPSULE

PRODUCTIVE SKIN

HABITATION CAPSULE

RECYCLED PLASTIC

WASTE WATER
DISTRIBUTION SYSTEM

CIRCULATION

ALGAE PURIFICATION
POCKETS

BIOFUEL & FOOD
PRODUCTION MODULE

WASTE WATER
PURIFICATION SYSTEM

50
m

HEALING MATRIX

Jie Liu
Wen Sun
Hewen Suo

Canada

BACKGROUND

Research has shown that crime has closely related to personality disorders. Conventional correction centre usually conveys a feeling of suffering for the inmates. Limited sunlight and tight space has negative psychological impact on the inmates. Personality disorder tends to be aggravated in the custody process, rendering the inmates difficult to effectively reform or being corrected. The Healing Matrix is trying to break the ordinary design of a correction centre; it is attempting to address this social issue from an architectural perspective.

PILOT PROJECT LOCATION

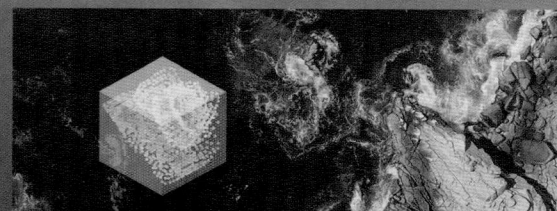

This is a global research project. The ultimate goal is to research novel ways of reducing global criminal rate. We are striving to modify the current prison system model and create a state-of-art architectural space to eventually reach our goal. This research project is located in a public area without border restrictions; free unlimited access is granted to criminals and researchers from all over the world. Mutual exchange of experiment data and results are promoted. Once this pilot project becomes more mature, this new concept of correction centre design can be implemented into cities of all countries.

PERSONALITY DISORDER HEALING ANALYSIS

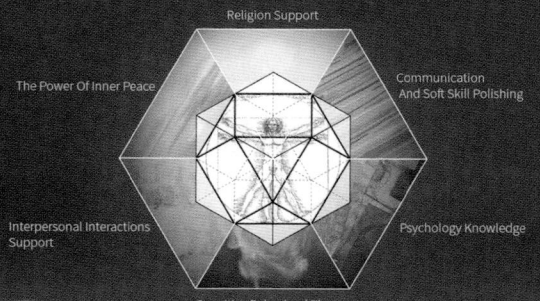

Research has shown that crime has closely related to personality disorders. Conventional correction center usually conveys a feeling of suffering for the inmates. Limited sunlight and tight space has negative psychological impact on the inmates. In this building, newly defined healing cluster-space has replaced the traditional detention space to facilitate the healing of personality disorders, and meet the needs of inmates in different stages of the healing process. To achieve crime prevention and psychological and cognitive rehabilitation, other than the setup of a conventional correction center, six independent yet related types of spaces are created here. Each space has its own function and approach towards self-healing and self-correction. Each space is a cluster of several cubes. Different needs of inmates with distinct personalities are addressed here. Spaces are divided as such: Praying

MATRIX PATHWAY

0583

3M

HEALING COORDINATE

In this building, newly defined healing cluster-space has replaced the traditional detention space to facilitate the healing of personality disorders, and meet the needs of inmates in different stages of the healing process. During the entire sentence, under the arrangement by the Command Centre of the building, inmates will interact with each other according to their instant need. Inmates will also be able to look inside to discover their inner spirit and interact with the architectural space itself, through a multi-layer treatment approach, therefore fundamentally cure the personality disorder and achieve the goal of complete healing.

UNIT AND MATRIX

Each inmate has his/her own independent space (each space is a cube with dimension of 3m*3m*3m). Inmates' life and privacy are appropriately respected and protected. Inmates' instant need is transmitted through feeling receptors to the Command Centre of the Building. The matrix network would then automatically match and transfer the inmate to a "best fit" space to optimize the healing effect. In order to ensure the free multi-directional movement each unit, the building itself has an inner matrix space which allows for three dimensional movement. The mobility of the space has not only created diverse environmental experience for the inmates, but also has realized the frequent interactions between inmates hence promoting the healing effect.

PRAYING SPACE
religion support

MEDITATION SPACE
the power of inner peace
ACCOMPANIMENT SPACE
interpersonal interactions/support
ANGER/DEPRESSION MANAGEMENT SPACE
cognitive behavioral therapy
SOCIAL TRAINING SPACE
communication and soft skill polishing
EDUCATION
psychology knowledge

MATRIX AND HEALING SPACE

To achieve crime prevention and psychological and cognitive rehabilitation, other than the setup of a conventional correction centre, six independent yet related types of spaces are created here. Each space has its own function and approach towards self-healing and self-correction. Each space is a cluster of several cubes. Different needs of inmates with distinct personalities are addressed here.

[HEALING MATRIX]

Life path and the meaning of space are being revolutionarily redefined here in the Healing Matrix, a system trying to break the ordinary design of a correction centre.

CHANGING APPERANCE

In terms of the appearance, due to the changing needs of the inmates to the healing space, the inner form of the building is kept dynamic and adaptive. At different times, by observing the location and volume of the clusters formed by different cells, inmates' current psychological status and the needs for particular space could be identified.

ACCOMPANYING MODE   SOCIAL TRAINING MODE   EDUCATING MODE   PRAYING MODE

Space (religion support), Meditation Space (the power of inner peace), Accompaniment Space (interpersonal interactions and support), Anger/Depression Management Space (cognitive behavioral therapy), and Social Training Space (communication and soft skill polishing)Each inmate has his/her own independent space (each space is a cube with dimension of 3m*3m*3m). Inmates' life and privacy are appropriately respected and protected. Inmates' instant need is transmitted through feeling receptors to the Command Centre of the Building. The matrix network would then automatically match and transfer the inmate to a "best fit" space to optimize the healing effect. In order to ensure the free multi-directional movement each unit, the building itself has an inner matrix space, which allows for three-dimensional movement. The mobility of the space has not only created diverse environmental experience for the

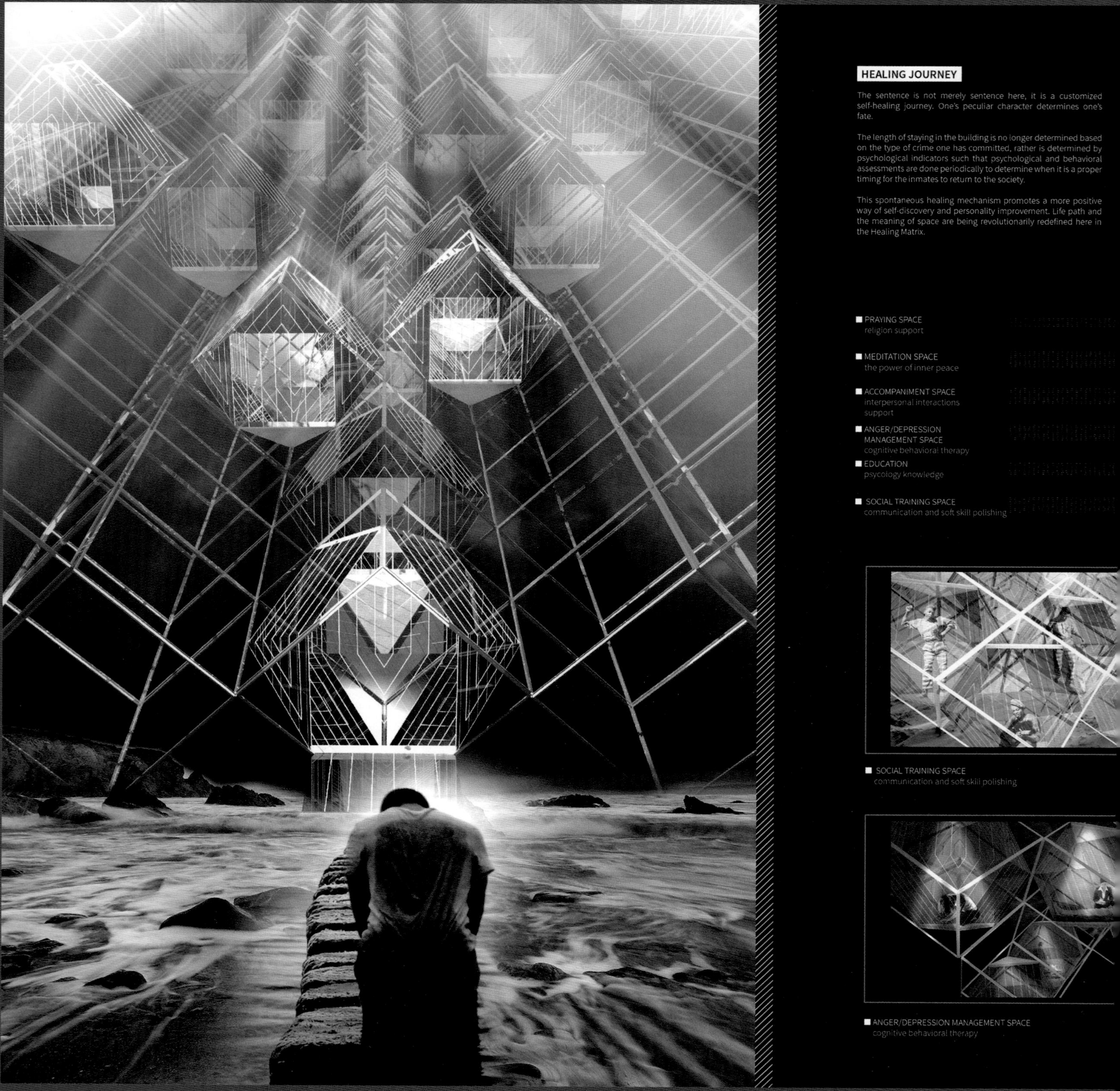

HEALING JOURNEY

The sentence is not merely sentence here, it is a customized self-healing journey. One's peculiar character determines one's fate.

The length of staying in the building is no longer determined based on the type of crime one has committed, rather is determined by psychological indicators such that psychological and behavioral assessments are done periodically to determine when it is a proper timing for the inmates to return to the society.

This spontaneous healing mechanism promotes a more positive way of self-discovery and personality improvement. Life path and the meaning of space are being revolutionarily redefined here in the Healing Matrix.

■ PRAYING SPACE
religion support

■ MEDITATION SPACE
the power of inner peace

■ ACCOMPANIMENT SPACE
interpersonal interactions
support

■ ANGER/DEPRESSION
MANAGEMENT SPACE
cognitive behavioral therapy

■ EDUCATION
psycology knowledge

■ SOCIAL TRAINING SPACE
communication and soft skill polishing

■ SOCIAL TRAINING SPACE
communication and soft skill polishing

■ ANGER/DEPRESSION MANAGEMENT SPACE
cognitive behavioral therapy

inmates, but also has realized the frequent interactions between inmates hence promoting the healing effect. Rather than being differentiated through conventional parameters, inmates are identified and distinguished by the types of personality disorders they are suffering from. Each inmate's experience of space and healing path is determined in accordance with their unique personalities and healing needs. The sentence is not merely sentence here; it is a customized self-healing journey. One's peculiar character determines one's fate. The length of staying in the building is no longer determined based on the type of crime one has committed, rather is determined by psychological indicators such that psychological and behavioral assessments are done periodically to determine when it is a proper timing for the inmates to return to the society.

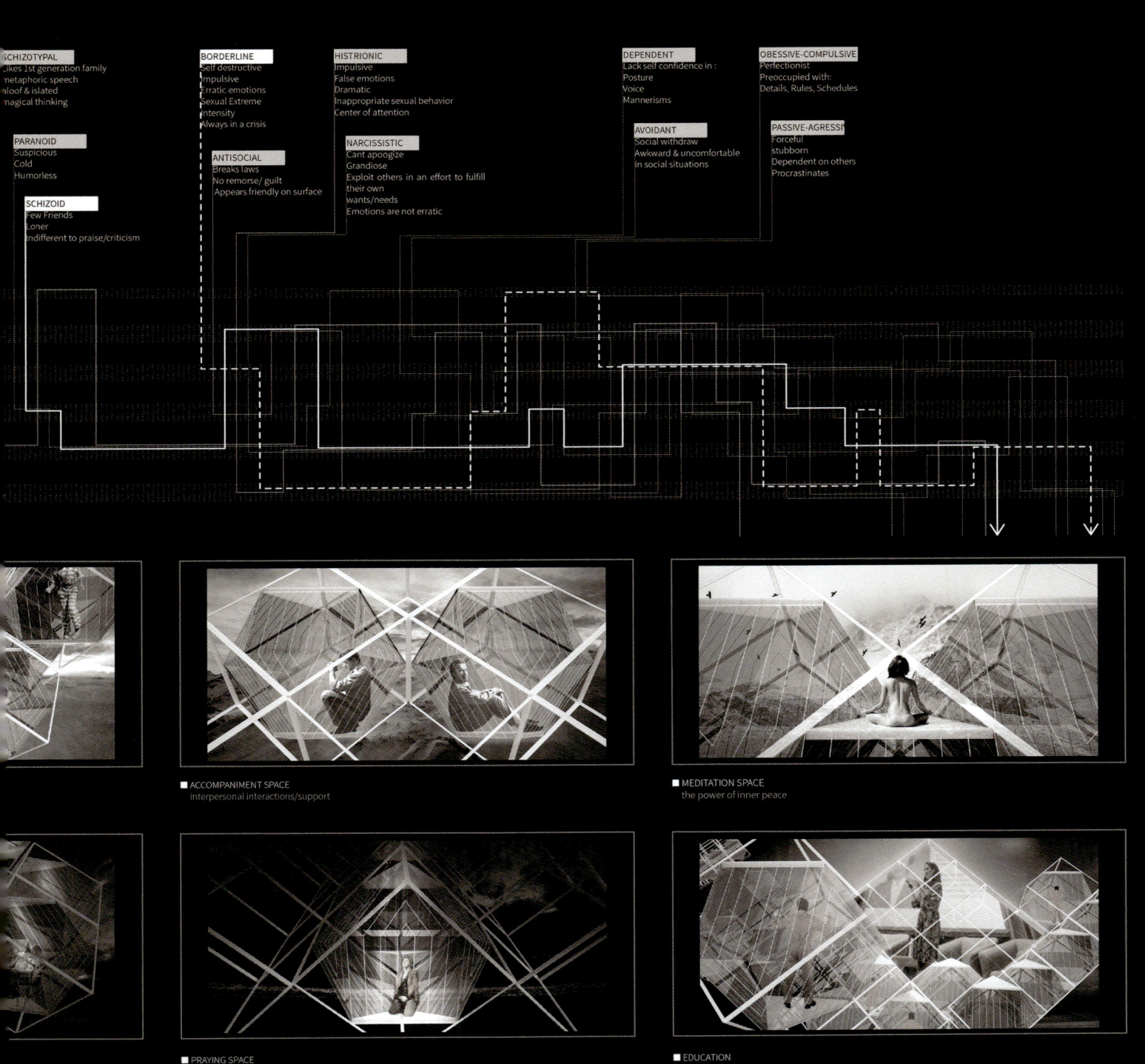

0583

SCHIZOTYPAL
Likes 1st generation family
metaphoric speech
aloof & isolated
magical thinking

BORDERLINE
Self destructive
Impulsive
Erratic emotions
Sexual Extreme
intensity
Always in a crisis

HISTRIONIC
Impulsive
False emotions
Dramatic
Inappropriate sexual behavior
Center of attention

DEPENDENT
Lack self confidence in :
Posture
Voice
Mannerisms

OBSESSIVE-COMPULSIVE
Perfectionist
Preoccupied with:
Details, Rules, Schedules

PARANOID
Suspicious
Cold
Humorless

ANTISOCIAL
Breaks laws
No remorse/ guilt
Appears friendly on surface

NARCISSISTIC
Cant apoogize
Grandiose
Exploit others in an effort to fulfill
their own
wants/needs
Emotions are not erratic

AVOIDANT
Social withdraw
Awkward & uncomfortable
in social situations

PASSIVE-AGRESSIV
Forceful
stubborn
Dependent on others
Procrastinates

SCHIZOID
Few Friends
Loner
Indifferent to praise/criticism

■ ACCOMPANIMENT SPACE
interpersonal interactions/support

■ MEDITATION SPACE
the power of inner peace

■ PRAYING SPACE
religion support

■ EDUCATION
psycology knowledge

RE-BIRTH SKYSCRAPER

Alessa Engalan

Philippines

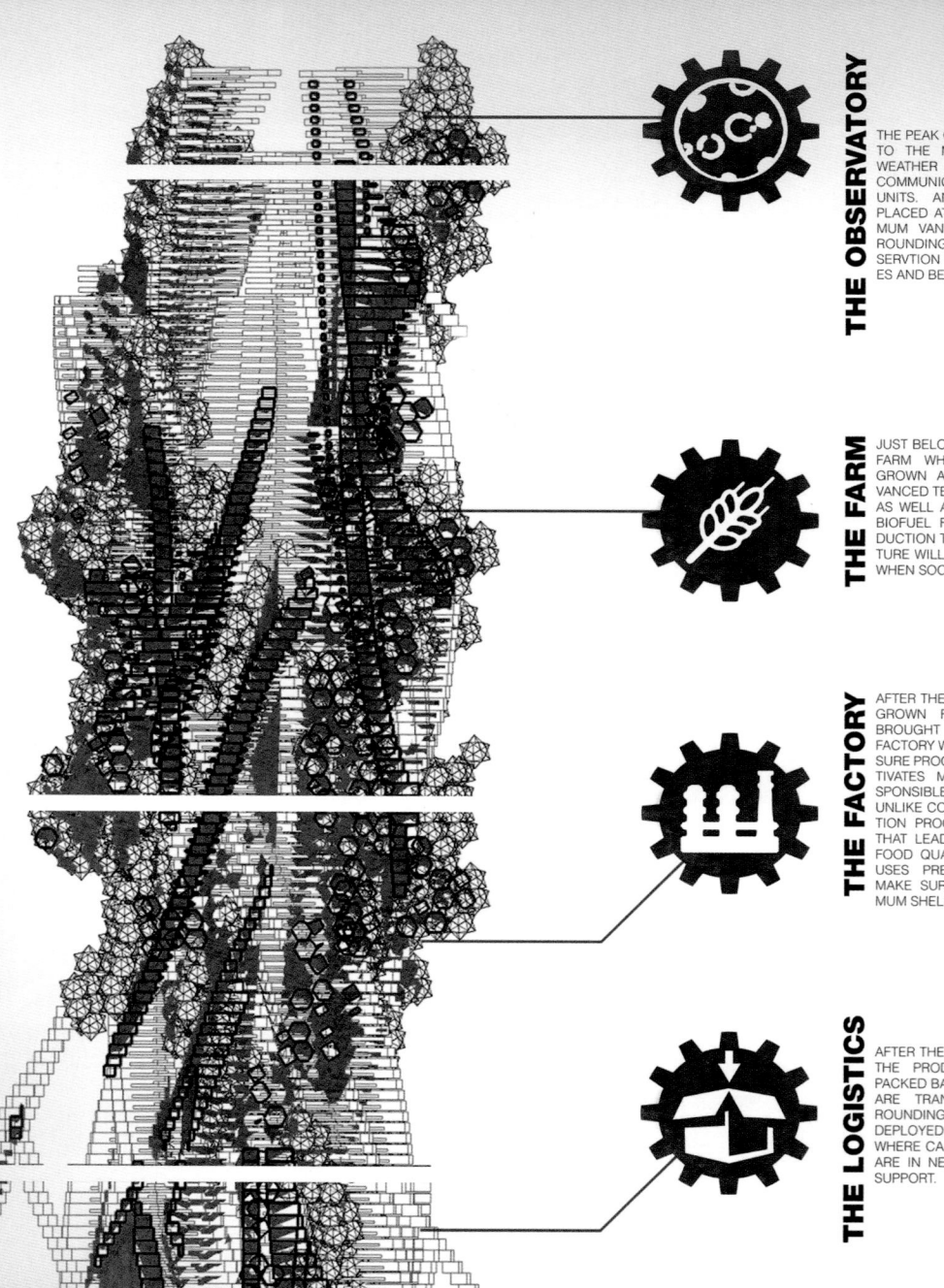

THE OBSERVATORY

THE PEAK OF THE TOWER IS DEDICATED TO THE MONITORING OF OUTDOOR WEATHER CONDITIONS AS WELL AS COMMUNICATIONS WITH SURVIVING UNITS. AN OBSERVATORY IS ALSO PLACED AT THE TOP TO HAVE A MAXIMUM VANTAGE POINT OF THE SURROUNDING AREAS AND A DETAILED OBSERVTION OF ASTRONOMICAL SCIENCES AND BEHAVIORS.

THE FARM

JUST BELOW THE OBSERVATORY IS THE FARM WHERE FOOD IS NATURALLY GROWN AND PRODUCED USING ADVANCED TECHNIQUES OF AQUAPONICS. AS WELL AS THE MANUFACTURING OF BIOFUEL FROM SURPLUS FOOD PRODUCTION TO ENSURE THAT THE STRUCTURE WILL BE ABLE TO SUSTAIN ITSELF WHEN SOCIETY BREAKS DOWN.

THE FACTORY

AFTER THE HARVESTING OF NATURALLY GROWN FOOD IS FINISHED, IT IS BROUGHT STRAIGHT INTO THE MRE FACTORY WHICH UTILIZES A HIGH PRESSURE PROCESSING SYSTEM THAT DEACTIVATES MICROBES WHICH ARE RESPONSIBLE FOR FOOD SPOILAGE. UNLIKE CONVENTIONAL MRE PRODUCTION PROCESSES WHICH USES HEAT, THAT LEADS TO THE DIMINISHING OF FOOD QUALITY AND FRESHNESS, HPP USES PRESSURIZED HYDROGEN TO MAKE SURE MRES HAVE THEIR MAXIMUM SHELF LIFE.

THE LOGISTICS

AFTER THE PRODUCTION OF THE MRES, THE PRODUCTS ARE STORED AND PACKED BACK INTO THE MODULES AND ARE TRANSPORTED INTO TE SURROUNDING DOCKS TO WAITING TO BE DEPLOYED AND DELIVERED TO AREAS WHERE CALAMITIES HAVE STRUCK AND ARE IN NEED OF RELIEF GOODS AND SUPPORT.

RE//BIRTH

A major destructive earthquake is predicted to shake the city of Tehran in the near future. To mitigate the damage from such earthquakes it is necessary to find relevant risk factors of Tehran by assessing the social and urban response to such catastrophes.

Our proposal for a safe and temporary infrastructure in the event of an earthquake consists of a network of urban links that lead to central core or "stackable" shelter pockets. We have strategically selected the Deh-Vanak area of Tehran as our scenario location due to its high urban density of buildings at high risk of collapsing and its lack of open public spaces.

The proposed central safety nods are based on the antisismic properties of and consist of clusters of sliding sphere geometries. Mixed use clusters that cover basic needs are allocated around a core public

0662

LandEscape

space and key transportation nods. These nods are capable of serving as shelter by aggregating the mobile sphere units that navigate the network.

The proposed network in Deh-Vanak analyses threats and opportunities of the site and efficient trajectories not only at pedestrian level and but also along clearances of low rise and mid-rise buildings. Through this analysis we are able to deploy minimal infrastructure to reach safety and optimize the number and location of these central safety nods.

The geometry of the sphere allows the minimum friction and the maximum freedom of movement hence minimizing structural tension during the repercussions that follow in the aftermath of an earthquake. A selection of spheres are fixed to compose central pockets that serve as public spaces

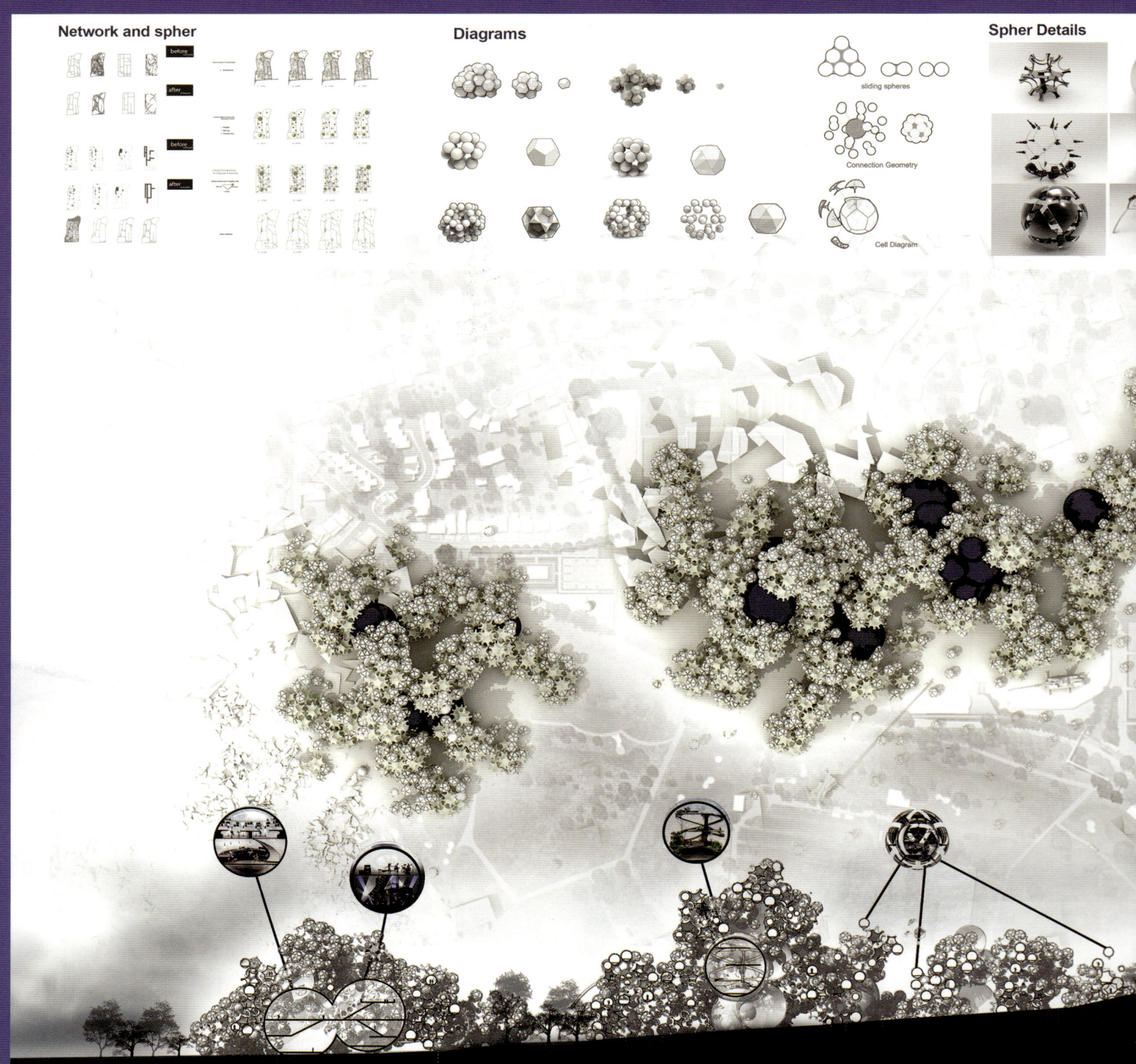

Network and spher

Diagrams

Spher Details

sliding spheres

Connection Geometry

Cell Diagram

while other spheres characterized by their double shell act as mobile units to host diverse functions from information points to first aid checkpoints to food and clean water distribution centers. The shells of these mobile spheres have the capacity to ensemble into emergent shelters.

   Supporting infrastructure such as water and waste canals feed along main links into the core public space and key stations. Connectivity between spheres in shelter pockets is possible through connecting joints.

Conection

before

0662

time

site plan

after

andEscape

THE CATHEDRAL AND SEVEN WONDERS

Dan Zhu
Changhao Xin

China
United States

THE CATHEDRAL AND SEVEN WONDERS

A Tale of a Glorious City in Desert

Once upon a time, an unexpected cataclysm swept through the globe, ravaging and devastating cities large and small, leaving most of the earth a barely habitable wasteland. Very few humans survived the initial firestorm, and even fewer were able to establish small communities capable of subsisting through the first long winter, with whatever remnants of modern civilization they could salvage.

I was born almost three decades after the event, in a small village along one of the newly established trading routes. Every day brought new merchants peddling their goods and workers bartering their skills, a trickle of humanity drifting from villages to small cities back and forth. Every night brought the villagers and transients together around the purifying pyre, elders and visitors trading stories of the world that was and the world now emerging, about the losses and the hardships, about the forbidden zones, and about the fragile shoots of hope sprouting far and few.

One day a troupe of artists settled for the evening, telling tales of distant cities, and mesmerizing all with stories of magic and rebirth through the night. I ate it all up. And fist time, I heard about The Cathedral, a glorious city in a distant desert. Immense. A truly three-dimensional city. Shaped like a cathedral of yore, resonant with harmony, brimming with joy, the impossible dream. Cradling a crescent of magnificent pearls, seven biospheres sparkling in the sun, shining under the moon, each nurturing a unique ecosystem with its own microclimate, all at once mementoes of times passed, monuments mourning human folly, and seeds for a better future. Tales of The Cathedral hypnotized me.

The next morning I left behind all I had known, I was drawn to The Cathedral like a parched soul to an oasis in the desert. And this is what this city was, an oasis of creation and love in a bare landscape, scorched by human destructiveness. It was a dangerous trip, crossing endless wasteland with extreme weathers. The journey might have been the reward but my eyes were transfixed by the city, undulating in the distance like a mirage. I felt to my knees awed by its size, majesty and splendor.

Golden afternoon light struck the massive structure, coating it with a multitude of warm and earthy colors. As I approached it, details came into focus: a pair of tall towers held a facade with three arched gates and circular windows of rose flower pattern; a row of giant but slim towers flanking on each side, rigid and cold. Finally reaching the gate, I crossed the threshold beaming with excitement: it was a true metropolis! How surprisingly bright inside! Light shining through countless stained glass windows combined with light emanating from the biospheres and from some of the supporting structures, bridges, aqueducts, piazzas, pedestrian spaces, buildings, courtyards, malls and skyscrapers.

The Cathedral was pulsating with life every minute, people flowing ant-like in and out of buildings and space and ground transportation, and a ballet of flying vehicles navigating through space like birds. Seven spectacular structures were suspended in the air. Their bottoms were a maze of intricate and dense metal structures, pipes and machineries supporting platforms covered by glowing geodesic domes; vine-like bridges spreading among and connecting these biospheres, the Seven Wonders! The atmosphere permeating the city was one of poise and peace, resolve and determination to achieve spiritual fulfillment rather than material accumulation.

residential district

solar collector

aqueduct

secondary traffic

Once upon a time, an unexpected cataclysm swept through the globe, ravaging and devastating cities large and small, leaving most of the earth a barely habitable wasteland. Very few humans survived the initial firestorm, and even fewer were able to establish small communities capable of subsisting through the first long winter, with whatever remnants of modern civilization they could salvage. I was born almost three decades after the event, in a small village along one of the newly established trading routes. Every day brought new merchants peddling their goods and workers bartering their skills, a trickle of humanity drifting from villages to small cities back and forth. Every night brought the villagers and transients together around the purifying pyre, elders and visitors trading stories of the world that was and the world now emerging, about the losses and the hardships, about the forbidden zones, and about the

0677

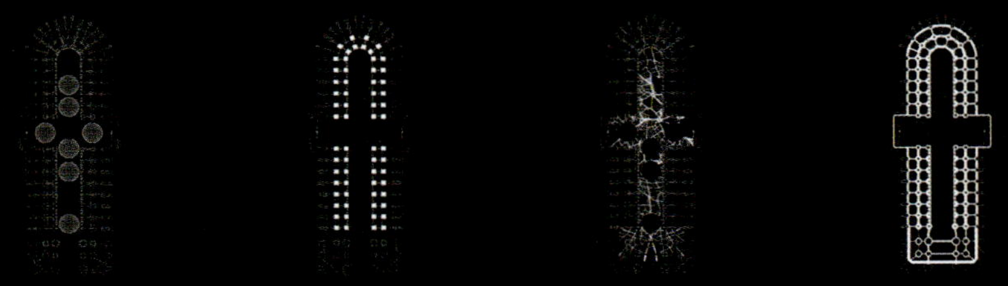

seven wonders   main bridges   charging station   main traffic

fragile shoots of hope sprouting far and few. One day a troupe of artists settled for the evening, telling tales of distant cities, and mesmerizing all with stories of magic and rebirth through the night. I ate it all up. And fist time, I heard about The Cathedral, a glorious city in a distant desert – immense, a truly three-dimensional city. Shaped like a cathedral of yore, resonant with harmony, brimming with joy, the impossible dream. Cradling a crescent of magnificent pearls, seven biospheres sparkling in the sun, shining under the moon, each nurturing a unique ecosystem with its own microclimate, all at once mementoes of times passed, monuments mourning human folly, and seeds for a better future. Tales of The Cathedral hypnotized me. The next morning I left behind all I had known, I was drawn to The Cathedral like a parched soul to an oasis in the desert. And this is what this city was, an oasis of creation and love in a bare landscape, scorched by human destructiveness. It was a dangerous trip, crossing

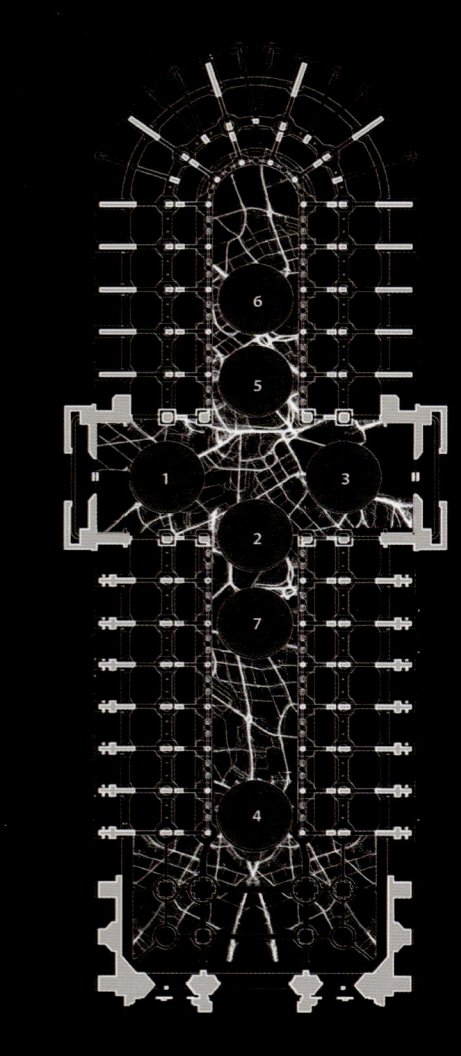

MASTER PLAN

LONGITUDINAL SECTION

In the cathedral, diligent and wise human beings put last precious spices and land-scapes into seven domes to pre-serve and wor-ship our memoir of beautiful earth.

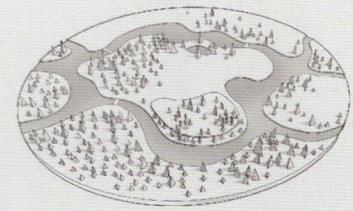

1 FOREST

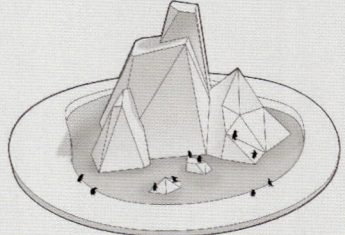

2 SNOW MOUNTAIN

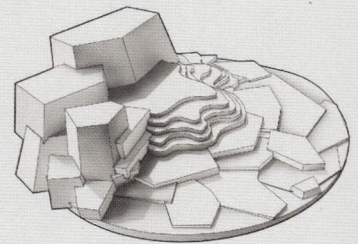

3 MOUNTAIN & VALLEY

endless wasteland with extreme weathers. The journey might have been the reward but my eyes were transfixed by the city, undulating in the distance like a mirage. I felt to my knees awed by its size, majesty and splendor. Golden afternoon light struck the massive structure, coating it with a multitude of warm and earthy colors. As I approached it, details came into focus: a pair of tall towers held a facade with three arched gates and circular windows of rose flower pattern; a row of giant but slim towers flanking on each side, rigid and cold. Finally reaching the gate, I crossed the threshold beaming with excitement: it was a true metropolis! How surprisingly bright inside! Light shining through countless stained glass windows combined with light emanating from the biospheres and from some of the supporting structures. The Cathedral was pulsating with life every minute.

Super spherical solar power collector absorbs solar energy during daytime, and the energy is converted into electricity and stored in the city power station.

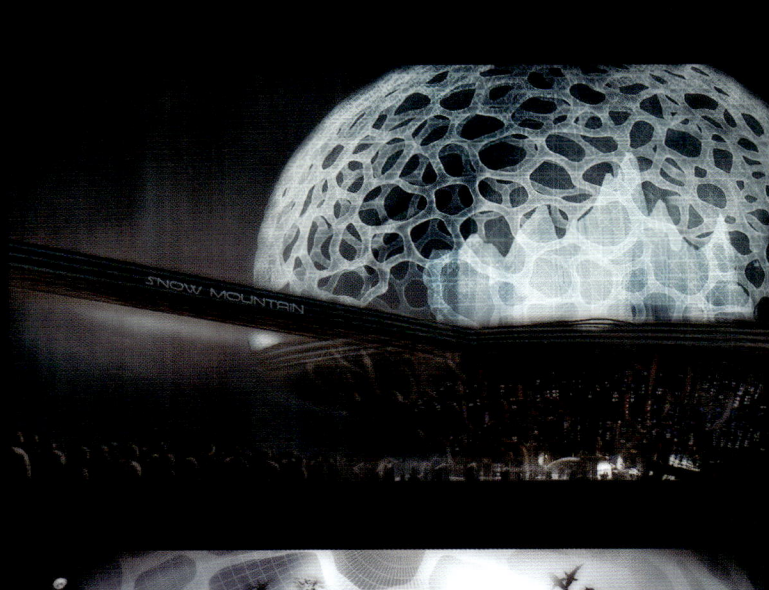

0677

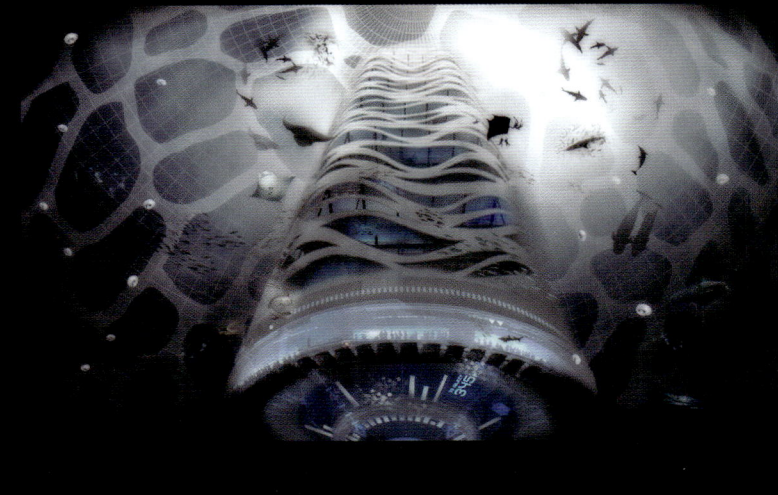

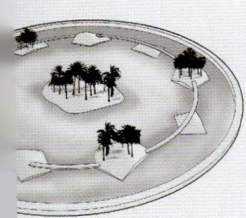

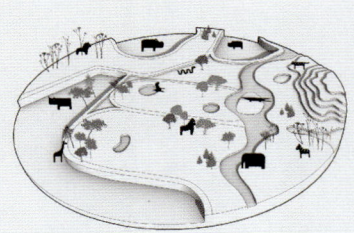

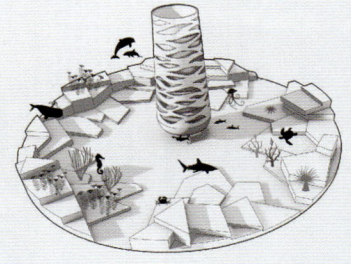

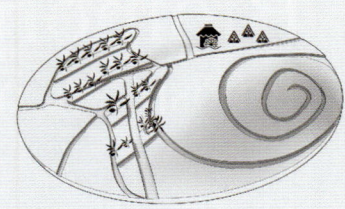

4   BEACH

5   ZOO

6   AQUARIUM

7   FARM & ORCHARD

BIOMORPHOR: ATMOSPHERE OF THE SPACE

Jayong Shim
Dailong Ma
Tai Feng

United States

Biomorph
atmosphere of the place

New York City is a city of large high-density buildings that sets a trend for people's life and goals. A lot of people are still trying to come to the city with a utopian dream. However, at same time, people are running out of town because of they struggle with urban life causing little social diversity. There are countless skyscrapers in NYC but people cannot recognize existence of the places because the buildings don't have specific features.

A definition of a place is a particular portion of space, whether of definite or indefinite extent. However, in the building, the space is not limited by the fundamental dimensions of "place". The place is a space people can feel the existence and specific emotion. The morphosis design of organic creature integrates diverse experience that blurs the boundary between spatial relationships. The space uses

Atmosphere

0758

New York City is a city of large high density buildings that sets a trend for people's life and goals. A lot of people are still trying to come to the city with utopia dream. However, at same time, people are running out of town because of they struggle with urban life causing little social diversity. There are countless skyscrapers in NY but people cannot recognize existence of the places because the buildings don't have specific features.

A definition of a place is a particular portion of space, whether of definite or indefinite extent. However, in the building, the space is not limited by the fundamental dimensions of "place". The place is a space people can feel the existence and specific emotion. The morphosis design of organic creature integrates diverse experience that blurs the boundary between spatial relationships. The space uses the city's landscape as a background, and façade as an experimental symbol which is stunning the society and evoking people's thought to explore more value of the community. Spatial atmosphere also creates an opportunity to experience some special interior phenomenon and moment which people may get inspired and surprised. It can be considered as a chance to provoke people's passion about aesthetic urban life and turn those passions into a diverse way of thinking. In the façade, morphosis design of organic creature make many different diffuse light qualities which can produce various interior atmospheres.

When people experience the space, the bright light lead and gather people who are losing way from dark area, then the dark zone attracts people who are holding a strong curiosity. The contrast of small scale rooms and large scale atriums gives people various spatial inspirations on the difference of urban scale. The entire project does not only synthesize the fundamental function with morphology of the building design, but also consider large scale urban environment as an experimental field to explore and provoke people's diversity.

Plan

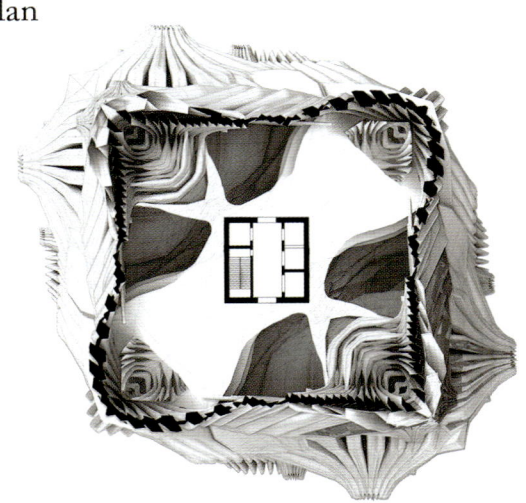

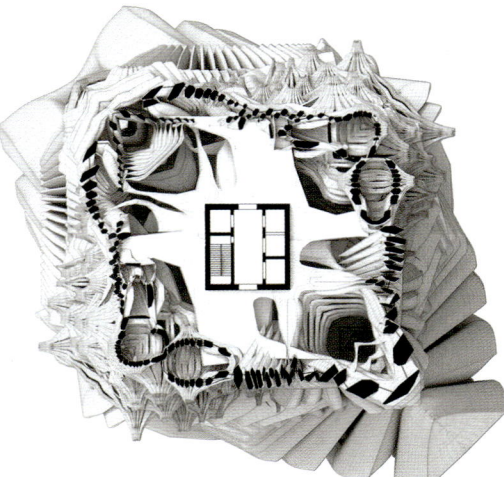

Morphosis

Dandelion structure   Connection of petals   Accumulation   Variation

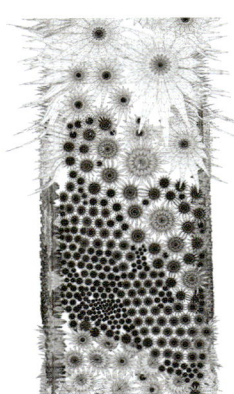

the city's landscape as a background, and façade as an experimental symbol, which is stunning the society and evoking people thought to explore more value of the community. Spatial atmosphere also creates an opportunity to experience some special interior phenomenon and moment which people may get inspired and surprised with. It can be considered as a chance to provoke people's passion about aesthetic urban life and turn those passions into a diverse way of thinking.

In the façade, morphosis design of organic creature makes many different diffuse light qualities, which can produce various interior atmospheres. When people experience the space, the bright light lead and gather people who are losing way from dark area, then the dark zone attracts people who are holding a strong curiosity. The contrast of small-scale rooms and large-scale atriums gives people various spatial

inspirations on the difference of urban scale.

The entire project does not only synthesize the fundamental function with morphology of the building design, but also consider large-scale urban environment as an experimental field to explore and provoke people's diversity.

0758

Elevation   Section

PLAQUES AND TANGLES

Jillian Blakey
Mara Marcu (advisor)

United States

PLAQUES AND TANGLES
STRUCTURES FOR REMEMBERING

Disintegration of the brain in our increasingly aging population is addressed relentlessly in medical research but largely neglected in environmental experiment. Our lifespan has been elongated due to a growing body of knowledge in health and medicine, and still a third of seniors will live with Alzheimer's or another dementia. Plaques and Tangles is driven by an investigation into the formal, spatial, and societal potential of extended memory care in the vertical environment.

Typical retirement communities and full time care facilities are developed as sprawling patterns in remote corners. Within this proposed Manhattan context, the project gives dementia a physical urban presence and offers an opportunity for a dynamic community. A programmatically rich and site sensitive armature is systematically populated by a flexible, structural unit. The aggregate's inherently radial patterns produce a legible datum while formally reflecting the sponge-like quality of plaques and tangles common to an Alzheimer's brain.

The structural unit is intended to multiply and mutate, as need rises and medical knowledge progresses. Plaques and Tangles seeks to create an architectural system that considers the complexities of overpopulation and maximizes prosperity in the final stage of life.

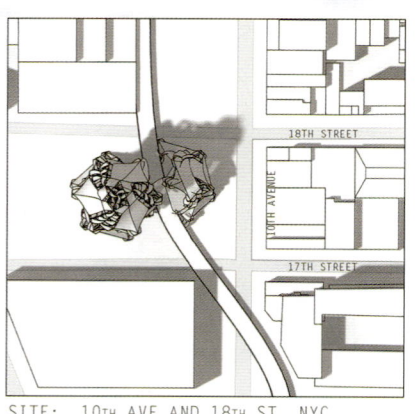

SITE: 10TH AVE AND 18TH ST, NYC

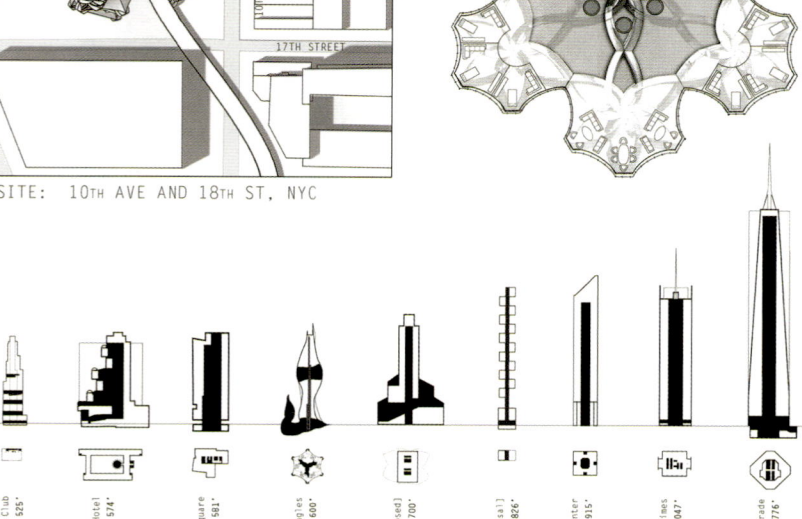

Disintegration of the brain in our increasingly aging population is addressed relentlessly in medical research but largely neglected in environmental experiment. Our lifespan has been elongated due to a growing body of knowledge in health and medicine, and still a third of seniors will live with Alzheimer's or another dementia. Plaques and Tangles is driven by an investigation into the formal, spatial, and societal potential of extended memory care in the vertical environment.

Typical retirement communities and full time care facilities are developed as sprawling patterns in remote corners. Within this proposed Manhattan context, the project gives dementia a physical urban presence and offers an opportunity for a dynamic community. A programmatically rich and site sensitive armature is systematically populated by a flexible, structural unit. The aggregate's inherently radial

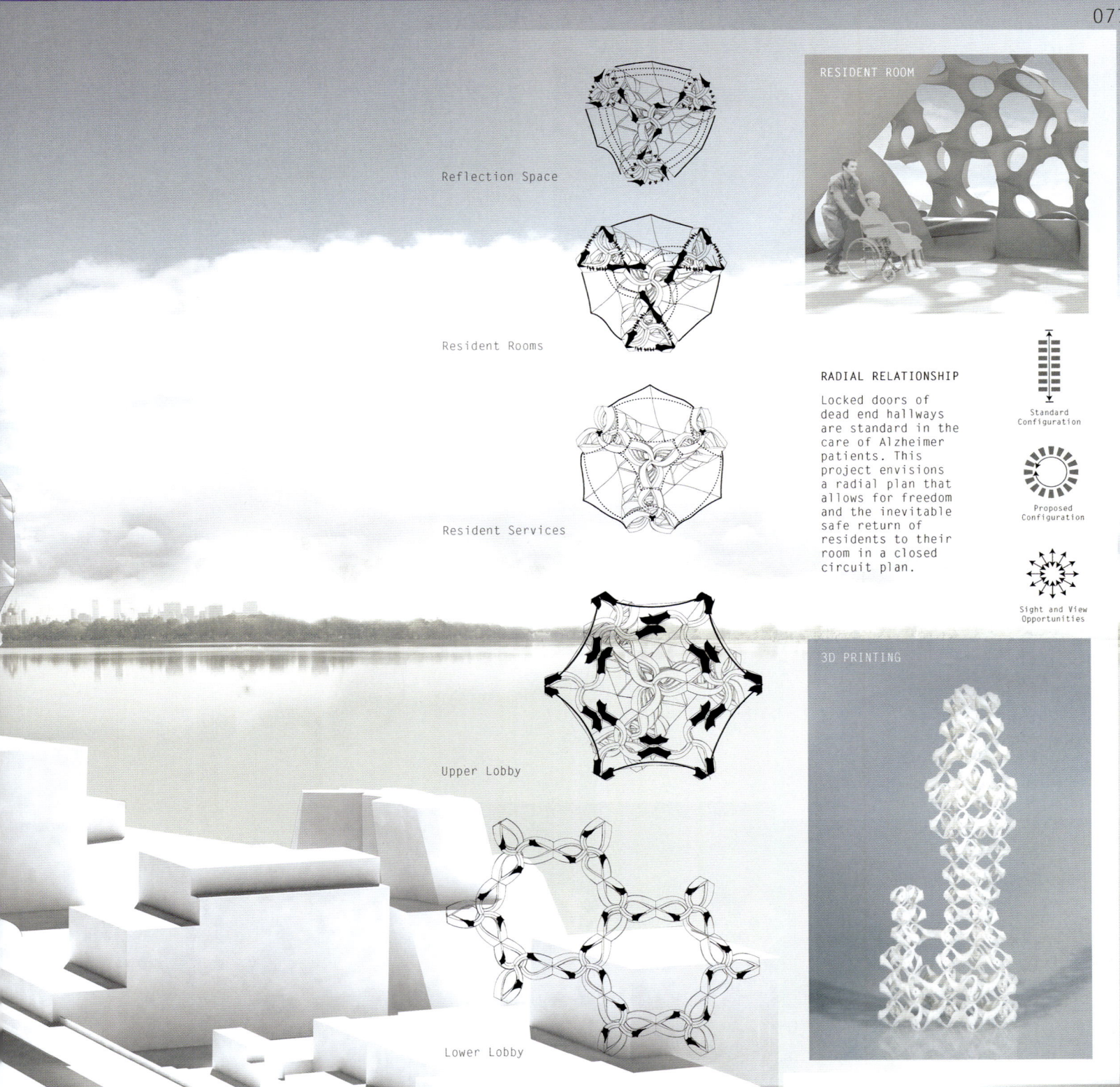

0775

Reflection Space

Resident Rooms

Resident Services

Upper Lobby

Lower Lobby

RESIDENT ROOM

RADIAL RELATIONSHIP

Locked doors of dead end hallways are standard in the care of Alzheimer patients. This project envisions a radial plan that allows for freedom and the inevitable safe return of residents to their room in a closed circuit plan.

Standard Configuration

Proposed Configuration

Sight and View Opportunities

3D PRINTING

patterns produce a legible datum while formally reflecting the sponge-like quality of plaques and tangles common to an Alzheimer's brain.

    Two primary lobbies serve as cultural hubs for residents of the building and local community members alike. They include space for theaters, galleries, restaurants, and commercial development. One wing is reserved for outpatient care and further medical research into memory loss and recovery. Residential units are designed as one or two person dwellings, however equal space is reserved for communal gathering and reflection. Transportation systems in the building are exclusively elevators and escalators to maximize mobility of residents.

    The structural unit is intended to multiply and mutate, as need rises and medical knowledge

UPPER LOBBY

REFLECTION

PLAQUES
STRUCTURES

ENVELOPE SY

ENVELOPE FRAME

STRUCTURAL UNIT

FLEXIBLE ENVELOPE

A single unit, aggregated within a programmatic armature defines the form of this building. Smaller cells populate the unit to create an envelope system for unique resident rooms.

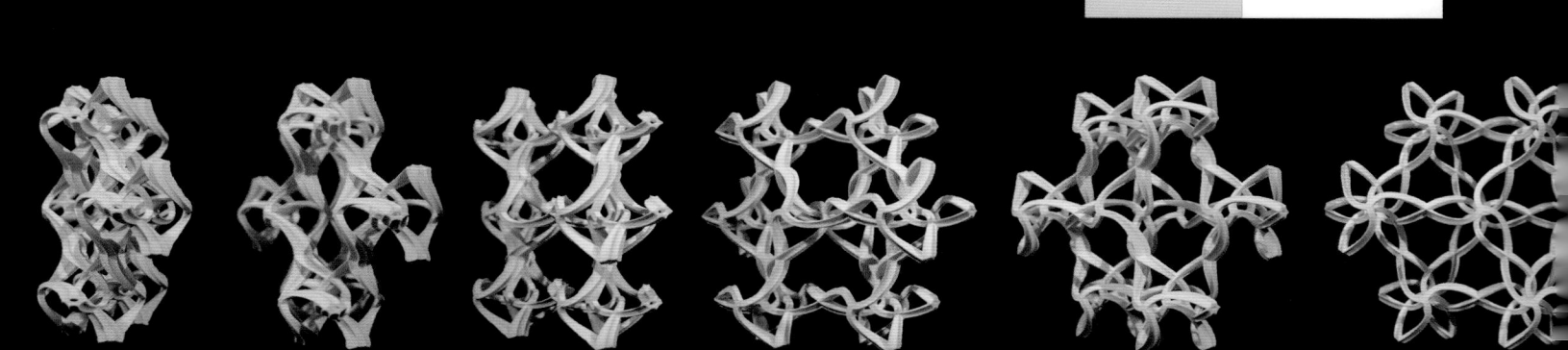

progresses. Plaques and Tangles seeks to create an architectural system that considers the complexities of overpopulation and maximizes prosperity in the final stage of life.

0775

ND TANGLES
OR REMEMBERING

500'

SPIRE
475'

PENTHOUSE
445'

STAGE 3 CARE
415'

STAGE 2 CARE
380'

STAGE 1 CARE
340'

UPPER LOBBY
240'

STAGE 1 CARE
200'

ENVELOPE CELL

165'

STAGE 2 CARE
165'

STAGE 3 CARE
135'

STAGE 2 CARE
105'

STAGE 1 CARE
70'

OUTPATIENT CARE
50'

HIGH LINE
30'

GROUND
0'

LOWER LOBBY
-75'

3D PRINTING
STRUCTURAL BAY

5,687 ft.

5,280 ft.

12.2 psi atmosphere

MOUNTAIN PARK

RETAIL WORLD 3

VERTICAL FARMS

RESIDENCE 5

RESIDENCE 4

REDWOOD PARK

RETAIL WORLD 2

SOUTH BEACH

VIEW AT 5000 FT

URBAN THEORIES & STRATEGIES 6

VOLUMETRIC URBANISM

Bill Or Man Oiu

Hong Kong

VOLUMETRIC URBANISM

Urban Design | 3D City | Biomimetics

UP TO TODAY MANY TOOLS FOR URBAN PLANNING HAVE BEEN PROPOSED, AS WE CAN ANALYZE THE CITIES BY DIFFERENT ASPECTS SUCH AS SOCIAL, DENSITY, ECONOMIC, SUSTAINABILITY, ETC. IN THIS PROJECT, THE URBAN CONNECTION IS THE MAIN ASPECT THAT WILL BE ANALYZE IN THE BEGINNING.

ACCORDINGLY, CITIES AND REGIONS ARE PLANNED FROM TWO-DIMENSIONAL POINT OF VIEW. HOWEVER, WITH THE RISE OF THE GLOBAL POPULATION AND TECHNOLOGICAL DEVELOPMENTS, THREE-DIMENSIONAL PLANNING METHODS WILL INCREASINGLY INVADING URBAN DEVELOPMENTS IN THE FUTURE.

THEREFORE, THIS PROJECT TAKES AN EVOLUTIONARY STANDPOINT TO 'READ URBAN STRUCTURE FROM A URBAN CONNECTIVITY STANDPOINT AND STUDYING VOLUMETRIC URBAN SPATIAL PLANNING AS A NEW URBAN TYPOLOGY FOR FUTURE CITY EXPANSION.' A KEY ASPECT IN THIS PERSPECTIVE LIES IN HOW TO INTERPRET THE CONCEPT OF URBAN CONNECTIVITY FOR THREE-DIMENSIONAL URBAN PLANNING. WHAT IS MEANT BY URBAN CONNECTIVITY AT THE LEVEL OF URBAN PLANNING, AND HOW IS IT USED FOR THE PURPOSE OF INVENTING AND PLANNING VOLUMETRIC CITY. HOW CAN WE TRANSLATE THE CONCEPT OF URBAN CONNECTIVITY FROM TWO-DIMENSION INTO THREE-DIMENSION? HOW TO PERFORM THE TRANSLATION TO COMPUTER APPLICATIONS DEALING WITH THE PROBLEM OF THREE-DIMENSION PLANNING?

AFTER VARIOUS STUDIES OF THE URBAN STRUCTURE, IT TAKES AN EXPERIMENTAL WAY TO EXAMINE THE POSSIBILITY OF NEW URBAN TYPOLOGIES FOR A VOLUMETRIC URBANISM IN THE FUTURE DEVELOPMENT. THE INTEGRATED MULTI-DIMENSIONS CONNECTED NETWORK AND ELEVATED URBAN EXPERIENCE ARE THE ESSENTIAL ELEMENTS WHICH PRESENTED IN THIS VOLUMETRIC URBAN MODEL.

01 INWARD URBAN EXPANSION FORCES

02 TRADITIONAL INWARD VERTICAL CITY PROPOSAL WITHOUT URBAN CONTEXT

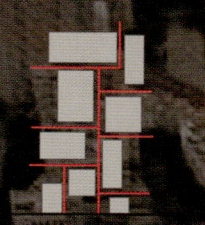

03 BREAK DOWN INTO COMMUNITY SIZE AND CREATE OUTWARD URBAN SPACE

04 SPREADING OUT TO MAXIMIZE THE VISUAL CONTACT TO OTHER COMMUNITIES

05 RECON PLACE TO PUBLIC S STREET

Up until today, many tools for urban planning have been proposed, as we can analyze cities by different aspects such as society, density, economics, sustainability, etc. In this project, the urban connection is the main aspect that will be analyzed in the beginning.

Accordingly, cities and regions are planned from A two-dimensional point of view. However, with the rise of the global population and technological developments, three-dimensional planning methods will increasingly invade urban developments in the future.

Therefore, this project takes an evolutionary standpoint to read urban structure from an urban connectivity standpoint and studying volumetric urban spatial planning as a new urban typology for future city expansion. A key aspect in this perspective lies in how to interpret the concept of urban

0068

TING THE
OVIDE
E AND

connectivity for three-dimensional urban planning. What is meant by urban connectivity at the level of urban planning, and how is it used for the purpose of inventing and planning a volumetric city. How can we translate the concept of urban connectivity from two-dimensions into three-dimensions? How to perform the translation to computer applications dealing with the problem of three-dimensional planning?

After various studies of the urban structure, it takes an experimental way to examine the possibility of new urban typologies for a volumetric urbanism in future development. The integrated, multi-dimensional, connected network and elevated urban experience are the essential elements, which are presented, in this volumetric urban model.

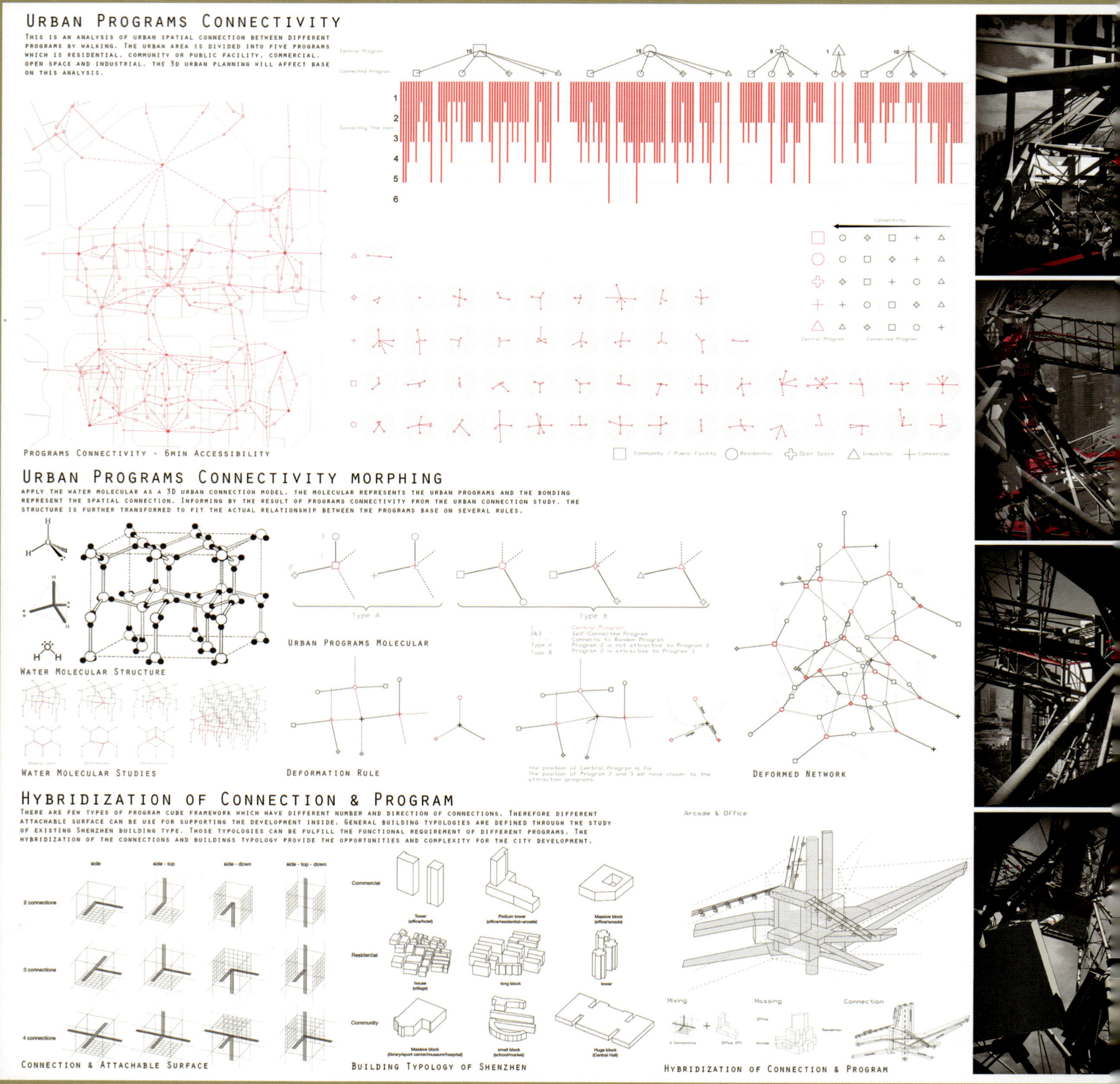

URBAN PROGRAMS CONNECTIVITY

THIS IS AN ANALYSIS OF URBAN SPATIAL CONNECTION BETWEEN DIFFERENT PROGRAMS BY WALKING. THE URBAN AREA IS DIVIDED INTO FIVE PROGRAMS WHICH IS RESIDENTIAL, COMMUNITY OR PUBLIC FACILITY, COMMERCIAL, OPEN SPACE AND INDUSTRIAL. THE 3D URBAN PLANNING WILL AFFECT BASE ON THIS ANALYSIS.

PROGRAMS CONNECTIVITY - 6MIN ACCESSIBILITY

URBAN PROGRAMS CONNECTIVITY MORPHING

APPLY THE WATER MOLECULAR AS A 3D URBAN CONNECTION MODEL. THE MOLECULAR REPRESENTS THE URBAN PROGRAMS AND THE BONDING REPRESENT THE SPATIAL CONNECTION. INFORMING BY THE RESULT OF PROGRAMS CONNECTIVITY FROM THE URBAN CONNECTION STUDY. THE STRUCTURE IS FURTHER TRANSFORMED TO FIT THE ACTUAL RELATIONSHIP BETWEEN THE PROGRAMS BASE ON SEVERAL RULES.

WATER MOLECULAR STRUCTURE

WATER MOLECULAR STUDIES

URBAN PROGRAMS MOLECULAR

DEFORMATION RULE

DEFORMED NETWORK

HYBRIDIZATION OF CONNECTION & PROGRAM

THERE ARE FEW TYPES OF PROGRAM CUBE FRAMEWORK WHICH HAVE DIFFERENT NUMBER AND DIRECTION OF CONNECTIONS. THEREFORE DIFFERENT ATTACHABLE SURFACE CAN BE USE FOR SUPPORTING THE DEVELOPMENT INSIDE. GENERAL BUILDING TYPOLOGIES ARE DEFINED THROUGH THE STUDY OF EXISTING SHENZHEN BUILDING TYPE. THOSE TYPOLOGIES CAN BE FULFILL THE FUNCTIONAL REQUIREMENT OF DIFFERENT PROGRAMS. THE HYBRIDIZATION OF THE CONNECTIONS AND BUILDINGS TYPOLOGY PROVIDE THE OPPORTUNITIES AND COMPLEXITY FOR THE CITY DEVELOPMENT.

CONNECTION & ATTACHABLE SURFACE

BUILDING TYPOLOGY OF SHENZHEN

HYBRIDIZATION OF CONNECTION & PROGRAM

0068

Building

Connections

Attaching Grid

Skeleton

Spatial Framework

Grid & Columns

THE NEW TOWER OF BABEL

Petko Stoevski

Germany

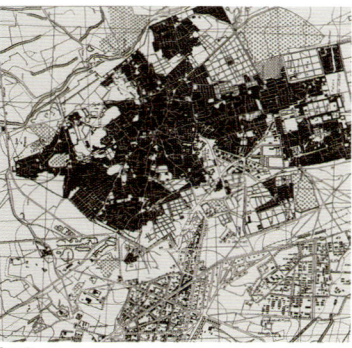

Image 01

Image 02

Image 03

Image 04

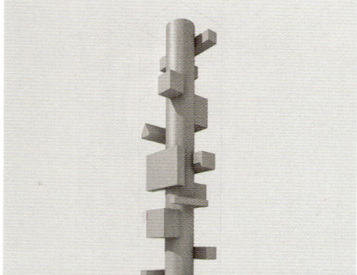

Image 04

Image 05

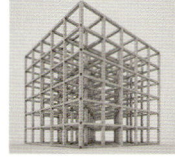

Image 06

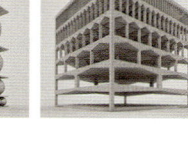

Image 07

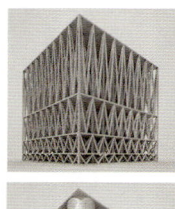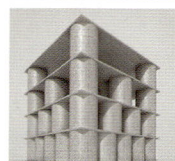

Image 08

"The New Tower of Babel"

Cities are strongly influenced by their landscapes resulting in various spaces and unique structures which define the inhabitants' way of life. Some cities have open, free spatial structures while others evolve vertically following a particular grid. (*image 01*).

A steel construction is built over the desert surface (field dimensions: 7x 7 km) so that multiple levels can be planned depending on the landscape's topology. (*image 02*)

The top two panels are made of glass, and the air contained in between is warmed up by the sunlight. The structure is slightly tilted upwards which leads the air to the middle of the tower (1000x 200x 200 m) into an inner cylindrical cavity (diameter 100 m). The updraft power channels the warm air into the chimney tower, propelling the wind turbines located in the base of the building, thus converting kinetic energy into electrical power. (*image 18*)

Under the glass panels, protected from adverse weather conditions, dust, and debris, are located photovoltaic panels. They generate electricity while at the same time reflecting the sun rays thereby further increasing the temperature of the air contained between the glass. Underneath, the levels are transformable and can be utilized in different ways, such as the transportation of people and goods as well as the transmission of water, gas or electricity. Moreover, the photovoltaic panels cast a shadow which cools down the land's surface. This newly created microclimate allows the creation of residential and recreational areas as well as the development of agriculture. (*image 09*)

The individual spatial elements create a common body and allow the use of space in different ways. (*image 05-08*)
The elements follow the principles of statics: by gradually decreasing the weight of the structures moving from the base up. (*image 03*)

Different solutions of the open spaces break off the continuity of inner spaces and create places with unique identity. (*image 04, 10-17*)

The Tower of Babel establishes a new landscape which makes use of the natural forces of an upwind power plant and therefore stretches from the horizontal to the vertical. The environment is decided as an open city, with maximum freedom. The building is characterized by many different spaces and leaves their use open to improvisation. Therefore, life develops in different places with different intensity. The project reinforces the principles of sustainability which allow long term economic, social, and ecological development. (image 19)

The concept of "The New Tower of Babel" is conceived with the idea of uniting people with diverse cultural backgrounds, occupations and ideas and thus imparting a new meaning to the myth.

Cities are strongly influenced by their landscapes resulting in various spaces and unique structures, which define its inhabitants' way of life. Some cities have open, free spatial structures while others evolve vertically following a particular grid.

The New Tower of Babel is a steel construction built over the desert surface with multiple levels planned depending on the landscape's topology. The top two panels are made of glass, and the air contained in between is warmed up by the sunlight. The structure is slightly tilted upwards, which leads the air to the middle of the tower into an inner cylindrical. The updraft power channels the warm air into the chimney tower, propelling the wind turbines located in the base of the building, thus converting kinetic energy into electrical power. Under the glass panels, protected from adverse weather conditions,

0369

Image 09

dust, and debris, photovoltaic panels are placed. They generate electricity while reflecting the sunrays thereby further increasing the temperature of the air contained between the glasses. Underneath, the floor plates are transformable and can be utilized in different ways, including the transportation of people and goods as well as the transmission of water, gas or electricity. Moreover, the photovoltaic panels cast a shadow, which cools down the land's surface. This newly created microclimate allows the creation of residential and recreational areas as well as the development of agriculture.

The individual spatial elements create a common body and allow the use of space in different ways. The elements follow the principles of statics: by gradually decreasing the weight of the structures moving from the base up. Different solutions of the open spaces break off the continuity of inner spaces and

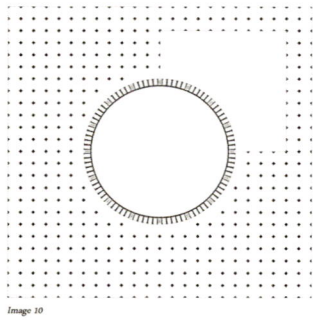

Image 10

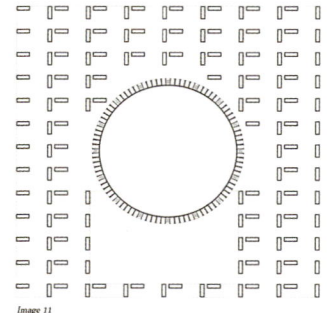

Image 11

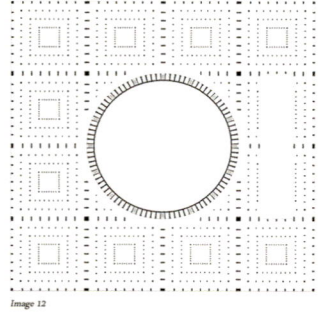

Image 12

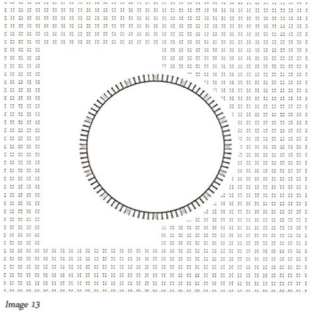

Image 13

Image 14

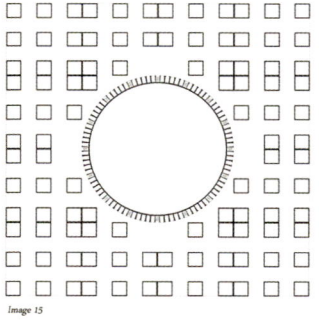

Image 15

Image 16

Image 17

Image 18

create places with unique identity. The Tower of Babel establishes a new landscape, which makes use of the natural forces of an upwind power plant and therefore stretches from the horizontal to the vertical. The environment is decided as an open city, with maximum freedom. The building is characterized by many different spaces and leaves their use open to improvisation. Therefore, life develops in different places with different intensity. The project reinforces the principles of sustainability, which allow long term economic, social, and ecological development.

0369

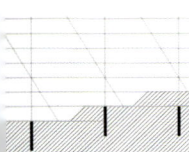

Image 19

GERRIDAE: SETTLING THE TIDES

Joe Shi

Canada

GERRIDAE
SETTLING THE TIDES

The Water Strider

As our need for infrastructure and resources increases with the ever rising population, the dilemma for mankind's growth is ever present. The foundation of our cities rests on the same grounds as our natural resources, thus as one grows, the other must inevitably recede. We are in a constant state of preserving one region of resource while forfeiting another for continuing development. Amidst this balancing act, it would seem appropriate that we look to our largest body of resource, the oceans. To inhabit a variable entity so different from our current environment, one must rethink the way settlements are built, both to adapt and to effectively preserve our most essential resource. Take the commonly dubbed water strider, effortlessly skimming along the water's surface by virtue of the hydrophobic hair lining its limbs. It is able to be in constant interaction with its most needed reserve, yet its physical presence is hardly felt, leaving no impression of its stay once it leaves. It is from this organism that the project derives its taxonomic name, "Gerridae".

Expansion and Integration

Gerridae addresses the issue of our perpetually increasing footprint on land mass and natural resources by expanding human settlement onto the bodies of water that comprise the majority of our planet's surface. With particular emphasis on self-sustainability and minimizing permanent ecological impact, especially the potential adverse effects of permanent densified human activity on aquatic life, Gerridae allows for a state of semi-nomadism as it is subtly guided and nourished by the tides on which it rests. Meanwhile, the typical model of a city is inverted in Gerridae's architecture where a Life Hub - the center of ecological resources - is upheld and sustained by connected residential limbs that steadily collect and transfer water through their pointed contact with the ocean below. This configuration is also employed to take full advantage of naturally occurring phenomena, where better access to sunlight and stronger winds at higher altitudes allow a circumference of specialized solar and wind power generators around the Life Hub to be utilized at utmost efficiency. In addition, distributed contact with the waves below make the most of each residential limb's tidal power generators.

While settlement of the oceans would provide a vast supply of inhabitable estate, an essential component of Gerridae's design is also to improve the current relationship between the built city and the natural world by reducing the physical footprint of our occupation. As such, Gerridae relies on the mass distribution properties of its form in conjunction with the buoyant properties of water. The central mass of the Life Hub is distributed along a dome formation of 3 to 6 modular residential limbs, each of which distributes its load among 4 Stabilizing Arms which then finally transfer the load to tripod formations atop air-filled platform buoys on the water's surface. This tiered system of mass distribution aids the reduction of point loads and stress on any one part of the the structure, allowing it to stay afloat while occupying a minute portion of the water's surface area. Gerridae is able to house up to 15,000 occupants by virtue of its adaptable Life Hub on a physical yet nomadic footprint of just 0.025 square kilometers when the maximum of 6 residential limbs are attached. For comparison, New York City has an average density of 10,500 occupants per square kilometer where most of the surface area is covered by structural foundations. Unlike the stacking of traditional high-rise buildings, Gerridae's Residential Halos are held together by a structural frame that also functions as a green wall on each limb, allowing for improved ventilation and light permeation through every residential level.

By essentially introducing a new layer of sustainable natural resources 500 meters above the surface of the ocean, Gerridae becomes a unique model of autonomous and highly unobstrusive human development that actively pursues a more organic integration between the natural and built environment.

Comparing Support Systems

We face the ever-diminishing supply of our natural resources as a result of rapid urban expansion on land. And while modern technology has allowed us to erect structures at greater scales along the vertical plane, inhabiting just 30% of the planet's surface will eventually find its limitation. Inspired by the organic properties of the water strider, "Gerridae" is a highly sustainable and autonomous model for the urban expansion of highly dense cities into large nearby bodies of water that also allows for the propagation of increased resource cultivation.

Inverting the common model of the built foundation, Gerridae places an ecological "Life Hub" 500 meters above the ocean's surface supported and fed by modular "residential limbs" that are precariously balanced and stabilized at small points along the water's surface, extracting steady flows of collected

0471

water from the ocean below like the maxillae of an insect. In effect, the residential portion of the architecture acts as a conduit connecting two layers of ecological resources while tidal buoys and high altitude allow for the effective implementation and flow of solar, wind, and wave energy technologies that make the architecture self-sustaining.

Gerridae also speaks to porosity and preserving the state of our most precious resource. Specifically, the effort to create small points of contact while elevating the structure's ecological platform ensures that minimal impact is had on the aquatic life below, including its access to natural sunlight. Each residential limb is also deceptively hollow with units occupying the outer perimeter of every level around a highly light and air permeable core that allows the architecture to "breathe". Such a living model reinforces the

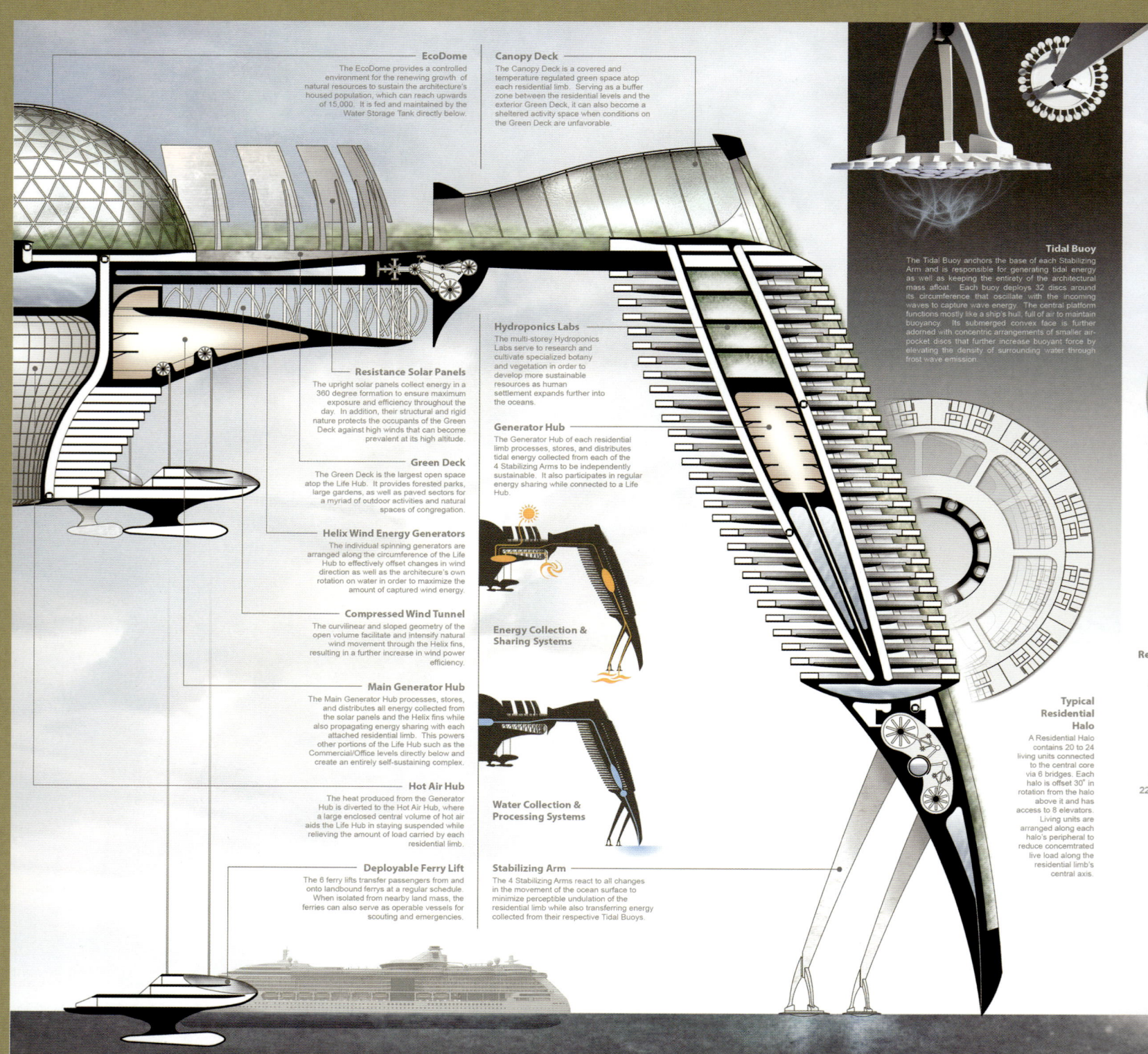

EcoDome
The EcoDome provides a controlled environment for the renewing growth of natural resources to sustain the architecture's housed population, which can reach upwards of 15,000. It is fed and maintained by the Water Storage Tank directly below.

Canopy Deck
The Canopy Deck is a covered and temperature regulated green space atop each residential limb. Serving as a buffer zone between the residential levels and the exterior Green Deck, it can also become a sheltered activity space when conditions on the Green Deck are unfavorable.

Tidal Buoy
The Tidal Buoy anchors the base of each Stabilizing Arm and is responsible for generating tidal energy as well as keeping the entirety of the architectural mass afloat. Each buoy deploys 32 discs around its circumference that oscillate with the incoming waves to capture wave energy. The central platform functions mostly like a ship's hull, full of air to maintain buoyancy. Its submerged convex face is further adorned with concentric arrangements of smaller air-pocket discs that further increase buoyant force by elevating the density of surrounding water through frost wave emission.

Resistance Solar Panels
The upright solar panels collect energy in a 360 degree formation to ensure maximum exposure and efficiency throughout the day. In addition, their structural and rigid nature protects the occupants of the Green Deck against high winds that can become prevalent at its high altitude.

Hydroponics Labs
The multi-storey Hydroponics Labs serve to research and cultivate specialized botany and vegetation in order to develop more sustainable resources as human settlement expands further into the oceans.

Green Deck
The Green Deck is the largest open space atop the Life Hub. It provides forested parks, large gardens, as well as paved sectors for a myriad of outdoor activities and natural spaces of congregation.

Generator Hub
The Generator Hub of each residential limb processes, stores, and distributes tidal energy collected from each of the 4 Stabilizing Arms to be independently sustainable. It also participates in regular energy sharing while connected to a Life Hub.

Helix Wind Energy Generators
The individual spinning generators are arranged along the circumference of the Life Hub to effectively offset changes in wind direction as well as the architecure's own rotation on water in order to maximize the amount of captured wind energy.

Compressed Wind Tunnel
The curvilinear and sloped geometry of the open volume facilitate and intensify natural wind movement through the Helix fins, resulting in a further increase in wind power efficiency.

Energy Collection & Sharing Systems

Main Generator Hub
The Main Generator Hub processes, stores, and distributes all energy collected from the solar panels and the Helix fins while also propagating energy sharing with each attached residential limb. This powers other portions of the Life Hub such as the Commercial/Office levels directly below and create an entirely self-sustaining complex.

Hot Air Hub
The heat produced from the Generator Hub is diverted to the Hot Air Hub, where a large enclosed central volume of hot air aids the Life Hub in staying suspended while relieving the amount of load carried by each residential limb.

Water Collection & Processing Systems

Deployable Ferry Lift
The 6 ferry lifts transfer passengers from and onto landbound ferrys at a regular schedule. When isolated from nearby land mass, the ferries can also serve as operable vessels for scouting and emergencies.

Stabilizing Arm
The 4 Stabilizing Arms react to all changes in the movement of the ocean surface to minimize perceptible undulation of the residential limb while also transferring energy collected from their respective Tidal Buoys.

Typical Residential Halo
A Residential Halo contains 20 to 24 living units connected to the central core via 6 bridges. Each halo is offset 30° in rotation from the halo above it and has access to 8 elevators. Living units are arranged along each halo's peripheral to reduce concentrated live load along the residential limb's central axis.

Res
2

22.4

idea that rather than a building, Gerridae functions more as an ecological organism, drifting and thriving with the ebb and flow of the tide.

MADE IN NEW YORK

Stuart Beattie

United Kingdom

MADE IN NEW YORK

THE VERTICAL FACTORY

Exploring the potential of vertical urban industry in inner city New York as a premise for a re-localisation of manufacturing.

In the past few decades the world economy has seen a global shift of industry and manufacturing eastwards to the emerging markets of China and India purely for economic efficiency and not innovation. The rate at which urban populations are expanding will impact upon how we perceive the strategies of sustaining our cities with regards to supply and demand. The rise of global cargo shipping has seen the ability of local enterprises to move their businesses to areas of low labour costs but sharp rises in oil prices is only enhancing the argument of more localised production.

1964	29%
1980	20%
2005	~4%

New York City population employed in the manufacturing sector

The population of New York City is expected to grow to 9.4 million people in the next two decades and in addition with a declining manufacturing industry, not aided by recent rezonings, the pressure to support the proposed influx will only grow exponentially with an ever increasing reliance on imports. Dense cities such as New York, with a substantial inventory of older factory structures have the capability to look at the new innovative and flexible industrial methods to revive manufacturing locally and regionally.

In constrained, urban environments could certain import-reliant industries be designed to act vertically to prevent unnecessary horizontal expanses of manufacturing ultimately as a stimulus for urban and economic growth?

How can an paradigmatic architectural approach be adopted to support and promote local and city wide manufacturing as a precedent for a new industrial urbanism?

The project aims to investigate, in a world of free trade and rapid globalisation, the possibility of flexible alternatives to inefficient industrial sprawl by considering the prospect of vertical manufacturing towers.

Vertiginous manufacturing structures would be proposed in former areas of prominent industrial activity; where struggling businesses are being forced further away from their consumers due to higher rents and potential re-zoning uncertainty - Williamsburg, Long Island City, Newtown Creek and Red Hook amongst others. The manufacturing hubs would intend to act as a physical socio-political barrier to counter-act the adverse affects of the current administration's inadequate industrial assistance and the onset of encroaching residential and commercial developments in nearby Long Island City and Williamsburg.

Three 158m high towers perched on the Newtown Creek peninsula in Queens aim to create a new paradigmatic urbanism within the eclectic idiosyncrasy of the city. The repeatable industrial cluster provides a range of flexible manufacturing spaces that can accommodate small/ large scale industries, be they labour intensive or entirely mechanical, that would choose to locate in inner city New York. A vertical assembly line running up the south of each tower accommodates large mechanical industries that would otherwise have a huge footprint. An exterior megastructural frame, variable large floor to ceiling heights and exterior structural lift cores allow for maximum spatial allowance and adaptability. A reintroduction of the iconic finger pier has been utilised in order to re-establish alternate distribution methods that have become uncommon in the city with 90m high projections into the East River to enable waterbourne traffic to once again freely interact directly with a large agglomeration of manufacturers on a small footprint in the heart of the city.

With an average of 10 floors, each tower has 70,000 sqft of rentable space in each tower with the potential for over 1000 employees or the equivalent of 40 local businesses. Over 3000 jobs/ 120 manufacturers can be accommodated through the development of each manufacturing node.

The former Bloomberg administration had the largest agenda of re-zonings since the zoning resolution of 1961, however the amount of land retained for manufacturing has decreased by 20% and with dwindling financial aid to support the promotion and relocation of industry, local manufacturers can only hope that the new de Blasio administration can build-upon what has already been achieved as futher catalyst for the retention of industry in New York.

Proposed 'vertical manufacturing' nodes along the East River - Newtown Creek, Queens, New York City

April 2013

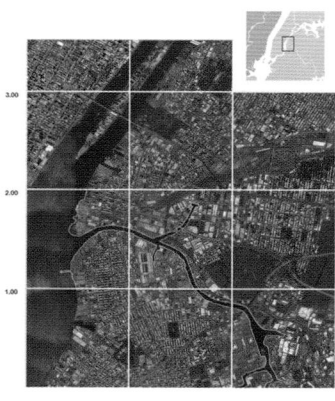

Newtown Creek, Long Island City

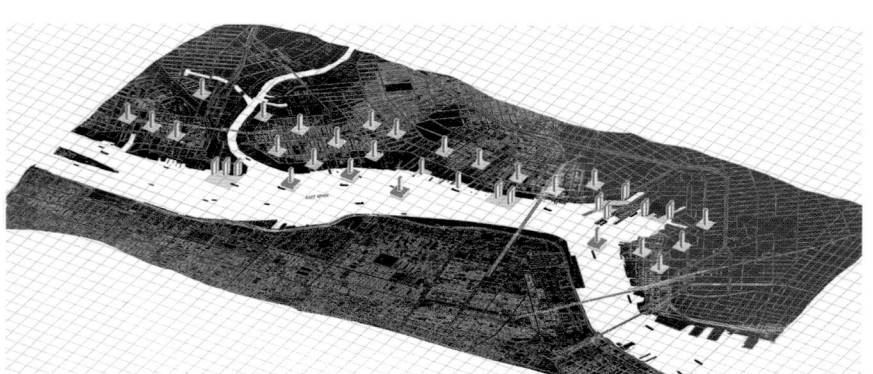

Industrial Agglomeration Proposal, Masterplan, Brooklyn, New York

Exploring the potential of vertical urban industry in inner city New York as a premise for a re-localisation of manufacturing. The project aims to investigate, in a world of free trade and rapid globalisation, the possibility of flexible alternatives to inefficient industrial sprawl by considering the prospect of vertical manufacturing towers.

Vertiginous manufacturing structures would be proposed in former areas of prominent industrial activity; where struggling businesses are being forced further away from their consumers due to higher rents and potential re-zoning uncertainty - Williamsburg, Long Island City, Newtown Creek and Red Hook amongst others. The manufacturing hubs would intend to act as a physical socio-political barrier to counter-act the adverse affects of the current administration's inadequate industrial assistance and the onset of encroaching residential and commercial developments in nearby Long Island City and Williamsburg.

0639

Looking west towards Manhattan from Newtown Creek Manufacturing Node #001

Three 158m high towers perched on the Newtown Creek peninsula in Queens aim to create a new paradigmatic urbanism within the eclectic idiosyncrasy of the city. The repeatable industrial cluster provides a range of flexible manufacturing spaces that can accommodate small/ large scale industries, be they labour intensive or entirely mechanical, that would choose to locate in inner city New York. A vertical assembly line running up the south of each tower accommodates large mechanical industries that would otherwise have a huge footprint. An exterior megastructural frame, variable large floor to ceiling heights and exterior structural lift cores allow for maximum spatial allowance and adaptability. A reintroduction of the iconic finger pier has been utilised in order to re-establish alternate distribution methods that have become uncommon in the city with 90m high projections into the East River to enable waterbourne traffic to once again freely interact directly with a

MADE IN NEW YORK

THE VERTICAL FACTORY

large agglomeration of manufacturers on a small footprint in the heart of the city. With an average of 10 floors, each tower has 70,000 sqft of rentable space in each tower with the potential for over 1000 employees or the equivalent of 40 local businesses. Over 3000 jobs/ 120 manufacturers can be accommodated through the development of each manufacturing node.

The former Bloomberg administration had the largest agenda of re-zonings since the zoning resolution of 1961, however the amount of land retained for manufacturing has decreased by 20% and with dwindling financial aid to support the promotion and relocation of industry, local manufacturers can only hope that the new de Blasio administration can build-upon what has already been achieved as further catalyst for the retention of industry in New York.

THE END OF URBANIZATION

Unha Park
Gyuyoung Lee
Donguk Choi
Myunghyun Bae
Chanrae Noh
Hyunwoo Park

South Korea

THE END OF URBANIZATION

Global Urbanization

In the modern society where productivity and efficiency are emphasized, urbanization is an inevitable social issue. According to Population Reference Bureau (PRB), the urban population which was 5% of the whole population in the 1800s has soared up to 50% in the 2000s. This tendency is only accelerating. Taking an example of South Korea, in particular, once was a developing country, 39.15% urbanization rate in the 60s rose over 90% in 2000. These kinds of big cities are either flourishing or declining and causing a lot of social and environmental problems such as traffic jams, population concentration, the gap between the rich and poor, and changes in natural terrain. The efforts to solve these problems ironically also in turn cause other problems. In other words, the history of cities built by humans is standing at the turning point.

Expansion of Seoul City

Seoul, the capital of Korea, which experienced rapid urbanization, explicitly shows the problems of urbanization. The quality level of space and land in Seoul is well behind the quality level of economy and life quality of the city. Since the 1970s, full scale industrialization and urbanization have changed the spatial structure of the country. Especially, a lot of things have been focused in Seoul. In other words, rural to urban migration has moved the center to Seoul. This migration has accelerated year by year and as a result, the overcrowded metropolitan area has drawn a lot of social attention to itself since the late 1960s. Urbanization which took about 250 years in other developed cities happened in 100 years in this country, mostly in Seoul and its surrounding area. Seoul, therefore, the city that has faced a rapid expansion and biased development which none of the other counterparts have experienced, is now steadily getting worse due to poor infrastructure that can't sustain its population.

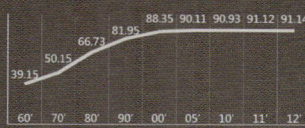

39.15 50.15 66.73 81.95 88.35 90.11 90.93 91.12 91.14
60' 70' 80' 90' 00' 05' 10' 11' 12'

 1910    1940    1965    1985

The Problem of Urbanization

A rapid change of a city causes a lot of problems. A city with small land and a lot of people has to establish enough infrastructures. However, since there is no room for new infrastructures, these cities are now in a situation in which they can't easily cope with changes in population and life style. Finally, big cities have an inherent structure where political, administrative, economic, social, spatial, and environmental problems frequently happen. These problems in turn can only offer unequal opportunities. Eventually in this capitalist society, people with money live in a good environment whereas poor people are pushed out to a poor environment. That is to say, big cities make the gap between the rich and poor worse.

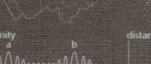
opportunity
distance

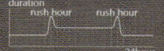
distance
industry area
time

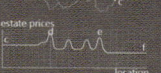
duration rush hour rush hour
24hour

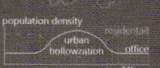
estate prices
location

population density residential urban hollowization office
time

area man-made topography natural topography time

Culture

The concentration of culture is also an urban problem. Cultural centers often exist in the center of a city. In most planned cities, the cultural center is focused in the center and this is where museums and galleries exist. This means that people living near the cultural center can easily benefit from their geographical advantage while those who live far from the center have less opportunity to enjoy culture. This concentration of culture influences the life quality of people living in cities.

Industry

Our lifestyle has also affected the urban form a lot. After the first and second industrial revolution, information-oriented society has come and made cities smarter and more compact. Due to this phenomenon, agricultural and industrial complexes are pushed out of the city and people who make a living out of them also had to move themselves out of the city. These industries are getting further and further away from the cities.

Transportation

Cities where we live have traffic jams. Current cities are made horizontally that space for transportation is poorly managed. In addition, the growth rate of roads is far behind the increasing rate of vehicles. Increase of roads also means not enough space for pedestrians. People living in satellite cities around a big central city commute suffer from insufficient transportation infrastructures when they commute and same goes for the people living the central city.

The gap between the rich and poor

While city area is limited, increasing population makes property prices rise up continuously. Only wealthy people can afford good houses close to the center or good areas and exchanges between these people help them keep their wealth to themselves. This eventually makes people living outskirts poorer and the gap gets worse.

Urban Hollowization

Things tend to be densely concentrated in big cities due to their functions. Cities where residential and business areas are separated show hollowization. During working hours, people are mostly in business areas while they go back to their residential areas after that. This makes the city as if it is hollowed out and also makes the business areas slums.

Environment

Horizontal expansion of cities has a huge effect on its environment. For their convenience, people level mountains and hills. This eliminates contour lines and causes a big change in the geography. And this change links to natural disasters in the city.

Idea

The purpose of this project is to suggest solutions to the problems caused by the horizontal expansion of cities. Currently, cities suggest concentrated skyscrapers in order to avoid the horizontal expansion. However, this can only reduce the horizontal expansion rate but is not a fundamental solution. Our suggestion is about reorganizing the horizontally expanding city by making a certain point of the city vertical. This three-dimensional vertical city has a new and different structure from two-dimensional horizontal cities. Taking advantage of this vertical structure of the city, we are to solve the complicated problems that conventional cities were facing.

Lotte Wolrd Tower
555m / 123 floors

In modern society, where productivity and efficiency are emphasized, urbanization is an inevitable social issue. South Korea, in particular, once was a developing country, 39.15% urbanization rate in the 60's rose over 90% in 2000. These kinds of big cities are either flourishing or declining and causing a lot of social and environmental problems such as traffic jams, population concentration, the gap between the rich and poor, and changes in natural terrain. The efforts to solve these problems ironically also in turn cause other problems. In other words, the history of cities built by humans is standing at the turning point.

Seoul, the capital of South Korea, which experienced rapid urbanization, explicitly shows the problems of urbanization. The quality level of space and land in Seoul is well behind the quality level of

0654

economy and life quality of the city. Since the 1970s, full-scale industrialization and urbanization have changed the spatial structure of the country. Especially, a lot of things have been focused in Seoul. In other words, rural to urban migration has moved the center to Seoul. This migration has accelerated year by year and as a result, the overcrowded metropolitan area has drawn a lot of social attention to itself since the late 1960s. Urbanization, which took about 250 years in other developed cities, happened in 100 years in this country, mostly in Seoul and its surrounding area. Seoul, therefore, the city that has faced a rapid expansion and biased development which none of the other counterparts have experienced, is now steadily getting worse due to poor infrastructure that can't sustain its population.

Finally, big cities have an inherent structure where political, administrative, economic, social, spatial, and environmental problems frequently happen. These problems in turn can only offer unequal

Residential Unit

Housing 75%

Office 10%
Cultural 5%
Commercial 5%

Etc 5%

Office, Cultural and Commercial districts are concentrated on the Central Floor

Axonometric Plan
Center Floor

opportunities. Eventually in this capitalistic society, people with money live in a good environment whereas poor people are pushed out to a poor environment. That is to say, big cities make the gap between the rich and poor worse. The purpose of this project is to suggest solutions to the problems caused by the horizontal expansion of cities. Currently, cities suggest concentrated skyscrapers in order to avoid the horizontal expansio¬n. However, this can only reduce the horizontal expansion rate but is not a fundamental solution. Our suggestion is about reorganizing the horizontally expanding city by making a certain point of the city vertical. This three-dimensional vertical city has a new and different structure from two-dimensional horizontal cities. Taking advantage of this vertical structure of the city, we are to solve the complicated problems that conventional cities were facing.

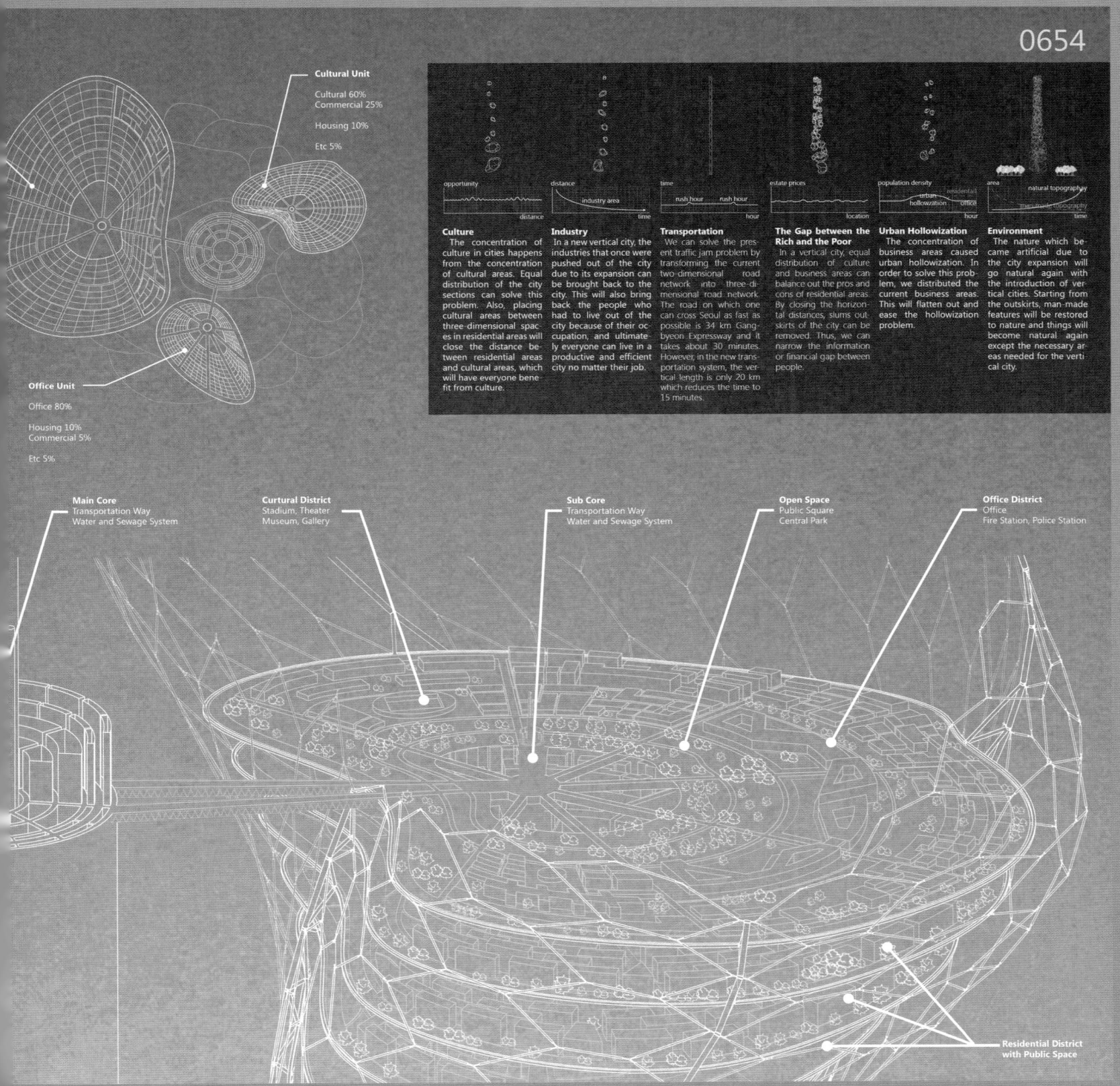

0654

Cultural Unit

Cultural 60%
Commercial 25%

Housing 10%

Etc 5%

Office Unit

Office 80%

Housing 10%
Commercial 5%

Etc 5%

Culture
The concentration of culture in cities happens from the concentration of cultural areas. Equal distribution of the city sections can solve this problem. Also, placing cultural areas between three-dimensional spaces in residential areas will close the distance between residential areas and cultural areas, which will have everyone benefit from culture.

Industry
In a new vertical city, the industries that once were pushed out of the city due to its expansion can be brought back to the city. This will also bring back the people who had to live out of the city because of their occupation, and ultimately everyone can live in a productive and efficient city no matter their job.

Transportation
We can solve the present traffic jam problem by transforming the current two-dimensional road network into three-dimensional road network. The road on which one can cross Seoul as fast as possible is 34 km Gangbyeon Expressway and it takes about 30 minutes. However, in the new transportation system, the vertical length is only 20 km which reduces the time to 15 minutes.

The Gap between the Rich and the Poor
In a vertical city, equal distribution of culture and business areas can balance out the pros and cons of residential areas. By closing the horizontal distances, slums outskirts of the city can be removed. Thus, we can narrow the information or financial gap between people.

Urban Hollowization
The concentration of business areas caused urban hollowization. In order to solve this problem, we distributed the current business areas. This will flatten out and ease the hollowization problem.

Environment
The nature which became artificial due to the city expansion will go natural again with the introduction of vertical cities. Starting from the outskirts, man-made features will be restored to nature and things will become natural again except the necessary areas needed for the vertical city.

Main Core
Transportation Way
Water and Sewage System

Curtural District
Stadium, Theater
Museum, Gallery

Sub Core
Transportation Way
Water and Sewage System

Open Space
Public Square
Central Park

Office District
Office
Fire Station, Police Station

**Residential District
with Public Space**

CAR OR SHELL

Mark Talbot
Daniel Markiewicz

United States

2ND PLACE / 2014

CAR and SHELL
or MARINETTI'S MONSTER

My partner and I have been awake all morning, out faces aglow in front of brightly burning screens, our fingers feverishly clicking to keep pace with our racing thoughts. Frantically driven by decades of fear, themselves perpetuated by an avalanche of numbers and an onslaught of "better world" fantasies born of an endless stream of technological innovation, our mission is clear: rescue Detroit from being rescued. In a world whose only acceptable path is the immediate betterment of our own existence, my partner and I demand the discipline to let it die and live another day. Sweating and panting with the knowledge that our current society's insatiable and nearsighted appetite for growth, innovation and development is strangling the whispers of life out of the very future it hopes to serve, my partner and I can no longer stand idly by and watch our cities consume themselves with an anxious need for expansion. Our society has been poisoned by the belief that a city in decline is a city in need of resurrection.

MANIFESTO:

1. Revolt! Let us use the efficient machines inefficiently, for pleasure and not production. Loops where once there were straight lines. Deadends where before there were connections.

2. Why not revel in the punishment of a relentless technology? Like a fighter leaning into an opponent's blow, Let us incite provoke and encourage our own urban desertion. From rust to silicon. From silicon to.....

3. We shall weep for the dark ages, in the presence o the gleaming Renaissance Tower before us. Our royal Detroit we shall serve the rightful King. Long live the king. The king is dead. Long live the King.

4. Throw off the shackles of the endless sprawl ever encroaching on the lakes, streams and fields of this country! Revive the American landscape of boundless freedom and the pleasures of the open road!

5. Commute has become a dirty word. Why? I say commute your decaying suburb for a city in the sky!

SUBURBAN HOMES
These suburban homes from the ground have been placed into the lower forming a dense and vibrant community of those remaining residents.

SCENIC BYWAYS
Enjoy a simple pleasure that our culture has forgotten from the comfort of your car, a great view.

NEW SUBURBAN GRID
As Detroit's population declines and those residents left behind move into the massive structure, the city-grid is slowly picked away allowing for nature to take hold again. Those who choose to live in the suburbs, live in a wilderness.

INTERSTATE 94
Access this road for a cross country drive or access to downtown.

RENAISSANCE CENTER
General Motors world headquarters, an all glass complex of interconnected skyscrapers shines brightly over the remains of Detroit... The industry that built this monument of re-birth left this city to die.

ACCELERATED URBAN FABRIC DECAY
The emptiness of the suburbs has led to myriad problems, crime, poverty, decline in basic services. To save the city, de-densification has been accelerated. The suburbs have been returned to nature.

DOWNTOWN DETROIT
Downtown is booming, new mixed use development is revitalizing the core of Detroit. The outlying areas, tragically, have not been so fortunate.

NEW TECH HUBS
As the old industries die out and the fabric decays, new industries move in. Tech hubs are formed in clusters accessible by automobile. What were once the bland and forgettable drives of daily commuters are transformed by the wilderness into pleasurable experiences.

This project proposes a city in the sky for Detroit, MI. The new city is conceived as a vertical suburban neighborhood equipped with recreational and commercial areas where three main grids (streets, pedestrian pathways, and structure) are intertwined to create a box-shaped wireframe. Traditional and contemporary houses and other diverse programs plug in the structure to create a rich vertical urban fabric.

My partner and I have been awake all morning, out faces aglow in front of brightly burning screens, our fingers feverishly clicking to keep pace with our racing thoughts. Franticly driven by decades of fear, themselves perpetuated by an avalanche of numbers and an onslaught of "better world" fantasies born of an endless stream of technological innovation, our mission is clear: rescue Detroit from being

0697

PARKING TOWERS

PEDESTRIAN PIERS

BIG BOX PROGRAM

HIGHWAY OFF RAMPS
Sitting this massive structure above the highway interchange allows residents to move directly between work and home in one fluid arc.

PEDESTRIAN OFF RAMPS
Residents can experience the bucolic lifestyle afforded by the new wilderness. The access ramps spread out to each of the four "quadrants" imposed by the intersection of the highways.

rescued. In a world whose only acceptable path is the immediate betterment of our own existence, my partner and I demand the discipline to let it die and live another day. Sweating and panting with the knowledge that our current society's insatiable and nearsighted appetite for growth, innovation and development is strangling the whispers of life out of the very future it hopes to serve, my partner and I can no longer stand idly by and watch our cities consume themselves with an anxious need for expansion. Our society has been poisoned by the belief that a city in decline is a city in need of resurrection.

MANIFESTO
1. Revolt! Let us use the efficient machines inefficiently, for pleasure and not production. Loops where

once there were straight lines. Dead-ends where before there were connections.

2. Why not revel in the punishment of a relentless technology? Like a fighter leaning into an opponent's blow, Let us incite, provoke, and encourage our own urban desertion. From rust to silicon, from silicon to…

3. We shall weep for the dark ages, in the presence of the gleaming Renaissance Tower before us. Our royal Detroit, we shall serve the rightful King. Long live the king. The king is dead. Long live the King.

4. Throw off the shackles of the endless sprawl ever encroaching on the lakes, streams and fields of this country! Revive the American landscape of boundless freedom and the pleasures of the open road!

5. Commute has become a dirty word. Why? I say commute your decaying suburb for a city in the sky!

0697

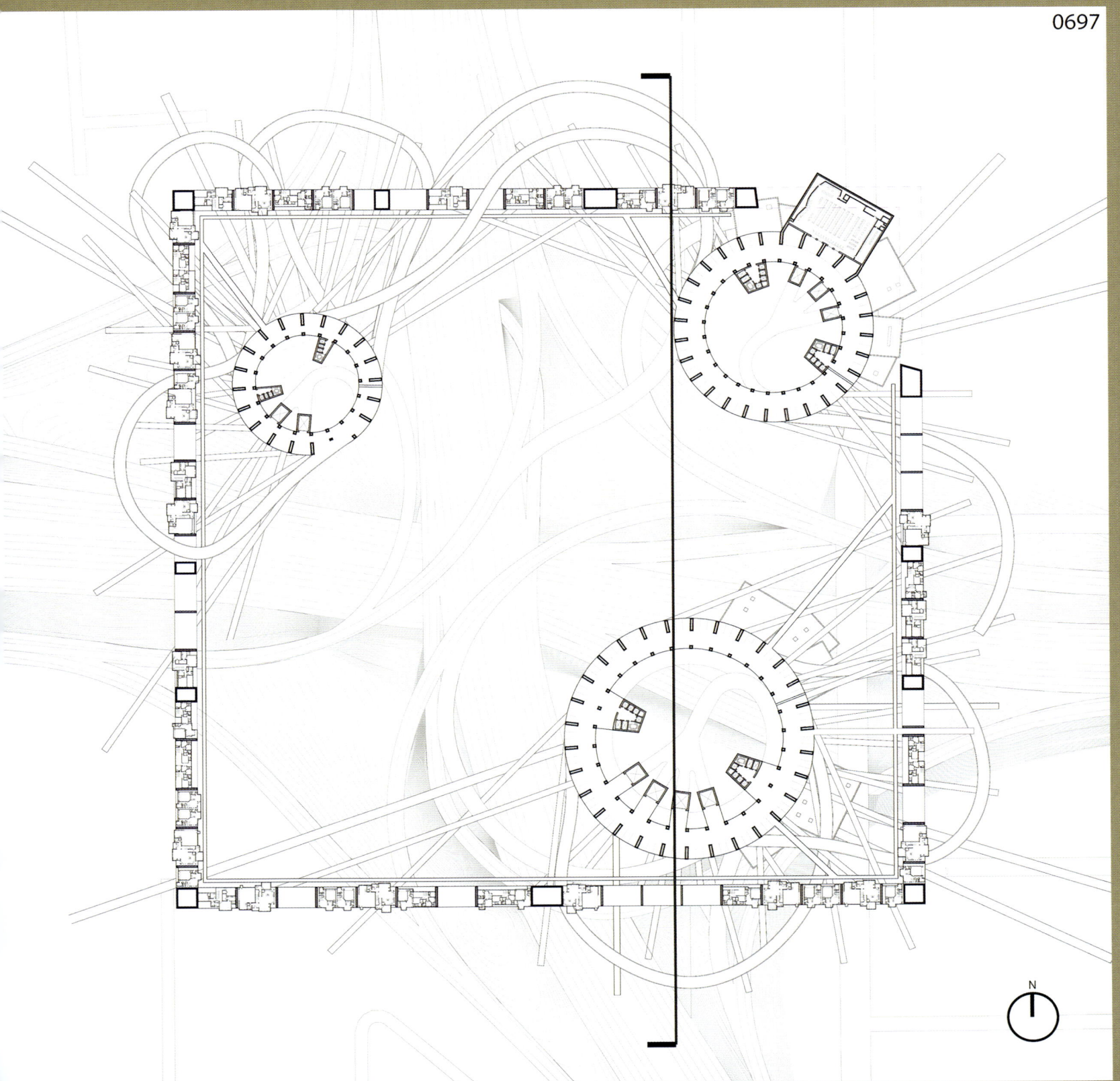

SKYVILLAGE FOR LOS ANGELES

Ziwei Song

United States

SKYVILLAGE FREEWAY INTERCHANGE

VISION STATEMENT

Los Angeles freeway segregates the city fabrics and the urban activity is restricted to single area. Vertical towers exacerbate the condition of segregation instead of encouraging integration. The envisioned vertical city —skyvillage—would bridge over freeway interruptions and connect the four quadrants around 101&110 as one architectural organism. It would boost cultural exchange and urban activities with intense social interaction.

URBAN PROBLEMS

The interchange 101&110 break Los Angeles urban fabrics into disconnected four quadrants-Downtown, Chinatown, echo park and Temple Beaudry. The four quadrants have distinct cultural and social differences, lacking a coherent urban tissue to connect. Moreover, the leftover junk space around the four-level stacking freeway reaches over 27 acre, leaving vast land of urban tissue into Terrain Vague, the in-between abandoned space between freeway infrastructure and urban center.Skyvillage aims to reclaim the terrain vague, by providing green filtering towers to clean freeway pollutions and a multitude of programs to revitalize the disconnected urban fabric.

PROPOSAL SKYVILLAGE

Skyvillage encourages a car free lifestyle by incoporating multi-use program in a single architecture organism. Besides fulfilling the daily function of office, housing, school and hotels, it provides another level of interactive space to bridge those sub communities together. Those interactive space (entertainment, gym, restaurants, bars, swimming pools, theater, music clubs, shopping mall, urban park) breaks the segregation of traditional skyscrapers. It brings people from different social groups together (work, study, visit) and enables a creative social pattern. People could walk throughout skyvillage fulfilling their daily functions without the necessity to drive around the city. It also integrates the four quadrants by providing interactive service programs which is lacking around the freeway.

Skyvillage hybridizes all programs needed for great living experience together. US metropolis often has singular program building, with strict zoning specifically for residential, office, commercial and entertainment etc. This project aims to break the singularity and embraces multiplicity of programs , enabling people to get access to other programs within a comfortable walking distance (1/2 mile). Skyvillage highlights the potential of urban lives' performance- —the ability to play,work, live, socialize, eat, entertain and study within walking distance of great convenience.

The formal language of Skyvillage helps to articulate the core social/urban concept. The single geometry module has great potential to grow, expand and develop into a complex architectural organism. It has great flexibility as well as capability to accommodate the complex functional program relationships. How each program typology interact with each other and how the people using them scheduled their daily lives are interrelated with the formal organism. The formal organisation illustrates the program relationship and interaction patterns. The vertical modules supports the building, both structurally and ecologically. They are green filtration space with specifically chosen pollution filtering plants. It helps to absorb freeway pollution. The horizontal modules connecting vertical modules constitute of various programs for creating great vertical living performance.

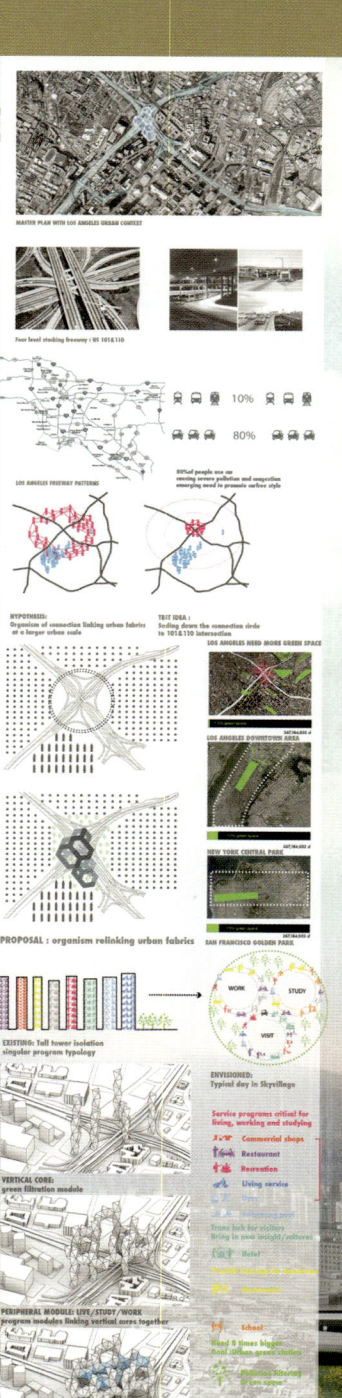

LosAngeles US 101&110 Interchange
Reclaiming freeway terrain vague

Los Angele's freeway system segregates the city's fabric, restricting urban activities to single locations. Similarly, skyscrapers exacerbate this condition of segregation instead of encouraging urban integration. The envisioned vertical city would bridge over freeway interruptions and connect the four quadrants around 101 and 110 freeways as a single architectural organism while boosting cultural exchange, urban activities, and social interaction.

The interchange 101 and 110 breaks Los Angeles east urban fabric into four disconnected quadrants: Downtown, Chinatown, Echo Park, and Temple Beaudry. The four quadrants have distinct cultural and social differences, lacking a coherent urban tissue. Moreover, the leftover space around the freeways reaches over 27 acre. Skyvillage aims to reclaim this terrain vague and provide green filtering

0698

towers to clean the freeways and also articulate various programs to revitalize the disconnected urban fabric.

The Skyvillage is designed as a cluster of seven skyscrapers positioned in the residual space of the freeways interchange. These towers house a mixed-use program of housing and commercial areas. In the top floors the skyscrapers are interconnected by horizontal structures that contain recreational programs. The structural skin is designed as a faceted structure of tubular steel members that allow open floor plans without inside columns. Although the project has been designed for a specific location in Los Angeles, the system could be replicated anywhere in the world.

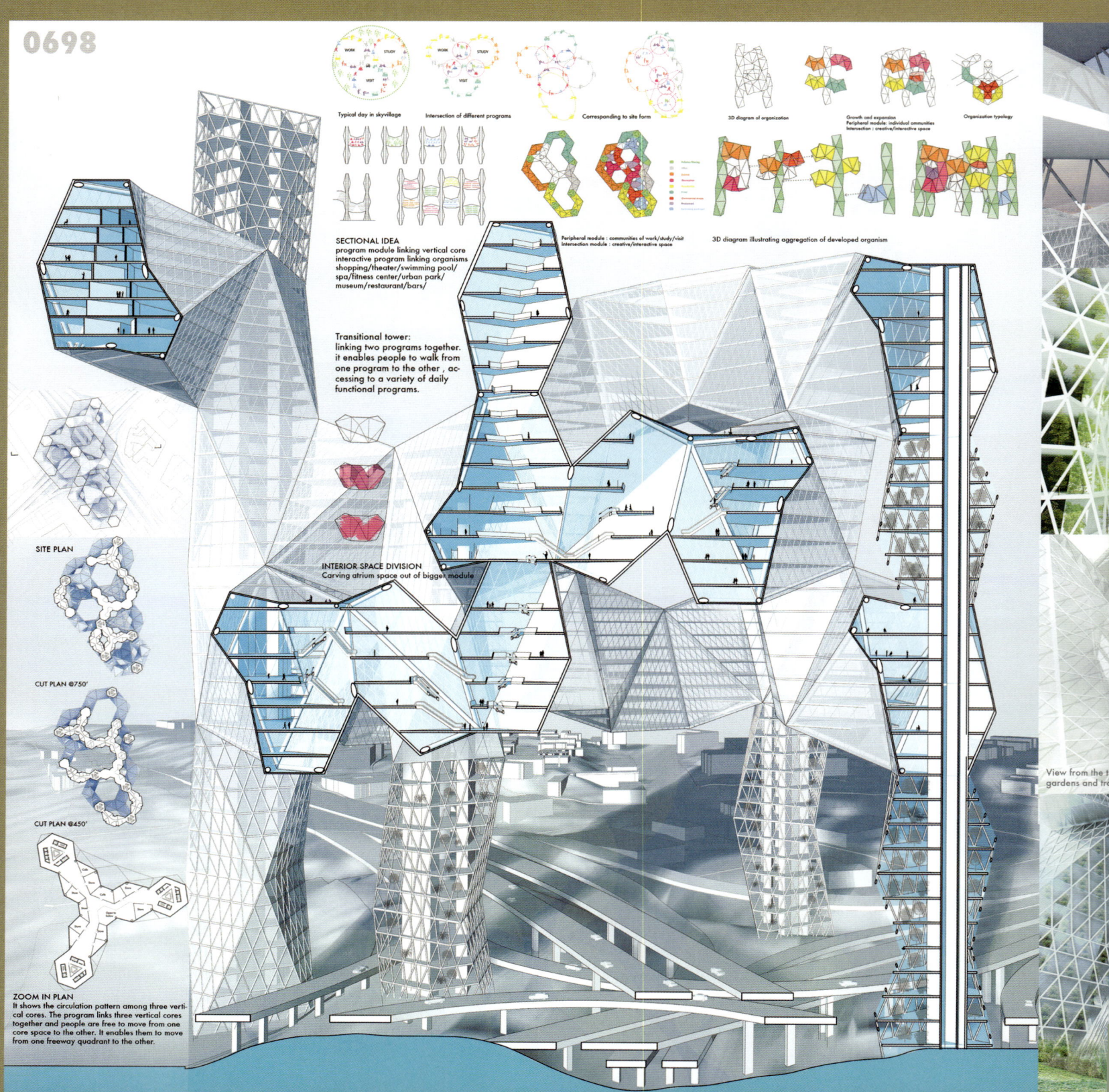

LOOKING OUT TO DOWNTOWN
Peripheral corner of Skyvillage with downtown skyline

View from the freeway to Chinatown

ng the landscape roof
d freeway green space

LOOKING OUT TO DOWNTOWN
The interconnected architecture organism has
rich spatial effects with view to downtown

RE-SILIENCE SKYSCRAPER

Diego Espinosa Figueroa
Javiera Valenzuela Gonzalez

Chile

RE - SILIENCE
re - juvenation
re - structuring
SKYSCRAPER

Biomass reduction

It is estimated that over 80% of the global population lives in an urban entity, the growth of cities and the massive expansion brought great progress but major setbacks on the level of land use.
The overloads of the soil through our urban developments have caused extinction of species, fertile land reduction, and poor distribution of it among others.

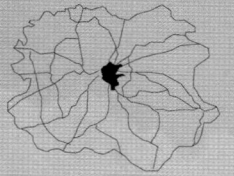 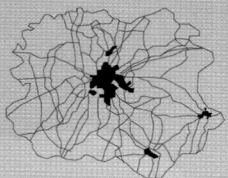 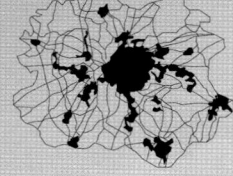 

Urban growth scheme

Realizing that the soil, their biomass and what it conceives, is a limited resource, it gives a glimpse of how we should live to preserve and improve our living environments, which we are helping to des troy.

Re-silience therefore looks for an answer to that, proposing a new organization and resources distribution, soil and biomass, this by observing the natural forms, like wild honeycombs, coral reefs, ant's nests, and other kinds of architecture constructed by species which contributing, coexisting and forming a major part of the cycle of life.

The way of building nowadays sets a null relationship with its surroundings, so having no more than 1 or 2 interrelations happening in one place, Re-silience allows to cross the threshold and reorganize this behavior through optimally interrelate resources, soil and biomass as part of the same

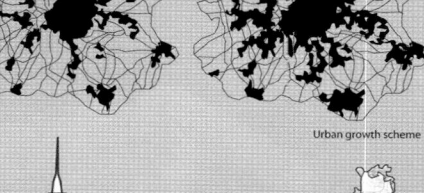

common skyscraper   Re-silience skyscraper

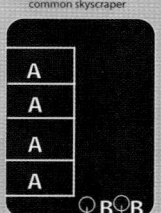  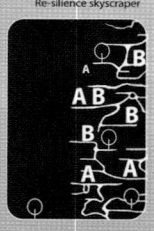

Comparative scheme
Distribution of biomass

It is estimated that over 50% of the global population lives in an urban settlement. The growth of cities and their massive expansion brought great progress but major setbacks on the level of land use. The overloads of the soil through our urban developments have caused extinction of animal and plant species, fertile land reduction, and poor distribution of biomass.

Realizing that the soil, its biomass, and what it conceives is a limited resource, gives us a glimpse of how we should live to preserve and improve our natural environment. Re-Silence Skyscraper looks for an answer by proposing a new organization and resources distribution of the soil and its biomass through the observation of natural forms such as honeycombs, coral reefs, and ant nests.

Our buildings today set a null relationship with its surroundings having no more than one or two

0711

Adaptable structure

Through a new form of reorganization, Re-silence manages to take advantage of better use of space in relation to inhabitant per square meter, besides being an adaptable entity to the surrounding environment and eventually being one with the environment.

interrelations in one place. Whereas Re-Silience allows us to cross the threshold and reorganize this behavior through an optimal use of soil and biomass.

The Re-silience skyscraper was designed to generate the larger possible natural environment. Its design is based on natural forms ranging from the efficient organization of a honeycomb to the functional beauty of stony corals. Thus inhabitants can appreciate and enjoy a friendly environment based on natural principles as well as perfectly functional structure.

The structure of the skyscraper consists of a complex platforms system combined with vertical capsules in which the residential and commercial areas are located. Vertical capsules are the main circulation of the building and provide a clean and efficient transportation system.

RE - SILIENCE
re - juvenation
re - structuring
SKYSCRAPER

Recreational Interior area

Pathway surrounded by nature

Upward view of the platforms

400 m

Habitable area

0 m

Production and storage area

-150 m

Front view

Vertical capsules are the backbone of the Re-silience skyscraper, coming from underground up high in the sky

Recreational areas

Natural Skyscraper

The Re-silience skyscraper was desic is based on natural forms ranging fr Thus inhabitants can appreciate and structure.

Schematics Plans

0711

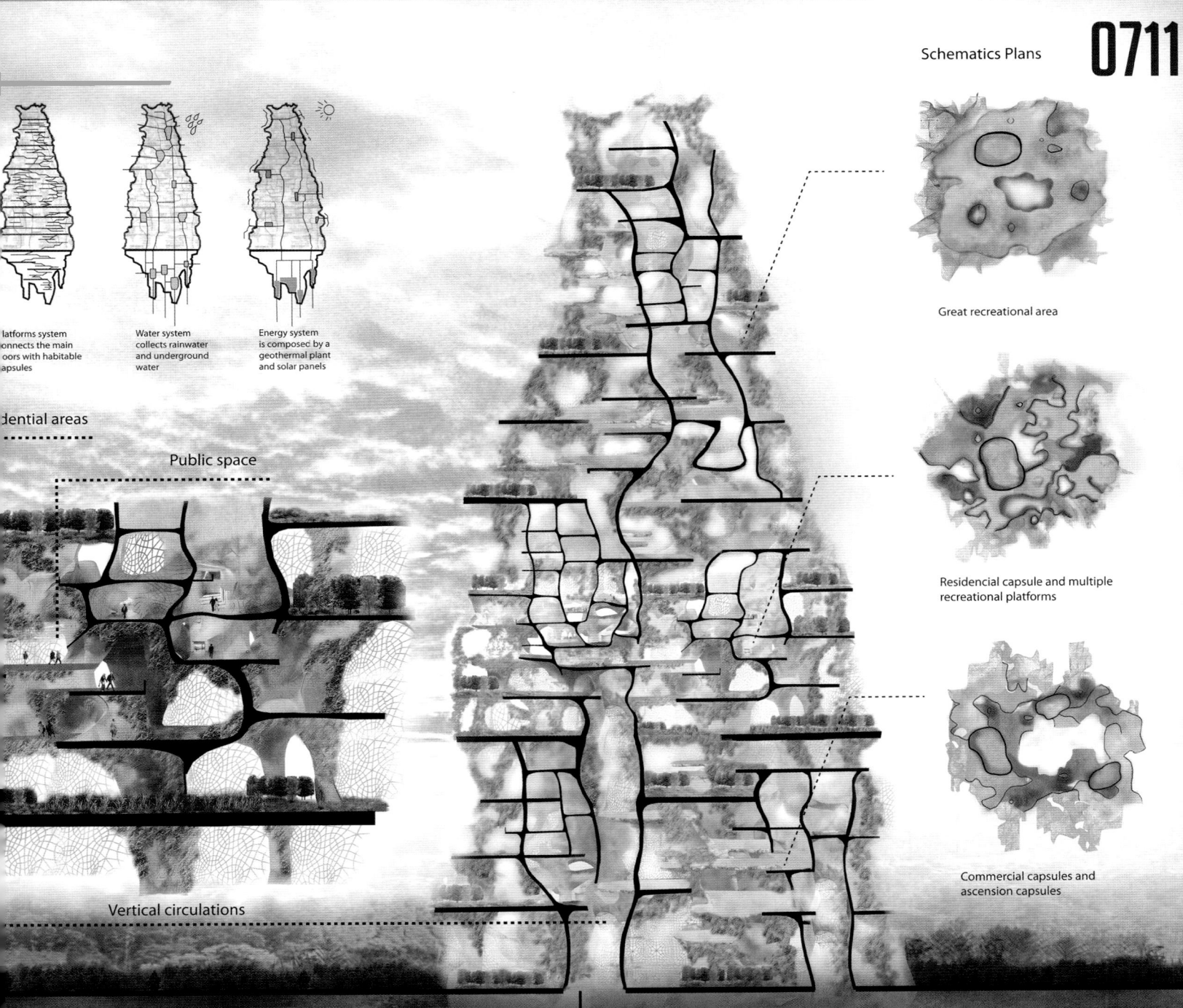

platforms system connects the main oors with habitable apsules

Water system collects rainwater and underground water

Energy system is composed by a geothermal plant and solar panels

dential areas

Public space

Vertical circulations

Great recreational area

Residencial capsule and multiple recreational platforms

Commercial capsules and ascension capsules

Main structure

The Re-silience skyscraper structure consists in a complex platforms system combined with vertical capsules in which is located the residencial and commercial areas.
Also vertical capsules are the main circulations of the building, which are composed by a clean and efficient transport system.

o generate the most natural environment possible. Its design
e organization of a honeycomb to the beauty of stony corals.
y a friendly environment with nature, as well as a fully functional

REVERSAL STRATEGY

Luigi Bertazzoni
Paolo Giacomo Vasino

Italy

PHASE 0 existing typical city blocks composed of reinforced concrete structure buildings will be at collapsing risk within 30 years

PHASE 1 construction of a new vertical land on street walkways thin carbon concrete structures that leave unaffected the old blocks

PHASE 2 completion with urban infrastructure, vertical transportation, housing shells and a dense network of "artificial photosynthesis leafs"

PHASE 3 local inhabitants can move to the new housing facilities, old damaged buildings finally empty can be demolishes

Reversal Strategy is one answer to multiple emerging global questions. A single synchronic action can reverse the collapse of human habitat to a better scenario. The decomposing process of Carbonation makes reinforced concrete structures unstable in 70/80 years. Almost 60% of global concrete structure buildings were built in the 20 years after WW2. This means that in the next decades an impressive number of heavy and expensive structural refurbishments or reconstructions must occur. The collapsing risk of most concrete cities is increasing year by year. It is necessary to think new durable construction systems to reverse the collapsing trend and to substitute existing exhausted buildings. It is important to find a "new construction land" to build before moving people and functions. Then, it is possible to demolish what is substituted. Planet Earth deserves a reversal strategy to change the proportion

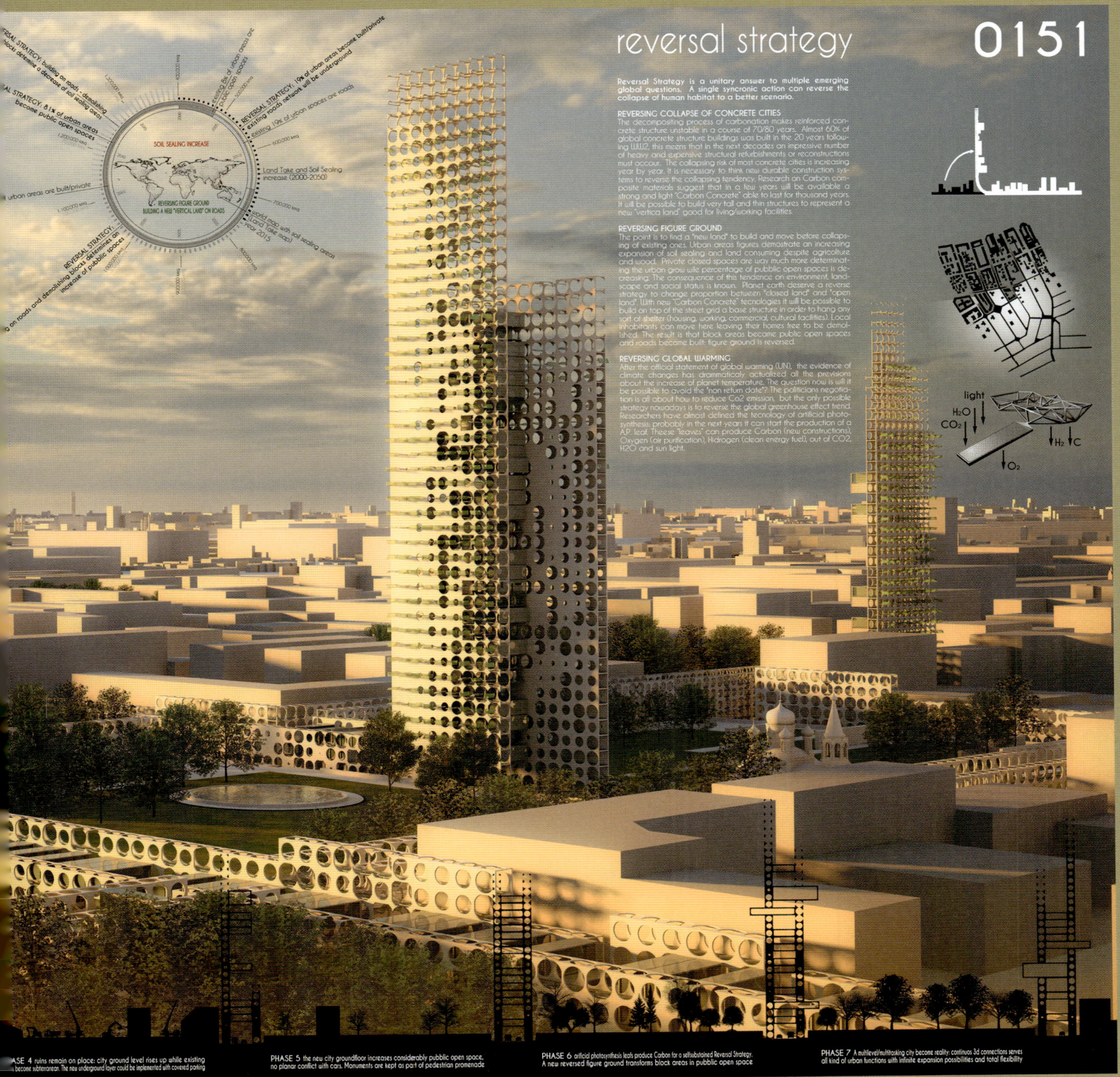

reversal strategy

0151

Reversal Strategy is a unitary answer to multiple emerging global questions. A single synchronic action can reverse the collapse of human habitat to a better scenario.

REVERSING COLLAPSE OF CONCRETE CITIES
The decomposing process of carbonation makes reinforced concrete structure unstable in a course of 70/80 years. Almost 60% of global concrete structure buildings was built in the 20 years following WW2, this means that in the next decades an impressive number of heavy and expensive structural refurbishments or reconstructions must occour. The collapsing risk of most concrete cities is increasing year by year. It is necessary to think new durable construction systems to reverse the collapsing tendency. Research on Carbon composite materials suggest that in a few years will be available a strong and light "Carbon Concrete" able to last for thousand years. It will be possible to build very tall and thin structures to represent a new "vertical land" good for living/working facilities.

REVERSING FIGURE GROUND
The point is to find a "new land" to build and move before collapsing of existing ones. Urban areas figures demostrate an increasing expansion of soil sealing and land consuming despite agriculture and wood. Private closed spaces are way much more determinating the urban grow while percentage of pubblic open spaces is decreasing. The consequence of this tendency on environment, landscape and social status is known. Planet earth deserve a reversal strategy to change proportion between "closed land" and "open land". With new "Carbon Concrete" tecnologies it will be possible to build on top of the street grid a basic structure in order to hang any sort of shelter (housing, working, commercial, cultural facilities). Local inhabitants can move here, leaving their homes free to be demolished. The result is that block areas became public open spaces and roads became built: figure ground is reversed.

REVERSING GLOBAL WARMING
After the official statement of global warming (UN), the evidence of climate changes has dramatically actualized, all the previsions about the increase of planet temperature. The question now is will it be possible to avoid the "non return date"? The politicians negotiation is all about how to reduce Co2 emission, but the only possible strategy nowadays is to reverse the global greenhouse effect trend. Researchers have almost defined the tecnology of artificial photosynthesis: probably in the next years it can start the production of a A.P. leaf. These "leaves" can produce Carbon (new constructions), Oxygen (air purification), Hidrogen (clean energy fuel), out of CO2, H2O and sun light.

PHASE 4 ruins remain on place: city ground level rises up while existing become subterranean. The new underground layer could be implemented with covered parking

PHASE 5 the new city groundfloor increases considerably public open space, no planar conflict with cars. Monuments are kept as part of pedestrian promenade

PHASE 6 artificial photosinthesis leafs produce Carbon for a selfsubstained Reversal Strategy. A new reversed figure ground transforms block areas in public open space

PHASE 7 A multilevel/multitasking city become reality: continuos 3d connections serves all kind of urban functions with infinite expansion possibilities and total flexibility between "closed land" and "open land". How can one "substitute" a massive amount of buildings with new ones without urbanizing open land? A possible answer is to build on the top of the urban mobility network. Narrow structures can rise on the side of roads, just on the edge of urban blocks. These structural walls will became "the new construction land" leaving vehicles circulating at ground floor. Then infinite combinations of shell units can be hung onto the main structure. At this point local inhabitants can move to their new accommodation facilities, leaving the old ones free to be safely demolished. Ruins will rise up to ground floor level, while roads and parking will become underground. Former block areas freed of constructions will create a continuous sequence of public open spaces, parks, squares, or even cultivated land, exclusively for pedestrian use. Cities' figure ground diagram is now completely reversed:

old blocks are public open space; old streets are covered with buildings. A photo-catalyst based on copper oxide or another molecular catalyzer, will make possible, in a few years, the production of an Artificial Photosynthesis Leaf. The process, already prototyped, uses solar light, CO_2, H_2O to produce Hydrogen, Carbon, and Oxygen. This would not only remove carbon dioxide from the environment, but would also turn it into solid carbonates that could be used for building construction. At the same time, the water-splitting process will produce Hydrogen for all energy needs through Fuel Cells technology. Research on Carbon composite materials suggest that in a few years, strong and light "Carbon Concrete" able to last for a thousand years, will be available. It will be possible to build very tall and thin structures to represent a new "vertical land", good for living/working facilities.

0151

VIEW OF A HORIZONTAL CONNECTION

HEIGHT VS DENSITY height of new vertical lands depends on density of former nearby blocks. low density will result low towers. high density will result high towers. Population of urban areas wouldn't change. It will only increase open public space.

VIEW FROM TOP

VIEW FROM RAISED FORMER BLOCK LEVEL WHEAT CULTIVATED, ON UNDERGROUD LEVEL THE VEHICLES FLUX

MADE IN NEW YORK

Stuart Beattie

United Kingdom

MADE IN NEW YORK

THE VERTICAL FACTORIES OF GREENPOINT, NY

Exploring the potential of vertical urban industry in inner city New York as a premise for an introduction of an innovative manufacturing archetype in the form of a vertical factory cluster within Greenpoint

In the past few decades the world economy has seen a global shift of industry and manufacturing eastwards to the emerging markets of China and India purely for economic efficiency but not innovation. The rate at which urban populations are expanding will impact upon how we perceive the strategies of sustaining our cities with regards to supply and demand. The rise of global cargo shipping has seen the ability of local industries to move their production to areas of low labour, tax and land costs. However, the onset of rising labour costs in East Asia, higher transportation costs, a weaker dollar, rising U.S. productivity and cheaper energy are only enhancing the argument for more localised production that is closer to the consumer.

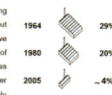

1964	29%
1980	20%
2005	~4%

Percentage of New York's population employed in the manufacturing sector

The population of New York City is forecast to grow by 12% to 9.4 million people in the next two decades resulting in a current city-wide acute affordable housing shortage. Manufacturing land in the city is perceived by planners as a viable outlet for the expansion of residential development, forcing a gradual decentralisation and extinction of local industries which are inherent to a wider network of urban ecologies within New York.

In addition to a declining manufacturing sector, not aided by recent re-zonings or passive policy measures, the pressure on manufacturers to relocate in the face of development-led socio-spatial conflicts will only grow exponentially with a burgeoning population and an ever increasing reliance on imports. Economically diverse cities such as New York, with a substantial inventory of old, functionally unsuitable factory structures have the capacity to look at the new innovative and flexible industrial methods to revive manufacturing locally and regionally. However, the assumption that the city's manufacturers are a dying breed or an anachronism epitomises the enormous challenge that the sector faces.

This project investigates the possibility of an alternative to inefficient horizontal industrial sprawl by considering the prospect of a new vertiginous architectural typology in the form of a vertical factory devoted to the stabilisation and re-integration of manufacturing into inner city Brooklyn. These interventions aim to act as a compromise to residential development aspirations and the shortage of suitable industrial land. The new typological approach speculates the re-establishment of the once prominent manufacturing economy in the face of malign policy neglect and the City's focus to sustain New York's economy primarily through finance, insurance and real-estate initiatives.

Arrayed along the Greenpoint coastline and orientated to the formalised Cartesian street grid, the agglomeration of 21 towers are manifested as an archipelago of site-specific interventions which are encompassed by an essential infrastructural network of highways, trainlines and ports that aids the stability of the industrial ecology. Acting as a spatial clustering of industry, the proposal aims to incubate and augment current inter-urban relationships emphasising the importance of local knowledge on steady growth and innovation. Each tower can accomodate from 52 - 81 small industries providing a maximum of 103,950 sqft of manufacturing space and potentially more than 1000 jobs. Maximum spatial allowance and flexibility within the factory nodes are achieved through an exoskeletal structural system and column free floorplates served by exterior lift cores that provide lateral stability to the overall tower. The floorplate dimensions of the proposal are not designated towards any particular industry but serve to provide a series of intimate, generic industrial spatial volumes which local 21st century manufacturers can occupy. Although as an ideological interpretation, the scheme is intended to provoke discussion as to an alternate approach to retain the local manufacturing sector and how these small industries can be encouraged in the face of alternative urban, political and neoliberal economic imperatives.

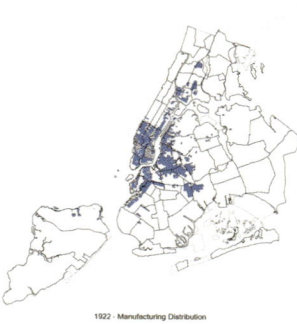

1922 - Manufacturing Distribution

2012 - Manufacturing Distribution

Vertical Factory Masterplan

Looking South along West Street, Greenpoint

In the past few decades the world economy has seen a global shift of industry and manufacturing eastwards to the emerging markets of China and India purely for economic efficiency but not innovation. The rate at which urban populations are expanding will impact upon how we perceive the strategies of sustaining our cities with regards to supply and demand. The rise of global cargo shipping has seen the ability of local industries to move their production to areas of low labor, tax and land costs. However, the onset of rising labor costs in East Asia, higher transportation costs, a weaker dollar, rising U.S. productivity and cheaper energy are only enhancing the argument for more localized production that is closer to the consumer.

    This project investigates the possibility of an alternative to inefficient horizontal industrial sprawl

0215

Looking south at Manufacturing Hub #001 arrayed along the Greenpoint coastline

by considering the prospect of a new vertiginous architectural typology in the form of a vertical factory devoted to the stabilization and re-integration of manufacturing into inner city Brooklyn. These interventions aim to act as a compromise to residential development aspirations and the shortage of suitable industrial land. The new typological approach speculates the re-establishment of the once prominent manufacturing economy in the face of malign policy neglect and the City's focus to sustain New York's economy primarily through finance, insurance and real estate initiatives. Arrayed along the Greenpoint coastline and orientated to the formalized Cartesian street grid, the agglomeration of 21 towers are manifested as an archipelago of site-specific interventions which are encompassed by an essential infrastructural network of highways, train lines and ports that aids the stability of the industrial ecology. Acting as a spatial clustering of industry, the proposal aims to incubate and augment

MADE IN NEW YORK

THE VERTICAL FACTORIES OF GREENPOINT, NY

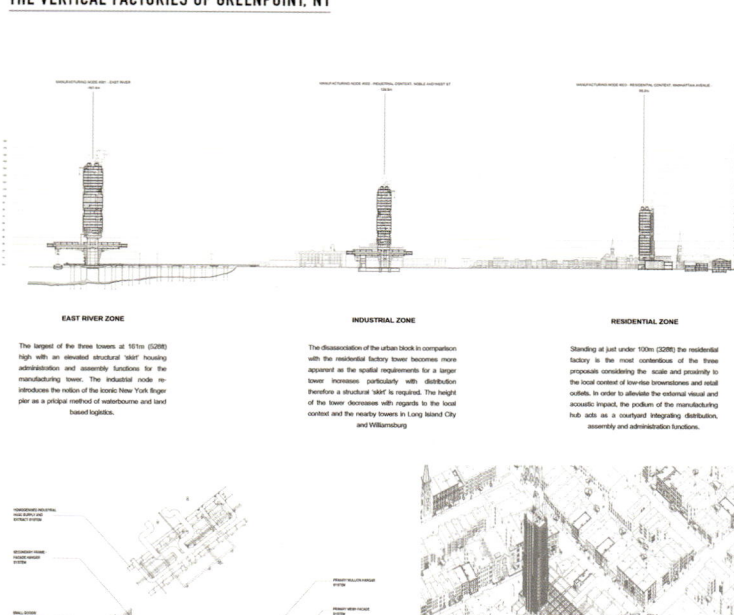

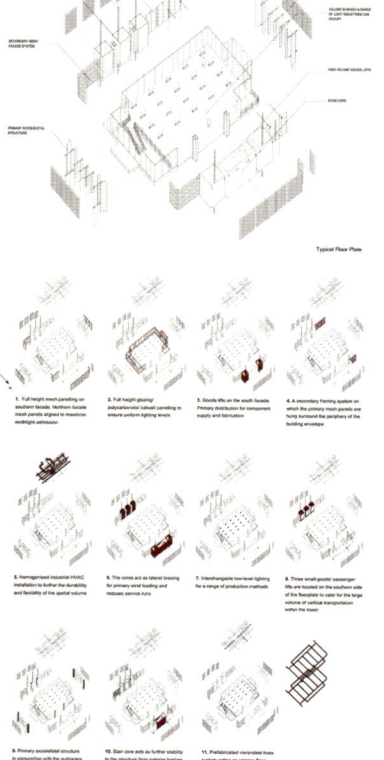

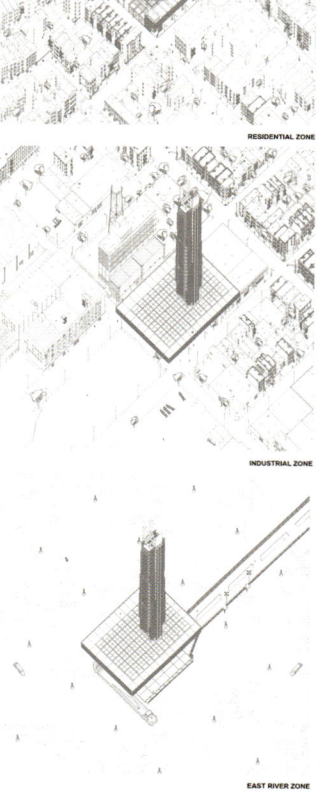

current inter-urban relationships emphasizing the importance of local knowledge on steady growth and innovation. Each tower can accommodate from 52 - 81 small industries providing a maximum of 103,950 sq. ft. of manufacturing space and potentially more than 1000 jobs. Maximum spatial allowance and flexibility within the factory nodes are achieved through an exoskeletal structural system and column free floor plates served by exterior lift cores that provide lateral stability to the overall tower. The floor plate dimensions of the proposal are not designated towards any particular industry but serve to provide a series of intimate, generic industrial spatial volumes, which local 21st century manufacturers can occupy. Although as an ideological interpretation, the scheme is intended to provoke discussion as to an alternate approach to retain the local manufacturing sector and how these small industries can be encouraged in the face of alternative urban, political and neoliberal economic imperatives.

0215

CONTENT +
HUMANIZE

Daniel Tiong Wei Wen

Malaysia

Conter

Modular residential units

Steel structure
Allow adaptability to future expansion
or reassemble of materials.

Interactive multimedia facade

Wind block
An improved gizmo from conventional ventilation block.
30% more efficient than conventional vent. block
in improving wind flow rate to reduce indoor air humidity.
Responding to prevailing wind and also as a shading device.

Fire s

With the current urban development in Malaysia, high-rise buildings have been an essential solution in the economic and population boom. This single point block buildings are often wrongly planned and lack a response to the urban situation, therefore allowing more high rise offices or monotonous towers to fail and becomes an unoccupied urban monolith. Architecturally, high-rises in Malaysia only respond in their form, but the content of the building is usually lacking. Therefore, this proposal is trying to emphasize more on its content rather than its form, and hopefully demonstrate how this content can contribute to the social sustainability of the site.

This proposal is located at PJ section 13 in Selangor, Malaysia. It is a place going through transformation from its past as an industrial usage area into a new mixed-use development and the

0340

PROPOSED MASTERPLAN

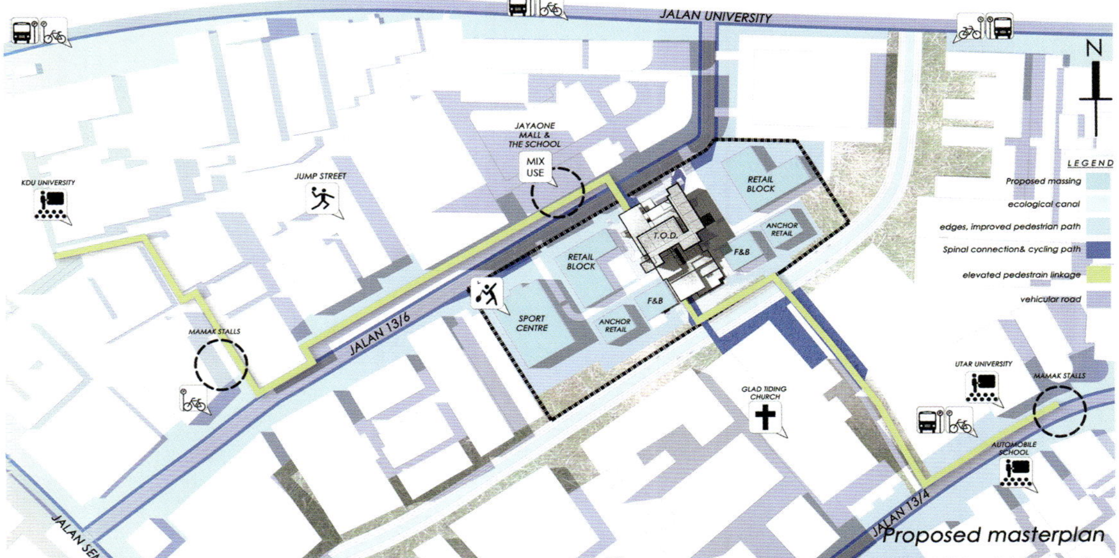

Proposed masterplan

The main aim of this masterplan proposal is to create accessibility to infill the missing connection within middle of PJsection 13, and connecting different places of interest with institute area. Besides proposing dedicated elevated pedestrian path, more bus stop and bicycle sharing dock will be places near by institute and place of interest as the main focal user group in PJsection 13 is the students. The masterplan site is approximate 5 acres with main retail perimeter blocks facing the traffic frontage to generate feasible interest while smaller point blocks with f&B and anchor retail will be facing the water canal, this strategy is to harmonize the scale of buildings along the water canal as the water canal will be reform into a recreational ecological canal for public use. Finally, the heart of the masterplan will be the transit hub which provide bike sharing system and free shuttle bus pick up to the nearest LRT station.

PROGRAMS, CONCEPTS AND DESIGN DEVELOPMENT

SIGN UP   SWIPE OUT   RIDE!   DOCK

MAIN SERVICE PROGRAM:
BIKE SHARING FOR STUDENTS

The idea to optimize the accesibility in PJ section 13 is through both pedestrain and cycling. This program will utilize students ID card to get an access to a bike and deposit will be return upon docking back the bike. Bike is great in term of accessing places within distance of 4km which is about PJsection 13 land area diameter, and this will be the provision to reduce the carparking by students as this program will incorporate free shuttle bus from PJsection 13 to nearest LRT station. Hence, this proposal will add value to the proposed transit hub in PJsection 13.

Concepts and ideas

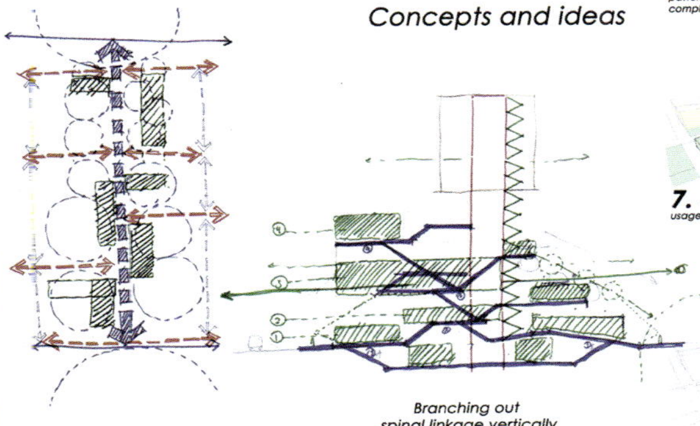

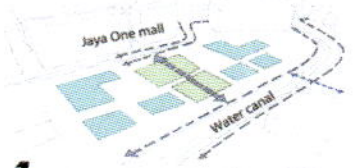

1. Connecting missing internal link and using waterway as connector.
2. Proposed building massing and dedicated elevated linkage. 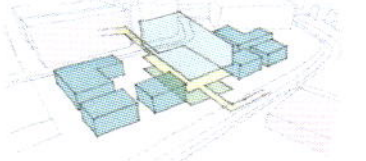
3. Double frontage facing Jayaone and water canal. 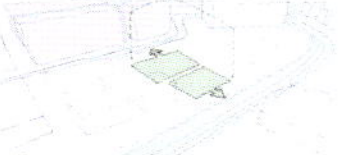
4. Linear spine connecting movement pattern, common spaces and compliment activities. 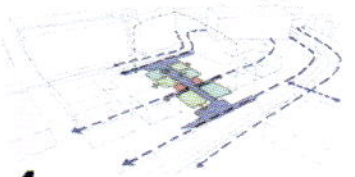
5. Allowing more permeability to other proposed blocks. 
6. Common spaces on dedicated floors for other users on upper level. 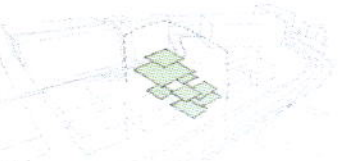
7. Vertical activites response to building usages around the site. 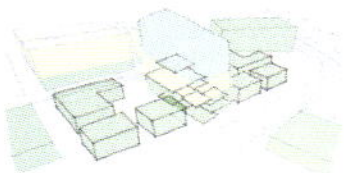 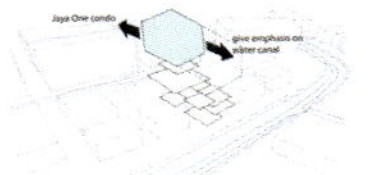
8. Residential block is push facing towards private residential direction (urban scale)allowing more openess and emphasis on water canal(human scale). 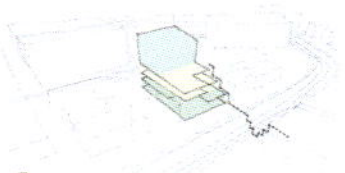
9. Allowing semi open common spaces facing the canal, stepping down towards the canal to visually harmonize the building scale while the facade facing the Jayao One will remain more solid.
10. Volumetric entrance to emphasize the legibility of entry and welcoming public space. 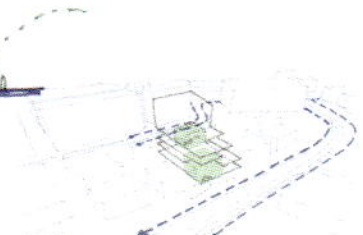
11. Application of 'Gizmo' at certain crucial facade to improve indoor thermal comfort. 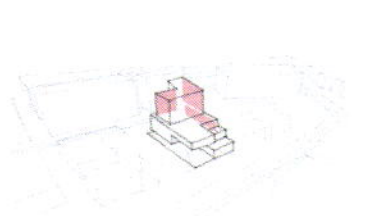

Porous Spinal link

Branching out spinal linkage vertically

+ Humanize
optimmizing accessibility in PJsection 13

Statement

...rrent urban development in Malaysia, high rise buildings has been ...ential solutions in economic and population boom. This single point ...buildings are often wrongly planned and lack of respond to urban ...n , therefore allowing more high rise offices or monotonous tower ...and becomes an unoccupied urban monolith.

...ecturally, high rises in Malaysia only respond in its form, but the con... the building is lacking. Therefore, this proposal is trying to empha... ...re on its content rather than its form, and hopefully demonstrate ...ese content can contribute to the social sustainability of the site.

...oposal is located at PJsection 13 in Selangor, Malaysia. It is a place ...through transformation from its past as an industrial use area into a ...ix used development and the biggest issue this site is facing is it's ...internal access and connections in between buildings. The major ...older of that area is the college students and they have the diffi...f reaching the point of interest scattered throughout PJsection 13; ...s missing internal linkage created additional issue such as carpark-...cause the tenant has no alternative option other than car to ...the places within the site.

...oposal hopes to optimize accessibility of the proposed high rise and ...ounding through legible access, connection and common spaces; ...chieving social sustainability through the interaction between the ...ic user group which is the students. Access to different common ...are link together through a series of spinal movement pattern and ...ing out vertically to create legibility of access and the use of ...Elevated pedestrian and cycling path for student's use is inte-...to connect specific place of interest to encourage more walking ...ing over vehicular car.

...oposal as a mix use high rise will consist of bicycle oriented transit ...the anchor program aim to improve the accessibility and connec-...ithin PJsection 13 and to its nearest train station. The proposed bike ...m will offer the students alternative mean of public transportation ...table environment to encourage more use of bicycle and pedes-...access the place of interest in PJsection 13.

...oposed program will be focusing on the students as the primary ...oup as they are the major stakeholder which creates vibrancy and ...of activities. Therefore, this proposal will also include compliment-...gram such as student central, workshop, seminar, classes, art ...and temporal events collaborate with existing art college for the ...ts to elevate the robustness of PJsection 13.

...e as architecture expression.

biggest issue this site is facing is its missing internal access and connections in between buildings. The major stakeholders of that area are the college students and they have the difficulty of reaching the point of interest scattered throughout PJ section 13; and this missing internal linkage created additional issues such as car parking because the tenant has no alternative option other than car to access the places within the site. This proposal hopes to optimize accessibility of the proposed high-rise and its surrounding through tangible access, connection and common spaces; while achieving social sustainability through the interaction between the dynamic user group which is students. Access to different common spaces are linked together through a series of spinal movement patterns and branching out vertically to create a legibility of access and the use of spaces. Elevated pedestrian and cycling paths for student's use are integrated to connect specific places of interest and to encourage

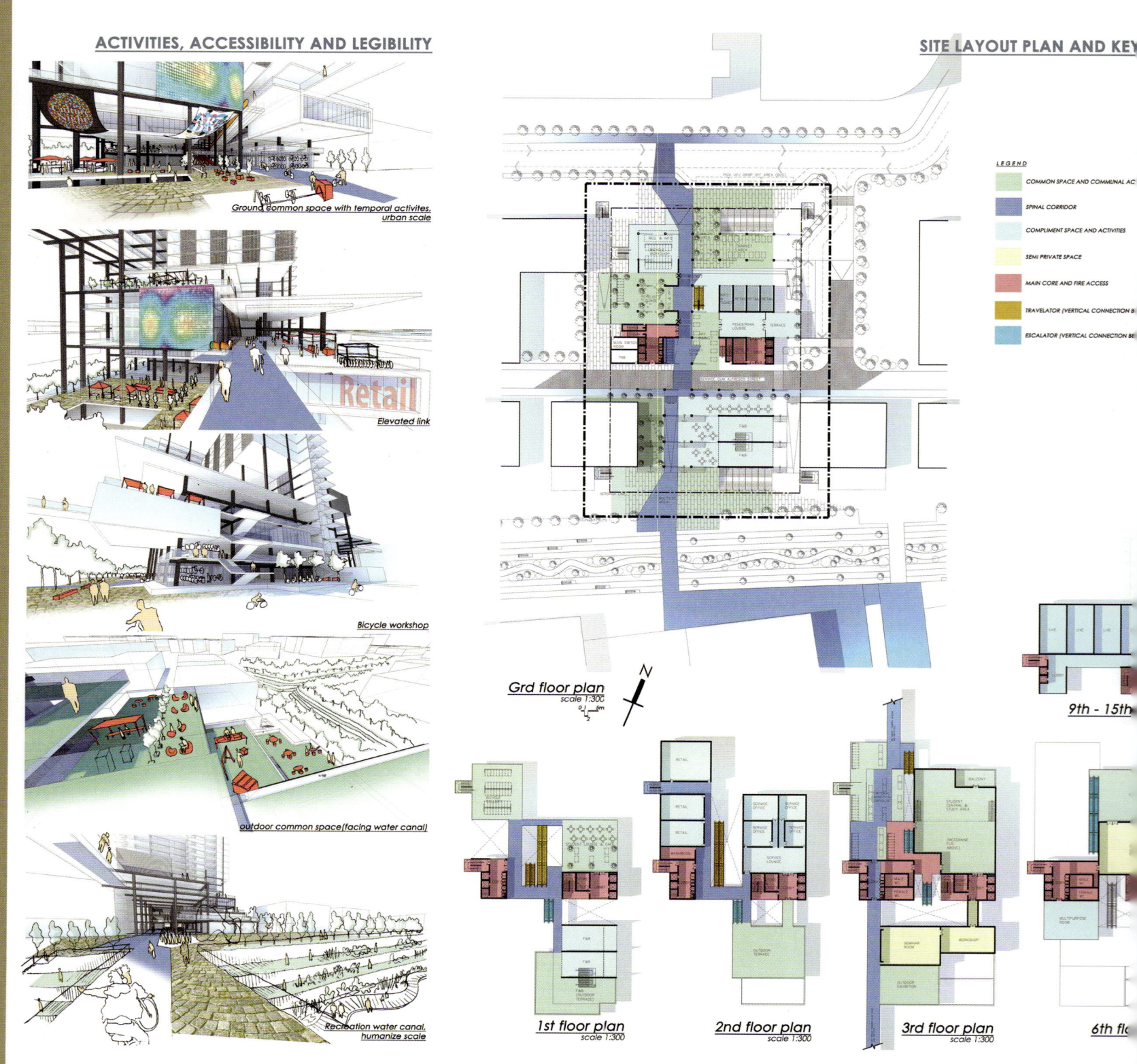

ACTIVITIES, ACCESSIBILITY AND LEGIBILITY

Ground common space with temporal activites, urban scale

Elevated link

Bicycle workshop

outdoor common space (facing water canal)

Recreation water canal, humanize scale

SITE LAYOUT PLAN AND KEY

LEGEND

COMMON SPACE AND COMMUNAL AC
SPINAL CORRIDOR
COMPLIMENT SPACE AND ACTIVITIES
SEMI PRIVATE SPACE
MAIN CORE AND FIRE ACCESS
TRAVELATOR (VERTICAL CONNECTION B
ESCALATOR (VERTICAL CONNECTION BE

Grd floor plan
scale 1:300

9th - 15th

1st floor plan
scale 1:300

2nd floor plan
scale 1:300

3rd floor plan
scale 1:300

6th flo

more walking or cycling over vehicular traffic. This proposal as a mixed-use high-rise will consist of a bicycle oriented transit hub as the anchor program, aimed to improve the accessibility and connectivity within PJ section 13 and to its nearest train station. The proposed bike program will offer the students an alternative means of public transportation and a suitable environment to encourage more usage of bicycles and pedestrians to access the places of interest in PJ section 13. The proposed program will be focusing on the students as the primary user group as they are the major stakeholders, which create vibrancy and the need of activities. Therefore, this proposal will also include a complimentary program such as a student center, workshop, seminar, classes, art market and temporal events collaborating with existing art colleges for the students to elevate the robustness of PJ section 13.

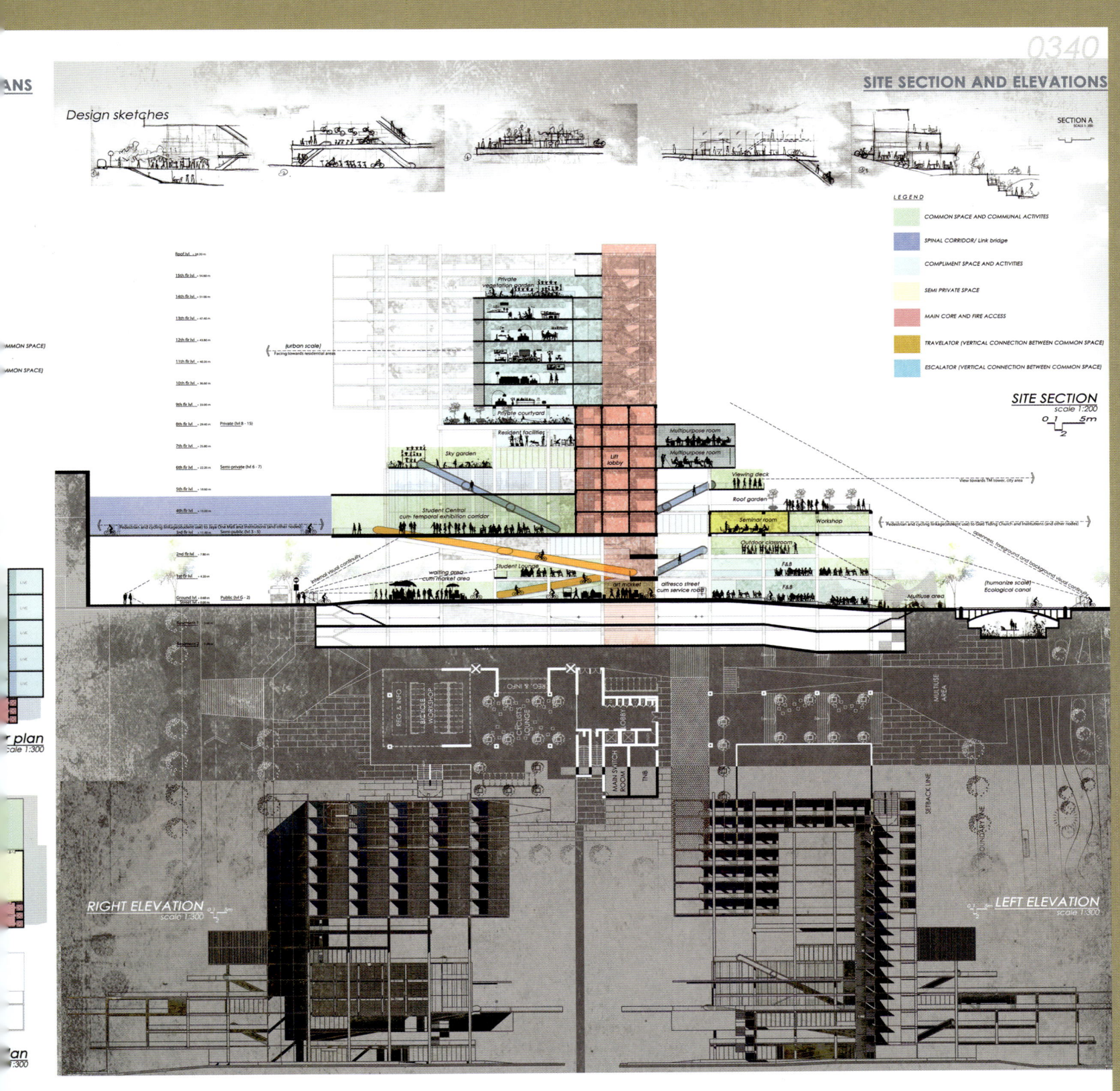

SUCCESSIONAL SKYSCRAPER

Petr Kolacek
Jiri Vitek

Czech Republic

solar impact on cells and spikes

succesional structure

Branches cells (working, culture, sports)

The spikes as residential layer

structural growth from primary roots system
structural patterns in plans > roots, middle part, top part. Cores does not just goes strait upwards, a part of the

The main goal of the Successional Skyscraper is to research and develop a coherent structural system with complex differentiation and the potential of growth urbanism. Trees have a magnificent optimizing strategy. Their system of roots searches for water sources and static stabilization. The trunk typically contains woody tissue for strength, and vascular tissue transfer nutrient's from one part of the tree to another. With most trees a layer of bark, which serves as a protective barrier, surrounds the trunk. Below the ground, the roots branch and spread out widely, serving to anchor the tree and extract moisture and nutrients from the soil. The supply channels do not just go straight upwards to the core, a part of them goes in a spiral shape to avoid the centralization of the network. Above the ground, the branches divide into smaller branches and shoots. The shoots typically bear leaves, which capture solar energy and

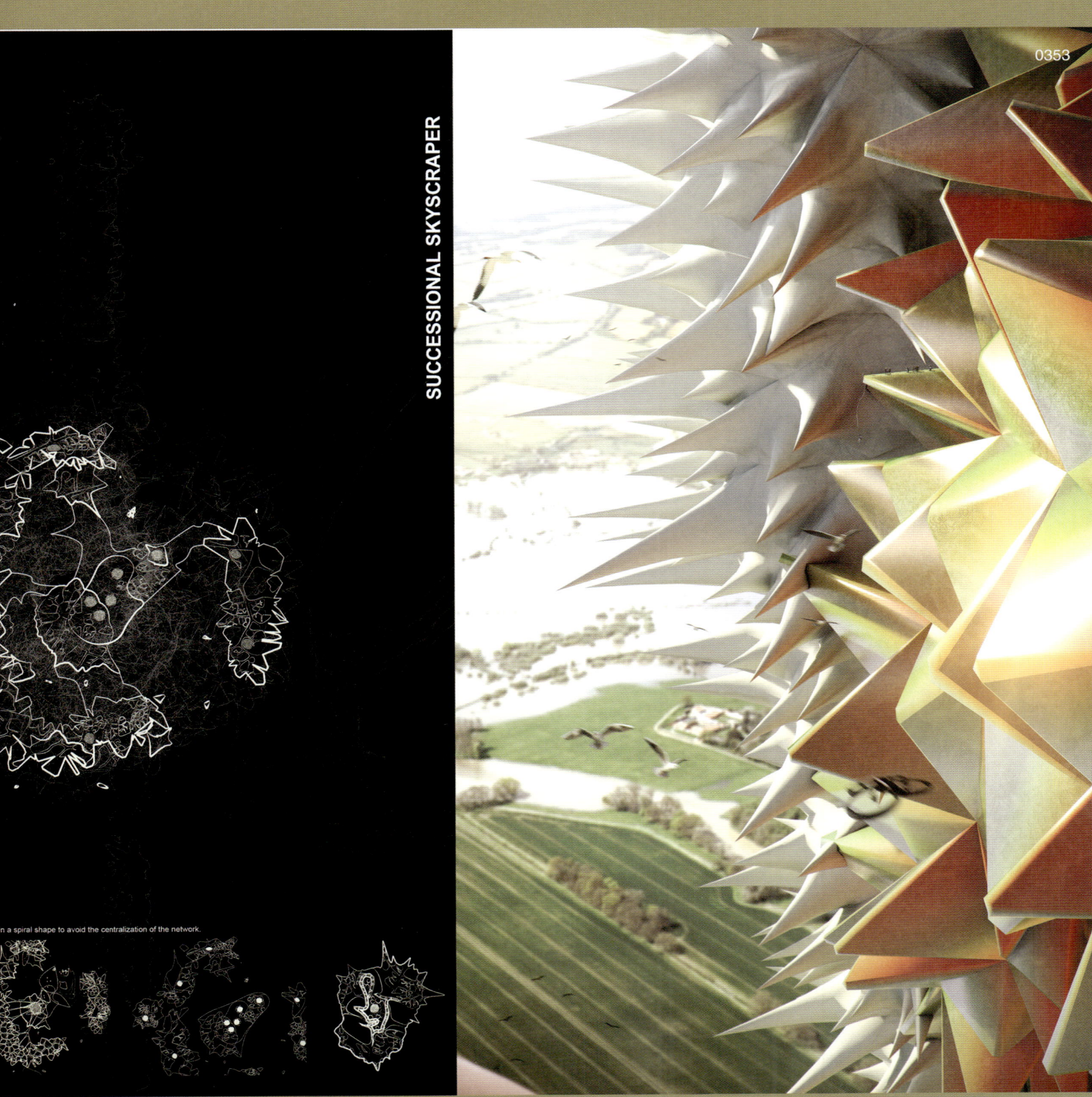

0353

SUCCESSIONAL SKYSCRAPER

in a spiral shape to avoid the centralization of the network.

convert it into sugars by photosynthesis, providing the food for the tree's growth and development. Trees play a significant role in reducing erosion and moderating the climate. They remove carbon dioxide from the atmosphere and store large quantities of carbon their tissues. Trees and forests provide a habitat for many species of animals and plants. They grow constantly only if in a good condition. For creating leaves or conifer needles a lot of energy is needed, so the tree always responds to the actual balance of energy. It calculates if it has enough energy to grow new leaves or if its better to invest energy in different parts. According to that we can observe differentiation in the cellular system and growing patterns. In our project, this root system represents the structural stability and the main frame. Roots provide a balanced network, which could serve as a low-rise city network with a very moderate pattern of transition between open landscape and a dense city core. The frame is not defined only in the horizontal plane, but also in

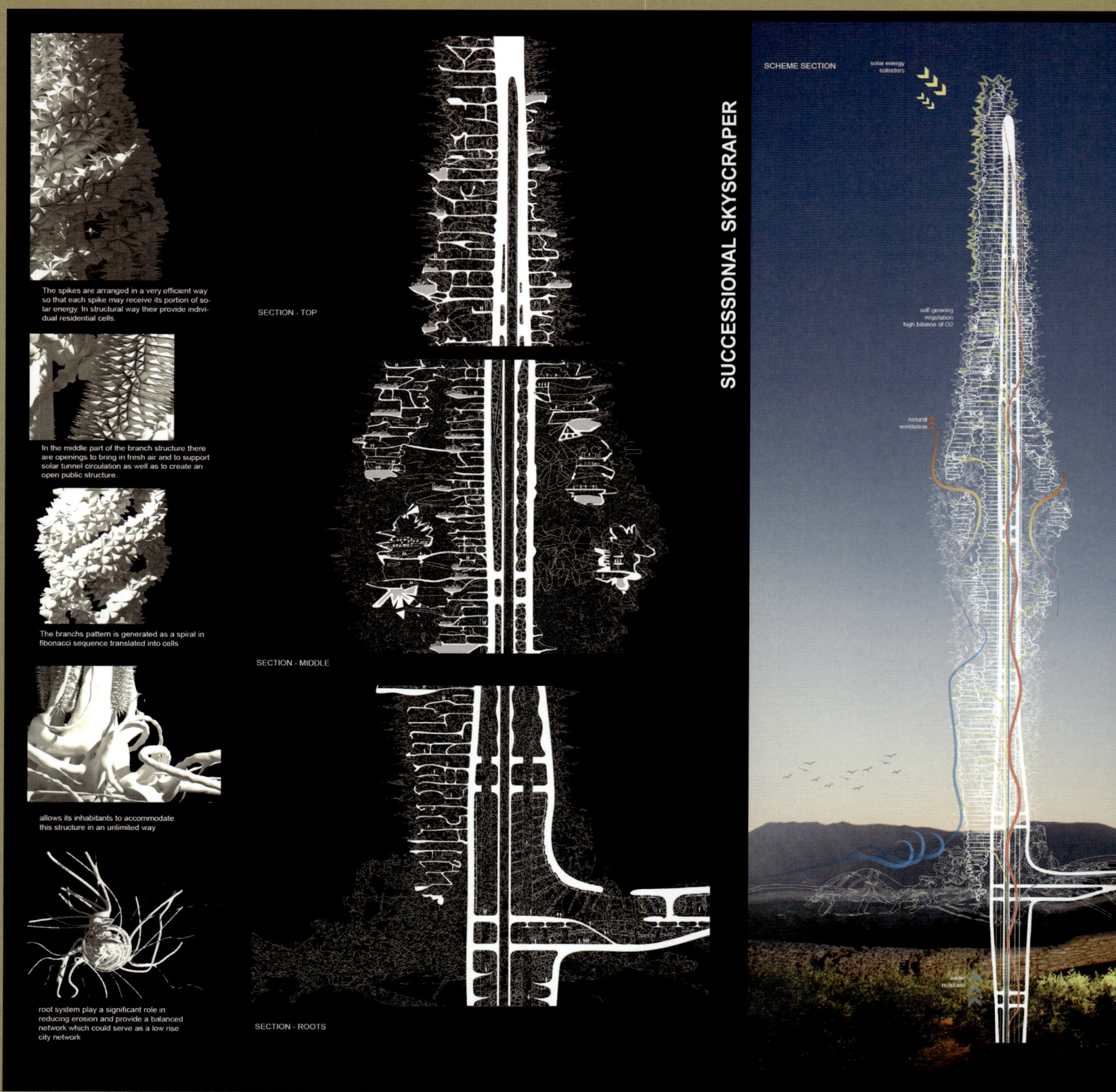

The spikes are arranged in a very efficient way so that each spike may receive its portion of solar energy. In structural way their provide individual residential cells.

In the middle part of the branch structure there are openings to bring in fresh air and to support solar tunnel circulation as well as to create an open public structure.

The branchs pattern is generated as a spiral in fibonacci sequence translated into cells

allows its inhabitants to accommodate this structure in an unlimited way

root system play a significant role in reducing erosion and provide a balanced network which could serve as a low rise city network

SECTION - TOP

SECTION - MIDDLE

SECTION - ROOTS

SUCCESSIONAL SKYSCRAPER

SCHEME SECTION

solar energy collectors

self-growing vegetation high balance of O2

natural ventilation

the vertical dimension, which allows its inhabitants to accommodate this structure in an unlimited way. The main goal of the research is the relationship between individual and collective patterns. When we create a structural system in a certain way, we get a great variability of patterns with both coherence and difference, observing obvious similarity with an ancient self-growing city. The branch's pattern is generated as a spiral in fibonacci sequence translated into cells with the size from 3 to 12 m. In the middle part of the branch structure there are openings to bring in fresh air and to support solar tunnel circulation as well as to create an open public structure. The plan clearly presents a visible tendency to self-organization with the generation of individual complex units, which are, however, connected with the core and between each other.

0353

THERE WAS A MAN, WHO HAD DESIRE FOR FREEDOM AND LIFE WITHOUT FACTORIES, CARS, POLUTION, RUSH, NOISE, AND ALL THE HABITS OF 21.TH CENTRURY

HE LEFT FROM SICK CITY AND RUN OFF TO THE FOREST, FIRSTLY HE WAS LOST ....IN HIS THOUGHTS.... THAN HE FINALLY FOUND OLD TREE OF WISDOM.... VERY NICE IDEA WAS SEND TO HIM. PLANT A BIG TREE. THE TREE WHICH CAN GIVE YOU FRAME OF FREEDOM, COLLECT SUN ENERGY, WATER AND OTHERS NUTRIENTS, FRUITS AND EVEN IT IS ABLE TO CREATE YOUR HOME...

YOU CAN IMAGINE WHATEVER.....SCIENCE, AGES OF RESEARCH, MATERIAL INTELLIGENCE BEHAVIOR RESEARCH, EVEN MAGIC IF YOU WANT... ....BUT ONE DAY ....HUMANKIND REALIZE THAT SEQUIA CELL IS MUCH STRONGER THAN ANY CONCRETE.... AND TREE STRUCTURE IS SO OPTIMISED THAT ITS PROVIDE GREAT OPPORTUNITY TO LIVE IN.

...SO INSTEAD OF CUTTING, BURNING AND HARVESTING...WE REALIZE THAT WE ARE ABLE TO COMMUNICATE IN CONSCIOUSNESS WAY WITH NATURE ....

AFTER SOME TIME THAT THE SEED HAD BEEN PLANTED...

.... AND SUCESSIONAL SKYSCAPER WAS BORN...

INTERVENTION VERTICAL NEIGHBORHOOD

Bocong Chen

United States

INTERVETION VERTICAL NEIGHBORHOOD

Morphological Skyscraper in Highline-Park
Meatpacking District, Manhattan, New York City

The city, as idea and fact, has become the location for some of the most significant theoretical discourse and experimental design in a wide range of disciplines that have been increasingly converging in recent decades. What are the contemporary possibilities of Le Corbusier's Maison Domino? Subtractive cuts in floor plates allow for connection and create potential spatial figures as voids. Continuously differentiated non-oriented surfaces such as a Moebius strip or Klein bottle reveal surfaces of complex ambiguity. There can be no stable understanding of what is inside or outside. A lively and communicative neighborhood is no longer conventionally horizontal, but comes out in a vertical typology under an intervention field impact.

Opposed to the skyscraper that sadly will never touch the sky while leaving behind its only real grounding in the world, this project develops strategies to displace, lift, bend, warp, and multiply ground so that it becomes a fully three dimensional reality always engaged within structures tending towards significant height. The relationship between horizontal slabs and mega morphological surface produces more potential and unexpected section possibilities and spatial connections between both horizontal and vertical. In this way, the sky goes into the skyscraper and coexists with the human habitat. Ramps and tilted planes also create continuous surfaces that obviate distinctions between levels or between the very idea of horizontal and vertical with their problematic corollary associations that distinguish and separate landscape from building.

ROOF GARDENT
Open sky space for the community resident;
Ecological property to the roof cooling down

RESIDENTIAL UNITS
Residential housing units;
Day-care center; healthy center; etc.

COMMUNITY PLATFORM
Community activity event;
Entertainment facilities;
Outdoor performing space; etc.

RESIDENTIAL UNITS
Residential housing units, day-care center;
Healthy center; etc.

ARTIST BUBBLE
Community performing theater; mini cinema;
Banquet; exhibition hall

HIGHLINE PARK
Regional historic landmark;
Great crowd of tourists

ENTRANC
Outdoor pub
Free artists p

The site is in the Meat Packing District of New York City and is currently occupied by parking. The High Line bisects the site. This is an area that has rapidly gentrified over the past years. The surrounding area, the Chelsea Neighborhood, is well known for its artistic and cultural activities, and many desirable high-end boutiques and restaurants. This project will bring back the needed affordable housing, places of work and production, small start up businesses, artist studios, edgy clubs, public as well as private recreational facilities, experimental theater in order to make this area a dynamic and lively context.

A lively and communicative neighborhood is no longer conventionally horizontal, but comes out in a vertical typology under an intervention field impact. Opposed to the skyscraper that sadly will never touch the sky while leaving behind its only real grounding in the world, this project develops strategies to displace, lift, bend, warp, and multiply ground so that it becomes a fully three dimensional reality always engaged within structures tending towards significant height. The relationship between horizontal slabs and mega morphological surface produces more potential and unexpected section possibilities and spatial connections between horizontal and vertical. In this way, the sky goes into the skyscraper and coexists with the human habitat. Ramps and tilted planes also create continuous surfaces that obviate distinctions between levels or between the very idea of horizontal and vertical with their problematic

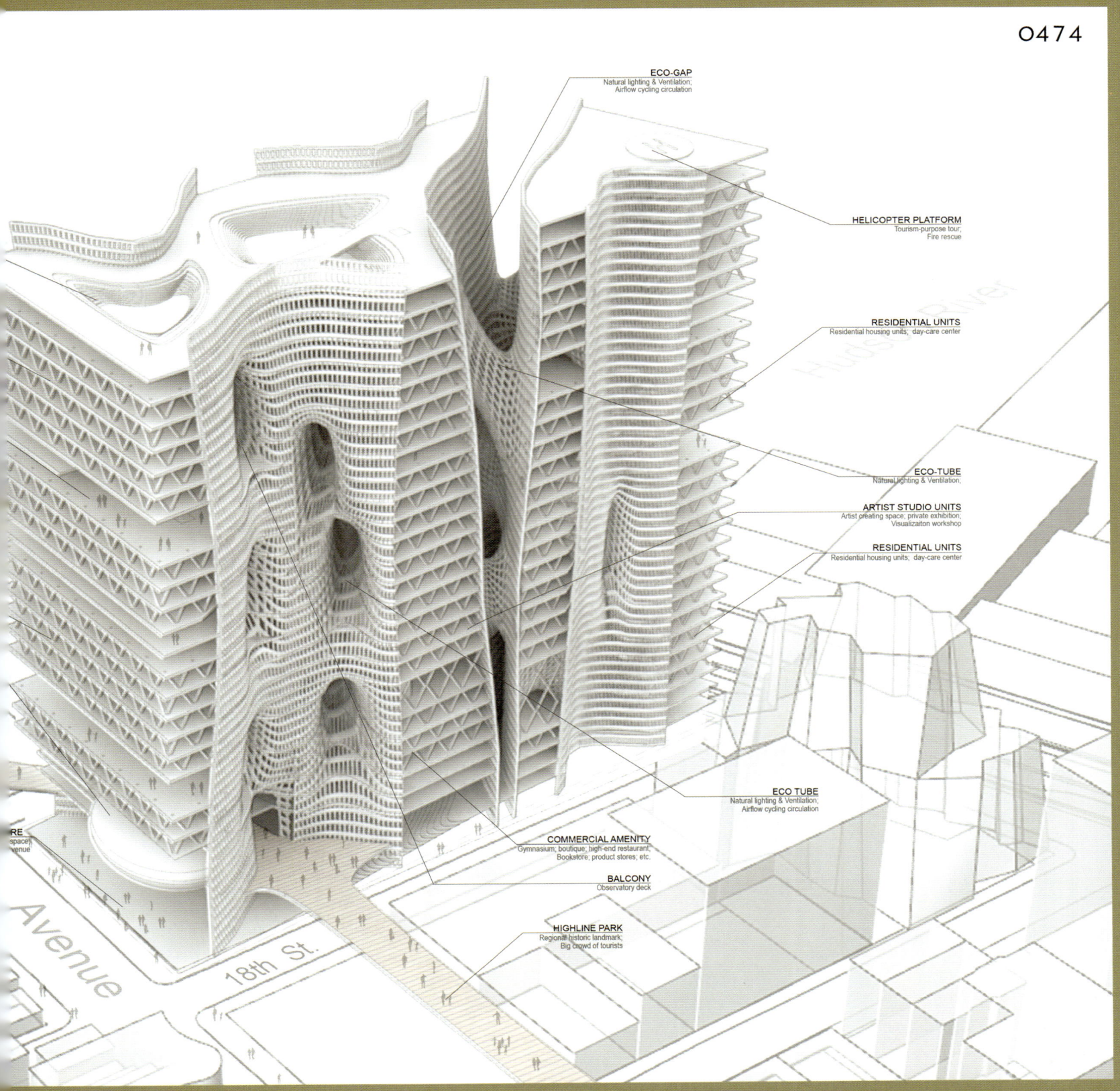

O474

ECO-GAP
Natural lighting & Ventilation;
Airflow cycling circulation

HELICOPTER PLATFORM
Tourism-purpose tour;
Fire rescue

RESIDENTIAL UNITS
Residential housing units; day-care center

ECO-TUBE
Natural lighting & Ventilation;

ARTIST STUDIO UNITS
Artist creating space; private exhibition;
Visualizaiton workshop

RESIDENTIAL UNITS
Residential housing units; day-care center

ECO TUBE
Natural lighting & Ventilation;
Airflow cycling circulation

COMMERCIAL AMENITY
Gymnasium; boutique; high-end restaurant;
Bookstore; product stores; etc.

BALCONY
Observatory deck

HIGHLINE PARK
Regional historic landmark;
Big crowd of tourists

corollary associations that distinguish and separate landscape from building. The site is in the Meat Packing District of New York City and is currently occupied by parking. The High Line bisects the site. This is an area that has rapidly gentrified over the past years. The surrounding area, the Chelsea Neighborhood, is well known for its artistic and cultural activities, and many desirable high-end boutiques and restaurants. This project will bring back the needed affordable housing; places of work and production, small start up businesses, artist studios, edgy clubs, public as well as private recreational facilities, experimental theater in order to make this area a dynamic and lively context. Based on this background, the responsibility of the prospective building is to seek and create a morphological form that has the potential to produce many opportunities about urban life and urban space. Programs will also be intersecting under this diverse mix spatial system, where ecological passive strategy will also

Model Test_image1

Model Test_image 2

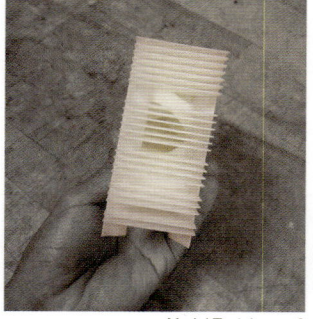

Model Test_image 3

Model Test_detail portion

PERSPECTIVE VIEW
Chelsea Neighborhood, Manhattan, N

SECTION DIAGRAM_
Experiment on the Potential Morphology of the Section

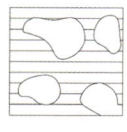
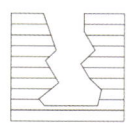
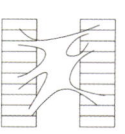
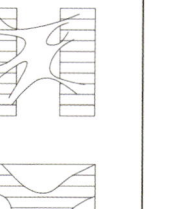

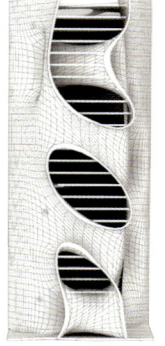
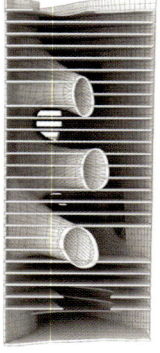

A-A SECTION   B-B SECTION   C-C SECTION

SPILT-UP MODEL DISPLAY_
Continuously non-oriented surfaces between inside and outside

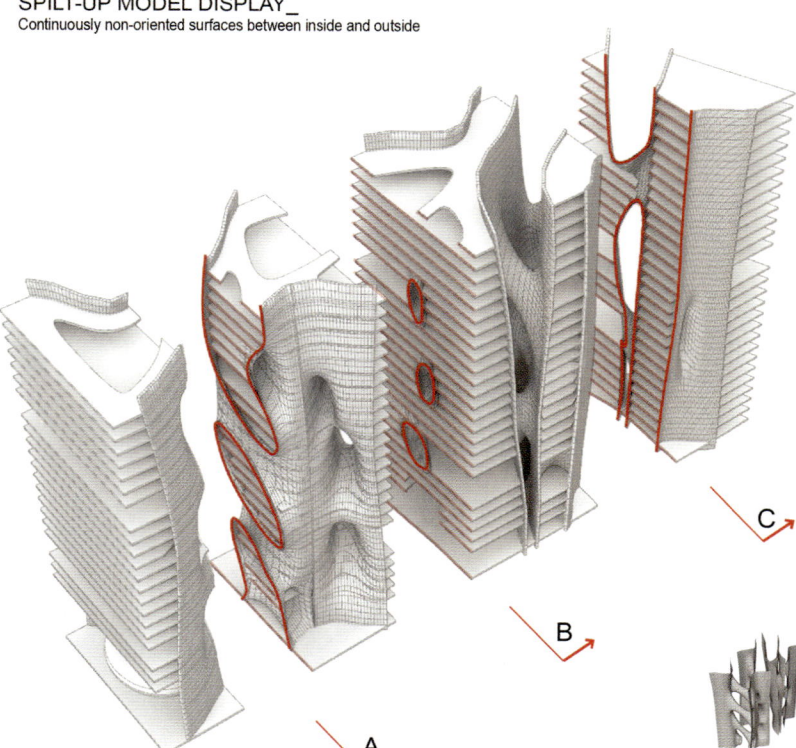

C

B

A

primary structure   slab system   integration mass

SECTION CONCEPT:

1.   The free section becomes even more interesting than the free plan because it implicates actions in full three dimensional space. Benefiting from the combination of the slabs and morphological surface, variable possibilities of section iterate between the surfaces, and there can be no stable definition of what is outside or inside.

2.   Mega intersected tubes create opportunities for connection, programmatically and ecologically. Here liminal space surrounding freely deployed figures in section can be the place of unrestricted movement, a complex plenum for light and air, or other forms of habitation.

3.   Radical subtraction of floor plates and other stabilizing field structures might be wrapped with a topologic surface that itself is habitable on all sides creating an opportunistic gap between systems. The outcome of this ambiguous spatial construct has substantial implications for larger questions of how humans inhabit the world.

CONTEXTURALIZED
Section cutting along the 10th Avenue
Manhattan, New York City

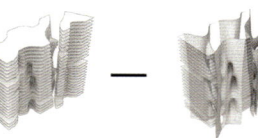
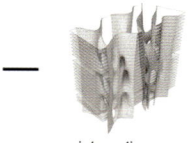

operate. The free section becomes even more interesting than the free plan because it implicates actions in full three-dimensional space. Benefiting from the combination of the slabs and morphological surface, variable possibilities of section iterate between the surfaces, and there can be no stable definition of what is outside or inside. Mega intersected tubes create opportunities for connection, programmatically and ecologically. Here liminal space surrounding freely deployed figures in section can be the place of unrestricted movement, a complex plenum for light and air, or other forms of habitation. Radical subtraction of floor plates and other stabilizing field structures might be wrapped with a topologic surface that itself is habitable on all sides creating an opportunistic gap between systems. The outcome of this ambiguous spatial construct has substantial implications for larger questions of how humans inhabit the world.

OM THE HIGHLINE-PARK DECK
 City

O474

PASSIVE STRATEGY:
The mega morphological tubes in one way iconically bring unique interior spatial experience and come out a distinct architectural typology, in other way it also contribute to the ecological value to the inside building space.
Passive ventilation would keep operating to always renew the interior airflow. And natural lighting will provide the interior space with mild and steay illuminance environment.

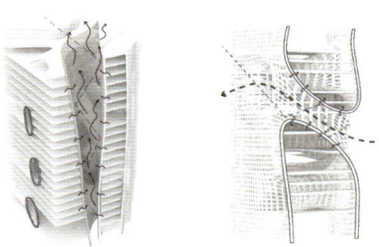

AN ELEVATION
e Park

URBAN FOREST TOWER

Baoyi Mao

New Zealand

DESIGN INTENT

THE MAIN IDEA IS TO DESIGN AN URBAN FOREST SKYSCRAPER WHICH WILL BE POSITIONED IN THE CENTRE OF BEIJING, THE CAPITAL CITY OF CHINA. THE SKYSCRAPER DESIGN PROVIDES AN ECOLOGICAL SYSTEM THAT PRODUCE FOODS AND REDUCES THE POLLUTION OF THE CITY CENTRE WHILST ALSO CREATING RECREATIONAL OPPORTUNITIES FOR THE SURROUNDING ENVIRONMENT.

SUSTAINABLE CONTINUUM

FROM POPULATION ESTIMATES IN 2014, APPROXIMATELY 50% OF THE WORLDS POPULATION RESIDES IN AN URBAN ENVIRONMENT. THIS IS SET TO INCREASE TO 70-80% BY 2050 THEREFORE OUR AIM IS TO DESIGN A SELF-SUFFICIENT SUSTAINABLE LIVING ENVIRONMENT THAT INCORPORATES AGRICULTURE BASED FOOD SYSTEMS TO PROVIDE A FOOD SOURCE FOR THE IMMEDIATE OCCUPANTS AND SURROUNDING METROPOLITAN AREA THAT SEAMLESSLY INTEGRATES WITH THE CITY.

URE
ARCHIT

THE "URB
COUNTRY.
THE URBA
FLOORS O
HAS A LAR

The main idea is to design an Urban Forest Skyscraper, which will be positioned in the centre of Beijing, the capital city of China. The skyscraper design provides an Ecological system that produces food and reduces the pollution of the city centre whilst also creating recreational opportunities for the surrounding environment.

From population estimates in 2014, approximately 50% of the world's population resides in an urban environment. This is set to increase to 70-80% by 2050 therefore our aim is to design a self-sufficient sustainable living environment that incorporates agriculture based food systems to provide a food source for the immediate occupants and surrounding metropolitan area that seamlessly integrates with the city.

Architecture has to perform as an ecosystem within the organic tissue of the city. The "Urban Forest

0482-1

˥ FOREST TOWER

˥RE HAS TO PERFORM AS AN ECOSYSTEM WITHIN THE ORGANIC TISSUE OF THE CITY

˥REST TOWERS" IS DESIGNED TO BECOME A LOGICAL CONTINUATION OF THE MOUNTAINOUS LANDSCAPE OF THE
˥ ARE THREE TOWERS FLOATING ON THE RIVER SIDE, AND FOUR DIRECTIONAL PEDESTRIAN PATHS LEADING TO
˥EST TOWERS. THE MAIN CONSTRUCTION IS DESIGNED AS A CYLINDRICAL SKYSCRAPER MADE FROM MULTIPLE
˥ERENT SHAPES AND SIZE WHICH HAVE BEEN LAYERED SLIGHTLY OFF-CENTRE FROM ONE OTHER. EACH FLOOR
˥ASS GALLERY WHICH IS VERY CONVENIENT IN EXPERIENCING THE URBAN PANORAMA.

Towers" is designed to become a logical continuation of the mountainous landscape of the country. There are three towers floating on the riverside, and four directional pedestrian paths leading to the Urban Forest Towers. The main construction is designed as a cylindrical skyscraper made from multiple floors of different shapes and size which have been layered slightly off-center from one other. Each floor has a large glass gallery, which is very convenient in experiencing the urban panorama. The structural skin exhibits an organic pattern based on cellular configurations. The result comes from the analysis of mathematical systems that optimize the best weight to strength ration. This skin performs a playful movement as it goes in an out the building while creating interior spatial pockets and outdoor balconies of different shapes and sizes – each with a distinct function. Habitable horizontal bridges that provide

SECTIONAL   ELEVATION

LEVELS OF SLABS   VORONOR FORM STRUCTURE   SKIN TRUSSES FORM

STRUCTURE EXPLORATION

START WITH A BASE SLAB TOWER FORM AND TWISTING TO DEFINED THE SHAPES. THAN BY COMPOUND WITH VORONOR SHAPE STRUCTURE TC CREATE SPACE INBT- WEEN. THE VORONOR FORM ALSO AS THE GROWTH SYSTEM AND WATER CATCHMENT THAT TRANSFER FOR THE HOLD TOWER USE TO PLATING.

TOWER 1   TOWER 2   TOWER 3   BASE INFRASTRUCTURE PLAN   PLAN

auxiliary programs to the inhabitants interconnect the three towers. These bridges are located in seven levels.

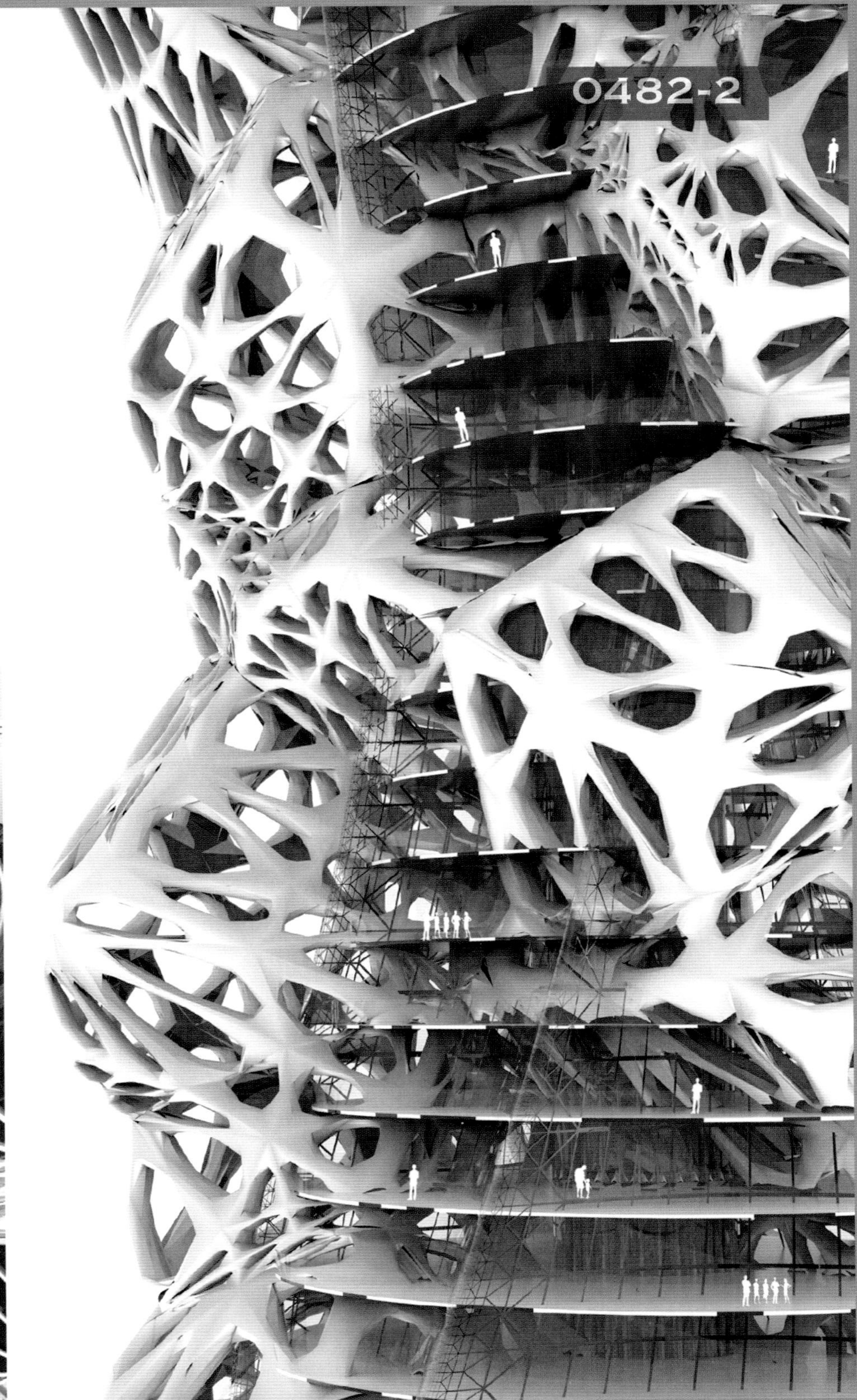

0482-2

HIGH-RISE

See Jia Ho

United States

H I G H - R I S E

{The world as floor}

This is a re-imagination of the Duxton Plain Public Housing Project in Singapore for which an international competition was held in 2001. The built entry consisted of seven 50-storey towers linked by two sky bridges (the Pinnacle@Duxton), the towers themselves composed of conventional double-loaded corridors opening onto apartments.

In this re-imagination, the building is made of 41 towers, either 50 or 100 stories tall. Each tower is composed of major "world floors" at every fifth storey from which the apartments are accessed, each tower having five 4-storey apartments that open their front doors into the major floor. Each major floor of the highrise reflects the context of the kampongs (villages) of old Singapore, where the world was not divided into one-storey slices stacked and fractured by the elevator system but where a whole community is accessed on one floor.

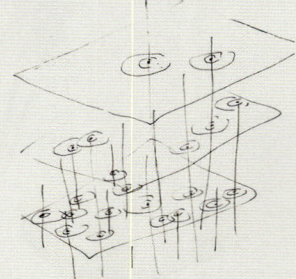

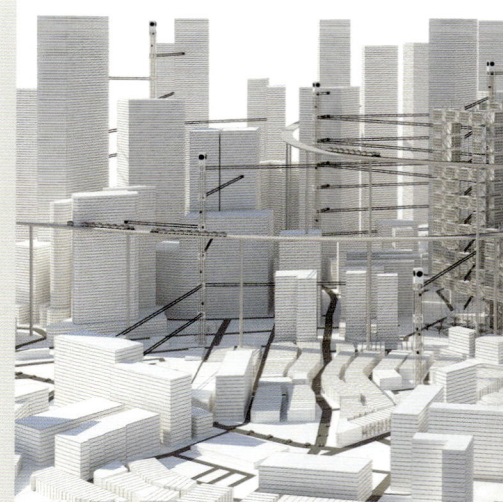

World: floor

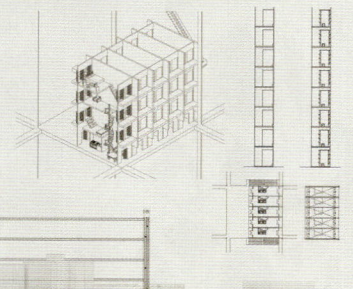

Table of Contents

WORLD : FLOOR

Do high-rises dream of technicolor floors?

180

good at everything.

Singapore is too small. It is what I thought for a long time. Too small for what? Its economy is doing well for the most part. In terms of governance, the small size is an advantage. Crime rate is low. Employment rate is decent. Home ownership is the pride of the country. Too small for what?

181   186

Too small for dreams.

The smallness of the land is the most apparent— half the size of Los Angeles, two thirds the size of New York City, half the size of London, two thirds the size of Hong Kong and one third the size of Tokyo.) It is an with no hinterland.

In a large country, if one travels for a long time would arrive at an entirely different place eventual so here. You reach the sea—

To go anywhere further, one needs a passport — is no middle ground between staying and going. Th a sense of loss that only a person from a small place comprehend.

Afterword

In the Fall semester before I entered my thesis preparation, I thought about what I wanted to do. Throughout my undergraduate architectural studies in Singapore, the predominant so-called problem was 'what is a Singapore architecture?' The kind of problem that troubled American architects in earlier times. The more I think about the idea of a "Singapore style," the more distasteful and empty the proposition. There are two issues: Singapore is too young a country for any historical architectural precedent. Singapore is a mixture of cultures that originated in China, India and Southeast Asia. Any attempt to discover a Singapore architecture leads to either a climatic design (tropical response, sun shades, etc) or an ethno-cultural influenced design (Chinese, Indian, Malay, etc.) I had thought that all these are ok; if it is a contrived architecture, then that is the Singapore style. If the problem is the lack of a style, one need not worry, for that by itself is also a style. The problem is that these are not good enough for Singapore. Suffering from a paranoid attitude of being too small and weak in a big world, it had been constantly trying to be

"The him! What a queer idea!"
"But if you don't let him," I said, "he will wander off some and get lost."
My friend broke into another peal of laughter:
"But where do you think he would go?"
"Anywhere. Straight ahead of him."
Then the little prince said, earnestly:
"That doesn't matter. Where I live, everything is so small!"
And, with perhaps a hint of sadness, he added:
"Straight ahead of him, nobody can go very far..."
- Antoine de Saint-Exupéry, The Little Prince

The dominant typology in Singapore is the hig Almost 70% of the people live in government-built go housing blocks ranging from four to fifty stories.

52

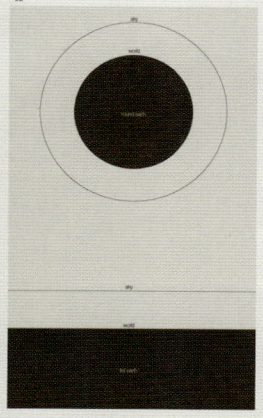

The world is a floor.

53

54

The LORD said to Abram, after Lot had separated from him, "Now lift up your eyes and look from the place where you are, northward and southward and eastward and westward; for all the land which you see, I will give it to you and to your descendants forever.
(Genesis 13:13-14)

Your world is what you see.

"Arise, walk about the land through its length and breadth; for I will give it to you."
(Genesis 16:17)

Your world is what you walk on.

55

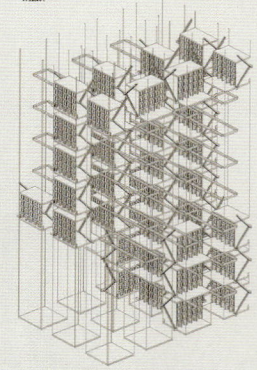

World Floor

Worldfloor is a world read as a continuous plane of floor planes without any gaps in between each plane. Conventionality, worldfloor is simplified to the visualization of only major strata, one at every 40 feet.

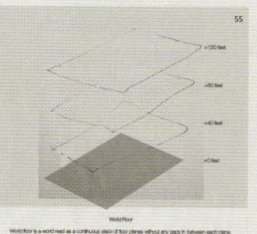

Major Floor

High-rise strata ripples in each major floor.

56

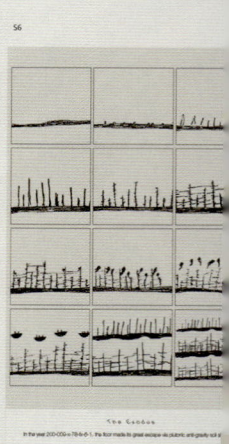

The London

Growing up in Singapore, I never liked high-rises. I didn't know exactly why; it could be the unmistakable verticality and the obviousness of human effort, but far more than aesthetic appearances and questions of style it seemed to me that there was something limiting about the world they contain. In setting out to define what a world is, I could not deny the horizontality of man's vision and movement, both of which created 'the world experienced as floor', be it the flat earth of ancient times or the skyscraper floors stacked and accessed by the elevator core. The fracturing of experience in the skyscraper floors results in limited worlds each one story tall and experienced only one at a time. This phenomenon is supported by the mechanism of the elevator which functions more or less like a teleportation machine: from one unique world we step into a box through a pair of doors, and two seconds later we step out the same

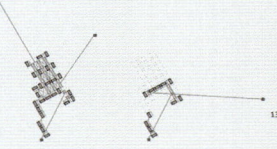

0628

Death of the High-Rise

The high-rise is dead, and no one is mourning. Conceived and birthed by a young urban context, it was murdered by the elevator in its infancy. Its carcass was cloned and piled up, sometimes with earnestness, sometimes with callous indifference, sometimes with swiss precision, nonetheless like pancakes. The elevator that murdered the high-rise did it over and over again, placing the carcasses on display like an obsessive serial killer with a penchant for arrangement and artistic expression - masterpieces wrapped in shiny material as if to hide the ultimate lifelessness and futility of the effort; like a rain soaked cigarette butt on the pavement it is no longer able to invent any future. The elevator has one quest: height. It is a psychopath unable to deal with emotions, sympathy or context. Lacking the ability to dream of anything other than height, it created taller and taller pancake towers, sometimes constructing gymnastically impressive pancake towers. Its accomplice and hustler is the square foot price. Prestige and status are its ancient lovers and patrons.

The Elevator

There is no high-rise building. The only thing that rises is the elevator, skewering through stacks of single-storey worlds. Each floor is lifted from the ground like a baby with its umbilical cord still attached. The elevator has always suffered from an inferiority complex - it is the unoverachieving sibling of the teleport machine. The reigning king of worlds survives on cables and maintenance men and can hardly yet deviate from the straight line, but it does its job. It does not matter that the floors are stacked vertically: if the 3rd floor is in Antarctica and the 72nd floor is on Venus, we are in still in a high-rise, unless our eyes (these days we can trick them) tell us that we have moved a hundred million kilometers between two worlds.

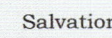

skyscrapers are found in the central business district. If there is anywhere to start making Singapore into a place where dreams could live (a bigger world?) it in the high-rise.

72nd Floor Pizza Place
: A whole new world

If the world at the 72nd floor is complete, man does not have to go down to the ground floor. If the world at the ground floor is complete, man does not have to go up to the 72nd floor. There are fractured worlds in a high-rise but each world is not a vacuum. If you live on pizza on the 72nd floor for the rest of your life, someone would have to deliver it to your door from the ground floor, human or android. If the pizza place is on the 72nd floor someone would have to deliver the ingredients from the ground floor. If the ingredients are on the 72nd floor someone would have to grow the wheat somewhere in the world on the ground floor. If the wheat field is on the 72nd floor then we have a whole new world.

Changing Worlds

Certainly, I decided, that a dog sees the world quite differently than I do, or any humans do. And then I began to think, Maybe each human being lives in a unique world, a private world, a world different from those inhabited and experienced by all other humans. And that led me to wonder, if reality differs from person to person, can we speak of reality singular, or shouldn't we really be talking about plural realities? (How to How to Build a Universe That Doesn't Fall Apart Two Days Later, Philip K. Dick)

What is a world? In Strange Days (1995), one man's mundane and desperate existence is another man's technicolor. People pay big bucks to procure black market 'experience tapes', living the moments of another person's life (or perhaps their own in a better age), seeing the world through a different set of eyes, touching what another touched, feeling what they felt. In Dollhouse (2009-2010), worlds are fully imprinted into a person's brain, one day she is a negotiator with nine successful hostage situations under her belt, the next day she is a hitchhiking pilgrim born blind. These may appear to be fantastical science fic-

tion, but movies and television show us possible (albeit extreme) extrapolations of strands of reality. The entire show business industry thrives on creating, describing, articulating, filling with details, live-actioning and visualizing dreams of a better (or at least more interesting) world for a humanity that feeds on hopes and dreams: Strange Days without the touching.

Salvation

It is argued that human beings cannot fly. This is a serious hindrance to the resurrection of the highrise, post elevator. There is a need for human beings to live in highrises where the demand for land exceeds the supply. (Where there is no need, there is no argument - like a copycat murder the motive is only an attempt to achieve the original's fame.) The limited physical potential of human beings with regards to stair-climbing created the ancient scenario of servant attics and wealthy ground floor parlors. No sooner had the poor hailed the elevator as a new saving power that destroyed the 'airy graves', it revealed itself to be a false messiah came only to lift the rich above the clouds. But even for them it is a spurious salvation; there are no worlds up there, only observation decks.

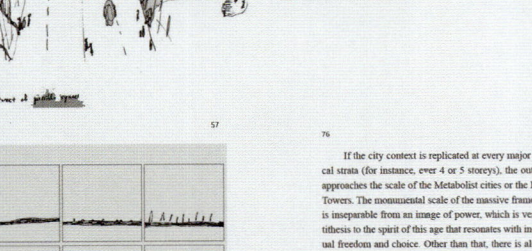

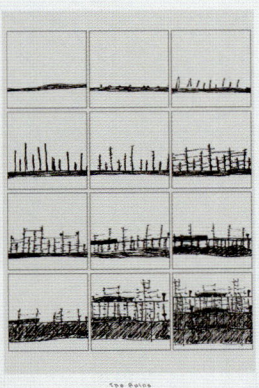

If the city context is replicated at every major vertical strata (for instance, ever 4 or 5 storeys), the outcome approaches the scale of the Metabolist cities or the Hyper Towers. The monumental scale of the massive framework is inseparable from an image of power, which is very antithesis to the spirit of this age that resonates with individual freedom and choice. Other than that, there is also the question of material consumption and cost of construction.

The Anti-Hyper Tower
The anti-Hyper Tower expands horizontally as much as it expands vertically.

BUILDING SCALE
At the scale of the building, each floor is expanded vertically (see "EXPANDING THE WORLD/FLOOR, METHOD 1", p.59); each floor contains a world (see "1 DEFINITIONS", p.20).

TOWN SCALE
At the scale of the town, bridges link each world(floor) to adjacent existing buildings at the same strata to create an extended world(floor) (see "EXPANDING THE WORLD(FLOOR), METHOD 1", p.59).

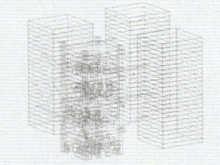

At a further point in time, new buildings are built with a similar concept. As with existing buildings, bridges link each floor to create an extended world(floor).

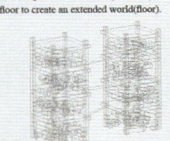

CITY SCALE
The city gradually transforms.

{The Anti-Hyper Tower}

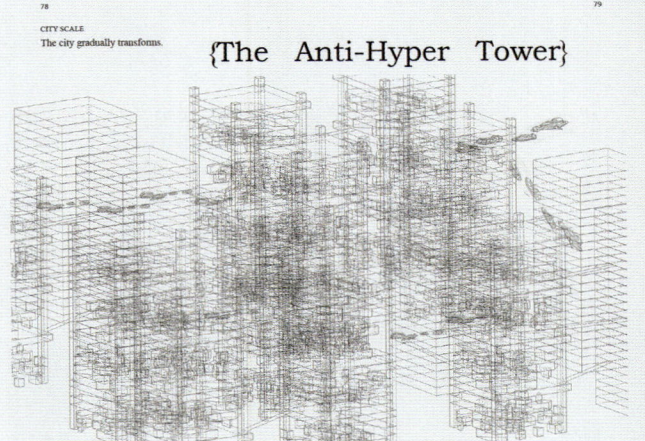

way into another world.

In this project, I imagined a Singapore high-rise where the phenomenon of fractured worlds in a high-rise is countered by forming extensive visual porosity between floors, and expanding the height of each floor to five stories. Each apartment is four stories tall and open onto the "major floors" in a setting that brings to mind the kampungs (villages) of old where community was accessed near one's front door.

The elevators of this project are not embedded in the building core, but are instead pulled away from the building. There are four elevator towers, each located at a major node in the city fabric: two subway stations, one major road, and one multi-story carpark. These transportation nodes then become the entry-point of the building, which is no longer a sculpture in space, but a continuation of the city.

World: floor

{Singapore highrise}

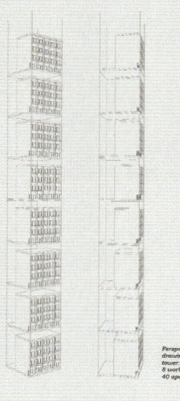

Perspective drawings of one tower: 40 stories, 8 world(floor)s, 40 apartments.

World: floor

Proposal

Using the idea of the anti-Hyper Tower (p.76), this proposal for Duxton Plain Public Housing is made of 41 towers (each either 40 or 80 stories tall) linked by bridges every five stories.

Tower

There are 41 towers (16 towers are 40 stories tall, the rest are 80 stories tall). Each tower has a 50' by 50' foot print that contains the floor plan of five apartments (p.159). This plan is replicated in each tower every five storeys.

Apartment

Each apartment is a four-storey tall interior with only one floor (see Section a-a, p.159) and a default configuration of kitchen and bathroom (see Level +5, p.159). The idea is that when young families move in, they might only need

to live on one floor; when the family expands, additional floors and stairs can be added inside the apartment envelope. Anticipating this, windows openings are provided for the future 2nd, 3rd and 4th floors. This gives an unlimited amount of choice to apartment owners for interior configuration.

Each apartment sits on a world(floor) level, with its front door opening into a walkway (like the five-floor-way of shophouses) that is shared by all five apartments of one tower in one world(floor). The 41 towers link to one another by bridges on world(floor) levels.

Building

STAGE 1 - FILIGREE

The highrise building complex is made up of the 41 towers on site, laid out in a grid following the grain of the adjacent shophouses (p.161-87) and Duxton Plain Park (p.164). They are laid out in a density that satisfies the required number of apartments and the stated maximum height of 500 feet. There is a degree of filigree caused by the sheer number of apartments, their windows, the space containing facade (five-floor way and balconies), the vertical gaps between towers and the horizontal gaps between world(floor)s. A first sign of toile is present in the ground floor adjacent to Duxton Plain Park, where blocks are removed to create a continuation of the park (p.166).

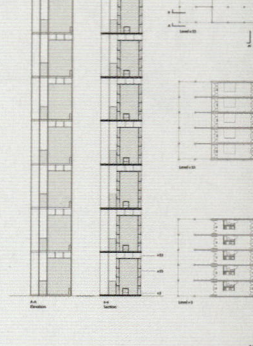

STAGE 2 - DOUBLING THE BUILDING HEIGHT

In Stage 1, any subtraction operation on the building (filigree, etc.) is impossible as it would not leave enough apartments. The building doubles itself in height.

STAGE 3 - SUBTRACTION

A major portion of the building is removed to expose more apartments to light.

STAGE 4 - FURTHER SUBTRACTION

Holes are cut through the building to further expose more apartments to light. There is now an element of toile where the larger holes are noticed before the smaller building gaps.

STAGE 5 - ELEVATOR TOWERS

The building is not served by embedded elevators, but elevator towers are inserted at four points. Elevator A

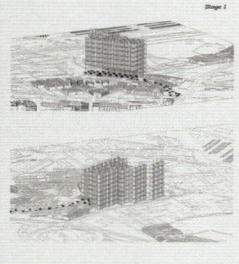

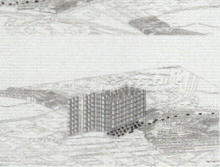

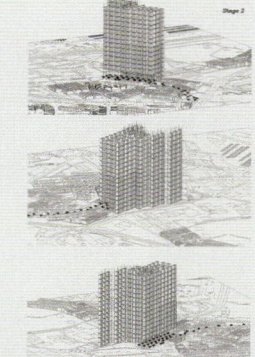

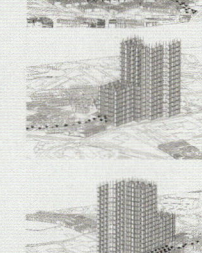

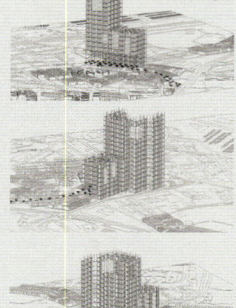

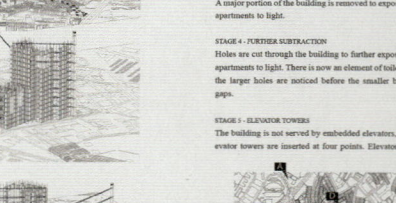

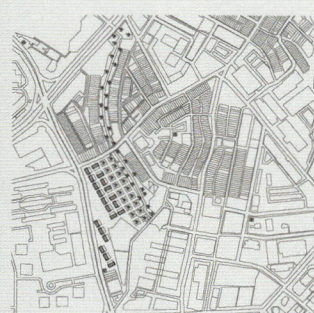

Amiens Cathedral Flipbook

{Filigree & Toile}

The Case of the Gothic Cathedral

In the making of a highrise, a big question is what does the facade do? This series of images strip away the ornament on the facade of Amiens Cathedral a little at a time, starting with the wall relief and details, moving on to the sculptures, and finally taking away even the hierarchy of the apertures and the silhouette of the towers. The generic facade that is generated is subsequently subdivided further to achieve a certain detail density that mirrors the original, but here we can bring into focus the phenomena of "filigree" and "toile", which differentiates the last image from the first.

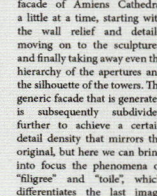

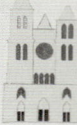

0628

176

C are situated at the two nearest subway stations, Outram Park MRT and Tanjong Pagar MRT. Bridges from these elevator towers then bridge into the apartment complex at every two world(floor) levels. From the entry world(floor), residents can then use the stairs within the complex. Elevator D is situated at an existing carpark which will be extended underground for the new apartment's lots. Elevator B is close to the south tip of the complex and can be used by residents who wish to travel only within the complex and its adjacent ground floor context.

The Anti-Teleportation Elevator

The elevators here counter the teleportation syndrome (p.131) caused by traditional elevators in two ways: First, at the subway station, users emerge in transparent elevators that provide views outside: they are aware of the vertical passing of scenery. Second, extended away from the building they serve, the threshold between elevator portal and world(floor) is increased from the null of traditional elevators to a whole city context.

World(floor) Entry Point

The elevator towers are the beginnings of a future city-scale World(floor) system, acting as entry nodes situated at every subway station (the transportation backbone in Singapore.) The entry from the subway into the city is no longer monopolized by the ground floor (p.179).

177

(Non)Conclusion

When asked what the most shocking thing he saw was, the photographer says it was a beautiful Cathay Pacific air hostess, in full uniform, wheeling her suitcase through the filthy streets.

- An internet magazine interview, 2014 tangbang-museum.org

Greg Girard, the famed photographer of Kowloon Walled City, never forgot the air stewardess he saw more than two decades ago. A shining light in a dark city – a pristine uniform in dirty streets: it isn't the dirt or the darkness that we admire when we dream about the Walled City, and ultimately it is not even the incomprehensible maze of internal streets... it is the human in the architecture.

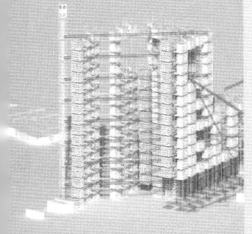
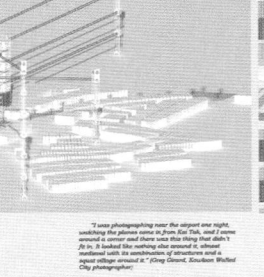

The Anti-Teleportation {Elevator}

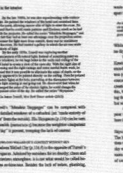

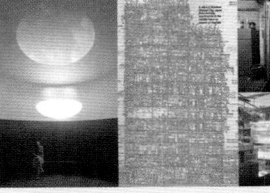

O n
Ornament

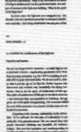

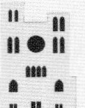

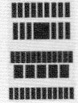

ALREADY THERE

Ramiro Chiriotti Alvarez

Spain

"Already there"

3D URBAN PLANNING SYSTEM

Why we still design cities by dividing the ground in urban plots and defining heights for each building? Why don't we think our cities as a whole, planning them from the three dimensions scale at the same time, allowing us to define positions freely for our constructions in the space (x,y,z axes).

Let's think and create new cities in a three dimensional development system that won't consider the ground as the main one, and will permit to have several of them "floating" on air. That would allow the creation of new green areas on the rooftops, creating new forms of living, working, circulation... and public space relationships.

Thinking about cities through a three dimensional point of view could be a good way of hyper-densifying cities even when they are extremely dense without affecting negatively the existing living conditions. This is the case I examine, taking as an example of a very dense urban fabric: area in the Haizu district in the city of Guangzhou in China.

In many Asian cities, urban development has come about extremely quickly in the last decades, promoting overly dense areas with very low living standards, making life significantly harder for inhabitants.

These zones reflect the culture and history of the country and demonstrate the growing trends in Asia to live in close proximity with small spaces. However these situations are sometimes negative in many aspects and ask for solutions, local way of living cannot be changed overnight doing a complete "tabula rasa". That's why considering examples that took the general 20 planning method, with a complete anarchy resulted into "incredible" monsters like the Kowloon city. Thinking the cities as a whole won't let that happen but will permit a very dense fabric with good quality of air conditions, light, green space access, mobility...

HYPER BUILDING

The "Hyper building" hasn't come out from subjective interests or aesthetics preferences. The project is a direct use and re-interpretation of the existing urban fabric geometry. While it responds to a certain subjective approach, the main concept that shapes the "Hyper building" is that the final form appeared from a parametric composition made by the superposition of existing site layers, extracted from the footprints of the urban fabric connected in a way that every floor is different from the others.

In order to maintain and build new housing and activities structures the project imagines a development where the inhabitants of the existing site will be involved in the decisions of the future city; which buildings will stay, which will be taken down, and how the city performs on a larger scale. The result of that proces would be a mutable and adaptable tower cluster that emerges from the existing conditions to establish a spatial net of buildings and green spaces.

The Hyper building is conceived from the idea of being almost an independent city, with its typology will allow different use distributions, creating and keeping all kind of activities together (commercial spaces, production, offices, schools, health centers, small farming spaces, warehouses...) to maximize the quality of living of its inhabitants.

The overall guiding concept is that the "Hyper building" emerges from the existing fabric like the roots of a tree emerge from the ground. This building develops different density conditions and through this process of increasing build spaces, the building cluster expand horizontally and begins to increase in height, transforming into a tower.

This 3D participation planning system could be adapted to the existing urban fabric of the neighboring areas, as well as in many other Chinese cities, which all have similar conditions and seem to be overlooked as potential interesting sites for new urban poles.

Existing urban fabric

Torn down buildings and creation of new urban plazas

Cores to conect and support the tower clu

Thinking about cities through a three dimensional point of view could be a good way of hyper-densifying cities even when they are extremely dense without negatively affecting the existing living conditions. This is the case to be examined, taking as an example a very dense urban fabric: in the Haizu district in the city of Guangzhou, China. In many Asian cities, urban development has come about extremely quickly in the last decades, promoting overly dense areas with very low standards of living, making life significantly harder for inhabitants. These zones reflect the culture and history of the country and demonstrate the growing trends in Asia to live in close proximity with small spaces. One must keep in mind the local way of living cannot be changed overnight with a complete "tabula rasa". That is why, considering examples that took the general 2D planning method with complete anarchy, resulted in incredible monsters like

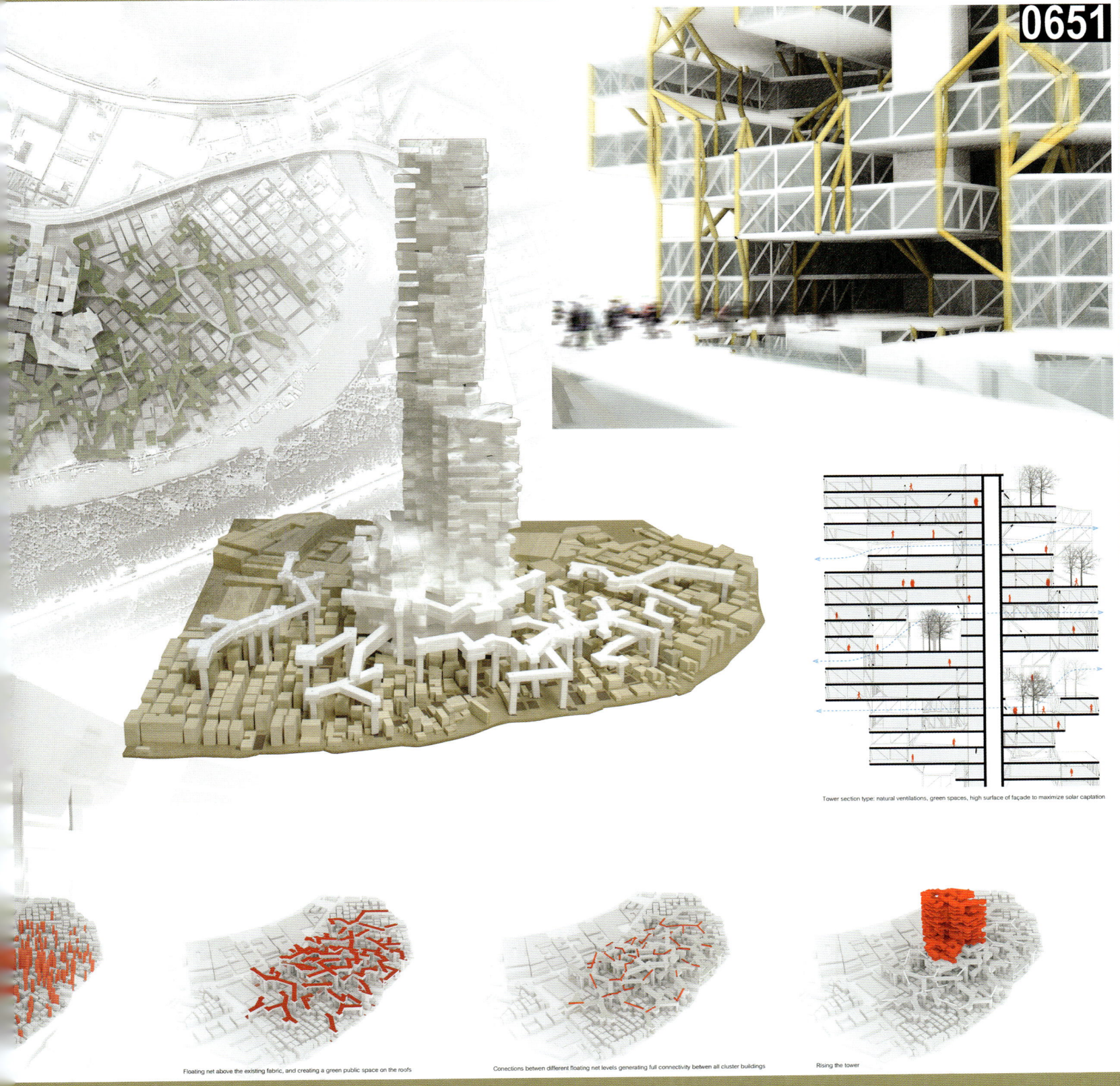

0651

Tower section type: natural ventilations, green spaces, high surface of façade to maximize solar captation

Floating net above the existing fabric, and creating a green public space on the roofs

Conections between different floating net levels generating full connectivity between all cluster buildings

Rising the tower

Kowloon city. Thinking of the cities as a whole would prevent that from happening, and rather permit a very dense fabric while attaining good quality of air conditions, light, green space access, mobility. This 'hyper building' has not come to be from subjective interests or aesthetics preferences. The project is a direct use and re-interpretation of the existing urban fabric geometry. While it responds to a certain subjective approach, the main concept that shapes the 'hyper building' is that the final form appeared from a parametric composition made by the superposition of existing site layers, extracted from the footprints of the urban fabric, connecting them in such a way that each floor is different from the other.

In order to maintain and build new housing and activities structures, the project imagines a development where the inhabitants of the existing site will be involved in the decisions of the future city; which buildings will stay, which will be taken down, and how the city performs on a larger scale.

The base

The base of the hyper building consists of a series of buildings that emerge from the existing fabric by substituting some of the existing buildings through vertical circulation cores.
On top of theses cores, a new series of floor plates appear, connecting the footprints projected in the z coordinates, and establish a new typology that "floats" above the existing fabric.
The original site conditions lack any form of green areas or even a single square meter of open space which greatly detracts from the living conditions of the inhabitants of the island.
The main challenge of the project was to increase the density of the island by adding new buildings while at the same time, maintaining part of the existent and working upon improving its qualities. Also, as part of this process of cleaning up the city, vegetation is incorporated in several places in the exiting fabric.
Vegetation represents a significant factor in the process of cleaning up the city and is incorporated in several locations in the existing fabric such as in the creation of roof top parks on the buildings that rise on the tower's perimeter as well as open gardens in the cavities between floors.

The result of that process would be a malleable and adaptable tower cluster that emerges from the existing conditions to establish a spatial network of buildings and green spaces. The 'hyper building' is conceived from the idea of being an almost entirely independent city, as its typology allows for different use distributions, creating and keeping all kind of activities together (commercial spaces, production, offices, schools, health centers, small farming spaces, warehouses, etc.) to maximize the quality of living for its inhabitants. The overall guiding concept is that the 'hyper building' emerges from the existing fabric like the roots of a tree emerge from the ground. This building develops different density conditions and through this process, the building cluster expands horizontally and begins to increase in height, transforming into a tower.

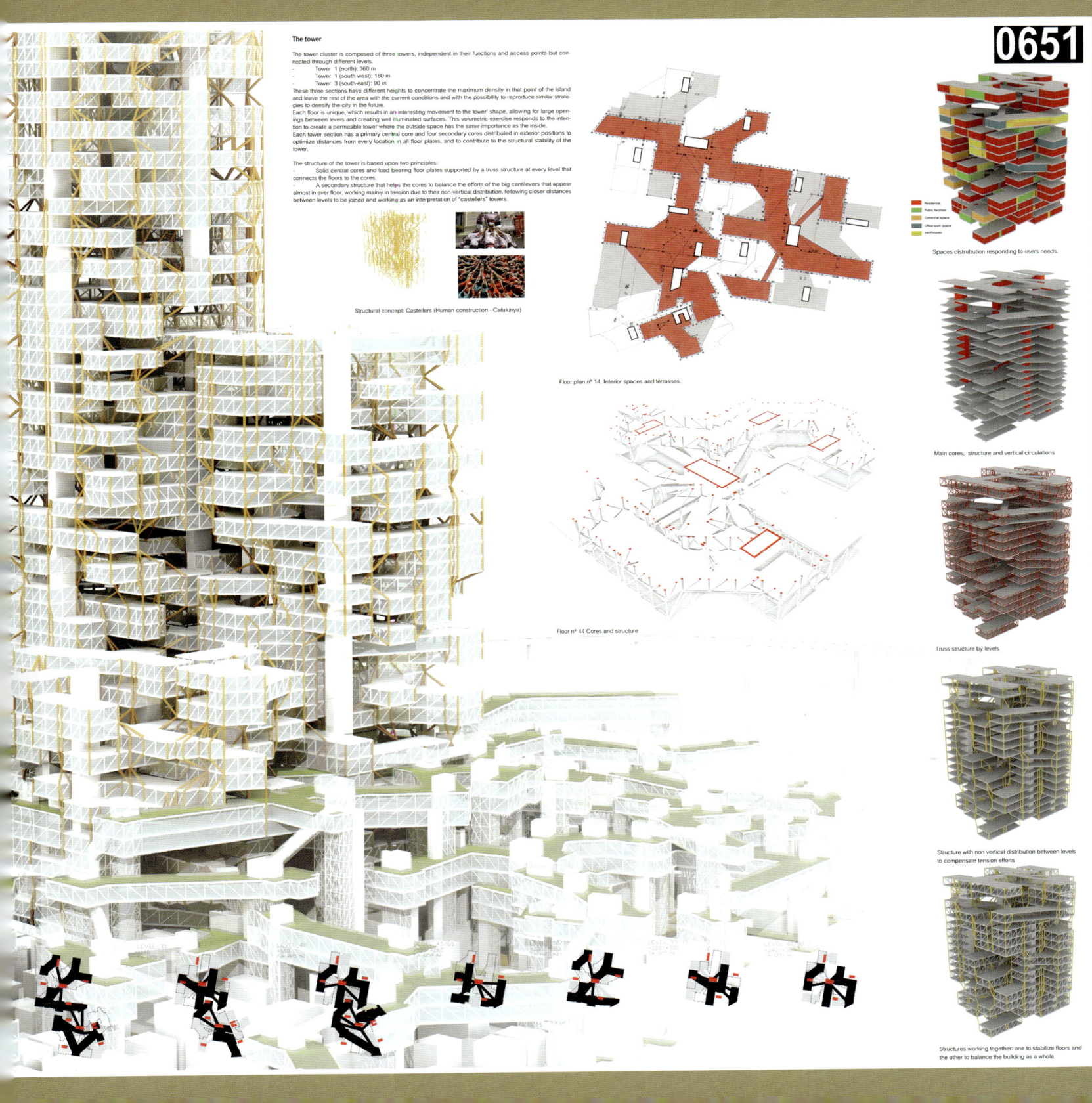

The tower

The tower cluster is composed of three towers, independent in their functions and access points but connected through different levels.
- Tower 1 (north): 360 m
- Tower 1 (south-west): 180 m
- Tower 3 (south-east): 90 m

These three sections have different heights to concentrate the maximum density in that point of the island and leave the rest of the area with the current conditions and with the possibility to reproduce similar strategies to densify the city in the future.
Each floor is unique, which results in an interesting movement to the tower' shape, allowing for large openings between levels and creating well illuminated surfaces. This volumetric exercise responds to the intention to create a permeable tower where the outside space has the same importance as the inside.
Each tower section has a primary central core and four secondary cores distributed in exterior positions to optimize distances from every location in all floor plates, and to contribute to the structural stability of the tower.

The structure of the tower is based upon two principles:
- Solid central cores and load bearing floor plates supported by a truss structure at every level that connects the floors to the cores.
- A secondary structure that helps the cores to balance the efforts of the big cantilevers that appear almost in ever floor, working mainly in tension due to their non-vertical distribution, following closer distances between levels to be joined and working as an interpretation of "castellers" towers.

Structural concept: Castellers (Human construction - Catalunya)

0651

Floor plan nº 14: Interior spaces and terrasses.

Floor nº 44 Cores and structure

Spaces distribution responding to users needs.

Main cores, structure and vertical circulations

Truss structure by levels

Structure with non vertical distribution between levels to compensate tension efforts

Structures working together: one to stabilize floors and the other to balance the building as a whole.

TIMES SQUARED 3015

Blake Freitas
Grace Chen
Alexi Kararavokiris

United States

times squared 3015

Financial district
+ governers mansion

RETAIL - 1
+ 25 floor
+ 800 store

RESIDENT CITY 3 - residence population 12,000
2,800 - 1 bed room
1,800 - 2 bed room
1,800 - 3 bed room

RESIDENT CITY 2 - residence population 12,000
2,800 - 1 bed room
1,800 - 2 bed room
1,800 - 3 bed room

RESIDENT CITY 1 - residence population 8,000
1,800 - 1 bed room
1,000 - 2 bed room
1,000 - 3 bed room

RESIDENCE AMENITIES
- 16 PARKS
- 4 MUSEUMS
- 12 GROCERY STORES
- 50 RESTAURANTS
- 40 SHOPS (mom and pop)
- 3 THEATERS
- 2 ELEMENTARY SCHOOLS
- 4 ATHLETIC FACILITIES
- 4,000 ACRES FARM PLOTS

EMPIRE STATE BUILDING

CAMPUS - 1
+ 35 floor
+ 5,000 private offices
+ campus amenities

RETAIL - 1
+ 25 floor
+ 800 store
+ Red wood forest 1

VIEW AT 400 FT

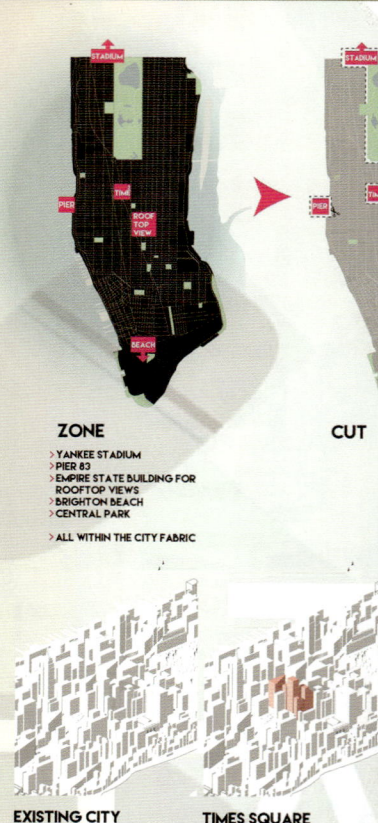

ZONE   CUT

> YANKEE STADIUM
> PIER 83
> EMPIRE STATE BUILDING FOR
  ROOFTOP VIEWS
> BRIGHTON BEACH
> CENTRAL PARK

> ALL WITHIN THE CITY FABRIC

EXISTING CITY   TIMES SQUARE

TIMES SQUARED 3015 EMBRACES THE PROBLEMS OF OVERPOPULATION, FARM PRODUCTION, OXYGEN GENERATION, AND THE REPURPOSING OF OBSOLETE INFRASTRUCTURE. AS POPULATION LEVELS CONTINUE TO EXPLODE, THIS TOWER EXPLORES THE SPATIAL, ENVIRONMENTAL, AND EXPERIMENTAL POSSIBILITIES OF VERTICAL LIVING IN THE FUTURE.

THE TOWER GROUNDS ITSELF IN THE HEART OF THE CITY THAT NEVER SLEEPS: TIMES SQUARE, NEW YORK CITY. THE EXISTING FRAMEWORK OF TIMES SQUARE TAKES ON A DIFFERENT, THREE-DIMENSIONAL FORM, AS THE TOWER RISES ABOVE IT, DRIVING THE CONCEPT OF MANHATTANIZATION TO NEW HEIGHTS. PEAKING OVER A MILE ABOVE THE CITY, THE TOWER PUSHES THE BOUNDARIES OF HOW VERTICAL A SKYSCRAPER CAN BE. WHEN FULLY TAKEN ADVANTAGE OF, TIMES SQUARED 3015 PROVES THE SKYSCRAPER TYPOLOGY CAPABLE OF FITTING AN ENTIRE CITY WITHIN ITSELF.

As our planet continues to overpopulate, 'Times Squared 3015' is an opportunity to explore the spatial, environmental, and experimental possibilities of vertical living. This tower embraces the problems of overpopulation, farm production, oxygen generation, and the re-purposing of obsolete infrastructure.

The tower grounds itself in the heart of the city that never sleeps: Times Square, New York City.   The existing framework of Times Square takes on a different, three-dimensional form, as the tower rises above it, driving the concept of Manhattanization to new heights.   Peaking over a mile above the city, the tower pushes the boundaries of how vertical a skyscraper can be.   When fully taken advantage of, 'Times Squared 3015' proves the skyscraper typology capable of fitting an entire city within itself.

Vertical farming, a beach, a mountain range, a stadium, a redwood forest, housing, and offices -

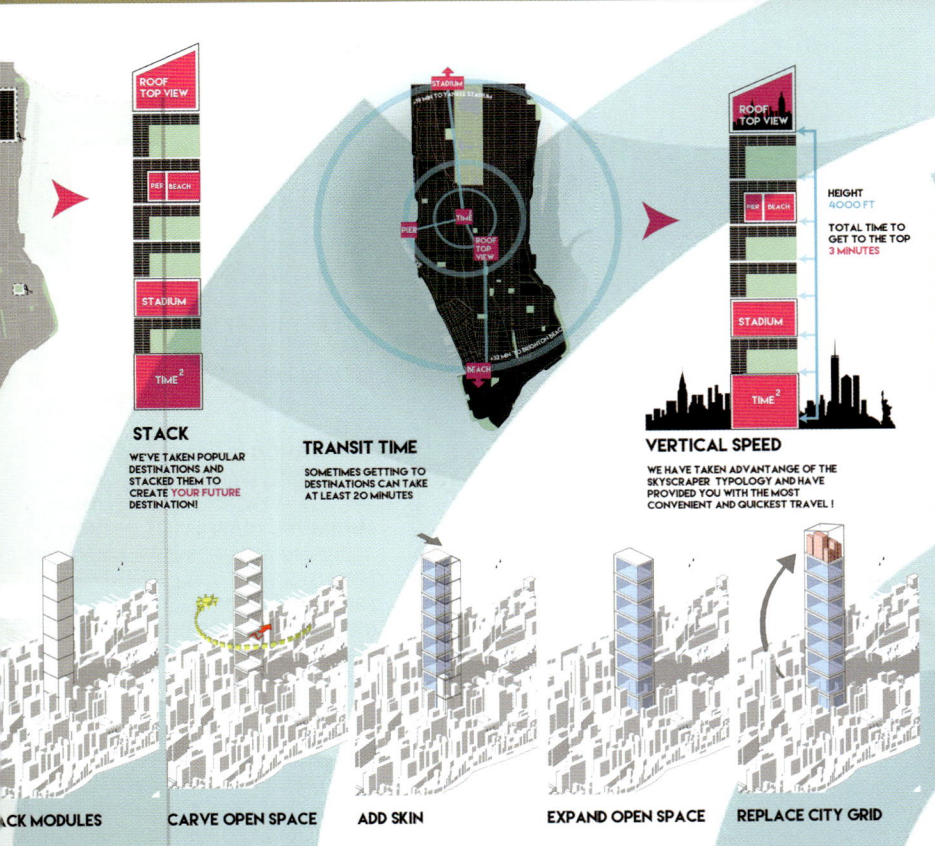

MOUNTAIN MODULE + 4500 FT

VERTICAL FARMING, A BEACH, A MOUNTAIN RANGE, A STADIUM, A REDWOOD FOREST, HOUSING, AND OFFICES -- DESTINATIONS THAT ARE NORMALLY FARTHER APART, ARE NOW STACKED VERTICALLY. EACH ONE OF THESE DESTINATION ZONES CONSISTS OF AN INDIVIDUALIZED BLOCK OR MODULE, MUCH LIKE THE DIFFERENT DISTRICTS IN A HORIZONTAL CITY. OPEN SPACE IS CARVED OUT OF THE THE SOUTH-FACING SIDE OF THE MODULE FOR MAXIMUM SOLAR EXPOSURE, REGULATING THE DESTINATION ENVIRONMENTS WITHIN. THIS CREATES A SERIES OF L-SHAPED 'LIVING' CLUSTERS -- THE CITY FABRIC -- THAT SURROUND AND INTEGRATE WITH THE NATURAL ENVIRONMENT.

REDWOOD FOREST MODULE + 2500 FT

SKY CITY + 5500 FT

destinations that are normally farther apart - are now stacked vertically.   Each one of these destination zones consists of an individualized block or module, much like ¬the different districts in a horizontal city. Open space is carved out of the south-facing side of the module for maximum solar exposure, regulating the destination environments within. This creates a series of L-shaped 'living' clusters - the city fab¬ric - that surround and integrate with the natural environment.

  Located above and below the residential/destination modules are a series of retail-themed entertainment modules or 'sky malls' that draw upon the vitality of Times Square and extend the same excitement and energy vertically throughout the tower.   Finally, using the idea of the skyscraper as makeshift observation deck, an enclosed city in the sky resides at the very top of the tower, providing

5,687 ft.

5,280 ft.
12.2 psi atmosphere

MOUNTAIN PARK

RETAIL WORLD 3

VERTICAL FARMS

RESIDENCE 5

RESIDENCE 4

REDWOOD PARK

RETAIL WORLD 2

SOUTH BEACH

VIEW AT 5000 FT

LOCATED ABOVE AND BELOW THE RESIDENTIAL / DESTINATION MODULES ARE A SERIES OF RETAIL-THEMED ENTERTAINMENT MODULES OR 'SKY MALLS' THAT DRAW UPON THE VITALITY OF TIMES SQUARE AND EXTEND THE SAME EXCITEMENT AND ENERGY VERTICALLY THROUGHOUT THE TOWER. FINALLY, USING THE IDEA OF THE SKYSCRAPER AS MAKESHIFT OBSERVATION DECK, AN ENCLOSED CITY IN THE SKY RESIDES AT THE VERY TOP OF THE TOWER, PROVIDING DIZZYING VIEWS OF THE CITY WITHIN A CITY.

CIRCULATION IS HANDLED BY THE MAIN CORE, A MASSIVE ELEVATOR SYSTEM / VERTICAL SUBWAY THAT MINIMIZES TRAVEL TIME BY ONLY STOPPING AT THE TWELVE MAJOR MODULES THAT MAKE UP THE TOWER. FROM THERE, TRAVELERS NEED ONLY USE A SERIES OF SECONDARY ELEVATORS / STAIRS TO JOURNEY VERTICALLY WITHIN EACH MODULE.

THIS VERTICAL ORGANIZATION INTRODUCES A NEW KIND OF DAILY LIFE. FARMERS TEND TO VERTICAL FARMS THAT TAKE ADVANTAGE OF SOUTHERN EXPOSURE AND PROVIDE OXYGEN AND SUSTENANCE TO THE TOWER'S COMMUNITY. RESIDENTS HAVE A BEACH OR A REDWOOD FOREST RIGHT IN THEIR OWN BACKYARD. A SHOPPING MALL OR THE LATEST FOOTBALL GAME ARE JUST AN ELEVATOR RIDE AWAY. ALL OF THESE FACTORS COMBINE TO CREATE A LIVELY AND DYNAMIC SELF-SUSTAINING CITY EXPERIENCE FOR A RAPIDLY GROWING FUTURE POPULATION.

dizzing views of the city within a city.

   Circulation is handled by the main core, a massive elevator system/vertical subway that minimizes travel time by only stopping at the twelve major modules that make up the tower.   From there, travelers need only use a series of secondary elevators / stairs to journey vertically within each module.

   This vertical organization introduces a new kind of daily life. Farmers tend to vertical farms that take advantage of southern exposure and provide oxygen and sustenance to the tower's community. Residents have a beach or a redwood forest right in their own backyard. A shopping mall or the latest football game are just an elevator ride away. All of these factors combine to create a lively and dynamic self-sustaining city experience for a rapidly growing future population.

0745

WORLD'S LARGEST CORPORATE CAMPUS

VERTICAL FARMING / OXYGEN GENERATION

WORLD'S ONLY INDOOR REDWOOD FOREST

CITY IN THE SKY

SOUTH BEACH

GIANTS STADIUM

'TIMES SQUARE²' ENTERTAINMENT BLOCK

THE DISPLACEMENT SKYSCRAPER
Ko Anthony Chun Ming

Hong Kong

'a building **inherits** buildings'

boats and ships perform the salvation by moving the abandoned from their origin to Harumi in Tokyo Bay, an artificial island where the project took place, the displaced are then processed through the factory on-site, granting them a new aura relationship while inheriting their memories as well. the whole architecture is an empty framework sitting on the site. through the architectural salvation, it will continually be infilled with the reclaimed objects and buildings in phases and in the end it attains saturation. it is an architecture that inherits buildings, not hiding what we abandoned, but acknowledging their efforts to create our memories.

THE '**DISPLACEMENT**' / 'There are **values** more than the object is priced of.'

project statement

In this 21st century, the act of cities throwing away architectures and everything that contributed to their present scene is no longer strange to the eyes. Everyday there are buildings being torn down, immeasurable amount of objects being abandoned and sent to landfill sites in an overwhelming rate. Our neighborhood changed progressively, eventually it became a place we are no longer familiar with.

In Japan, the government created artificial islands within Tokyo Bay as a method to bury the evidence of earthquakes debris and also, indirectly reduce landfills. Unwanted objects are then hidden beneath as reclaimed lands; their aura, existence and contribution to the city are obscured.

It is urgent that a revolt is needed to criticize on the erasing actions of human and cities without considering the true values of the removed.

The 'Displacement' is to evoke the nostalgic emotion of mankind, through architectural salvage to regenerate the abandoned and hence turnaround their fate to be forgotten. Boats and ships perform the salvation by moving the abandoned from their origin to Harumi in Tokyo Bay, an artificial island where the project took place.

The salvaged are then processed through the factory on-site, granting them a new aura relationship while inheriting their memories as well. The whole architecture is an empty framework sitting on this site. Through the architectural salvation, it will continually be infilled with the reclaimed objects and buildings in phases and in the end it attains saturation. It is an architecture that inherits buildings, Not hiding what we abandoned, but acknowledging their efforts to create our memories.

In the 21st Century, the act of cities throwing away architectures and everything that contributed to their present scene is no longer strange to the eyes. Everyday there are buildings being torn down, immeasurable amount of objects being abandoned and sent to landfills at an overwhelming rate. Neighborhoods change progressively, eventually becoming a place we are no longer familiar with.

In Japan, the government created artificial islands within Tokyo Bay as a method to bury the evidence of earthquakes debris and also, indirectly reduce landfills. Unwanted objects are then hidden beneath as reclaimed lands. Their existence and contribution to the city are obscured.

It is urgent; a revolt is needed to criticize on the erasing actions of human and cities without considering the true values of what it is demolished.

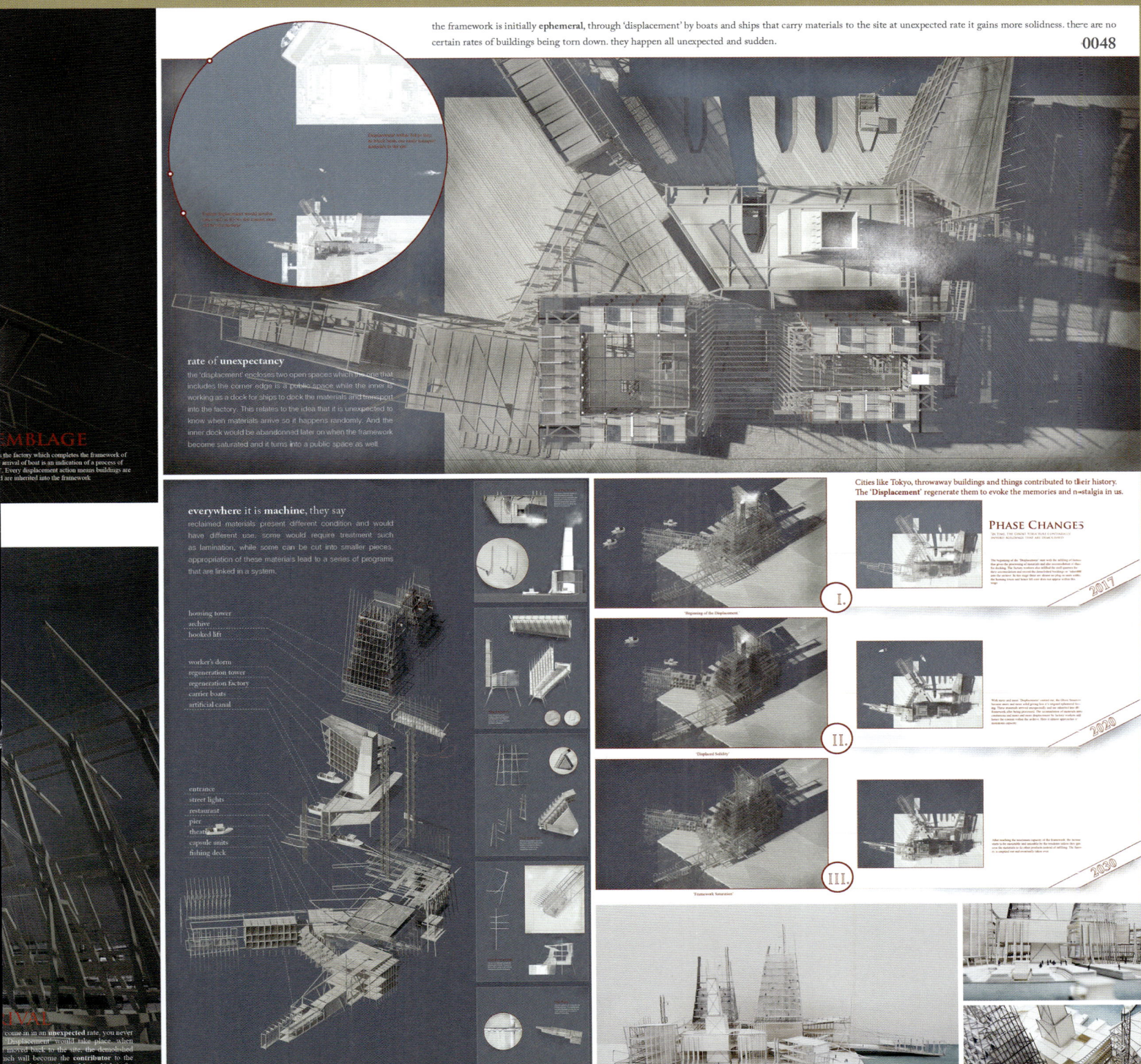

THE DISPLACEMENT

The 'Displacement' is to evoke the nostalgic emotion of mankind, through architectural salvage to regenerate the abandoned and hence turnaround their fate to be forgotten. Boats and ships perform the salvation by moving the abandoned from their origin to Harumi in Tokyo Bay, an artificial island where the project took place.

The salvaged are then processed through the factory on-site, granting them a new aura relationship while inheriting their memories as well. The whole architecture is an empty framework sitting on the site. Through the architectural salvation, it will continually be infilled with the reclaimed objects and buildings in phases and in the end it attains saturation. It is an architecture that inherits buildings. Not hiding what we abandoned, but acknowledging their efforts to create our memories.

the 'Displacement' first introduces scheme that boats or ships carry demolished and forgotten buildings or objects across Tokyo Bay to the artificial island site in Tokyo, Harumi, then on site, it regenerate the collected ones by inheriting into this megastructure which is a 'ghosted structure' giving different scale of displaced activities.

the framework gives a sense of **ephemeral and emptiness** and when displacement start to take place it 'fills up' the framework with the reclaimed objects as it became more and more solid, the whole event is not only a revolt of the abandoned, it also gently evoke our nostalgia, which is how do we value things that are not 'valuable' but culturally important or important to us personally due to memories of us.

0048

register to the 'displacement'

when people move in as residence, the action that they bring in the '**flatpack units**' by the **hooked lift** and assemble their house with **structures recycled from construction sites** and materials from the 'displacement' become an act of infilling of framework, which re-aura the materials that lost their identity and use and meaning.

人造の島

Memories and **the evidence of our life is lost. We are no more nostalgic.**

There is always something more valuable than what it is priced.

'Hard Edge' of islands, make us lose touch to our environment.

Tokyo Gov. 'Re-claim' to boost their Economics since WWII.

Dematerialize the collected objects to make 'Nostalgic' but not to provoke melancholic.

Objects are 'defamiliarized' to give new 'Attachment' or 'Aura' to it.

  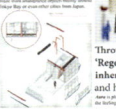

the **everyday** culture of people's **oblivion** at **21**st century, is an **implication** of *our* losing **attachment** to where we belong.

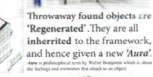  

in Tokyo Bay

The DISPLACEMENT, is 'culturally sustainable'. People are 'registered' or 'participated' in the event as they move in.

to the *mistrust* of land of the *metabolist* : - kiyonori kikutake -

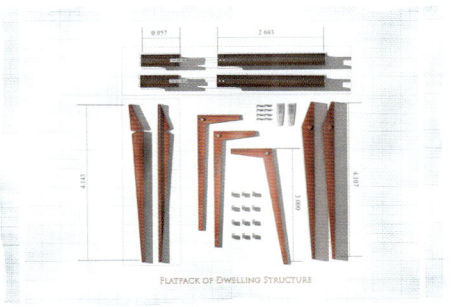

flatpack

the idea of **flatpack** is to enhance the way plug-in units can be set up in the framework. to smoothen the setting up, flatpack can allow users to carry their units easily through the lifts with hook that can then carry all these skeletal structures to the floors theirs want to live in.

FLATPACK OF DWELLING STRUCTURE

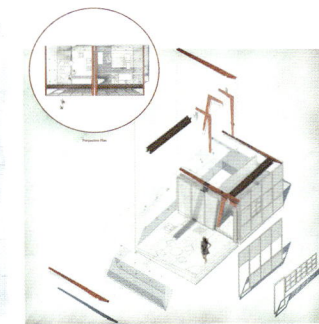

fast assemble units

skeletal structures refer to **jean prouve**'s units that look 8 minutes by 3 people to construct a livable units. the design is a '**found object**' by workers carry out 'displacement'.

SENSORY SKYSCRAPER

Alexandr Pincov
Heng Chang

China, Moldova

SEN

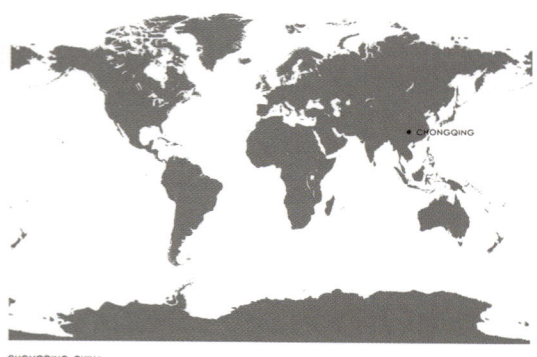

CHONGQING, CHINA

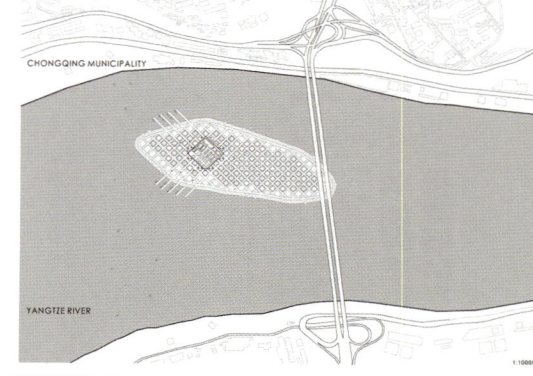

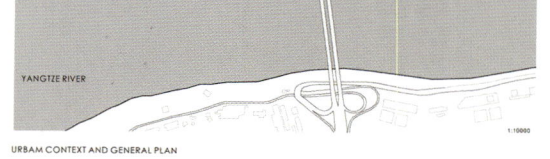

URBAM CONTEXT AND GENERAL PLAN

1:10060

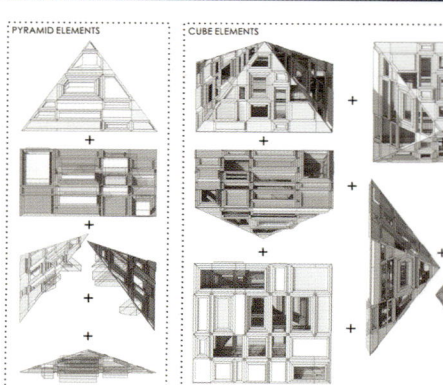

"SENSORY" COMPOSITION ELEMENTS - 3D SCHEME

PYRAMID ELEMENTS

CUBE ELEMENTS

Modernization and globalization symbolize human advancement in the 21st Century, but life in big "modern" cities is difficult and focuses only on work. Modernization, despite of all the conveniences it brings, it also devours people's feelings, sensory information and emotions.

The Sensory Skyscraper was conceived for an island in the Yangtze River in the Chongqing Municipality, China. Landform, environment and climate deprive the local society of perceptual experiences. This project is a multifunctional laboratory of scientific exploration on human senses, perceptions, rehabilitation of sensory information, rehabilitation of experience effects, and rehabilitation of motivations and expectations.

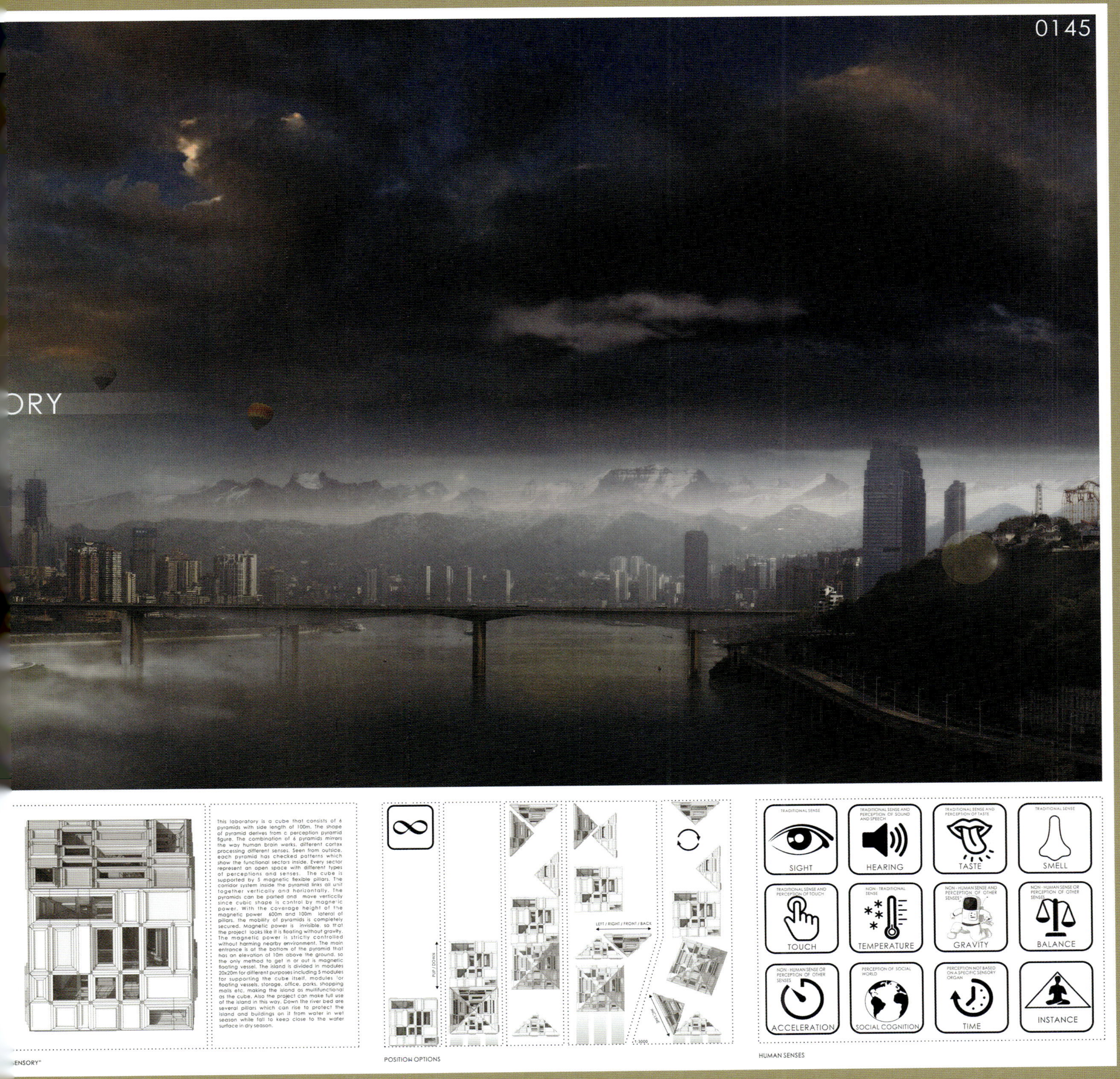

0145

...ORY

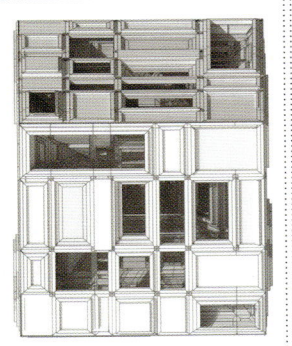

This laboratory is a cube that consists of 6 pyramids with side length of 100m. The shape of pyramid derives from a perception pyramid figure. The combination of 6 pyramids mirrors the way human brain works, different cortex processing different senses. Seen from outside, each pyramid has checked patterns which show the functional sectors inside. Every sector represent an open space with different types of perceptions and senses. The cube is supported by 5 magnetic flexible pillars. The corridor system inside the pyramids links all unit together vertically and horizontally. The pyramids can be parallel and move vertically since cubic shape is control by magnetic power. With the coverage height of the magnetic power 600m and 100m lateral of pillars, the mobility of pyramids is completely secured. Magnetic power is invisible, so that the project looks like it is floating without gravity. The magnetic power is strictly controlled without harming nearby environment. The main entrance is at the bottom of the pyramid that has an elevation of 10m above the ground, so the only method to get in or out is magnetic floating vessel. The island is divided in modules 20x20m for different purposes including 5 modules for supporting the cube itself, modules for floating vessels, storage, office, parks, shopping malls etc, making the island as multifunctional as the cube. Also the project can make full use of the island in this way. Down the river bed are several pillars which can rise to protect the island and buildings on it from water in wet season while fall to keep close to the water surface in dry season.

"SENSORY"

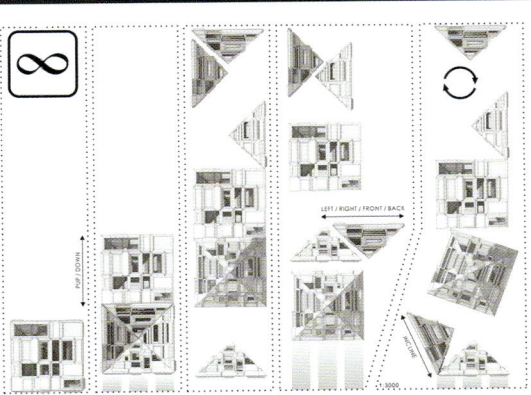

POSITION OPTIONS

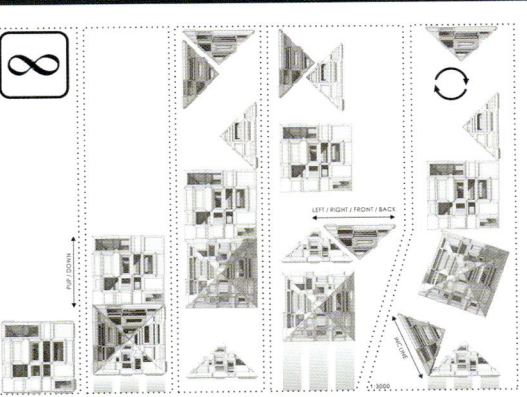

LEFT / RIGHT / FRONT / BACK

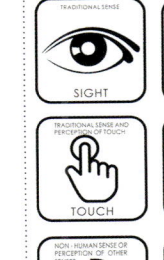

CLOSE

SIGHT

HEARING

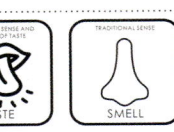

TASTE

SMELL

TOUCH

TEMPERATURE

GRAVITY

BALANCE

ACCELERATION

SOCIAL COGNITION

TIME

INSTANCE

HUMAN SENSES

This laboratory is a cube that consists of 6 pyramids with a side length of 100 meters. The combination of 6 pyramids mirrors the way human brain works, different cortex process different senses. Seen from outside, each pyramid has specific patterns which show the functional sectors inside. Every sector represents an open space for different types of perceptions and senses and five magnetic flexible pillars support the cubes. The corridor system inside the pyramid links all the units together both vertically and horizontally.

The pyramids can be parted and move vertically since the cubic shape is controlled by magnetic power. With a coverage height of the magnetic power to 600 meters and 100 meters laterally from the pillars, the mobility of the pyramids is completely secured. The main entrance is at the bottom of the

"SENSORY"

NON - TRADITIONAL SENSE "BALANCE, ACCELERATION, TEMPERATURE ETC." • NON - HUMAN SENSES "GRAVITY" • NON - SENSORY ORGAN PERCEPTION "TIME" • PERCEPTION OF OTHER SENSES

TRADITIONAL SENSES "TASTE AND SMELL" AND PERCEPTION OF TASTE

TRADITIONAL SENSE "TOUCH" AND PERCEPTION OF TOUCH

BASE PLAN - TRADITIONAL SENSE "SIGHT"

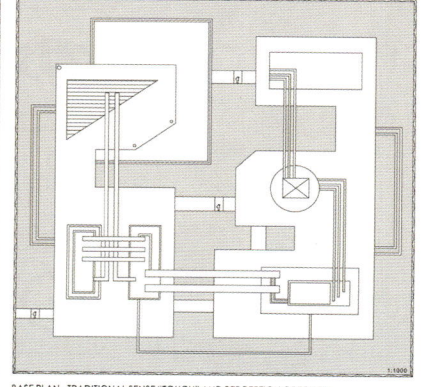

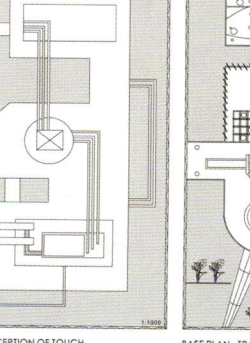

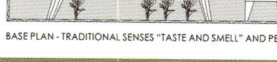

BASE PLAN - TRADITIONAL SENSE "TOUCH" AND PERCEPTION OF TOUCH

BASE PLAN - TRADITIONAL SENSES "TASTE AND SMELL" AND PERCEPTION OF TASTE

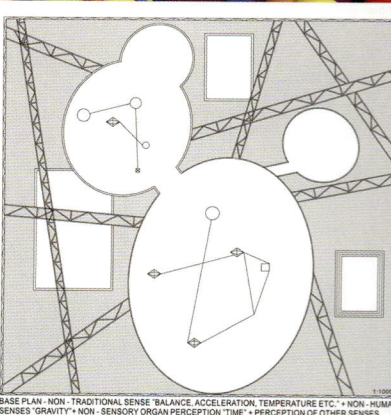

BASE PLAN - NON - TRADITIONAL SENSE "BALANCE, ACCELERATION, TEMPERATURE ETC." • NON - HUMAN SENSES "GRAVITY" • NON - SENSORY ORGAN PERCEPTION "TIME" • PERCEPTION OF OTHER SENSES

pyramid that has an elevation of 10 meters above the ground and the only way to get in or out is through a magnetic floating vessel. The island is divided in modules of 20 x20 meters for different purposes including 5 modules for supporting the cube itself, modules for floating vessels, storage, office, parks, and shopping malls.

Once humans regain their sensory perceptions they can better understand their origins, potentials, and natural environment, thus get rid of the downside of modernization and enjoy life.

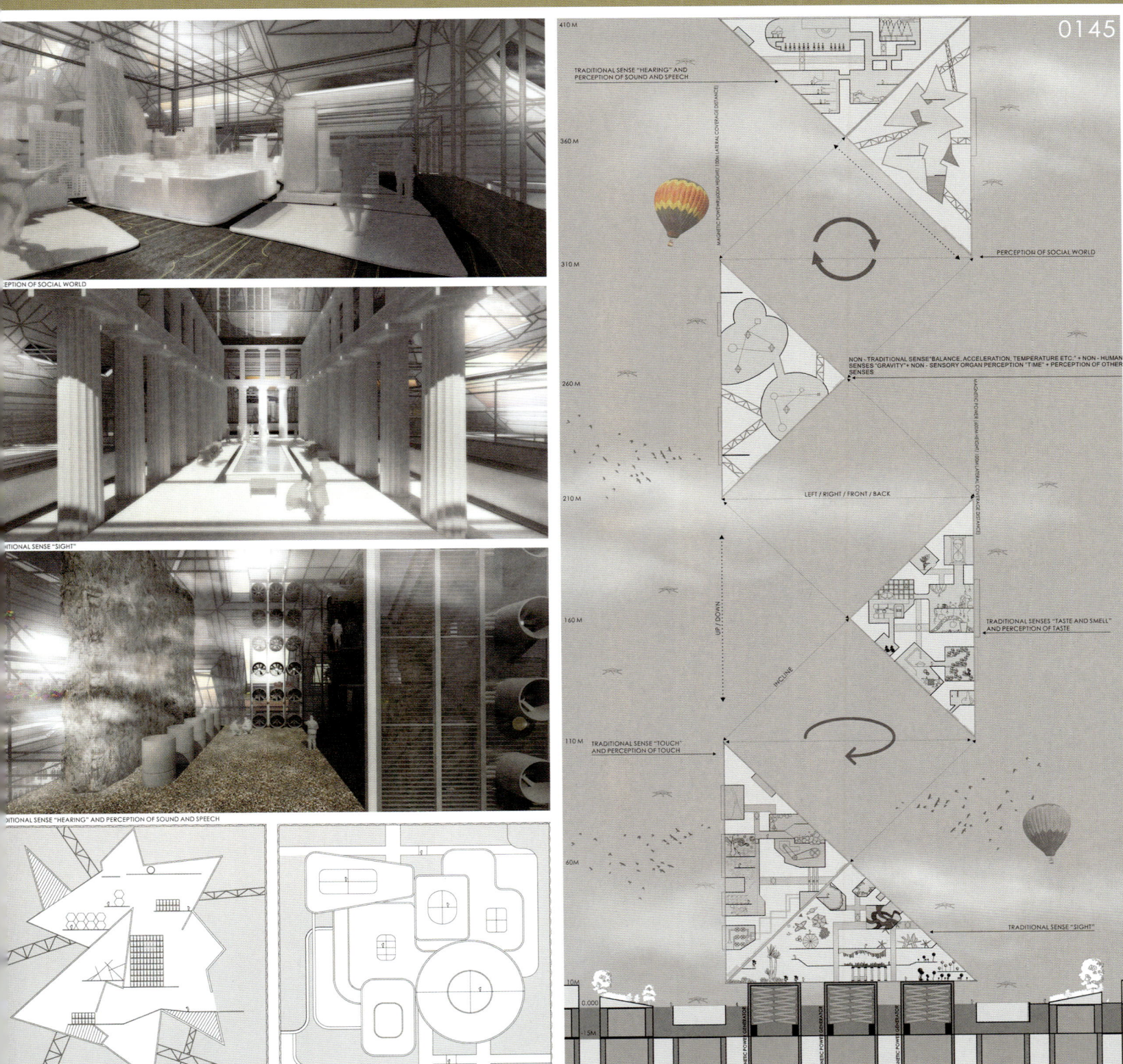

TOWARDS UNITY
SUTURING CYPRUS

Lin Rujia

China

"Towards U

—— Suturing "UN Buf

Cyprus, an island in the Mediterranean is a divided country between Greeks and Turks. Nicosia is the capital of Cyprus and it's the only city divided in two in the world since 1974.

The demographic composition of Nicosia consists of Turks who live in northern cities and Greeks who live in southern cities.   There were lots of public spaces and facilities in the "UN Buffer Zone" before Cyprus was divided and people needed them. But at the same time, the "UN Buffer Zone" became a barrier between the two parts because of it's a limit of height. Both Turks and Greeks in Nicosia are looking forward to a unified country.

This project changes the horizontal "UN Buffer Zone" and public spaces near it to a vertical direction. Both Turks and Greeks ordinary life will have an intersection in the new skyscrapers.

0202

Background

1. Cyprus , an island in the Mediterranean , which is a divided country . Cyprus is divided by Turkey and Greece . Nicosia is the capital of Cyprus and it's the only one divided city in the world now .
2. "UN Buffer Zone" is the boundaries between the northern area and the southern area of Cyprus .
3. All the people in Cyprus are looking forward to unifying .

Concept Diagram

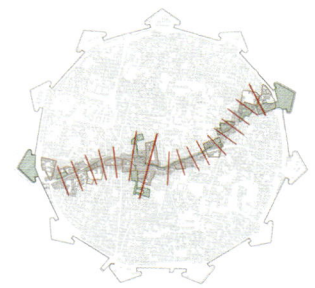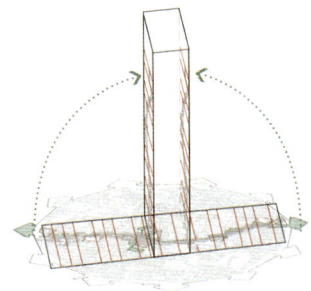

Nicosia is the capital of Cyprus and it is the only one divided city in the world which was split into two parts since 1974 . Two parts were divided by "UN Buffer Zone" which was made up of buildings , fences , walls and so on .
The demographic composition of nicosia consist of Turks who live in northern cities and Greeks who live in southern cities . There were lots of public spaces and facilities in the "UN Buffer Zone" before Cyprus were divided and people needed them . But at the same time , the "UN Buffer Zone" became a barrier between the two parts because of it's a limit of height . Both Turks and Greek in Nicosia are looking forward to a unified country very much but the "UN Buffer Zone" seems that it can't be overstepped .
So I decided to change the horizontal " UN Buffer Zone " and public spaces near it to vertical direction , and then the limit of height would be broken . Both Turks' and Greek's ordinary life will have intersection in the skyscrapers and the connection can't be limited any more . So we can suturing Cyprus !
There're three design points of the "Unify Monument" skyscrapers :
1. Looking at it for each time , people in Cyprus could remember those periods that Cyprus were split into two parts .
2. Water is one of the most important elements for people in Nicosia . Water in vertical " UN Buffer Zone " can make people know that we connected the two parts with " water " , and this is an important function of the skyscrapers .
3. These skyscrapers distribute in all the main areas of Cyprus which are passed through by the " UN Buffer Zone " . So the whole Cyprus will be "sutured" by these skyscrapers because all the people will go into them for public spaces .

All main cities in Cyprus will build one skyscraper like Nicosia and each one will set up a corresponding relationship with the part of " UN Buffer Zone " in each city , and then , the whole country will be sutured by these skyscrapers .
In conclusion , the skyscraper is a silent announcement to Cyprus's Unity .

Function Diagram

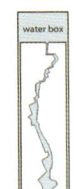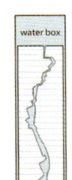

Suture Cyprus By The Skyscrapers - "Towards Unity"

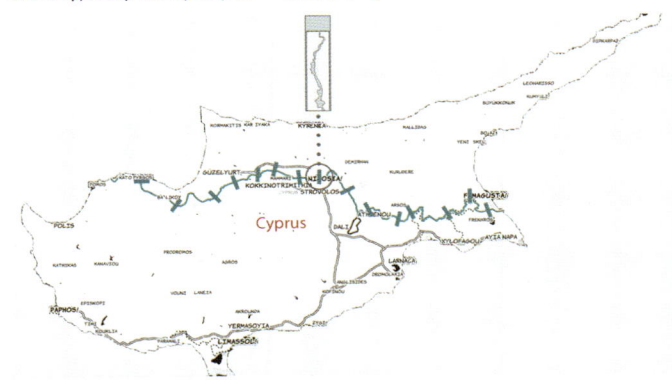

ity" — Suturing Cyprus

one" in Cyprus by skyscrapers along it

There are three design points of the "Unify Monument" skyscrapers:

1) Looking at it for each time, people in Cyprus could remember those periods that Cyprus were split into two parts.

2) Water is one of the most important elements for people in Nicosia. Water in vertical "UN Buffer Zone" can make people know that we connected the two parts with "water", and this is an important function of the skyscrapers.

3) These skyscrapers distribute in all the main areas of Cyprus, which are passed through by the "UN Buffer Zone".

So the whole Cyprus will be "sutured" by these skyscrapers because all the people will go into them

[Freshwater System]
In rainy days , the freshwater system designed can collect rainwater and store it . At the same time , the freshwater system can get seawater transported from the sea and desalinate .

[City Public Spaces]
For attracting citizen to gather into the skyscrapers , I extracted all the main elements of public spaces of Cyprus like theaters , zoos , factories , gardens and so on .

[Monument : Unity]
As a monument for unifying , I designed two vertical rivers in the elevations of each skyscraper . The reversal strategy can emphasize the moral of unifying .

[Nature Landscapes]
Cities in Cyprus have some nature landscapes but they are not enough for morden city life . So I add more nature landscapes into the bottom of these skyscrapers .

[Viewing Rampway]
The rampways between up and down floors are not only connecting structures but also viewing platforms in the skyscrapers . People can even see the whole country on the top of the skyscrapers .

[Atrium Space]
The atrium spaces in the skyscraper can make the space between up and down floors more abundant . At the same time , people can get a wide field of vision when they are near the atrium spaces .

Plans & Freshwater System Structure

City Public Spaces Plan   City Park Plan   Church Space Plan   Nature Landscapes Plan

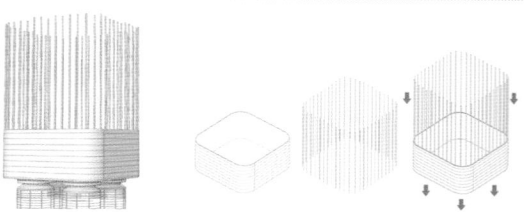

[Water Collecting Center] : It's a water collecting equipment on the top of the skyscraper . It's connected with the " water treatment center " by tubes on the bottom of the collecting boxes . The water collecting center consist of two parts :
1. The collecting box on the bottom of the water collecting center is used to store rainwater for a little time and then the water will be transported to the water treatment center .
2. Thin tubes on the top can increase the area of collecting rainwater .

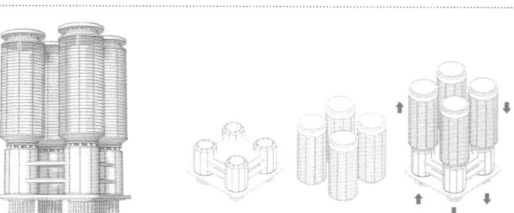

[Water Treatment Center] : It's the most important part in the top of the skyscraper . Rainwater and sea water that is transported here can be collected and stored here , and then , water here can be purified .
1. The vertical "UN Buffer Zone" is full of water and the water is provided by the water treatment center continuously .
2. Cities can get enough water to use for citizen's lives or industry at any time .

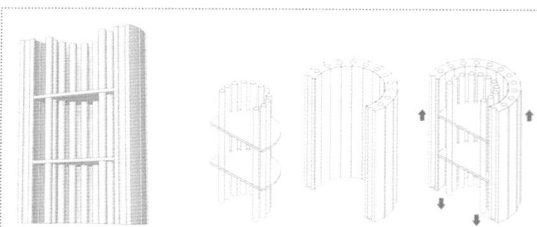

[Vertical Transport Center] : It's the main parts to transport water from "water treatment center". The shape of water transport center comes from plant screen and at the same time the shape has its' own advantages on transporting water .
1. The inner tubes mainly transport water from the top of the skyscraper to the bottom of it and then , the water will be transported to cities .
2. The outer tubes mainly transport seawater to the top for desalination .

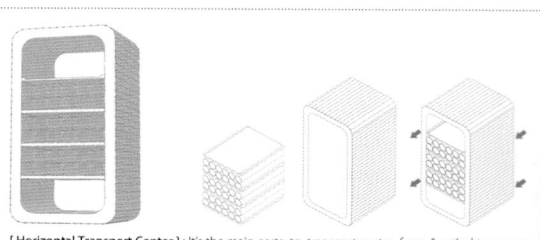

[Horizontal Transport Center] : It's the main parts to transport water from "vertical transport center" to cities . The tubes are divided into three parts in three floors . There are thick shells wrapped the tubes so they can get enough spaces to transport a lot of water in high speed .
1. Tubes have equipments to control the speed of water in them so the water can meet the water pressure demands of different city users .
2. Different tubes transport water to different city users like lives , industry and public services .

for public spaces.

All main cities in Cyprus will build one skyscraper like Nicosia and each one will set up a corresponding relationship with the part of "UN Buffer Zone" in each city, and then, the whole country will be sutured by these skyscrapers.

Section - For example , Nicosia's Skyscraper

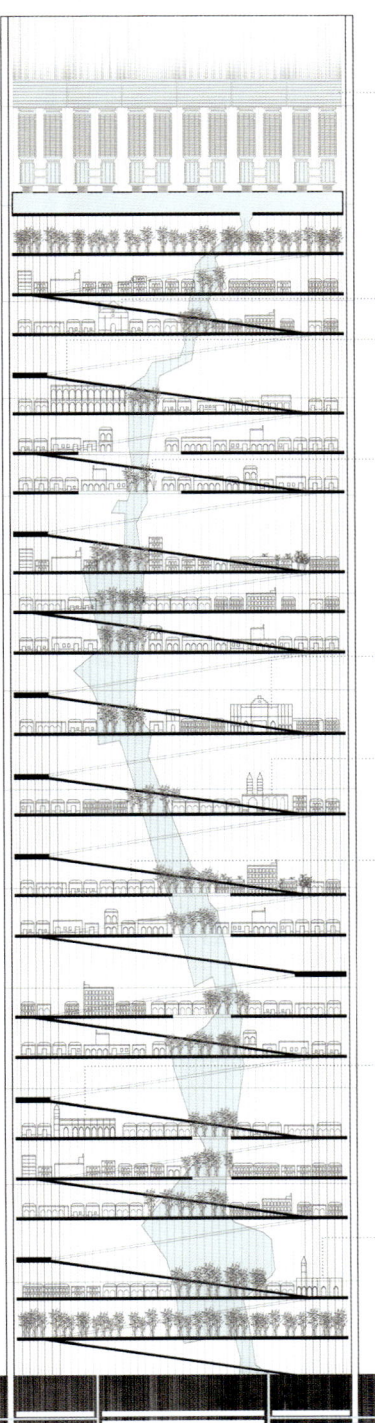

825.000m ▼

[Symbol 01] :
The height of the skyscraper is 825m and it's a symbol of the radius of old nicosia city .

[Symbol 02] :
The " river " on the surface of the skyscraper is a symbol of "UN Buffer Zone".
At the same time , it's a sym -bol of the split country for over 40 years .

[Symbol 03] :
Houses in the skyscraper are the city buildings near the " UN Buffer Zone " changed into vertical direction and it is the symbol of unifying by non-destructive methods .

[Thunder Strom]
The rainwater is one of the main water sources for the whole Cyprus .

[Nicosia's Reservoir]
The reservoir is one of the main ways to store fresh water by natural methods for the whole country .

[Holy Cross Catholic Church]
The Holy Cross Catholic Church is one of the main church near the western boundary of Nicosia .

[Buyuk Han]
Buyuk Han is the largest caravansarai on the island of Cyprus .

[Monument]
The monument is located on the " UN Buffer Zone " and it repersents the wish that all people in Cyprus are looking forward to unifying .

[Belediye Pazari]
Belediye Pazari is one of the oldest and biggest market in the center of old Nicosia .

[Selimiye Mosque]
The Selimiye Mosque is the biggest and oldest mosque in Nicosia .

[E.Cetin Street]
The Cetin Street is one of the most famous business street near the " UN Buffer Zone " . It has hundreds of years history .

[St. Catherine Kilisesi]
The St . Catherine Kilisesi is one of the most famous church in the Nicosia's old city .

[Panagia Chrysaliniotissa Church]
Panagia Chrysaliniotissa Ch -urch is a famous church in Nicosia's old city .

0202

City Public Spaces

Nature Landscapes

TAIWAN BABEL

Lu Te Hsin

China

TAIWAN BABEL:
CULTURE, SOCIETY AND ECONOMY

If there is a need for a monument in this city, let there be one. This monument will become a slice of the contemporary world, and the ideology of citizens will be revealed on the tower. With a massive collage of culture symbols, the tower is a reality for everyone in the city.

Taipei is a great city where people of different classes from different countries are living and working. Mysterious games are played by everyone, while the winners accumulate huge capitals and others lose everything they have. It is not a gamble though; some people are born to win while others never have a chance. With population rising and more foreign culture are imported to the city, the game will be played by more people with franzy pace.

Taipei is made of a diverse set of buildings, categorized by different groups and classes. Like all other colonized cities, the urbanscape is an agglomeration of different influences and developments. Citizens have no say on how the city looks.

To represent the city and its people, the government started a project to create a monument that is also a tremendous housing. Having no more land to use in the already crowded city, the only way to go is up. A colossal height is expected, and the design becomes a task of vertical urban-planning.

A megastructure in architecture as well as a superstructure in the sense of Marx theories, this monument / housing complex is an embodiment of economy, culture and society.

The infrastructure of the architecture is designed to allow various builders to construct different buildings within the tower for different needs. Huge elevators are erected to provide vertical transportation. While wealthy people purchase luxury high level residences, the lower levels and the ground floor becomes a slum that is not that different to the surrounded urban areas: chaotic and immense. The Tower becomes not only a monument for the city, but a representation of the city itself.

If there is a need for a monument in this city, let there be one. This monument will become a slice of the contemporary world, and the ideology of citizens will be revealed with a massive collage of culture symbols. Taipei is a great city where people of different classes from different countries are living. Mysterious games are played by everyone, while the winners accumulate huge capitals and others lose everything they have. Some people are born to win while others never have a chance. With population rising and more foreign culture are imported to the city, the game will be played by more people with frenzy pace. The Dutch, the Spanish, the Chinese and the Japanese people in modern history have colonized Taiwan. A diverse political and cultural heritage has rendered Taiwan a country without clear root or origin. Taiwan thus becomes a blender that accepts most influences from other cultures. The

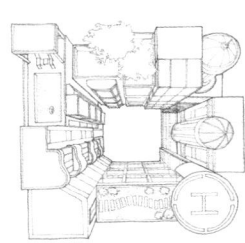

THE RICH
The most powerful and wealthiest people live in this level. Everything here is beyond imagination of lower level residents. Only a few people have seen any part of the level, while the residents remain mysterious for they rarely show up in other parts of the tower.

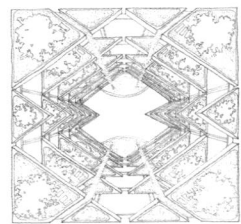

GARDENS
Gardens are the symbol of power of upper level residents. The favorable conditions on the top levels allows plants and flowers to flourish, which are to entertain the residents wealthy enough to live beyond this section.

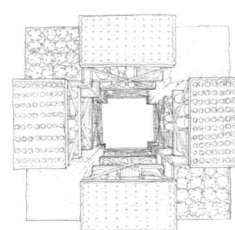

FARMS
Aside from providing food in the tower, farms also serves to divide the middle and upper floors. The higher levels allow farms to acquire enough sunlight and rains.

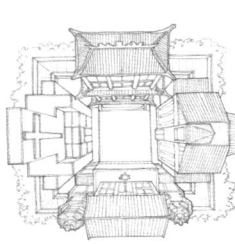

TEMPLES
The tower is scattered with places that provides religious services. Buddhist temples and Christian churches are the most prevailing ones. The same consuming power also determines the sizes of religious places: small temples are often hidden behind narrow alleys, while great ones are easily seen on upper levels. High visibility allows big religion places to draw great crowds to gain substantial profits.

0266

Phase 1: A superstructure starts to develop under the supervision of the government. Verticality is a strategy to densify the use of space and to accumulate the population.

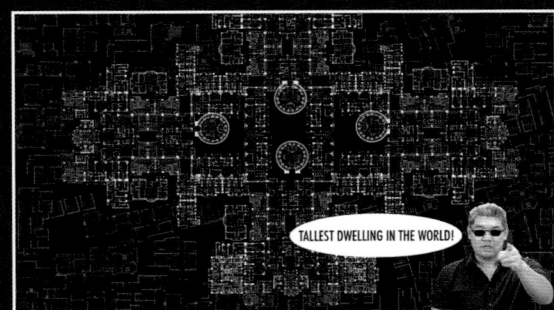

TALLEST DWELLING IN THE WORLD!

Phase 2: Real estate dealers start to advertise on the "tallest dwelling in the world" even before the structure is finished. Lured by the view and the sunlight accompanied with the height, middle-class buyers flock toward the mid- and upper sections of the tower.

Phase 3: As the tower continues to grow, people starts to move in. Newcomers guadually finds that the tower is self-supplied; residents don't need to get down and out for their daily needs. Many never leave the tower ever again.

NOT AGAIN...

Phase 4: But making the tower become self- supplied needs huge amount of manpower to accomplish. Residents of upper floor assemble a management committee, and announce a policy to ground floor: low levels of the tower is now open for labors to move in, houses and job opportunities are offered. Labors (mostly the poor) influx into the tower soon after.

mixture also represents in the build environment. The infrastructure of the architecture is designed to allow various builders to construct different buildings within the tower for different needs. Huge elevators are erected to provide vertical transportation. While wealthy people purchase luxury high level residences, the lower levels and the ground floor becomes a slum that is not that different to the surrounded urban areas: chaotic and immense. The Tower becomes not only a monument for the city, but a representation of the city itself.

Seven Phases of Tower Building

1. A superstructure starts to develop under the supervision of the government. Verticality is a strategy to densify the use of space. 2. Real estate dealers start to advertise on the "tallest dwelling in the world".

TAIWAN BABEL
CULTURE, SOCIETY AND ECONOMY

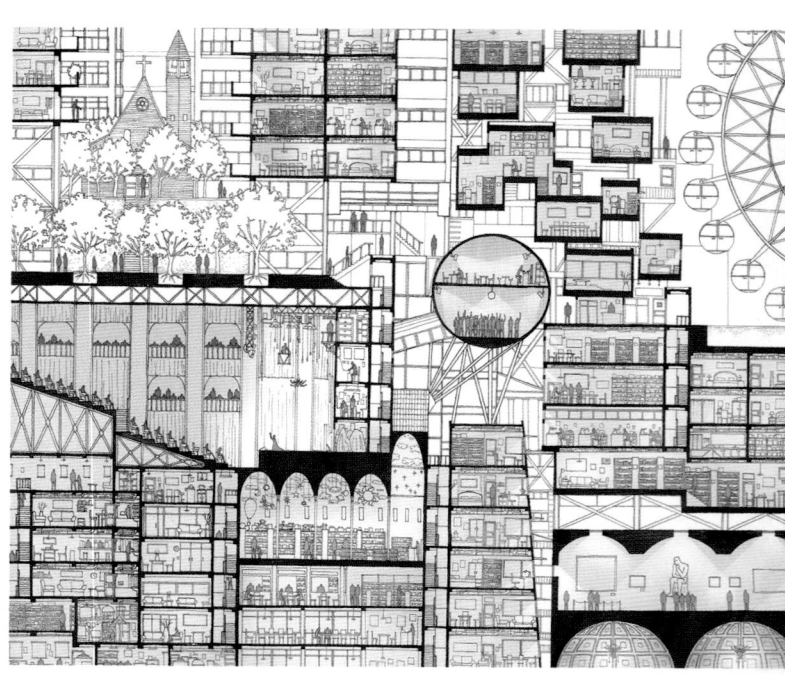

Lured by the view and the sunlight accompanied with the height, buyers flock toward the mid- and upper sections of the tower. 3. As the tower continues to grow, people starts to move in. Newcomers gradually find that the tower is self-supplied. 4. A huge amount of labor force is needed to sustain the tower. The lower levels are open for workers to move in. 5. The possibility of lower level residents working their way up to the upper level threatens the stability of the power structure. A separate management is established for the lower levels to cut away connections with the top. 6. The capacity and influence of tower expands rapidly. The difference between the three sections deepens. The lower levels fall into a slum condition while the top floors become more luxurious, and the middle-class working people caught in between spend much effort to keep up. 7. The infrastructure of the tower keeps expanding, as if the tower would never reach a limit.

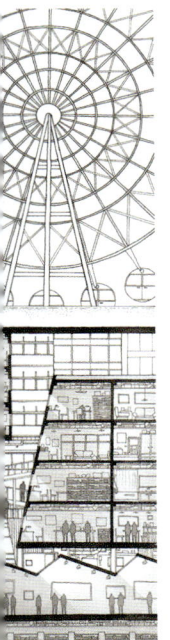

About culture collage //

Taiwan has been colonized by the Dutch, the Spanish, the Chinese the Japanese people in modern history. The current government was established in 1945. A diverse political and cultural heritage has rendered Taiwan a country without clear root or origin. Taiwan thus becomes a blender that accepts most influences from other cultures, whether from China, Japan, the US or other regions. The mixture also represents in the build environment. Taiwan has find ways to incorporate different cultural aspects, whether traditional or modern, western or eastern. While the Tower represents the city of Taipei, it is also a miniature of the society of Taiwan,

Left: Upper floor section
Down: Ground floor section

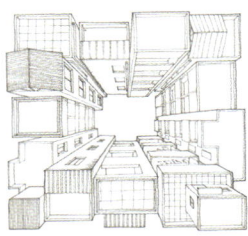

THE MIDDLE
The 3-bedroom apartment type (with a dining and a living room) is the most prevailing, if not the only housing type for the middle-class families.

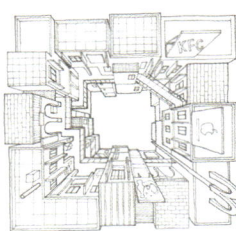

SHOPS
Commercial services are provided all over the tower. Depending on the locations and the levels, the shops develops into different scales and classes; the higher, the bigger. Consuming power is the shop size indicator.

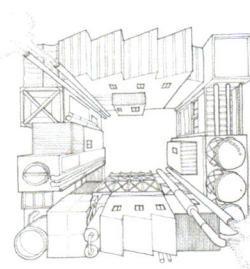

FACTORIES
The Factory sections separates the Poor with other parts of the tower. Labor workers take the elevator up to work everyday, providing all the physical needs to the tower.

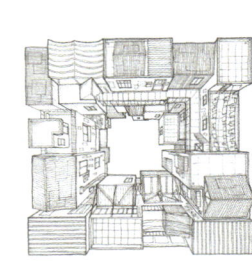

THE POOR
Slum houses with tight footprints and illegal extensions occupies the ground floor which authority ignores. Lack of public service causes messy look and dirty environments. Usual use of space includes: small workshop, illegal gambling, pigeon farms (for pigeon race and gambling), etc.

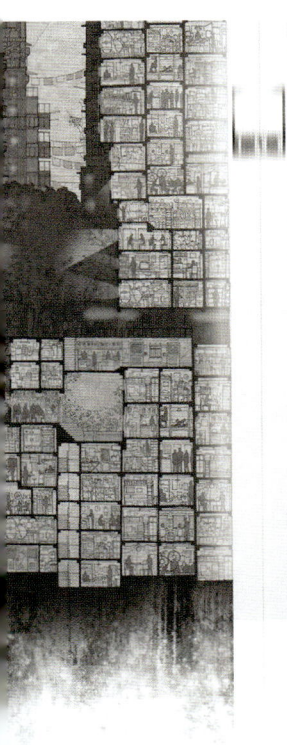

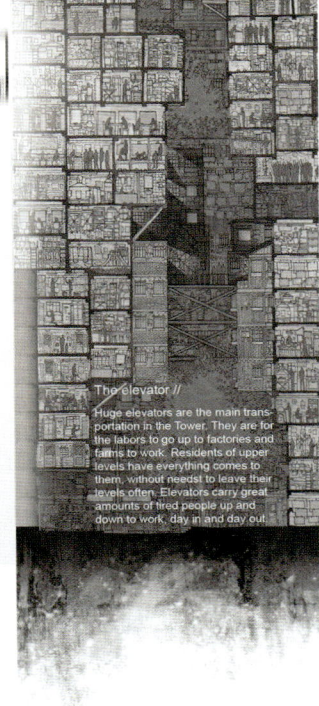

The elevator //
Huge elevators are the main transportation in the Tower. They are for the labors to go up to factories and farms to work. Residents of upper levels have everything comes to them, without needst to leave their levels often. Elevators carry great amounts of tired people up and down to work, day in and day out.

0266

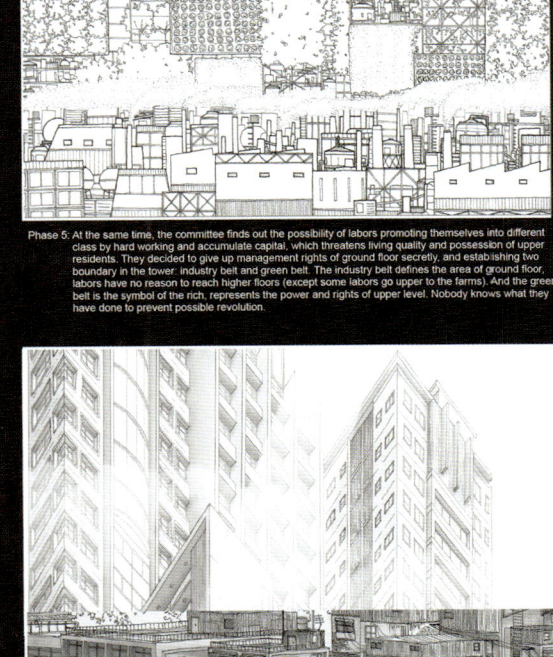

Phase 5: At the same time, the committee finds out the possibility of labors promoting themselves into different class by hard working and accumulate capital, which threatens living quality and possession of upper residents. They decided to give up management rights of ground floor secretly, and establishing two boundary in the tower: industry belt and green belt. The industry belt defines the area of ground floor, labors have no reason to reach higher floors (except some labors go upper to the farms). And the green belt is the symbol of the rich, represents the power and rights of upper level. Nobody knows what they have done to prevent possible revolution.

Phase 6. The tower gets taller and taller, and expands very fast. The difference between three sections becomes more severe after committee made the decision. Ground floor becomes a huge messy slum, on top lives the rich and powerful people in good condition, in between is the middle-class working hard, trying to go up and not to fall to the ground floor.

Phase 7: The tower is still being built. People still influx into the tower like crazy, they jump into the game rules of tower trying to win. Nobody know how tall this tower will get. As different people start living in the tower, it become harder to tell how the tower really look like. The tower has become a great hybrid of groups and classes.

OSTEON CUMULUS: VERTICAL CITY

Layton Reid
Adrian Jimenez Escarfullery
Sakib Hasan
Bryan Ruiz
Milot Pivera

United Kingdom

Site. The prototypical site in China, Wuxi City, Jiansu Province, allows the exploration of issues of displacement and cultural identity as well as those of community and diversity as defined by architectural form.

Concept. The banyan tree deposits additional downward branches to stabilize its imposed load much in the manner of this structure, Osteon city maximizes the potential of a small footprint, touching the earth lightly, whilst providing the maximum in amenity, at times appearing as a cumulo-nimbus cloud formation, and at others as a floating forest.

Ethos. The proposition consider the nature of the skyscraper as a 210 floor community, where work, retail, hospitality , leisure and residential accommodation form an aerial community serviced

0507

OSTEON CUMULUS VERTICAL CITY,
Kilometre high city

SITE

The prototypical site in China , Wuxi City , Jiansu Province , allows the exploration of issues of displacement and cultural identity as well as those of community and diversity as defined by architectural form , The smart city leverages both passive and active technologies in its formation this includes the local , as a definition of connectivity , with off grid networks owned by the inhabitants. It is proposed that the physical and material qualities of this construct should manifest itself in a porus coral like form , these can either appear as slices joined together to form a more conventional urban grain or as in this instance become a stacked series of evolving circumstances defined by the consequence of the internal and external environment.

horizontally by driverless cars and bicycles swegeways and pedestrian routes.

Structure and Form. The diagrid is re purposed to a waffle format, much like a radiator, the interleaving structural elements; join together to form a self-supporting yet extremely strong and flexible structure. The elements which make up the structure are porous lightweight and analogous to bone osteo, it is envisaged that the construction will make use of rapid prototyping techniques on an industrial scale with integrated services technology.

Vertical Farms. Within the leisure zoned tower additional atria are created to house a range of agricultural activities thus making the aim of self sustainability an achievable goal when allied to the range of personal and communal garden solutions allowed by the proposal.

Sustainability, Energy, Microclimate. The aims of a building of this type are to act as an energy generator, hence the form mimicking that of radiator. The blade like surfaces of the structure house micro turbines and solar surfaces in the porous blade like structure these are used to drive local amenities, energy generated is stored and exchanged through the structure and surface of the building.
Plan. The ground level structure defines a series of light filled plazas, whilst the upper levels show the range of spatial configurations, which include crescents and squares, roads and land bridges.

0507

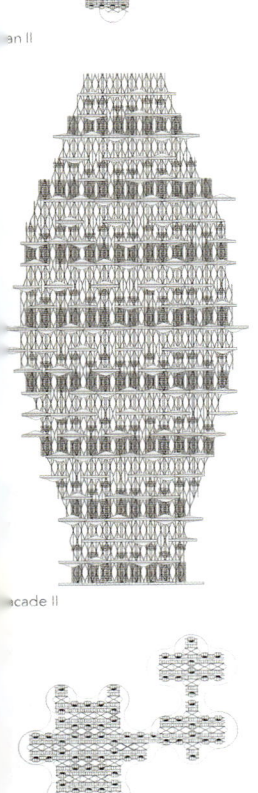

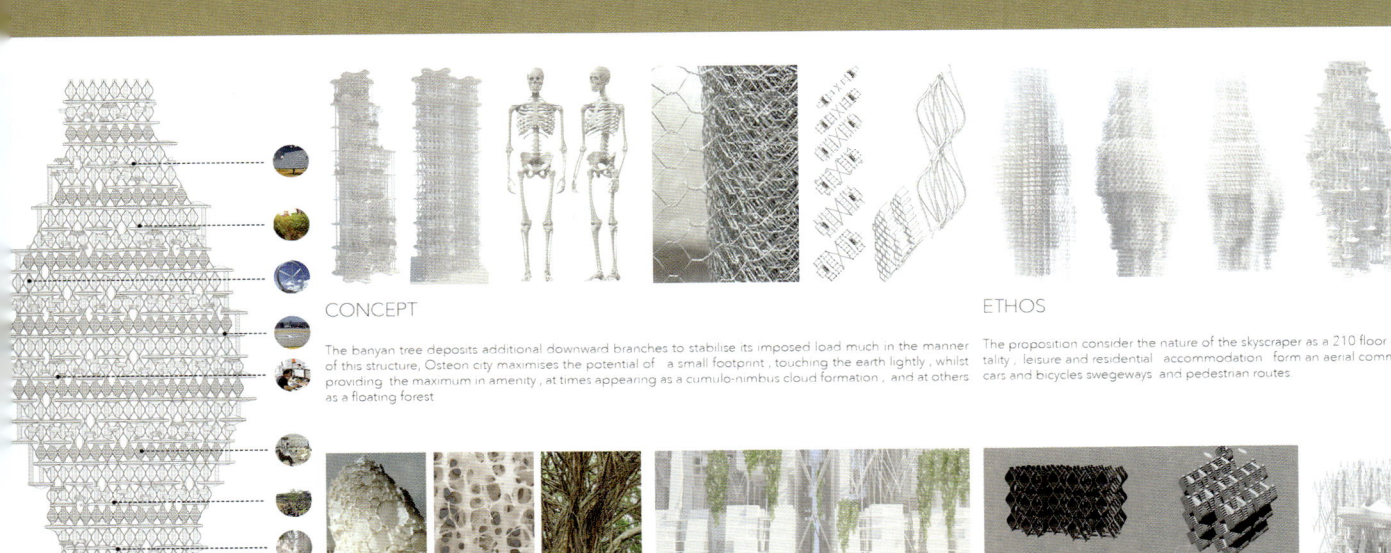

CONCEPT

The banyan tree deposits additional downward branches to stabilise its imposed load much in the manner of this structure, Osteon city maximises the potential of a small footprint, touching the earth lightly, whilst providing the maximum in amenity, at times appearing as a cumulo-nimbus cloud formation, and at others as a floating forest

ETHOS

The proposition consider the nature of the skyscraper as a 210 floor community, where work, retail, hospitality, leisure and residential accommodation form an aerial community serviced horizontally by driverless cars and bicycles swegeways and pedestrian routes

STRUCTURE AND FORM

The diagrid is re purposed to a waffle format, much like a radiator, the interleaving structural elements, join together to form a self supporting yet extremely strong and flexible structure. The elements which make up the structure are porus lightweight and analogous to bone " osteo, it is envisaged that the construction will make use of rapid prototyping techniques on an industrial scale with integrated services technology. These elements are then horizontally braced with walkways and lift cores

VERTICAL FARMS

Within the leisure zoned tower additional atria are created to house a range of agricultural activities thus making the aim of self sustainability an achievable goal when allied to the range of personal and communal garden solutions allowed by the proposal.

Facade II

AERIAL PARKS AND LANDSCAPE

These areas, provide respite and a sense of localism to the towers inhabitants, the voids allow light to penetrate deep into the structure, whose surfaces act as sun scoops illuminating the inner areas of the tower

Sustainability, energy, micro climate

The aims of a building of this type is to act as an energy generator, hence the form mimicking that of radiator The blade like surfaces of the structure house micro turbines and solar surfaces in the porous blade like structure these are used to drive local amenities, energy generated is stored and exchanged through the structure and surface of the building, at its highest levels temperature differentials, create precipitate, which can be encouraged, dissuaded used immediately, or stored for re use as directed by the control mechanisms contained within each zone.

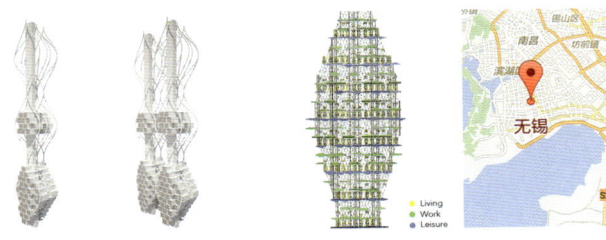

ZONING

The three main elements of residential, leisure and work located within the vertical elements of then tower, whilst retail sits within the landscape mounds which appear to rise and descend from the aerial parks Residential elements are disposed within the diagrid structure, cradled such that they can be interconnected to form more or less complex arrangements as required

PLAN

The ground level structure defines a series of light filled plazas, whilst the upper levels show the range of spatial configurations which include crescents and squares, roads and land bridges

AGORÀ

Alessandro Arcangeli
Filippo Fiorani

The Netherlands

Agorà

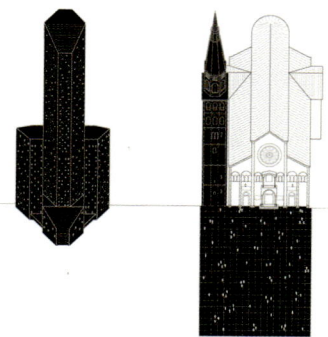

Landmark vs Selfmark

The Architectural product of the capitalist age is the Skyscraper, and its mania for reaching the sky. The Skyscraper is the XX century's Babel tower.
Towers where people work, speaking different languages, distancing themselves from the city, from other people and from the real world. The Skyscraper "steals" people from the city.

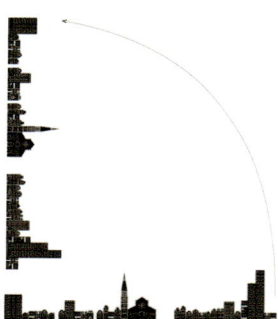

Power to the people

Assuming that every spatial choice is political, and every political choice is spatial, we want to reverse the idea of the skyscraper, giving back the tower to the people. We take the street, the 'public' space and we flip it, arranging in vertical all the spaces we walk through when we go for a stroll in town. Then we base our design on the connection within public and private space.

Typologies through the ages

We access the tower arising on a new Parliament, where the community decides for itself in a new form of free and collaborative democracy. From this political theatre we walk up to the working spaces, to end up in the library, conceived as an ascent, through books, datas and theories to the last level, which we called the labyrinth: a space where people lose themselves and meet in small squares scattered on the top of the tower.

Modern capitalism has been the 20th Century's religion, and finance is its product. This system created utter inequality, the final stage of class struggle, where 1% of the population controls more than 40% of world's wealth. Growing inequality is the flip side of something else: shrinking opportunity. Whenever we diminish equality of opportunity, it means that we are not using some of our most valuable assets— our people—in the most productive way possible. In 2008 financial capitalism collapsed. This collapse aroused the crowds, breathing life into a new political and economical approach, which we call Socialism 2.0. The upcoming neo-socialist economy requires a collective action, it is based on the certainty that paying attention to everyone else's self-interest-in other words, the common welfare-is in fact a precondition for one's own ultimate well being. Assuming that every spatial choice is political, and every

0562

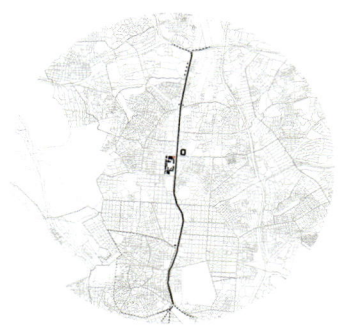

The project focuses on the analysis of the most paradoxical tower: the Skyscraper in Europe. The site of *Agorà*, is in Madrid, along the arterial road of "La Castellana". Between the city centre and the financial district.

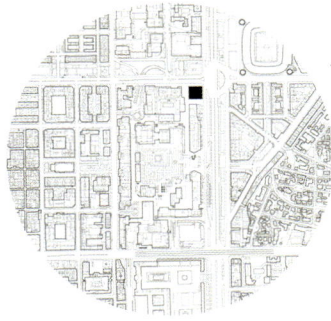

Agorà wants to be a new *landmark* for the city, juxtapose a new idea of *the tower* to the classic financial, private building.

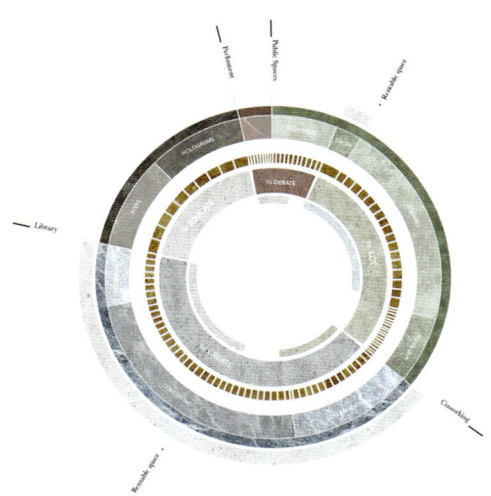

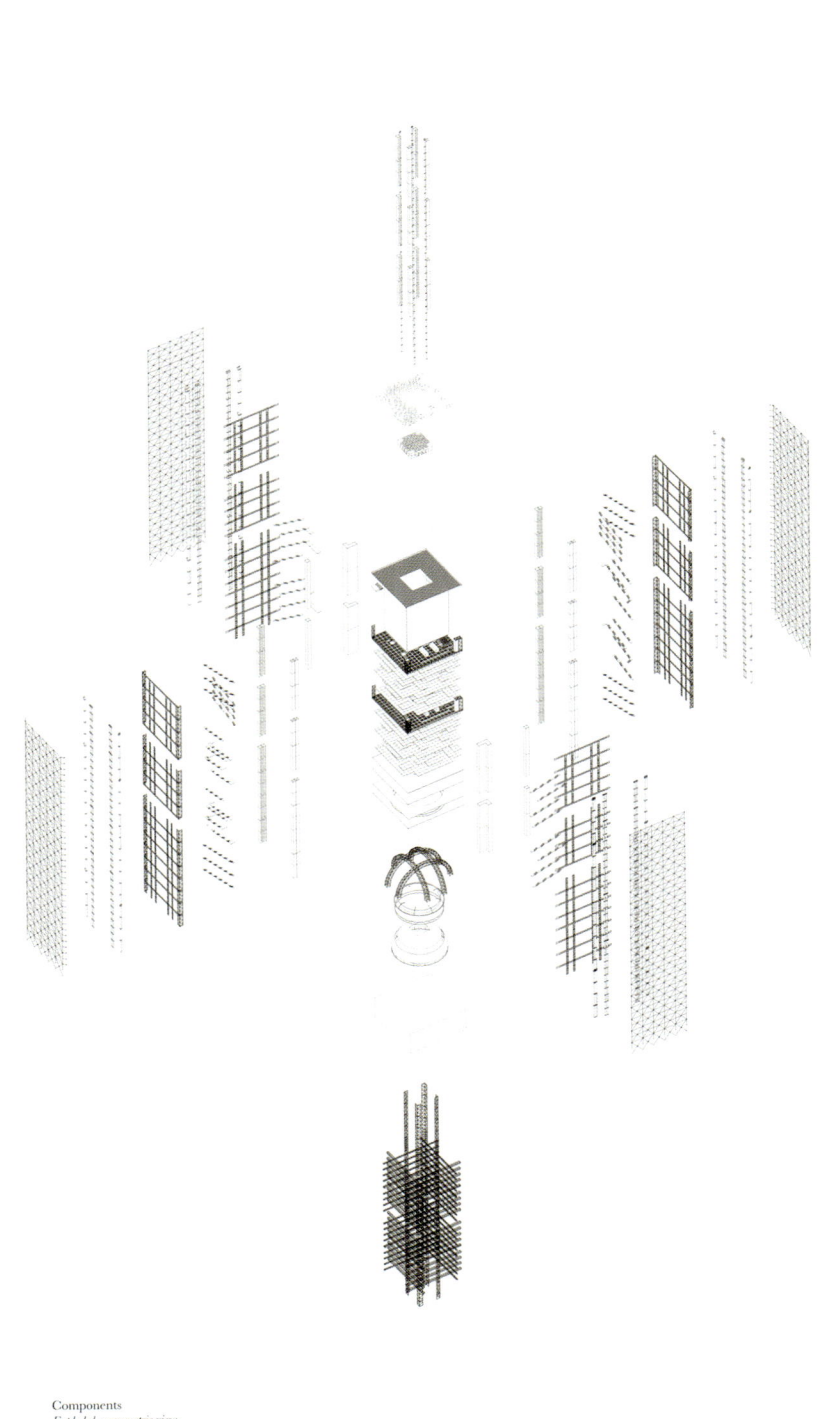

Components
Exploded axonometric view

political choice is spatial, we want to reverse the idea of the skyscraper, giving back the tower to the public. Most of the hybrid buildings we know failed, resulting in structures where different functions and spaces just stand in top or in front of each other, without interacting. We tried to create a space where functions and spaces interact, rather than co-exist, basing our design on the distinction that Aristoteles first, than Hannah Arendt, made, between the two verbs act and work. A space where people act rather than work. Action goes on directly between men, corresponding to the human condition of plurality, to the fact that men, not man, live the earth. Plurality and connectivity are the natural conditions of Agorà. We take the street and we flip it, arranging in vertical all the spaces we walk through when we go for a stroll in town. We base our design on the connection within public and private spaces. The

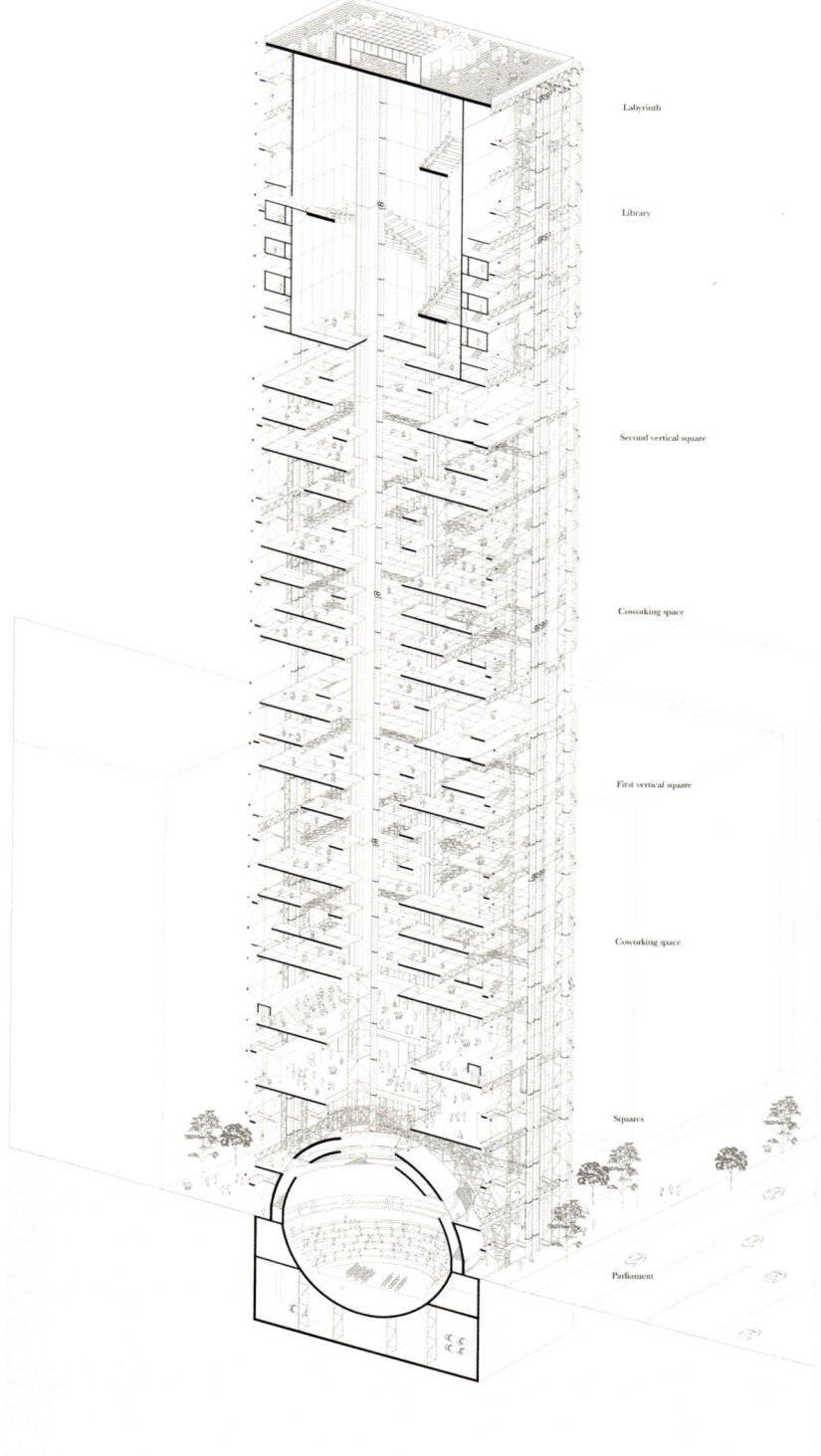

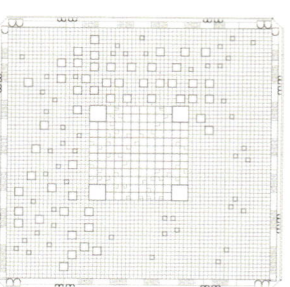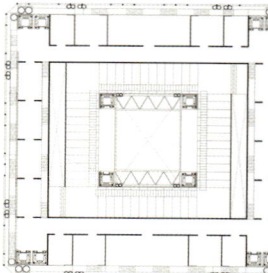

Labyrinth - Library
Plans sc. 1:500

On top we conceived a library as a series of steps around the empty core that runs from the sky to the earth. From this library there is access to the bordering rooms, where holograms and 3d representations support the content of the good old books. The rooftop is conceived as a labyrinth of monoliths, the last stage of the *homo ludens*, a square where people can gather, manifestate, play and also find a spriritual spot for meditate.

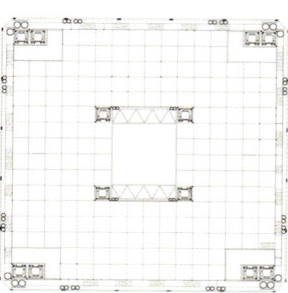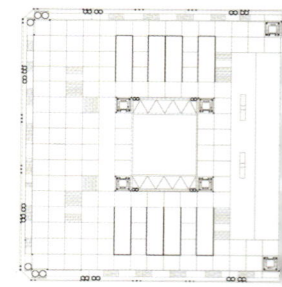

Coworking - Vertical Square
Plans sc. 1:500

The coworking space module is divided in three parts: at the bottom an open space, where people gather, exchange ideas, collaborate; where young workers and startupper can rent a table and few chairs instead of expensive offices in the financial district. Above, we find two floors of more private space, rentable by group of workers as meeting rooms. Two vertical squares, with shops and skateparks break the rhythm of the tower.

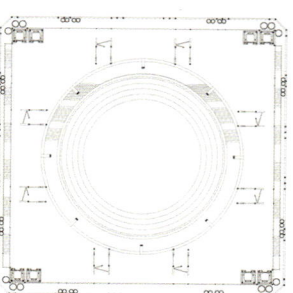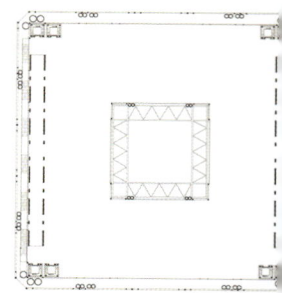

Parliament - Square
Plans sc. 1:500

The re-invented parliament, on which the tower arises, is conceived as a sphere, a sort of *public arena*, where people can easily assist, interact, debate and partecipate, in a new form of continuous ex-tempore referendum. On top of the sphere, two squares are conceived as places of debate, encounters, meeting and dialogue.

former will be distributed along the three dimensions of the tower, the latter will be literally re-invented: a new flexible working space, based on interactions between spaces and people, where sharing is the keyword: sharing services, workforce, ideas. From the city of Madrid, we access the tower arising on the new Spanish parliament, where the community decides for itself in a new form of free and collaborative democracy. From this political theatre we walk up to two squares that introduce the working spaces. This space is conceived for young workers, start uppers, students, who have the possibility to rent a just a cheap table, enjoying the possibility of sharing the cost of common services and more important: to meet other people, potential collaborators and teammates. The whole building is conceived as a spiritual and social path, running from the crowded arena, to the spiritual, intimate, religious labyrinth.

0562

Library
Perspective Section

Labyrinth
Perspective Section

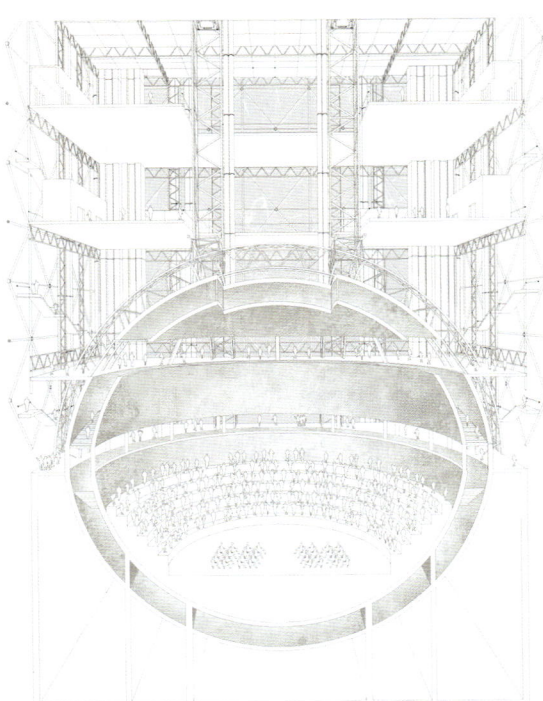

Democratic parliament
Perspective Section

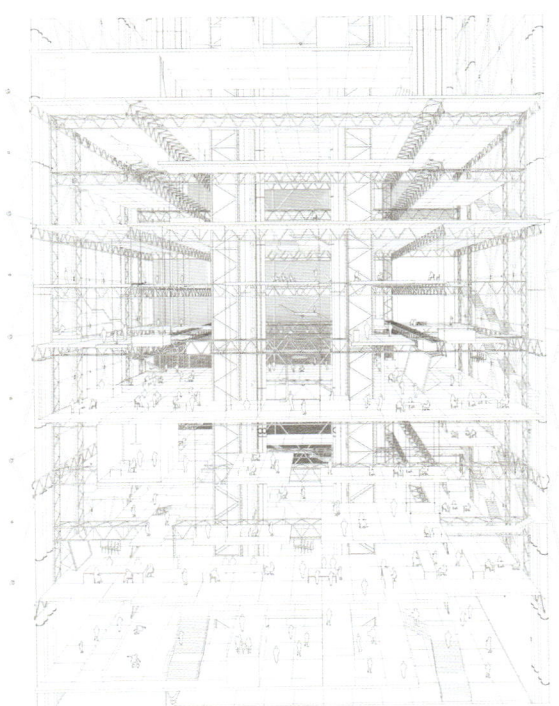

Coworking space
Perspective Section

NEW YORK HORIZON

Yitan Sun
Jianshi Wu

United States

1ST PLACE / 2016

As the busiest and most densely populated county in America, Manhattan has always been a big fan of skyscrapers. Limited by its street grid, however, buildings in New York City are often skinny and tall. Rather than constructing another slim tower by building upwards, "New York Horizon" envisions a new paradigm by digging downward to Central Park's bedrock, which will reveal the park's rugged natural terrain while also creating a continuous wall of skyscrapers around its periphery to house habitable spaces with unobstructed views of the new underground park. The project was conceived to contrast against the city's densely constructed buildings and towering skyscrapers, as well as, to provide New Yorkers with a natural environment that they could enjoy and use as an escape from their busy urban lives. Consequently, the soil removed from the park would be used to add a more dynamic landscape

NEW YORK HORIZON

0579

Statement

As the busiest and most densely populated county in America, Manhattan has always been a big fan of skyscrapers. Limited by its street grid, however, space in New York City is often skinny and tall. One exception being the Central Park, a 1.3 square mile urban park, giving New Yorkers a change to escape the busy urban life. However, only a fraction of them can enjoy Central Park's natural environment on a daily basis, and most of the population either live or work beyond the walking distance from it.

Is there a way to make Central Park available to more people? Our proposal is a hybrid multi-functional mega structure. Not by building up, but by digging down, it reveals the bedrock(mountain) that was hidden under the Central Park, and creates space along the new cliff. The ambition is to reverse the traditional relationship between landscape and architecture, in a way that every occupable space has direct connection to the nature

The 1000-feet tall, 100-feet deep mega structure provides a total floor area of 7 square miles, which is about 80 times greater than the Empire State Building. Wrapping all four sides of the new central park. This system breaks the traditional perception of large scale skyscrapers without taking valuable ground area of Manhattan

The soil removed from the original park is relocated to various neighborhoods, which will be demolished and moved into the new structure. This creates a new urban condition, where landscape can serve as an inherent part of the city

With its highly reflective glass cover on all sides, the landscape inside the new park can reach beyond physical boundaries, creating an illusion of infinity. In the heart of New York City, a New Horizon is born

Plan

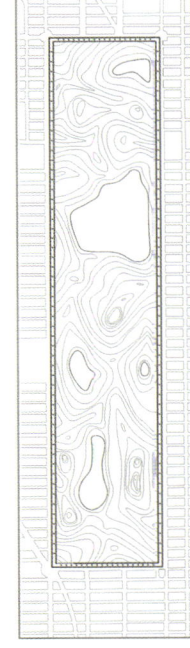

Concept

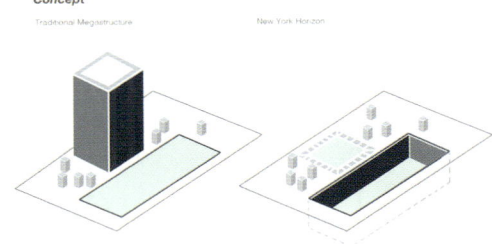

Traditional Megastructure   New York Horizon

Storyboard

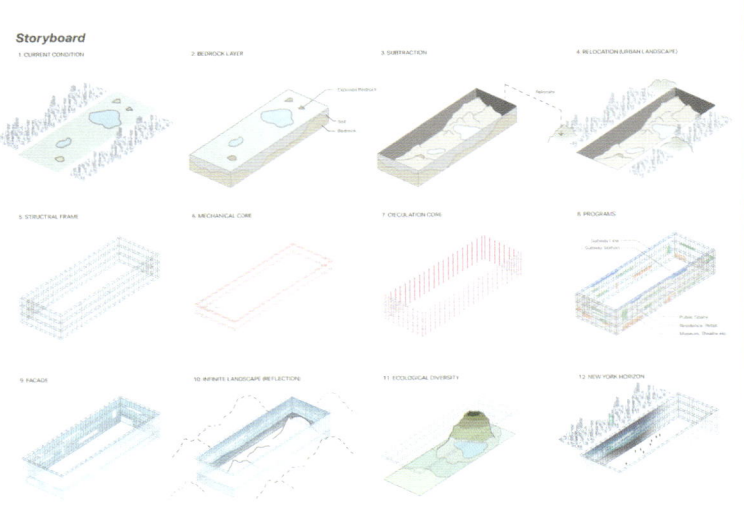

(mini-mountains, hills etc.) to underdeveloped plots all over Manhattan. This would create a new urban condition, where the newly constructed landscape becomes a cohesive part of the city. This reimagined parkland would allow for hiking, climbing, swimming and other outdoor activities. And finally, the reflective glass façade canvassing the wall of skyscrapers will reflect the park's natural terrain and create the illusion of a never-ending natural world within the heart of Manhattan's concrete jungle, while also offering New Yorkers' a perspective of the landscape that is not limited by the park's physical boundaries. The 1000 feet tall, 100 feet wide wall of skyscrapers/mega-structure would create 7 square miles (80 times greater than the Empire State Building) of habitable indoor space, while introducing more natural diversity and verticality to the once flat 1.3 square mile Central Park. The seven-mile-perimeter wraparound mega-structure would contain apartments, retails, museums, libraries, etc. within the

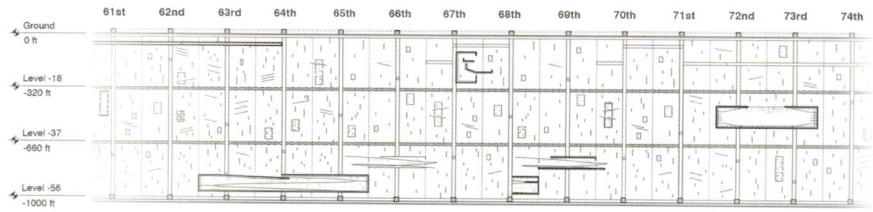

Partial Section

"The Mountain is Already There"

According to geological researches, the bedrock in Central Park is generally deeper than Midtown and Downtown Manhattan, which is part of the reason why Central Park is established at where it is now, as deeper bedrock is not ideal for skyscrapers to anchor themselves to the ground. One the other hand, deeper bedrock means there are more removable soil above it, making our proposal possible.

Built in 19th Century, Central Park was designed with the existing underground geology in mind. Our strategy is to take the original design one step further, remove and relocate the soil above the bedrock in Central Park, revealing the "mountains" underneath. It accommodates the development of the city since the Central Park was first established, and proposes an exciting new urban planning paradigm for the centuries to follow.

100 feet deep inhabitable walls, with an unobstructed view and connection to the park. Following Manhattan's city grid, there are main circulation cores (elevators) that would align with every single street from 59th to 110th street to transfer people down to the park, as well as to other various floors. Secondary circulation (ramps, stairs) would connect separate spaces in various scales between the cores. The goal of the concept is to reverse the traditional relationship between landscape and architecture. Instead of building distant, flat landscapes to surround and complement individual architectural buildings, the natural landscape is now the centerpiece. In this case, the dynamic landscape is surrounded by characterless architecture that tries to be nothing but mirror that reflects nature. In the heart of New York City's concrete jungle, a New Horizon is born.

0579

Geology Diagram

Experience

Before

After

Entrance

POROSITY SKYSCRAPER

Mok Chit Yan Paul

Hong Kong

Porosity shall emerge as a new residential-towers typology in tropical and sub-tropical regions.

Most high-dense residential towers would inevitably confront the tension between smaller repetitive residential units and larger public programs. In contrast with typical podium-tower typology where the public programs and residential units are totally segregated, a proposed tower allocates public programs along the core of the tower while residential modules along the periphery. These cubic rooms are separated from each other, forming a perforated 8-feet deep façade.

Unlike the curtain-wall system where exterior and interior are only separated by 6 inches of construction materials, along a porous tower the exterior is diffused into the core through the gaps between the "floating" residential modules. Most of the public programs could therefore be semi-exterior

0593

P O R O S I T Y

with natural ventilation and self-shading.

In terms of spatial quality, corridors of typical residential towers are very often value-less. They are nothing but the enclosed, inevitable transition zones between the elevators and the rooms. The porose tower embraces the programing complexity of a tower design by juxtaposing residential units and public programs adjacent to each other. Though circulation systems of the public programs and residential units are separated, the semi-exterior corridors connecting the residential rooms are visually open to the double-heighted portions of public programs.

The facades of residential modules take up 50% of tower's façade. They are the only portions of façade that confront the exterior directly. Smaller-scaled façade systems such as double-brick-wall and

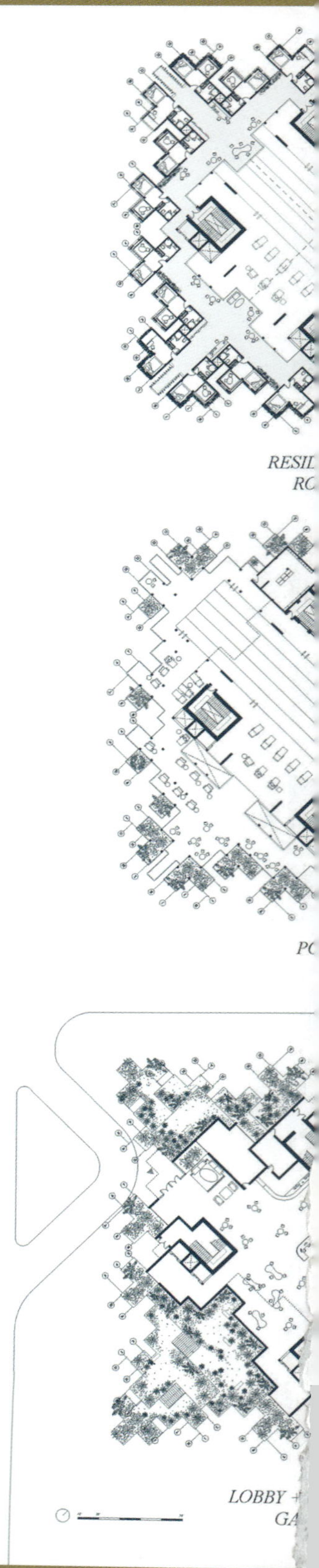

roof top greenhouse
▼

skydeck + greenhouse lab
▼

black box theatre
▼

pool + thermal baths
▼

gallery + exhibition
▼

conference + restaurant
▼

RESIL
RO

PO

LOBBY +
GA

SECTION

100 feet deep inhabitable walls, with an unobstructed view and connection to the park. Following Manhattan's city grid, there are main circulation cores (elevators) that would align with every single street from 59th to 110th street to transfer people down to the park, as well as to other various floors. Secondary circulation (ramps, stairs) would connect separate spaces in various scales between the cores. The goal of the concept is to reverse the traditional relationship between landscape and architecture. Instead of building distant, flat landscapes to surround and complement individual architectural buildings, the natural landscape is now the centerpiece. In this case, the dynamic landscape is surrounded by characterless architecture that tries to be nothing but mirror that reflects nature. In the heart of New York City's concrete jungle, a New Horizon is born.

0579

Geology Diagram

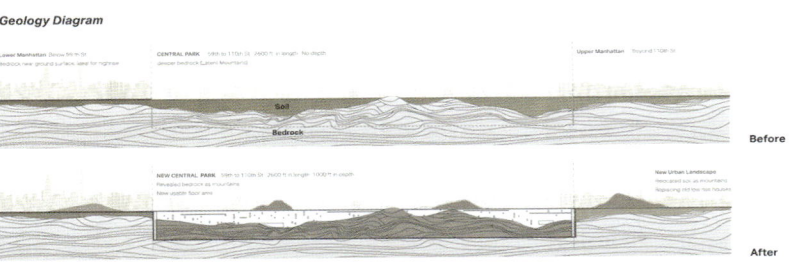

Experience

Before

After

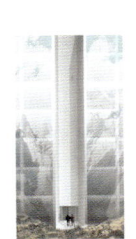

Entrance

Interior

POROSITY
SKYSCRAPER

Mok Chit Yan Paul

Hong Kong

Porosity shall emerge as a new residential-towers typology in tropical and sub-tropical regions.

Most high-dense residential towers would inevitably confront the tension between smaller repetitive residential units and larger public programs. In contrast with typical podium-tower typology where the public programs and residential units are totally segregated, a proposed tower allocates public programs along the core of the tower while residential modules along the periphery. These cubic rooms are separated from each other, forming a perforated 8-feet deep façade.

Unlike the curtain-wall system where exterior and interior are only separated by 6 inches of construction materials, along a porous tower the exterior is diffused into the core through the gaps between the "floating" residential modules. Most of the public programs could therefore be semi-exterior

0593

P O R O S I T Y

with natural ventilation and self-shading.

In terms of spatial quality, corridors of typical residential towers are very often value-less. They are nothing but the enclosed, inevitable transition zones between the elevators and the rooms. The porose tower embraces the programing complexity of a tower design by juxtaposing residential units and public programs adjacent to each other. Though circulation systems of the public programs and residential units are separated, the semi-exterior corridors connecting the residential rooms are visually open to the double-heighted portions of public programs.

The facades of residential modules take up 50% of tower's façade. They are the only portions of façade that confront the exterior directly. Smaller-scaled façade systems such as double-brick-wall and

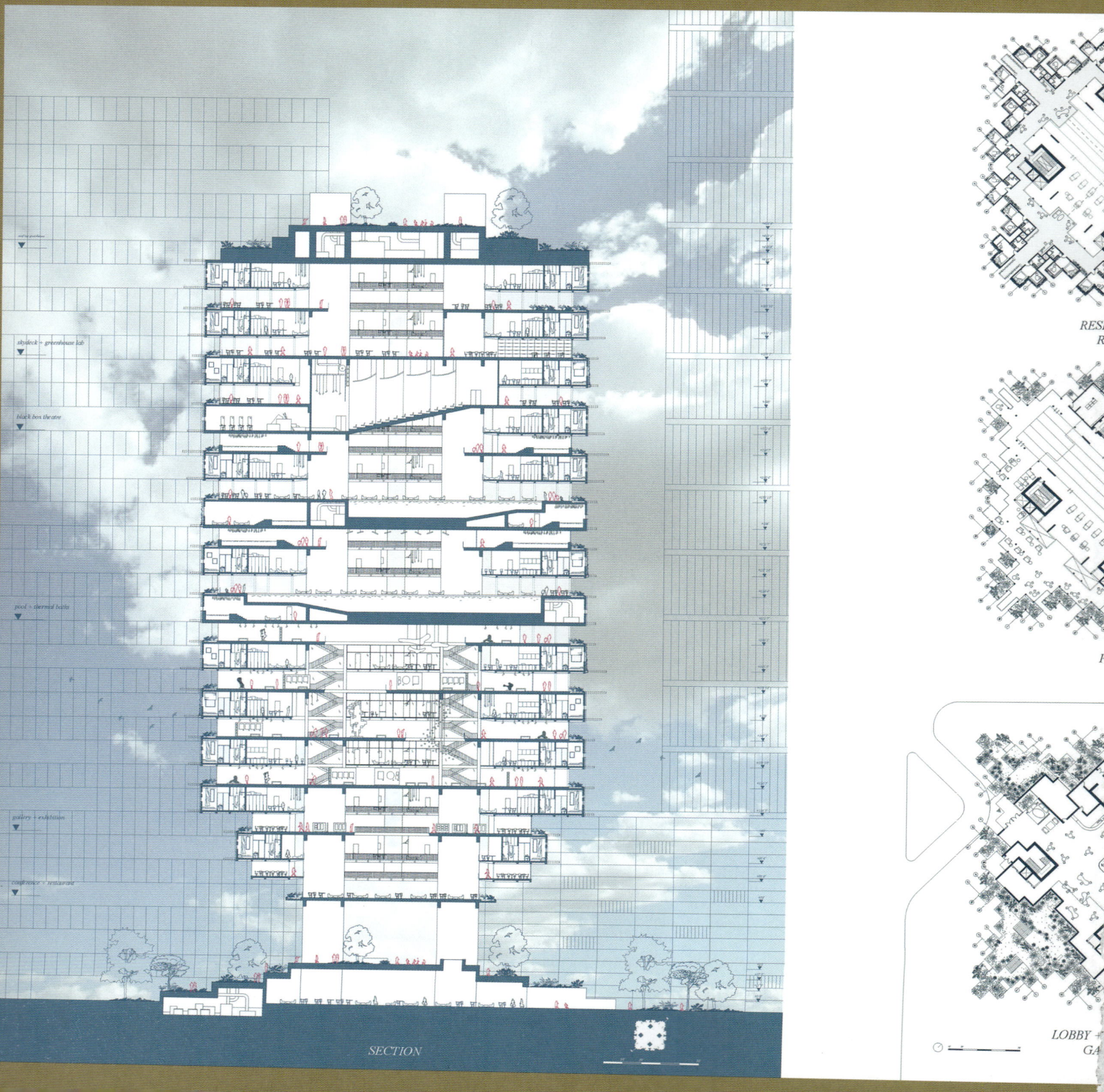

SECTION

window screens inspired by antique window arts are adopted.

Porosity shall emerge as a new tower typology that addresses the programing complexity of modern residential towers, and negotiate better between exterior and interior environments in topical and sub-tropical climates.

0593

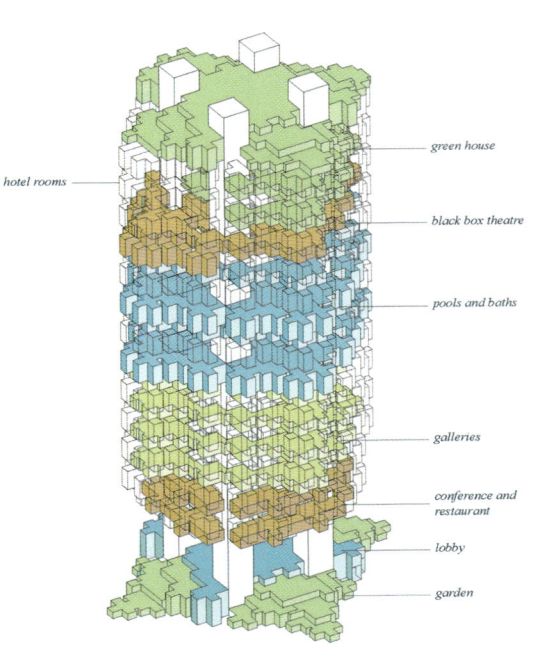

hotel rooms

green house

black box theatre

pools and baths

galleries

conference and restaurant

lobby

garden

PROGRAMS

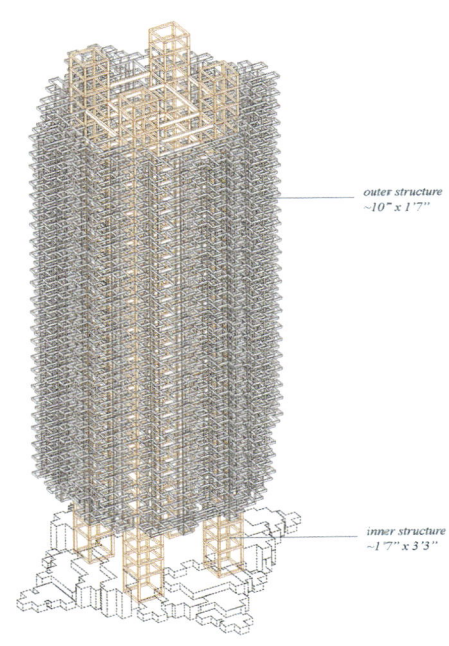

outer structure
~10" x 1'7"

inner structure
~1'7" x 3'3"

STRUCTURE

residential capsules / semi-exterior corridors

public programs

residential capsules / semi-exterior corridors

public programs

TYPICAL FRAGMENT

ICONOCLAST OR THE KINGDOM OF CHOICE

Thomas S. Krall
Quentin Rihoux

Denmark
France

ICONOCLAST ABOVE THE SEA OF FOG

I AM THE ICONOCLAST

THE ICONOCLAST IS THE VIRTUAL HUMAN

THE ICONOCLAST IS THE PERFECT WORLD

THE ICONOCLAST IS THE ARTIFICIAL APOTHEOSIS

THE ICONOCLAST IS THE KINGDOM OF CHOICE

NOW FOLLOW ME ON MY JOURNEY...

The Iconoclast is the physical manifestation of the Virtual World. It is home to the Dreamer, the virtual descendant of our current existence. This post human being has the ability of living in absolute self-fulfillment, regardless his or her gender, social status, race or sexuality in the physical world. There are no mundane responsibilities anymore, no redundant boundaries of morality or society. The digital human is free to do whatever it desires to do, the Virtual World is the technological realization of Garden Eden. The Iconoclast itself is a modular mega structure fully independent from the physical world. The most promising technologies of the near future make its self-sufficiency possible. It is controlled by an artificial intelligence, keeping it maintained and protected by machines. Fusion reactors generate enough energy for the Iconoclast and its super-servers, which are generating the Virtual World. Nutrition cells,

0639

ANONYMOUS

In our current lifes in the **OLD WORLD** we vegetate alone in anonymity, torn apart in the schizophrenia of more digital connection and social isolation at the same time

DEVOURER

We have lost the link to our planet, we exploit its resources without regrets, destroying the ecosystem and thereby the foundation of all the generations to come

SUPPRESSOR

We suppress each other for our own benefit, the rich and powerful take advantage of the weak, enslaving them to gain wealth and power born in injustice

DESTROYER

We will never end war, terrorism and violence, as we still watch each other as enemies and threat our own kind with weapons capable of destroying he planet

ARRIVAL

The **ICONOCLAST** is the only escape, it gives us the chance for the perfect life, a life without fear, poverty, inequality, illness and suffering

REFLECTION

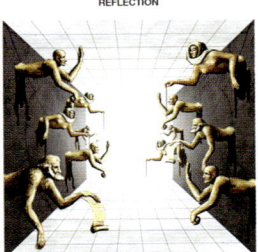

To finally achieve perfection we let the Old World behind us, but on our way will be confronted with all the consequences of our decision, to proof our true will

TESTING

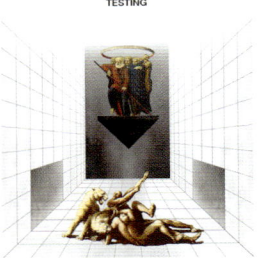

To protect itself, the Iconoclast will neutralize the ones with bad intentions, everyone who is willing to bring harm to it will fail the testing and is annihilated

SARCOPHAGUS

As we pass the test, we will sleep in the Iconoclast, the Sarcophagus will carry us into the dream of Garden Eden, shared by entire mankind

PERFECTION

We finally rise to perfection, in the **VIRTUAL WORLD** we are without any flaws and diseases, absolutely creative and beautiful, omnipotent and immortal

UTOPIA

We live in absolute harmony with the New World, there is no need for pollution, exploitation and slaughter anymore, as all of our life is only a dream

EQUALITY

Here we are all the same, it doesn't matter if we were born black or white, female or male, rich or poor, as these things do not exist here

PEACE

There are no conflicts in the Virtual World anymore, there is only harmony, as everybody has everything and there is no limit in virtual wealth

RETURN

We can return to our former life whenever we want to, as soon as we get tired of dreaming, we go back and enter the **NEW WORLD**

RENEWAL

What we find there is a regenerating ecosystem, as almost entire mankind decides to dream of perfection the planet outside can begin to restore

FREEDOM

There is no war or inequality here anymore, because everyone who is suppressed can join the dream in the Iconoclast, and so the New World becomes livable again

CHOICE

The Iconoclast is the future, the virtual utopia, and it is every human being's birthright to decide in which world to live in, as all of us are part of this **KINGDOM OF CHOICE**

a densified way of food production, are cultured for the inhabitants of the Virtual World. All machines, server elements and structural components are produced there, using advanced three-dimensional printing. Drones maintain the logistics of the human storages. They assemble the Sarcophagi, the artifacts containing the bodies of the Dreamers, in systems similar to high-bay warehouses. Thereby, the highest density of human life can be generated, defining a new typology of post-urban efficiency. The Sarcophagus is the physical presence of the human being in the Iconoclast. It is its machine body, an artificial womb, protecting and feeding the sleeping Dreamer inside of it. It reacts to individual needs and monitors vital functions, and it is the connection between the human being and the Virtual World. Thereby it also is the physical and virtual interface of the society inside of the Iconoclast.

PROCESS I

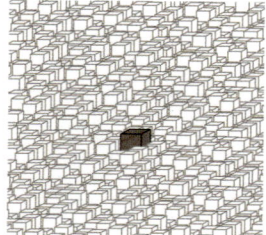

The **ICONOCLAST** generates a virtual reality, creating a livable and perfect world for everybody. It is a self-sufficient system, fully independent from the outside world

Population: 1.000.000
800ft x 800ft x 800ft

PROCESS II

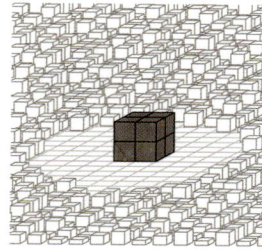

It's independence is made possible by a controlling artificial intelligence, regulating all internal processes as well as the extension of the Iconoclast, if a higher capacity is needed

Population: 8.000.000
1.600ft x 1.600ft x 1.600ft

PROCESS III

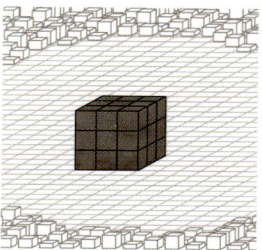

While it increases in size it cannibalizes the city, which is being abandoned by its inhabitants, by reusing urban materials for the construction of new modules

Population: 27.000.000
2.400ft x 2.400ft x 2.400ft

PROCESS IV

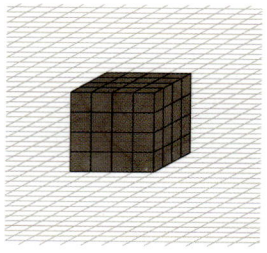

At the end of this process the Iconoclast has fully replaced the urban landscape. It is mankind's new city, and the regeneration of the New World can begin

Population: 64.000.000
3.200ft x 3.200ft x 3.200ft

FUSION REACTOR

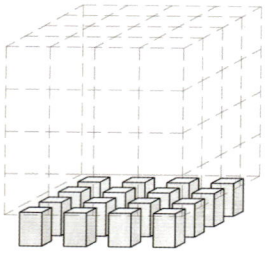

The Iconoclast is powered by fusion reactors, located and protected in its foundations, they are a key element for Iconoclast's independence from the outside world

STRUCTURE + VENTILATION

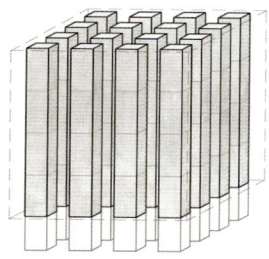

The vertical structure above works as cooling and ventilation towers, exhaling excess heat and used air while bringing fresh oxygen into the structure

SUPPLY

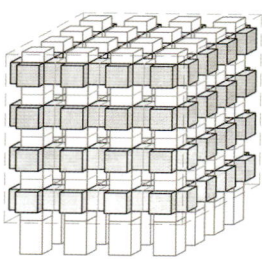

In the horizontal structure all supplying systems are located, such as nutrition production, fabrication, drone control and the server stations

HUMAN STORAGE

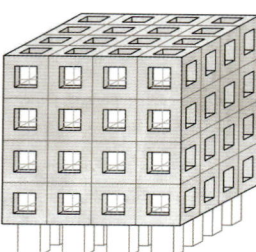

The open space in between those structural elements is filled with the Sarcophagi, the sleeping cells of those who decide to live in the Virtual World

INFRASTRUCTURE

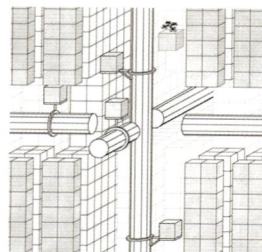

The highest density of the Sarcophagi is achieved by using the methods of high-bay warehouses, allowing efficient stacking and the connection to supply functions

NUTRITION

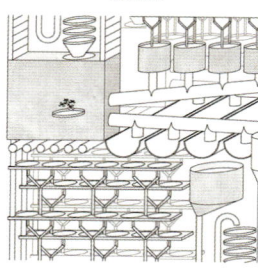

Eating and drinking is replaced by cellular nutrition, cultured inside of the Iconoclast, as all elements needed for adequate human nutrition can be artificially created

PRODUCTION

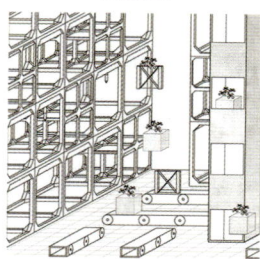

As the Iconoclast is fully independent from the outside world, every single necessary element is fabricated in internal machine plants

SERVER

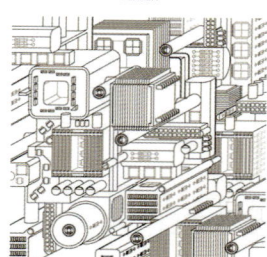

The server stations are the heart of the Iconoclast, every human being inside of it is connected to this supercomputer as it is generating the Virtual World

CONNECTION

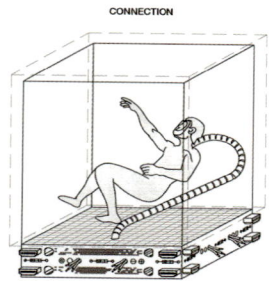

This connection is established by the **SARCOPHAGUS**, which maintains the vital functions of the Dreamer. The virtual environment is projected directly into his mind

RECEPTORS

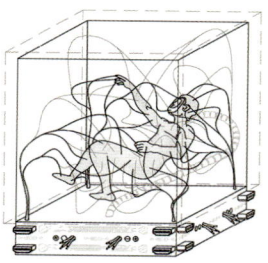

To make this world further authentic, thousands of sensory receptors are connected to the Dreamer, making a complete sensual perception of the Virtual World possible

FLUID

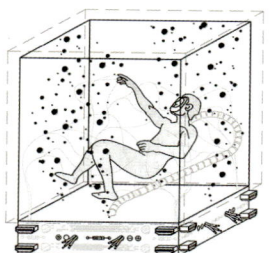

At any time the human being is surrounded by an supplying fluid, which contains all the nutrition and oxygen needed for maintaining live functions of the Dreamer

ENVELOPE

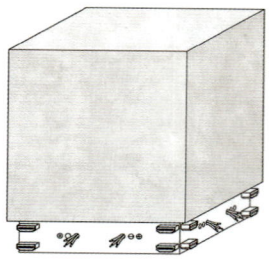

The Sarcophagus is the physical body of the human being in the Iconoclast and constructed to endure for decades, allowing the Dreamer to safely live his perfect life

The Sarcophagus is connected to the brain and nervous system of the Dreamer, making the direct implementation of the simulated environment into his mind possible. By stimulating sensory organs, the Virtual World becomes an equivalent to the physical world. Nutrition and medical treatments are transferred over the liquid surrounding the Dreamer. Physical exercise takes place while not being consciously perceived, to keep the human body physically functional. This is a necessity, as the dream in the Iconoclast is neither absolute nor infinite. Whenever the human being wants to, it is enabled to return into the physical world. This world we originally left behind for the virtual existence benefits from the Iconoclast as well. With the disappearance of a high percentage of human population, it is no longer polluted and exploited. Thereby it has the chance to start the process of environmental regeneration.

0639

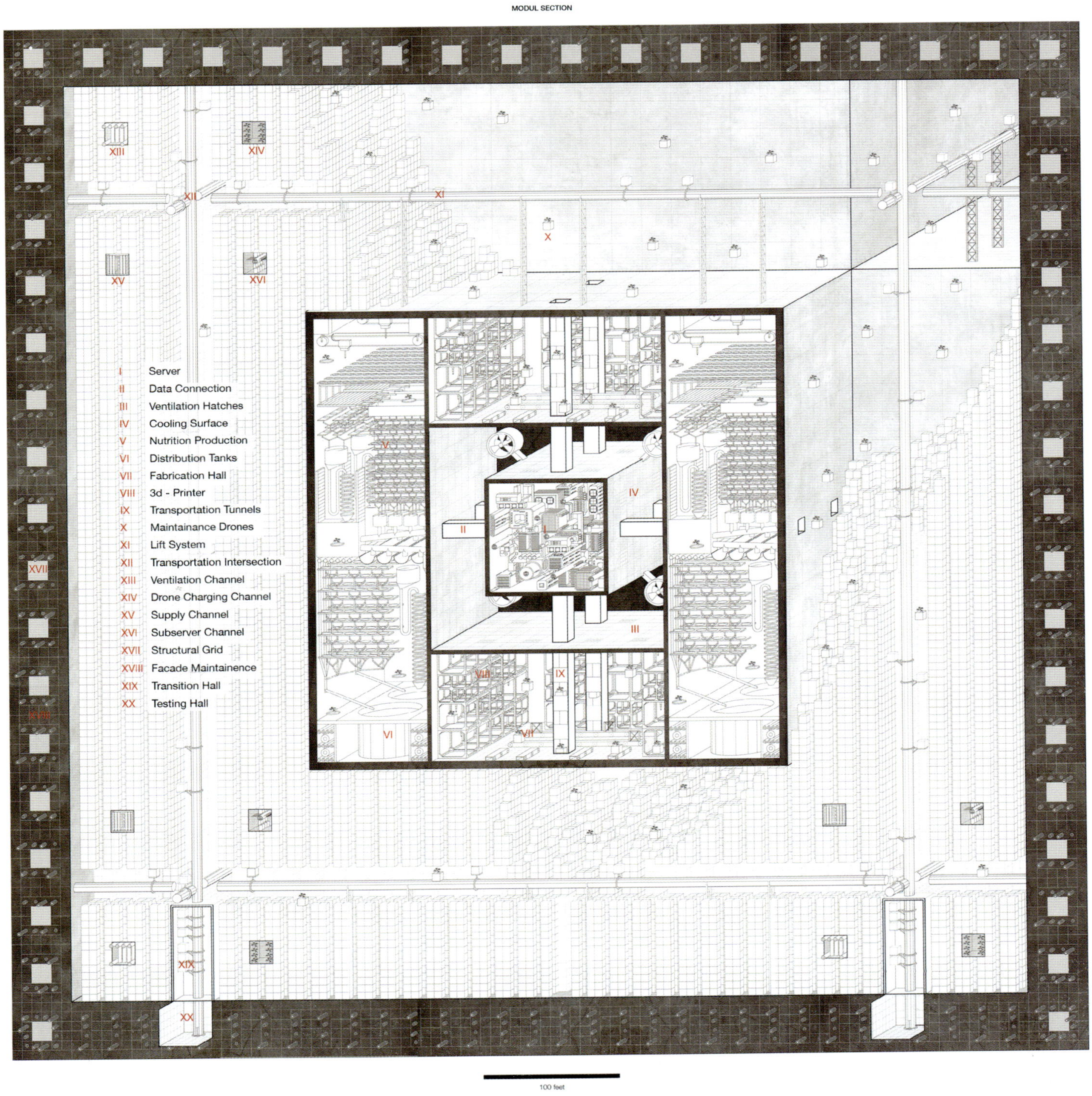
MODUL SECTION
XIII
XIV
XII
XI
X
XV
XVI
I Server
II Data Connection
III Ventilation Hatches
IV Cooling Surface
V Nutrition Production
VI Distribution Tanks
VII Fabrication Hall
VIII 3d - Printer
IX Transportation Tunnels
X Maintainance Drones
XI Lift System
XII Transportation Intersection
XIII Ventilation Channel
XIV Drone Charging Channel
XV Supply Channel
XVI Subserver Channel
XVII Structural Grid
XVIII Facade Maintainence
XIX Transition Hall
XX Testing Hall
XVII
II
IV
III
V
VI
VII
VIII
IX
XIX
XX
100 feet

LINK-SCAPE

Antonius Richard Rusli
Alexander Octa
Raymond San
Tika Dwiputri

Indonesia

LINK - SCAPE

Singapore is a leading global city in Southeast Asia and the world's only island city-state. Despite lacking natural resources and a hinterland, the nation developed rapidly as an Asian tiger economy, based on external trade and its human capital. With total population of 5.54 million (Jun 2015, Department of Statistics, Singapore), Singapore becomes the second densest sovereign state in the world, after the microstate Monaco.

As the nation develops intensively through of growth in services and construction, employment continued to rise. Overall employment grew by 16,400 in the third quarter of 2015, faster than in the last quarter. There were 3,644,000 persons in employment in September 2015, which means more than 65% of the total population is workers.

Singapore's Vision on Sustainable and Livable Country

Often being referred as Garden City, Singapore has its own long-term vision on achieving green and sustainable country. The government made a conscious decision and strategies to make the country green. They have started back in 1960s before environmental issues became a global concern and as the result, Singapore is recognized as a livable and sustainable country. In 2011, a Siemens-Economist Intelligence Unit study ranked Singapore as Asia's greenest city.

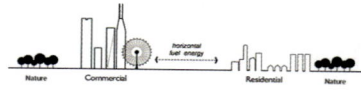

Link-Scape Tower is proposed to bring people into the nature, as part of the mission is to demonstrate how humans can dwell in the world without destroying life sustaining ecosystems. To provide a high quality living environment, the use of limited land must be prioritized between competing national needs such as housing, transport and commercial uses. The main goal for Link-Scape Tower is to create a balance relationship between urban dwelling and nature in the garden city of Singapore.

Exposing Nature, Enclosing Human Activity

Reconnecting habitats – nature conquers over manmade structures
The initial idea is to connect the existing green points in Singapore, with tower that spans from one green point to another. Link-Scape Tower act as bridges that connect habitats, showing more affection to nature and wildlife. On top portion of the building, a dense rainforest jungle is created in order to restore the original state of nature. Link-scape Towers are constructed over the dense city area to allow wildlife to live all over Singapore. Therefore, the balanced life between human and nature can be achieved.

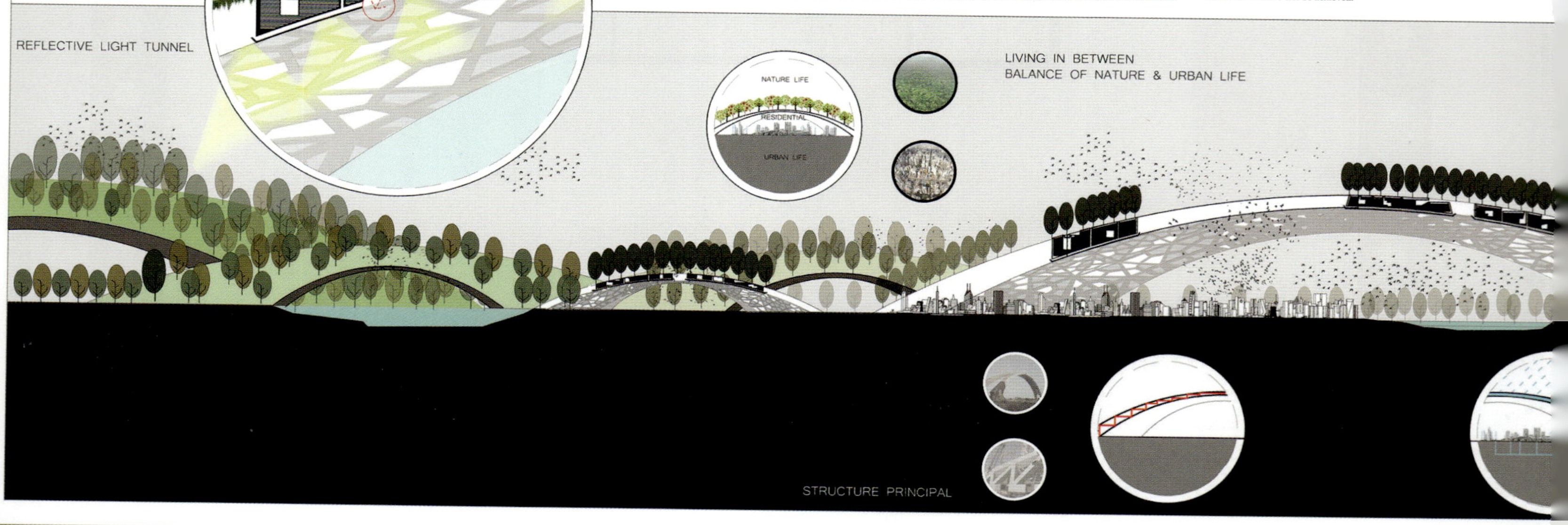

REFLECTIVE LIGHT TUNNEL

NATURE LIFE
RESIDENTIAL
URBAN LIFE

LIVING IN BETWEEN
BALANCE OF NATURE & URBAN LIFE

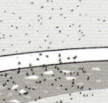

STRUCTURE PRINCIPAL

Often being referred as Garden City, Singapore has its own long-term vision on achieving green and sustainable country. The government made a conscious decision and strategies to make the country green. They have started back in 1960s before environmental issues became a global concern and as the result, Singapore is recognized as a livable and sustainable city. Singapore's ambitious goal as stated in the Sustainable Singapore Blueprint 2015 is to continuously provide greenery, including park spaces and water-bodies. Singapore's sustainable land planning principles: Develop an efficient city and adopt innovative ideas to improve our living environment and optimize land use. Promote the use of public transport by providing an extensive rail network and intensifying land use around rail stations. Decentralize commercial centers to provide more jobs near homes, as well as to reduce the need to

Singapore's ambitious goal as stated in the Sustainable Singapore Blueprint 2015 is to continuously provide greenery, including park spaces and water-bodies. Singapore's sustainable land planning principles:

- Develop an efficient city and adopt innovative ideas to improve our living environment and optimize land use
- Promote the use of public transport by providing an extensive rail network and intensifying land use around rail stations
- Decentralize commercial centers to provide more jobs near homes, as well as to reduce the need to travel and peak hour traffic congestion
- Provide a quality living environment by offering a wide variety of housing choices and comprehensive amenities within each new town
- Conserve our natural and built heritage by safeguarding Nature Reserves and Nature Areas and carefully conserving buildings with outstanding architecture and historical significance
- Foster community spirit through the provision of public spaces and by facilitating active civic participation in sustainable development

Citizens with a high level of productivity and workplace are concentrated in certain areas, making commuter gathered at a certain point at the same time. As a result, working spaces, green and blue spaces are centralized at certain area due to unequal zonings.

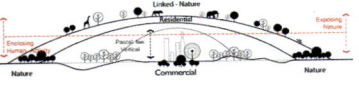

Balancing between commercial and residential zoning
Dwelling for residents are combined into the Link-Scape Tower and to be spreaded at various areas in Singapore, including at city area near offices and commercial centres. The intention is to reduce the need to travel and peak hour traffic congestion. Vibrant share spaces and communal facilities are located within residential areas at Link-Scape Tower to facilitate the residents' needs.

Adopt innovative ideas to improve living environment and optimize land use

- Link-scape tower act as massive water harvesting, which rain water falls down to the rainforest above and being distributed along the arc surface. The pressure which comes from gravity of rainwater downpipe is utilized for the elevator system from the residential units to the city area underneath. Residential units which located at above will get the primary supply, then after a recycling process, it will flow to city area (secondary). The rest will flow into the water tank as back up supply.
- A layer of reflective ceiling is implemented to allow sun light to come into the residential units and common spaces in between. Thus every spaces will get sufficient natural light.

0714

EXPOSING NATURE - ENCLOSING URBANISM

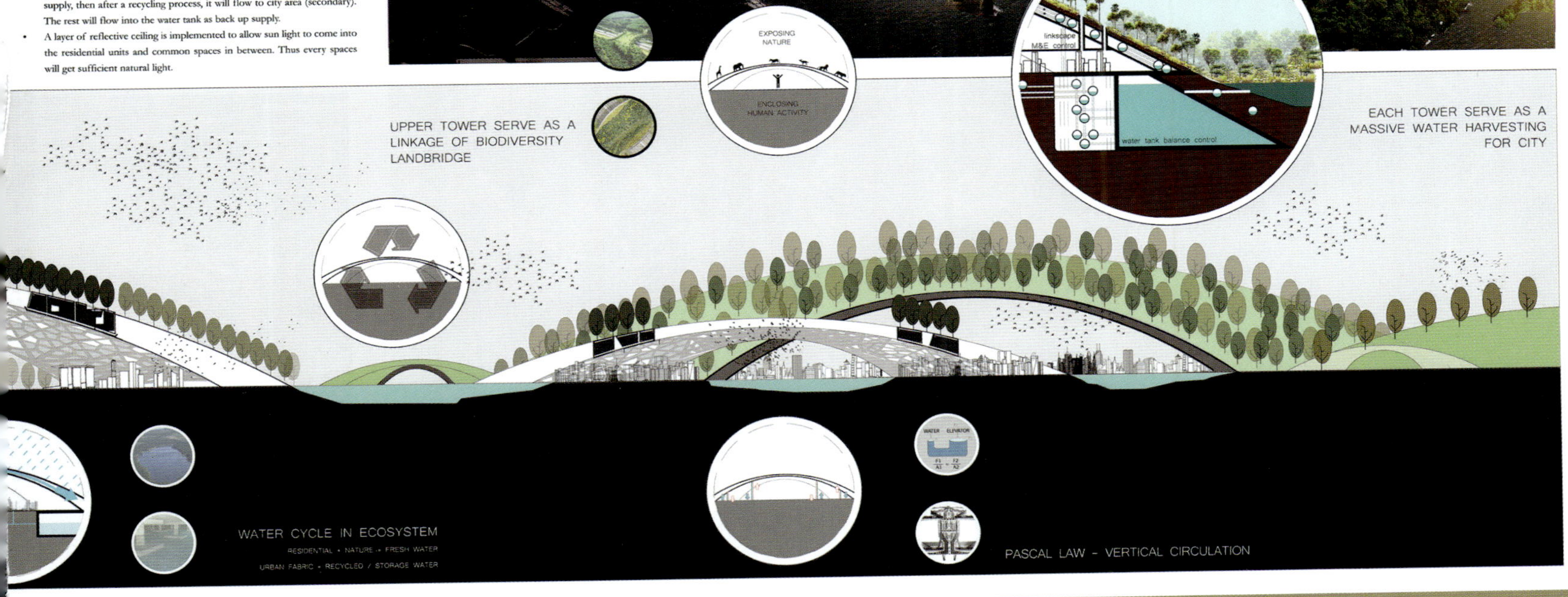

UPPER TOWER SERVE AS A
LINKAGE OF BIODIVERSITY
LANDBRIDGE

EXPOSING
NATURE

ENCLOSING
HUMAN ACTIVITY

EACH TOWER SERVE AS A
MASSIVE WATER HARVESTING
FOR CITY

WATER CYCLE IN ECOSYSTEM
RESIDENTIAL · NATURE · FRESH WATER
URBAN FABRIC · RECYCLED / STORAGE WATER

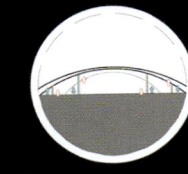

PASCAL LAW - VERTICAL CIRCULATION

travel and peak hour traffic congestion. Provide a quality living environment by offering a wide variety of housing choices and comprehensive amenities within each new town. Conserve our natural and built heritage by safeguarding Nature Reserves and Nature Areas and carefully conserving buildings with outstanding architecture and historical significance. Foster community spirit through the provision of public spaces and by facilitating active civic participation in sustainable development. Citizens with a high level of productivity and workplace are concentrated in certain areas, making commuter gathered at a certain point at the same time. As a result, working spaces, green and blue spaces are centralized at certain area due to unequal zonings. Link-Scape Tower is proposed to bring people into the nature, as part of the mission is to demonstrate how humans can dwell in the world without destroying life-

North-South Massing for Link-Scape Towers

Link-scape design approach is to treat building as landscape, with North-South direction for massing pattern, which means the tower allow its largest opening to face North and South. The residential units and common areas will get sufficient natural lighting into their areas.

sustaining ecosystems. To provide a high quality living environment, the use of limited land must be prioritized between competing national needs such as housing, transport and commercial uses. The initial idea is to connect the existing green points in Singapore, with tower that spans from one green point to another. Link-Scape Tower act as bridges that connect habitats, showing more affection to nature and wildlife. Dwelling for residents are combined into the Link-Scape Tower and to be distributed at various areas in Singapore, including at city area near offices and commercial centers. The intention is to reduce the need to travel and peak hour traffic congestion. Adopt innovative ideas to improve living environment and optimize land use. Link-scape Tower act as massive water harvesting, which rain water falls down to the rainforest above and being distributed along the arc surface.

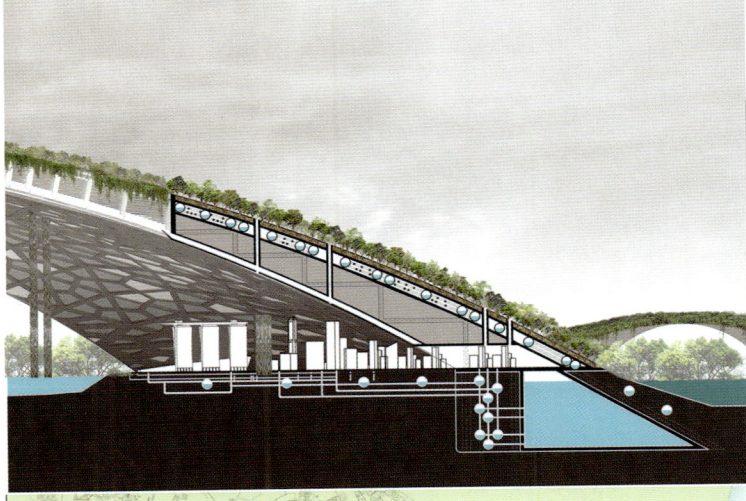

NEW ARCADIA

Joseph Konrad Kosmas Schneider
Vincent Johann Moller

Germany

NEW ARCADIA

The 22nd century

Humankind succeeded in avoiding the dangers of the
21st century's Technological Singularity. Through great
efforts and extensive preparation the crucial moment
of the awakening of a self-improving *Artificial Super
Intelligence (ASI)* could be predicted and controlled.
Mankind was able to stay the most powerful yet not the
most intelligent species on the planet while *ASI* became
its god-like slave - forever bound to serve humanity in
its needs.
Induced by *ASI*, unimaginable, all-embracing progress
throughout the entire research was achieved, lifting the
human state of knowledge to uncharted heights.

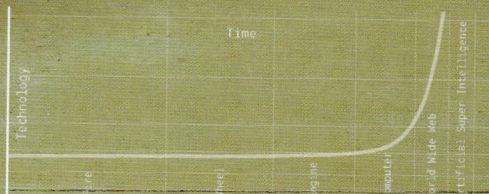

Exponential growth of technological advance throughout human history

Step by step the the human biological body was technically
modified and, through the immortality of its digital mind,
eventually made redundant. Biological evolution merged
with technology. All boundaries between the human being
and the digital realm were torn down. Human communication
changed into the medium of electromagnetic radiation,
eventually the human mind was transcended into technical
units and merged with *ASI*. A total integration happened.
The shift of human reality from the physical to the
digital world was completed.

Although physical reality is the basis of everything,
being in it became obsolete. Within the physical
constraints, energy and matter became shapeable and the
possibility arised to create any kind of matter at any
given time at any given place.
The appearance of the digital world is beyond our current
understanding of time and space - its only dimension is
the speed of communication, the speed of data transfer.
Cartesian locations loose their importance. The digital
world is not a world of movement - it's a world of calling
up.

Since being in this digital world differs entirely from
human's former nature a new desire towards the physical
reality arose. Just like humanist artists used to depict
the ideal ancient landscape of *Arcadia* in their paintings,
mankind transformed the physical world into the world of
NEW ARCADIA. For reasons of nostalgia human minds would
materialize into a favored biological body to experience
this physical world's truth.
The Tower of New Arcadia situates everything that used to
constitute human life.
It defines a place where people can meet and enjoy the
beauty of physical world's sensations.

The 22nd Century
Humankind succeeded in avoiding the dangers of the 21st Century's Technological Singularity. Through great efforts and extensive preparation the crucial moment of the awakening of a self-improving Artificial Super Intelligence (ASI) could be predicted and controlled. Mankind was able to stay the most powerful yet not the most intelligent species on the planet while ASI became its god-like slave - forever bound to serve humanity in its needs.

Induced by ASI, unimaginable, all-embracing progress throughout the entire research was achieved, lifting the human state of knowledge to uncharted heights.
Step by step the human biological body was technically modified. Biological evolution merged with

0798

Humanist artists used to depict
the ideal ancient landscape of Arcadia in their paintings.
Mankind transformed the physical world into
the world of NEW ARCADIA.

Technical Unit

technology. Human communication changed into the medium of electromagnetic radiation, eventually the human mind was transcended into technical units and merged with ASI. A total integration happened. The human body was, through the immortality of its digital mind, eventually made redundant. Although physical reality is the basis of everything, being in it became obsolete. The shift of human reality from the physical to the digital world was completed.

The appearance of this digital world is beyond our current understanding of time and space - its only dimension is the speed of communication, the speed of data transfer. Cartesian locations loose their importance. The digital world is not a world of movement – it is a world of calling up.

Floorplans 1:500

Elevation   Section

A place of t
A place of pr
To st

Since being in this digital world differs entirely from human's former nature, a new desire towards the physical reality arose at a certain point. Just like humanist artists used to depict the ideal ancient landscape of Arcadia in their paintings, mankind made the physical world into their world of NEW ARCADIA. For reasons of nostalgia human minds would then materialize into a favored biological body to experience this physical world's truth. The Tower of New Arcadia situates everything that used to constitute human life. It defines a place where people can meet and enjoy the beauty of physical world's sensations. A place of touch, sight, sound, smell and taste. A place of pristine human interaction and feelings. To stroll our so-called Real World.

0798

+900 ft

+10 ft

ouch, sight, sound, smell and taste.
stine human interaction and feeling.
ll our so called *Real World.*

eVolo